"What does every Bible chapter say..."

THE ULTIMATE BIBLE OUTLINE/THEME BOOK

"What does every Bible chapter say..."

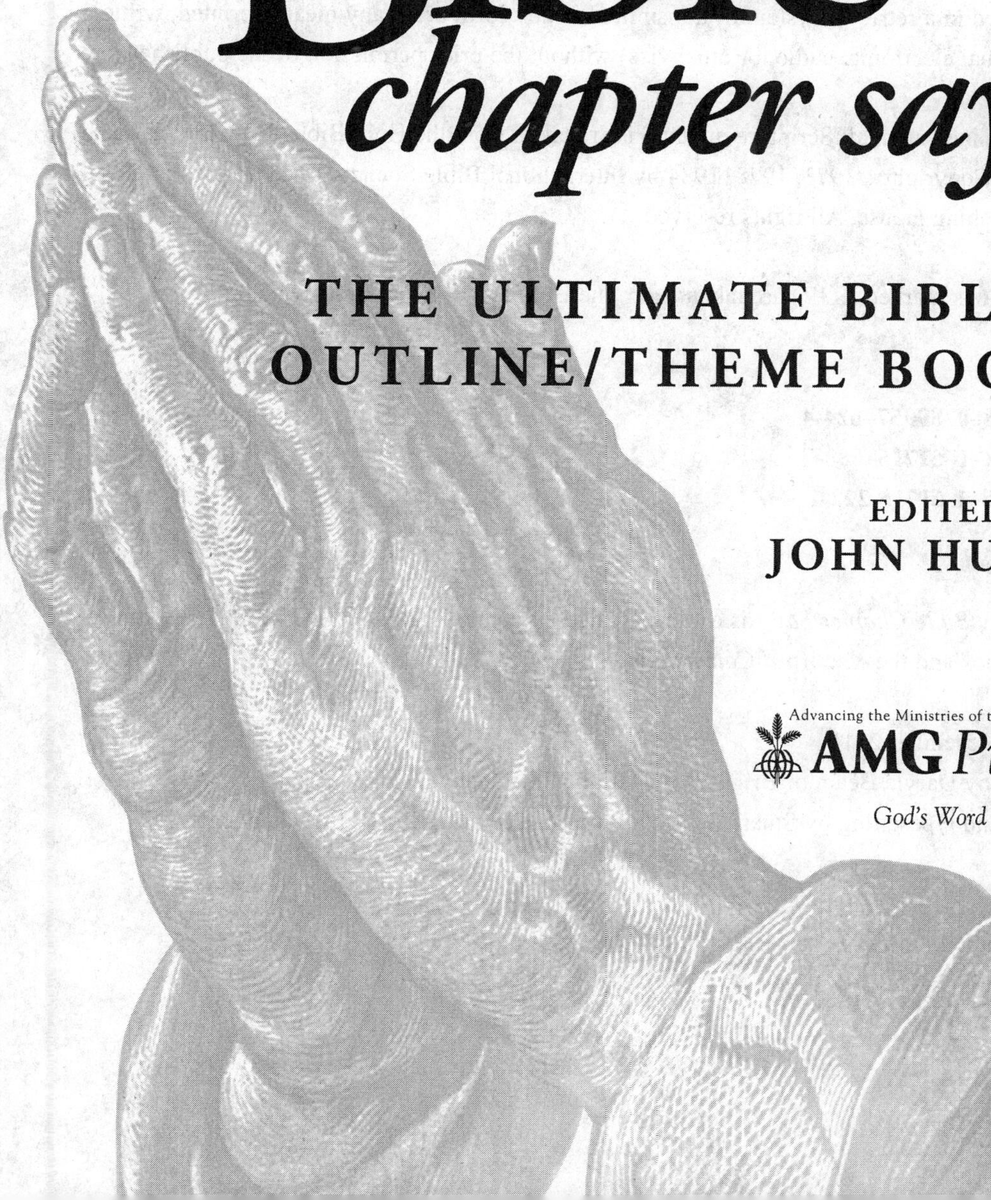

THE ULTIMATE BIBLE OUTLINE/THEME BOOK

EDITED BY:
JOHN HUNT

Advancing the Ministries of the Gospel
AMG Publishers
God's Word to you is our highest calling.

What Does Every Bible Chapter Say...

Published by AMG Publishers
6815 Shallowford Rd.
Chattanooga, Tennessee 37421–1755

Print ISBN: 978–0–89957–624-4
ePub ISBN: 978–1–61715–080-7
Mobi ISBN: 978–1-61715-222-1

What Does Every Bible Chapter Say... is a work created by combining two AMG titles: *The Ultimate Bible Outline Book* and the *Key Word Commentary*

First printing—December 2011
Cover designed by Daryle Beam of Bright Boy Design, Chattanooga, Tennessee
Interior design and typesetting by Stuart Davies, France and Jennifer Ross of Chattanooga, TN.

Printed in the United States of America
17 16 15 14 13 12 –R– 7 6 5 4 3 2 1

Contents

Introduction

The Bible was written in order to be understood. *The Ultimate Bible Outline Book* enables the first-time reader of the Bible to appreciate the main themes of each of the sixty-six Bible books, as well as every chapter within each book. The seasoned Bible student will find *The Ultimate Bible Outline Book* to be a treasure trove of seemingly endless Bible study material on each Bible book.

The whole Bible is covered in this book, including every Old Testament book. When people ask the question: "Why bother with the Old Testament?" Professor G.A. Smith's reply is worth recalling: "For us the supreme sanction of the Old Testament is that which it derived from Christ Himself. What was indispensable to the Redeemer must always be indispensable to the redeemed."

A closed book

One of the main reasons for the Bible not being understood today is that we do not read the Bible. For most people — Christians included — the Bible remains a formidable, unread book. There is no excuse for this. We are blessed today with accurately translated Bibles in our mother tongue. One of the great aims of the Reformation was to produce such Bibles so that ordinary people, for the first time, were able to read the Bible for themselves. So why does the Bible remain a closed book? *The Ultimate Bible Outline Book* has been compiled because the publishers are convinced that we all need assistance as we delve into the large unknown tracts of the Bible. *The Ultimate Bible Outline Book* is one gigantic do-it-yourself Bible study course. But it has been broken up into hundreds of short easily managed studies. Each Bible book is considered under the following four major headings:

1. Book by book: introduction to each Bible book
2. Helpful summaries
3. Chapter by chapter: outline of every chapter in the Bible
4. Select bibliography

Additional material

Some extra material is also found in the book consisting of important gems from the past which still greatly illuminate the Bible for us today. One such example is Martin Luther's introduction to his *Commentary on Galatians*. It presents, like no other of Luther's writings, the central thought of Christianity, the justification of a sinner through faith in Jesus' work alone.

1. Book by book: introduction to each Bible book

Introduction

Each Bible book begins with an introduction. These introductions include scholarly information about the author of the book, the date when it was probably written, and its first readers. They are edited versions of the introductions to each Bible book found in the massive one volume Bible commentary: *Commentary Critical and Explanatory on the Whole Bible (1871)*, authored by Robert Jamieson, A. R. Faussett and David Brown.

In addition to these introductions many books of the Bible have an entry which serves to shed extra light on the contents of the Bible book:

Old Testament

- Entries about the contents of the Bible book by James Orr, M.A., D.D, from his *International Standard Bible Encyclopedia, for the following:*

Contents of Genesis
Contents of Exodus
Contents of Deuteronomy
Contents of Judges
Contents of 1 and 2 Samuel
Contents of 1 and 2 Kings
Contents of 1 and 2 Chronicles
Contents of Esther
Contents of Job
Contents of Ecclesiastes
History of Interpretation of Song of Songs
Contents of Ezekiel
Contents of Amos
Contents of Micah
Contents of Nahum

- Entries about the contents of the Bible book by M.G. Easton M.A., D.D., from his *Illustrated Bible Dictionary,* for the following:

Contents of Leviticus
Contents of Numbers
Contents of Joshua

- Entries about the contents of the Bible book by C. F. Keil and F. Delitzsch, for the following:

Contents of Ruth
Contents of Ezra
Contents of Nehemiah

- An entry about the contents of the Bible book by Dr William Smith, from his *Smith's Bible Dictionary*, for the following:

Psalms

Entries by John Calvin, for the following:
John Calvin's introduction to Daniel
John Calvin's introduction to Hosea
John Calvin's introduction to Joel
John Calvin's introduction to Obadiah
John Calvin's introduction to Jonah
John Calvin's introduction to Habakkuk
John Calvin's introduction to Zephaniah
John Calvin's introduction to Haggai
John Calvin's introduction to Zechariah
John Calvin's introduction to Malachi

New Testament

Following the introduction to Matthew, Dr. Philip Schaff on the Resurrection of Jesus
Following the introduction to Romans, Martin Luther's Preface to Romans
Following the introduction to Revelation, Louis Berkof on the Contents of Revelation

Detailed outline

The introduction to each Bible book is followed by a detailed breakdown of the outline of all the chapters in the book. This breakdown of all the sections within each book enables the reader to view the topics covered in any particular Bible book.

2. Helpful summaries

Bird's eye view

A one or two sentence summary of each book of the Bible starts off this section of helpful summaries.

Reading plan

By following this reading plan for each Old Testament book you will read through the whole of the Old Testament in a year. By following the reading plan for each New Testament book you will also read through the whole of the New Testament in a year.

So to read the whole Bible in one year, one day's worth of readings from both the Old Testament and the New Testament need to be covered.

If you wish to take Jesus' words in John 8:31–32 to heart: "Jesus therefore was saying to those Jews who had believed him, 'If you abide in My word, you are truly disciples of Mine; and you shall know the truth, and the truth shall make you free,'" then the best place to start is by reading the chapters of the Bible for yourself. This should have priority over reading even the best Bible commentaries.

Verse/verses to memorize

One or more verses from each Bible book that are ideal for memorizing have been selected. The value of memorizing Scripture is hard to overestimate.

"I know of no other single practice in the Christian life more rewarding, practically speaking, than memorizing Scripture. That's right. No other single exercise pays greater spiritual dividends! Your prayer life will be strengthened. Your witnessing will be sharper and much more effective. Your attitudes and outlook will begin to change. Your mind will become alert and observant. Your confidence and assurance will be enhanced. Your faith will be solidified." – Charles Swindoll.

Corrie ten Boom concurs: "Gather the riches of God's promises. Nobody can take away from you those texts from the Bible which you have learned by heart."

Statistics

Statistics about each Bible book give the reader a little information about the book's size and where it comes in the Bible.

Famous sayings found in (each Bible book)

It is interesting to note that many common sayings and phrases with which we are familiar today can be traced back to different Bible books.

Names/titles given, and quotes about (each Bible book)

The different names the books of the Bible have been given over the centuries are set out here.

Where they exist, the Hebrew title and the Greek title in the Septuagint are supplied for the Bible books. Jerome (c. 347–420), who was known as one of the Latin Church Fathers for his outstanding theological understanding, was also the author of the *Vulgate*. Jerome made this Latin translation of the Bible for ordinary people to read. It became the standard Bible and was used throughout the Middle Ages. The titles used in the *Vulgate* for each Bible book are included here also.

Helpful keys to note in understanding (each Bible book)

Key word/words/phrase/phrases
It is surprising how knowing a key word or phrase in a Bible book can shed so much light on the whole book as one studies it.

Key verse/verses
There are many verses that could be called "key" verses in different Bible books. At least one such "key" verse from each Bible book is highlighted in this section.

Key people/key events
The key people and key events that occur in the long historical Old Testament books are listed here.

Themes to study
Each Bible book can be studied by theme as well as by chapter by chapter. Some of the most important themes found in each Bible book are listed here.

Unusual events and miracles
Unique and special items from particular Bible books are listed and/or explained in this section.

Jesus is found and referred to in many different ways in the Old Testament books. The following two sub-headings focus on such instances.
Jesus in (each Old Testament book)
Jesus in (each Old Testament book) gives a one line summary about how Jesus is found in that book.

Types of Jesus in (each Old Testament book)
Types of Jesus in (each Old Testament book) In the Bible the word "type" is used of historical facts which serve as illustrations of spiritual truths. This section gives numerous instances of such Messianic types. An obvious example of this comes in the book of Exodus where the Passover shows how Jesus is a "type" of the Passover Lamb.

Lessons to learn from (each Bible book)
Life Application Bibles have been popular for many years because they seek to apply the truths of God's Word to our daily lives. The *Lessons to learn from* sections in *The Ultimate Bible Outline Book* suggest a number of salient lessons from every Bible book which we can benefit from.

3. Chapter by chapter: outline of every chapter in the Bible

No greater reason for Bible study can be found than in the following words of Jesus:

"Jesus therefore was saying to those Jews who had believed Him, 'If you abide in My word, you are truly disciples of Mine; and you shall know the truth, and the truth shall make you free.'" John 8:31–32.

The second main section of *The Ultimate Bible Outline Book* gives the reader an opportunity to dwell on every chapter in each Bible book.

Matthew Henry's introduction

Matthew Henry's introduction gives an introduction to each chapter in each Bible book. His overviews of the chapter often include an element of comment or exposition in them, as well as a devotional thought.

Dr Adam Clarke's analysis of each New Testament chapter

In the New Testament section of *The Ultimate Bible Outline Book* the additional heading *Dr. Adam Clarke's analysis of chapter* appears. It is taken from Dr. Adam Clarke's *Commentary on the Bible.* As there are often so many detailed themes packed into the chapters of the New Testament the material found in Clarke's analysis contains a more detailed breakdown of each chapter than *Matthew Henry's introduction* does. However, Clark's analysis is simply a list of the events in the chapter, and, unlike Henry's, has no notes or comments.

Clarke's analysis of the breakdown of each New Testament chapter is an ideal place to refer to if one wants to gain the gist of any Bible chapter.

4. Select bibliography

A bibliography for each Bible book is found in this section.

In addition to these commentaries there are also a number of most useful Bible commentaries which are whole Bible commentaries or one-volume commentaries on the Bible. Such commentaries cover all of the Bible books, and so are not listed under each Bible book in the bibliography section, but appear below:

Whole Bible commentaries

Adam Clarke's Bible Commentary

Calvin's Commentaries on the Whole Bible, John Calvin

Commentary Critical and Explanatory on the Whole Bible, Robert Jamieson, A. R. Faussett and David Brown, 1871.

Matthew Henry Commentary on the Whole Bible, 1706
John Gill's Exposition of the Bible
People's New Testament, 1891, B.W. Johnson
The 1599 Geneva Study Bible
Wesley's Explanatory Notes, John Wesley, 1754–1765.

One volume commentaries on the Bible

New Bible Commentary: 21st Century Edition, Inter-Varsity, 1994, R. T. France, J. A. Motyer, G. J. Wenham, and D. A. Carson.
New Bible Commentary, Eerdmans, 1970, D. Guthrie, J. A. Motyer, A. M. Stibbs, and D. J. Wiseman

Conclusion

The Bible is different from every other book. It is much more than a collection of facts to be mastered. Jesus even gave a warning against the wrong type of Bible study. ". . . nor does his word dwell in you, for you do not believe the one he sent. You diligently study the Scriptures because you think that by them you possess eternal life. These are the Scriptures that testify about me, yet you refuse to come to me to have life" (John 5:38–40). All Bible study should help us to know Jesus better. *The Ultimate Bible Outline Book* seeks to assist every reader in this lifelong quest.

Part One
Old Testament Books

Genesis

1. Book by book: Introduction to Genesis

Introduction

The Pentateuch

The Pentateuch, the name by which the first five books of the Bible are designated, is derived from two Greek words, *pente*, "five," and *teuchos*, a "volume," thus signifying the fivefold volume. Originally these books formed one continuous work, as in the Hebrew manuscripts they are still connected in one unbroken roll. At what time they were divided into five portions, each having a separate title, is not known, but it is certain that the distinction dates at or before the time of the Septuagint translation. The names they bear in our English version are borrowed from the Septuagint, and they were applied by those Greek translators as descriptive of the principal subjects—the leading contents of the respective books. In the later Scriptures they are frequently referred to under the general title, The Law or The Book of the Law. since, to give a detailed account of the preparations for and the delivery of, the divine code, with all the civil and sacred institutions that were peculiar to the ancient economy, is the object to which they are exclusively devoted.

They have always been placed at the beginning of the Bible, not only on account of their priority in point of time, but as forming an appropriate and indispensable introduction to the rest of the sacred books. The numerous and oft-recurring references made in the later Scriptures to the events, the ritual, and the doctrines of the ancient Church would have not only lost much of their point and significance, but would have been absolutely unintelligible without the information which these five books contain. They constitute the groundwork or basis on which the whole fabric of revelation rests, and a knowledge of the authority and importance that is thus attached to them will sufficiently account for the determined assaults that infidels have made on these books, as well as for the zeal and earnestness which the friends of the truth have displayed in their defense.

Author

The Mosaic origin of the Pentateuch is established by the concurring voices both of Jewish and Christian tradition; and their unanimous testimony is supported by the internal character and statements of the work itself. That Moses did keep a written record of the important transactions relative to the Israelites is attested by his own express affirmation. For in relating the victory over the Amalekites, which he was commanded by divine authority to record, the language employed, "write this for a memorial in a book" (Hebrew, "the book"), (Exodus 17:14), shows that that narrative was to form part of a register already in progress, and various circumstances combine to prove that this register was a continuous history of the special goodness and care of divine providence in the choice, protection, and guidance of the Hebrew nation.

First, there are the repeated assertions of Moses himself that the events which checkered the experience of that people were written down as they occurred (see Exodus 24:4–7; 34:27; Numbers 33:2).

Secondly, there are the testimonies borne in various parts of the later historical books to the Pentateuch as a work well known, and familiar to all the people (see Joshua 1:8; 23:6; 24:26; 1 Kings 2:3, etc.)

Thirdly, frequent references are made in the works of the prophets to the facts recorded in the books of Moses (compare Isaiah 1:9 with Genesis 19:1; Isaiah 12:2 with Exodus 15:2; Isaiah 51:2 with Genesis 12:2; Isaiah 54:9 with Genesis 8:21,22; compare Hosea 9:10 with Numbers 25:3; Hosea 11:8 with Genesis 19:24; Hosea 12:4 with Genesis 32:24,25; Hosea 12:12 with Genesis 28:5; 29:20; compare Joel 1:9 with Numbers 15:4–7; 28:7–14; Deuteronomy 12:6, 7; 16:10,11; compare Amos 2:9 with Numbers 21:21; Amos 4:4 with Numbers 28:3; Amos 4:11 with Genesis 19:24; Amos 9:13 with Leviticus 26:5; compare Micah 6:5 with Numbers 22:25; Micah 6:6 with Leviticus 9:2; Micah 6:15 with Leviticus 26:16, etc.)

Fourthly, the testimony of Christ and the Apostles is repeatedly borne to the books of Moses (Matthew 19:7; Luke 16:29; 24:27; John 1:17; 7:19; Acts 3:22; 28:23; Romans 10:5). Indeed the references are so numerous, and the testimonies so distinctly borne to the existence of the Mosaic books throughout the whole history of the Jewish nation, and the unity of character, design, and style pervading these books is so clearly perceptible, notwithstanding the rationalistic assertions of their forming a series of separate and unconnected fragments, that it may with all safety be said, there is immensely stronger and more varied evidence in proof of their being the authorship of Moses than of any of the Greek or Roman classics being the productions of the authors whose names they bear.

But admitting that the Pentateuch was written by Moses, an important question arises, as to whether the books which compose it have reached us in an authentic form; whether they exist genuine and entire as they came from the hands of their author. In answer to this question, it might be sufficient to state that, in the public and periodical rehearsals of the law in the solemn religious assemblies of the people, implying the existence of numerous copies, provision was made for preserving the integrity of "The Book of the Law." But besides this, two remarkable facts, the one of which occurred before and the other after the captivity, afford conclusive evidence of the genuineness and authenticity of the Pentateuch.

The first is the discovery in the reign of Josiah of the autograph copy which was deposited by Moses in the ark of the testimony, and the second is the schism of the Samaritans, who erected a temple on

Mount Gerizim, and who, appealing to the Mosaic law as the standard of their faith and worship equally with the Jews, watched with jealous care over every circumstance that could affect the purity of the Mosaic record.

There is the strongest reason, then, for believing that the Pentateuch, as it exists now, is substantially the same as it came from the hands of Moses. The appearance of a later hand, it is true, is traceable in the narrative of the death of Moses at the close of Deuteronomy, and some few interpolations, such as inserting the altered names of places, may have been made by Ezra, who revised and corrected the version of the ancient Scriptures. But, substantially, the Pentateuch is the genuine work of Moses, and many, who once impugned its claims to that character, and looked on it as the production of a later age, have found themselves compelled, after a full and unprejudiced investigation of the subject, to proclaim their conviction that its authenticity is to be fully relied on.

Inspiration and canonical authority

The genuineness and authenticity of the Pentateuch being admitted, the inspiration and canonical authority of the work follow as a necessary consequence. The admission of Moses to the privilege of frequent and direct communion with God (Exodus 25:22; 33:3; Numbers 7:89; 9:8); his repeated and solemn declarations that he spoke and wrote by command of God; the submissive reverence that was paid to the authority of his precepts by all classes of the Jewish people, including the king himself (Deuteronomy 17:18; 27:3); and the acknowledgment of the divine mission of Moses by the writers of the New Testament, all prove the inspired character and authority of his books. The Pentateuch possessed the strongest claims on the attention of the Jewish people, as forming the standard of their faith, the rule of their obedience, the record of their whole civil and religious polity. But it is interesting and important to all mankind, inasmuch as besides revealing the origin and early development of the divine plan of grace, it is the source of all authentic knowledge, giving the true philosophy, history, geography, and chronology of the ancient world.

Finally, the Pentateuch "is indispensable to the whole revelation contained in the Bible; for Genesis being the legitimate preface to the law; the law being the natural introduction to the Old Testament; and the whole a prelude to the gospel revelation, it could not have been omitted. What the four Gospels are in the New, the five books of Moses are in the Old Testament."

Robert Jamieson

Contents of Genesis

The Book of Genesis treats the history of the kingdom of God on earth from the time of the creation of the world down to the beginning of Israel's stay in Egypt and to the death of Joseph; and it treats these subjects in such a way that it narrates in the first part (Genesis 1:1–11:26) the history of humankind; and in the second part (Genesis 11:27–50:26) the history of families; and this latter part is at the same time the beginning of the history of the chosen people, which history itself begins with Exodus. 1.

Though the introduction, Genesis 1–11, with its universal character, includes all humankind in the promise given at the beginning of the history of Abraham (12:1–3), it is from the outset distinctly declared that God, even if He did originally set apart one man and his family (Gen. 12–50), and after that a single nation (Exodus 1), nevertheless intends that this particularistic development of the plan of salvation is eventually to include all humankind. The manner in which salvation is developed historically is particularistic, but its purposes are universal.

Link with the next Bible books

The history of the chosen people, which begins with Exodus 1, at the very outset and with a clear purpose, refers back to the history as found in Genesis (compare Exodus 1:1–6,8 with Genesis 46:27; 50:24), although hundreds of years had elapsed between these events; which years are ignored, because they were in their details of no importance for the religious history of the people of God. But to Abraham in Genesis 12:1–3 the promise had been given, not only that he was to be the father of a mighty nation that would recognize him as their founder, and the earliest history of which is reported in Exodus and the following books of the Pentateuch, but also that the Holy Land had been promised him.

In this respect, the Book of Joshua, which gives the story of the capture of this land, is also a continuation of the historical development begun in Genesis. The blessing of God pronounced over Abraham, however, continued to be efficacious also in the later times among the people who had descended from him. In this way Genesis is an introduction to all of the books of the Old Testament that follow it, which in any way have to do with the fate of this people, and originated in its midst as the result of the special relation between God and this people. But in so far as this blessing of God was to extend to all the nations of the earth (Genesis 12:3), the promises given can be entirely fulfilled only in Christ, and can expand only in the work and success of Christian missions and in the blessings that are found within Christianity.

Accordingly, this book treats first of beginnings and origins, in which, as in a kernel, the entire development of the kingdom of God down to its consummation is contained.

Orr, James, M.A., D.D. General Editor, International Standard Bible Encyclopedia

Detailed outline

- I. The history of humanity: 1:1–11:26
  - A. Creation: 1:1–2:25
  - B. The fall of man: 3:1–4:26
    - 1. Adam and Eve: 3:1–24
    - 2. Cain and Abel: 4:1–26
  - C. Genealogy from the fall to the flood: 5:1–32
  - D. The flood: 6:1–9:29
    - 1. The wickedness of man: 6:1–4
    - 2. God's decision: 6:5–7
    - 3. Noah: 6:8–10

4. God speaks to Noah: 6:11–21
5. Noah's response: 6:22
6. God speaks to Noah: 7:1–4
7. Noah's response: 7:5–16
8. Life in the ark: 7:17–24
9. Release from the ark: 8:1–19
10. God's covenant: 9:1–17
11. Generations of Noah: 9:18–19
12. Sins of Noah's family: 9:20–29

E. From the flood to Abraham: 10:1–11:26
1. Generations of the sons of Noah: 10:1–32
2. The tower of Babel: 11:1–9
3. Generations of Shem: 11:10–26
4. Generations of Terah: 11:27–32

II. The patriarchal history of Israel: 11:27–50:26

A. Abraham: 11:27–25:10
1. Abraham's birth and ancestry: 11:26–30
2. His wanderings: 11:31–13:1
(a) From Ur to Haran: 11:31–32
(b) From Haran to Canaan: 12:1–9
(c) To Egypt and back: 12:10–13:1
3. Abraham and Lot: 13:2–14:24
(a) Dispute and division: 13:2–13
(b) God's promise to Abraham: 13:14–18
(c) Lot captured by the kings of the east: 14:1–24
4. The covenant: 15:1–20
5. Ishmael: 16:1–16
6. Circumcision: 17:1–27
7. A promised son: 18:1–15
8. Sodom and Gomorrah: 18:16–19:38
9. Abraham visits Abimelech: 20:1–18
10. Isaac born and Ishmael driven out: 21:1–21
11. Abraham and Abimelech: 21:22–34
12. Proposed sacrifice of Isaac: 22:1– 19
13. The death and burial of Sarah: 23:1–20
14. Marriage of Isaac and Rebekah: 24:1–67
15. Abraham and Keturah: 25:1–6
16. Abraham's death and burial: 25:7–10

B. Isaac: 25:11–35:29
1. Birth of Isaac: 21:1–8
2. Marriage to Rebekah: 24
3. Isaac and his sons: 25:19–35:29
4. Covenant renewed: 26:1–5
5. Deception of Abimelech: 26:6–33
6. Marriage to Judith and Bashemath: 26:34–35
7. Isaac deceived by Jacob: 27:1–45
8. Jacob's flight to Haran: 27:46–28:5
9. Death of Isaac: 35:27–29

C. Jacob: 28:10–36:43
1. His birth: 25:19–26
2. Rivalry between Jacob and Esau: 25:27–45
(a) The birthright: 25:27–34
(b) The blessing: 27:1–45
3. The flight to Haran: 27:46–29:14
4. Jacob's marriages to Leah and Rachel: 29:15–30
5. Life in Haran: 29:31–30:43
6. Return to Canaan: 31:1–55
7. Preparations to meet Esau: 32:1–23
8. Jacob's wrestling match: 32:24–32
9. Peace with Esau: 33:1–17

10. Jacob and his family in Canaan: 33:18–45:28
11. Jacob's final days and death: 46:1–50:14

D. Joseph: 37:1–50:26
1. Joseph's early life: 37:1–36
(a) His coat: 37:1–4
(b) His dreams: 37:5–11
(c) Sold into slavery: 37:12–36
(d) The sin of Judah: 38:1–30
2. Joseph the slave: 39:1–40:23
(a) In Potiphar's house: 39:1–20
(b) In prison: 39:21–40:23
3. Joseph the prime minister: 41:1–45:28
(a) Preparation for famine: 41:1–57
(b) Joseph and his brothers: 42:1–45:28
(c) Joseph and his family in Egypt: 46:1–50:21
(d) Joseph's death: 50:22–26

2. Helpful summaries of Genesis

Bird's eye view

God provides redemption to remedy humanity's sin by providing a covenant and a chosen race.

Reading plan

The following reading plan, taking one reading per day, enables you to read through Genesis in twenty-four days.

Genesis 1–2
Genesis 3–5
Genesis 6–7
Genesis 8–10
Genesis 11–12
Genesis 13–15
Genesis 16–18
Genesis 19–20
Genesis 21–22
Genesis 23–24
Genesis 25
Genesis 26–27
Genesis 28–29
Genesis 30
Genesis 31–32
Genesis 33–34
Genesis 35–36
Genesis 37–38
Genesis 39–40
Genesis 41–42
Genesis 43–44
Genesis 45–46
Genesis 47–48
Genesis 49–50

Verses to memorize

Genesis 1:1
In the beginning God created the heaven and the earth.

Genesis 9:13
I have set my rainbow in the clouds and it will be the sign of the covenant between me and the earth.

Genesis 50:20a
But as for you, ye thought evil against me; but God meant it unto good. kjv

Statistics

First Old Testament book
50 chapters

1,533 verses
38,267 words

Famous sayings found in Genesis

"Sweat of your brow" Genesis 3:19
"My brother's keeper" Genesis 4:9
"Dust of the earth" Genesis 13:16

Names/titles given

First book of Moses
First book of the Law
First book of the Pentateuch
("Pentateuch" means "five books/scrolls.)
Hebrew title: Bereshith: "In the beginning."
Greek title in Septuagint: Genesis: "origin, source, generation, beginning."
Latin title in Vulgate: "The book of generations"

3. Helpful keys to turn to in understanding Genesis

Key words/phases

"Beginning"
beginning of the world. 1.1–2.25.
beginning of sin. 3.1–24.
beginning family. 4.1–26.
beginning of God's work to restore humankind. 11.27–12.3.

Key verses

Genesis 1:1; 3:15; 12:3

Key people

Adam
Eve
Cain
Abel
Seth
Noah
Flood
Babel
Abraham
Sarah
Lot
Sodom
Hagar
Ishmael
Isaac
Rebekah
Jacob
Esau
Laban
Rachel
Leah
Bilhah
Zilpah
12 sons of Jacob
Dinah
Joseph
Potiphar
Manasseh
Ephraim

Key people/events

Creation
The Fall
The Flood
The Tower of Babel
Abraham
Isaac
Jacob
Joseph

Themes to study

- Election: The leading figures in Genesis, Abel, Noah, Abraham, Jacob, and Joseph are all called by God.
- Worship: see Genesis 4:1–7; 28:10–22.
- Satan: see Genesis 3:1–7.
- Salvation: see Genesis 3:15; 4:4; 22:8.
- Marriage: see Genesis 2:18–25.
- Work and rest: see Genesis 1:28; 3:17–19.

Important people who are grouped with each other

Adam and Eve
Cain and Abel
Abraham and Lot
Isaac and Ishmael
Esau and Jacob
Joseph and his eleven brothers

Generations

Genesis has eleven units, focusing on the word "generations," in the phrase, "these are the generations."

1. Introduction to generations: 1:1–2:3
2. Creation of heaven and earth: 2:4–4:26
3. Adam: 5:1–6:8
4. Noah: 6:9–9:29
5. Noah's sons: 10:1–11:9
6. Shem: 11:10–26
7. Terah: 11:27–25:11
8. Ishmael: 25:12–18
9. Isaac: 25:19–35:29
10. Esau: 36:1–37:1
11. Jacob: 37:2–50:26

Genealogies in Genesis

After the prologue where we find the true beginning of all things, we discover ten genealogies, each of which is introduced by the same Hebrew word meaning generation, account or record (Hebrew: Toledot).

- 1:1–2:3 Prologue

  In the beginning God created the heavens and the earth. (Genesis 1:1).
- 2:4–4:26 The generations of Heaven and Earth

  This is the account of the heavens and the earth when they were created, in the day that the Lord made earth and heaven. (Genesis 2:4).
- 5:1–6:8 The generations of Adam

  This is the book of the generations of Adam. In the day when God created man, He made him in the likeness of God. (Genesis 5:1).
- 6:9–9:29 The generations of Noah

  These are the records of the generations of Noah... (Genesis 6:9).
- 10:1–11:19 The generations of the sons of Noah

  Now these are the records of the generations of Shem, Ham, and Japheth, the sons of Noah; and sons were born to them after the flood. (Genesis 10:1).
- 11:10–26 The generations of Shem

  These are the records of the generations of Shem. (Genesis 11:10).
- 11:27–25:11 The generations of Terah

  Now these are the records of the generations of Terah. (Genesis 11:27).

- 25:12–18 The generations of Ishmael
  Now these are the records of the generations of Ishmael, Abraham's son, whom Hagar the Egyptian, Sarah's maid, bore to Abraham; (Genesis 25:12).
- 25:19–35:29 The generations of Isaac
  Now these are the records of the generations of Isaac, Abraham's son: (Genesis 25:19).
- 36:1–37:1 The generations of Esau
  Now these are the records of the generations of Esau (that is, Edom). (Genesis 36:1).
- 37:2–50:26 The generations of Jacob
  These are the records of the generations of Jacob. Joseph, ... (Genesis 37:2).

These series of genealogies show how God's promise and line of godly descendants pass down through the generations. Both Luke and Matthew use the genealogical accounts to trace Jesus' descendants.

Matthew traces Jesus Christ's genealogy back to Abraham. Luke, however, goes right back to the son of Seth, the son of Adam, the son of God!

"The book of the genealogy of Jesus Christ, the son of David, the son of Abraham." (Matthew 1:1).

"... the son of Enosh, the son of Seth, the son of Adam, the son of God." (Luke 3:38).

Five covenants in Genesis

1. The creation covenant: Genesis 1:26–28.
2. Covenant with Adam: Genesis 3:14–19.
3. Covenant with Noah: Genesis 8:20–9:6.
4. Covenant with Abraham: Genesis 12:1–3.
5. Covenant about Palestine: Genesis 15:18–21.

Genesis in the rest of the Bible

- No other book in the Bible is referred to or quoted so much in other books as is Genesis.
- There are more than 200 references to the book of Genesis in the New Testament.
- Only three New Testament books do not have any allusions to Genesis: Philemon and 1 & 2 John; yet, both of these authors, Paul and John, frequently quote from Genesis in their other writings.
- Jacob is mentioned in 22 other books of the Old Testament.
- Jacob is also mentioned 23 times in 7 New Testament books.

Genesis themes in the New Testament

- God in the beginning
  Gen. 1:1; cf. John 1:1
- Beginning of the world
  Gen. 1:1; cf. 2 Timothy 1:9; Titus 1:2; Hebrews 11:3; 1:10
- Creation of male and female
  Gen. 1:26–27; cf. Mark 10:6–7
- Humankind made in God's image
  Gen. 1:26–27; cf. Colossians 3:10; 1 Corinthians 11:7
- Creation attributed to God
  Gen. 1:31; cf. Acts 17:24; Ephesians 3:9; John 1:10; Revelation 4:11
- Death comes into the world through sin
  Gen. 2:17; cf. Romans 5:12
- End of death and pain
  Gen. 3:18–19 ; cf. Revelation 21:4
- Abel's superior sacrifice
  Gen. 4:3–5; cf.Hebrews 11:4
- The blood of Abel

Gen. 4:10; cf.Luke 11:51; Hebrews 12:24

- All die in Adam
  Gen. 5:5 ; cf. 1 Corinthians 15:22
- The days of Noah
  Gen. 6:12–13; cf. Luke 17:26
- Noah and the ark
  Gen. 7:13–16; cf. Matthew 24:38
- The flood
  Gen. 7:17–18 ; cf. Matthew 24:39
- Abraham's faith
  Gen. 12:4; cf. Hebrews 11:8
- Melchizedek and Abraham
  Gen. 14:18–20; cf. Hebrews 7:1, 4–7
- Faith and righteousness
  Gen. 15:6; cf. Romans 4:3,5,9,22
- Circumcision
  Gen. 17:11, 13; cf. Acts 7:8; Romans 4:11
- Sodom and Gomorrah
  Gen. 18:20; cf. Matthew 10:15
- Lot's wife
  Gen. 19:26 ; cf. Luke 17:32
- Abraham offering Isaac
  Gen. 22:1–3 ; cf. Hebrews 11:17
- The God of Abraham, Isaac, and Jacob
  Gen. 31:42; cf. Matthew 22:32
- Joseph
  Gen. 37–41; cf. Acts 7:9–14
- Joseph's death
  Gen. 50:24–26; cf. Hebrews 11:22

Unusual events and miracles in Genesis

- God's creation of the universe, 1:1–27
- Seth's birth, 4:25,26
- Enoch's translation, 5:24
- Noah building an ark, 6:8–9:17
- The Flood, 6:5–17; 7:11,12,34
- Punishment of Ham, 9:20–27
- Erection of Tower of Babel, 11:1–4
- Destruction of Tower of Babel and confusion of tongues, 11:5–9
- Abraham chosen and called by God, 4:4–5
- Birth of Isaac, 17:15–19
- Sodomites blinded, 19:11
- Sodom and Gomorrah destroyed, 19:24–25
- Lot's wife turned into a pillar of salt, 19:26
- Ram caught in a thicket, 22:13
- Joseph's God-given ability to interpret Pharaoh's dream, 41:14–44
- Famine, which caused Joseph to be reunited to his family, 41:47; 45:4–11

Prayers in Genesis:

- Adam and Eve talk with God, Gen.3:8–19
- Cain prays for Mercy, Gen 4:13–15
- God talks to Noah, Gen.6:12–7:5
- God's Covenant with Noah, Gen.9:1–17
- God calls Abraham, the call, Gen.12:1–5
- Abraham prays for a son and for land, the covenant, Gen.15:1–18
- The covenant of circumcision, Abraham prays for Ishmael, Gen.17:1–26
- Abraham pleads for Sodom, Gen.18:20–33
- Abraham prays for Abimelech, Gen.20:17
- Hagar consoled, Gen.21:14–20
- Abraham's servant prays for success and guidance, Gen.24:17–19
- Prayer of Isaac for his barren wife, Gen.25:21
- Prayer of understanding of Rebekah, Gen.25:22–25
- God talks to Jacob, Gen.28:10–15
- Jacob prays for deliverance from Esau,

Gen.32:9–12

- Jacob wrestles with God all night, Gen.32:22–31

Jesus in Genesis

In Genesis Jesus is our Creator God.

Messianic predictions in Genesis

Jesus is the Seed of the woman, 3:15
Jesus is from the line of Seth, 4:25
Jesus is the son of Shem, 9:27
Jesus is a descendant of Abraham, 12:3
Jesus is a descendant of Isaac, 21:12
Jesus is a descendant of Jacob, 25:23
Jesus is from the tribe of Judah, 49:10

Types of Jesus in Genesis

(In the Bible the word "type" is used of historical facts which serve as illustrations of spiritual truths.)

- Adam is said to be a type of him who was to come, Rom. 5:14.
- Abel offered an acceptable sacrifice, pointing to Jesus' sacrifice of himself.
- Melchizedek is said to be make like the Son of God, Heb. 7:3.
- The tree of life: Gen. 2:9 with Rev. 2:7.
- Noah, who pleased God: Gen. 6:8,9 with Matthew 3:17.
- Noah's ark, as an ark of safety: Gen. 7:1, 7; with 1 Peter 3:20, 21.
- Abraham, as head of many nations: Gen. 17:5 with Gal. 3:6–9.
- Joseph's life is also a type of Jesus.

Lessons to learn from Genesis

- Our relationship to God should be characterized by obedience, belief, and trust.
- Our relationship to our family should be characterized by having no favorites, honesty with each other, and faithfulness to each other.
- In our relationship to the world we should care for the world's resources.
- Remember that everything is created by God.

4. Chapter by chapter: outline of every chapter of Genesis

Genesis 1

Matthew Henry's introduction

The foundation of all religion being laid in our relation to God as our Creator, it was fit that the book of divine revelations which was intended to be the guide, support, and rule, of religion in the world, should begin, as it does, with a plain and full account of the creation of the world–in answer to that first enquiry of a good conscience, "Where is God my Maker?" (Job 35:10).

About this the pagan philosophers wretchedly blundered, and became vain in their imaginations, some asserting the world's eternity and self-existence, others ascribing it to a fortuitous concourse of atoms: thus "the world by wisdom knew not God," but took a great deal of pains to lose him. The holy scripture therefore, designing by revealed religion to maintain and improve natural religion lays down, at first, this principle of the unclouded light of nature, That this world was, in the beginning of time, created by a Being of infinite wisdom and power, who was himself before all time and all worlds. The entrance into God's word gives this light, Ps. 119:130. The first verse of the Bible gives us a surer and better, a more satisfying and useful, knowledge of the origin of the universe, than all the volumes of the philosophers. The lively faith of humble Christians understands this matter better than the elevated fancy of the greatest wits, Heb. 11:3.

We have three things in this chapter:

I. A general idea given us of the work of creation vv. 1, 2.

II. A particular account of the several days' work, registered, as in a journal, distinctly and in order. The creation of the light the first day, vv. 3–5; of the firmament the second day, vv. 6–8; of the sea, the earth, and its fruits, the third day, vv. 9–13; of the lights of heaven the fourth day, vv. 14–19; of the fish and fowl the fifth day, vv. 20–23; of the beasts, vv. 24, 25; of man, vv. 26–28; and of food for both the sixth day, vv. 29, 30.

III. The review and approbation of the whole work, v. 31.

A detailed analysis of chapter

God creates heaven and earth. (1,2)
The creation of light. (3–5)
God separates the earth from the waters, and makes it fruitful. (6–13)
God forms the sun, moon, and stars. (14–19)
Animals created. (20–25)
Man created in the image of God. (26–28)
Food is given. (29,30)
The work of creation ended and approved. (31)

Key verse

Verse 1: "In the beginning God created the heaven and the earth."

Key word / key phrase

Verse 1, "beginning."

Key event / key person / key theme

God's creation explains the origin of the earth and the heavens.

Key thought

Everything that God created was good. Note how this is repeatedly stated in this chapter.

Key thing to look out for

Man was made in the image of God, verses 26,27.

Key Bible cross-reference

Read the opening chapter of John's Gospel alongside this chapter.

Key "by way of explanation"

The Bible never attempts to explain, justify, or defend God as the Creator of the universe. The truth is boldly stated as a fact and is affirmed by Bible poetry, Psalm 102:25, and Bible prophecy, Isaiah 40:21.

Key "Quotable Quote"

"Whatever view is taken of the relationship of the two accounts of creation, in chapters 1 and 2, it is clear that the former is written from God's standpoint, while man is the center of the latter."

H. L. Ellison

Genesis 2

Matthew Henry's introduction

This chapter is an appendix to the history of the creation, more particularly explaining and enlarging on that part of the history which relates immediately to man, the favorite of this lower world. We have in it,

I. The institution and sanctification of the Sabbath, which was made for man, to further his holiness and comfort (vv. 1–3).

II. A more particular account of man's creation, as the center and summary of the whole work (vv. 1–7).

III. A description of the garden of Eden, and the placing of man in it under the obligations of a law and covenant (vv. 8–17).

IV. The creation of the woman, her marriage to the man, and the institution of the ordinance of marriage (v. 18, etc.).

A detailed analysis of chapter

The first Sabbath. (1–3)
Details about the creation. (4–7)
The planting of the garden of Eden. (8–14)
Man is placed in it. (15)
God's command. (16,17)
The animals named, the making of woman, the divine institution of marriage. (18–25)

Key verse

Verse 1: "Thus the heavens and the earth were finished, and all the host of them."

Key word / key phrase

Verse 1, "The heavens and the earth."

Key event / key person / key theme

God completed his creation.

Key thought

Verse 2. The "seventh day" was special, and was especially blessed by God.

Key thing to look out for

Verse 15. What responsibilities have been given to humankind?

Key Bible cross-reference

Verse 9, "Tree of life." See 3:22; Revelation 2:7; 22:2, 14.

Key "by way of explanation"

Verse 7, "And the Lord God formed man from the dust of the ground." The Hebrew word translated "formed" is used of a potter and his work: Isaiah 45:9; Jeremiah 18:6. God "formed" humans and animals: verse 19; 1:21,25.

Key "Quotable Quote"

"If man is the head, she [woman] is the crown, a crown to her husband, the crown of visible creation. The man was dust refined, but the woman was dust double-refined."

Matthew Henry's Commentary on the Bible (on Genesis 2:21–25).

Genesis 3

Matthew Henry's introduction

The story of this chapter is perhaps as sad a story (all things considered) as any we have in all the Bible. In the previous chapters we have had the pleasant view of the holiness and happiness of our first parents, the grace and favor of God, and the peace and beauty of the whole creation, all good, very good; but here the scene is altered. We have here an account of the sin and misery of our first parents, the wrath and curse of God against them, the peace of the creation disturbed, and its beauty stained and sullied, all bad, very bad. "How has the gold become dim, and the most fine gold changed!" O that our hearts were deeply affected with this record! For we are all nearly concerned in it; let it not be as a tale that is told. The general contents of this chapter we have (Rom. 5:12), "By one man sin entered into the world, and death by sin; and so death passed on all men, for that all have sinned." More particularly, we have here,

I. The innocent tempted, vv. 1–5.
II. The tempted transgressing, vv. 6–8.
III. The transgressors arraigned, vv. 9, 10.
IV. On their arraignment, convicted, vv. 11–13.
V. On their conviction, sentenced, vv. 14–19.
VI. After sentence, reprieved, vv. 20, 21.
VII. Notwithstanding their reprieve, execution in part done, vv. 22–24. And, were it not for the gracious intimations here given of redemption the promised seed, they, and all their degenerate guilty race, would have been left to end less despair.

A detailed analysis of chapter

The serpent deceives Eve. (1–5)
Adam and Eve break the divine command, and fall into sin and misery. (6–8)
God calls upon Adam and Eve to answer. (9–13)
The serpent cursed, and the promised Seed. (14,15)
The punishment of humankind. (16–19)
The first clothing of humankind. (20,21)
Adam and Eve are driven out of paradise. (22–24)

Key verse

Verse 6: "And when the woman saw that the tree was good for food, and that it was pleasant to the eyes, and a tree to be desired to make one wise, she took of the fruit thereof, and did eat, and gave also unto her husband with her; and he did eat."

Key word / key phrase

Verse 17, "cursed."

Key event / key person / key theme

The Fall

Key thought

Both Adam and Eve gave way to temptation. "Many a dangerous temptation comes to us in fine gay colors, that are but skin-deep."

Matthew Henry

Key thing to look out for

"There is a kind of foreshadowing of the whole gospel in Genesis 3:15."

D. Martyn Lloyd-Jones

Key Bible cross-reference

Verse 6 shows three aspects of temptation: see 1 John 2:16; Luke 4:3, 5, 9.

Key "by way of explanation"

Verse 1. The "serpent" is a reference to the devil. He is also described as "that ancient serpent" Revelation 12:9.

Key "Quotable Quote"

"Jesus assumes the thorns, that he may cancel the sentence; for this cause also was he buried in the earth, that the earth which had been cursed might receive the blessing instead of a curse."

Cyril of Jerusalem, Catechetical Lectures

Genesis 4

Matthew Henry's introduction

In this chapter we have both the world and the church in a family, in a little family, in Adam's family, and an example given of the character of both in all ages, to the end of time. As all humankind was represented in Adam, so that great distinction of humankind into saints and sinners, godly and wicked, the children of God and the children of the wicked one, was here represented in Cain and Abel, and an early instance is given of the enmity which was put between the seed of the woman and the seed of the serpent. We have here,

I. The birth, names, and callings, of Cain and Abel, vv. 1, 2.

II. Their religion, and different success in it, vv. 3, 4, and part of v. 5.

III. Cain's anger at God and the reproof of him for that anger, vv. 5–7.

IV. Cain's murder of his brother, and the process against him for that murder. The murder committed, v. 8. The proceedings against him.

A. His arraignment, v. 9, former part.

B. His plea, v. 9, latter part.

C. His conviction, v. 10.

D. The sentence passed on him, vv. 11, 12.

E. His complaint against the sentence, vv. 13, 14.

F. The ratification of the sentence, v. 15.

G. The execution of the sentence, vv. 15, 16.

V. The family and posterity of Cain, vv. 17–24.

VI. The birth of another son and grand son of Adam, vv. 25, 26.

A detailed analysis of chapter

The birth, work, and religion of Cain and Abel. (1–7)

Cain murders Abel, and the curse of Cain. (8–15)

The behavior of Cain, his family. (16–18)

Lamech and his wives, and the skill of Cain's descendants. (19–24)

The birth of another son and grandson of Adam. (25,26)

Key verse

Verse 8: "And Cain talked with Abel his brother: and it came to pass, when they were in the field, that Cain rose up against Abel his brother, and slew him."

Key word / key phrase

Verse 5, "anger."

Key event / key person / key theme

The first murder recorded in the Bible.

Key thought

Verse 8. Cain was deliberately deceitful.

Key thing to look out for

Verse 24. The extent of personal revenge can be contrasted with Jesus' teaching about the extent of our forgiving, see Matthew 18:21, 22.

Key Bible cross-reference

Verse 10. See Luke 11:50, 51; Hebrews 11:4; 12:24.

Key "by way of explanation"

Verse 7, "sin is crouching at your door." Sin is pictured here, crouching, and waiting to pounce on Cain.

Key "Quotable Quote"

"Original sin may be defined as hereditary corruption and depravity of our nature, extending to all the parts of the soul, which first makes us obnoxious to the wrath of God, and then produces in us works which in Scripture are termed works of the flesh."

John Calvin,
The Institutes of Christian Religion

Genesis 5

Matthew Henry's introduction

This chapter is the only authentic history extant of the first age of the world from the creation to the flood, containing (according to the verity of the Hebrew text) 1656 years, as may easily be computed by the ages of the patriarchs. This is one of those which the apostle calls "endless genealogies" (1 Tim. 1:4), for Christ, who was the end of the Old Testament law, was also the end of the Old Testament genealogies; towards him they looked, and in him they centered. The genealogy here recorded is inserted briefly in the pedigree of our Savior (Luke 3:36–38), and is of great use to show that Christ was the "seed of the woman" that was promised. We have here an account,

I. About Adam, vv. 1–5.
II. Seth, vv. 6–8.
III. Enos, vv. 9–11.
IV. Cainan, vv. 12–14.
V. Mahalaleel, vv. 15–17.
VI. Jared, vv. 18–20.
VII. Enoch, vv. 21–24.
VIII. Methuselah, vv. 25–27.
IX. Lamech and his son Noah, vv. 28–32. All scripture, being given by inspiration of God, is profitable, though not all alike profitable.

A detailed analysis of chapter

Adam and Seth. (1–5)
The patriarchs from Seth to Enoch. (6–20)
Enoch. (21–24)
Methuselah to Noah. (25–32)

Key verse

Verse 5: "This is the book of the generations of Adam."

Key word / key phrase

Verse 23, "walked."

Key event / key person / key theme

Account of Adam's descendants

Key thought

Verse 3. Adam was made in God's perfect image, but because of the Fall, Adam's son was born with Adam's fallen nature.

Key thing to look out for

If the number of years each person lived for is taken literally, then Methuselah died in the same year as the flood. The figures in verses 27 and 25, 28, and 7:6 make 969.

Key Bible cross-reference

Verse 23. The only other person whom the Bible records as being translated directly to heaven without dying is Elijah. See 2 Kings 2:10; Hebrews 11:5.

Key "by way of explanation"

Verse 31, "777." Lamech is said to have lived for 777 years. Seven stands for completeness, so 777 would be a number emphasizing completeness.

Key "Quotable Quote"

"Someone once quipped that the doctrine of original sin is the only philosophy empirically validated by thirty-five centuries of recorded human history."

Charles Colson

Genesis 6

Matthew Henry's introduction

The most remarkable thing we have on record about the old world is the destruction of it by the universal deluge, the account of which commences in this chapter, in which we have,

I. The abounding iniquity of that wicked world, vv. 1–5, and vv. 11, 12.

II. The righteous God's just resentment of that abounding iniquity, and his holy resolution to punish it, vv. 6, 7.

III. The special favor of God to his servant Noah.

A. In the character given of him, vv. 8–10.

B. In the communication of God's purpose to him, vv. 13, 17.

C. In the directions he gave him to make an ark for his own safety, vv. 14–16.

D. In the employing of him for the preservation of the rest of the creatures, vv. 18–21.

Lastly, Noah's obedience to the instructions given him, v. 22. And this about the old world is written for our admonition, on whom the ends of the new world have come.

A detailed analysis of chapter

The wickedness of the world, which provoked God's wrath. (1–7)

Noah finds grace. (8–11)

Noah warned of the flood, and the directions about the ark. (12–21)

Noah's faith and obedience. (22)

Key verse

Verse 8: "But Noah found grace in the eyes of the Lord."

Key word / key phrase

Verse 5, "wickedness."

Key event / key person / key theme

The Flood

Key thought

Verses 11, 12. The Flood event pictures God's wrath and attitude to human sin.

Key thing to look out for

Verse 9. Noah's character.

Key Bible cross-reference

Verse 18. God rescuing Noah from the flood is a picture of God's salvation. See Hebrews 11:7; 2 Peter 2:5.

Key "by way of explanation"

Verse 17, "Destroy all life." From this some argue that the flood was universal. Others, however, argue that such universal language is also used elsewhere, such as 41:54, 57, where it was not intended to be interpreted as having a global dimension.

Key "Quotable Quote"

"Noah was the first of many individuals who, apparently single-handed, have been used by God to carry out his purpose and to make a crucial difference to the world. Even today people famous and people unknown are making a difference in the world simply by trying to obey God. They have refused to be bullied into believing that what they do makes no difference."

Stephen Travis

Genesis 7

Matthew Henry's introduction

In this chapter we have the performance of what was foretold in the previous chapter, both about the destruction of the old world and the salvation of Noah; for we may be sure that no word of God shall fall to the ground. There we left Noah busy about his ark, and full of care to get it finished in time, while the rest of his neighbors were laughing at him for his pains. Now here we see the purpose of his work as well as their carelessness. And this famous period of the old world gives us some idea of the state of things when the world that now is shall be destroyed by fire, as that was by water. See 2 Pet. 3:6, 7. We have, in this chapter,

I. God's gracious call to Noah to come into the ark (v. 1), and to bring the creatures that were to be preserved alive along with him (vv. 2, 3), in consideration of the deluge at hand, v. 4.

II. Noah's obedience to this heavenly vision, v. 5. When he was six hundred years old, he came with his family into the ark (vv. 6, 7), and brought the creatures along with him (vv. 8, 9), an account of which is repeated (vv. 13–16), to which is added God's tender care to shut him in.

III. The coming of the threatened deluge (v. 10); the causes of it (vv. 11, 12): the prevalence of it, vv. 17–20.

IV. The dreadful desolations that were made by it in the death of every living creature on earth, except those that were in the ark, vv. 21–23.

V. The continuance of it in full sea, before it began to ebb, one hundred and fifty days, v. 24.

A detailed analysis of chapter

Noah, his family, and the living creatures enter the ark, and the flood begins. (1–12)

Noah shut in the ark. (13–16)

The flood rises for forty days. (17–20)

All flesh is destroyed by the flood. (21–24)

Key verse

Verse 5: "And Noah did according unto all that the Lord commanded him."

Key word / key phrase

Verse 5, "commanded."

Key event / key person / key theme

Noah obeys God.

Key thought

Verse 16, "God . . . commanded . . . the Lord shut." This verse illustrates how God takes the initiative in salvation, how humankind should obey, and how God acts.

Key thing to look out for

Verse 4, "Forty days and forty nights." This period of time is mentioned at other key moments in the Bible: see Deuteronomy 9:11; Matthew 4:1–11.

Key Bible cross-reference

Verse 13. See 1 Peter 3:20 and 2 Peter 2:5.

Key "by way of explanation"

Verse 2, "Take with you seven of every kind of clean animal, a male and its mate, and two of every kind of unclean animal." The ceremonially clean animals would be needed as sacrifices after the Flood.

Key "Quotable Quote"

"God, if he has freely justified you by faith in his Son, and given you his Spirit, has sealed you to be his; and has secured you, as surely as he secured Noah, when he locked him in the ark."

George Whitefield

Genesis 8

Matthew Henry's introduction

In the close of the previous chapter we left the world in ruins and the church in straits; but in this chapter we have the repair of the one and the enlargement of the other. Now the scene alters, and another face of things begins to be presented to us, and the brighter side of that cloud which there appeared so black and dark; for, though God contend long, he will not contend for ever, nor be always wrath. We have here,

I. The earth made anew, by the recess of the waters, and the appearing of the dry land, now a second time, and both gradual.

A. The increase of the waters is stayed, vv. 1, 2.

B. They begin sensibly to abate, v. 3.

C. After sixteen days' ebbing, the ark rests, v. 4.

D. After sixty days' ebbing, the tops of the mountains appeared above water, v. 5.

E. After forty days' ebbing, and twenty days before the mountains appeared, Noah began to send out his spies, a raven and a dove, to gain intelligence, vv. 6–12.

F. Two months after the appearing of the tops of the mountains, the waters had gone, and the face of the earth was dry (v. 13), though not dried so as to be fit for man till almost two months after v. 14.

II. Man placed anew on the earth, in which,

A. Noah's discharge and departure out of the ark, vv. 15–19.

B. His sacrifice of praise, which he offered to God on his enlargement, v. 20.

C. God's acceptance of his sacrifice, and the promise he made there on not to drown the world again, vv. 21, 22. And thus, at length, mercy rejoices against judgment.

A detailed analysis of chapter

God remembers Noah, and dries up the waters. (1–3)

The ark rests on Ararat. Noah sends out a raven and a dove. (4–12)

Noah being commanded, goes out of the ark. (13–19)

Noah offers sacrifices, God promises never again to destroy all living creatures. (20–22)

Key verse

Verse 1: "And God remembered Noah."

Key word / key phrase

Verse 20, "sacrificed."

Key event / key person / key theme

Noah leaves the ark.

Key thought

Worship is the appropriate way to acknowledge God's goodness.

Key thing to look out for

Verse 14. The length of time Noah and his family were in the ark, even after the rain had stopped.

Key Bible cross-reference

Verse 8. Note how God remembers his people on this occasion, and, "with favor," on other occasions: see Nehemiah 5:19; 13:31.

Key "by way of explanation"

Verse 11, "olive leaf." Olives do not grow at the tops of mountains, but at lower altitudes. So the waters must have receded.

Key "Quotable Quote"

"Nature is God's tongue."

Henry Ward Beecher

Genesis 9

Matthew Henry's introduction

Both the world and the church were now again reduced to a family, the family of Noah. From this family we are all descendants. Here is,

I. The covenant of providence settled with Noah and his sons, vv. 1–11. In this covenant,

A. God promises them to take care of their lives, so that, They should replenish the earth, vv. 1, 7. They should be safe from the insults of the brute-creatures, which should stand in awe of them, v. 2. They should be allowed to eat flesh for the support of their lives; only they must not eat blood, vv. 3, 4. The world should never be drowned again, vv. 8–11.

B. God requires of them to take care of one another's lives, and of their own, vv. 5, 6.

II. The seal of that covenant, namely, the rainbow, vv. 12–17.

III. A particular passage of story about Noah and his sons,

A. Noah's sin and shame, vv. 20, 21.

B. Ham's impudence and impiety, v. 22.

C. The pious modesty of Shem and Japheth, v. 23.

D. The curse of Canaan, and the blessing of Shem and Japheth, vv. 21–27.

IV. The age and death of Noah, vv. 28, 29.

A detailed analysis of chapter

God blesses Noah, and grants flesh for food. (1–3)

Murder forbidden. (4–7)

God's covenant and the sign of the rainbow. (8–17)

Noah plants a vineyard gets drunk and is mocked by Ham. (18–23)

Noah curses Canaan, blesses Shem, and prays for Japheth. Noah's death. (24–29)

Key verse

Verse 13: "I do set my bow in the cloud, and it shall be for a token of a covenant between me and the earth."

Key word / key phrase

Verse 15, "never again."

Key event / key person / key theme

God's covenant with Noah

Key thought

Verse 12. The covenant "sign" pointed to God's love in making the covenant.

Key thing to look out for

Noah's first actions on leaving the ark.

Key Bible cross-reference

Verse 6. See Exodus 21:12–14; Numbers 35:16–32; Romans 13:3,4; 1 Peter 2:13,14.

Key "by way of explanation"

Verse 12, "Rainbow." There is no suggestion that rainbows did not exist before the Flood. But now they have been given special significance.

Key "Quotable Quote"

"If you say, 'Would there were no wine' because of the drunkards, then you must say, going on by degrees, 'Would there were no steel,' because of the murderers, 'Would there were no night,' because of the thieves, 'Would there were no light,' because of the informers, and 'Would there were no women,' because of adultery."

John Chrysostom, Homilies

Genesis 10

Matthew Henry's introduction

This chapter shows more particularly what was said in general (9:19), about the three sons of Noah, that "of them was the whole earth overspread;" and the fruit of that blessing (9:1, 7), "replenish the earth." This is the only certain account extant of the origin of nations; and yet perhaps there is no nation but the Jews that can be confident from which of these seventy fountains (for so many there are here) it derives its streams. Through the lack of early records, the mixtures of people, the revolutions of nations, and distance of time, the knowledge of the lineal descent of the present inhabitants of the earth is lost; nor were any genealogies preserved but those of the Jews, for the sake of the Messiah, only in this chapter we have a brief account,

I. Of the posterity of Japheth, vv. 2–5.

II. The posterity of Ham (vv. 6–20), and in this particular notice is taken of Nimrod, vv. 8–10.

III. The posterity of Shem, v. 21, etc.

A Detailed analysis of chapter

The sons of Noah, of Japheth, of Ham. (1–7)

Nimrod the first ruler. (8–14)

The descendants of Canaan, and the sons of Shem. (15–32)

Key verse

Verse 1: "Now these are the generations of the sons of Noah, Shem, Ham, and Japheth: and unto them were sons born after the flood."

Key word / key phrase

Verse 32, "flood."

Key event / key person / key theme

The record of family trees

Key thought

God is the Author of all human life.

Key thing to look out for

The Bible is full of history, not fairy tales.

Key Bible cross-reference

Verse 12. The "great city" here is most probably Nineveh, see Jonah 1:2; 3:2; 4:11.

Key "by way of explanation"

Verse 29, "Ophir." Much of Solomon's gold came from here, 1 Kings 9:28.

Key "Quotable Quote"

"Peace in society depends upon peace in the family."

Augustine of Hippo

Genesis 11

Matthew Henry's introduction

The old distinction between the sons of God and the sons of men (professors and profane) survived the flood, and now appeared again, when men began to multiply: according to this distinction we have, in this chapter,

I. The dispersion of the sons of men at Babel (vv. 1–9), where we have,

A. Their presumptuous provoking design, which was to build a city and a tower,

vv. 1–4.

B. The righteous judgment of God on them in disappointing their design, by confounding their language, and so scattering them, vv. 5–9.

II. The pedigree of the sons of God down to Abraham (vv. 10–26), with a general account of his family, and removal out of his native country, v. 27, etc.

A Detailed analysis of chapter

One language in the world, and the building of Babel. (1–4)

The confusion of tongues, and the builders of Babel scattered. (5–9)

The descendants of Shem. (10–26)

Terah, father of Abram, grandfather of Lot, they move to Haran. (27–32)

Key verse

Verse 4: "And they said, Go to, let us build us a city and a tower, whose top may reach unto heaven; and let us make us a name, lest we be scattered abroad upon the face of the whole earth."

Key word / key phrase

Verse 4, "scattered."

Key event / key person / key theme

Building the tower of Babel

Key thought

Abram is introduced.

Key thing to look out for

God sees everything, even hidden motives.

Key Bible cross-reference

Verse 30. Sarah being barren was a most important event: 15:2–3; 17:5, 17.

Key "by way of explanation"

Verse 3, "brick instead of stone." As stones were so scarce in Mesopotamia, bricks made of mud and bitumen were used as building materials.

Key "Quotable Quote"

"The only Bible-honoring conclusion is, of course, that Genesis 1–11 is actual historical truth, regardless of any scientific or chronological problems thereby entailed."

Dr Henry Morris, President ICR, 1972

Genesis 12

Matthew Henry's introduction

The pedigree and family of Abram we had an account of in the previous chapter; here the Holy Spirit enters on his story, and henceforward Abram and his seed are almost the only subject of the sacred history. In this chapter we have,

I. God's call of Abram to the land of Canaan, vv. 1–3.

II. Abram's obedience to this call, vv. 4, 5.

III. His welcome to the land of Canaan, vv. 6–9.

IV. His journey to Egypt, with an account of what happened to him there. Abram's flight and fault, vv. 10–13. Sarai's danger and deliverance, vv. 14–20.

A Detailed analysis of chapter

God calls Abram, and blesses him with a promise about Christ. (1–3)

Abram departs from Haran. (4,5)
He travels through Canaan, and worships God in that land. (6–9)
Abram is driven by a famine into Egypt, he pretends that his wife is his sister. (10–20)

Key verse

Verse 1: "Now the Lord had said unto Abram, Get thee out of thy country, and from thy kindred, and from thy father's house, unto a land that I will show thee."

Key word / key phrase

Verse 2, "bless."

Key event / key person / key theme

The call of Abram

Key thought

From one person, God chose a great people who would be his followers.

Key thing to look out for

Verse 7. The Lord often appeared to Abram, even though he did not appear in all his glory.

Key Bible cross-reference

Verses 2–3. See verses 7; 15:2–21; 17:4–8; 18:18,19; 22:17,18.

Key "by way of explanation"

Verses 2–3. God reaffirmed his covenant and blessing to Isaac, 26:2–4, and to Jacob, 28:13–15, and to Moses, Exodus 3:6–8.

Key "Quotable Quote"

"Election is God's eternal choice of some persons unto everlasting life – not because of foreseen merit in them, but of his sheer mercy in Christ – in consequence of which choice they are called, justified, and glorified."

James Boyce

Genesis 13

Matthew Henry's introduction

In this chapter we have a further account about Abram.

I. In general, of his condition and behavior in the land of promise, which was now the land of his pilgrimage.
  A. His removes, vv. 1, 3, 4, 18.
  B. His riches, v. 2.
  C. His devotion, vv. 4, 18.

II. A particular account of a quarrel that happened between him and Lot.
  A. The unhappy occasion of their strife vv. 5, 6.
  B. The parties concerned in the strife, with the aggravation of it, v. 7.

III. The making up of the quarrel, through Abram's prudence, vv. 8, 9.

IV. Lot's departure from Abram to the plain of Sodom, vv. 10–13.

V. God's appearance to Abram, to confirm the promise of the land of Canaan to him, v. 14, etc.

A detailed analysis of chapter

Abram returns from of Egypt with great riches. (1–4)
Strife between the herdsmen of Abram and Lot.

Abram gives Lot his choice of the country. (5–9)
Lot chooses to live at Sodom. (10–13)
God renews his promise to Abram, who moves to Hebron. (14–18)

Key verse

Verse 7: "And there was a strife between the herdmen of Abram's cattle and the herdmen of Lot's cattle: and the Canaanite and the Perizzite dwelled then in the land."

Key word / key phrase

Verse 8, "quarrelling."

Key event / key person / key theme

Abram and Lot separate.

Key thought

Lot was asking for trouble by going close to the wicked people of Sodom.

Key thing to look out for

Abram shows his generous nature to Lot in allowing him to choose first where to live.

Key Bible cross-reference

Verse 16. See 28:14; 2 Chronicles 1:9.

Key "by way of explanation"

Verse 10, "well watered." Archaeological findings show that this area, which is now desert, was indeed once full of people who had good water supplies.

Key "Quotable Quote"

"God judged it better to bring good out of evil than to suffer no evil to exist."

Augustine of Hippo

Genesis 14

Matthew Henry's introduction

We have four things in the story of this chapter.

I. A war with the king of Sodom and his allies, vv. 1–11.
II. The captivity of Lot in that war, v. 12.
III. Abram's rescue of Lot from that captivity, with the victory he won over the conquerors, vv. 13–16.
IV. Abram's return from the expedition, v. 17, with an account of what passed,
  A. Between him and the king of Salem, vv. 18–20.
  B. Between him and the king of Sodom, vv. 21–24. So that here we have that promise to Abram in part fulfilled, that God would make his name great.

A detailed analysis of chapter

The battle of the kings, Lot is taken prisoner. (1–12)
Abram rescues Lot. (13–16)
Melchizedek blesses Abram. (17–20)
Abram restores the spoil. (21–24)

Key verse

Verse 18: "And Melchizedek king of Salem brought forth bread and wine: and he was the priest of the most high God."

Key word / key phrase

Verse 18, "Melchizedek."

Key event / key person / key theme

Abram rescues Lot.

Key thought

In the Bible, God is frequently identified as the Creator, see verse 19.

Key thing to look out for

Abraham's great wealth is indicated in many ways. See verse 14.

Key Bible cross-reference

Verse 18. See Psalm 110:4; Hebrews 7:11

Key "by way of explanation"

Verse 20. A tenth was the amount given to a king. See 1 Samuel 8: 15,17.

Key "Quotable Quote"

"By faith we are convinced that the signs of permanence, order, progress, which we observe in nature are true."

B.F. Westcott

Genesis 15

Matthew Henry's introduction

In this chapter we have a solemn treaty between God and Abram about a covenant that was to be established between them. In the previous chapter we had Abram in the field with kings; here we find him in the mount with God; and, though there he looked great, yet, I think, here he looks much greater: that honor have the great men of the world, but "this honor have all the saints." The covenant to be settled between God and Abram was a covenant of promises; accordingly, here is,

I. A general assurance of God's kindness and good-will to Abram, v. 1.

II. A particular declaration of the purposes of his love about him, in two things:

A. That he would give him many descendants, vv. 2–6.

B. That he would give him Canaan for an inheritance, vv. 7–21. Either an estate without an heir, or heir without an estate, would have been but a partial comfort to Abram. But God promises both to him; and that which made these two, the promised seed and the promised land, comforts indeed to this great believer was that they were both typical of those two invaluable blessings, Christ and heaven; and so, we have reason to think, Abram saw them.

A detailed analysis of chapter

God encourages Abram. (1)

The divine promise, Abraham is justified by faith. (2–6)

God promises Canaan to Abraham for an inheritance. (7–11)

The promise confirmed in a vision. (12–16)

The promise confirmed by a sign. (17–21)

Key verse

Verse 6: "And he believed in the Lord; and he counted it to him for righteousness."

Key word / key phrase

Verse 8, "Sovereign."

Key event / key person / key theme

God's covenant with Abram

Key thought

The first reference to anyone exercising faith in God's promises comes in verse 6.

Key thing to look out for

The greatness of God is seen in the number of stars. 8,000 stars can be seen in a clear Near-Eastern night sky.

Key Bible cross-reference

Verse 17. This symbolizes God's presence: see Exodus 3:2; 14:24; 19:18; 1 Kings 18: 38: Acts 2:3,4.

Key "by way of explanation"

Verse 9, "three years old." This was the specified age of most sacrificial animals, 1 Samuel 1:24.

Key "Quotable Quote"

"Our faith was prefigured in Abraham. He was the patriarch of our faith, and, as it were, the prophet of it, as the apostle very fully taught, when he says in the epistle to the Galatians: 'Even as Abraham believed God, and it was accounted unto him for righteousness. Know ye therefore, that they which are of faith, the same are the children of Abraham.' [Abraham's] faith and ours are one and the same."

Irenaeus

Genesis 16

Matthew Henry's introduction

Hagar is the main person in this chapter, an obscure Egyptian woman, whose name and story we never should have heard of if Providence had not brought her into the family of Abram. About her, we have four things in this chapter:

I. Her marriage to Abram her master, vv. 1–3.

II. Her misbehavior towards Sarai her mistress, vv. 4–6.

III. Her conversation with an angel that met her in her flight, vv. 7–14.

IV. Her delivery of a son, vv. 15, 16.

Analysis of chapter

Sarai gives Hagar to Abram. (1–3)

Hagar's misbehavior towards Sarai. (4–6)

The Angel commands Hagar to return, and the promise about the birth of Ishmael. (7–16)

Key verse

Verse 1: "Now Sarai Abram's wife bare him no children: and she had an handmaid, an Egyptian, whose name was Hagar."

Key word / key phrase

Verse 5, "despises."

Key event / key person / key theme

Hagar and Ishmael

Key thought

God cares for people, especially rejects of society.

Key thing to look out for

Sara's infertility illustrates that even in the most trying of situations God watches over his people.

Key Bible cross-reference

Angels are the Lord's messengers. See 19:1, 21; 31:11; Zechariah 3:1–6.

Key "by way of explanation"

Verse 5, "May the Lord judge between you and me," was a saying that indicated hatred, hostility, or suspicion. See 31:53.

Key "Quotable Quote"

"Afflictions make the heart more deep, more experimental, more knowing and profound, and so, more able to hold, to contain, and bear more."

John Bunyan

Genesis 17

Matthew Henry's introduction

This chapter contains articles of agreement covenanted between the great Jehovah, the Father of mercies, on the one part, and pious Abram, the father of the faithful, on the other part. Abram is therefore called "the friend of God," not only because he was the man of his counsel, but because he was the man of his covenant; both these secrets were with him. Mention was made of this covenant (15:18), but here it is particularly drawn up, and put into the form of a covenant, that Abram might have strong consolation. Here are,

I. The circumstances of the making of this covenant, the time and manner (v. 1), and the posture Abram was in, v. 3.

II. The covenant itself. In the general scope of it, v. 1. And, afterwards, in the particular instances.

A. That he should be the father of many nations (vv. 4, 6), and, to show this, his name was changed, v. 5.

B. That God would be a God to him and his seed, and would give them the land of Canaan, vv. 7, 8. And the seal of this part of the covenant was circumcision, vv. 9–14.

C. That he should have a son by Sarai, and so her name was changed, vv. 15, 16. This promise Abram received, v. 17. And his request for Ishmael, (v. 18) was answered, vv. 19–22.

III. The circumcision of Abram and his family, according to God's appointment, v. 23, etc.

A detailed analysis of chapter

God renews the covenant with Abram. (1–6)
Circumcision instituted. (7–14)
Sarai's name changed, Isaac promised. (15–22)
Abraham and his family are circumcised. (23–27)

Key verse

Verse 10: "This is my covenant, which ye shall keep, between me and you and thy seed after thee; Every man child among you shall be circumcised."

Key word / key phrase

Verse 11, "circumcision."

Key event / key person / key theme

The giving of circumcision as the sign of the covenant

Key thought

Verse 7. While we may break God's covenant, it still remains an everlasting covenant.

Key thing to look out for

God always requires his people to respond to his love: see verse 9.

Key Bible cross-reference

Verse 7. See Jeremiah 24:7; Ezekiel 24:30,31; Hosea 2:23 and Zechariah 8:8.

Key "by way of explanation"

Verse 19, God is referred to as "God Almighty." The Hebrew word here is "El-Shaddai," referring to God's power, and was the special name through which God revealed himself to the patriarchs.

Key "Quotable Quote"

"God defined: 'The One who loves.'"

Karl Barth

Genesis 18

Matthew Henry's introduction

We have an account in this chapter of another interview between God and Abraham, probably within a few days after the former, as the reward of his cheerful obedience to the law of circumcision. Here is,

I. The kind visit which God made him, and the entertainment which Abraham provided, vv. 1–8.

II. Their conversation.

A. The purposes of God's love about Sarah, vv. 9–15.

B. The purposes of God's wrath about Sodom. God's purpose in destroying Sodom, vv. 16–22. The intercession Abraham made for Sodom, v. 23, etc.

A detailed analysis of chapter

The Lord appears to Abraham. (1–8)

Sarah's unbelief reproved. (9–15)

God reveals to Abraham the destruction of Sodom. (16–22)

Abraham's intercession for Sodom. (23–33)

Key verse

Verse 32: "And he said, Oh let not the Lord be angry, and I will speak yet but this once: Peradventure ten shall be found there. And he said, I will not destroy it for ten's sake."

Key word / key phrase

Verse 25, "Judge."

Key event / key person / key theme

Abraham entertains three visitors.

Key thought

God's followers should always pray, no matter how bad the circumstances are.

Key thing to look out for

Abraham's persistence in many things, and here, his persistence in prayer.

Key Bible cross-reference

Verse 17. Abraham is said to have been God's friend: see 2 Chronicles 20:7; James 2:23.

Key "by way of explanation"

Verse 2 says there were "three men." At least two of these "men" were angels, see 19:1. That the third "man" was the Lord himself is supported by verse 18:19.

Key "Quotable Quote"

"Our valleys may be filled with foes and tears; but we can lift our eyes to the hills to see God and the angels, heaven's spectators, who support us according to God's infinite wisdom as they prepare our welcome home."

Billy Graham

Genesis 19

Matthew Henry's introduction

In this chapter we find, 2 Pet. 2:6–8, that "God, turning the cities of Sodom and Gomorrah into ashes, condemned them with an overthrow, and delivered just Lot." It is the history of Sodom's ruin, and Lot's rescue from that ruin. We read (ch. 18) of God's coming to take a view of the present state of Sodom, what its wickedness was, and what righteous people there were in it: now here we have the result of that enquiry.

I. It was found, on trial, that Lot was very good (vv. 1–3), and it did not appear that there was any more of the same character.

II. It was found that the Sodomites were very wicked and vile, vv. 4–11.

III. Special care was therefore taken for the securing of Lot and his family, in a place of safety, vv. 12–23.

IV. Mercy having rejoiced therein, justice shows itself in the ruin of Sodom and the death of Lot's wife (vv. 24–26), with a general repetition of the story, vv. 27–29.

V. A foul sin that Lot was guilty of, in committing incest with his two daughters, v. 30, etc.

A detailed analysis of chapter

The destruction of Sodom, and the deliverance of Lot. (1–29)

The sin and disgrace of Lot. (30–38)

Key verse

Verse 26: "But his wife looked back from behind him, and she became a pillar of salt."

Key word / key phrase

Verse 13, "destroy."

Key event / key person / key theme

The destruction of Sodom

Key thought

The blatant wickedness of the people of Sodom comes under God's judgment.

Key thing to look out for

Lot's initial reaction to the angel's command to flee was one of hesitation, verses 16–18.

Key Bible cross-reference

Lot's wife "looking back" became proverbial: see Luke 17:32.

Key "by way of explanation"

Verse 26, "a pillar of salt." Strange shapes from dried salt are seen to this day at the southern end of the Dead Sea.

Key "Quotable Quote"

"Moses here records the wonderful judgment of God, by which the wife of Lot was transformed into a statue of salt."

John Calvin

Genesis 20

Matthew Henry's introduction

We are here returning to the story of Abraham; yet that part of it which is here recorded is not to his honor. The fairest marbles have their flaws, and, while there are spots in the sun, we must not expect any thing spotless under it. The scripture is impartial in relating the blemishes even of its most celebrated characters. We have here,

I. Abraham's sin in denying his wife, and Abimelech's sin thereon in taking her, vv. 1, 2.

II. God's conversation with Abimelech in a dream, in which he shows him his error (v. 3), accepts his plea (vv. 4–6), and directs him to make restitution, v. 7.

III. Abimelech's conversation with Abraham, in which he chides him for the cheat he had put on him (vv. 8–10), and Abraham excuses it as well as he can, vv. 11–13.

IV. The good issue of the story, in which Abimelech restores Abraham his wife (vv. 14–16), and Abraham, by prayer, prevails with God for the removal of the judgment Abimelech was under, vv. 17, 18.

A detailed analysis of chapter

Abraham's stay at Gerar, Sarah is taken by Abimelech. (1–8)

Abimelech's rebuke to Abraham. (9–13)

Abimelech restores Sarah. (14–18)

Key verse

Verse 17: "So Abraham prayed unto God: and God healed Abimelech, and his wife, and his maidservants; and they bare children."

Key word / key phrase

Verse 5, "clear conscience."

Key event / key person / key theme

Abraham visits Abimelech.

Key thought

Sometimes God's followers are less righteous than those who do not profess to know God.

Key thing to look out for

The Bible's portraits of people includes "warts and all."

Key Bible cross-reference

In the Old Testament God often used dreams to reveal his will. See Numbers 12:6; Judges 7:13; Daniel 2:3.

Key "by way of explanation"

Verse 7. Abraham is the first person in the Bible to be given the title of prophet.

Key "Quotable Quote"

"It is profitable for the pious to be unsettled on earth, lest, by setting their minds on a commodious and quiet habitation, they should lose the inheritance of heaven."

John Calvin, commentating on Genesis 20:1

Genesis 21

Matthew Henry's introduction

In this chapter we have,

I. Isaac, the child of promise born into Abraham's family, vv. 1–8.

II. Ishmael, the son of the slave woman, cast out of it, vv. 9–21.

III. Abraham's pact with his neighbor Abimelech, vv. 22–32.

IV. His devotion to his God, v. 33.

A detailed analysis of chapter

Birth of Isaac, Sarah's joy. (1–8)

Ishmael mocks Isaac. (9–13)

Hagar and Ishmael are ejected, and they are comforted by an angel. (14–21)

Abimelech's covenant with Abraham. (22–34)

Key verse

Verse 2: "For Sarah conceived, and bare Abraham a son in his old age, at the set time of which God had spoken to him."

Key word / key phrase

Verse 1, "promised."

Key event / key person / key theme

The birth of Isaac

Key thought

God very often works "against all the odds."

Key thing to look out for

Behind what may be read as a story or historical event, the Bible writers expect us to detect God's providential hand.

Key Bible cross-reference

Verse 23, "kindness" is seen as an act of friendship. See verse 27; 20:14.

Key "by way of explanation"

Verse 8. It was quite normal for toddlers in the ancient Near East, as it is in Africa today, not to be weaned before they were two or three years old.

Key "Quotable Quote"

"The family should be a place where each new human being can have an early atmosphere conducive to the development of constructive creativity."

Edith Schaeffer

Genesis 22

Matthew Henry's introduction

We have here the famous story of Abraham's offering up his son Isaac, that is, his offering to offer him, which is justly looked on as one of the wonders of the church. Here is,

I. The strange command which God gave to Abraham about it, vv. 1, 2.

II. Abraham's strange obedience to this command, vv. 3–10.

III. The strange result of this trial.

A. The sacrificing of Isaac was countermanded, vv. 11, 12.
B. Another sacrifice was provided, vv. 13, 14.
C. The covenant was renewed with Abraham hereon, vv. 15–19. Lastly, an account of some of Abraham's relations, v. 20, etc.

A detailed analysis of chapter

God commands Abraham to sacrifice Isaac. (1, 2)
Abraham's faith and obedience to the divine command. (3–10)
Another sacrifice is provided in the place of Isaac. (11–14)
The covenant with Abraham renewed. (15–19)
The family of Nahor. (20–24)

Key verse

Verse 2: "And he said, Take now thy son, thine only son Isaac, whom thou lovest, and get thee into the land of Moriah; and offer him there for a burnt offering upon one of the mountains which I will tell thee of."

Key word / key phrase

Verse 8, "God himself will provide."

Key event / key person / key theme

Abraham's faith is tested.

Key thought

God asks Abraham to give up his most prized possession.

Key thing to look out for

Note how this event depicts the resurrection.

Key Bible cross-reference

Verse 8 says God provided a ram. Jesus was God's sacrificial lamb. See John 1:29, 36.

Key "by way of explanation"

Verse 13, "He went over and took the ram and sacrificed it as a burnt offering instead of his son." This is the first time that the concept of substitutionary sacrifice is mentioned in the Bible. See Mark 10:45.

Key "Quotable Quote"

"For family devotions, Martin Luther once read the account of Abraham offering Isaac on the altar in Genesis 22. His wife, Katie, said, 'I do not believe it. God would not have treated his son like that!' 'But, Katie,' Luther replied, 'he did.'"

Warren Wiersbe

Genesis 23

Matthew Henry's introduction

Here is,

I. Abraham a mourner for the death of Sarah, vv. 1, 2.
II. Abraham a purchaser of a burying-place for Sarah.
A. The purchase humbly proposed by Abraham, vv. 3, 4.
B. A fair deal, and agreed to, with a great deal of mutual civility and respect, vv. 5–16.
C. The purchase-money paid, v. 16.
D. The premises conveyed and secured to

Abraham, vv. 17, 18, 20.

E. Sarah's funeral, v. 19.

A detailed analysis of chapter

The death of Sarah. Abraham buys a burial place. (1–13)

Sarah's burial place. (14–20)

Key verse

Verse 2: "And Sarah died in Kirjatharba."

Key word / key phrase

Verse 6, "tomb/s."

Key event / key person / key theme

Sarah's death

Key thought

Abraham bought land in "the land of Canaan," verse 19, and so showed his faith in God's promise that Canaan would be his new homeland.

Key thing to look out for

The purchase of the cave of Machpelah, verse 9, became important later on. See 25:8–10; 49:30, 31; 50:12, 13.

Key Bible cross-reference

Verse 4. The patriarchs often referred to themselves as "aliens" or "strangers." See 1 Chronicles 29:15; Psalm 39:12.

Key "by way of explanation"

Verses 10–16. Abraham was coaxed into paying a high price for the land. But Abraham did not mind, as this land became the first part of a great inheritance.

Key "Quotable Quote"

"Faith has to do with things that are not seen, and hope with things that are not in hand."

Thomas Aquinas

Genesis 24

Matthew Henry's introduction

Marriages and funerals are the changes of families, and the common news among the inhabitants of the villages. In the previous chapter we had Abraham burying his wife, here we have him marrying his son. These stories about his family, with their minute circumstances, are related in detail, while the histories of the kingdoms of the world then in being, with their revolutions, are buried in silence; for the Lord knows those who are his. The subjoining of Isaac's marriage to Sarah's funeral shows us that as "one generation passes away another generation comes." Here is,

I. Abraham's care about his son's marriage, and the charge he gave to his servant about it, vv. 1–9.

II. His servant's journey into Abraham's country, to seek a wife for his young master among his own relations, vv. 10–14.

III. The providence which brought him to find Rebekah, whose father was Isaac's cousin, vv. 15–28.

IV. The treaty of marriage with her relations, vv. 29–49.

V. Their consent obtained, vv. 50–60.

VI. The happy meeting and marriage between Isaac and Rebekah, v. 61, etc.

A detailed analysis of chapter

Abraham's concern for Isaac's marriage. (1–9)

The journey of Abraham's servant to Mesopotamia, his meeting with Rebekah. (10–28)

Rebekah and her relatives consent to her marriage. (29–53)

The happy meeting and marriage of Isaac and Rebekah. (54–67)

Key verse

Verse 3: "And I will make thee swear by the Lord, the God of heaven, and the God of the earth, that thou shalt not take a wife unto my son of the daughters of the Canaanites, among whom I dwell."

Key word / key phrase

Verse 7, "promised."

Key event / key person / key theme

Rebekah becomes Isaac's wife.

Key thought

This chapter revolves around the faith and faithfulness of an unnamed servant.

Key thing to look out for

The unnamed servant was not ashamed to acknowledge God. "I praised the Lord," verse 48.

Key Bible cross-reference

Verse 40. See 5:22; 6:8, 9; 17:1.

Key "by way of explanation"

Verse 11. Women went out to wells "towards evening," as that was the coolest part of the day.

Key "Quotable Quote"

"Faithfulness in little things is a big thing."

John Chrysostom

Genesis 25

Matthew Henry's introduction

The sacred historian, in this chapter,

I. Takes his leave of Abraham, with an account,

A. Of his children by another wife, vv. 1–4.

B. Of his last will and testament, vv. 5, 6.

C. Of his age, death, and burial, vv. 7–10.

II. He takes his leave of Ishmael, with a short account,

A. Of his children, vv. 12–16.

B. Of his age and death, vv. 17, 18.

III. He begins the history of Isaac.

A. His prosperity, v. 11.

B. The conception and birth of his two sons, with the oracle of God about them, vv. 19–26.

C. Their different characters, vv. 27, 28.

D. Esau's selling his birthright to Jacob, vv. 29–34.

A detailed analysis of chapter

Abraham's family by Keturah, his death and burial. (1–10)

God blesses Isaac, and the descendants of Ishmael. (11–18)

The birth of Esau and Jacob. (19–26)

The different characters of Esau and Jacob. (27, 28)

Esau despises and sells his birthright. (29–34)

Key verse

Verse 8: “Then Abraham gave up the ghost, and died in a good old age, an old man, and full of years; and was gathered to his people.”

Key word / key phrase

Verse 24, “birth.”

Key event / key person / key theme

Abraham’s death

Key thought

When Rebekah was barren “Isaac prayed to the Lord,” verse 21.

Key thing to look out for

Verse 23 states that the elder will serve the younger and this illustrates God’s love in his election of anyone for salvation.

Key Bible cross-reference

“Esau despised his birthright,” verse 34, thus showing his godlessness. See Hebrews 12:16.

Key “by way of explanation”

Verse 26, “Jacob.” This name means “he grasps the heel.” Figuratively speaking it means “to deceive.” Jacob became a proverbial name for a deceptive person.

Key “Quotable Quote”

“Dare to be true:
Nothing can need a lie;
A fault, which needs it most, grows two thereby.”

George Herbert

Genesis 26

Matthew Henry’s introduction

In this chapter we have,

I. Isaac in adversity, because of a famine in the land, which,
  A. Obliges him to change his quarters, v. 1.
  B. But, God visits him with direction and comfort, vv. 2–5.
  C. He foolishly denies his wife, and is reproved for it by Abimelech, vv. 6–11.

II. Isaac in prosperity, by the blessing of God on him, vv. 12–14. And,
  A. The Philistines were envied him, vv. 14–17.
  B. He continued industrious in his business, vv. 18–23.
  C. God appeared to him, and encouraged him, and he devoutly acknowledged God, vv. 24, 25.
  D. The Philistines made a covenant with him, vv. 26–33.
  E. The disagreeable marriage of his son Esau was an alloy to the comfort of his prosperity, vv. 34, 35.

A detailed analysis of chapter

Isaac, because of famine, goes to Gerar. (1–5)

He denies his wife and is reproved by Abimelech. (6–11)

Isaac grows rich, and the Philistines envy him. (12–17)

Isaac digs wells and God blesses him. (18–25)

Abimelech makes a covenant with Isaac. (26–33)

Esau’s wives. (34, 35)

Key verse

Verse 2: "And the Lord appeared unto him, and said, Go not down into Egypt; dwell in the land which I shall tell thee of."

Key word / key phrase

Verse 3, "bless."

Key event / key person / key theme

Isaac meets Abimelech.

Key thought

God's promises are always spiritually reviving. See verse 3.

Key thing to look out for

Esau showed his godlessness by marrying a Hittite, that is, Canaanite woman, verse 34.

Key Bible cross-reference

Verse 20. There were frequent disputes about wells and water rights where water was so scarce. See 13:6–11; 21:25; 36:7.

Key "by way of explanation"

Verse 30, "feast." Covenant agreements often concluded with a feast or shared meal, which was a further token of friendship between the two parties. See 31:54; Exodus 24:11.

Key "Quotable Quote"

"The Christian's faith is strengthened as he keeps the promises of God before him and considers, not the difficulties in the way of the things promised, but the character and resources of God who has made the promise."

Paul Little

Genesis 27

Matthew Henry's introduction

In this chapter we return to the typical story of the struggle between Esau and Jacob. Esau had profanely sold the birthright to Jacob; but Esau hopes not to loose out as he preserves his interest in his father's affections, and so secures the blessing. Here therefore we find how he was justly punished for his contempt of the birthright, with the loss of the blessing, of which Jacob fraudulently deprives him. Thus this story is explained, Heb. 12:16, 17, "Because he sold the birthright, when he would have inherited the blessing he was rejected." For those that make light of the name and profession of religion, and throw them away for a trifle, forfeit its powers and privileges. We have here,

I. Isaac's desire to bless Esau, vv. 1–5.

II. Rebekah's plot to procure it for Jacob, vv. 6–17.

III. Jacob's success in obtaining the blessing, vv. 18–29.

IV. Esau's resentment of this, in which,

A. His great importunity with his father to obtain a blessing, vv. 30–40.

B. His great enmity towards his brother for defrauding him of the first blessing, v. 41, etc.

A detailed analysis of chapter

Isaac sends Esau for venison. (1–5)

Rebekah tells Jacob how to obtain the blessing. (6–17)

Jacob, pretending to be Esau, obtains the blessing. (18–29)

Isaac's fear, Esau's importunity. (30–40)

Esau threatens Jacob's life, Rebekah sends Jacob away. (41–46)

Key verse

Verse 3: "Now therefore take, I pray thee, thy weapons, thy quiver and thy bow, and go out to the field, and take me some venison."

Key word / key phrase

"Bless" or "blessing" come twenty-four times in this chapter.

Key event / key person / key theme

Jacob obtains Isaac's blessing through deceit.

Key thought

To live by deception brings people down.

Key thing to look out for

Rebekah's favoritism among her children reaped a terrible harvest. See 25:28.

Key Bible cross-reference

Verse 27. Jesus was also betrayed with a kiss. See Matthew 26:48, 49.

Key "by way of explanation"

Verse 1. Blindness among old people was even more common then than now. See 48:10; 1 Samuel 4:15.

Key "Quotable Quote"

"We are experts at deceiving others and ourselves too!"

Erwin W. Lutzer

Genesis 28

Matthew Henry's introduction

We have here,

I. Jacob parting with his parents, to go to Padan-aram; the charge his father gave him (vv. 1, 2), the blessing he sent him away with (vv. 3, 4), his obedience to the orders given him (vv. 5, 10), and the influence this had on Esau, vv. 6–9.

II. Jacob meeting with God, and his communion with him by the way. And there,

A. His vision of the ladder, vv. 11, 12.

B. The gracious promises God made him, vv. 13–15.

C. The impression this made on him, vv. 16–19.

D. The vow he made to God, on this occasion, v. 20, etc.

A detailed analysis of chapter

Isaac sends Jacob to Padan-aram. (1–5)

Esau marries the daughter of Ishmael. (6–9)

Jacob's vision. (10–15)

The stone of Bethel. (16–19)

Jacob's vow. (20–22)

Key verse

Verse 5: "And Isaac sent away Jacob: and he went to Padanaram unto Laban, son of Bethuel the Syrian, the brother of Rebekah, Jacob's and Esau's mother."

Key word / key phrase

Verse 12, "dream."

Key event / key person / key theme

Jacob's famous dream

Key thought

Verse 15. God promises to bless us, despite our failings.

Key thing to look out for

Verse 20. Jacob, despite his past deception, now seeks to honor God.

Key Bible cross-reference

Verse 12. See what Jesus had to say about this: John 1:51. Also see John 14:6 and 1 Timothy 2:5.

Key "by way of explanation"

Verse 4. Paul applied this verse to Christians. See Galatians 3:14.

Key "Quotable Quote"

"What greater insult . . . can there be to God, than not to believe his promises?"

Martin Luther

Genesis 29

Matthew Henry's introduction

This chapter gives us an account of God's providences about Jacob, pursuant to the promises made to him in the previous chapter.

I. How he was brought in safety to his journey's end, and directed to his relations there, who bade him welcome, vv. 1–14.

II. How he was comfortably disposed of in marriage, vv. 15–30.

III. How his family was built up in the birth of four sons, vv. 31–35. The affairs of princes and mighty nations that were then in being are not recorded in the book of God, but are left to be buried in oblivion; while these small domestic concerns of holy Jacob are particularly recorded with their minute circumstances, that they may be in everlasting remembrance. For "the memory of the just is blessed."

A detailed analysis of chapter

Jacob comes to the well of Haran. (1–8)

Jacob meets Rachel, Laban entertains him. (9–14)

Jacob's covenant for Rachel, Laban's deceit. (15–30)

Leah's sons. (31–35)

Key verse

Verse 6: "Rachel his daughter cometh with the sheep."

Key word / key phrase

Verse 20, "love."

Key event / key person / key theme

Jacob marries Leah before he can marry Rachel.

Key thought

The great deceiver is himself deceived.

Key thing to look out for

Through the many ups and downs of his life Jacob experienced God's providential care.

Key Bible cross-reference

Verse 22. It was not uncommon for feasts to last up to seven days: see verses 27,28; Judges 14:10, 12.

Key "by way of explanation"

Verse 9. Rachel is called a "shepherdess" as the work of shepherding flocks was done by both men and women then.

Key "Quotable Quote"

"Many times divine providence intervenes in our matters, to make us correct ourselves."

Basil the Great

Genesis 30

Matthew Henry's introduction

In this chapter we have an account of the increase,

I. Of Jacob's family. Eight children more we find registered in this chapter; Dan and Naphtali by Bilhah, Rachel's maid, vv. 1–8. Gad and Asher by Zilpah, Leah's maid, vv. 9–13. Issachar, Zebulun, and Dinah, by Leah, vv. 14–21. And, last of all, Joseph, by Rachel, vv. 22–24.

II. Of Jacob's estate. He makes a new bargain with Laban, vv. 25–34. And in the six years' further service he did to Laban God wonderfully blessed him, so that his stock of cattle became very considerable, vv. 35–43. Herein was fulfilled the blessing with which Isaac dismissed him (28:3), "God make thee fruitful, and multiply thee." Even these small matters about Jacob's house and field, though they seem inconsiderable, are improvable for our learning. For the scriptures were written, not for princes and statesmen, to instruct them in politics; but for all people, even the meanest, to direct them in their families and callings: yet some things are here recorded about Jacob, not for imitation, but for admonition.

A detailed analysis of chapter

A further account of Jacob's family. (1–13)
Rachel bears Joseph. (14–24)
Jacob's new agreement with Laban to serve him for cattle. (25–43)

Key verse

Verse 1: "And when Rachel saw that she bare Jacob no children, Rachel envied her sister; and said unto Jacob, Give me children, or else I die."

Key word / key phrase

Verse 31, "flocks."

Key event / key person / key theme

Jacob's flocks increase, and so his wealth.

Key thought

Although Jacob was one of the patriarchs, he continued to live by deception.

Key thing to look out for

God does not withhold his blessings just because we are unholy.

Key Bible cross-reference

Verse 27, "divination." See Ezekiel 21:21; Acts 16:16; Leviticus 19:26; Deuteronomy 18:10, 14.

Key "by way of explanation"

Verse 23. Barrenness was thought to be a disgrace and a sign of God's disfavor.

Key "Quotable Quote"

"We all bow down before wealth. It is a homage resulting from a profound faith that with wealth we may do all things."

Augustine of Hippo

Genesis 31

Matthew Henry's introduction

Jacob was a very honest good man, a man of great devotion and integrity, yet he had more trouble and vexation than any of the patriarchs. He left his father's house in a fright, went to his uncle's in distress, very hard usage he met with there, and now is going back surrounded with fears. Here is,

I. His resolution to return, vv. 1–16.
II. His clandestine departure, vv. 17–21.
III. Laban's pursuit of him in displeasure, vv. 22–25.
IV. The hot words that passed between them, vv. 26–42.
V. Their amicable agreement at last, v. 43, etc.).

A detailed analysis of chapter

Jacob leaves secretly. (1–21)
Laban pursues Jacob. (23–35)
Jacob's complaint and Laban's response. (36–42)
Their covenant at Galeed. (43–55)

Key verse

Verse 3: "And the Lord said unto Jacob, Return unto the land of thy fathers, and to thy kindred; and I will be with thee."

Key word / key phrase

Verse 11, "dream."

Key event / key person / key theme

Jacob leaves Laban.

Key thought

God does not always tell people to do things they do not want to do.

Key thing to look out for

God frequently promises that his presence will go with his servants.

Key Bible cross-reference

Verse 48. See Joshua 22:10–12, 34.

Key "by way of explanation"

Verse 19. "Household gods" belonged to a pagan belief that these small, portable, gods could bring "good luck" to their owners.

Key "Quotable Quote"

"The best of all is, God is with us."

John Wesley

Genesis 32

Matthew Henry's introduction

We have here Jacob still on his journey towards Canaan. Never did so many memorable things occur in any march as in this of Jacob's little family. By the way he meets,

I. With good tidings from his God, vv. 1, 2.

II. With bad tidings from his brother, to whom he sent a message to notify his return, vv. 3–6. In his distress,

A. He divides his company, vv. 7, 8.

B. He makes his prayer to God, vv. 9–12.

C. He sends a present to his brother, vv. 13–23.

D. He wrestles with the angel, vv. 24–32.

A detailed analysis of chapter

Jacob's vision at Mahanaim, his fear of Esau. (1–8)

Jacob's earnest prayer for deliverance, he prepares a present for Esau. (9–23)

He wrestles with the angel. (24–32)

Key verse

Verse 25: "And when he saw that he prevailed not against him, he touched the hollow of his thigh; and the hollow of Jacob's thigh was out of joint, as he wrestled with him."

Key word / key phrase

Verse 26, "bless."

Key event / key person / key theme

Jacob wrestles with God.

Key thought

God met Jacob at the critical points in his life.

Key thing to look out for

Jacob had something physically wrong with him to remind him of God's presence.

Key Bible cross-reference

Verse 12. See 28:14; 22:17.

Key "by way of explanation"

Verse 30. It was thought that if you saw God you would die. That is why, in a symbolic sense, only God's "back" Exodus 33:23, or "feet" Exodus 24:10 might be seen.

Key "Quotable Quote"

"Fear imprisons, faith liberates; fear paralyzes, faith empowers; fear disheartens, faith encourages; fear sickens, faith heals; fear makes useless, faith makes serviceable; most of all, fear puts hopelessness at the heart of life, while faith rejoices in its God."

H.E. Fosdick

Genesis 33

Matthew Henry's introduction

We read, in the previous chapter, how Jacob had power with God, and prevailed; here we find what power he had with men too, and how his brother Esau was mollified, and, on a sudden, reconciled to him; for so it is written, Prov. 16:7, "When a man's ways please the Lord, he maketh even his enemies to be at peace with him." Here is,

I. A very friendly meeting between Jacob and Esau, vv. 1–4.

II. Their conversation at their meeting, in which they vie with each other in civil and kind expressions. Their conversation is,

A. About Jacob's family, vv. 5–7.

B. About the present he had sent, vv. 8–11.

C. About the progress of their journey, vv. 12–15.

III. Jacob's settlement in Canaan, his house, ground, and altar, vv. 16–20.

A detailed analysis of chapter

The friendly meeting between Jacob and Esau. (1–16)

Jacob comes to Succoth and Shechem, he builds an altar. (17–20)

Key verse

Verse 1: "And Jacob lifted up his eyes, and looked, and, behold, Esau came, and with him four hundred men"

Key word / key phrase

Verse 3, "bowed down."

Key event / key person / key theme

Jacob meets Esau.

Key thought

Reconciliation should never be ruled out.

Key thing to look out for

Jacob took great pains to make amends for his previous evil behavior.

Key Bible cross-reference

Verse 18, "Shechem." See 12:6; John 4:5–6. There is a well to this day at Shechem.

Key "by way of explanation"

Verse 3. Bowing down seven times is documented in the texts discovered at Tell el-Amarna in Egypt, and indicates total submission.

Key "Quotable Quote"

"All who strive for reconciliation seek to listen rather than to convince, to understand rather than to impose themselves."

Brother Roger of Taizé

Genesis 34

Matthew Henry's introduction

At this chapter begins the story of Jacob's afflictions in his children, which were very great, and are recorded to show, The vanity of this world. That which is dearest to us may prove our greatest vexation, and we may meet with the greatest crosses in those things of which we said, "This same shall comfort us." The common griefs of good people. Jacob's children were circumcised, were well taught, and prayed for, and had very good examples set them; yet some of them proved very untoward. "The race is not to the swift, nor the battle to the strong." Grace does not run in the blood, and yet the interrupting of the entail of grace does not cut off the entail of profession and visible church-privileges: nay, Jacob's sons, though they were his grief in some things, yet were all taken into covenant with God. In this chapter we have,

I. Dinah debauched, vv. 1–5.

II. A treaty of marriage between her and Shechem who had defiled her, vv. 6–19.

III. The circumcision of the Shechemites, pursuant to that treaty, vv. 20–24.

IV. The perfidious and bloody revenge which Simeon and Levi took on them, vv. 25–31.

A detailed analysis of chapter

Dinah defiled by Shechem. (1–19)

The Shechemites murdered by Simeon and Levi. (20–31)

Key verse

Verse 5: "And Jacob heard that he had defiled Dinah his daughter."

Key word / key phrase

Verse 2, "raped."

Key event / key person / key theme

Dinah is raped.

Key thought

The name of God comes in the last verse of chapter 33, and it starts chapter 35, but it is absent from this horrific chapter.

Key thing to look out for

Sin leads to sin. The revenge exacted for Shechem's evil deed seems disproportionate. See verses 25–31.

Key Bible cross-reference

Verse 2, "Shechem." The person was probably named after the city of that name. See 33:19.

Key "by way of explanation"

Verse 20, "the gate of their city." The gate of a city acted as a meeting place for business and as an open-air courtroom.

Key "Quotable Quote"

"Man must evolve for all human conflict a method which rejects revenge, aggression and retaliation. The foundation of such a method is love."

Martin Luther King, Jr.

Genesis 35

Matthew Henry's introduction

In this chapter we have three communions and three funerals.

I. Three communions between God and Jacob.

A. God ordered Jacob to Beth-el; and, in obedience to that order, he purged his house of idols, and prepared for that journey, vv. 1–5.

B. Jacob built an altar at Beth-el, to the honor of God that had appeared to him, and in performance of his vow, vv. 6, 7.

C. God appeared to him again, and confirmed the change of his name and covenant with him (vv. 9–13), of which appearance Jacob made a grateful acknowledgment, vv. 14, 15.

II. Three funerals.

A. Deborah's, v. 8.

B. Rachel's, vv. 16–20.

C. Isaac's, vv. 27–29. Here is also Reuben's incest (v. 22), and an account of Jacob's sons, vv. 23–26.

A detailed analysis of chapter

God commands Jacob to go to Bethel, he puts away idols from his family. (1–5)

Jacob builds an altar, the death of Deborah. God blesses Jacob. (6–15)

Death of Rachel. (16–20)

Reuben's crime, and the death of Isaac. (21–29)

Key verse

Verse 1: "And God said unto Jacob, Arise, go up to Bethel, and dwell there: and make there an altar unto God, that appeared unto thee when thou fleddest from the face of Esau thy brother."

Key word / key phrase

Verse 1, "Bethel."

Key event / key person / key theme

Rachel and Isaac die.

Key thought

Jacob insists that the people be pure before God.

Key thing to look out for

Once again God reassures Jacob of his presence.

Key Bible cross-reference

Verse 4, "rings." See Hosea 2:13. Rings here were worn as pagan charms.

Key "by way of explanation"

Verse 10. To the name "Jacob" is now added "Israel." See 32:28. For other instances of name-changing compare 21:31 with 26:33, and 28:19 with 35:15.

Key "Quotable Quote"

"You will never be able to pray everywhere all the time until you have learned to pray somewhere some of the time."

Dalrymple

Genesis 36

Matthew Henry's introduction

In this chapter we have an account of the posterity of Esau, who, from him, were called Edomites, that Esau who sold his birthright, and lost his blessing, and was not loved of God as Jacob was. Here is a brief register kept of his family for some generations. Because he was the son of Isaac, for whose sake this honor is put on him. Because the Edomites were neighbors to Israel, and their genealogy would shed light to the following stories of what passed between them. It is to show the performance of the promise to Abraham, that he should be "the father of many nations," and of that answer which Rebekah had from the oracle she consulted, "Two nations are in thy womb," and of the blessing of Isaac, "Thy dwelling shall be the fatness of the earth." We have here,

I. Esau's wives, vv. 1–5.

II. His move to mount Seir, vv. 6–8.

III. The names of his sons, vv. 9–14.

IV. Those who descended from his sons, vv. 15–19.

V. The leaders of the Horites, vv. 20–30.

VI. The kings and leaders of Edom, vv. 31–43. Little more is recorded than their names, because the history of those that were out of the church would have been of little use in divinity. It is in the church that the memorable instances are found of special grace, and special providence. This chapter is abridged, 1 Chron. 1:35, etc.

A detailed analysis of chapter

Esau and his descendants. (1–43)

Key verse

Verse 1: "Now these are the generations of Esau, who is Edom."

Key word / key phrase

Verse 1, "Esau."

Key event / key person / key theme

Esau's descendants

Key thought

Our times are in God's hands.

Key thing to look out for

Christians are supposed to care for their close family.

Key Bible cross-reference

As Eliphaz, verse 11, was also the name of one of Job's so-called comforters, and since Job was from the land of Uz, Job 1:1, it has been thought that Job may have lived in Edom. See verses 28, 34.

Key "by way of explanation"

Verses 10–14 and verses 15–19 have a list of identical names in them. The first list is of Esau's descendants and the second is a list of the tribal chiefs.

Key "Quotable Quote"

"He who loves not his wife and children feeds a lioness at home and broods a nest of sorrows."

Jeremy Taylor

Genesis 37

Matthew Henry's introduction

At this chapter begins the story of Joseph, who, in every subsequent chapter but one to the end of this book, is the leading figure. He was Jacob's eldest son by his beloved wife Rachel, born, as many eminent men were, of a mother that had been long barren. His story is so remarkably divided between his humiliation and his exaltation that we cannot avoid seeing something of Christ in it, who was first humbled and then exalted, and, in many instances, is the type of Joseph. It also shows the lot of Christians, who must through many tribulations enter into the kingdom. In this chapter we have,

I. The malice his brethren bore against him. They hated him,
   - A. Because he informed his father of their wickedness, vv. 1, 2.
   - B. Because his father loved him, vv. 3, 4.
   - C. Because he dreamed of his dominion over them, vv. 5–11.

II. The mischiefs his brethren designed and did to him.
   - A. The kind visit he made gave an opportunity, vv. 12–17.
   - B. They designed to slay him, but determined to starve him, vv. 18–24.
   - C. They changed their purpose, and sold him for a slave, vv. 25–28.
   - D. They made their father believe that he was torn in pieces, vv. 29–35.
   - E. He was sold into Egypt to Potiphar, v. 36.

   And all this was working together for good.

A detailed analysis of chapter

Joseph is loved by Jacob, but hated by his brothers. (1–4)

Joseph's dreams. (5–11)

Jacob sends Joseph to visit his brothers, and they plot to kill him. (12–22)

Joseph's brothers sell him. (23–10)

Jacob deceived, and Joseph sold to Potiphar. (31–36)

Key verse

Verse 5: "And Joseph dreamed a dream."

Key word / key phrase

Verse 5, "dream," which comes nine times in this chapter.

Key event / key person / key theme

Joseph the dreamer

Key thought

There is no suggestion in this chapter that Joseph was showing off.

Key thing to look out for

Joseph knew, with hindsight, that God was looking after him. See verse 36.

Key Bible cross-reference

Verse 3. There have been many suggestions about the meaning of the Hebrew word, translated in the *King James Version* as "of many colors." The coat was certainly a mark of his father's favoritism. See 2 Samuel 13:18.

Key "by way of explanation"

Verse 1, "Canaan." Jacob made his home in Canaan, the promised land, and was buried there, 49:29–30; 50:13. Joseph also ensured that he was buried there, 50:24, 25.

Key "Quotable Quote"

"Every Christian family ought to be, as it were, a little church consecrated to Christ, and wholly influenced and governed by his rules."

Jonathan Edwards

Genesis 38

Matthew Henry's introduction

This chapter gives us an account of Judah and his family, and such an account it is that one would wonder that, of all Jacob's sons, our Lord should spring out of Judah, Heb. 7:14. If we were to form a character of him by this story, we should not say, "Judah, thou art he whom thy brethren shall praise," 49:8. But God will show that his choice is of grace and not of merit, and that Christ came into the world to save sinners, even the chief, and is not ashamed, on their repentance, to be allied to them, also that the worth and worthiness of Jesus Christ are personal, of himself, and not derived from his ancestors. Humbling himself to be "made in the likeness of sinful flesh," he was pleased to descend from some that were infamous. We have, in this chapter,

I. Judah's marriage and issue, and the untimely death of his two eldest sons, vv. 1–11.

II. Judah's incest with his daughter-in- law Tamar, without his knowing it, vv. 12–23.

III. His confusion, when it was discovered, vv. 24–26.

IV. The birth of his twin sons, in whom his family was built up, v. 27, etc.

A detailed analysis of chapter

The profligate behavior of Judah and his family. (1–30)

Key verse

Verse 1: "And it came to pass at that time, that Judah went down from his brethren."

Key word / key phrase

Verse 18, "seal."

Key event / key person / key theme

Judah treats his daughter-in-law, Tamar, as a prostitute.

Key thought

Judge not and you will not be judged.

Key thing to look out for

Jesus spoke out strongly against hypocrites.

Key Bible cross-reference

Verse 8 refers to levirate marriage. See Deuteronomy 25:5, 6; Matthew 22:24; Ruth 4:5.

Key "by way of explanation"

Verse 14. Prostitutes often positioned themselves along a roadside. See Jeremiah 3:2.

Key "Quotable Quote"

"The knowledge of God, and the remembrance of his all-seeing presence, are the most powerful means against hypocrisy."

Richard Baxter

Genesis 39

Matthew Henry's introduction

At this chapter we return to the story of Joseph. We have him here,

I. A servant, a slave in Potiphar's house (v. 1), and yet there greatly honored and favored,

A. By the providence of God, which made him, in effect, a master, vv. 2–6.

B. By the grace of God, which made him more than a conqueror over a strong temptation to uncleanness, vv. 7–12.

II. We have him here a sufferer, falsely accused (vv. 13–18), imprisoned (vv. 19, 20), and yet his imprisonment made both honorable and comfortable by the tokens of God's special presence with him, vv. 21–23. And herein Joseph was a type of Christ, "who took on him the form of a servant," and yet then did that which made it evident that "God was with him," who was tempted by Satan, but overcame the temptation, who was falsely accused and bound, and yet had all things committed to his hand.

A detailed analysis of chapter

Joseph is chosen by Potiphar. (1–6)
Joseph resists temptation. (7–12)
Joseph is falsely accused by his master's wife. (13–18)
He is thrown into prison, God is with him there. (19–23)

Key verse

Verse 1: "And Joseph was brought down to Egypt."

Key word / key phrase

Verse 19, "prison."

Key event / key person / key theme

Joseph resists Potiphar's wife's advances.

Key thought

Doing right does not always seem to pay.

Key thing to look out for

Verse 21. Even in prison Joseph experienced the Lord's kindness.

Key Bible cross-reference

Verse 6. Joseph is said to have been given full responsibility on two other occasions. See verses 22, 23 and 41:41.

Key "by way of explanation"

Verse 2. In the account of Joseph it is often stressed that the Lord was with him. See verses 3, 21, 23, and 26:3, and Acts 7:9.

Key "Quotable Quote"

"The one and only infallible way to go safely through all the difficulties, trials, temptations, dryness, or opposition of our own evil tempers is this: It is to expect nothing from ourselves, to trust to nothing in ourselves, but in everything to expect and depend upon God for relief."

William Law

Genesis 40

Matthew Henry's introduction

In this chapter things are working, though slowly, towards Joseph's advancement.

I. Two of Pharaoh's servants are committed to prison, and there to Joseph's care, and so become witnesses of his extraordinary conduct, vv. 1–4.

II. They each dreamed a dream, which Joseph interpreted (vv. 5–19), and the event verified the interpretation (vv. 20–22), and so they became witnesses of his extraordinary skill.

III. Joseph recommends his case to one of them, whose preferment he foresaw (vv. 14, 15), but in vain, v. 23.

A detailed analysis of chapter

Pharaoh's chief butler and baker in prison, and their dreams interpreted by Joseph. (1–19)
The ingratitude of the chief butler. (20–23)

Key verse

Verse 23: "Yet did not the chief butler remember Joseph, but forgat him."

Key word / key phrase

Verse 16, "interpretation."

Key event / key person / key theme

The cupbearer and the baker

Key thought

Waiting is not easy for anyone. The cupbearer forgot about Joseph for two years.

Key thing to look out for

Verse 15. Joseph was more than once a victim of injustice.

Key Bible cross-reference

Verse 8 states that only God can correctly interpret dreams. See 41:16, 25, 28; Daniel 2:28.

Key "by way of explanation"

Verse 5. People in the ancient Near East believed that dreams had meanings.

Key "Quotable Quote"

"The dungeon became to me as it were a palace."

Perpetua, the Christian martyr

Genesis 41

Matthew Henry's introduction

Two things Providence is here bringing about:

I. The advancement of Joseph.

II. The maintenance of Jacob and his family in a time of famine; for the eyes of the Lord run to and fro through the earth, and direct the affairs of the children of men for the benefit of those few whose hearts are upright with him. In order to these, we have here,

A. Pharaoh's dreams, vv. 1–8.

B. The recommendation of Joseph to him for an interpreter, vv. 9–13.

C. The interpretation of the dreams, and the prediction of seven years of plenty and seven years of famine in Egypt, with the prudent advice given to Pharaoh thereon, vv. 14–36.

D. The preferment of Joseph to a place of the highest power and trust in Egypt, vv. 37–45.

E. The accomplishment of Joseph's prediction, and his fidelity to his trust, v. 46, etc.

A detailed analysis of chapter

Pharaoh's dreams. (1–8)

Joseph interprets Pharaoh's dreams. (9–32)

Joseph's counsel, and his promotion. (33–45)

Joseph's children, and the beginning of the famine. (46–57)

Key verse

Verse 14: "Then Pharaoh sent and called Joseph, and they brought him hastily out of the dungeon: and he shaved himself, and changed his raiment, and came in unto Pharaoh."

Key word / key phrase

Verse 8, "dreams," mentioned thirteen times in this chapter.

Key event / key person / key theme

Joseph is released from prison.

Key thought

Verse 38. Pharaoh recognized God's Spirit at work in Joseph.

Key thing to look out for

Verse 16. Joseph made sure that Pharaoh knew that his ability to interpret dreams was God-given.

Key Bible cross-reference

Verse 16. See 40:4; Daniel 2:27, 28, 30; 2 Corinthians 3:5.

Key "by way of explanation"

Verse 40. Pharaoh ordered that people should "submit" to Joseph. Literally this means to kiss his hands and feet, as a sign of giving him homage. See Psalm 2:12.

Key "Quotable Quote"

"Someone defined responsibility as 'our response to God's ability.'"

Warren Wiersbe

Genesis 42

Matthew Henry's introduction

We had, in the previous chapter, the fulfilling of the dreams which Joseph had interpreted: in this and the following chapters we have the fulfilling of the dreams which Joseph himself had dreamed, that his father's family should do homage to him. The story is very largely and particularly related of what happened between Joseph and his brethren, not only because it is an entertaining story, and probably was much talked of, both among the Israelites and among the Egyptians, but because it is very instructive, and it gave occasion for the removal of Jacob's family into Egypt, on which so many great events afterwards depended. We have, in this chapter,

I. The humble application of Jacob's sons to Joseph to buy corn, vv. 1–6.

II. The fright Joseph put them into, for their trial, vv. 7–20.

III. The conviction they were now under of their sin about Joseph long before, vv. 21–24.

IV. Their return to Canaan with corn, and he great distress their good father was in on hearing the account of their expedition, v. 25, etc.

A detailed analysis of chapter

Jacob sends ten sons to buy corn. (1–6)

Joseph's treatment of his brothers. (7–20)

Their remorse, Simeon detained. (21–24)

The rest return with corn. (25–28)

Jacob refuses to send Benjamin to Egypt. (29–38)

Key verse

Verse 2: "And he said, Behold, I have heard that there is corn in Egypt: get you down thither, and buy for us from thence; that we may live, and not die."

Key word / key phrase

Verse 5, "famine."

Key event / key person / key theme

Joseph's brothers go to Egypt in search of food.

Key thought

The circumstances in which Joseph's first dreams would come true were taking shape.

Key thing to look out for

Verse 21. The brothers' sense of guilt.

Key Bible cross-reference

Verse 15, "As surely as Pharaoh lives." It was

common for solemn oaths to be taken in the name of rulers, Psalm 16:4, or of the Lord himself, Judges 8:19; 1 Samuel 14:39, 45.

Key "by way of explanation"

Verse 4. Jacob would "not send Benjamin." Rachel was dead, 35:19, Jacob thought that Joseph was dead, 37:33. Jacob could not bear to be parted from the only other son of his beloved Rachel.

Key "Quotable Quote"

"If you can't change circumstances, change the way you respond to them."

Tim Hansel

Genesis 43

Matthew Henry's introduction

Here the story of Joseph's brethren is carried on, and very particularly related.

I. Their melancholy parting with their father Jacob in Canaan, vv. 1–14.

II. Their pleasant meeting with Joseph in Egypt, v. 15, etc. For on this occasion nothing occurs there but what is agreeable and pleasant.

A detailed analysis of chapter

Jacob is persuaded to send Benjamin into Egypt. (1–14)

Joseph's reception of his brothers, their fears. (15–25)

Joseph makes a feast for his brothers. (26–34)

Key verse

Verse 2: "And it came to pass, when they had eaten up the corn which they had brought out of Egypt, their father said unto them, Go again, buy us a little food."

Key word / key phrase

Verse 34, "Benjamin."

Key event / key person / key theme

Joseph's brothers go to Egypt a second time.

Key thought

Joseph's determination to ensure that his father comes to Egypt is clear.

Key thing to look out for

Verse 30. There are a number of pointers to Joseph's great love for his family.

Key Bible cross-reference

Verse 11, "a gift." See 1 Samuel 16:20; 17:18; 2 Kings 5:15.

Key "by way of explanation"

Verse 3, "Judah said." Judah acted as the leader and spokesman of the remaining brothers, 8–10; 44:14–34; 46:28; and he became Jesus' ancestor, Matthew 1:2, 17; Luke 3:23, 33.

Key "Quotable Quote"

"I believe the family was established long before the Church, and my duty is to my family first."

D.L. Moody

Genesis 44

Matthew Henry's introduction

Joseph, having entertained his brethren, dismissed them; but here we have them brought back in a greater fright than any they had been in yet. Observe,

I. What method he took both to humble them further and also to try their affection to his brother Benjamin, by which he would be able to judge of the sincerity of their repentance for what they had done against himself, of which he was desirous to be satisfied before he manifested his reconciliation to them. This he contrived to do by bringing Benjamin into distress, vv. 1–17.

II. The success of the experiment; he found them all heartily concerned, and Judah particularly, both for the safety of Benjamin and for the comfort of their aged father, v. 18, etc.

A detailed analysis of chapter

Joseph's plan to detain his brothers, and test their affection for Benjamin. (1–17)
Judah's plea to Joseph. (18–34)

Key verse

Verse 2: "And put my cup, the silver cup, in the sack's mouth of the youngest, and his corn money."

Key word / key phrase

Verse 12, "cup."

Key event / key person / key theme

Joseph's silver cup is found in Benjamin's sack.

Key thought

Verse 34. The brothers now show concern for their father.

Key thing to look out for

Joseph's plan to keep Benjamin and so bring Jacob to Egypt.

Key Bible cross-reference

Verse 14. See 37:7, 9; 42:6; 43:26, 28.

Key "by way of explanation"

Verse 30. In 1 Samuel 18:1 a similar statement is made about David and Jonathan's close friendship.

Key "Quotable Quote"

"You don't choose your family. They are God's gift to you, as you are to them."

Desmond Tutu

Genesis 45

Matthew Henry's introduction

It is a pity that this chapter and the previous should be separated. There we had Judah's intercession for Benjamin, with which, we may suppose, the rest of his brethren signified their concurrence; Joseph let him go on without interruption, heard all he had to say, and then answered it all in one word, "I am Joseph." Now he found his brethren humbled for their sins, mindful of himself (for Judah had mentioned him twice in his speech), respectful to their father, and very tender of their brother Benjamin; now they were ready for the comfort he designed them, by making himself known to them, the story of which we have in this chapter. It was to Joseph's brethren as clear shining after rain, nay, it was to them as life from the dead. Here is,

I. Joseph's revealing of himself to his brethren, and his conversation with them on that occasion, vv. 1–15.

II. The orders Pharaoh gave to fetch Jacob and his family down to Egypt, and Joseph's sending back of his brothers to his father with those orders, vv. 16–24.

III. The joyful tidings of this brought to Jacob, v. 25, etc.

A detailed analysis of chapter

Joseph comforts his brothers, and sends for his father. (1–15)

Pharaoh confirms Joseph's invitation, Joseph's gifts to his brothers. (16–24)

Jacob receives the news of Joseph being alive. (25–28)

Key verse

Verse 1: "And there stood no man with him, while Joseph made himself known unto his brethren."

Key word / key phrase

Verse 26, "alive."

Key event / key person / key theme

Joseph reveals himself to his brothers.

Key thought

Verse 5 summarizes Joseph's response to all the harm his brothers had done to him.

Key thing to look out for

Joseph's genuine love for his family is clearly illustrated in this chapter.

Key Bible cross-reference

Verse 14. See 42:23.

Key "by way of explanation"

Verse 5. See Acts 7:9; 2:23; 4:28.

Key "Quotable Quote"

"God is the first object of our love. Its next office is to bear the defects of others. And we should begin the practice of this amid our own household."

John Wesley

Genesis 46

Matthew Henry's introduction

Jacob is here moving to Egypt in his old age, forced by a famine, and invited by a son. Here,

I. God sends him thither, vv. 1–4.

II. All his family goes with him, vv. 5–27.

III. Joseph bids him welcome, vv. 28–34.

A detailed analysis of chapter

God's promises to Jacob. (1–4)

Jacob and his family go to Egypt. (5–27)

Joseph meets his father and his brothers. (28–34)

Key verse

Verse 1: "And Israel took his journey with all that he had, and came to Beersheba, and offered sacrifices unto the God of his father Isaac."

Key word / key phrase

Verse 1, "Israel."

Key event / key person / key theme

Jacob goes to Egypt.

Key thought

Jacob could hardly take it in that Joseph was really still alive.

Key thing to look out for

Joseph took great pains to ensure that his large family would be very well cared for in Egypt.

Key Bible cross-reference

Verse 1. See 21:33; 26:23–25.

Key "by way of explanation"

Verse 4. Jacob knew from experience that the Lord himself went with him on his journeys. See 28:15; 15:6; 48:21.

Key "Quotable Quote"

"If your father and mother, your sister and brother, if the very cat and dog in the house, are not happier for your being Christian, it is a question whether you really are."

James Hudson Taylor

Genesis 47

Matthew Henry's introduction

In this chapter we have instances,

I. Of Joseph's kindness and affection to his relations, presenting his brethren first and then his father to Pharaoh (vv. 1–10), settling them in Goshen, and providing for them there (vv. 11, 12), and paying his respects to his father when he sent for him, vv. 27–31.

II. Of Joseph's justice between prince and people in a very critical affair, selling Pharaoh's corn to his subjects with reasonable profits to Pharaoh, and yet without any wrong to them, v. 13, etc. Thus he approved him self wise and good, both in his private and in his public capacity.

A detailed analysis of chapter

Joseph presents his brothers to Pharaoh. (1–6)

Jacob blesses Pharaoh. (7–12)

Joseph's dealings with the Egyptians during the famine. (13–26)

Jacob's age. His desire to be buried in Canaan. (27–31)

Key verse

Verse 14: "And Joseph gathered up all the money that was found in the land of Egypt, and in the land of Canaan, for the corn which they bought: and Joseph brought the money into Pharaoh's house."

Key word / key phrase

Verse 13, "famine."

Key event / key person / key theme

Joseph's role in providing food for Egypt

Key thought

Without Joseph's administrative skills Egypt would have starved.

Key thing to look out for

The relationship of respect between Pharaoh and Jacob.

Key Bible cross-reference

Verse 27. See 35:11, 12; 46:3.

Key "by way of explanation"

Verse 13. Joseph ensured that Egypt had food, but the price the people had to pay for this involved their money, their livestock, their land, and themselves. See 14, 15, 16, 17, 20, 21.

Key "Quotable Quote"

"He that respects not is not respected."

George Herbert

Genesis 48

Matthew Henry's introduction

The time is drawing close when Israel must die, having, in the previous chapter, given order about his burial, in this he takes leave of his grand-children by Joseph, and in the next of all his children. Thus Jacob's dying words are recorded, because he then spoke by a spirit of prophecy; Abraham's and Isaac's are not. God's gifts and graces shine forth much more in some saints than in others on their death-beds. The Spirit, like the wind, blows where it listeth. In this chapter,

I. Joseph, hearing of his father's sickness, goes to visit him, and takes his two sons with him, vv. 1, 2.

II. Jacob solemnly adopts his two sons, and takes them for his own, vv. 3–7.

III. He blesses them, vv. 8–16.

IV. He explains and justifies the crossing of his hands in blessing them, vv. 17–20.

V. He leaves a particular legacy to Joseph, vv. 21, 22.

A detailed analysis of chapter

Joseph visits his dying father. (1–7)

Jacob blesses Joseph's sons. (8–22)

Key verse

Verse 21: "And Israel said unto Joseph, Behold, I die: but God shall be with you, and bring you again unto the land of your fathers"

Key word / key phrase

Verse 3, "blessed."

Key event / key person / key theme

Jacob blesses Manasseh and Ephraim.

Key thought

God's grace is illustrated in the way Jacob puts Manasseh and Ephraim on a par with his own two firstborn.

Key thing to look out for

God's deliverance includes physical deliverance as well as forgiveness of sins.

Key Bible cross-reference

Verse 15. See Psalm 23:1; 49:24.

Key "by way of explanation"

Verse 20. Joseph enables the younger son of Joseph, Ephraim, to take precedence over the elder son, Manasseh.

Key "Quotable Quote

"There is a famine in America. Not a famine of food, but of love, of truth, of life."

Mother Teresa of Calcutta

Genesis 49

Matthew Henry's introduction

This chapter is a prophecy; the closest to it we

have met with was that of Noah, 9:25, etc. Jacob is here on his death-bed, making his will. He put it off till now, because dying men's words are apt to make deep impressions, and to be remembered long: what he said here, he could not say when he would, but as the Spirit gave him utterance, who chose this time, that divine strength might be perfected in his weakness. The twelve sons of Jacob were, in their day, men of renown, but the twelve tribes of Israel, which descended and were denominated from them, were much more renowned; we find their names on the gates of the New Jerusalem, Rev. 21:12. In the prospect of this their dying father says something remarkable of each son, or of the tribe that bore his name. Here is,

I. The preface, vv. 1, 2.
II. The prediction about each tribe, vv. 3–28.
III. The charge repeated about his burial, vv. 29–32.
IV. His death, v. 33.

A detailed analysis of chapter

Jacob calls his sons to bless them. (1, 2)
Reuben, Simeon, Levi. (3–7)
Judah. (8–12)
Zebulun, Issachar, Dan. (13–18)
Gad, Asher, Naphtali. (19–21)
Joseph and Benjamin. (22–27)
Jacob's charge about his burial, his death. (28–33)

Key verse

Verse 1: "And Jacob called unto his sons, and said, Gather yourselves together, that I may tell you that which shall befall you in the last days."

Key word / key phrase

Verse 26, "blessings."

Key event / key person / key theme

Jacob blesses his sons.

Key thought

In fulfillment of his dreams, Joseph is referred to as "the prince among his brothers," verse 26.

Key thing to look out for

God does not bestow the same blessings on everyone.

Key Bible cross-reference

Verses 2–27. See further poetic blessings in Genesis in 9:26, 27; 14:19, 20; 27:27–29; 27:39, 40; 48:15, 16; 48:20.

Key "by way of explanation"

Verses 2–27 is the longest poem in Genesis. Jacob's blessings were intended for the descendants of the twelve brothers and not just for the twelve themselves

Key "Quotable Quote"

"Justice–When you get what you deserve.
Mercy–When you don't get what you deserve.
Grace–When you get what you don't deserve."

Author unknown

Genesis 50

Matthew Henry's introduction

Here is,

I. The preparation for Jacob's funeral, vv. 1–6.
II. The funeral itself, vv. 7–14.

III. The settling of a good understanding between Joseph and his brethren after the death of Jacob, vv. 15–21.

IV. The age and death of Joseph, vv. 22–26. Thus the book of Genesis, which began with the origin of light and life, ends with nothing but death and darkness; so sad a change has sin made.

A detailed analysis of chapter

The mourning for Jacob. (1–6)

His funeral. (7–14)

Joseph's brothers beg for his pardon, he comforts them. (15–21)

Joseph's instructions about his bones, his death. (22–26)

Key verse

Verse 26: "So Joseph died, being an hundred and ten years old: and they embalmed him, and he was put in a coffin in Egypt."

Key word / key phrase

Verse 17, "forgive."

Key event / key person / key theme

Joseph dies.

Key thought

Verse 17. The brothers show that they still do not fully believe that Joseph's love for them is total and genuine.

Key thing to look out for

How God provided for a slave in a foreign country.

Key Bible cross-reference

Verse 25. See Exodus 13:19; Joshua 24:32; Genesis 33:19.

Key "by way of explanation"

Verse 20. This summarizes God's grace in Joseph's heart, despite all the ill will his brothers had shown him.

Key "Quotable Quote"

"Our blessed Lord reveals himself to his people more in the valleys, in the shades, in the deeps, than he does anywhere else."

C.H. Spurgeon

5. Select bibliography for Genesis

Aalders, G. Charles. *Genesis. Bible Student's Commentary*. Grand Rapids: Zondervan, 1981.

Delitzsch, Franz. *A New Commentary on Genesis*. Translated by Sophia Taylor. Edinburgh: T. & T. Clark, 1888.

Kidner, Derek. *Genesis: An Introduction and Commentary*. London: Tyndale, 1967.

Thomas, W. H. Griffith. *Genesis: A Devotional Commentary*. Grand Rapids: Eerdmans, 1946.

Wenham, Gordon J. *Genesis*: Word Books, 1987. (two vols.)

Exodus

1. Book by book: Introduction to Exodus

Introduction

Exodus, a "going forth," derives its name from its being occupied principally with the departure of the Israelites from Egypt, and the incidents that immediately preceded as well as followed that memorable migration. Its authorship by Moses is asserted by himself (Exodus 24:4), as well as by our Lord (Mark 12:26; Luke 20:37). Besides, the thorough knowledge it exhibits of the institutions and usages of the ancient Egyptians and the minute geographical details of the journey to Sinai, establish in the clearest manner the authenticity of this book.

Robert Jamieson

Contents of Exodus

In seven parts, after the Introduction (Exodus 1:1–7), which furnishes the connection of the contents with Genesis, the book covers the following topics:

(1) the sufferings of Israel in Egypt, for which mere human help is insufficient (Exodus 1:8–7:7), while Divine help through human mediatorship is promised;

(2) the power of Yahweh, which, after a preparatory miracle, is glorified through the ten plagues inflicted on Pharaoh and which thus forces the exodus (Exodus 7:8–13:16);

(3) the love of Yahweh for Israel, which exhibits itself in a most brilliant manner, in the guidance of the Israelites to Mt. Sinai, even when the people complain (Exodus 13:17–18:27);

(4) making the covenant at Mt. Sinai together with the revelation of the Ten Words (Exodus 20:1) and of the legal ordinances (Exodus 21:1) as the condition of making the Covenant (Exodus 19:1–24:18);

(5) the directions for the building of the Tabernacle, in which Yahweh is to dwell in the middle of His people (Exodus 24:18–31:18);

(6) the renewal of the Covenant on the basis of new demands after Israel's great apostasy in the worship of the Golden Calf, which seemed for the time being to make doubtful the realization of the promises mentioned in (5) above (Exodus 32:1–35:3);

(7) the building and erection of the Tabernacle of Revelation (or Tent of Meeting) and its dedication by the entrance of Yahweh (Exodus 35:4–40:38).

As clearly as these seven parts are separated from one another, so clearly again are they most closely connected and constitute a certain progressive whole.

In the case of the last four, the separation is almost self-evident. The first three as separate parts are justified by the ten plagues standing between them, which naturally belong together and cause a division between that which precedes and that which follows. Thus in the first part we already find predicted the hardening of the heart of Pharaoh, the miracles of Yahweh and the demonstrations of His power down to the slaying of the firstborn, found in the 2nd part (compare Exodus 2:23–7:7).

In part 3, the infatuation of Pharaoh and the demonstration of the power of Yahweh are further unfolded in the narrative of the catastrophe in the Red Sea (Exodus 14:4,17). Further the directions given with reference to the Tabernacle presuppose the Decalogue; compare Exodus 25:16,21; 31:18; as again the 6th section (Exodus 32) presupposes the 5th part, which had promised the continuous presence of God (compare Exodus 32:34; 33:3,5,7; 33:12,14–17; 34:9, with 25:8; 29:45; compare also the forty days in 34:28 with those in 24:18) as in 34:1,28 and 34:11–27 refers back to the 4th part, namely, 20:1; 21:1; 24:7 (Decalogue; Books of the Covenant; Making the Covenant). In the same way the last section presupposes the third, since the cloud in Exodus 40:34 is regarded as something well known (compare 13:21; 14:19 and 14:24) .

The entire contents of the Book of Exodus are summarized in an excellent way in the word of God to Israel spoken through Moses about the making of the covenant:

"Ye have seen what I did unto the Egyptians, and how I bare you on eagles' wings, and brought you unto myself." Now therefore, if ye will obey my voice indeed, and keep my covenant, then ye shall be mine own possession from among all peoples: for all the earth is mine: and ye shall be unto me a kingdom of priests, and a holy nation" (Exodus 19:4–6).

Here reference is made to the powerful deeds of God done to the Egyptians, to His deeds of loving-kindness done to Israel in the history of how He led them to Sinai, to the selection of Israel, and to the conditions attached to the making of the covenant, to God's love, which condescended to meet the people, and to His holiness, which demands the observance of His commandments; but there is also pointed out here the punishment for their transgression. The whole book is built on one word in the preface to the ten commandments: "I am Yahweh thy God, who brought thee out of the land of Egypt, out of the house of bondage" (Exodus 20:2; compare 29:45).

Link with the other books of the Pentateuch

The events which are described in the Book of Exodus show a certain contrast to those in Genesis. In the first eleven chapters of this latter book we have the history of humankind; then beginning with 11:27, a history of families, those of Abraham, Isaac and Jacob. In Exodus we have following this the beginning of the history of the chosen people. Exodus 1:1–7 connects the history of the people as found in Exodus with the family history of Genesis, by narrating how the seventy descendants of Jacob that had migrated to Egypt (compare Exodus 1:5; Genesis 46:27) had come to be the people of Israel, and that God, who offers Himself as a liberator to Moses and the people, is also the God of those fathers, of whom Genesis spoke (compare Exodus 3:6; 3:13; 3:15; 4:5; 6:3). Indeed, His covenant with the fathers and His promises to them are the reasons why He at all cares for Israel (Exodus 2:24), and when Moses intercedes for the sinful people, his most effective motive is found in the promises made to the patriarchs (Exodus 32:13).

As is the case with Genesis, Exodus stands in the closest connection also with the succeeding books of the Pentateuch. Israel is certainly not to remain at Sinai, but is to come into the promised land (3:17; 6:8; 23:20; 32:34; 33:1; 33:12; 34:9; compare also the many ordinances of the Books of the Covenant, 21:1; 34:11). In this way the narratives of the following books, which begin again in Numbers 10:11 with the story of the departure from Sinai, continue the history in Exodus. But the legislation in Leviticus also is a necessary continuation and supplement of the Book of Exodus, and is prepared for and pointed to in the latter. The erection of the burnt-offering altar (27:1; 38:1), as well as mention of the different kinds of sacrifices, such as the burnt sacrifices and the sin offering (29:18,14) and of the fellowship offering (29:28), point to the promulgation of a law of sacrifices such as we find in Leviticus 1–7. The directions given in regard to the consecration of the priests (Exodus 29) are carried out in Leviticus 8. The indefinite commands of Exodus 30:10 in reference to the atonement on the horn of the incense altar once every year renders necessary the special ritual of the Day of Atonement in Leviticus 16 as its supplement. The more complete enlargement in reference to the bread of the presence mentioned in Exodus 25:30 is found in Leviticus 24:5–9; and even the repetitions in references to the candlesticks (Exodus 25:31; Leviticus 24:1–4; Numbers 8:1–4), as also the daily sacrifices (compare Numbers 28:3–8 with Exodus 29:38–42), point to a certain connection between Exodus and the following books. Then there is the link between Deuteronomy and Exodus, both in regard to the historical narratives and also to their legal portions: compare the Decalogue and the Books of the Covenant.

Orr, James, M.A., D.D. General Editor, International Standard Bible Encyclopedia

Detailed outline

- I. The nation of Israel in Egypt: 1:1 12:36
  - A. Egyptian bondage: 1:1–22
  - B. God prepares a deliverer: Moses: 2:1–4:31
  - C. The dialogue with Pharaoh: 5:1–11:10
  - D. The Passover: 12:1–30
  - E. Deliverance from Egypt: 12:31–36
- II. Israel in the wilderness: 12:37–18:27
  - A. The Exodus and the pursuit by the Egyptians: 12:37–15:21
  - B. The journey to Sinai: 15:22–17:16
  - C. The visit of Jethro: 18:1–27
- III. Israel at Sinai: 19:1–40:38
  - A. The giving of the law: 19:1–25
  - B. Laws governing moral life: 19–22
  - C. Laws governing social life: 22–23
  - D. Laws governing religious life: 24:1–31:18
  - E. The tabernacle: 24:12–40:38
    1. Instructions about the tabernacle and the priests: 24:12–31:18
    2. The golden calf and renewal of the covenant: 32:1–34:35
    3. Building the tabernacle and institution of the priesthood: 35:1–40:38

2. Helpful summaries of Exodus

Bird's eye view

Israel's history from the death of Joseph to the building of the tabernacle.

Reading plan

The following reading plan, taking one reading per day, enables you to read through Exodus in nineteen days.

Exodus 1–3
Exodus 4–5
Exodus 6–8
Exodus 9
Exodus 10–12
Exodus 13–14
Exodus 15–16
Exodus 17–19
Exodus 20–21
Exodus 22–23
Exodus 24–25
Exodus 26–27
Exodus 28–29
Exodus 30–31
Exodus 32–33
Exodus 34–35
Exodus 36–37
Exodus 38–39
Exodus 40

Verses to memorize

Exodus 14:13

Do not be afraid. Stand firm and you will see the deliverance the Lord will bring you today.

Exodus 14:14

The Lord will fight for you; you need only to be still.

Exodus 33:14

The Lord replied, "My Presence will go with you, and I will give you rest".

Statistics

Second Old Testament book
40 chapters
1,213 verses
32,692 words

Famous sayings found in Exodus

"Eye for an eye" Exodus 21:24
"Golden calf" Exodus 32

Names/titles given

Hebrew title: We'elleh Shemoth: "These are the names."

Greek title in Septuagint: Exodus: "Going out, departure, exit."

Latin title in Vulgate: Liber Exodus: "The Book of Departure."

3. Helpful keys to turn to in understanding Exodus

Key words

Redemption
Pass over you

Key verses

Exodus 6:6; 12:23; 19:5–6

Key people/events

Moses
Aaron
Ten Plagues
Passover
Journey to Sinai
Ten Commandments
Book of the Covenant
Tabernacle

Themes to study

The Exodus is the key event in this book. See Exodus 19:1; Luke 9:31 and 2 Peter 1:15.

The book of Exodus has three main topics:

1. Moses: Moses' life, from his birth to the Exodus.
2. The Law: The giving of the ten commandments.
3. Worship: The building of the chest for the ten commandments, the building of the tent (tabernacle) and instructions about worship.

Feasts

Two pilgrimage feasts
The feast of the Passover: Exodus 12
The feast of Tabernacles: Exodus 15–18

The Tabernacle

The purpose of the Tabernacle is stated in Exodus 25:8: "Then have them make a sanctuary for me, and I will dwell among them."

The typical meaning of the Tabernacle comes in Hebrews 9:24: "For Christ did not enter a man-made sanctuary that was only a copy of the true one; he entered heaven itself, now to appear for us in God's presence."

Exodus in the New Testament

There are about two hundred references to the Exodus in the New Testament.

Jesus is presented as the new Moses, the new Israel and the Passover Lamb. His birth as the firstborn, His going down to Egypt, His baptism in the Jordan and His testing for forty days in the wilderness replay the events of the old Exodus. His death is the Passover. His death in Jerusalem is also called "His exodus," Luke 9:31, in the Greek. ("They spoke about his departure, which he was about to bring to fulfillment at Jerusalem." NIV)

Exodus quoted in the New Testament

- There arose another king over Egypt, who knew not Joseph.
  Ex. 1:8 quoted in Acts 7:18
- Who made thee a ruler and a judge over us?
  Ex. 2:14 quoted in Acts 7:27–28 and Acts 7:35
- An angel appeared to him in the wilderness of mount Sinai
  Ex. 3:2 quoted in Acts 7:30
- Loose the shoes from thy feet
  Ex. 3:5–10 quoted in Acts 7:33–34
- I am the God of Abraham
  Ex. 3:6 quoted in Matt. 22:32, Mark 12:26, Luke 20:37, Acts 3:13 and Acts 7:32
- The affliction of my people . . . I will send thee
  Ex. 3:7–10 quoted in Acts 7:34
- And serve me in this place
  Ex. 3:12 quoted in Acts 7:7

- I am the God of Abraham
  Ex. 3:15 quoted in Matt. 22:32, Mark 12:26 and Acts 3:13
- My name might be published abroad in all the earth
  Ex. 9:16 quoted in Rom. 9:17
- A bone of him shall not be broken
  Ex. 12:46 quoted in John 19:36
- Sanctify to me every firstborn
  Ex. 13:2 quoted in Luke 2:23
- Thou shalt sanctify the males to the Lord
  Ex. 13:12 quoted in Luke 2:23
- The males to the Lord
  Ex. 13:15 quoted in Luke 2:32
- He that gathered much had nothing over
  Ex. 16:18 quoted in 2 Cor. 8:15
- A royal priesthood
  Ex. 19:6 quoted in 1 Pet. 2:9
- If even a beast touch the mountain, it shall be stoned
  Ex. 19:12–13 quoted in Heb. 12:20
- Honor thy father and thy mother
  Ex. 20:12 quoted in Matt. 15:4, Mark 7:10 and Eph. 6:2–3
- Thou knowest the commandments
  Ex. 20:12–16 quoted in Matt. 19:18–19, Mark 10:19 and Luke 18:20
- Thou shalt not kill
  Ex. 20:13 quoted in Matt. 5:21 and James 2:11
- Thou shalt not commit adultery
  Ex. 20:13–15 quoted in Rom. 13:9
- Thou shalt not commit adultery
  Ex. 20:14 quoted in Matt. 5:27 and James 2:11
- Thou shalt not covet
  Ex. 20:17 quoted in Rom. 7:7
- He that speaketh evil of father or mother, let him die the death
  Ex. 21:17 quoted in Matt. 15:4 and Mark 7:10
- An eye for an eye, and a tooth for a tooth
  Ex. 21:24 quoted in Matt. 5:38
- Thou shalt not speak evil of a ruler of thy people
  Ex. 22:28 quoted in Acts 23:5
- This is the blood of the covenant
  Ex. 24:8 quoted in Heb. 9:20
- See that thou make all things according to the pattern
  Ex. 25:40 quoted in Heb. 8:5
- Arise, and make us gods
  Ex. 32:1 quoted in Acts 7:40
- The people sat down to eat and drink, and rose up to play
  Ex. 32:6 quoted in 1 Cor. 10:7
- We know not what is become of him
  Ex. 32:23 quoted in Acts 7:40
- I will have mercy on whom I will have mercy
  Ex. 33:19 quoted in Rom. 9:15

Prayers in Exodus

- God spoke with Moses over 100 times in Exodus.
- Israelites pray for deliverance, Ex 2:23–25; 3:7
- Moses and God talk at the burning bush, Ex.3:1–22, 4:1–17
- Moses prays for Pharaoh, Ex.8:9–15
- God talks to Moses in each of the ten plagues, Exodus 7–11

- Moses prays for pure water, Ex.15:22–25
- Moses receives manna and quails from God, Ex.16:1–55
- Water from the rock, Ex.17:3–7
- Moses prays for Israel, Ex.32:30–35

The Ten Commandments

And God spoke all these words:

"I am the Lord your God, who brought you out of Egypt, out of the land of slavery.

1. "You shall have no other gods before me.
2. "You shall not make for yourself an idol in the form of anything in heaven above or on the earth beneath or in the waters below. You shall not bow down to them or worship them; for I, the Lord your God, am a jealous God, punishing the children for the sin of the fathers to the third and fourth generation of those who hate me, but showing love to a thousand {generations} of those who love me and keep my commandments.
3. "You shall not misuse the name of the Lord your God, for the Lord will not hold any one guiltless who misuses his name.
4. "Remember the Sabbath day by keeping it holy. Six days you shall labor and do all your work, but the seventh day is a Sabbath to the Lord your God. On it you shall not do any work, neither you, nor your son or daughter, nor your manservant or maidservant, nor your animals, nor the alien within your gates. For in six days the Lord made the heavens and the earth, the sea, and all that is in them, but he rested on the seventh day. Therefore the Lord blessed the Sabbath day and made it holy.
5. "Honor your father and your mother, so that you may live long in the land the Lord your God is giving you.
6. "You shall not murder.
7. "You shall not commit adultery.
8. "You shall not steal.
9. "You shall not give false testimony against your neighbor.
10. "You shall not covet your neighbor's house. You shall not covet your neighbor's wife, or his manservant or maidservant, his ox or donkey, or anything that belongs to your neighbor." Exodus 20:1–17

Unusual events and miracles in Exodus

- The burning bush which was not destroyed, 3:2
- Moses' staff turning into a snake and back into a staff, 4:2–5
- Moses' hand become leprous and is cured, 4:6–7
- Aaron's staff turns into a snake, 7:10–12
- The ten plagues
- The First Plague (Exodus 7:14–24)
- All of the water in Egypt turned to blood, causing all the fish to die.
- The Second Plague (Exodus 8:1–15)
- Infestation of frogs.
- The Third Plague (Exodus 8:16–19)
- Swarms of gnats tormented both people and animals.
- The Fourth Plague (Exodus 8:20–32)
- Swarms of flies.
- The Fifth Plague (Exodus 9:1–7)
- Disease on Egyptian livestock.
- The Sixth Plague (Exodus 9:8–12)

- Boils on people and animals.
- The Seventh Plague (Exodus 9:13–35)
- Hail storms with hail stones that killed people.
- The Eighth Plague (Exodus 10:1–20)
- Swarms of locusts.
- The Ninth Plague (Exodus 10:21–29)
- Darkness over the entire land for three days, although the Israelites had light in Goshen.
- The Tenth Plague (Exodus 11:1–10, 12:1–42)
- Death of the firstborn.
- The cloud by day and pillar of fire by night, 13:20–21
- The Red Sea divided, 14:21,30–31
- The waters of Marah made sweet, 15:23,25; 16:14–35
- The Ten Commandments, 31:18; 32:16–18

Jesus in Exodus

In Exodus Jesus is our Passover Lamb.

Types of Jesus in Exodus

Moses' life is a type of Jesus

- Moses and Jesus were preserved in childhood: Ex. 2:2 with Matt. 2.14,15.
- Moses and Jesus fought against evil: Ex. 7:11 with Matt. 4:1.
- Moses and Jesus fasted for forty days: Ex. 34:28 with Matt. 4:2.
- Moses and Jesus tamed the sea: Ex. 14:21 with Mt. 8:26.
- Moses and Jesus fed crowds of people: Ex. 16:15 with Mt. 14:20.
- Moses and Jesus had shining faces: Ex. 34:35 with Mt. 17:2.
- Moses and Jesus put up with grumbling: Ex. 15:24 with Mk. 7:2.
- Moses and Jesus were rejected by their own homes: Ex. 12:1 with John 7:5.

Other types of Jesus in Exodus

- The Passover shows how Jesus in the Passover Lamb.
- The seven feasts of Exodus depict aspects of Jesus' ministry.
- The Exodus is a type of baptism, Rom. 6:2–3.
- The manna is a type of Jesus.
- The water is a type of Jesus, 1 Cor. 10:3–4.
- The tabernacle and its furnishings are types of Jesus and his redemption.
- The high priest is a type of Jesus, who is our Great High Priest, Heb. 4:14–16.

Lessons to learn from Exodus

God is holy and requires that we are holy.

God provides our daily needs.

God is sovereign and everything is in his hands.

God promises to guide us.

God expects us to worship him.

4. Chapter by chapter: outline of every chapter of Exodus

Exodus 1

Matthew Henry's introduction

We have here,

I. God's kindness to Israel, in multiplying them exceedingly, (vv. 1–7).

II. The Egyptians' wickedness to them,

A. Oppressing and enslaving them, (vv. 8–14).

B. Murdering their children, (vv. 15–22).

Thus whom the court of heaven blessed

the country of Egypt cursed, and for that reason.

A detailed analysis of chapter

The children of Israel increase in Egypt after the death of Joseph. (8–14)

They are oppressed, but multiply exceedingly. (1–7)

The baby boys destroyed. (15–22)

Key verse

Verse 8: "Now there arose up a new king over Egypt, which knew not Joseph."

Key word / key phrase

Verse 15, "Hebrew."

Key event / key person / key theme

A new Pharaoh

Key thought

When is it right to obey God and disobey men?

Key thing to look out for

The history of the Israelites and Pharaoh's motives.

Key Bible cross-reference

Verse 7. See Acts 7:17; Genesis 1:28; Genesis 8:17; Genesis 17:2, 6; Genesis 26:4 and 48:4.

Key "by way of explanation"

Verse 1, "Israel." Jacob had been given this additional name by God. See Genesis 32:28; 35:10.

Key "Quotable Quote"

"History is a story written by the finger of God."

C.S. Lewis

Exodus 2

Matthew Henry's introduction

This chapter begins the story of Moses, that man of renown, famed for his intimate acquaintance with Heaven and his eminent usefulness on earth, and the most remarkable type of Christ, as a prophet, savior, lawgiver, and mediator, in all the Old Testament. The Jews have a book among them of the life of Moses, which tells a great many stories concerning him, which we have reason to think are mere fictions; what he has recorded concerning himself is what we may rely upon, for we know that his record is true; and it is what we may be satisfied with, for it is what Infinite Wisdom thought fit to preserve and transmit to us. In this chapter we have,

I. The perils of his birth and infancy, vv. 1–4.

II. His preservation through those perils, and the preferment of his childhood and youth, vv. 5–10.

III. The pious choice of his adult life years, when he owned the people of God.

A. He offered them his service at present, if they would accept it, vv. 11–14.

B. He retired, that he might reserve himself for further service hereafter, vv. 15–22.

IV. The dawning of the day of Israel's deliverance, v. 23, etc.

A detailed analysis of chapter

Moses is born, and exposed on the river. (1–4)

He is found, and brought up by Pharaoh's daughter. (5–10)

Moses kills an Egyptian, and flees to Midian. (11–15)

Moses marries the daughter of Jethro. (16–22)

God hears the Israelites. (23–25)

Key verse

Verse 3: "And when she could not longer hide him, she took for him an ark of bulrushes, and daubed it with slime and with pitch, and put the child therein; and she laid it in the flags by the river's brink."

Key word / key phrase

Verse 10, "Moses."

Key event / key person / key theme

Moses is born.

Key thought

A mother's love and a princess' compassion combine to save one baby.

Key thing to look out for

God's greatest leaders are frequently misunderstood.

Key Bible cross-reference

Verse 2. See Acts 7:20; Hebrews 11:23.

Key "by way of explanation"

Verse 3, "papyrus basket." Moses' waterproof cradle was a tiny version of a papyrus boat. See Isaiah 18:2.

Key "Quotable Quote"

"The Church does not need brilliant personalities but faithful servants of Jesus and the brethren."

Dietrich Bonhoeffer

Exodus 3

Matthew Henry's introduction

As prophecy had ceased for many ages before the coming of Christ, that the revival and perfection of it in that great prophet might be the more remarkable, so vision had ceased among the patriarchs for some ages before the coming of Moses, that God's appearances to him for Israel's salvation might be the more welcome; and in this chapter we have God's first appearance to him in the bush and the conversation between God and Moses in that vision. Here is,

I. The discovery God was pleased to make of his glory to Moses at the bush, to which Moses was forbidden to approach too near, vv. 1–5.

II. A general declaration of God's grace and good-will to his people, who were beloved for their fathers' sakes, v. 6.

III. A particular notification of God's purpose concerning the deliverance of Israel out of Egypt.

A. He assures Moses it should now be done, vv. 7–9.

B. He gives him a commission to act in it as his ambassador both to Pharaoh, (v. 10) and to Israel, v. 16.

C. He answers the objection Moses made of his own unworthiness, vv. 11, 12.

D. He gives him full instructions what to say both to Pharaoh and to Israel, vv. 13–18.
E. He tells him beforehand what the issue would be, v. 19, etc.

A detailed analysis of chapter

God appears to Moses in a burning bush. (1–6)
God sends Moses to deliver Israel. (7–10)
The name of God. (11–15)
The deliverance of the Israelites promised. (16–22)

Key verse

Verse 2: "And the angel of the Lord appeared unto him in a flame of fire out of the midst of a bush: and he looked, and, behold, the bush burned with fire, and the bush was not consumed."

Key word / key phrase

Verse 3, "bush."

Key event / key person / key theme

The burning bush

Key thought

Moses learns about God's holiness.

Key thing to look out for

Initially, Moses shows himself to be a most reluctant leader.

Key Bible cross-reference

Verse 4. See 1 Samuel 3:4; Isaiah 6:8; Jeremiah 1:4, 5; Ezekiel 2:1–8.

Key "by way of explanation"

Verse 8. God is also said to come down in judgment in Genesis 11:5–9; 18:21.

Key "Quotable Quote"

"How beautiful, how beautiful
The sight of thee must be,
Thine endless wisdom, boundless power,
And awful purity!"

F.W. Faber

Exodus 4

Matthew Henry's introduction

This chapter,

I. Continues and concludes God's discourse with Moses at the bush concerning this great affair of bringing Israel out of Egypt.
   A. Moses objects the people's unbelief (v. 1), and God answers that objection by giving him power to work miracles, to turn his rod into a serpent, and then into a rod again, vv. 2–5. To make his hand leprous,and then whole again, vv. 6–8. To turn the water into blood, v. 9.
   B. Moses objects his own slowness of speech (v. 10), and begs to be excused (v. 13); but God answers this objection, By promising him his presence, vv. 11, 12. By joining Aaron in commission with him, vv. 14–16. By putting an honor upon the very staff in his hand, v. 17.
II. It begins Moss's execution of his commission.
   A. He obtains leave of his father-in-law to return to Egypt, v. 18.
   B. He receives further instructions and

encouragements from God, vv. 19, 21–23.

C. He hastens his departure, and takes his family with him, v. 20.

D. He meets with some difficulty about the circumcising of his son, vv. 24–26.

E. He has the satisfaction of meeting his brother Aaron, vv. 27, 28.

F. He produces his commission before the elders of Israel, to their great joy, vv. 29–31. And thus the wheels were set a going towards that great deliverance.

A detailed analysis of chapter

God gives Moses power to work miracles. (1–9)

Moses does not want to be sent, Aaron is to assist him. (10–17)

Moses leaves Midian, God's message to Pharaoh. (18–23)

God's displeasure with Moses, Aaron meets him, and the people believe them. (24–31)

Key verse

Verse 18: "And Moses went and returned to Jethro his father in law, and said unto him, Let me go, I pray thee, and return unto my brethren which are in Egypt, and see whether they be yet alive."

Key word / key phrase

Verse 30, "signs."

Key event / key person / key theme

Moses goes back to Egypt.

Key thought

God's plans are not thwarted by anyone.

Key thing to look out for

The excuses made by Moses.

Key Bible cross-reference

Verse 21. See 7:3; 9:12; 10:1,20,27; 11:10; 14:4,8; Romans 9:17,18.

Key "by way of explanation"

Verse 22, "firstborn son." This phrase is a figure of speech used to show Israel's unique relationship with God. See Jeremiah 31:9; Hosea 11:1.

Key "Quotable Quote"

"Evidence of our hardness is that we are more concerned about our sufferings than our sins."

Matthew Henry

Exodus 5

Matthew Henry's introduction

Moses and Aaron are here dealing with Pharaoh, to ask his permission to go and worship in the wilderness.

I. They demand to leave in the name of God (v. 1), and he answers their demand with a defiance of God, v. 2.

II. They beg to leave in the name of Israel (v. 3), and he answers their request with further orders to oppress Israel, vv. 4–9. These cruel orders were,

A. Carried out by the task-masters, vv. 10–14.

B. Complained of to Pharaoh, but in vain, vv. 15–19.

C. Complained of by the people to Moses vv. 20, 21), and by him to God, vv. 22, 23.

A detailed analysis of chapter

Pharaoh's displeasure, he increases the tasks of the Israelites. (1–9)

The sufferings of the Israelites, Moses' complaint to God. (10–23)

Key verse

Verse 18: "Go therefore now, and work; for there shall no straw be given you, yet shall ye deliver the tale of bricks."

Key word / key phrase

Verse 7, "bricks."

Key event / key person / key theme

Bricks but no straw

Key thought

Moses has a most unpromising start as Israel's great leader and deliverer.

Key thing to look out for

Strong criticism from his own people was part of the price Moses had to pay for being a leader.

Key Bible cross-reference

Verse 21. See Genesis 16:5; 31:49.

Key "by way of explanation"

Verse 7. Straw was essential in making bricks as it helped to bind the clay together and so give the bricks strength.

Key "Quotable Quote"

"A man would do nothing, if he waited until he could do it so that no one would find fault with what he has done."

John Henry Newman

Exodus 6

Matthew Henry's introduction

Great efforts were made to bring Moses to his work, and when the ice was broken, some difficulty having occurred in carrying it on, there was no less effort made to put him forward in it. Witness this chapter, in which,

I. God satisfies Moses himself in an answer to his complaints in the close of the foregoing chapter, v. 1.

II. He gives him fuller instructions than had yet been given him what to say to the children of Israel, for their satisfaction (vv. 2–8), but to little purpose, v. 9.

III. He sends him again to Pharaoh, vv. 10, 11. But Moses objects (v. 12), upon which a very strict charge is given to him and his brother to carry out their commission with vigor, v. 13.

IV. Here is an abstract of the genealogy of the tribes of Reuben and Simeon, to introduce that of Levi, that the pedigree of Moses and Aaron might be cleared (vv. 14–25), and then the chapter concludes with a repetition of so much of the preceding story as was necessary to make way for the following chapter.

A detailed analysis of chapter

God renews his promise. (1–9)

Moses and Aaron again sent to Pharaoh. (10–13)
The parentage of Moses and Aaron. (14–30)

Key verse

Verse 1: "Then the LORD said unto Moses, Now shalt thou see what I will do to Pharaoh: for with a strong hand shall he let them go, and with a strong hand shall he drive them out of his land."

Key word / key phrase

Verse 5, "covenant."

Key event / key person / key theme

Aaron

Key thought

Aaron had totally different gifts from Moses, but was essential to God's plan.

Key thing to look out for

Moses' whole ministry is underpinned with God's promises.

Key Bible cross-reference

Verse 7. See 19:5, 6; Jeremiah 31:33.

Key "by way of explanation"

Verse 6. Redemption included deliverance for Israel, but judgment for Egypt.

Key "Quotable Quote"

"I will not glory because I am righteous but because I am redeemed, not because I am clear of sin, but because my sins are forgiven."

Ambrose

Exodus 7

Matthew Henry's introduction

In this chapter,

I. The dispute between God and Moses finishes, and Moses applies himself to the execution of his commission, in obedience to God's command, vv. 1–7.

II. The dispute between Moses and Pharaoh begins, and a famous trial of skill it was. Moses, in God's name, demands Israel's release; Pharaoh denies it. The contest is between the power of the great God and the power of a proud prince; and it will be found, in the issue, that when God judges he will overcome.

A. Moses confirms the demand he had made to Pharaoh, by a miracle, turning his rod into a serpent; but Pharaoh hardens his heart against this conviction, vv. 8–13.

B. He chastises his disobedience by a plague, the first of the ten, turning the waters into blood; but Pharaoh hardens his heart against this correction, v. 14, etc.

A detailed analysis of chapter

Moses and Aaron encouraged. (1–7)
The staffs turned into serpents, Pharaoh's heart is hardened. (8–13)
The river is turned into blood, and the distress of the Egyptians. (14–25)

Key verse

Verse 20: "And Moses and Aaron did so, as the LORD commanded; and he lifted up the rod, and smote the waters that were in the river, in the sight of Pharaoh, and in the sight of his servants; and all the waters that were in the river were turned to blood."

Key word / key phrase

Verse 9, "miracle."

Key event / key person / key theme

Aaron's ministry

Key thought

Nothing is so hard as the human heart.

Key thing to look out for

The greatest miracle is someone turning to God in repentance.

Key Bible cross-reference

Verse 17. See Psalm 78:44; 105:29.

Key "by way of explanation"

Verse 14. One way of viewing the first nine plagues is to put them into three groups, with three plagues in each group: 7:14–8:19; 8:20–9:12; 9:13–10:29.

Key "Quotable Quote"

"I never have any difficulty believing in miracles, since I experienced the miracle of a change in my own heart."

Augustine of Hippo

Exodus 8

Matthew Henry's introduction

Three more of the plagues of Egypt are related in this chapter,

I. That of the frogs, which is,

A. Threatened, vv. 1–4.

B. Inflicted, vv. 5, 6.

C. Mimicked by the magicians, v. 7.

D. Removed, at the humble request of Pharaoh (vv. 8–14), who yet hardens his heart, and, notwithstanding his promise while the plague was upon him (v. 8), refuses to let Israel go, v. 15.

II. The plague of lice (vv. 16, 17), by which,

A. The magicians were baffled (vv. 18, 19), and yet,

B. Pharaoh was hardened, v. 19.

III. That of flies.

A. Pharaoh is warned of it before (vv. 20, 21), and told that the land of Goshen should be exempt from this plague, vv. 22, 23.

B. The plague is brought, v. 24.

C. Pharaoh treats with Moses about the release of Israel, and humbles himself, vv. 25–29.

D. The plague is thereupon removed (v. 31), and Pharaoh's heart hardened, v. 32.

A detailed analysis of chapter

The plague of frogs. (1–15)
The plague of lice. (16–19)
The plague of flies. (20–32)

Key verse

Verse 16: "And the Lord said unto Moses, Say unto Aaron, Stretch out thy rod, and smite the dust of the land, that it may become lice throughout all the land of Egypt."

Key word / key phrase

Verse 5, “frogs.”

Key event / key person / key theme

Plagues

Key thought

Hardness of heart is not limited to a Pharaoh.

Key thing to look out for

Moses and his prayer life.

Key Bible cross-reference

Verse 19, “finger of God.” See 31:18; Psalm 83; Luke 11:20.

Key “by way of explanation”

Verse 22, “deal differently.” God made a distinction between the Egyptians and the Israelites in most of the plagues, illustrating how he preserves some people and judges other people.

Key “Quotable Quote”

“Prayer is the highest activity of the human soul, and therefore it is at the same time the ultimate test of a man’s true spiritual condition.”

D. Martyn Lloyd-Jones

Exodus 9

Matthew Henry’s introduction

In this chapter we have an account of three more of the plagues of Egypt.

I. Murrain among the cattle, which was fatal to them, vv. 1–7.

II. Boils upon man and beast, vv. 8–12.

III. Hail, with thunder and lightning.

- A. Warning is given of this plague, vv. 13–21.
- B. It is inflicted, to their great terror, vv. 22–26.
- C. Pharaoh, in a fright, renews his treaty with Moses, but instantly breaks his word, v. 27, etc.

A detailed analysis of chapter

The plague on the livestock. (1–7)

The plague of boils. (8–12)

The plague of hail threatened. (13–21)

The plague of hail inflicted. (22–35)

Key verse

Verse 23: “And Moses stretched forth his rod toward heaven: and the Lord sent thunder and hail, and the fire ran along upon the ground; and the Lord rained hail upon the land of Egypt.”

Key word / key phrase

Verse 18, “hailstorm.”

Key event / key person / key theme

More plagues

Key thought

God is never seen to be in a hurry.

Key thing to look out for

The plague on the livestock would be seen as an attack on Egyptian religion, in which bull-gods were worshiped.

Key Bible cross-reference

Verse 29. See 1 Kings 8:22, 38, 54; 2 Chronicles 6:12, 13, 29; Ezra 9:5.

Key "by way of explanation"

Verse 16. The apostle Paul used this verse to illustrate God's sovereignty. See Romans 9:17.

Key "Quotable Quote"

"Of all the doctrines of the Bible, none is so offensive to human nature as the doctrine of God's sovereignty."

J.C. Ryle

Exodus 10

Matthew Henry's introduction

The eighth and ninth of the plagues of Egypt, that of locusts and that of darkness, are recorded in this chapter.

I. Concerning the plague of locusts,

A. God instructs Moses in the meaning of these amazing dispensations of his providence, vv. 1, 2.

B. He threatens the locusts, vv. 3–6.

C. Pharaoh, at the persuasion of his servants, is willing to treat again with Moses (vv. 7–9), but they cannot agree, vv. 10, 11.

D. The locusts come, vv. 12–15.

E. Pharaoh cries Peccavi—I have offended (vv. 16, 17), whereupon Moses prays for the removal of the plague, and it is done; but Pharaoh's heart is still hardened, vv. 18–20.

II. Concerning the plague of darkness,

A. It is inflicted, vv. 21–23.

B. Pharaoh again treats with Moses about a surrender, but the treaty breaks off in a heat, v. 26, etc.

A detailed analysis of chapter

The plague of locusts threatened, Pharaoh, moved by his servants, inclines to let the Israelites go. (1–11)

The plague of locusts. (12–20)

The plague of thick darkness. (21–29)

Key verse

Verse 13: "And Moses stretched forth his rod over the land of Egypt, and the LORD brought an east wind upon the land all that day, and all that night; and when it was morning, the east wind brought the locusts."

Key word / key phrase

Verse 13, "locusts."

Key event / key person / key theme

More plagues

Key thought

It is not hard to be half-hearted.

Key thing to look out for

The last verse of this chapter points to a momentous event.

Key Bible cross-reference

Verse 4. See Joel 1:4–7; 2:1–11; Amos 7:1–3.

Key "by way of explanation"

Verse 2. God ensured that his acts would

never be forgotten. See 12:26, 27; 13:8, 14, 15; Deuteronomy 4:9; Psalm 77:11–20.

Key "Quotable Quote"

"Half-hearted Christianity is worse than no Christianity."

Johann Heinrich Arnold

Exodus 11

Matthew Henry's introduction

Pharaoh had told Moses to get out of his presence (ch. 10:28), and Moses had promised this should be the last time he would trouble him, yet he resolves to say out what he had to say, before he left him; accordingly, we have in this chapter,

I. The instructions God had given to Moses, which he was now to pursue (vv. 1, 2), together with the interest Israel and Moses had in the esteem of the Egyptians, v. 3.

II. The last message Moses delivered to Pharaoh, concerning the death of the firstborn, vv. 4–8.

III. A repetition of the prediction of Pharaoh's hardening his heart, (v. 9), and the event answering to it, v. 10.

A detailed analysis of chapter

God's last instructions to Moses about Pharaoh and the Egyptians. (1–3)

The death of the firstborn threatened. (4–10)

Key verse

Verse 5: "And all the firstborn in the land of Egypt shall die."

Key word / key phrase

Verse 5, "firstborn."

Key event / key person / key theme

Death of Egypt's firstborn

Key thought

God's judgments may appear to be harsh, but what about human sin?

Key thing to look out for

Verse 9. God is in control all the time.

Key Bible cross-reference

Verse 5. See Psalm 78:51; 105:36; 135:8.

Key "by way of explanation"

Verse 5, "firstborn." When God's judgment fell on the firstborn, it was judgment on whole families and the whole Egyptian community.

Key "Quotable Quote"

"God examines both rich and poor, not according to their lands and houses, but according to the riches of their hearts."

Augustine of Hippo

Exodus 12

Matthew Henry's introduction

This chapter gives an account of one of the most memorable ordinances, and one of the most memorable providences, of all that are recorded in the Old Testament.

I. Not one of all the ordinances of the Jewish church was more eminent than that of the Passover, nor is any one more frequently mentioned in the New Testament; and we have here an account of the institution to it. The ordinance consisted of three parts:

A. The killing and eating of the paschal lamb, vv. 1–6, 8–11.
B. The sprinkling of the blood upon the door-posts, spoken of as a distinct thing (Heb. 9:28), and peculiar to this first Passover (v. 7), with the reason for it, v. 13.
C. The feast of unleavened bread for seven days following; this points rather at what was to be done afterwards, in the observance of this ordinance, vv. 14–20. This institution is communicated to the people, and they are instructed in the observance, Of this first Passover, vv. 21–23. Of the subsequent Passovers, vv. 24–27. And the Israelites' obedience to these orders, v. 28.

II. Not one of all the providences of God concerning the Jewish church was more illustrious, or is more frequently mentioned, than the deliverance of the children of Israel out of Egypt.

A. The firstborn of the Egyptians are slain, vv. 29, 30.
B. Orders are given immediately for their discharge, vv. 31–33.
C. They begin their march.
   Loaded with their own effects, v. 34.
   Enriched with the spoils of Egypt, vv. 35, 36.
   Attended with a mixed multitude, vv. 37, 38.
   Put to their shifts for present supply, v. 39. The event is dated, vv. 40–42.
   Lastly, A recapitulation in the close,
   1. Of this memorable ordinance, with some additions, vv. 43–49.
   2. Of this memorable providence, vv. 50, 51.

A detailed analysis of chapter

The beginning of the year changed, and the Passover instituted. (1–20)

The people instructed how to observe the Passover. (21–28)

The death of the firstborn of the Egyptians. The Israelites urged to leave the land of Egypt. (29–36)

The Israelites' first journey to Succoth. (37–42)

Ordinance about the Passover. (43–51)

Key verse

Verse 17: "And ye shall observe the feast of unleavened bread; for in this selfsame day have I brought your armies out of the land of Egypt: therefore shall ye observe this day in your generations by an ordinance for ever."

Key word / key phrase

Verse 21, "Passover."

Key event / key person / key theme

The initiation of the Passover

Key thought

The idea of the Passover is central to the Lord's Supper.

Key thing to look out for

God explained profound spiritual truth through ordinary things everyone knew about.

Key Bible cross-reference

Verse 22 and sprinkling. See Leviticus 14:4, 6, 49, 51, 52; Hebrews 9:19.

Key "by way of explanation"

Verse 21. For Christians, the "Passover lamb" is Jesus, 1 Corinthians 5:7, who died once for all according to Hebrews 7:27.

Key "Quotable Quote"

"He was condemned, that thou mightest be justified, and was killed, that thou mightest live."

John Bunyan

Exodus 13

Matthew Henry's introduction

In this chapter we have,

I. The commands God gave to Israel,

A. To sanctify all their firstborn to him, vv. 1, 2.

B. To be sure to remember their deliverance out of Egypt (vv. 3, 4), and, in remembrance of it, to keep the feast of unleavened bread, vv. 5–7.

C. To transmit the knowledge of it with all possible care to their children, vv. 8–10.

D. To set apart unto God the firstlings of their cattle, (vv. 11–13), and to explain that also to their children, vv. 14–16.

II. The care God took of Israel, when he had brought them out of Egypt.

A. Choosing their way for them, vv. 17, 18.

B. Guiding them in the way, vv. 20–22.

III. And Their care of Joseph's bones, v. 19.

A detailed analysis of chapter

The firstborn sanctified to God. The Passover must be commemorated. (1–10)

The firstborn of beasts set apart. (11–16)

Joseph's bones carried with the Israelites, and they come to Etham. (17–20)

God guides the Israelites by a pillar of cloud and a pillar of fire. (21, 22)

Key verse

Verse 21: "And the LORD went before them by day in a pillar of a cloud, to lead them the way; and by night in a pillar of fire, to give them light; to go by day and night."

Key word / key phrase

Verse 7, "unleavened."

Key event / key person / key theme

The pillar of cloud and the pillar of fire

Key thought

The meal of unleavened bread was never meant to be a mere empty ritual. See verse 14.

Key thing to look out for

God never leaves his people without the guidance they need.

Key Bible cross-reference

Verse 13 and redemption. See Genesis 22:12; Numbers 3:39–51; Romans 12:1.

Key "by way of explanation"

Verse 21. God often spoke to his people from a

cloud. See Numbers 12:5, 6; Deuteronomy 31:15, 16; Psalm 99:6, 7.

Key "Quotable Quote"

"One drop of Christ's blood is worth more than heaven and earth."

Martin Luther

Exodus 14

Matthew Henry's introduction

The departure of the children of Israel out of Egypt (which was indeed the birth of the Jewish church) is made yet more memorable by further works of wonder, which were wrought immediately upon it. Witness the records of this chapter, the contents whereof, together with a key to it, we have, Heb. 11:29. "They passed through the Red Sea as by dry land, which the Egyptians assaying to do were drowned;" and this they did by faith, which intimates that there was something typical and spiritual in it. Here is,

I. The extreme distress and danger that Israel was in at the Red Sea.
   A. Notice was given of it to Moses before, vv. 1–4.
   B. The cause of it was Pharaoh's violent pursuit of them, vv. 5–9.
   C. Israel was in a great consternation upon it, vv. 10–12.
   D. Moses endeavors to encourage them, vv. 13, 14.

II. The wonderful deliverance that God wrought for them out of this distress.
   A. Moses is instructed concerning it, vv. 15–18.
   B. Lines that could not be forced are set between the camp of Israel and Pharaoh's camp, vv. 19, 20.
   C. By the divine power the Red Sea is divided (v. 31), and is made, A lane to the Israelites, who marched safely through it, vv. 22, 29. But, To the Egyptians it was made,
      1. An ambush into which they were drawn, vv. 23–25. And,
      2. A grave in which they were all buried, vv. 26–28.

III. The impressions this made upon the Israelites, vv. 30, 31.

A detailed analysis of chapter

God directs the Israelites to Pihahiroth, Pharaoh pursues them. (1–9)

The Israelites murmur, Moses comforts them. (10–14)

God instructs Moses, and the cloud between the Israelites and the Egyptians. (15–20)

The Israelites pass through the Red Sea, which drowns the Egyptians. (21–31)

Key verse

Verse 29: "But the children of Israel walked upon dry land in the midst of the sea; and the waters were a wall unto them on their right hand, and on their left."

Key word / key phrase

Verse 17, "glory."

Key event / key person / key theme

Crossing the Red Sea

Key thought

God is the God of the impossible.

Key thing to look out for

God is Judge.

Key Bible cross-reference

Verse 31. See Joshua 24:29; 1 Samuel 3:10; 2 Samuel 3:18.

Key "by way of explanation"

Verse 22. This event was never to be forgotten, and was frequently spoken of in the Psalms. See Psalm 66:6; 106:9; 136:13, 24.

Key "Quotable Quote"

"What have we our time and strength for, but to lay them out for God? What is a candle made for, but to be burned?"

Richard Baxter

Exodus 15

Matthew Henry's introduction

In this chapter,

I. Israel looks back upon Egypt with a song of praise for their deliverance. Here is,

A. The song itself, vv. 1–19.

B. The solemn singing of it, vv. 20, 21.

II. Israel marches forward in the wilderness (v. 22), and there,

A. Their discontent at the waters of Marah (vv. 23, 24), and the relief granted them, vv. 25, 26.

B. Their satisfaction in the waters of Elam, v. 27.

A detailed analysis of chapter

The song of Moses for the deliverance of Israel. (1–21)

The bitter waters at Marah, and the Israelites come to Elim. (22–27)

Key verse

Verse 1: "Then sang Moses and the children of Israel this song unto the LORD, and spake, saying, I will sing unto the LORD, for he hath triumphed gloriously: the horse and his rider hath he thrown into the sea."

Key word / key phrase

Verse 2, "sing."

Key event / key person / key theme

The Song of Moses

Key thought

Thanksgiving is essential.

Key thing to look out for

Much of the Bible is taken up with recalling God's goodness.

Key Bible cross-reference

Verse 1. See Judges 5:3; Psalm 89:1; 101:1; 108:1.

Key "by way of explanation"

Verse 20. Prophetesses were not unknown in the Bible. See Numbers 12:1, 2; Judges 4:4; 2 Kings 22:14; Nehemiah 6:14; Luke 2:36, Acts 21:9.

Key "Quotable Quote"

"No duty is more urgent than that of returning thanks."

Ambrose

Exodus 16

Matthew Henry's introduction

This chapter gives us an account of the feeding of the camp of Israel.

I. Their complaint for want of bread, vv. 1–3.
II. The notice God gave them beforehand of the provision he intended to make for them, vv. 4–12.
III. The sending of the manna, vv. 13–15.
IV. The laws and orders concerning the manna.
  A. That they should gather it daily for their daily bread, vv. 16–21.
  B. That they should gather a double portion on the sixth day, vv. 22–26.
  C. That they should expect none on the seventh day, vv. 27–31.
  D. That they should preserve a pot of it for a memorial, v. 32, etc.

A detailed analysis of chapter

The Israelites come to the desert of Sin. They murmur for food, God promises bread from heaven. (1–12)
God sends quails and manna. (13–21)
Details about the manna. (22–31)
An omer of manna to be preserved. (32–36)

Key verse

Verse 15: "And when the children of Israel saw it, they said one to another, It is manna: for they wist not what it was. And Moses said unto them, This is the bread which the LORD hath given you to eat."

Key word / key phrase

Verse 12, "grumbling."

Key event / key person / key theme

God's provision through manna and quail

Key thought

God shows his kindness despite human failures and sins.

Key thing to look out for

God's commands are given for our benefit.

Key Bible cross-reference

Verse 34. See 31:18; 32:15; 34:29; Hebrews 9:4.

Key "by way of explanation"

Verse 4. For Christians Jesus is the "bread from heaven." See John 6:32, 33, 35, 48.

Key "Quotable Quote"

"All plenty which is not my God is poverty to me."

Augustine of Hippo

Exodus 17

Matthew Henry's introduction

Two passages of story are recorded in this chapter,

I. The watering of the host of Israel.
  A. In the wilderness they wanted water, v. 1.
  B. In their want they chided Moses, vv. 2, 3.

C. Moses cried to God, v. 4.

D. God ordered him to smite the rock, and fetch water out of that; Moses did so, vv. 5, 6.

E. The place named from it, v. 7.

II. The defeating of the host of Amalek.

A. The victory obtained by the prayer of Moses, vv. 8–12.

B. By the sword of Joshua, v. 13.

C. A record kept of it, vv. 14, 16. And these things which happened to them are written for our instruction in our spiritual journey and warfare.

A detailed analysis of chapter

The Israelites murmur for water at Rephidim, God provides it from the rock. (1–7)

Amalek overcome, and the prayers of Moses. (8–16)

Key verse

Verse 6: "Behold, I will stand before thee there upon the rock in Horeb; and thou shalt smite the rock, and there shall come water out of it, that the people may drink. And Moses did so in the sight of the elders of Israel."

Key word / key phrase

Verse 7, "quarreled."

Key event / key person / key theme

Water from the rock

Key thought

God hates grumblers.

Key thing to look out for

Wars in the Bible can be seen as an illustration of the spiritual battle every Christian faces.

Key Bible cross-reference

Verse 6. See 1 Corinthians 10:4; Hebrews 11:24–26.

Key "by way of explanation"

Verse 11. Hands were held up as a symbol of appealing to God for his help. See 9:22; 10:12.

Key "Quotable Quote"

"When afflicted, love can allow thee to groan, but not to grumble."

William Gurnall

Exodus 18

Matthew Henry's introduction

This chapter is concerning Moses himself, and the affairs of his own family.

I. Jethro his father-in-law brings to him his wife and children, vv. 1–6.

II. Moses entertains his father-in-law with great respect (v. 7), with good discourse (vv. 8–11), with a sacrifice and a feast, v. 12.

III. Jethro advises him about the management of his business as a judge in Israel, to take inferior judges in to his assistance (vv. 13–23), and Moses, after some time, takes his counsel (vv. 24–26), and so they part, v. 27.

A detailed analysis of chapter

Jethro brings to Moses his wife and two sons. (1–6)

Moses entertains Jethro. (7–12)

Jethro's counsel to Moses. (13–27)

Key verse

Verse 5: "And Jethro, Moses' father in law, came with his sons and his wife unto Moses into the desert, where he encamped at the mount of God."

Key word / key phrase

Verse 1, "Jethro."

Key event / key person / key theme

Jethro visits Moses.

Key thought

Jethro is delighted to hear all that God did, verse 9.

Key thing to look out for

Shared leadership and delegation are essential in Christian work.

Key Bible cross-reference

Verse 11. See 2 Kings 5:15.

Key "by way of explanation"

Verse 15. God's will was sought by going to a place of worship, Genesis 25:22, and by visiting a prophet, 1 Samuel 9:9.

Key "Quotable Quote"

"We never find a presbyter in the singular in the New Testament. He is always a member of a team."

E.M.B. Green

Exodus 19

Matthew Henry's introduction

This chapter introduces the solemnity of the giving of the law upon mount Sinai, which was one of the most striking appearances of the divine glory that ever was in this lower world. We have here,

I. The circumstances of time and place, vv. 1, 2.

II. The covenant between God and Israel settled in general. The gracious proposal God made to them (vv. 3–6), and their consent to the proposal, vv. 7, 8.

III. Notice given three days before of God's design to give the law out of a thick cloud, v. 9. Orders given to prepare the people to receive the law (vv. 10–13), and care taken to carry out those orders, vv. 14, 15.

IV. A terrible appearance of God's glory upon mount Sinai, vv. 16–20.

V. Silence proclaimed, and strict charges given to the people to observe decorum while God spoke to them, v. 21, etc.

A detailed analysis of chapter

The people come to Sinai, God's message to them, and their answer. (1–8)

The people told to prepare to hear the law. (9–15)

The presence of God on Sinai. (16–25)

Key verse

Verse 20: "And the LORD came down upon mount Sinai, on the top of the mount: and the LORD called Moses up to the top of the mount; and Moses went up."

Key word / key phrase

Verse 10, "consecrate."

Key event / key person / key theme

Moses meets the Lord on top of Mount Sinai.

Key thought

God's holiness should never be forgotten.

Key thing to look out for

Moses was content to do what God ordered.

Key Bible cross-reference

Verse 6. See Deuteronomy 7:6; 14:2; 26:18; Psalm 135:4.

Key "by way of explanation"

Verse 6. The point about priests is that they are meant to be wholly consecrated to the service of God. See Isaiah 61:6; 1 Peter 2:5.

Key "Quotable Quote"

"Nothing shall be lost that is done for God or in obedience to him."

John Owen

Exodus 20

Matthew Henry's introduction

All things being prepared for the solemn promulgation of the divine law, we have, in this chapter,

I. The ten commandments, as God himself spoke them upon mount Sinai (vv. 1–17), as remarkable a portion of scripture as any in the Old Testament.

II. The impressions made upon the people thereby, vv. 18–21.

III. Some particular instructions which God gave privately to Moses, to be by him communicated to the people, relating to his worship, v. 22, etc.

A detailed analysis of chapter

The preface to the Ten Commandments. (1, 2)
Commandments 1 to 4: our duty to God. (3–11)
Commandments 5–10: our relationship with others. (12–17)
The fear of the people. (18–21)
Idolatry again forbidden. (22–26)

Key verse

Verse 1: "And God spake all these words, saying, I am the LORD thy God, which have brought thee out of the land of Egypt, out of the house of bondage."

Key word / key phrase

Verse 1, "spoke."

Key event / key person / key theme

God gives the Ten Commandments.

Key thought

The Ten Commandments never go out of date.

Key thing to look out for

The Ten Commandments explain how we are to love God and our fellow human beings in our daily lives.

Key Bible cross-reference

Verses 1–17. See Deuteronomy 5:6–21; Matthew 5:21, 27; 19:17–19.

Key "by way of explanation"

Verse 4, "idol." The problem with idols is that they aim to represent God, yet God has no visible form. So all idols misrepresent God. See Deuteronomy 4:12, 15–18.

Key "Quotable Quote"

"The only things which ought to be painted or sculptured, are things which can be presented to the eye; the majesty of God, which is far beyond the reach of any eye, must not be dishonored by unbecoming representations."

John Calvin

Exodus 21

Matthew Henry's introduction

The laws recorded in this chapter relate to the fifth and sixth commandments; and though they are not accommodated to our constitution, especially in point of servitude, nor are the penalties annexed binding on us, yet they are of great use for the explanation of the moral law, and the rules of natural justice. Here are several enlargements,

I. Upon the fifth commandment, which concerns particular relations.
   A. The duty of masters towards their servants, their men-servants (vv. 2–6), and the maidservants, vv. 7–11.
   B. The punishment of disobedient children that strike their parents (v. 15), or curse them, v. 17.

II. Upon the sixth commandment, which for bids all violence offered to the person of a man. Here is,
   A. Concerning murder, vv. 12–14.
   B. Man-stealing, v. 16.
   C. Assault and battery, vv. 18, 19.
   D. Correcting a servant, vv. 20, 21.
   E. Hurting a woman with child, vv. 22, 23.
   F. The law of retaliation, vv. 24, 25.
   G. Maiming a servant, vv. 26, 27.
   H. An ox goring, vv. 28–32.
   I. Damage by opening a pit, vv. 33, 34.
   J. Cattle fighting, vv. 35, 36.

A detailed analysis of chapter

Laws about servants. (1–11)
Laws about personal injuries. (12–36)

Key verse

Verse 1: "Now these are the judgments which thou shalt set before them."

Key word / key phrase

Verse 2, "servant."

Key event / key person / key theme

How to treat slaves

Key thought

God's kindness extends to everyone.

Key thing to look out for

Laws are meant to benefit the wronged.

Key Bible cross-reference

Verses 12–15. See Numbers 35:16–34; Deuteronomy 19:1–13.

Key "by way of explanation"

Verse 32. The price of a slave was the same as

the payment Judas received for betraying Jesus, see Matthew 26:14, 15.

Key "Quotable Quote"

"*Lex mala, lex nulla*. An evil law, is no law."

Thomas Aquinas

Exodus 22

Matthew Henry's introduction

The laws of this chapter relate,

I. To the eighth commandment, concerning theft (vv. 1–4), trespass by cattle (v. 5), damage by fire (v. 6), trusts (vv. 7–13), borrowing cattle (vv. 14, 15), or money, vv. 25–27.

II. To the seventh commandment. Against fornication (vv. 16, 17), bestiality, v. 19.

III. To the first table, forbidding witchcraft (v. 18), idolatry, v. 20. Commanding to offer the first fruits, vv. 29, 30.

IV. To the poor, vv. 21–24.

V. To the civil government, v. 28.

VI. To the peculiarity of the Jewish nation, v. 31.

A detailed analysis of chapter

Laws about protection of property. (1–15)

Laws about social responsibility. (16–31)

Key verse

Verse 31: "And ye shall be holy men unto me."

Key word / key phrase

Verse 7, "pay back."

Key event / key person / key theme

Moral and religious laws

Key thought

God's laws extend to every area of life.

Key thing to look out for

God's laws come from a compassionate heart, verse 27.

Key Bible cross-reference

Verses 21–27. See Psalm 10:14, 17, 18; 68:5; 82:3; 146:9.

Key "by way of explanation"

Verse 20. Total destruction of idols and those who worshiped idols was commanded by God. See Numbers 21:2.

Key "Quotable Quote"

"One has not only a legal but a moral responsibility to obey just laws . Conversely, one has a moral responsibility to disobey unjust laws."

Martin Luther King, Jr.

Exodus 23

Matthew Henry's introduction

This chapter continues and concludes the acts that passed in the first session (if I may so call it) upon mount Sinai. Here are,

I. Some laws of universal obligation, relating especially to the ninth commandment, against bearing false witness (v. 1), and giving false judgment, vv. 2, 3, 6–8. Also a law of doing good to our enemies (vv. 4, 5), and not oppressing strangers, v. 9.

II. Some laws peculiar to the Jews. The sabbatical year (vv. 10, 11), the three annual feasts

(vv. 14–17), with some laws pertaining thereto.

III. Gracious promises of the completing of the mercy God had begun for them, upon condition of their obedience. That God would conduct them through the wilderness (vv. 20–24), that he would prosper all they had (vv. 25, 26), that he would put them in possession of Canaan, vv. 27–31. But they must not mingle themselves with the nations, vv. 32, 33.

A detailed analysis of chapter

Laws against falsehood and injustice. (1–9)

The year of rest, and the Sabbath, and the three festivals. (10–19)

God promises to take the Israelites to Canaan. (20–33)

Key verse

Verse 32: "Thou shalt make no covenant with them, nor with their gods."

Key word / key phrase

Verse 2, "crowd."

Key event / key person / key theme

Laws about justice and mercy

Key thought

Following the crowd very often means following evil.

Key thing to look out for

Righteousness exalts a nation.

Key Bible cross-reference

Verse 1. See Leviticus 19:16; Deuteronomy 23:13–19.

Key "by way of explanation"

Verse 7. This verse is often illustrated in the Bible. See 1 Kings 21:10–13.

Key "Quotable Quote"

"Justice is truth in action."

Joseph Joubert

Exodus 24

Matthew Henry's introduction

Moses, as mediator between God and Israel, having received divers laws and ordinances from God privately in the three foregoing chapters, in this chapter,

I. Comes down to the people, acquaints them with the laws he had received, and takes their consent to those laws (v. 3), writes the laws, and reads them to the people, who repeat their consent (vv. 4–7), and then by sacrifice, and the sprinkling of blood, ratifies the covenant between them and God, vv. 5, 6, 8.

II. He returns to God again, to receive further directions. When he was dismissed from his former attendance, he was ordered to attend again, vv. 1, 2. He did so with seventy of the elders, to whom God made a discovery of his glory, vv. 9–11. Moses is ordered up into the mount (vv. 12, 13); the rest are ordered down to the people, v. 14. The cloud of glory is seen by all the people on the top of mount Sinai (vv. 15–17), and Moses is therewith God forty days and forty nights, v. 18.

A detailed analysis of chapter

Moses is called up into the mountain, and the people promise obedience. (1–8)

The glory of the Lord appears. (9–11)

Moses goes up into the mountain. (12–18)

Key verse

Verse 7: "And he took the book of the covenant, and read in the audience of the people: and they said, All that the LORD hath said will we do, and be obedient."

Key word / key phrase

Verse 17, "glory."

Key event / key person / key theme

The covenant is confirmed.

Key thought

Moses alone was allowed to approach God, as he was the mediator of the covenant.

Key thing to look out for

Jesus' new covenant was sealed with his own blood. See Matthew 26:28.

Key Bible cross-reference

Verse 7. See 20:22–23:19; 20:2–17; 23:20–33.

Key "by way of explanation"

Verse 17. Every glimpse of God's glory is like a blinding light. During Jesus' transfiguration his clothes looked like the most brilliant white.

Key "Quotable Quote"

"Grace is but glory begun, and glory is but grace perfected."

Jonathan Edwards

Exodus 25

Matthew Henry's introduction

At this chapter begins an account of the orders and instructions God gave to Moses upon the mount for the erecting and furnishing of a tabernacle to the honor of God. We have here.

I. Orders given for a collection to be made among the people for this purpose, vv. 1–9.

II. Particular instructions,

A. Concerning the ark of the covenant, vv. 10–22.

B. The table of showbread, vv. 23–30.

C. The golden candlestick, v. 31, etc.

A detailed analysis of chapter

What the Israelites were to offer for making the tabernacle. (1–9)

The ark. (10–22)

The table, with its furniture. (23–30)

The candlestick. (31–40)

Key verse

Verse 10: "And they shall make an ark of shittim [acacia] wood."

Key word / key phrase

Verse 21, "ark."

Key event / key person / key theme

The ark

Key thought

Nothing is more important than worshiping God.

Key thing to look out for

Verses 8, 22. The purpose of the ark.

Key Bible cross-reference

Verse 30. See 33:14, 15; Isaiah 63:9.

Key "by way of explanation"

The ark was a wooden box covered with gold. Its lid (KJV "mercy seat") was made of pure gold. At either end of the lid was a golden cherubim.

Key "Quotable Quote"

"'Divine service' is not a thing of a few hours and a few places, but when all life becomes holiness unto the Lord, and every place and thing, as consecrated as the tabernacle."

C.H. Spurgeon

Exodus 26

Matthew Henry's introduction

Moses here receives instructions,

I. Concerning the inner curtains of the tent or tabernacle, and the coupling of those curtains, vv. 1–6.

II. Concerning the outer curtains which were of goats' hair, to strengthen the former, vv. 7–13.

III. Concerning the case or cover which was to secure it from the weather, v. 14.

IV. Concerning the boards which were to be reared up to support the curtains, with their bars and sockets, vv. 15–30.

V. The partition between the holy place and the most holy, vv. 31–35.

VI. The veil for the door, vv. 36, 37. These particulars, thus largely recorded, seem of little use to us now; yet, having been of great use to Moses and Israel, and God having thought fit to preserve down to us the remembrance of them, we ought not to overlook them. Even the antiquity renders this account venerable.

A detailed analysis of chapter

The curtains of the tabernacle. (1–6)

The curtains of goats' hair. (7–14)

The boards, sockets, and bars. (15–30)

The curtain (veil) in front of the holy of holies, and for the entrance. (31–37)

Key verse

Verse 1: "Moreover thou shalt make the tabernacle with ten curtains of fine twined linen, and blue, and purple, and scarlet: with cherubims of cunning work shalt thou make them."

Key word / key phrase

Verse 1, "tabernacle."

Key event / key person / key theme

Instructions for making the tabernacle

Key thought

Is it not amazing that humans can have fellowship with God?

Key thing to look out for

God wishes humans to worship him.

Key Bible cross-reference

Verse 1. In John 1:14 John says that Jesus "made his dwelling among us." The word used here means "tabernacled," or, "pitched his tent" among us.

Key "by way of explanation"

Verse 31. This curtain was dramatically torn from top to bottom at Jesus' crucifixion, Mark 15:38, indicating that access to God was now possible.

Key "Quotable Quote"

"What God chooses, he cleanses.
What God cleanses, he molds.
What God molds, he fills.
What God fills, he uses."

J.S. Baxter

Exodus 27

Matthew Henry's introduction

In this chapter directions are given,

I. Concerning the brazen altar for burnt-offerings, vv. 1–8.

II. Concerning the court of the tabernacle, with the hangings of it, vv. 9–19.

III. Concerning oil for the lamp, vv. 20, 21.

A detailed analysis of chapter

The altar of burnt offerings. (1–8)
The court of the tabernacle. (9–19)
The oil for the lamps. (20, 21)

Key verse

Verse 20: "And thou shalt command the children of Israel, that they bring thee pure oil olive beaten for the light, to cause the lamp to burn always."

Key word / key phrase

Verse 1, "altar."

Key event / key person / key theme

Some of the furniture for the temple

Key thought

Every item of "furniture" in the temple was full of significant symbolism.

Key thing to look out for

Nothing was thought to be too costly if needed in God's service.

Key Bible cross-reference

Verse 21. See 29:42, 43.

Key "by way of explanation"

Verse 2. The "horns" at each corner of the altar were symbols of help and refuge. See 1 Kings 1:50.

Key "Quotable Quote"

"Often, what passes for religious experience is a communal emotion felt in church services, in meetings, in singing or contrived fellowship. Few Christians would know God on their own."

Os Guinness

Exodus 28

Matthew Henry's introduction

Orders being given for the fitting up of the place of worship, in this and the following chapter care is taken about the priests that were to minister in this holy place, as the menial servants of the God of Israel. He hired servants, as a token of his purpose to reside among them. In this chapter,

I. He pitches upon the persons who should be his servants, v. 1.

II. He appoints their livery; their work was holy, and so must their garments be, and unanswerable to the glory of the house which was now to be erected, vv. 2–5.

A. He appoints the garments of his head-servant, the high priest, which were very rich.

An ephod and girdle, vv. 6–14.

A breast-plate of judgment (vv. 15–29), in which must be put the urim and thummim, v. 30.

The robe of the ephod, vv. 31–35.

The miter, vv. 36–39.

B. The garments of the inferior priests, vv. 40–43. And these also were shadows of good things to come.

A detailed analysis of chapter

Aaron and his sons set apart for the priest's office, and their garments. (1–5)

The ephod. (6–14)

The breastpiece, and the Urim and Thummim. (15–30)

The robe of the ephod (a sleeveless garment), and the plate of gold. (31–39)

The garments for Aaron's sons. (40–43)

Key verse

Verse 15: "And thou shalt make the breastplate of judgment with cunning work."

Key word / key phrase

Verse 15, "breastpiece."

Key event / key person / key theme

Clothes for the priests

Key thought

The garments the priests wore were to reflect the special work they were engaged in.

Key thing to look out for

If worship does not emphasize God's holiness, verse 36, there is something wrong with it.

Key Bible cross-reference

Verse 6. See Judges 8:27; 18:17; Hosea 3:4.

Key "by way of explanation"

Verse 30, "Urim and Thummim," were sacred lots which were cast in order to discover God's will. See Numbers 27:21.

Key "Quotable Quote"

"He humbled himself for us; let us glorify him."

Augustine of Hippo

Exodus 29

Matthew Henry's introduction

Particular orders are given in this chapter,

I. Concerning the consecration of the priests, and the sanctification of the altar, vv. 1–37.

II. Concerning the daily sacrifice, vv. 38–41. To which gracious promises are annexed that God would own and bless them in all their services, v. 42, etc.

A detailed analysis of chapter

The sacrifice and ceremony for the consecration of the priests. (1–37)

The continual burnt offerings, God's promise to live among the Israelites. (38–46)

Key verse

Verse 44: "And I will sanctify the tabernacle of the congregation, and the altar: I will sanctify also both Aaron and his sons, to minister to me in the priest's office."

Key word / key phrase

Verse 43, "glory."

Key event / key person / key theme

The consecration of the priests

Key thought

Worship and God's glory should always be linked. See verse 43.

Key thing to look out for

God's presence was never restricted to the tabernacle. See verse 45.

Key Bible cross-reference

Verse 14. See Hebrews 13:11–13.

Key "by way of explanation"

Verse 20. The right ears symbolize listening to God; the right hands and right feet symbolize serving others for God's sake.

Key "Quotable Quote"

"There are few individuals in this life, and perhaps even none, who sufficiently understand how much we hinder and keep God from doing what he desires in our souls."

Ignatius of Loyola

Exodus 30

Matthew Henry's introduction

Moses is, in this chapter, further instructed,

I. Concerning the altar of incense, vv. 1–10.

II. Concerning the ransom-money which the Israelites were to pay, when they were numbered, vv. 11–16.

III. Concerning the laver of brass, which was set for the priests to wash in, vv. 17–21.

IV. Concerning the making up of the anointing oil, and the use of it, vv. 22–33.

V. Concerning the incense and perfume which were to be burned on the golden altar, v. 34, etc.

A detailed analysis of chapter

The altar of incense. (1–10)

The ransom of souls. (11–16)

The bronze laver. (17–21)

The holy anointing oil, and the perfume. (22–38)

Key verse

Verse 16: "And thou shalt take the atonement money of the children of Israel, and shalt appoint it for the service of the tabernacle of the congregation; that it may be a memorial unto the children of Israel before the LORD, to make an atonement for your souls."

Key word / key phrase

Verse 15, “atone.”

Key event / key person / key theme

More furniture for the temple

Key thought

Washing with water is often used in the Bible to symbolize God washing away our sins.

Key thing to look out for

When a person or object was anointed with oil he, she, or it, was set apart for God’s use.

Key Bible cross-reference

Verse 12. See Numbers 1:2; 26:2.

Key “by way of explanation”

Verse 1. Incense stood for prayers. See Psalm 141:2; Luke 1:10; Revelation 5:8.

Key “Quotable Quote”

“If you are talking of atonement, the means by which we sinners can be reconciled to the God of holy love, why then, yes, I don’t think we can escape the truth of the divine substitution.”

John R.W. Stott

Exodus 31

Matthew Henry’s introduction

God is here drawing towards a conclusion of what he had to say to Moses upon the mount, where he had now been with him forty days and forty nights; and yet no more is recorded of what was said to him in all that time than what we have read in the six chapters foregoing. In this,

I. He appoints what workmen should be employed in the building and furnishing of the tabernacle, vv. 1–11.

II. He repeats the law of the Sabbath, and the religious observance of it, vv. 12–17.

III. He delivers to him the two tables of the testimony at parting, v. 18.

A detailed analysis of chapter

Bezalel and Oholiab are appointed and qualified for the work of the tabernacle. (1–11)

The observance of the Sabbath. (12–17)

Moses receives the tablets of the law. (18)

Key verse

Verse 14: “Ye shall keep the Sabbath therefore; for it is holy unto you.”

Key word / key phrase

Verse 3, “skill.”

Key event / key person / key theme

Bezalel and Oholiab

Key thought

Every talent can be used in God’s service.

Key thing to look out for

The Sabbath was God’s gift to humankind.

Key Bible cross-reference

Verse 18, “two tablets.” See 25:21.

Key “by way of explanation”

Verse 18. The covenant came from God with

his instructions, so it was said to be inscribed with God's finger.

Key "Quotable Quote"

"I feel as if God had, by giving the Sabbath, given fifty-two springs in every year."

Samuel Taylor Coleridge

Exodus 32

Matthew Henry's introduction

It is a very lamentable interruption which the story of this chapter gives to the record of the establishment of the church, and of religion among the Jews. Things went on admirably well towards that happy settlement: God had shown himself very favorable, and the people also had seemed to be pretty tractable. Moses had now almost completed his forty days upon the mount, and, we may suppose, was pleasing himself with the thoughts of the very joyful welcome he should have to the camp of Israel at his return, and the speedy setting up of the tabernacle among them. But, behold, the measures are broken, the sin of Israel turns away those good things from them, and puts a stop to the current of God's favors; the sin that did the mischief (would you think it?) was worshipping a golden calf. The marriage was ready to be solemnized between God and Israel, but Israel plays the harlot, and so the match is broken, and it will be no easy matter to piece it again. Here is,

I. The sin of Israel, and of Aaron particularly, in making the golden calf for a god (vv. 1–4), and worshipping it, vv. 5, 6.

II. The notice which God gave of this to Moses, who was now in the mount with him, (vv. 7, 8), and the sentence of his wrath against them, vv. 9, 10.

III. The intercession which Moses immediately made for them in the mount (vv. 11–13), and the result of that intercession, v. 14.

IV. His coming down from the mount, when he became an eye-witness of their idolatry (vv. 15–19), in abhorrence of which, and as an expression of just indignation, he broke the tables (v. 19), and burnt the golden calf, v. 20.

V. The examination of Aaron about it, vv. 21–24.

VI. Execution done upon the ring-leaders in the idolatry, vv. 25–29.

VII. The further intercession Moses made for them, to turn away the wrath of God from them (vv. 30–32), and a reprieve granted thereupon, reserving them for a further reckoning, v. 33, etc.

A detailed analysis of chapter

The people tell Aaron to make a golden calf. (1–6)

God's displeasure, and the intercession of Moses. (7–14)

Moses breaks the tablets of the law. He destroys the golden calf. (15–20)

Aaron's excuse, and the idolaters killed. (21–29)

Moses prays for the people. (30–35)

Key verse

Verse 4: "And he received them at their hand, and fashioned it with a graving tool, after he had made it a molten calf: and they said, These be thy gods, O Israel, which brought thee up out of the land of Egypt."

Key word / key phrase

Verse 4, "idol."

Key event / key person / key theme

Making an idol in the shape of a golden calf

Key thought

Idleness led to idolatry.

Key thing to look out for

None of God's people are exempt from being tempted to sin against God.

Key Bible cross-reference

Verse 14. See Psalm 106:45; Amos 7:1–6; James 5:16.

Key "by way of explanation"

Verse 9. To be "stiff-necked" was to behave like some unbending and unresponsive ox which would not go the way it was being directed. See Jeremiah 27:11, 12.

Key "Quotable Quote"

"We think it unlawful to give a visible shape to God, because God himself has forbidden it, and because it cannot be done without, in some degree, tarnishing his glory."

John Calvin,
The Institutes of Christian Religion

Exodus 33

Matthew Henry's introduction

In this chapter we have a further account of the mediation of Moses between God and Israel, for the making up of the breach that sin had made between them.

I. He brings a very humbling message from God to them (vv. 1–3, 5), which has a good effect upon them, and helps to prepare them for mercy, vv. 4, 6.

II. He settles a correspondence between God and them, and both God and the people signify their approbation of that correspondence, God by descending in a cloudy pillar, and the people by worshipping at the tent doors, vv. 7–11.

III. He is earnest with God in prayer, and prevails,

A. For a promise of his presence with the people, vv. 12–17.

B. For a sight of his glory for himself, v. 18, etc.

A detailed analysis of chapter

The Lord refuses to go with Israel. (1–6)

The "tent of meeting" set up outside the camp. (7–11)

Moses desires to see the glory of God. (12–23)

Key verse

Verse 14: "And he said, My presence shall go with thee, and I will give thee rest."

Key word / key phrase

Verse 18, "glory."

Key event / key person / key theme

God's people are told to move on from Mount Sinai.

Key thought

No one deserves God's mercy.

Key thing to look out for

God is compassionate and so showers his love on everyone.

Key Bible cross-reference

Verse 17. See Matthew 17:5; Hebrews 3:1–6.

Key "by way of explanation"

The tabernacle was in the midst of the camp; the tent of meeting was a temporary structure until the tabernacle was finished.

Key "Quotable Quote"

"Man may dismiss compassion from his heart, but God never will."

William Cowper

Exodus 34

Matthew Henry's introduction

God having in the foregoing chapter intimated to Moses his reconciliation to Israel, here gives proofs of it, proceeding to settle his covenant and communion with them. Four instances of the return of his favor we have in this chapter:

I. The orders he gives to Moses to come up to the mount, the next morning, and bring two tables of stone with him, vv. 1–4.

II. His meeting him there, and the proclamation of his name, vv. 5–9.

III. The instructions he gave him there, and his converse with him for forty days together, without intermission, vv. 10–28.

IV. The honor he put upon him when he sent him down with his face shining, vv. 29–35. In all this God dealt with Moses as a public person, and mediator between him and Israel, and a type of the great Mediator.

A detailed analysis of chapter

The tablets of the law renewed. (1–4)

The name of the Lord proclaimed, and the entreaty of Moses. (5–9)

God's covenant. (10–17)

The festivals. (18–27)

The veil of Moses. (28–35)

Key verse

Verse 4: "And he hewed two tables of stone like unto the first; and Moses rose up early in the morning, and went up unto mount Sinai, as the LORD had commanded him, and took in his hand the two tables of stone."

Key word / key phrase

Verse 6, "faithfulness."

Key event / key person / key theme

A replacement set of stone tablets

Key thought

It is not possible to hide the fact that one has been in God's presence.

Key thing to look out for

The revelation which the Bible gives about God's character.

Key Bible cross-reference

Verses 6, 7. See Numbers 14:18; Nehemiah 9:17; Jonah 4:2.

Key "by way of explanation"

Verse 13. "Asherah poles" were erected in honor of Asherah, the partner of the main Canaanite god, El.

Key "Quotable Quote"

"The infinite-personal God, the God who is Trinity, has spoken. He is there, and he is not silent."

Francis A. Schaeffer

Exodus 35

Matthew Henry's introduction

What should have been said and done upon Moses' coming down the first time from the mount, if the golden calf had not broken the measures and put all into disorder, now at last, when with great difficulty reconciliation was made, begins to be said and done; and that great affair of the setting up of God's worship is put into its former channel again, and goes on now without interruption.

I. Moses gives Israel those instructions, received from God, which required immediate observance.

A. Concerning the Sabbath, vv. 1–3.

B. Concerning the contribution that was to be made for the erecting of the tabernacle, vv. 4–9.

C. Concerning the framing of the tabernacle and the utensils of it, vv. 10–19.

II. The people bring in their contributions, vv. 20–29.

III. The head-workmen are nominated, v. 30, etc.

A detailed analysis of chapter

The Sabbath to be observed. (1–3)

The free gifts for the tabernacle. (4–19)

The willingness of the people to present offerings. (20–29)

Bezalel and Oholiab called to the work. (30–35)

Key verse

Verse 31: "And he hath filled him with the spirit of God, in wisdom, in understanding, and in knowledge, and in all manner of workmanship."

Key word / key phrase

Verse 5, "offering."

Key event / key person / key theme

More items for the tabernacle

Key thought

God loves a generous heart.

Key thing to look out for

All service for God is meant to be carried out willingly.

Key Bible cross-reference

35:4–39:43. See 25–28; 30:1–5; 31:1–11.

Key "by way of explanation"

Verse 5 emphasizes the voluntary nature of serving God. See verses 21, 26, 29; 36:2, 3.

Key "Quotable Quote"

"Everybody can be great . . . because anybody can serve."

Martin Luther King, Jr.

Exodus 36

Matthew Henry's introduction

In this chapter,

I. The work of the tabernacle is begun, vv. 1–4.

II. A stop is put to the people's contributions, vv. 5–7.

III. A particular account is given of the making of the tabernacle itself; the fine curtains of it, vv. 8–13. The coarse ones, vv. 14–19. The boards, vv. 20–30. The bars, vv. 31–34. The partition veil, vv. 35, 36. And the hanging for the door, v. 37, etc.

A detailed analysis of chapter

The making of the tabernacle. The liberality of the people restrained. (1–38)

Key verse

Verse 8: "And every wise hearted man among them that wrought the work of the tabernacle made ten curtains of fine twined linen, and blue, and purple, and scarlet: with cherubims of cunning work made he them."

Key word / key phrase

Verse 8, "tabernacle."

Key event / key person / key theme

Items made for the tabernacle.

Key thought

Any service for God is honorable.

Key thing to look out for

God calls specific people to serve him in specific ways.

Key Bible cross-reference

Verses 1–38. See 35:4–39:43.

Key "by way of explanation"

Verse 7. The enthusiasm of God's people was so great that Moses had to ask them not to bring in anything more for the sanctuary.

Key "Quotable Quote"

"Dislike of enthusiasm is to quench the Spirit."

D. Martyn Lloyd-Jones

Exodus 37

Matthew Henry's introduction

Bezaleel and his workmen are still busy, making

I. The ark with the mercy-seat and the cherubim, vv. 1–9.

II. The table with its vessels, vv. 10–16.

III. The candlestick with its appurtenances, vv. 17–24.

IV. The golden altar for incense, vv. 25–28.

V. The holy oil and incense, v. 29. The particular appointment concerning each of which we had before the 25th and 30th chapters.

A detailed analysis of chapter

The making of the ark, and the furniture of the tabernacle. (1–29)

Key verse

Verse 1: "And Bezalel made the ark of shittim [acacia] wood: two cubits and a half was the length of it, and a cubit and a half the breadth of it, and a cubit and a half the height of it."

Key word / key phrase

Verse 1, "ark."

Key event / key person / key theme

Making the furniture for the tabernacle

Key thought

The design of the ark, with all its gold, would have emphasized God's holiness.

Key thing to look out for

All the tabernacle furnishings in some way reflected an aspect of God's greatness.

Key Bible cross-reference

Verses 1–9. See Exodus 25:10–20.

Key "by way of explanation"

Verse 1. As Bezalel was the chief craftsman he was given the privilege of making the most sacred object for the tabernacle, the ark.

Key "Quotable Quote"

"Now, if you will prove that your ceremonies proceed from faith, and do please God, you must prove that God in expressed words has commanded them; or else you shall never prove that they proceed from faith, nor yet that they please God; but they are sin, and do displease him, according to the words of the apostle, 'Whatsoever is not of faith is sin.'"

John Knox

Exodus 38

Matthew Henry's introduction

Here is an account,

I. Of the making of the brazen altar (vv. 1–7), and the laver, v. 8.

II. The preparing of the hangings for the enclosing of the court in which the tabernacle was to stand, vv. 9–20.

III. A summary of the gold, silver, and brass, that was contributed to, and used in, the preparing of the tabernacle, v. 21, etc.

A detailed analysis of chapter

The bronze altar and basin. (1–8)

The courtyard. (9–20)

The offerings of the people. (21–31)

Key verse

Verse 1: "And he made the altar of burnt offering of shittim [acacia] wood: five cubits was the length thereof, and five cubits the breadth thereof; it was foursquare; and three cubits the height thereof."

Key word / key phrase

Verse 1, "altar of burnt offering."

Key event / key person / key theme

Making the altar for the burnt offerings

Key thought

Everyone contributed financially to the cost of building the tabernacle.

Key thing to look out for

The tabernacle was constructed so it could be dismantled, transported, and then erected again.

Key Bible cross-reference

Verse 26, "603,550 men." See Numbers 1:21–43; 2:4–31.

Key "by way of explanation"

Verse 8. Mirrors were not made of glass in ancient times, but a reflection was obtained by looking into bronze mirrors.

Key "Quotable Quote"

"Act wisely, as a good steward, holding everything as lent to you who have been made God's steward."

Catherine of Siena

Exodus 39

Matthew Henry's introduction

This chapter gives us an account of the finishing of the work of the tabernacle.

I. The last things prepared were the holy garments. The ephod and its curious girdle, vv. 1–5. The onyx-stones for the shoulders, vv. 6, 7. The breastplate with the precious stones in it, vv. 8–21. The robe of the ephod, vv. 22–26. The coats, bonnets, and breeches, for the inferior priests, vv. 27–29. And the plate of the holy crown, vv. 30, 31.

II. A summary account of the whole work, as it was presented to Moses when it was all finished, v. 32, etc.

A detailed analysis of chapter

The priests' garments. (1–31)

The tabernacle completed. (32–43)

Key verse

Verse 2: "And he made the ephod of gold, blue, and purple, and scarlet, and fine twined linen."

Key word / key phrase

Verse 8, "breastpiece."

Key event / key person / key theme

Making the special clothes for the priests

Key thought

Nothing but the best was good enough for God. So pure gold was always used.

Key thing to look out for

The Israelites, verse 32, were most conscientious in the way they carried out God's orders for building the tabernacle.

Key Bible cross-reference

Verse 32. See Genesis 2:1–3.

Key "by way of explanation"

Verse 30. The plate on the turbans worn by the priests was given the name of the "sacred diadem."

Key "Quotable Quote"

"By perseverance the snail reached the ark."

C.H. Spurgeon

Exodus 40

Matthew Henry's introduction

In this chapter,

I. Orders are given for the setting up of the tabernacle and the fixing of all the appurtenances of it in their proper places (vv. 1–8), and the consecrating of it (vv. 9–11), and of the priests, vv. 12–15.

II. Care is taken to do all this, and as it was appointed to be done, vv. 16–33.

III. God takes possession of it by the cloud, v. 34, etc.

A detailed analysis of chapter

The tabernacle is to be set up, Aaron and his sons to be sanctified. (1–15)

Moses performs all as directed. (16–33)

The glory of the Lord fills the tabernacle. (34–38)

Key verse

Verse 34: "Then a cloud covered the tent of the congregation, and the glory of the LORD filled the tabernacle."

Key word / key phrase

Verse 34, "glory."

Key event / key person / key theme

Setting up and dedicating the tabernacle

Key thought

The whole of the tabernacle cried out, "Glory to God."

Key thing to look out for

God's presence and glory so filled the tabernacle that Moses was unable to enter.

Key Bible cross-reference

Verse 16. See Matthew 7:21.

Key "by way of explanation"

Verse 34. The climax to the book of Exodus is the glory of the Lord filling the tabernacle.

Key "Quotable Quote"

"Afflictions are light when compared with what we really deserve. They are light when compared with the sufferings of the Lord Jesus. But perhaps their real lightness is best seen by comparing them with the weight of glory which is awaiting us."

Arthur W. Pink

5. Select bibliography for Exodus

Armerding, Carl. *Exodus* (NIBC), Hendrickson, 2001.

Bush, George. *Notes on Exodus*. 2 Vols. Reprint. Minneapolis: James and Klock, 1976.

Cole, R. A. *Exodus: An Introduction and Commentary*. (Tyndale Old Testament Commentaries) Downers Grove, Ill.: InterVarsity, 1973.

Ellison, H. L. *Exodus. The Daily Study Bible.* Philadelphia: Westminster, 1982.

Kaiser, Walter Jr., "Exodus" in *Expositor's Bible*

Commentary, Zondervan, 1990.

Keil, C. F., and Delitzsch, Franz. *The Pentateuch*. KD. Translated by James Martin. Vols. 1 and 2. Reprint. Grand Rapids: Eerdmans, 1956.

Lange, John Peter. *Exodus*. Translated by Charles M. Mead. Reprint. Grand Rapids: Zondervan, 1960.

Youngblood, Ronald F. Exodus. Chicago: Moody, 1983.

Leviticus

1. Book by book: Introduction to Leviticus

Introduction

The book of Leviticus derives its name from its treatment of the laws relating to the ritual, the services, and sacrifices of the Jewish religion, overseen by the Levitical priesthood. It is chiefly, however, the duties of the priests, "the sons of Aaron," which this book describes; and its claim to be the work of Moses is established by the following passages: 2 Chronicles 30:16; Nehemiah 8:14; Jeremiah 7:22–23; Ezekiel 20:11; Matthew 8:4; Luke 2:22; John 8:5 Romans 10:4; 13:9; 2 Corinthians 6:16; Galatians 3:12; 1 Peter 1:16.

Robert Jamieson

Contents of Leviticus

In the first section of the book (1–17), which exhibits the worship itself, there is, a series of laws (1–7) regarding sacrifices, burnt-offerings, meat-offerings, and thank-offerings (1–3), sin-offerings and trespass-offerings (4; 5), followed by the law of the priestly duties in connection with the offering of sacrifices (6; 7). An historical section (8–10) follows, giving an account of the consecration of Aaron and his sons (8); Aaron's first offering for himself and the people (9); Nadab and Abihu's presumption in offering "strange fire before Jehovah," and their punishment (10). Laws about purity, and the sacrifices and ordinances for putting away impurity are found in the next chapters (11–16). Then follows laws for the sanctification of the people (18–20), laws about the personal purity of the priests (21–22); laws about sanctification in worship (23–24), laws about sanctification in the land of Canaan (25–26) and laws about sanctification through vows in the last chapter (27).

Link with the other books of the Pentateuch

Leviticus stands in the same relation to Exodus, that the Epistles do to the Gospels. Exodus is the record of redemption, and lays the foundation of the cleansing, worship, and service of a redeemed people. Leviticus gives the detail of the walk, worship, and service of that people. In Exodus God speaks from the mount to which approach was forbidden; in Leviticus He speaks out of the tabernacle in which He dwells in the middle of His people, to tell them what is appropriate for His holiness in their approach to, and communion with, Himself.

No book contains more of the very words of God. He is almost throughout the whole of it the direct speaker. This book is a prophecy of things to come, a shadow of the substance is Christ and his kingdom. The principles on which it is to be interpreted are laid down in the Epistle to the Hebrews. It contains in its complicated ceremonial the gospel of the grace of God.

M.G. Easton, M.A., D.D., Illustrated Bible Dictionary

Detailed outline

I. Laws about sacrifices: 1:1–7:38
- A. Introduction: 1:1–2
- B. The burnt offering: 1:3–17
- C. The meal offering: 2:1–16
- D. The peace offering: 3:1–17
- E. The sin offering: 4:1–5:13
- F. The trespass offering: 5:14–17

II. Laws and incidents about the priests: 8–10
- A. Prescriptions for consecration: 8:1–9:24
- B. Punishment for violation: 10:1–20

III. Laws of purification: 11:1–15:33
- A. Clean and unclean food: 11:1–47
- B. Purification after childbirth: 12:1–8
- C. Leprosy: 13:1–14:57
- D. Sexual impurities and cleansings: 15:1–33

IV. The day of Atonement: 16:1–34
- A. Aaron's preparation: 16:1–10
- B. The sin offering for the priests: 16:11–14
- C. The sin offering for the people: 16:15–19
- D. The scapegoat: 16:20–22
- E. The offering completed: 16:23–28
- F. The solemnity of the day: 16:29–34

V. The holiness code: 17:1–27:34
- A. Prohibitions: 17:1–22:33
  1. Holiness on the part of the people: 17:1–20:27
  2. Holiness on the part of the priests: 21:1–22:33
- B. Religious festivals: 23:1–44
  1. The Sabbath: 23:1–3
  2. Passover and unleavened bread: 23:4–14
  3. Feast of weeks, or Pentecost: 23:15–22
  4. Feast of trumpets: 23:23–25
  5. Day of Atonement: 23:25–32
  6. Feast of tabernacles: 23:33–44
- C. Religious symbols: 24:1–23
- D. Sabbatical year and jubilee: 25:1–26:2
- E. Promises and warnings: 26:3–46
  1. The necessity for right relationship to God: 26:1–2
  2. The blessings of obedience to God: 26:1–2
  3. The chastisements for disobedience: 26:14–39
  4. God's faithfulness to His covenant: 26:40–45
  5. Summary statement: 26:46
- F. Vows and tithes: 27:1–34
  1. Vows to people: 27:2–8
  2. Vows of domestic animals: 27:9–1.
  3. Vows of houses and fields: 27:14–25
  4. The tithe: 27:30–33
     (a) First among beasts: 27:26–27

(b) Devoted things: 27:28–29

(c) The tithe: 27:30–33

2. Helpful summaries of Leviticus

Bird's eye view

How the holy Lord God provided the way for humankind to have fellowship with him.

Reading plan

The following reading plan, taking one reading per day, enables you to read through Leviticus in fourteen days.

Leviticus 1–4
Leviticus 5–6
Leviticus 7–8
Leviticus 9–10
Leviticus 11–12
Leviticus 13
Leviticus 14–15
Leviticus 16–17
Leviticus 18–19
Leviticus 20–22
Leviticus 23
Leviticus 24–25
Leviticus 26
Leviticus 27

Verse to memorize

Leviticus 26:12

I will walk among you and be your God and you will be my people.

Statistics

Third Old Testament book
27 chapters
859 verses
24,546 words

Famous saying found in Leviticus

"Eye for an eye" Leviticus 24:20

Names/titles given

Hebrew title: *Wayyiqra*: "And he called."

Greek title in Septuagint: *Leuitikon*: "About the Levites."

Latin title in Vulgate: Leviticus.

"Law of the Priests," and, "Law of Offerings," references found in the Talmud to Leviticus.

"A wilderness book"

3. Helpful keys to turn to in understanding Leviticus

Key words

Holiness, 87 times
Holy, 65 times
Be ye holy, for I am holy

Key verses

Leviticus 17:11; 19:2; 20:7–8

Key people/events

Nadab
Abihu
Day of Atonement
Sabbatical Year
Jubilee Year

Themes to study

There are two main parts to the book of Leviticus.

1. The rules about sacrifice.
2. The rules about how to live as God's people.

Sandwiched between these two parts, in chapter 16, is the chapter about the Day of Atonement.

Laws of the sacrifices in Leviticus

These laws describe the technical aspects of the sacrificial rituals. They belong to the context of worship in which prayer, hymns, and other forms of liturgy were integral parts.

1. Burnt offering (Leviticus 1; 6:8–13)
   This offering indicates the desire of the offerer to be in complete harmony with God.
2. Grain offering (Leviticus 2; 6:14–23)
   The grain offering was also known as the meal or cereal offering. It demonstrated Israel's dependence on God.
3. Peace or fellowship offering (Leviticus 3; 7:11–36)
   The peace offering symbolized reconciliation.
4. Sin offering (Leviticus 4:1–5:13; 6:24–30)
   This offering was made by those who had sinned unintentionally.
5. Guilt offering (Leviticus 5:14–6:7; 7:1–10)
   This offering was for those who had committing a violation against the Lord (Leviticus 5:14–19).

The seven feasts of Leviticus 23

1. The Passover, 23:4–5; see 1 Cor. 5:7.
2. Unleavened Bread, 23:6–8; see 1 Thess. 4:3–7.
3. First fruits, 23:9–14; see 1 Cor. 15:20.
4. Pentecost, 23:15–22; see Acts 2:1–4.
5. Trumpets, 23:23–25.
6. Atonement, 23:26–32; see 2 Cor. 7:10.
7. Tabernacles, 23:33–34; wee Col. 1:13–14.

Leviticus quoted in the New Testament

- A pair of turtledoves, or two young pigeons
  Lev. 12:8 quoted in Luke 2:24
- He that doeth them shall live therein
  Lev. 18:5 quoted in Rom. 10:5 and Gal. 3:12
- Ye shall be holy, for I am holy
  Lev. 19:2 quoted in 1 Pet. 1:16
- Thou shalt not forswear thyself
  Lev. 19:12 quoted in Matt. 5:33
- Thou shalt love thy neighbor as thyself
  Lev. 19:18 quoted in Matt. 5:43, 19:19, 22:39, Mark 12:31, 12:33, Luke 10:27, Rom. 13:9, Gal. 5:14 and James 2:8
- Every soul that shall not hearken to that prophet, shall be utterly destroyed from among the people
  Lev. 23:29 quoted in Acts 3:23
- An eye for an eye, and a tooth for a tooth
  Lev. 24:20 quoted in Matt. 5:38
- I will be their God, and they shall be my people
  Lev. 26:12 quoted in 2 Cor. 6:16

Unusual events and miracles in Leviticus

- Aaron's sons consumed by fire
- The Year of Jubilee, 25:8–16, held every fifty years, when slaves were liberated and debts cancelled.

Jesus in Leviticus

In Leviticus Jesus is our sacrifice for sin.

Types of Jesus in Leviticus

- The five offerings in Leviticus are types of Jesus' ministry.
- The seven feasts in Leviticus are types of Jesus' ministry.
- The first high priest, Aaron, is contrasted with Jesus, our eternal High Priest.

Lessons to learn from Leviticus

Living a holy life includes:

- obeying and worshipping God;
- protecting one's family;
- providing for the poor;
- having no dealings with the occult.

4. Chapter by chapter: outline of every chapter of Leviticus

Leviticus 1

Matthew Henry's introduction

This book begins with the laws concerning sacrifices, of which the most ancient were the burnt-offerings, about which God gives Moses instructions in this chapter. Orders are here given how that sort of sacrifice must be managed.

I. If it was a bullock out of the herd, vv. 3–9.

II. If it was a sheep or goat, a lamb or kid, out of the flock, vv. 10–13.

III. If it was a turtle-dove or a young pigeon, vv. 14–17. And whether the offering was more or less valuable in itself, if it was offered with an upright heart, according to these laws, it was accepted of God.

A detailed analysis of chapter

The offerings. (1, 2)

From the herds. (3–9)

From the flocks, and birds. (10–17)

Key verse

Verse 1: "And the LORD called unto Moses, and spake unto him out of the tabernacle of the congregation."

Key word / key phrase

Verse 4, "burnt offering."

Key event / key person / key theme

Offering sacrifices which were burnt whole

Key thought

Verse 1. God is the speaker in the book of Leviticus.

Key thing to look out for

The offerings, which are "without defect," verse 3, are types of Jesus' offering of himself. See Hebrews 9:14; 1 Peter 1:19.

Key Bible cross-reference

Verse 9, "aroma pleasing to the LORD." See Ephesians 5:2; Philippians 4:18.

Key "by way of explanation"

Jews called the book of Leviticus the "priests law." It consists of laws connected with the worship and ritual of the tabernacle, and so gives a background to the other books in the Bible.

Key "Quotable Quote"

"Read the Old Testament, and to get reacquainted

with the character of God."

R.C. Sproul

Leviticus 2

Matthew Henry's introduction

In this chapter we have the law concerning the meat-offering.

I. The matter of it; whether of raw flour with oil and incense (v. 1), or baked in the oven (v. 4), or upon a plate (vv. 5, 6), or in a frying pan, v. 7.

II. The management of it, of the flour (vv. 2, 3), of the cakes, vv. 8–10.

III. Some particular rules concerning it, That leaven and honey must never be admitted (vv. 11, 12), and salt never omitted in the meat-offering, v. 13.

IV. The law concerning the offering of first fruits in the ear, v. 14, etc.

A detailed analysis of chapter

The meat offering of flour. (1–11)

The offering of first fruits. (12–16)

Key verse

Verse 4: "And if thou bring an oblation of a meat offering baken in the oven, it shall be unleavened cakes of fine flour mingled with oil, or unleavened wafers anointed with oil."

Key word / key phrase

Verse 4, "flour."

Key event / key person / key theme

Grain offerings

Key thought

Each offering symbolized a reason for coming to worship God.

Key thing to look out for

All the offerings detailed in the Old Testament express the worshiper's devotion to God.

Key Bible cross-reference

Verse 1. See 6:14–23; 7:9,10.

Key "by way of explanation"

Verse 4. Grain offerings were made to thank God for his provision.

Key "Quotable Quote"

"Worship is our occupation with God himself, with the greatness of his being."

Ray Stedman

Leviticus 3

Matthew Henry's introduction

In this chapter we have the law concerning the peace-offerings, whether they were,

I. Of the heard, a bullock or a heifer, vv. 1–5. Or,

II. Of the flock, either a lamb (vv. 6–11) or a goat, vv. 12–17. The ordinances concerning each of these are much the same, yet they are repeated, to show the care we ought to take that all our services be done according to the appointment and the pleasure God takes in the services that are so performed. It is likewise to intimate what need we have of precept upon precept, and line upon line.

A detailed analysis of chapter

The peace offering of the herd. (1–5)

The peace offering of the flock. (6–17)

Key verse

Verse 1: "And if his oblation be a sacrifice of peace offering, if he offer it of the herd; whether it be a male or female, he shall offer it without blemish before the LORD."

Key word / key phrase

Verse 6, "fellowship offering."

Key event / key person / key theme

Fellowship offerings

Key thought

The traditional name for this fellowship offering was "peace offering." This came from the Hebrew word for peace, *shalom*, which also means wholeness.

Key thing to look out for

God is the focal point of all the Old Testament offerings.

Key Bible cross-reference

Verse 1. See 7:11–21, 28–34

Key "by way of explanation"

Verse 6. Fellowship offerings were motivated by the desire to give thanks to God.

Key "Quotable Quote"

"One act of thanksgiving when things go wrong with us is worth a thousand thanks when things are agreeable to our inclination."

John Jewell

Leviticus 4

Matthew Henry's introduction

This chapter is concerning the sin-offering, which was properly intended to make atonement for a sin committed through ignorance,

I. By the priest himself, vv. 1–12.

Or,

II. By the whole congregation, vv. 13–21.

Or,

III. By a ruler, vv. 22–26.

Or,

IV. By a private person, v. 27, etc.

A detailed analysis of chapter

The sin offering of ignorance for the priest. (1–12)

For the whole congregation. (13–21)

For a ruler. (22–26)

For any of the people. (27–35)

Key verse

Verse 2: "Speak unto the children of Israel, saying, If a soul shall sin through ignorance against any of the commandments of the LORD concerning things which ought not to be done, and shall do against any of them."

Key word / key phrase

Verse 20, "atonement."

Key event / key person / key theme

Offerings for unintentional sins

Key thought

Note "will be forgiven" which comes nine times in chapter 4, 5, and 6.

Key thing to look out for

There are two types of sin offering to note. See verses 3–21 for the first one, and 4:22–5:13 for the second one.

Key Bible cross-reference

Verse 20. See Exodus 29:36; 32:30; Romans 3:25.

Key "by way of explanation"

Verse 3. Sin offerings had to be made for specific unintentional sins. Unlike fellowship offerings they were not voluntary.

Key "Quotable Quote"

"What can I give him,
Poor as I am?
If I were a shepherd,
I would bring a lamb,
If I were a Wise Man,
I would do my part –
Yet what can I give him?
Give my heart."

Christina Rossetti

Leviticus 5

Matthew Henry's introduction

This chapter, and part of the next, concern the trespass-offering. The difference between this and the sin-offering lay not so much in the sacrifices themselves, and the management of them, as in the occasions of the offering of them. They were both intended to make atonement for sin; but the former was more general, this applied to some particular instances. Observe what is here said,

I. Concerning the trespass. If a man sin,
  A. In concealing his knowledge, when he is adjured, v. 1.
  B. In touching an unclean thing, vv. 2, 3.
  C. In swearing, v. 4.
  D. In embezzling the holy things, vv. 14–16.
  E. In any sin of infirmity, vv. 17–19. Some other cases there are, in which these offerings were to be offered, ch. 6:2–4; 14:12; 19:21; Num. 6:12.

II. Concerning the trespass-offerings,
  A. Of the flock, vv. 5, 6.
  B. Of fowls, vv. 7–10.
  C. Of flour, vv. 11–13; but chiefly a ram without blemish, v. 15, etc.

A detailed analysis of chapter

Various trespasses. (1–13)
Trespasses against the Lord. (14–19)

Key verse

Verse 16: "And he shall make amends for the harm that he hath done in the holy thing."

Key word / key phrase

Verse 15, "guilt offering."

Key event / key person / key theme

Repayment offerings

Key thought

"There is a way back to God from the dark path of sin."

Key thing to look out for

Verse 5, "he must confess." The guilty person had to confess his sin before he could be forgiven.

Key Bible cross-reference

Verse 15. See Isaiah 53:10.

Key "by way of explanation"

The sin offering and guilt offering were similar, but the former related more to the sinner's relationship to God; the latter involved making compensation for damage done.

Key "Quotable Quote"

"The confession of evil works is the first beginning of good works."

Augustine of Hippo

Leviticus 6

Matthew Henry's introduction

The first seven verses of this chapter might fitly have been added to the foregoing chapter, being a continuation of the law of the trespass-offering, and the putting of other cases in which it was to be offered; and with this end the instructions God gave concerning the several kinds of sacrifices that should be offered: and then at v. 8 (which in the original begins a new section of the law) he comes to appoint the several rites and ceremonies concerning these sacrifices which had not been mentioned before.

I. The burnt-offering, vv. 8–13.

II. The meat-offering (vv. 11–18), particularly that at the consecration of the priest, vv. 19–23.

III. The sin-offering, v. 24, etc.

A detailed analysis of chapter

Trespasses against our neighbor. (1–7)

The burnt offering. (8–13)

The meat offering. (14–23)

The sin offering. (24–30)

Key verse

Verses 24, 25: "And the LORD spake unto Moses, saying, Speak unto Aaron and to his sons, saying, This is the law of the sin offering."

Key word / key phrase

Verse 5, "offering."

Key event / key person / key theme

More regulations about offerings

Key thought

These offerings catered for the whole range of sins.

Key thing to look out for

Dealing with personal sin is essential for any kind of spiritual life.

Key Bible cross-reference

Verse 25, "sin offering." See 4:1–5:13.

Key "by way of explanation"

Verses 9, 12. As well as the private offerings made by the people, a public burnt offering was made every morning and evening.

Key "Quotable Quote"

"The deadliest sin were the consciousness of no sin."

Thomas Carlyle

Leviticus 7

Matthew Henry's introduction

Here is,

I. The law of the trespass-offering (vv. 1–7), with some further directions concerning the burnt-offering and the meat-offering, vv. 8–10.

II. The law of the peace-offering. The eating of it (vv. 11–21), on which occasion the prohibition of eating fat or blood is repeated (vv. 22–27), and the priests' share of it, vv. 28–34.

III. The conclusion of those institutions, v. 35, etc.

A detailed analysis of chapter

The trespass offering. (1–10)

The peace offering. (11–27)

The fellowship offering. (28–34)

The conclusion of these institutions. (35–38)

Key verse

Verse 11: "And this is the law of the sacrifice of peace offerings, which he shall offer unto the LORD."

Key word / key phrase

Verse 11, "fellowship offering."

Key event / key person / key theme

Further regulations about the three types of fellowship offerings.

Key thought

Every worship service should include thanksgiving.

Key thing to look out for

Note how seriously the Bible takes sin.

Key Bible cross-reference

Verse 26. Not eating the blood. See 3:17; 19:26; Ezekiel 33:25.

Key "by way of explanation"

Verse 20. Some people were in danger of being cut off from God's covenant.

Key "Quotable Quote"

"Not to think of God is grievously to offend him. Not to praise him day by day for all he is and has done is in itself terrible sin."

D. Martyn Lloyd-Jones

Leviticus 8

Matthew Henry's introduction

This chapter gives us an account of the solemn consecration of Aaron and his sons to the priest's office.

I. It was done publicly, and the congregation was called together to be witnesses of it, vv. 1–4.

II. It was done exactly according to God's appointment, v. 5.

A. They were washed and dressed, vv. 6–9, 13.

B. The tabernacle and the utensils of it were anointed, and then the priests, vv. 10–12.

C. A sin-offering was offered for them, vv. 14–17.

D. A burnt-offering, vv. 18–21.

E. The ram of consecration, vv. 22–30.

F. The continuance of this solemnity for seven days, v. 31, etc.

A detailed analysis of chapter

The consecration of Aaron and his sons. (1–13)

The offerings of consecration. (14–36)

Key verse

Verse 2: "Take Aaron and his sons with him, and the garments, and the anointing oil, and a bullock for the sin offering, and two rams, and a basket of unleavened bread."

Key word / key phrase

Verse 12, "anointing."

Key event / key person / key theme

Ordination of Aaron and his sons

Key thought

Aaron had a special work to do for God and so was anointed with oil.

Key thing to look out for

Aaron and his sons were happy to obey God, even though their instructions came through Moses.

Key Bible cross-reference

Verse 2. See Exodus 39:1–31; 40:12–16.

Key "by way of explanation"

Verse 14. During Aaron's consecration service a sin offering for atonement was offered.

Key "Quotable Quote"

"There is need of a great revival of spiritual life, of truly fervent devotion to our Lord Jesus, of entire consecration to his service."

Andrew Murray

Leviticus 9

Matthew Henry's introduction

Aaron and his sons, having been solemnly consecrated to the priesthood, are in this chapter entering upon the execution of their office, the very next day after their consecration was completed.

I. Moses (no doubt by direction from God) appoints a meeting between God and his priests, as the representatives of his people, ordering them to attend him, and assuring them that he would appear to them, vv. 1–7.

II. The meeting is held according to the appointment.

A. Aaron attends on God by sacrifice, offering a sin-offering and burnt-offering for himself (vv. 8–14), and then the offerings for the people, whom he blessed in the name of the Lord, vv. 15–22.

B. God signifies his acceptance, of their persons, by showing them his glory, v. 23. Of their sacrifices, by consuming them with fire from heaven, v. 24.

A detailed analysis of chapter

The first offerings of Aaron for himself and the

people. (1–21)
Moses and Aaron bless the people. Fire comes on the altar from the Lord. (22–24)

Key verse
Verse 22: "And Aaron lifted up his hand toward the people, and blessed them, and came down from offering of the sin offering, and the burnt offering, and peace offerings."

Key word / key phrase
Verse 4, "sacrifice."

Key event / key person / key theme
Aaron offers sacrifices.

Key thought
Only those blessed by God are capable of passing on any blessing from God.

Key thing to look out for
Aaron's threefold blessing.

Key Bible cross-reference
Verse 24, "fire." See 10:2; 1 Kings 18:38.

Key "by way of explanation"
Verse 23. The "glory of the Lord" is seen again, as it was when the tabernacle was erected, Exodus 40:34,35.

Key "Quotable Quote"
"*Soli Deo Gloria,*" (Only to God be the glory).
J.S. Bach, often wrote these words at the end of his musical compositions.

Leviticus 10

Matthew Henry's introduction
The story of this chapter is as sad an interruption to the institutions of the levitical law as that of the golden calf was to the account of the erecting of the tabernacle. Here is,

I. The sin and death of Nadab and Abihu, the sons of Aaron, vv. 1, 2.
II. The quieting of Aaron under this sore affliction, v. 3.
III. Orders given and observed about the funeral and mourning, vv. 4–7.
IV. A command to the priests not to drink wine when they went in to minister, vv. 8–11.
V. The care Moses took that they should go on with their work, notwithstanding the agitation produced by this event, v. 12, etc.

A detailed analysis of chapter
The sin and death of Nadab and Abihu. (1, 2)
Aaron and his sons forbidden to mourn for Nadab and Abihu. (3–7)
Priests are forbidden to drink when serving in the tabernacle. (8–11)
Eating the holy things. (12–20)

Key verse
Verse 2: "And there went out fire from the LORD, and devoured them, and they died before the LORD."

Key word / key phrase
Verse 13, "holy."

Key event / key person / key theme
Nadab and Abihu die as a result of their sin.

Key thought

We cannot over-emphasize the importance of God's holiness.

Key thing to look out for

God's teaching must be passed on to the next generation.

Key Bible cross-reference

Verse 2. See a comparable incident in Acts 5:1–11.

Key "by way of explanation"

Verse 2, "died before the Lord." While this incident may seem harsh, one lesson it teaches is that God's people had to remember that they existed for God's glory.

Key "Quotable Quote"

"God, being infinitely holy, has an infinite hatred of sin."

Jerry Bridges

Leviticus 11

Matthew Henry's introduction

The ceremonial law is described by the apostle (Heb. 9:9, 10) to consist, not only "in gifts and sacrifices," which hitherto have been treated of in this book, but "in meats, and drinks, and divers washings" from ceremonial uncleanness, the laws concerning which begin with this chapter, which puts a difference between some sorts of flesh-meat and others, allowing some to be eaten as clean and forbidding others as unclean. "There is one kind of flesh of men." Nature startles at the thought of eating this, and none do it but such as have arrived at the highest degree of barbarity, and become but one remove from brutes; therefore there needed no law against it. But there is "another kind of flesh of beasts," concerning which the law directs here (vv. 1–8), "another of fishes" (vv. 9–12), "another of birds" (vv. 13–19), and "another of creeping things," which are distinguished into two sorts, flying creeping things (vv. 20–28) and creeping things upon the earth, vv. 29–43. And the law concludes with the general rule of holiness, and reasons for it, v. 44, etc.

A detailed analysis of chapter

What animals were clean (i.e. could be sacrificed, and could be eaten) and unclean. (1–47)

Key verse

Verse 2: "These are the beasts which ye shall eat among all the beasts that are on the earth."

Key word / key phrase

Verse 4, "unclean."

Key event / key person / key theme

Animals which may and may not be eaten.

Key thought

Verse 45. This refrain, "brought . . . out of Egypt" comes 18 times in this book.

Key thing to look out for

The word "holiness" appears more frequently in the book of Leviticus than in any other book of the Bible.

Key Bible cross-reference

Verse 2. See Deuteronomy 14:3–21.

Key "by way of explanation"

Verse 44. "Be holy." Holiness, the most important theme in Leviticus, hinges on God's own holiness.

Key "Quotable Quote"

"There is a danger of forgetting that the Bible reveals, not first the love of God, but the intense, blazing holiness of God, with his love as the center of that holiness."

Oswald Chambers

Leviticus 12

Matthew Henry's introduction

After the laws concerning clean and unclean food come the laws concerning clean and unclean persons; and the first is in this chapter concerning the ceremonial uncleanness of women in child-birth, vv. 1–5. And concerning their purification from that uncleanness, v. 6, etc.

A detailed analysis of chapter

Ceremonial purification. (1–8)

Key verse

Verse 8: "And if she be not able to bring a lamb, then she shall bring two turtles, or two young pigeons."

Key word / key phrase

Verse 2, "ceremonially unclean."

Key event / key person / key theme

Purifying women after childbirth

Key thought

Being ceremonially unclean underlines the importance of remembering God's holiness.

Key thing to look out for

It would appear that Mary and Joseph were poor, or else they would have offered a lamb.

Key Bible cross-reference

Verse 8. See 1:14–17; 5:7–10; Luke 2:24.

Key "by way of explanation"

Verse 2. The uncleanness was not due to the birth of the baby, but to the bleeding. The word translated leprosy refers to a wide variety of skin disorders, not all malignant, and also to mildew in clothing and houses.

Key "Quotable Quote"

"The will of God is the purification and sanctification of the heart that comes about through fully experienced and conscious participation in the perfect and divine Spirit."

Makarios of Egypt

Leviticus 13

Matthew Henry's introduction

The next ceremonial uncleanness is that of the leprosy, concerning which the law was very large and particular; we have the discovery of it in this chapter, and the cleansing of the leper in the next. Scarcely any one thing in all the levitical law takes up so much room as this.

I. Rules are here given by which the priest must judge whether the man had the leprosy or no, according as the symptom was that appeared.
   A. If it was a swelling, a scab, or a bright spot, vv. 1–17.
   B. If it was a bile, vv. 18–23.
   C. If it was in inflammation, vv. 24–28.
   D. If it was in the head or beard, vv. 29–37.
   E. If it was a bright spot, vv. 38, 39.
   F. If it was in a bald head, vv. 40–44.

II. Direction is given how the leper must be disposed of, vv. 45, 46.

III. Concerning the leprosy in garments, v. 47, etc.

A detailed analysis of chapter

Directions to the priest to judge concerning leprosy. (1–17)
Further directions. (18–44)
How the leper must be treated. (45,46)
The mildew in garments. (47–59)

Key verse

Verse 46: "All the days wherein the plague shall be in him he shall be defiled; he is unclean: he shall dwell alone; without the camp shall his habitation be."

Key word / key phrase

Verse 2, "infectious skin disease."

Key event / key person / key theme

Regulations about infectious skin diseases

Key thought

These regulations were intended to provide a way for a healed person to be officially declared "clean."

Key thing to look out for

Just as some people needed physical healing, everyone needs spiritual healing.

Key Bible cross-reference

Verse 2. See 22:4; Numbers 5:2.

Key "by way of explanation"

Verses 45, 46. Nobody who was ceremonially unclean was allowed into the Israelite camp, as God's presence was there.

Key "Quotable Quote"

"God heals, and the doctor takes the fee."

George Herbert

Leviticus 14

Matthew Henry's introduction

The former chapter directed the priests how to convict a leper of ceremonial uncleanness. No prescriptions are given for his cure; but, when God had cured him, the priests are in this chapter directed how to cleanse him. The remedy here is only adapted to the ceremonial part of his disease; but the authority Christ gave to his ministers was to cure the lepers, and so to cleanse them. We have here,

I. The solemn declaration of the leper's being clean, with the significant ceremony attending it, vv. 1–9.

II. The sacrifices which he was to offer to God

eight days after, vv. 10–32.

III. The management of a house in which appeared signs of a leprosy, vv. 33–53. And the conclusion and summary of this whole matter, v. 54, etc.

A detailed analysis of chapter

Of declaring the leper to be clean. (1–9)
The sacrifices to be offered by him. (10–32)
The mildew in a house. (33–53)
Summary of the law about leprosy. (54–57)

Key verse

Verse 3: "And the priest shall go forth out of the camp."

Key word / key phrase

Verse 57, "unclean."

Key event / key person / key theme

Purification after having a skin disease

Key thought

Disease was often used as a picture of sin.

Key thing to look out for

The pains that were taken to declare that a person was physically cured.

Key Bible cross-reference

Verse 7. See Psalm 51:7.

Key "by way of explanation"

Verse 45. A house with mildew had to be "torn down" or it would continue to be a serious health risk.

Key "Quotable Quote"

"There is a great market for religious experience in our world . . . there is little inclination to sign up for the long apprenticeship in what earlier generations of Christians called holiness."

Eugene H. Peterson

Leviticus 15

Matthew Henry's introduction

In this chapter we have laws concerning other ceremonial uncleanness contracted either by bodily disease like that of the leper, or some natural incidents, and this either,

I. In men, vv. 1–18.

Or,

II. In women, vv. 19–33. We need not be at all curious in explaining these antiquated laws, it is enough if we observe the general intention; but we have need to be very cautious lest sin take occasion by the commandment to become more exceedingly sinful; and exceedingly sinful it is when lust is kindled by sparks of fire from God's altar. The case is bad with the soul when it is putrefied by that which should purify it.

A detailed analysis of chapter

Laws about ceremonial uncleanness. (1–33)

Key verse

Verse 31: "Thus shall ye separate the children of Israel from their uncleanness; that they die not in their uncleanness, when they defile my tabernacle that is among them."

Key word / key phrase

Verse 2, "bodily discharge."

Key event / key person / key theme

Unclean bodily discharges

Key thought

Spiritual purity is even more important that physical purity.

Key thing to look out for

God has provided the solution to the worst impurity.

Key Bible cross-reference

Verse 25. See Matthew 9:20.

Key "by way of explanation"

Verse 31. This verse summarizes the teaching about the need to keep unclean people and objects away from God. It prepares the way for the teaching about atonement (chapter 16).

Key "Quotable Quote"

"Religion that is merely ritual and ceremonial can never satisfy. Neither can we be satisfied by a religion that is merely humanitarian or serviceable to mankind. Man's craving is for the spiritual."

Samuel M. Shoemaker

Leviticus 16

Matthew Henry's introduction

In this chapter we have the institution of the annual solemnity of the day of atonement, or expiation, which had as much gospel in it as perhaps any of the appointments of the ceremonial law, as appears by the reference the apostle makes to it, Heb. 9:7, &c. We had before divers laws concerning sin-offerings for particular persons, and to be offered upon particular occasions; but this is concerning the stated sacrifice, in which the whole nation was interested. The whole service of the day is committed to the high priest.

I. He must never come into the most holy place but upon this day, vv. 1, 2.

II. He must come dressed in linen garments, v. 4.

III. He must bring a sin-offering and a burnt-offering for himself (v. 3), offer his sin-offering (vv. 6–11), then go within the veil with some of the blood of his sin-offering, burn incense, and sprinkle the blood before the mercy-seat, vv. 12–14.

IV. Two goats must be provided for the people, lots cast upon them, and,

- A. One of them must be a sin-offering for the people (vv. 5, 7–9), and the blood of it must be sprinkled before the mercy-seat (vv. 15–17), and then some of the blood of both the sin-offerings must be sprinkled upon the altar, vv. 18, 19.
- B. The other must be a scapegoat (v. 10), the sins of Israel must be confessed over him, and then he must be sent away into the wilderness (vv. 20–22), and he that brought him away must be ceremonially unclean, v. 26.

V. The burnt-offerings were then to be offered, the fat of the sin-offerings burnt on the altar, and their flesh burnt without the camp, vv. 23–25, 27, 28.

VI. The people were to observe the day religiously by a holy rest and holy mourning for sin; and this was to be a statute for ever, v. 29, etc.

A detailed analysis of chapter

The great Day of Atonement. (1-14)

The sacrifices on it, and the scapegoat. (15-34)

Key verse

Verse 6: "And Aaron shall offer his bullock of the sin offering, which is for himself, and make an atonement for himself, and for his house."

Key word / key phrase

Verse 6, "atonement."

Key event / key person / key theme

The Day of Atonement

Key thought

Without atonement we remain dead in our sins.

Key thing to look out for

The different elements which make up the Day of Atonement as they are detailed in this chapter.

Key Bible cross-reference

Verses 20-22 describe substitutionary atonement. See Leviticus 1:4; 3:8; 4:4.

Key "by way of explanation"

According to verse 34 atonement was made once a year. Jesus' atonement was made once and for all time. See Hebrews 9:11–10:14.

Key "Quotable Quote"

"I must die or get somebody to die for me. If the Bible doesn't teach that, it doesn't teach anything. And that is where the atonement of Jesus Christ comes in."

D.L. Moody

Leviticus 17

Matthew Henry's introduction

After the law concerning the atonement to be made for all Israel by the high priest, at the tabernacle, with the blood of bulls and goats, in this chapter we have two prohibitions necessary for the preservation of the honor of that atonement.

I. That no sacrifice should be offered by any other than the priests, nor any where but at the door of the tabernacle, and this upon pain of death, vv. 1–9.

II. That no blood should be eaten, and this under the same penalty, v. 10, etc.

A detailed analysis of chapter

All sacrifices to be offered at the tabernacle. (1-9)

Eating of blood, or of animals which died a natural death, forbidden. (10-16)

Key verse

Verse 11: "For the life of the flesh is in the blood: and I have given it to you upon the altar to make an atonement for your souls: for it is the blood that maketh an atonement for the soul."

Key word / key phrase

Verse 6, "blood."

Key event / key person / key theme

Animals offered in sacrifice.

Key thought

Do not eat blood.

Key thing to look out for

The central role of blood in the sacrifices.

Key Bible cross-reference

Verse 11. For teaching on substitutionary atonement, see verse 6; 1:5; 3:2; 4:6,25; 7:2.

Key "by way of explanation"

Verse 11, "the life of a creature is in the blood." As blood symbolized life it had to be treated with great respect, especially in all the sacrifices.

Key "Quotable Quote"

"An atonement that does not regenerate is not an atonement in which men can be asked to believe."

James Denney

Leviticus 18

Matthew Henry's introduction

Here is,

I. A general law against all conformity to the corrupt usages of the heathen, vv. 1–5.

II. Particular laws,

A. Against incest, vv. 6–18.

B. Against beastly lusts, and barbarous idolatries, vv. 19–23.

III. The enforcement of these laws from the ruin of the Canaanites, vv. 24–30.

A detailed analysis of chapter

Unlawful marriages and unlawful sexual relations. (1-30)

Key verse

Verse 3: "After the doings of the land of Egypt, wherein ye dwelt, shall ye not do: and after the doings of the land of Canaan, whither I bring you, shall ye not do: neither shall ye walk in their ordinances."

Key word / key phrase

Verse 4, "obey."

Key event / key person / key theme

Forbidden sexual relations

Key thought

Sex is a gift from God.

Key thing to look out for

As God is the Creator he knows best about every aspect of our behavior.

Key Bible cross-reference

Verse 18 "live." See Ezekiel 20:11, 13, 21; Romans 10:5; Galatians 3:12.

Key "by way of explanation"

Verse 2. The phrase "I am the Lord," coming 42 times in chapters 18–26, underlines the fact that it is God and his authority that stands behind these instructions.

Key "Quotable Quote"

"No country can be happy while the walls may still be standing but the morals are collapsing."

Augustine of Hippo

Leviticus 19

Matthew Henry's introduction

Some ceremonial precepts there are in this chapter, but most of them are moral. One would wonder that when some of the lighter matters of the law are greatly enlarged upon (witness two long chapters concerning the leprosy) many of the weightier matters are put into a little compass: divers of the single verses of this chapter contain whole laws concerning judgment and mercy; for these are things which are manifest in every man's conscience; men's own thoughts are able to explain these, and to comment upon them.

I. The laws of this chapter, which were peculiar to the Jews, are,

A. Concerning their peace-offerings, vv. 5–8.

B. Concerning the gleanings of their fields, vv. 9, 10.

C. Against mixtures of their cattle, seed, and cloth, v. 19.

D. Concerning their trees, vv. 23–25.

E. Against some superstitious usages, vv. 26–28. But,

II. Most of these precepts are binding on us, for they are expositions of most of the ten commandments.

A. Here is the preface to the ten commandments, "I am the Lord," repeated fifteen times.

B. A sum of the ten commandments. All the first table in this, "Be you holy," v. 2. All the second table in this, "Thou shalt love thy neighbor" (v. 18), and an answer to the question, "Who is my neighbor?" vv. 33, 34.

C. Something of each commandment.

The first commandment implied in that which is often repeated here, "I am your God." And here is a prohibition of enchantment (vv. 26) and witchcraft (v. 31), which make a god of the devil.

Idolatry, against the second commandment, is forbidden, v. 4.

Profanation of God's name, against the third, v. 12.

Sabbath-sanctification is pressed, vv. 3, 30.

Children are required to honor their parents (v. 3), and the aged, v. 32.

Hatred and revenge are here forbidden, against the sixth commandment, vv. 17, 18.

Adultery (vv. 20–22), and whoredom, v. 29.

Justice is here required in judgment (v. 15), theft forbidden (v. 11), fraud and withholding dues (v. 13), and false weights, vv. 35, 36.

Lying, v. 11. Slandering, v. 14.

Talebearing, and false-witness bearing, v. 16.

The tenth commandment laying a restraint upon the heart, so does that (v. 17), "Thou shalt not hate thy brother in thy heart." And here is a solemn charge to observe all these statutes, v. 37.

> Now these are things which need not much help for the understanding of them, but require constant care and watchfulness for the observing of them. "A good understanding have all those that do these commandments."

A detailed analysis of chapter

Various laws, dealing with many aspects of daily life. (1-17)

Key verse

Verse 2: "Ye shall be holy: for I the Lord your God am holy."

Key word / key phrase

Verse 32, "revere."

Key event / key person / key theme

Detailed expansion of some of the Ten Commandments

Key thought

A prohibition can be very positive.

Key thing to look out for

How happy a society would be if it followed these commands.

Key Bible cross-reference

Verse 26, "sorcery." See Exodus 22:18; Deuteronomy 18:14; 1 Samuel 28:9; Isaiah 47:12-14.

Key "by way of explanation"

Verse 35, "dishonest standards." Dishonesty in business was a way of life. See Deuteronomy 25:13-16.

Key "Quotable Quote"

"It is the perfection of holiness to do what God loves, and to love what God does."

William Bates, Puritan

Leviticus 20

Matthew Henry's introduction

The laws which before were made are in this chapter repeated and penalties annexed to them, that those who would not be deterred from sin by the fear of God might be deterred from it by the fear of punishment. If we will not avoid such and such practices because the law has made them sin (and it is most acceptable when we go on that principle of religion), surely we shall avoid them when the law has made them death, from a principle of self-preservation. In this chapter we have,

I. Many particular crimes that are made capital.
   A. Giving their children to Moloch, vv. 1–5.
   B. Consulting witches, vv. 6, 27.
   C. Cursing parents, v. 9.
   D. Adultery, v. 10.
   E. Incest, vv. 11, 12, 14, 17, 19–21.
   F. Unnatural lusts, vv. 13, 15, 16, 18.

II. General commands given to be holy, vv. 7, 8, 22–26.

A detailed analysis of chapter

Law against sacrificing children to Moloch. Children who curse their parents. (1-9)

Laws repeated. Holiness commanded. (10-27)

Key verse

Verse 7: "Sanctify yourselves therefore, and be ye holy: for I am the LORD your God."

Key word / key phrase

Verse 13, "detestable."

Key event / key person / key theme

Penalties for going against God's morality

Key thought

In God's book evil will be punished.

Key thing to look out for

The distinction between right and wrong is not at all blurred.

Key Bible cross-reference

Verse 5. See 17:7.

Key "by way of explanation"

Verse 6. It was sinful to be a medium, and it was also sinful to consult one.

Key "Quotable Quote"

"Moral collapse follows upon spiritual collapse."

C.S. Lewis

Leviticus 21

Matthew Henry's introduction

This chapter might borrow its title from Mal. 2:1, "And now, O you priests, this commandment is for you." It is a law obliging priests with the utmost care and jealousy to preserve the dignity of their priesthood.

I. The inferior priests are here charged both concerning their mourning and concerning their marriages and their children, vv. 1–9.

II. The high priest is restrained more than any of them, vv. 10–15.

III. Neither the one nor the other must have any blemish, v. 16, etc.

A detailed analysis of chapter

Laws about the priests. (1-24)

Key verse

Verse 8: "Thou shalt sanctify him therefore; for he offereth the bread of thy God: he shall be holy unto thee: for I the LORD, which sanctify you, am holy."

Key word / key phrase

Verse 1, "priests."

Key event / key person / key theme

The holiness of priests

Key thought

God's servants should be holy.

Key thing to look out for

Priests had to be separate from any kind of ceremonial uncleanness.

Key Bible cross-reference

Verse 1. See Numbers 19:11; 14.

Key "by way of explanation"

Verse 5. In pagan religions worshipers disfigured their bodies in an effort to gain the attention of their deities. See 1 Kings 18:28.

Key "Quotable Quote"

"God makes me pure in heart; I must make myself pure in conduct."

Oswald Chambers

Leviticus 22

Matthew Henry's introduction

In this chapter we have divers laws concerning the priests and sacrifices all for the preserving of the honor of the sanctuary.

I. That the priests should not eat the holy things in their uncleanness, vv. 1–9.

II. That no stranger who did not belong to some family of the priests should eat of the holy things (vv. 10–13), and, if he did it unwittingly, he must make restitution, vv. 14–16.

III. That the sacrifices which were offered must be without blemish, vv. 17–25.

IV. That they must be more than eight days old (vv. 26–28), and that the sacrifices of thanksgiving must be eaten the same day they were offered, v. 29, etc.

A detailed analysis of chapter

Laws about the priests and sacrifices. (1-33)

Key verse

Verse 32: "Neither shall ye profane my holy name."

Key word / key phrase

Verse 2, "offerings."

Key event / key person / key theme

The holiness of the offerings

Key thought

The idea of restitution is promoted.

Key thing to look out for

God's name must be acknowledged among the ungodly.

Key Bible cross-reference

Key "by way of explanation"

Verse 3. Being cut off from the Lord's presence and being excluded from the fellowship with God's people are almost identical.

Key "Quotable Quote"

"He does not believe that does not live according to his belief."

Thomas Fuller

Leviticus 23

Matthew Henry's introduction

Hitherto the levitical law had been chiefly conversant about holy persons, holy things, and holy places; in this chapter we have the institution of holy times, many of which had been mentioned occasionally before, but here they are all put together, only the new moons are not mentioned. All the rest of the feasts of the Lord are,

I. The weekly feast of the Sabbath, v. 3.

II. The yearly feasts,

A. The Passover, and the feast of unleavened bread (vv. 4–8), to which was annexed the offering of the sheaf of first fruits, vv. 9–14.

B. Pentecost, vv. 15–22. 3. The solemnities of the seventh month. The feast of trumpets on the first day (vv. 23–25), the day of atonement on the tenth day (vv. 26–32), and the feast of tabernacles on the fifteenth, v. 33, etc.

A detailed analysis of chapter

The feasts of the Lord, and the Sabbath. (1–3)

The Passover, and the offering of first-fruits. (4–14)

The feast of Pentecost. (15–22)

The feast of Trumpets, and the Day of Atonement. (23–32)

The feast of Tabernacles. (33–44)

Key verse

Verse 6: "And on the fifteenth day of the same month is the feast of unleavened bread unto the Lord: seven days ye must eat unleavened bread."

Key word / key phrase

Verse 27, "Day of Atonement."

Key event / key person / key theme

The religious festivals

Key thought

Should we observe more Christian festivals?

Key thing to look out for

God's followers spent a great deal of time in worshiping the Lord.

Key Bible cross-reference

Verse 27. See Hebrews 9:7; 13:11,12.

Key "by way of explanation"

Verse 27. The Jewish *Yom Kippur*, Day of Atonement, comes from the Hebrew words *yom* (day) and *kipper* (to atone).

Key "Quotable Quote"

"Worship is celebration."

Clement of Alexander

Leviticus 24

Matthew Henry's introduction

In this chapter we have,

I. A repetition of the laws concerning the lamps and the show-bread, vv. 1–9.

II. A violation of the law against blasphemy, with the imprisonment, trial, condemnation, and execution, of the blasphemer, vv. 10–14, with v. 23.

III. The law against blasphemy reinforced (vv. 15, 16), with sundry other laws, v. 17, etc.

A detailed analysis of chapter

Oil for the lamps, and the shew-bread. (1–9)

The law of blasphemy, blasphemer is stoned. (10–23)

Key verse

Verse 17: "And he that killeth any man shall surely be put to death."

Key word / key phrase

Verse 2, "light."

Key event / key person / key theme

Taking care of the lamps

Key thought

An eye for an eye limited retribution.

Key thing to look out for

The seriousness of blasphemy could not be plainer.

Key Bible cross-reference

Verse 20. See Exodus 21:23–25; Matthew 5:38–42.

Key "by way of explanation"

Verse 8. The bread represented a gift from all the twelve tribes of Israel and so symbolized God sustaining them.

Key "Quotable Quote"

"Special vengeance will be executed on those who have taken the name of God in vain."

John Calvin

Leviticus 25

Matthew Henry's introduction

The law of this chapter concerns the lands and estates of the Israelites in Canaan, the occupying and transferring of which were to be under the divine direction, as well as the management of religious worship; for, as the tabernacle was a holy house, so Canaan was a holy land; and upon that account, as much as any thing, it was the glory of all lands. In token of a peculiar title which God had to this land, and a right to dispose of it, he appointed,

I. That every seventh year should be a year of rest from occupying the land, a sabbatical year, vv. 1–7. In this God expected from them extraordinary instances of faith and obedience, and they might expect from God extraordinary instances of power and goodness in providing for them, vv. 18–22.

II. That every fiftieth year should be a year of jubilee, that is,

A. A year of release of debts and mortgages, and return to the possession of their alienated lands, vv. 8–17. Particular directions are given, Concerning the sale and redemption of lands, vv. 23–28. Of houses in cities and villages, with a proviso for Levite cities, vv. 29–34.

B. A year of release of servants and bondslaves. Here is inserted a law for the kind usage of poor debtors, vv. 35–38. Then comes the law for the discharge of all Israelites that were sold for servants, in the year of jubilee, if they were not redeemed before.

1. If they were sold to Israelites, vv. 39–46. And,
2. If sold to proselytes, vv. 47–55. All these appointments have something moral and of perpetual obligation in them, though in the letter of them they were not only peculiar to the Jews, but to them only while they were in Canaan.

A detailed analysis of chapter

The Sabbath of rest for the land in the seventh year. (1–7)

The jubilee of the fiftieth year. Oppression forbidden. (8–22)

Redemption of the land and houses. (23–34)

Compassion toward the poor. (35–38)
Laws about the poor. Oppression forbidden. (39–55)

Key verse

Verse 8: "And thou shalt number seven Sabbaths of years unto thee, seven times seven years; and the space of the seven Sabbaths of years shall be unto thee forty and nine years."

Key word / key phrase

Verse 4, "seventh year."

Key event / key person / key theme

The Sabbath year

Key thought

God's commands extend to the business world.

Key thing to look out for

God, as a God of justice and kindness, wants his followers to be just and kind.

Key Bible cross-reference

Verse 10. See Isaiah 61:1, 2; Luke 4:16–21.

Key "by way of explanation"

Verse 13. The principle here is that the Lord did not allow the poor to be exploited as an individual accumulated property.

Key "Quotable Quote"

"As a fresh start, the Church should give away all her endowments to the poor and needy."

Dietrich Bonhoeffer

Leviticus 26

Matthew Henry's introduction

This chapter is a solemn conclusion of the main body of the levitical law. The precepts that follow in this and the following book either relate to some particular matters or are repetitions and explications of the foregoing institutions. Now this chapter contains a general enforcement of all those laws by promises of reward in case of obedience on the one hand, and threatening of punishment for disobedience on the other hand, the former to work upon hope, the latter on fear, those two handles of the soul, by which it is taken hold of and managed. Here is,

I. A repetition of two or three of the principal of the commandments, vv. 1, 2.
II. An inviting promise of all good things, if they would but keep God's commandments, vv. 3–13.
III. A terrible threatening of ruining judgments which would be brought upon them if they were refractory and disobedient, vv. 14–39.
IV. A gracious promise of the return of mercy to those of them that would repent and reform, v. 40, etc. Deut. 28 is parallel to this.

A detailed analysis of chapter

Promises on keeping the precepts. (1–13)
Warnings against disobedience. (14–39)
God promises to remember those who repent. (40–46)

Key verse

Verse 45: "But I will for their sakes remember the covenant of their ancestors, whom I brought forth out of the land of Egypt in the sight of the heathen, that I might be their God: I am the LORD."

Key word / key phrase
Verse 14, "commands."

Key event / key person / key theme
Obedience and disobedience are contrasted

Key thought
Obedience brings blessing.

Key thing to look out for
Disobedience brings punishment.

Key Bible cross-reference
Verse 14. See Deuteronomy 28:15–29.

Key "by way of explanation"
Verse 30. The word "high places" at first meant a hill-top, and later an idolatrous shrine built on a hill-top.

Key "Quotable Quote"
"Disobedience and sin are the same thing, for there is no sin but disobedience."

Theologia Germanica

Leviticus 27

Matthew Henry's introduction
The last verse of the foregoing chapter seemed to close up the statute-book; yet this chapter is added as an appendix. Having given laws concerning instituted services, here he directs concerning vows and voluntary services, the free-will offerings of their mouth. Perhaps some devout serious people among them might be so affected with what Moses had delivered to them in the foregoing chapter as in a pang of zeal to consecrate themselves, or their children, or estates to him: this, because honestly meant, God would accept; but, because men are apt to repent of such vows, he leaves room for the redemption of what had been so consecrated, at a certain rate. Here is,

I. The law concerning what was sanctified to God, persons (vv. 2–8), cattle, clean or unclean (vv. 9–13), houses and lands (vv. 15–25), with an exception of firstlings, vv. 26, 27.
II. Concerning what was devoted, vv. 28, 29.
III. Concerning tithes, v. 30, etc.

A detailed analysis of chapter
The law about vows. About people and animals. (1–13)
Vows about houses and land. (14–25)
Devoted things not to be redeemed. (26–33)
Conclusion. (34)

Key verse
Verse 34: "These are the commandments, which the LORD commanded Moses for the children of Israel in mount Sinai."

Key word / key phrase
Verse 9, "acceptable."

Key event / key person / key theme
Law about gifts given to the Lord

Key thought

Servants, houses and land were given to the Lord.

Key thing to look out for

Money was also given to the Lord.

Key Bible cross-reference

Verse 30. See Numbers 18:21–29; Deuteronomy 12:6–18.

Key "by way of explanation"

Verse 34 is taken to support Moses' authorship of this book, as well as its divine origin.

Key "Quotable Quote"

"The tithe can be a beginning way to acknowledge God as the owner of all things, but it is only a beginning and not an ending."

Richard J. Foster

5. Select bibliography for Leviticus

Bonar, Andrew A. *A Commentary on Leviticus*. 1861. Reprint. London: Banner of Truth, 1966.

Calvin, John. *Commentaries on the Four Last Books of Moses*. Reprint. 1852 Translation. Grand Rapids: Eerdmans, n.d.

Harrison, R. K. *Leviticus: An Introduction and Commentary*. (Tyndale Old Testament Commentaries) Downers Grove, Ill.: InterVarsity, 1980.

Keil, C. F. *The Pentateuch*. Vol. 2. Reprint. Grand Rapids: Eerdmans, 1951.

Payne, J. Barton. *Leviticus. The Biblical Expositor*. Vol. 1. Edited by C. F. H. Henry. London: Pickering & Inglis, 1960.

Schultz, Samuel J., *Leviticus: God among His People*, Moody, 1983.

Wenham, Gordon J., *Leviticus* (NICOT), Eerdmans, 1994.

Numbers

1. Book by book: Introduction to Numbers

Introduction

This book is so called because it contains an account of the numbering and arrangement of the Israelites. The early part of it, from the first through the tenth chapters, appears to be a supplement to Leviticus, being occupied with relating the appointment of the Levites to the sacred offices. The journal of the march through the wilderness is then given as far as Numbers 21:20; after which the early incidents of the invasion are narrated. One direct quotation only from this book (Numbers 16:5) is made in the New Testament (2 Timothy 2:19); but indirect references to it by the later sacred writers are very numerous.

Robert Jamieson

Contents of Numbers

This book is of special historical interest as furnishing us with details as to the route of the Israelites in the wilderness and their principal encampments. It may be divided into three parts:

1. The numbering of the people at Sinai, and preparations for their resuming their march (1:1–10:10). The sixth chapter gives an account of the vow of a Nazarite.

2. An account of the journey from Sinai to Moab, the sending out of the spies and the report they brought back, and the murmurings (eight times) of the people at the hardships by the way (10:11–21:20).

3. The transactions in the plain of Moab before crossing the Jordan (21:21–ch. 36).

The period covered in the history extends from the second month of the second year after the Exodus to the beginning of the eleventh month of the fortieth year, in all about thirty-eight years and ten months; a period of wanderings, during which that disobedient generation all died in the wilderness. They were fewer in number at the end of their wanderings than when they left the land of Egypt. We see in this history, on the one hand, the unceasing care of the Almighty over his chosen people during their wanderings; and, on the other hand, the murmurings and rebellions by which they offended their heavenly Protector, drew down repeated marks of his displeasure, and provoked him to say that they should "not enter into his rest" because of their unbelief (Heb. 3:19).

M.G. Easton, M.A., D.D., Illustrated Bible Dictionary

Detailed outline

- I. Preparation for departure from Sinai: 1:1–10:10
  - A. The people numbered: 1:1–54
  - B. The camp arranged: 2:1–34
  - C. The priest and Levites instructed: 3:1–4:49
  - D. The people protected: 5:1–31
  - E. The vow of the Nazarite: 6:1–27
  - F. Gifts of the princes: 7:1–89
  - G. Lighting of the tabernacle lamps: 8:1–4
  - H. Cleansing of the Levites: 8:5–26
  - I. Observance of the Passover: 9:1–14
  - J. Guidance of the camp: 9:15–23
  - K. Calling an assembly and moving the camp: 10:1–10
- II. The journey from Mt. Sinai to Kadesh-Barnea: 10:11–12:15
  - A. Mobilizing for the march: 10:11–28
  - B. Hobab refuses service: 10:29–32
  - C. A continuing cloud: 10:34–36
  - D. A fiery judgment: 11:1–3
  - E. A murmuring multitude: 11:4–9
  - F. A provoked prophet: 11:10–15
  - G. A deadly diet: 11:31–34
  - H. A suffering sister: 12:1–15
- III. Israel at Kadesh-Barnea: 13:1–14:45
  - A. Spying out the land: 13:1–25
  - B. The reports and response: 13:26–14:10
  - C. The judgment of God: 14:11–34
- IV. Events during the wilderness wandering: 20:1–35:34

A. Stoning of a Sabbath breaker: 15:32–36
B. The rebellion of Korah: 16:1–32
C. The budding of Aaron's rod: 17:1–13
D. Instructions to Aaron: 18:1–19:22
E. The death of Miriam: 20:1
F. The sin of Moses: 20:1–13
G. A request refused: 20:14–22
H. Aaron's death: 20:23–29
I. Serpents among the people: 21:5–9
J. A perverted prophet: 22:1–24:25
K. A patriotic priest: 25:1–18
L. Miscellaneous instructions: 26:1–31:54
M. Territorial distribution in East Jordan: 32:1–42
N. Record of the journey from Egypt: 33:1–56
O. Instructions prior to entering Canaan: 34:1–36:13

2. Helpful summaries of Numbers

Bird's eye view

The account of Israel's forty years of wandering in the desert before they entered the Promised Land.

Reading plan

The following reading plan, taking one reading per day, enables you to read through Numbers in twenty days.

Numbers 1–2
Numbers 3–4
Numbers 5–6
Numbers 7
Numbers 8
Numbers 9–10
Numbers 11–13
Numbers 14
Numbers 15–16
Numbers 17–18
Numbers 19–20
Numbers 21–22
Numbers 23–24
Numbers 25–26
Numbers 27–28
Numbers 29–30
Numbers 31
Numbers 32–33
Numbers 34–35
Numbers 36

Verses to memorize

Numbers 6:24–25

The Lord bless you and keep you; the Lord make his face shine on you and be gracious to you.

Numbers 12:3

(Now Moses was a very humble man, more humble than anyone on the face of the earth.)

Statistics

Fourth Old Testament book
36 chapters
1,288 verses
32,902 words

Names/titles given

Hebrew title: *Wayyedabber*: "And he said."
Title in Jewish writings: *Bemidbar* "In the wilderness" the fifth Hebrew word in Numbers.

Greek title in Septuagint: *Arithmoi*: "Numbers."

Latin title in Vulgate: *Liber Numeri*: "Book of Numbers."

The book of murmurings

The book of wanderings

The book of journeys

Two "numbering" of the Israelites are recorded in chapters 1 and 26. Hence the title of the book.

3. Helpful keys to turn to in understanding Numbers

Key word

Alien

Key verses

Numbers 14:22–23; 20:12; 33:1

Key people/events

Miriam

12 spies

Korah

Aaron's rod

Edom

Bronze serpent

Balaam

Phineas

Sihon and Og

Meribah

Joshua

City of refuge

Themes to study

God's provision and guidance

God is a God of order.

Numbers quoted in the New Testament

A bone of him shall not be broken
Num. 9:12 quoted in John 19:36

The Lord knoweth them that are his
Num. 16:5 quoted in 2 Tim. 2:19

Thou shalt not forswear thyself
Num. 30:2 quoted in Matt. 5:33

Unusual events and miracles in Numbers

- Cloud by day, pillar of fire by night, 9:15–23
- Fire from the Lord, 11:1–3
- Quails provided, 11:4–6
- Severe plague, 11:31–34
- Miriam's leprosy, 12:1–15
- Earth swallowed up Korah and his followers, 16:30–35
- 14,700 died in plague, 16:41–50
- Aaron's rod buds, blossoms and bears almonds, 17:1–8
- Water comes from the rock, 20:7–11
- Venomous snake bites cured by looking at bronze snake, 21:5–9
- Balaam's speaking ass, 22:21–31

Seven complaints in Numbers

1. About the way, 11:1–3
2. About their food, 11:4–6
3. About giant opposition, 13:33–14:2
4. About their own leaders, 16:3
5. About God's judgments, 20:2–5
6. About manna, for the second time, 21:5

Jesus in Numbers

In Numbers Jesus the One who is lifted up.

Types of Jesus in Numbers

- The bronze snake, Num. 21:4–9.
- The rock, 1 Cor. 10:4.
- The manna, John 6:31–33.
- Balaam's prophecy about Jesus' reign, Num. 24:17.
- The pillar of cloud and fire are types of Jesus' guidance.
- The six cities of refuge have been seen as types of Jesus.
- The red heifer sacrifice, Lev. 19, and Jesus' sacrifice are linked.

Lessons to learn from Numbers

- Christians receive salvation in order to serve God and humanity.
- God's people often sin through unbelief.
- Caleb and Joshua show us how to be faithful to God through great trials.

4. Chapter by chapter: outline of every chapter of Numbers

Numbers 1

Matthew Henry's introduction

Israel was now to be formed into a commonwealth, or rather a kingdom; for "the Lord was their King" (1 Sam. 12:12), their government a theocracy, and Moses under him was king in Jeshurun, Deut. 33:5. Now, for the right settlement of this holy state, next to the institution of good laws was necessary the institution of good order; and account therefore must be taken of the subjects of this kingdom, which is done in this chapter, where we have,

I. Orders given to Moses to number the people, vv. 1–4.

II. People nominated to assist him herein, vv. 5–16.

III. The particular number of each tribe, as it was given in to Moses, vv. 17–43.

IV. The sum total of all together, vv. 44–46.

V. An exception of the Levites, v. 47, etc.

A detailed analysis of chapter

The numbering of the Israelites. (1-43)

The number of the people. (44-46)

The Levites not numbered with the rest. (47-54)

Key verse

Verse 2: "Take ye the sum of all the congregation of the children of Israel, after their families, by the house of their fathers, with the number of their names, every male by their poll."

Key word / key phrase

Verse 2, "census."

Key event / key person / key theme

The first census of Israel

Key thought

God's people came from one man who was childless.

Key thing to look out for

The Exodus was so important to God's people that events were cited in relation to it.

Key Bible cross-reference

Verse 46. See Exodus 12:27; 38:26.

Key "by way of explanation"

In the book of Leviticus we are told over one hundred times in twenty different ways that God spoke to and through Moses.

Key "Quotable Quote"

"O God, give me the grace to be faithful in my actions, but indifferent to success."

François Fénelon

Numbers 2

Matthew Henry's introduction

The thousands of Israel, having been mustered in the previous chapter, in this are marshaled, and a regular disposition is made of their camp, by a divine appointment. Here is,

I. A general order about it, vv. 1, 2.

II. Particular directions for the posting of each of the tribes, in four distinct squadrons, three tribes in each squadron.

A. In the van-guard on the east were posted Judah, Issachar, and Zebulun, vv. 3–9.

B. In the right wing, southward, Reuben, Simeon, and Gad, vv. 10–16.

C. In the rear, westward, Ephraim, Manasseh, and Benjamin, vv. 18–24.

D. In the left wing, northward, Dan, Asher, and Naphtali, vv. 25–31.

E. The tabernacle in the center, v. 17.

III. The conclusion of this appointment, v. 32, etc.

A detailed analysis of chapter

The arrangement of the tribes in their tents. (1-34)

Key verse

Verse 2: "Every man of the children of Israel shall pitch by his own standard, with the ensign of their father's house: far off about the tabernacle of the congregation shall they pitch."

Key word / key phrase

Verse 2, "camp."

Key event / key person / key theme

The arrangement of the tribes in camp

Key thought

There is nothing wrong with things being done decently and in order.

Key thing to look out for

Worship is central for the followers of God.

Key Bible cross-reference

Verse 2. See Ezekiel 1:10; Revelation 4:7.

Key "by way of explanation"

Verse 17. The tabernacle, representing God's presence, is at the center of the camp.

Key "Quotable Quote"

"The humblest and the most unseen activity in the world can be the true worship of God."

William Barclay

Numbers 3

Matthew Henry's introduction

This chapter and the next are about the tribe of Levi, which was to be mustered and marshaled by itself, and not in common with the other tribes, intimating the particular honor put on them and the particular duty and service required from them. The Levites are in this chapter considered,

I. As attendants on, and assistants to, the priests in the temple-service. And so we have an account,

A. Of the priests themselves (vv. 1–4) and their work, v. 10.

B. Of the gift of the Levites to them (vv. 5–9), in order to which they are mustered (vv. 14–16), and the sum of them taken, v. 39. Each particular family of them is mustered, has its place assigned and its charge, the Gershonites (vv. 17–26), the Kohathites (vv. 27–32), the Merarites, vv. 33–39.

II. As equivalents for the first-born, vv. 11–13.

A. The first-born are numbered, and the Levites taken instead of them, as far as the number of the Levites went, vv. 40–45.

B. What first-born there were more than the Levites were redeemed, v. 46, etc.

A detailed analysis of chapter

The sons of Aaron, and the Levites taken instead of the firstborn. (1–13)

The Levites numbered by their families, and their duties. (14–39)

The firstborn are numbered. (40–51)

Key verse

Verse 6: "Bring the tribe of Levi near, and present them before Aaron the priest, that they may minister unto him."

Key word / key phrase

Verse 2, "Aaron's sons."

Key event / key person / key theme

The Levites are appointed to serve the priests.

Key thought

God has a special work for each of his followers to do.

Key thing to look out for

Money is important in God's work.

Key Bible cross-reference

Verse 4. See 1 Samuel 2:12-17, 22-25, 27-36; 3:11-14.

Key "by way of explanation"

Verse 1. Aaron precedes Moses in this verse because it is Aaron's sons who are about to be given directions.

Key "Quotable Quote"

"The living Church ought to be dependent on its living members."

Thomas Barnardo

Numbers 4

Matthew Henry's introduction

In the previous chapter an account was taken of the whole tribe of Levi, in this we have an account of those of that tribe who were in the prime of their time for service, betwixt thirty and fifty years old.

I. The serviceable men of the Kohathites are ordered to be numbered, and their charges are given them, vv. 2–20.

II. Of the Gershonites, vv. 24–28.

III. Of the Merarites, vv. 29–33.

IV. The numbers of each, and the sum total at last, are recorded, v. 34, etc.

A detailed analysis of chapter

The Levites' service. (1–3)

The duties of the Kohathites. (4–20)

The duties of the Gershonites and Merarites. (21–33)

The numbers of the serviceable Levites. (34–49)

Key verse

Verse 46: "All those that were numbered of the Levites, whom Moses and Aaron and the chief of Israel numbered, after their families, and after the house of their fathers."

Key word / key phrase

Verse 2, "Kohathite."

Key event / key person / key theme

The duties of the Levite clan of Kohath

Key thought

Purity is essential in God's holy eyes.

Key thing to look out for

Jesus taught that inner purity is vital.

Key Bible cross-reference

Verse 16. See 3:12; 6:8.

Key "by way of explanation"

Verse 4. God's own holiness is underlined here as the Kohathites were not allowed even to look on the holy things, let alone touch them.

Key "Quotable Quote"

"Purity of heart and simplicity are of great force with Almighty God, who is in purity most singular, and of nature most simple."

Gregory the Great

Numbers 5

Matthew Henry's introduction

In this chapter we have,

I. An order, pursuant to the laws already made, for the removing of the unclean out of the camp, vv. 1–4.

II. A repetition of the laws about restitution, in case of wrong done to a neighbor (vv. 5–8), and about the appropriating of the hallowed things to the priests, vv. 9, 10.

III. A new law made about the trial of a wife suspected of adultery, by the waters of jealousy, v. 11, etc.

A detailed analysis of chapter

The unclean to be taken out of the camp.

Restitution to be made for trespasses. (1–10)

The trial of jealousy. (11–31)

Key verse

Verse 6: "When a man or woman shall commit any sin that men commit, to do a trespass against the LORD, and that person be guilty."

Key word / key phrase

Verse 3, "defile."

Key event / key person / key theme
Purity among God's people

Key thought
Wrongs need to be put right.

Key thing to look out for
Faithfulness to God and in relationships is commanded by God.

Key Bible cross-reference
Verse 2. See Leviticus 13:2; Luke 5:12–16.

Key "by way of explanation"
Verse 2. Anything that made a person ceremonially "unclean" such as contact with a dead body, meant that the person was separated from the community until he was cleansed.

Key "Quotable Quote"
"To be true to ourselves, we must be true to others."

Jimmy Carter

Numbers 6

Matthew Henry's introduction
In this chapter we have,

I. The law about Nazarites,

A. What it was to which the vow of a Nazarite obliged him, vv. 1–8.

B. A remedial law in case a Nazarite happened to be polluted by the touch of a dead body, vv. 9–12.

C. The solemnity of his discharge when his time was up, vv. 13–21.

II. Instructions given to the priests how they should bless the people, v. 22, etc.

A detailed analysis of chapter
The law about the Nazirites. (1–21)
The form of blessing the people. (22–27)

Key verse
Verse 25: "The Lord make his face shine upon thee, and be gracious unto thee."

Key word / key phrase
Verse 2, "Nazirite."

Key event / key person / key theme
Rules for Nazirites

Key thought
These vows were made to God, not for show.

Key thing to look out for
God's blessings are to be sought daily.

Key Bible cross-reference
Verse 6. See 5:2; Leviticus 21:1–3.

Key "by way of explanation"
Verses 24–26. Note how Aaron's blessing calls on God's name three times, and how each verse mentions two blessings.

Key "Quotable Quote"
"Moody did not have a monopoly on God, God had a monopoly on Moody."

Author unknown

Numbers 7

Matthew Henry's introduction

God having set up house (as it were) in the midst of the camp of Israel, the princes of Israel here come a visiting with their presents, as tenants to their landlord, in the name of their respective tribes.

I. They brought presents,

A. On the dedication of the tabernacle, for the service of that, vv. 1–9.

B. On the dedication of the altar, for the use of that, vv. 10–88. And,

II. God graciously signified his acceptance of them, v. 89. The two previous chapters were the records of additional laws which God gave to Israel, this is the history of the additional services which Israel performed to God.

A detailed analysis of chapter

The offerings of the princes at the dedication of the tabernacle. (1–9)

The offerings of the princes at the dedication of the altar. (10–89)

Key verse

Verse 1: "And it came to pass on the day that Moses had fully set up the tabernacle, and had anointed it, and sanctified it, and all the instruments thereof, both the altar and all the vessels thereof, and had anointed them, and sanctified them."

Key word / key phrase

Verse 1, "finished."

Key event / key person / key theme

The offerings at the dedication of the tabernacle

Key thought

The people are blessed and they respond by giving back to God.

Key thing to look out for

We have nothing that God did not give us.

Key Bible cross-reference

Verses 12–78. See 1:5–15; 2:3–32.

Key "by way of explanation"

Verses 84–88 act as a summary, giving the totals of all the twelve sets of gifts.

Key "Quotable Quote"

"Gratitude is the fairest blossom which springs from the soul."

Henry Ward Beecher

Numbers 8

Matthew Henry's introduction

This chapter is about the lamps or lights of the sanctuary.

I. The burning lamps in the candlestick, which the priests were charged to tend, vv. 1–4.

II. The living lamps (if I may so call them), The Levites, who as ministers were burning and shining lights. The ordination of the priests we had an account of, Lev. 8. Here we have an account of the ordination of the Levites, the inferior clergy.

A. How they were purified, vv. 5–8.

B. How they were parted with by the people, vv. 9, 10.
C. How they were presented to God in lieu of the firstborn, vv. 11–18.
D. How they were consigned to Aaron and his sons, to be ministers to them, v. 19.
E. How all these orders were duly carried out, vv. 20–22. And, lastly, the age appointed for their ministration, v. 23, etc.

A detailed analysis of chapter

The lamps of the sanctuary. (1–4)

Consecration of the Levites, and their service. (5–26)

Key verse

Verse 6: "Take the Levites from among the children of Israel, and cleanse them."

Key word / key phrase

Verse 5, "Levites."

Key event / key person / key theme

Purification and dedication of the Levites

Key thought

Everyone needs to be dedicated to God.

Key thing to look out for

God gives special responsibilities to some of his followers.

Key Bible cross-reference

Verse 2. See Exodus 25:37; 27:21.

Key "by way of explanation"

Verses 5–26. There is a striking similarity between the cleansing of the Levites and the ordination of Aaron's sons. See Leviticus 8.

Key "Quotable Quote"

"If I can stop one heart from breaking,
I shall not live in vain;
If I can ease one life the aching,
Or cool one pain,
Or help one fainting robin
Unto his nest again,
I shall not live in vain."

Emily Dickinson

Numbers 9

Matthew Henry's introduction

This chapter is,

I. About the great ordinance of the Passover;
  A. Orders given for the observance of it, at the return of the year, vv. 1–5.
  B. Provisos added in regard to such as should be ceremonially unclean, or other wise disabled, at the time when the Passover was to be kept, vv. 6–14.

II. About the great favor of the pillar of cloud, which was a guide to Israel through the wilderness, v. 15, etc.

A detailed analysis of chapter

The Passover. (1–14)

The cloud about the tabernacle. (15–23)

Key verse

Verse 2: "Let the children of Israel also keep the Passover at his appointed season."

Key word / key phrase

Verse 2, "Passover."

Key event / key person / key theme

The second Passover

Key thought

The Lord knows how we suffer from lapse of memory.

Key thing to look out for

All that the Passover continues to stand for.

Key Bible cross-reference

Verse 13. See 1 Corinthians 11:28–30.

Key "by way of explanation"

Verse 12. Jesus is our Passover Lamb and his bones were not broken. See 1 Corinthians 5:7.

Key "Quotable Quote"

"Here, O my Lord, I see thee face to face."

Horatius Bonar

Numbers 10

Matthew Henry's introduction

In this chapter we have,

I. Orders given about the making and using of silver trumpets, which seems to have been the last of all the commandments God gave on mount Sinai, and one of the least, yet not without its significance, vv. 1–10.

II. The history of the removal of Israel's camp from mount Sinai, and their orderly march into the wilderness of Paran, vv. 11–28.

III. Moses' treaty with Hobab, his brother-in-law, vv. 29–32.

IV. Moses' prayer at the removing and resting of the ark, v. 33, etc.

A detailed analysis of chapter

The silver trumpets. (1–10)

The Israelites move from Sinai to Paran. (11–28)

Hobab entreated by Moses to continue. (29–32)

The blessing pronounced by Moses. (33–36)

Key verse

Verse 13: "And they first took their journey according to the commandment of the Lord by the hand of Moses."

Key word / key phrase

Verse 13, "set out."

Key event / key person / key theme

The Israelites leave their camp

Key thought

God always leads his people onwards.

Key thing to look out for

Trumpets alert us to God himself and his actions.

Key Bible cross-reference

Verses 14–27. See 1:5–15; 2:3–31; 7:12– 83.

Key "by way of explanation"

Verse 35. This verse starts Psalm 68's celebration of God's march from Sinai to Jerusalem.

Key "Quotable Quote"

"Unfurl the sails, and let God steer us where God will."

Bede

Numbers 11

Matthew Henry's introduction

Hitherto things had gone pretty well in Israel; little interruption had been given to the methods of God's favor to them since the matter of the golden calf; the people seemed teachable in marshalling and purifying the camp, the princes devout and generous in dedicating the altar, and there was good hope that they would be in Canaan presently. But at this chapter begins a melancholy scene; the measures are all broken, God has turned to be their enemy, and fights against them—and it is sin that makes all this mischief.

I. Their murmurings kindled a fire among them, which yet was soon quenched by the prayer of Moses, vv. 1–3.

II. No sooner was the fire of judgment quenched than the fire of sin breaks out again, and God takes occasion from it to magnify both his mercy and his justice.

A. The people fret for want of flesh, vv. 4–9.

B. Moses frets for want of help, vv. 10–15. Now,

God promises to gratify them both, to appoint help for Moses (vv. 16, 17), and to give the people flesh, vv. 18–23. And, He presently makes good both these promises. For,

1. The Spirit of God qualifies the seventy elders for the government, vv. 24–30.
2. The power of God brings quails to feast the people, vv. 31, 32. Yet
3. The justice of God plagued them for their murmurings, v. 33, etc.

A detailed analysis of chapter

The burning at Taberah. (1–3)

The people long for meat, and loathe the manna. (4–9)

Moses complains about his charge. (10–15)

Elders appointed to divide the charge. Meat promised. (16–23)

The Spirit rests on the elders. (24-30)

Quails are given. (31–35)

Key verse

Verse 1: ". . . the fire of the LORD burnt among them, and consumed them that were in the uttermost parts of the camp."

Key word / key phrase

Verse 16, "seventy."

Key event / key person / key theme

Moses chooses seventy leaders.

Key thought

Complaining is one of our besetting sins.

Key thing to look out for

God's goodness is clear for all to see.

Key Bible cross-reference

Verse 25. See 1 Samuel 10:5, 6; 18:10; 19:20–24.

Key "by way of explanation"

Verse 21. It appears from this verse that there were over two million Israelites on the march.

Key "Quotable Quote"

"God is so good that he only awaits our desire to overwhelm us with the gift of himself."

François Fénelon

Numbers 12

Matthew Henry's introduction

In the previous chapter we had the vexation which the people gave to Moses; in this we have his patience tried by his own relations.

I. Miriam and Aaron, his own brother and sister, affronted him, vv. 1–3.

II. God called them to an account for it, vv. 4–9.

III. Miriam was smitten with a leprosy for it, v. 10.

IV. Aaron submits, and Moses meekly intercedes for Miriam, vv. 11–13.

V. She is healed, but put to shame for seven days, vv. 14–16. And this is recorded to show that the best people and families have both their follies and their crosses.

A detailed analysis of chapter

God rebukes the murmuring of Aaron and Miriam. (1–9)

Miriam struck with leprosy, and healed by the prayer of Moses. (10–16)

Key verse

Verse 1: "And Miriam and Aaron spake against Moses because of the Ethiopian woman whom he had married: for he had married an Ethiopian woman."

Key word / key phrase

Verse 1, "Miriam."

Key event / key person / key theme

Miriam is punished.

Key thought

Casting doubt on what God has said was the trick the serpent played on Eve.

Key thing to look out for

Punishment for wrongdoing can bring about most positive results.

Key Bible cross-reference

Verse 4. See Job 22:10; Isaiah 47:11; Jeremiah 4:20.

Key "by way of explanation"

Verse 5. The words "came down" are often used in connection with God making himself known.

Key "Quotable Quote"

"Man punishes the action, but God the intention."

Thomas Fuller

Numbers 13

Matthew Henry's introduction

It is a memorable and very melancholy story which is related in this and the following chapter, of the turning back of Israel from the borders of Canaan, when they were just ready to set foot in it, and the sentencing of them to wander and perish in the wilderness for their unbelief and murmuring. It is referred to Ps. 95:7, etc., and improved for warning to Christians, Heb. 3:7, etc. In this chapter we have,

I. The sending of twelve spies before them into Canaan, vv. 1–16.
II. The instructions given to these spies, vv. 17–20.
III. Their executing their commission according to their instructions, and their return from the search, vv. 21–25.
IV. The report they brought back to the camp of Israel, v. 26, etc.

A detailed analysis of chapter

Twelve men sent to search the land of Canaan, and their instructions. (1–20)
Their exploration of the land. (21–25)
Their account of the land. (26–33)

Key verse

Verse 2: "Send thou men, that they may search the land of Canaan, which I give unto the children of Israel."

Key word / key phrase

Verse 1, "explore."

Key event / key person / key theme

The spies

Key thought

There is much land still to be captured.

Key thing to look out for

God's gifts are always totally satisfying.

Key Bible cross-reference

Verse 22. See Genesis 13:14–18; 14:13; 23:2; 25:9; 50:13.

Key "by way of explanation"

Verse 16. This verse paves the way for the later importance of Joshua.

Key "Quotable Quote"

"He who blesses most is blest."

John Greenleaf Whittier

Numbers 14

Matthew Henry's introduction

This chapter gives us an account of that fatal quarrel between God and Israel on which, for their murmuring and unbelief, he swore in his wrath that they should not enter into his rest. Here is,

I. The mutiny and rebellion of Israel against God, on the report of the evil spies, vv. 1–4.
II. The fruitless endeavor of Moses and Aaron, Caleb and Joshua, to still the tumult, vv. 5–10.
III. Their utter ruin justly threatened by an offended God, vv. 11, 12.
IV. The humble intercession of Moses for them, vv. 13–19.
V. A mitigation of the sentence in answer to the prayer of Moses; they shall not all be cut off, but the decree goes forth ratified with an oath, published to the people, again and again repeated, that this whole congregation should perish in the wilderness, and none of them enter Canaan but Caleb and Joshua only, vv. 20–35.

VI. The present death of the evil spies, vv. 36–39.

VII. The rebuke given to those who attempted to go forward notwithstanding, vv. 40–45. And this is written for our admonition, that we "fall not after the same example of unbelief."

A detailed analysis of chapter

The people murmur at the report of the spies. (1–4)

Joshua and Caleb attempt to calm the people. (5–10)

The divine warnings, and the intercession of Moses. (11–19)

The murmurers forbidden to enter the promised land. (20–35)

Death of the evil spies. (36–39)

Defeat of the people, who now want to invade the land. (40–45)

Key verse

Verse 44: "But they presumed to go up unto the hill top: nevertheless the ark of the covenant of the LORD, and Moses, departed not out of the camp."

Key word / key phrase

Verse 2, "grumbled."

Key event / key person / key theme

More complaints from God's people

Key thought

When things go wrong some will immediately grumble.

Key thing to look out for

Christian leaders need to know how to deal with grumblers.

Key Bible cross-reference

Verse 22. See Exodus 14–17; 32; Numbers 11 and 14.

Key "by way of explanation"

Verse 10. This was undoubtedly a theophany, a manifestation of God's glory.

Key "Quotable Quote"

"Murmur at nothing."

C.C. Colton

Numbers 15

Matthew Henry's introduction

Here is,

I. The law about the meat-offerings and drink-offerings (vv. 1–12) both for Israelites and for strangers (vv. 13–16), and a law about the heave-offerings of the first of their dough, vv. 17–21.

II. The law about sacrifices for sins of ignorance, vv. 22–29.

III. The punishment of presumptuous sins (vv. 30, 31), and an instance given in the Sabbath-breaker, vv. 32–36.

IV. A law about fringes, for memorandums, on the borders of their garments, v. 37, etc.

A detailed analysis of chapter

The law of the meat-offering and the drink-offering. The stranger under the same law. (1–21)

The sacrifice for the sin of ignorance. (22–29)
The punishment of presumption The Sabbath-breaker stoned. (30–36)
The law for tassels on garments. (37–41)

Key verse

Verse 27: "And if any soul sin through ignorance, then he shall bring a she goat of the first year for a sin offering."

Key word / key phrase

Verse 6, "offering."

Key event / key person / key theme

Laws about sacrifice

Key thought

God gave things to help his people to obey him.

Key thing to look out for

Whenever we read about God punishing sin we should take heed.

Key Bible cross-reference

Verse 38. See Deuteronomy 6:4–9.

Key "by way of explanation"

Verse 2. God's punishments and God's grace should always be held in balance.

Key "Quotable Quote"

"Punishment is justice for the unjust."

Augustine of Hippo

Numbers 16

Matthew Henry's introduction

Here is,

I. A daring and dangerous rebellion raised against Moses and Aaron, by Korah, Dathan, and Abiram, vv. 1–15.
  A. Korah and his accomplices contend for the priesthood against Aaron, v. 3. Moses reasons with them, and appeals to God for a decision of the controversy, vv. 4–11.
  B. Dathan and Abiram quarrel with Moses, and refuse to obey his summons, which greatly grieves him, vv. 12–15.

II. A solemn appearance of the pretenders to the priesthood before God, according to order, and a public appearance of the glory of the Lord, which would have consumed the whole congregation if Moses and Aaron had not interceded, vv. 16–22.

III. The deciding of the controversy, and the crushing of the rebellion, by the cutting off of the rebels.
  A. Those in their tents were buried alive, vv. 23–34.
  B. Those at the door of the tabernacle were consumed by fire (v. 35), and their censers preserved for a memorial, vv. 37–40.

IV. A new insurrection of the people, vv. 41–43.
  A. God stayed in the insurrection by a plague, v. 45.
  B. Aaron stayed the plague by offering incense, vv. 46–50. The manner and method of recording this story plainly show the ferment to have been very great.

A detailed analysis of chapter

The rebellion of Korah, Dathan, and Abiram. Korah contends for the priesthood. (1–11)
Disobedience of Dathan and Abiram. (12–15)
The glory of the Lord appears. The intercession of Moses and Aaron. (16–22)
The earth swallows up Dathan and Abiram. (23–34)
The company of Korah consumed. (35–40)
The people murmur. A plague sent. (41–50)

Key verse

Verse 1: "Now Korah, the son of Izhar, the son of Kohath, the son of Levi, and Dathan and Abiram, the sons of Eliab, and On, the son of Peleth, sons of Reuben, took me."

Key word / key phrase

Verse 2, "rose up against."

Key event / key person / key theme

Rebellion against Moses' leadership

Key thought

It is easier to rebel than to remain faithful.

Key thing to look out for

God does not take rebellion lightly.

Key Bible cross-reference

Verse 1. See Jude 11.

Key "by way of explanation"

Verse 49. The census lists in Numbers are huge, so 14,700 people dying is quite possible.

Key "Quotable Quote"

"The curse of infidelity is sensuality."

Richard Cecil

Numbers 17

Matthew Henry's introduction

I. The matter is put on trial by the bringing of twelve rods, one for each prince, before the LORD, vv. 1–7.
II. On trial, the matter is determined by the miraculous blossoming of Aaron's rod, vv. 8, 9.
III. The decision of the controversy is registered by the preservation of the rod, vv. 10, 11.
IV. The people acquiesce in it with some reluctance, vv. 12, 13.

A detailed analysis of chapter

Twelve staffs laid up before the Lord. (1–7)
Aaron's staff buds, and is kept for a memorial. (8–13)

Key verse

Verse 8: ". . . the rod of Aaron for the house of Levi was budded, and brought forth buds, and bloomed blossoms, and yielded almonds."

Key word / key phrase

Verse 8, "almonds."

Key event / key person / key theme

Aaron's rod produces ripe almonds

Key thought

Nothing is too hard for the Lord.

Key thing to look out for

Yet again Moses' obedience to God is highlighted.

Key Bible cross-reference

Verse 10. See Exodus 16:33, 34; Hebrews 9:4.

Key "by way of explanation"

Verse 10. Aaron's staff is given a place of special honor and this contrasts with the dreadful grumbling of the Israelites.

Key "Quotable Quote"

"Become a good manager of those things given you by God."

John Chrysostom

Numbers 18

Matthew Henry's introduction

Aaron being now fully established in the priesthood abundantly to his own satisfaction, and to the satisfaction of the people (which was the good that God brought out of the evil opposition made to him), in this chapter God gives him full instructions about his office or rather repeats those which he had before given him. He tells him,

I. What must be his work and the care and charge committed to him, and what assistance he should have the Levites in that work, vv. 1–7.

II. What should be his and the Levites' wages for this work.

A. The perquisites or fees peculiar to the priests, vv. 8–19.

B. The settled maintenance of the Levites, vv. 20–24.

III. The portion which must be paid to the priests out of the Levites' maintenance, vv. 25–32. Thus every one knew what he had to do, and what he had to live on.

A detailed analysis of chapter

The charge of the priests and Levites. (1–7)

The priests' portion. (8–19)

The Levites' portion. (20–32)

Key verse

Verse 18: "And I, behold, I have taken your brethren the Levites from among the children of Israel: to you they are given as a gift for the LORD, to do the service of the tabernacle of the congregation."

Key word / key phrase

Verse 2, "Levites."

Key event / key person / key theme

The duties of the priests and Levites

Key thought

All service for God is a privilege and responsibility.

Key thing to look out for

There is a right way and a wrong way to act in God's service.

Key Bible cross-reference

Verses 1–7. See Psalm 99:6–8.

Key "by way of explanation"

Verse 7. Serving in the priesthood is specifically said to be God's gift.

Key "Quotable Quote"

"Love God, serve God; everything is in that."

Clare of Assisi

Numbers 19

Matthew Henry's introduction

This chapter is only about the preparing and using of the ashes which were to impregnate the water of purification. The people had complained of the strictness of the law, which forbade their near approach to the tabernacle, 17:13. In answer to this complaint, they are here directed to purify themselves, so as that they might come as far as they had occasion without fear. Here is,

I. The method of preparing these ashes, by the burning of a red heifer, with a great deal of ceremony, vv. 1–10.

II. The way of using them.

A. They were designed to purify people from the pollution contracted by a dead body, vv. 11–16.

B. They were to be put into running water (a small quantity of them), with which the person to be cleansed must be purified, vv. 17–22. And that this ceremonial purification was a type and figure of the cleansing of the consciences of believers from the pollutions of sin appears by the apostle's discourse, Heb. 9:13, 14, where he compares the efficacy of the blood of Christ with the sanctifying virtue that was in "the ashes of a heifer sprinkling the unclean."

A detailed analysis of chapter

The ashes of a heifer. (1–10)

Used to purify the unclean. (11–22)

Key verse

Verse 9: "And a man that is clean shall gather up the ashes of the heifer, and lay them up without the camp in a clean place, and it shall be kept for the congregation of the children of Israel for a water of separation: it is a purification for sin."

Key word / key phrase

Verse 2, "red heifer."

Key event / key person / key theme

Ashes of the red cow

Key thought

God has provided a way for us to be presented clean before him.

Key thing to look out for

No matter how unclean a person may have become in God's sight, there is a way back to God.

Key Bible cross-reference

Verse 9. See Hebrews 9:13.

Key "by way of explanation"

Verse 18. The idea behind sprinkling with a hyssop branch is explained here.

Key "Quotable Quote"

"The Church should be the Society of the Forgiven and Forgiving."

William George Spencer

Numbers 20

Matthew Henry's introduction

At this chapter begins the history of the fortieth year (which was the last year) of the Israelites' wandering in the wilderness. And since the beginning of their second year, when they were sentenced to perform their quarantine in the desert, there to wear away the tedious revolution of forty years, there is little recorded about them till this last year, which brought them to the borders of Canaan, and the history of this year is almost as large as the history of the first year. This chapter gives an account of,

I. The death of Miriam, v. 1.

II. The fetching of water out of the rock, in which observe,

A. The distress Israel was in, for want of water, v. 2.

B. Their discontent and murmuring in that distress, vv. 3–5.

C. God's pity and power engaged for their supply with water out of the rock, vv. 6–9.

D. The infirmity of Moses and Aaron on this occasion, vv. 10, 11.

E. God's displeasure against them, vv. 12, 13.

III. The negotiation with the Edomites. Israel's request (vv. 14–17), and the repulse the Edomites gave them, vv. 18–21.

IV. The death of Aaron the high priest on Mount Hor, the installment of Eleazar in his room, and the people's mourning for him, v. 22, etc.

A detailed analysis of chapter

The people come to Zin, and they grumble about the lack of water. Moses is told to hit the rock, and the infirmity of Moses and Aaron. (1–13)

The Israelites are refused a route through Edom. (14–21)

Aaron hands on the priest's office to Eleazar, and dies on Mount Hor. (22–29)

Key verse

Verse 11: "And Moses lifted up his hand, and with his rod he smote the rock twice: and the water came out abundantly, and the congregation drank, and their beasts also."

Key word / key phrase

Verse 1, "Kadesh."

Key event / key person / key theme

Events at Kadesh

Key thought

Water from a rock illustrates God's power to do the impossible.

Key thing to look out for

God's people have always met with opposition.

Key Bible cross-reference

Verse 28. See Exodus 29:29; Numbers 33:38.

Key "by way of explanation"

Verse 24. "Gathered to his people," was a euphemistic way of referring to death.

Key "Quotable Quote"

"Lord, grant that my last hour may be my best hour."

Author unknown, Old English prayer

Numbers 21

Matthew Henry's introduction

The armies of Israel now begin to emerge out of the wilderness, and to come into a land inhabited, to enter on action, and take possession of the frontiers of the land of promise. A glorious campaign this chapter gives us the history of, especially in the latter part of it. Here is,

I. The defeat of Arad the Canaanite, vv. 1–3.

II. The chastisement of the people with fiery serpents for their murmurings, and the relief granted them on their submission by a brazen serpent, vv. 4–9.

III. Several marches forward, and some occurrences by the way, vv. 10–20.

IV. The celebrated conquest of Sihon king of the Amorites (vv. 21–32), and of Og king of Bashan (vv. 33–35), and possession taken of their land.

A detailed analysis of chapter

The Canaanites of Arad destroyed. (1–3)

The people murmur. The plague of poisonous snakes. The people repent and are healed through the bronze snake. (4–9)

Further journeys of the Israelites. (10–20)

Sihon and Og overcome, and their land possessed. (21–35)

Key verse

Verse 8: "And the LORD said unto Moses, Make thee a fiery serpent, and set it upon a pole: and it shall come to pass, that every one that is bitten, when he looketh upon it, shall live."

Key word / key phrase

Verse 8, "snake."

Key event / key person / key theme

Making a bronze snake

Key thought

God's way of dealing with sin may look strange to outsiders.

Key thing to look out for

The principle of looking in faith to the bronze snake illustrates repentance and faith in God.

Key Bible cross-reference

Verse 9. See John 3:14.

Key "by way of explanation"

Verse 7. Moses only ordered the bronze snake to be made after the people had confessed their sins.

Key "Quotable Quote"

"Confession of sin;
Shame for sin;
Hatred for sin;
Turning from sin."

Thomas Watson

Numbers 22

Matthew Henry's introduction

At this chapter begins the famous story of Balak and Balaam, their attempt to curse Israel, and the baffling of that attempt; God's people are long afterwards told to remember what Balak the king of Moab consulted, and what Balaam the son of Beor answered him, that they might know the righteousness of the Lord, Mic. 6:5. In this chapter we have,

I. Balak's fear of Israel, and the plot he had to get them cursed, vv. 1–4.

II. The embassy he sent to Balaam, a conjurer, to fetch him for that purpose, and the disappointment he met with in the first embassy, vv. 5–14.

III. Balaam's coming to him on his second message, vv. 15–21.

IV. The opposition Balaam met with by the way, vv. 22–35.

V. The interview at length between Balak and Balaam, v. 36, etc.

A detailed analysis of chapter

Balak's fear of Israel. He sends for Balaam. (1–14)

Balaam goes to Balak. (15–21)

Balaam's donkey. (22–35)

Balaam and Balak meet. (36–41)

Key verse

Verse 28: "And the LORD opened the mouth of the ass, and she said unto Balaam, What have I done unto thee, that thou hast smitten me these three times?"

Key word / key phrase

Verse 8, "the answer the Lord gives me."

Key event / key person / key theme

Balaam is sent for by the king of Moab

Key thought

God uses all kinds of means to direct us along his paths.

Key thing to look out for

It seems hard to believe that a dumb animal should speak. Is it not harder to believe that humans should be so brute-like in their disobedience?

Key Bible cross-reference

Verse 35. See 23:12, 20, 26.

Key "by way of explanation"

Verse 23. Balaam's donkey could see more spiritual reality than Balaam.

Key "Quotable Quote"

"Only he who believes is obedient. Only he who is obedient, believes."

Dietrich Bonhoeffer

Numbers 23

Matthew Henry's introduction

Here is,

I. The first attempt to curse Israel.

A. The preparation made for it by sacrifice, vv. 1–3.

B. The contrary instruction God gave Balaam, vv. 4, 5.

C. The blessing Balaam was compelled to pronounce on Israel, instead of a curse, vv. 7–10.

D. The great disappointment of Balak, vv. 11, 12.

II. The second attempt, in the same manner made, and in the same manner frustrated, vv. 13–26.

III. Preparations made for a third attempt (vv. 27–30), the issue of which we have in the next chapter.

A detailed analysis of chapter

Balak's sacrifice. Balaam pronounces a blessing instead of a curse. (1–10)

Balak's disappointment, and second sacrifice. Balaam again blesses Israel. (11–30)

Key verse

Verse 12: "Must I not take heed to speak that which the LORD hath put in my mouth?"

Key word / key phrase

Verse 1, "Balaam."

Key event / key person / key theme

Balaam's three prophesies

Key thought

Obedience to God is never easy.

Key thing to look out for

Following the crowd and pleasing men is easy.

Key Bible cross-reference

Verse 21. See Psalm 32:2, 5; 85:2.

Key "by way of explanation"

Verse 8. God prevented Balaam from cursing God's people, even though he had been hired for that purpose.

Key "Quotable Quote"

"A truly intelligent man has only one care – wholeheartedly to obey Almighty God and to please him."

Antony the Great

Numbers 24

Matthew Henry's introduction

This chapter continues and concludes the history of the defeat of the counsels of Balak and Balaam against Israel, not by might, nor by power, but by the Spirit of the Lord of hosts; and as great an instance it is of God's power over the children of men, and his favor towards his own children, as any of the victories recorded in the book of the wars of the Lord. What preparation was made the third time for the cursing of Israel we read of in the close of the previous chapter. In this chapter we are told,

I. What the blessing was into which that intended curse was turned, vv. 1–9.

II. How Balak dismissed Balaam from his service thereon, vv. 10–13.

III. The predictions Balaam left behind him about Israel, and some of the neighboring nations, v. 14, etc.

A detailed analysis of chapter

Balaam, abandoning sorcery, prophesies the happiness of Israel. (1–9)

Balak dismisses Balaam in anger. (10–14)
Balaam's prophesies. (15-25)

Key verse

Verse 1: "And when Balaam saw that it pleased the LORD to bless Israel, he went not, as at other times, to seek for enchantments, but he set his face toward the desert."

Key word / key phrase

Verse 2, "the Spirit of God."

Key event / key person / key theme

Balaam's final prophesies

Key thought

Balaam was now determined to carry out God's will.

Key thing to look out for

The graphic imagery Balaam uses in his oracles.

Key Bible cross-reference

Verse 9. See Genesis 12:3; 49:9.

Key "by way of explanation"

Verse 1. Balaam had come a long way from the times when he had indulged in sorcery.

Key "Quotable Quote"

"Absolutely reject all divination, fortune-telling, sacrifices to the dead, prophecies in groves or by fountains, amulets, incantations, sorcery (i.e.: evil spells), and all those sacrilegious practices that used to go on in your country."

Gregory III

Numbers 25

Matthew Henry's introduction

Here is,

I. The sin of Israel; they were enticed by the daughters of Moab both to whoredom and to idolatry, vv. 1–3.

II. The punishment of this sin by the hand of the magistrate (vv. 4, 5) and by the immediate hand of God, v. 9.

III. The pious zeal of Phinehas in slaying Zimri and Cozbi, two impudent sinners, vv. 6, 8, 14, 15.

IV. God's commendation of the zeal of Phinehas, vv. 10–13.

V. Enmity put between the Israelites and the Midianites, their tempters, as at first between the woman and the serpent, v. 16, etc.

A detailed analysis of chapter

The Israelites enticed by the daughters of Moab and Midian. (1–5)
Phinehas puts Zimri and Cozbi to death. (6–15)
The Midianites to be punished. (16–18)

Key verse

Verse 2: "And they called the people unto the sacrifices of their gods: and the people did eat, and bowed down to their gods."

Key word / key phrase

Verse 3, "Baal of Peor."

Key event / key person / key theme

The people of Israel at Peor

Key thought

Nobody is beyond temptation.

Key thing to look out for

The same temptations kept on defeating God's people.

Key Bible cross-reference

Verse 11. See Exodus 20:4–6; Leviticus 10:1–3.

Key "by way of explanation"

Verses 1–18. It only becomes clear in 31:8, 16 who is behind this temptation of God's people: Balaam.

Key "Quotable Quote"

"The devil's snare does not catch you unless you are first caught by the devil's bait."

St. Ambrose

Numbers 26

Matthew Henry's introduction

This book is called Numbers, from the numberings of the children of Israel, of which it gives an account. Once they were numbered at Mount Sinai, in the first year after they came out of Egypt, which we had an account of, ch. 1 and 2. And now a second time they were numbered in the plains of Moab, just before they entered Canaan, and of this we have an account in this chapter. We have,

I. Orders given for the doing of it, vv. 1–4.

II. A register of the families and numbers of each tribe (vv. 5–50), and the sum total, v. 51.

III. Direction given to divide the land among them, vv. 52–56.

IV. The families and numbers of the Levites by themselves, vv. 57–62.

V. Notice taken of the fulfilling of the threatening in the death of all those that were first numbered, vv. 63–65), and to this there seems to have been a special regard in the taking and keeping of this account.

A detailed analysis of chapter

Numbering of Israel in the plains of Moab. (1–51)

The division of the land. (52–56)

Number of the Levites. (57–62)

None remaining of the first numbering. (63–65)

Key verse

Verse 2: "Take the sum of all the congregation of the children of Israel, from twenty years old and upward, throughout their fathers' house, all that are able to go to war in Israel."

Key word / key phrase

Verse 2, "census."

Key event / key person / key theme

The second census

Key thought

God provides against all the odds.

Key thing to look out for

God uses his followers, even though they have let him down in the past.

Key Bible cross-reference

Verses 1-51. See 1:1-46.

Key "by way of explanation"

Verse 51, "601,730" is very close to the number in the first census. That God's people had not been greatly reduced in size was due to his mercy.

Key "Quotable Quote"

"The house of my soul is too small for you to come to it. May it be enlarged by you. It is in ruins; restore it."

Augustine of Hippo

Numbers 27

Matthew Henry's introduction

Here is,

I. The case of Zelophehad's daughters determined, vv. 1–11.

II. Notice given to Moses of his death approaching, vv. 12–14.

III. Provision made of a successor in the government,

A. By the prayer of Moses, vv. 15–17.

B. By the appointment of God, v. 18, etc.

A detailed analysis of chapter

The daughters of Zelophehad ask for an inheritance, and the law of inheritances. (1–11)

Moses warned of his death. (12–14)

Joshua appointed to succeed Moses. (15–23)

Key verse

Verse 18: "And the LORD said unto Moses, Take thee Joshua the son of Nun, a man in whom is the spirit, and lay thine hand upon him."

Key word / key phrase

Verse 22, "Joshua."

Key event / key person / key theme

Joshua is chosen to succeed Moses

Key thought

God is never tied to one leader.

Key thing to look out for

God provides leadership in every generation.

Key Bible cross-reference

Verse 18. See Exodus 17:9–14; 24:13; 32:17.

Key "by way of explanation"

Verse 16. After Moses is reminded of his own sin he is very positive and prayerfully asks about his successor.

Key "Quotable Quote"

"No man safely rules but he who loves to be subject. No man safely commands but he who loves to obey."

Thomas à Kempis

Numbers 28

Matthew Henry's introduction

Now that the people were numbered, orders given for the dividing of the land, and a general of the forces nominated and commissioned, one would have expected that the next chapter should begin the history of the campaign, or at least should give us an account of the ordinances of war; no, it contains the ordinances of worship, and provides that now, as they were on the point of entering Canaan, they should be sure to take their religion along with them, and not forget this, in the prosecution of their wars, vv. 1, 2. The laws are here repeated and summed up about the sacrifices that were to be offered,

I. Daily, vv. 3–8.

II. Weekly, vv. 9, 10.

III. Monthly, vv. 11–15.

IV. Yearly.

A. At the Passover, vv. 16–25.

B. At Pentecost, vv. 26–31. And the next chapter is about the annual solemnities of the seventh month.

A detailed analysis of chapter

Offerings, and the daily sacrifice. (1–8)

The offering on the Sabbath and new moons. (9–15)

Offerings at the Passover, and on the day of firstfruits. (16–31)

Key verse

Verses 16,17: "And in the fourteenth day of the first month is the Passover of the LORD. And in the fifteenth day of this month is the feast: seven days shall unleavened bread be eaten."

Key word / key phrase

Verse 16, "the Lord's Passover."

Key event / key person / key theme

Differing offerings

Key thought

The Day of Atonement is given pride of place.

Key thing to look out for

Compare the Day of Atonement with the death of Jesus.

Key Bible cross-reference

Verses 1–8. See Exodus 29:38–41; Leviticus 1–7.

Key "by way of explanation"

Verses 1-31. These verses illustrate the centrality of sacrifice and the work of the priests to the life of the Israelites.

Key "Quotable Quote"

"Christ died for all men; I am a man: therefore, Christ died for me."

John Owen

Numbers 29

Matthew Henry's introduction

This chapter appoints the offerings that were to be made by fire unto the Lord in the three great solemnities of the seventh month.

I. In the feast of trumpets on the first day of that month, vv. 1–6.

II. In the day of atonement on the tenth day, vv. 7–11.

III. In the feast of tabernacles on the fifteenth day and the seven days following, vv. 12–38. And then the conclusion of these ordinances, vv. 39, 40.

A detailed analysis of chapter

The offering at the Feats of Trumpets, and on the Day of Atonement. (1–11)

Offerings at the Feast of Tabernacles. (12–40)

Key verse

Verse 11: "One kid of the goats for a sin offering; beside the sin offering of atonement, and the continual burnt offering, and the meat offering of it, and their drink offerings."

Key word / key phrase

Verse 2, "offering."

Key event / key person / key theme

Offerings made to God

Key thought

Moses thought of himself as the Lord's messenger.

Key thing to look out for

Doing what God commands always pleases him. See verse 6.

Key Bible cross-reference

Verses 1–6. See Leviticus 23:23–25.

Key "by way of explanation"

Verses 7–11. The Feast of Trumpets led into the Day of Atonement with its confession of sin and celebration of God's redemption.

Key "Quotable Quote"

"Put aside your own will so as to go to war under Christ the Lord, the real King, picking up the keen and glittering weapons of obedience."

Benedict

Numbers 30

Matthew Henry's introduction

In this chapter we have a law about vows, which had been mentioned in the close of the previous chapter.

- I. Here is a general rule laid down that all vows must be carefully performed, vv. 1, 2.
- II. Some particular exceptions to this rule.
  - A. That the vows of daughters should not be binding unless allowed by the father, vv. 3–5. Nor,
  - B. The vows of wives unless allowed by the husband, v. 6, etc.

A detailed analysis of chapter

Vows to be kept. (1, 2)

The reasons why vows might be waived. (3–16)

Key verse

Verse 2: "If a man vow a vow unto the LORD, or swear an oath to bind his soul with a bond; he shall not break his word, he shall do according to all that proceedeth out of his mouth."

Key word / key phrase

Verse 2, "vow."

Key event / key person / key theme

Rules about vows

Key thought

Vows made to God should not be broken.

Key thing to look out for

Vows should not be entered into lightly. See Ecclesiastes 5:1–7.

Key Bible cross-reference

Verses 10–15. See 27:1–11; Matthew 5:33–37.

Key "by way of explanation"

Verses 1–16. This is the main biblical passage on taking vows. See also Deuteronomy 23:21–23.

Key "Quotable Quote"

"We ought not to be weary of doing little things for the love of God, who regards not the greatness of the work, but the love with which it is performed."

Brother Lawrence

Numbers 31

Matthew Henry's introduction

This chapter belongs to "the book of the wars of the Lord," in which it is probable it was inserted. It is the history of a holy war, a war with Midian. Here is,

I. A divine command for the war, vv. 1, 2.

II. The undertaking of the war, vv. 3–6.

III. The glorious success of it, vv. 7–12.

IV. Their triumphant return from the war.

A. The respect Moses paid to the soldiers, v. 13.

B. The rebuke he gave them for sparing the women, vv. 14–18.

C. The directions he gave them for the purifying of themselves and their effects, vv. 19–24.

D. The distribution of the spoil they had taken, one half to the soldiers, the other to the congregation, and a tribute to the Lord out of each, vv. 25–47.

E. The free-will offering of the officers, v. 48, etc.

A detailed analysis of chapter

War with Midian. (1–6)

Balaam killed. (7–12)

Those killed who caused sin. (13–38)

Purification of the Israelites. (39–24)

Division of the spoil. (25–47)

Offerings. (48–54)

Key verse

Verses 1,2: "And the Lord spake unto Moses, saying, Avenge the children of Israel of the Midianites: afterward shalt thou be gathered unto thy people."

Key word / key phrase

Verse 2, "Midianites."

Key event / key person / key theme

God's war against Midian

Key thought

Personal revenge is forbidden.

Key thing to look out for

Human attributes like petulant anger should never be attributed to God.

Key Bible cross-reference

Verses 19–24. Because this was a holy war

everything had to be cleansed. See 19:11–13.

Key "by way of explanation"

Verses 1–24. Moses engaged in this war, not out of personal anger, but because it was "the Lord's vengeance," verse 3, since the Midianites has led the Israelites into idolatry.

Key "Quotable Quote"

"God's wrath is God's punishment of sin and evil. It is a mighty declaration that God has done what he has always said he would do, namely, that he would punish sin, and the wages of sin is death."

D. Martyn Lloyd-Jones

Numbers 32

Matthew Henry's introduction

In this chapter we have,

I. The humble request of the tribes of Reuben and Gad for an inheritance on that side Jordan where Israel now lay encamped, vv. 1–5.

II. Moses' misinterpretation of their request, vv. 6–15.

III. Their explication of it, and stating it aright, vv. 16–19.

IV. The grant of their petition under the provisos and limitations which they themselves proposed, v. 20, etc.

A detailed analysis of chapter

The tribes of Reuben and Gad request an inheritance on the east of Jordan. (1–5)

Moses reproves the Reubenites and Gadites. (6–15)

They explain their views. Moses consents. (16–27)

They take possession of the land to the east of Jordan. (28–42)

Key verse

Verse 1: "Now the children of Reuben and the children of Gad had a very great multitude of cattle: and when they saw the land of Jazer, and the land of Gilead, that, behold, the place was a place for cattle."

Key word / key phrase

Verse 5, "Jordan."

Key event / key person / key theme

The tribes east of the Jordan

Key thought

Wholeheartedness in following God is held up as the ideal.

Key thing to look out for

Moses could listen to reasonable arguments and change his mind.

Key Bible cross-reference

Verses 8–9. See Numbers 13:17–33.

Key "by way of explanation"

Verse 2. Moses did not want the tribes to be separated as that might encourage rebellion.

Key "Quotable Quote"

"God will put up with a great many things in the human heart, but there is one thing he will not put up with – a second place."

John Ruskin

Numbers 33

Matthew Henry's introduction

In this chapter we have,

I. A particular account of the removals and encampments of the children of Israel, from their escape out of Egypt to their entrance into Canaan, forty-two in all, with some remarkable events that happened at some of those places, vv. 1–49.

II. A strict command given them to drive out all the inhabitants of the land of Canaan, which they were not going to conquer and take possession of, vv. 50–56. So that the former part of the chapter looks back on their march through the wilderness, the latter looks forward to their settlement in Canaan.

A detailed analysis of chapter

Stages in Israel's journey. (1–49)

The Canaanites to be destroyed. (50–56)

Key verse

Verse 2: "And Moses wrote their goings out according to their journeys by the commandment of the LORD: and these are their journeys according to their goings out."

Key word / key phrase

Verse 1, "stages in the journey."

Key event / key person / key theme

The Israelites' journey from Egypt to Moab

Key thought

After the great victory of escaping from Egypt the Israelites just wandered in the desert.

Key thing to look out for

After some spiritual victory in the Christian life Christians are most vulnerable to temptation.

Key Bible cross-reference

Verse 38. See Numbers 20:22–28.

Key "by way of explanation"

Verses 1–49. The Israelites wandered in the desert for forty years. These verses list forty places visited by the Israelites during this time.

Key "Quotable Quote"

"Faithfulness in little things is a big thing."

John Chrysostom

Numbers 34

Matthew Henry's introduction

In this chapter God directs Moses, and he is to direct Israel,

I. About the bounds and borders of the land of Canaan, vv. 1–15.

II. About the division and distribution of it to the tribes of Israel, v. 16, etc.

A detailed analysis of chapter

The boundaries of the promised land. (1–15)

Those appointed to divide the land. (16–29)

Key verse

Verse 2: "Command the children of Israel, and say unto them, When ye come into the land of

Canaan; (this is the land that shall fall unto you for an inheritance, even the land of Canaan with the coasts thereof:)"

Key word / key phrase
Verse 1, "Canaan."

Key event / key person / key theme
The boundaries of the land in Canaan

Key thought
The earth and all its land belongs to God.

Key thing to look out for
As one leader from each tribe is chosen to divide the land, impartiality is ensured.

Key Bible cross-reference
Verses 16–29. See 1:5–16.

Key "by way of explanation"
Verses 3–12. The size of the land listed underlines God's great generosity.

Key "Quotable Quote"
"Seek to distinguish yourself from others only in your generosity."

Clement

Numbers 35

Matthew Henry's introduction
Orders having been given before for the dividing of the land of Canaan among the lay-tribes (as I may call them), care is here taken for a competent provision for the clergy, the tribe of Levi, which ministered in holy things.

I. Forty-eight cities were to be assigned them, with their suburbs, some in every tribe, vv. 1–8.

II. Six cities out of these were to be for cities of refuge, for any man that killed another unawares, vv. 9–15. In the law about these observe,

A. In what case sanctuary was not allowed, namely, that of willful murder, vv. 16–21.

B. In what cases it was allowed, vv. 22–24.

C. What was the law about those that took shelter in these cities of refuge, v. 25, etc.

A detailed analysis of chapter
The cities of the Levites. (1–8)
The cities of refuge, and the laws about murder. (9–34)

Key verse
Verse 6: "And among the cities which ye shall give unto the Levites there shall be six cities for refuge, which ye shall appoint for the manslayer, that he may flee thither: and to them ye shall add forty and two cities."

Key word / key phrase
Verse 6, "cities of refuge."

Key event / key person / key theme
Cities of refuge

Key thought
The psalmist thought of God as his refuge.

Key thing to look out for

The existence of these cities of refuge curbed angry revenge and promoted justice.

Key Bible cross-reference

Verses 9–34. See Deuteronomy 19:1–13; Joshua 20:1–9.

Key "by way of explanation"

Verse 33. The land is held to be sacred. So murder pollutes the land.

Key "Quotable Quote"

"God's freedom from bias does not mean that he maintains neutrality in the struggle for justice."

Ronald J. Sider

Numbers 36

Matthew Henry's introduction

We have in this chapter the determination of another question that arose on the case of the daughters of Zelophehad. God had appointed that they should inherit, 27:7. Now here,

I. An inconvenience is suggested, in case they should marry into any other tribe, vv. 1–4.

II. It is prevented by a divine appointment that they should marry in their own tribe and family (vv. 5–7), and this is settled for a rule in like cases (vv. 8, 9); and they did marry accordingly to some of their own relations (vv. 10–12), and with this the book concludes, v. 13.

5. Select bibliography for Numbers

Bush, George. *Notes on Numbers*. Reprint of 1856 edition. Minneapolis: James & Klock, 1976.

Harrison, Roland K. *Numbers.* Baker, 1990.

Keil, C. F. *Biblical Commentary on the Old Testament: The Pentateuch*. Vol. 3. KD. Translated by James Martin. Grand Rapids: Eerdmans, n.d.

Wenham, Gordon J. *Numbers: An Introduction and Commentary*. Downers Grove, Ill., and Leicester, England: InterVarsity Press, 1981.

Deuteronomy

1. Book by book: Introduction to Deuteronomy

Introduction

Deuteronomy, the second law, a title which plainly shows what is the object of this book, namely, a recapitulation of the law. It was given in the form of public addresses to the people; and as Moses spoke in the prospect of his speedy removal, he enforced obedience to it by many forcible appeals to the Israelites, about their long and varied experience both of the mercies and the judgments of God. The minute notices of the heathen people with whom they had come in contact, but who afterward disappeared from the pages of history, as well as the accounts of the fertility and products of Canaan, and the counsels respecting the conquest of that country, fix the date of this book and the time of its composition by the hand of Moses. The close, however, must have been added by another; and, indeed, it is supposed by some to have formed the original preface to the Book of Joshua.

Robert Jamieson

Contents of Deuteronomy

Deuteronomy is made up of three discourses, followed by three short appendices:

Deuteronomy 1:1–4:43, historical; a review of God's dealings with Israel, specifying in great detail where and when delivered (Deuteronomy 1:1–5), recounting in broad outlines the main events in the nation's experience from Horeb to Moab (Deuteronomy 1:6–3:29), on which the author bases an earnest appeal to the people to be faithful and obedient, and in particular to keep clear of all possible idolatry (Deuteronomy 4:1–40).

Appended to this first discourse is a brief note (Deuteronomy 4:41–43) about Moses' appointment of three cities of refuge on the East side of the Jordan.

Deuteronomy 4:44–26:19, hortatory and legal; introduced by a superscription (Deuteronomy 4:44–49), and consisting of a resume of Israel's moral and civil statutes, testimonies and judgments. Analyzed in greater detail, this second discourse is composed of two main sections:

(a) chapters 5–11, an extended exposition of the Ten Commandments on which theocracy was based;

(b) chapters 12–26, a code of special statutes about worship, purity, tithes, the three annual feasts, the administration of justice, kings, priests, prophets, war, and the private and social life of the people. The spirit of this discourse is most ethical and religious. The tone is that of a father no less than that of a legislator. A spirit of humanity pervades the entire discourse. Holiness is its ideal.

Deuteronomy 27:1–31:30. The subject of this third discourse being "the blessings of obedience and the curses of disobedience." This section begins with directions to inscribe these laws on stones to be set up on Mt. Ebal (Deuteronomy 27:1–10), to be ratified by an antiphonal ritual of blessings and cursings from the two adjacent mountains, Gerizim and Ebal (Deuteronomy 27:11–26). These are followed by solemn warnings against disobedience (Deuteronomy 28:1–29:1), and fresh exhortations to accept the terms of the new covenant made in Moab, and to choose between life and death (Deuteronomy 29:2–30:20). Moses' farewell charge to Israel and his formal commission of Joshua close the discourse (Deuteronomy 31). The section is filled with predictions, which were woefully verified in Israel's later history.

The appendices are in Moses' song (Deuteronomy 32), which the great Lawgiver taught the people; Moses' blessing (Deuteronomy 33); Moses is praised in Israel (Deuteronomy 34:10–12).

Orr, James, M.A., D.D. General Editor, International Standard Bible Encyclopedia

Detailed outline

I. Moses' first sermon: 1:1–4:43
- A. Historical introduction: 1:1–5
- B. Review of the journey from Horeb to Moab: 1:6–3:29
- C. Appeal to the new generation to keep the law: 4:1–40
- D. Account of the appointment of the cities of refuge: 4:41–43
- E. Summary of the law of Moses: 4:44–49

II. Moses' second sermon: 5:1–26:19
- A. Exposition of the ceremonial laws: 12:1–16:17
- B. Exposition of the civil laws: 16:18–20:20
- C. Exposition of the social laws: 21:1–22:30

III. Moses' third sermon: 27:1–30:20
- A. Inscription of laws on stone, and blessings and curses: 27:1–26
- B. Prediction of blessings and curses: 28:1–68
- C. Exhortations to holiness: 29:1–30:20

IV. Historical appendix: 31:1–34:12
- A. Moses' final words and appointment of Joshua: 31:1–30
- B. Moses' song and exhortation: 32:1–47
- C. God's final words to Moses: 32:48–52
- D. Moses' parting blessing on the tribes: 33:1–29
- E. The death and burial of Moses: 34:1–12

2. Helpful summaries of Deuteronomy

Bird's eye view

Deuteronomy repeats and emphasizes the God's covenant and his laws given to the Israelites.

Reading plan

The following reading plan, taking one reading per day, enables you to read through Deuteronomy in thirteen days.

Deuteronomy 1–2
Deuteronomy 3–4
Deuteronomy 5–6
Deuteronomy 7–9
Deuteronomy 10–11
Deuteronomy 12–14
Deuteronomy 15–17
Deuteronomy 18–20
Deuteronomy 21–22
Deuteronomy 23–25
Deuteronomy 26–27
Deuteronomy 28–29
Deuteronomy 30–31
Deuteronomy 32–34

Verses to memorize

Deuteronomy 6:4–5

Hear, O Israel: The Lord our God, the Lord is one. Love the Lord your God with all your heart and with all your soul and with all your strength.

Deuteronomy 30:14

The word is near you, it is in your mouth and in your heart, so you may obey it.

Statistics

Fifth Old Testament book
34 chapters
958 verses
28,461 words

Famous sayings found in Deuteronomy

"Apple of my eye" Deuteronomy 2:10

"Man shall not live by bread alone" Deuteronomy 8:3

"Eye for an eye" Deuteronomy 19:21

Names/titles given

Hebrew title: *Haddebharim*: "The words."

Greek title in Septuagint: *To Deuteronimion Touto*: "This second law."

Latin title in Vulgate: *Deuteronimion:* "Second law."

Five fifths of the Law, as it completes the five books of Moses.

Book of remembrance.

3. Helpful keys to note in understanding Deuteronomy

Key words

Possess

Obedience

Remember

Remember

Deuteronomy says eight things should never be forgotten.

1. The Law, 4:9–10
2. God's covenant, 4:23
3. Their previous slavery, 5:15
4. Their wonderful deliverance, 7:18
5. The Lord's provision for them, 8:2–6
6. Their past sins, 9:7
7. God's judgments, 24:9
8. Their past, 32:7

Key verses

Deuteronomy 6:5; 10:12–13

Key people/events

Moses' first sermon

The Shema (Deut. 6)

Three feasts: Passover, Feast of Weeks, Tabernacles

Themes to study

God's love

God's faithfulness

Following the Lord and his law.

Deuteronomy quoted in the New Testament

- There is none other but he
  Deut. 4:35 quoted in Mark 12:32
- Honor thy father and thy mother
  Deut. 5:16 quoted in Matt. 15:4, Mark 7:10, and Eph. 6:2–3
- Thou shalt not kill, Thou shalt not commit adultery
  Deut. 5:16–20 quoted in Matt. 19:18–19, Mark 10:19 and Luke 18:20
- Thou shalt not kill
  Deut. 5:17 quoted in Matt. 5:21 and James 2:11
- Thou shalt not commit adultery
  Deut. 5:17–19, 21 quoted in Rom. 13:9
- Thou shalt not commit adultery
  Deut. 5:18 quoted in Matt. 5:27
- Thou shalt not covet
  Deut. 5:21 quoted in Rom. 7:7
- He is one
  Deut. 6:4 quoted in Mark 12:32
- Hear, O Israel

Deut. 6:4–5 quoted in Mark 12:29–30

- Thou shalt love the Lord thy God
  Deut. 6:5 quoted in Matt. 22:37, Mark 12:33, and Luke 10:27
- Thou shalt worship the Lord thy God, and him only shalt thou serve
  Deut. 6:13 quoted in Matt. 4:10 and Luke 4:8
- Thou shalt not tempt the Lord thy God
  Deut. 6:16 quoted in Matt. 4:7 and Luke 4:12
- Man shall not live by bread alone
  Deut. 8:3 quoted in Matt. 4:4 and Luke 4:4
- Speak not in thine heart
  Deut. 9:4 quoted in Rom. 10:6
- I exceedingly fear
  Deut. 9:19 quoted in Heb. 12:21
- Put away the wicked man from among yourselves
  Deut. 17:7 quoted in 1 Cor. 5:13
- A prophet shall God raise up unto you
  Deut. 18:15 quoted in Acts 7:37
- To him shall ye hearken in all things
  Deut. 18:15–16 quoted in Acts 3:22
- Every soul that shall not hearken to that prophet
  Deut. 18:19 quoted in Acts 3:23
- At the mouth of two witnesses or three
  Deut. 19:15 quoted in Matt. 18:16 and 2 Cor. 13:1
- Eye for eye, tooth for tooth
  Deut. 19:21 quoted in Matt. 5:38
- Cursed is every one that hangeth on a tree
  Deut. 21:23 quoted in Gal. 3:13
- Let him give here a writing of divorcement
  Deut. 24:1 quoted in Matt. 5:31 and Matt. 19:1
- Write a bill of divorcement
  Deut. 24:1, 3 quoted in Mark 10:4
- Thou shalt not muzzle the ox when he treadeth out the corn
  Deut. 25:4 quoted in 1 Cor. 9:9 and 1 Tim 5:18
- If a man's brother die
  Deut. 25:5 quoted in Matt. 22:24, Mark 12:19, and Luke 20:28
- Cursed is everyone who continueth not
  Deut. 27:26 quoted in Gal. 3:10
- Eyes that they should not see
  Deut. 29:4 quoted in Rom. 11:8
- The word is nigh thee
  Deut. 30:12–14 quoted in Rom. 10:6–8
- I will in no wise fail thee
  Deut. 31:6, 8 quoted in Heb. 13:5
- I will provoke you to jealousy
  Deut. 32:21 quoted in Rom. 10:19
- Vengeance is mine
  Deut. 32:35 quoted in Rom. 12:19
- The Lord shall judge his people
  Deut. 32:35, 36 quoted in Heb. 10:30
- Rejoice, ye Gentiles, with his people
  Deut. 32:43 quoted in Rom. 15:10
- Let all the angels of God worship him
  Deut. 32:43 quoted in Heb. 1:6

Unusual events and miracles in Deuteronomy

Deuteronomy has a review of the miracles and signs God gave to his people in the desert.

Moses' unusual death, 34:5–6

Jesus in Deuteronomy

In Deuteronomy Jesus is our true prophet.

Types of Jesus in Deuteronomy

Moses is a type of Jesus, as he was a prophet,

priest, and a ruler.

Lessons to learn from Deuteronomy

- We must have a personal relationship with God.
- This relationship should effect all areas of our lives.
- Our worship of God must be from our hearts and should be joyful. It must exclude any pagan customs.

4. Chapter by chapter: outline of every chapter of Deuteronomy

Deuteronomy 1

Matthew Henry's introduction

The first part of Moses' farewell sermon to Israel begins with this chapter, and is continued to the latter end of the fourth chapter. In the first five verses of this chapter we have the date of the sermon, the place where it was preached (vv. 1, 2, 5), and the time when, vv. 3, 4. The narrative in this chapter reminds them,

I. Of the promise God made them of the land of Canaan, vv. 6–8.

II. Of the provision made of judges for them, vv. 9–18.

III. Of their unbelief and murmuring on the report of the spies, vv. 19–33.

IV. Of the sentence passed on them for it, and the ratification of that sentence, v. 34, etc.

A detailed analysis of chapter

The words Moses spoke to Israel in the plains of Moab, and the promise of Canaan. (1–8)

Judges provided for the people. (9–18)

The spies are sent. God's anger over their unbelief and disobedience. (19–46)

Key verse

Verse 1: "These be the words which Moses spake unto all Israel on this side Jordan in the wilderness, in the plain over against the Red sea, between Paran, and Tophel, and Laban, and Hazeroth, and Dizahab."

Key word / key phrase

Verse 22, "spy."

Key event / key person / key theme

Spies sent out

Key thought

Caleb's devotion to God is most instructive, verse 36.

Key thing to look out for

Even a great leader like Moses had clay feet.

Key Bible cross-reference

Verse 31. See Isaiah 40:11; Jeremiah 31:10; Ezekiel 34:11–16.

Key "by way of explanation"

Verse 10. God is the prime mover in Israel's history.

Key "Quotable Quote"

"It is very difficult to be humble if you are always successful, so God chastises us with failure at times in order to humble us, to keep us in a state of humility."

D. Martyn Lloyd-Jones

Deuteronomy 2

Matthew Henry's introduction

Moses, in this chapter, proceeds in the rehearsal of God's providences about Israel in their way to Canaan, yet preserves not the record of any thing that happened during their tedious march back to the Red Sea, in which they wore out almost thirty-eight years, but passes that over in silence as a dark time, and makes his narrative to begin again when they faced about towards Canaan (vv. 1–3), and drew towards the countries that were inhabited, about which God here gives them direction,

I. What nations they must not give any disturbance to.

A. Not to the Edomites, vv. 4–8.

B. Not to the Moabites (v. 9), of the antiquities of whose country, with that of the Edomites, he gives some account, vv. 10–12. And here comes in an account of their passing the river Zered, vv. 13–16.

C. Not to the Ammonites, of whose country here is some account given, vv. 17–23.

II. What nations they should attack and conquer. They must begin with Sihon, king of the Amorites, vv. 24, 25. And accordingly,

A. They had a fair occasion of quarrelling with him, vv. 26–32.

B. God gave them a complete victory over him, v. 33, etc.

A detailed analysis of chapter

The Edomites to be spared. (1–7)

The Moabites and Ammonites to be spared. (8–23)

The Amorites to be destroyed. (24–37)

Key verse

Verse 1: "Then we turned, and took our journey into the wilderness by the way of the Red sea, as the LORD spake unto me: and we compassed mount Seir many days."

Key word / key phrase

Verse 1, "desert."

Key event / key person / key theme

Wandering in the desert

Key thought

All victories in the Christian life should be attributed to God.

Key thing to look out for

God's plans are never permanently thwarted by human disobedience.

Key Bible cross-reference

Verse 34. See 3:7; Joshua 8:2.

Key "by way of explanation"

Verse 5. The tribes of Lot and Esau were given land, just as the Israelites were.

Key "Quotable Quote"

"Let no man think to kill sin with few, easy, or gentle strokes."

John Owen

Deuteronomy 3

Matthew Henry's introduction

Moses, in this chapter, relates,

I. The conquest of Og, king of Bashan, and

the seizing of his country, vv. 1–11.

II. The distribution of these new conquests to the two tribes and a half, vv. 12–17. Under certain provisos and limitations, vv. 18–20.

III. The encouragement given to Joshua to carry on the war which was so gloriously begun, vv. 21, 22.

IV. Moses' request to go over into Canaan (vv. 23–25), with the denial of that request, but the grant of an equivalent, v. 26, etc.

A detailed analysis of chapter

The conquest of Og king of Bashan. (1–11)

The land of Gilead and Bashan. (12–20)

Moses encourages Joshua. (21–29)

Key verse

Verse 18: "And I commanded you at that time, saying, The LORD your God hath given you this land to possess it: ye shall pass over armed before your brethren the children of Israel, all that are meet for the war."

Key word / key phrase

Verse 12, "land."

Key event / key person / key theme

The land is divided up

Key thought

Moses' single sin had unforeseen consequences.

Key thing to look out for

All kinds of rest, verse 20, come from the Lord's hand.

Key Bible cross-reference

Verses 23–25. See 1:37; 31:2.

Key "by way of explanation"

Verse 22. These events are recorded in such a way that it is clear that God himself lay behind each advance and victory.

Key "Quotable Quote"

"Thou hast made us for thyself, O Lord, and our hearts are restless until they find their rest in thee."

Augustine of Hippo

Deuteronomy 4

Matthew Henry's introduction

In this chapter we have,

I. A most earnest and pathetic exhortation to obedience, both in general, and in some particular instances, backed with a great variety of very pressing arguments, repeated again and again, and set before them in the most moving and affectionate manner imaginable, vv. 1–40.

II. The appointing of the cities of refuge on that side Jordan, vv. 41–43.

III. The particular description of the place where Moses delivered the following repetition of the law, v. 44, etc.

A detailed analysis of chapter

Earnest exhortations to obedience, and warnings against idolatry. (1–23)

Warnings against disobedience, and promises of mercy. (24–40)

Cities of refuge appointed. (41–49)

Key verse

Verse 34: "Or hath God assayed to go and take him a nation from the midst of another nation, by temptations, by signs, and by wonders, and by war, and by a mighty hand, and by a stretched out arm, and by great terrors, according to all that the LORD your God did for you in Egypt before your eyes?"

Key word / key phrase

Verse 16, "idol."

Key event / key person / key theme

The sin of idolatry

Key thought

God's faithful followers learn from their failures.

Key thing to look out for

Out of God's kindness the cities of refuge are set up.

Key Bible cross-reference

Verse 20. See 1 Kings 8:51; Jeremiah 11:4; Isaiah 48:10.

Key "by way of explanation"

Verse 25. This verse shows a pattern of events repeated in this book: rebellion, expulsion, repentance, and restoration.

Key "Quotable Quote"

"The purpose of revelation is restoration, the renewal in us of that likeness to God which man lost by sin."

Stephen Neill

Deuteronomy 5

Matthew Henry's introduction

In this chapter we have the second edition of the ten commandments.

I. The general intent of them; they were in the nature of a covenant between God and Israel, vv. 1–5.

II. The particular precepts are repeated (vv. 6–21), with the double delivery of them, both by word and writing, v. 22.

III. The settling of the correspondence thence forward between God and Israel, by the mediation and ministry of Moses.

A. It was Israel's humble petition that it might be so, vv. 23–27.

B. It was God's gracious grant that it should be so, vv. 28–31. And hence he infers the obligation they were under to obedience, vv. 32, 33.

A detailed analysis of chapter

The covenant in Horeb. (1–5)

The Ten Commandments repeated. (6–22)

The request of the people that the law might be delivered through Moses. (23–33)

Key verse

Verse 4: "The LORD talked with you face to face in the mount out of the midst of the fire."

Key word / key phrase

Verse 22, "commandments."

Key event / key person / key theme

The Ten Commandments

Key thought

The Ten Commandments have not dated.

Key thing to look out for

Prosperity follows from obedience.

Key Bible cross-reference

Verse 2. See Jeremiah 31:31–34.

Key "by way of explanation"

Verses 16–21. The Ten Commandments form the basis of God's relationship with his people.

Key "Quotable Quote"

"If men will not be governed by the Ten Commandments, they shall be governed by the ten thousand commandments."

G.K. Chesterton

Deuteronomy 6

Matthew Henry's introduction

Moses, in this chapter, goes on with his charge to Israel, to be sure to keep up their religion in Canaan. It is much the same with ch.4.

I. His preface is a persuasive to obedience, vv. 1–3.

II. He lays down the great principles of obedience. The first truth to be believed, That God is one, v. 4. The first duty to be done, To love him with all our heart, v. 5.

III. He prescribes the means for keeping up religion, vv. 6–9.

IV. He cautions them against those things which would be the ruin of religion—abuse of plenty (vv. 10–12), inclination to idolatry (vv. 14, 15), and gives them some general precepts, vv. 13, 16–18.

V. He directs them what instructions to give their children, v. 20, etc.

A detailed analysis of chapter

A persuasive to obedience. (1–3)
An exhortation to obedience. (4, 5)
Obedience taught. (6–16)
General precepts. Instructions to be given to their children. (17–25)

Key verse

Verse 6: "And thou shalt love the LORD thy God with all thine heart, and with all thy soul, and with all thy might."

Key word / key phrase

Verse 5, "love."

Key event / key person / key theme

Loving God

Key thought

Keeping God's commandments involves fearing God, loving God, but not putting God to the test.

Key thing to look out for

Obedience is essential in the Christian life.

Key Bible cross-reference

Verse 2. See 4:40; 5:16,33.

Key "by way of explanation"

Verse 6. One of the characteristics of the new covenant was to be having God's laws in the heart, not just on stone tablets.

Key "Quotable Quote"

"There are no disappointments to those whose wills are buried in the will of God."

F.W. Faber

Deuteronomy 7

Matthew Henry's introduction

Moses in this chapter exhorts Israel,

I. In general, to keep God's commandments, vv. 11, 12.

II. In particular, and in order to that, to keep themselves pure from all communion with idolaters.

A. They must utterly destroy the seven devoted nations, and not spare them, or make leagues with them, vv. 1, 2, 16, 24.

B. They must by no means marry with the remainders of them, vv. 3, 4.

C. They must deface and consume their altars and images, and not so much as take the silver and gold of them to their own use, vv. 5, 25, 26. To enforce this charge, he shows that they were bound to do so,

1. In duty. Considering

a. Their election to God, v. 6.

b. The reason of that election, vv. 7, 8.

c. The terms they stood on with God, vv. 9, 10.

2. In interest. It is here promised,

a. In general, that, if they would serve God, he would bless and prosper them, vv. 12–15.

b. In particular, that if they would drive out the nations, that they might not be a temptation to them, God would drive them out, that they should not be any vexation to them, v. 17, etc.

A detailed analysis of chapter

Driving out the nations. (1–11)

The promises of obedience. (12–26)

Key verse

Verse 1: "When the Lord thy God shall bring thee into the land whither thou goest to possess it, and hath cast out many nations before thee."

Key word / key phrase

Verse 7, "choose."

Key event / key person / key theme

Taking possession of the land

Key thought

God does not love us on account of any merit on our part.

Key thing to look out for

Spiritual power comes from obeying God, verse 24.

Key Bible cross-reference

Verse 9. See Psalm 103:3.

Key "by way of explanation"

Verse 4. God did not forbid mixed marriages on racial grounds, but on religious grounds. He wanted to avoid apostasy.

Key "Quotable Quote"

"Though Christians be not kept altogether from falling, yet they are kept from falling altogether."

William Secker

Deuteronomy 8

Matthew Henry's introduction

In this chapter Moses gives the Israelites,

I. General exhortations to obedience, vv. 1, 6.

II. A review of the great things God had done for them in the wilderness, as a good argument for obedience, vv. 2–5, 15, 16.

III. A prospect of the good land into which God would now bring them, vv. 7–9.

IV. A necessary caution against the temptations of a prosperous condition, vv. 10–14, and 17, 18.

V. A fair warning of the fatal consequences of apostasy from God, vv. 19, 20.

A detailed analysis of chapter

Exhortations and warnings, enforced by the Lord's former dealings with Israel, and his promises. (1–9)

Exhortations and warnings further enforced. (10–20)

Key verse

Verse 19: "And it shall be, if thou do at all forget the LORD thy God, and walk after other gods, and serve them, and worship them, I testify against you this day that ye shall surely perish."

Key word / key phrase

Verse 2, "remember."

Key event / key person / key theme

Do not forget the Lord.

Key thought

God's discipline should be welcomed.

Key thing to look out for

God's goodness is to be recalled.

Key Bible cross-reference

Verse 3. See Matthew 4:4; Luke 4:4.

Key "by way of explanation"

Verses 7–9. These verses give a good description of the land that God's followers were about to enter.

Key "Quotable Quote"

"The purpose of Christ's redeeming work was to make it possible for bad men to become good deeply, radically, and finally."

A.W. Tozer

Deuteronomy 9

Matthew Henry's introduction

The design of Moses in this chapter is to convince the people of Israel of their utter unworthiness to receive from God those great favors that were now to be conferred on them, writing this, as it were, in capital letters at the head of their charter, "Not for your sake, be it known unto you," Ezek. 36:32.

I. He assures them of victory over their enemies, vv. 1–3.

II. He cautions them not to attribute their successes to their own merit, but to God's justice, which was engaged against their enemies, and his faithfulness, which was engaged to their fathers, vv. 4–6.

III. To make it evident that they had no reason to boast of their own righteousness, he mentions their faults, shows Israel their transgressions, and the house of Jacob their sins. In general, they had been all along a provoking people, vv. 7–24. In particular,
   A. In the matter of the golden calf, the story of which he largely relates, vv. 8–21.
   B. He mentions some other instances of their rebellion, vv. 22, 23. And,
   C. Returns, at v. 25, to speak of the intercession he had made for them at Horeb, to prevent their being ruined for the golden calf.

A detailed analysis of chapter

The Israelites should not think their success came by their own merit. (1–6)

Moses reminds the Israelites of their rebellions. (7–29)

Key verse

Verse 16: "And I looked, and, behold, ye had sinned against the LORD your God, and had made you a molten calf: ye had turned aside quickly out of the way which the LORD had commanded you."

Key word / key phrase

Verse 16, "an idol cast in the shape of a calf."

Key event / key person / key theme

The golden calf

Key thought

No group of God's people are beyond falling into temptation.

Key thing to look out for

The body is willing but the spirit is weak.

Key Bible cross-reference

Verse 6. See 10:16; 31:27.

Key "by way of explanation"

Verse 19. Moses' prayer resulted in the survival of the Israelites.

Key "Quotable Quote"

"Apostasy begins in the closet. No man ever backslid from the life and power of Christianity who continued constant and fervent in private prayer. He who prays without ceasing is likely to rejoice evermore."

Adam Clark

Deuteronomy 10

Matthew Henry's introduction

Moses having, in the previous chapter, reminded them of their own sin, as a reason why they should not depend on their own righteousness, in this chapter he sets before them God's great mercy to them, notwithstanding their provocations, as a reason why they should be more obedient for the future.

I. He mentions divers tokens of God's favor and reconciliation to them, never to be forgotten.
   A. The renewing of the tables of the covenant, vv. 1–5.
   B. Giving orders for their progress towards

Canaan, vv. 6, 7.

C. Choosing the tribe of Levi for his own, vv. 8, 9.

D. And continuing the priesthood after the death of Aaron, v. 6.

E. Owning and accepting the intercession of Moses for them, vv. 10, 11.

II. Hence he infers what obligations they lay under to fear, and love, and serve God, which he presses on them with many motives, v. 12, etc.

A detailed analysis of chapter

God's mercies to Israel after their rebellion. (1–11)

An exhortation to obedience. (12–22)

Key verse

Verse 1: "At that time the LORD said unto me, Hew thee two tables of stone like unto the first, and come up unto me into the mount, and make thee an ark of wood."

Key word / key phrase

Verse 4, "Ten Commandments."

Key event / key person / key theme

Moses receives the Ten Commandments again

Key thought

Moses is given a clear command by the Lord about what he has to do, verse 11.

Key thing to look out for

The correct reaction to seeing God's greatness is humility in his presence.

Key Bible cross-reference

Verse 16. See 9:6,13; 31:27.

Key "by way of explanation"

Verses 1–3. Different Bible versions use a variety of words such as "box," or "chest,"for what was traditionally translated as "ark."

Key "Quotable Quote"

"Wherever the fear of God rules in the heart, it will appear both in works of charity and piety, and neither will excuse us from the other."

Matthew Henry

Deuteronomy 11

Matthew Henry's introduction

With this chapter Moses concludes his preface to the repetition of the statutes and judgments which they must observe to do. He repeats the general charge (v. 1), and, having in the close of the previous chapter begun to mention the great things God had done among them, in this,

I. He specifies several of the great works God had done before their eyes, vv. 2–7.

II. He sets before them, for the future, life and death, the blessing and the curse, according as they did, or did not, keep God's commandments, that they should certainly prosper if they were obedient, should be blessed with plenty of all good things (vv. 8–15), and with victory over their enemies, and the enlargement of their coast thereby, vv. 22–25. But their disobedience would undoubtedly be their ruin, vv. 16, 17.

III. He directs them what means to use that they might keep in mind the law of God, vv. 18–21. And,

IV. Concludes all with solemnly charging them to choose which they would have, the blessing or the curse, v. 26, etc.

A detailed analysis of chapter

The great work God performed for Israel. (1–7)

Promises and warnings. (8–17)

Careful study of God's word is necessary. (18–25)

The blessings and the curse are set out. (26–32)

Key verse

Verse 26: "Behold, I set before you this day a blessing and a curse."

Key word / key phrase

Verse 9, "milk and honey."

Key event / key person / key theme

The blessings of the promised land

Key thought

The more the Lord is loved the more he will be obeyed.

Key thing to look out for

God's promises and blessings are more than we can imagine.

Key Bible cross-reference

Verse 28. See 13:2, 6, 13; 28:64.

Key "by way of explanation"

Verse 14. The main season for rain in Palestine is between October and April.

Key "Quotable Quote"

"Fear the Lord and you will do everything well."

Shepherd of Hermas

Deuteronomy 12

Matthew Henry's introduction

Moses at this chapter comes to the particular statues which he had to give in charge to Israel, and he begins with those which relate to the worship of God, and particularly those which explain the second commandment, about which God is in a special manner jealous.

I. They must utterly destroy all relics and remains of idolatry, vv. 1–3.

II. They must keep close to the tabernacle, vv. 4, 5. The former precept was intended to prevent all false worship, the latter to preserve the worship God had instituted. By this latter law,

A. They are commanded to bring all their offerings to the altar of God, and all their holy things to the place which he should choose, vv. 6, 7, 11, 12, 14, 18, 26–28.

B. They are forbidden, in general, to do as they now did in the wilderness (vv. 8–11), and as the Canaanites had done (vv. 29–32), and, in particular, to eat the hallowed things at their own houses (vv. 13, 17, 18), or to forsake the instituted ministry, v. 19.

C. They are permitted to eat flesh as common food at their own houses, provided they do not eat the blood, vv. 15, 16, and again, vv. 20–26.

A detailed analysis of chapter

Monuments of idolatry to be destroyed. (1–4)
The place of God's service to be kept. (5–32)

Key verse

Verse 2: "Ye shall utterly destroy all the places, wherein the nations which ye shall possess served their gods, upon the high mountains, and upon the hills, and under every green tree."

Key word / key phrase

Verse 2, "worship."

Key event / key person / key theme

The one place for worship

Key thought

Idolatry remains a temptation for God's followers.

Key thing to look out for

The Lord tolerates no rivals.

Key Bible cross-reference

Verse 5. See 14:23,24; 16:2.

Key "by way of explanation"

Verse 12. Joy was meant to characterize God's followers.

Key "Quotable Quote"

"Joy is the great note all through the Bible."

Oswald Chambers

Deuteronomy 13

Matthew Henry's introduction

Moses is still on that necessary subject about the peril of idolatry. In the close of the previous chapter he had cautioned them against the peril that might arise from their predecessors the Canaanites. In this chapter he cautions them against the rise of idolatry from among themselves; they must take heed lest any should draw them to idolatry,

I. By the pretense of prophecy, vv. 1–5.
II. By the pretense of friendship and relation, vv. 6–11.
III. By the pretense of numbers, vv. 12–18. But in all these cases the temptation must be resolutely resisted and the tempters punished and cut off.

A detailed analysis of chapter

People who entice others to idolatry to be put to death. (1–5)
Relatives who entice to idolatry not to be spared. (6–11)
Idolatrous cities not to be spared. (12–18)

Key verse

Verse 5: "So shalt thou put the evil away from the midst of thee."

Key word / key phrase

Verse 6, "other gods."

Key event / key person / key theme

Warning against idolatry

Key thought

Evil and goodness do not mix.

Key thing to look out for

Idolatry requires drastic action if it is to be eliminated.

Key Bible cross-reference

Verse 13. See 1 Samuel 1:16; 2:12; 25:17.

Key "by way of explanation"

Verse 5. Evil as well as those who promoted evil had to be thrown out of the land.

Key "Quotable Quote"

"You don't have to go to heathen lands today to find false gods. America is full of them. Whatever you love more than God is your idol."

D.L. Moody

Deuteronomy 14

Matthew Henry's introduction

Moses in this chapter teaches them,

I. To distinguish themselves from their neighbors by a singularity,

A. In their mourning, vv. 1, 2.

B. In their meat, vv. 3–21.

II. To devote themselves unto God, and, in token of that, to give him his dues out of their estates, the yearly tithe, and that every third year, for the maintenance of their religious feasts, the Levites, and the poor, v. 22, etc.

A detailed analysis of chapter

The Israelites to be different from other nations. (1–21)

About making tithes. (22–29)

Key verse

Verse 3: "Thou shalt not eat any abominable thing."

Key word / key phrase

Verse 4, "animals."

Key event / key person / key theme

Clean and unclean animals

Key thought

God's regulations are for our benefit.

Key thing to look out for

God is concerned about every aspect of life, including health and hygiene.

Key Bible cross-reference

Verses 22–29. See Numbers 18:21–29.

Key "by way of explanation"

Verse 2. The Israelites had to separate themselves from anything that was ceremonially unclean.

Key "Quotable Quote"

"If you do not give the tenth part to God, he will take the nine parts."

Ambrose

Deuteronomy 15

Matthew Henry's introduction

In this chapter Moses gives orders,

I. About the release of debts, every seventh year (vv. 1–6), with a caution that this should be no hindrance to charitable lending, vv. 7–11.

II. About the release of servants after seven years' service, vv. 12–18.

III. About the sanctification of the firstlings of cattle to God, v. 19, etc.

A detailed analysis of chapter

The year of release. (1–11)

The release of servants. (12–18)

About the firstborn of cattle. (19–23)

Key verse

Verse 1: "At the end of every seven years thou shalt make a release."

Key word / key phrase

Verse 1, "debts."

Key event / key person / key theme

The year for canceling debts

Key thought

Money matters are constantly taught in the Bible.

Key thing to look out for

The importance of a generous heart is underlined in verse 10.

Key Bible cross-reference

Verse 1. See Exodus 23:10,11; Leviticus 25:1–7.

Key "by way of explanation"

Verse 4. If the Israelites followed the orders of God that are set out in this chapter then there would be no poor people in their number.

Key "Quotable Quote"

"God prizes generosity, especially joyful generosity."

Charles R. Swindoll

Deuteronomy 16

Matthew Henry's introduction

In this chapter we have,

I. A repetition of the laws about the three yearly feasts; in particular, that of the Passover, vv. 1–8. That of Pentecost, vv. 9–12. That of tabernacles, vv. 13–15. And the general law about the people's attendance on them, vv. 16, 17.

II. The institution of an inferior magistracy, and general rules of justice given to those that were called into office, vv. 18–20.

III. A caveat against groves and images, vv. 21, 22.

A detailed analysis of chapter

The yearly feasts. (1–17)

About judges. Sacred stones and images forbidden. (18–22)

Key verse

Verse 1: "Observe the month of Abib, and keep the Passover unto the LORD thy God: for in the month of Abib the LORD thy God brought thee forth out of Egypt by night."

Key word / key phrase

Verse 1, "Passover."

Key event / key person / key theme

The Passover and other festivals

Key thought

Celebrating these festivals was meant to help the Israelites never to forget the Lord.

Key thing to look out for

Different festivals emphasized different aspects of God's character.

Key Bible cross-reference

Verses 1–8. See Exodus 12:1–28; 13:1–16.

Key "by way of explanation"

Verse 16. The Israelites were ordered to attend these three festivals each year.

Key "Quotable Quote"

"The life of man consists in beholding God."

Irenaeus

Deuteronomy 17

Matthew Henry's introduction

The charge of this chapter is,

I. About the purity and perfection of all those animals that were offered in sacrifice, v. 1.

II. About the punishment of those that worshipped idols, vv. 2–7.

III. About appeals from the inferior courts to the great Sanhedrim, vv. 8–13.

IV. About the choice and duty of a king, v. 14, etc.

A detailed analysis of chapter

All sacrifices to be perfect. Idolaters must be killed. (1–7)

Difficult controversies. (8–13)

The choice of a king. His duties. (14–20)

Key verse

Verse 8: "If there arise a matter too hard for thee in judgment, between blood and blood, between plea and plea, and between stroke and stroke, being matters of controversy within thy gates: then shalt thou arise, and get thee up into the place which the LORD thy God shall choose."

Key word / key phrase

Verse 11, "do not turn aside."

Key event / key person / key theme

Law courts

Key thought

Contempt should not be part of the character of God's followers.

Key thing to look out for

The importance of having leaders who obey God.

Key Bible cross-reference

Verse 6. See Numbers 35:30.

Key "by way of explanation"

Verse 14. Although the Lord did not want the Israelites to have a king, Moses is here anticipating a time when they will seek one.

Key "Quotable Quote"

"Dost thou wish to rise? Begin by descending."

Augustine of Hippo

Deuteronomy 18

Matthew Henry's introduction

In this chapter,

I. The rights and revenues of the church are settled, and rules given about the Levites' ministration and maintenance, vv. 1–8.

II. The caution against the idolatrous abominable customs of the heathen is repeated, vv. 9–14.

III. A promise is given them of the spirit of prophecy to continue among them, and to center at last in Christ the great prophet, vv. 15–18.

IV. Wrath threatened against those that despise prophecy (v. 19) or counterfeit it (v. 20), and a rule given for the trial of it, vv. 21, 22.

A detailed analysis of chapter

A provision about Levites. (1–8)

The abominations of the Canaanites to be avoided. (9–14)

Christ the great Prophet. (15–22)

Key verse

Verse 15: "The LORD thy God will raise up unto thee a Prophet from the midst of thee, of thy brethren, like unto me; unto him ye shall hearken."

Key word / key phrase

Verse 9, "detestable ways."

Key event / key person / key theme

Warning against pagan practices

Key thought

Our society is so godless that it is hardly possible to escape being influenced by it.

Key thing to look out for

Sorcery is out for God's followers.

Key Bible cross-reference

Verse 4. See Exodus 23:19; 34:26.

Key "by way of explanation"

Verse 9. This verse gives the Bible's most detailed list of magical things forbidden by the Bible.

Key "Quotable Quote"

"Magic is not mere superstition. It can corrupt people."

Andrew Murray

Deuteronomy 19

Matthew Henry's introduction

The laws which Moses had hitherto been repeating and urging mostly concerned the acts of religion and devotion towards God; but here he comes more fully to press the duties of righteousness between man and man. This chapter relates,

I. To the sixth commandment, "Thou shalt not kill," vv. 1–13.

II. To the eighth commandment, "Thou shalt not steal," v. 14.

III. To the ninth commandment, "Thou shalt not bear false witness," v. 15, etc.

A detailed analysis of chapter

The cities of refuge, the man-slayer, and the murderer. (1–13)

Landmarks not to be removed. (14)

The punishment of false witnesses. (15–21)

Key verse

Verse 15: "One witness shall not rise up against a man for any iniquity, or for any sin, in any sin that he sinneth: at the mouth of two witnesses, or at the mouth of three witnesses, shall the matter be established."

Key word / key phrase

Verse 4, "flees."

Key event / key person / key theme

The cities of refuge

Key thought

God is deeply concerned about us, especially when things go wrong.

Key thing to look out for

God is a God of justice.

Key Bible cross-reference

Verses 1–13. See 4:41–43; Numbers 35:9–28.

Key "by way of explanation"

Verse 14. To move a boundary stone was to rob someone of part of their property.

Key "Quotable Quote"

"The Bible tells us to love our neighbors, and also to love our enemies; probably because they are generally the same people."

G.K. Chesterton

Deuteronomy 20

Matthew Henry's introduction

This chapter settles the militia, and establishes the laws and ordinances of war,

I. Relating to the soldiers.

A. Those must be encouraged that were drawn up to battle, vv. 1–4.

B. Those must be dismissed and sent back again whose private affairs called for their attendance at home (vv. 5–7), or whose weakness and timidity unfitted them for service in the field, vv. 8, 9.

II. Relating to enemies they made war with.

A. The treaties they must make with the cities that were far off, vv. 10–15.

B. The destruction they must make of the people into whose land they were going, vv. 16–18.

C. The care they must take, in besieging cities, not to destroy the fruit trees, vv. 19, 20.

A detailed analysis of chapter

Exhortation and proclamation about those who went to war. (1–9)

Peace to be offered.Which cities were to be devoted. (10–20)

Key verse

Verse 1: "When thou goest out to battle against

thine enemies, and seest horses, and chariots, and a people more than thou, be not afraid of them: for the LORD thy God is with thee, which brought thee up out of the land of Egypt."

Key word / key phrase

Verse 1, "war."

Key event / key person / key theme

Going to war

Key thought

Marriage is placed above war.

Key thing to look out for

Evil has to be destroyed or else it takes us over.

Key Bible cross-reference

Verse 11. See Genesis 9:25.

Key "by way of explanation"

Verses 5–8. Israelites were not to rely on the size of their army but on the Lord.

Key "Quotable Quote"

"All that is necessary for the triumph of evil is that good men do nothing."

Edmund Burke

Deuteronomy 21

Matthew Henry's introduction

In this chapter provision is made,

I. For the putting away of the guilt of blood from the land, when he that shed it had fled from justice, vv. 1–9.

II. For the preserving of the honor of a captive maid, vv. 10–14.

III. For the securing of the right of a first-born son, though he were not a favorite, vv. 15–17.

IV. For the restraining and punishing of a rebellious son, vv. 18–21.

V. For the maintaining of the honor of human bodies, which must not be hanged in chains, but decently buried, even the bodies of the worst malefactors, vv. 22, 23.

A detailed analysis of chapter

The expiation of uncertain murder. (1–9)

Marrying a captive woman. (10–14)

The firstborn not to be disinherited for private affection. (15–17)

A stubborn son to be stoned. (18–21)

Bodies of criminals not to be left hanging on a tree all night. (22,23)

Key verse

Verse 8: "Be merciful, O LORD, unto thy people Israel, whom thou hast redeemed, and lay not innocent blood unto thy people of Israel's charge. And the blood shall be forgiven them."

Key word / key phrase

Verse 22, "capital offense."

Key event / key person / key theme

Justice

Key thought

The death penalty was given for a capital offense.

Key thing to look out for

To be hung on a tree was thought to be a total disgrace.

Key Bible cross-reference

Verse 22. See Genesis 40:19.

Key "by way of explanation"

Verse 23. A body hung on a tree was under God's condemnation. Hence the significance of Jesus' death by crucifixion on a tree. See Galatians 3:13.

Key "Quotable Quote"

"He was condemned, that thou mightest be justified, and was killed, that thou mightest live."

John Bunyan

Deuteronomy 22

Matthew Henry's introduction

The laws of this chapter provide,

I. For the preservation of charity in the care of strayed or fallen cattle, vv. 1–4.

II. For the preservation of order and distinction, that men and women should not wear one another's clothes (v. 5), and that other needless mixtures should be avoided, vv. 9–11.

III. For the preservation of birds, vv. 6, 7.

IV. Of life, v. 8.

V. Of the commandments, v. 12.

VI. Of the reputation of a wife abused, if she were innocent (vv. 13–19), but for her punishment if guilty, vv. 20, 21.

VII. For the preservation of the chastity of wives, v. 22. Virgins betrothed (vv. 23–27), or not betrothed, vv. 28, 29. And, lastly, against incest, v. 30.

A detailed analysis of chapter

Humility towards brethren. (1–4)

Various precepts. (5–12)

Against impurity. (13–30)

Key verse

Verse 4: "Thou shalt not see thy brother's ass or his ox fall down by the way, and hide thyself from them: thou shalt surely help him to lift them up again"

Key word / key phrase

Verse 4, "donkey."

Key event / key person / key theme

Further laws to ensure a humanitarian and just society.

Key thought

We are not meant to pass by on the other side.

Key thing to look out for

We are meant to be on the look-out for the safety of other people.

Key Bible cross-reference

Verse 15. See 25:7.

Key "by way of explanation"

Verse 5. God made men and women and it is his intention that the differences between the sexes should be maintained.

Key "Quotable Quote"

"Faith and works should travel side by side, step answering to step, like the legs of men walking. First faith, and then works; and then faith again, and then works again – until you can scarcely distinguish which is the one and which is the other."

William Booth

Deuteronomy 23

Matthew Henry's introduction

The laws of this chapter provide,

I. For the preserving of the purity and honor of the families of Israel, by excluding such as would be a disgrace to them, vv. 1–8.

II. For the preserving of the purity and honor of the camp of Israel when it was abroad, vv. 9–14.

III. For the encouraging and entertaining of slaves who fled to them, vv. 15, 16.

IV. Against whoredom, vv. 17, 18.

V. Against usury, vv. 19, 20.

VI. Against the breach of vows, vv. 21–23.

VII. What liberty a man might take in his neighbor's field and vineyard, and what not, vv. 23, 25.

A detailed analysis of chapter

Who are excluded from the congregation. (1–8)

Cleanliness commanded. (15–25)

About fugitive servants. Usury, and other precepts. (9–14)

Key verse

Verse 24: "When thou comest into thy neighbor's vineyard, then thou mayest eat grapes thy fill at thine own pleasure; but thou shalt not put any in thy vessel."

Key word / key phrase

Verse 24 "vineyard."

Key event / key person / key theme

The just society

Key thought

We are never meant to take advantage of our neighbor.

Key thing to look out for

God is the one who protects us.

Key Bible cross-reference

Verse 6. See Ezekiel 25:1–11; Zephaniah 2:8–11.

Key "by way of explanation"

Verses 9–14. Rules about hygiene were crucial, especially during a war.

Key "Quotable Quote"

"Divine love not only repeatedly commands us to love our neighbors, but also itself produces this love and pours it out into our hearts."

Francis de Sales

Deuteronomy 24

Matthew Henry's introduction

In this chapter we have,

I. The toleration of divorce, vv. 1–4.

II. A discharge of new-married men from the war, v. 5.

III. Laws about pledges, vv. 6, 10–13, 17.
IV. Against man-stealing, v. 7.
V. About the leprosy, vv. 8, 9.
VI. Against the injustice of masters towards their servants, vv. 14, 15. Judges in capital causes (v. 16), and civil concerns, vv. 17, 18.
VII. Of charity to the poor, v. 19, etc.

A detailed analysis of chapter

About divorce. (1–4)
About newly-weds, thieves, and pledges. (5–13)
Justice and generosity. (14–22)

Key verse

Verse 22: "And thou shalt remember that thou wast a bondman in the land of Egypt: therefore I command thee to do this thing."

Key word / key phrase

Verse 1, "marries."

Key event / key person / key theme

Divorce and remarriage

Key thought

The importance of helping newly-weds is clear from verse 5.

Key thing to look out for

Kindness should extend to people who are in debt to us.

Key Bible cross-reference

Verses 1–4. See Leviticus 21:7, 14; Matthew 5:31, 32; 19:3–9.

Key "by way of explanation"

Verses 1–4. Although divorce was allowed in the books of Moses, it was severely restricted.

Key "Quotable Quote"

"Kindness is an essential part of God's work and ours here on earth."

Billy Graham

Deuteronomy 25

Matthew Henry's introduction

Here is,

I. A law to moderate the scourging of male factors, vv. 1–3.
II. A law in favor of the ox the treads out the corn, v. 4.
III. For the disgracing of him that refused to marry his brother's widow, vv. 5–10.
IV. For the punishment of an immodest woman, vv. 11, 12.
V. For just weights and measures, vv. 13–16.
VI. For the destroying of Amalek, v. 17, etc.

A detailed analysis of chapter

Extent of punishment. (1–3)
The ox that treads the corn. (4)
Marriage of a brother's wife. (5–12)
Dishonest weights. (13–16)
War against Amalek. (17–19)

Key verse

Verse 1: "If there be a controversy between men, and they come unto judgment, that the judges may judge them; then they shall justify the righteous, and condemn the wicked."

Key word / key phrase

Verse 5, "brothers."

Key event / key person / key theme

Duty to a dead brother

Key thought

Cruelty must never be part of punishment.

Key thing to look out for

Duty to family should take a very high priority.

Key Bible cross-reference

Verse 4. See 1 Corinthians 9:9, 10; 1 Timothy 5:17, 18.

Key "by way of explanation"

Verse 23. A limit was put on corporal punishment.

Key "Quotable Quote"

"The foundations of civilization are no stronger and no more enduring than the corporate integrity of the homes on which they rest. If the home deteriorates, civilization will crumble and fall."

Billy Graham

Deuteronomy 26

Matthew Henry's introduction

With this chapter Moses concludes the particular statutes which he thought fit to give Israel in charge at his parting with them; what follows is by way of sanction and ratification. In this chapter,

I. Moses gives them a form of confession to be made by him that offered the basket of his first-fruits, vv. 1–11.

II. The protestation and prayer to be made after the disposal of the third year's tithe, vv. 12–15.

III. He binds on all the precepts he had given them,

A. By the divine authority: "Not I, but the Lord thy God has commanded thee to do these statutes," v. 16.

B. By the mutual covenant between God and them, v. 17, etc.

A detailed analysis of chapter

Confession in offering the first-fruits. (1–11)

The prayer after disposal of the third year's tithe. (12–15)

The covenant between God and the people. (16–19)

Key verse

Verse 12: "When thou hast made an end of tithing all the tithes of thine increase the third year, which is the year of tithing, and hast given it unto the Levite, the stranger, the fatherless, and the widow, that they may eat within thy gates, and be filled."

Key word / key phrase

Verse 2, "firstfruits."

Key event / key person / key theme

Harvest offerings

Key thought

We are meant to show our gratitude to God.

Key thing to look out for

Rejoicing in God's goodness should be our daily delight. See verse 11.

Key Bible cross-reference

Verse 2. See 18:4.

Key "by way of explanation"

Verse 5. The "wandering Aramean" refers to Jacob and his journeys.

Key "Quotable Quote"

"Whether God gives us something or withholds it from us, he acts for our good, even if we, like children, are not aware of this."

Peter of Damaskos

Deuteronomy 27

Matthew Henry's introduction

Moses having very largely and fully set before the people their duty, both to God and one another, in general and in particular instances,—having shown them plainly what is good, and what the law requires of them,—and having in the close of the previous chapter laid them under the obligation both of the command and the covenant, he comes in this chapter to prescribe outward means,

I. For the helping of their memories, that they might not forget the law as a strange thing. They must write all the words of this law on stones, vv. 1–10.

II. For the moving of their affections, that they might not be indifferent to the law as a light thing. Whey they came into Canaan, the blessings and curses which were the sanctions of the law, were to be solemnly pronounced in the hearing of all Israel, who were to say Amen to them, vv. 11–26. And if such a solemnity as this would not make a deep impression on them, and affect them with the great things of God's law, nothing would.

A detailed analysis of chapter

The law to be written on stones in the promised land. (1–10)

The curses to be pronounced on Mount Ebal. (11–26)

Key verse

Verse 15: "Cursed be the man that maketh any graven or molten image, an abomination unto the LORD, the work of the hands of the craftsman, and putteth it in a secret place. And all the people shall answer and say, Amen."

Key word / key phrase

Verse 15, "cursed."

Key event / key person / key theme

God's curses on disobedience

Key thought

Obedience to God is not an optional extra.

Key thing to look out for

As we sow, so shall we reap.

Key Bible cross-reference

Verse 15. See 4:28; 5:6–10; 31:29.

Key "by way of explanation"

Verse 26. Galatians 3:10 quotes this verse to show that no one can keep all of God's laws.

Key "Quotable Quote"

"We are God's glory, when we follow his ways."

Florence Nightingale

Deuteronomy 28

Matthew Henry's introduction

In this chapter Moses,

I. Describes the blessings that should come on them if they were obedient; personal, family, and especially national, for in that capacity especially they are here treated with, vv. 1–14.

II. He more largely describes the curses which would come on them if they were disobedient; such as would be,

A. Their extreme vexation, vv. 15–44.

B. Their utter ruin and destruction at last, vv. 45–68. This chapter is much to the same purport with Lev. 26, setting before them life and death, good and evil; and the promise, in the close of that chapter, of their restoration, on their repentance, is here likewise more largely repeated, ch. 30.

A detailed analysis of chapter

The blessings for obedience. (1–14)
The curses for disobedience. (15–44)
Their ruin, if disobedient. (45–68)

Key verse

Verse 9: "The LORD shall establish thee an holy people unto himself, as he hath sworn unto thee, if thou shalt keep the commandments of the LORD thy God, and walk in his ways."

Key word / key phrase

Verse 1, "obey."

Key event / key person / key theme

Blessings for obedience

Key thought

God gave us his laws for our good.

Key thing to look out for

Obeying God may seem tough but that does not mean that we should disobey God.

Key Bible cross-reference

Verse 12. See Job 38:22; Psalm 135:7.

Key "by way of explanation"

Compare verses 3–6 with 16–19 to see how blessings are the opposite of curses.

Key "Quotable Quote"

"Our first resurrection begins when we first show obedience to God."

Baldwin of Canterbury

Deuteronomy 29

Matthew Henry's introduction

The first words of this chapter are the contents of it, "These are the words of the covenant" (v. 1), that is, these that follow. Here is,

I. A recital of God's dealings with them, in order to the bringing of them into this covenant, vv. 2–8.
II. A solemn charge to them to keep the covenant, v. 9.
III. An abstract of the covenant itself, vv. 12, 13.
IV. A specification of the people taken into the covenant, vv. 10, 11, 14, 15.
V. An intimation of the great design of this covenant against idolatry, in a parenthesis, vv. 16, 17.
VI. A most solemn and dreadful denunciation of the wrath of God against such people as promise themselves peace in a sinful way, vv. 18–28.
VII. The conclusion of this treaty, with a distinction between things secret and things revealed, v. 29.

A detailed analysis of chapter

Moses recalls Israel's mercies. (1–9)
The divine wrath on those who bask in their wickedness. (10–21)
The ruin of the Jewish nation. (22–28)
Secret things belong to God. (29)

Key verse

Verse 4: "Yet the LORD hath not given you an heart to perceive, and eyes to see, and ears to hear, unto this day."

Key word / key phrase

Verse 1, "covenant."

Key event / key person / key theme

God's covenant in the land of Moab

Key thought

Time taken to reflect on God's past blessings is time well spent.

Key thing to look out for

We are meant to take great care in following God's commands.

Key Bible cross-reference

Verse 23. See Genesis 19:24, 25.

Key "by way of explanation"

God has revealed to us what we need to know. This does not mean to say that God has revealed everything to us. See verse 29.

Key "Quotable Quote"

"The essence of obedience lies in the hearty love which prompts the deed rather than in the deed itself."

C.H. Spurgeon

Deuteronomy 30

Matthew Henry's introduction

Here we have,

I. Exceedingly great and precious promises made to them, on their repentance and return to God, vv. 1–10.
II. The righteousness of faith set before them in the plainness and easiness of the commandment that was now given them, vv. 11–14.
III. A fair reference of the whole matter to their choice, v. 15, etc.

A detailed analysis of chapter

Mercies promised to the repentant. (1–10)

The commandment is clear. (11–14)

The choice between death and life. (15–20)

Key verse

Verse 9: ". . . for the LORD will again rejoice over thee for good, as he rejoiced over thy fathers."

Key word / key phrase

Verse 16, "walk in his ways."

Key event / key person / key theme

Choosing between life and death

Key thought

Every day we face a choice in how we follow God.

Key thing to look out for

Hearts can grow cold.

Key Bible cross-reference

Verse 19. See 31:28; 32:1.

Key "by way of explanation"

Verse 20. To choose the Lord is to choose life.

Key "Quotable Quote"

"Good and evil both increase at compound interest. That is why the little decisions you and I make every day are of such infinite importance."

C.S. Lewis

Deuteronomy 31

Matthew Henry's introduction

In this chapter Moses, having finished his sermon,

I. Encourages both the people who were now to enter Canaan (vv. 1–6), and Joshua who was to lead them, vv. 7, 8, 23. And,

II. He takes care for the keeping of these things always in their remembrance after his decease,

A. By the book of the law which was,

Written.

Delivered into the custody of the priests, vv. 9, and 24–27.

Ordered to be publicly read every seventh year, vv. 10–13.

B. By a song which God orders Moses to prepare for their instruction and admonition.

He calls Moses and Joshua to the door of the tabernacle, vv. 14, 15.

He foretells the apostasy of Israel in process of time, and the judgments they would thereby bring on themselves, vv. 16–18.

He prescribes the following song to be a witness against them, vv. 19–21.

Moses wrote it, v. 22. And delivered it to Israel, with an intimation of the design of it, as he had received it from the Lord, v. 28, etc.

A detailed analysis of chapter

Moses encourages the people, and Joshua. (1–8)

The Law to be read every seventh year. (9–13)

The Israelites' apostasy foretold. A song given to be witness against them. (14–22)
The Law given to the Levites. (22–30)

Key verse

Verse 7: "And Moses called unto Joshua, and said unto him in the sight of all Israel, Be strong and of a good courage: for thou must go with this people unto the land which the LORD hath sworn unto their fathers to give them; and thou shalt cause them to inherit it."

Key word / key phrase

Verse 7, "Joshua."

Key event / key person / key theme

Joshua will succeed Moses

Key thought

We need to pray for the Lord's strength if we are to be strong.

Key thing to look out for

Moses reminds Joshua that his most important asset will be the Lord's presence.

Key Bible cross-reference

Verse 6. See Joshua 1:6, 7, 9, 18.

Key "by way of explanation"

Verse 2. Moses' age did not stop him being Israel's leader, but his sin did. See 1:37; 3:23–27.

Key "Quotable Quote"

"When God is our strength, it is strength indeed; when our strength is our own, it is only weakness."

Augustine of Hippo

Deuteronomy 32

Matthew Henry's introduction

In this chapter we have,

I. The song which Moses, by the appointment of God, delivered to the children of Israel, for a standing admonition to them, to take heed of forsaking God. This takes up most of the chapter, in which we have,

A. The preface, vv. 1, 2.

B. A high character of God, and, in opposition to that, a bad character of the people of Israel, vv. 3–6.

C. A rehearsal of the great things God had done for them, and in opposition to that an account of their ill carriage towards him, vv. 7–18.

D. A prediction of the wasting destroying judgments which God would bring on them for their sins, in which God is here justified by the many aggravations of their impieties, vv. 19–33.

E. A promise of the destruction of their enemies and oppressors at last, and the glorious deliverance of a remnant of Israel, vv. 36–43.

II. The exhortation with which Moses delivered this song to them, vv. 41–47.

III. The orders God gives to Moses to go up to Mount Nebo and die, v. 48, etc.

A detailed analysis of chapter

The song of Moses. (1, 2)

The character of God, and the character of Israel. (3–6)
The great things God had done for Israel. (7–14)
The wickedness of Israel. (19–25)
The judgments which would come on them because of their sins. (15–18)
Deserved vengeance withheld. (26–38)
God's deliverance for his people. (39–43)
The exhortation with which the song was delivered. (44–47)
Moses to go up Mount Nebo to die. (48–52)

Key verse

Verse 9: "For the LORD'S portion is his people; Jacob is the lot of his inheritance."

Key word / key phrase

Verse 1, "I will speak."

Key event / key person / key theme

The Song of Moses

Key thought

Recalling God's goodness is the most positive thing we can do today.

Key thing to look out for

Using a prayer like this can be our way of sharing in Moses' delight in the Lord.

Key Bible cross-reference

Verse 4. See verses 15, 18, 30, 31.

Key "by way of explanation"

Verse 10. This refers to God's protection of us, just as the pupil is kept safe by the rest of the eye.

Key "Quotable Quote"

"Just the word thanksgiving prompts the spirit of humility."

Charles R. Swindoll

Deuteronomy 33

Matthew Henry's introduction

In this chapter Moses,

I. pronounces them all blessed in what God had done for them already, especially in giving them his law, vv. 2–5.
II. He pronounces a blessing on each tribe, which is both a prayer for and a prophecy of their felicity.
   A. Reuben, v. 6.
   B. Judah, v. 7.
   C. Levi, vv. 8–11.
   D. Benjamin, v. 42.
   E. Joseph, vv. 13–17.
   F. Zebulun and Issachar, vv. 18, 19.
   G. Gad, vv. 20, 21.
   H. Dan, v. 22.
   I. Naphtali, v. 23.
   J. Asher, vv. 24, 25.
III. He pronounces them all in general blessed on the account of what God would be to them, and do for them if they were obedient, v. 26, etc.

A detailed analysis of chapter

The glorious majesty of God. (1–5)
The blessings of the twelve tribes. (6–23)
Strength to believers. (24, 25)
The excellency of Israel. (26–29)

Key verse

Verse 1: "And this is the blessing, wherewith Moses the man of God blessed the children of Israel before his death."

Key word / key phrase

Verse 1, "blessing."

Key event / key person / key theme

Moses blesses the tribes

Key thought

Moses starts his blessings by recalling God's great love.

Key thing to look out for

Everyone may not be blessed in the same way, but each has his or her special blessing from the Lord.

Key Bible cross-reference

Verse 16. See Exodus 3:1–6.

Key "by way of explanation"

Verse 9. The book of the Law was kept in the ark. The ark was kept in the tabernacle. The Levites looked after the tabernacle, and so are said to watch over the Lord's word.

Key "Quotable Quote"

"God is more anxious to bestow his blessings on us than we are to receive them."

Augustine of Hippo

Deuteronomy 34

Matthew Henry's introduction

We have had an account of Moses' dying words, here we have an account of his dying work, and that is work we must all do shortly, and it had need be well done. Here is,

I. The view Moses had of the land of Canaan just before he died, vv. 1–4.
II. His death and burial, vv. 5, 6.
III. His age, v. 7.
IV. Israel's mourning for him, v. 8.
V. His successor, v. 9.
VI. His character, v. 10, etc.

A detailed analysis of chapter

Moses views the promised land from Mount Nebo. (1–4)

The death and burial of Moses. The people mourn. (5–8)

Joshua succeeds Moses, and the praise of Moses. (9–12)

Key verse

Verse 5: "So Moses the servant of the LORD died there in the land of Moab, according to the word of the LORD."

Key word / key phrase

Verse 5, "died."

Key event / key person / key theme

The death of Moses

Key thought

No greater prophet than Moses ever came.

Key thing to look out for

Moses' greatness lay in the fact that he experienced God face to face.

Key Bible cross-reference

Verse 10. See Numbers 12:8.

Key "by way of explanation"

Verse 5. The words "servant of the Lord" refer to someone the Lord has taken into his service.

Key "Quotable Quote"

"One drop of water helps to swell the ocean; a spark of fire helps to give light to the world. None are too small, too feeble, too poor to be of service. Think of this and act."

Hannah More

5. Select bibliography for Deuteronomy

Craigie, Peter C. *The Book of Deuteronomy* (NICOT), Eerdmans, 1976.

Christensen, Duane L. *Deuteronomy* (Word, 2 Vols.), Word Books, 2000.

Schultz, Samuel J. *Deuteronomy: The Gospel of Love*. Chicago: Moody, 1971.

Smith, G. A. *The Book of Deuteronomy*. The Cambridge Bible. Cambridge: University Press, 1918.

Thompson, J. A. *Deuteronomy*. (Tyndale Old Testament Commentary) London: InterVarsity, 1974.

Wright, Christopher J. H. *Deuteronomy* (NIBC), Hendrickson, 1996.

Joshua

1. Book by book: Introduction to Joshua

Introduction

The title of this book is derived from the godly and courageous leader whose achievements it relates and who is commonly supposed to have been its author. The objections to this idea are founded chiefly on the clause, "unto this day," which occurs several times (Joshua 4:9; 6:25; 8:28). But this, at least in the case of Rahab, is no valid reason for rejecting the idea of his authorship; for assuming what is most probable, that this book was composed toward the close of Joshua's long career, or compiled from written documents left by him, Rahab might have been still alive. A more simple and satisfactory way of accounting for the frequent insertion of the clause, "unto this day," is the opinion that it was a comment introduced by Ezra, when revising the sacred canon; and this difficulty being removed, the direct proofs of the book having been produced by a witness of the transactions related in it, the strong and vivid descriptions of the passing scenes, and the use of the words "we" and "us," (Joshua 5:1–6), viewed in connection with the fact, that, after his farewell address to the people, Joshua "wrote these words in the book of the law of God" (Joshua 24:26)—all afford strong presumptive proof that the entire book was the work of that eminent individual. Its inspiration and canonical authority are fully established by the repeated testimonies of other Scripture writers (compare Joshua 6:26 with 1 Kings 16:34; compare Joshua 10:13 with Habakkuk 3:11; Joshua 3:14 with Acts 7:45; Joshua 6:17–23 with Hebrews 11:30; Joshua 2:1–24 with James 2:25; Psalm 44:2; 68:12–14; 78:54–55). As a narrative of God's faithfulness in giving the Israelites possession of the promised land, this history is most valuable, and bears the same character as a sequel to the Pentateuch, that the Acts of the Apostles do to the Gospels.

Robert Jamieson

Contents of Joshua

Joshua contains a history of the Israelites from the death of Moses to that of Joshua. It consists of three parts:

The history of the conquest of the land (1–12).

The allotment of the land to the different tribes, with the appointment of cities of refuge, the provision for the Levites (13–22), and the dismissal of the eastern tribes to their homes. This section has been compared to the Doomsday Book of the Norman conquest.

The farewell addresses of Joshua, with an account of his death (23, 24).

This book stands first in the second of the three sections, (1) the Law, (2) the Prophets, (3) the "other writings" = *Hagiographa*, into which the Jewish Church divided the Old Testament. There is every reason for concluding that the uniform tradition of the Jews is correct when they assign the authorship of the book to Joshua, all except the concluding section; the last verses (24:29–33) were added by some other hand.

Two difficulties

There are two difficulties connected with this book which have given rise to much discussion, (1.) The miracle of the standing still of the sun and moon on Gibeon. The record of it occurs in Joshua's impassioned prayer of faith, as quoted (Josh. 10:12–15) from the "Book of Jasher" (q.v.). There are many explanations given of these words. They need, however, present no difficulty if we believe in the possibility of God's miraculous interposition on behalf of his people. Whether it was caused by the refraction of the light, or how, we know not.

(2.) Another difficulty arises out of the command given by God utterly to exterminate the Canaanites. "Shall not the Judge of all the earth do right?" It is enough that Joshua clearly knew that this was the will of God, who employs his terrible agencies, famine, pestilence, and war, in the righteous government of this world. The Canaanites had sunk into a state of immorality and corruption so foul and degrading that they had to be rooted out of the land with the edge of the sword. "The Israelites' sword, in its bloodiest executions, wrought a work of mercy for all the countries of the earth to the very end of the world."

Historical events

This book resembles the Acts of the Apostles in the number and variety of historical incidents it records, and in its many references to persons and places; and as in the latter case the epistles of Paul. confirm its historical accuracy by their incidental allusions and "undesigned coincidences," so in the former modern discoveries confirm its historicity. The Amarna tablets are among the most remarkable discoveries of the age. Dating from about 1480 b.c. down to the time of Joshua, and consisting of official communications from Amorite, Phoenician, and Philistine chiefs to the king of Egypt, they afford a glimpse into the actual condition of Palestine prior to the Hebrew invasion, and illustrate and confirm the history of the conquest.

M.G. Easton, M.A., D.D., Illustrated Bible Dictionary

Detailed outline

I. Entering the land: 1:1–5:15
- A. Joshua commissioned: 1:1–9
- B. Preparation to cross the Jordan: 1:10–2:24
- C. Jordan crossed: 3:1–4:24
- D. Gilgal occupied: 5:1–15

II. Conquering the land: 6:1–12:24
- A. Jericho and Ai taken: 6:1–8:29
- B. Joshua's altar: 8:30–35
- C. The Gibeonites received: 9:1–27
- D. Southern Canaan conquered: 10:1–43
- E. Northern Canaan conquered: 11:1–15
- F. The conquest summarized: 11:16–12:24

III. Settling in the land: 13:1–22:34
- A. Joshua instructed: 13:1–7
- B. The eastern tribes assigned: 13:8–33
- C. The western tribes assigned: 14:1–19:51
- D. The cities of refuge: 20:1–9
- E. Levitical towns: 21:1–45
- F. Eastern tribes sent home: 22:1–34

IV. Joshua's farewell address and death: 23:1–24:33
- A. He reminds them of God's goodness: 23:3–10
- B. He warns them about disobedience: 23:11–13
- C. He reviews this history: 24:1–13
- D. He challenges them to serve God: 24:14–18
- E. He completes the book that bears his name: 24:26–28
- F. Joshua and Eleazar die: 24:29–33

2. Helpful summaries of Joshua

Bird's eye view

Joshua is an historical record about God keeping his promise to bring his people into the Promised Land.

Reading plan

The following reading plan, taking one reading per day, enables you to read through Joshua in ten days.

Joshua 1–4
Joshua 5–7
Joshua 8–9
Joshua 10–12
Joshua 13–14
Joshua 15–16

Joshua 17–18
Joshua 19–20
Joshua 21–22
Joshua 23–24

Verses to memorize

Joshua 1:8

Do not let this Book of the Law depart from your mouth; meditate on it day and night, so that you may be careful to do everything written in it. Then you will be prosperous and successful.

Joshua 1:9

Be strong and courageous, do not be terrified; do not be discouraged, for the Lord your God will be with you wherever you go.

Joshua 21:45

Not one of all the Lord's good promises to the house of Israel failed; every one was fulfilled.

Statistics

Sixth Old Testament book
24 chapters
658 verses
18,858 words

Names/titles given

Hebrew title: *Hoshea*: "salvation."
Greek title in Septuagint:
Iesous Naus: "Joshua the son of Nun."
Latin title in Vulgate: *Liber Josue*:
"Book of Joshua."

3. Helpful keys to turn to in understanding Joshua

Key word

Possess

Key verses

Joshua 1:8; 21:44,45

Key people/events

Joshua
Rahab
Ark of the Covenant
Battle of Jericho
Crossing the Jordan
Battle of Ai
Achan
The Gibeonites
Shiloh
Eastern Tribes: Reuben, Gad, half tribe of Manasseh
The altar

Themes to study

- Winning life's battles.
- Positive lessons to learn from Joshua's character.
- Obeying God's Word.

Unusual events and miracles in Joshua

The River Jordan divided, 3:14–17
An angel appearing to Joshua, 5:13–15
The walls of Jericho collapsing, 6:1–20
The storm of hailstones, 10:11
The sun and the moon standing still, 10:12–14

Jesus in Joshua

In Joshua Jesus is the Lord of our salvation.

Types of Jesus in Joshua

- Joshua is a type of Jesus, Heb. 2:10; 2 Cor 2:14.
- "The Commander of the army of the Lord" Num. 5:13–15 is taken to refer to Jesus himself.
- Rahab's scarlet cord is linked to safety through Jesus' blood.

Lessons to learn from Joshua

- We must recognize and deal with the spiritual forces that oppose our progress in the Christian life.
- We must obey God's Word in our daily lives.
- We should be able to testify to God's work I our lives.

4. Chapter by chapter: outline of every chapter of Joshua

Joshua 1

Matthew Henry's introduction

The book begins with the history, not of Joshua's life (many remarkable passages of that we had before in the books of Moses) but of his reign and government. In this chapter,

I. God appoints him to the government in the stead of Moses, gives him an ample commission, full instructions, and great encouragements, vv. 1–9.

II. He accepts the government, and addresses himself immediately to the business of it, giving orders to the officers of the people in general, vv. 10, 11, and particularly to the two tribes and a half, vv. 12–15.

III. The people agree to it, and take an oath of fealty to him, vv. 16–18. A reign which thus began with God could not but be honorable to the prince and comfortable to the subject. The last words of Moses are still verified, "Happy art thou, O Israel! Who is like unto thee, O people?" Deut. 33:29.

A detailed analysis of chapter

The Lord appoints Joshua to succeed Moses. (1–4)

God promises to assist Joshua. (5–9)

Preparation to cross over Jordan. (10–15)

The people promise to obey Joshua. (16–18)

Key verse

Verse 7: "Only be thou strong and very courageous, that thou mayest observe to do according to all the law, which Moses my servant commanded thee: turn not from it to the right hand or to the left, that thou mayest prosper whithersoever thou goest."

Key word / key phrase

Verse 2, "cross the Jordan River"

Key event / key person / key theme

Joshua is told to conquer Canaan.

Key thought

Conquering the promised land was not Joshua's idea.

Key thing to look out for

The Book of the Law was to be in Joshua's mind all the time.

Key Bible cross-reference

Verse 1. See Exodus 24:13; 33:11; Deuteronomy 1:38.

Key "by way of explanation"

Verse 8, the "Book of the Law." This must have been made up of some of the laws given at Mount Sinai that had already been written down.

Key "Quotable Quote"

"Listen less to your own thoughts and more to God's thoughts."

François Fénelon

Joshua 2

Matthew Henry's introduction

In this chapter we have an account of the scouts that were employed to bring an account to Joshua of the posture of the city of Jericho. Observe here,

I. How Joshua sent them, v. 1.

II. How Rahab received them, and protected them, and told a lie for them (vv. 2–7), so that they escaped out of the hands of the enemy.

III. The account she gave them of the present posture of Jericho, and the panic-fear they were struck with on the approach of Israel, vv. 8–11.

IV. The bargain she made with them for the security of herself and her relations in the ruin she saw coming on her city, vv. 12–21.

V. Their safe return to Joshua, and the account they gave him of their expedition, vv. 22–24. And that which makes this story most remarkable is that Rahab, the person principally concerned in it, is twice celebrated in the New Testament as a great believer (Heb. 11:31) and as one whose faith proved itself by good works, James 2:25.

A detailed analysis of chapter

Rahab receives and hides two Israelites. (1–7)

Rahab and the spies. (8–21)

The return of the spies. (22–24)

Key verse

Verse 1: "And Joshua the son of Nun sent out of Shittim two men to spy secretly, saying, Go view the land, even Jericho."

Key word / key phrase

Verse 1, "Rahab."

Key event / key person / key theme

Rahab and the spies

Key thought

God cares for individuals.

Key thing to look out for

There is no greater privilege than to serve God.

Key Bible cross-reference

Verse 1. See Judges 7:10, 11; 1 Samuel 26:16.

Key "by way of explanation"

Verse 18. The scarlet cord acted as a marker,

just as the blood on doorposts did at the first Passover.

Key "Quotable Quote"

"The most eloquent prayer is the prayer through hands that heal and bless. The highest form of worship is the worship of unselfish Christian service. The greatest form of praise is the sound of consecrated feet seeking out the lost and helpless."

Billy Graham

Joshua 3

Matthew Henry's introduction

This chapter, and that which follows it, give us the history of Israel's passing through Jordan into Canaan, and a very memorable history it is.

I. The people are directed to follow the ark, vv. 2–4.

II. They are commanded to sanctify themselves, v. 5.

III. The priests with the ark are ordered to lead the van, v. 6.

IV. Joshua is magnified and made commander in chief, vv. 7, 8.

V. Public notice is given of what God is about to do for them, vv. 9–13.

IV. The thing is done, Jordan is divided, and Israel brought safely through it, vv. 14–17. This was the Lord's doing, and it is marvelous in our eyes.

A detailed analysis of chapter

The Israelites come to Jordan. (1–6)

The Lord encourages Joshua. Joshua encourages the people. (7–13)

The Israelites pass over the River Jordan on dry land. (14–17)

Key verse

Verse 5: "And Joshua said unto the people, Sanctify yourselves: for to morrow the LORD will do wonders among you."

Key word / key phrase

Verse 14, "Jordan."

Key event / key person / key theme

The Israelites cross over the River Jordan

Key thought

Consecration to God should take place before engaging on any important action.

Key thing to look out for

It is crucial to listen to God's word and God's words, verse 9.

Key Bible cross-reference

Verse 3. See Numbers 10:33–36.

Key "by way of explanation"

Verse 7. Through God's miracle at the River Jordan Joshua's leadership was vindicated.

Key "Quotable Quote"

"Hear the true Word of God; lay hold of it, and spend your days not in raising hard questions, but in feasting upon precious truth."

C.H. Spurgeon

Joshua 4

Matthew Henry's introduction

This chapter gives a further account of the miraculous passage of Israel through Jordan.

I. The provision that was made at that time to preserve the memorial of it, by twelve stones set up in Jordan (v. 9) and other twelve stones taken up out of Jordan, vv. 1–8.

II. The march of the people through Jordan's channel, the two tribes first, then all the people, and the priests that bore the ark last, vv. 10–14.

III. The closing of the waters again on their coming up with the ark, vv. 15–19.

IV. The erecting of the monument in Gilgal, to preserve the remembrance of this work of wonder to posterity, vv. 20–24.

A detailed analysis of chapter

Stones taken out of Jordan. (1–9)
The people pass through Jordan. (10–19)
The twelve stones placed in Gilgal. (20–24)

Key verse

Verse 8: "And the children of Israel did so as Joshua commanded, and took up twelve stones out of the midst of Jordan, as the LORD spake unto Joshua, according to the number of the tribes of the children of Israel, and carried them over with them unto the place where they lodged, and laid them down there."

Key word / key phrase

Verse 2, "twelve stones."

Key event / key person / key theme

Memorial stones are set up.

Key thought

Without the faithful obedience of countless unnamed Israelites God's plans would not have been carried out.

Key thing to look out for

God's nature is seen to be powerful. The people should therefore reverence him.

Key Bible cross-reference

Verse 6. See 24:26; 1 Samuel 7:12.

Key "by way of explanation"

Verse 6. These stones were to act as a reminder to future generations of God's actions.

Key "Quotable Quote"

"Every man naturally desires knowledge; but what good is knowledge without fear of God?"

Thomas à Kempis

Joshua 5

Matthew Henry's introduction

Israel have now got over Jordan, and the waters which had opened before them, to favor their march forward, are closed again behind them, to forbid their retreat backward. They have now got footing in Canaan, and must apply themselves to the conquest of it, in order to which this chapter tells us,

I. How their enemies were dispirited, v. 1.

II. What was done at their first landing to assist and encourage them.

A. The covenant of circumcision was renewed, vv. 2–9.
B. The feast of the Passover was celebrated, v. 10.
C. Their camp was provided with the corn of the land, whereon the manna ceased, vv. 11, 12.
D. The captain of the Lord's host himself appeared to Joshua to animate and direct him, vv. 13–15.

A detailed analysis of chapter

The Canaanites are afraid. Circumcision renewed. (1–9)

The Passover at Gilgal. The manna ceases. (10–12)

The Captain of the Lord's host appears to Joshua. (13–15)

Key verse

Verse 15: "And the captain of the LORD'S host said unto Joshua, Loose thy shoe from off thy foot; for the place whereon thou standest is holy. And Joshua did so."

Key word / key phrase

Verse 2, "circumcise."

Key event / key person / key theme

Circumcision at Gilgal

Key thought

God's people are meant to be marked out by holy lives.

Key thing to look out for

God's provision of manna lasted until they could eat food from Canaan.

Key Bible cross-reference

Verse 11. See Exodus 12:15; Leviticus 23:6.

Key "by way of explanation"

Verse 2. Circumcision was given as a way of showing that people belonged to God. See Genesis 17:10, 11.

Key "Quotable Quote"

"Baptized, re-baptized, circumcised, confirmed, fed upon sacraments, and buried in consecrated ground – you shall all perish except you believe in Christ."

C.H. Spurgeon

Joshua 6

Matthew Henry's introduction

Joshua opened the campaign with the siege of Jericho, a city which could not trust so much to the courage of its people as to act offensively, and to send out its forces to oppose Israel's landing and encamping, but trusted so much to the strength of its walls as to stand on its defence, and not to surrender, or desire conditions of peace. Now here we have the story of the taking of it,

I. The directions and assurances which the captain of the Lord's host gave about it, vv. 1–5.
II. The trial of the people's patient obedience in walking round the city six days, vv. 6–14.
III. The wonderful delivery of it into their hands the seventh day, with a solemn charge

to them to use it as a devoted thing, vv. 15–21 and 24.

IV. The preservation of Rahab and her relations, vv. 22, 23, 25.

V. A curse pronounced on the man that should dare to rebuild this city, vv. 26, 27. An abstract of this story we find among the trophies of faith, Heb. 11:30. "By faith the walls of Jericho fell down, after they were compassed about seven days."

A detailed analysis of chapter

The siege of Jericho. (1–5)

The city is surrounded. (6–16)

Jericho is taken, Rahab and her family are saved. (17–27)

Key verse

Verse 2: "And the LORD said unto Joshua, See, I have given into thine hand Jericho, and the king thereof, and the mighty men of valor."

Key word / key phrase

Verse 1, "Jericho."

Key event / key person / key theme

Jericho is captured.

Key thought

God's people had to exercise faith in him before Jericho would fall.

Key thing to look out for

Spiritual victories are impossible without the help of God's Spirit.

Key Bible cross-reference

Verse 25. See Hebrews 11:31; James 2:25.

Key "by way of explanation"

Verse 4. The blowing of "rams' horns" announced God's presence.

Key "Quotable Quote"

"In God We Trust."

This motto first appeared on U.S. 2-cent coins after April 22, 1864. On July 30, 1956, it became the national motto.

Joshua 7

Matthew Henry's introduction

We have here,

I. The sin of Achan in meddling with the accursed thing, v. 1.

II. The defeat of Israel before Ai thereon, vv. 2–5.

III. Joshua's humiliation and prayer on occasion of that sad disaster, vv. 6–9.

IV. The directions God gave him for the putting away of the guilt which had provoked God thus to contend with them, vv. 10–15.

V. The discovery, trial, conviction, condemnation, and execution, of the criminal, by which the anger of God was turned away, vv. 16–26. And by this story it appears that, as the laws, so Canaan itself, "made nothing perfect," the perfection both of holiness and peace to God's Israel is to be expected in the heavenly Canaan only.

A detailed analysis of chapter

The Israelites defeated at Ai. (1–5)

Joshua's humiliation and prayer. (6–9)
God instructs Joshua what to do. (10–5)
Achan is detected, and is destroyed. (16–26)

Key verse

Verse 6: "And Joshua rent his clothes, and fell to the earth upon his face before the ark of the LORD until the eventide, he and the elders of Israel, and put dust upon their heads."

Key word / key phrase

Verse 1, "acted unfaithfully."

Key event / key person / key theme

Achan's sin

Key thought

God demands wholehearted obedience from his followers.

Key thing to look out for

It is never difficult to rationalize about taking a different course of action from the one we know God has chosen.

Key Bible cross-reference

Verse 15. See Deuteronomy 22:21; 2 Samuel 13:12.

Key "by way of explanation"

Verse 11. One person's sin can affect the whole fellowship.

Key "Quotable Quote"

"The deceitfulness of sin is seen in that it is modest in its first proposals but when it prevails it hardens men's hearts, and brings them to ruin."

John Owen

Joshua 8

Matthew Henry's introduction

The embarrassment which Achan's sin gave to the affairs of Israel being over, we have them here in a very good posture again, the affairs both of war and religion. Here is,

I. The glorious progress of their arms in the taking of Ai, before which they had lately suffered disgrace.
  A. God encourages Joshua to attack it, with the assurance of success, and directs him what method to take, vv. 1, 2.
  B. Joshua gives orders accordingly to the men of war, vv. 3–8.
  C. The stratagem is managed as it was projected, and succeeds as it was desired, vv. 9–22.
  D. Joshua becomes master of this city, puts all the inhabitants to the sword, burns it, hangs the king, but gives the plunder to the soldiers, vv. 23–29.

II. The great solemnity of writing and reading the law before a general assembly of all Israel, drawn up for that purpose on the two mountains of Gerizim and Ebal, according to an order which Moses had received from the Lord, and delivered to them, vv. 30–35. Thus did they take their work before them, and make the business of their religion to keep pace with their secular business.

A detailed analysis of chapter

God encourages Joshua. (1,2)

The taking of Ai. (3–22)

The destruction of Ai and its king. (23–29)

The law read on Ebal and Gerizim. (30–35)

Key verse

Verse 34: "And afterward he read all the words of the law, the blessings and cursings, according to all that is written in the book of the law."

Key word / key phrase

Verse 1, "do not be discouraged."

Key event / key person / key theme

Ai is destroyed.

Key thought

After failure God issues fresh orders.

Key thing to look out for

Recovery from failure is always possible with God's help.

Key Bible cross-reference

Verse 1. See 1:3–5; 3:11–13.

Key "by way of explanation"

Verse 34. Joshua promoted God's word among God's people.

Key "Quotable Quote"

"Emulate the tiny ant; be an ant of God. Listen to the word of God and hide it in your heart. Collect plenty of food during the happy days of your spiritual summers."

Augustine of Hippo

Joshua 9

Matthew Henry's introduction

Here is in this chapter,

I. The impolite confederacy of the kings of Canaan against Israel, vv. 1, 2.

II. The polite confederacy of the inhabitants of Gibeon with Israel,

A. How it was subtly proposed and petitioned for by the Gibeonites pretending to come from a far country, vv. 3–13.

B. How it was unwarily consented to by Joshua and the Israelites, to the disgust of the congregation when the fraud was discovered, vv. 14–18.

C. How the matter was adjusted to the satisfaction of all sides, by giving these Gibeonites their lives because they had covenanted with them, yet depriving them of their liberties because the covenant was not fairly obtained, vv. 19–27.

A detailed analysis of chapter

The kings unite against Israel. (1,2)

The Gibeonites ask for peace. (3–13)

They obtain peace, but are soon detected. (14–21)

The Gibeonites are to be servants. (22–27)

Key verse

Verse 15: "And Joshua made peace with them, and made a league with them, to let them live: and the princes of the congregation sware unto them."

Key word / key phrase

Verse 14, "did not enquire of the Lord."

Key event / key person / key theme

The Gibeonites deceive Joshua.

Key thought

Godless standards common in the world are not to be followed.

Key thing to look out for

Deceit is no small matter.

Key Bible cross-reference

Verse 15. See Exodus 20:7; Leviticus 19:12.

Key "by way of explanation"

Verse 4. If the Gibeonites had trusted God they would not have needed to resort to this deception.

Key "Quotable Quote"

"The commandment of absolute truthfulness is really only another name for the fullness of discipleship."

Dietrich Bonhoeffer

Joshua 10

Matthew Henry's introduction

We have in this chapter an account of the conquest of the kings and kingdoms of the southern part of the land of Canaan, as, in the next chapter, of the reduction of the northern parts, which together completed the glorious successes of the wars of Canaan. In this chapter we have an account,

I. Of the routing of their forces in the field, in which observe,

A. Their confederacy against the Gibeonites, vv. 1–5.

B. The Gibeonites' request to Joshua to assist them, v. 6.

C. Joshua's speeds march under divine encouragement for their relief, vv. 7–9.

D. The defeat of the armies of these confederate kings, vv. 10, 11.

E. The miraculous prolonging of the day by the standing still of the sun in favor of the conquerors, vv. 12–14.

II. Of the execution of the kings that escaped out of the battle, vv. 15–27.

III. Of the taking of the particular cities, and the total destruction of all that were found in them. Makkedah, v. 28. Libnah, vv. 29, 30. Lachish, vv. 31, 32, and the king of Gezer that attempted its rescue, v. 33. Eglon, vv. 34, 35. Hebron, vv. 36, 37. Debir, vv. 38, 39. And the bringing of all that country into the hands of Israel, vv. 40–42. And, lastly, the return of the army to the head-quarters, v. 43.

A detailed analysis of chapter

Five kings fight against Gibeon. (1–6)

Joshua succors Gibeon. The sun and moon stand still. (7–14)

The kings are taken, their armies defeated, and they are put to death. (15–27)

Seven other kings defeated and killed. (28–43)

Key verse

Verse 13: "And the sun stood still, and the moon stayed, until the people had avenged themselves upon their enemies."

Key word / key phrase

Verse 12, "sun."

Key event / key person / key theme

The day the sun stood still.

Key thought

Conversion is the greatest miracle.

Key thing to look out for

The different ways in which God revealed his mighty power.

Key Bible cross-reference

Verse 11. See Judges 5:20; Job 38:22.

Key "by way of explanation"

Verse 13. There are a number of history books mentioned in the Old Testament, such as the "Book of Jashar" which we no longer have.

Key "Quotable Quote"

"True conversion will involve the mind, the affection, and the will."

Billy Graham

Joshua 11

Matthew Henry's introduction

This chapter continues and concludes the history of the conquest of Canaan; of the reduction of the southern parts we had an account in the previous chapter, after which we may suppose Joshua allowed his forces some breathing-time; now here we have the story of the war in the north, and the happy success of that war.

I. The confederacy of the northern crowns against Israel, vv. 1–5.

II. The encouragement which God gave to Joshua to engage them, v. 6.

III. His victory over them, vv. 7–9.

IV. The taking of their cities, vv. 10–15.

V. The destruction of the Anakim, vv. 21, 22.

VI. The general conclusion of the story of this war, vv. 16–20, 23.

A detailed analysis of chapter

Various kings overcome at the Waters of Merom. (1–9)

Hazor is taken and burned. (10–14)

All that country subdued, and the Anakites cut off. (15–23)

Key verse

Verse 6: "And the LORD said unto Joshua, Be not afraid because of them: for to morrow about this time will I deliver them up all slain before Israel: thou shalt hough their horses, and burn their chariots with fire."

Key word / key phrase

Verse 8, "defeated."

Key event / key person / key theme

Northern kings defeated.

Key thought

The battle belongs to the Lord.

Key thing to look out for

If we experience peace that is God's gift.

Key Bible cross-reference

Verse 20. See Exodus 8:32; 9:12.

Key "by way of explanation"

Verse 13. "Mounds" were formed by successive towns being built on one site.

Key "Quotable Quote"

"We rest on thee, our shield and our defender!
Thine is the battle, thine shall be the praise;
When passing through the gates of pearly splendor,
Victors, we rest with thee, through endless days."

Edith Gilling Cherry

Joshua 12

Matthew Henry's introduction

This chapter is a summary of Israel's conquests.

I. Their conquests under Moses, on the other side Jordan (for we now suppose ourselves in Canaan) eastward, which we had the history of, Num. 21:24, etc. And here the abridgment of that history, vv. 1–6.

II. Their conquests under Joshua, on this side Jordan, westward.

A. The country they reduced, vv. 7, 8.

B. The kings they subdued, thirty-one in all, vv. 9–24. And this comes in here, not only as a conclusion of the history of the wars of Canaan (that we might at one view see what they had got), but as a preface to the history of the dividing of Canaan, that all that might be put together which they were not to make a distribution of.

A detailed analysis of chapter

The two kings conquered by Moses. (1–6)

The kings whom Joshua defeated. (7–24)

Key verse

Verse 1: "Now these are the kings of the land, which the children of Israel smote"

Key word / key phrase

Verse 1, "kings."

Key event / key person / key theme

Kings defeated by Moses and Joshua.

Key thought

Paul often pictured the Christian life as one long battle.

Key thing to look out for

Count your blessings, name them one by one.

Key Bible cross-reference

Verse 4. See Nehemiah 9:22; Psalm 135:11.

Key "by way of explanation"

Verse 1 gives the boundaries of the conquered territories.

Key "Quotable Quote"

"Christians have overcome, but they are still fighting."

D. Martyn Lloyd-Jones

Joshua 13

Matthew Henry's introduction

In this chapter,

I. God informs Joshua what parts of the country that were intended in the grant to Israel yet remained unconquered, and not got in possession, vv. 1–6.
II. He appoints him, notwithstanding, to make a distribution of what was conquered, v. 7.
III. To complete this account, here is a repetition of the distribution Moses had made of the land on the other side Jordan; in general (vv. 8–14), in particular, the lot of Reuben (vv. 15–23), of Gad (vv. 24–28), of the half tribe of Manasseh, vv. 29–33.

A detailed analysis of chapter

Boundaries of the land not yet conquered. (1–6)
Inheritance of Reuben. (7–33)

Key verse

Verse 1: "Now Joshua was old and stricken in years; and the LORD said unto him, Thou art old and stricken in years, and there remaineth yet very much land to be possessed."

Key word / key phrase

Verse 1, "land."

Key event / key person / key theme

Land still to be taken

Key thought

Paul pressed on even at the end of his life.

Key thing to look out for

Jesus told his followers to aim for perfection.

Key Bible cross-reference

Verse 33. See Deuteronomy 18:1–8.

Key "by way of explanation"

Verse 1. Joshua was between ninety and a hundred years old. For Caleb's age, see 14:10.

Key "Quotable Quote"

"We ought to persevere to the end in good works."

Anselm

Joshua 14

Matthew Henry's introduction

Here is,

I. The general method that was taken in dividing the land, vv. 1–5.
II. The demand Caleb made of Hebron, as his by promise, and therefore not to be put into the lot with the rest, vv. 6–12. And Joshua's grant of that demand, vv. 13–15. This was done at Gilgal, which was as yet their head-quarters.

A detailed analysis of chapter

The inheritance of the nine and a half tribes. (1–5)
Caleb is given Hebron. (6–15)

Key verse

Verse 1: "And these are the countries which the children of Israel inherited in the land of Canaan, which Eleazar the priest, and Joshua the son of Nun, and the heads of the fathers of the tribes of the children of Israel, distributed for inheritance to them."

Key word / key phrase
Verse 614 "inheritance."

Key event / key person / key theme
Hebron is given to Caleb.

Key thought
God's promises never fail.

Key thing to look out for
Experienced Christians should be valued for their wisdom.

Key Bible cross-reference
Verse 6. See Numbers 13:30; Deuteronomy 1:34–36.

Key "by way of explanation"
Verse 1. Eleazar was in charge of casting lots.

Key "Quotable Quote"
"The next best thing to being wise oneself is to live in a circle of those who are."

C.S. Lewis

Joshua 15

Matthew Henry's introduction
Though the land was not completely conquered, yet being (as was said in the close of the previous chapter) at rest from war for the present, and their armies all drawn out of the field to a general rendezvous at Gilgal, they began to divide the land, though the work was afterwards perfected at Shiloh, 18:1, etc. In this chapter we have the lot of the tribe of Judah, which in this, as in other things, had the precedence.

I. The borders or bounds of the inheritance of Judah, vv. 1–12.
II. The particular assignment of Hebron and the country thereabout to Caleb and his family, vv. 13–19.
III. The names of the several cities that fell within Judah's lot, vv. 20–63.

A detailed analysis of chapter
The boundaries of the lot of Judah. (1–12)
Caleb's portion. His daughter's blessing. (13–19)
The cities of Judah. (20–63)

Key verse
Verse 1: "This then was the lot of the tribe of the children of Judah by their families; even to the border of Edom the wilderness of Zin southward was the uttermost part of the south coast."

Key word / key phrase
Verse 2, "boundary."

Key event / key person / key theme
Caleb's daughter

Key thought
All possessions are given from God.

Key thing to look out for
We are tenants not owners.

Key Bible cross-reference
Verse 1. See Genesis 49:8–12; 2 Kings 17:18.

Key "by way of explanation"

Verse 17. Othniel's work as judge is recorded in Judges 3:7–11.

Key "Quotable Quote"

"A Church of comfort, property, privilege, and position stands in sharp contrast with the Bible which describes the people of God as aliens, exiles, pilgrims and strangers."

Jim Wallis

Joshua 16

Matthew Henry's introduction

It is a pity that this and the next chapter should be separated, for both of them give us the lot of the children of Joseph, Ephraim and Manasseh, who, next to Judah, were to have the post of honor, and therefore had the first and best portion in the northern part of Canaan, as Judah now had in the southern part. In this chapter we have,

I. A general account of the lot of these two tribes together, vv. 1–4.

II. The borders of the lot of Ephraim in particular, vv. 5–10. That of Manasseh following in the next chapter.

A detailed analysis of chapter

The territory given to Ephraim. (1–10)

Key verse

Verse 4: "So the children of Joseph, Manasseh and Ephraim, took their inheritance."

Key word / key phrase

Verse 10, "Canaanites."

Key event / key person / key theme

Territory for Ephraim and Manasseh

Key thought

A failure is recorded in verse 10.

Key thing to look out for

What matters is how we are viewed in God's eyes.

Key Bible cross-reference

Verse 10. See 1 Kings 9:15,16; 2 Samuel 5:25.

Key "by way of explanation"

Verse 1. After Judah; Joseph's tribes (the tribes of his two sons) are given priority.

Key "Quotable Quote"

"Your reputation is what people say about you. Your character is what God and your wife know about you."

William Ashley (Billy) Sunday

Joshua 17

Matthew Henry's introduction

The half tribe of Manasseh comes next to be provided for; and here we have,

I. The families of that tribe that were to be portioned, vv. 1–6.

II. The country that fell to their lot, vv. 7–13.

III. The joint request of the two tribes that descended from Joseph, for the enlargement of their lot, and Joshua's answer to that request, vv. 14–18.

A detailed analysis of chapter

The lot of Manasseh. (1–6)

The boundaries of Manasseh, and the Canaanites not driven out. (7–13)

Joseph desires a larger portion. (14–18)

Key verse

Verse 1: "There was also a lot for the tribe of Manasseh; for he was the firstborn of Joseph; to wit, for Machir the firstborn of Manasseh, the father of Gilead: because he was a man of war, therefore he had Gilead and Bashan."

Key word / key phrase

Verse 14, "only one allotment."

Key event / key person / key theme

A request for more land

Key thought

Our inheritance comes from God.

Key thing to look out for

Our inheritance is God himself.

Key Bible cross-reference

Verse 1. See Genesis 48:14,19.

Key "by way of explanation"

Verse 16. Anybody who had an iron chariot had the latest in weapons and would be feared.

Key "Quotable Quote"

"A conscience void of offence before God and man is an inheritance for eternity."

Daniel Webster

Joshua 18

Matthew Henry's introduction

In this chapter we have,

I. The setting up of the tabernacle at Shiloh, v. 1.

II. The stirring up of the seven tribes that were yet unsettled to look after their lot, and the putting of them in a method for it, by Joshua, vv. 2–7.

III. The distributing of the land into seven lots, by certain men employed for that purpose, vv. 8, 9.

IV. The determining of these seven portions to the seven tribes yet unprovided for by lot, v. 10.

V. The particular lot of the tribe of Benjamin, the borders of it, vv. 11–20. And the cities contained in it, vv. 21–28. The other six tribes we shall find well provided for in the next chapter.

A detailed analysis of chapter

The tabernacle set up at Shiloh. (1)

The remainder of the land described and divided. (2–10)

The boundaries of Benjamin. (11–28)

Key verse

Verse 3: "And Joshua said unto the children of Israel, How long are ye slack to go to possess the land, which the LORD God of your fathers hath given you?"

Key word / key phrase

Verse 2, "inheritance."

Key event / key person / key theme

Division of the rest of the land

Key thought

An inheritance gained from this world may be valueless.

Key thing to look out for

God keeps our inheritance for us in heaven.

Key Bible cross-reference

Verse 7. See Deuteronomy 18:1–8.

Key "by way of explanation"

Verse 3. After victory, the people had to settle in the land before they would experience it as theirs.

Key "Quotable Quote"

"It does not take great men to do great things; it only takes consecrated men."

Phillips Brooks

Joshua 19

Matthew Henry's introduction

In the description of the lots of Judah and Benjamin we have an account both of the borders that surrounded them and of the cities contained in them. In that of Ephraim and Manasseh we have the borders, but not the cities; in this chapter Simeon and Dan are described by their cities only, and not their borders, because they lay very much within Judah, especially the former; the rest have both their borders described and their cities names, especially frontiers. Here is,

I. The lot of Simeon, vv. 1–9.

II. Of Zebulun, vv. 10–16.

III. Of Issachar, vv. 17–23.

IV. Of Asher, vv. 24–31.

V. Of Naphtali, vv. 32–39.

VI. Of Dan, vv. 40–48. Lastly, The inheritance assigned to Joshua himself and his own family, vv. 49–51.

A detailed analysis of chapter

The lot of Simeon. (1–9)

The lot of Zebulun. (10–16)

The lot of Issachar, Asher, Naphtali, and Dan. (17–51)

Key verse

Verse 1: "And the second lot came forth to Simeon, even for the tribe of the children of Simeon according to their families: and their inheritance was within the inheritance of the children of Judah."

Key word / key phrase

Verse 49, "allotted portions."

Key event / key person / key theme

More territory assigned

Key thought

All our faculties are God's gifts.

Key thing to look out for

Any influence we have comes from God.

Key Bible cross-reference

Verse 49. See Numbers 13:30; 14:6.

Key "by way of explanation"

Verse 49. Joshua is the last one to receive any inheritance, which is most fitting for a servant of God.

Key "Quotable Quote"

"Make it a rule, and pray to God to help you to keep it, never, if possible, to lie down at night without being able to say: 'I have made one human being at least a little wiser, or a little happier, or at least a little better this day.'"

Charles Kingsley

Joshua 20

Matthew Henry's introduction

This short chapter is about the cities of refuge, which we often read of in the writings of Moses, but this is the last time that we find mention of them, for now that matter was thoroughly settled. Here is,

I. The law God gave about them, vv. 1–6.

II. The people's designation of the particular cities for that use, vv. 7–9. And this remedial law was a figure of good things to come.

A detailed analysis of chapter

The law about the cities of refuge. (1–6)

The cities appointed as refuges. (7–9)

Key verse

Verse 2: "Speak to the children of Israel, saying, Appoint out for you cities of refuge, whereof I spake unto you by the hand of Moses."

Key word / key phrase

Verse 2, "cities of refuge."

Key event / key person / key theme

Cities of refuge

Key thought

Revenge is never to be indulged in.

Key thing to look out for

God cared for his people in countless different ways.

Key Bible cross-reference

Verse 3. See Ruth 3:9; Psalm 19:14.

Key "by way of explanation"

Verse 9. Foreigners were looked after by the people of Israel.

Key "Quotable Quote"

"The more familiar we are with sickness or hunger, the greater will be our compassion for others who are sick or hungry."

Bernard of Clairvaux

Joshua 21

Matthew Henry's introduction

It had been often said that the tribe of Levi should have "no inheritance with their brethren," no particular part of the country assigned them, as the other tribes had, no, not the country about Shiloh, which one might have expected to be appropriated to them as the lands of the church; but, though they were not thus cast into a country by themselves, it appears, by the provision made for them in this chapter, that they were no losers, but the rest of the tribes were very much gainers, by their being dispersed. We have here,

I. The motion they made to have their cities assigned them, according to God's appointment, vv. 1, 2.
II. The nomination of the cities accordingly out of the several tribes, and the distribution of them to the respective families of this tribe, vv. 3–8.
III. A catalogue of the cities, forty-eight in all, vv. 9–42.
IV. A receipt entered in full of all that God had promised to his people Israel, vv. 43–45.

A detailed analysis of chapter

Cities for the Levites. (1–8)

The cities allotted to the Levites. (9–42)

God gave the land and rest to the Israelites, according to his promise. (43–45)

Key verse

Verse 4: "And the lot came out for the families of the Kohathites"

Key word / key phrase

Verse 8, "Levites."

Key event / key person / key theme

Towns for the Levites

Key thought

God never breaks any of his promises.

Key thing to look out for

We need to appropriate God's promises.

Key Bible cross-reference

Verses 43–45. See Genesis 15:18–21.

Key "by way of explanation"

Verse 43–45. These verses are a summary of how God fulfilled his promise and provided land for the Israelites.

Key "Quotable Quote"

"The stars may fall, but God's promises will stand and be fulfilled."

J.I. Packer

Joshua 22

Matthew Henry's introduction

Many particular things we have read about the two tribes and a half, though nothing separated them from the rest of the tribes except the river Jordan, and this chapter is wholly about them.

I. Joshua's dismissing of the militia of those tribes from the camp of Israel, in which the had served as auxiliaries, during all the wars of Canaan, and their return thereon to their own country, vv. 1–9.
II. The altar they built on the borders of Jordan, in token of their communion with the land of Israel, v. 10.
III. The offence which the rest of the tribes took at this altar, and the message they sent thereon, vv. 11–20.
IV. The apology which the two tribes and a half made for what they had done, vv. 21–29.
V. The satisfaction which their apology gave to the rest of the tribes, vv. 30–34. And (which is strange), whereas in most differences that happen there is a fault on both sides, on this there was fault on no side; none (for aught that appears) were to be blamed, but all to be praised.

A detailed analysis of chapter

Reuben and Gad, with the half tribe of Manasseh, dismissed to their homes. (1–9)
They build an altar of testimony. (10–20)
The answer of the Reubenites. (21–29)
The children of Israel satisfied. (30–34)

Key verse

Verse 1: "Then Joshua called the Reubenites, and the Gadites, and the half tribe of Manasseh"

Key word / key phrase

Verse 6, "sent them away."

Key event / key person / key theme

Joshua sends the eastern tribes home

Key thought

Nobody is beyond benefiting from a warning.

Key thing to look out for

Experiencing God's presence is the greatest possible daily blessing.

Key Bible cross-reference

Verse 12. See Deuteronomy 13:12–18; Judges 20.

Key "by way of explanation"

Verse 5. Like Moses, Joshua knew that God needed to be loved from the heart.

Key "Quotable Quote"

"I longed to be a flame of fire continually glowing in the divine service and building up of Christ's kingdom to my last and dying breath."

David Brainerd

Joshua 23

Matthew Henry's introduction

In this and the next chapter we have two farewell sermons that Joshua preached to the people of Israel a little before his death. Had he designed to gratify the curiosity of succeeding ages, he would rather have recorded the method of Israel's settlement in their new conquests, their husbandry, manufacturers, trade, customs, courts of justice, and the constitutions of their infant commonwealth, which one would wish to be informed of; but that which he intended in the registers of this book was to entail on posterity a sense of religion and their duty to God; and therefore, overlooking these things which are the usual subjects of a common history, he here transmits to his reader the methods he took to persuade Israel to be faithful to their covenant with their God, which might have a good influence on the generations to come who should read those reasonings, as we may hope they had on that generation which then heard them. In this chapter we have,

I. A convention of the states called (vv. 1, 2), probably to consult about the common concerns of their land, and to set in order that which, after some years' trial, being left to their prudence, was found wanting.

II. Joshua's speech to them as the opening, or perhaps at the concluding, of the sessions, to hear which was the principal design of their coming together. In it,

A. Joshua reminds them of what God had done for them (vv. 3, 4, 9, 14), and what he was ready to do yet further, vv. 5, 10.

B. He exhorts them carefully and resolutely

to persevere in their duty to God, vv. 6, 8, 11.

III. He cautions them against all familiarity with their idolatrous neighbors, v. 7.

IV. He gives them fair warning of the fatal consequences of it, if they should revolt from God and turn to idols, vv. 12, 13, 15, 16. In all this he showed himself zealous for his God, and jealous over Israel with a godly jealousy.

A detailed analysis of chapter

Joshua's exhortation before his death. (1–10)

Joshua warns the people of idolatry. (11–16)

Key verse

Verse 2: "I am old and stricken in age . . ."

Key word / key phrase

Verse 2, "leaders."

Key event / key person / key theme

Joshua's farewell words to the leaders

Key thought

Leaders need leadership.

Key thing to look out for

The advice to rely on God's strength.

Key Bible cross-reference

Verse 6. See 1:7, 8; 22:5.

Key "by way of explanation"

Verse 12. Joshua includes a severe warning in his encouraging last words.

Key "Quotable Quote"

"No gift is more precious than good advice."

Desiderius Erasmus

Joshua 24

Matthew Henry's introduction

This chapter concludes the life and reign of Joshua, in which we have,

I. The great care and pains he took to confirm the people of Israel in the true faith and worship of God, that they might, after his death, persevere therein. In order to this he called another general assembly of the heads of the congregation of Israel (v. 1) and dealt with them.

A. By way of narrative, recounting the great things God had done for them and their fathers, vv. 2–13.

B. By way of charge to them, in consideration thereof, to serve God, v. 14.

C. By way of treaty with them, in which he aims to bring them,

To make religion their deliberate choice; and they did so, with reasons for their choice, vv. 15–18. (2.)

To make it their determinate choice, and to resolve to adhere to it, vv. 19–24.

By way of covenant on that treaty, vv. 25–28.

II. The conclusion of this history, with,

A. The death and burial of Joshua (vv. 29, 30) and Eleazar (v. 33), and the mention of the burial of Joseph's bones on that occasion, v. 32.

B. A general account of the state of Israel at that time, v. 31.

A detailed analysis of chapter

God's benefits to their fathers. (1–13)

Joshua renews the covenant between the people and God. (14–28)

Joshua's death, Joseph's bones buried, and the state of Israel. (29–33)

Key verse

Verse 29: "And it came to pass after these things, that Joshua the son of Nun, the servant of the LORD, died, being an hundred and ten years old."

Key word / key phrase

Verse 29, "died."

Key event / key person / key theme

Joshua is buried in the promised land

Key thought

View your life from the day after you are dead.

Key thing to look out for

We have only one life to live.

Key Bible cross-reference

Verse 22. See Deuteronomy 30:19.

Key "by way of explanation"

Verse 19. Joshua contrasts the people's inability to serve God in their own strength with God's wonderful character.

Key "Quotable Quote"

"A life spent in communion with God, is the pleasantest life in the world."

Matthew Henry, his last words

5. Select bibliography for Joshua

Calvin, J. *Commentaries on the Book of Joshua.* Grand Rapids: Eerdmans, 1949.

Goslinga, C. J. *Joshua, Judges, Ruth.* Bible Student's Commentary. Grand Rapids: Zondervan, 1986.

Hess, Richard S. *Joshua: An Introduction and Commentary* (Tyndale, 6), 1996.

Keil, C. F., and Delitzsch, F. *Joshua, Judges, Ruth*. Grand Rapids: Eerdmans, 1950.

Judges

1. Book by book: Introduction to Judges

Introduction

This book is called the book of Judges because it contains the history of those non-regal rulers who governed the Hebrews from the time of Joshua to that of Eli, and whose functions in time of peace consisted chiefly in the administration of justice, although they occasionally led the people in their wars against their public enemies.

The date and authorship of this book are not precisely known. It is certain, however, that it preceded the Second Book of Samuel (compare Judges 9:35 with 2 Samuel 11:21), as well as the conquest of Jerusalem by David (compare Judges 1:21 with 2 Samuel 5:6).

Its author was in all probability Samuel, the last of the judges (see Judges 19:1 21:25), and the date of the first part of it is fixed in the reign of Saul, while the five chapters at the close might not have been written till after' David's establishment as king in Israel (see Judges 18:31). It is a fragmentary history, being a collection of important facts and signal deliverances at different times and in various parts of the land, during the intermediate period of three hundred years between Joshua and the establishment of the monarchy. The inspired character of this book is confirmed by allusions to it in many passages of Scripture (compare Judges 4:2; 6:14 with 1 Samuel 12:9–12; Judges 9:53 with 2 Samuel 11:21; Judges 7:25 with Psalms 83:11; compare Judges 5:4,5 with Psalms 7:5; Judges 13:5; 16:17 with Matthew 2:13–23; Acts 13:20; Hebrews 11:32).

Robert Jamieson

Contents of Judges

The book of Judges provides a link between the military leader Joshua and the first kings of Israel, Saul and David. During the times of the judges Israel gradually began to act as a single nation, rather than twelve separate tribes.

The Book of Judges consists of 3 main parts or divisions, which are easily distinguished.

(1) Introductory, Judges 1:1–2:5.

A brief summary and recapitulation of the events of the conquest of Western Palestine, for the most part parallel to the narrative of Joshua, but with a few additional details and some divergences from the earlier account, in particular emphasizing (Judges 1:27–36) the general failure of the Israelites to expel completely the original inhabitants of the land, which is described as a violation of their covenant with Yahweh (Judges 2:1–3), entailing on them suffering and permanent weakness. The introductory verse (Judges 1:1), which refers to the death of Joshua as having already taken place, seems to be intended as a general indication of the historical period of the book as a whole; for some at least of the events narrated in Judges 1:1–2:5 took place during Joshua's lifetime.

(2) The Central and Main Portion, Judges 2:6–16.

A series of narratives of 12 "judges," each of whom in turn, by his devotion and prowess, was enabled to deliver Israel from thralldom and oppression, and for a longer or shorter term ruled over the people whom he had thus saved from their enemies. Each successive repentance on the part of the people, however, and their deliverance are followed, on the death of the judge, by renewed apostasy, which entails on them renewed misery and servitude, from which they are again rescued when in response to their prayer the Lord "raises up" for them another judge and deliverer. Thus the entire history is set as it were in a recurrent framework of moral and religious teaching and warning; and the lesson is enforced that it is the sin of the people, their abandonment of Yahweh and persistent idolatry, which entails on them calamity, from which the Divine longsuffering and forbearance alone makes for them a way of escape.

(a) Judges 2:6–3:6:

A second brief introduction, conceived entirely in the spirit of the following narratives, which seems to attach itself to the close of the Book of Joshua, and in part repeats almost verbally the account there given of the death and burial of Israel's leader (Judges 2:6–9 parallel Joshua 24:28–31), and proceeds to describe the condition of the land and people in the succeeding generation, ascribing their misfortunes to their idolatry and repeated neglect of the warnings and commands of the judges; closing with an enumeration of the peoples left in the land, whose presence was to be the test of Israel's willingness to obey Yahweh and at the same time to prevent the nation from sinking into a condition of lethargy and ease.

(b) Judges 3:7–3:11:

Judgeship of Othniel who delivered Israel from the hand of Cushan-rishathaim.

(c) Judges 3:12–30:

Victory of Ehud over the Moabites, to whom the Israelites had been in servitude 18 years. Ehud slew their king Eglon, and won for the nation a long period of tranquility.

(d) Judges 3:31:

In a few brief words Shamgar is named as the deliverer of Israel from the Philistines. The title of "judge" is not accorded to him, nor is he said to have exercised authority in any way. It is doubtful, therefore, whether the writer intended him to be regarded as one of the judges.

(e) Judges 4; 5:

Victory of Deborah and Barak over Jabin the Canaanite king, and death of Sisera, captain of his army, at the hands of Jael, the wife of Kenite chief; followed by a song of triumph, descriptive and commemorative of the event.

(f) Judges 6–8:

A 7–year oppression at the hands of the Midianites, which is described as peculiarly severe, so that the land became desolate on account of the perpetual raids to which it was subject. After a period of hesitation and delay, Gideon defeats the combined forces of the Midianites and Amalekites and the "children of the east," i.e. the wandering Bedouin bands from the eastern deserts, in the valley of Jezreel. The locality and course of the battle are traced by the sacred writer, but it is not possible to follow his account in detail because of our inability to identify the places named. After the victory, Gideon is formally offered the position of ruler for himself and his descendants, but refuses; nevertheless, he seems to have exercised a measure of restraining influence over the people until his death, although he himself and his family apparently through covetousness fell away from their faithfulness to Yahweh (Judges 8:27,33).

(g) Judges 9:

Episode of Abimelech, son of Gideon by a concubine, who by the murder of all but one of his brethren, the legitimate sons of Gideon, secured the throne at Shechem for himself, and for 3 years ruled Israel. After successfully stamping out a revolt at Shechem against his authority, he is himself killed when engaged in the siege of the citadel or tower of Thebez by a stone thrown by woman.

(h) (i) Judges 10:1–5:

Tola and Jair are briefly named as successive judges of Israel for 23 and 22 years respectively.

(j) Judges 10:6–12:7:

Oppression of Israel for 18 years by the Philistines and Ammonites. The national deliverance is effected by Jephthah, who is described as an illegitimate son of Gilead who had been on that account driven out from his home and had become the captain of a band of outlaws. Jephthah stipulates with the elders of Gilead that if he undertakes to do battle on their behalf with the Ammonites, he is afterward to be recognized as their ruler; and in accordance with the agreement, when the victory has been won, he becomes judge over Israel (Judges 11:9; 12:7).

(k) (l) (m) Judges 12:8–15:

Three of the so-called "minor" judges, Ibzan, Elon and Abdon, judged Israel in succession for 7, 10 and 8 years respectively. As they are not said to have delivered the nation from any calamity or oppression, it is perhaps to be understood that the whole period was a time of rest and tranquility.

(n) Judges 13–16:

The history of Samson.

(3) An Appendix, Judges 17–21.

The final section, in the nature of an appendix, consisting of two narratives. They contain no indication of date, except the statement 4 times repeated that "in those days there was no king in Israel" Judges 6; 18:1; 19:1; 21:25. No name of a judge appears, however, and there is no direct reference to the office or to any central or controlling authority.

(a) Judges 17–18:

The episode of Micah the Ephraimite and the young Levite who is consecrated as priest in his house. A war party, however, during a migration northward, by threats and promises induced the Levite to accompany them, taking with him the priestly ephod, the household goods of his patron, and a costly image which Micah had caused to be made. These Micah in vain endeavors to recover from the Danites. The latter sack and burn Laish in the extreme North of Palestine, rebuilding the city on the same site and renaming it "Dan." There they set up the image which they had stolen, and establish a rival priesthood and worship, which is said to have endured "all the time that the house of God was in Shiloh" (18:31).

(b) Judges 19–21:

Outrage of the Benjamites of Gibeah against the concubine of a Levite staying for a night in the city on his way from Bethlehem to the hill country of Ephraim. The united tribes, after twice suffering defeat at the hands of the men of Benjamin, exact full vengeance; the tribe of Benjamin is almost annihilated, and their cities, including Gibeah, are destroyed. In order that the tribe may not utterly perish, peace is declared with the 600 survivors, and they are provided with wives, the Israelites having taken a solemn vow not to permit intermarriage between their own daughters and the members of the guilty tribe.

Orr, James, M.A., D.D. General Editor, International Standard Bible Encyclopedia

Detailed outline

I. Introduction to the period of the judges: 1:1–2:5
- A. Political conditions from Joshua to the time of the judges: 1:1–36
- B. Religious conditions from Joshua to the time of the judges: 2:1–5

II. The period of the judges: 2:6–16:31
- A. Summary of religious conditions of the entire period: 2:6–3:6
- B. List of the judges: 3:7–16:31
  1. Othniel of Judah: 3:7–11
  2. Ehud of Benjamin: 3:12–30
  3. Shamgar: 3:31
  4. Deborah of Ephraim and Barak of Naphtali: 4:1–5:31
  5. Gideon of Manasseh and Abimelech: 6:1–9:57
  6. Tola of Issachar: 10:1–2
  7. Jair of Gilead: 10:3–5
  8. Jephthah of Gilead: 10:6–12:7
  9. Ibzan of Zebulon: 12:8–10
  10. Elon of Zebulon: 12:11–12
  11. Abdon of Ephraim: 12:13–15
  12. Samson of Dan: 13:1–16:31

III. Historical appendix: 17:1–21:25
- A. The idolatry of Micah and the Danites: 17:1–18:31
  1. Micah and his personal priest: 17:1–13
  2. The Danites join the idolatry: 18:1–31
- B. Israel's immorality: 19:1–30
  1. Personal immorality: 19:1–10
  2. Tribal immorality: 19:11–30
- C. War between the tribes: 20:1–21:25
  1. War between Dan and Israel: 20:1–48
  2. Israel's failure after the war: 21:1–25

2. Helpful summaries of Judges

Bird's eye view

Israel's history under the leadership of fourteen judges.

Linked New Testament book

Galatians

Both Judges and Galatians are about the dangers of backsliding.

Reading plan

The following reading plan, taking one reading per day, enables you to read through Judges in nine days.

Judges 1–3
Judges 4–5
Judges 6–7
Judges 8–9
Judges 10
Judges 11–13
Judges 14–16
Judges 17–19
Judges 20–21

Verse to memorize

Judges 5:31

So may all your enemies perish, oh Lord!
But may they who love you be like the sun
when it rises in its strength.

Statistics

Seventh Old Testament book
21 chapters
618 verses
18,976 words

Names/titles given

- Hebrew title: *Shophetim*: "rulers, judges, saviors."
- Greek title in Septuagint: *Kritai*: "judges."
- Latin title in Vulgate: *Liber Judicum* "Book of Judges."
- "The book of failure."

3. Helpful keys to turn to in understanding Judges

Key word

Delivered, 28 times

Key verses

Judges 2:20–21; 21:25

Themes to study

- Learning lessons from Deborah, Gideon, Jephthah, and Samson.
- How a nation is successful in God's sight.

Unusual events and miracles in Judges

- Fire from a rock, 6:17–23
- Gideon's fleece, 6:36
- Gideon's drastically reduced army being victorious, 7:1–8
- Jephthah's rash vow, 11:29–40
- Water from a jawbone, 15:19
- Samson's strength, 14–16

Key people/events

Ehud
Eglon
Deborah
Barak
Sisera
Jael
Gideon
Signs given to Gideon
Abimelech
Jotham
Jephthah
Samson
Delilah
Micah and the Danites
The Levite and his concubine

Jesus in Judges

In Judges Jesus is our Deliverer.

Types of Jesus in Judges

The judges have a similar role to Jesus', as savior-kings.

Lessons to learn from Judges

- If we live without God we end up in great trouble.
- God is always willing to forgive.
- We are judged and delivered by God, not by

human beings.

4. Chapter by chapter: outline of every chapter of Judges

Judges 1

Matthew Henry's introduction

This chapter gives us a particular account what sort of progress the several tribes of Israel made in the reducing of Canaan after the death of Joshua. He did (as we say) break the neck of that great work, and put it into such a posture that they might easily have perfected it in due time, if they had not been wanting to themselves; what they did in order hereunto, and where they came short, we are told.

I. The united tribes o Judah and Simeon did bravely.
   A. God appointed Judah to begin, vv. 1, 2.
   B. Judah took Simeon to act in conjunction with him, v. 3.
   C. They succeeded in their enterprises against Bezek (vv. 4–7), Jerusalem, v. 8. Hebron and Debir (vv. 9–15), Hormah, Gaza, and other places, vv. 17–19.
   D. Yet where there were chariots of iron their hearts failed them, v. 19. Mention is made of the Kenites settling among them, v. 16.

II. The other tribes, in comparison with these, acted a cowardly part.
   A. Benjamin failed, v. 21.
   B. The house of Joseph did well against Beth-el (vv. 22–26), but in other places did not improve their advantages, nor Manasseh (vv. 27, 28), nor Ephraim, v. 29.
   C. Zebulun spared the Canaanites, v. 30.
   D. Asher truckled worse than any of them to the Canaanites, vv. 31, 32.
   E. Naphtali was kept out of the full possession of several of his cities, v. 33.
   F. Dan was straitened by the Amorites, v. 34.
   No account is given of Issachar, nor of the two tribes and a half on the other side Jordan.

A detailed analysis of chapter

Events among the tribes of Judah and Simeon. (1–8)

Hebron and other cities taken. (9–20)

The events among the other tribes. (21–36)

Key verse

Verse 1: "Now after the death of Joshua it came to pass, that the children of Israel asked the LORD, saying, Who shall go up for us against the Canaanites first, to fight against them?"

Key word / key phrase

Verse 8, "Jerusalem."

Key event / key person / key theme

Jerusalem and Hebron conquered

Key thought

God's people should have nothing to do with brutal practices.

Key thing to look out for

Some of the practices of God's people are recorded as examples for us, others as warnings for us to heed.

Key Bible cross-reference

Verse 20. See Numbers 14:24; Joshua 14:9–14.

Key "by way of explanation"

Verse 8. Jerusalem was conquered but the Israelites did not occupy it until David reconquered it.

Key "Quotable Quote"

"We can do nothing unless divine aid support us."

Bonaventure

Judges 2

Matthew Henry's introduction

In this chapter we have,

I. A particular message which God sent to Israel by an angel, and the impression it made on them, vv. 1–5.

II. A general idea of the state of Israel during the government of the judges, in which observe,

A. Their adherence to God while Joshua and the elders lived, vv. 6–10.

B. Their revolt afterwards to idolatry, vv. 11–13.

C. God's displeasure against them, and his judgments on them for it, vv. 14, 15.

D. His pity towards them, shown in raising them up deliverers, vv. 16–18.

E. Their relapse into idolatry after the judgment was over, vv. 17–19.

F. The full stop God in anger put to their successes, vv. 20–23. These are the contents, not only of this chapter, but of the whole book.

A detailed analysis of chapter

The angel of the Lord rebukes the people. (1–5)

The wickedness of the new generation after Joshua. (6–23)

Key verse

Verse 4: "And it came to pass, when the angel of the LORD spake these words unto all the children of Israel, that the people lifted up their voice, and wept."

Key word / key phrase

Verse 2, "yet you have disobeyed me."

Key event / key person / key theme

The death of Joshua

Key thought

There is no higher station in life than being God's servant.

Key thing to look out for

The Israelites were constantly violating God's covenant, yet God never gave up on them.

Key Bible cross-reference

Verse 8. See Isaiah 41:8,9; 42:1.

Key "by way of explanation"

The judges were tribal leaders. Some of them led the people to victory over their enemies.

Key "Quotable Quote"

"Beware of Christian activities instead of Christian being."

Oswald Chambers

Judges 3

Matthew Henry's introduction

In this chapter,

I. A general account of Israel's enemies is premised, and of the mischief they did them, vv. 1–7.

II. A particular account of the brave exploits done by the first three of the judges.

A. Othniel, whom God raised up to fight Israel's battles, and plead their cause against the king of Mesopotamia, vv. 8–11.

B. Ehud, who was employed in rescuing Israel out of the hands of the Moabites, and did it by stabbing the king of Moab, vv. 12–30.

C. Shamgar, who signalized himself in an encounter with the Philistines, v. 31.

A detailed analysis of chapter

The nations left to test Israel. (1–7)
Othniel delivers Israel. (8–11)
Ehud delivers Israel from Eglon. (12–30)
Shamgar delivers and judges Israel. (31)

Key verse

Verse 12: "And the children of Israel did evil again in the sight of the LORD: and the LORD strengthened Eglon the king of Moab against Israel, because they had done evil in the sight of the LORD."

Key word / key phrase

Verse 9,15 "they cried to the LORD."

Key event / key person / key theme

Othniel, Ehud

Key thought

God's people slowly settled down in the promised land, thanks to God's charismatic leaders.

Key thing to look out for

The results of doing evil.

Key Bible cross-reference

Verse 10. See 6:34; 1 Samuel 16:13.

Key "by way of explanation"

Verse 15. Because Ehud was left-handed he was able to conceal his dagger without anyone suspecting him of carrying his lethal weapon.

Key "Quotable Quote"

"We are each born into a world in which it is easy for us to do evil and hard for us to do good."

Bishop Kallistos Ware

Judges 4

Matthew Henry's introduction

The method of the history of Deborah and Barak (the heroes in this chapter) is the same with that before Here is,

I. Israel revolted from God, v. 1.

II. Israel oppressed by Jabin, vv. 2, 3.

III. Israel judged by Deborah, vv. 4, 5.

IV. Israel rescued out of the hands of Jabin.

A. Their deliverance is concerted between Deborah and Barak, vv. 6, 9.

B. It is accomplished by their joint-agency. Barak takes the field, v. 10. Sisera, Jabin's general, meets him, vv. 12, 13. Deborah encourages him, v. 14. And God gives him a complete victory. The army routed, vv. 15, 16. The general forced to flee, v. 17. And where he expected shelter he had his life stolen from him by Jael while he was asleep (vv. 18–21), which completes Barak's triumph (v. 22) and Israel's deliverance, vv. 23, 24.

A detailed analysis of chapter

Israel again rebels, and is oppressed by Jabin. (1–3)

Deborah plans their deliverance with Barak. (4–9)

Sisera defeated. (10–16)

Sisera put to death by Jael. (17–24)

Key verse

Verse 4: "And Deborah, a prophetess, the wife of Lapidoth, she judged Israel at that time."

Key word / key phrase

Verse 6, "the Lord commands you."

Key event / key person / key theme

Judge Deborah

Key thought

God used men and women judges.

Key thing to look out for

God spoke through prophets and prophetesses.

Key Bible cross-reference

Verse 14. See 1 Samuel 8:20; Exodus 15:3.

Key "by way of explanation"

Chapter 4 celebrates victory over Sisera in prose and chapter 5 celebrates the same victory, but in a poem.

Key "Quotable Quote"

"I expect to pass through the world but once. Any good therefore that I can do, or any kindness or abilities that I can show to any fellow creature, let me do it now. Let me not defer or neglect it, for I shall not pass this way again."

William Penn

Judges 5

Matthew Henry's introduction

This chapter contains the triumphal song which was composed and sung on occasion of that glorious victory which Israel won over the forces of Jabin king of Canaan and the happy consequences of that victory. Probably it was usual then to publish poems on such occasions, as now; but this only is preserved of all the poems of that age of the judges, because dictated by Deborah a prophetess, designed for a psalm of praise then, and a pattern of praise to after-ages, and it gives a great deal of light to the history of these times.

I. It begins with praise to God, vv. 2, 3.

II. The substance of this song transmits the memory of this great achievement.

A. Comparing God's appearances for them on this occasion with his appearances to them on Mount Sinai, vv. 4, 5.

B. Magnifying their deliverance from the consideration of the calamitous condition they had been in, vv. 6–8.

C. Calling those to join in praise that shared in the benefits of the success, vv. 9–13.

D. Reflecting honor on those tribes that were forward and active in that war, and disgrace on those that declined the service, vv. 14–19, 23.

E. Taking notice how God himself fought for them, vv. 20–22.

F. Celebrating particularly the honor of Jael, that slew Sisera, on which head the song is very large, vv. 24–30. It concludes with a prayer to God, v. 31.

A detailed analysis of chapter

Praise and glory given to God. (1–5)
The distress and deliverance of Israel. (6–11)
Some commended, others censured. (12–23)
Sisera's mother disappointed. (24–31)

Key verse

Verse 1: "Then sang Deborah and Barak the son of Abinoam on that day . . ."

Key word / key phrase

Verse 31, "the land had peace."

Key event / key person / key theme

Victory

Key thought

Praise is given to the Lord, rather than to the people who fought.

Key thing to look out for

Singing God's praises gives an added dimension to saying God's praises.

Key Bible cross-reference

Verses 4–5. See Deuteronomy 33:2; Psalm 68:7, 8.

Key "by way of explanation"

Verses 1–31. The Israelites frequently celebrated their victories in song. See Exodus 15:1–18; Numbers 21:27–30.

Key "Quotable Quote"

"Sing lustily and with a good courage. Beware of singing as if you were half dead, or half asleep; but lift up your voice with strength."

John Wesley

Judges 6

Matthew Henry's introduction

This chapter presents us with Gideon in the field, commanding the army of Israel, and routing the army of the Midianites, for which great exploit we found in the previous chapter how he was prepared by his converse with God and his conquest of Baal. We are here told,

I. What direction God gave to Gideon for the modeling of his army, by which it was reduced to 300 men, vv. 1, 8.

II. What encouragement God gave to Gideon to attack the enemy, by sending him secretly into their camp to hear a Midianite tell his dream, vv. 9–15.

III. How he formed his attack on the enemy's camp with his 300 men, not to fight them, but to frighten them, vv. 16–20.

IV. The success of this attack; it put them to flight, and gave them a total rout, the disbanded forces, and their other neighbors, then coming in to his assistance, vv. 21–25. It is a story that shines very brightly in the book of the wars of the Lord.

A detailed analysis of chapter

Israel oppressed by Midianites. (1–6)
Israel rebuked by a prophet. (7–10)
Gideon told to deliver Israel. (11–24)
Gideon destroys Baal's altar. (25–32)
Signs given him. (33–40)

Key verse

Verse 11: "And there came an angel of the LORD, and sat under an oak which was in Ophrah, that pertained unto Joash the Abiezrite: and his son Gideon threshed wheat by the winepress, to hide it from the Midianites."

Key word / key phrase

Verse 14, "Go in the strength you have."

Key event / key person / key theme

After the Israelites had ignored God, he raised up a new leader to guide them back into his ways.

Key thought

God looks on the heart, not on outward appearances.

Key thing to look out for

Sometimes things have to be torn down before anything can be built up.

Key Bible cross-reference

Verse 25. See Exodus 34:13; Deuteronomy 7:5.

Key "by way of explanation"

Verse 15. God often called the lowly to serve him. See Genesis 25:23; 1 Samuel 9:21.

Key "Quotable Quote"

"The curse of much modern Christian work is its determination to preserve itself."

Oswald Chambers

Judges 7

Matthew Henry's introduction

This chapter gives us a further account of Gideon's victory over the Midianites, with the residue of the story of his life and government.

I. Gideon prudently pacifies the offended Ephraimites, vv. 1–3.
II. He bravely pursues the flying Midianites, vv. 4, 10–12.
III. He justly chastises the insolence of the men of Succoth and Penuel, who basely abused him (vv. 5–9), and were reckoned with for it, vv. 13–17.
IV. He honorably slays the two kings of Midian, vv. 18–21.
V. After all this he modestly declines the government of Israel, vv. 22, 23.
VI. He foolishly gratified the superstitious humor of his people by setting up an ephod in his own city, which proved a great snare, vv. 24–27.
VII. He kept the country quiet for forty years, v. 28.
VIII. He died in honor, and left a numerous family behind him, vv. 29–32.
IX. Both he and his God were soon forgotten by ungrateful Israel, vv. 33–35.

A detailed analysis of chapter

Gideon's army reduced. (1–8)

Gideon is encouraged. (9–15)

The defeat of the Midianites. (16–22)

The Ephraimites take Oreb and Zeeb. (23–25)

Key verse

Verse 8: "So the people took victuals in their hand, and their trumpets: and he sent all the rest of Israel every man unto his tent, and retained those three hundred men: and the host of Midian was beneath him in the valley."

Key word / key phrase

Verse 2, "that Israel may not boast."

Key event / key person / key theme

The Midianites are defeated by Gideon.

Key thought

Numbers do not have the final say in God's kingdom.

Key thing to look out for

One plus God is a majority.

Key Bible cross-reference

Verse 13. See 2 Kings 7:1.

Key "by way of explanation"

Verse 6. The point about the numbers being reduced to 300 is that this made it clear that the battle was won by God and not by the power of a vast army of Israelites.

Key "Quotable Quote"

"God's part is to put forth power; our part is to put forth faith."

Andrew A. Bonar

Judges 8

Matthew Henry's introduction

This chapter gives us a further account of Gideon's victory over the Midianites, with the residue of the story of his life and government.

I. Gideon prudently pacifies the offended Ephraimites, vv. 1–3.

II. He bravely pursues the flying Midianites, vv. 4, 10–12.

III. He justly chastises the insolence of the men of Succoth and Penuel, who basely abused him (vv. 5–9), and were reckoned with for it, vv. 13–17.

IV. He honorably slays the two kings of Midian, vv. 18–21.

V. After all this he modestly declines the government of Israel, vv. 22, 23.

VI. He foolishly gratified the superstitious humor of his people by setting up an ephod in his own city, which proved a great snare, vv. 24–27.

VII. He kept the country quiet for forty years, v. 28.

VIII. He died in honor, and left a numerous family behind him, vv. 29–32.

IX. Both he and his God were soon forgotten by ungrateful Israel, vv. 33–35.

A detailed analysis of chapter

Gideon pacifies the Ephraimites. (1–3)

Succoth and Penuel refuse to relieve Gideon. (4–12)
Succoth and Penuel punished. (13–17)
Gideon avenges his brethren. (18–21)
Gideon declines to govern, but allows idolatry. (22–28)
Gideon's death, Israel's ingratitude. (29–35)

Key verse

Verse 32: "And Gideon the son of Joash died in a good old age, and was buried in the sepulcher of Joash his father, in Ophrah of the Abiezrites."

Key word / key phrase

Verse 23, "The LORD will rule over you."

Key event / key person / key theme

The final defeat of the Midianites.

Key thought

Victories often come in stages.

Key thing to look out for

There are no spiritual victories where God is not given the glory.

Key Bible cross-reference

Verse 3. See Proverbs 15:1.

Key "by way of explanation"

Verse 28, "forty years" often represents a round number in the Bible, such as a generation.

Key "Quotable Quote"

"Be thou therefore ready for the conflict, if thou wilt have the victory."

Thomas à Kempis

Judges 9

Matthew Henry's introduction

The apostasy of Israel after the death of Gideon is punished, not as the former apostasies by a foreign invasion, or the oppressions of any neighboring power, but by intestine broils among themselves, which in this chapter we have the story of; and it is hard to say whether their sin or their misery appears most in it. It is an account of the usurpation and tyranny of Abimelech, who was base son to Gideon; so we must call him, and not more modishly his natural son: he was so unlike him. We are here told,

I. How he thrust himself into the government at Shechem, his own city, by subtlety and cruelty, particularly by the murder of all his brethren, vv. 1–6.
II. How his doom was read in a parable by Jotham, Gideon's youngest son, vv. 7–21.
III. What strifes there were between Abimelech and his friends the Shechemites, vv. 22–41.
IV. How this ended in the ruin of the Shechemites (vv. 42–49), and of Abimelech himself, vv. 50–57. Of this meteor, this ignis fatuus of a prince, that was not a protector but a plague to his country, we may say, as once was said of a great tyrant, that he came in like a fox, ruled like a lion, and died like a dog. "For the transgression of a land, such are the princes thereof."

A detailed analysis of chapter

Abimelech murders his brethren, and is made king. (1–6)

Jotham rebukes the Shechemites. (7–21)

The Shechemites conspire against Abimelech. (22–29)

Abimelech destroys Shechem. (30–49)

Abimelech is killed. (50–57)

Key verse

Verse 56: "Thus God rendered the wickedness of Abimelech, which he did unto his father, in slaying his seventy brethren."

Key word / key phrase

Verse 56. "God repaid the wickedness."

Key event / key person / key theme

Abimelech received God's punishment for his wicked ways in his lifetime.

Key thought

Many evil people become rulers.

Key thing to look out for

God does not abdicate just because an ungodly person is in power.

Key Bible cross-reference

Verse 15. See Isaiah 30:2,3; Lamentations 4:20.

Key "by way of explanation"

Verse 1–57. Abimelech and Gideon can be studied together as they are such contrasting characters.

Key "Quotable Quote"

"Those who will not be governed by God, will be ruled by tyrants."

William Penn

Judges 10

Matthew Henry's introduction

In this chapter we have,

I. The peaceable times Israel enjoyed under the government of two judges, Tola and Jair, vv. 1–5.

II. The troublesome times that ensued.

A. Israel's sin that brought them into trouble, v. 6.

B. The trouble itself they were in, vv. 7–9.

III. Their repentance and humiliation for sin, their prayers and reformation, and the mercy they found with God thereon, vv. 10–16.

IV. Preparation made for their deliverance out of the hand of their oppressors, vv. 17, 18.

A detailed analysis of chapter

Tola and Jair judge Israel. (1–5)

The Philistines and Ammonites oppress Israel. (6–9)

Israel's repentance. (10–18)

Key verse

Verse 6: "And the children of Israel did evil again in the sight of the LORD, and served Baalim, and Ashtaroth, and the gods of Syria, and the gods of Zidon, and the gods of Moab, and the gods of the children of Ammon, and the gods of the Philistines, and forsook the LORD, and served not him."

Key word / key phrase

Verse 16, "foreign gods."

Key event / key person / key theme

More judges

Key thought

Rulers come and go, but God reigns forever.

Key thing to look out for

Evangelism needs to take place in times of war as well as in times of peace.

Key Bible cross-reference

Verse 6. See 1 Kings 11:7; Leviticus 18:21.

Key "by way of explanation"

Verse 11. The Lord is always aware of any unfaithfulness.

Key "Quotable Quote"

"When the sovereign God brings us to nothing, it is to reroute our lives, not to end them."

Charles R. Swindoll

Judges 11

Matthew Henry's introduction

This chapter gives as the history of Jephthah, another of Israel's judges, and numbered among the worthies of the Old Testament, that by faith did great things (Heb. 11:32), though he had not such an extraordinary call as the rest there mentioned had. Here we have,

I. The disadvantages of his origin, vv. 1–3.

II. The Gileadites' choice of him to be commander-in-chief against the Ammonites, and the terms he made with them, vv. 4–11.

III. His treaty with the king of Ammon about the rights of the two nations, that the matter might be determined, if possible, without bloodshed, vv. 12–28.

IV. His war with the Ammonites, which he enters on with a solemn vow (vv. 29–31), prosecutes with bravery (v. 32), and ends with a glorious victory, v. 33.

V. The straits he was brought into at his return to his own house by the vow he had made, vv. 34–40.

A detailed analysis of chapter

Jephthah and the Gileadites. (1–11)

He attempts to make peace. (12–28)

Jephthah's vow. He vanquishes the Ammonites. (29–40)

Key verse

Verse 1: "Now Jephthah the Gileadite was a mighty man of valor."

Key word / key phrase

Verse 130 "vow."

Key event / key person / key theme

Jephthah

Key thought

Righteousness exalts a nation.

Key thing to look out for

Evil never has the last word.

Key Bible cross-reference

Verse 11. See 1 Samuel 11:15; Rehoboam, 1 Kings 12:1.

Key "by way of explanation"

Verse 34. Dancing women often greeted successful armies as they returned home. See Exodus 15:20.

Key "Quotable Quote"

"Suppose a nation in some distant region should take the Bible for their only Law Book, and every member should regulate his conduct by the precepts there exhibited . . . What a paradise would this region be!"

John Adams

Judges 12

Matthew Henry's introduction

In this chapter we have,

I. Jephthah's rencounter with the Ephraimites, and the blood shed on that unhappy occasion (vv. 1–6), and the conclusion of Jephthah's life and government, v. 7.

II. A short account of three other of the judges of Israel: Ibzan (vv. 8–10), Elon (vv. 11, 12), Abdon, vv. 13–15.

A detailed analysis of chapter

Ephraimites quarrel with Jephthah. (1–7)

Ibzan, Elon, and Abdon judge Israel. (8–15)

Key verse

Verse 7: "And Jephthah judged Israel six years. Then died Jephthah the Gileadite, and was buried in one of the cities of Gilead."

Key word / key phrase

Verse 1, "men of Ephraim."

Key event / key person / key theme

Jephthah and the Ephraimites

Key thought

Peter was told that his accent gave him away and that it showed that he was a friend of Jesus.

Key thing to look out for

How we speak can bring glory to God.

Key Bible cross-reference

Verse 1. See 14:15; 20:48.

Key "by way of explanation"

Verse 6. By listening to how people pronounced the word "Shibboleth" you could tell which region they came from.

Key "Quotable Quote"

"Happy the man whose words come from the Holy Spirit and not from himself!"

Anthony of Padua

Judges 13

Matthew Henry's introduction

At this chapter begins the story of Samson, the last of the judges of Israel whose story is recorded in this book, and next before Eli. The passages related about him are, from first to last, very surprising and uncommon. The figure he makes in this history is really great, and yet vastly different from that of his predecessors. We never find him at the head either of a court or of an army, never on the throne of judgment nor in the field of battle, yet, in his own proper person, a great patriot of his country, and a terrible scourge and check to its enemies and oppressors; he was an eminent believer (Heb. 11:32) and a glorious type of him who with his own arm wrought salvation. The history of the rest of the judges commences from their advancement to that station, but Samson's begins with his birth, nay, with his conception, no less than an angel from heaven ushers him into the world, as a pattern of what should be afterwards done to John Baptist and to Christ. This is related in this chapter.

I. The occasion of raising up this deliverer was the oppression of Israel by the Philistines, v. 1.
II. His birth is foretold by an angel to his mother, vv. 2–5.
III. She relates the prediction to his father, vv. 6, 7.
IV. They both together have it again from the angel (vv. 8–14), whom they treat with respect (vv. 15–18), and who, to their great amazement, discovers his dignity at parting, vv. 19–23.
V. Samson is born, vv. 24, 25.

A detailed analysis of chapter

The Philistines, Samson announced. (1–7)
The angel appears to Manoah. (8–14)
Manoah's sacrifice. (15–23)
Birth of Samson. (24,25)

Key verse

Verse 24: "And the woman bare a son, and called his name Samson: and the child grew, and the LORD blessed him."

Key word / key phrase

Verse 1, "Philistines."

Key event / key person / key theme

The birth of Samson

Key thought

Every birth is a miracle.

Key thing to look out for

God has loved us from before we were born.

Key Bible cross-reference

Verse 5. See 1 Samuel 7:10–14; 2 Samuel 5:17–25; 8:1.

Key "by way of explanation"

Verse 5. "Nazirite" comes from a word meaning "dedicated." Samson's Nazirite calling differed from the vow described in Numbers 6:1–21 in that his was not voluntary, and was to be for a lifetime.

Key "Quotable Quote"

"The good pleasure of God is an act of the divine will freely and effectively determining all things."

William Ames

Judges 14

Matthew Henry's introduction

The idea which this chapter gives us of Samson is not what one might have expected about one who, by the special designation of heaven, was a Nazarite to God and a deliverer of Israel; and yet really he was both. Here is,

I. Samson's courtship of a daughter of the Philistines, and his marriage to her, vv. 1–5, 7, 8.

II. His conquest of a lion, and the prize he found in the carcass of it, vv. 5, 6, 8, 9.

III. Samson's riddle proposed to his companions (vv. 10–14) and discovered by the treachery of his wife, vv. 15–18.

IV. The occasion this gave him to kill thirty of the Philistines (v. 19) and to break off his new alliance, v. 20.

A detailed analysis of chapter

Samson desires a wife of the Philistines. (1–4)
Samson kills a lion. (5–9)
Samson's riddle. (10–20)

Key verse

Verse 1: "And Samson went down to Timnath, and saw a woman in Timnath of the daughters of the Philistines."

Key word / key phrase

Verse 2, "wife."

Key event / key person / key theme

Samson's marriage

Key thought

Marriages need a better foundation than this one.

Key thing to look out for

Countless marriages between Christians also break up.

Key Bible cross-reference

Verse 6. See 13:25; 14:19; 15:14.

Key "by way of explanation"

Verse 12. Riddles were often posed at feasts as part of the entertainment.

Key "Quotable Quote"

"Temptations, when we meet them at first, are as the lion that reared upon Samson; but if we overcome them, the next time we see them we shall find a nest of honey within them."

John Bunyan

Judges 15

Matthew Henry's introduction

Samson, when he courted an alliance with the Philistines, did but seek an occasion against them, 14:4. Now here we have a further account of the occasions he took to weaken them, and to avenge, not his own, but Israel's quarrels, on them. Everything here is surprising; if any thing be thought incredible, because impossible, it must be remembered that with God nothing is impossible, and it was by the Spirit of the Lord coming on him that he was both directed to and strengthened for those unusual ways of making war.

I. From the perfidiousness of his wife and her father, he took occasion to burn their corn, vv. 1–5.

II. From the Philistines' barbarous cruelty to his wife and her father, he took occasion to smite them with a great slaughter, vv. 6–8.

III. From the treachery of his countrymen, who delivered him bound to the Philistines, he took occasion to kill 1000 of them with the jaw-bone of an ass, vv. 9–17.

IV. From the distress he was then in for want of water, God took occasion to show him favor in a seasonable supply, vv. 18–20.

A detailed analysis of chapter

Samson is denied his wife. He kills the Philistines. (1–8)

Samson kills a thousand of the Philistines with a jaw-bone. (9–17)

His distress from thirst. (18–20)

Key verse

Verse 16: "And Samson said, With the jawbone of an ass, heaps upon heaps, with the jaw of an ass have I slain a thousand men."

Key word / key phrase

Verse 3, "get even with."

Key event / key person / key theme

Samson takes his revenge on the Philistines.

Key thought

Revenge never succeeds in pleasing God.

Key thing to look out for

Taking revenge usually only increases hatred between the opposing factions.

Key Bible cross-reference

Verse 15. See 3:31.

Key "by way of explanation"

Verse 19. God provided water for Samson just as he had for the Israelites in the desert.

Key "Quotable Quote"

"Let us learn humility from Christ, humiliation from David, and from Peter to cry over what has happened; but let us also learn to avoid the despair of Samson, Judas, and the wisest of men, Solomon."

Hesychois of Sinai

Judges 16

Matthew Henry's introduction

Samson's name (we have observed before) signifies a little sun (sol parvus); we have seen this sun rising very bright, and his morning ray strong and clear; and, nothing appearing to the contrary, we take it for granted that the middle of the day was proportionally illustrious, while he judged Israel twenty years; but the melancholy story of this chapter gives us such an account of his evening as did not commend his day. This little sun set under a cloud, and yet, just in the setting, darted forth one such strong and glorious beam as made him even then a type of Christ, conquering by death. Here is,

I. Samson greatly endangered by his familiarity with one harlot, and hardly escaping, vv. 1–3.

II. Samson quite ruined by his familiarity with another harlot, Delilah. Observe,

A. How he was betrayed to her by his own lusts, v. 4.

B. How he was betrayed by her to his sworn enemies, the Philistines, who,

By her means got it out of him at last where his great strength lay, vv. 5–17.

Then robbed him of his strength, by taking from his head the crown of his separation, vv. 18–20.

Then seized him, blinded him, imprisoned him, abused him, and, at a solemn festival, made a show of him, vv. 21–25.

But, lastly, he avenged himself of them by pulling down the theatre on their heads, and so dying with them, vv. 26–31.

A detailed analysis of chapter

Samson's escape from Gaza. (1–3)

Samson enticed to reveal the source of his strength. (4–17)

The Philistines take Samson, and put out his eyes. (18–21)

Samson's strength is renewed. (22–24)

He destroys many of the Philistines. (25–31)

Key verse

Verse 4: "And it came to pass afterward, that he loved a woman in the valley of Sorek, whose name was Delilah."

Key word / key phrase

Verse 15, "day after day."

Key event / key person / key theme

Samson and Delilah

Key thought

Not to know that God's Spirit had left Samson was a terrible state to have arrived at.

Key thing to look out for

Samson had great strengths and great weaknesses.

Key Bible cross-reference

Verse 21. See 1 Samuel 11:2; 2 Kings 25:7.

Key "by way of explanation"

Verses 19,20. From these verses it is clear that God was the source of Samson's strength.

Key "Quotable Quote"

"As Samson fell asleep in Delilah's lap, so many have fallen so fast asleep in the lap of prosperity, that they have never awaked till they have been in hell."

Thomas Watson

Judges 17

Matthew Henry's introduction

All agree that what is related in this and the rest of the chapters to the end of this book was not done, as the narrative occurs, after Samson, but long before, even soon after the death of Joshua, in the days of Phinehas the son of Eleazar, 20:28. But it is cast here into the latter part of the book that it might not interrupt the history of the Judges. That it might appear how happy the nation was in the judges it is here shown how unhappy they were when there was none.

I. Then idolatry began in the family of Micah, ch. 17.

II. Then it spread itself into the tribe of Dan, ch. 18.

III. Then villainy was committed in Gibeah of Benjamin, ch. 19.

IV. Then that whole tribe was destroyed for

countenancing it, ch. 20.

V. Then strange expedients were adopted to keep up that tribe, ch. 21. Therefore blessed be God for the government we are under! In this chapter we are told how Micah an Ephraimite furnished himself,

A. With an image for his god, vv. 1–6.

B. With a Levite, such a one as he was, for his priest, vv. 7–13.

A detailed analysis of chapter

The beginning of idolatry in Israel, Micah and his mother. (1–6)

Micah hires a Levite to be his priest. (7–13)

Key verse

Verse 5: "And the man Micah had an house of gods, and made an ephod, and teraphim, and consecrated one of his sons, who became his priest."

Key word / key phrase

Verse 6, "everyone did as he saw fit."

Key event / key person / key theme

Micah

Key thought

Modern forms of idolatry are easy to take on board.

Key thing to look out for

John told his readers, in the last verse of the last chapter of his first letter, to beware of idols.

Key Bible cross-reference

Verse 6. See 18:1; 19:1; 21:25.

Key "by way of explanation"

Verse 5. This verse indicates how low the Israelites had sunk. They made and worshiped idols.

Key "Quotable Quote"

"I confess Jesus Christ, the son of God, with my whole being. Those whom you call gods are idols; they are made by hands."

Alban, first British martyr

Judges 18

Matthew Henry's introduction

How idolatry crept into the family of Micah we read in the preceding chapter, how it was translated thence into the tribe of Dan we have an account in this chapter, and how it gained a settlement in a city of note; for how great a matter does a little fire kindle! The tribe of Dan had their lot assigned them last of all the tribes, and, it happening to be too strait for them, a considerable city in the utmost corner of Canaan northward was added to it. "Let them get it, and take it;" it was called Laish or Leshem, Josh. 19:47. Now here we are told,

I. How they sent spies to bring them an account of the place, who, by the way, got acquainted with Micah's priest, vv. 1–6.

II. What an encouraging report these spies brought back, vv. 7–10.

III. What forces were sent to conquer Laish, vv. 11–13.

IV. How they, by the way, plundered Micah of his gods, vv. 14–26.

V. How easily they conquered Laish (vv. 27–29), and, when they had it, set up the graven image in it, vv. 30, 31.

A detailed analysis of chapter

The Danites seek to enlarge their inheritance, and rob Micah. (1–31)

Key verse

Verse 31: "And they set them up Micah's graven image, which he made, all the time that the house of God was in Shiloh."

Key word / key phrase

Verse 1, "had no king."

Key event / key person / key theme

Micah and the tribe of Dan

Key thought

If a man is essentially evil he will do little good no matter how highly he is promoted.

Key thing to look out for

Evil can rule individuals as well as groups.

Key Bible cross-reference

Verse 31. See Joshua 18:1.

Key "by way of explanation"

Verse 31. Shiloh was eventually destroyed: see Psalm 78:60; Jeremiah 7:12,14; 26:6.

Key "Quotable Quote"

"Someone once asked Billy Graham, 'If Christianity is valid, why is there so much evil in the world?' Billy Graham replied, 'With so much soap, why are there so many dirty people in the world? Christianity, like soap, must be personally applied if it is to make a difference in our lives.'"

Billy Graham

Judges 19

Matthew Henry's introduction

The three remaining chapters of this book contain a most tragic story of the wickedness of the men of Gibeah, patronized by the tribe of Benjamin, for which that tribe was severely chastised and almost entirely cut off by the rest of the tribes. This seems to have been done not long after the death of Joshua, for it was when there was no king, no judge, in Israel (vv. 1, and 21:25), and Phinehas was then high priest, 20:28. These particular iniquities, the Danites' idolatry, and the Benjamites' immorality, let in that general apostasy, 3:7. The abuse of the Levite's concubine is here very particularly related.

I. Her adulterous elopement from him, vv. 1, 2.
II. His reconciliation to her, and the journey he took to fetch her home, v. 3.
III. Her father's kind entertainment of him, vv. 4–9.
IV. The abuse he met with at Gibeah, where, being benighted, he was forced to stop.
  A. He was neglected by the men of Gibeah (vv. 10–15) and entertained by an Ephraimite that sojourned among them, vv. 16–21.
  B. They set on him in his quarters, as the Sodomites did on Lot's quests, vv. 22–24.
  C. They villainously forced his concubine to death, vv. 25–28.

V. The course he took to send notice of this to all the tribes of Israel, vv. 29, 30.

A detailed analysis of chapter

The wickedness of the men of Gibeah. (1–30)

Key verse

Verse 1: "And it came to pass in those days, when there was no king in Israel, that there was a certain Levite sojourning on the side of mount Ephraim, who took to him a concubine out of Bethlehemjudah."

Key word / key phrase

Verse 23, "vile."

Key event / key person / key theme

A Levite and his concubine

Key thought

If God is left out of any society it is doomed.

Key thing to look out for

Without God men live like the animals in the jungle.

Key Bible cross-reference

Verse 14. See Hosea 9:9; 10:9.

Key "by way of explanation"

This chapter illustrates the moral degradation to which the Israelites had sunk.

Key "Quotable Quote"

"Back to the Bible or back to the jungle."

Luis Palau

Judges 20

Matthew Henry's introduction

Into the book of the wars of the Lord the story of this chapter must be brought, but it looks as sad and uncomfortable as any article in all that history; for there is nothing in it that looks in the least bright or pleasant but the pious zeal of Israel against the wickedness of the men of Gibeah, which made it on their side a just and holy war; but otherwise the obstinacy of the Benjamites in protecting their criminals, which was the foundation of the war, the vast loss which the Israelites sustained in carrying on the war, and (though the righteous cause was victorious at last) the issuing of the war in the almost utter extirpation of the tribe of Benjamin, make it, from first to last, melancholy. And yet this happened soon after the glorious settlement of Israel in the land of promise, on which one would have expected every thing to be prosperous and serene. In this chapter we have,

I. The Levite's cause heard in a general convention of the tribes, vv. 1–7.

II. A unanimous resolve to avenge his quarrel on the men of Gibeah, vv. 8–11.

III. The Benjamites appearing in defense of the criminals, vv. 12–17.

IV. The defeat of Israel in the first and second day's battle, vv. 18–25.

V. Their humbling themselves before God on that occasion, vv. 26–28.

VI. The total rout they gave the Benjamites in the third engagement, by a stratagem, by which they were all cut off, except 600 men, vv. 29–48. And all this the effect of the indignities done to one poor Levite and his wife; so little do those that do iniquity consider what will be the end thereof.

A detailed analysis of chapter

The tribe of Benjamin nearly wiped out. (1–48)

Key verse

Verse 1: "Then all the children of Israel went out, and the congregation was gathered together as one man, from Dan even to Beersheba, with the land of Gilead, unto the LORD in Mizpeh."

Key word / key phrase

Verse 18, "enquired of God."

Key event / key person / key theme

War against the Benjamites

Key thought

All wrongs may not be put right in our lifetime.

Key thing to look out for

In heaven there will not be room for any injustice.

Key Bible cross-reference

Verse 16. See 3:15; 1 Samuel 17:49.

Key "by way of explanation"

Verse 1. Speaking about "Dan to Beersheba" was a way of referring to the whole of the country, from its northern tip to its most southerly point.

Key "Quotable Quote"

"Christianity is a warfare, and Christians are spiritual soldiers."

Robert Southwell

Judges 21

Matthew Henry's introduction

The ruins of the tribe of Benjamin we read of in the previous chapter; now here we have,

I. The lamentation which Israel made over these ruins, vv. 1–4, 6, 15.

II. The provision they made for the repair of them out of the 600 men that escaped, for whom they procured wives,

A. Of the virgins of Jabesh-Gilead, when they destroyed that city for not sending its forces to the general rendezvous, vv. 5, 7–14.

B. Of the daughters of Shiloh, vv. 16–25. And so this melancholy story concludes.

A detailed analysis of chapter

The Israelites mourn for the Benjamites. (1–25)

Key verse

Verse 25: "In those days there was no king in Israel: every man did that which was right in his own eyes."

Key word / key phrase

Verse 25, "as he saw fit."

Key event / key person / key theme

Wives for the tribe of Benjamin

Key thought

Evil may be eradicated but it often leaves a terrible legacy.

Key thing to look out for

The fight against evil never stops.

Key Bible cross-reference

Verse 2. See 20:18, 26, 27.

Key "by way of explanation"

Verse 25. The last verse of this book shows how rudderless the Israelites were. They should have been satisfied with God as their ruler.

Key "Quotable Quote"

"Christianity introduced no new forms of government, but a new spirit, which totally transformed the old ones."

John E.E D. Acton

5. Select bibliography for Judges

Bowling, Andrew C. "Judges." *Evangelical Commentary on the Bible.* Edited by Walter A. Elwell. Grand Rapids: Baker, 1989.

Cundall, Arthur E., and Morris, Leon. *Judges, Ruth*. Chicago: InterVarsity, 1968.

Faussett, Andrew R. *Judges* (Geneva), Banner of Truth, 1999.

Keil, C. F., and Delitzsch, F. *Joshua, Judges, Ruth.* KD. 1887. Reprint. Grand Rapids: Eerdmans, 1950.

Ruth

1. Book by book: Introduction to Ruth

Introduction

Ruth may be accurately viewed as a supplement to the preceding book, to which, in fact, it was appended in the ancient Jewish canon. Although it relates an episode belonging to the time of the Judges, its precise date is unknown. It appears certain, however, that it could not have been written prior to the time of Samuel (see Ruth 4:17–22), who is generally supposed to have been its author; and this opinion, in addition to other reasons on which it rests, is confirmed by Ruth 4:7, where it is evident that the history was not compiled till long after the transactions recorded. The inspiration and canonical authority of the book is attested by the fact of Ruth's name being inserted by Matthew in the Savior's genealogy (Matthew 1:5).

Robert Jamieson

Contents of Ruth

The book of Ruth is set in the time of the Judges. It shows how Jesus the Messiah had a non-Jew, Ruth, in his ancestral family.

Ruth Goes with Naomi to Bethlehem. Ch. 1.

In the time of the judges Elimelech emigrated from Bethlehem in Judah into the land of Moab, along with his wife Naomi, and his two sons Mahlon and Chilion, because of a famine in the land (vv. 1, 2).

There Elimelech died; and his two sons married Moabitish women, named Orpah and Ruth. But in the course of ten years they also died, so that Naomi and her two daughters-in-law were left by themselves (vv. 3–5). When Naomi heard that the Lord had once more blessed the land of Israel with bread, she set out with Orpah and Ruth to return home. But on the way she entreated them to turn back and remain with their relations in their own land; and Orpah did so (vv. 6–14). But Ruth declared that she would not leave her mother-in-law, and went with her to Bethlehem (vv. 15–22).

Ruth Gleans in the Field of Boaz. Ch. 2.

Ruth went to the field to glean ears of corn, for the purpose of procuring support for herself and her mother-in-law, and came by chance to the field of Boaz, a relative of Naomi, who, when he heard that she had come with Naomi from Moabitis, spoke kindly to her, and gave her permission not only to glean ears in his field and even among the sheaves, but to appease her hunger and thirst with the food and drink of his reapers (vv. 1–16), so that in the evening she returned to her mother-in-law with a plentiful gleaning, and told her of the gracious reception she had met with from this man, and then learned from her that Boaz was a relation of her own (vv. 17–23).

Ruth Seeks for Marriage with Boaz. Ch. 3.

After the harvest Naomi advised Ruth to visit Boaz on a certain night, and ask him to marry her as redeemer (vv. 1–5). Ruth followed this advice, and Boaz promised to fulfill her request, provided the nearer redeemer who was still living would not perform this duty (vv. 6–13), and sent her away in the morning with a present of wheat, that she might not return empty to her mother-in-law (vv. 14–18).

Boaz Marries Ruth. Ch. 4.

To redeem the promise he had given to Ruth, Boaz went the next morning to the gate of the city, and calling to the nearer redeemer as he passed by, asked him, before the elders of the city, to redeem the piece of land which belonged to Elimelech and had been sold by Naomi; and if he did this, at the same time to marry Ruth, to establish the name of the deceased on his inheritance (vv. 1–5). But as he renounced the right of redemption on account of the condition attached to the redemption of the field, Boaz undertook the redemption before the assembled people, together with the obligation to marry Ruth (vv. 6–12). The marriage was blessed with a son, who became the father of Jesse, the father of David (vv. 13–17). The book closes with a genealogical proof of the descent of David from Perez (vv. 18–22).

C. F. Keil and F. Delitzsch

Detailed outline

I. Moab: 1:1–5

A. Journey to Moab: 1:1–2

1. When the story occurs: 1:1

2. Why they went to Moab: 1:1

3. Introduction of the family: 1:2

B. Tragedy in Moab: 1:3–5

1. Naomi's husband dies: 1:3

2.Naomi's sons marry 1:4

3. Naomi's sons die: 1:5

II. Return to Bethlehem: 1:6–18

A. Naomi plans to return: 1:6–9

B. Their appeal to stay: 1:10
C. Naomi's answer: 1:11–13
D. Their response: 1:14
E. Ruth's declaration: 1:16–18
1. She does not want to leave Naomi: 1:16
2. She will go where Naomi goes: 1:16
3. She will live where Naomi lives: 1:16
4. Naomi's people shall be hers: 1:16
5. Naomi's God shall be her God: 1:16
6. She will remain faithful to death: 1:17

III. Arrival in Bethlehem: 1:19–22
A. Reception by the city: 1:19
B. Naomi's response: 1:20–21
C. The timing of the return: 1:22

IV. Ruth in the fields of Boaz: 2:1–17
A. Gleaning in the fields: 2:1–3
B. Boaz's recognition: 2:4–13
C. Mealtime with Boaz: 2:14
D. Gleaning the best: 2:15–17
E. Return from the fields: 2:18–23

V. A special plan: 3:1–18
A. Naomi's plan: 3:1–5
B. The results: 3:6–15
C. The return to Naomi: 3:16–18

VI. The redemption: 4:1–13
A. The process: 4:1–12
B. The union of Ruth and Boaz: 4:13–17
C. The blessing: 4:14–16

VII. David's genealogy: 4:17–22

2. Helpful summaries of Ruth

Bird's eye view

The account of how a Gentile woman became the ancestor of David and Jesus.

Reading plan

The following reading plan, taking one reading per day, enables you to read through Ruth in two days.

Ruth 1–2

Ruth 3–4

Verse to memorize

Ruth 1:16

But Ruth replied, "Don't urge me to leave you or to turn back from you. Where you go I will go, and where you stay I will stay. Your people will be my people and your God my God."

Statistics

Eighth Old Testament book

4 chapters

85 verses

2,578 words

The book of Ruth is one of only two Bible books written by a woman (the other one being the book of Esther).

Names/titles given

Hebrew title: *Ruth*: from the Hebrew word *reuit* which means "friendship."

Greek title in Septuagint: *Routh*.

Latin title in Vulgate: *Ruth*.

3. Helpful keys to turn to in understanding Ruth

Key word/words

Goel, Kinsman-Redeemer, 13 times

Key /verses

Ruth 1:16; 4:14

Themes to study

Human loyalty

God's providential care

Key people/events

Naomi

Ruth

Boaz

Obed

Jesus in Ruth

In Ruth Jesus is our Kinsman-Redeemer, *goel*.

Lessons to learn from Ruth

- Never despise giving or receiving practical help.
- God overrules in our lives, even when we are unaware of it.

4. Chapter by chapter: outline of every chapter of Ruth

Ruth 1

Matthew Henry's introduction

In this chapter we have Naomi's afflictions.

I. As a distressed housekeeper, forced by famine to remove into the land of Moab, vv. 1, 2.

II. As a mournful widow and mother, bewailing the death of her husband and her two sons, vv. 3–5.

III. As a careful mother-in-law, desirous to be kind to her two daughters, but at a loss how to be so when she returns to her own country, vv. 6–13. Orpah she parts with in sorrow, v. 14. Ruth she takes with her in fear, vv. 15–18.

IV. As a poor woman sent back to the place of her first settlement, to be supported by the kindness of her friends, vv. 19–22. All these things were melancholy and seemed against her, and yet all were working for good.

A detailed analysis of chapter

Elimelech and his sons die in the land of Moab. (1–5)

Naomi returns home. (6–14)

Orpah stays behind, but Ruth goes with Naomi. (15–18)

They come to Bethlehem. (19–22)

Key verse

Verse 16: "And Ruth said, Entreat me not to leave thee, or to return from following after thee: for whither thou goest, I will go; and where thou lodgest, I will lodge: thy people shall be my people, and thy God my God."

Key word / key phrase

Verse 2, "Naomi."

Key event / key person / key theme

Tragedy wiping out Naomi's family

Key thought

Ruth was not an Israelite.

Key thing to look out for

Ruth's selflessness was amazing.

Key Bible cross-reference

Verse 22. See 2:2,6,21; 4:5,10.

Key "by way of explanation"

Verse 1. This account of Ruth's life is set in the time of the judges.

Key "Quotable Quote"

"Set a high value on spontaneous kindness."

Samuel Johnson

Ruth 2

Matthew Henry's introduction

There is scarcely any chapter in all the sacred history that stoops so low as this to take cognizance of so mean a person as Ruth, a poor Moabitish widow, so mean an action as her gleaning corn in a neighbor's field, and the minute circumstances thereof. But all this was in order to her being grafted into the line of Christ and taken in among his ancestors, that she might be a figure of the espousals of the Gentile church to Christ, Is. 54:1. This makes the story remarkable; and many of the passages of it are instructive and very improvable. Here we have,

I. Ruth's humility and industry in gleaming corn, Providence directing her to Boaz's field, vv. 1–3.

II. The great favor which Boaz showed to her in many instances, vv. 4–16.

III. The return of Ruth to her mother-in-law, vv. 18–23.

A detailed analysis of chapter

Ruth gleans in the field of Boaz. (1–3)

The kindness of Boaz to Ruth. (4–16)

Ruth returns to her mother-in-law. (17–23)

Key verse

Verse 12: "The LORD recompense thy work, and a full reward be given thee of the LORD God of Israel, under whose wings thou art come to trust."

Key word / key phrase

Verse 20, "kindness."

Key event / key person / key theme

Ruth works in Boaz's field

Key thought

There is no such thing as a "chance" meeting.

Key thing to look out for

God can bring hope out of every desperate situation.

Key Bible cross-reference

Verse 1. See Matthew 1:5; Luke 3:32.

Key "by way of explanation"

Verse 20, "kinsman-redeemers." Such people could redeem a slave who had been sold into slavery or redeem land that a poor relative had been forced to sell.

Key "Quotable Quote"

"No creature that deserved redemption would need to be redeemed."

C.S. Lewis

Ruth 3

Matthew Henry's introduction

We found it very easy, in the previous chapter, to applaud the decency of Ruth's behavior, and to show what good use we may make of the account given us of it; but in this chapter we shall have much ado to vindicate it from the imputation of indecency, and to save it from having an ill use made of it; but the goodness of those times was such as saved what is recorded here from being ill done, and yet the badness of these times is such as that it will not justify any now in doing the like. Here is,

I. The directions Naomi gave to her daughter-in-law how to claim Boaz for her husband, vv. 1–5.

II. Ruth's punctual observance of those directions, vv. 6, 7.

III. The kind and honorable treatment Boaz gave her, vv. 8–15.

IV. Her return to her mother-in-law, vv. 16–18.

A detailed analysis of chapter

The directions given to Ruth by Naomi. (1–5)

Boaz acknowledges the duty of a kinsman. (6–13)

Ruth's return to her mother-in-law. (14–18)

Key verse

Verse 13: "Tarry this night, and it shall be in the morning, that if he will perform unto thee the part of a kinsman, well; let him do the kinsman's part: but if he will not do the part of a kinsman to thee, then will I do the part of a kinsman to thee, as the LORD liveth: lie down until the morning."

Key word / key phrase

Verse 9, "kinsman-redeemer."

Key event / key person / key theme

Ruth finds a husband.

Key thought

Ruth had never dreamed that she would find a husband in the foreign land of her mother-in-law.

Key thing to look out for

God's loving care for those who trust him.

Key Bible cross-reference

Verse 3. See Isaiah 9:3; 16:9,10.

Key "by way of explanation"

Verse 9. This was probably an indirect way of asking someone to marry you. See Ezekiel 38:13–30.

Key "Quotable Quote"

"God moves in a mysterious way
his wonders to perform;
he plants his footsteps in the sea
And rides upon the storm."

William Cowper

Ruth 4

Matthew Henry's introduction

In this chapter we have the wedding between Boaz and Ruth, in the circumstances of which there was something uncommon, which is kept on record for the illustration, not only of the law about the marrying of a brother's widow (Deut. 25:5, etc.), for cases help to expound laws, but of the gospel too, for from this marriage descended David, and the Son of David, whose espousals to the Gentile church were hereby typified. We are here told,

I. How Boaz got clear of his rival, and fairly shook him off, vv. 1–8.

II. How his marriage with Ruth was publicly solemnized, and attended with the good wishes of his neighbors, vv. 9–12.

III. The happy issue that descended from this marriage, Obed, the grandfather of David, vv. 13–17. And so the book concludes with the pedigree of David, vv. 18–22. Perhaps it was to oblige him that the blessed Spirit directed the inserting of this story in the sacred canon, he being desirous that the virtues of his great-grandmother Ruth, together with her Gentile extraction and the singular providences that attended her, should be transmitted to posterity.

A detailed analysis of chapter

The kinsman refuses to redeem Ruth's inheritance. (1–8)

Boaz marries Ruth. (9–12)

Birth of Obed. (13–22)

Key verse

Verse 22: "And Obed begat Jesse, and Jesse begat David."

Key word / key phrase

Verse 13, "wife."

Key event / key person / key theme

Boaz marries Ruth.

Key thought

God's providence is clear throughout these chapters.

Key thing to look out for

The book ends with the most amazing genealogy.

Key Bible cross-reference

Verses 18–22. See Matthew 1:3–6; Luke 3:31–33.

Key "by way of explanation"

Verses 18–22. Business was conducted at the town gate.

Key "Quotable Quote"

"Man proposes, but God disposes."

Thomas à Kempis

5. Select bibliography for Ruth

Atkinson, David, *The Message of Ruth: The Wings of Refuge* (The Bible Speaks Today), InterVarsity, 1983.

Hubbard Robert L. Jr., *The Book of Ruth* (NICOT), Eerdmans, 1989.

Keil, C. F., and F. Delitzsch, *Biblical Commentary on the Old Testament: Joshua, Judges, Ruth*. Reprint edition. Translated by James Martin. Grand Rapids: Eerdmans, 1956.

1 and 2 Samuel

1. Book by book: Introduction to 1 and 2 Samuel

Introduction

These two books were, by the ancient Jews, linked so that they made one book, and in that form could be called the Book of Samuel with more propriety than now, the second being wholly occupied with the relation of transactions that did not take place till after the death of that eminent judge. Accordingly, in the Septuagint and the Vulgate, it is called the First and Second Books of Kings. The early portion of the First Book, down to the end of the twenty-fourth chapter, was probably written by Samuel; while the rest of it and the whole of the Second, are commonly ascribed to Nathan and Gad, founding the opinion on 1 Chronicles 29:29. Commentators, however, are divided about this, some supposing that the statements in 1 Samuel 2:26; 3:1, indicate the hand of the judge himself, or a contemporary; while some think, from 1 Samuel 6:18; 12:5; 27:6, that its composition must be referred to a later age. It is probable, however, that these supposed marks of an after-period were interpolations of Ezra. This uncertainty, however, as to the authorship does not affect the inspired authority of the book, which is indisputable, being quoted in the New Testament (1 Samuel 13:14 in Acts 13:22, and 2 Samuel 7:14 in Hebrews 1:5), as well as in many of the Psalms.

Robert Jamieson

Contents of 1 and 2 Samuel

1 Samuel gives selected stories about the lives of Samuel, Saul, and David.

2 Samuel is just about King David.

The narrative of the two Books of Samuel covers a period of about a hundred years, from the close of the unsettled era of the Judges to the establishment and consolidation of the kingdom under David. It is therefore a record of the changes, national and constitutional, which accompanied this growth and development of the national life, at the close of which the Israelites found themselves a united people under the rule of a king to whom all owed allegiance, controlled and guided by more or less definitely established institutions and laws. This may be described as the general purpose and main theme of the books, to trace the advance of the people under divine guidance to a state of settled prosperity and union in the promised land, and to give prominence to theocratic rule which was the essential condition of Israel's life as the people of God under all the changing forms of early government. The narrative therefore centers itself around the lives of the three men, Samuel, Saul and David, who were chiefly instrumental in the establishment of the monarchy, and to whom it was due more than to any others that Israel emerged from the depressed and disunited state in which the tribes had remained during the period of the rule of the Judges, and came into possession of a combined and effective national life. If the formal separation therefore into two books be disregarded, the history of Israel as it is narrated in "Samuel" is most naturally divided into three parts, which are followed by an appendix recording words and incidents which for some reason had not found a place in the general narrative:

A. The life and rule of Samuel (1 Samuel 1–15) (death 1 Samuel 25:1).

B. The life, reign and death of Saul (1 Samuel 16–2 Samuel 1).

C. The reign and acts of David to the suppression of the two rebellions of Absalom and Sheba (2 Samuel 2–20).

D. Appendix; other incidents in the reign of David, the names of his chief warriors and his So or Psalm of Praise (2 Samuel 21–24).

Orr, James, M.A., D.D. General Editor, International Standard Bible Encyclopedia

Detailed outline of 1 Samuel

I. Samuel: The last of the judges: 1:1–7:17
- A. Samuel's birth and childhood: 1:1–2:10
- B. Eli's rejection and Samuel's call: 2:11–3:21
- C. The ark among the Philistines: 4:1–7:1
- D. Samuel's activities as judge: 7:2–17

II. Saul: The first of the kings: 8:1–15:35
- A. Israel's demand for a king: 8:1–22
- B. The choice of Saul: 9:1–11:15
- C. Samuel's farewell address: 12:1–25
- D. Saul's war against the Philistines: 13:1–14:52
- E. Saul's disobedience and rejection: 15:1–35

III. Saul and David: 16:1–31:13
- A. David's anointing and call: 16:1–23
- B. David's victory over Goliath: 17:1–58
- C. David's flight from Saul: 18:1–20:42
- D. David's wanderings: 21:1–30:31
- E. Saul's death: 31:1–13

Detailed outline of 2 Samuel

I. The triumphs of David: 1:1–10:19
- A. The lament of David over Saul and Jonathan: 1:1–27
- B. David's coronation over Judah: 2:1–7
- C. David establishes national and religious unity: 2:8–6:23
- D. The Davidic covenant: 7:1–29
- E. David's conquests: 8:1–10:19

II. The troubles of David: 11:1–24:25
- A. David's sin and repentance: 11:1–12:31
- B. Amnon and Absalom's crimes: 13:1–18:33
- C. David's restoration to power: 19:1–20:26
- D. The famine and revenge of the Gibeonites: 21:1–14
- E. Heroes in the war with the Philistines: 21:15–22
- F. David's song and last words: 22:1–23:7
- G. David's heroes: 23:8–39
- H. David's census and punishment: 24:1–25

2. Helpful summaries of 1 and 2 Samuel

Bird's eye view

I Samuel outlines the lives of Samuel, David, and Saul; while 2 Samuel concentrates only on King David.

Reading plan

The following reading plan, taking one reading per day, enables you to read through 1 and 2 Samuel in twenty-three days.

1 Samuel 1–3
1 Samuel 4–6
1 Samuel 7–9
1 Samuel 10–12
1 Samuel 13–14
1 Samuel 15–16
1 Samuel 17
1 Samuel 18–19
1 Samuel 20–22
1 Samuel 23–24
1 Samuel 25–26
1 Samuel 27–29
1 Samuel 30–31
2 Samuel 1–3
2 Samuel 4–6
2 Samuel 7–10
2 Samuel 11–12
2 Samuel 13–14
2 Samuel 15–16
2 Samuel 17–18
2 Samuel 19–20
2 Samuel 21–22
2 Samuel 23–24

Verses to memorize

1 Samuel 2:2

There is no one holy like the Lord, there is no one besides you; there is no Rock like our God.

1 Samuel 16:7

But the Lord said to Samuel, "Do not consider his appearance or his height, for I have rejected him. The Lord does not look at the things man looks at. Man looks at the outward appearance, but the Lord looks at the heart."

2 Samuel 22:7

In my distress I called to the Lord; I called out to my God. From his temple he heard my voice; my cry came to his ears.

2 Samuel 22:33–34

God is my strength and power; and he maketh my way perfect. He maketh my feet like hinds' feet; and setteth me on my high places. kjv

Statistics

1 Samuel

Ninth Old Testament book
31 chapters
810 verses
25,061 words

2 Samuel

Tenth Old Testament book
24 chapters
695 verses
20,612 words

Famous sayings found in 1 Samuel

"How are the mighty fallen" 1 Samuel 1:19–27
"A man after his own heart" 1 Samuel 13:14

Names/titles given

Hebrew title: "The book of Samuel," referring to a single book which included 1 Samuel and 2 Samuel.

Greek title in Septuagint: *Bibloi Basileion:* "Books of Kingdoms," as the Septuagint split the single Hebrew book into the two books of 1 Samuel and 2 Samuel. The "kingdoms" refer to the later kingdoms of Israel and Judah.

Basileion Alpha: "First kingdoms," refers to 1 Samuel.

Basileion Beta: 2 Samuel is called the "Second kingdom."

Latin title in Vulgate: *Libri Regum:* "Book of Kings." This title applied to 1 and 2 Samuel, and to 1 and 2 Kings.

Liber 1 Samuelis, was a later title adopted by the Latin Bible, combining the Hebrew title and the Latin titles, giving us, "First book of Samuel/First Samuel."

Liber II Samuelis: "Second book of Samuel/Second Samuel."

3. Helpful keys to turn to in understanding 1 and 2 Samuel

Key words

1 Samuel

King/kingdom

Prayed

2 Samuel

King

Key verses

1 Samuel 10:25; 13:14

2 Samuel 7:12–13; 5:12

Themes to study

1 Samuel

- Praising God
- Using one's spiritual gifts
- Principles about serving God
- Paths deviating from God's law which brought trouble:
- Polygamy, 1 Samuel 1:6
- Indulgence of parents, 1 Samuel 2:22–25; 8:1– 5
- Trusting sacred objects, 1 Samuel 4:3
- Impatience, 1 Samuel 13:8–9
- Disobedience, 1 Samuel chapter 15

2 Samuel

- The Lord's holiness
- Human unfaithfulness

1 Samuel quoted in the New Testament

A man after my heart

1 Sam. 13:14 quoted in Acts 13:22

2 Samuel quoted in the New Testament

I will be to him a father

2 Sam. 7:14 quoted in 2 Cor. 6:18 and Heb. 1:5.

I will give praise unto thee among the Gentiles

2 Sam. 22:50 quoted in Rom. 15:9

Unusual events and miracles in 1 Samuel

- Dagon falling on its face before the Ark
- Plague of tumors on the Philistines, 6:1–12
- The men of Beth-shemesh struck down for looking into the ark, 6:19
- A thunderstorm causing confusion among

the Philistine army, 7:9–13

- Thunder and rain during harvest time, 12:16–19
- David's successful use of his sling against the giant Goliath

Unusual events and miracles in 2 Samuel

Uzzah struck down, 6:7

Results of five departures from God's law in 1 Samuel

Polygamy, 1:6

Bad parenting, 2:22–25

Faith in idols, 4:3

Being impatient, 13:8–9

Less than total obedience, chapter 15

Key people/events

1 Samuel

Hannah

Samuel

Elkanah

Penninah

Eli

Hophni

Phineas

The Ark and the Philistines

Saul

Jonathan

Agag

David

Goliath

Michal

Ahimelech

Abiathar

Doeg

Abigail

Nabal

Gad

Achish

Abner

Ishbaal

Joab

Hebron

2 Samuel

Rechab and Baanah

Jerusalem

Uzzah

Bathsheba

Uriah

Nathan

Solomon

Tamar

Absalom

Story of Absalom's rebellion

Ahithophel

Mephibosheth

Rizpah

David's census

Jesus in 1 and 2 Samuel

In 1 and 2 Samuel Jesus is our King.

Types of Jesus in 1 and 2 Samuel

- The life of David is the greatest type of Jesus in the Old Testament. See Rom. 1:3; Rev. 22:16.
- The Lord's covenant with David, 2 Samuel 7:4–17, looks forward to Jesus the king.

Lessons to learn from 1 and 2 Samuel

1 Samuel

- It is God's will that we should pray to him.
- Praying for others is a Christian ministry.
- Being right with God should be our number one priority.

2 Samuel

- Discipline is required in families.
- It is normal for Christians to be tempted.

4. Chapter by chapter: outline of every chapter of 1 and 2 Samuel

1 Samuel 1

Matthew Henry's introduction

The history of Samuel here begins as early as that of Samson did, even before he was born, as afterwards the history of John the Baptist and our blessed Savior. Some of the scripture-worthies drop out of the clouds, as it were, and their first appearance is in their full growth and luster. But others are accounted for from the birth, and from the womb, and from the conception. What God says of the prophet Jeremiah is true of all: "Before I formed thee in the belly I knew thee," Jer. 1:5. But some great men were brought into the world with more observation than others, and were more early distinguished from common people, as Samuel for one. God, in this matter, acts as a free agent. The story of Samson introduces him as a child of promise, Judg. 13. But the story of Samuel introduces him as a child of prayer. Samson's birth was foretold by an angel to his mother; Samuel was asked of God by his mother. Both together intimate what wonders are produced by the word and prayer. Samuel's mother was Hannah, the principal person concerned in the story of this chapter.

I. Here is her affliction—she was childless, and this affliction aggravated by her rival's insolence, but in some measure balanced by her husband's kindness, vv. 1–8.

II. The prayer and vow she made to God under this affliction, in which Eli the high priest at first censured her, but afterwards encouraged her, vv. 9–18.

III. The birth and nursing of Samuel, vv. 19–23.

IV. The presenting of him to the Lord, vv. 24–28.

A detailed analysis of chapter

Elkanah and his family. (1–8)

Hannah's prayer. (9–18)

Samuel, Hannah presents him to the Lord. (19–28)

Key verse

Verse 11: "And she vowed a vow, and said, O LORD of hosts, if thou wilt indeed look on the affliction of thine handmaid, and remember me, and not forget thine handmaid, but wilt give unto thine handmaid a man child, then I will give him unto the LORD all the days of his life, and there shall no razor come upon his head."

Key word / key phrase

Verse 10, "Hannah wept and prayed."

Key event / key person / key theme

The birth of Samuel

Key thought

Here is another example of God's power to do the seemingly impossible.

Key thing to look out for

Hannah's response to suffering and to blessing.

Key Bible cross-reference

Verse 21. See Leviticus 7:16; Psalm 50:14.

Key "by way of explanation"

Verse 3. At "Shiloh" the ark of the covenant was kept. See Joshua 18:1; Judges 21:19.

Key "Quotable Quote"

"*Nil sine Numine*, Nothing without providence."

Motto of the State of Colorado

1 Samuel 2

Matthew Henry's introduction

In this chapter we have,

I. Hannah's song of thanksgiving to God for his favor to her in giving her Samuel, vv. 1–10.

II. Their return to their family, with Eli's blessing, vv. 11, 20. The increase of their family, v. 21. Samuel's growth and improvement (vv. 11, 18, 21, 26), and the care Hannah took to clothe him, v. 19.

III. The great wickedness of Eli's sons, vv. 12–17, 22.

IV. The over-mild reproof that Eli gave them for it, vv. 23–25.

V. The justly dreadful message God sent him by a prophet, threatening the ruin of his family for the wickedness of his sons, vv. 27–36.

A detailed analysis of chapter

Hannah's song of thanksgiving. (1–10)

The wickedness of Eli's sons, Samuel's ministry. (11–26)

The prophecy against Eli's family. (27–36)

Key verse

Verse 1: "And Hannah prayed, and said, My heart rejoiceth in the LORD, mine horn is exalted in the LORD: my mouth is enlarged over mine enemies; because I rejoice in thy salvation."

Key word / key phrase

Verse 1, "prayed."

Key event / key person / key theme

Hannah's prayer

Key thought

Hannah began her prayer by rejoicing in the Lord.

Key thing to look out for

Hannah's reasons for praising God.

Key Bible cross-reference

Verse 1. See Psalm 72:20.

Key "by way of explanation"

Verse 1. As there are a number of similarities between this prayer and that of Mary's, see Luke 1:46–55, it is unsurprising that it has been called the "Magnificat of the Old Testament."

Key "Quotable Quote"

"You can do more than pray after you've prayed, but you cannot do more than pray until you have prayed."

John Bunyan

1 Samuel 3

Matthew Henry's introduction

In the previous chapter we had Samuel a young priest, though by birth a Levite only, for he ministered before the Lord in a linen ephod; in this chapter we have him a young prophet, which was more, God in an extraordinary manner revealing himself to him, and in him reviving, if not commencing, prophecy in Israel. Here is,

I. God's first manifestation of himself in an extraordinary manner to Samuel, vv. 1–10.

II. The message he sent by him to Eli, vv. 11–14.

III. The faithful delivery of that message to Eli, and his submission to the righteousness of God in it, vv. 15–18.

IV. The establishment of Samuel to be a prophet in Israel, vv. 19–21.

A detailed analysis of chapter

The word of the Lord first revealed to Samuel. (1–10)

God tells Samuel about the destruction of Eli's house. (11–18)

Samuel established to be a prophet. (19–21)

Key verse

Verse 10: "And the LORD came, and stood, and called as at other times, Samuel, Samuel. Then Samuel answered, Speak; for thy servant heareth."

Key word / key phrase

Verse 1, "the word of the Lord was rare."

Key event / key person / key theme

Samuel's call

Key thought

God's call often goes unrecognized and is more often recognized, than followed.

Key thing to look out for

Verses 12,13. The judgment against Eli's family did not come without prior warning.

Key Bible cross-reference

Verse 3. See Exodus 27:20,21; 30:7,8.

Key "by way of explanation"

Verse 1. Throughout the period of the judges the word of the Lord did appear to be "rare" as we only know of two prophets. See Judges 4:4; 6:8.

Key "Quotable Quote"

"Christian spirituality begins with listening to God call us, heal us, forgive us."

Eugene H. Peterson

1 Samuel 4

Matthew Henry's introduction

The predictions in the previous chapters about the ruin of Eli's house here begin to be fulfilled; how long after does not appear, but certainly not long. Such sinners God often makes quick work with. Here is,

I. The disgrace and loss Israel sustained in an encounter with the Philistines, vv. 1, 2.

II. Their foolish project to fortify themselves by bringing the ark of God into their camp on the shoulders of Hophni and Phinehas (vv. 3, 4), which made them secure (v. 5) and struck a fear into the Philistines, but such a fear as roused them, vv. 6–9.

III. The fatal consequences of it: Israel was beaten, and the ark taken prisoner, vv. 10, 11.

IV. The tidings of this brought to Shiloh, and the sad reception of those tidings.
- A. The city was put into confusion, vv. 12, 13.
- B. Eli fainted away, fell, and broke his neck, vv. 14–18.
- C. On hearing what had occurred his daughter-in-law fell in labor, bore a son, but died immediately, vv. 19–22. These were the things which would make the ears of those that heard them to tingle.

A detailed analysis of chapter

The Israelites overcome by the Philistines. (1–9)
The ark taken. (10,11)
The death of Eli. (12–18)
The birth of Ichabod. (19–22)

Key verse

Verse 11: "And the ark of God was taken."

Key word / key phrase

Verse 2, "defeated."

Key event / key person / key theme

The death of Eli

Key thought

Eli's children did not follow in the ways of their godly father.

Key thing to look out for

Eli must take some of the blame for his wayward children.

Key Bible cross-reference

Verse 12. This describes signs of grief and mourning. See Joshua 7:6; 2 Samuel 1:2.

Key "by way of explanation"

Verse 18. The death of Eli brings an era to a close. See Joshua 24:29, 31; 2 Samuel 7:11.

Key "Quotable Quote"

"People who really want help may attack you if you help them. Help them anyway."

Mother Teresa of Calcutta

1 Samuel 5

Matthew Henry's introduction

We are told in this chapter,

I. How the Philistines triumphed over the ark (vv. 1, 2), and,

II. How the ark triumphed over the Philistines,
- A. Over Dagon their god, vv. 3–5.
- B. Over the Philistines themselves, who were sorely plagued with tumors, and made weary of the ark; the men of Ashdod first (vv. 6, 7), then the men of Gath (vv. 8, 9), and lastly those of Ekron, which forced them at length on a resolution to send the ark back to the land of Israel; for when God judgeth he will overcome.

A detailed analysis of chapter

Dagon is broken before the ark. (1–5)
The Philistine killed. (6–12)

Key verse

Verse 4: "Dagon was fallen upon his face to the ground before the ark of the LORD."

Key word / key phrase

Verse 1, "ark."

Key event / key person / key theme

The ark with the Philistines

Key thought

God is stronger than evil.

Key thing to look out for

If God is against us it does not matter who is for us.

Key Bible cross-reference

Verse 2. See Judges 16:21,23,26.

Key "by way of explanation"

Verse 6. God would not allow the Philistines to think that their capture of the ark meant that they had power over the Israelites.

Key "Quotable Quote"

"Power is never good, unless the one who has it is good."

King Alfred

1 Samuel 6

Matthew Henry's introduction

In this chapter we have the return of the ark to the land of Israel, whither we are now gladly to attend it, and observe,

I. How the Philistines dismissed it, by the advice of their priests (vv. 1–11), with rich presents to the God of Israel, to make an atonement for their sin (vv. 3–5), and yet with a project to bring it back, unless Providence directed the kine, contrary to their inclination, to go to the land of Israel, vv. 8, 9.

II. How the Israelites entertained it.

A. With great joy and sacrifices of praise, vv. 12–18.

B. With an over-bold curiosity to look into it, for which many of them were struck dead, the terror of which moved them to send it forward to another city, vv. 19–21.

A detailed analysis of chapter

The Philistines decide to send back the ark. (1–9)

They bring it to Bethshemesh. (10–18)

The people killed for looking into the ark. (19–21)

Key verse

Verse 1: "And the ark of the LORD was in the country of the Philistines seven months."

Key word / key phrase

Verse 20, "the presence of the Lord."

Key event / key person / key theme

The ark is returned to Israel

Key thought

What if God still punished us today for our irreverence, as he did in verse 19?

Key thing to look out for

Even non-believers have consciences and often know when they have done wrong.

Key Bible cross-reference

Verse 2. See Deuteronomy 18:10; Isaiah 2:6; Ezekiel 21:21.

Key "by way of explanation"

Verse 6. God's action among the Egyptians was known about far and wide.

Key "Quotable Quote"

"God's created beings cannot help without him, but he can help without them."

Matthew Henry

1 Samuel 7

Matthew Henry's introduction

In this chapter we have,

I. The eclipsing of the glory of the ark, by its privacy in Kirjath-jearim for many years, vv. 1, 2.

II. The appearing of the glory of Samuel in his public services for the good of Israel, to whom he was raised up to be a judge, and he was the last that bore that character. This chapter gives us all the account we have of him when he was in the prime of his time; for what we had before was in his childhood (ch. 2 and 3.); what we have of him after was in his old age, 8:1. We have him here active,

A. In the reformation of Israel from their idolatry, vv. 3, 4.

B. In the reviving of religion among them, vv. 5, 6.

C. In praying for them against the invading Philistines (vv. 7–9), over whom God, in answer to his prayer, gave them a glorious victory, vv. 10, 11.

D. In erecting a thankful memorial of that victory, v. 12.

E. In the improvement of that victory, vv. 13, 14.

F. In the administration of justice, vv. 15–17. And these were the things for which God was preparing the designing him, in the early care of his grace to him.

A detailed analysis of chapter

The ark moved to Kiriath Jearim. (1–4)

The Israelites solemnly repent. (5,6)

The Lord defeats the Philistines. (7–12)

They are subdued, Samuel judges Israel. (13–17)

Key verse

Verse 1: "And the men of Kirjathjearim came, and fetched up the ark of the LORD"

Key word / key phrase

Verse 2, "mourned."

Key event / key person / key theme

Samuel rules Israel.

Key thought

Samuel gives a clear choice in verse 4.

Key thing to look out for

The Israelites were so fearful that they asked Samuel to pray for them.

Key Bible cross-reference

Verse 3. See 12:10; Judges 2:13; 3:7.

Key "by way of explanation"

Verse 6. This was a symbolic way of showing deep repentance.

Key "Quotable Quote"

"The desire to rule is the mother of heresies."

John Chrysostom

1 Samuel 8

Matthew Henry's introduction

Things went so very well with Israel, in the chapter before, under Samuel's administration, that, methinks, it is a pity to find him so quickly, as we do in this chapter, old, and going off, and things working towards a revolution. But so it is; Israel's good days seldom continue long. We have here,

I. Samuel decaying, v. 1.

II. His sons degenerating, vv. 2, 3.

III. Israel discontented with the present government and anxious to see a change. For

A. They petition Samuel to set a king over them, vv. 4, 5.

B. Samuel brings the matter to God, v. 6.

C. God directs him what answer to give them, by way of reproof (vv. 7, 8), and by way of remonstrance, setting forth the consequences of a change of the government, and how uneasy they would soon be under it, vv. 9–18.

D. They insist on their petition, vv. 19, 20.

E. Samuel promises them, from God, that they shall shortly be gratified, vv. 21, 22.

Thus hard is it for people to know when they are well off.

A detailed analysis of chapter

The evil government of Samuel's sons. (1–3)

The Israelites ask for a king. (4–9)

The behavior of their future king. (10–22)

Key verse

Verse 6: "Give us a king to judge us."

Key word / key phrase

Verse 6, "king."

Key event / key person / key theme

To choose a king means to choose trouble.

Key thought

It is clear that asking for a king meant that the Israelites were rejecting God.

Key thing to look out for

Rejecting good advice is most unwise.

Key Bible cross-reference

Verse 18. See 1 Kings 12:4; Jeremiah 22:13–17.

Key "by way of explanation"

Verse 5. The Israelites longed to be like the surrounding nations. This motivated their request for a king.

Key "Quotable Quote"

"God considers not the action, but the spirit of the action."

Peter Abelard

1 Samuel 9

Matthew Henry's introduction

Here is,

I. A short account of Saul's parentage and person, vv. 1, 2.

II. A large and particular account of the bringing of him to Samuel, to whom he had been before altogether a stranger.

A. God, by revelation, had told Samuel to expect him, vv. 15, 16.

B. God, by providence, led him to Samuel.

1.Being sent to seek his father's asses, he was at a loss, vv. 3–5.

2. By the advice of his servant, he determined to consult Samuel, vv. 6–10.

3. By the direction of the young maidens, he found him out, vv. 11–14.

4. Samuel, being informed of God about him (v. 17), treated him with respect in the gate (vv. 18–21), in the dining room (vv. 22–24), and at length in private, where he prepared him to hear the surprising news that he must be king, vv. 25–27. And these beginnings would have been very hopeful and promising if it had not been that the sin of the people was the spring of this great affair.

A detailed analysis of chapter

Saul is brought to Samuel. (1–10)

Samuel is told about Saul. (11–17)

Samuel's treatment of Saul. (18–27)

Key verse

Verse 2: "And he had a son, whose name was Saul, a choice young man, and a goodly: and there was not among the children of Israel a goodlier person than he: from his shoulders and upward he was higher than any of the people."

Key word / key phrase

Verse 2, "an impressive young man."

Key event / key person / key theme

Samuel anoints Saul.

Key thought

Samuel was known as "the man of God."

Key thing to look out for

Who would have thought that Saul could end up being such an evil person?

Key Bible cross-reference

Verse 12. See Leviticus 26:30.

Key "by way of explanation"

Verse 16. Although priests were also anointed the phase "the anointed of the Lord" now referred to the king.

Key "Quotable Quote"

"It is evidently a falling away from the faith, and a proof of great presumption, to neglect any part of what is written, or to introduce anything that is not written in the Scriptures."

Basil

1 Samuel 10

Matthew Henry's introduction

We left Samuel and Saul walking together, probably some private way over the fields down from Ramah, perhaps in the paths of the vineyards, and Saul expecting to hear from Samuel the word of God. Now here we have,

I. The anointing of Saul then and there, v. 1. The signs Samuel gave him, vv. 2–6. And instructions, vv. 7–8.
II. The accomplishment of those signs to the satisfaction of Saul, vv. 9–13.
III. His return to his father's house, vv. 14–16.
IV. His public election by lot, and solemn inauguration, vv. 17–25.
V. His return to his own city, vv. 26, 27. It is a great work that is here a doing, the setting up not only of a monarch, but of monarchy itself, in Israel; and therefore in all the advances towards it much of God is seen.

A detailed analysis of chapter

Samuel anoints Saul. (1–8)
Saul prophesies. (9–16)
Saul chosen king. (17–27)

Key verse

Verse 1: "Then Samuel took a vial of oil, and poured it upon his head."

Key word / key phrase

Verse 9, "God changed Saul's heart."

Key event / key person / key theme

Saul is made king.

Key thought

Settling for second best is never a good idea.

Key thing to look out for

Some people, verse 27, can never be satisfied.

Key Bible cross-reference

Verse 24. See 2 Samuel 16:16.

Key "by way of explanation"

Verse 25. Samuel tried to ensure that Saul's reign would not be incompatible with God's rule over his people.

Key "Quotable Quote"

"I have never met a soul who has set out to satisfy the Lord and has not been satisfied himself."

Watchman Nee

1 Samuel 11

Matthew Henry's introduction

In this chapter we have the first-fruits of Saul's government, in the glorious rescue of Jabesh-Gilead out of the hands of the Ammonites. Let not Israel thence infer that therefore they did well to ask a king (God could and would have saved them without one); but let them admire God's goodness, that he did not reject them when they rejected him, and acknowledge his wisdom in the choice of the person whom, if he did not find fit, yet he made fit, for the great trust he called him to, and enabled, in some measure, to merit the crown by his public services, before it was fixed on his head by the public approbation. Here is,

I. The great extremity to which the city of Jabesh-Gilead, on the other side of Jordan, was reduced by the Ammonites, vv. 1–3.
II. Saul's great readiness to come to their relief, whereby he signalized himself, vv. 4–10.

III. The good success of his attempt, by which God signalized him, v. 11.

IV. Saul's tenderness, notwithstanding this, towards those that had opposed him, vv. 12, 13.

V. The public confirmation and recognition of his election to the government, vv. 14, 15.

A detailed analysis of chapter

Jabesh Gilead delivered. (1–11)
Saul confirmed in his kingdom. (12–15)

Key verse

Verse 15: "And all the people went to Gilgal; and there they made Saul king before the LORD in Gilgal."

Key word / key phrase

Verse 14, "reaffirm the kingship."

Key event / key person / key theme

Saul is confirmed as king.

Key thought

Spiritual power only comes from the Lord.

Key thing to look out for

Without the Spirit there is no spiritual life.

Key Bible cross-reference

Verse 6. See 10:6,10; Judges 14:6.

Key "by way of explanation"

Verses 14,15. Samuel is affirming the Lord's rule over Saul.

Key "Quotable Quote"

"The means by which we live have outdistanced the ends for which we live. Our scientific power has outrun our spiritual power. We have guided missiles and misguided men."

Martin Luther King, Jr.

1 Samuel 12

Matthew Henry's introduction

We left the general assembly of the states together, in the close of the previous chapter; in this chapter we have Samuel's speech to them, when he resigned the government into the hands of Saul, in which,

I. He clears himself from all suspicion or imputation of mismanagement, while the administration was in his hands, vv. 1–5.

II. He reminds them of the great things God had done for them and for their fathers, vv. 6–13.

III. He sets before them good and evil, the blessing and the curse, vv. 14, 15.

IV. He awakens them to regard what he said to them, by calling to God for thunder, vv. 16–19.

V. He encourages them with hopes that all should be well, vv. 20–25. This is his farewell sermon to that august assembly and Saul's coronation sermon.

A detailed analysis of chapter

Samuel testifies his integrity. (1–5)
Samuel reproves the people. (6–15)
Thunder sent in harvest time. (16–25)

Key verse

Verse 1: "And Samuel said unto all Israel, Behold, I have hearkened unto your voice in all that ye said unto me, and have made a king over you."

Key word / key phrase

Verse 7, "Confront."

Key event / key person / key theme

Samuel's farewell speech

Key thought

Breaking God's covenant always brings down God's judgment.

Key thing to look out for

The people were in no mood to listen to Samuel's timely warnings.

Key Bible cross-reference

Verse 14. See Exodus 19:5,6; Joshua 24:20.

Key "by way of explanation"

Verse 25. Samuel warned the people that if they broke God's covenant they themselves would be broken by God.

Key "Quotable Quote"

"Where there is charity and wisdom, there is neither fear nor ignorance."

Francis of Assisi

1 Samuel 13

Matthew Henry's introduction

I. Saul appears here a very silly prince.

A. Infatuated in his counsels, vv. 1–3.

B. Invaded by his neighbors, vv. 4, 5.

C. Deserted by his soldiers, vv. 6, 7.

D. Disordered in his own spirit, and sacrificing in confusion, vv. 8–10.

E. Chidden by Samuel, vv. 11–13.

F. Rejected of God from being king, v. 14.

II. The people appear hear a very miserable people.

A. Disheartened and dispersed, vv. 6, 7.

B. Diminished, vv. 15, 16.

C. Plundered, vv. 17, 18.

D. Disarmed, vv. 19–23. This they got by casting off God's government, and making themselves like the nations: all their glory departed from them.

A detailed analysis of chapter

The invasion of the Philistines. (1–7)

Saul sacrifices. He is reproved by Samuel. (8–14)

The policy of the Philistines. (15–23)

Key verse

Verse 9: "And Saul said, Bring hither a burnt offering to me, and peace offerings. And he offered the burnt offering."

Key word / key phrase

Verse 19, "blacksmith."

Key event / key person / key theme

War against the Philistines

Key thought

Saul and Jonathan make a great team.

Key thing to look out for

Saul knew that he had acted wrongly, but showed no sign of repentance.

Key Bible cross-reference

Verse 13. See 2 Samuel 24:10.

Key "by way of explanation"

Verse 19. If you had a blacksmith it meant you had the great advantage of knowing about how to make weapons of war from iron.

Key "Quotable Quote"

"Whoever delays his repentance does in effect pawn his soul with the devil."

Thomas Manton

1 Samuel 14

Matthew Henry's introduction

In this chapter we have,

I. The host of the Philistines trampled on, and triumphed over, by the faith and courage of Jonathan, who unknown to his father (vv. 1–3), with his armor-bearer only, made a brave attack on them, encouraging himself in the Lord his God, vv. 4–7. He challenged them (vv. 8–12), and, on their acceptance of the challenge, charged them with such fury, or rather such faith, that he put them to flight, and set them one against another (vv. 13–15), which gave opportunity to Saul and his forces, with other Israelites, to follow the blow, and gain a victory, vv. 16–23.

II. The host of Israel troubled and perplexed by the rashness and folly of Saul, who adjured the people to eat no food till night, which

A. Brought Jonathan to a præmunire, vv. 24–30.

B. Was a temptation to the people, when the time of their fast had expired, to eat with the blood,, vv. 31–35. Jonathan's error, through ignorance, had like to have been his death, but the people rescued him, vv. 36–46.

III. In the close we have a general account of Saul's exploits (vv. 47, 48) and of his family, vv. 49–52.

A detailed analysis of chapter

Jonathan attacks the Philistines. (1–15)

Their defeat. (16–23)

Saul forbids the people to eat until evening. (24–35)

Jonathan pointed out by lot. (36–46)

Saul's family. (47–52)

Key verse

Verse 13: "And Jonathan climbed up upon his hands and upon his feet, and his armor bearer after him: and they fell before Jonathan; and his armor bearer slew after him."

Key word / key phrase

Verse 13, "climbed."

Key event / key person / key theme

Jonathan acts courageously.

Key thought

Saul is motivated by a personal vendetta more than by the glory of God.

Key thing to look out for

Saul reveals that he does not have the right character to be a good king.

Key Bible cross-reference

Verse 41. See 10:20,21; Joshua 7:14–18.

Key "by way of explanation"

Verse 24. Saul's order that his men should fast before a battle only weakened them for the fight.

Key "Quotable Quote"

"If I take care of my character, my reputation will take care of itself."

Dwight Moody

1 Samuel 15

Matthew Henry's introduction

In this chapter we have the final rejection of Saul from being king, for his disobedience to God's command in not utterly destroying the Amalekites. By his wars and victories he hoped to magnify and perpetuate his own name and honor, but, by his mismanagement of them, he ruined himself, and laid his honor in the dust. Here is,

I. The commission God gave him to destroy the Amalekites, with a command to do it utterly, vv. 1–3.

II. Saul's preparation for this expedition, vv. 4–6.

III. His success, and partial execution of this commission, vv. 7–9.

IV. His examination before Samuel, and sentence passed on him, notwithstanding the many frivolous pleas he made to excuse himself, vv. 10–31.

V. The slaying of Agag, vv. 32, 33.

VI. Samuel's final farewell to Saul, vv. 34, 35.

A detailed analysis of chapter

Saul sent to destroy Amalek. (1–9)

Saul excuses and commends himself. (10–23)

Saul's imperfect confession. (24–31)

Agag put to death, Samuel and Saul part. (32–35)

Key verse

Verse 3: "Now go and smite Amalek, and utterly destroy all that they have."

Key word / key phrase

Verse 22, "obey."

Key event / key person / key theme

The Lord rejects Saul as king.

Key thought

If we reject God's word God rejects us.

Key thing to look out for

Rebellion and divination are put on the same level.

Key Bible cross-reference

Verse 29. See Psalm 89:17; Isaiah 13:19.

Key "by way of explanation"

Verse 22. Samuel is not speaking against making sacrifices, but points out how useless they are if they are not accompanied by devotion in the heart.

Key "Quotable Quote"

"Obey God in the thing he is at present showing

you, and instantly the next thing is opened up."

Oswald Chambers

1 Samuel 16

Matthew Henry's introduction

At this chapter begins the story of David, one that makes as great a figure in the sacred story as almost any of the worthies of the Old Testament, one that both with his sword and with his pen served the honor of God and the interests of Israel as much as most ever did, and was as illustrious a type of Christ. Here

I. Samuel is appointed and commissioned to anoint a king among the sons of Jesse at Bethlehem, vv. 1–5.

II. All his elder sons are passed by and David the youngest is pitched on and anointed, vv. 6–13.

III. Saul growing melancholy, David is pitched on to relieve him by music, vv. 14–23. Thus small are the beginnings of that great man.

A detailed analysis of chapter

Samuel sent to Bethlehem to Jesse. (1–5)
David is anointed. (6–13)
Saul troubled with an evil spirit, is calmed by David. (14–23)

Key verse

Verse 13: "Then Samuel took the horn of oil, and anointed him in the midst of his brethren: and the Spirit of the LORD came upon David from that day forward."

Key word / key phrase

Verse 13, "David."

Key event / key person / key theme

David is anointed by Samuel.

Key thought

God's plans are never tied to one person if he or she should prove unfaithful.

Key thing to look out for

David has many God-given talents.

Key Bible cross-reference

Verse 11. See 2 Samuel 7:7, 8; Psalm 78:71, 72.

Key "by way of explanation"

Verse 14. On whom God's Spirit stayed became the critical point in the history of Israel.

Key "Quotable Quote"

"When the Spirit leaves me, I am like dry gunpowder. Oh for a sense of this!"

Robert Murray M'Cheyne

1 Samuel 17

Matthew Henry's introduction

In the story observe,

I. What a noble figure Goliath made, and how daringly he challenged the armies of Israel, vv. 1–11.

II. What a mean figure David made, when Providence brought him to the army, vv. 12–30.

III. The unparalleled bravery wherewith David undertook to encounter this Philistine, vv. 31–39.

IV. The pious resolution with which he attacked him, vv. 40–47.

V. The glorious victory he won over him with a sling and a stone, and the advantage which the Israelites thereby gained against the Philistines, vv. 48–54.

VI. The great notice which was hereon taken of David at court, vv. 55–58.

A detailed analysis of chapter

Goliath's challenge. (1–11)
David comes to the camp. (12–30)
David undertakes to fight Goliath. (31–39)
and goes to meet him. (40–47)
He kills Goliath. (48–58)

Key verse

Verse 4: "And there went out a champion out of the camp of the Philistines, named Goliath, of Gath, whose height was six cubits and a span."

Key word / key phrase

Verse 45, "the Lord Almighty."

Key event / key person / key theme

David defeats Goliath.

Key thought

The power of the world is puny against Almighty God.

Key thing to look out for

David's quiet confidence came from his trust in God.

Key Bible cross-reference

Verse 46. See Exodus 7:17; 9:14, 16, 29; Joshua 2:10, 11.

Key "by way of explanation"

The stones for the sling were about the size of a base ball ball.

Key "Quotable Quote"

"When a man has no strength, if he leans on God, he becomes powerful."

D.L. Moody

1 Samuel 18

Matthew Henry's introduction

In the course of the previous chapter we left David in triumph; now in this chapter we have,

I. The improvement of his triumphs; he soon became,
   A. Saul's constant attendant, v. 2.
   B. Jonathan's covenant friend, vv. 1, 3, 4.
   C. The darling of his country, vv. 5, 7, 16.

II. The allays of his triumphs. This is the vanity that accompanies even a right work, that "for it a man is envied," Eccl. 4:4. So David was by Saul.
   A. He hated him, and sought to kill him himself, vv. 8–11.
   B. He feared him, and contrived how he might have some mischief done him, vv. 12–17. He proposed to marry his daughter to him; but, cheated him of the eldest to provoke him (v. 19), and, gave him the younger, on conditions which would endanger his life, vv. 20–25. But David performed his conditions bravely (vv. 26, 27), and grew to be more and more esteemed, vv. 28–30. Still David is rising, but (as all that aim at the crown of

life must expect) he had a great deal of difficulty and opposition to grapple with.

A detailed analysis of chapter

Jonathan's friendship with David. (1–5)
Saul seeks to kill David. (6–11)
Saul's fear of David. (12–30)

Key verse

Verse 1: "And it came to pass, when he had made an end of speaking unto Saul, that the soul of Jonathan was knit with the soul of David, and Jonathan loved him as his own soul."

Key word / key phrase

Verse 8, "galled him."

Key event / key person / key theme

Saul becomes jealous of David

Key thought

Jealousy can ruin relationships.

Key thing to look out for

The contrast between the characters of Saul and David.

Key Bible cross-reference

Verse 4. See 20:14,15,31; 23:17.

Key "by way of explanation"

Verse 7. When women sang about David killing "tens of thousands" it was a poetic way of referring to thousands. See Deuteronomy 32:30; Psalm 91:7.

Key "Quotable Quote"

"In jealousy there is more self-love than love."

François duc de La Rochefoucauld

1 Samuel 19

Matthew Henry's introduction

Immediately after David's marriage, which one would have hoped would secure him Saul's affection, we find his troubles coming on him faster than ever and Saul's enmity to him the cause of all. His death was vowed, and four fair escapes of his from the hurtful sword of Saul we have an account of in this chapter:
the first by the prudent mediation of Jonathan (vv. 1–7), the second by his own quickness (vv. 8–10), the third by Michal's fidelity (vv. 11–17), the fourth by Samuel's protection, and a change, for the present, wrought on Saul, vv. 18–24. Thus God has many ways of preserving his people. Providence is never at a loss.

A detailed analysis of chapter

Jonathan reconciles his father to David, Saul again tries to kill him. (1–10)
David flees to Samuel. (11–24)

Key verse

Verse 2: "But Jonathan Saul's son delighted much in David: and Jonathan told David, saying, Saul my father seeketh to kill thee"

Key word / key phrase

Verse 9, "spear."

Key event / key person / key theme

Saul attempts to kill David.

Key thought

It can be a short step from jealousy and anger to murder.

Key thing to look out for

Contrast Jonathan's character with that of his father Saul.

Key Bible cross-reference

Verse 1. See 18:13, 17, 25.

Key "by way of explanation"

Verse 9. The phrase "An evil spirit from the Lord" indicates that even evil spirits are not out of God's control. See Judges 9:23; 1 Kings 22:19–23.

Key "Quotable Quote"

"Sow a thought and you reap an act;
Sow an act and you reap a habit;
Sow a habit and you reap a character;
Sow a character and you reap a destiny."

Samuel Smiles

1 Samuel 20

Matthew Henry's introduction

I. David complains to Jonathan of his present distress, and engages him to be his friend, vv. 1–8.

II. Jonathan faithfully promises to get and give him intelligence how his father stood affected to him, and renews the covenant of friendship with him, vv. 9–23.

III. Jonathan, on trial, finds, to his grief, that his father was implacably enraged against David, vv. 24–34.

IV. He gives David notice of this, according to the appointment between them, vv. 35–42.

A detailed analysis of chapter

David consults Jonathan. (1–10)
Jonathan's covenant with David. (11–23)
Saul seeks to kill Jonathan. (24–34)
Jonathan and David part. (35–42)

Key verse

Verse 4: "Then said Jonathan unto David, Whatsoever thy soul desireth, I will even do it for thee."

Key word / key phrase

Verse 41, "wept together."

Key event / key person / key theme

David and Jonathan's friendship

Key thought

Jonathan had to choose between his friend and his father.

Key thing to look out for

Jonathan and David's friendship was profound.

Key Bible cross-reference

Verse 5. See Leviticus 23:24, 25; Numbers 29:1–6.

Key "by way of explanation"

Verse 31. Saul tries to turn Jonathan against David by saying that David will take the throne from him.

Key "Quotable Quote"

"No medicine is more valuable, none more efficacious, none better suited to the cure of all our temporal ills than a friend to whom we may turn for consolation in time of trouble, and with whom we may share our happiness in times of joy."

Aelred Rievaulx

1 Samuel 21

Matthew Henry's introduction

The example of the suffering Jesus was a copy without a blot, that of David was not so; witness the records of this chapter, where we find David in his flight,

I. Imposing on Abimelech the priest, to get from him both victuals and arms, vv. 1–9.

II. Imposing on Achish, king of Gath, by feigning himself mad, vv. 10–15. Justly are troubles called temptations, for many are by them drawn into sin.

A detailed analysis of chapter

David with Ahimelech. (1–9)

David at Gath pretends to be mad. (10–15)

Key verse

Verse 1: "Then came David to Nob to Ahimelech the priest."

Key word / key phrase

Verse 1, "trembled."

Key event / key person / key theme

David at Nob and Gath

Key thought

David was a fugitive on the run.

Key thing to look out for

Note how Doeg, verse 7, plays a key role in the next chapter.

Key Bible cross-reference

Verse 1. See 22:10, 15.

Key "by way of explanation"

Verse 4. Jesus referred to this verse and taught that ceremonial law should not be viewed in a legalistic way. See Matthew 12:3, 4.

Key "Quotable Quote"

"When I am in the cellar of affliction, I look for the Lord's choicest wines."

Samuel Rutherford

1 Samuel 22

Matthew Henry's introduction

David, being driven from Achish, returns into the land of Israel to be hunted by Saul.

I. David sets up his standard in the cave of Adullam, entertains his relations (v. 1), enlists soldiers (v. 2), but removes his aged parents to a more quiet settlement (vv. 3, 4), and has the prophet Gad for his counselor, v. 5.

II. Saul resolves to pursue him and find him out, complains of his servants and Jonathan (vv. 6–8), and, finding by Doeg's information that Ahimelech had been kind to David, he ordered him and all the priests that were with him, eighty-five in all, to be put to death, and all that belonged to them destroyed (vv. 9–19) from the barbarous execution of which sentence Abiathar escaped to David, vv. 20–23.

A detailed analysis of chapter

David at Adullam. Many come to him. (1–5)

Saul destroys the priests of Nob. (6–19)

Abiathar escapes to David. (20–23)

Key verse

Verse 1: "David therefore departed thence, and escaped to the cave Adullam."

Key word / key phrase

Verse 18, "struck them down."

Key event / key person / key theme

Saul slaughters the priests.

Key thought

A Doeg type of a person and a tyrant go together.

Key thing to look out for

Saul's evil now knows no bounds.

Key Bible cross-reference

Verse 7. See 8:14.

Key "by way of explanation"

Verse 7. As Saul was himself a Benjamite he hoped for tribal loyalty from his officials from the same tribe.

Key "Quotable Quote"

"My child, flee from every evil and everything that resembles it."

Didache

1 Samuel 23

Matthew Henry's introduction

Saul, having made himself drunk with the blood of the priests of the Lord, is here, in this chapter, seeking David's life, who appears here doing good, and suffering ill, at the same time. Here is,

I. The good service he did to his king and country, in rescuing the city of Keilah out of the hands of the Philistines, vv. 1–6.

II. The danger he was thereby brought into from the malice of the prince he served and the treachery of the city he saved, and his deliverance, by divine direction, from that danger, vv. 7–13.

III. David in a wood and his friend Jonathan visiting him there and encouraging him, vv. 14–18.

IV. The information which the Ziphites brought to Saul of David's haunts, and the expedition Saul made, in pursuit of him, vv. 19–25. The narrow escape David had of falling into his hands, vv. 26–29. "Many are the troubles of the righteous, but the Lord delivereth them out of them all."

A detailed analysis of chapter

David rescues Keilah. (1–6)

God warns him to escape from Keilah. (7–13)

Jonathan comforts David. (14–18)

He is rescued from Saul by an invasion of the Philistines. (19–29)

Key verse

Verse 16: "And Jonathan Saul's son arose, and

went to David into the wood, and strengthened his hand in God."

Key word / key phrase

Verse 8, "besiege."

Key event / key person / key theme

Saul pursues David

Key thought

Jonathan does not resent David' ascendancy.

Key thing to look out for

Evil, once let loose, overtakes people and situations.

Key Bible cross-reference

Verse 17. See 18:8.

Key "by way of explanation"

Verse 2. David used Urim and Thummim to discover the Lord's will. See verses 6, 9.

Key "Quotable Quote"

"The perfect person does not only try to avoid evil. Nor does he do good for fear of punishment, still less in order to qualify for the hope of a promised reward. The perfect person does good through love."

Clement of Alexandria

1 Samuel 24

Matthew Henry's introduction

We have hitherto had Saul seeking an opportunity to destroy David, and, to his shame, he could never find it. In this chapter David had a fair opportunity to destroy Saul, and, to his honor, he did not make use of it; and his sparing Saul's life was as great an instance of God's grace in him as the preserving of his own life was of God's providence over him. Observe,

I. How maliciously Saul sought David's life, vv. 1, 2.

II. How generously David saved Saul's life (when he had him at an advantage) and only cut off the skirt of his robe, vv. 3–8.

III. How pathetically he reasoned with Saul, on this to bring him to a better temper towards him, vv. 9–15.

IV. The good impression this made on Saul for the present, vv. 16–22.

A detailed analysis of chapter

David spares Saul's life. (1–7)

David shows his innocence. (8–15)

Saul acknowledges his fault. (16–22)

Key verse

Verse 4: "Then David arose, and cut off the skirt of Saul's robe privily."

Key word / key phrase

Verse 5, "conscience-stricken."

Key event / key person / key theme

David spares Saul's life.

Key thought

Even though he was being hounded David followed his conscience.

Key thing to look out for

Saul showed remorse but not repentance.

Key Bible cross-reference

Verse 16. See 26:21.

Key "by way of explanation"

Verse 6. David was determined not to act as if he, rather than the Lord, controlled everything.

Key "Quotable Quote"

"Conscience is the perfect interpreter of life."

Karl Barth

1 Samuel 25

Matthew Henry's introduction

We have here some intermission of David's troubles by Saul. Providence favored him with a breathing time, and yet this chapter gives us instances of the troubles of David. If one vexation seems to be over, we must not be secure; a storm may arise from some other point, as here to David.

I. Tidings of the death of Samuel could not but trouble him, v. 1. But,

II. The abuse he received from Nabal is more largely recorded in this chapter.

A. The character of Nabal, vv. 2, 3.

B. The humble request sent to him, vv. 4–9.

C. His churlish answer, vv. 10–12.

D. David's angry resentment of it, vv. 13, 21, 22.

E. Abigail's prudent care to prevent the mischief it was likely to bring on her family, vv. 14–20.

F. Her address to David to pacify him, vv. 23–31.

G. David's favorable reception of her, vv. 32–35.

H. The death of Nabal, vv. 36–38.

I. Abigail's marriage to David, vv. 39–44.

A detailed analysis of chapter

Death of Samuel. (1)

David's request; Nabal's churlish refusal. (2–11)

David's intention to kill Nabal. (12–17)

Abigail takes a present to David. (18–31)

He is pacified. Nabal dies. (32–39)

David takes Abigail as his wife. (39–44)

Key verse

Verse 1: "And Samuel died."

Key word / key phrase

Verse 11, "Why should I?"

Key event / key person / key theme

David and Abigail

Key thought

Nabal and Abigail show how different they are.

Key thing to look out for

David shows that he was open to changing his mind.

Key Bible cross-reference

Verse 3. See 24:12, 14, 15.

Key "by way of explanation"

Verse 25, "Fool." In this instance the meaning of Nabal's name exactly reflected his character. Names were often chosen to do this in ancient times.

Key "Quotable Quote"

"The greatest thing a man can do for his heavenly Father is to be kind to some of his other children."

Henry Drummond

1 Samuel 26

Matthew Henry's introduction

I. The Ziphites informed him where David was (v. 1), and thereon he marched out with a considerable force in quest of him, vv. 2, 3.

II. David gained intelligence of his motions (v. 4), and took a view of his camp, v. 5.

III. He and one of his men ventured into his camp in the night and found him and all his guards fast asleep, vv. 6, 7.

IV. David, though much urged to it by his companions, would not take away Saul's life, but only carried off his spear and his cruse of water, vv. 8–12.

V. He produced these as a further witness for him that he did not design any ill to Saul, and reasoned with him on his conduct, vv. 13–20.

VI. Saul was hereby convinced of his error, and once more desisted from persecuting David, vv. 21–25

A detailed analysis of chapter

Saul goes after David, who again spares Saul's life. (1–12)

David exhorts Saul. (13–20)

Saul acknowledges his sin. (21–25)

Key verse

Verse 2: "Then Saul arose, and went down to the wilderness of Ziph, having three thousand chosen men of Israel with him, to seek David in the wilderness of Ziph."

Key word / key phrase

Verse 21, "acted like a boy."

Key event / key person / key theme

David spares Saul's life again.

Key thought

Verses 10, 23, David's actions are based on his knowledge of God's character.

Key thing to look out for

Saul ignores another opportunity to repent.

Key Bible cross-reference

Verse 20. See 24:14.

Key "by way of explanation"

Verse 12. By taking his spear and water jug David thought that Saul would realize that he did not seek to kill him.

Key "Quotable Quote"

"If we hope for mercy we must show mercy."

Peter Chrysologus

1 Samuel 27

Matthew Henry's introduction

I. We find, to his praise, that he prudently took care of his own safety and his family's (vv. 2–4) and valiantly fought Israel's battles against the Canaanites (vv. 8–9), yet,

II. We find, to his dishonor,

A. That he began to despair of his deliverance, v. 1.

B. That he deserted his own country, and went to dwell in the land of the Philistines, vv. 1, 5–7.

C. That he imposed on Achish with an equivocation, if not a lie, about his expedition, vv. 10–12.

A detailed analysis of chapter

David retires to Gath. (1–7)
David deceives Achish. (8–12)

Key verse

Verse 1: "And David said in his heart, I shall now perish one day by the hand of Saul: there is nothing better for me than that I should speedily escape into the land of the Philistines; and Saul shall despair of me, to seek me any more in any coast of Israel: so shall I escape out of his hand."

Key word / key phrase

Verse 1, "escape."

Key event / key person / key theme

David among the Philistines

Key thought

David feels that Saul gave him no option but to go over to the Philistines.

Key thing to look out for

Some of David's most moving psalms were written in times of despair.

Key Bible cross-reference

Verse 7. See 2 Samuel 1:1; 2:1–3.

Key "by way of explanation"

Verse 1. The verse probably shows that David was beginning to doubt his own faith in the Lord.

Key "Quotable Quote"

"The kingdom of God is not attained by enduring one or two troubles, but many!"

Elder Anthony of Optina

1 Samuel 28

Matthew Henry's introduction

Preparations are herein making for that war which will put an end to the life and reign of Saul, and so make way for David to the throne. In this war,

I. The Philistines are the aggressors and Achish their king makes David his confidant, vv. 1, 2.

II. The Israelites prepare to receive them, and Saul their king makes the devil his privy-counselor, and thereby fills the measure of his iniquity. Observe,

A. The despairing condition which Saul was in, vv. 3–6.

B. The application he made to a witch, to bring him up Samuel, vv. 7–14.
C. His conversation with the apparition, vv. 15–19. The damp it struck on him, vv. 20–25.

A detailed analysis of chapter

Achish puts confidence in David, Saul's fear. (1–6)
Saul consults a witch at Endor. (7–19)
Saul's terror. (20–25)

Key verse

Verse 3: "Now Samuel was dead, and all Israel had lamented him, and buried him in Ramah, even in his own city."

Key word / key phrase

Verse 7, "medium."

Key event / key person / key theme

Saul consults a medium.

Key thought

Going against God's commands leads to evil.

Key thing to look out for

The Bible is categorical in its condemnation of mediums.

Key Bible cross-reference

Verse 7. See verse 3; Leviticus 19:26.

Key "by way of explanation"

Verse 14. Saul recalls that this description fits the kind of clothes Samuel used to wear.

Key "Quotable Quote"

"How absurd would it be that in satisfying men you should incur the displeasure of him for whose sake you obey men themselves!"

John Calvin

1 Samuel 29

Matthew Henry's introduction

How Saul, who was forsaken of God, when he was in a strait was more and more perplexed and embarrassed with his own counsels, we read in the previous chapter. In this chapter we find how David, who kept close to God, when he was in a strait was extricated and brought off by the providence of God, without any contrivance of his own. We have him,

I. Marching with the Philistines, vv. 1, 2.
II. Excepted against by the lords of the Philistines, vv. 3–5.
III. Happily dismissed by Achish from that service which did so ill become him, and which yet he knew not how to decline, vv. 6–11.

A detailed analysis of chapter

The Philistines object to having David with them. (1–5)
He is dismissed by Achish. (6–11)

Key verse

Verse 3: "Then said the princes of the Philistines, What do these Hebrews here? And Achish said unto the princes of the Philistines, Is not this David, the servant of Saul the king of Israel, which hath been with me these days, or these years, and I have found no fault in him since he fell unto me unto this day?"

Key word / key phrase

Verse 3, "what about these Hebrews?"

Key event / key person / key theme

David is rejected by the Philistines.

Key thought

David could not have forever stayed with the Philistines.

Key thing to look out for

The events of this chapter help David to be free of the Philistines.

Key Bible cross-reference

Verse 4. See 27:6.

Key "by way of explanation"

Verse 3. David was an accomplished tactician and fighter.

Key "Quotable Quote"

"God never does anything to you that isn't for you."

Elizabeth Elliott

1 Samuel 30

Matthew Henry's introduction

Now here we are told,

I. What a melancholy posture he found the city in, all laid waste by the Amalekites, and what distress it occasioned him and his men, vv. 1–6.

II. What course he took to recover what he had lost. He enquired of God, and took out a commission from him (vv. 7, 8), pursued the enemy (vv. 9, 10), gained intelligence from a straggler (vv. 11–15), attacked and routed the plunderers (vv. 16, 17), and recovered all that they had carried off, vv. 18–20.

III. What method he observed in the distribution of the spoil, vv. 21–31.

A detailed analysis of chapter

Ziklag defeated by the Amalekites. (1–6)
David overtakes the Amalekites. (7–15)
He recovers what had been lost. (16–20)
David's distribution of the spoil. (21–31)

Key verse

Verse 10: "But David pursued, he and four hundred men: for two hundred abode behind, which were so faint that they could not go over the brook Besor."

Key word / key phrase

Verse 24, "all shall share alike."

Key event / key person / key theme

David destroys the Amalekites.

Key thought

The Lord knows about every part of our lives.

Key thing to look out for

A great deal of David's life was full of danger.

Key Bible cross-reference

Verse 1. See 27:8.

Key "by way of explanation"

Verse 23. David attributes their success to the Lord.

Key "Quotable Quote"

"How often has providence convinced believers, upon a sober recollection of the events of their lives, that if the Lord had left them to their own counsels they had as often been their own tormentors, if not executioners!"

John Flavel

1 Samuel 31

Matthew Henry's introduction

Here is,

I. His army routed, v. 1.

II. His three sons slain, v. 2.

III. Himself wounded (v. 3), and slain by his own hand, v. 4. The death of his armor-bearer (v. 5) and all his men, v. 6.

IV. His country possessed by the Philistines, v. 7. His camp plundered, and his dead body deserted, v. 8. His fall triumphed in, v. 9. His body publicly exposed (v. 10) and with difficulty rescued by the men of Jabesh-Gilead, vv. 11–13. Thus fell the man that was rejected of God.

A detailed analysis of chapter

Saul's defeat and death. (1–7)

Saul's body rescued by the men of Jabesh Gilead. (8–13)

Key verse

Verse 6: "So Saul died, and his three sons, and his armor bearer, and all his men, that same day together."

Key word / key phrase

Verse 1, "slain."

Key event / key person / key theme

Saul's death

Key thought

Death-bed repentances are rare.

Key thing to look out for

Saul's life failed to live up to its early promise.

Key Bible cross-reference

Verse 13. See 2 Samuel 21:12–14.

Key "by way of explanation"

Verse 4, "abuse me." It was common practice for captured prisoners to be mutilated. See Judges 16:23–25.

Key "Quotable Quote"

"The divine providence, which is sufficient to deliver us in our utmost, is equally necessary to our preservation in the most peaceful situation."

John Newton

2 Samuel 1

Matthew Henry's introduction

In the close of the previous book (with which this is connected as a continuation of the same history) we had Saul's exit; he went down slain to the pit, though we was the terror of the mighty in the land of the living. We are now to look towards the rising sun, and to enquire where David is, and what he is doing. In this chapter we have,

I. Tidings brought him to Ziklag of the death of Saul and Jonathan, by an Amalekite, who undertook to give him a particular narrative of it, vv. 1–10.

II. David's sorrowful reception of these tidings, vv. 11, 12.

III. Justice done on the messenger, who boasted that he had helped Saul to dispatch himself, vv. 13–16.

IV. An elegy which David penned on this occasion, vv. 17–27. And in all this David's breast appears very happily free from the sparks both of revenge and ambition, and he observes a very suitable demeanor.

A detailed analysis of chapter

News brought to David of the death of Saul. (1–10)

The Amalekite is put to death. (11–16)

David's lamentation for Saul and Jonathan. (17–27)

Key verse

Verse 11: "Then David took hold on his clothes, and rent them; and likewise all the men that were with him."

Key word / key phrase

Verse 17, "lament."

Key event / key person / key theme

David mourns for Saul and Jonathan.

Key thought

Saul may have hounded David but David still genuinely mourned his passing.

Key thing to look out for

David's love for Jonathan is openly expressed, verse 26.

Key Bible cross-reference

Verse 1. See Joshua 1:1; Judges 1:1.

Key "by way of explanation"

Verse 28. When well-known people died or were killed it was normal for a lament to be written for them.

Key "Quotable Quote"

"Grief is itself a medicine."

William Cowper

2 Samuel 2

Matthew Henry's introduction

David had paid due respect to the memory of Saul his prince and Jonathan his friend, and what he did was as much his praise as theirs; he is now considering what is to be done next. Saul is dead, now therefore David arise.

I. By direction from God he went up to Hebron, and was there anointed king, vv. 1–4.

II. He returned thanks to the men of Jabesh Gilead for burying Saul, vv. 5–7.

III. Ishbosheth, the son of Saul, is set up in opposition to him, vv. 8–11.

IV. A warm encounter happens between David's party and Ishbosheth's, in which,

A. Twelve of each side engaged hand to hand and were all slain, vv. 12–16.
B. Saul's party was beaten, v. 17.
C. Asahel, on David's side, was slain by Abner, vv. 18–23.
D. Joab, at Abner's request, sounds a retreat, vv. 24–28.
E. Abner makes the best of his way (v. 29), and the loss on both sides is computed, vv. 30–32. So that here we have an account of a civil war in Israel, which, in process of time, ended in the complete settlement of David on the throne.

A detailed analysis of chapter

David made king in Hebron. (1–7)
Abner makes Ish-Bosheth king. Battle between Abner's men and those of Joab. (8–17)
Both parties retreat. (18–24)
Asahel killed by Abner. (25–32.)

Key verse

Verse 4: "And the men of Judah came, and there they anointed David king over the house of Judah."

Key word / key phrase

Verse 1, "enquired of the LORD."

Key event / key person / key theme

David is made king of Judah

Key thought

The Lord raises the humble.

Key thing to look out for

Qualities such as kindness and faithfulness need fostering.

Key Bible cross-reference

Verse 3. See 1 Samuel 22:2; 23:13; 30:3, 9.

Key "by way of explanation"

Verse 28. "Joab blew the trumpet." The trumpet was the main means of communication between troops and their leader in a battle situation.

Key "Quotable Quote"

"Conquer evil men by your gentle kindness."

Isaac from Syria

2 Samuel 3

Matthew Henry's introduction

The battle between Joab and Abner did not end the controversy between the two houses of Saul and David, but it is in this chapter working towards a period. Here is,

I. The gradual advance of David's interest, v. 1.
II. The building up of his family, vv. 2–5.
III. Abner's quarrel with Ish-bosheth, and his treaty with David, vv. 6–12.
IV. The preliminaries settled, vv. 13–16.
V. Abner's undertaking and attempt to bring Israel over to David, vv. 17–21.
VI. The treacherous murder of Abner by Joab, when he was carrying on this matter, vv. 22–27.
VII. David's great concern and trouble for the death of Abner, vv. 28–39.

A detailed analysis of chapter

David's power increases his family. (1–6)

Abner goes over to David. (7–21)

Joab kills Abner. David mourns for him. (22–39)

Key verse

Verse 1: "Now there was long war between the house of Saul and the house of David: but David waxed stronger and stronger, and the house of Saul waxed weaker and weaker."

Key word / key phrase

Verse 9, "what the LORD promised him."

Key event / key person / key theme

Abner's death

Key thought

Hatred kills.

Key thing to look out for

Verse 32. David, who was not yet king of all Israel, felt that his position was insecure.

Key Bible cross-reference

Verse 25. See 2:18, 23; 3:27.

Key "by way of explanation"

Verse 17. The "elders of Israel" were the leaders of Israel who ruled their nation. See 1 Samuel 8:4; 2 Samuel 5:3.

Key "Quotable Quote"

"The devil does not care who you hate, even if it's himself."

Metropolitan Anthony

2 Samuel 4

Matthew Henry's introduction

When Abner was slain David was at a loss for a friend to perfect the reduction of those tribes that were yet in Ish-bosheth's interest. Which way to adopt for the accomplishment of it he could not tell; but here Providence brings it about by the removal of Ish-bosheth.

I. Two of his own servants slew him, and brought his head to David, vv. 1–8.

II. David, instead of rewarding them, put them to death for what they had done, vv. 9–12.

A detailed analysis of chapter

Ish-Bosheth murdered. (1–7)

David puts to death the murderers. (8–12)

Key verse

Verse 6: "And they came thither into the midst of the house, as though they would have fetched wheat; and they smote him under the fifth rib."

Key word / key phrase

Verse 1, "lost courage."

Key event / key person / key theme

Ish-Bosheth is murdered.

Key thought

Man's inhumanity to man appears in every generation.

Key thing to look out for

Verse 40. What happened to Jonathan's son.

Key Bible cross-reference

Verse 4. See 9:1–13; 16:1–4; 19:24–30.

Key "by way of explanation"

Verse 8. The murderers of Ish-Bosheth couched their deed in pious language but that did not please David.

Key "Quotable Quote"

"Anger is a weed. Hate is the tree."

Augustine of Hippo

2 Samuel 5

Matthew Henry's introduction

Here is,

I. David anointed king by all the tribes, vv. 1–5.

II. Making himself master of the strong-hold of Zion, vv. 6–10.

III. Building himself a house and strengthening himself in his kingdom, vv. 11, 12.

IV. His children that were born after this, vv. 13–16.

V. His victories over the Philistines, vv. 17–25.

A detailed analysis of chapter

David king over all Israel. (1–5)
He captures Jerusalem. (6–10)
David's kingdom established. (11–16)
He defeats the Philistines. (17–25)

Key verse

Verse 3: "So all the elders of Israel came to the king to Hebron; and king David made a league with them in Hebron before the LORD: and they anointed David king over Israel."

Key word / key phrase

Verse 6, "Jebusites."

Key event / key person / key theme

Seven years after the death of Saul, the northern tribes invite David to be their king.

Key thought

Rulers are meant to be like shepherds.

Key thing to look out for

David's success is attributed to the Lord Almighty.

Key Bible cross-reference

Verse 2. See 1 Samuel 13:13, 14; 16:1, 13.

Key "by way of explanation"

Verse 6. The "Jebusites" lived in the region of Jerusalem and were a Canaanite people. See Genesis 10:15, 16. Since Jerusalem had been controlled neither by the northern nor southern tribes it made a perfect capital city for David.

Key "Quotable Quote"

"The United States was founded upon a Christian consensus. We today should bring Judeo-Christian principles into play in regard to government."

Francis A. Schaeffer

2 Samuel 6

Matthew Henry's introduction

I. The plan was well laid, vv. 1, 2. But,

A. They were guilty of an error in carrying it in a cart, vv. 3–5.

B. They were punished for that error by the sudden death of Uzzah (vv. 6, 7), which was a great terror to David (vv. 8, 9) and put a stop to his proceedings, vv. 10, 11.

II. The great joy and satisfaction with which it was at last done, vv. 12–15. And,

A. The good understanding between David and his people, vv. 17–19.

B. The uneasiness between David and his wife on that occasion, vv. 16, 20–23. And, when we consider that the ark was both the token of God's presence and a type of Christ, we shall see that this story is very instructive.

A detailed analysis of chapter

The ark moved from Kirjath Jearim. (1–5)
Uzzah killed for touching the ark. Obed-Edom blessed. (6–11)
David brings the ark to Zion. (12–19)
Michal's evil behavior. (20–23)

Key verse

Verse 7: "And the anger of the LORD was kindled against Uzzah; and God smote him there for his error; and there he died by the ark of God."

Key word / key phrase

Verse 2, "ark."

Key event / key person / key theme

The ark is brought to Jerusalem.

Key thought

God's holiness cannot be ignored.

Key thing to look out for

Michal's and David's characters are set in great contrast to each other.

Key Bible cross-reference

Verse 7. See Exodus 25:15; Numbers 4:5, 6:15.

Key "by way of explanation"

Verse 7. The death of Uzzah would have brought home to the Israelites that they must serve the Lord with all their hearts.

Key "Quotable Quote"

"If I hate or despise any one man in the world, I hate something which God cannot hate, and despise that which he loves."

William Law

2 Samuel 7

Matthew Henry's introduction

Still the ark is David's care as well as his joy. In this chapter we have,

I. His consultation with Nathan about building a house for it; he signifies his purpose to do it (vv. 1, 2) and Nathan approves his purpose, v. 3.

II. His communion with God about it.

A. A gracious message God sent him about it, accepting his purpose, countermanding the performance, and promising him an entail of blessings on his family, vv. 4–17.

B. A very humble prayer which David offered up to God in return to that gracious message, thankfully accepting God's promises to him, and earnestly praying for the performance of them, vv. 18–29. And, in both these, there is an eye to the Messiah and his kingdom.

A detailed analysis of chapter

David's care for the ark. (1–3)

God's covenant with David. (4–17)

His prayer and thanksgiving. (18–29)

Key verse

Verse 3: "And Nathan said to the king, Go, do all that is in thine heart; for the LORD is with thee."

Key word / key phrase

Verses 12, 13, "house."

Key event / key person / key theme

Nathan's message to David

Key thought

David reveals his trust in God in his prayer.

Key thing to look out for

God's promises to David.

Key Bible cross-reference

Verse 2. See 12:1–14; 1 Kings 1.

Key "by way of explanation"

Verse 3. David may have acted rightly in consulting Nathan the prophet, but the prophet did not consult the Lord before pronouncing the Lord's will.

Key "Quotable Quote"

"Where God finds charity with its loving concern, there he recognizes the reflection of his own fatherly care."

Leo the Great

2 Samuel 8

Matthew Henry's introduction

David having sought first the kingdom of God and the righteousness thereof, settling the ark as soon as he was himself well settled, we are here told how all other things were added to him. Here is an account,

I. Of his conquests. He triumphed,
  A. Over the Philistines, v. 1.
  B. Over the Moabites, v. 2.
  C. Over the king of Zobah, vv. 3, 4.
  D. Over the Syrians, vv. 5–8, 13.
  E. Over the Edomites, v. 14.

II. Of the presents that were brought him and the wealth he got from the nations he subdued, which he dedicated to God, vv. 9–12.

III. Of his court, the administration of his government (v. 15), and his chief officers, vv. 16–18. This gives us a general idea of the prosperity of David's reign.

A detailed analysis of chapter

David subdues the Philistines, the Moabites, and the Syrians. (1–8)

The spoil dedicated. (9–14)

David's government and officers. (15–18)

Key verse

Verse 1: "And after this it came to pass, that David smote the Philistines, and subdued them."

Key word / key phrase
Verse 1, "subdued."

Key event / key person / key theme
David's military victories

Key thought
You don't have to be king to promote justice and right living.

Key thing to look out for
Everything we have should be dedicated to the Lord.

Key Bible cross-reference
Verse 2. See Genesis 19:37; 1 Samuel 14:47.

Key "by way of explanation"
Verse 15. Justice and right actions are two characteristics of a godly king.

Key "Quotable Quote"
"God does not desire "something" from us – he desires us, ourselves; not our works, but our personality, our will, our heart."
Emil Brunner

2 Samuel 9

Matthew Henry's introduction
The only thing recorded in this chapter is the kindness David showed to Jonathan's seed.

I. The kind enquiry he made after the remains of the house of Saul, and his discovery of Mephibosheth, vv. 1–4.
II. The kind reception he gave to Mephibosheth, when he was brought to him, vv. 5–8.
III. The kind provision he made for him and his, vv. 9–13.

A detailed analysis of chapter
David sends for Mephibosheth. (1–8)
And provides for him. (9–13)

Key verse
Verse 7: "And David said unto him, Fear not: for I will surely show thee kindness for Jonathan thy father's sake, and will restore thee all the land of Saul thy father; and thou shalt eat bread at my table continually."

Key word / key phrase
Verse 1, "for Jonathan's sake."

Key event / key person / key theme
David shows kindness to Mephibosheth.

Key thought
David deliberately sets out to be kind.

Key thing to look out for
Should our society show positive discrimination toward the disabled?

Key Bible cross-reference
Verse 1. See 1 Samuel 20:15, 42.

Key "by way of explanation"
Verse 8. Mephibosheth shows his genuine humility before David by calling himself a "dead dog."

Key "Quotable Quote"

"I thank God for my handicaps for, through them, I have found myself, my work, and my God."

Helen Keller

2 Samuel 10

Matthew Henry's introduction

I. David sent a friendly embassy to Hanun king of the Ammonites, vv. 1, 2.

II. He, on a base surmise that it was ill intended, abused David's ambassadors, vv. 3, 4.

III. David resenting it (v. 5), and the Ammonites prepared for war against him, v. 6.

IV. David carried the war into their country, sent against them. Joab and Abishai, who addressed themselves to the battle with a great deal of conduct and bravery, vv. 7–12.

V. The Ammonites, and the Syrians their allies, were totally routed, vv. 13, 14.

VI. The forces of the Syrians, which rallied again, were a second time defeated, vv. 15–19. Thus did David advance his own reputation for gratitude, in returning kindness, and for justice, in repaying injuries.

A detailed analysis of chapter

David's messengers ill-treated by Hanun. (1–5)
The Ammonites defeated. (6–14)
The Syrians defeated. (15–19)

Key verse

Verse 5: "When they told it unto David, he sent to meet them, because the men were greatly ashamed: and the king said, Tarry at Jericho until your beards be grown, and then return."

Key word / key phrase

Verse 2, "I will show kindness."

Key event / key person / key theme

David defeats the Ammonites and Arameans.

Key thought

Verse 3. The Ammonite nobles created a problem. It could have been solved if the king had listened to David's men. How often wars and feuds are caused by suspicion and misunderstanding.

Key thing to look out for

Joab's courage and trust in God.

Key Bible cross-reference

Verse 4. See Isaiah 20:4.

Key "by way of explanation"

Verse 4. To shave off his beard was one of the most insulting things you could do to a man.

Key "Quotable Quote"

"Your actions in passing, pass not away, for every good work is a grain of seed for eternal life."

Bernard of Clairvaux

2 Samuel 11

Matthew Henry's introduction

I. He committed adultery with Bath-sheba, the wife of Uriah, vv. 1–5.

II. He endeavored to father the spurious brood on Uriah, vv. 6–13.

III. When that project failed, he plotted the death of Uriah by the sword of the children of Ammon, and effected it, vv. 14–25.

IV. He married Bath-sheba, vv. 26, 27. Is this David? Is this the man after God's own heart? How is his behavior changed, worse than it was before Ahimelech! How has this gold become dim! Let him that readeth understand what the best of men are when God leaves them to themselves.

A detailed analysis of chapter

David's adultery. (1–5)

He tries to conceal his sin. (6–13)

Uriah murdered. (14–27)

Key verse

Verse 4: "And David sent messengers, and took her; and she came in unto him, and he lay with her."

Key word / key phrase

Verse 1, "David remained in Jerusalem."

Key event / key person / key theme

David and Bathsheba

Key thought

Thou shalt not commit adultery.

Key thing to look out for

One evil leads on to another evil.

Key Bible cross-reference

Verse 5. See Leviticus 20:10; Deuteronomy 22:22.

Key "by way of explanation"

Verse 15. David arranged for Uriah to be killed in battle so he could then marry Bathsheba.

Key "Quotable Quote"

"I've committed adultery in my heart many times. This is something that God recognizes I do and I have done it and God forgives me for it."

Jimmy Carter

2 Samuel 12

Matthew Henry's introduction

The previous chapter gave us the account of David's sin; this gives us the account of his repentance. Though he fell, he was not utterly cast down, but, by the grace of God, recovered himself, and found mercy with God. Here is,

I. His conviction, by a message Nathan brought him from God, which was a parable that obliged him to condemn himself (vv. 1–6), and the application of the parable, in which Nathan charged him with the sin (vv. 7–9) and pronounced sentence on him, vv. 10–12.

II. His repentance and remission, with a proviso, vv. 13, 14.

III. The sickness and death of the child, and his behavior while it was sick and when it was dead (vv. 15–23), in both which David gave evidence of his repentance.

IV. The birth of Solomon, and God's gracious message about him, in which God gave an evidence of his reconciliation to David, vv. 24, 25.

V. The taking of Rabbah (vv. 26–31), which is mentioned as a further instance that God did not deal with David according to his sins.

A detailed analysis of chapter

Nathan's parable. David confesses his sin. (1–14)

The birth of Solomon. (15–25)
David's severity to the Ammonites. (26–31)

Key verse
Verse 1: "And the LORD sent Nathan unto David."

Key word / key phrase
Verse 7, "You are the man."

Key event / key person / key theme
Nathan rebukes David.

Key thought
Parables can be most effective in conveying truth.

Key thing to look out for
David repented.

Key Bible cross-reference
Verse 13. See Psalm 51:8,12.

Key "by way of explanation"
Verse 20. David shows his willingness to accept whatever punishment God would give him as a result of his sin.

Key "Quotable Quote"
"True repentance brings an urge to be different."
Florence Allshorn

2 Samuel 13

Matthew Henry's introduction
In this chapter we have,

I. Amnon ravishing Tamar, assisted in his plot to do it by Jonadab his kinsman, and villainously executing it, vv. 1–20.

II. Absalom murdering Amnon for it, vv. 21–39. Both were great griefs to David, and the more because he was unwittingly made accessory to both, by sending Tamar to Amnon and Amnon to Absalom.

A detailed analysis of chapter
Amnon's violence to his sister. (1–20)
Absalom murders his brother Ammon. (21–29)
David's grief. Absalom flees to Geshur. (30–39)

Key verse
Verse 14: "Howbeit he would not hearken unto her voice: but, being stronger than she, forced her, and lay with her."

Key word / key phrase
Verse 1, "Tamar."

Key event / key person / key theme
Amnon and Tamar

Key thought
Uncontrolled lust ruins lives.

Key thing to look out for
Revenge solves nothing.

Key Bible cross-reference
Verse 19. See Jeremiah 2:37.

Key "by way of explanation"
Verse 15. This verse proves that Amnon never loved Tamar in the first place.

Key "Quotable Quote"

"Lust is felt even by fleas and lice."

Martin Luther

2 Samuel 14

Matthew Henry's introduction

I. Joab, by bringing a feigned issue (as the lawyers speak) to be tried before him, in the case of a poor widow of Tekoah, gains from him a judgment in general, That the case might be so as that the putting of a murderer to death ought to be dispensed with, vv. 1–20.

II. On the application of this, he gains from him an order to bring Absalom back to Jerusalem, while yet he was forbidden the court, vv. 21–24.

III. After an account of Absalom, his person, and family, we are told how at length he was introduced by Joab into the king's presence, and the king was thoroughly reconciled to him, vv. 25–33.

A detailed analysis of chapter

Joab procures Absalom's recall. (1–20)
Absalom recalled. (21–24)
His personal beauty. (25–27)
He is admitted to his father's presence. (28–33)

Key verse

Verse 1: "Now Joab the son of Zeruiah perceived that the king's heart was toward Absalom."

Key word / key phrase

Verse 1, "longed for."

Key event / key person / key theme

Joab arranges for Absalom to return.

Key thought

Absalom reveals his nasty character.

Key thing to look out for

David shows weakness in not seeking justice or Absalom's repentance and apology.

Key Bible cross-reference

Verse 8. See Deuteronomy 19:4–6.

Key "by way of explanation"

Verse 32. There is nothing here to indicate that Absalom was repentant for what he had done.

Key "Quotable Quote"

"A stiff apology is a second insult."

G.K. Chesterton

2 Samuel 15

Matthew Henry's introduction 15

The story of Absalom's rebellion begins with this chapter, but we must go over three or four more before we see the end of it. In this chapter we have,

I. The arts Absalom used to insinuate himself into the people's affections, vv. 1–6.

II. His open avowal of his pretensions to the crown at Hebron, whither he went under color of a vow, and the strong party that appeared for him there, vv. 7–12.

III. The notice brought of this to David, and his flight from Jerusalem thereon, vv. 13–18. In his flight we are told,

A. What passed between him and Ittai, vv. 19–22.

B. The concern of the country for him, v. 23.

C. His conversation with Zadok, vv. 24–29.
D. His tears and prayers on this occasion, vv. 30–31.
E. Matters concerted by him with Hushai, vv. 32–37. Now the word of God was fulfilled, that he would "raise up evil against him out of his own house," 12:11.

A detailed analysis of chapter

Absalom's ambition. (1–6)
His conspiracy. (7–12)
David leaves Jerusalem. (13–23)
David sends back the ark. (24–30)
He prays against Ahithophel's counsel. (31–37)

Key verse

Verse 12: "And the conspiracy was strong; for the people increased continually with Absalom."

Key word / key phrase

Verse 14, "we must flee."

Key event / key person / key theme

Absalom's conspiracy

Key thought

Absalom was a thief.

Key thing to look out for

David had so many ups and downs in his life. Here he is on the run again.

Key Bible cross-reference

Verse 21. See Ruth 1:16, 17.

Key "by way of explanation"

Verse 31. In deep trouble, David turns to the Lord in prayer.

Key "Quotable Quote"

"Prayer and helplessness are inseparable. Only he who is helpless can truly pray."

O. Hallesby

2 Samuel 16

Matthew Henry's introduction

In the close of the previous chapter we left David flying from Jerusalem, and Absalom entering into it; in this chapter,

I. We are to follow David in his melancholy flight; and there we find him,
  A. Cheated by Ziba, vv. 1–4.
  B. Cursed by Shimei, which he bears with wonderful patience, vv. 5–14.

II. We are to meet Absalom in his triumphant entry; and there we find him,
  A. Cheated by Hushai, vv. 15–19.
  B. Counseled by Ahithophel to go in unto his father's concubines, vv. 20–23.

A detailed analysis of chapter

Ziba's falsehood. (1–4)
David cursed by Shimei. (5–14)
Ahithophel's counsel. (15–23)

Key verse

Verse 1: "And when David was a little past the top of the hill, behold, Ziba the servant of Mephibosheth met him."

Key word / key phrase

Verse 20, "your advice."

Key event / key person / key theme

Treachery

Key thought

Why did David believe Ziba's lies?

Key thing to look out for

It takes a wise person to know which advice to take.

Key Bible cross-reference

Verse 2. See 9:7–10.

Key "by way of explanation"

Verses 20,21. By following Ahithopheh's advice Absolom announced his open rebellion on David.

Key "Quotable Quote"

"Knowledge without wisdom may be soon discerned; it is usually curious and censorious."

Thomas Manton

2 Samuel 17

Matthew Henry's introduction

The contest between David and Absalom is now hasting towards a crisis. It must be determined by the sword, and preparation is made accordingly in this chapter.

I. Absalom calls a council of war, in which Ahithophel urges dispatch (vv. 1–4), but Hushai recommends deliberation (vv. 5–13); and Hushai's counsel is agreed to (v. 14), for vexation at which Ahithophel hangs himself, v. 23.

II. Secret intelligence is sent to David (but with much difficulty) of their proceedings, vv. 15–21.

III. David marches to the other side Jordan (vv. 22–24), and there his camp is fed by some of his friends in that country, vv. 27–29.

IV. Absalom and his forces march after him into the land of Gilead on the other side Jordan, vv. 25, 26. There we shall, in the next chapter, find the cause decided by a battle: hitherto, every thing has looked black on poor David, but now the day of his deliverance begins to dawn.

A detailed analysis of chapter

Ahithophel's counsel overthrown. (1–21)

He hangs himself. Absalom pursues David. (22–29)

Key verse

Verse 4: "And the saying pleased Absalom well, and all the elders of Israel."

Key word / key phrase

Verse 5, "Summon also Hushai the Arkite."

Key event / key person / key theme

Hushai, the mole in Absalom's court

Key thought

Absalom failed to take God into account as he made his plans.

Key thing to look out for

The courage and loyalty of David's friends.

Key Bible cross-reference

Verse 5. See 16:16–19.

Key "by way of explanation"

Verse 14. This verse indicates that David's prayer was answered. See 15:31.

Key "Quotable Quote"

"Catastrophe can be a means of grace."

Eugune H. Peterson

2 Samuel 18

Matthew Henry's introduction

This chapter puts a period to Absalom's rebellion and life, and so makes way for David to his throne again, whither the next chapter brings him back in peace and triumph. We have here,

I. David's preparations to engage the rebels, vv. 1–5.

II. The total defeat of Absalom's party and their dispersion, vv. 6–8.

III. The death of Absalom, and his burial, vv. 9–18.

IV. The bringing of the tidings to David, who tarried at Mahanaim, vv. 19–32.

V. His bitter lamentation for Absalom, v. 33.

A detailed analysis of chapter

Absalom's army defeated. (1–8)

He is killed. (9–18)

David's great sorrow. (19–33)

Key verse

Verse 14: "Then said Joab, I may not tarry thus with thee. And he took three darts in his hand, and thrust them through the heart of Absalom, while he was yet alive in the midst of the oak."

Key word / key phrase

Verse 53, "Oh my son Absalom!"

Key event / key person / key theme

Absalom's death

Key thought

David loved his wicked son to the end.

Key thing to look out for

David's great sadness was brought on him by his own inaction and sin, as well as by Absalom's rebellion.

Key Bible cross-reference

Verse 6. See 15:13; 16:15.

Key "by way of explanation"

Verse 5. David could not bear the thought that Absalom would come to any harm.

Key "Quotable Quote"

"We never know the love of the parent until we become parents ourselves."

Henry Ward Beecher

2 Samuel 19

Matthew Henry's introduction

We left David's army in triumph and yet David himself in tears: now here we have,

I. His return to himself, by the persuasion of Joab, vv. 1–8.

II. His return to his kingdom from his present banishment.

A. The men of Israel were forward of themselves to bring him back, vv. 9, 10.

B. The men of Judah were dealt with by David's agents to do it (vv. 11–14) and did it, v. 15.

III. At the king's coming over Jordan, Shimei's treason is pardoned (vv. 16–23), Mephibosheth's failure is excused (vv. 24–30), and Barzillai's kindness is thankfully owned, and recompensed to his son, vv. 31–39.

IV. The men of Israel quarreled with the men of Judah, for not calling them to the ceremony of the king's restoration, which occasioned a new rebellion, an account of which we have in the next chapter, vv. 40–43.

A detailed analysis of chapter

Joab helps David to stop mourning. (1–8)

At David's instigation the elders of Judah invite him back. (9–15)

He pardons Shimei. (16–23)

David withholds judgment on Mephibosheth. (24–30)

David's parting with Barzillai. (31–40)

David's homecoming; the leaders of Israel quarrel with the leaders of Judah. (41–43)

Key verse

Verse 8: "Then the king arose, and sat in the gate. And they told unto all the people, saying, Behold, the king doth sit in the gate. And all the people came before the king: for Israel had fled every man to his tent."

Key word / key phrase

Verse 14, "return."

Key event / key person / key theme

David returns to Jerusalem

Key thought

Mephibosheth is a picture of loyalty.

Key thing to look out for

People in places of responsibility can be guilty of betraying people.

Key Bible cross-reference

Verse 24. See 9:6–13.

Key "by way of explanation"

Verse 20. The "house of Joseph" refers to the northern tribes, whose most important parts were Ephraim and Manasseh.

Key "Quotable Quote"

"Our loyalty is due not to our species but to God . . . it is spiritual, not biological, kinship that counts."

C.S. Lewis

2 Samuel 20

Matthew Henry's introduction

How do the clouds return after the rain! No sooner is one of David's troubles over than another arises, as it were out of the ashes of the former, in which the threatening is fulfilled, that the sword should never depart from his house.

I. Before he reaches Jerusalem a new rebellion is raised by Sheba, vv. 1, 2.

II. His first work, when he comes to Jerusalem, is to condemn his concubines to perpetual imprisonment, v. 3.

III. Amass, whom he entrusts to raise an army against Sheba, is too slow in his motions, which puts him into a fright, vv. 4–6.

IV. One of his generals barbarously murders the other, when they are taking the field, vv. 7–13.

V. Sheba is at length shut up in the city of Abel (vv. 14, 15), but the citizens deliver him up to Joab, and so his rebellion is crushed, vv. 16–22. The chapter concludes with a short account of David's great officers, vv. 23–26.

A detailed analysis of chapter

Sheba's rebellion. (1–3)

Amasa killed by Joab. (4–13)

Sheba takes refuge in Abel Beth Maacah where he is killed. (14–22)

David's officers. (23–26)

Key verse

Verse 2: "So every man of Israel went up from after David, and followed Sheba."

Key word / key phrase

Verse 1, "troublemaker."

Key event / key person / key theme

Sheba rebels against David

Key thought

Joab was no stranger to committing murder in order to secure his own position.

Key thing to look out for

The part played by the wise woman.

Key Bible cross-reference

Verse 19. See Jeremiah 50:12; Galatians 4:26.

Key "by way of explanation"

Verse 19. The phrase "a mother in Israel" refers to a city that produced people who became faithful Israelites.

Key "Quotable Quote"

"The least-used words by an unselfish person are I, me, my, and mine."

Charles R. Swindoll

2 Samuel 21

Matthew Henry's introduction

We have here,

I. The Gibeonites avenged,

A. By a famine in the land, v. 1.

B. By the putting of seven of Saul's posterity to death (vv. 2–9), care, however, being taken of their dead bodies, and of the bones of Saul, vv. 10–14.

II. The giants of the Philistines slain in several battles, vv. 15–22.

A detailed analysis of chapter

The Gibeonites avenged. (1–9)

Rizpah's care for the bodies of Saul's descendants. (10–14)

Battles with the Philistines. (15–22)

Key verse

Verse 7: "But the king spared Mephibosheth, the son of Jonathan the son of Saul, because of the LORD's oath that was between them, between David and Jonathan the son of Saul."

Key word / key phrase

Verse 1, "famine."

Key event / key person / key theme

Saul's descendants are killed

Key thought

Trials drive us to the Lord as times of ease do not.

Key thing to look out for

Verse 1. When trouble came, what was David's purpose in praying?

Key Bible cross-reference

Verse 4. See Exodus 22:21; Leviticus 19:34.

Key "by way of explanation"

Verse 12. David shows his respect for King Saul and his love for Jonathan by taking charge of their bones.

Key "Quotable Quote"

"Troubles are often the tools by which God fashions us for better things."

Henry Ward Beecher

2 Samuel 22

Matthew Henry's introduction

Here is,

I. The title of the psalm, v. 1.

II. The psalm itself, in which, with a very warm devotion and very great fluency and copiousness of expression,

A. He gives glory to God.

B. He takes comfort in him; and he finds matter for both,

In the experiences he had of God's former favors.

In the expectations he had of his further favors. These are intermixed through out the whole psalm.

A detailed analysis of chapter

David's psalm of thanksgiving. (1–51)

Key verse

Verse 1: "And David spake unto the LORD the words of this song in the day that the LORD had delivered him out of the hand of all his enemies, and out of the hand of Saul."

Key word / key phrase

Verse 1, "sang."

Key event / key person / key theme

David's song of praise

Key thought

David's heart is full of thanksgiving.

Key thing to look out for

For a man who suffered so much it is noteworthy that he can give thanks to the Lord so much.

Key Bible cross-reference

Verse 1. See Psalm 18.

Key "by way of explanation"

Verse 2. It is most instructive to see the first name David gives to his Lord in this psalm: it is "rock."

Key "Quotable Quote"

"Praise focuses our hearts on God. The problem or need about which we pray may seem overwhelming, but we must see God infinitely greater than our problem, able to meet all our need."

Wesley Duewel

2 Samuel 23

Matthew Henry's introduction

The historian is now drawing towards a conclusion of David's reign, and therefore gives us an account here,

I. Of some of his last words, which he spoke by inspiration, and which seem to have reference to his seed that was to be for evermore, spoken of in the close of the previous chapter, vv. 1–7.

II. Of the great men, especially the military men, that were employed under him, the first three (vv. 8–17), two of the next three (vv. 18–23), and then the thirty, vv. 24–39.

A detailed analysis of chapter

David's last words. (1–7)

David's mighty men. (8–39)

Key verse

Verse 1: "Now these be the last words of David."

Key word / key phrase

Verse 10, "the LORD brought about."

Key event / key person / key theme

David's last words

Key thought

David saw how much righteousness means to the Lord.

Key thing to look out for

The different ways in which people can be "mighty."

Key Bible cross-reference

Verse 1. See 1 Kings 2:1–10.

Key "by way of explanation"

David's mighty men are subdivided into the Three and Thirty.

Key "Quotable Quote"

"We should not give the impression in our practice that, just because they are expressed in traditional Christian terminology, all religious concepts are on a graduated, quantitative spectrum – that, in regard to central doctrine, no chasm exists between right and wrong."

Francis A. Schaeffer

2 Samuel 24

Matthew Henry's introduction

The last words of David, which we read in the chapter before, were admirably good, but in this chapter we read of some of his last works, which were none of the best; yet he repented, and did his first works again, and so he finished well. We have here,

I. His sin, which was numbering the people

in the pride of his heart, vv. 1–9.
II. His conviction of the sin, and repentance for it, v. 10.
III. The judgment inflicted on him for it, vv. 11–15.
IV. The staying of the judgment, vv. 16, 17.
V. The erecting of an altar in token of God's reconciliation to him and his people, vv. 18–25.

A detailed analysis of chapter

David numbers the people. (1–9)
He chooses the plague. (10–15)
The plague is stopped. (16,17)
David's sacrifice, and the plague lifted. (18–25)

Key verse

Verse 1: "And again the anger of the LORD was kindled against Israel, and he moved David against them to say, Go, number Israel and Judah."

Key word / key phrase

Verse 1, "census."

Key event / key person / key theme

David takes a census

Key thought

David is quick to take the blame.

Key thing to look out for

David's humility and confession of sin before the Lord rectifies the situation.

Key Bible cross-reference

Verse 1. See 24:1.

Key "by way of explanation"

Verse 1. It appears that the taking of this particular census showed that David was trusting in human power rather than in God's power.

Key "Quotable Quote"

"There is nothing morbid about the confession of sins, so long as we go on to give thanks for the forgiveness of sins."

John R.W. Stott

5. Select bibliography for 1 and 2 Samuel

Baldwin, Joyce G. *1 & 2 Samuel.* Downers Grove: InterVarsity, 1988.

Gordon, Evans, Mary J. *1 And 2 Samuel* (New International Biblical Commentary: OT Series, 6), Hendrickson, 2000.

Gordon, Robert P. *I and II Samuel: An Exegetical Commentary*, Zondervan, 1988.

Keil, C. F., and F. Delitzsch. *Biblical Commentary on the Books of Samuel.* Grand Rapids: Eerdmans, 1956.

1 and 2 Kings

1. Book by book: Introduction to 1 and 2 Kings

Introduction

The first and second books of Kings, in the ancient copies of the Hebrew Bible, constitute one book. Various titles have been given them; in the Septuagint and the Vulgate they are called the Third and Fourth Books of Kings. The authorship of these books is unknown; but the prevailing opinion is that they were compiled by Ezra, or one of the later prophets, from the ancient documents that are so frequently referred to in the course of the history as of public and established authority. Their inspired character was acknowledged by the Jewish Church, which ranked them in the sacred canon; and, besides, it is attested by our Lord, who frequently quotes from them (compare 1 Kings 17:9; 2 Kings 5:14 with Luke 4:24–27; 1 Kings 10:1 with Matthew 12:42).

Robert Jamieson

Contents of 1 and 2 Kings

1 and 2 Kings give the history of the Israelites over a four hundred year period, from David's death to their deportation to Babylon.

The Books of Kings contain 47 chapters (I, 22 chs; II, 25 chs), and cover the period from the conspiracy of Adonijah and the accession of Solomon (975 B.C.) to the liberation of Jehoiachin after the beginning of the Exile (561 B.C.).

The chief aim of these books is didactic, the imparting of great moral lessons backed up by well-known illustrations from the nation's history and from the lives of its heroes and leaders. Accordingly, we have here a sort of historical archipelago, more continuous than in the Pentateuch.

The Books of Kings contain much historical material, yet the historical is not their primary purpose. What in our English Bibles pass for historical books are in the Hebrew Canon prophetic books, the Books of Joshua, Judges, 1 Samuel, 2 Samuel, 1 Kings and 2 Kings being classed as the "Earlier Prophets."

(1) Solomon and his times (1 Kings 1–11);

(2) Israel and Judah to the fall of Israel (1 Kings 12–2 Kings 17);

(3) the captivity to the liberation of Jehoiachin (561 B.C.) (2 Kings 18–25).

Above all, there are three features in the history, which, in the mind of the author, are of prime importance as shown by the prominence he gives them in his narrative.

(1) The dynasty of David is invested with peculiar dignity. This had two aspects. It pointed back to the Divine election of the nation in the past, and gave the guaranty of indefinite national perpetuity in the future. The promise of the `sure mercies of David' was a powerful uniting influence in the Exile.

(2) The Temple and its service, for which the writer had such special regard, contributed greatly to the phase of national character of subsequent times. With all the drawbacks and defacements of pure worship here was the stated regular performance of sacred rites, the development and regulation of priestly order and ritual law, which stamped themselves so firmly on later Judaism.

(3) Above all, this was the period of bloom of Old Testament prophecy. Though more is said of men like Elijah and Elisha, who have left no written words, we must not forget the desires of pre-exilic prophets, whose writings have come down to us—men who, against the opposition of rulers and the indifference of the people, testified to the moral foundation on which the nation was constituted, vindicated Divine righteousness, rebuked sin, and held up the ideal to which the nation was called." Robertson, Temple

Orr, James, M.A., D.D. General Editor, International Standard Bible Encyclopedia

Detailed outline of 1 Kings

1:1–1:27	The Struggle for the Succession
1:28–1:53	The Accession of Solomon
2:1–2:9	David's Instruction to Solomon
2:10–2:12	Death of David
2:13–2:46	Solomon Consolidates His Reign
3:1–3:15	Solomon's Prayer for Wisdom
3:16–3:28	Solomon's Wisdom in Judgment
4:1–4:19	Solomon's Administrative Officers
4:20–4:28	Magnificence of Solomon's Rule
4:29–4:34	Fame of Solomon's Wisdom
5:1–5:18	Preparations and Materials
6:1–6:22	Solomon Builds the Temple
6:23–6:38	The Furnishings of the Temple
7:1–7:12	Solomon's Palace and Other Buildings
7:13–7:51	Products of Hiram the Bronze worker
8:1–8:21	Dedication of the Temple
8:22–8:53	Solomon's Prayer of Dedication
8:54–8:61	Solomon Blesses the Assembly
8:62–8:66	Solomon Offers Sacrifices
9:1–9:14	God Appears Again to Solomon
9:15–9:25	Other Acts of Solomon
9:26–9:28	Solomon's Commercial Activity
10:1–10:29	Visit of the Queen of Sheba
11:1–11:13	Solomon's Errors
11:14–11:25	Adversaries of Solomon
11:26–11:40	Jeroboam's Rebellion
11:41–11:43	Death of Solomon
12:1–12:19	The Northern Tribes Secede
12:20–12:24	First Dynasty: Jeroboam Reigns over Israel
12:25–12:33	Jeroboam's Golden Calves
13:1–13:34	A Man of God from Judah

14:1–14:18 Judgment on the House of Jeroboam
14:19–14:20 Death of Jeroboam
14:21–14:31 Rehoboam Reigns over Judah

15:1–15:8 Abijam Reigns over Judah: Idolatry and War
15:9–15:15 Asa Reigns over Judah
15:16–15:24 Alliance with Aram against Israel
15:25–15:32 Nadab Reigns over Israel
15:33–16:7 Second Dynasty: Baasha Reigns over Israel

16:8–16:14 Elah Reigns over Israel
16:15–16:20 Third Dynasty: Zimri Reigns over Israel
16:21–16:23 Fourth Dynasty: Omri Reigns over Israel
16:24–16:28 Samaria the New Capital
16:29–16:30 Ahab Reigns over Israel
16:31–16:34 Ahab Marries Jezebel and Worships Baal

17:1–17:7 Elijah Predicts a Drought
17:8–17:16 The Widow of Zarephath
17:17–17:24 Elijah Revives the Widow's Son

18:1–18:19 Elijah's Message to Ahab
18:20–18:40 Elijah's Triumph over the Priests of Baal
18:41–18:46 The Drought Ends

19:1–19:10 Elijah Flees from Jezebel
19:11–19:18 Elijah Meets God at Horeb
19:19–19:21 Elisha Becomes Elijah's Disciple

20:1–20:12 Ahab's Wars with the Arameans
20:13–20:22 Prophetic Opposition to Ahab
20:23–20:34 The Arameans are Defeated
20:35–20:43 A Prophet Condemns Ahab

21:1–21:16 Naboth's Vineyard
21:17–21:28 Elijah Pronounces God's Sentence

22:1–22:12 Joint Campaign with Judah against Aram
22:13–22:28 Micaiah Predicts Failure
22:29–22:40 Defeat and Death of Ahab
22:41–22:50 Jehoshaphat Reigns over Judah
22:51–22:53 Ahaziah Reigns over Israel

Detailed outline of 2 Kings

Part one: The divided kingdom: 1:1–17:41

1:1–1:16 Elijah Denounces Ahaziah
1:17–1:18 Death of Ahaziah

2:1–2:12 Elijah Ascends to Heaven
2:13–2:18 Elisha Succeeds Elijah
2:19–2:25 Elisha Performs Miracles

3:1–3:3 Jehoram Reigns over Israel
3:4–3:27 War with Moab

4:1–4:7 Elisha and the Widow's Oil
4:8–4:37 Elisha Raises the Shunammite's Son
4:38–4:41 Elisha Purifies the Pot of Stew
4:42–4:44 Elisha Feeds One Hundred Men

5:1–5:19 The Healing of Naaman
5:20–5:27 Gehazi's Greed

6:1–6:23 The Miracle of the Ax Head
6:24–7:2 Ben-hadad's Siege of Samaria

7:3–7:20 The Arameans Flee

8:1–8:6 The Shunammite Woman's Land Restored
8:7–8:15 Death of Benhadad
8:16–8:24 Jehoram Reigns over Judah
8:25–8:29 Ahaziah Reigns over Judah

9:1–9:13 Anointing of Jehu
9:14–9:26 Joram of Israel Killed
9:27–9:29 Ahaziah of Judah Killed
9:30–9:37 Jezebel's Violent Death

10:1–10:17 Massacre of Ahab's Descendants
10:18–10:31 Slaughter of Worshipers of Baal
10:32–10:36 Death of Jehu

11:1–11:3 Athaliah Reigns over Judah
11:4–11:12 Jehoiada Anoints the Child Joash
11:13–11:21 Death of Athaliah

12:1–12:16 The Temple Repaired
12:17–12:18 Hazael Threatens Jerusalem
12:19–12:21 Death of Joash

13:1–13:9 Jehoahaz Reigns over Israel
13:10–13:13 Jehoash Reigns over Israel
13:14–13:21 Death of Elisha
13:22–13:25 Israel Recaptures Cities from Aram
14:1–14:29 Amaziah Reigns over Judah

15:1–15:7 Azariah Reigns over Judah
15:8–15:12 Zechariah Reigns over Israel
15:13–15:16 Shallum Reigns over Israel
15:17–15:22 Menahem Reigns over Israel
15:23–15:26 Pekahiah Reigns over Israel
15:27–15:31 Pekah Reigns over Israel
15:32–15:38 Jotham Reigns over Judah

16:1–16:20 Ahaz Reigns over Judah

17:1–17:4 Hoshea Reigns over Israel
17:5–17:23 Israel Carried Captive to Assyria
17:24–17:41 Assyria Resettles Samaria

Part two: The surviving kingdom of Judah: 18:1–25:30

18:1–18:12 Hezekiah's Reign over Judah
18:13–18:37 Sennacherib Invades Judah

19:1–19:7 Hezekiah Consults Isaiah
19:8–19:13 Sennacherib's Threat
19:14–19:34 Hezekiah's Prayer
19:35–19:37 Sennacherib's Defeat and Death

20:1–20:11 Hezekiah's Illness
20:12–20:19 Envoys from Babylon
20:20–20:21 Death of Hezekiah

21:1–21:18 Manasseh Reigns over Judah
21:19–21:26 Amon Reigns over Judah

22:1–22:2 Josiah Reigns over Judah

22:3–22:20 Hilkiah Finds the Book of the Law
23:1–23:20 Josiah's Reformation
23:21–23:27 The Passover Celebrated
23:28–23:30 Josiah Dies in Battle
23:31–23:35 Reign and Captivity of Jehoahaz
23:36–23:37 Jehoiakim Reigns over Judah

24:1–24:7 Judah Overrun by Enemies
24:8–24:12 Reign and Captivity of Jehoiachin
24:13–24:17 Capture of Jerusalem
24:18–24:20 Zedekiah Reigns over Judah

25:1–25:21 The Fall and Captivity of Judah
25:22–25:26 Gedaliah Made Governor of Judah
25:27–25:30 Jehoiachin Released from Prison

2. Helpful summaries of 1 and 2 Kings

Bird's eye view

The history of Israel and Judah, from the end of Ahaziah's reign in Israel, and from the reign of Jehoram in Judah, until the kingdoms were captured.

Reading plan

The following reading plan, taking one reading per day, enables you to read through 1 and 2 Kings in twenty-five days.

1 Kings 1
1 Kings 2–3
1 Kings 4–5
1 Kings 6
1 Kings 7–8
1 Kings 9
1 Kings 10–11
1 Kings 12–13
1 Kings 14–15
1 Kings 16–17
1 Kings 18–19
1 Kings 20–21
1 Kings 22
2 Kings 1–3
2 Kings 4–5
2 Kings 6–7
2 Kings 8–9
2 Kings 10–11
2 Kings 12–14
2 Kings 15–16
2 Kings 17
2 Kings 18–19
2 Kings 20–22
2 Kings 23–24
2 Kings 25

Verses to memorize

1 Kings 8:58

May he turn our hearts to him, to walk in all his ways and keep the commands, decrees, and regulations he gave our fathers.

2 Kings 20:5

I have heard your prayer and seen your tears; I will heal you.

Statistics

1 Kings

Eleventh Old Testament book
22 chapters
816 verses
24,524 words

2 Kings
Twelfth Old Testament book
22 chapters
719 verses
23,532 words

Famous saying found in 2 Kings
"Put your house in order" 2 Kings 20:1

Names/titles given
Hebrew title: *Melechim*: from the first word in 1 Kings 1:1, *Vehamelech*: "Now king." In the Hebrew Bible 1 and 2 Kings were a single book.
Greek title in Septuagint: The Septuagint split the single Hebrew book into two book, 1 and 2 Kings. It gave the name of "First and Second Kingdoms" to 1 and 2 Samuel, and "Third and Fourth Kingdoms" to 1 and 2 Kings.
Latin title in Vulgate: *Liber Regum Tertius et Quartus:* "Third and Fourth Book of Kings."

3. Helpful keys to turn to in understanding 1 and 2 Kings

Key words
1 Kings
Royalty
David his father
2 Kings
Evil

Key verses
1 Kings 9:4–5; 11:11
2 Kings 10:10; 23:27

Themes to study
1 Kings
The Lord's sovereignty
The Lord's righteousness
Human weaknesses
2 Kings
Hezekiah's reforms
Lessons about leadership
Evil is punished, righteousness is rewarded.

1 Kings quoted in the New Testament
I alone am left, and they seek my life
1 Kgs. 19:10, 14 quoted in Rom. 11:3
Who have not bowed the knee to Baal
1 Kgs. 19:18 quoted in Rom. 11:4

Unusual events and miracles in 1 Kings
- Solomon's request for wisdom, 3:5–15
- Solomon's judgment over two women claiming to be the mother of the same baby, 3:16–28
- Jeroboam's hand shriveled up, and later restored, 13:4–13
- Drought, 17:1
- Elijah fed by ravens, 17:2–6
- The widow's flour and oil not running out, 17:10–16
- The raising of the widow's son, 17:17–24
- The Lord's fire burning up the sacrifice, 18:38
- Rain at the end of the drought, 18:41–45
- Elijah fed by an angel, 19:1–8
- City wall falling on Syrian troops, 20:28–30

Unusual events and miracles in 2 Kings
- Ahaziah's men consumed by fire, 1:9–12
- The River Jordan divided, 2:8,14

- Chariot of fire taking Elijah to heaven, 2:11
- Waters of Jericho made drinkable, 2:19–22
- Mocking youths mauled by bears, 2:24
- Water provided for large army, 3:16–20
- Moabites mistake reflection of sunset for blood, 3:21–24
- The widow's oil does not run out, 4:1–7
- The Shunammite woman having a son, 4:14–17
- The widow's son raised from the dead, 4:32–36
- One hundred men fed with twenty loaves, 4:42–44
- Naaman's leprosy healed, 5:10–14
- Gehazi becomes a leper, 5:24–27
- Axe head floats, 6:6
- Elijah's servant sees the Lord's army, 6:13–17
- Syrian army blinded, and have sight restored, 6:18–20
- Dead man brought back to life after contact with Elisha's bones, 13:20–21
- Sennacherib's army destroyed, in answer to prayer, 29:35
- Hezekiah given fifteen more years of life, 20:1–7
- The sun goes backwards, 20:8–11

Key people/ events

1 Kings

Abiathar

Zadok

Adonijah

Solomon

Solomon's actions to secure the throne

Temple

Rehoboam

Jeroboam (I)

Dan and Bethel

Omri

Samaria

Ahab

Jezebel

Elijah

Baal

Contest on Mt. Carmel

Elijah at Horeb

Naboth

2 Kings

Elisha

Shunammite woman

Naaman

Jehu

Athaliah

Jeroboam (II)

Hoshea

Sennacherib

Hezekiah and Assyria

Merodach-Baladan

Manasseh

Josiah

Huldah

"Book of the Law"

Nebuchadnezzar

Zedekiah

Gedaliah

List of kings of Israel

1 Kings

Jeroboam I, 1 Kgs. 11:28

Nadab, 1 Kgs. 14:20

Baasha, 1 Kgs. 15:16

Elah, 1 Kgs. 16:8
Zimri, 1 Kgs. 16:15
Omri, 1 Kgs. 16:16
Ahab, 1 Kgs. 16:29
Ahaziah, 1 Kgs.22:40
Jehoram/Joram, 2 Kgs. 1:17
Jehu, 1 Kgs. 19:16

2 Kings

Jehoahaz, 2 Kgs. 10:35
Jehoash, 2 Kgs.13:10
Jeroboam II, 2 Kgs.14:23
Zechariah, 2 Kgs. 14:29
Shallum, 2 Kgs. 15:10
Menahem, 2 Kgs. 15:14
Pekahiah, 2 Kgs. 15:23
Pekah, 2 Kgs.15:25
Hoshea, 2 Kgs. 15:30

List of kings of Judah

1 Kings

Rehoboam, 1 Kgs. 11:43
Abijah [Abijam] , 1 Kgs. 14:31
Asa, 1 Kgs. 15:8
Jehoshaphat, 1 Kgs. 15:24
[Jehoram, 2 Chr. 21:1]

2 Kings

Ahaziah, 2 Kgs. 8:25
Queen Athaliah, 2 Kgs. 8:26
Joash [Jehoash] , 2 Kgs. 11:2
Amaziah, 2 Kgs. 14:1
Azariah [Uzziah] , 2 Kgs. 14:21
Jotham, 2 Kgs. 15:5
Ahaz, 2 Kgs. 15:38
Hezekiah, 2 Kgs. 16:20
Manasseh, 2 Kgs.21:1
Amon, 2 Kgs.21:19
[Josiah, 1 Kgs. 13:2]
Jehoahaz [Shallum], 2 Kgs. 23:30
Jehoiakim, 2 Kgs. 23:34
Jehoiachin [Jeconiah] , 2 Kgs.24:6
Zedekiah [Mattaniah] , 2 Kgs. 24:17

Jesus in 1 and 2 Kings

In 1 and 2 Kings Jesus is the King of kings and Lord of lords.

Types of Jesus in 1 and 2 Kings

1 Kings

- Solomon is seen as a type of Jesus because of his renowned wisdom, see 1 Cor. 1:30; and because of the wealth and glory of his earthly kingdom which mirrored Jesus' heavenly kingdom, see Matt. 12:42.

2 Kings

- Jesus is a direct descendant of David's line.
- Elijah is a type of John the Baptist, see Matt. 11:14, the forerunner of Jesus.

Lessons to learn from 1 and 2 Kings

1 Kings

- Elijah shows how God's servants should be faithful to God, and trust in God and his Word.
- The temple emphasizes with importance of worship.
- Helping God's servants is a Christian ministry.

2 Kings

- God chose an infinite variety of people to serve him.
- Faith and action are both required in serving God.

4. Chapter by chapter: outline of every chapter of 1 and 2 Kings

1 Kings 1

Matthew Henry's introduction

In this chapter we have,

I. David declining in his health, vv. 1–4.

II. Adonijah aspiring to the kingdom, and treating his party, in order to it, vv. 5–10.

III. Nathan and Bathsheba contriving to secure the succession to Solomon, and prevailing for an order from David for the purpose, vv. 11–31.

IV. The anointing of Solomon accordingly, and the people's joy therein, vv. 32–40.

V. The effectual stop this put to Adonijah's usurpation, and the dispersion of his party thereon, vv. 41–49.

VI. Solomon's dismissing of Adonijah on his good behavior, vv. 50–53.

A detailed analysis of chapter

David's old age. (1–4)

Adonijah aspires to the throne. (5–10)

David makes Solomon king. (11–31)

Solomon is anointed king, and Adonijah's usurpation stopped. (32–53)

Key verse

Verse 1: "Now king David was old and stricken in years; and they covered him with clothes, but he gat no heat."

Key word / key phrase

Verse 30, "Carry out."

Key event / key person / key theme

David appoints Solomon to succeed him as king.

Key thought

David never seemed to be far from some rebellion against him.

Key thing to look out for

Solomon shows his wisdom in a difficult situation.

Key Bible cross-reference

Verse 31. See Nehemiah 2:3; Daniel 2:4; 3:9; 5:10.

Key "by way of explanation"

Verse 5. David's fourth son, Adonijah, attempts to ensure that he will succeed to David's throne.

Key "Quotable Quote"

"He will not be a wise man who does not study the human heart. "

C.H. Spurgeon

1 Kings 2

Matthew Henry's introduction

In this chapter we have David setting and Solomon at the same time rising.

I. The conclusion of David's reign with his life.

A. The charge he gives to Solomon on his death-bed, in general, to serve God (vv. 1–4), in particular, about Joab, Barzillai, and Shimei, vv. 5–9.

B. His death and burial, and the years of his reign, vv. 10, 11.

II. The beginning of Solomon's reign, v. 12. Though he was to be a prince of peace, he began his reign with some remarkable acts of justice,

A. On Adonijah, whom he put to death for his aspiring pretensions, vv. 13–25.

B. On Abiathar, whom he deposed from the high priesthood for siding with Adonijah, vv. 26, 27.

C. On Joab, who he put to death for his late treasons and former murders, vv. 28–35.

D. On Shimei, whom, for cursing David, he confined to Jerusalem (vv. 36–38), and three years after, for transgressing the rules, put to death, vv. 39–46.

A detailed analysis of chapter

David's dying charge to Solomon. (1–4)
David's charge to Joab and others. (5–11)
Solomon reigns. Adonijah aspiring to the throne is put to death. (12–25)
Abiathar banished. Joab put to death. (26–34)
Shimei is put to death. (35–46)

Key verse

Verse 1: "Now the days of David drew nigh that he should die; and he charged Solomon his son . . ."

Key word / key phrase

Verse 1, "die."

Key event / key person / key theme

David's last instructions to Solomon

Key thought

Solomon knew that David's overriding concern was that he should be faithful to God.

Key thing to look out for

Solomon was also told to whom he should show kindness.

Key Bible cross-reference

Verse 4. See Deuteronomy 4:29; 6:5.

Key "by way of explanation"

Verse 22. Solomon saw that this request was a thinly disguised attempt to take the throne away from him.

Key "Quotable Quote"

"I do not pray for success, I ask for faithfulness."

Mother Teresa of Calcutta

1 Kings 3

Matthew Henry's introduction

Solomon's reign looked bloody in the previous chapter, but the necessary acts of justice must not be called cruelty; in this chapter it appears with another face. We must not think the worse of God's mercy to his subjects for his judgments on rebels. We have here,

I. Solomon's marriage to Pharaoh's daughter, v. 1.

II. A general view of his religion, vv. 2–4.

III. A particular account of his prayer to God for wisdom, and the answer to that prayer, vv. 5–15.

IV. A particular instance of his wisdom in deciding the controversy between the two harlots, vv. 16–28. And very great he looks here, both at the altar and on the bench, and therefore on the bench because at the altar.

A detailed analysis of chapter

Solomon's marriage. (1–4)

His vision. His prayer for wisdom. (5–15)

The judgment of Solomon. (16–28)

Key verse

Verse 9: "Give therefore thy servant an understanding heart to judge thy people, that I may discern between good and bad: for who is able to judge this thy so great a people?"

Key word / key phrase

Verse 9, "discerning heart."

Key event / key person / key theme

Solomon asks for wisdom

Key thought

God reads our hearts.

Key thing to look out for

Wisdom comes from God.

Key Bible cross-reference

Verse 13. See Luke 12:31.

Key "by way of explanation"

Verse 9, "discerning." This comes from the Hebrew word meaning "listen"–"a listening heart."

Key "Quotable Quote"

"Knowledge is horizontal. Wisdom is vertical – it comes down from above."

Billy Graham

1 Kings 4

Matthew Henry's introduction

An instance of the wisdom God granted to Solomon we had in the close of the previous chapter. In this we have an account of his wealth and prosperity, the other branch of the promise there made him. We have here,

I. The magnificence of his court, his ministers of state (vv. 1–6), and the purveyors of his household (vv. 7–19), and their office, vv. 27, 28.

II. The provisions for his table, vv. 22, 23.

III. The extent of his dominion, vv. 21–24.

IV. The numbers, case, and peace, of his subjects, vv. 20–25. V. His stables, v. 26.

VI. His great reputation for wisdom and learning, vv. 29–34. Thus great was Solomon, but our Lord Jesus was greater than he (Matt. 12:42), though he took on him the form of a servant; for divinity, in its lowest humiliation, infinitely transcends royalty in its highest elevation.

A detailed analysis of chapter

Solomon's court. (1–19)

Solomon's dominions. His daily provision. (20–28)

The wisdom of Solomon. (29–34)

Key verse

Verse 29: "And God gave Solomon wisdom and understanding exceeding much, and largeness of heart, even as the sand that is on the sea shore."

Key word / key phrase
Verse 22, “daily provisions.”

Key event / key person / key theme
Solomon’s prosperous reign

Key thought
Material prosperity is a gift from God.

Key thing to look out for
In what ways did Solomon reveal his wisdom?

Key Bible cross-reference
Verse 1. See 2 Samuel 8:15.

Key “by way of explanation”
Verse 32. Some of the “three thousand proverbs” of Solomon have been preserved in the Old Testament book of Proverbs.

Key “Quotable Quote”
“A wise man cares not for what he cannot have.”
George Herbert

1 Kings 5

Matthew Henry’s introduction

I. Hiram congratulated him on his accession to the throne, v. 1.
II. Solomon signified to him his design to build the temple and desired him to furnish him with workmen, vv. 2–6.
III. Hiram agreed to do it, vv. 7–9.
IV. Solomon’s work was accordingly well done and Hiram’s workmen were well paid, vv. 10–18.

A detailed analysis of chapter
Solomon’s agreement with Hiram. (1–9)
Solomon’s workmen for the temple. (10–18)

Key verse
Verse 1: “And Hiram king of Tyre sent his servants unto Solomon; for he had heard that they had anointed him king in the room of his father: for Hiram was ever a lover of David.”

Key word / key phrase
Verse 5, “build a temple.”

Key event / key person / key theme
Preparations are made to build the temple

Key thought
Friendship between nations can be mutually beneficial.

Key thing to look out for
Skilled craftsmen were used at each stage of the temple’s building.

Key Bible cross-reference
Verse 3. See 1 Chronicles 22:2–5.

Key “by way of explanation”
Verse 13. This forced labor eventually resulted in rebellion after Solomon died.

Key “Quotable Quote”
“We can express our worship to God in many ways. But if we love the Lord and are led by his Holy Spirit, our worship will always bring a delighted sense of admiring awe and a

sincere humility on our part."

A.W. Tozer

1 Kings 6

Matthew Henry's introduction

Here is,

I. The time when it was built (v. 1), and how long it was in the building, vv. 37, 38.
II. The silence with which it was build, v. 7.
III. The dimensions of it, vv. 2, 3.
IV. The message God sent to Solomon, when it was in the building, vv. 11–13.
V. The particulars: windows (v. 4), chambers (vv. 5, 6, 8–10), the walls and flooring (vv. 15–18), the oracle (vv. 19–22), the cherubim (vv. 23–30), the doors (vv. 31–35), and the inner court, v. 36.

A detailed analysis of chapter

The building of Solomon's temple. (1–10)
Promise given about the temple. (11–14)
Details about the temple. (15–38)

Key verse

Verse 2: "And the house which king Solomon built for the LORD, the length thereof was threescore cubits, and the breadth thereof twenty cubits, and the height thereof thirty cubits."

Key word / key phrase

Verse 1, "build."

Key event / key person / key theme

Solomon builds the temple

Key thought

Solomon is reassured that his own family will succeed him.

Key thing to look out for

The building materials used indicate the great care that was taken to ensure that the temple was fit to be "the house of the Lord."

Key Bible cross-reference

Verse 19. See Exodus 25:16, 21.

Key "by way of explanation"

Verse 14. Much more attention is paid to Solomon building the temple, and completing it, than to the buildings he erected for himself.

Key "Quotable Quote"

"We should dedicate ourselves to becoming in this life the most perfect worshipers of God we can possibly be, as we hope to be through all eternity."

Brother Lawrence

1 Kings 7

Matthew Henry's introduction

In this chapter we have,

I. His fitting up several buildings for himself and his own use, vv. 1–12.
II. His furnishing the temple which he had built for God,
   A. With two pillars, vv. 13–22.
   B. With a molten sea, vv. 23–26.
   C. With ten basins of brass (vv. 27–37), and ten layers on them, vv. 38, 39.

D. With all the other utensils of the temple, vv. 40–50.

E. With the things that his father had dedicated, v. 51.

A detailed analysis of chapter

Solomon's buildings. (1–12)

Furniture of the temple. (13–47)

Furniture made from gold. (48–51)

Key verse

Verse 1: "But Solomon was building his own house thirteen years, and he finished all his house."

Key word / key phrase

Verse 14, "craftsman."

Key event / key person / key theme

The furniture for the temple

Key thought

From this chapter what can we learn about our own lives and service for God?

Key thing to look out for

The beauty of the temple must have been mind-blowing.

Key Bible cross-reference

Verse 23. See Exodus 30:17–21.

Key "by way of explanation"

Verse 13, "Huram." Huram, a half-Israelite, was indeed highly skilled. While his expertise is not directly attributed to God's Spirit, he nevertheless reminds one of Bezalel. See Exodus 31:4.

Key "Quotable Quote"

"We have lost our spirit of worship and our ability to withdraw inwardly to meet God in adoring silence."

A.W. Tozer

1 Kings 8

Matthew Henry's introduction

I. The representatives of all Israel were called together (vv. 1, 2), to keep a feast to the honor of God, for fourteen days, v. 65.

II. The priests brought the ark into the most holy place, and fixed it there, vv. 3–9.

III. God took possession of it by a cloud, vv. 10, 11.

IV. Solomon, with thankful acknowledgments to God, informed the people touching the occasion of their meeting, vv. 12–21.

V. In a long prayer he recommended to God's gracious acceptance all the prayers that should be made in or towards this place, vv. 22–53.

VI. He dismissed the assembly with a blessing and an exhortation, vv. 54–61.

VII. He offered abundance of sacrifices, on which he and his people feasted, and so parted, with great satisfaction, vv. 62–66. These were Israel's golden days, days of the Son of man in type.

A detailed analysis of chapter

The ark is brought into the temple. (1–11)

The occasion. (12–21)

Solomon's prayer. (22–53)
His blessing and exhortation. (54–61)
Solomon's peace-offerings. (62–66)

Key verse

Verse 10: "And it came to pass, when the priests were come out of the holy place, that the cloud filled the house of the LORD."

Key word / key phrase

Verse 1, "ark."

Key event / key person / key theme

The ark is brought to the temple.

Key thought

The symbol of God's presence arriving in "God's city" must have been a most memorable day.

Key thing to look out for

The requests that Solomon made in his prayer of dedication.

Key Bible cross-reference

Verse 40. See Deuteronomy 5:29; 6:1–2.

Key "by way of explanation"

The ark symbolized God's presence.

Key "Quotable Quote"

"To my God a heart of flame;
To my fellow men a heart of love;
To myself a heart of steel."

Augustine of Hippo

1 Kings 9

Matthew Henry's introduction

In this chapter we have,

I. The answer which God, in a vision, gave to Solomon's prayer, and the terms he settled with him, vv. 1–9.
II. The interchanging of grateful kindnesses between Solomon and Hiram, vv. 10–14.
III. His workmen and buildings, vv. 15–24.
IV. His devotion, v. 25.
V. His trading navy, vv. 26–28.

A detailed analysis of chapter

God's answer to Solomon. (1–9)
The presents of Solomon and Hiram. (10–14)
Solomon's buildings. His trade. (15–28)

Key verse

Verse 4: "And if thou wilt walk before me, as David thy father walked, in integrity of heart, and in uprightness, to do according to all that I have commanded thee, and wilt keep my statutes and my judgments."

Key word / key phrase

Verse 2, "appeared."

Key event / key person / key theme

The Lord appears to Solomon.

Key thought

The Lord reminds Solomon about the need to stay faithful to him.

Key thing to look out for

Solomon ensured that all the temple regulations

for correct worship and all the sacrifices were carried out.

Key Bible cross-reference

Verse 28. See 2 Chronicles 8:18; Job 28.

Key "by way of explanation"

Verse 4,5. With the coming of prosperity this warning not to break God's covenant was especially timely.

Key "Quotable Quote"

"We do the works, but God works in us the doing of the works."

Augustine of Hippo

1 Kings 10

Matthew Henry's introduction

I. What abundance of wisdom there was there appears from the application the queen of Sheba made to him, and the great satisfaction she had in her entertainment there (vv. 1–13), and others likewise, v. 24.

II. What abundance of wealth there was there appears here by the gold imported, with other things, yearly (vv. 14, 15), and in a triennial return, v. 22. Gold presented (v. 25), and gold used in targets and shields (vv. 16, 17), and vessels, v. 21. A stately throne made, vv. 18–20. His chariots and horsemen, v. 26. His trade with Egypt, vv. 28, 29. And the great plenty of silver and cedars among his people, v. 27.

A detailed analysis of chapter

The Queen of Sheba's visit to Solomon. (1–13)
Solomon's wealth. (14–29)

Key verse

Verse 1: "And when the queen of Sheba heard of the fame of Solomon concerning the name of the LORD, she came to prove him with hard questions."

Key word / key phrase

Verse 1, "queen of Sheba."

Key event / key person / key theme

The Queen of Sheba visits Solomon.

Key thought

The Queen of Sheba appreciated both Solomon's possessions and his wisdom.

Key thing to look out for

The Queen of Sheba attributed all that Solomon had to the eternal love of the Lord.

Key Bible cross-reference

Verse 22. See verse 11; 9:26–28.

Key "by way of explanation"

It has been suggested that the Queen of Sheba came on a trade mission because Solomon's sea trade was in competition with the lucrative overland trade routes which brought prosperity to the little kingdom of Sheba.

Key "Quotable Quote"

"Wealth is like a viper that is harmless if a man

knows how to take hold of it; but if he does not, it will twine round his hand and bite him."

Clement

1 Kings 11

Matthew Henry's introduction

I. The glory of his piety is stained by his departure from God and his duty, in his latter days, marrying strange wives and worshipping strange gods, vv. 4–8.

II. The glory of his prosperity is stained by God's displeasure against him and the fruits of that displeasure.

A. He sent him an angry message, vv. 9–13.

B. He stirred up enemies, who gave him disturbance, Hadad (vv. 14–22), Rezon, vv. 23–25.

C. He gave away ten tribes of his twelve, from his posterity after him, to Jeroboam, whom therefore he sought in vain to slay (vv. 26–40), and this is all that remains here to be told about Solomon, except his death and burial (vv. 41–43), for there is nothing perfect under the sun, but all is so above the sun.

A detailed analysis of chapter

Solomon's wives and concubines. His idolatry. (1–8)

God's anger. (9–13)

Solomon's adversaries. (14–25)

Jeroboam's promotion. (26–40)

The death of Solomon. (41–43)

Key verse

Verse 3: "And he had seven hundred wives, princesses, and three hundred concubines: and his wives turned away his heart."

Key word / key phrase

Verse 1, "foreign women."

Key event / key person / key theme

Solomon's wives

Key thought

Solomon's unfaithfulness in marrying non-Israelites was his undoing.

Key thing to look out for

Verse 4 categorically states that Solomon's heart was turned away from the Lord by his foreign wives.

Key Bible cross-reference

Verse 4. See 8:61.

Key "by way of explanation"

Verse 5. Worshiping the pagan deities of Molech and Milcom sometimes involved the evil practice of child sacrifice.

Key "Quotable Quote"

"Collapse in the Christian life is rarely a blow out. It's usually a slow leak."

George Sweeting

1 Kings 12

Matthew Henry's introduction

Here is,

I. Rehoboam's accession to the throne and Jeroboam's return out of Egypt, vv. 1, 2.

II. The people's petition to Rehoboam for the redress of grievances, and the rough answer he gave, by the advice of his young counselors, to that petition, vv. 3–15.

III. The revolt of the ten tribes thereon, and their setting up Jeroboam, vv. 16–20.

IV. Rehoboam's attempt to reduce them and the prohibition God gave to that attempt, vv. 21–24.

V. Jeroboam's establishment of his government on idolatry, vv. 25–33. Thus did Judah become weak, being deserted by their brethren, and Israel, by deserting the house of the Lord.

A detailed analysis of chapter

Rehoboam's accession, and the people's request. His rough answer. (1–15)

Ten tribes rebel. (16–24)

Jeroboam's idolatry. (25–33)

Key verse

Verse 1: "And Rehoboam went to Shechem: for all Israel were come to Shechem to make him king."

Key word / key phrase

Verse 4, "a heavy yoke."

Key event / key person / key theme

The northern tribes revolt

Key thought

Rehoboam, Solomon's son and successor, made an unwise choice in the advice he accepted.

Key thing to look out for

Verse 28. the disastrous spiritual consequences of the revolt.

Key Bible cross-reference

Verse 29. See Genesis 12:8; Judges 20:26–28.

Key "by way of explanation"

From now on the nation is divided into two: Israel, comprising the ten northern tribes; and Judah and Benjamin, centered on Jerusalem.

Key "Quotable Quote"

"Like many political leaders he tried to harness the power of religion to bolster his own regime."

Stephen Travis

1 Kings 13

Matthew Henry's introduction

In the close of the previous chapter we left Jeroboam attending his altar at Beth-el, and there we find him in the beginning of this, when he received a testimony from God against his idolatry and apostasy. This was sent to him by a prophet, a man of God that lived in Judah, who is the principal subject of the story of this chapter, where we are told,

I. What passed between him and the new king.

A. The prophet threatened Jeroboam's altar (vv. 1, 2), and gave him a sign (v. 3), which immediately came to pass, v. 5.

B. The king threatened the prophet, and was himself made another sign, by the withering of his hand (v. 4), and the restoring of it on his submission and the prophet's intercession, v. 6.

C. The prophet refused the kindness offered him thereon, vv. 7–10.

II. What passed between him and the old prophet.

A. The old prophet fetched him back by a lie, and gave him entertainment, vv. 11–19.

B. He, for accepting it, in disobedience to the divine command, is threatened with death, vv. 20–22. And,

C. The threatening is carried out, for he is slain by a lion (vv. 23, 24), and buried at Bethel, vv. 25–32.

d. Jeroboam is hardened in his idolatry, vv. 33, 34. "Thy judgments, Lord, are a great deep."

A detailed analysis of chapter

Jeroboam's sin reproved. (1–10)

The prophet deceived. (11–22)

The disobedient prophet is killed. Jeroboam's obstinacy. (23–34)

Key verse

Verse 1: "And, behold, there came a man of God out of Judah by the word of the LORD unto Bethel: and Jeroboam stood by the altar to burn incense."

Key word / key phrase

Verse 1, "Bethel."

Key event / key person / key theme

The elderly prophet of Bethel

Key thought

Age is of little consequence in God's service.

Key thing to look out for

Some people seem to be so intent on evil that they are impossible to change.

Key Bible cross-reference

Verse 6. See 2:3; Genesis 27:20.

Key "by way of explanation"

Verse 3. A "sign" meant the immediate fulfillment of a prophecy.

Key "Quotable Quote"

"God does not so much need people to do extraordinary things as he needs people who do ordinary things extraordinarily well."

William Barclay

1 Kings 14

Matthew Henry's introduction

In this chapter we have,

I. The prophecy of the destruction of Jeroboam's house, vv. 7–16. The sickness of his child was the occasion of it (vv. 1–6), and the death of his child the earnest of it (vv. 17, 18), together with the conclusion of his reign, vv. 19, 20.

II. The history of the declension and diminution of Rehoboam's house and kingdom (vv. 21–28) and the conclusion of his reign, vv. 29–31. In both we may read the mischievous consequences of sin and the calamities it brings on kingdoms and families.

A detailed analysis of chapter

Abijah being sick, his mother consults Ahijah. (1–6)

The destruction of Jeroboam's family. (7–20)

Rehoboam's wicked reign. (21–31)

Key verse

Verse 1: "At that time Abijah the son of Jeroboam fell sick."

Key word / key phrase

Verse 6, "Why this pretence?"

Key event / key person / key theme

King Rehoboam of Judah

Key thought

Some kind of idolatry seems to have been the besetting sin of God's people in nearly every generation.

Key thing to look out for

The reasons why Rehoboam was condemned.

Key Bible cross-reference

Verse 22. See 2 Chronicles 11–12.

Key "by way of explanation"

Verses 23, 24. Moses had warned God's people to have nothing at all to do with the "male shrine-prostitutes" but his voice was not heeded now.

Key "Quotable Quote"

"All sin is a kind of lying."

Augustine of Hippo

1 Kings 15

Matthew Henry's introduction

In this chapter we have an abstract of the history,

I. Of two of the kings of Judah, Abijam, the days of whose reign were few and evil (vv. 1–8), and Asa, who reigned well and long, vv. 9–24.

II. Of two of the kings of Israel, Nadab the son of Jeroboam, and Baasha the destroyer of Jeroboam's house, vv. 25–34.

A detailed analysis of chapter

Wicked reign of Abijam, king of Judah. (1–8)

Good reign of Asa, king of Judah. (9–24)

The evil reigns of Nadab and Baasha in Israel. (25–34)

Key verse

Verse 1: "Now in the eighteenth year of king Jeroboam the son of Nebat reigned Abijam over Judah."

Key word / key phrase

Verse 1, "Abijah."

Key event / key person / key theme

King Abijah of Judah

Key thought

Life father like son . . .

Key thing to look out for

Lack of wholeheartedness in following the Lord ends in disaster.

Key Bible cross-reference

Verse 7. See 2 Chronicles 13.

Key "by way of explanation"

Verse 3. David may have sinned in dreadful ways. But his heart was not divided between serving the Lord and worshiping pagan idols.

Key "Quotable Quote"

"What God asks is a will which will no longer be divided between him and any creature."

François Fénelon

1 Kings 16

Matthew Henry's introduction

In this chapter we have,

I. The ruin of Baasha's family, after it had been but twenty-six years a royal family, foretold by a prophet (vv. 1–7), and carried out by Zimri, one of his captains, vv. 8–14.

II. The seven days' reign of Zimri, and his sudden fall, vv. 15–20.

III. The struggle between Omri and Tibni, and Omri's prevalence, and his reign, vv. 21–28.

IV. The beginning of the reign of Ahab, of whom we shall afterwards read much, vv. 29–33.

V. The rebuilding of Jericho, v. 34. All this while, in Judah, things went well.

A detailed analysis of chapter

The reigns of Baasha and Elah in Israel. (1–14)
Reigns of Zimri and Omri in Israel. (15–28)
Ahab's wickedness, Hiel rebuilds Jericho. (29–34)

Key verse

Verse 8: "In the twenty and sixth year of Asa king of Judah began Elah the son of Baasha to reign over Israel in Tirzah, two years."

Key word / key phrase

Verse 1, "Baasha."

Key event / key person / key theme

Kings of Israel

Key thought

The end does not justify the means.

Key thing to look out for

A series of evil rulers does not mean that God is no longer in ultimate control in the world.

Key Bible cross-reference

Verse 3. See 14:10; 21:21.

Key "by way of explanation"

Verse 7. Baasha did kill off the house of Jeroboam, but in an evil way.

Key "Quotable Quote"

"Order your soul; reduce your wants; live in charity; associate in Christian community; obey the laws; trust in providence."

Augustine of Hippo

1 Kings 17

Matthew Henry's introduction

In this chapter we have,

I. Elijah's prediction of a famine in Israel, through the want of rain, v. 1.

II. The provision made for him in that famine,

A. By the ravens at the brook Cherith, vv. 2–7.

B. When that failed, by the widow at Zarephath, who received him in the name of a prophet and had a prophet's reward; for

1. He multiplied her meal and her oil, vv. 8–16.
2. He raised her dead son to life, vv. 17–24. Thus his story begins with judgments and miracles, designed to awaken that stupid generation that had to deeply corrupted themselves.

A detailed analysis of chapter

Elijah fed by ravens. (1–7)
Elijah sent to Zarephath. (8–16)
Elijah raises the widow's son to life. (17–24)

Key verse

Verse 6: "And the ravens brought him bread and flesh in the morning, and bread and flesh in the evening; and he drank of the brook."

Key word / key phrase

Verse 1, "the Lord whom I serve."

Key event / key person / key theme

Elijah and the drought

Key thought

God provides by one means or another.

Key thing to look out for

God is on the side of the poor.

Key Bible cross-reference

Verse 21. See Romans 4:17; Hebrews 11:19.

Key "by way of explanation"

Verse 16. A non-Israelite was prepared to risk her life for Elijah.

Key "Quotable Quote"

"The cruse of oil and the barrel of meal overflow because the widow has firm faith."

Agathias Scholasticus

1 Kings 18

Matthew Henry's introduction

We have here,

I. Elijah's interview with Obadiah, one of Ahab's servants, by whom he sends notice to Ahab of his coming, vv. 2–16.
II. His interview with Ahab himself, vv. 17–20.
III. His interview with all Israel on Mount Carmel, in order to a public trial of titles between the Lord and Baal; a most distinguished solemnity it was, in which,
   A. Baal and his prophets were confounded.
   B. God and Elijah were honored, vv. 21–39.
IV. The execution he did on the prophets of Baal, v. 40.
V. The return of the mercy of rain, at the word of Elijah, vv. 41–46. It is a chapter in which are many things very observable.

A detailed analysis of chapter

Elijah sends Ahab notice of his coming. (1–16)
Elijah meets Ahab. (17–20)
Elijah's trial with the false prophets. (21–40)
Elijah, by prayer, obtains rain. (41–46)

Key verse

Verse 1: "And it came to pass after many days,

that the word of the LORD came to Elijah in the third year, saying, Go, show thyself unto Ahab; and I will send rain upon the earth."

Key word / key phrase

Verse 17, "You troubler of Israel."

Key event / key person / key theme

God sends down fire.

Key thought

Elijah prayed and God answered.

Key thing to look out for

Elijah had God's glory at the forefront of his thinking.

Key Bible cross-reference

Verse 24. See Psalm 104:3; 29:3–9.

Key "by way of explanation"

Verse 21. Elijah made the people choose between good and evil, between following the Lord God and following Baal.

Key "Quotable Quote"

"God has not always answered my prayers. If he had, I would have married the wrong man – several times!"

Ruth Bell Graham

1 Kings 19

Matthew Henry's introduction

Observe,

I. How he was driven into banishment by the malice of Jezebel his sworn enemy, vv. 1–3.

II. How he was met, in his banishment, by the favor of God, his covenant friend.

A. How God fed him, vv. 4–8.

B. How he conversed with him, and manifested himself to him (vv. 9, 11–13), heard his complaint (vv. 10–14), directed him what to do (vv. 15–17), and encouraged him, v. 18.

III. How his hands were strengthened, at his return out of banishment, by the joining of Elisha with him, vv. 19–21.

A detailed analysis of chapter

Elijah flees to the desert. (1–8)

God manifests himself to Elijah. (9–13)

God's answer to Elijah. (14–18)

The call of Elisha. (19–21)

Key verse

Verse 8: "And he arose, and did eat and drink, and went in the strength of that meat forty days and forty nights unto Horeb the mount of God."

Key word / key phrase

Verse 4, "I have had enough, Lord."

Key event / key person / key theme

Elijah on Mount Sinai hears God in a gentle whisper.

Key thought

Elijah felt like committing suicide.

Key thing to look out for

Elijah was revived with very ordinary physical things.

Key Bible cross-reference

Verse 4. See Jonah 4:3, 8.

Key "by way of explanation"

Verse 10. Elijah felt that he was the only faithful follower of the Lord left on earth.

Key "Quotable Quote"

"The ultimate cause of all spiritual depression is unbelief. For if it were not for unbelief even the devil could do nothing. It is because we listen to the devil instead of listening to God that we go down before him and fall before his attacks."

D. Martyn Lloyd-Jones

1 Kings 20

Matthew Henry's introduction

Here is,

I. Ben-hadad's descent on Israel, and his insolent demand, vv. 1–11.

II. The defeat Ahab gave him, encouraged and directed by a prophet, vv. 12–21.

III. The Syrians rallying again, and the second defeat Ahab gave them, vv. 22–30.

IV. The covenant of peace Ahab made with Ben-hadad, when he had him at his mercy (vv. 31–34), for which he is reproved and threatened by a prophet, vv. 35–43.

A detailed analysis of chapter

Benhadad besieges Samaria. (1–11)
Benhadad's defeat. (12–21)
The Syrians again defeated. (22–30)
Ahab makes peace with Benhadad. (31–43)

Key verse

Verse 1: "And Benhadad the king of Syria gathered all his host together: and there were thirty and two kings with him, and horses, and chariots: and he went up and besieged Samaria, and warred against it."

Key word / key phrase

Verses 13, 28, "You will know that I am the Lord."

Key event / key person / key theme

Ben-Hadad attacks Samaria

Key thought

God sends his blessings pressed down and running over.

Key thing to look out for

Our God is in charge, no matter what is happening on the world stage.

Key Bible cross-reference

Verse 35, "sons of the prophets." See 2 Kings 2:3, 5, 7, 15.

Key "by way of explanation"

Verse 30. Not only did Israel's army beat the Assyrians, but the Lord inflicted further disaster on twenty-seven thousand of them.

Key "Quotable Quote"

"All history is incomprehensible without Christ."

Joseph Ernest Renan

1 Kings 21

Matthew Henry's introduction

Ahab is still the unhappy subject of the sacred history; from the great affairs of his camp and kingdom this chapter leads us into his garden, and gives us an account of some ill things (and ill indeed they proved to him) relating to his domestic affairs.

I. Ahab is sick for Naboth's vineyard, vv. 1–4.
II. Naboth dies by Jezebel's plot, that the vineyard may escheat to Ahab, vv. 5–14.
III. Ahab goes to take possession, vv. 15–16.
IV. Elijah meets him, and denounces the judgments of God against him for his injustice, vv. 17–24.
V. On his humiliation a reprieve is granted, vv. 25–29.

A detailed analysis of chapter

Ahab covets Naboth's vineyard. (1–4)

Naboth murdered by Jezebel. (5–16)

Elijah denounces judgments against Ahab. (17–29)

Key verse

Verse 2: "And Ahab spake unto Naboth, saying, Give me thy vineyard."

Key word / key phrase

Verse 2, "Let me have."

Key event / key person / key theme

Naboth's vineyard

Key thought

Greed is a killer.

Key thing to look out for

Grown-ups as well as children behave like spoilt toddlers.

Key Bible cross-reference

Verse 10. See Numbers 35:30; Deuteronomy 17:6.

Key "by way of explanation"

Verse 19. Ahab was guilty of committing murder, even though Jezebel had arranged for Naboth to be killed. Numbers 36:7–9 forbad the selling of land one has inherited.

Key "Quotable Quote"

"Nothing enslaves us more to the devil, as the desire for more and love for greed."

John Chrysostom

1 Kings 22

Matthew Henry's introduction

This chapter finishes the history of Ahab's reign. It was promised in the close of the previous chapter that the ruin of his house should not come in his days, but his days were soon at an end. His war with the Syrians at Ramoth-Gilead is that which we have an account of in this chapter.

I. His preparations for that war. He consulted,
  A. His privy-council, vv. 1–3.
  B. Jehoshaphat, v. 4.
  C. His prophets.
    1. His own, who encouraged him to go on this expedition (vv. 5, 6), Zedekiah particularly, vv. 11, 12.
    2. A prophet of the Lord, Micaiah, who

was desired to come by Jehoshaphat (vv. 7, 8), sent for (vv. 9, 10–13, 14), upbraided Ahab with his confidence in the false prophets (5:15), but foretold his fall in this expedition (vv. 16–18), and gave him an account how he came to be thus imposed on by his prophets, vv. 19–23. He is abused by Zedekiah (vv. 24, 25), and imprisoned by Ahab, vv. 26–28.

II. The battle itself, in which,
 A. Jehoshaphat is exposed. But,
 B. Ahab is slain, vv. 29–40. In the close of the chapter we have a short account,
  1. Of the good reign of Jehoshaphat king of Judah, vv. 41–50.
  2. Of the wicked reign of Ahaziah king of Israel, vv. 51–53.

A detailed analysis of chapter

Jehoshaphat makes a pact with Ahab. (1–14)
Micaiah predicts the death of Ahab. (15–28)
Death of Ahab. (29–40)
Jehoshaphat's good reign over Judah. (41–50)
Ahaziah's evil reign over Israel. (51–53)

Key verse

Verse 37: "So the king died, and was brought to Samaria; and they buried the king in Samaria."

Key word / key phrase

Verse 5, "first seek."

Key event / key person / key theme

Micaiah prophesies against Ahab

Key thought

Even the most wicked ruler will die.

Key thing to look out for

The lure of idolatry succeeds in capturing countless hearts.

Key Bible cross-reference

Verse 17. See Numbers 27:16, 17; Zechariah 13:7.

Key "by way of explanation"

Verse 23. The prophets lied because they had chosen to speak from their own evil hearts rather than to follow the truth.

Key "Quotable Quote"

"In the time we have it is surely our duty to do all the good we can to all the people we can in all the ways we can."

William Barclay

2 Kings 1

Matthew Henry's introduction

We here find Ahaziah, the genuine son and successor of Ahab, on the throne of Israel. His reign continued not two years; he died by a fall in his own house, of which, after the mention of the revolt of Moab (v. 1), we have here an account.

I. The message which, on that occasion, he sent to the god of Ekron, v. 2.
II. The message he received from the God of Israel, vv. 3–8.
III. The destruction of the messengers he sent to seize the prophet, once and again, vv. 9–12.

IV. His compassion to, and compliance with, the third messenger, on his submission, and the delivery of the message to the king himself, vv. 13–16.

IV. The death of Ahaziah, vv. 17, 18. In the story we may observe how great the prophet looks and how little the prince.

A detailed analysis of chapter

The rebellion of Moab. Sickness of Ahaziah, king of Israel. (1–8)

Fire called from heaven by Elijah. Death of Ahaziah. (9–18)

Key verse

Verse 8: "And they answered him, He was an hairy man, and girt with a girdle of leather about his loins. And he said, It is Elijah the Tishbite."

Key word / key phrase

Verse 3, "the angel of the LORD."

Key event / key person / key theme

Failure to consult God

Key thought

Elijah followed angelic advice.

Key thing to look out for

Elijah was fearless and outspoken in the messages he delivered.

Key Bible cross-reference

Verse 8. See Mark 1:6.

Key "by way of explanation"

Verse 10. Just as God had answered by fire at Mount Carmel, so here the Lord authenticates his own prophet by answering with fire.

Key "Quotable Quote"

"True will power and courage are not on the battlefield, but in every day conquests over our inertia, laziness, boredom."

Dwight Moody

2 Kings 2

Matthew Henry's introduction

In this chapter we have,

I. That extraordinary event, the translation of Elijah. In the close of the previous chapter we had a wicked king leaving the world in disgrace, here we have a holy prophet leaving it in honor; the departure of the former was his greatest misery, of the latter his greatest bliss: men are as their end is. Here is,

A. Elijah taking leave of his friends, the sons of the prophets, and especially Elisha, who kept close to him, and walked with him through Jordan, vv. 1–10.

B. Elijah taken into heaven by the ministry of angels (v. 11), and Elisha's lamentation of the loss this earth has of him, v. 12.

II. The manifestation of Elisha, as a prophet in his room.

A. By the dividing of Jordan, vv. 13, 14.

B. By the respect which the sons of the prophets paid him, vv. 15–18.

C. By the healing of the unwholesome waters of Jericho, vv. 19–22.

D. By the destruction of the children of Bethel that mocked him, vv. 23–25. This revolution in prophecy makes a greater figure than the revolution of a kingdom.

A detailed analysis of chapter

Elijah divides Jordan. (1–8)
Elijah is taken up into heaven. (9–12)
Elisha is manifested to be Elijah's successor. (13–18)
Elisha heals the waters of Jericho, and those that mocked Elisha are destroyed. (19–25)

Key verse

Verse 8: "And Elijah took his mantle, and wrapped it together, and smote the waters, and they were divided hither and thither, so that they two went over on dry ground."

Key word / key phrase

Verse 1, "heaven."

Key event / key person / key theme

Elijah is taken up to heaven.

Key thought

Elijah had served the Lord in many unusual ways and he left earth in an unusual way.

Key thing to look out for

God's work does not end just because one person's ministry comes to an end.

Key Bible cross-reference

Verse 11. See Genesis 5:24.

Key "by way of explanation"

Verse 9. When Elisha asked to "inherit a double portion" from Elijah he was not asking for twice as much as Elijah possessed, but rather that he might inherit Elijah's ministry. A "double portion" was the inheritance a firstborn son received on the death of his father.

Key "Quotable Quote"

"We are all in a lifetime of 'ministry.'"

John R.W. Stott

2 Kings 3

Matthew Henry's introduction

We are now called to attend the public affairs of Israel, in which we shall find Elisha concerned. Here is,

I. The general character of Jehoram, king of Israel, vv. 1–3.
II. A war with Moab, in which Jehoram and his allies were engaged, vv. 4–8.
III. The straits which the confederate army were reduced to in their expedition against Moab, and their consulting Elisha in that distress, with the answer of peace he gave them, vv. 9–19.
IV. The glorious issue of this campaign (vv. 20–25) and the barbarous method the king of Moab took to oblige the confederate army to retire, vv. 26, 27. The house of Ahab is doomed to destruction; and, though in this chapter we have both its character and its condition better than before, yet the threatened ruin is not far off.

A detailed analysis of chapter

Jehoram, king of Israel. (1–5)

War with Moab, and the intercession of Elisha. (6–19)

Water supplied, Moab overcome. (20–27)

Key verse

Verse 1: "Now Jehoram the son of Ahab began to reign over Israel in Samaria the eighteenth year of Jehoshaphat king of Judah, and reigned twelve years."

Key word / key phrase

Verse 11, "enquire of the LORD."

Key event / key person / key theme

God's miraculous provision of water.

Key thought

The Old Testament prophets were messengers passing on what the Lord had told them.

Key thing to look out for

An unusual way to win a battle.

Key Bible cross-reference

Verse 13. See 1 Kings 22:6.

Key "by way of explanation"

Verse 15. The music was probably to calm everyone down.

Key "Quotable Quote"

"Prophets are the beating hearts of the Old Testament."

W. Rauschenbusch

2 Kings 4

Matthew Henry's introduction

I. Elisha multiplied the poor widow's oil, vv. 1–7.

II. He won for the good Shunammite the blessing of a son in her old age, vv. 8–17.

III. He raised that child to life when it was dead, vv. 18–27.

IV. He healed the deadly pottage, vv. 38–41.

V. He fed 100 men with twenty small loaves, vv. 42–44.

A detailed analysis of chapter

Elisha multiplies the widow's oil. (1–7)

The Shunammite receives a son. (8–17)

The Shunammite's son restored to life. (18–37)

The miracle of healing the stew, and of feeding the sons of the prophets. (38–44)

Key verse

Verse 6: "And it came to pass, when the vessels were full, that she said unto her son, Bring me yet a vessel. And he said unto her, There is not a vessel more. And the oil stayed."

Key word / key phrase

Verse 14, "What can be done for her?"

Key event / key person / key theme

Elisha comes to the rescue of a people in need.

Key thought

God's prophets were instantly recognizable.

Key thing to look out for

To be able to say, "everything is all right" in the

middle of a seeming tragedy displays great faith. See verse 26.

Key Bible cross-reference

Verse 1. See Exodus 21:1, 2; Leviticus 25:39–41.

Key "by way of explanation"

The chapter gives a picture of everyday life at that time.

Key "Quotable Quote"

"Do not worry why problems exist in the world. Just respond to people's needs."

Mother Teresa

2 Kings 5

Matthew Henry's introduction

Two more of Elisha's miracles are recorded in this chapter.

I. The cleansing of Naaman, a Syrian, a stranger, from his leprosy, and there,

A. The badness of his case, v. 1.

B. The providence that brought him to Elisha, the intelligence given him by a captive maid, vv. 2–4. A letter from the king of Syria to the king of Israel, to introduce him, vv. 5–7. And the invitation Elisha sent him, v. 8.

C. The method prescribed for his cure, his submission, with much ado, to that method, and his cure thereby, vv. 9–14.

D. The grateful acknowledgments he made to Elisha hereon, vv. 15–19.

II. The smiting of Gehazi, his own servant, with that leprosy.

A. Gehazi's sins, which were belying his master to Naaman (vv. 20–24), and lying to his master when he examined him, v. 25.

B. His punishment for these sins. Naaman's leprosy was entailed on his family, vv. 26, 27.

A detailed analysis of chapter

Naaman's leprosy. (1–8)
His cure from leprosy. (9–14)
Elisha refuses Naaman's gifts. (15–19)
Gehazi's covetousness and falsehood. (20–27)

Key verse

Verse 1: "Now Naaman, captain of the host of the king of Syria, was a great man with his master, and honorable, because by him the LORD had given deliverance unto Syria: he was also a mighty man in valor, but he was a leper."

Key word / key phrase

Verse 1, "leprosy."

Key event / key person / key theme

The leper Naaman is healed.

Key thought

Naaman had to come off his high horse before he could be cured.

Key thing to look out for

The role of a young servant girl.

Key Bible cross-reference

Verse 3. See verse 9; 2:25; 6:19.

Key "by way of explanation"

Verse 14. Naaman's healing can be seen as a message to disobedient Israel who needed to behave like Naaman and trust and obey God if they were to receive God's blessing.

Key "Quotable Quote"

"We are all healers who can reach out and offer health, and we are all patients in constant need of help."

Henri Nouwen

2 Kings 6

Matthew Henry's introduction

In this chapter we have,

I. A further account of the wondrous works of Elisha.
   A. His making iron to swim, vv. 1–7.
   B. His disclosing to the king of Israel the secret counsels of the king of Syria, vv. 8–12.
   C. His saving himself out of the hands of those who were sent to apprehend him, vv. 13–23.

II. The besieging of Samaria by the Syrians and the great distress the city was reduced to, vv. 24–33.

A detailed analysis of chapter

The sons of the prophets enlarge their habitations. Iron made to float. (1–7)

Elisha discloses the counsels of the Syrians. (8–12)

Syrians sent to seize Elisha. (13–23)

Samaria besieged. A famine, and the king sends to kill Elisha. (24–33)

Key verse

Verse 1: "And the sons of the prophets said unto Elisha, Behold now, the place where we dwell with thee is too strait for us."

Key word / key phrase

Verse 16, "Those who are with us are more than those who are with them."

Key event / key person / key theme

Elisha's ministry

Key thought

The Lord calls some people to a very varied ministry.

Key thing to look out for

Elisha exemplifies the proverb that the Lord's followers should be as shrewd as snakes.

Key Bible cross-reference

Verse 16. See 2 Chronicles 32:7, 8. 1 John 4:4.

Key "by way of explanation"

Verse 6. This miracle shows God's concern for his faithful follower.

Key "Quotable Quote"

"Think of it! Multitudes of angels, indescribably mighty, performing the commands of heaven."

Billy Graham

2 Kings 7

Matthew Henry's introduction

Relief is here brought to Samaria and her king,

when the case is, in a manner, desperate, and the king despairing.

I. It is foretold by Elisha, and an unbelieving lord shut out from the benefit of it, vv. 1, 2.

II. It is brought about,

A. By an unaccountable fright into which God put the Syrians (v. 6), which caused them to retire precipitately, v. 7.

B. By the seasonable discovery which four lepers made of this (vv. 3–5), and the account which they gave of it to the court, vv. 8–11.

C. By the cautious trial which the king made of the truth of it, vv. 12–15.

III. The event answered the prediction both in the sudden plenty (v. 16), and the death of the unbelieving lord (vv. 17–20); for no word of God shall fall to the ground.

A detailed analysis of chapter

Elisha prophesies plenty. (1,2)

The flight of the Syrian army. (3–11)

Samaria plentifully supplied. (12–20)

Key verse

Verse 1: "Then Elisha said, Hear ye the word of the LORD; Thus saith the LORD, To morrow about this time shall a measure of fine flour be sold for a shekel, and two measures of barley for a shekel, in the gate of Samaria."

Key word / key phrase

Verse 5, "not a man was there."

Key event / key person / key theme

Elijah's prophecies

Key thought

Good news is for sharing.

Key thing to look out for

God's prophecies all come true.

Key Bible cross-reference

Verse 2. See verse 19; Genesis 8:2; Isaiah 24:18.

Key "by way of explanation"

Verse 3. These four lepers were at the "entrance of the city gate" as the law did not allow them to live with the healthy people.

Key "Quotable Quote"

"God gave the prophecies, not to gratify men's curiosity by enabling them to foreknow things, but that after they were fulfilled they might be interpreted by the event, and his own providence, not the interpreter's, be thereby manifested to the world."

Isaac Newton

2 Kings 8

Matthew Henry's introduction

The passages of story recorded in this chapter oblige us to look back.

I. We read before of a Shunammite woman that was a kind benefactor to Elisha; now here we are told how she fared the better for it, afterwards, in the advice Elisha gave her, and the favor the king showed her for his sake, vv. 1–6.

II. We read before of the designation of Hazael to be king of Syria (1 Kings 19:15), and here we have an account of his elevation to that throne and the way he forced for himself to it, by killing his master, vv. 7–15.

III. We read before of Jehoram's reigning over Judah in the room of his father Jehoshaphat (1 Kings 22:50), now here we have a short and sad history of his short and wicked reign (vv. 16–24), and the beginning of the history of the reign of his son Ahaziah, vv. 25–29.

A detailed analysis of chapter

A famine in Israel, and the Shunammite receives her land. (1–6)

Elisha consulted by Hazael. Death of Benhadad. (7–15)

Jehoram's wicked reign in Judah. (16–24)

Ahaziah's wicked reign in Judah. (25–29)

Key verse

Verse 1: "Then spake Elisha unto the woman, whose son he had restored to life, saying, Arise, and go thou and thine household, and sojourn wheresoever thou canst sojourn: for the LORD hath called for a famine; and it shall also come upon the land seven years."

Key word / key phrase

Verse 13, "the LORD has shown me."

Key event / key person / key theme

Elisha and King Benhadad

Key thought

Power corrupts. Seeking power can completely dominate lives.

Key thing to look out for

He was equally at ease with the poor and the powerful.

Key Bible cross-reference

Verse 12. See 9:14–16; 10:31; 12:17,18.

Key "by way of explanation"

Verse 10. Faced with the tears of the prophet and the dreadful prophecies Hazael shows no sign of repentance.

Key "Quotable Quote"

"Two heads are better than one, not because either is infallible, but because they are unlikely to go wrong in the same direction."

C. S. Lewis

2 Kings 9

Matthew Henry's introduction

I. A commission is sent to Jehu by the hand of one of the prophets, to take on him the government, and destroy the house of Ahab, vv. 1–10.

II. Here is his speedy execution of this commission.

  A. He communicates it to his captains, vv. 11–15.

  B. He marches directly to Jezreel (vv. 16–20), and there dispatches

    1. Joram king of Israel, vv. 21–26.
    2. Ahaziah king of Judah, vv. 27–29.
    3. Jezebel, vv. 30–37.

A detailed analysis of chapter

Elisha sent to anoint Jehu. (1–10)

Jehu and the captains. (11–15)

Joram and Ahaziah killed by Jehu. (16–29)

Jezebel eaten by dogs. (30–37)

Key verse

Verse 1: "And Elisha the prophet called one of the children of the prophets, and said unto him, Gird up thy loins, and take this box of oil in thine hand, and go to Ramothgilead."

Key word / key phrase

Verse 2, "Jehu."

Key event / key person / key theme

Jehu is anointed king.

Key thought

When Jehu was anointed he was given a specific work to accomplish.

Key thing to look out for

The role of the prophet was to do what the Lord said, not to do what he felt he would like to do.

Key Bible cross-reference

Verse 7. See verses 25, 26; 1 Kings 21:21–24.

Key "by way of explanation"

Verse 11. God's prophets often had to suffer in different ways. Here Elisha is referred to as "this madman."

Key "Quotable Quote"

"In doing what we ought we deserve no praise."

Augustine of Hippo

2 Kings 10

Matthew Henry's introduction

We have in this chapter,

I. A further account of Jehu's execution of his commission. He cut off,

A. All Ahab's sons, vv. 1–10.

B. All Ahab's kindred, vv. 11–14, 17.

C. Ahab's idolatry: his zeal against this he took Jonadab to be witness to (vv. 15, 16), summoned all the worshippers of Baal to attend (vv. 18–23) and slew them all (vv. 24, 25), and then abolished that idolatry, vv. 26–28.

II. A short account of the administration of his government.

A. The old idolatry of Israel, the worship of the calves, was retained, vv. 29–31.

B. This brought God's judgments on them by Hazael, with which his reign concludes, vv. 32–36.

A detailed analysis of chapter

Ahab's sons and Ahaziah's brethren put to death. (1–14)

Jehu destroys the worshipers of Baal. (15–28)

Jehu follows Jeroboam's sins. (29–36)

Key verse

Verse 27: "And they brake down the image of Baal, and brake down the house of Baal, and made it a draught house unto this day."

Key word / key phrase

Verse 18, "Baal."

Key event / key person / key theme

Baal worshipers killed.

Key thought

It is easy to be driven by mixed motives.

Key thing to look out for

To serve the Lord only does not come easily.

Key Bible cross-reference

Verse 29. See 1 Kings 12:26–32; 13:33, 34.

Key "by way of explanation"

Verses 30,31. Jehu is commended for bringing God's judgment on the house of Ahab. But he went too far and so was condemned in Hosea 1:4 for the "massacre at Jezreel."

Key "Quotable Quote"

"O Lord, grant that I may do thy will as if it were my will; so that thou mayest do my will as if it were thy will."

Augustine of Hippo

2 Kings 11

Matthew Henry's introduction

I. Athaliah usurps the government and destroys all the seed-royal, v. 1.
II. Joash, a child of a year old, is wonderfully preserved, vv. 2, 3.
III. At six years' end he is produced, and, by the agency of Jehoiada, made king, vv. 4–12.
IV. Athaliah is slain, vv. 13–16.
V. Both the civil and religious interests of the kingdom are well settled in the hands of Joash, vv. 17–21.

A detailed analysis of chapter

Athaliah usurps the government of Judah. Jehoash made king. (1–12)
Athaliah put to death. (13–16)
The worship of the Lord restored. (17–21)

Key verse

Verse 1: "And when Athaliah the mother of Ahaziah saw that her son was dead, she arose and destroyed all the seed royal."

Key word / key phrase

Verse 3, "hidden."

Key event / key person / key theme

Queen Athaliah of Judah

Key thought

The Lord's covenants were meant to be followed all the time.

Key thing to look out for

To ignore God's instructions brings personal and national disaster.

Key Bible cross-reference

Verse 17. See Exodus 19:5, 6; Deuteronomy 4:20.

Key "by way of explanation"

Verse 14. The two pillars outside the temple were called Jakin and Boaz. See 23:3; 1 Kings 7:15–22.

Key "Quotable Quote"

"The commands of God are all designed to

make us more happy than we can possibly be without them."

Thomas Wilson

2 Kings 12

Matthew Henry's introduction 12

This chapter gives us the history of the reign of Joash, which does not answer to that glorious beginning of it which we had an account of in the previous chapter; he was not so illustrious at forty years old as he was at seven, yet his reign is to be reckoned one of the better sort, and appears much worse in Chronicles (2 Chron. 24.) than it does here, for there we find the blood of one of God's prophets laid at his door; here we are only told,

I. That he did well while Jehoiada lived, vv. 1–3.

II. That he was careful and active to repair the temple, vv. 4–16.

III. That after a mean compact with Hazael (vv. 17, 18) he died ingloriously, vv. 19–21.

A detailed analysis of chapter

Jehoash orders the repair of the temple. (1–16)
He is killed by his servants. (17–21)

Key verse

Verse 2: "And Jehoash did that which was right in the sight of the LORD all his days wherein Jehoiada the priest instructed him."

Key word / key phrase

Verse 2, "did what was right."

Key event / key person / key theme

King Joash of Judah

Key thought

Repairing the temple symbolized making good the spiritual lives of God's people.

Key thing to look out for

The Lord's work has to be financed.

Key Bible cross-reference

Verse 16. See Leviticus 5:16; 6:5.

Key "by way of explanation"

Verse 5. The "treasurers" were the officials who handled the money given in connection with the sacrifices, on behalf of the priests.

Key "Quotable Quote"

"Separation from Jesus means sadness. Restoration of fellowship means joy."

John Piper

2 Kings 13

Matthew Henry's introduction

This chapter brings us again to the history of the kings of Israel, and particularly of the family of Jehu. We have here an account of the reign,

I. Of his son Jehoahaz, which continued seventeen years.

A. His bad character in general (vv. 1, 2), the trouble he was brought into (v. 3), and the low ebb of his affairs, v. 7.

B. His humiliation before God, and God's compassion towards him, vv. 4, 5, and 23.

C. His continuance in his idolatry notwithstanding, v. 6.

D. His death, vv. 8, 9.

II. Of his grandson Joash, which continued sixteen years. Here is a general account of his reign in the usual form (vv. 10–13), but a particular account of the death of Elisha in his time.

A. The kind visit the king made him (v. 14), the encouragement he gave the king in his wars with Syria, vv. 15–19.

B. His death and burial (v. 20), and a miracle wrought by his bones, v. 21. And, lastly, the advantages Joash gained against the Syrians, according to his predictions, vv. 24, 25.

A detailed analysis of chapter

Reign of Jehoahaz. (1–9)

Jehoash, king of Israel. Elisha dying. (10–19)

Elisha's death, and the victories of Jehoash. (20–25)

Key verse

Verse 1: "In the three and twentieth year of Joash the son of Ahaziah king of Judah Jehoahaz the son of Jehu began to reign over Israel in Samaria, and reigned seventeen years."

Key word / key phrase

Verse 3, "the LORD'S anger."

Key event / key person / key theme

Jehoahaz king of Israel

Key thought

Eradication of idolatry is never easy.

Key thing to look out for

It is the devil's ploy to make sin look more attractive than godliness.

Key Bible cross-reference

Verse 2. See 1 Kings 12:26–32; 13:33, 34.

Key "by way of explanation"

Verse 6. The "Asherah pole" was an idol which had been set up by Ahab.

Key "Quotable Quote"

"It does not take great men to do great things; it only takes consecrated men."

Phillips Brooks

2 Kings 14

Matthew Henry's introduction

This chapter continues the history of the succession in the kingdoms both of Judah and Israel.

I. In the kingdom of Judah here is,

A. The entire history (as much as is recorded in this book) of Amaziah's reign

1. His good character, vv. 1–4.
2. The justice he carried out on the murderers of his father, vv. 5, 6.
3. His victory over the Edomites, v. 7.
4. His war with Joash, and his defeat in that war, vv. 8–14.
5. His fall, as last, by a conspiracy against him, vv. 17–20.

B. The beginning of the history of Azariah, vv. 21, 22.

II. In the kingdom of Israel, the conclusion of the reign of Joash (vv. 15, 16), and the entire history of Jeroboam his son, the second of that name, vv. 23–29. How many great men are made to stand in a little compass in God's book!

A detailed analysis of chapter

Amaziah's good reign. (1–7)

Amaziah provokes Jehoash king of Israel, and is overcome. (8–14)

He is killed by conspirators. (15–22)

Wicked reign of Jeroboam II. (23–29)

Key verse

Verse 1: "In the second year of Joash son of Jehoahaz king of Israel reigned Amaziah the son of Joash king of Judah."

Key word / key phrase

Verse 26, "the LORD has seen."

Key event / key person / key theme

Amaziah King of Judah

Key thought

Wholeheartedness in following him is what the Lord asks for.

Key thing to look out for

We are not meant to stand in judgment over the lives of these kings but to learn from them.

Key Bible cross-reference

Verse 3. See 2 Chronicles 15:14–16.

Key "by way of explanation"

Verse 8. In this instance the phrase, "meet me face to face" amounted to a virtual declaration of war.

Key "Quotable Quote"

"There, but for the grace of God, goes John Bradford."

John Bradford, as he saw criminals being taken off to be executed.

2 Kings 15

Matthew Henry's introduction

In this chapter,

I. The history of two of the kings of Judah is briefly recorded:

A. Of Azariah, or Uzziah, vv. 1–7.

B. Of Jotham his son, vv. 32–38.

II. The history of many of the kings of Israel that reigned at the same time is given us in short, five in succession, all of whom, except one, went down slain to the pit, and their murders were their successors.

A. Zachariah, the last of the house of Jehu, reigned six months, and then was slain and succeeded by Shallum, vv. 8–12.

B. Shallum reigned one month, and then was slain and succeeded by Menahem, vv. 13–15.

C. Menahem reigned ten years, or tyrannized rather, such were his barbarous cruelties (v. 16) and unreasonable exactions (v. 20), and then died in his bed, and left his son to succeed him first, and then suffer for him, vv. 16–22.

D. Pekahiah reigned two years, and then was slain and succeeded by Pekah, vv. 23–26.

E. Pekah reigned twenty years, and then was slain and succeeded by Hoshea, the last of all the kings of Israel (vv. 27–31) for things were now working and hastening apace towards the final destruction of that kingdom.

A detailed analysis of chapter

Reign of Azariah, king of Judah. (1–7)

The latter kings of Israel and invasion of Assyria. (8–31)

Jotham, king of Judah. (32–38)

Key verse

Verse 1: "In the twenty and seventh year of Jeroboam king of Israel began Azariah son of Amaziah king of Judah to reign."

Key word / key phrase

Verses 9, 18, 24, 28, "did evil."

Key event / key person / key theme

Tiglath Pileser, King of Assyria

Key thought

It is easier to please men than to please the Lord.

Key thing to look out for

Azariah (Uzziah) was a good king. See the significance of his death for Isaiah (Isaiah 6:1, 11).

Key Bible cross-reference

Verse 29. See 16:5–9; 2 Chronicles 28:16–21.

Key "by way of explanation"

In 734 Tiglath Pileser overran Gilead and Galilee burning and destroying the towns.

Key "Quotable Quote"

"A far-reaching reformation of the Church is a prerequisite if it is to commit itself to Jesus' mission of liberating the oppressed."

Ronald J. Sider

2 Kings 16

Matthew Henry's introduction

This chapter is wholly taken up with the reign of Ahaz; and we have quite enough of it, unless it were better. He had a good father, and a better son, and yet was himself one of the worst of the kings of Judah.

I. He was a notorious idolater, vv. 1–4.

II. With the treasures of the temple, as well as his own, he hired the king of Assyria to invade Syria and Israel, vv. 5–9.

III. He took pattern from an idol's altar which he saw at Damascus for a new altar in God's temple, vv. 10–16.

IV. He abused and embezzled the furniture of the temple, vv. 17, 18. And so his story ends, vv. 19, 20.

A detailed analysis of chapter

Ahaz, king of Judah. His wicked reign. (1–9)

Ahaz copies an idol's altar. (10–16)

Ahaz robs the temple. (17–20)

Key verse

Verse 2: "Twenty years old was Ahaz when he began to reign, and reigned sixteen years in Jerusalem, and did not that which was right in the sight of the LORD his God, like David his father."

Key word / key phrase

Verse 34, "did what was right."

Key event / key person / key theme

Verse 37. Danger threatened from the north.

Key thought

Morality and belief in God are bound up with each other.

Key thing to look out for

Temple improvements

Key Bible cross-reference

Verse 3. See Leviticus 18:21.

Key "by way of explanation"

Verse 4. The "high places" were originally sites where the pagan Baal was worshiped. Later immoral pagan practices took place on these sites.

Key "Quotable Quote"

"There is no true and abiding morality that is not founded in religion."

Henry Ward Beecher

2 Kings 17

Matthew Henry's introduction

This chapter gives us an account of the captivity of the ten tribes, and so finishes the history of that kingdom, after it had continued about 265 years, from the setting up of Jeroboam the son of Nebat. In it we have,

I. A short narrative of this destruction, vv. 1–6.

II. Remarks on it, and the causes of it, for the justifying of God in it and for warning to others, vv. 7–23.

III. An account of the nations which succeeded them in the possession of their land, and the mongrel religion set up among them, vv. 24–41.

A detailed analysis of chapter

Reign of Hoshea in Israel, and the Israelites carried captives by the Assyrians. (1–6)

Captivity of the Israelites. (7–23)

The nations placed in the land of Israel. (24–41)

Key verse

Verse 18: "Therefore the LORD was very angry with Israel, and removed them out of his sight: there was none left but the tribe of Judah only."

Key word / key phrase

Verse 24, "Samaria."

Key event / key person / key theme

The fall of Samaria

Key thought

People sin despite being told not to.

Key thing to look out for

The writer's summary of the reasons for the fall of Israel.

Key Bible cross-reference

Verse 23. See Hosea 10:1–7; Amos 5:27.

Key "by way of explanation"

The fall of Samaria took place in the winter of

722/721. The King of Assyria resettled the conquered lands with people of other races. This led to a syncretistic religion. It was the beginning of the Samaritans so hated by later orthodox Jews.

Key "Quotable Quote"

"The basic sin is that we usurp God's place at the center of our lives."

David Watson

2 Kings 18

Matthew Henry's introduction

Hezekiah is here on the throne,

I. Reforming his kingdom, vv. 1–6.

II. Prospering in all his undertakings (vv. 7, 8), and this at the same time when the ten tribes were led captive, vv. 9–12.

III. Yet invaded by Sennacherib, the king of Assyria, v. 13.

A. His country put under contribution, vv. 14–16.

B. Jerusalem besieged, v. 17.

C. God blasphemed, himself reviled, and his people solicited to revolt, in a virulent speech made by Rabshakeh, vv. 18–37. But how well it ended, and how much to the honor and comfort of our great reformer, we shall find in the next chapter.

A detailed analysis of chapter

Good reign of Hezekiah in Judah. Idolatry. (1–8)
Sennacherib invades Judah. (9–16)
Rabshakeh's blasphemies. (17–37)

Key verse

Verse 7: "And the LORD was with him; and he prospered whithersoever he went forth: and he rebelled against the king of Assyria, and served him not."

Key word / key phrase

Verse 17, "Jerusalem."

Key event / key person / key theme

Sennachrib besieges Jerusalem

Key thought

Our extremity is God's opportunity.

Key thing to look out for

The extreme desperation of the situation, but the people's refusal to capitulate (verse 36).

Key Bible cross-reference

Verse 19. See Psalm 47:2; 48:2; 95:3.

Key "by way of explanation"

In Sennacherib's own account of this invasion, he says Hezekiah was trapped "like a bird in a cage."

Key "Quotable Quote"

"When you reach rock bottom, that rock is Jesus."

Author unknown

2 Kings 19

Matthew Henry's introduction

I. Hezekiah, in great concern, sent to the prophet Isaiah, to desire his prayers (vv. 1–5) and received from him an answer of peace, vv. 6, 7.

II. Sennacherib sent a letter to Hezekiah to fright him into a surrender, vv. 8–13.

III. Hezekiah thereon, by a very solemn prayer, recommended his case to God, the righteous Judge, and begged help from him, vv. 14–19.

IV. God, by Isaiah, sent him a very comfortable message, assuring him of deliverance, vv. 20–34.

V. The army of the Assyrians was all cut off by an angel and Sennacherib himself slain by his own sons, vv. 35–37. And so God glorified himself and saved his people.

A detailed analysis of chapter

Messengers sent to Isaiah asking for prayer. Isaiah's reply. (1–7)

Sennacherib's letter. (8–19)

His fall is prophesied. (20–34)

The Assyrian army destroyed. Sennacherib killed. (35–37)

Key verse

Verse 1: "And Hezekiah received the letter of the hand of the messengers, and read it: and Hezekiah went up into the house of the LORD, and spread it before the LORD."

Key word / key phrase

Verse 5, "Do not be afraid."

Key event / key person / key theme

Isaiah predicts Sennacherib's fall

Key thought

The Lord answers prayers that come from the heart and answers in amazing ways.

Key thing to look out for

Hezekiah's reasons for asking for God's help (verses 15–19).

Key Bible cross-reference

Verse 18. See Psalm 115:3–8; 135:15–18.

Key "by way of explanation"

Verse 25. Israel's God not only rules his own people but he is the God of history for every nation.

Key "Quotable Quote"

"By prayer the Christian can open his heart to God, as to a friend, and obtain fresh testimony of God's friendship to him."

John Bunyan

2 Kings 20

Matthew Henry's introduction

In this chapter we have,

I. Hezekiah's sickness, and his recovery from that, in answer to prayer, in performance of a promise, in the use of means, and confirmed with a sign, vv. 1–11.

II. Hezekiah's sin, and his recovery from that, vv. 12–19. In both of these, Isaiah was God's messenger to him.

III. The conclusion of his reign, vv. 20, 21.

A detailed analysis of chapter

Hezekiah's sickness. His recovery in answer to prayer. (1–11)

Hezekiah shows his treasures to the ambassadors from Babylon. His death. (12–21)

Key verse

Verse 9: "And Isaiah said, This sign shalt thou have of the LORD, that the LORD will do the thing that he hath spoken: shall the shadow go forward ten degrees, or go back ten degrees?"

Key word / key phrase

Verses 5, 6, "heal . . . deliver."

Key event / key person / key theme

Hezekiah's illness

Key thought

Miracles are meant to support the faith of God's people.

Key thing to look out for

Trusting in God should not make people naïve (verses 12–15).

Key Bible cross-reference

Verse 5. See Psalm 139:16 Ephesians 1:11.

Key "by way of explanation"

Verse 20. There was no river in Jerusalem. The tunnel, cut through rock to the spring, would ensure a water supply during a siege.

Key "Quotable Quote"

"Prayer is not a substitute for work, thinking, watching, suffering, or giving; prayer is a support for all other efforts."

George Buttrick

2 Kings 21

Matthew Henry's introduction

In this chapter we have a short but sad account of the reigns of two of the kings of Judah, Manasseh and Amon.

I. About Manasseh, all the account we have of him here is,

A. That he devoted himself to sin, to all manner of wickedness, idolatry, and murder, vv. 1–9 and 16.

B. That therefore God devoted him, and Jerusalem for his sake, to ruin, vv. 10–18. In the book of Chronicles we have an account of his troubles, and his repentance.

II. About Amon we are only told that he lived in sin (vv. 19–22), died quickly by the sword, and left good Josiah his successor, vv. 23–26. By these two reigns Jerusalem was much debauched and much weakened, and so hastened apace towards its destruction, which slumbered not.

A detailed analysis of chapter

Wicked reign of Manasseh. (1–9)

The prophetic denunciations against Judah. (10–18)

Wicked reign and death of Amon. (19–26)

Key verse

Verse 2: "And he did that which was evil in the sight of the LORD, after the abominations of the heathen, whom the LORD cast out before the children of Israel."

Key word / key phrase

Verse 1, "Manasseh."

Key event / key person / key theme

King Manasseh of Judah

Key thought

Some people are evil through and through.

Key thing to look out for

Evil needs to be resisted or else it just takes over.

Key Bible cross-reference

Verse 2. See 18:3–5; 16:3.

Key "by way of explanation"

Verse 13. A "measuring line" and a "plumb-line" were usually used to help with constructing a building. In this instance they are going to be used in the destruction of a building, symbolizing God's judgment.

Key "Quotable Quote"

"What greater work is there than training the mind and forming the habits of the young?"

John Chrysostom

2 Kings 22

Matthew Henry's introduction

Here, after his general character (vv. 1, 2), we have a particular account of the respect he paid

I. To God's house, which he repaired, vv. 3–7

II. To God's book, which he was much affected with the reading of, vv. 8–11

III. To God's messengers, whom he thereon consulted, vv. 12–14 And by whom he received from God an answer threatening Jerusalem's destruction (vv. 15–17), but promising favor to him (vv. 18–20), on which he set about that glorious work of reformation which we have an account of in the next chapter.

A detailed analysis of chapter

Josiah's good reign, his care for repairing the temple, and the Book of the Law found. (1–10)
Josiah consults Huldah the prophetess. (11–20)

Key verse

Verse 1: "Josiah was eight years old when he began to reign, and he reigned thirty and one years in Jerusalem."

Key word / key phrase

Verse 1, "Josiah."

Key event / key person / key theme

The discovery of the Book of the Law

Key thought

The Lord never left his people without clear commandments.

Key thing to look out for

The Book of the Law gives instructions to nations and individuals.

Key Bible cross-reference

Verse 8. See Deuteronomy 31:24, 26; 2 Chronicles 34:14.

Key "by way of explanation"

Verse 2. Josiah was the last king in David's line who faithfully followed the Lord, prior to the Exile.

Key "Quotable Quote"

"No man is uneducated who knows the Bible and no one is wise who is ignorant of its teachings."

Samuel Chadwick

2 Kings 23

Matthew Henry's introduction

We have here,

I. The happy continuance of the goodness of Josiah's reign, and the progress of the reformation he began, reading the law (vv. 1, 2), renewing the covenant (v. 3), cleansing the temple (v. 4), and rooting out idols and idolatry, with all the relics thereof, in all places, as far as his power reached (vv. 5–20), keeping a solemn Passover (vv. 21–23), and clearing the country of witches (v. 24); and in all this acting with extraordinary vigor, v. 25

II. The unhappy conclusion of it in his untimely death, as a token of the continuance of God's wrath against Jerusalem, vv. 26–30

III. The more unhappy consequences of his death, in the bad reigns of his two sons Jehoahaz and Jehoiakim, that came after him, vv. 31–37

A detailed analysis of chapter

Josiah reads the law, and renews the covenant. (1–3)

He destroys idolatry. (4–14)

The reformation extended to Israel. A Passover kept. (15–24)

Josiah killed by Pharaoh Neco. (25–30)

Wicked reigns of Jehoahaz and Jehoiakim. (31–37)

Key verse

Verse 2: "And the king went up into the house of the LORD, and all the men of Judah and all the inhabitants of Jerusalem with him, and the priests, and the prophets, and all the people, both small and great: and he read in their ears all the words of the book of the covenant which was found in the house of the LORD."

Key word / key phrase

Verse 2, "the Book of the Covenant."

Key event / key person / key theme

Josiah renews the covenant.

Key thought

Some things need to be destroyed if good is to prevail.

Key thing to look out for

After evil has been eradicated goodness needs to step in, or else there will be a vacuum.

Key Bible cross-reference

Verse 3. See Exodus 24:3–8; Deuteronomy 1:34.

Key "by way of explanation"

Verse 21. Celebrating the Passover and following the teaching of the Book of the Law went hand in hand.

Key "Quotable Quote"

"They err who look not to the bright rays of the divine Scriptures, because they walk in darkness."

John Chrysostom

2 Kings 24

Matthew Henry's introduction

Things are here ripening for, and hastening towards, the utter destruction of Jerusalem. We left Jehoiakim on the throne, placed there by the king of Egypt: now here we have,

I. The troubles of his reign, how he was brought into subjection by the king of Babylon, and severely chastised for attempting to shake off the yoke (vv. 1–6), and how Egypt also was conquered by Nebuchadnezzar, v. 7.

II. The desolations of his son's reign, which continued but three months; and then he and all his great men, being forced to surrender at discretion, were carried captives to Babylon, vv. 8–16.

III. The preparations for the next reign (which was the last of all) for the utter ruin of Jerusalem, which the next chapter will give us an account of, vv. 17–20.

A detailed analysis of chapter

Jehoiakim subdued by Nebuchadnezzar. (1–7)

Jehoiachin captured in Babylon. (8–20)

Key verse

Verse 1: "In his days Nebuchadnezzar king of Babylon came up, and Jehoiakim became his servant three years: then he turned and rebelled against him."

Key word / key phrase

Verse 10, "Nebuchadnezzar."

Key event / key person / key theme

Nebuchadnezzar captures Jerusalem

Key thought

Even in the face of calamity many refuse to turn to God.

Key thing to look out for

God punishes evil and sin.

Key Bible cross-reference

Verse 15. See Jeremiah 22:24–27.

Key "by way of explanation"

Verse 19. Zedekiah had been given plenty of warnings about the need to repent. See Jeremiah 38:5, 19.

Key "Quotable Quote"

"The Scripture moveth us, in sundry places to acknowledge and confess our manifold sins and wickedness."

Book of Common Prayer

2 Kings 25

Matthew Henry's introduction

In this chapter we have,

I. The utter destruction of Jerusalem by the Chaldeans, the city besieged and taken (vv. 1–4), the houses burnt (vv. 8, 9), and wall broken down (v. 10), and the inhabitants carried away into captivity, vv. 11, 12. The glory of Jerusalem was,

A. That it was the royal city, where were set "the thrones of the house of David;" but that glory has now departed, for the prince is made a most miserable prisoner, the seed royal is destroyed (vv. 5–7), and the principal officers are put to death, vv. 18–21.

B. That it was the holy city, where was the testimony of Israel; but that glory has departed, for Solomon's temple is burnt to the ground (v. 9) and the sacred vessels that remained are carried away to Babylon, vv. 13–17. Thus has Jerusalem become as a widow, Lam. 1.

1. Ichabod—Where is the glory?
2. The distraction and dispersion of the remnant that was left in Judah under Gedaliah, vv. 22–26.
3. The countenance which, after thirty-seven years' imprisonment, was given to Jehoiachin the captive king of Judah, vv. 27–30.

A detailed analysis of chapter

Jerusalem besieged, Zedekiah taken. (1–7)

The temple burnt, and the people carried into captivity. (8–21)

The rest of the Jews flee into Egypt, Evil-merodach relieves the captivity of Jehoiachin. (22–30)

Key verse

Verse 1: "And it came to pass in the ninth year of his reign, in the tenth month, in the tenth day of the month, that Nebuchadnezzar king of Babylon came, he, and all his host, against Jerusalem, and pitched against it; and they built forts against it round about."

Key word / key phrase

Verse 1, "Jerusalem."

Key event / key person / key theme

The fall of Jerusalem

Key thought

Jerusalem need never have fallen.

Key thing to look out for

What can be learned from the fall of Jerusalem?

Key Bible cross-reference

Verse 1. See Jeremiah 39:1; 52:4.

Key "by way of explanation"

Verse 7. Zedekiah could have prevented God's judgment on Jerusalem if he had only done what Jeremiah told him to do. See Jeremiah 38:14–28. Jerusalem fell in the summer of 586 BC.

Key "Quotable Quote"

"God can turn any tragedy into a triumph, if only you will wait and watch."

Max Lucado

5. Select bibliography for 1 and 2 Kings

Edersheim, Alfred. *The Bible History, Old Testament* . 7 vols. in 2 vols. Grand Rapids: Eerdmans, 1956.

Keil, C. F., and Delitzsch, F. *Biblical Commentary on the Old Testament: The Books of the Kings*. KD. Grand Rapids: Eerdmans, 1954.

Provan, Iain W. *1 and 2 Kings* (New International Biblical Commentary), Hendrickson, 1995.

Wiseman, Donald J. *1 & 2 Kings* (Tyndale), InterVarsity, 1993.

1 and 2 Chronicles

1. Book by book: Introduction to 1 and 2 Chronicles

Introduction

The first and second books of Chronicles were considered as one by the ancient Jews, who called them "words of days," that is, diaries or journals, being probably compiled from those registers that were kept by the king's historiographers of passing occurrences. In the Septuagint the title given them is *Paraleipomenon*, "of things omitted," that is, the books are supplementary because many things unnoticed in the former books are here recorded; and not only the omissions are supplied, but some narratives extended while others are added.

The authorship is commonly ascribed to Ezra, whose leading object seems to have been to show the division of families, possessions, etc., before the captivity, with a view to the exact restoration of the same order after the return from Babylon. Although many things are restated and others are exact repetitions of what is contained in Kings, there is so much new and important information that, as Jerome has well said, the Chronicles furnish the means of comprehending parts of the New Testament, which must have been unintelligible without them. They are frequently referred to by Christ and the Apostles as forming part of "the Word of God" (see the genealogies in Matthew 1:1–16; Luke 3:23–38; compare 2 Chronicles 19:7 with 1 Peter 1:17; 2 Chronicles 24:19–21 with Matthew 23:32–35).

Robert Jamieson

Contents of 1 and 2 Chronicles

1 Chronicles acts as a supplement to 1 and 2 Samuel and 1 and 2 Kings.

1 Chronicles is a history book mainly taken up with the reign of King David.

2 Chronicles continues the story of 1 Chronicles, with the reign of King Solomon and then traces four hundred years of the history of God's people until they are exiled.

The books of Chronicles are the last books of the Hebrew Bible. So the genealogies in 1 Chronicles 1–9 may be seen as an introduction to the genealogy of Jesus found in Matthew 1, the first chapter of the New Testament.

The contents the Books of Chronicles are naturally divided into three parts.

The first part is preliminary, consisting mostly of genealogical matters with accompanying facts and incidents (1 Chr. 1–9).

The second part is an account of the accession and reign of David (1 Chr. 10–29).

The third part is an account of the events under David's successors in the dynasty (2 Ch).

Genealogies

The genealogies begin with Adam (1 Chronicles 1:1) and extend to the latest Old Testament times (1 Chronicles 9; compare Nehemiah 11, and the latest names in the genealogical lines, e. g. 1 Chronicles 3:19). The events incidentally mentioned in connection with them are more numerous and of more importance than the casual reader would imagine. They are some dozens of them. Some of them are repeated from the parts of the Old Testament from which the Chronicler draws as sources—for example, such statements as that Nimrod was a mighty one, or that in the time of Peleg the earth was divided, or the details about the kings of Edom (1 Chronicles 1:10,19,43; compare Genesis 10:8,25; 36:31). Others are instances which the Chronicler has taken from other sources than the Old Testament—for instance, the story of Jabez, or the accounts of the Simeonite conquests of the Meunim and of Amalek (1 Chronicles 4:9, 10, 38–43).

David's reign

The account in Chronicles of the reign of David divides itself into three parts. The first part (1 Chr. 10–21) is a series of sections giving a general view, including the death of Saul, the crowning of David over the twelve tribes, his associates, his wars, the bringing of the ark to Jerusalem, the great Davidic promise, the plague that led to the purchase of the threshing-floor of Ornan the Jebusite. The second part (1 Chr. 22:1–29:22) deals with one particular event and the preparations for it. The event is the making Solomon king, at a great public assembly (1 Chronicles 23:1; 28:1). The preparations for it include arrangements for the site and materials and labor for the temple that is to be built, and the organizing of Levites, priests, singers, doorkeepers, captains, for the service of the temple and the kingdom.

David's successors

The third part (1 Chronicles 29:20–30) is a brief account of Solomon's being made king "a second time" (compare 1 Kings 1). 2 Chronicles recounts the reign of Solomon and the reigns of the kings of Judah: Rehoboam, Abijah, Asa, Jehoshaphat, Jehoram, Ahaziah, Athaliah, Joash, Amaziah, Uzziah, Jotham, Ahar, Hezekiah, Manasseh, Amon, Josiah, Jehoahaz, Jehoiakim, Jehoiachin, and Zedekiah.

2 Chronicles opens with a description of Solomon's glorious temple, and ends with Cyrus' edit to rebuild the temple, more than four hundred years later.

Orr, James, M.A., D.D. General Editor, International Standard Bible Encyclopedia

Detailed outline of 1 Chronicles

Part one: David's royal line: 1:1–9:44

1:1–1:27	From Adam to Abraham
1:28–1:54	From Abraham to Jacob
2:1–2:55	The Sons of Israel and the Descendants of Judah
3:1–3:24	Descendants of David and Solomon
4:1–4:23	Descendants of Judah
4:24–4:43	Descendants of Simeon
5:1–5:10	Descendants of Reuben
5:11–5:22	Descendants of Gad
5:23–5:26	The Half-Tribe of Manasseh
6:1–6:30	Descendants of Levi
6:31–6:53	Musicians Appointed by David
6:54–6:81	Settlements of the Levites
7:1–7:5	Descendants of Issachar
7:6–7:12	Descendants of Benjamin
7:13	Descendants of Naphtali
7:14–7:19	Descendants of Manasseh
7:20–7:29	Descendants of Ephraim
7:30–7:40	Descendants of Asher
8:1–9:2	Descendants of Benjamin
9:3–9:9	Inhabitants of Jerusalem
9:10–9:13	Priestly Families
9:14–9:34	Levitical Families
9:35–9:44	The Family of King Saul

Part two: David's reign: 10:1–29:30

10:1–10:14	Death of Saul and His Sons
11:1–11:3	David Anointed King of All Israel
11:4–11:9	Jerusalem Captured
11:10–11:47	David's Mighty Men and Their Exploits
12:1–12:22	David's Followers in the Wilderness
12:23–12:40	David's Army at Hebron
13:1–13:14	The Ark Brought from Kiriath-Jearim
14:1–14:7	David Established at Jerusalem
14:8–14:17	Defeat of the Philistines
15:1–15:29	The Ark Brought to Jerusalem
16:1–16:6	The Ark Placed in the Tent
16:7–16:36	David's Psalm of Thanksgiving
16:37–16:43	Regular Worship Maintained
17:1–17:15	God's Covenant with David
17:16–17:27	David's Prayer
18:1–18:13	David's Kingdom Established and Extended
18:14–18:17	David's Administration
19:1–19:19	Defeat of the Ammonites and Arameans
20:1–20:3	Siege and Capture of Rabbah
20:4–20:8	Exploits against the Philistines

21:1–21:17 The Census and Plague
21:17–21:27 David's Altar and Sacrifice
21:28–22:1 The Place Chosen for the Temple

22:2–22:5 David Prepares to Build the Temple
22:6–22:19 David's Charge to Solomon and the Leaders

23:1–23:32 Families of the Levites and Their Functions

24:1–24:19 Divisions of the Priests
24:20–24:31 Other Levites

25:1–25:31 The Temple Musicians
26:1–26:19 The Gatekeepers
26:20–26:32 The Treasurers, Officers, and Judges

27:1–27:15 The Military Divisions
27:16–27:24 Leaders of Tribes
27:25–27:34 Other Civic Officials

28:1–28:21 Solomon Instructed to Build the Temple

29:1–29:9 Offerings for Building the Temple
29:10–29:22 David's Praise to God
29:22–29:25 Solomon's Anointed King
29:16–29:30 Summary of David's Reign

Detailed outline of 2 Chronicles

1:1–1:13 Solomon Requests Wisdom
1:14–1:17 Solomon's Military and Commercial Activity

2:1–2:2 Preparations for Building the Temple
2:3–2:18 Alliance for Building the Temple

3:1–3:17 Solomon Builds the Temple

4:1–5:1 Furnishings of the Temple

5:2–5:14 The Ark Brought into the Temple

6:1–6:11 Dedication of the Temple
6:12–6:42 Solomon's Prayer of Dedication

7:1–7:11 Solomon Dedicates the Temple
7:12–7:22 God's Second Appearance to Solomon

8:1–8:18 Various Activities of Solomon

9:1–9:12 Visit of the Queen of Sheba
9:13–9:28 Solomon's Great Wealth
9:29–9:31 Death of Solomon

10:1–10:19 The Revolt against Rehoboam

11:1–11:12 Judah and Benjamin Fortified
11:13–11:17 Priests and Levites Support Rehoboam
11:18–11:23 Rehoboam's Marriages

12:1–12:12 Egypt Attacks Judah
12:13–12:16 Death of Rehoboam

13:1–13:22 Abijah Reigns over Judah

14:1–14:8 Asa Reigns
14:9–15:19 Ethiopian Invasion Repulsed

16:1–16:10 Alliance with Aram Condemned
16:11–16:14 Asa's Disease and Death

17:10–17:19 Jehoshaphat's Reign

18:1–18:27 Micaiah Predicts Failure
18:28–19:3 Defeat and Death of Ahab

19:4–19:11 The Reforms of Jehoshaphat

20:1–20:4 Invasion from the East
20:5–20:30 Jehoshaphat's Prayer and Victory
20:31–20:37 The End of Jehoshaphat's Reign

21:1–21:7 Jehoram's Reign
21:8–21:10 Revolt of Edom
21:11–21:17 Elijah's Letter
21:18–21:20 Disease and Death of Jehoram

22:1–22:9 Ahaziah's Reign
22:10–23:7 Athaliah Seizes the Throne

23:8–23:11 Joash Crowned King
23:12–23:21 Athaliah Murdered

24:1–24:14 Joash Repairs the Temple
24:15–24:22 Apostasy of Joash
24:23–24:27 Death of Joash

25:1–25:4 Reign of Amaziah
25:5–25:16 Slaughter of the Edomites
25:17–25:24 Israel Defeats Judah
25:25–25:28 Death of Amaziah

26:1–26:15 Reign of Uzziah
26:16–26:23 Pride and Apostasy

27:1–27:9 Reign of Jotham

28:1–28:4 Reign of Ahaz
28:5–28:7 Aram and Israel Defeat Judah
28:8–28:15 Intervention of Oded
28:16–28:21 Assyria Refuses to Help Judah
28:22–28:27 Apostasy and Death of Ahaz

29:1–29:2 Reign of Hezekiah
29:3–29:19 The Temple Cleansed
29:20–29:36 Temple Worship Restored

30:1–30:27 The Great Passover

31:1–31:10 Pagan Shrines Destroyed
31:11–31:21 Reorganization of Priests and Levitess

32:1–32:19 Sennacherib's Invasion
32:20–32:23 Sennacherib's Defeat and Death
32:24–32:26 Hezekiah's Sickness
32:27–32:33 Hezekiah's Prosperity and Achievements

33:1–33:9 Reign of Manasseh
33:10–33:17 Manasseh Restored after Repentance
33:18–33:20 Death of Manasseh
33:21–33:25 Amon's Reign and Death

34:1–34:7 Reign of Josiah
34:8–34:21 Discovery of the Book of the Law
34:22–34:28 The Prophet Huldah Consulted

34:29–34:33 The Covenant Renewed

35:1–35:19 Celebration of the Passover
35:20–35:27 Defeat by Pharaoh Neco and Death of Josiah

36:1–36:4 Reign of Jehoahaz
36:5–36:8 Reign and Captivity of Jehoiakim
36:9–36:10 Reign and Captivity of Jehoiachin
36:11–36:14 Reign of Zedekiah
36:15–36:21 The Fall of Jerusalem
36:22–36:23 Cyrus Proclaims Liberty for the Exiles

2. Helpful summaries of 1 and 2 Chronicles

Bird's eye view

I Chronicles records the spiritual history of Israel under King David's reign.

2 Chronicles continues the history of Israel under Solomon and its successive kings until its capital is destroyed in 587 b.c..

Reading plan

The following reading plan, taking one reading per day, enables you to read through 1 and 2 Chronicles in twenty-eight days.

1 Chronicles 1–2
1 Chronicles 3–4
1 Chronicles 5
1 Chronicles 6
1 Chronicles 7–8
1 Chronicles 9–10
1 Chronicles 11
1 Chronicles 12–14
1 Chronicles 15–16
1 Chronicles 17–19
1 Chronicles 20–22
1 Chronicles 23–24
1 Chronicles 25–26
1 Chronicles 27–29
2 Chronicles 1–2
2 Chronicles 3–5
2 Chronicles 6–8
2 Chronicles 9–11
2 Chronicles 12–14
2 Chronicles 15–17
2 Chronicles 18–20
2 Chronicles 21–23
2 Chronicles 24–25
2 Chronicles 26–28
2 Chronicles 29–31
2 Chronicles 32–33
2 Chronicles 34–35
2 Chronicles 36

Verses to memorize

1 Chronicles 16:11

Look to the Lord and his strength; seek his face always. Remember the wonders he has done.

2 Chronicles 7:14

if my people, who are called by my name, will humble themselves and pray and seek my face and turn from their wicked ways, then will I hear from heaven and will forgive their sin and will heal their land.

2 Chronicles 16:9

For the eyes of the Lord range throughout the earth to strengthen those whose hearts are fully committed to him.

2 Chronicles 20:6
O Lord, God of our fathers, you rule over all the kingdoms of the nations. Power and might are in your hand.

Statistics

1 Chronicles
Thirteenth Old Testament book
29 chapters
941 verses
20,369 words

2 Chronicles
Fourteenth Old Testament book
36 chapters
822 verses
26,074 words

Names/titles given

Hebrew title: *Dibere Hyyamim:*
"The words/events/accounts of the days," that is: "The events of the times."

In the Hebrew Bible 1 and 2 Chronicles are a single book. The Septuagint divided it into two books.

Greek title in Septuagint: *Paraleipomenon:*
"Of things omitted." That is, the things left out of the books of Samuel and Kings.

Paraleipomenon Primus: "The first book of things omitted" was the name of 1 Chronicles.

Latin title in Vulgate: *Chronicorum Liber:*
"The book of Chronicles"

"Chronicle of the whole of sacred history," Jerome

A supplement to 1 and 2 Samuel, and 1 and 2 Kings

3. Helpful keys to turn to in understanding 1 and 2 Chronicles

Key words

1 Chronicles
Reigned

2 Chronicles
Established

Key verses

1 Chronicles 15:2; 29:11
2 Chronicles 7:14; 20:20

Themes to study

1 Chronicles
Prayer
God's election of us
Buildings erected for the Lord
Failure
Service and giving to the Lord's work

2 Chronicles
Guidance
Suffering
Wisdom
Praise
Giving to the Lord

Five reforms in 2 Chronicles, in the time of:

1. King Asa, chapter 15
2. King Jehoshaphat, 17:6–10
3. Jehoiada the priest, and King Joash, 23:16–19
4. King Hezekiah, chapters 29–31
5. King Josiah, chapters 34–35

Jesus in 1 and 2 Chronicles

In 1 and 2 Chronicles Jesus is the King of kings and Lord of lords.

Lessons to learn from 1 and 2 Chronicles

1 Chronicles

Our worship should be characterized by:
Reverence,
Celebration
Thanksgiving expressed in music
Adoration of God himself.

2 Chronicles

God is in charge of the whole world and every nation in it.
Worship should lead to a life of purity, praise, and obedience.
Christians should aim to be totally dedicated in their discipleship.

4. Chapter by chapter: outline of every chapter of 1 and 2 Chronicles

1 Chronicles 1

Matthew Henry's introduction

This chapter and many that follow it repeat the genealogies we have hitherto met with in the sacred history, and put them all together, with considerable additions. We may be tempted, it may be, to think it would have been well if they had not been written, because, when they come to be compared with other parallel places, there are differences found, which we can scarcely accommodate to our satisfaction; yet we must not therefore stumble at the word, but bless God that the things necessary to salvation are plain enough. And since the wise God has thought fit to write these things to us, we should not pass them over unread. All scripture is profitable, though not all alike profitable; and we may take occasion for good thoughts and meditations even from those parts of scripture that do not furnish so much matter for profitable remarks as some other parts. These genealogies,

1. Were then of great use, when they were here preserved, and put into the hands of the Jews after their return from Babylon; for the captivity, like the deluge, had put all into confusion, and they, in that dispersion and despair, would be in danger of losing the distinctions of their tribes and families. This therefore revives the ancient landmarks even of some of the tribes that were carried captive into Assyria. Perhaps it might invite the Jews to study the sacred writings which had been neglected, to find the names of their ancestors, and the rise of their families in them.
2. They are still of some use for the illustrating of the scripture-story, and especially for the clearing of the pedigrees of the Messiah, that it might appear that our blessed Savior was, according to the prophecies which went before of him, the son of David, the son of Judah, the son of Abraham, the son of Adam. And, now that he has come for whose sake these registers were preserved, the Jews since have so lost all their genealogies that even that of the priests, the most sacred of all, is forgotten, and they know not of any one man in the world that can prove himself of the house of Aaron. When the building is reared the scaffolds are removed. When the

promised Seed has come the line that was to lead to him is broken off. In this chapter we have an abstract of all the genealogies in the book of Genesis, till we come to Jacob.

I. The descents from Adam to Noah and his sons, out of Gen. 5:1–4.
II. The posterity of Noah's sons, by which the earth was repeopled, out of Gen. 10., vv. 5–23.
III. The descents from Shem to Abraham, out of Gen. 11:24–28.
IV. The posterity of Ishmael, and of Abraham's sons by Keturah, out of Gen. 25:29–35.
V. The posterity of Esau, out of Gen. 36:36–54. These, it is likely, were passed over lightly in Genesis; and therefore, according to the law of the school, we are made to go over that lesson again which we did not learn well.

A detailed analysis of chapter

Genealogies, Adam to Abraham. (1–27)

The descendants of Abraham. (28–54)

Key verse

Verse 1: "Adam, Seth, Enosh . . ."

Key word / key phrase

Verse 1, "Adam."

Key event / key person / key theme

Genealogy from Adam to Abraham

Key thought

God has his providential hand over all his people.

Key thing to look out for

The orderly arrangement of names has been likened to a garden divided into separate beds.

Key Bible cross-reference

Verses 5–23. See Genesis 10:2–29.

Key "by way of explanation"

1 and 2 Chronicles were written after the exile to Babylon. In Hebrew Bibles they make up one book and this book is included, not among the historical books, but in the section called the Writings.

Key "Quotable Quote"

"The history of the Church ought properly to be called the history of truth."

Blaise Pascal

1 Chronicles 2

Matthew Henry's introduction

We have now come to what was principally intended, the register of the children of Israel, that distinguished people, that were to "dwell alone, and not be reckoned among the nations." Here we have,

I. The names of the twelve sons of Israel, vv. 1, 2.
II. An account of the tribe of Judah, which has the precedence, not so much for the sake of David as for the sake of the Son of David, our Lord, who sprang out of Judah, Heb. 7:14.
A. The first descendants from Judah, down to Jesse, vv. 3–12.
B. The children of Jesse, vv. 13–17.

C. The posterity of Hezron, not only through Ram, from whom David came, but through Caleb (vv. 18–20), Segub (vv. 21–24), Jerahmeel (5:25–33), and more by Caleb (vv. 42–49), with the family of Caleb the son of Hur, vv. 50–55.

A detailed analysis of chapter

Israel's sons. (1–2)

The line of Judah. (3–55)

Key verse

Verse 1: "These are the sons of Israel."

Key word / key phrase

Verse 1, "Israel."

Key event / key person / key theme

Genealogy from Jacob to David

Key thought

God is the God of the individual.

Key thing to look out for

Verse 20. In this list, the Chronicler includes the craftsman Bezalel, who master-minded the building of the tabernacle.

Key Bible cross-reference

Verses 1, 2. See Genesis 29:31–30:24.

Key "by way of explanation"

In 1 and 2 Chronicles the writer's emphasis is on the priesthood, the temple, and worship.

Key "Quotable Quote"

"God, so great an artificer in great things, is not less great in small things."

Augustine of Hippo

1 Chronicles 3

Matthew Henry's introduction

Of all the families of Israel none was so illustrious as the family of David. That is the family which was mentioned in the previous chapter, v. 15. Here we have a full account of it.

I. David's sons, vv. 1–9.

II. His successors in the throne as long as the kingdom continued, vv. 10–16.

III. The remains of his family in and after the captivity, vv. 17–24. From this family, "as about the flesh, Christ came."

A detailed analysis of chapter

The line of David. (1–24)

Key verse

Verse 1: "Now these were the sons of David, which were born unto him in Hebron."

Key word / key phrase

Verse 1, "David."

Key event / key person / key theme

Genealogy from David to the captivity

Key thought

Jesus was happy to be recognized as the son of David.

Key thing to look out for

Despite his many faults David was Israel's greatest king.

Key Bible cross-reference

Verses 1–9. See 2 Samuel 3:2–5; 5:13–16; 13:1.

Key "by way of explanation"

The Chronicler has lifted material from the archives. Slight variations in the lists here and in Kings and Luke 3 probabaly indicate different ways of recording inter-marriages.

Key "Quotable Quote"

"Man moves himself, but God leads him."

François Fénelon

1 Chronicles 4

Matthew Henry's introduction

In this chapter we have,

I. A further account of the genealogies of the tribe of Judah, the most numerous and most famous of all the tribes. The posterity of Shobal the son of Hur (vv. 1–4), of Ashur the posthumous son of Hezron (who was mentioned, 2:24), with something particular about Jabez (vv. 5–10), of Chelub and others (vv. 11–20), of Shelah, vv. 21–23.

II. An account of the posterity and cities of Simeon, their conquest of Gedon, and of the Amalekites in Mount Seir, vv. 24–43.

A detailed analysis of chapter

Southern tribal lists. (1–43)

Key verse

Verse 1: "The sons of Judah; Pharez, Hezron, and Carmi, and Hur, and Shobal."

Key word / key phrase

Verse 1, "Judah."

Key event / key person / key theme

Genealogy of Judah and Simeon

Key thought

To turn to the Lord in prayer expresses faith and dependence.

Key thing to look out for

Verse 10. God loves to answer prayers.

Key Bible cross-reference

Verse 13. See Joshua 15:17; Judges 1:13; 3:9–11.

Key "by way of explanation"

Verses 9,10. These two verses are an example of the short historical notes which intersperse the list of names in these genealogies.

Key "Quotable Quote"

"I have no doubt that the world stands because of the prayers of Christians."

Aristides of Athens

1 Chronicles 5

Matthew Henry's introduction

This chapter gives us some account of the two tribes and a half that were seated on the other side Jordan.

I. Of Reuben, vv. 1–10.

II. Of Gad, vv. 11–17.
III. Of the half-tribe of Manasseh, vv. 23, 24.
IV. About all three acting in conjunction we are told,
  A. How they conquered the Hagarites, vv. 18–22.
  B. How they were, at length, themselves conquered, and made captives, by the king of Assyria, because they had forsaken God, vv. 25, 26.

A detailed analysis of chapter

The line of Reuben. (1–10)
The line of Gad. (11–22)
The half-tribe of Manasseh (23–26)

Key verse

Verse 1: "Now the sons of Reuben the firstborn of Israel."

Key word / key phrase

Verse 1, "Reuben."

Key event / key person / key theme

Genealogy of the tribes who lived across the Jordan.

Key thought

Verse 22. God helped his people in their victories.

Key thing to look out for

Anything that is good in our lives we should attribute to God.

Key Bible cross-reference

Verses 1–26. See Numbers 32:33–42.

Key "by way of explanation"

Verse 6. "Tiglath-Pileser" was the Assyrian king who attacked Israel. His personal name was "Pul" and he kept this name as king of Babylon. But as ruler of Assyria he was known as "Tiglath-Pileser."

Key "Quotable Quote"

"It is most certain that, where the grace of God reigns, there is also the readiness to obey."

John Calvin

1 Chronicles 6

Matthew Henry's introduction

Though Joseph and Judah shared between them the forfeited honors of the birthright, yet Levi was first of all the tribes, dignified and distinguished with an honor more valuable than either the precedence or the double portion, and that was the priesthood. That tribe God set apart for himself; it was Moses's tribe, and perhaps for his sake was thus favored. Of that tribe we have an account in this chapter.

I. Their pedigree, the first fathers of the tribe (vv. 1–3), the line of the priests, from Aaron to the captivity (vv. 4–15), and of some other of their families, vv. 16–30.
II. Their work, the work of the Levites (vv. 31–48), of the priests, vv. 49–53.
III. The cities appointed them in the land of Canaan, vv. 54–81.

A detailed analysis of chapter

Descendants of the high priests. (1–15)

Other descendants of Levi. (16–30)

Temple musicians. (31–48)

Descendants of Aaron. (49–53)

Levite territory. (54–80)

Key verse

Verse 1: "The sons of Levi."

Key word / key phrase

Verse 1, "Levi."

Key event / key person / key theme

Genealogy of Levi

Key thought

The inclusion in the list of temple musicians shows the importance of music in the worship of the Israelites.

Key thing to look out for

Verse 31. David, himself a singer and musician, established a guild of musicians.

Key Bible cross-reference

Verses 31–38. See 15:16, 27; 25:1–31.

Key "by way of explanation"

Verse 4–15. These verses give a shortened list of the high priests from the time of Eleazar to the Exile.

Key "Quotable Quote"

"Pastors have neglected their rightful oversight of worship, including the doctrinal content of the music."

Alliance of Confessing Evangelicals,
The Cambridge Declaration

1 Chronicles 7

Matthew Henry's introduction

In this chapter we have some account of the genealogies,

I. Of Issachar, vv. 1–5.
II. Of Benjamin, vv. 6–12.
III. Of Naphtali, v. 13.
IV. Of Manasseh, vv. 14–19.
V. Of Ephraim, vv. 20–29.
VI. Of Asher, vv. 30–40. Here is no account either of Zebulun or Dan. Why they only should be omitted we can assign no reason; only it is the disgrace of the tribe of Dan that idolatry began in that colony of the Danites which fixed in Laish, and called Dan, and there one of the golden calves was set up by Jeroboam. Dan is omitted, Rev. 7.

A detailed analysis of chapter

Issachar's descendants. (1–5)

Descendants of Benjamin, Dan, and Naphtali. (6–13)

Descendants of Manasseh. (14–19)

Descendants of Ephraim. (20–29).

Descendants of Asher. (30–40)

Key verse

Verse 1: "Now the sons of Issachar were, Tola, and Puah, Jashub, and Shimrom, four."

Key word / key phrase

Verse 1, "Issachar."

Key event / key person / key theme

Genealogy of Issachar, Benjamin, Naphtali, Manasseh, Ephraim, and Asher

Key thought

Every Christian is a member of God's family.

Key thing to look out for

Verse 40. How would we wish our descendants to be described?

Key Bible cross-reference

Verses 1–5. See Genesis 46:13; Numbers 1:28; 26:23–25.

Key "by way of explanation"

Verse 15. The daughters of Zelophehad are linked to the teaching on the inheritance rights of women found in Numbers 26:29–34; 27:1–11.

Key "Quotable Quote"

"Every Christian community must realize that not only do the weak need the strong, but also that the strong cannot exist without the weak. The elimination of the weak is the death of the fellowship."

Dietrich Bonhoeffer

1 Chronicles 8

Matthew Henry's introduction

We had some account given us of Benjamin in the previous chapter; here we have a larger catalogue of the great men of that tribe.

1. Because of that tribe Saul came, the first king of Israel, to the story of whom the sacred writer is hastening, 10:1.
2. Because that tribe clave to Judah, inhabited much of Jerusalem, was one of the two tribes that went into captivity, and returned back; and that story also he has an eye to, 9:1. Here is,

I. Some of the heads of that tribe named, vv. 1–32.

II. A more particular account of the family of Saul, vv. 33–40.

A detailed analysis of chapter

Descendants of Benjamin. (1–32)

Family of King Saul. (33–40)

Key verse

Verse 1: "Now Benjamin begat Bela his firstborn, Ashbel the second, and Aharah the third."

Key word / key phrase

Verse 1, "Benjamin."

Key event / key person / key theme

Genealogy of Benjamin

Key thought

Life itself is a gift from God.

Key thing to look out for

Families are meant to encourage their members to love the Lord.

Key Bible cross-reference

Verse 33. See 1 Samuel 14:49; 31:2.

Key "by way of explanation"

Verses 6–27. These verses are among the few verses that are unique to Chronicles.

Key "Quotable Quote"

"Behind every saint stands another saint."

Friedrich von Hugel

1 Chronicles 9

Matthew Henry's introduction

This chapter intimates to us that one end of recording all these genealogies was to direct the Jews, now that they had returned out of captivity, with whom to incorporate and where to reside; for here we have an account of those who first took possession of Jerusalem after their return from Babylon, and began the rebuilding of it on the old foundation.

I. The Israelites, vv. 2–9.
II. The priests, vv. 10–13.
III. The Levites and other Nethinim, vv. 14–26.
IV. Here is the particular charge of some of the priests and Levites, vv. 27–34.
V. A repetition of the genealogy of king Saul, vv. 35–44.

A detailed analysis of chapter

Returned captives in Jerusalem. (1–9)
Priests and Levites in Jerusalem. (10–16)
Temple guards and other Levites in Jerusalem. (17–34)
Genealogy of King Saul (35–44)

Key verse

Verse 1: "So all Israel were reckoned by genealogies; and, behold, they were written in the book of the kings of Israel and Judah, who were carried away to Babylon for their transgression."

Key word / key phrase

Verse 22, "positions of trust."

Key event / key person / key theme

The work of the Levites

Key thought

Christians should excel at being members of a team.

Key thing to look out for

Verse 33. Musicians offered praise to God night and day.

Key Bible cross-reference

Verses 10–13. See Nehemiah 11:10–14.

Key "by way of explanation"

Verses 22–27. A pool of 212 gatekeepers guarded Jerusalem. Seventy-two gatekeepers were on duty each week.

Key "Quotable Quote"

"The great cannot exist without the less, nor the less without the great."

Clement of Rome

1 Chronicles 10

Matthew Henry's introduction

The design of Ezra, in these books of the Chronicles, was to preserve the records of the house of David, which, though much sunk and lessened in a common eye by the captivity, yet grew more and more illustrious in the eyes of those that lived by faith by the nearer approach of the Son of David. And therefore he repeats, not the history of Saul's reign, but only of his death, by which way was made for David to the throne. In this chapter we have,

I. The fatal rout which the Philistines gave to Saul's army, and the fatal stroke which he gave himself, vv. 1–7.
II. The Philistines' triumph therein, vv. 8–10.
III. The respect which the men of Jabesh Gilead showed the royal corpse, vv. 11, 12.
IV. The reason of Saul's rejection, vv. 13, 14.

(For 1 Chronicles chapter 10, see 1 Samuel 31.)

1 Chronicles 11

Matthew Henry's introduction

In this chapter is repeated,

I. The elevation of David to the throne, immediately on the death of Saul, by common consent, vv. 1–3.
II. His gaining the castle of Zion out of the hands of the Jebusites, vv. 4–9.
III. The catalogue of the worthies and great men of his kingdom, vv. 10–47.

(For 1 Chronicles chapter 11, see 2 Samuel 5:1–3, 6–10; 23:8–39.)

1 Chronicles 12

Matthew Henry's introduction

What the mighty men did towards making David king we read in the previous chapter. Here we are told what the many did towards it. It was not all at once, but gradually, that David ascended the throne. His kingdom was to last; and therefore, like fruits that keep longest, it ripened slowly. After he had long waited for the vacancy of the throne, it was at two steps and those above seven years distant, that he ascended it. Now we are here told,

I. What help came in to him to Ziklag, to make him king of Judah, vv. 1–22.
II. What help came in to him in Hebron, to make him king over all Israel, above seven years after, vv. 23–40.

A detailed analysis of chapter

Those who came to David at Ziklag (where he was still an outlaw). (1–22)

Those who came to Hebron to proclaim him king. (23–40)

Key verse

Verse 1: "Now these are they that came to David to Ziklag, while he yet kept himself close because of Saul the son of Kish: and they were among the mighty men, helpers of the war."

Key word / key phrase

Verse 18, "your God will help you."

Key event / key person / key theme

David's followers

Key thought

So many hundreds of thousands of people were united by their love and loyalty for one man: this ought to be a picture of the Church.

Key thing to look out for

The many varied gifts of David's followers.

Key Bible cross-reference

Verses 38–40. David's great feast has been taken as a picture of the future Messianic feast. Messianic times are often pictured in terms of a feast. See Matthew 25:1–13; Luke 22:28–30.

Key "by way of explanation"

Verses 23–37. Sometimes the Hebrew word for "thousand" stands for a group of men with its own commander. See 13:1.

Key "Quotable Quote"

"Imprudent is he whoever arranges only his earthly will and not his heavenly one."

Basil the Great

1 Chronicles 13

Matthew Henry's introduction

In the previous chapter we have David made king, by which the civil government was happily settled. In this chapter care is taken about religion.

I. David consults with the representatives of the people about bringing up the ark out of its obscurity into a public place; and it is resolved on, vv. 1–4.

II. With a great deal of solemnity and joy, it is carried from Kirjath-jearim, vv. 5–8.

III. Uzza is struck dead for touching it, which, for the present, spoils the solemnity and stops the proceedings, vv. 9–14.

(For 1 Chronicles chapter 13, see 2 Samuel 6:1–12.)

1 Chronicles 14

Matthew Henry's introduction

In this chapter we have,

I. David's kingdom established, vv. 1, 2.

II. His family built up, vv. 3–7.

III. His enemies, the Philistines, routed in two campaigns, vv. 8–17. This is repeated here from 2 Sam. 5:11, etc.

(For 1 Chronicles chapter 14, see 2 Samuel 5:11–25.)

1 Chronicles 15

Matthew Henry's introduction

The bringing in of the ark to the city of David was a very good work; it was resolved on (13:4), and attempted, but not perfected; it lay by the way in the house of Obed-edom. Now this chapter gives us an account of the completing of that good work.

I. How it was done more regularly than before.

A. A place was prepared for it, v. 1.

B. The priests were ordered to carry it, vv. 2–15.

C. The Levites had their offices assigned them in attending on it, vv. 16–24.

II. How it was done more successfully than before, v. 25.

A. The Levites made no mistake in their work, v. 26.

B. David and the people met with no damp on their joy, vv. 27, 28. As for Michal's despising David, it was nothing, v. 29.

A detailed analysis of chapter

Preparations for the removal of the ark. (1–24)

The removal of the ark. (25–29)

Key verse

Verse 3: "And David gathered all Israel together to Jerusalem, to bring up the ark of the LORD unto his place, which he had prepared for it."

Key word / key phrase

Verse 1, "ark."

Key event / key person / key theme

The ark is brought to Jerusalem

Key thought

Worship is meant to be at the heart of the Christian fellowship.

Key thing to look out for

What was the matter with Michal?

Key Bible cross-reference

Verses 1–29. See Psalm 132.

Key "by way of explanation"

Verse 12. The consecration referred to in this verse means ritual washings and all other activities commanded to avoid ceremonial uncleanness.

Key "Quotable Quote"

"Visualize the Lord high and lifted up filling the sanctuary with his presence."

Richard Foster

1 Chronicles 16

Matthew Henry's introduction

This chapter concludes that great affair of the settlement of the ark in the royal city, and with it the settlement of the public worship of God during the reign of David. Here is,

I. The solemnity with which the ark was fixed, vv. 1–6.

II. The psalm David gave to be sung on this occasion, vv. 7–36.

III. The settling of the stated public worship of God in order thenceforward, vv. 37–43.

A detailed analysis of chapter

The ark is set down inside the tent with great solemnity. (1–6)

David's psalm of praise. (7–36)

Setting in order the worship of God. (37–43)

Key verse

Verse 1: "So they brought the ark of God, and set it in the midst of the tent that David had pitched for it: and they offered burnt sacrifices and peace offerings before God."

Key word / key phrase

Verse 8, "give thanks."

Key event / key person / key theme

David's song of praise

Key thought

Praise and thanksgiving should be part of the daily life of God's people.

Key thing to look out for

The reasons why God is to be praised.

Key Bible cross-reference

Verses 8–36. See Psalm 105:1–15; 96; 106:1, 47, 48.

Key "by way of explanation"

Verse 1–3. David is here linked with the priests as he supervised their sacrifices and blessed the people.

Key "Quotable Quote"

"Remember the perfections of that God whom you worship, that he is most holy, pure, and jealous, and therefore to be purely worshipped; and that he is still present with you, and all things are naked and open to him with whom we have to do."

Richard Baxter

1 Chronicles 17

Matthew Henry's introduction

This excellent chapter is the same with 2 Sam. 7. It will be worth while to look back on what was there said on it. Two things in general we have in it:

(For 1 Chronicles chapter 17, see 2 Samuel 7:1–29)

1 Chronicles 18

Matthew Henry's introduction

David's piety and his prayer we had an account of in the previous chapter; here follows immediately that which one might reasonably expect, an account of his prosperity; for those that seek first the kingdom of God and the righteousness thereof, as David did, shall have other things added to them as far as God sees good for them. Here is,

I. His prosperity abroad. He conquered the Philistines (v. 1), the Moabites (v. 2), the king of Zobah (vv. 3, 4), the Syrians (vv. 5–8), made the king of Hamath his tributary (vv. 9–11), and the Edomites, vv. 12, 13.

II. His prosperity at home. His court and kingdom flourished, vv. 14–17. All this we had an account of before, 2 Sam. 8.

(For 1 Chronicles chapter 18 see 2 Samuel 8:1–18.)

1 Chronicles 19

Matthew Henry's introduction

The story is here repeated of David's war with the Ammonites and the Syrians their allies, and the victories he won over them, which we read just as it is here related, 2 Sam. 10. Here is,

I. David's civility to the king of Ammon, in sending an embassy of condolence to him on occasion of his father's death, vv. 1, 2.

II. His great incivility to David, in the base usage he gave to his ambassadors, vv. 3, 4.

III. David's just resentment of it, and the war which broke out thereon, in which the Ammonites acted with policy in bringing the Syrians to their assistance (vv. 6, 7), Joab did bravely (vv. 8–13), and Israel was once and again victorious, vv. 14–19.

(For 1 Chronicles chapter 19, see 2 Samuel 10.)

1 Chronicles 20

Matthew Henry's introduction

Here is a repetition of the story of David's wars,

I. With the Ammonites, and the taking of Rabbah, vv. 1–3.

II. With the giants of the Philistines, vv. 4–8.

(For 1 Chronicles chapter 20, see 2 Samuel 12:29–31; 21:15–22.)

1 Chronicles 21

Matthew Henry's introduction

As this rehearsal makes no mention of David's sin in the matter of Uriah, so neither of the troubles of his family that followed on it; not a word of Absalom's rebellion, or Sheba's. But David's sin, in numbering the people, is here related, because, in the atonement made for that sin, an intimation was given of the spot of ground on which the temple should be built. Here is,

I. David's sin, in forcing Joab to number the people, vv. 1–6.

II. David's sorrow for what he had done, as soon as he perceived the sinfulness of it, vv. 7, 8.

III. The sad dilemma (or trilemma rather) he was brought to, when it was put to him to choose how he would be punished for this sin, and what rod he would be beaten with, vv. 9–13.

IV. The woeful havoc which was made by the pestilence in the country, and the narrow escape which Jerusalem had from being laid waste by it, vv. 14–17.

V. David's repentance, and sacrifice, on this occasion, and the staying of the plaque thereon, vv. 18–30. This awful story we met with, and meditated on, 2 Sam. 24.

(For 1 Chronicles chapter 21, see 2 Samuel 24.)

1 Chronicles 22

Matthew Henry's introduction

"Out of the eater comes forth meat." It was on occasion of the terrible judgment inflicted on Israel for the sin of David that God gave intimation of the setting up of another altar, and of the place where he would have the temple to be built, on which David was excited with great vigor to make preparation for that great work, in which, though he had long since designed it, it should seem, he had, of late, grown remiss, till awakened by the alarm of that judgment. The tokens of God's favor he received after those of his displeasure,

I. Directed him to the place, v. 1.

II. Encouraged and quickened him to the work.

A. He set himself to prepare for the building, vv. 2–5.

B. He instructed Solomon, and gave him a charge about this work, vv. 6–16.

C. He commanded the princes to assist him in it, vv. 17–19.

There is a great deal of difference between the frame of David's spirit in the beginning of the previous chapter and in the beginning of this. There, in the pride of his heart, he was numbering the people; here, in his humility, preparing for the service of God. There corruption was uppermost (but the well of living water in the soul, though it may be muddied, will work itself clear again); grace here has recovered the upper hand.

A detailed analysis of chapter

David's preparations for the temple. (1–5)

David's instructions to Solomon. (6–16)

The leaders of Israel commanded to assist. (17–19)

Key verse

Verse 5: "So David prepared abundantly before his death."

Key word / key phrase

Verse 1, "house of the Lord."

Key event / key person / key theme

Preparations for building the temple

Key thought

Many different skills were needed to build the temple.

Key thing to look out for

Verse 19. A crucial instruction.

Key Bible cross-reference

Verses 8, 9. See 1 Kings 5:3.

Key "by way of explanation"

Verses 8, 9. David's constant preoccupation with war left him defiled so that he was in no state to build the temple.

Key "Quotable Quote"

"In a Christian community, everything depends upon whether each individual is an indispensable link in a chain. Only when even the smallest link is securely interlocked is the chain unbreakable."

Dietrich Bonhoeffer

1 Chronicles 23

Matthew Henry's introduction

David, having given charge about the building of the temple, in this and the following chapters settles the method of the temple-service and puts into order the offices and officers of it. In the late irregular times, and during the wars in the beginning of his reign, we may suppose that, though the Levitical ordinances were kept up, yet it was not in the order, nor with the beauty and exactness, that were desirable. Now David, being a prophet, as well as a prince, by divine warrant and direction, "set in order the things that were wanting." In this chapter we are informed,

I. He declared Solomon to be his successor, v. 1.

II. He numbered the Levites, and appointed them to their respective offices, vv. 2–5.

III. He took an account of the several families of the Levites, vv. 6–23.

IV. He made a new reckoning of them from twenty years old, and appointed them their work, vv. 24–32. And in this he prepared for the temple as truly as when he laid up gold and silver for it; for the place is of small account in comparison with the work.

A detailed analysis of chapter

David declares Solomon his successor. (1)

The Levites, their family and work. (2–32)

Key verse

Verse 1: "So when David was old and full of days, he made Solomon his son king over Israel."

Key word / key phrase

Verse 2, "Levites."

Key event / key person / key theme

The work of the Levites

Key thought

No job should be too small to do in God's service.

Key thing to look out for

The many jobs performed by the Levites.

Key Bible cross-reference

Verse 3. See Numbers 4:1–3.

Key "by way of explanation"

The Levites were assistants to the priests, and were also in charge of the music (verse 30).

Key "Quotable Quote"

"I count that part of my life lost which I spent not in communion with God, or in doing good."

John Donne

1 Chronicles 24

Matthew Henry's introduction

This chapter gives us a more particular account of the distribution of the priests and Levites into their respective classes, for the more regular discharge of the duties of their offices, according to their families.

I. Of the priests, vv. 1–19.

II. Of the Levites, vv. 20–31.

A detailed analysis of chapter

Work given to the priests. (1–19)

The rest of the Levites listed. (20–31)

Key verse

Verse 1: "Now these are the divisions of the sons of Aaron. The sons of Aaron; Nadab, and Abihu, Eleazar, and Ithamar."

Key word / key phrase

Verse 1, "sons of Aaron."

Key event / key person / key theme

Work given to the priests

Key thought

Every Christian can serve the Lord in a unique way.

Key thing to look out for

Verse 5. There should be no rivalry or jealousy among the Lord's servants.

Key Bible cross-reference

1–19. See 6:3–15; Ezra 2:36–39.

Key "by way of explanation"

Verse 4. The priests serving in the temple were divided into twenty-four teams or divisions and were chosen by lots.

Key "Quotable Quote"

"Blessed is the servant who esteems himself no more highly when he is praised and exalted by people than when he is considered worthless, foolish, and to be despised; since what a man is before God, that he is and nothing more."

Francis of Assisi

1 Chronicles 25

Matthew Henry's introduction

David, having settled the courses of these Levites that were to attend the priests in their ministrations, proceeds, in this chapter, to put those into a method that were appointed to be singers and musicians in the temple. Here is,

I. The people that were to be employed, Asaph, Heman, and Jeduthun (v. 1), their sons (vv. 2–6), and other skilful people, v. 7.

II. The order in which they were to attend determined by lot, vv. 8–31.

A detailed analysis of chapter

The temple musicians (all Levites). (1–31)

Key verse

Verse 1: "Moreover David and the captains of the host separated to the service of the sons of Asaph, and of Heman, and of Jeduthun, who should prophesy with harps, with psalteries, and with cymbals."

Key word / key phrase

Verse 1, "harps, lyres and cymbals."

Key event / key person / key theme

The temple musicians

Key thought

Music and singing should be an integral part of Christian worship.

Key thing to look out for

Here and elsewhere in Chronicles the temple officials had a ministry of prophesying (compare Ehesians 5:18, 19).

Key Bible cross-reference

Verse 1. See 2 Chronicles 20:14–17; 35:15.

Key "by way of explanation"

Verse 1. David's great interest in music would have made him ideal for organizing the singers and musicians in the temple.

Key "Quotable Quote"

"The aim and final end of all music should be none other than the glory of God and the refreshment of the soul. If heed is not paid to this, it is not true music but a diabolical bawling and twanging."

J.S. Bach

1 Chronicles 26

Matthew Henry's introduction

We have here an account of the business of the Levites. That tribe had made but a very small figure all the time of the judges, till Eli and

Samuel appeared. But when David revived religion the Levites were, of all men, in the greatest reputation. And happy it was that they had Levites who were men of sense, fit to support the honor of their tribe. We have here an account,

I. Of the Levites that were appointed to be porters, vv. 1–19.

II. Of those that were appointed to be treasurers and storekeepers, vv. 20–28.

III. Of those that were officers and judges in the country, and were entrusted with the administration of public affairs, vv. 29–32.

A detailed analysis of chapter

The temple guards. (1–19)

Other temple duties. (20–28)

Duties of other Levites (29–32)

Key verse

Verse 1: "Concerning the divisions of the porters: From the Korhites was Meshelemiah the son of Kore, of the sons of Asaph."

Key word / key phrase

Verse 1, "gatekeepers."

Key event / key person / key theme

The temple guards

Key thought

God's word needs guarding in the sense that it should be taught faithfully.

Key thing to look out for

Christian fellowships should guard against being infiltrated by false teachers.

Key Bible cross-reference

Verses 1–19. See 9:17–27; 16:37, 38.

Key "by way of explanation"

Verse 29. Work outside Jeruselem. The officers collected tithes for the temple; the judges gave judgment about the application of the law.

Key "Quotable Quote"

"False teachers tear the Bible to pieces, scourge and crucify it, and subject it to all manner of torture until they stretch it sufficiently to apply to their heresy, meaning, and whim."

Martin Luther

1 Chronicles 27

Matthew Henry's introduction

In this chapter we have the civil list, including the military,

I. The twelve captains for every separate month of the year, vv. 1–15.

II. The princes of the several tribes, vv. 16–24.

III. The officers of the court, vv. 25–34.

A detailed analysis of chapter

David's military force. (1–15)

Leaders and officers. (16–34)

Key verse

Verse 1: "Now the children of Israel after their number, to wit, the chief fathers and captains of thousands and hundreds, and their officers that served the king in any matter of the courses, which came in and went out month by month throughout all the months of the year, of every course were twenty and four thousand."

Key word / key phrase

Verse 1, "commanders of thousands."

Key event / key person / key theme

Government officials

Key thought

The desire for unity is meant to be one of the characteristics of Christian workers.

Key thing to look out for

Verse 24. When does counting numbers arouse God's anger?

Key Bible cross-reference

Verses 1–15. See 2 Samuel 23:23–37.

Key "by way of explanation"

Verses 32–34. In these verses David's inner circle of leaders is detailed.

Key "Quotable Quote"

"It is not our business to succeed, but to do right: when you have done so, the rest lies with God."

C.S. Lewis

1 Chronicles 28

Matthew Henry's introduction

The account we have of David's exit, in the beginning of the first book of Kings, does not make his sun nearly so bright as that given in this and the following chapter, where we have his solemn farewell both to his son and his subjects, and must own that he finished well. In this chapter we have,

I. A general convention of the states summoned to meet, v. 1.

II. A solemn declaration of the divine entail both of the crown and of the honor of building the temple on Solomon, vv. 2–7.

III. An exhortation both to the people and to Solomon to make religion their business, vv. 8–10.

IV. The model and materials delivered to Solomon for the building of the temple, vv. 11–19.

V. Encouragement given him to undertake it and proceed in it, vv. 20, 21.

A detailed analysis of chapter

David exhorts the people to fear of the Lord. (1–10)

He gives instructions for the temple. (11–21)

Key verse

Verse 8: "Now therefore in the sight of all Israel the congregation of the LORD, and in the audience of our God, keep and seek for all the commandments of the LORD your God: that ye may possess this good land, and leave it for an inheritance for your children after you for ever."

Key word / key phrase

Verse 1, "David."

Key event / key person / key theme

David's last words to his officials and to Solomon

Key thought

God's power should always be the basis for any Christian work.

Key "by way of explanation"

Verse 5. Here Asa is said to have "removed the high places." But in 1 Kings 15:14 he is said not to have removed the high places. In the early part of his reign Asa did try to remove them but did not completely succeed, so by the end of his reign the pagan worship still existed.

Key "Quotable Quote"

"To be united to Christ by faith is to throw off the thralldom of hostile powers, to enjoy perfect freedom, to gain the mastery over the dominion of evil – because Christ's victory is ours."

F.F. Bruce

2 Chronicles 15

Matthew Henry's introduction

Asa and his army were now returning in triumph from the battle, laden with spoils and adorned with the trophies of victory, the pious prince, we may now suppose, studying what he should render to God for this great favor. He knew that the work of reformation, which he had begun in his kingdom, was not perfected; his enemies abroad were subdued, but there were more dangerous enemies at home that were yet unconquered—idols in Judah and Benjamin: his victory over the former emboldened him vigorously to renew his attack on the latter. Now here we have,

I. The message which God sent to him, by a prophet, to engage him to, and encourage him in, the prosecution of his reformation, vv. 1–7.

II. The life which this message put into that good cause, and their proceedings in pursuance of it. Idols removed, v. 8. The spoil dedicated to God, vv. 9–11. A covenant made with God, and a law for the punishing of idolaters, vv. 12–15. A reformation at court, v. 16. Dedicated things brought into the house of God, v. 18. All well, but that the high places were permitted, v. 17. And the effect of this was great peace, v. 19.

A detailed analysis of chapter

Asa's reforms. (1–19)

Key verse

Verse 1: "And the Spirit of God came upon Azariah the son of Oded."

Key word / key phrase

Verse 1, "the Spirit of God."

Key event / key person / key theme

King Asa's reforms

Key thought

Nobody who seeks God will fail to find him.

Key thing to look out for

Whoever decides to forsake God will find himself forsaken by God.

Key Bible cross-reference

Verse 12. See Deuteronomy 29:1; 1 Samuel 11:14.

Key "by way of explanation"

Verse 3. Priests not only carried out the sacrifices in the temple but also were meant to teach the people.

Key thing to look out for

Verses 9, 10. David's reasons for urging Solomon to serve God wholeheartedly.

Key Bible cross-reference

Verse 19. See Exodus 25:40; 27:8; 31:18.

Key "by way of explanation"

Verse 20. The key to David's advice to Solomon comes in this verse with its emphasis on the power and reliability of the Lord.

Key "Quotable Quote"

"In God's faithfulness lies eternal security."

Corrie ten Boom

1 Chronicles 29

Matthew Henry's introduction

David has said what he had to say to Solomon. But he had something more to say to the congregation before he parted with them.

I. He pressed them to contribute, according to their ability, towards the building and furnishing of the temple, vv. 1–5.

II. They made their presents accordingly with great generosity, vv. 6–9.

III. David offered up solemn prayers and praises to God on that occasion (vv. 10–20), with sacrifices, vv. 21, 22.

IV. Solomon was hereon enthroned, with great joy and magnificence, vv. 23–25.

V. David, soon after this finished his course, vv. 26–30. And it is hard to say which shines brighter here, the setting sun or the rising sun.

A detailed analysis of chapter

David induces the leaders and people to offer willingly. (1–9)

His thanksgiving and prayer. (10–19)

Solomon enthroned. (20–25)

David's reign and death. (26–30)

Key verse

Verse 6: "Then the chief of the fathers and princes of the tribes of Israel, and the captains of thousands and of hundreds, with the rulers of the king's work, offered willingly."

Key word / key phrase

Verse 1, "King David."

Key event / key person / key theme

Summary of David's reign

Key thought

David nearly always praised God when he prayed.

Key thing to look out for

Verse 14. Why were the people so generous?

Key Bible cross-reference

Verses 2–9. See Exodus 25:1–8; 35:4–9, 20–20.

Key "by way of explanation"

Verse 7. A "daric" was a Persian coin, named after King Darius I.

Key "Quotable Quote"

"Let us sing how the eternal God, the author of all marvels, first created the heavens for the sons of men as a roof to cover them, and how their almighty Protector gave them the earth to live in."

Caedmon

2 Chronicles 1

Matthew Henry's introduction

In the close of the previous book we read how God magnified Solomon and Israel obeyed him; God and Israel concurred to honor him. Now here we have an account,

I. How he honored God by sacrifice (vv. 1–6) and by prayer, vv. 7–12.

II. How he honored Israel by increasing their strength, wealth, and trade, vv. 13–17.

(For 2 Chronicles chapter 1, see 1 Kings 3:4–15; 10:26–29.)

2 Chronicles 2

Matthew Henry's introduction

Solomon's trading, which we read of in the close of the previous chapter, and the encouragement he gave both to merchandise and manufacturers, were very commendable. But building was the work he was designed for, and to that business he is here applying himself. Here is,

I. Solomon's determination to build the temple and a royal palace, and his appointing laborers to be employed herein, vv. 1, 2, 17, 18.

II. His request to Huram king of Tyre to furnish him both with artists and materials, vv. 3–10.

III. Huram's obliging answer to, and compliance with, his request, vv. 11–16.

(For 2 Chronicles chapter 2, see 1 Kings 5.)

2 Chronicles 3

Matthew Henry's introduction

It was a much larger and more particular account of the building of the temple which we had in the book of Kings than is here in this book of Chronicles. In this chapter we have,

I. The place and time of building the temple, vv. 1, 2.

II. The dimensions and rich ornaments of it, vv. 3–9.

III. The cherubim in the most holy place, vv. 10–13.

IV. The veil, v. 14.

V. The two pillars, vv. 15–17. Of all this we have already and an account, 1 Kings 6, 7.

(For 2 Chronicles chapter 3, see 1 Kings 6.)

2 Chronicles 4

Matthew Henry's introduction

We have here a further account of the furniture of God's house.

I. Those things that were of brass. The altar for burnt-offerings (v. 1), the sea and lavers to hold water (vv. 2–6), the plates with which the doors of the court were overlaid (v. 9), the vessels of the altar, and other things, vv. 10–18.

II. Those that were of gold. The candlesticks and tables (vv. 7, 8), the altar of incense (v. 19), and the appurtenances of each of these, vv. 20–22. All these, except the brazen altar (v. 1), were accounted for more largely, 1 Kings 7:23, etc.

A detailed analysis of chapter

Furnishings of the temple. (1–22)

Key verse

Verse 2: "Also he made a molten sea of ten cubits from brim to brim, round in compass, and five cubits the height thereof; and a line of thirty cubits did compass it round about."

Key word / key phrase

Verse 1, "made."

Key event / key person / key theme

Making the furnishings for the temple

Key thought

All this craftsmanship was fashioned to bring glory to God.

Key thing to look out for

The New Testament speaks of these ceremonies as foreshadowing the cleansing and forgiveness that Christ brought.

Key Bible cross-reference

Verse 2. See Exodus 30:18.

Key "by way of explanation"

Verse 4. It is likely that the twelve bulls which held up the great Sea represented the twelve tribes of Israel. They had also surrounded the tabernacle with three on each side.

Key "Quotable Quote"

"The Old Testament does not occupy itself with how Israel thought of God. Its concern is with how Israel ought to think of God. The fundamental note of the Old Testament is revelation."

Benjamin B. Warfield

2 Chronicles 5

Matthew Henry's introduction

The temple being built and furnished for God, we have here,

I. Possession given to him, by bringing in the dedicated things (v. 1), but especially the ark, the token of his presence, vv. 2–10.

II. Possession taken by him, in a cloud, vv. 11–14. For if any man open the door of his heart to God he will come in, Rev. 3:20.

A detailed analysis of chapter

The ark placed in the temple. (1–10)

The temple filled with God's glory. (11–14)

Key verse

Verse 14: "So that the priests could not stand to minister by reason of the cloud: for the glory of the LORD had filled the house of God."

Key word / key phrase

Verse 2, "ark."

Key event / key person / key theme

The ark is brought to the temple

Key thought

The ark symbolized the presence of God.

Key thing to look out for

How did people celebrate one of the greatest events in their history?

Key Bible cross-reference

Verse 2. See 1 Chronicles 15:1–16:6.

Key "by way of explanation"

Verse 10. In addition to the two stone tablets the ark had contained Aaron's staff and a gold jar of manna. Nobody knows what happened to these items.

Key "Quotable Quote"

"Faith is the eye through which the light of God's presence and the vigor of his power stream into the soul."

Andrew Murray

2 Chronicles 6

Matthew Henry's introduction

The glory of the Lord, in the vehicle of a thick cloud, having filled the house which Solomon built, by which God manifested his presence there, he immediately improves the opportunity, and addresses God, as a God now, in a peculiar manner, nigh at hand.

I. He makes a solemn declaration of his intention in building this house, to the satisfaction of the people and the honor of God, both of whom he blessed, vv. 1–11.

II. He makes a solemn prayer to God that he would please graciously to accept and answer all the prayers that should be made in, or towards, that house, vv. 12–42. This whole chapter we had before, with very little variation (1 Kings 8:12–53), to which it may not be amiss here to look back.

A detailed analysis of chapter

Solomon speaks to the people. (1–11)

Solomon's prayer. (12–42)

Key verse

Verse 1: "Then said Solomon, The LORD hath said that he would dwell in the thick darkness."

Key word / key phrase

Verse 1, "Solomon."

Key event / key person / key theme

Solomon's prayer of dedication

Key thought

God keeps his promises.

Key thing to look out for

Recalling our own personal histories with gratitude before God is a healthy spiritual exercise.

Key Bible cross-reference

Verses 8, 9. See 1 Chronicles 28:2, 3.

Key "by way of explanation"

Verses 34, 35. The Chronicler often states that God gave his people victory in answer to prayer.

Key "Quotable Quote"

"God is my being, my me, my strength, my beatitude, my good, my delight."

Catherine of Genoa

2 Chronicles 7

Matthew Henry's introduction

In this chapter we have God's answer to Solomon's prayer.

I. His public answer by fire from heaven, which consumed the sacrifices (v. 1), with which the priests and people were much affected, vv. 2, 3. By that token of God's acceptance they were encouraged to continue the solemnities of the feast for fourteen days, and Solomon was encouraged to pursue all his designs for the honor of God, vv. 4–11.

II. His private answer by word of mouth, in a dream or vision of the night, vv. 12–22. Most of these things we had before, 1 Kings 8 and 9

(For 2 Chronicles chapter 7, see 1 Kings 8:62–66; 9:1–19.)

2 Chronicles 8

Matthew Henry's introduction

In this chapter we are told,

I. What cities Solomon built, vv. 1–6.

II. What workmen Solomon employed, vv. 7–10.

III. What care he took about a proper settlement for his wife, v. 11.

IV. What a good method he put the temple service into, vv. 12–16.

V. What trading he had with foreign countries, vv. 17, 18.

(For 2 Chronicles chapter 8, see 1 Kings 9:10–28.)

2 Chronicles 9

Matthew Henry's introduction

Solomon here continues to appear great both at home and abroad. We had this account of his grandeur, 1 Kings 10. Nothing is here added; but his defection towards his latter end, which we have there (ch. 11), is here omitted, and the close of this chapter brings him to the grave with an unstained reputation. Perhaps none of the chapters in the Chronicles agree so much with a chapter in the Kings as this does with 1 Kings 10 verse for verse, only that the first two verses there are put into one here, and verse 25 here is taken from 1 Kings 4:26, and the last three verses here from 1 Kings 11:41–43. Here is,

I. The honor which the queen of Sheba did to Solomon, in the visit she made him to hear his wisdom, vv. 1–12.

II. Many instances given of the riches and splendor of Solomon's court, vv. 13–28.

III. The conclusion of his reign, vv. 29–31.

(For 2 Chronicles chapter 9, see 1 Kings 10:1–29; 11:41–43.)

2 Chronicles 10

Matthew Henry's introduction

This chapter is copied almost verbatim from 1 Kings 12:1–19, where it was opened at large. Solomon's defection from God was not repeated, but the defection of the ten tribes from his family is, in this chapter, where we find,

I. How foolish Rehoboam was in his treating with them, vv. 1, 5–14.

II. How wicked the people were in complaining of Solomon (vv. 2–4) and forsaking

Rehoboam, vv. 16–19.

III. How just and righteous God was in all this, v. 15. His counsel was thereby fulfilled. With him are strength and wisdom; both the deceived and the deceiver (the fool and the knave) are his (Job 12:16), that is, are made use of by him to suit his purposes.

(For 2 Chronicles chapter 10, see 1 Kings 12:1–24.)

2 Chronicles 11

Matthew Henry's introduction

We are here going on with the history of Rehoboam.

I. His attempt to recover the ten tribes he has lost, and the letting fall of that attempt in obedience to the divine command, vv. 1–4.

II. His successful endeavors to preserve the two tribes that remained, vv. 5–12.

III. The resort of the priests and Levites to him, vv. 13–17.

IV. An account of his wives and children, vv. 18–23.

A detailed analysis of chapter

Rehoboam forbidden to fight against Israel. (1–12)

The priests and Levites find refuge in Judah. (13–23)

Key verse

Verse 4: "Thus saith the LORD, Ye shall not go up, nor fight against your brethren: return every man to his house: for this thing is done of me."

Key word / key phrase

Verse 1, "Rehoboam."

Key event / key person / key theme

Rehoboam fortifies the cities of Judah

Key thought

Choosing to follow God's ways is to vote against evil ways.

Key thing to look out for

Anything which strengthens goodness should be positively supported.

Key Bible cross-reference

Verses 13–17. See 1 Kings 12:26–33.

Key "by way of explanation"

Verses 16, 17. When the northern tribes rebelled and formed the separate nation of Israel, many people came south to worship in Jerusalem and support Rehoboam.

Key "Quotable Quote"

"Man has two great spiritual needs One is for forgiveness. The other is for goodness."

Billy Graham

2 Chronicles 12

Matthew Henry's introduction

This chapter gives us a more full account of the reign of Rehoboam than we had before in Kings and it is a very melancholy account. Methinks we are in the book of Judges again; for,

I. Rehoboam and his people did evil in the sight of the Lord, v. 1.

II. God thereon sold them into the hands of Shishak, king of Egypt, who greatly oppressed them, vv. 2–4.
III. God sent a prophet to them, to expound to them the judgment and to call them to repentance, v. 5.
IV. They thereon humbled themselves, v. 6.
V. God, on their repentance, turned from his anger (vv. 7, 12) and yet left them under the marks of his displeasure, vv. 8–11.
Lastly, Here is a general character of Rehoboam and his reign, with the conclusion of it, vv. 13–16.

A detailed analysis of chapter

Shishak attacks Jerusalem. (1–12)

Summary of Rehoboam's reign. (13–16)

Key verse

Verse 2: "And it came to pass, that in the fifth year of king Rehoboam Shishak king of Egypt came up against Jerusalem."

Key word / key phrase

Verse 2, "Shishak."

Key event / key person / key theme

Shishak, king of Egypt, attacks Jerusalem

Key thought

Every time we humble ourselves before the Lord we grow spiritually.

Key thing to look out for

God's purpose in allowing Judah to become a vassal nation of Egypt (verse 8).

Key Bible cross-reference

Verse 1. See 9:30; 10:16; 11:13; 11:3.

Key "by way of explanation"

Verse 2. The Chronicler often includes notes which are not found in 1 and 2 Kings. See 11:17; 15:10,19; 16:1,12,13; 17:7: 21:20; 25:15, 17, 23.

Key "Quotable Quote"

"It is only with the heart that one can see rightly; what is essential is invisible to the eye."

Antoine of St Exupery

2 Chronicles 13

Matthew Henry's introduction

We have here a much fuller account of the reign of Abijah, the son of Rehoboam, than we had in the Kings. There we found that his character was no better than his father's—he "walked in the sins of his father, and his heart was not right with God," 1 Kings 15:2, 3. But here we find him more brave and successful in war than his father was. He reigned but three years, and was chiefly famous for a glorious victory he won over the forces of Jeroboam. Here we have,

I. The armies brought into the field on both sides, v. 3.
II. The remonstrance which Abijah made before the battle, setting forth the justice of his cause, vv. 4–12.
III. The distress which Judah was brought into by the policy of Jeroboam, vv. 13, 14.
IV. The victory they won notwithstanding, by the power of God, vv. 15–20.
V. The conclusion of Abijah's reign, vv. 21, 22.

A detailed analysis of chapter

Abijah overcomes Jeroboam. (1–22)

Key verse

Verse 1: "Now in the eighteenth year of king Jeroboam began Abijah to reign over Judah."

Key word / key phrase

Verse 1, "Abijah."

Key event / key person / key theme

Abijah goes to war against Jeroboam

Key thought

In their extremity, Judah cried out to the Lord.

Key thing to look out for

Verse 10. How the people showed that they had not forsaken God.

Key Bible cross-reference

Verse 3. See 1 Chronicles 21:5.

Key "by way of explanation"

Verse 8. This verse shows how David's kingdom stood for the "kingdom of the Lord."

Key "Quotable Quote"

"There is no point in us traveling abroad to find the kingdom of heaven, or crossing the sea in search of virtue. As the Lord has already told us, God's kingdom is within you."

Antony of Egypt

2 Chronicles 14

Matthew Henry's introduction

In this and the two following chapters we have the history of the reign of Asa, a good reign and a long one. In this chapter we have,

I. His piety, vv. 1–5.

II. His policy, vv. 6–8.

III. His prosperity, and particularly a glorious victory he won over a great army of Ethiopians that came out against him, vv. 9–15.

A detailed analysis of chapter

Asa's piety. He strengthens his kingdom. (1–15)

Key verse

Verse 2: "And Asa did that which was good and right in the eyes of the LORD his God."

Key word / key phrase

Verse 2, "Asa."

Key event / key person / key theme

King Asa of Judah defeats the vast Cushite army

Key thought

We should never underestimate the power of evil, and its insidious hold on us.

Key thing to look out for

What happens when we rely only on God (verses 11, 12).

Key Bible cross-reference

Verse 5. See 17:6; 20:33.

I. His accession to and establishment in the throne, vv. 1, 2, 5.
II. His persona piety, vv. 3, 4, 6.
III. The course he took to promote religion in his kingdom, vv. 7–9.
IV. The mighty sway he bore among the neighbors, vv. 10, 11.
V. The great strength of his kingdom, both in garrisons and standing forces, vv. 12–19. Thus was his prosperity the reward of his piety and his piety the brightest grace and ornament of his prosperity.

A detailed analysis of chapter

Jehoshaphat becomes king. (1–9)
Jehoshaphat's greatness. (10–19)

Key verse

Verse 1: "And Jehoshaphat his son reigned in his stead, and strengthened himself against Israel."

Key word / key phrase

Verse 4, "sought God."

Key event / key person / key theme

King Jehoshaphat of Judah

Key thought

Jehoshaphat's heart was in the right place.

Key thing to look out for

Right actions stem from being right with the Lord.

Key Bible cross-reference

17:1–21:3. See 1 Kings 22:1–46.

Key "by way of explanation"

Verses 7–9. God's Law was not just taught by priests and prophets, but also by officials appointed by the king.

Key "Quotable Quote"

"Let our hearts and souls burst with love!"

Catherine of Siena

2 Chronicles 18

Matthew Henry's introduction

The story of this chapter we had just as it is here related in the story of the reign of Ahab king of Israel, 1 Kings 22. There it looks more creditable to Ahab than any thing else recorded of him that he was in league with so good a man as Jehoshaphat; here it is a great blemish in the reign of Jehoshaphat that he thus connected himself with so bad a man as Ahab. Here is,

I. The alliance he contracted himself with Ahab, v. 1.
II. His consent to join with him in his expedition for the recovery of Ramoth Gilead out of the hands of the Syrians, vv. 2, 3.
III. Their consulting with the prophets, false and true, before they went, vv. 4–27.
IV. The success of their expedition. Jehoshaphat hardly escaped (vv. 28–32) and Ahab received his death's wound, vv. 33, 34.

(For 2 Chronicles chapter 18, see 1 Kings 22.)

2 Chronicles 19

Matthew Henry's introduction

We have here a further account of the good reign of Jehoshaphat,

I. His return in peace to Jerusalem, v. 1.
II. The reproof given him for his league with Ahab, and his acting in conjunction with him, vv. 2, 3.
III. The great care he took thereon to reform his kingdom, v. 4.
IV. The instructions he gave to his judges, both those in the country towns that kept the inferior courts (vv. 5–7), and those in Jerusalem that sat in the supreme judicature of the kingdom, vv. 8–11.

A detailed analysis of chapter

Jehoshaphat is reprimanded. (1–3)
Jehoshaphat's reforms. (4–11)

Key verse

Verse 2: "And Jehu the son of Hanani the seer went out to meet him, and said to king Jehoshaphat, Shouldest thou help the ungodly, and love them that hate the LORD?"

Key word / key phrase

Verse 2, "wholeheartedly."

Key event / key person / key theme

Micaiah prophecies against Ahab

Key thought

A prophet needed courage as well as spiritual insight.

Key thing to look out for

How a person reacts to wise advice tells you much about his state of heart.

Key Bible cross-reference

Verse 1. See 22:10–23:21.

Key "by way of explanation"

Verse 1. In 19:2–3 the prophet condemns the marriage alliance Jehoshaphat made with Ahab.

Key "Quotable Quote"

"Watch over your heart."

Jean Pierre de Caussade

2 Chronicles 20

Matthew Henry's introduction

We have here,

I. The great danger and distress that Jehoshaphat and his kingdom were in from a foreign invasion, vv. 1, 2.
II. The pious course he took for their safety, by fasting, and praying, and seeking God, vv. 3–13.
III. The assurance which God, by a prophet, immediately gave them of victory, vv. 14–17.
IV. Their thankful believing reception of those assurances, vv. 18–21.
V. The defeat which God gave to their enemies thereon, vv. 22–25.
VI. A solemn thanksgiving which they kept for their victory, and for a happy consequences of it, vv. 26–30.
VII. The conclusion of the reign of Jehoshaphat, not without some blemishes, vv. 31–37.

A detailed analysis of chapter

The danger and distress of Judah. (1–13)
Jahaziel's prophecy of victory. (14–19)

The thanksgiving of Judah. (20–30)
Jehoshaphat's alliance with Ahaziah. (31–37)

Key verse

Verse 3: "And Jehoshaphat feared, and set himself to seek the LORD, and proclaimed a fast throughout all Judah."

Key word / key phrase

Verse 15, "the battle . . . is God's."

Key event / key person / key theme

Jehoshaphat defeats Moab and Ammon

Key thought

How a person is in his or her prayers is how a person is.

Key thing to look out for

God's people, equipped with God's Spirit, can face an army.

Key Bible cross-reference

Verse 1. See 26:7; 1 Chronicles 4:41.

Key "by way of explanation"

Verses 5–12. Jehoshaphat's prayer reveals that his heart is devoted to the Lord.

Key "Quotable Quote"

"God made us and God is able to empower us to do whatever he calls us to do."

Warren Wiersbe

2 Chronicles 21

Matthew Henry's introduction

Never surely did any kingdom change its king so much for the worse as Judah did, when Jehoram, one of the vilest, succeeded Jehoshaphat, one of the best. Thus were they punished for not making a better use of Jehoshaphat's good government, and their disaffectedness (or coldness at least) to his reformation, 20:33. Those that knew not now to value a good king are justly plagued with a bad one. Here is,

I. Jehoram's elevation to the throne, vv. 1–3.
II. The wicked course he took to establish himself in it, by the murder of his brethren, v. 4.
III. The idolatries and other wickedness he was guilty of, vv. 5, 6, 11.
IV. The prophecy of Elijah against him, vv. 12–15.
V. The judgments of God on him, in the revolt of his subjects from him (vv. 8–10) and the success of his enemies against him, vv. 16, 17.
VI. His miserable sickness and inglorious exit, vv. 18–20.
VII. The preservation of the house of David notwithstanding, v. 7.

A detailed analysis of chapter

The wicked reign of Jehoram. (1–11)
Jehoram's miserable end. (12–20)

Key verse

Verse 4: "Now when Jehoram was risen up to the kingdom of his father, he strengthened himself, and slew all his brethren with the sword, and divers also of the princes of Israel."

Key word / key phrase

Verse 20, "to no one's regret."

Key event / key person / key theme

King Jehoram of Judah

Key thought

Not to walk in God's ways always brings down God's judgment.

Key thing to look out for

To be a faithful prophet was a tough calling.

Key Bible cross-reference

Verse 2. See 11:18–22; 1 Chronicles 25:5.

Key "by way of explanation"

Verses 12–15. While 1 Kings and 2 Kings record much information about the prophet Elijah these verses with their reference to a letter from Elijah are the only ones about the prophet in 1 and 2 Chronicles.

Key "Quotable Quote"

"It's going to be quite a revealing thing at the last judgment when we see everyone standing naked before God."

Billy Graham

2 Chronicles 22

Matthew Henry's introduction

We read, in the previous chapter, of the carrying away of Jehoram's sons and his wives; but here we find one of his sons and one of his wives left, his son Ahaziah and his wife Athaliah, both reserved to be the shame and plague of his family.

I. Ahaziah was the shame of it as a partaker,
 A. In the sin, and,
 B. In the destruction, of the house of Ahab, vv. 1–9.

II. Athaliah was the plague of it, for she destroyed all the seed-royal, and usurped the throne, vv. 10–12.

(For 2 Chronicles chapters 22, 23, see 1 Kings 8:25–29; 9:21–29; 11:1–21.)

2 Chronicles 23

Matthew Henry's introduction

Six years bloody Athaliah had tyrannized; in this chapter we have her deposed and slain, and Joash, the rightful heir, enthroned. We had the story before nearly as it is here related, 2 Kings 11:4, etc.

I. Jehoiada prepared the people for the king, acquainted them with his design, armed them, and appointed them their posts, vv. 1–10.

II. He produced the king to the people, crowned him, and anointed him, v. 11.

III. He slew the usurper, vv. 12–15.

IV. He reformed the kingdom, re-established religion, and restored the civil government, vv. 16–21.

(For 2 Chronicles chapters 22, 23, see 1 Kings 8:25–29; 9:21–29; 11:1–21.)

2 Chronicles 24

Matthew Henry's introduction

We have here the history of the reign of Joash,

the progress of which, and especially its termination, were not of a piece with its beginning, nor shone with so much luster. How wonderfully he was preserved for the throne, and placed in it, we read before; now here we are told how he began in the spirit, but ended in the flesh.

I. In the beginning of his time, while Jehoiada lived, he did well; particularly, he took care to put the temple in good repair, vv. 1–14.

II. In the latter end of his time, after Jehoiada's death, he apostatized from God, and his apostasy was his ruin.

A. He set up the worship of Baal again (vv. 15–18), though warned to the contrary, v. 19.

B. He put Zechariah the prophet to death because he reproved him for what he had done, vv. 20–22.

C. The judgments of God came on him for it. The Syrians invaded him, vv. 23, 24. He was struck with sore diseases; his own servants conspired against him and slew him; and, as a mark of infamy on him, he was not buried in the burying-place of the kings, vv. 25–27.

A detailed analysis of chapter

Joash, of Judah, and the temple repaired. (1–14)

Joash falls into idolatry. He is killed by his servants. (15–27)

Key verse

Verse 4: "And it came to pass after this, that Joash was minded to repair the house of the LORD."

Key word / key phrase

Verse 17, "After the death of Jehoiada."

Key event / key person / key theme

Joash repairs the temple

Key thought

Within one chapter Joash is commended and condemned.

Key thing to look out for

Remaining faithful to the Lord throughout one's life challenges all of God's followers.

Key Bible cross-reference

Verse 3. See verse 27.

Key "by way of explanation"

Verse 19. The destruction of Israel can be traced back to their rejection of the Lord's prophets. See 36:16.

Key "Quotable Quote"

"Perseverance in faith, devotion, and virtue is assured by three things: prayer, fasting, and mercy. Prayer knocks at the door, fasting gains entrance, mercy receives. These three things, prayer, fasting, and mercy, are all one and they give life to each other."

Peter Chrysologus

2 Chronicles 25

Matthew Henry's introduction

Amaziah's reign, recorded in this chapter, was not one of the worse and yet for from good. Most of the passages in this chapter we had before more briefly related, 2 Kings 14. Here we find Amaziah,

I. A just revenger of his father's death, vv. 1–4.

II. An obedient observer of the command of God, vv. 5–10.

III. A cruel conqueror of the Edomites, vv. 11–13.

IV. A foolish worshipper of the gods of Edom and impatient of reproof for it, vv. 14–16.

V. Rashly challenging the king of Israel, and smarting for his rashness, vv. 17–24. And, lastly, ending his days ingloriously, vv. 25–28.

A detailed analysis of chapter

Amaziah, king of Judah. (1–13)
Amaziah worships the idols of Edom. (14–16)
Amaziah's rash challenge. (17–28)

Key verse

Verse 1: "Amaziah was twenty and five years old when he began to reign, and he reigned twenty and nine years in Jerusalem."

Key word / key phrase

Verse 16, "God had determined."

Key event / key person / key theme

King Amaziah of Judah

Key thought

How many people have fallen because they "would not listen," verse 20?

Key thing to look out for

What turns a seemingly godly person into one who stops following the Lord?

Key Bible cross-reference

Verses 5–16. See 2 Kings 14:7.

Key "by way of explanation"

Verses 1–28. Amaziah's life can be studied in two parts: his good years, verses 1–13, and his bad years, verses 14–28.

Key "Quotable Quote"

"Those who fall away have never been thoroughly imbued with the knowledge of Christ but only had a slight and passing taste of it."

John Calvin

2 Chronicles 26

Matthew Henry's introduction

This chapter gives us an account of the reign of Uzziah (Azariah he was called in the Kings) more fully than we had it before, though it was long, and in some respects illustrious, yet it was very briefly related, 2 Kings 14:21; 15:1, etc. Here is,

I. His good character in general, vv. 1–5.

II. His great prosperity in his wars, his buildings, and all the affairs of his kingdom, vv. 6–15.

III. His presumption in invading the priests' office, for which he was struck with a leprosy, and confined by it (vv. 16–21) even to his death, vv. 22, 23.

A detailed analysis of chapter

Uzziah's good reign in Judah. (1–15)

Uzziah's attempt to burn incense. (16–23)

Key verse

Verse 16: "But when he was strong, his heart was lifted up to *his* destruction: for he transgressed against the LORD his God, and went into the temple of the LORD to burn incense upon the altar of incense."

Key word / key phrase

Verse 16, "pride."

Key event / key person / key theme

King Uzziah of Judah

Key thought

Leprosy often stands for sin in the Bible.

Key thing to look out for

All of God's judgments do not take place in this life.

Key Bible cross-reference

Verse 19. See 16:12; 21:12–15.

Key "by way of explanation"

Verses 2, 16–21. In 2 Kings 15:5 Uzziah's leprosy is just mentioned. But in 2 Chronicles it is stated that this disease came on Uzziah because of his unfaithfulness to God.

Key "Quotable Quote"

"The Christian's battle is first of all with sin."

C.H. Spurgeon

2 Chronicles 27

Matthew Henry's introduction

Here is a very short account of the reign of Jotham, a pious prosperous prince, of whom one would wish to have known more: but we may better dispense with the brevity of his story because that which lengthened the history of the last three kings was their degeneracy in their latter end, of which we have had a faithful account; but there was no occasion for such a melancholy conclusion of the history of this reign, which is only an account,

I. Of the date and continuance of this reign, vv. 1, 8.

II. The general good character of it, vv. 2, 6.

III. The prosperity of it, vv. 3–5.

IV. The period of it, vv. 7, 9.

A detailed analysis of chapter

Jotham's reign in Judah. (1–9)

Key verse

Verse 3: "He built the high gate of the house of the LORD, and on the wall of Ophel he built much."

Key word / key phrase

Verse 6, "walked steadfastly."

Key event / key person / key theme

King Jotham of Judah

Key thought

Walking with God was also used to describe Enoch's relationship with the Lord.

Key thing to look out for

To walk with the Lord implies that the person is in step with the Lord in every part of his or her life.

Key Bible cross-reference

Verse 7. See 2 Kings 15:37.

Key "by way of explanation"

Verses 3–6. Here faithfulness to God results in blessings from God.

Key "Quotable Quote"

"Quietness and peace before God are more important than any influence a position may seem to give, for we must stay in step with God to have the power of the Holy Spirit."

Francis A. Schaeffer

2 Chronicles 28

Matthew Henry's introduction

This chapter is the history of the reign of Ahaz the son of Jotham; a bad reign it was, and which helped to augment the fierce anger of the Lord. We have here,

I. His great wickedness, vv. 1–4.

II. The trouble he brought himself into by it, vv. 5–8.

III. The reproof which God sent by a prophet to the army of Israel for trampling on their brethren of Judah, and the obedient ear they gave to that reproof, vv. 9–15.

IV. The many calamities that followed to Ahaz and his people, vv. 16–21.

V. The continuance of his idolatry notwithstanding (vv. 22–25), and so his story ends, vv. 26, 27.

(For 2 Chronicles chapter 28, see 2 Kings 16.)

2 Chronicles 29

Matthew Henry's introduction

We are here entering on a pleasant scene, the good and glorious reign of Hezekiah, in which we find more of God and religion than perhaps in any of the good reigns we have yet met with; for he was a very zealous, devout, good man. In this chapter we have an account of the work of reformation which he set about with vigor immediately after his accession to the crown. Here is,

I. His exhortation to the priests and Levites, when he put them in possession of the house of God again, vv. 1–11.

II. The care and pains which the Levites took to cleanse the temple, and put things in order there, vv. 12–19.

III. A solemn revival of God's ordinances that had been neglected, in which atonement was made for the sins of the last reign, and the wheels were set a-going again, to the great satisfaction of king and people, vv. 20–36.

A detailed analysis of chapter

Hezekiah's good reign in Judah. (1–19)

Hezekiah's sacrifice of atonement. (20–36)

Key verse

Verse 1: "Hezekiah began to reign when he was five and twenty years old, and he reigned nine and twenty years in Jerusalem."

Key word / key phrase

Verse 5, "consecrate."

Key event / key person / key theme

Hezekiah purifies the temple

Key thought

To encourage people to be faithful to God is a great privilege and responsibility.

Key thing to look out for

Godly people rejoice at the sight of godliness.

Key Bible cross-reference

Verse 35. See 7:4–6.

Key "by way of explanation"

Verses 7, 18, 35. Hezekiah has been called a "second Solomon" because of all the arrangements he made for temple worship, as well as because of his wealth and power.

Key "Quotable Quote"

"If missions languish, it is because the whole life of godliness is feeble."

A.T. Pierson

2 Chronicles 30

Matthew Henry's introduction

In this chapter we have an account of the solemn Passover which Hezekiah kept in the first year of his reign.

I. The consultation about it, and the resolution he and his people came to for the observance of it, vv. 2–5.

II. The invitation he sent to Judah and Israel to come and keep it, vv. 1, 6–12.

III. The joyful celebration of it, vv. 13–27. By this the reformation, set on foot in the previous chapter, was greatly advanced and established, and that nail in God's holy place clenched.

A detailed analysis of chapter

Hezekiah's Passover. (1–12)

The Passover celebrated. (13–20)

The Feast of Unleavened Bread. (21–27)

Key verse

Verse 1: "And Hezekiah sent to all Israel and Judah, and wrote letters also to Ephraim and Manasseh, that they should come to the house of the LORD at Jerusalem, to keep the Passover unto the LORD God of Israel."

Key word / key phrase

Verse 20, "heard . . . healed."

Key event / key person / key theme

Hezekiah celebrates the Passover

Key thought

Celebrating the Passover reminded God's people that he was their Redeemer.

Key thing to look out for

The Lord's Supper reminds us that Jesus is our Redeemer.

Key Bible cross-reference

Verses 18, 19. See Mark 7:1–23; John 7:22, 23.

Key "by way of explanation"

Verse 8. The Passover was one of the three annual festivals that had to be celebrated at the temple. See Numbers 28:9–29:39.

Key "Quotable Quote"

"The reason my sins are forgiven so easily is because the redemption cost God so much."

Oswald Chambers

2 Chronicles 31

Matthew Henry's introduction

We have here a further account of that blessed reformation of which Hezekiah was a glorious instrument, and of the happy advances he made in it.

I. All the remnants of idolatry were destroyed and abolished, v. 1.

II. The priests and Levites were set to work again, every man in his place, v. 2.

III. Care was taken for their maintenance.

A. The royal bounty to the clergy, and for the support of the temple service, was duly paid, v. 3.

B. Orders were given for the raising of the people's quota, v. 4.

C. The people, thereon, brought in their dues abundantly, vv. 5–10.

D. Commissioners were appointed for the due distribution of what was brought in, vv. 11–19.

Lastly, Here is the general praise of Hezekiah's sincerity in all his under takings, vv. 20, 21.

A detailed analysis of chapter

Hezekiah destroys idolatry. (1–21)

Key verse

Verse 1: "Now when all this was finished, all Israel that were present went out to the cities of Judah, and brake the images in pieces, and cut down the groves, and threw down the high places and the altars out of all Judah and Benjamin, in Ephraim also and Manasseh, until they had utterly destroyed them all."

Key word / key phrase

Verse 20, "good and right and faithful."

Key event / key person / key theme

Hezekiah reforms religious life

Key thought

Lead by example.

Key thing to look out for

Praising the Lord and giving thanks to people go hand in hand.

Key Bible cross-reference

Verse 2. See 8:14.

Key "by way of explanation"

Verse 3. The example of King Hezekiah giving from "his own possessions" inspired the people to be generous as well.

Key "Quotable Quote"

"God has given us two hands – one to receive with and the other to give with."

Billy Graham

2 Chronicles 32

Matthew Henry's introduction

This chapter continues and concludes the history of the reign of Hezekiah.

I. The descent which Sennacherib made on him, and the care he took to fortify himself, his city, and the minds of his people, against that enemy, vv. 1–8.

II. The insolent blasphemous letters and messages which Sennacherib sent him, vv. 9–19.

III. The real answer God gave to Sennacherib's blasphemies, and to Hezekiah's prayers, in the total rout of the Assyrian army, to the shame of Sennacherib and the honor of Hezekiah, vv. 20–23.

IV. Hezekiah's sickness and his recovery from that, his sin and his recovery from that, with the honors that attended him living and dead, vv. 24–33.

A detailed analysis of chapter

The invasion of Sennacherib. His defeat. (1–23) Hezekiah's sickness. His prosperous reign, and death. (24–33)

Key verse

Verse 1: "After these things, and the establishment thereof, Sennacherib king of Assyria came, and entered into Judah, and encamped against the fenced cities, and thought to win them for himself."

Key word / key phrase

Verse 8, "with us is the Lord our God."

Key event / key person / key theme

Sennacherib threatens Jerusalem

Key thought

The time of God's miracles is in God's sovereign hands.

Key thing to look out for

Hezekiah was not devoid of pride.

Key Bible cross-reference

Verse 18. See 2 Kings 18:26–28; Isaiah 36:11–13.

Key "by way of explanation"

Verses 25, 26. For all his good qualities Hezekiah's disobedience to the Lord is not skated over.

Key "Quotable Quote"

"Pride alienates man from heaven; humility leads to heaven."

Bridget of Sweden

2 Chronicles 33

Matthew Henry's introduction

In this chapter we have the history of the reign,

I. Of Manasseh, who reigned long.

A. His wretched apostasy from God, and revolt to idolatry and all wickedness, vv. 1–10.

B. His happy return to God in his affliction; his repentance (vv. 11–13), his reformation (vv. 15–17), and prosperity (v. 14), with the conclusion of his reign, vv. 18–20.

II. Of Amon, who reigned very wickedly (vv. 21–23), and soon ended his days unhappily, vv. 24, 25.

A detailed analysis of chapter

Manasseh's evil reign. (1–20)

Amon's wicked reign in Judah. (21–25)

Key verse

Verse 13: "And prayed unto him: and he was entreated of him, and heard his supplication, and brought him again to Jerusalem into his kingdom. Then Manasseh knew that the LORD he *was* God."

Key word / key phrase

Verse 13, "when he prayed."

Key event / key person / key theme

King Manasseh of Judah

Key thought

Idolatry and sorcery are often linked.

Key thing to look out for

Knowing that the Lord is God, verse 13, was the best thing that ever happened to Manasseh.

Key Bible cross-reference

Verses 1–20. See 2 Kings 21:1–18.

Key "by way of explanation"

Verse 11–17. Defeat is seen as the consequences of Manasseh's evil, while his repentance brings about his restoration.

Key "Quotable Quote"

"Oh, the fullness, pleasure, sheer excitement of knowing God on earth! I care not if I never raise my voice again for him, if only I may love him, please him."

Jim Elliot

2 Chronicles 34

Matthew Henry's introduction

Before we see Judah and Jerusalem ruined we shall yet see some glorious years, while good Josiah sits at the helm. By his pious endeavors for reformation God tried them yet once more; if they had known in this their day, the day of their visitation, the things that belonged to their peace and improved them, their ruin might have been prevented. But after this reign they were hidden from their eyes, and the next reigns brought an utter desolation on them. In this chapter we have,

I. A general account of Josiah's character, vv. 1, 2.

II. His zeal to root out idolatry, vv. 3–7.

III. His care to repair the temple, vv. 8–13.

IV. The finding of the book of the law and the good use made of it, vv. 14–28.

V. The public reading of the law to the people and their renewing their covenant with God thereon, vv. 29–33. Much of this we had 2 Kings 22.

(For 2 Chronicles chapter 34, see 2 Kings 22;1–20; 23:1–20.)

2 Chronicles 35

Matthew Henry's introduction

We are here to attend Josiah,

I. To the temple, where we see his religious care for the due observance of the ordinance of the Passover, according to the law, vv. 1–19.

II. To the field of battle, where we see his rashness in engaging with the king of Egypt, and how dearly it cost him, vv. 20–23.

III. To the grave, where we see him bitterly lamented, vv. 24–27. And so we must take our leave of Josiah.

A detailed analysis of chapter

The Passover kept by Josiah. (1–19)

Josiah killed in battle. (20–27)

Key verse

Verse 1: "Moreover Josiah kept a passover unto the LORD in Jerusalem: and they killed the passover [lamb] on the fourteenth day of the first month."

Key word / key phrase

Verse 3, "now serve the Lord."

Key event / key person / key theme

Josiah celebrates the Passover

Key thought

Worshiping the Lord was a great celebration in the Old Testament.

Key thing to look out for

The thought of seven days of worship seems alien today.

Key Bible cross-reference

Verse 4. See 7:10; 11:17.

Key "by way of explanation"

Verse 25. The laments Jeremiah composed for Josiah no longer exist. But the fact that Jeremiah did compose such laments is evidence for Jeremiah's authorship of the book of Lamentations.

Key "Quotable Quote"

"Mission is the overflow of our delight in God because mission is the overflow of God's delight in being God."

John Piper

2 Chronicles 36

Matthew Henry's introduction

We have here,

I. A short but sad account of the utter ruin of Judah and Jerusalem within a few years after Josiah's death.

A. The history of it in the unhappy reigns of Jehoahaz for three months (vv. 1–4), Jehoiakim (vv. 5–8) for eleven years, Jehoiachin in three months (vv. 9, 10), and Zedekiah eleven years, v. 11. Additions were made to the national guilt, and advances towards the national destruction, in each of those reigns. The destruction was, at length, completed in the slaughter of multitudes (v. 17), the plundering and burning of the temple and all the palaces, the desolation of the city (vv. 18, 19), and the captivity of the people that remained, v. 20.

B. Some remarks on it—that herein sin was punished, Zedekiah's wickedness (vv. 12, 13), the idolatry the people were guilty of

(v. 14), and their abuse of God's prophets, vv. 15, 16. The word of God was herein fulfilled, v. 21.

II. The dawning of the day of their deliverance in Cyrus's proclamation, vv. 22, 23.

(For 2 Chronicles chapter 36, see 2 Kings 23:28–24:20; 25:1–21; Ezra 1:1–3.)

5. Select bibliography for 1 and 2 Chronicles

Keil, C. F. *The Books of the Chronicles*. KD. Grand Rapids: Eerdmans, 1950.

Sailhamer, John H. *First and Second Chronicles*, Moody, 1981.

Selman, Martin J. *1 Chronicles* (Tyndale), InterVarsity, 1994.

Wilcock, Michael. *The Message of Chronicles* (The Bible Speaks Today), InterVarsity, 1987.

Ezra

1. Book by book: Introduction to Ezra

Introduction

Ezra was, along with Nehemiah, reckoned one book by the ancient Jews, who called them the First and Second Books of Ezra, and they are still designated by Roman Catholic writers the First and Second Books of Esdras.

This book naturally divides itself into two parts or sections, the one contained in the first six chapters, and which relates the circumstances connected with the return of the first detachment of Babylonian exiles under Zerubbabel with the consequent rebuilding of the temple and the re-establishment of the divine service. The other part, embraced in the four concluding chapters, narrates the journey of a second caravan of returning captives under the conduct of Ezra himself, who was invested with powers to restore, in all its splendor, the entire system of the Jewish ritual.

The general opinion of the Church in every succeeding age has been that Ezra was the author of this book. The chief objection is founded on Ezra 5:4, where the words, "Then said we unto them after this manner, What are the names of the men that make this building?" have occasioned a surmise that the first portion of the book was not written by Ezra, who did not go to Jerusalem for many years after. But a little attention will show the futility of this objection, as the words in question did not refer to the writer, but were used by Tatnai and his associates (Ezra 5:3). The style and unity of object in the book clearly prove it to have been the production of but one author. The canonical authority of this book is well established; but another under the name of Ezra is rejected as apocryphal.

Robert Jamieson

Contents of Ezra

Ezra continues the story of the Israelites set out in 1 and 2 Chronicles and records how God's people returned from Babylonia back to Jerusalem.

I. The return of the Jews from Babylon under Cyrus. restoration of the temple and of the worship of God at Jerusalem. Chapters 1–6.

When the seventy years of the Babylonian captivity had elapsed, King Cyrus, by an edict published in the first year of his rule over Babylon, gave permission to all the Jews in his whole realm to return to their native land, and called on them to rebuild the temple of God at Jerusalem. The execution of this royal and gracious decree by the Jews forms the subject of the first part of this book.

Chapters 1 and 2 treating of the return of a considerable number of families of Judah, Benjamin, and Levi, under the conduct of Zerubbabel the prince and Joshua the high priest, to Jerusalem and Judaea; the remaining chapters, 3–6, of the restoration of the worship of God, and of the rebuilding of the temple.

II. The return of Ezra the scribe from Babylon to Jerusalem, and his official duties there. Chapters 7–10.

In the seventh year of the reign of King Artaxerxes Longimanus, Ezra the priest and scribe returned with certain priests, Levites, and other Israelites from Babylon to Jerusalem, furnished with a royal commission to provide for the worship of God, and the observance of the law, according to the ordinance of God, by the community, ch. 7 and 8. This mission he began to carry out by sending away the heathen women who were married to Israelites, ch. 9 and 10.

C. F. Keil and F. Delitzsch

Detailed outline

- I. Restoration under Zerubbabel: 1:1–6:22
  - A. First return of exiles: 1:1–2:70
    - 1. Edict of Cyrus: 1:1–11
      - (a) The writing of the edict: 1:2–4
      - (b) The desire of the people: 1:5–11
    - 2. List of exiles: 2:1–70
  - B. Restoration of public worship : 3:1–6:22
    - 1. Rebuilding of temple: 3:1–6:15
      - (a) Worship reinstated in Jerusalem: 3:1–7
      - (b) Work on the temple: 3:8–13
      - (c) Hindrances to the work: 4:1–24
      - (d) The prophets come to help: 5:1–2
      - (e) The governor's questions: 5:3–5
      - (f) The letter to Darius: 5:6–17
      - (g) he search: 6:1–12
      - (h) Tatnai's response: 6:13–15
    - 2. Dedication of temple: 6:16–22
- II. Reforms under Ezra: 7:1–10:44
  - A. Second Return of Exiles 7:1–8:36
    - 1. Ezra's background and preparation: 7:1–10
    - 2. The letter of Artaxerxes: 7:11–26
    - 3. The response of Ezra: 7:27–28
  - B. Correction of social evils: 9:1–10:44
    - 1. God's people compromising: 9:1–2
    - 2. Ezra's supplication: 9:3–15

3. Conviction settles on the people: 10:1–8
4. Confession and repentance: 10:9–16
5. The list of offenders: 10:18–44

2. Helpful summaries of Ezra

Bird's eye view

Ezra records the Jews returning from exile in Babylon to Jerusalem.

Reading plan

The following reading plan, taking one reading per day, enables you to read through Ezra in three days.

Ezra 1–3
Ezra 4–6
Ezra 7–10

Verses to memorize

Ezra 3:11

And all the people gave a great shout of praise to the Lord because the foundation of the house of the Lord was laid.

Ezra 7:10

For Ezra had devoted himself to the study and observance of the Law of the Lord, and to teaching its decrees and laws in Israel.

Statistics

Fifteenth Old Testament book
10 chapters
280 verses
7,441 words

Names/titles given

The books of Ezra and Nehemiah originally formed one bound book, as Chronicles, Ezra and Nehemiah were seen as one history.

Hebrew title: *ezer* is the Hebrew word based on the Aramaic word *Ezra*, meaning "Jehovah helps."

Greek title in Septuagint: *Esdras Deuteron:* "Second Esdras." There was an apocryphal book called "Books of Esdras." The combined book of Ezra-Nehemiah was called *Esdras Deuteron* in the Septuagint.

Latin title in Vulgate: *Liber Primus Esdrae:* "First book of Ezra." The Latin Bible called the book of Nehemiah, "Second Ezra."

3. Helpful keys to turn to in understanding Ezra

Key word

Build

Key verses

Ezra 1:5; 7:10

Key people/events

Cyrus
Zerubbabel
Ezra

Themes to study

Ambition
Failure
Purity

Jesus in Ezra

In Ezra Jesus is our Restorer.

Types of Jesus in Ezra

- The whole book of Ezra portrays Jesus' work of restoration.
- Zerubbabel, grandson of Jeconiah, (that is Jehoiachin of 1 Chronicles 3:17–19) is an ancestor of Jesus.

Lessons to learn from Ezra

- God, not dictators, controls world events.
- The Christian church should be united in the Spirit.
- Giving money and doing practical work is part of Christian discipleship.

4. Chapter by chapter: outline of every chapter of Ezra

Ezra 1

Matthew Henry's introduction

In this chapter we have,

I. The proclamation which Cyrus, king of Persia, issued out for the release of all the Jews that he found captives in Babylon, and the building of their temple in Jerusalem, vv. 1–4.

II. The return of many thereon, vv. 5, 6.

III. Orders given for the restoring of the vessels of the temple, vv. 7–11. And this is the dawning of the day of their deliverance.

A detailed analysis of chapter

The proclamation of Cyrus for the rebuilding of the temple. (1–4)

The people provide for their return. (5–11)

Key verse

Verse 1: "Now in the first year of Cyrus king of Persia, that the word of the LORD by the mouth of Jeremiah might be fulfilled, the LORD stirred up the spirit of Cyrus king of Persia"

Key word / key phrase

Verse 1, "Cyrus."

Key event / key person / key theme

Cyrus enables the exiles to return to Jerusalem

Key thought

God had never forgotten his people during their exile.

Key thing to look out for

All kinds of unlikely people are used by God to fulfill his will.

Key Bible cross-reference

Verse 5. See 2:59.

Key "by way of explanation"

Verse 2. Out of the twenty-two occurrences of the phrase "God of heaven" in the Old Testament, it comes seventeen times in Ezra. Cyrus came to the throne and issued his edict in March 538 BC.

Key "Quotable Quote"

"The believer is never the victim of the powers of nature or fate. Chance is eliminated."

G.C. Berkouwer

Ezra 2

Matthew Henry's introduction

That many returned out of Babylon on Cyrus's proclamation we were told in the previous chapter; we have here a catalogue of the several families that returned, v. 1.

I. The leaders, v. 2.
II. The people, vv. 3–35.
III. The priests, Levites, and retainers to the temple, vv. 35–63.
IV. The sum total, with an account of their retinue, vv. 64–67.
V. Their offerings to the service of the temple, vv. 68–70.

A detailed analysis of chapter

The number of people who returned. (1–35)
The numbers of the priests and Levites. (36–63)
The offerings for the temple. (64–70)

Key verse

Verse 1: "Now these are the children of the province that went up out of the captivity, of those which had been carried away, whom Nebuchadnezzar the king of Babylon had carried away unto Babylon, and came again unto Jerusalem and Judah, every one unto his city"

Key word / key phrase

Verse 1, "exiles."

Key event / key person / key theme

Lists of the exiles who returned

Key thought

Jeremiah had prophesied that his people would return to Jerusalem after seventy years in exile.

Key thing to look out for

God always keeps his promises.

Key Bible cross-reference

Verses 1–70. See Nehemiah 7:6–73.

Key "by way of explanation"

Verse 2. "Jeshua" means "the Lord saves." It is an Aramaic version of the Hebrew word for "Joshua." In Greek this name is "Jesus."

Key "Quotable Quote"

"No one is safe by his own strength, but he is safe by the grace and mercy of God."

Cyprian

Ezra 3

Matthew Henry's introduction

I. They set up an altar, and offered sacrifices on it, kept the feasts, and contributed towards the rebuilding of the temple, vv. 1–7.
II. They laid the foundation of the temple with a mixture of joy and sorrow, vv. 8–13. This was the day of small things, which was not to be despised, Zech. 4:10.

A detailed analysis of chapter

The altar and festivals. (1–7)
Rebuilding begns. (8–13)

Key verse

Verse 10: "And when the builders laid the foundation of the temple of the LORD, they set the priests in their apparel with trumpets, and the

Levites the sons of Asaph with cymbals, to praise the LORD, after the ordinance of David king of Israel."

Key word / key phrase

Verse 11 "his love to Israel endures."

Key event / key person / key theme

The foundations of the temple are laid.

Key thought

The rebuilding of the temple is the central feature of Ezra.

Key thing to look out for

Verses 11–13. A variety of emotions are expressed as the foundations for rebuilding the temple are laid.

Key Bible cross-reference

Verse 7. The Phoenicians supplied timbers and craftsmen, as they had for building the original temple. See 1 Chronicles 14:1.

Key "by way of explanation"

Verses 12, 13. It was clear that the new temple would lack the magnificence of the first temple, built in the golden era of Solomon.

Key "Quotable Quote"

"In the Dark Ages, reform did not arise from the state but from communities of those who remained uncompromising in a compromising age."

Charles Colson

Ezra 4

Matthew Henry's introduction

I. They offered to be partners in the building of it, that they might have it in their power to retard it; but they were refused, vv. 1–3.

II. They discouraged them in it, and dissuaded them from it, vv. 4, 5.

III. They basely misrepresented the undertaking, and the undertakers, to the king of Persia, by a memorial they sent him, vv. 6–16.

IV. They obtained from him an order to stop the building (vv. 17–22), which they immediately put in execution, vv. 23, 24.

A detailed analysis of chapter

The adversaries of the temple. (1–5)

The building of the temple is hindered. (6–24)

Key verse

Verse 3: "But Zerubbabel, and Jeshua, and the rest of the chief of the fathers of Israel, said unto them, Ye have nothing to do with us to build an house unto our God; but we ourselves together will build unto the LORD God of Israel, as king Cyrus the king of Persia hath commanded us."

Key word / key phrase

Verse 1, "enemies."

Key event / key person / key theme

Opposition is encountered to rebuilding the temple

Key thought

Christian activity usually does meet opposition.

Key thing to look out for

The reason why the Jewish leaders refused to offer of help was because the worship of these enemies (later called Samaritans) was syncretistic.

Key Bible cross-reference

Verse 15. See 5:17; 6:1; Esther 2:23; 6:1–2.

Key "by way of explanation"

4:8–6:18 and 7:12–26 are not written in Hebrew, as is nearly all of the Old Testament, but in Aramaic. In the Persian period Aramaic was the international language.

Key "Quotable Quote"

"They that know anything in this world know that, as the first great opposition of hell, the world, and corrupt nature, is against faith to God by Christ; so the next great opposition made against us, is against our love."

John Owen

Ezra 5

Matthew Henry's introduction

We left the temple-work at a full stop; but, being God's work, it shall be revived, and here we have an account of the reviving of it. It was hindered by might and power, but it was set a-going again "by the Spirit of the Lord of hosts." Now here we are told how that blessed Spirit,

I. Warmed its cool-hearted friends and excited them to built, vv. 1, 2.

II. Cooled its hot-headed enemies, and brought them to better tempers; for, though they secretly disliked the work as much as those in the previous chapter, yet,

A. They were more mild towards the builders, vv. 3–5.

B. They were more fair in their representation of the matter to the king, of which we have here an account, vv. 6–17.

A detailed analysis of chapter

The leaders encourage the building of the temple. (1,2)

Letter against the Jews. (3–17)

Key verse

Verse 2: "Then rose up Zerubbabel the son of Shealtiel, and Jeshua the son of Jozadak, and began to build the house of God which is at Jerusalem: and with them were the prophets of God helping them."

Key word / key phrase

Verse 2, "rebuild."

Key event / key person / key theme

Rebuilding work on the temple continues

Key thought

God's prophets knew that the people needed encouragement to rebuild the temple.

Key thing to look out for

The prophets did not just shout at the people, they helped them, verses 2.

Key Bible cross-reference

Verse 11. See 1 Kings 6:1, 38.

Key "by way of explanation"

Verse 5. While the inquiry was taking place the Jews were given the benefit of the doubt and their work was not stopped.

Key "Quotable Quote"

"To pray when one ought to be working is as much a sin as to work when one ought to be praying."

Dorothy L. Sayers

Ezra 6

Matthew Henry's introduction

We have here,

I. A recital of the decree of Cyrus for the building of the temple, vv. 1–5.

II. The enforcing of that decree by a new order from Darius for the perfecting of that work, vv. 6–12.

III. The finishing of it thereon, vv. 13–15.

IV. The solemn dedication of it when it was built (vv. 16–18), and the hand selling of it (as I may say) with the celebration of the Passover, vv. 19–22. And now we may say that in Judah and Jerusalem things went well, very well.

A detailed analysis of chapter

The decree for completing the temple. (1–12)
The temple is finished. (13–22)

Key verse

Verse 1: "Then Darius the king made a decree, and search was made in the house of the rolls, where the treasures were laid up in Babylon."

Key word / key phrase

Verse 3, "Cyrus."

Key event / key person / key theme

Cyrus' decree is rediscovered

Key thought

God sometimes helps his people through the goodwill of those who are not his followers.

Key thing to look out for

The rebuilt temple was dedicated to God and joy was the memorable thing about that day, verse 16.

Key Bible cross-reference

Verse 3. See 3:12; Haggai 2:3.

Key "by way of explanation"

Verse 15. The date for the completion of the rebuilding was March 12th, 516 BC.

Key "Quotable Quote"

"Christ is not only a remedy for your weariness and trouble, but he will give you an abundance of the contrary, joy and delight."

Jonathan Edwards

Ezra 7

Matthew Henry's introduction

Here is,

I. An account, in general, of Ezra himself, and of his expedition to Jerusalem for the public good, vv. 1–10.

II. A copy of the commission which Artaxerxes gave him, vv. 11–26.

III. His thankfulness to God for it, vv. 27, 28. The next chapter will give us a more particular narrative of his associates, his journey, and his arrival at Jerusalem.

A detailed analysis of chapter

Ezra goes up to Jerusalem. (1–10)
The commission to Ezra. (11–26)
Ezra blesses God for his favor. (27,28)

Key verse

Verse 10: "For Ezra had prepared his heart to seek the law of the LORD, and to do it, and to teach in Israel statutes and judgments."

Key word / key phrase

Verse 28, "the hand of the Lord my God was on me."

Key event / key person / key theme

Ezra arrives in Jerusalem

Key thought

Verse 10 remains a great example for any pastor or Bible teacher today.

Key thing to look out for

Verse 25. The commission given to Ezra.

Key Bible cross-reference

Verse 10. See Nehemiah chapter 8.

Key "by way of explanation"

Verse 28. For the first time in this book the word "me" is used, indicating that Ezra's memoirs begin at 7:27. They end at 9:15.

Key "Quotable Quote"

"No preacher can at one and the same time give the impression that he is clever and that Jesus is great and wonderful."

James Denney

Ezra 8

Matthew Henry's introduction

This chapter gives us a more particular narrative of Ezra's journey to Jerusalem, of which we had a general account in the previous chapter.

I. The company that went up with him, vv. 1–20.
II. The solemn fast which he kept with his company, to implore God's presence with them in this journey, vv. 21–23.
III. The care he took of the treasure he had with him, and the charge he gave about it to the priests, to whose custody he committed it, vv. 24–30.
IV. The care God took of him and his company in the way, v. 31.
V. Their safe arrival at Jerusalem, where they delivered their treasure to the priests (vv. 32–34), their commissions to the kings lieutenants (v. 36), offered sacrifices to God (v. 35), and then applied to their business.

A detailed analysis of chapter

The companions of Ezra. (1–20)
Ezra implores God's blessing. (21–23)
Treasures committed to the priests. (24–30)
Ezra arrives at Jerusalem. (31–36)

Key verse

Verse 1: "These are now the chief of their

fathers, and this is the genealogy of them that went up with me from Babylon, in the reign of Artaxerxes the king."

Key word / key phrase

Verse 1, "came up with me."

Key event / key person / key theme

Safe arrival in Jerusalem

Key thought

Verses 22, 23. Ezra was determined to rely only on God for protection as a public witness to the power of God.

Key thing to look out for

In the book of Ezra no blame is attached to those who did not return to Jerusalem with Ezra, but the excitement of being involved in doing the Lord's work is obvious.

Key Bible cross-reference

Verse 32. See Nehemiah 2:11.

Key "by way of explanation"

The 900-mile journey took four months. The people were in great danger from wild beasts and armed robbers.

Key "Quotable Quote"

"It is God who gives our prayer its value and its character, not our interior dispositions, not our fervor, not our lucidity."

Jacques Ellul

Ezra 9

Matthew Henry's introduction

We have here,

I. A complaint brought to Ezra of the many marriages that had been made with strange wives, vv. 1, 2.

II. The great trouble which he, and others influenced by his example, were in on this information, vv. 3, 4.

III. The solemn confession which he made of this sin to God, with godly sorrow, and shame, vv. 5–15.

A detailed analysis of chapter

Ezra mourns for the Jews' behavior. (1–4)

Ezra's confession of sins. (5–15)

Key verse

Verse 4: "Then were assembled unto me every one that trembled at the words of the God of Israel, because of the transgression of those that had been carried away; and I sat astonied until the evening sacrifice."

Key word / key phrase

Verse 1, "not kept themselves separate."

Key event / key person / key theme

Ezra's reaction to news about mixed marriages

Key thought

Ezra's response to the crisis was to pray.

Key thing to look out for

Ezra was not left unaffected by sin.

Key Bible cross-reference

Verse 6. See 8:22.

Key "by way of explanation"

Verse 2. Marrying people who did not belong to God was seen as an act of unfaithfulness to God.

Key "Quotable Quote"

"Prayer is the central avenue God uses to transform us."

Richard J. Foster

Ezra 10

Matthew Henry's introduction

In this chapter we have that grievance redressed which was complained of and lamented in the previous chapter. Observe,

I. How the people's hearts were prepared for the redress of it by their deep humiliation for the sin, v. 1.

II. How it was proposed to Ezra by Shechaniah, vv. 2–4.

III. How the proposal was put in execution.

A. The great men were sworn to stand to it, v. 5.

B. Ezra appeared first in it, v. 6.

C. A general assembly was called, vv. 7–9.

D. They all, in compliance with Ezra's exhortation, agreed to the reformation, vv. 10–14.

E. Commissioners were appointed to sit "de die in diem"—day after day, to enquire who had married strange wives and to oblige them to put them away, which was done accordingly (vv. 15–17), and a list of the names of those that were found guilty given in, vv. 18–44.

A detailed analysis of chapter

Ezra encourages reformation. (1–6)

He assembles the people. (7–15)

Reformation effected. (16–44)

Key verse

Verse 1: "Now when Ezra had prayed, and when he had confessed, weeping and casting himself down before the house of God, there assembled unto him out of Israel a very great congregation of men and women and children: for the people wept very sore."

Key word / key phrase

Verse 1, "confessing."

Key event / key person / key theme

The people confess their sins

Key thought

Not everyone indulged in mixed marriages, see verse 14.

Key thing to look out for

Holiness involves being separate from evil.

Key Bible cross-reference

Verse 4. See 1 Chronicles 22:16.

Key "by way of explanation"

Verse 1. Ezra threw himself to the ground. Other prophets also acted out their feelings in order to impress their teaching upon the people. See

Isaiah 7:3; Jeremiah 13:1–11; Ezekiel 4:1–5:4.

Key "Quotable Quote"

"Sometimes truth is lost first in a church, and then holiness and sometimes the decay or hatred of holiness is the cause of the loss of truth. But if either is rejected, the other will not abide."

John Owen

5. Select bibliography for Ezra

More recent commentaries

Clines, D. J. A. *Ezra, Nehemiah, Esther*. Grand Rapids: Eerdmans, 1984.

Keil, C. F. *The Books of Ezra, Nehemiah and Esther*. Biblical Commentary on the Old Testament. KD. Grand Rapids: Eerdmans, n.d.

Kidner, D. *Ezra-Nehemiah*. Leicester and Downers Grove: InterVarsity, 1979.

Turnbull, R. G. *The Book of Nehemiah*. Grand Rapids: Baker, 1968.

Williamson, H. G. M. *Ezra, Nehemiah*. Waco: Word, 1985.

Yamauchi, Edwin. "Ezra Nehemiah" *in Expositor's Bible Commentary*, 4, Zondervan, 1988.

Nehemiah

1. Book by book: Introduction to Nehemiah

Introduction

Nehemiah appears to have been the author of this book, from his usually writing in his own name, and indeed, except in those parts which are unmistakably later editions or borrowed from public documents, he usually employs the first person. The major portion of the book is occupied with a history of Nehemiah's twelve years' administration in Jerusalem, after which he returned to his duties in Shushan. At a later period he returned with new powers and commenced new and vigorous measures of reform, which are detailed in the later chapters of the book.

Robert Jamieson

Contents of Nehemiah

While Nehemiah's contemporary, Ezra, concentrated on bringing spiritual revival to the returned exiles, Nehemiah set about rebuilding the walls of Jerusalem, as well as focusing on their spiritual restoration.

I. Nehemiah's journey to Jerusalem, and the restoration of the walls of Jerusalem. ch. 1–6.

Nehemiah, cup-bearer to King Artaxerxes, is plunged into deep sadness by the account which he receives from Judah about the condition of his countrymen who had returned to Jerusalem and Judah. He prays with fasting to the Lord for mercy (ch. 1), and entreats the king and queen for permission to make a journey to Jerusalem, and for the necessary authority to repair its ruined walls. His request being granted, he travels as governor to Jerusalem, provided with letters from the king, and escorted by captains of the army and horsemen (Neh. 2:1–10). Soon after his arrival, he surveys the condition of the walls and gates, summons the rulers of the people and the priests to set about building the wall, and in spite of the obstacles he encounters from the enemies of the Jews, accomplishes this work (2:11–6:19). In describing the manner in which the building of the walls was carried on, he first enumerates in succession (3) the individuals and companies engaged in restoring the walls surrounding the city (3), and then relates the obstacles and difficulties encountered (3:33–6:19).

II. Nehemiah's further exertions on behalf of the community. 7:1–12:43.

The building of the wall being now concluded, Nehemiah first made arrangements for securing the city against hostile attacks (Neh. 7:1–3); then took measures to increase the inhabitants of Jerusalem (7:4–73 and 11:1 and 2); and finally endeavored to fashion domestic and civil life according to the precepts of the law (ch. 8–10), and, on the occasion of the solemn dedication of the wall, to set in order the services of the Levites (ch. 12).

III. Nehemiah's work during his second stay in Jerusalem. 12:44–13:31.

The joint efforts of Nehemiah and Ezra succeeded both in restoring the enactments of the law for the performance and maintenance of the public worship, and in carrying out the separation of the community from strangers, especially by the dissolution of unlawful marriages (Neh 12:44–13:3). When Nehemiah, however, returned to the king at Babylon, in the thirty-second year of Artaxerxes, and remained there some time, the abuses which had been abolished were again allowed by the people. During Nehemiah's absence, Eliashib the priest prepared a chamber in the forecourt of the temple, as a dwelling for his son-in-law Tobiah the Ammonite. The delivery of their dues to the Levites (the first-fruits and tenths) was omitted, and the Sabbath desecrated by field-work and by buying and selling in Jerusalem; Jews married Ashdodite, Ammonitish, and Moabitish wives; even a son of the high priest Joiada allying himself by marriage with Sanballat the Horonite. All these illegal acts were energetically opposed by Nehemiah at his return to Jerusalem, when he strove both to purify the congregation from foreigners, and to restore the appointments of the law with respect to divine worship (13:4–31).

C. F. Keil and F. Delitzsch

Detailed outline

I. Introduction: 1:1–11
  A. Bad news from Jerusalem: 1:1–3
  B. Nehemiah's response: 1:4–11
II. Preparation for the task: 2:1–20
  A. With the King: 2:1–8
  B. With the governors: 2:9–10
  C. In Jerusalem: 2:11–15
  D. With the leaders of the people: 2:15–20
III. Restoration of the walls: 3:1–6:19
  A. List of builders and organization: 3:1–32
  B. External and internal opposition:

4:1–6:14

C. The wall is finished: 6:15–19

IV. Control and census: 7:1–73

A. City controls established: 7:1–4

B. Census of returning exiles: 7:5–73

V. Religious reforms by Ezra and Nehemiah: 8:1–13:31

A. Reading of the law: 8:1–8:18

B. Confession and prayer: 9:1–37

C. Renewal of the covenant: 9:38–10:39

D. List of residents: 11:1–12:26

E. Dedication of the wall: 12:27–47

F. Reforms of Nehemiah: 13:1–31

2. Helpful summaries of Nehemiah

Bird's eye view

The book of Nehemiah records how the walls of Jerusalem were rebuilt under the leadership of Nehemiah.

Reading plan

The following reading plan, taking one reading per day, enables you to read through Nehemiah in seven days.

Nehemiah 1–2

Nehemiah 3–4

Nehemiah 5–6

Nehemiah 7

Nehemiah 8–9

Nehemiah 10–11

Nehemiah 12–13

Verses to memorize

Nehemiah 1:4

When I heard these things, I sat down and wept. For some days I mourned and fasted and prayed before the God of heaven.

Nehemiah 9:5

Stand up and praise the Lord your God who is from everlasting to everlasting.

Statistics

Sixteenth Old Testament book

13 chapters

406 verses

10,483 words

Names/titles given

Hebrew title: *Nehemyah:* Nehemiah, that is, "Comfort of Jehovah."

Greek title in Septuagint: *Esdras Deuteron:* "Second Esdras." See "Names/titles given" under Ezra.

Latin title in Vulgate: *Liber Secundus Esdrae:* "Second book of Ezra," Ezra being the "First book of Ezra."

Later it was named: *Liber Nehemiae:* "Book of Nehemiah."

3. Helpful keys to turn to in understanding Nehemiah

Key words

Work

Prayer

Key verses

Nehemiah 1:8,9; 8:8

Key people/events

• Nehemiah

- Sanballat and Tobiah
- The rebuilding of the temple and city of Jerusalem

Themes to study

Nehemiah prayed:

Earnestly, 1:4

Hopefully, 1:5–6

Humbly, 1:6–8

Believingly, 1:9

Unselfishly, 1:10–11

Inspirationally, 2:4–5

Successfully, 2:8

Giving glory to God, 2:8

Nehemiah's dedication and perseverance.

Jesus in Nehemiah

In Nehemiah Jesus is our Restorer.

Lessons to learn from Nehemiah

Prayer and hard work go together.

Christian work is often opposed and attacked.

Perseverance is a key to Christian living.

4. Chapter by chapter: outline of every chapter of Nehemiah

Nehemiah 1

Matthew Henry's introduction

Here we first meet with Nehemiah at the Persian court, where we find him,

I. Inquisitive about the state of the Jews and Jerusalem, vv. 1, 2.

II. Informed of their deplorable condition, v. 3.

III. Fasting and praying thereon (v. 4), with a particular account of his prayer, vv. 5–11.

Such is the rise of this great man, by piety, not by policy.

A detailed analysis of chapter

Nehemiah's distress for the misery of Jerusalem. (1–4)

Nehemiah's prayer. (5–11)

Key verse

Verse 4: "And it came to pass, when I heard these words, that I sat down and wept, and mourned certain days, and fasted, and prayed before the God of heaven."

Key word / key phrase

Verse 3, "trouble and disgrace."

Key event / key person / key theme

Nehemiah's prayer

Key thought

Nehemiah combines prayer and action throughout this book.

Key thing to look out for

All that can be learned from Nehemiah's prayer about coming to God to pray for success.

Key Bible cross-reference

Verse 6. See Psalm 42:3; Jeremiah 9:1.

Key "by way of explanation"

Verse 4. Nehemiah shows how profoundly affected he was by the news about Jerusalem. He sat down, wept, mourned, fasted and prayed for three months.

Key "Quotable Quote"

"Do what you can and then pray that God will give you the power to do what you cannot."

Augustine of Hippo

Nehemiah 2

Matthew Henry's introduction

I. Nehemiah prevailed with the king to send him to Jerusalem with a commission to build a wall about it, and grant him what was necessary for it, vv. 1–8.

II. He prevailed against the enemies that would have obstructed him in his journey (vv. 9–11) and laughed him out of his undertaking, vv. 19, 20.

III. He prevailed on his own people to join with him in this good work, viewing the desolations of the walls (vv. 12–16) and then gaining them to lend every one a hand towards the rebuilding of them, vv. 17, 18. Thus did God own him in the work to which he called him.

A detailed analysis of chapter

Nehemiah's request to the king. (1–8)
Nehemiah comes to Jerusalem. (9–18)
The opposition of the adversaries. (19,20)

Key verse

Verse 5: "And I said unto the king, If it please the king, and if thy servant have found favor in thy sight, that thou wouldest send me unto Judah, unto the city of my fathers' sepulchers, that I may build it."

Key word / key phrase

Verse 2, "so the king asked."

Key event / key person / key theme

Artaxerxes sends Nehemiah to Jerusalem

Key thought

Nehemiah trusted God in his desire to go to Jerusalem.

Key thing to look out for

Nehemiah only shared his God-given task with a few trustworthy people.

Key Bible cross-reference

Verse 6. See 5:14.

Key "by way of explanation"

Verse 4. Nehemiah was a great one for "arrow" prayers. See 1:4; 4:4, 9; 5:19; 6:9, 14; 13:14, 22; 29, 31. It is probable that Ezra went to Jerusalem in 458 BC, and Nehemiah went about eighteen years later.

Key "Quotable Quote"

"Prayer is not so much an act as it is an attitude – an attitude of dependency, dependency upon God."

Arthur W. Pink

Nehemiah 3

Matthew Henry's introduction

This chapter gives an account of two things:

I. The names of the builders, which are recorded here to their honor, for they were such as herein discovered a great zeal for

God and their country, both a pious and a public spirit, a great degree both of industry and courage; and what they did was fit to be thus largely registered, both for their praise and for the encouragement of others to follow their example.

II. The order of the building; they took it before them, and ended where they began. They repaired,
   A. From the sheep-gate to the fish-gate, vv. 1, 2.
   B. Thence to the old-gate, vv. 3–5.
   C. Thence to the valley-gate, vv. 6–12.
   D. Thence to the dung-gate, vv. 13, 14.
   E. Thence to the gate of the fountain, v. 15.
   F. Thence to the water-gate, vv. 16–26.
   G. Thence by the horse-gate to the sheepgate again, where they began (vv. 27–32), and so they brought their work quite round the city.

A detailed analysis of chapter

Rebuilding the walls of Jerusalem. (1–16)
Levites who worked on the wall. (17–21)
Priests who worked on the wall. (22–26)
Other builders. (27–32)

Key verse

Verse 2: "And next unto him builded the men of Jericho. And next to them builded Zaccur the son of Imri."

Key word / key phrase

Verse 1, "rebuilt."

Key event / key person / key theme

Rebuilding the walls of Jerusalem

Key thought

The faithful work of each team member enabled the repairs to be made.

Key thing to look out for

Each group of people doing the rebuilding work had a definite but limited aim.

Key Bible cross-reference

Verse 3. See 12:39; 2 Chronicles 33:14; Zephaniah 14:10.

Key "by way of explanation"

Verses 1–32. Ten gates are mentioned, as these were the places where people attacking a city concentrated their effort.

Key "Quotable Quote"

"The filling with the Spirit happens for the sake of service."

D. Martyn Lloyd-Jones

Nehemiah 4

Matthew Henry's introduction

I. Their enemies reproached and ridiculed their undertaking, but their scoffs they answered with prayers: they heeded them not, but went on with their work notwithstanding, vv. 1–6.

II. They formed a bloody design against them, to hinder them by force of arms, vv. 7, 8, 10–12. To guard against this Nehemiah prayed (v. 9), set guards (v. 13), and encouraged them to fight (v. 14), by which the design was broken (v. 15), and so the work was carried on with all needful precaution against a surprise, vv. 16–23. In all this Nehemiah approved himself a man of great wisdom and courage, as well as great piety.

A detailed analysis of chapter

Sanballat and others redicule the builders. (1–6)
The builders hear of death threats. (7–15)
Nehemiah's precautions. (16–23)

Key verse

Verse 1: "But it came to pass, that when Sanballat heard that we builded the wall, he was wroth, and took great indignation, and mocked the Jews."

Key word / key phrase

Verse 14, "remember the LORD."

Key event / key person / key theme

Opposition to the rebuilding work

Key thought

There are always people who will laugh at work being done for God.

Key thing to look out for

Opposition sometimes comes in the form of delaying tactics.

Key Bible cross-reference

Verse 14. See Deuteronomy 3:22; 20:3.

Key "by way of explanation"

Verse 9 is another example of Nehemiah as a man of prayer and at the same time a man of action.

Key "Quotable Quote"

"In our case [as Christians] we are hated for our name."

Athenagoras

Nehemiah 5

Matthew Henry's introduction

Here is,

I. The complaint which the poor made to him of the great hardships which the rich (of whom they were forced to borrow money) put on them, vv. 1–5.

II. The effectual course which Nehemiah took both to reform the oppressors and to relieve the oppressed, vv. 6–13.

III. The good example which he himself, as governor, set them of compassion and tenderness, vv. 14–19.

A detailed analysis of chapter

The Jews complain of grievances. (1–5)
Nehemiah redresses the grievances. (6–13)
Nehemiah's forbearance. (14–19)

Key verse

Verse 1: "And there was a great cry of the people and of their wives against their brethren the Jews."

Key word / key phrase

Verse 6, "outcry."

Key event / key person / key theme

Nehemiah helps the poor

Key thought

Before taking action Nehemiah found why some people were so poor and then took to task those who were to blame.

Key thing to look out for

Nehemiah acted to remedy the need of the poor.

Key Bible cross-reference

Verse 9. See Proverbs 14:31; 1 Peter 2:12–15.

Key "by way of explanation"

Verse 6. See Mark 11:15–18; Ephesians 4:26. In the face of dreadful social injustice anger is the appropriate reaction.

Key "Quotable Quote"

"Although it is right to campaign for social justice and to expect to improve society further, in order to make it more pleasing to God, we know that we should never perfect it."

John R.W. Stott

Nehemiah 6

Matthew Henry's introduction

I. When the Jews' enemies asked Nehemiah for an interview, with design to do him a mischief, he would not stir, vv. 1–4.

II. When they would have made him believe his undertaking was represented as seditious and treasonable, he regarded not the insinuation, vv. 5–9.

III. When they hired pretended prophets to advise him to retire into the temple for his own safety, still he kept his ground, vv. 10–14.

IV. Notwithstanding the secret correspondence that was kept up between them and some false and treacherous Jews, the work was finished in a short time, vv. 15–19. Such as these were the struggles between the church and its enemies. But great is God's cause and it will be prosperous and victorious.

A detailed analysis of chapter

Sanballat's plot to hinder Nehemiah. (1–9)
False prophets try to frighten Nehemiah. (10–14)
The wall finished, and treachery of some of the Jews. (15–19)

Key verse

Verse 5: "Then sent Sanballat his servant unto me in like manner the fifth time with an open letter in his hand."

Key word / key phrase

Verse 15, "the wall was completed."

Key event / key person / key theme

More opposition to the rebuilding work

Key thought

Fear has caused much of God's work to grind to a halt.

Key thing to look out for

When any service for God is completed it is important that glory is only given to God.

Key Bible cross-reference

Verse 12. See Deuteronomy 18:20; Isaiah 8:19, 20.

Key "by way of explanation"

Verse 4. Opposition can be persistent. The only remedy is to be equally persistent.

Key "Quotable Quote"

"When your enemies see that you are so determined that neither sickness, fancies, poverty, life, death, nor sins discourage you, but that you will continue to seek the love of Jesus and nothing else, by continuing your prayer and other spiritual works, they will grow enraged and will not spare you the most cruel abuse."

Walter Hilton

Nehemiah 7

Matthew Henry's introduction

The success of one good design for God and our generation should encourage us to proceed and form some other; Nehemiah did so, having fortified Jerusalem with gates and walls, his next care is,

I. To see the city well kept, vv. 1–4.

II. To see it well peopled, in order to which he here reviews and calls over the register of the children of the captivity, the families that returned at first, and records it, vv. 5–73. It is the same, in effect, with that which we had, Ezra 2. What use he made of it we shall find afterwards, when he brought one of ten to live in Jerusalem, 11:1.

A detailed analysis of chapter

Hananiah and Hanani put in charge of Jerusalem. (1–4)

Register of those who first returned. (5–73)

Key verse

Verse 2: "I gave my brother Hanani, and Hananiah the ruler of the palace, charge over Jerusalem: for he was a faithful man, and feared God above many."

Key word / key phrase

Verse 5, "my God put it into my heart."

Key event / key person / key theme

The exiles who returned to Jerusalem

Key thought

God's people in returning to Jerusalem were being given a second chance to be faithful to him there.

Key thing to look out for

Nehemiah makes it clear that the initiative for this return came from the Lord, and not from himself, verse 5.

Key Bible cross-reference

Verses 6–73. See Ezra 2.

Key "by way of explanation"

Verse 3. The gates of Jerusalem were not to be opened at dawn, as would have been normal, in order to guard against any attack taking place while the people were still asleep.

Key "Quotable Quote"

"What is sought from Christians is the motivation for selfless service, which once distinguished the Christian heritage."

Klaus Bockmühl

Nehemiah 8

Matthew Henry's introduction

I. The public and solemn reading and expounding of the law, vv. 1–8.
II. The joy which the people were ordered to express on that occasion, vv. 9–12.
III. The solemn keeping of the feast of tabernacles according to the law, vv. 13–18.

A detailed analysis of chapter

The reading and expounding of the Law. (1–8)
The people called upon to be joyful. (9–12)
The Feast of Tabernacles, and the joy of the people. (13–18)

Key verse

Verse 8: "And Ezra the priest brought the law before the congregation both of men and women, and all that could hear with understanding, upon the first day of the seventh month."

Key word / key phrase

Verse 1, "The Book of the Law."

Key event / key person / key theme

Ezra reads the Law

Key thought

God's word brings reform and revival.

Key thing to look out for

Verse 10 says that the source of strength for God's followers is the joy of the Lord.

Key Bible cross-reference

Verse 3. See Exodus 24:7; Acts 8:30.

Key "by way of explanation"

Verse 6. The intensity of the feelings of the people is conveyed in the way they repeat the word, "Amen!"

Key "Quotable Quote"

"We cannot make too much of the word of God."

E.M. Bounds

Nehemiah 9

Matthew Henry's introduction

We have here an account.

I. How this fast was observed, vv. 1–3.
II. What were the heads of the prayer that was made to God on that occasion, in which they made a thankful acknowledgment of God's mercies, a penitent confession of sin, and a humble submission to the righteous hand of God in the judgments that were brought on them, concluding with a solemn resolution of new obedience, vv. 4–38.

A detailed analysis of chapter

A solemn fast. (1–3)
Prayer and confession of sin. (4–38)

Key verse

Verse 4: "Then stood up upon the stairs, of the Levites, Jeshua, and Bani, Kadmiel, Shebaniah,

Bunni, Sherebiah, Bani, and Chenani, and cried with a loud voice unto the LORD their God."

Key word / key phrase

Verse 1, "fasting and wearing sackcloth."

Key event / key person / key theme

The Israelites confess their sins

Key thought

Nothing is more spiritually therapeutic than confession of sin.

Key thing to look out for

God's purpose in giving the Spirit (verse 20).

Key Bible cross-reference

Verse 20. See Exodus 31:3.

Key "by way of explanation"

Verse 21. The fact that the clothes of the people in the desert did not wear out is given as evidence of God's care for them.

Key "Quotable Quote"

"All Word and no Spirit, we dry up; all Spirit and no Word, we blow up; both Word and Spirit, we grow up."

David Watson

Nehemiah 10

Matthew Henry's introduction

Here we have,

I. The names of those that set their hands and seals to it, vv. 1–27.

II. An account of those who signified their consent and concurrence, vv. 28, 29.

III. The covenant itself, and the articles of it in general, that they would "keep God's commandments" (v. 29); in particular, that they would not marry with the heathen (v. 30), nor profane the Sabbath, nor be rigorous with their debtors (v. 31), and that they would carefully pay their church-dues, for the maintenance of the temple service, which they promise faithfully to adhere to, vv. 32–39.

A detailed analysis of chapter

The covenant, and those who signed it. (1–29)

A commitment to keep specific parts of the Law recently neglected. (30–39)

Key verse

Verse 29: "They clave to their brethren, their nobles, and entered into a curse, and into an oath, to walk in God's law, which was given by Moses the servant of God, and to observe and do all the commandments of the LORD our Lord, and his judgments and his statutes."

Key word / key phrase

Verse 1, "sealed."

Key event / key person / key theme

The agreement made by the people

Key thought

The people promise to live according to God's laws.

Key thing to look out for

The link between sin and offerings and atonement is constantly made in the Old Testament. See verse 33.

Key Bible cross-reference

Verse 35. See Exodus 23:19; Ezekiel 44:30.

Key "by way of explanation"

Verse 35. Provisions were given to the priests and Levites as they did not have time to earn a living for themselves.

Key "Quotable Quote"

"The greatest good in this life is the union of will between creature and Creator."

Ignatius of Loyola

Nehemiah 11

Matthew Henry's introduction

Jerusalem was walled round, but it was not as yet fully inhabited, and therefore was weak and despicable. Nehemiah's next care is to bring people into it; of that we have here an account.

I. The methods taken to replenish it, vv. 1, 2.

II. The principal people that resided there, of Judah and Benjamin (vv. 3–9), of the priests and Levites, vv. 10–19.

III. The several cities and villages of Judah and Benjamin that were peopled by the rest of their families, vv. 20–36.

A detailed analysis of chapter

The people who lived in Jerusalem. (1–24)

People in other cities and towns. (25–36)

Key verse

Verse 1: "And the rulers of the people dwelt at Jerusalem: the rest of the people also cast lots, to bring one of ten to dwell in Jerusalem the holy city, and nine parts to dwell in other cities."

Key word / key phrase

Verse 1, "Jerusalem."

Key event / key person / key theme

The people who lived in Jerusalem

Key thought

The resettling of God's people in Jerusalem was one of the high points in the Old Testament. The Lord provided a place for his people to live.

Key thing to look out for

Verse 2. God's work is done by some people who are told to do it as well as those who volunteer.

Key Bible cross-reference

Verse 1. See Isaiah 48:2; Revelation 11:2.

Key "by way of explanation"

Compare 11:1 with 7:4. The city was underpopulated.

Key "Quotable Quote"

"We ought not to be weary of doing little things for the love of God, who regards not the greatness of the work, but the love with which it is performed."

Brother Lawrence

Nehemiah 12

Matthew Henry's introduction

In this chapter are preserved on record,

I. The names of the chief of the priests and the Levites that came up with Zerubbabel, vv. 1–9.

II. The succession of the high priests, vv. 10, 11.

III. The names of the next generation of the other chief priests, vv. 12–21.

IV. The eminent Levites that were in Nehemiah's time, vv. 22–26.

V. The solemnity of dedicating the wall of Jerusalem, vv. 27–43.

VI. The settling of the offices of the priests and Levites in the temple, vv. 44–47.

A detailed analysis of chapter

The priests and Levites who returned. (1–26)
The dedication of the wall. (27–43)
The officers of the temple settled. (44–47)

Key verse

Verse 27: "And at the dedication of the wall of Jerusalem they sought the Levites out of all their places, to bring them to Jerusalem, to keep the dedication with gladness, both with thanksgivings, and with singing, with cymbals, psalteries, and with harps."

Key word / key phrase

Verse 27, "dedication."

Key event / key person / key theme

The dedication of the wall of Jerusalem

Key thought

God's people have always been given ways in which they are to serve God.

Key thing to look out for

God gives different talents and different spiritual gifts to his people so we should expect people to be serving God in a great variety of ways.

Key Bible cross-reference

Verse 43. See 1 Chronicles 29:2.

Key "by way of explanation"

Verse 30. In times of revival the Levites purified the temple itself as well as everything that was sacred in the temple.

Key "Quotable Quote"

"God insists that he set up his throne in the heart, and reign in it, without a rival. If we keep him from his right, it will not matter by what competitor."

William Wilberforce

Nehemiah 13

Matthew Henry's introduction

I. Nehemiah removed from Israel the mixed multitude, the Moabites and Ammonites especially, vv. 1–3. With a particular indignation, he expelled Tobiah out of the lodgings he had got in the court of the temple, vv. 4–9.

II. He secured the maintenance of the priests and Levites to them more firmly than it had been, vv. 10–14.

III. He restrained the profanation of the Sabbath day, and provided for the due sanctification of it, vv. 15–22.

IV. He checked the growing mischief of marrying strange wives, vv. 23–31.

A detailed analysis of chapter

Nehemiah throws out Tobiah's household goods. (1–9)

Nehemiah's reform in the house of God. (10–14)

Sabbath-breaking restrained. (15–22)

Marriage to foreign women denounced. (23–31)

Key verse

Verse 11: "Then contended I with the rulers, and said, Why is the house of God forsaken?"

Key word / key phrase

Verse 9, "orders."

Key event / key person / key theme

Nehemiah's reforms

Key thought

Following God's laws often proves very hard.

Key thing to look out for

Nehemiah kept helping God's people to live in ways that pleased the Lord.

Key Bible cross-reference

Verse 8. See verses 24, 25; 5:6, 7.

Key "by way of explanation"

As previously agreed (see 2:5) Nehemiah had returned to Artaxerxes in Babylon. When he later came back to resume his work as governor of Jerusalem he was furious to discover the negligence of the people.

Key "Quotable Quote"

"Perhaps there cannot be a better way of judging of what manner of spirit we are of, than to see whether the actions of our life are such as we may safely commend them to God in our prayers."

William Law

5. Select bibliography for Nehemiah

See Select bibliography for Ezra.

Esther

1. Book by book: Introduction to Esther

Introduction

Esther derives its name from the Jewess, who, having become wife of the king of Persia, employed her royal influence to effect a memorable deliverance for the persecuted Church of God. Various opinions are embraced and supported as to the authorship of this book, some ascribing it to Ezra, to Nehemiah, or to Mordecai. The preponderance of authorities is in favor of the last. The historical character of the book is undoubted, since, besides many internal evidences, its authenticity is proved by the strong testimony of the feast of Purim, the celebration of which can be traced up to the events which are described in this book. Its claim, however, to canonical authority has been questioned on the ground that the name of God does not once occur in it. But the uniform tradition both of the Jewish and the Christian Churches supports this claim, which nothing in the book tends to shake; while it is a record of the superintending care of divine providence over his chosen people, with which it is of the utmost importance the Church should be furnished.

The name of God is strangely enough omitted, but the presence of God is felt throughout the history; and the whole tone and tendency of the book is so decidedly subservient to the honor of God and the cause of true religion that it has been generally received by the Church in all ages into the sacred canon.

Robert Jamieson

Contents of Esther

The book is characterized by supreme dramatic power. The scene is "Shushan the palace," that part of the ancient Elamitic capital which formed the fortified residence of the Persian kings. The book opens with the description of a major festival. All the notabilities of the kingdom are present, together with their retainers, both small and great. To grace the occasion, Vashti is summoned to appear before the king's guests; and, to the dismay of the great assembly, the queen refuses to obey. A council is immediately summoned. Vashti is degraded; and a decree is issued that every man bear rule in his own house (Esther 1). To find a successor to Vashti, the fairest damsels in the empire are brought to Shushan; and Hadassah, the cousin and adopted daughter of Mordecai, is of the number. Esther (2) closes with two incidents:

(1) the coronation of Hadassah (now and henceforth named "Esther") as queen;

(2) Mordecai's discovery of a palace plot to assassinate the king.

Chapter 3 introduces another leading person, Haman, the son of Hammedatha, whose seat the king had set "above all the princes that were with him." All the king's servants who are at the king's gates prostrate themselves before the powerful favorite. Mordecai, who is not a trained courtier but a God-fearing Jew, refrains. Though expostulated with, he will not conform. The matter is brought to Haman's notice for whose offended dignity Mordecai is too small a sacrifice. The whole Jewish people must perish. Lots are cast to find a lucky day for their extermination. The king's consent is obtained, and the royal decree is sent into all the provinces fixing the slaughter for the 13th day of the 12th month.

The publication of the decree is followed by universal mourning among the Jews (Esther 4). News of Mordecai's mourning is brought to Esther, who, through the messengers she sends to him, is informed of her own and her people's danger. She is urged to save herself and them. She eventually decides to seek the king s presence at the risk of her life. She presents herself (chapter 5) before the king and is graciously received. Here we breathe atmosphere of the place and time. Everything depends on the decision of one will—the king's. Esther does not attempt too much at first: she invites the king and Haman to a banquet. Here the king asks Esther what her petition is, assuring her that it shall be granted. In reply she requests his and Haman's presence at a banquet the following day. Haman goes forth in high elation. On his way home he passes Mordecai, who "stood not up nor moved for him." Haman passes on filled with rage, and unburdens himself to his wife and all his friends. They advise that a stake, fifty cubits high, be prepared for Mordecai's impalement; that on the morrow he obtain the royal permission for Mordecai's execution; and that he then proceed with a merry heart to banquet with the queen. The stake is made ready.

But (Esther 6) that night Xerxes cannot sleep. The chronicles of the kingdom are read before him. The reader has come to Mordecai's discovery of the plot, when the king asks what reward was given him. He is informed that the service had received no acknowledgment. It is now early morn, and Haman is waiting in the court for an audience to request Mordecai's life. He is summoned to the king's presence and asked what should be done to the man whom the king desires to honor. Believing that the king can be thinking only of him, he suggests that royal honors be paid him. He is appalled by the command to do so to Mordecai. Hurrying home from his lowly attendance on the hated Jew, he has hardly time to tell the mournful story to his wife and friends when he is summoned to Esther's banquet. There, at the king's renewed request to be told her desire, she begs life for herself and for her people (Esther 7). The king asks in astonishment, who he is, and where he is, who dared to injure her and them. The reply is that Haman is the adversary. Xerxes, filled with indignation, rises from the banquet and passes into the palace garden. He returns and discovers that Haman, in the madness of his fear, has thrown himself on the queen's couch, begging for his life. That act seals his doom. He is led away to be impaled on the very stake he had prepared for the Jew. The seal of the kingdom is transferred to Mordecai (Esther 8). Measures are immediately taken to avert the consequence of Haman's plot (Esther 9–10). The result is deliverance and honor for the Jews. These resolve that the festival of Purim should be instituted and be ever after observed by Jews and proselytes. The decision was confirmed by letters from Esther and Mordecai.

Orr, James, M.A., D.D. General Editor, International Standard Bible Encyclopedia

Detailed outline

I. Introduction: 1:1–22
- A. The great feasts: 1:1–9
- B. A domestic problem: 1:10–12
- C. A royal commandment: 1:13–22

II. A new queen: 2:1–21
- A. The search for a queen: 2:1–4
- B. Esther enters the competition: 2:5–11
  - 1. Mordecai's background: 2:5–6
  - 2. Esther's background: 2:7
- C. Esther in the custody of Hegai: 2:8–11
- D. The women presented before the king: 2:12–14
- E. Esther selected as queen: 2:15–17
- F. The feast for Esther: 2:18
- G. Esther's secret: 2:19

III. Two men, two plots: 2:21–3:15
- A. The plot overthrown by Mordecai:

2:22–23

1. Mordecai in the king's gate: 2:22–23
2. Mordecai aborts the plot: 2:21–22
3. The two criminals hanged: 2:23

B. The promotion and plot of Haman: 3:1–15

1. Haman promoted above all other princes: 3:1
2. The problem between Haman and Mordecai: 3:2–6
3. Haman's vengeful plot: 3:7–15

IV. Despair and deliverance: 4:1–7:10

A. Despair of the Jews: 4:1–3

B. Despair of the Queen: 4:4–9

C. A plan for deliverance: 4:10–5:14

1. The plan: 4:10–17
2. Before the King: 5:1–3
3. Invitation to a banquet: 5:4–8
4. Haman's pride: 5:9–14

D. Mordecai honored: 6:1–14

1. The king's reading: 6:1–3
2. Haman sought for advice: 6:4–5
3. Haman prideful response: 6:6–9
4. Haman's mortification as Mordecai is honored: 6:10–12
5. The response of Haman's family and friends: 6:13–14

E. The feast of Esther: 7:1–6

F. Haman punished: 7:7–10

V. The new kingdom order: 8:1–10:3

A. New orders from the king: 8:1–14

B. Mordecai honored: 8:15–17

C. Deliverance of the Jews: 9:1–11

D. House of Haman destroyed: 9:12–14

E. The feast of Purim: 9:15–32

F. Representation by Mordecai: 10:1–3

2. Helpful summaries of Esther

Bird's eye view

Esther, as queen of the Persian King Xerxes, saves her fellow Jews from extermination, by reversing the king's orders against the Jews.

Reading plan

The following reading plan, taking one reading per day, enables you to read through Esther in three days.

Esther 1–3

Esther 4–7

Esther 8–10

Verse to memorize

Esther 4:14

And who knows but that you have come to royal position for such a time as this?

Statistics

Seventeenth Old Testament book

10 chapters

167 verses

5,637 words

The book of Esther is one of only two Bible books written by a woman (the other one being the book of Ruth).

Names/titles given

Hebrew title: *Hadassah*, "myrtle" (Esther 2:7) was Esther's Hebrew name, but her Persian name was *Ester*, meaning "star."

Greek title in Septuagint: *Esther.*

Latin title in Vulgate: *Hester.*

"The Scroll of Esther," Jewish tradition.

3. Helpful keys to turn to in understanding Esther

Key word

Deliverance

Key verses

Esther 4:14; 8:17

Key people/events

Ahasuerus

Vashti

Esther

Mordecai

Haman

Feast of Purim

Themes to study

Study the characters of the three main people: Esther, Mordecai, and Haman

Three feasts

1. The Feast of Xerxes (Ahasuerus)
2. The Feast of Esther
3. The Feast of Purim

Jesus in Esther

In Esther Jesus our Advocate.

Lessons to learn from Esther

- We should place our trust in God knowing full well that he cares for us.
- Times come when we should stand up and be counted as disciples of Jesus.

4. Chapter by chapter: outline of every chapter of Esther

Esther 1

Matthew Henry's introduction

Several things in this chapter itself are very instructive and of great use; but the design of recording the story of it is to show how way was made for Esther to the crown, in order to her being instrumental to defeat Haman's plot, and this long before the plot was laid, that we may observe and admire the foresight and vast reaches of Providence. "Known unto God are all his works" before-hand. Ahasuerus the king,

I. In his height feasts all his great men, vv. 1–9.

II. In his heat he divorces his queen, because she would not come to him when he sent for her, vv. 10–22. This shows how God serves his own purposes even by the sins and follies of men, which he would not permit if he know not how to bring good out of them.

A detailed analysis of chapter

The royal feast of Ahasuerus. (1–9)

Vashti's refusal to appear, and the king's decree. (10–22)

Key verse

Verse 5: ". . . the king made a feast unto all the people that were present in Shushan the palace . . ."

Key word / key phrase

Verse 1, "Xerxes."

Key event / key person / key theme

Xerxes looks for a new queen

Key thought

Drunkenness is often not condemned in ungodly circles.

Key thing to look out for

Many other evils go uncensored in godless company.

Key Bible cross-reference

Verse 19. See 8:8; Daniel 6:8.

Key "by way of explanation"

Verse 3. Esther is full of feasts. There are ten banquets in this book. The story takes place in Persia when Xerxes ruled the Persian Empire (486–465 BC). Susa was his winter residence.

Key "Quotable Quote"

"There is practically nothing that men do not prefer to God. "

François Fénelon

Esther 2

Matthew Henry's introduction

Two things are recorded in this chapter, which were working towards the deliverance of the Jews from Haman's conspiracy:

I. The advancement of Esther to be queen instead of Vashti. Many others were candidates for the honor (vv. 1–4); but Esther, an orphan, a captive-Jewess (vv. 5–7), recommended herself to the king's chamberlain first (vv. 8–11) and then to the king (vv. 12–17), who made her queen, vv. 18–20.

II. The good service that Mordecai did to the king in discovering a plot against his life, vv. 21–23.

A detailed analysis of chapter

Esther chosen as queen. (1–20)

Mordecai discovers a plot against the king. (21–23)

Key verse

Verse 8: "So it came to pass, when the king's commandment and his decree was heard, and when many maidens were gathered together unto Shushan the palace, to the custody of Hegai, that Esther was brought also unto the king's house, to the custody of Hegai, keeper of the women."

Key word / key phrase

Verse 22, "plot."

Key event / key person / key theme

Esther becomes the new queen

Key thought

Loyalty is a wonderful characteristic.

Key thing to look out for

The word of "God" does not come in this book, but God's providential hand made the Jewess, Esther, Queen.

Key Bible cross-reference

Verse 8. See 2 Samuel 11:4.

Key "by way of explanation"

Verse 10. The fact that nobody knew Esther's background became very important later on, and it is merely mentioned twice, once in this verse and once in verse 20.

Key "Quotable Quote"

"Circumstances are constantly affecting us and their purpose is to produce our sanctification. Pleasant circumstances and unpleasant circumstances. We should therefore be observant and always watching for lessons, seeking and asking questions."

D. Martyn Lloyd-Jones

Esther 3

Matthew Henry's introduction

I. Haman is made the king's favorite, v. 1.
II. Mordecai refuses to give him the honor he demands, vv. 2–4.
III. Haman, for his sake, vows to be revenged on all the Jews, vv. 5, 6.
IV. He, on a malicious suggestion, obtains an order from the king to have the all massacred on a certain day, vv. 7–13.
V. This order is dispersed through the kingdom, vv. 14, 15.

A detailed analysis of chapter

Haman seeks to destroy the Jews. (1–6)
He obtains a decree against the Jews. (7–15)

Key verse

Verse 6: "Haman sought to destroy all the Jews that were throughout the whole kingdom of Ahasuerus, even the people of Mordecai."

Key word / key phrase

Verse 1, "Haman."

Key event / key person / key theme

Haman's plot to destroy the Jews

Key thought

The Lord had provided for the Jews before Haman tried to exterminate them.

Key thing to look out for

Evil is arrogant and callous.

Key Bible cross-reference

Verse 8. See 8:11, 17; 9:2, 12, 16, 19, 20, 28.

Key "by way of explanation"

Verses 8,9. Although the Jews did have their own laws they had not broken any of the king's laws.

Key "Quotable Quote"

"I think we do not attach sufficient importance to the restoration of the Jews."

C.H. Spurgeon

Esther 4

Matthew Henry's introduction

I. The Jews' friends lay to heart the danger and lament it, vv. 1–4.
II. Matters are concerted between Mordecai and Esther for the preventing of it.
  A. Esther enquires into this case, and receives a particular account of it, vv. 5–7.
  B. Mordecai urges her to intercede with the king for a revocation of the edict, vv. 8, 9.

III. Esther objects the danger of addressing the king uncalled, vv. 10–12.
IV. Mordecai presses her to venture, vv. 13, 14.
V. Esther, after a religious fast of three days, promises to do so (vv. 15–17).

A detailed analysis of chapter

The Jews lament their danger. (1–4)

Esther undertakes to plead for the Jews. (5–17)

Key verse

Verse 4: "Then was the queen exceedingly grieved; and she sent raiment to clothe Mordecai, and to take away his sackcloth from him: but he received it not."

Key word / key phrase

Verse 14, "royal position."

Key event / key person / key theme

Esther risks her life as she agrees to speak up for her people

Key thought

Sometimes it is not clear how God will use us in the future in his service.

Key thing to look out for

If Esther had become proud or fearful she would have acted differently.

Key Bible cross-reference

Verse 14. See Genesis 45:5–7.

Key "by way of explanation"

Verses 12–16. As God is sovereign he would have acted in some other way had Esther not cooperated with Mordecai's plan.

Key "Quotable Quote"

"To the Christian, love is the works of love."

Oswald Chambers

Esther 5

Matthew Henry's introduction

The last news we had of Haman left him in his cups, 3:15. Our last news of queen Esther left her in tears, fasting and praying. Now this chapter brings in,

I. Esther in her joys, smiled on by the king and honored with his company at her banquet of wine, vv. 1–8.
II. Haman on the fret, because he had not Mordecai's cap and knee, and with great indignation setting up a gallows for him, vv. 9–14.

A detailed analysis of chapter

Esther's request received. (1–8)

Haman prepares to hang Mordecai. (9–14)

Key verse

Verse 3: "Then said the king unto her, What wilt thou, queen Esther? and what is thy request? it shall be even given thee to the half of the kingdom."

Key word / key phrase

Verse 2, "held out to her the gold scepter."

Key event / key person / key theme

Esther dares to ask for an audience with the king

Key thought

The Lord overruled so that the king granted Esther's wish.

Key thing to look out for

The Lord also overruled in the timing of Haman's anger.

Key Bible cross-reference

Verses 12, 13. See Proverbs 16:18; 29:23.

Key "by way of explanation"

Verse 4. Esther does not tell the king at once the nature of her request. This heightens the tension in the whole story.

Key "Quotable Quote"

"Life appears to me too short to be spent in nursing animosity or registering wrong."

Charlotte Brontë

Esther 6

Matthew Henry's introduction

I. The providence of God recommend Mordecai in the night to the king's favor, vv. 1–3.

II. Haman, who came to incense the king against him, is employed as an instrument of the king's favor to him, vv. 4–11.

III. From this his friends read him his doom, which is carried out in the next chapter, vv. 12–14.

A detailed analysis of chapter

Providence recommends Mordecai to the king's favor. (1–3)

Haman's counsel honors Mordecai. (4–11)

Haman's friends tell him of his danger. (12–14)

Key verse

Verse 1: "On that night could not the king sleep, and he commanded to bring the book of records of the chronicles; and they were read before the king."

Key word / key phrase

Verse 3, "honor."

Key event / key person / key theme

Mordecai is honored

Key thought

The Lord overruled that the king could not sleep that night and so looked through his records.

Key thing to look out for

The Lord overruled that on the next day Haman wanted to make his request to the king.

Key Bible cross-reference

Verse 1. See Daniel 2:1; 6:18.

Key "by way of explanation"

Verse 2. The events the scribe was reading to the king had taken place five years previously. See 3:7 and 2:16.

Key "Quotable Quote"

"O love of God, how deep and great.
Far deeper than man's deepest hate."

Corrie ten Boom

Esther 7

Matthew Henry's introduction

We are now to attend the second banquet to which the king and Haman were invited: and there,

I. Esther presents her petition to the king for her life and the life of her people, vv. 1–4.

II. She plainly tells the king that Haman is the man who designed her ruin and the ruin of all her friends, vv. 5, 6.

III. The king thereon gave orders for the hanging of Haman on the gallows that he had prepared for Mordecai, which was done accordingly, vv. 7–10.

A detailed analysis of chapter

Esther accuses Haman. (1–6)

Haman hanged on his own gallows. (7–10)

Key verse

Verse 6: "And Esther said, The adversary and enemy is this wicked Haman."

Key word / key phrase

Verse 10, "gallows."

Key event / key person / key theme

Haman is hanged

Key thought

Many men like Haman do receive just rewards for their evil in this life.

Key thing to look out for

You do not have to be a follower of God to appreciate justice.

Key Bible cross-reference

Verse 4. See 3:9; 4:7.

Key "by way of explanation"

Verse 8. It was normal for meals to be eaten reclining on couches. See Amos 6:4–7; John 13:23.

Key "Quotable Quote"

"The day of grace ends with some men before God taketh them out of the world."

John Bunyan

Esther 8

Matthew Henry's introduction

We left the plotter hanging, and are now to see what becomes of his plot.

I. His plot was to raise an estate for himself; and all his estate, being confiscated for treason, is given to Esther and Mordecai, vv. 1, 2.

II. His plot was to ruin the Jews; and as to that,

A. Esther earnestly intercedes for the reversing of the edict against them, vv. 3–6.

B. It is in effect done by another edict, here published, empowering the Jews to stand up in their own defense against their enemies, vv. 7–14.

III. This occasions great joy to the Jews and all their friends, vv. 15–17.

A detailed analysis of chapter

Mordecai is advanced. (1, 2)

Esther pleads for the Jews. (3–14)

Mordecai honored, and the joy of the Jews. (15–17)

Key verse

Verse 2: "And the king took off his ring, which he had taken from Haman, and gave it unto Mordecai."

Key word / key phrase

Verse 8, "another decree."

Key event / key person / key theme

The king supports the Jews with his second edict

Key thought

The king was quick to see how he could save the Jews from their predicament, which he had unwittingly caused.

Key thing to look out for

What could have been an unmitigated tragedy ended in joy and happiness.

Key Bible cross-reference

Verse 5. See 4:11; 5:2.

Key "by way of explanation"

Verse 8. The king could not revoke his first edict. But he effectively did this by issuing the second edict.

Key "Quotable Quote"

"Christianity is a rescue religion."

John R.W. Stott

Esther 9

Matthew Henry's introduction

Here we are told,

I. What a glorious day it was, that year, to the Jews, and the two days following—a day of victory and triumph, both in the city Shushan and in all the rest of the king's provinces, vv. 1–19.

II. What a memorable day it was made to posterity, by an annual feast, in commemoration of this great deliverance, called "the feast of Purim," vv. 20–32.

A detailed analysis of chapter

The success of the Jews. (1–19)

The feast of Purim to commemorate this. (20–32)

Key verse

Verse 2: "The Jews gathered themselves together in their cities throughout all the provinces of the king Ahasuerus, to lay hand on such as sought their hurt: and no man could withstand them; for the fear of them fell upon all people."

Key word / key phrase

Verse 5, "The Jews struck down."

Key event / key person / key theme

The Festival of Purim

Key thought

The Lord's people should always show their gratitude to the Lord whenever anything good happens to them.

Key thing to look out for

The Festival of Purim ensured that the Jews would never forget God's deliverance.

Key Bible cross-reference

Verses 2, 3. See Genesis 12:3.

Key "by way of explanation"

Verses 18, 19. To this day Purim is celebrated on different days in different places. In Jerusalem it is celebrated on the 14th, but elsewhere on the 15th.

Key "Quotable Quote"

"Worship is the direct acknowledgment to God, of his nature, attributes, ways and claims, whether by the outgoing of the heart in praise and thanksgiving or by deed done in such acknowledgment."

W.E. Vine

Esther 10

Matthew Henry's introduction

This is but a part of a chapter; the rest of it, beginning at v. 4, with six chapters more, being found only in the Greek, is rejected as apocryphal. In these three verses we have only some short hints,

I. About Ahasuerus in the throne, what a mighty prince he was, vv. 1, 2.

II. About Mordecai his favorite, what a distinguished blessing he was to his people, vv. 2, 3.

A detailed analysis of chapter

Greatness of Ahasuerus. Mordecai's advancement. (1–3)

Key verse

Verse 3: "For Mordecai the Jew was next unto king Ahasuerus, and great among the Jews, and accepted of the multitude of his brethren, seeking the wealth of his people, and speaking peace to all his seed."

Key word / key phrase

Verse 3, "pre-eminent."

Key event / key person / key theme

Mordecai's greatness

Key thought

The Lord raises the humble.

Key thing to look out for

Mordecai's good actions are remembered.

Key Bible cross-reference

Verse 2. See 1 Chronicles s17:21.

Key "by way of explanation"

The word "Purim" came from the Assyrian word *puru*, a small stone, which was used when casting lots.

Key "Quotable Quote"

"I read somewhere that this young man, Jesus Christ, went about doing good. But I just go about."

Toyohiko Kagawa

5. Select bibliography for Esther

Baldwin, Joyce G. *Esther* (Tyndale), InterVarsity Press, 1984.

Bush, Frederic W. *Ruth, Esther*. (Word Biblical Commentary, 9), Word Books, 1996.

Keil, C. F. *The Books of Ezra, Nehemiah and Esther*. Biblical Commentary on the Old Testament. KD. 1888 Reprint. Grand Rapids: Eerdmans, 1956.

Job

1. Book by book: Introduction to Job

Introduction

Job a real person

It has been supposed by some that the book of Job is an allegory, not a real narrative, on account of the artificial character of many of its statements. Thus the sacred numbers, three and seven, often occur. He had seven thousand sheep, seven sons, both before and after his trials; his three friends sit down with him seven days and seven nights; both before and after his trials he had three daughters. So also the number and form of the speeches of the several speakers seem to be artificial. The name of Job, too, is derived from an Arabic word signifying repentance.

But Ezek. 14:14 (compare Ezek. 14:16, 20) speaks of "Job" in conjunction with "Noah and Daniel," real people. St. James (James 5:11) also refers to Job as an example of "patience," which he would not have been likely to do had Job been only a fictitious person. Also the names of people and places are specified with a particularity not to be looked for in an allegory. As to the exact doubling of his possessions after his restoration, no doubt the round number is given for the exact number, as the latter approached near the former; this is often done in undoubtedly historical books. As to the studied number and form of the speeches, it seems likely that the arguments were substantially those which appear in the book, but that the studied and poetic form was given by Job himself, guided by the Holy Spirit. He lived one hundred and forty years after his trials, and nothing would be more natural than that he should, at his leisure, mould into a perfect form the arguments used in the momentous debate, for the instruction of the Church in all ages. Probably, too, the debate itself occupied several sittings; and the number of speeches assigned to each was arranged by a prior agreement, and each was allowed the interval of a day or more to prepare carefully his speech and replies; this will account for the speakers bringing forward their arguments in regular series, no one speaking out of his turn. As to the name Job—repentance (supposing the derivation correct)—it was common in old times to give a name from circumstances which occurred at an advanced period of life, and this is no argument against the reality of the person.

Where Job lived

Uz, according to Gesenius, means a light, sandy soil, and was in the north of Arabia-Deserta, between Palestine and the Euphrates, called by Ptolemy (Geography, 19) Ausitai or Aisitai. In Gen. 10:23; 22:21; 36:28; and 1 Chr. 1:17, 42, it is the name of a man. In Jer. 25:20; Lam. 4:21; and Job 1:1, it is a country. Uz, in Gen. 22:21, is said to be the son of Nahor, brother of Abraham—a different person from the one mentioned (Gen. 10:23), a grandson of Shem. The probability is that the country took its name from the latter of the two; for this one was the son of Aram, from whom the Arameans take their name, and these dwelt in Mesopotamia, between the rivers Euphrates and Tigris. Compare as to the dwelling of the sons of Shem in Gen. 10:30, "a mount of the East," answering to "men of the East" (Job 1:3). Rawlinson, in his deciphering of the Assyrian inscriptions, states that "Uz is the prevailing name of the country at the mouth of the Euphrates." It is probable that Eliphaz the Temanite and the Sabeans dwelt in that quarter; and we know that the Chaldeans resided there, and not near Idumea, which some identify with Uz. The tornado from "the wilderness" (Job 1:19) agrees with the view of it being Arabia-Deserta. Job (Job 1:3) is called "the greatest of the men of the East"; but Idumea was not east, but south of Palestine: therefore in Scripture language, the phrase cannot apply to that country, but probably refers to the north of Arabia-Deserta, between Palestine, Idumea, and the Euphrates. So the Arabs still show in the Houran a place called Uz as the residence of Job.

When Job lived

Eusebius fixes it two ages before Moses, that is, about the time of Isaac: eighteen hundred years before Christ, and six hundred after the Deluge. Agreeing with this are the following considerations:

Job's length of life is patriarchal, two hundred years.

He alludes only to the earliest form of idolatry, namely, the worship of the sun, moon, and heavenly hosts (called Saba, whence arises the title "Lord of Sabaoth," as opposed to Sabeanism) (Job 31:26–28).

The number of oxen and rams sacrificed, seven, as in the case of Balaam. God would not have sanctioned this after the giving of the Mosaic law, though He might graciously accommodate Himself to existing customs before the law.

The language of Job is Hebrew, interspersed occasionally with Syriac and Arabic expressions, implying a time when all the Shemitic tribes spoke one common tongue and had not branched into different dialects, Hebrew, Syriac, and Arabic.

He speaks of the most ancient kind of writing, namely, sculpture. Riches also are reckoned by cattle. The Hebrew word, translated "a piece of money," ought rather be rendered "a lamb."

There is no allusion to the exodus from Egypt and to the miracles that accompanied it; nor to the destruction of Sodom and Gomorrah (Patrick, however, thinks there is); though there is to the Flood (Job 22:17); and these events, happening in Job's vicinity, would have been striking illustrations of the argument for God's interposition in destroying the wicked and vindicating the righteous, had Job and his friends known of them. Nor is there any undoubted reference to the Jewish law, ritual, and priesthood.

The religion of Job is that which prevailed among the patriarchs previous to the law; sacrifices performed by the head of the family; no officiating priesthood, temple, or consecrated altar.

Author

All the previous facts accord with Job himself having been the author. The style of thought, imagery, and manners, are such as we should look for in the work of an Arabian emir. There is precisely that degree of knowledge of primitive tradition (see Job 31:33, as to Adam) which was universally spread abroad in the days of Noah and Abraham, and which was subsequently embodied in the early chapters of Genesis. Job, in his speeches, shows that he was much more competent to compose the work than Elihu, to whom Lightfoot attributes it. The style forbids its being attributed to Moses, to whom its composition is by some attributed, "whilst he was among the Midianites, about 1520 b.c." But the fact, that it, though not a Jewish book, appears among the Hebrew sacred writings, makes it likely that it came to the knowledge of Moses during the forty years which he passed in parts of Arabia, chiefly near Horeb; and that he, by divine guidance, introduced it as a sacred writing to the Israelites, to whom, in their affliction, the patience and restoration of Job were calculated to be a lesson of especial utility. That it is inspired appears from the fact that Paul (1 Cor. 3:19) quotes it (Job 5:13) with the formula, "It is written." Our Savior, too, (Matt. 24:28), plainly refers to Job 29:30. Compare also James 4:10 and 1 Pet. 5:6 with Job 22:29; Rom. 11:34, 35 with Job 15:8. It is probably the oldest book in the world. It stands among the Hagiographa in the threefold division of Scripture into the Law, the Prophets, and the Hagiographa ("Psalms," Luke 24:44).

Purpose of book

It is a public debate in poetic form on an important question about the divine government; moreover the prologue and epilogue, which are in prose, shed the interest of a living history over the debate, which would otherwise be but a contest of abstract reasonings. To each speaker of the three friends three speeches are assigned. Job having no one to stand by him is allowed to reply to each speech of each of the three. Eliphaz, as the oldest, leads the way. Zophar, at his third turn, failed to speak, thus virtually owning himself overcome (Job 27:1–23). Therefore Job continued his reply, which forms three speeches (Job 26:1–14; 27:1–23; 28:1–28; 29:1–31:40). Elihu (Job 32:1–37:24) is allowed four speeches. Jehovah makes three addresses (Job 38:1–41:34). Thus, throughout there is a tripartite division. The whole is divided into three parts—the prologue, poem proper, and epilogue. The poem, into three—(1) The dispute of Job and his three friends; (2) The address of Elihu; (3) The address of God. There are three series in the controversy, and in the same order. The epilogue (Job 42:1–17) also is threefold; Job's justification, reconciliation with his friends, restoration. The speakers also in their successive speeches regularly advance from less to greater vehemence. With all this artificial composition, everything seems easy and natural.

The question to be solved, as exemplified in the case of Job, is, Why are the righteous afflicted consistently with God's justice? The doctrine of retribution after death, no doubt, is the great solution of the difficulty. And to it Job plainly refers in Job 14:14, and Job 19:25. The objection to this, that the explicitness of the language on the resurrection in Job is inconsistent with the obscurity on the subject in the early books of the Old Testament, is answered by the fact that Job enjoyed the divine vision (Job 38:1; 42:5), and therefore, by inspiration, foretold these truths. Next, the revelations made outside of Israel being few needed to be the more explicit; thus Balaam's prophecy (Num. 24:17) was clear enough to lead the wise men of the East by the star (Matt. 2:2); and in the age before the written law, it was the more needful for God not to leave Himself without witness of the truth. Still Job evidently did not fully realize the significance designed by the Spirit in his own words (compare 1 Pet. 1:11, 12). The doctrine, though existing, was not plainly revealed or at least understood. Hence he does not mainly refer to this solution. Yes, and even now, we need something in addition to this solution. David, who firmly believed in a future retribution (Ps. 16:10; 17:15), still felt the difficulty not entirely solved thereby (Ps. 83:1–18). The solution is not in Job's or in his three friends' speeches. It must, therefore, be in Elihu's. God will hold a final judgment, no doubt, to clear up all that seems dark in His present dealings; but He also now providentially and morally governs the world and all the events of human life. Even the comparatively righteous are not without sin which needs to be corrected. The justice and love of God administer the altogether deserved and merciful correction. Affliction to the godly is thus mercy and justice in disguise. The afflicted believer on repentance sees this. *"Via crucis, via salutis"* ("The way of the cross, the way of deliverance"). Though afflicted, the godly are happier even now than the ungodly, and when affliction has attained its end, it is removed by the Lord. In the Old Testament the consolations are more temporal and outward; in the New Testament, more spiritual; but in neither to the entire exclusion of the other. "Prosperity," says Bacon, "is the blessing of the Old Testament; adversity that of the New Testament, which is the mark of God's more especial favor. Yet even in the Old Testament, if you listen to David's harp, you shall hear as many hearse-like airs as carols; and the pencil of the Holy Spirit has labored more in describing the afflictions of Job than the felicities of Solomon. Prosperity is not without many fears and distastes; and adversity is not without comforts and hopes." This solution of Elihu is seconded by the addresses of God, in which it is shown God must be just (because He is God), as Elihu had shown how God can be just, and yet the righteous be afflicted. It is also acquiesced in by Job, who makes no reply. God reprimands the "three" friends, but not Elihu. Job's general course is approved; he is directed to intercede for his friends, and is restored to double his former prosperity.

Poetry

In all countries poetry is the earliest form of composition as being best retained in the memory. In the East especially it was customary for sentiments to be preserved in a terse, proverbial, and poetic form (called *maschal*). Hebrew poetry is not constituted by the rhythm or meter, but in a form peculiar to itself: 1. In an alphabetical arrangement somewhat like our acrostic. For instance, Lam. 1:1–22. 2. The same verse repeated at intervals; as in Ps. 42:1–11; 107:1–43. 3. Rhythm of gradation. Psalms of degrees, Ps. 120:1–134:3, in which the expression of the previous verse is resumed and carried forward in the next (Ps. 121:1–8). 4. The chief characteristic of Hebrew poetry is parallelism, or the correspondence of the same ideas in the parallel clauses. The earliest instance is Enoch's prophecy (Jude 14), and Lamech's parody of it (Gen. 4:23). Three kinds occur:

The synonymous parallelism, in which the second is a repetition of the first, with or without increase of force (Ps. 22:27; Is. 15:1); sometimes with double parallelism (Is. 1:15).

The antithetic, in which the idea of the second clause is the converse of that in the first (Prov. 10:1).

The synthetic, where there is a correspondence between different propositions, noun answering to noun, verb to verb, member to member, the sentiment, moreover, being not merely echoed, or put in contrast, but enforced by accessory ideas (Job 3:3–9). Also alternate (Is. 51:19). "Desolation and destruction, famine and sword," that is, desolation by famine, and destruction by the sword. Introverted; where the fourth answers to the first, and the third to the second (Matt. 7:6). Parallelism thus often affords a key to the interpretation. For fuller information, see Lowth (Introduction to Isaiah, and Lecture on Hebrew Poetry) and Herder (Spirit of Hebrew Poetry, translated by Marsh). The simpler and less artificial forms of parallelism prevail in Job—a mark of its early age.

A.R. Faussett

Contents of Job

The book of Job tackles the perennial question about why innocent people suffer. Job has discussions about this with four friends, Eliphaz, Bildad, Zophar, and Elihu, before being confronted with God himself and his sovereignty, at the close of the book.

To divide the story of Job into 42 parts, according to the 42 numbered chapters, is in the last degree arbitrary. Nothing comes of it except convenience in reading for those who wish to take their Job in little detached bits. The chapter division was no part of the original, and a very insignificant step in the later apprehension of the original. To divide according to the speeches of the interlocutors is better; it helps us realize how the conflict of views brought the various phases of the thought to expression; but this too, with its tempting, three-times-three, turns out to be merely a framework; it corresponds only imperfectly with the true inwardness of the story's movement; it is rather a scheme than a continuity. We are to bear in mind that this Book of Job is fundamentally the inner experience of one man, as he rises from the depths of spiritual gloom and doubt to a majestic table-land of new insight and faith; the other characters are but ancillary, helps and foils, whose function is subordinate and relative. Hence, mindful of this inwardness of Job's experience, I have ventured to trace the story in 5 main stages, naming them according to the landing-stage attained in each.

A) Job's Blessing and Curse

1. His "Autumn Days"

The story begins (Job 1:1–5) with a brief description of Job as he was before his trial began; the elements of his life, outer and inner, on which is to be raised the question of motive. A prosperous landholder of the land of Uz, distinguished far and wide as the greatest (i.e. richest) of the sons of the East, his inner character corresponds: to all appearance nothing lacking, a man "perfect and upright, and one that feared God, and turned away from evil." The typical Hebrew blessings of life were his to the full: wealth, honor, health, family. He is evidently set before us as the perfect example of the validity of the established Wisdom-tenet, that righteousness and Wisdom are identical and that this is manifest in its visible rewards. This period of his life Job describes afterward by retrospect as his "autumn days," when the friendship or intimacy of God was over his tent (see 29:4, and the whole chapter). Nor are we left without a glimpse into his heart: his constant attitude of worship, and his tender solicitude lest, in their enjoyment of the pleasures of life, his sons may have been disloyal to God (Job 1:4,5). It is easy to see that not Job alone, but Wisdom as embodied in Job, is postulated here for its supreme test.

2. The Wager in Heaven

Nor is the test delayed, or its ground ambiguous when it comes. Satan proposes it. Two scenes are given (Job 1:6–12; 2:1–6) from the court of God, wherever that is; for they are overheard by the reader, not seen, and of course neither Job nor any inhabitant of earth is aware of them. In these scenes the sons of God, the spirits who rejoiced over creation (38:7), are come together to render report, and Satan, uninvited, enters among them. He is a wandering spirit, unanchored to any allegiance, who roams through the earth, prying and criticizing. There is nothing, it would seem, in which he cannot find some flaw or discount. To Yahweh's question if he has considered Job, the man perfect and upright, he makes no denial of the fact, but raises the issue of motive: "Doth Job fear God for nought?" and urges that Job's integrity is after all only a transparent bargain, a paying investment with only reward in view. It is virtually an arraignment both of God's order and of the essential human character: of God's order in connecting righteousness so intimately with gain; and of the essential human character, virtually denying that there is such a thing as disinterested, intrinsic human virtue. The sneer strikes deep, and Job, the perfect embodiment of human virtue, is its designated victim. Satan proposes a wager, to the issue of which Yahweh commits Himself. The trial of Job is carried out in two stages: first against his property and family, with the stipulation that it is not to touch him; and then, this failing to detach him from his allegiance, against his person in sore disease, with the stipulation that his life is to be spared. Yahweh acknowledges that for once He is consenting to an injustice (2:3), and

Satan, liar that he is, uses instrumentalities that men have ascribed to God alone: the first time, tempest and lightning (as well as murderous foray), the second time, the black leprosy, a fell disease, loathsome and deadly, which, in men's minds meant the immediate punitive stroke of God. The evil is as absolute as was the reward; a complete reversal of the order in which men's wisdom had come to trust. But in the immediate result, Yahweh's faith in His noblest creature is vindicated. Urged by his wife in his extremity to "curse God and die," Job remains true to his allegiance; and in his staunch utterance, "Yahweh gave, and Yahweh hath taken away; blessed be the name of Yahweh," Job, as the writer puts it, `sinned not, nor attributed aught unbeseeming (*tiphalah*, literally, "tasteless") to God.' Such is the first onset of Job's affliction and its result. It remains to be seen what the long issue, days and months of wretchedness, will bring forth.

3. The Silent Friends

We are now to imagine the lapse of some time, perhaps several months (compare Job 7:3), during which Job suffers alone, an outcast from house and society, on a leper's ash-heap. Meanwhile three friends of his who have heard of his affliction make an appointment together and come from distant regions to give him sympathy and comfort (2:11–13). On arriving, however, they find things different from what they had expected; perhaps the ominous nature of his disease has developed since they started. What they find is a man wretched and outcast, with a disease (elephantiasis) which to them can mean nothing but the immediate vengeance of God. The awful sight gives them pause. Instead of condoling with him, they sit silent and dismayed, and for seven days and nights no word is spoken (compare Isaiah 53:3). What they were debating with themselves during that time is betrayed by the after-course of the story. How can they bless one whom God has stamped with His curse? To do so would be taking sides with the wicked. Is it not rather their duty to side with God, and be safe, and let sympathy go? By this introduction of the friends and their averted attitude, the writer with consummate skill brings a new element into the story, the element of the Wisdom-philosophy; and time will show whether as a theoretical thing, cold and intellectual, it will retain or repress the natural outpouring of human friendship. And this silence is ominous.

4. Whose Way Is Hid

The man who, in the first onset of trial, blessed Yahweh and set himself to bear in silence now opens his mouth to curse. His curse is directed, not against Yahweh nor against the order of things, but against the day of his birth. It is a day that has ceased to have meaning or worth for him. The day stands for life, for his individual life, a life that in the order of things should carry out the personal promise and fruitage for which it had been bestowed. And his quarrel with it is that he has lost its clue. Satan unknown to him has sneered because Yahweh had hedged him round with protection and favor (Job 1:10); but his complaint is that all this is removed without cause, and God has hedged him round with darkness. His way is hid (Job 3:23). Why then was life given at all? In all this, it will be noted, he raises no train of introspection to account for his condition; he assumes no sinfulness, nor even natural human depravity; the opposite rather, for a baffling element of his case is his shrinking sensitiveness against evil and disloyalty (compare Job 3:25, 26, in which the tenses should be past, with 1:5; see also 6:30; 16:17). His plight has become sharply, poignantly objective; his inner self has no part in it. Thus in this opening speech he strikes the keynote of the real, against which the friends' theories rage and in the end wreck themselves.

B) Job's Ultimatum of Protest

1. The Veiled Impeachment

With all the gentle regret of having to urge a disagreeable truth the friends, beginning with Eliphaz the wisest and most venerable, enter on their theory of the case. Eliphaz covers virtually the whole ground; the others come in mainly to echo or emphasize. He veils his reproof in general and implicatory terms, the seasoned terms of wisdom in which Job himself is expert (4:3–5); reminds him that no righteous man perishes, but that men reap what they sow (4:7, 8); adduces a vision that he had had which revealed to him that man, by the very fact of being mortal, is impure and iniquitous (4:17–19); implies that Job's turbulence of mind precludes him from similar revelations, and jeopardizes his soul (5:1, 2); advises him to commit his case to God, with the implication, however, that it is a case needing correction rather than justification, and that the result in view is restored comfort and prosperity. As Job answers with a more passionate and detailed portrayal of his wrong, Bildad, following, abandons the indirect impeachment and attributes the children's death to their sin (8:4), saying also that if Job were pure and upright he might supplicate and regain God's favor (8:5, 6). He then goes on to draw a lesson from the traditional Wisdom lore, to the effect that sure destruction awaits the wicked and sure felicity the righteous (Job 8:11–22). On Job's following this with his most positive arraignment of God's order and claim for light, Zophar replies with impetuous heat, averring that Job's punishment is less than he deserves (Job 11:6), and reproving him for his presumption in trying to find the secret of God (Job 11:7–12). All three of the friends, with increasing emphasis, end their admonitions in much the same way; promising Job reinstatement in God's favor, but always with the veiled implication that he must own to iniquity and entreat as a sinner.

2. Wisdom Insipid, Friends Doubtful

To the general maxims of Wisdom urged against him, with which he is already familiar (compare Job 13:2), Job's objection is not that they are untrue, but that they are insipid (Job 6:6, 7); they have lost their application to the case. Yet it is pain to him to think that the words of the Holy One should fail; he longs to die rather than deny them (Job 6:9, 10). One poignant element of his sorrow is that the intuitive sense is driven away from him; see Job 6:13. He is irritated by the insinuating way in which the friends beg the question of his guilt; longs for forthright and sincere words (6:25). It is this quality of their speech, in fact, which adds the bitterest drop to his cup; his friends, on whom he had counted for support, are deceitful like a dried-up brook (6:15–20); he feels, in his sick sensitiveness, that they are not sympathizing with him but using him for their cold, calculating purposes (6:27). Thus is introduced one of the most potent motives of the story, the motive of friendship; much will come of it when from the fallible friendships of earth he conquers his way by faith to a friendship in the unseen (compare 16:19; 19:27).

3. Crookedness of the Order of things

With the sense that the old theories have become stale and pointless, though his discernment of the evil of things is undulled by sin (Job 6:30), Job arrives at an extremely poignant realization of the hardness and crookedness of the world-order, the result both of what the friends are saying and of what he has always held in common with them. It is the view that is forced on him by the sense that he is unjustly dealt with by a God who renders no reasons, who on the score of justice vouchsafes to man neither insight nor recourse, and whose severity is out of all proportion to man's sense of worth (7:17) or right (9:17) or claim as a creature of His hand (10:8–14). Job 9, which contains Job's direct address to this arbitrary Being, is one of the most tremendous, not to say audacious conceptions in literature; in which a mortal on the threshold of death takes on himself to read God a lesson in godlikeness. In this part of the story Job reaches his ultimatum of protest; a protest amazingly sincere, but not blasphemous when we realize that it is made in the interest of the Godlike.

4. No Mediation in Sight

The great lack which Job feels in his arraignment of God is the lack of mediation between Creator and creature, the Oppressor and His victim. There is no umpire between them, who might lay his hand on both, so that the wronged one might have voice in the matter (9:32–35). The two things that an umpire might do: to remove God's afflicting hand, and to prevent God's terror from unmanning His victim (see 13:20–22, as compared with the passage just cited), are the great need to restore normal and reciprocal relations with Him whose demand of righteousness is so inexorable. This umpire or advocate idea, thus propounded negatively, will grow to a sublime positive conviction in the next stage of Job's spiritual progress (16:19; 19:25–27).

C) Job's Ultimatum of Faith

1. Detecting the Friends' False Note

As the friends finish their first round of speeches, in which a remote and arbitrary God is urged on him as everything, and man so corrupt and blind that he cannot but be a worm and culprit (compare Job 25:4–6), Job's eyes, which hitherto have seen with theirs, are suddenly opened. His first complaint of their professed friendship was that it was fallible; instead of sticking to him when he needed them most (Job 6:14), and in spite of his bewilderment (Job 6:26), they were making it virtually an article of traffic (Job 6:27), as if it were a thing for their gain. It was not sincere, not intrinsic to their nature, but an expedient. And now all at once he penetrates to its motive. They are deserting him in order to curry favor with God. That motive has prevented them from seeing true; they see only their theoretical God, and are respecting His person instead of responding to the inner dictate of truth and integrity. To his honest heart this is monstrous; they ought to be afraid of taking falseness for God (Obadiah 13:3–12). Nor does his inference stop with thus detecting their false note. If they are "forgers of lies" in this respect, what of all their words of wisdom? they have been giving him "proverbs of ashes" (Job 13:12); the note of false implication is in them all. From this point therefore he pays little attention to what they say; lets them go on to grossly exaggerated statement of their tenet, while he opens a new way of faith for himself, developing the germs of insight that have come to him.

2. Staking All on Integrity

Having cut loose from all countenancing of the friends' self-interested motives, Job now, with the desperate sense of taking his life in his hand and abandoning hope, resolves that come what will he will maintain his ways to God's face. This, as he believes, is not only the one course for his integrity, but his one plea of salvation, for no false one shall appear before him. How tremendous the meaning of this resolve, we can think when we reflect how he has just taken God in hand to amend His supposed iniquitous order of things; and that he is now, without mediator, pleading the privilege that a mediator would secure (13:20, 21; see 8, above) and urging a hearing on his own charges. The whole reach of his sublime faith is involved in this.

3. "If a Man Die"

In two directions his faith is reaching out; in both negatively at first. One, the belief in an Advocate, has already been broached, and is germinating from negative to positive. The other, the question of life after death, rises here in the same tentative way: using first the analogy of the tree which sprouts again after it is cut down (Job 14:7–9), and from it inquiring, `If a man die—might he live again?' and dwelling in fervid imagination on the ideal solution which a survival of death would bring (Job 14:13–17), but returning to his reluctant negative, from the analogy of drying waters (Job 14:11) and the slow wearing down of mountains (Job 14:18, 19). As yet he can treat the idea only as a fancy; not yet a hope or a grounded conviction.

4. The Surviving Next of Kin

The conviction comes by a nobler way than fancy, by the way of his personal sense of the just and God-like order. The friends in their second round of speeches have begun their lurid portrayals of the wicked man's awful fate; but until all have spoken again he is concerned with a far more momentous matter. Dismissing these for the present as an academic exercise composed in cold blood (Job 16:4, 5), and evincing a heart hid from understanding (Job 17:4), Job goes on to recount in the most bitter terms he has yet used the flagrancy of his wrong as something that calls out for expiation like the blood of Cain (16:18), and breaks out with the conviction that his witness and voucher who will hear his prayer for mediation is on high (16:19–21). Then after Bildad in a spiteful retort has matched his complaint with a description of the calamities of the wicked (an augmented echo of Eliphaz), and he has pathetically bewailed the treachery of earthly friends (19:13, 14, 21, 22), he mounts, as it were, at a bound to the sublime ultimatum of his faith in an utterance which he would fain see engraved on the rock forever (19:23–29). "I know that my Redeemer liveth," he exclaims; literally, my Go'el (go'ali), or next of kin, the person whose business in the old Hebrew idea was to maintain the rights of an innocent wronged one and avenge his blood. He does not recede from the idea that his wrong is from God (compare 19:6, 21); but over his dust stands his next of kin, and as the result of this one's intercession Job, in his own integral person, shall see God no more a stranger. So confident is he that he solemnly warns the friends who have falsely impeached him that it is they, not he, who are in peril (19:28, 29; compare 13:10, 11).

D) To Job's Verdict on Things as They Are

1. Climax and Subsidence of the Friends' Charge

That in this conviction of a living Redeemer Job's faith has reached firm and final ground is evident from the fact that he does not recur to his old doubts at all. They are settled, and settled right. But now, leaving them, he can attend to what the friends have been saying. Zophar, the third speaker, following, presses to vehement, extreme their iterated portrayal of the wicked man's terrific woes; it seems the design of the writer to make them outdo themselves in frantic overstatement of their thesis. As Zophar ceases, and Job has thus, as it were, drawn all their fire, Job refutes them squarely, as we shall presently see. Meanwhile, in the course of his extended refutation, the friends begin a third round of speeches. Eliphaz, who has already taken alarm at the tendency of Job's words, as those of a depraved skeptic and ruinous to devotion (15:4–6), now in the interests of his orthodoxy brings in his bill of particulars. It is the kind of theoretical cant that has had large prevalence in dogmatic religion, but in Job's case atrociously false. He accuses Job of the most heartless cruelties and frauds (22:5–11), and of taking occasion to indulge in secret wickedness when God was not looking (22:12–14); to this it is that he attributes the spiritual darkness with which Job is encompassed. Then in a beautiful exhortation—beautiful when we forget its unreal condition (22:23)—he ends by holding open to Job The way of reinstatement and peace. This is the last word of the friends that has any weight. Bildad follows Job's next speech indeed very briefly (Job 25), giving a last feeble echo of their doctrine of total depravity; a reply which Job ridicules and carries on in a kind of parody (Job 26). Zophar does not speak a third time at all. He has nothing to say. And this silence of his is the writer's way of making the friends' theory subside ingloriously.

2. The Real Cause of Job's Dismay

The idea that Job has a defensible cause or sees farther than they is wholly lost on the friends; to them he is simply a wicked man tormented by the consciousness of guilt, and they attribute the tumult of his thoughts to a wrath, or vexation, which blinds and imperils his soul (compare 5:2; 18:4). That is not the cause of his dismay at all, nor is it merely that his personal fate is inscrutable (compare 23:17 margin). He is confounded rather, even to horror, because the probable facts of the world-order prove the utter falsity of all that they allege. Leaving his case, the righteous man's, out of the account, he sees the wicked just as prosperous, just as secure, just as honored in life and death, as the righteous (21:5–15, 29–33). The friends ought to see so plain a fact as well as he (21:29). To all outward appearance there is absolutely no diversity of fate between righteous and wicked (21:23–26). The friends' cut-and-dried Wisdom-doctrine and their thrifty haste to justify God (compare 13:7, 8) have landed them in a lie; the truth is that God has left His times mysterious to men (24:1). They may as well own to the full the baffling fact of the impunity of wickedness; the whole of Job 24 is taken up with details of it. Wisdom, with its rigid law of reward and punishment, has failed to penetrate the secret. A hard regime of justice, work and wage, conduct and desert, does not sound the deep truth of God's dealings, either with righteous or wicked. What then? Shall Wisdom go, or shall it rise to a higher level of outlook and insight?

3. Manhood in the Ore

In some such dim inquiry as this, it would seem, Job goes on from where his friends sit silenced to figure some positive solution of things as they are. He begins with himself and his steadfastly held integrity, sealing his utterance by the solemn Hebrew oath (27:2–6), and as solemnly disavowing all part or sympathy with the wicked (27:7; compare 21:16). He has already found a meaning in his own searching experience; he is being tried for a sublime assay, in which all that is permanent and precious in him shall come out as gold (23:10). But this thought of manhood in the ore is no monopoly of his; it may hold for all. What then of the wicked? In a passage which some have deemed the lost third speech of Zophar (27:8–23), and which, indeed, recounts what all the friends have seen (27:12), he sets forth the case of the wicked in its true light. The gist of it is that the wicked have not the joy of God (27:10), or the peace of a permanent hope. It is in much the same tone as the friends' diatribes, but with a distinct advance from outward disaster toward tendency and futility. The ore is not being purged for a noble assay; and this will work their woe. Then finally, in the celebrated Job 28, comes up the summary of wisdom itself. That remains, after all this testing of motive, a thing intact and elemental; and man's part in it is just what Job's life has been, to fear God and shun evil (28:28).

4. Job Reads His Indictment

As the crowning pronouncement on things as they are, Job in his final and longest speech, describes in a beautiful retrospect his past life, from his "autumn days" when the friendship of God was over his tent and he was a counselor and benefactor among men (Job 29), through this contrasted time of his wretchedness and curse-betraying disease, when the most degraded despise him (Job 30), until now as he draws consciously near the grave, he recounts in solemn review the principles and virtues that have guided his conduct—a noble summary of the highest Hebrew ideals of character (Job 31). This he calls, in sublime irony, the indictment which his Adversary has written; and like a prince, bearing it on his shoulder and binding it to him like a crown, he is ready to take it with him beyond the bourn to the presence of his Judge. With this tremendous proposal, sanctioned Hebrew-fashion by a final curse if it prove false, the words of Job are ended.

E) The Denouncement

The friends are silenced, not enlightened. They have clung to their hard thesis to the stubborn end; postulating enough overt crime on Job's part to kill him (Job 22:5–9), and clinching their hypothesis with their theory of innate depravity (Job 4:18, 19; 15:14, 15; 25:4–6); but toward Job's higher level of honest integrity and exploring faith they have not advanced one inch; and here they lie, fossilized dogmatists, fixed and inveterate in their *odium theologicum*–a far cry from the friendship that came from afar to condole and console. Job, on the other hand, staking all on the issue of his integrity, has held on his way in sturdy consistency (compare 17:9), and stood his ground before the enigma of things as they are. Both parties have said their say; the story is evidently ready for its denouement. Job, too, is ready for the determining word, though it would seem he expects it to be spoken only in some unseen tribunal; the friends rather savagely wish that God would speak and reprove Job for his presumption (compare 11:5, 11). But how shall the solution be brought about in this land of Uz where all may see? And above all, how shall it affect the parties concerned? A skillfully told story should not leave this out.

1. The self-constituted interpreter

For this determining pronouncement the writer has chosen to have both parties definitely represented, apparently at their best. So, instead of proceeding at once to the summons from the whirlwind, he introduces here a new character, Elihu, a young man, who has listened with growing impatience to the fruitless discussion, and now must set both parties right or burst (Job 32:19). It is like the infusion of young blood into a theodicy too arrogant in its antiquity (compare Job 8:8–10; 15:10, 18; 12:12 margin, or better as question). This character of Elihu is conceived in a spirit of satire, not without a dash of grim humor. His self-confidence, not to say conceit, is strongly accentuated (Job 32:11–22); he assumes the umpire function for which Job has pleaded (33:6, 7; compare 9:33–35; 13:20–22); and is sure he represents the perfect in knowledge (36:2–4; 37:16). He speaks four times, addressing himself alternately to Job and the friends. His words, though designedly diffuse, are not without wisdom and beauty; he makes less of Job's deep-seated iniquity than do the friends, but blames him for speaking in the wicked man's idiom (34:7–9, 36, 37), and warns him against inclining more to iniquity than submission (36:21); but his positive contribution to the discussion is the view he holds of the chastening influence of dreams and visions (33:14–18; compare 7:13–15), and of the pains of disease (33:19–28), especially if the sufferer has an "angel (messenger) interpreter" to reveal its meaning, such a one perhaps as Elihu feels himself to be. As he proceeds in his speech, his words indicate that a storm is rising; and so long as it is distant he employs it to descant on the wonders of God in Nature, wonders which to him mean little more than arbitrary marvels of power; but as it approaches nearer and shows exceptional phenomena as of a theophany, his words become incoherent, and he breaks off with an abject attempt to disclaim his pretensions. Such is the effect, with him, of the near presence of God. It overwhelms, paralyzes, stops the presumptuous currents of life.

2. The Whirlwind and the Voice

The writer of the book has not committed the literary fatuity of describing the whirlwind, except as Elihu has seen its oncoming, first with conceit of knowledge, then with wild access of terror—a description in which his essentially vapid personality is reflected. For the readers the significance of the whirlwind is in the Voice it encloses, the thing it says. And here the writer has undertaken the most tremendous task ever attempted by the human imagination: to make the Almighty speak, and speak in character. The whole of the two discourses from the whirlwind is descriptive; a recounting of observable phenomena of created nature, from the great elemental things, earth and sea and light and star and storm, to the varied wonders of animal nature—all things in which the questing mind of man may share, laying hold in his degree on its meaning or mystery. Thus, in literary terms, it fails at no point of the Godlike. It begins with a peremptory dismissal of Elihu: "Who is this that darkeneth counsel by words without knowledge?" (Job 38:2). Then Job is bidden gird up his loins like a strong man, and listen and answer. The fact that Job alone, of all the company, can stand, as it were, on common terms with God is premonitory of the outcome. Of the two Divine discourses, the first (Job 38; 39) emphasizes more especially the unsearchable wisdom of creation; and the lesson it brings home to Job is that a being who is great enough—or presumptuous enough—to criticize and censure is great enough to resolve his own criticism (40:2). To this, of course, Job has no answer; he has presented his plea, which he neither adds to nor takes back (40:3–5). Resuming, then, the Voice in the second discourse (40:6–41:34) goes on to describe two great beasts, as it were, elemental monsters of Nature: Behemoth—probably the hippopotamus—vast in resisting and overcoming power, yet unaware of it; and Leviathan—probably the crocodile—beautifully adapted to its function in Nature, yet utterly malignant, untamable. And the lesson brought home to Job by this strange distribution of creative power is that he, who has called in question God's right to work as He does, had better undertake to lower human pride and "tread down the wicked where they stand" (40:12), thus demonstrating his ability to save himself and manage mankind (40:14). By this illuminating thought Job's trenchancy of demand is utterly melted away into contrition and penitence (42:1–6); but one inspiring effect is his, the thing indeed which he has persistently sought (compare 23:3): God is no more a hearsay, such as the friends have defended and his Wisdom has speculated about; his eye sees Him here on earth, and still in his affliction, no stranger, but a wise Friend, just as his confident faith had pictured he would, in some embodied sphere beyond suffering (19:27).

3. The Thing That Is Right

Two of the parties in the story have met the august theophany, and it has wrought its effect on them according to the spirit of the man. The self-constituted interpreter, Elihu, has collapsed as suddenly as he swelled up and exhibited himself. The man of integrity, Job, has reached the beatific goal of his quest. What now of the friends who came from far to confirm their Wisdom, and who were so sure they were defending the mind of God? they are not left without a sufficing word, addressed straight to their spokesman Eliphaz (Job 42:7); but their way to light is through the man whose honesty they outraged. Eliphaz' closing words had promised mediatorial power to Job if he would return from iniquity and acquaint himself with God (22:30); Job is now the mediator, though he has held consistently to the terms they reprobated. And the Divine verdict on them is: "Ye have not spoken of me the thing that is right, as my servant Job hath" (42:7). These are the words of the Being who acknowledged that in permitting this whole trial He was `swallowing Job up causelessly' (2:3). Job's honest and immensely revelatory words, anger, remonstrance, bold arraignment of God's way and all, were "the thing that is right." There is no more tremendous Divine pronouncement in all Scripture than this.

4. The Restored Situation

Here certain myopic students of the Book of Job think the story should end. It offends them, apparently, to see Satan's work undone; if they had had the making of the story they would have left Job still suffering, as if disinterested virtue could not be its own reward without it. The author, at least the final author, evidently did not think so; in the ideals and sanctions that prevailed in his age he knew better what he was about. It is not my business to cut the book to modern pattern, but to note what is there. Job is restored to health, to double his former wealth, to family and honor and a ripe old age. These were what the friends predicted for him on condition of his owning to guilt and calling injustice desert; but in no word of his has he intimated that worldly reinstatement was his wish or his object, the contrary rather. And what he sought he obtained, in richer measure than he sought; obtained it still in suffering, and on earth, "in the place where may see" (compare 34:26 margin). It is no discount to the value of this, nor on the other hand is it an essential addition, to express it not only in spiritual terms, but in terms current among men. And one fundamental thing this restored situation shows, or at least takes for granted, namely, that the quarrel has not been with Wisdom itself, its essence or its sanctions, but only with its encroaching false motive. Deepened, not invaded, its Newtonian law that it is well with the righteous, ill with the wicked, remains intact, an external sanction to live by, in spite of temporal exceptions. A spiritual principle of great significance, too, seems to be indicated, as it were, furtively, in the words, "And Yahweh turned the captivity of Job, when he prayed for his friends." He had stood on his integrity demanding his right, and became a self-loathing penitent; out of dust and ashes he prayed for his friends, and became again such a power in health and wealth as he had been in his "autumn days."

Orr, James, M.A., D.D. General Editor, International Standard Bible Encyclopedia

Detailed outline

I. Prologue: 1:1–2:13
- A. Introduction: 1:1–5
- B. Satan's first appearance and accusation: 1:6–12
- C. Job's trial: 1:13–22
- D. Satan's second appearance and accusation: 2:1–6
- E. Job's trial: 2:7–13

II. First cycle of speeches: 3:1–14:22
- A. Job's speech: 3:1–26
- B. Eliphaz's speech: 4:1–5:27

C. Job's reply: 6:1–7:21
D. Bildad's speech: 8:1–22
E. Job's reply: 9:1–10:22
F. Zophar's speech: 11:1–20
G. Job's reply: 12:1–14:22

III. Second cycle of speeches: 15:1–21:34
A. Eliphaz's speech: 15:1–35
B. Job's reply: 16:1–17:16
C. Bildad's speech: 18:1–21
D. Job's reply: 19:1–29
E. Zophar's speech: 20:1–29
F. Job's reply: 21:1–34

IV. Third cycle of speeches: 32:1–37
A. Eliphaz's final speech: 22:1–30
B. Job's reply: 23:1–24:25
C. Bildad's final speech: 25:1–6
D. Job's reply: 26:1–31:40

V. Elihu's speeches: 32:1–37:24
A. First speech: 32:1–33:33
B. Second speech: 34:1–37
C. Third speech: 35:1–16
D. Fourth speech 36:1–37:24

VI. God's answer: 38:1–42:6
A. First speech: 38:1–40:5
1. God questions Job from the realm of creation: 38:1–38
2. God questions Job from the realm of animals: 38:39–39:30
3. God demands an answer to His questions: 40:1–2
4. Job's first answer to God: 40:3–5

B. Second speech: 40:6–42:6
1. God tells Job to save himself: 40:6–14
2. God compares the power of Job with Behemoth: 40:15–24
3. God compares the power of Job with Leviathan: 41:1–34
4. Job's second answer to God: 42:1–6
(a) He confesses lack of understanding: 42:1–3
(b) He repents of His rebellion: 42:4–6

VII. Epilogue: 42:1–17
A. Divine rebuke of Job's three friends: 42:1–9
B. Job's restoration: 42:10–17

2. Helpful summaries of Job

Bird's eye view

The book of Job records how Job reacted to his severe afflictions.

Reading plan

The following reading plan, taking one reading per day, enables you to read through Job in eighteen days.

Job 1–3
Job 4–6
Job 7–8
Job 9–11
Job 12–13
Job 14–16
Job 17–19
Job 20–21
Job 22–23
Job 24–25
Job 26–27
Job 28–29
Job 30–31
Job 32–33
Job 34–36

Job 37–38
Job 39–40
Job 41–42

Verses to memorize

Job 9:10–11

He performs wonders that cannot be fathomed, miracles that cannot be counted. When he passes me, I cannot see him, when he goes by, I cannot perceive him. KJV

Job 19:25

For I know that my redeemer liveth, and that he shall stand at the latter day on the earth: KJV

Job 42:2

"I know that you can do all things; no plan of yours can be thwarted."

Statistics

Eighteenth Old Testament book
42 chapters
1,070 verses
10,102 words
Many biblical scholars think that Job may have been the oldest of all the Old Testament books.

Famous saying found in Job

"By the skin of our teeth" Job 19:20

Names/titles given

Hebrew title: *Iyyob:* may mean either, "persecuted one," or, "repent."
Greek title in Septuagint: *Iob.*
Latin title in Vulgate: *Iob.*

3. Helpful keys to turn to in understanding Job

Key word

Tried

Key verses

Job 23:10; 37:23–24

Themes to study

God's sovereignty
How to comfort others.
Faith in times of distress

Job quoted in the New Testament

- He that taketh the wise in their craftiness
  Job 5:13 quoted in 1 Cor. 3:19
- Who hath first given to him
  Job 41:11 quoted in Rom. 11:35

Jesus in Job

In Job Jesus is our Redeemer.

Types of Jesus in Job

Job calls out for a Mediator, Job 9:33; 25:4, and witnesses that his Redeemer is alive, Job 19:25–27.

Lessons to learn from Job

- There is a battle between good and evil spiritual forces going on in the world.
- Our attitude towards suffering is very important.
- God's ways are perfect, even if we fail to comprehend them.

4. Chapter by chapter: outline of every chapter of Job

Job 1

Matthew Henry's introduction

The history of Job begins here with an account,

I. Of his great piety in general (vv. 1), and in a particular instance, v. 5.

II. Of his great prosperity, vv. 2–4.

III. Of the malice of Satan against him, and the permission he obtained to try his constancy, vv. 6–12.

IV. Of the surprising troubles that befell him, the ruin of his estate (vv. 13–17), and the death of his children, vv. 18, 19.

V. Of his exemplary patience and piety under these troubles, vv. 20–22. In all this he is set forth for an example of suffering affliction, from which no prosperity can secure us, but through which integrity and uprightness will preserve us.

A detailed analysis of chapter

Job's great piety. (1)

His great prosperity. (2–4)

The malice of Satan against him, and the permission he obtained to test him. (6–12)

The surprising troubles that befell him, and the ruin of his estate. (13–17)

The death of his children. (18, 19)

His exemplary patience and piety under these troubles. (20–22)

Key verse

Verse 21, "And said, Naked came I out of my mother's womb, and naked shall I return thither; the LORD gave, and the LORD hath taken away; blessed be the name of the LORD"

Key word

Verse 1, "blameless."

Key event / key person / key theme

Satan's testing of Job's faith in God.

Key thought

The problem of why innocent people suffer is introduced.

Key thing to look out for

Job faces up to reality – but does not look for someone or something to blame. He praises God.

Key Bible cross-reference

Verse 21. See Ecclesiastes 5:15 and 1 Timothy 6:7.

Key "by way of explanation"

Verse 1, "Job . . . perfect and upright." Job may have been beyond reproach, but this verse does not mean that he was sinless.

Key "Quotable Quote"

"The greatest poem of ancient and modern times."

Alfred Tennyson (Rhyme is common in English-language poems, but it was rare in Hebrew poetry.)

Job 2

Matthew Henry's introduction

I. Satan moves for another trial, which should touch his bone and his flesh, vv. 1–5.

II. God, for holy ends, permits it, v. 6.

III. Satan smites him with a very painful and loathsome disease, vv. 7, 8.

IV. His wife tempts him to curse God, but he resists the temptation, vv. 9, 10.

V. His friends come to condole with him and to comfort him, vv. 11–13. And in this that good man is set forth for an example of suffering affliction and of patience.

A detailed analysis of chapter

Satan obtains leave to test Job. (1–6)
Job's sufferings. (7–10)
His friends come to comfort him. (11–13)

Key verse

Verse 6: "And the LORD said unto Satan, Behold, he is in thine hand; but save his life."

Key word / key phrase

Verse 1, "Satan."

Key event / key person / key theme

Job's second test

Key thought

Satan never rests.

Key thing to look out for

At this stage Job is still able to answer his wife in a good and positive way.

Key Bible cross-reference

Verse 3. See 38:2.

Key "by way of explanation"

Verse 9. Satan attempts to use Job's wife in the same way that he used Eve to tempt Adam.

Key "Quotable Quote"

"The riddles of God are more satisfying than the solutions of man."

G.K. Chesterton

Job 3

Matthew Henry's introduction

I. Complaining that he was born, vv. 1–10.

II. Complaining that he did not die as soon as he was born, vv. 11–19.

III. Complaining that his life was now continued when he was in misery, vv. 20–26.

A detailed analysis of chapter

Job complains that he was born. (1–10)
Job complaining. (11–19)
He complains of his life. (20–26)

Key verse

Verse 3: "Let the day perish wherein I was born, and the night in which it was said, There is a man child conceived."

Key word / key phrase

Verse 3, "may the day of my birth perish."

Key event / key person / key theme

Job speaks

Key thought

Job now curses the day he was born.

Key thing to look out for

Just because godly people commit some serious sin it does not mean that they will not later repent.

Key Bible cross-reference

Verses 21, 22. Job just wanted to die. See Revelation 9:6.

Key "by way of explanation"

Verse 8. In the east people used to pronounce curses on people, on days, and on objects.

Key "Quotable Quote"

"A believer may pass through much affliction, and yet secure very little blessing from it all. Abiding in Christ is the secret of securing all that the Father meant the chastisement to bring us."

Andrew Murray

Job 4

Matthew Henry's introduction

I. He bespeaks a patient hearing, v. 2.

II. He compliments Job with an acknowledgment of the eminence and usefulness of the profession he had made of religion, vv. 3, 4.

III. He charges him with hypocrisy in his profession, grounding his charge on his present troubles and his conduct under them, vv. 5, 6.

IV. To make good the inference, he maintains that man's wickedness is that which always brings God's judgments, vv. 7–11.

V. He corroborates his assertion by a vision which he had, in which he was reminded of the incontestable purity and justice of God, and the meanness, weakness, and sinfulness of man, vv. 12–21. By all this he aims to bring down Job's spirit and to make him both penitent and patient under his afflictions.

A detailed analysis of chapter

Eliphaz reproves Job. (4:1–6)

And maintains that God's judgments are for the wicked. (4:7–11)

The vision of Eliphaz. (4:12–21)

Eliphaz urges that the sin of sinners is their ruin. (5:1–5)

God is to be taken notice of in affliction. (5:6–16)

The happy end of God's correction. (5:17–27)

Key verse

Chapter 4, verse 1: "Then Eliphaz the Temanite answered."

Key word / key phrase

5:17, "Blessed is the man whom God corrects."

Key event / key person / key theme

Eliphaz replies

Key thought

It is easy to give unhelpful advice.

Key thing to look out for

It is wrong to always equate suffering and the Lord's punishment.

Key Bible cross-reference

4:1. See Genesis 36:11; Amos 1:12; Job 2:11.

Key "by way of explanation"

4:17–21. Eliphaz tells Job that he should be grateful that God is punishing him.

Key "Quotable Quote"

"Our affliction is not execution, but a correction."

Thomas Brooks

Job 5

Matthew Henry's introduction

Eliphaz, in the previous chapter, for the making good of his charge against Job, had vouched a word from heaven, sent him in a vision. In this chapter he appeals to those that bear record on earth, to the saints, the faithful witnesses of God's truth in all ages, v. 1. They will testify,

I. That the sin of sinners is their ruin, vv. 2–5.

II. That yet affliction is the common lot of mankind, vv. 6, 7.

III. That when we are in affliction it is our wisdom and duty to apply to God, for he is able and ready to help us, vv. 8–16.

IV. That the afflictions which are borne well will end well; and Job particularly, if he would come to a better temper, might assure himself that God had great mercy in store for him, vv. 17–27. So that he concludes his discourse in somewhat a better humor than he began it.

A detailed analysis of chapter

Eliphaz reproves Job. (4:1–6)

And maintains that God's judgments are for the wicked. (4:7–11)

The vision of Eliphaz. (4:12–21)

Eliphaz urges that the sin of sinners is their ruin. (5:1–5)

God is to be taken notice of in affliction. (5:6–16)

The happy end of God's correction. (5:17–27)

Key verse

Chapter 4, verse 1: "Then Eliphaz the Temanite answered."

Key word / key phrase

5:17, "Blessed is the man whom God corrects."

Key event / key person / key theme

Eliphaz replies

Key thought

It is easy to give unhelpful advice.

Key thing to look out for

It is wrong to always equate suffering and the Lord's punishment.

Key Bible cross-reference

4:1. See Genesis 36:11; Amos 1:12; Job 2:11.

Key "by way of explanation"

4:17–21. Eliphaz tells Job that he should be grateful that God is punishing him.

Key "Quotable Quote"

"Our affliction is not execution, but a correction."

Thomas Brooks

Job 6

Matthew Henry's introduction

I. Job shows that he had just cause to complain as he did of his troubles, and so it would appear to any impartial judge, vv. 2–7.
II. He continues his passionate wish that he might speedily be cut off by the stroke of death, and so be eased of all his miseries, vv. 8–13.
III. He reproves his friends for their uncharitable censures of him and their unkind treatment, vv. 14–30.

A detailed analysis of chapter

Job justifies his complaints. (6:1–7)
He longs for death. (6:8–13)
Job reproves his friends as unkind. (6:14–30)
Job's troubles. (7:1–6)
Job expostulates with God. (7:7–16)
He begs release. (7:17–21)

Key verse

Chapter 6, verse 2: "Oh that my grief were thoroughly weighed, and my calamity laid in the balances together!"

Key word / key phrase

6:2, "my anguish."

Key event / key person / key theme

Job's reply

Key thought

To accuse one's "comforters" gets you nowhere, see 6:27.

Key thing to look out for

As God knows everything about us it is pointless to justify ourselves before him.

Key Bible cross-reference

6:14, 15. See Galatians 6:1.

Key "by way of explanation"

Not having entered into the depths of Job's suffering, Eliphaz cannot say anything that will help.

Key "Quotable Quote"

"Let us learn like Christians to kiss the rod, and love it."

John Bunyan

Job 7

Matthew Henry's introduction

Job, in this chapter, goes on to express the bitter sense he had of his calamities and to justify himself in his desire of death.

I. He complains to himself and his friends of his troubles, and the constant agitation he was in, vv. 1–6.
II. He turns to God, and expostulates with him (v. 7, to the end), in which,
   A. He pleads the final period which death puts to our present state, vv. 7–10.
   B. He passionately complains of the miserable condition he was now in, vv. 11–16.
   C. He wonders that God will thus contend with him, and begs for the pardon of his sins and a speedy release out of his miseries, vv. 17–21. It is hard to methodize

the speeches of one who owned himself almost desperate, 6:26.

A detailed analysis of chapter

Job justifies his complaints. (6:1–7)

He longs for death. (6:8–13)

Job reproves his friends as unkind. (6:14–30)

Job's troubles. (7:1–6)

Job expostulates with God. (7:7–16)

He begs release. (7:17–21)

Key verse

Chapter 6, verse 2: "Oh that my grief were thoroughly weighed, and my calamity laid in the balances together!"

Key word / key phrase

6:2, "my anguish."

Key event / key person / key theme

Job's reply

Key thought

To accuse one's "comforters" gets you nowhere, see 6:27.

Key thing to look out for

As God knows everything about us it is pointless to justify ourselves before him.

Key Bible cross-reference

6:14, 15. See Galatians 6:1.

Key "by way of explanation"

Not having entered into the depths of Job's suffering, Eliphaz cannot say anything that will help.

Key "Quotable Quote"

"Let us learn like Christians to kiss the rod, and love it."

John Bunyan

Job 8

Matthew Henry's introduction

In this chapter Eliphaz endeavors to convince Job,

I. That he had spoken too passionately, v. 2.

II. That he and his children had suffered justly, vv. 3, 4.

III. That, if he were a true penitent, God would soon turn his captivity, vv. 5–7.

IV. That it was a usual thing for Providence to extinguish the joys and hopes of wicked men as his were extinguished; and therefore that they had reason to suspect him for a hypocrite, vv. 8–19.

V. That they would be abundantly confirmed in their suspicion unless God did speedily appear for his relief, vv. 20–22.

A detailed analysis of chapter

Bildad reproves Job. (1–7)

Hypocrites will be destroyed. (8–19)

Bildad applies God's just dealing to Job. (20–22)

Key verse

Verse 1: "Then answered Bildad the Shuhite"

Key word / key phrase

Verse 2, "a blustering wind."

Key event / key person / key theme

Bildad's advice

Key thought

Bildad is a hopeless comforter, calling Job an evildoer, verse 20.

Key thing to look out for

Bildad also accuses Job of being a hypocrite, verse 13.

Key Bible cross-reference

Verse 9. See 14:2; Psalm 102:11.

Key "by way of explanation"

Verse 3. Bildad is rather jumping the gun to ask Job the question, "Does God pervert justice?" when Job has not accused God of that.

Key "Quotable Quote"

"Brains can argue, but it takes heart to comfort."

Samuel Chadwick

Job 9

Matthew Henry's introduction

In this chapter we have,

I. The doctrine of God's justice laid down, v. 2.

II. The proof of it, from his wisdom, and power, and sovereign dominion, vv. 3–13.

III. The application of it, in which,

A. He condemns himself, as not able to contend with God either in law or battle, vv. 14–21.

B. He maintains his point, that we cannot judge of men's character by their outward condition, vv. 22–24.

C. He complains of the greatness of his troubles, the confusion he was in, and the loss he was at what to say or do, vv. 25–35.

A detailed analysis of chapter

Job acknowledges God's justice. (9:1–13)

He is not able to contend with God. (9:14–21)

Men are not to be judged by their outward condition. (9:22–24)

Job complains of troubles. (9:25–35)

Job complains of his hardships. (10:1–7)

He pleads with God as his Maker. (10:8–13)

He complains of God's severity. (10:14–22)

Key verse

Chapter 9, verse 13: "If God will not withdraw his anger, the proud helpers do stoop under him."

Key word / key phrase

9:1, "righteous before God."

Key event / key person / key theme

Job's reply

Key thought

When things are difficult it helps to think about God's characteristics.

Key thing to look out for

It does not help to question God's existence, especially if we are depressed.

Key Bible cross-reference

9:3. Note how Job uses courtroom vocabulary. See also 9:15, 32, 14, 15, 16, 19, 20, 24, 32.

Key "by way of explanation"

10:8–11 is a poetic description of a baby created by God in the womb. See Psalm 139:13–16.

Key "Quotable Quote"

"God does not comfort us to make us comfortable, but to make us comforters."

J.H. Jowett

Job 10

Matthew Henry's introduction

Job owns here that he was full of confusion (v. 15), and as he was so was his discourse: he knew not what to say, and perhaps sometimes scarcely knew what he said. In this chapter,

I. He complains of the hardships he was under (vv. 1–7), and then comforts himself with this, that he was in the hand of the God that made him, and pleads that, vv. 8–13.

II. He complains again of the severity of God's dealings with him (vv. 14–17), and then comforts himself with this, that death would put an end to his troubles, vv. 18–22.

A detailed analysis of chapter

Job acknowledges God's justice. (9:1–13)
He is not able to contend with God. (9:14–21)
Men are not to be judged by their outward condition. (9:22–24)
Job complains of troubles. (9:25–35)
Job complains of his hardships. (10:1–7)
He pleads with God as his Maker. (10:8–13)
He complains of God's severity. (10:14–22)

Key verse

Chapter 9, verse 13: "If God will not withdraw his anger, the proud helpers do stoop under him."

Key word / key phrase

9:1, "righteous before God."

Key event / key person / key theme

Job's reply

Key thought

When things are difficult it helps to think about God's characteristics.

Key thing to look out for

It does not help to question God's existence, especially if we are depressed.

Key Bible cross-reference

9:3. Note how Job uses courtroom vocabulary. See also 9:15, 32, 14, 15, 16, 19, 20, 24, 32.

Key "by way of explanation"

10:8–11 is a poetic description of a baby created by God in the womb. See Psalm 139:13–16.

Key "Quotable Quote"

"God does not comfort us to make us comfortable, but to make us comforters."

J.H. Jowett

Job 11

Matthew Henry's introduction

Poor Job's wound's were yet bleeding, his sore still runs and ceases not, but none of his friends bring him any oil, any balm; Zophar, the third, pours into them as much vinegar as the two former had done.

I. He exhibits a very high charge against Job, as proud and false in justifying himself, vv. 1–4.

II. He appeals to God for his conviction, and begs that God would take him to task (v. 5) and that Job might be made sensible,

A. Of God's unerring wisdom and his inviolable justice, v. 6.

B. Of his unsearchable perfections, vv. 7–9.

C. Of his incontestable sovereignty and uncontrollable power, v. 10.

D. Of the cognizance he takes of the children of men, vv. 11, 12.

III. He assures him that, on his repentance and reformation (vv. 13, 14), God would restore him to his former prosperity and safety (vv. 15–19); but that, if he were wicked it was in vain to expect it, v. 20.

A detailed analysis of chapter

Zophar reproves Job. (1–6)
God's perfections and almighty power. (7–12)
Zophar assures Job of blessings if he repents. (13–20)

Key verse

Verse 1: "Then answered Zophar the Naamathite."

Key word / key phrase

Verse 3, "your idle talk."

Key event / key person / key theme

Zophar's speech

Key thought

Zophar does not show any compassion toward Job.

Key thing to look out for

Zophar accuses Job of being guilty of thoughts and attitudes of which he is not guilty.

Key Bible cross-reference

Verses 8,9. See Ephesians 3:18.

Key "by way of explanation"

Verse 4. Job maintained that he was blameless. But Zophar accuses him of claiming to have reached the heights of sinless perfection.

Key "Quotable Quote"

"Comfort yourself with the sovereign Physician of both the soul and the body."

Brother Lawrence

Job 12

Matthew Henry's introduction

In this and the two following chapters we have Job's answer to Zophar's discourse, in which, as before, he first reasons with his friends (see 13:19) and then turns to his God, and directs his expostulations to him, from thence to the end of his discourse. In this chapter he addresses himself to his friends, and,

I. He condemns what they had said of him, and the judgment they had given of his character, vv. 1–5.

II. He contradicts and confronts what they had said of the destruction of wicked people in this world, showing that they often prosper, vv. 6–11.

III. He consents to what they had said of the wisdom, power, and sovereignty of God, and the dominion of his providence over the children of men and all their affairs; he confirms this, and enlarges on it, vv. 12–25.

A detailed analysis of chapter

Job reproves his friends. (12:1–5)

The wicked often prosper.(12:6–11)

Job speaks of the wisdom and power of God. (12:12–25)

Job reproves his friends. (13:1–12)

He professes his confidence in God. (13:13–22)

Job pleads to know his sins. (13:23–28)

Job speaks of man's life. (14:1–6)

Of man's death. (14:7–15)

By sin man is subject to corruption. (14:16–22)

Key verse

Chapter 12, verse 3: "But I have understanding as well as you; I am not inferior to you."

Key word / key phrase

12:3, "I am not inferior to you."

Key event / key person / key theme

Job's reply

Key thought

Job was helped by the silent sympathy of his friends, 13:5, but not by their advice.

Key thing to look out for

Job speaks to his three friends, 12:2–13:19, and then to God, 13:14–14:22.

Key Bible cross-reference

14:2. See Psalm 37:2; Isaiah 40:7, 24.

Key "by way of explanation"

12:20. Job's reaction to the advice of his friends is to reply with biting sarcasm.

Key "Quotable Quote"

"To comfort a sorrowful conscience is much better than to possess many kingdoms."

Martin Luther

Job 13

Matthew Henry's introduction

Job here comes to make application of what he had said in the previous chapter; and now we have him not in so good a temper as he was in then: for,

I. He is very bold with his friends, comparing himself with them, notwithstanding the mortifications he was under, vv. 1, 2. Condemning them for their falsehood, their forwardness to judge, their partiality and deceitfulness under color of pleading God's cause (vv. 4–8), and threatening them with the judgments of God for their so doing (vv. 9–12), desiring them to be silent (vv. 5, 13, 17), and turning from them to God, v. 3.

II. He is very bold with his God.

A. In some expressions his faith is very bold, yet that is not more bold than welcome, vv. 15, 16, 18. But,

B. In other expressions his passion is rather too bold in expostulations with God about the deplorable condition he was in (vv. 14, 19, etc.), complaining of the confusion he was in (vv. 20–22), and the loss he was at to find out the sin that provoked God thus to afflict him, and in short of the rigor of God's proceedings against him, vv. 23–28.

A detailed analysis of chapter

Job reproves his friends. (12:1–5)

The wicked often prosper.(12:6–11)

Job speaks of the wisdom and power of God. (12:12–25)

Job reproves his friends. (13:1–12)

He professes his confidence in God. (13:13–22)

Job pleads to know his sins. (13:23–28)

Job speaks of man's life. (14:1–6)

Of man's death. (14:7–15)

By sin man is subject to corruption. (14:16–22)

Key verse

Chapter 12, verse 3: "But I have understanding as well as you; I am not inferior to you."

Key word / key phrase

12:3, "I am not inferior to you."

Key event / key person / key theme

Job's reply

Key thought

Job was helped by the silent sympathy of his friends, 13:5, but not by their advice.

Key thing to look out for

Job speaks to his three friends, 12:2–13:19, and then to God, 13:14–14:22.

Key Bible cross-reference

14:2. See Psalm 37:2; Isaiah 40:7,24.

Key "by way of explanation"

12:20. Job's reaction to the advice of his friends is to reply with biting sarcasm.

Key "Quotable Quote"

"To comfort a sorrowful conscience is much better than to possess many kingdoms."

Martin Luther

Job 14

Matthew Henry's introduction

We have here an account,

I. Of man's life, that it is,

A. Short, v. 1.

B. Sorrowful, v.1.

C. Sinful, v. 4.

D. Stinted, vv. 5, 14.

II. Of man's death, that it puts a final period to our present life, to which we shall not again return (vv. 7–12), that it hides us from the calamities of life (v. 13), destroys the hopes of life (vv. 18, 19), sends us away from the business of life (v. 20), and keeps us in the dark about our relations in this life, how much soever we have formerly been in care about them vv. 21, 22.

III. The use Job makes of all this.

A. He pleads it with God, who, he thought, was too strict and severe with him (vv. 16, 17), begging that, in consideration of his frailty, he would not contend with him (v. 3), but grant him some respite, v. 6.

2. He engages himself to prepare for death (v. 14), and encourages himself to hope that it would be comfortable to him, v. 15. This chapter is proper for funeral solemnities; and serious meditations on it will help us both to get good by the death of others and to get ready for our own.

A detailed analysis of chapter

Job reproves his friends. (12:1–5)

The wicked often prosper.(12:6–11)

Job speaks of the wisdom and power of God. (12:12–25)

Job reproves his friends. (13:1–12)

He professes his confidence in God. (13:13–22)

Job pleads to know his sins. (13:23–28)

Job speaks of man's life. (14:1–6)

Of man's death. (14:7–15)

By sin man is subject to corruption. (14:16–22)

Key verse

Chapter 12, verse 3: "But I have understanding as well as you; I am not inferior to you."

Key word / key phrase

12:3, "I am not inferior to you."

Key event / key person / key theme

Job's reply

Key thought

Job was helped by the silent sympathy of his friends, 13:5, but not by their advice.

Key thing to look out for

Job speaks to his three friends, 12:2–13:19, and then to God, 13:14–14:22.

Key Bible cross-reference

14:2. See Psalm 37:2; Isaiah 40:7, 24.

Key "by way of explanation"

12:20. Job's reaction to the advice of his friends is to reply with biting sarcasm.

Key "Quotable Quote"

"To comfort a sorrowful conscience is much better than to possess many kingdoms."

Martin Luther

Job 15

Matthew Henry's introduction

Eliphaz here keeps close to the principles on which he had condemned Job, and,

I. He reproves him for justifying himself, and fathers on him many evil things which are unfairly inferred thence, vv. 2–13.

II. He persuades him to humble himself before God and to take shame to himself, vv. 14–16.

III. He reads him a long lecture about the woeful estate of wicked people, who harden their hearts against God and the judgments which are prepared for them, vv. 17–35. A good use may be made both of his reproofs (for they are plain) and of his doctrine (for it is sound), though both the one and the other are misapplied to Job.

A detailed analysis of chapter

Eliphaz reproves Job. (1–16)

The character of wicked men. (17–35)

Key verse

Verse 5: "For thy mouth uttereth thine iniquity, and thou choosest the tongue of the crafty."

Key word / key phrase

Verse 3, "useless words."

Key event / key person / key theme

Eliphaz's second speech

Key thought

Eliphaz again says that the wicked suffer because of their wickedness.

Key thing to look out for

Eliphaz does not allow the question, "Why do the innocent suffer?"

Key Bible cross-reference

Verse 5. See Matthew 15:11, 17–18.

Key "by way of explanation"

Verses 7–10. Eliphaz says that Job is guilty of thinking that he can sit alongside members of God's council when he is no wiser than the ordinary person.

Key "Quotable Quote"

"In Christ the heart of the Father is revealed, and higher comfort there cannot be than to rest in the Father's heart."

Andrew Murray

Job 16

Matthew Henry's introduction

This chapter begins Job's reply to that discourse of Eliphaz which we had in the previous chapter; it is but the second part of the same song of lamentation with which he had before bemoaned himself, and is set to the same melancholy tune.

I. He upbraids his friends with their unkind usage of him, vv. 1–5.

II. He represents his own case as very deplorable on all accounts, vv. 6–16.

III. He still holds fast his integrity, about which he appeals to God's righteous judgment from the unrighteous censures of his friends, vv. 14–22.

A detailed analysis of chapter

Job reproves his friends. (16:1–5)

He represents his case as deplorable. (16:6–16)

Job maintains his innocence. (16:17–22)

Job appeals from man to God. (17:1–9)

His hope is not in life, but in death. (17:10–16)

Key verse

Chapter 15, verse 11: "God hath delivered me to the ungodly, and turned me over into the hands of the wicked."

Key word / key phrase

16:1, "Job replied."

Key event / key person / key theme

Job's reply

Key thought

Job calls his three friends, "miserable comforters," 16:1.

Key thing to look out for

Job continues to maintain his innocence and to complain about his suffering.

Key Bible cross-reference

16:4. See Psalm 22:7; Jeremiah 48:27; Matthew 27:39.

Key "by way of explanation"

16:18–21. Job now feels that on earth he will

never be vindicated, so his only hope is that he will have a friend in heaven.

Key "Quotable Quote"

"Little things console us because little things afflict us."

Blaise Pascal

Job 17

Matthew Henry's introduction

In this chapter,

I. Job reflects on the harsh censures which his friends had passed on him, and looking on himself as a dying man (v. 1), he appeals to God, and begs of him speedily to appear for him, and right him, because they had wronged him, and he knew not how to right himself, vv. 2–7. But he hopes that, though it should be a surprise, it will be no stumbling-block, to good people, to see him thus abused, vv. 8, 9.

II. He reflects on the vain hopes they had fed him with, that he should yet see good days, showing that his days were just at an end, and with his body all his hopes would be buried in the dust, vv. 10–16.

A detailed analysis of chapter

Job reproves his friends. (16:1–5)
He represents his case as deplorable. (16:6–16)
Job maintains his innocence. (16:17–22)
Job appeals from man to God. (17:1–9)
His hope is not in life, but in death. (17:10–16)

Key verse

Chapter 15, verse 11: "God hath delivered me to the ungodly, and turned me over into the hands of the wicked."

Key word / key phrase

16:1, "Job replied."

Key event / key person / key theme

Job's reply

Key thought

Job calls his three friends, "miserable comforters," 16:1.

Key thing to look out for

Job continues to maintain his innocence and to complain about his suffering.

Key Bible cross-reference

16:4. See Psalm 22:7; Jeremiah 48:27; Matthew 27:39.

Key "by way of explanation"

16:18–21. Job now feels that on earth he will never be vindicated, so his only hope is that he will have a friend in heaven.

Key "Quotable Quote"

"Little things console us because little things afflict us."

Blaise Pascal

Job 18

Matthew Henry's introduction

I. Bildad sharply reproves Job as haughty and passionate, and obstinate in his opinion, vv. 1–4.

II. He enlarges on the doctrine he had before maintained, about the miser of wicked people and the ruin that attends them, vv. 5–21.

A detailed analysis of chapter

Bildad reproves Job. (1–4)

Ruin attends the wicked. (5–10)

The ruin of the wicked. (11–21)

Key verse

Verse 1: "Then answered Bildad the Shuhite."

Key word / key phrase

Verse 21, "an evil man."

Key event / key person / key theme

Bildad's second speech

Key thought

When a person pleads for comfort it is not a good time to start accusing him of wrongdoing.

Key thing to look out for

Bildad accuses Job of being full of self-pity.

Key Bible cross-reference

Verse 21. See Hosea 4:1–2, 6.

Key "by way of explanation"

Verses 5–21. Bildad treats Job to another poem about how the wicked suffer.

Key "Quotable Quote"

"The hill of comfort is the hill of Calvary; the house of consolation is built with the wood of the cross."

C.H. Spurgeon

Job 19

Matthew Henry's introduction

This chapter is Job's answer to Bildad's discourse in the previous chapter. Though his spirit was grieved and much heated, and Bildad was very peevish, yet he gave him leave to say all he designed to say, and did not break in on him in the midst of his argument; but, when he had done, he gave him a fair answer, in which,

I. He complains of unkind usage. And very unkindly he takes it.

A. That his comforters added to his affliction, vv. 2–7.

B. That his God was the author of his affliction, vv. 8–12.

C. That his relations and friends were strange to him, and shy of him, in his affliction, vv. 20–22.

II. He comforts himself with the believing hopes of happiness in the other world, though he had so little comfort in this, making a very solemn confession of his faith, with a desire that it might be recorded as an evidence of his sincerity, vv. 23–27.

III. He concludes with a caution to his friends not to persist in their hard censures of him, vv. 28, 29

A detailed analysis of chapter

Job complains of unkindness. (1–7)

God the Author of Job's afflictions. (8–22)

Job's belief in the resurrection. (23–29)

Key verse

Verse 6: "Know now that God hath overthrown me, and hath compassed me with his net."

Key word / key phrase

Verse 3, "you attack me."

Key event / key person / key theme

Job's reply

Key thought

Job knows that there is more to existence than just this life.

Key thing to look out for

Job is comforted by the thought that one day he will stand in the presence of his Redeemer.

Key Bible cross-reference

Verse 3. See Genesis 31:41; 1 Samuel 1:8.

Key "by way of explanation"

Verse 25. Despite all his difficulties Job still believes that his Redeemer will vindicate him against all his accusers.

Key "Quotable Quote"

"God made the body as well as the soul, and redemption is for the whole man."

Francis A. Schaeffer

Job 20

Matthew Henry's introduction

One would have thought that such an excellent confession of faith as Job made, in the close of the previous chapter, would satisfy his friends, or at least mollify them; but they do not seem to have taken any notice of it, and therefore Zophar here takes his turn, enters the lists with Job, and attacks him with as much vehemence as before.

I. His preface is short, but hot, vv. 2, 3.

II. His discourse is long, and all on one subject, the very same that Bildad was large on (ch. 18.), the certain misery of wicked people and the ruin that awaits them.

A. He asserts, in general, that the prosperity of a wicked person is short, and his ruin sure, vv. 4–9.

B. He proves the misery of his condition by many instances—that he should have a diseased body, a troubled conscience, a ruined estate, a beggared family, an infamous name and that he himself should perish under the weight of divine wrath: all this is most curiously described here in lofty expressions and lively similitudes; and it often proves true in this world, and always in another, without repentance, vv. 10–29.

A detailed analysis of chapter

Zophar speaks of the short joy of the wicked. (1–9)

The ruin of the wicked. (10–22)

The portion of the wicked. (23–29)

Key verse

Verse 1: "Then answered Zophar the Naamathite."

Key word / key phrase

Verse 3, “dishonors me.”

Key event / key person / key theme

Zophar’s second speech

Key thought

Zophar points to himself and his own prosperity as proof of his own righteousness.

Key thing to look out for

Do not make unhelpful comparisons when trying to bring comfort.

Key Bible cross-reference

Verse 18. See Ecclesiastes 2:18–23.

Key “by way of explanation”

Verse 29. Zophar’s speech is “remorselessly irrelevant to Job’s true situation” (David Clines).

Key “Quotable Quote”

“If we have not quiet in our minds, outward comfort will do no more for us than a golden slipper on a gouty foot.”

John Bunyan

Job 21

Matthew Henry’s introduction

I. Job’s preface here is designed for the moving of their affections, that he might gain their attention, vv. 1–6.

II. His discourse is designed for the convincing of their judgments and the rectifying of their mistakes. He owns that God does sometimes hang up a wicked man as it were in chains, in terrorem—as a terror to others, by some visible remarkable judgment in this life, but denies that he always does so; nay, he maintains that commonly he does otherwise, suffering even the worst of sinners to live all their days in prosperity and to go out of the world without any visible mark of his wrath on them.

A. He describes the great prosperity of wicked people, vv. 7–13.

B. He shows their great impiety, in which they are hardened by their prosperity, vv. 14–16.

C. He foretells their ruin at length, but after a long reprieve, vv. 17–21.

D. He observes a very great variety in the ways of God’s providence towards men, even towards bad men, vv. 22–26.

E. He overthrows the ground of their severe censures of him, by showing that the destruction of the wicked is reserved for the other world, and that they often escape to the last in this world (v. 27, to the end), and in this Job was clearly in the right.

A detailed analysis of chapter

Job entreats attention. (1–6)

The prosperity of the wicked. (7–16)

The dealings of God’s providence. (17–26)

The judgment of the wicked is in the world to come. (27–34)

Key verse

Verse 2: “Hear diligently my speech, and let this be your consolations.”

Key word / key phrase

Verse 34, "your nonesense."

Key event / key person / key theme

Job's reply

Key thought

Job points out that it is an observable fact that the wicked do prosper in this life.

Key thing to look out for

Job expresses his faith in God whom he knows is in control of the world.

Key Bible cross-reference

Verse 13. See Psalm 35:20.

Key "by way of explanation"

Verse 4. Job complains against God, blaming him for his present suffering.

Key "Quotable Quote"

"Sometimes a light surprises
The Christian while he sings;
It is the Lord who rises
With healing in his wings;
When comforts are declining,
He grants the soul again;
A season of clear shining,
To cheer it after rain."

William Cowper

Job 22

Matthew Henry's introduction

In this chapter,

I. Eliphaz checks him for his complaints of God, and of his dealings with him, as if he thought God had done him wrong, vv. 2–4.

II. He charges him with many high crimes and misdemeanors, for which he supposes God was now punishing him.

A. Oppression and injustice, vv. 5–11.

B. Atheism and infidelity, vv. 12–14.

III. He compares his case to that of the old world, vv. 15–20.

IV. He gives him very good counsel, assuring him that, if he would take it, God would return in mercy to him and he should return to his former prosperity, vv. 21–30.

A detailed analysis of chapter

Eliphaz shows that God does not rebuke piety. (1–4)

Job accused of wickedness. (5–14)

The world before the Flood. (15–20)

Eliphaz exhorts Job to repent. (21–30)

Key verse

Verse 2: "Can a man be profitable unto God, as he that is wise may be profitable unto himself?"

Key word / key phrase

Verse 21, "submit to God."

Key event / key person / key theme

Eliphaz's third speech

Key thought

Eliphaz continues to accuse Job of being wicked.

Key thing to look out for

Eliphaz thinks that all Job wants is the restoration of his prosperity.

Key Bible cross-reference

Verse 9. See 24:3; Isaiah 1:17.

Key "by way of explanation"

Chapters 22–26 contain the third round of speeches between Job and his three friends.

Key "Quotable Quote"

"God is our true Friend, who always gives us the counsel and comfort we need."

François Fénelon

Job 23

Matthew Henry's introduction

I. Job complains of his calamitous condition, and especially of God's withdrawings from him, so that he could not get his appeal heard (vv. 2–5), nor discern the meaning of God's dealings with him (vv. 8, 9), nor gain any hope of relief, vv. 13, 14. This made deep impressions of trouble and terror on him, vv. 15–17. But,

II. In the midst of these complaints he comforts himself with the assurance of God's clemency (vv. 6, 7), and his own integrity, which God himself was a witness to, vv. 10–12.

A detailed analysis of chapter

Job complains that God has withdrawn. (23:1–7)
He asserts his own integrity. (23:8–12)
Job is terrified. (23:13–17)
Wickedness is often unpunished. (24:1–12)
The wicked shun the light. (24:13–17)
Judgments for the wicked. (24:18–25)

Key verse

Chapter 23, verse 2: "Even to day is my complaint bitter: my stroke is heavier than my groaning."

Key word / key phrase

23:2, "my complaint is bitter."

Key event / key person / key theme

Job's reply

Key thought

Job points out how much injustice there is in the world.

Key thing to look out for

Job states that evil people rebel against the light, which is found in God's Law.

Key Bible cross-reference

24:20. See 21:26; Isaiah 14:11.

Key "by way of explanation"

23:8, 10. Job agrees that God is testing him, not in order to show up any wickedness in him but to demonstrate that he is pure as gold.

Key "Quotable Quote"

"All human comfort is vain and short."

Thomas à Kempis

Job 24

Matthew Henry's introduction

I. Those that openly do wrong to their poor neighbors are not reckoned with, nor the injured righted (vv. 2–12), though the former are very barbarous, vv. 21, 22.

II. Those that secretly practice mischief often go undiscovered and unpunished, vv. 13–17.

III. That God punished such by secret judgments and reserves them for future judgments (vv. 18–20, and 23–25), so that, on the whole matter, we cannot say that all who are in trouble are wicked; for it is certain that all who are in prosperity are not righteous.

A detailed analysis of chapter

Job complains that God has withdrawn. (23:1–7)
He asserts his own integrity. (23:8–12)
Job is terrified. (23:13–17)
Wickedness is often unpunished. (24:1–12)
The wicked shun the light. (24:13–17)
Judgments for the wicked. (24:18–25)

Key verse

Chapter 23, verse 2: "Even to day is my complaint bitter: my stroke is heavier than my groaning."

Key word / key phrase

23:2, "my complaint is bitter."

Key event / key person / key theme

Job's reply

Key thought

Job points out how much injustice there is in the world.

Key thing to look out for

Job states that evil people rebel against the light, which is found in God's Law.

Key Bible cross-reference

24:20. See 21:26; Isaiah 14:11.

Key "by way of explanation"

23:8, 10. Job agrees that God is testing him, not in order to show up any wickedness in him but to demonstrate that he is pure as gold.

Key "Quotable Quote"

"All human comfort is vain and short."

Thomas à Kempis

Job 25

Matthew Henry's introduction

Job in a few words shows the infinite distance there is between God and man, teaching us,

I. To think highly and honorably of God, vv. 2, 3, 5.

II. To think meanly of ourselves, vv. 4, 6. These, however misapplied to Job, are two good lessons for us all to learn.

A detailed analysis of chapter

Bildad shows that man cannot be justified before God. (1–6)

Key verse

Verse 4: "How then can man be justified with God?"

Key word / key phrase

Verse 6, "a maggot."

Key event / key person / key theme

Bildad's third speech

Key thought

Bildad repeats his previous thoughts. A comforter would do better to be silent than to continually repeat his advice.

Key thing to look out for

Bildad emphasizes the depravity of humankind.

Key Bible cross-reference

Verses 4–6. See 4:17–19; 15:14–16.

Key "by way of explanation"

Verse 3. Bildad states that everything has to submit to God's light.

Key "Quotable Quote"

"The broken and the jaded and the twisted are being ministered to by God through the saints who are not overcome by their own panic, who because of their oneness with him are absolutely at rest. Consequently he can work through them."

Oswald Chambers

Job 26

Matthew Henry's introduction

I. Job shows that Bildad's discourse was foreign to the matter he was discoursing of—though very true and good, yet not to the purpose, vv. 2–4.

II. That it was needless to the person he was discoursing with; for he knew it, and believed it, and could speak of it as well as he and better, and could add to the proofs which he had produced of God's power and greatness, which he does in the rest of his discourse (vv. 5–13), concluding that, when they had both said what they could, all came short of the merit of the subject and it was still far from being exhausted, v. 14.

A detailed analysis of chapter

Job reproves Bildad. (1–4)

Job acknowledges the power of God. (5–14)

Key verse

Verse 3: "How hast thou counseled him that hath no wisdom?"

Key word / key phrase

Verse 3, "without wisdom."

Key event / key person / key theme

Job's reply

Key thought

Job begins with a round of sarcasm.

Key thing to look out for

Verse 4. What spirit moved Bildad?

Key Bible cross-reference

Verse 5. See Proverbs 2:18; Isaiah 14:9; 26:14.

Key "by way of explanation"

Verses 5–14. Job is still able to speak of God's great power.

Key "Quotable Quote"

"You don't have to be alone in your hurt! Comfort is yours. Joy is an option. And it's all been made possible by your Savior."

Joni Eareckson Tada

Job 27

Matthew Henry's introduction

I. Job begins with a solemn protestation of his integrity and of his resolution to hold it fast, vv. 2–6.

II. He expresses the dread he had of that hypocrisy which they charged him with, vv. 7–10.

III. He shows the miserable end of wicked people, notwithstanding their long prosperity, and the curse that attends them and is entailed on their families, vv. 11–23.

A detailed analysis of chapter

Job protests his sincerity. (1–6)
The hypocrite is without hope. (7–10)
The miserable end of the wicked. (11–23)

Key verse

Verse 6: "My righteousness I hold fast."

Key word / key phrase

Verse 11, "I will teach you."

Key event / key person / key theme

Job's closing discourse

Key thought

Job continues to state his own innocence.

Key thing to look out for

Verses 1–6. What does Job hold on to?

Key Bible cross-reference

Verse 6. See 2:3.

Key "by way of explanation"

Verse 7. Job asks that his friends may be treated as if they were wicked men!

Key "Quotable Quote"

"It will greatly comfort you if you can see God's hand in both your losses and your crosses."

C.H. Spurgeon

Job 28

Matthew Henry's introduction

Job here shows,

I. About worldly wealth, how industriously that is sought for and pursued by the children of men, what pains they take, what contrivances they have, and what hazards they run to get it, vv. 1–11.

II. About wisdom, v. 12. In general, the price of it is very great; it is of inestimable value, vv. 15–19. The place of it is very secret, vv. 14, 20, 22. In particular, there is a wisdom which is hidden in God (vv. 23–27) and there is a wisdom which is revealed to the children of men, v. 28. Our enquiries into the former must be checked, into the latter quickened, for that is it which is our concern.

A detailed analysis of chapter

Worldly wealth. (1–11)
Wisdom is of inestimable value. (12–19)

Wisdom is the gift of God. (20–28)

Key verse

Verse 1: "Surely there is a vein for the silver, and a place for gold where they fine it."

Key word / key phrase

Verse 28, "wisdom."

Key event / key person / key theme

Interlude on wisdom

Key thought

Men and women look all over the world for wisdom.

Key thing to look out for

Wisdom can only be found in God.

Key Bible cross-reference

Verses 25–27. See Proverbs 8:22–31.

Key "by way of explanation"

Verses 1–11 give a description of mines in current times. "Wisdom" here means a full understanding of the universe. Although this wisdom is beyond humankind, practical down-to-earth wisdom is within human reach (verse 28).

Key "Quotable Quote"

"The beginning of divine wisdom is clemency and gentleness, which arise from greatness of soul and the bearing of infirmities of men."

Isaac of Nineveh

Job 29

Matthew Henry's introduction

In this chapter Job looks back to the days of his prosperity, and shows,

I. What comfort and satisfaction he had in his house and family, vv. 1–6.

II. What a great deal of honor and power he had in his country, and what respect was paid him by all sorts of people, vv. 7–10.

III. What abundance of good he did in his place, as a magistrate, vv. 11–17.

IV. What a just prospect he had of the continuance of his comfort at home (vv. 18–20) and of his interest abroad, vv. 21–25.

A detailed analysis of chapter

Job's former comforts. (1–6)

The honor paid to Job. His usefulness. (7–17)

His prospect of prosperity. (18–25)

Key verse

Verse 6: "When I washed my steps with butter, and the rock poured me out rivers of oil."

Key word / key phrase

Verse 21, "men listened to me."

Key event / key person / key theme

Job recalls his previous honor and blessing

Key thought

Job speaks about the time when he used to be a repected member of the city council.

Key thing to look out for

Verses 12, 13. Job reminds his friends that people

used to go to him for advice and practical help.

Key Bible cross-reference

Verse 14. See Isaiah 59:17; 61:10.

Key "by way of explanation"

In chapters 29–31 Job summarizes the position he is in.

Key "Quotable Quote"

"Down through the centuries in times of trouble and trial God has brought courage to the hearts of those who love him."

Billy Graham

Job 30

Matthew Henry's introduction

I. Job had lived in great honor, but now he had fallen into disgrace, and was as much vilified, even by the meanest, as ever he had been magnified by the greatest; this he insists much on, vv. 1–14.

II. He had had much inward comfort and delight, but now he was a terror and burden to himself (vv. 15, 16) and overwhelmed with sorrow, vv. 28–31.

III. He had long enjoyed a good state of health, but now he was sick and in pain, vv. 17–19, 29, 30.

IV. Time was when the secret of God was with him, but now his communication with heaven was cut off, vv. 20–22.

V. He had promised himself a long life, but now he saw death at the door, v. 23. One thing he mentions, which aggravated his affliction, that it surprised him when he looked for peace. But two things gave him some relief:

A. That his troubles would not follow him to the grave, v. 24.

B. That his conscience witnessed for him that, in his prosperity, he had sympathized with those that were in misery, v. 25.

A detailed analysis of chapter

Job's honor is turned into contempt. (1–14)

Job is a burden to himself. (15–31)

Key verse

Verse 5: "They were driven forth from among men."

Key word / key phrase

Verse 1, "mock me."

Key event / key person / key theme

Job's present dishonor and suffering

Key thought

Job remains very angry with God.

Key thing to look out for

The very great contrast between Job's past and present life.

Key Bible cross-reference

Verse 11. See 29:20.

Key "by way of explanation"

Verse 31. Job says that God has heaped burdens on him which he cannot bear.

Key "Quotable Quote"

"Human comfort and divine comfort are of different natures: human comfort consists in external, visible help, which a man may see, hold, and feel; divine comfort is only in words and promises, where there is neither seeing, hearing, nor feeling."

Martin Luther

Job 31

Matthew Henry's introduction

I. The sins from which he here acquits himself are,

A. Wantonness and uncleanness of heart, vv. 1–4.

B. Fraud and injustice in commerce, vv. 4–8.

C. Adultery, vv. 9–12.

D. Haughtiness and severity towards his servants, vv. 13–15.

E. Unmercifulness to the poor, the widows, and the fatherless, vv. 16–23.

F. Confidence in his worldly wealth, vv. 24, 25.

G. Idolatry, vv. 26–28.

H. Revenge, vv. 29–31.

I. Neglect of poor strangers, v. 32.

J. Hypocrisy in concealing his own sins and cowardice in conniving at the sins of others, vv. 33, 34.

K. Oppression, and the violent invasion of other people's rights, vv. 38–40. And towards the close, he appeals to God's judgment about his integrity, vv. 35–37.

A detailed analysis of chapter

Job declares his uprightness. (1–8)

His integrity. (9–15)

Job is merciful. (16–23)

Job is not guilty of covetousness or idolatry. (24–32)

Job is not guilty of hypocrisy and violence. (33–40)

Key verse

Verse 5: "If I have walked with vanity, or if my foot hath hasted to deceit."

Key word / key phrase

Verse 4, "Does he not see my ways?"

Key event / key person / key theme

Job protests his innocence

Key thought

Job continues to defend himself as if he is on trial in a courtroom.

Key thing to look out for

Job states that he is innocent of all the sins he lists.

Key Bible cross-reference

Verse 16. See 6:2; Proverbs 16:12.

Key "by way of explanation"

Verses 24–28. Greed and idolatry are both said to be evil in God's sight.

Key "Quotable Quote"

"The Bible is filled with assurances of God's help and comfort in every kind of trouble which might cause fears to arise in the human heart."

Billy Graham

Job 32

Matthew Henry's introduction

In this chapter we have,

I. Some account of him, his parentage, his presence at this dispute, and his sentiments about it, vv. 1–5.

II. The apology he made for his bold undertaking to speak to a question which had been so largely and learnedly argued by his seniors. He pleads,

A. That, though he had not the experience of an old man, yet he had the understanding of a man, vv. 6–10.

B. That he had patiently heard all they had to say, vv. 11–13.

C. That he had something new to offer, vv. 14–17.

D. That his mind was full of this matter, and it would be a refreshment to him to give it vent, vv. 18–20.

E. That he was resolved to speak impartially, vv. 21, 22.

A detailed analysis of chapter

Elihu is displeased at the dispute between Job and his friends. (32:1–5)

He reproves them. (32:6–14)

He speaks impartially. (32:15–22)

Elihu offers to reason with Job. (33:1–7)

Elihu blames Job for reflecting upon God. (33:8–13)

God calls men to repentance. (33:14–18)

God sends afflictions for good. (33:19–28)

Elihu entreats Job's attention. (33:29–33)

Key verse

Chapter 32, verse 1: "So these three men ceased to answer Job, because he was righteous in his own eyes."

Key word / key phrase

32:3, "angry with the three friends."

Key event / key person / key theme

Elihu's first speech

Key thought

Elihu talks to Job by name, which his other three friends did not.

Key thing to look out for

Elihu speaks about redemption being possible through a mediator.

Key Bible cross-reference

Verse 6. See Jeremiah 1:6–8; 1 Timothy 4:12.

Key "by way of explanation"

32:18. Elihu is indeed "full of words," and his four speeches continue to the end of chapter 37.

Verse 1. Job continued to maintain his innocence.

Key "Quotable Quote"

"I now possess not merely consolation, but the God of consolation."

Jeanne Guyon

Job 33

Matthew Henry's introduction

I. Elihu bespeaks Job's favorable acceptance of what he should say, and desires he would take him for that person whom he had so often wished for, that would plead with him, and receive his plea on God's behalf, vv. 1–7.

II. He does, in God's name, bring an action against him, for words which he had spoken, in the heat of disputation, reflecting on God as dealing hardly with him, vv. 8–11.

III. He endeavors to convince him of his fault and folly herein, by showing him,

A. God's sovereign dominion over man, vv. 12, 13.

B. The care God takes of man, and the various ways and means he uses to do his soul good, which we have reason to think he designs when he lays bodily afflictions on him, v. 14.

1. Job had sometimes complained of unquiet dreams, 7:14. "Why," says Elihu, "God sometimes speaks conviction and instruction to men by such dreams," vv. 15–18.
2. Job had especially complained of his sicknesses and pains; and, as to these, he shows largely that they were so far from being tokens of God's wrath, as Job took them, or evidences of Job's hypocrisy, as his friends took them, that they were really wise and gracious methods, which divine grace took for the increase of his acquaintance with God, to work patience, experience, and hope, vv. 19–30. And, lastly, he concludes with a request to Job, either to answer him or give him leave to go on, vv. 31–33.

A detailed analysis of chapter

Elihu is displeased at the dispute between Job and his friends. (32:1–5)
He reproves them. (32:6–14)
He speaks impartially. (32:15–22)
Elihu offers to reason with Job. (33:1–7)
Elihu blames Job for reflecting upon God. (33:8–13)
God calls men to repentance. (33:14–18)
God sends afflictions for good. (33:19–28)
Elihu entreats Job's attention. (33:29–33)

Key verse

Chapter 32, verse 1: "So these three men ceased to answer Job, because he was righteous in his own eyes."

Key word / key phrase

32:3, "angry with the three friends."

Key event / key person / key theme

Elihu's first speech

Key thought

Elihu talks to Job by name, which his other three friends did not.

Key thing to look out for

Elihu speaks about redemption being possible through a mediator.

Key Bible cross-reference

Verse 6. See Jeremiah 1:6–8; 1 Timothy 4:12.

Key "by way of explanation"

32:18. Elihu is indeed "full of words," and his

four speeches continue to the end of chapter 37.

Verse 1. Job continued to maintain his innocence.

Key "Quotable Quote"

"I now possess not merely consolation, but the God of consolation."

Jeanne Guyon

Job 34

Matthew Henry's introduction

I. Elihu speaks not only the audience, but the assistance of the company, vv. 2–4.

II. He charges Job with some more indecent expressions that had dropped from him, vv. 5–9.

III. He undertakes to convince him that he had spoken amiss, by showing very fully,

A. God's incontestable justice, vv. 10–12, 17, 19, 23.

B. His sovereign dominion, vv. 13–15.

C. His almighty power, vv. 20, 24.

D. His omniscience, vv. 21, 22, 25.

E. His severity against sinners, vv. 26–28.

F. His overruling providence, vv. 29, 30.

IV. He teaches him what he should say, vv. 31, 32. And then, lastly, he leaves the matter to Job's own conscience, and concludes with a sharp reproof of him for his peevishness and discontent, vv. 33–37.

A detailed analysis of chapter

Elihu accuses Job of charging God with injustice. (1–9)

God cannot be unjust. (10–15)

God's power and providence. (16–30)

Elihu reproves Job. (31–37)

Key verse

Verse 9: "For he hath said, It profiteth a man nothing that he should delight himself with God."

Key word / key phrase

Verse 4, "Let us discern."

Key event / key person / key theme

Elihu's second proposition

Key thought

Elihu does not like the way in which Job appeared to make the Lord the author of evil.

Key thing to look out for

Elihu champions God's glory.

Key Bible cross-reference

Verse 15. See Ecclesiastes 12:7.

Key "by way of explanation"

Verses 5, 9. Elihu attempts to correct what he deems to be Job's theological errors. 9:14–125; 16:11–17.

Key "Quotable Quote"

"God does not leave us comfortless, but we have to be in dire need of comfort to know the truth of his promise."

Peter Marshall

Job 35

Matthew Henry's introduction

I. Elihu had represented religion as an indifferent unprofitable thing, which God enjoins for his own sake, not for ours; Elihu evinces the contrary, vv. 1–8.

II. He had complained of God as deaf to the cries of the oppressed, against which imputation Elihu here justifies God, vv. 9–13.

III. He had despaired of the return of God's favor to him, because it was so long deferred, but Elihu shows him the true cause of the delay, vv. 14–16.

A detailed analysis of chapter

Elihu speaks of man's behavior. (1–8)

Why those who cry out under afflictions are not taken notice of. (9–13)

Elihu reproves Job's impatience. (14–26)

Key verse

Verse 2: "Thinkest thou this to be right, that thou saidst, My righteousness is more than God's?"

Key word / key phrase

Verse 2, "Cleared by God."

Key event / key person / key theme

Elihu's third proposition

Key thought

Elihu tells Job that he is wrong to accuse God of being silent.

Key thing to look out for

Elihu quite misses the point. He seems not to have been listening to what Job has actually been saying.

Key Bible cross-reference

Verse 2. See 13:18.

Key "by way of explanation"

Verse 9. Elihu includes Job among those who cry out to God but do not believe that he is the God of justice.

Key "Quotable Quote"

"Apt words have power to assuage
The tumors of a troubled mind
And are as balm to festered wounds."

John Milton

Job 36

Matthew Henry's introduction

Here we have,

I. His preface, vv. 2–4.

II. The account he gives of the methods of God's providence towards the children of men, according as they conduct themselves, vv. 5–15.

III. The fair warning and good counsel he gives to Job thereon, vv. 16–21.

IV. His demonstration of God's sovereignty and omnipotence, which he gives instances of in the operations of common providence, and which is a reason why we should all submit to him in his dealings with us, vv. 22–33. This he prosecutes and enlarges on in the following chapter.

A detailed analysis of chapter

Elihu desires Job's attention. (36:1–4)

The methods God uses to deal with people. (36:5–14)

Elihu counsels Job. (36:15–23)

The wonders in the works of creation. (36:24–33)

Elihu observes the power of God. (37:1–13)

Job required to explain the works of nature. (37:14–20)

God is great, and is to be feared. (37:21–24)

Key verse

36:3: "I will fetch my knowledge from afar, and will ascribe righteousness to my Maker."

Key word / key phrase

36:4, "my words are not false."

Key event / key person / key theme

Elihu's fourth proposition

Key thought

Elihu tells Job to avoid evil and so not come under God's judgment.

Key thing to look out for

Elihu points Job to God's magnificent creation.

Key Bible cross-reference

36:21. See 1:8; 2:3.

Key "by way of explanation"

36:6–9. In contrast to Job's assertions Elihu insists that God rewards the righteous and punishes sinners.

Key "Quotable Quote"

"Those who can sit in silence with their fellowman, not knowing what to say but knowing that they should be there, can bring new life in a dying heart."

Henri J.M. Nouwen

Job 37

Matthew Henry's introduction

Here Elihu observes the hand of God,

I. In the thunder and lightning, vv. 1–5.

II. In the frost and snow, the rains and wind, vv. 6–13.

III. He applies it to Job, and challenges him to solve the phenomena of these works of nature, that confessing his ignorance in them, he might own himself an incompetent judge in the proceedings of divine Providence, vv. 14–22. And then,

IV. Concludes with his principle, which he undertook to make out, That God is great and greatly to be feared, vv. 23, 24.

A detailed analysis of chapter

Elihu desires Job's attention. (36:1–4)

The methods God uses to deal with people. (36:5–14)

Elihu counsels Job. (36:15–23)

The wonders in the works of creation. (36:24–33)

Elihu observes the power of God. (37:1–13)

Job required to explain the works of nature. (37:14–20)

God is great, and is to be feared. (37:21–24)

Key verse

36:3: "I will fetch my knowledge from afar, and will ascribe righteousness to my Maker."

Key word / key phrase

36:4, "my words are not false."

Key event / key person / key theme

Elihu's fourth proposition

Key thought

Elihu tells Job to avoid evil and so not come under God's judgment.

Key thing to look out for

Elihu points Job to God's magnificent creation.

Key Bible cross-reference

36:21. See 1:8; 2:3.

Key "by way of explanation"

36:6–9. In contrast to Job's assertions Elihu insists that God rewards the righteous and punishes sinners.

Key "Quotable Quote"

"Those who can sit in silence with their fellowman, not knowing what to say but knowing that they should be there, can bring new life in a dying heart."

Henri J.M. Nouwen

Job 38

Matthew Henry's introduction

I. The Lord begins with an awakening challenge and demand in general, vv. 2, 3.

II. He proceeds in divers particular instances and proofs of Job's utter inability to contend with God, because of his ignorance and weakness: for,

A. He knew nothing of the founding of the earth, vv. 4–7.

B. Nothing of the limiting of the sea, vv. 8–11.

C. Nothing of the morning light, vv. 12–15.

D. Nothing of the dark recesses of the sea and earth, vv. 16–21.

E. Nothing of the springs in the clouds (vv. 22–27), nor the secret counsels by which they are directed.

F. He could do nothing towards the production of the rain, or frost, or lightning (vv. 28–30, 34, 35, 37, 38), nothing towards the directing of the stars and their influences (vv. 31–33), nothing towards the making of his own soul, v. 36. And lastly, he could not provide for the lions and the ravens, vv. 39–41.

A detailed analysis of chapter

God calls upon Job to answer. (38:1–3)
God questions Job. (38:4–11)
Light and darkness. (38:12–24)
Other mighty works. (38:25–41)
God asks Job about several animals. (39:1–30)

Key verse

38:1: "Then the LORD answered Job out of the whirlwind."

Key word / key phrase

38:2, "words without knowledge."

Key event / key person / key theme

God reminds Job about the amazing world of nature

Key thought

God's creatures point to God's sovereignty.

Key thing to look out for

Job is reminded that God cares for the animals.

Key Bible cross-reference

38:7. See Psalm 148:2, 3.

Key "by way of explanation"

God responds, not from a courtroom, but from a storm. Job is challenged to look again at the mystery of the world.

Key "Quotable Quote"

"You can look ahead with promise, hope, and joy."

Billy Graham

Job 39

Matthew Henry's introduction

God proceeds here to show Job what little reason he had to charge him with unkindness who was so compassionate to the inferior creatures and took such a tender care of them, or to boast of himself, and his own good deeds before God, which were nothing to the divine mercies. He shows him also what great reason he had to be humble who knew so little of the nature of the creatures about him and had so little influence on them, and to submit to that God on whom they all depend. He discourses particularly,

I. About the wild goats and hinds, vv. 1–4.
II. About the wild ass, vv. 5–8.
III. About the unicorn, vv. 9–12.
IV. About the peacock, v. 13.
V. About the ostrich, vv. 13–18.
VI. About the horse, vv. 19–25.
VII. About the hawk and the eagle, vv. 26–30.

A detailed analysis of chapter

God calls upon Job to answer. (38:1–3)
God questions Job. (38:4–11)
Light and darkness. (38:12–24)
Other mighty works. (38:25–41)
God asks Job about several animals. (39:1–30)

Key verse

38:1: "Then the LORD answered Job out of the whirlwind."

Key word / key phrase

38:2, "words without knowledge."

Key event / key person / key theme

God reminds Job about the amazing world of nature

Key thought

God's creatures point to God's sovereignty.

Key thing to look out for

Job is reminded that God cares for the animals.

Key Bible cross-reference

38:7. See Psalm 148:2, 3.

Key "by way of explanation"

God responds, not from a courtroom, but from a storm. Job is challenged to look again at the mystery of the world.

Key "Quotable Quote"

"You can look ahead with promise, hope, and joy."

Billy Graham

Job 40

Matthew Henry's introduction

Many humbling confounding questions God had put to Job, in the previous chapter; now, in this chapter,

I. He demands an answer to them, vv. 1, 2.

II. Job submits in a humble silence, vv. 3–5.

III. God proceeds to reason with him, for his conviction, about the infinite distance and disproportion between him and God, showing that he was by no means an equal match for God. He challenges him (vv. 6, 7) to vie with him, if he durst, for justice (v. 8), power (v. 9), majesty (v. 10), and dominion over the proud (vv. 11–14), and he gives an instance of his power in one particular animal, here called "Behemoth," vv. 15–24.

A detailed analysis of chapter

Job humbles himself to God. (1–5)

The Lord reasons with Job to show his righteousness, power, and wisdom. (6–14)

God's power shown in the behemoth. (15–24)

Key verse

Verse 4: "Behold, I am vile; what shall I answer thee?"

Key word / key phrase

Verse 3, "I am unworthy."

Key event / key person / key theme

Job replies to the Lord

Key thought

The Lord demolishes Job's attempts at self-justification.

Key thing to look out for

In the opening verses of this chapter God shows Job how feeble he is.

Key Bible cross-reference

Verses 11, 12. See Isaiah 13:11.

Key "by way of explanation"

Verse 15. This "behemoth" is not easy to identify, beyond the fact that it is a very large land animal.

Key "Quotable Quote"

"When the house doth sigh and weep,
And the world is drowned in sleep,
Yet mine eyes the watch do keep,
Sweet Spirit comfort me!"

Robert Herrick

Job 41

Matthew Henry's introduction

I. To convince Job of his own weakness he is here challenged to subdue and tame this leviathan if he can, and make himself master of him (vv. 1–9), and, since he cannot do this, he must own himself utterly unable to stand before the great God, v. 10.

II. To convince Job of God's power and terrible majesty several particular instances are here given of the strength and terror of the leviathan, which is no more than what God has given him, nor more than he has under his check, vv. 11, 12. The face of the leviathan is here described to be terrible (vv. 12, 14), his scales close (vv. 15–17), his breath sparkling (vv. 18–21), his flesh firm (vv. 22–24), his strength and spirit, when he is attacked, insuperable (vv. 25–30), his motions turbulent, and disturbing to the waters (vv. 31, 32), so that, on the whole, he is a very terrible creature, and man is no match for him, vv. 33, 34.

A detailed analysis of chapter

Leviathan. (1–34)

Key verse

Verse 1: "Canst thou draw out leviathan with an hook?"

Key word / key phrase

Verse 11, "everything . . . belongs to me."

Key event / key person / key theme

The Lord's second discourse

Key thought

No creatures are God's equal.

Key thing to look out for

The Lord is not impressed by the proud.

Key Bible cross-reference

Verse 11. See Romans 11:35.

Key "by way of explanation"

Verse 10. The leviathan is mightier than the behemoth. The Lord is mightier than the leviathan.

Key "Quotable Quote"

"My soul cannot be fully comforted or perfectly refreshed, except in God alone, who is the Comforter of the poor in spirit and the Embracer of the humble and low in heart."

Thomas à Kempis

Job 42

Matthew Henry's introduction

I. It has been a great trouble to us to see such a holy man as Job was so fretful, and peevish, and uneasy to himself, and especially to hear him quarrel with God and speak indecently to him; but, though he thus fall, he is not utterly cast down, for here he recovers his temper, comes to himself and to his right mind again by repentance, is sorry for what he has said amiss, unsays it, and humbles himself before God, vv. 1–6.

II. It has been likewise a great trouble to us to see Job and his friends so much at variance, not only differing in their opinions, but giving one another a great many hard words, and passing severe censures one on another, though they were all very wise and good men; but here we have this grievance redressed likewise, the differences between them happily adjusted, the quarrel taken up, all the peevish reflections they had cast on one another forgiven and forgotten, and all joining in sacrifices and prayers, mutually accepted of God, vv. 7–9.

III. It has troubled us to see a man of such eminent piety and usefulness as Job was so grievously afflicted, so pained, so sick, so poor, so reproached, so slighted, and made the very center of all the calamities of human life; but here we have this grievance redressed too, Job healed of all his ailments, more honored and beloved than ever, enriched with an estate double to what he had before, surrounded with all the comforts of life, and as great an instance of prosperity as ever he had been of affliction and patience, vv. 10–17. All this is written for our learning, that we, under these and the like discouragements that we meet with, through patience and comfort of this scripture may have hope.

A detailed analysis of chapter

Job humbly submits unto God. (1–6)
Job intercedes for his friends. (7–9)
His renewed prosperity. (10–17)

Key verse

Verse 5: "I have heard of thee by the hearing of the ear: but now mine eye seeth thee."

Key word / key phrase

Verse 6, "I . . . repent."

Key event / key person / key theme

Job repents

Key thought

No final "answer" to the problem of the suffering of the innocent is given.

Key thing to look out for

Job is content to rest in God's presence.

Key Bible cross-reference

Verse 5. See Isaiah 6:5.

Key "by way of explanation"

Verses 7,8. The phrase "my servant Job," repeated four times in these two verses, shows how the Lord viewed Job.

Key "Quotable Quote"

"When spiritual comfort is sent to you by God, take it humbly and give thanks meekly for it. But know for certain that it is the great goodness of God that sends it to you, and not because you deserve it."

Thomas à Kempis

5. Select bibliography for Job

Andersen, F. I. *Job, An Introduction and Commentary*. Downers Grove, Ill.: InterVarsity, 1976.

Calvin, J. *Sermons from Job*. Selected and translated by L. Nixon. Grand Rapids: Eerdmans, 1952.

Delitzsch, F. *Biblical Commentary on the Book of Job*. K. D. Reprint. Grand Rapids: Eerdmans, 1971.

Ellison, H. L. *From Tragedy to Triumph: The Message of the Book of Job*. Grand Rapids: Eerdmans, 1958.

Hubbard, David. *Job* (NIBC), Hendrickson, forthcoming.

Psalms

1. Book by book: Introduction to Psalms

Introduction

Title of whole book

The Hebrew title of this book is *Tehilim* ("praises" or "hymns"), for a leading feature in its contents is praise, though the word occurs in the title of only one Psalm (the hundred forty-fifth). The Greek title (in the Septuagint, a translation made two hundred years before Christ) is *psalmoi,* whence our word "Psalms." This corresponds to the Hebrew word *mizmoi* by which sixty-five Psalms are designated in their inscriptions, and which the Syriac, a language like the Hebrew, uses for the whole book. It means, as does also the Greek name, an ode, or song, whose singing is accompanied by an instrument, particularly the harp (compare 1 Chr. 16:4–8; 2 Chr. 5:12, 13). To some Psalms, the Hebrew word (*shir*) "a song," is prefixed. Paul seems to allude to all these terms in Eph. 5:19, "singing . . . in psalms, hymns, and spiritual songs."

Individual titles

To more than a hundred Psalms are prefixed inscriptions, which give one or more (and in one case, [Psalm 60], all) of these particulars: the direction to the musician, the name of the author or the instrument, the style of the music or of the poetry, the subject or occasion. The authority of these inscriptions has been disputed by some writers. They say that the earliest translators, as the Greek and Syriac, evince a disregard for their authority, by variations from a proper translation of some, altering others, and, in several instances, supplying titles to Psalms which, in Hebrew, had none. It is also alleged that the subject of a Psalm, as given in the title, is often inconsistent with its contents. But those translators have also varied from a right translation of many passages in the Bible, which all agree to be of good authority; and the alleged inconsistency may be shown, on more accurate investigation, not to exist. The admitted antiquity of these inscriptions, on the other hand, and even their obscurity, raise a presumption in their favor, while such prefaces to a composition accord with the usages of that age and part of the world (compare Is. 38:9).

"The Chief Musician" was the superintendent of music (compare "to oversee," 1 Chr. 15:21, Margin). "To" prefixed to this, means, "pertaining to" in his official character. This inscription is found in fifty-three Psalms and is attached to Habakkuk's prayer (Hab. 3:1–19). The same Hebrew preposition is prefixed to the name of the author and translated "of," as "a Psalm of David," "of Asaph," except that to "the sons of Korah," it is translated "for," which is evidently wrong, as the usual direction, "to the chief musician," is given, and no other authorship intimated. On the apparent exception to this last remark, see below, and see on Ps. 88:1, title. The explanations of other particulars in the titles will be given as they occur.

Authors

This book is often called "The Psalms of David," he being the only author mentioned in the New Testament (Luke 20:42) and his name appearing in more titles than that of any other writer. Besides about one-half of the Psalms in which it thus appears, Psalms 2 and 95 are ascribed to him (Acts 4:25 and Heb. 4:7). He was probably the author of many others which appear without a name. He used great efforts to beautify the worship of the sanctuary. Among the two hundred eighty-eight Levites he appointed for singing and performing instrumental music, we find mentioned the "sons of Korah" (1 Chr. 9:19); including Heman (1 Chr. 6:33–38); and also Asaph (1 Chr. 6:39–44); and Ethan (1 Chr. 15:17–19). God was doubtless pleased to endow these men with the inspiration of His Spirit, so that they used those poetic talents which their connection with the kindred art of music had led them to cultivate, in the production of compositions like those of their king and patron. To Asaph are ascribed twelve Psalms; to the sons of Korah, eleven, including the eighty-eighth, which is also ascribed to Heman, that being the only instance in which the name of the "son" (or descendant) is mentioned; and to Ethan, one. Solomon's name appears before the seventy-second and hundred twenty-seventh; and that of Moses before the ninetieth. Special questions respecting authorship will be explained as they arise.

Contents

As the book contains one hundred fifty independent compositions, it is not susceptible of any logical analysis. The Jews having divided it into five books, corresponding to the Five Books of Moses (First, Psalms 1–42; Second, Psalms 43–72; Third, Psalms 73–89; Fourth, Psalms 90–106; Fifth, Psalms 107–150), many attempts have been made to discover, in this division, some critical or practical value, but in vain. Sundry efforts have been made to classify the Psalms by subject. Angus' Bible Hand Book is perhaps the most useful, and is appended.

Still the Psalms have a form and character peculiar to themselves; and with individual diversities of style and subject, they all assimilate to that form, and together constitute a consistent system of moral truth. They are all poetical, and of that peculiar parallelism (see Introduction to the Poetical Books,) which distinguished Hebrew poetry. They are all lyrical, or songs adapted to musical instruments, and all religious lyrics, or such as were designed to be used in the sanctuary worship.

The distinguishing feature of the Psalms is their devotional character. Whether their matter be didactic, historical, prophetical, or practical, it is made the ground or subject of prayer, or praise, or both. The doctrines of theology and precepts of pure morality are here inculcated. God's nature, attributes, perfections, and works of creation, providence, and grace, are unfolded. In the sublimest conceptions of the most exalted verse, His glorious supremacy over the principalities of heaven, earth, and hell, and His holy, wise, and powerful control of all material and immaterial agencies, are celebrated. The great covenant of grace resting on the fundamental promise of a Redeemer, both alike the provisions of God's exhaustless mercy, is set forth in respect of the doctrines of regeneration by the Spirit, forgiveness of sins, repentance toward God, and faith toward Jesus Christ, while its glorious results, involving the salvation of men "from the ends of the earth" (Acts 13:47), are proclaimed in believing, prophetic prayer and thankful praise. The personal history of the authors, and especially David's in its spiritual aspects, is that of God's people generally. Christian biography is edifying only as it is truth illustrated in experience, such as God's Word and Spirit produce. It may be factitious in origin and of doubtful authenticity. But here the experience of the truly pious is detailed, under divine influence, and "in words which the Holy Ghost" taught (1 Cor. 2:13). The whole inner life of the pious man is laid open, and Christians of all ages have here the temptations, conflicts, perplexities, doubts, fears, penitent moanings, and overwhelming griefs on the one hand, and the joy and hope of pardoning mercy, the victory over the seductions of false-hearted flatterers, and deliverance from the power of Satan on the other, with which to compare their own spiritual exercises. Here, too, are the fruits of that sovereign mercy, so often sought in earnest prayer, and when found, so often sung in rapturous joy, exhibited by patience in adversity, moderation in prosperity, zeal for God's glory, love for man, justice to the oppressed, holy contempt for the proud, magnanimity towards enemies, faithfulness towards friends, delight in the prosperity of Zion, and believing prayer for her enlargement and perpetuity.

The historical summaries of the Psalms are richly instructive. God's choice of the patriarchs, the sufferings of the Israelites in Egypt, their exodus, temptations of God, rebellions and calamities in the wilderness, settlement in Canaan, backslidings and reformations, furnish illustrations of God's providential government of His people, individually and collectively, tending to exalt His adorable grace and abase human pride. But the promises and prophecies connected with these summaries, and elsewhere presented in the Psalms, have a far wider reach, exhibiting the relations of the book to the great theme of promise and prophecy:

The Messiah and his kingdom

David was God's chosen servant to rule His people, as the head at once of the State and the Church, the lineal ancestor, "according to the flesh" (Acts 2:30; Rom. 1:3), of His adorable Son, and His type, in His official relations, both in suffering and in triumph. Generally, David's trials by the ungodly depicted the trials of Christ, and his final success the success of Christ's kingdom. Typically, he uses language describing his feelings, which only finds its full meaning in the feelings of Christ. As such it is quoted and applied in the New Testament. And further, in view of the great promise (2Sa 7:12–16) to him and his seed, to which such frequent reference is made in the Psalms, David was inspired to know, that though his earthly kingdom should perish, his spiritual would ever endure, in the power, beneficence, and glory of Christ's. In repeating and amplifying that promise, he speaks not only as a type, but "being a prophet, and knowing that God had sworn with an oath to him, that of the fruit of his loins, according to the flesh, he would raise up Christ to sit on his throne," he "foretold the sufferings of Christ and the glory that should follow. His incarnation, humiliating sorrows, persecution, and cruel death are disclosed in the plaintive cries of a despairing sufferer; and His resurrection and ascension, His eternal priesthood, His royal dignity, His prophetical office, the purchase and bestowal of the gifts of the Spirit, the conversion of the nations, the establishment, increase, and perpetuity of the Church, the end of time, and the blessedness of the righteous who acknowledge, and the ruin of the wicked who reject this King in Zion, are predicted in the language of assured confidence and joy." While these great themes have supplied the people of God with a popular theology and a guide in religious experience and Christian morality, clothed in the language of devotion, they have provided an inspired liturgy in which the pious, of all creeds and sects, have, for nearly three thousand years, poured out their prayers and praises. The pious Jew, before the coming of Christ, mourned over the adversity, or celebrated the future glories, of Zion, in the words of her ancient king. Our Savior, with His disciples, sang one of these hymns on the night on which He was betrayed (Matt. 26:30); He took from one the words in which He uttered the dreadful sorrows of His soul (Matt. 27:46), and died with those of another on His lips (Luke 23:46). Paul and Silas in the dungeon (Acts 16:25), primitive Christians in their covert places of worship, or the costly churches of a later day, and the scattered and feeble Christian flocks in the prevalence of darkness and error through the Middle Ages, fed their faith and warmed their love with these consoling songs. Now, throughout the Christian world, in untold forms of version, paraphrase, and imitation, by Papists and Protestants, Prelatists and Presbyterians, Independents, Baptists, Methodists—men of all lands and all creeds, in public and private worship, God is still adored in the sentiments expressed in these venerable Psalms. From the tone of sorrow and suffering which pervade their earlier portions we are gradually borne on amid alternate conflicts and triumphs, mournful complaints and awakening confidence; as we approach the close the tones of sorrow grow feebler, and those of praise wax louder and stronger—till, in the exulting strains of the last Psalm, the chorus of earth mingles with the hallelujahs of the multitude, which no man can number, in the sanctuary above.

A.R. Faussett

Contents of Psalms

The psalms are songs of worship which were originally accompanied by a musical instrument. They were the hymnbook of the Israelites in their temple.

Division of the Psalms

The book contains 150 psalms, and may be divided into five great divisions or books, which must have been originally formed at different periods.

Book I is, by the superscriptions, entirely Davidic nor do we find in it a trace of any but David's authorship. We may well believe that the compilation of the book was also David's work.

Book II appears by the date of its latest psalm, (Psalms 46:1) to have been compiled in the reign of King Hezekiah. It would naturally comprise, firstly, several or most of the Levitical psalms anterior to that date; and secondly, the remainder of the psalms of David previously uncompiled. To these latter the collector after properly appending the single psalm of Solomon has affixed the notice that "the prayers of David the son of Jesse are ended." (Psalms 72:20)

Book III, the interest of which centers in the times of Hezekiah stretches out, by its last two psalms, to the reign of Manasseh: it was probably compiled in the reign of Josiah. It contains seventeen psalms, from Psalms 73–89 eleven by Asaph, four by the sons of Horah, one (86) by David, and one by Ethan.

Book IV contains the remainder of the psalms up to the date of the captivity, There are seventeen, from Psalms 90–106, one by Moses, two by David, and the rest anonymous.

Book V, the psalms of the return, contains forty-four, from Psalms 107–150, fifteen by David, one by Solomon and the rest anonymous.

Smith, William, Dr. Smith's Bible Dictionary

Detailed outline

Part one: Book one: 1–41

1:1–1:6 The Two Ways

2:1–2:11 God's Promise to His Anointed

3:1–3:8 Trust in God under Adversity

4:1–4:8 Confident Plea for Deliverance from Enemies

5:1–5:12 Trust in God for Deliverance from Enemies

6:1–6:10 Prayer for Recovery from Grave Illness

7:1–7:17 Plea for Help against Persecutors

8:1–8:9 Divine Majesty and Human Dignity

9:1–9:20 God's power and Justice

10:1–10:18 Prayer for Deliverance from Enemies

11:1–11:7 Song of Trust in God

12:1–12:8 Plea for Help in Evil Times

13:1–13:6 Prayer for Deliverance from Enemies

14:1–14:7 Denunciation of Godlessness

15:1–15:5 Who Shall Abide in God's Sanctuary?

16:1–16:11 Song of Trust and Security in God

17:1–17:15 Prayer for Deliverance from Persecutors

18:1–18:50 Royal Thanksgiving for Victory

19:1–19:14 God's Glory in Creation and the Law

20:1–20:9 Prayer for Victory

21:1–21:13 Thanksgiving for Victory

22:1–22:31 Plea for Deliverance from Suffering and Hostility

23:1–23:6 The Divine Shepherd

24:1–24:10 Entrance into the Temple

25:1–25:22 Prayer for Guidance and for Deliverance

26:1–26:12 Plea for Justice and Declaration of Righteousness

27:1–27:14 Triumphant Song of Confidence

28:1–28:9 Prayer for Help and Thanksgiving for It

29:1–29:11 The Voice of God in a Great Storm

30:1–30:12	Thanksgiving for Recovery from Grave Illness
31:1–31:24	Pray and Praise for Deliverance from Enemies
32:1–32:11	The Joy of Forgiveness
33:1–33:22	The Greatness and Goodness of God
34:1–34:22	Praise for Deliverance from Trouble
35:1–35:28	Prayer for Deliverance from Enemies
36:1–36:12	Human Wickedness and Divine Goodness
37:1–37:40	Exhortation to Patience and Trust of David
38:1–38:22	A Penitent Sufferer's Plea for Healing
39:1–39:13	Prayer for Wisdom and Forgiveness
40:1–40:17	Thanksgiving for Deliverance and Prayer for Help
41:1–41:13	Assurance of God's Help and a Plea for Healing

Part two: Book two: Psalms 42–72

42:1–42:11	Longing for God and His Help in Distress
43:1–43:5	Prayer to God in Time of Trouble
44:1–44:26	National Lament and Prayer for Help
45:1–45:17	Ode for a Royal Wedding
46:1–46:11	God's Defense of His City and People
47:1–47:9	God's Rule over the Nations
48:1–48:14	The Glory and Strength of Zion
49:1–49:20	The Folly of Trust in Riches
50:1–50:23	The Acceptable Sacrifice
51:1–51:19	Prayer for Cleansing and Pardon
52:1–52:9	Judgment on the Deceitful
53:1–53:6	Denunciation of Godlessness
54:1–54:7	Prayer for Vindication
55:1–55:23	Complaint about a Friend's Treachery
56:1–56:13	Trust in God under Persecution
57:1–57:11	Praise and Assurance under Persecution
58:1–58:11	Prayer for Vengeance
59:1–59:17	Prayer for Deliverance from Enemies
60:1–60:12	Prayer for National Victory after Defeat
61:1–61:8	Assurance of God's Protection
62:1–62:12	Song of Trust in God Alone
63:1–63:11	Comfort and Assurance in God's Presence
64:1–64:10	Prayer for Protection from Enemies
65:1–65:13	Thanksgiving for Earth's Bounty
66:1–66:20	Praise for God's Goodness to Israel
67:1–67:7	The Nations Called to Praise God
68:1–68:35	Praise and Thanksgiving
69:1–69:36	Prayer for Deliverance from Persecution
70:1–70:5	Prayer for Deliverance from Enemies
71:1–71:24	Prayer for Lifelong Protection and Help
72:1–72:20	Prayer for Guidance and Support for the King

Part three: Book three: 73–89

73:1–73:28 Plea for Relief from Oppressors
74:1–74:23 Plea for Help in Time of National Humiliation
75:1–75:10 Thanksgiving for God's Wondrous Deeds
76:1–76:16 Israel's God–Judge of All the Earth
77:1–77:20 God's Mighty Deeds Recalled
78:1–78:72 God's Goodness and Israel's Ingratitude
79:1–79:13 Plea for Mercy for Jerusalem
80:1–80:19 Prayer for Israel's Restoration
81:1–81:16 God's Appeal to Stubborn Israel
82:1–82:8 A Plea for Justice
83:1–83:18 Prayer for Judgment on Israel's Foes
84:1–84:12 The Joy of Worship in the Temple
85:1–85:13 Prayer for the Restoration of God's Favor
86:1–86:17 Supplication for Help against Enemies
87:1–87:7 The Joy of Living in Zion
88:1–88:18 Prayer for Help in Despondency
89:1–89:52 God's Covenant with David

Part four: book four: 90–106

90:1–90:17 God's Eternity and Human Frailty
91:1–91:16 Assurance of God's Protection
92:1–92:15 Thanksgiving for Vindication
93:1–93:5 The Majesty of God's Rule
94:1–94:23 God the Avenger of the Righteous
95:1–95:11 A Call to Worship and Obedience
96:1–96:13 Praise to God Who Comes in Judgment
97:1–97:12 The Glory of God's Reign
98:1–98:9 Praise the Judge of the World
99:1–99:9 Praise to God for His Holiness
100:1–100:5 All Lands Summoned to Praise God
101:1–101:8 A Sovereign's Pledge of Integrity and Justice
102:1–102:28 Prayer to the Eternal King for Help
103:1–103:22 Thanksgiving for God's Goodness
104:1–104:35 God the Creator and Provider
105:1–105:45 God's Faithfulness to Israel
106:1–106:48 A Confession of Israel's Sins

Part five: Book five: 107–150

107:1–107:43 Thanksgiving for Deliverance from Many Troubles
108:1–108:13 Praise and Prayer for Victory
109:1–109:31 Prayer for Vindication and Vengeance
110:1–110:7 Assurance of Victory for God's Priest-king
111:1–111:10 Praise for God's Wonderful Works
112:1–112:10 Blessings of the Righteous
113:1–113:9 God the Helper of the Needy
114:1–114:8 God's Wonders at the Exodus
115:1–115:18 The Impotence of Idols and the Greatness of God
116:1–116:19 Thanksgiving for Recovery from Illness
117:1–117:2 Universal Call to Worship
118:1–118:29 A Song of Victory

119:1–119:176 The Glories of God's Law
120:1–120:7 Prayer for Deliverance from Slanderers
121:1–121:8 Assurance of God's Protection
122:1–122:9 Song of Praise and Prayer for Jerusalem
123:1–123:4 Supplication for Mercy
124:1–124:8 Thanksgiving for Israel's Deliverance
125:1–125:5 The Security of God's People
126:1–126:6 A Harvest of Joy
127:1–127:5 God's Blessings in the Home
128:1–128:6 The Happy Home of the Faithful
129:1–129:8 Prayer for the Downfall of Israel's Enemies
130:1–130:8 Waiting for Divine Redemption
131:1–131:3 Song of Quiet Trust
132:1–132:18 The Eternal Dwelling of God in Zion
133:1–133:3 The Blessedness of Unity
134:1–134:3 Praise in the Night
135:1–135:21 Praise for God's Goodness and Might
136:1–136:26 God's Work in Creation and in History
137:1–137:9 Lament over the Destruction of Jerusalem
138:1–138:8 Thanksgiving and Praise of David
139:1–139:24 The Inescapable God
140:1–140:13 Prayer for Deliverance from Enemies
141:1–141:10 Prayer for Preservation from Evil
142:1–142:7 Prayer for Deliverance from Persecutors
143:1–143:12 Prayer for Deliverance from Enemies
144:1–144:15 Prayer for National Deliverance and Security
145:1–145:21 The Greatness and the Goodness of God
146:1–146:10 Praise for God's Help
147:1–147:20 Praise for God's Care for Jerusalem
148:1–148:14 Praise for God's Universal Glory
149:1–149:9 Praise for God's Goodness to Israel
150:1–150:6 Praise for God's Surpassing Greatness

2. Helpful summaries of Psalms

Bird's eye view

The Psalms were Israel's hymnbook, and contains one hundred and fifty spiritual songs.

Reading plan

The following reading plan, taking one reading per day, enables you to read through the Psalms in forty-one days.

Psalms 1–4
Psalms 5–8
Psalms 9–12
Psalms 13–16
Psalms 17–20
Psalms 21–24
Psalms 25–28
Psalms 29–32
Psalms 33–35
Psalms 36–39

Psalms 40–42
Psalms 43–46
Psalms 47–48
Psalms 49–51
Psalms 52–54
Psalms 55–56
Psalms 57–61
Psalms 62–66
Psalms 67–69
Psalms 70–72
Psalms 73–75
Psalms 76–77
Psalms 78–79
Psalms 80–84
Psalms 85–88
Psalms 89–90
Psalms 91–94
Psalms 95–101
Psalms 102–103
Psalms 104–105
Psalms 106
Psalms 107–109
Psalms 110–114
Psalms 115–118
Psalm 119:1–48
Psalm 119:49–120
Psalm 119:121–176
Psalms 120–135
Psalms 136–139
Psalms 140–144
Psalms 145–150

Verses to memorize

Psalm 1:1–3

1. Blessed is the man that walketh not in the counsel of the ungodly, nor standeth in the way of sinners, nor sitteth in the seat of the scornful.

2. But his delight is in the law of the Lord; and in his law doth he meditate day and night.

3. And he shall be like a tree planted by the rivers of water, that bringeth forth his fruit in his season; his leaf also shall not wither; and whatsoever he doeth shall prosper. KJV

Psalm 19:1

The heavens declare the glory of God; and the firmament sheweth his handywork. KJV

Psalm 19:7–9

7. The law of the Lord is perfect, converting the soul: the testimony of the Lord is sure, making wise the simple.

8. The statutes of the Lord are right, rejoicing the heart: the commandment of the Lord is pure, enlightening the eyes.

9. The fear of the Lord is clean, enduring for ever: the judgments of the Lord are true and righteous altogether. KJV

Psalm 19:14

Let the words of my mouth, and the meditation of my heart, be acceptable in thy sight, O Lord, my strength, and my redeemer. KJV

Psalm 27:1

The Lord is my light and my salvation, whom shall I fear? The Lord is my stronghold of my life, of whom shall I be afraid?

Psalm 27:14

Wait on the Lord: be of good courage, and he shall strengthen thine heart: wait, I say, on the Lord. KJV

Psalm 28:7

The Lord is my strength and my shield; my

heart trusted in him, and I am helped: therefore my heart greatly rejoiceth; and with my song will I praise him. KJV

Psalm 34:4

I sought the Lord, and he heard me, and delivered me from all my fears. KJV

Psalm 46:1

God is our refuge and strength, a very present help in trouble. KJV

Psalm 66:18

If I regard iniquity in my heart, the Lord will not hear me: KJV

Psalm 95:1

O come, let us sing unto the Lord: let us make a joyful noise to the rock of our salvation. KJV

Psalm 118:8

It is better to trust in the Lord than to put confidence in man. KJV

Psalm 119:11

Thy word have I hid in mine heart, that I might not sin against thee. KJV

Psalm 147:3

He healeth the broken in heart, and bindeth up their wounds. KJV

Statistics

Nineteenth Old Testament book

150 chapters

2,461 verses

43,743 words

The Psalms are the most often quoted Old Testament book in the New Testament.

The Psalms are the longest book in the Bible.

Famous sayings found in the Psalms

"Out of the mouths of babes" Psalm 8:2

"At my wit's end" Psalm 107:27

Names/titles given

Hebrew title: *Sepher tehillim:* "Book of Praises."

Greek title in Septuagint: *Psalmoi:* indicating that they were poems sung to musical accompaniment.

Latin title in Vulgate: *Liber Psalmorum:* "Book of Psalms."

Psalterium: "A collection of songs." This is the word that *Psalter* comes from.

3. Helpful keys to turn to in understanding Psalms

Key word

Praise, over 150 times

Key verses

Psalm 19:14; 95:1

Themes to study

Psalms of praise ideal for using today.

Different aspects of prayer

Blessings promised in the psalms.

Psalms quoted in the New Testament

- Why did the Gentiles rage?
  Ps. 2:1–2 quoted in Acts 4:25–26
- Thou art my Son, this day have I begotten thee
  Ps. 2:7 quoted in Acts 13:33, Heb. 1:5, and Heb. 5:5

- Be ye angry, and sin not
  Ps. 4:4 quoted in Eph. 4:26
- Their throat is an open sepulcher
  Ps. 5:9 quoted in Rom. 3:13
- Out of the mouth of babes
  Ps. 8:2 quoted in Matt. 21:16
- What is man, that thou art mindful of him?
  Ps. 8:4–6 quoted in Heb. 2:6–8
- He put all things in subjection under his feet
  Ps. 8:6 quoted in 1 Cor. 15:27
- Whose mouth is full of cursing and bitterness
  Ps. 10:7 quoted in Rom. 3:14
- They are together become unprofitable
  Ps. 14:1–3 quoted in Rom. 3:10–12
- Thou wilt not leave my soul unto Hades
  Ps. 16:8–11 quoted in Acts 2:25–28
- Neither was he left unto Hades
  Ps. 16:10 quoted in Acts 2:31
- Thou wilt not give thy Holy One to see destruction
  Ps. 16:10 quoted in Acts 13:35
- Therefore will I give praise unto thee among the Gentiles
  Ps. 18:49 quoted in Rom. 15:9
- Their sound went out into all the earth
  Ps. 19:4 quoted in Rom. 10:18
- My God, my God, why hast thou forsaken me?
  Ps. 22:1 quoted in Matt. 27:46 and Mark 15:34
- They parted my garments among them
  Ps. 22:18 quoted in John 19:24
- I will declare thy name unto my brethren
  Ps. 22:22 quoted in Heb. 2:12
- The earth is the Lord's, and the fullness thereof
  Ps. 24:1 quoted in 1 Cor. 10:26
- Into thy hands I commend my spirit
  Ps. 31:5 quoted in Luke 23:46
- Blessed are those whose iniquities are forgiven
  Ps. 32:1–2 quoted in Rom. 4:7–8
- He that would love life, and see good days
  Ps. 34:12–14 quoted in 1 Pet. 3:10–12
- They hated me without a cause
  Ps. 35:19 quoted in John 15:25
- There is no fear of God before their eyes
  Ps. 36:1 quoted in Rom. 3:18
- Sacrifice and offering thou wouldest not
  Ps. 40:6–8 quoted in Heb. 10:5–7
- He that eateth my bread lifted up his heel against me
  Ps. 41:9 quoted in John 13:18
- For thy sake we are killed all the day long
  Ps. 44:22 quoted in Rom. 8:36
- Thy throne, O God, is for ever and ever
  Ps. 45:6–7 quoted in Heb. 1:8–9
- That thou mightest be justified in thy words
  Ps. 51:4 quoted in Rom. 3:4
- They are together become unprofitable
  Ps. 53:1–3 quoted in Rom. 3:10–12
- They hated me without a cause
  Ps. 69:4 quoted in John 15:25
- Zeal for thy house shall eat me up
  Ps. 69:9 quoted in John 2:17 and Rom. 15:3
- Let their table be made a snare
  Ps. 69:22–23 quoted in Rom. 11:9–10
- Let his habitation be made desolate
  Ps. 69:25 quoted in Acts 1:20
- I will open my mouth in parables
  Ps. 78:2 quoted in Matt. 13:35
- He gave them bread out of heaven to eat
  Ps. 78:24 quoted in John 6:31

- I said, ye are gods
  Ps. 82:6 quoted in John 10:34
- I have found David
  Ps. 89:20 quoted in Acts 13:22
- He shall give his angels charge concerning thee
  Ps. 91:11–12 quoted in Matt. 4:6 and Luke 4:10–11
- The Lord knoweth the reasonings of the wise
  Ps. 94:11 quoted in 1 Cor. 3:20
- Today, if ye shall hear his voice
  Ps. 95:7–8 quoted in Heb. 3:15
- Today, if ye shall hear his voice
  Ps. 95:7–11 quoted in Heb. 3:7–11 and Heb. 4:7
- As I sware in my wrath, They shall not enter into my rest
  Ps. 95:11 quoted in Heb. 4:3, 5
- And they all shall wax old as doth a garment
  Ps. 102:25–27 quoted in Heb. 1:10–12
- Who maketh his angels winds
  Ps. 104:4 quoted in Heb. 1:7
- His office let another take
  Ps. 109:8 quoted in Acts 1:20
- The Lord said to my Lord
  Ps. 110:1 quoted in Matt. 22:44, Matt. 26:64, Mark 12:36, Mark 14:62, Luke 20:42–43, Luke 22:69, Acts 2:34–35, and Heb. 1:13
- Thou art a priest for ever
  Ps. 110:4 quoted in Heb. 5:6 and Heb. 7:17, 21
- He hath scattered abroad, he hath given to the poor
  Ps. 112:9 quoted in 2 Cor. 9:9
- I believed, and therefore did I speak
  Ps. 116:10 quoted in 2 Cor. 4:13
- Praise the Lord, all ye Gentiles
  Ps. 117:1 quoted in Rom. 15:11
- The Lord is my helper
  Ps. 118:6 quoted in Heb. 13:6
- The stone which the builders rejected
  Ps. 118:22 quoted in Luke 20:17, Acts 4:11, and 1 Pet. 2:7
- This was from the Lord, and it is marvelous in our eyes
  Ps. 118:22–23 quoted in Matt. 21:42 and Mark 12:10–11
- Blessed is he that cometh in the name of the Lord
  Ps. 118:26 quoted in Matt. 23:39, Luke 13:35 and Luke 19:38
- Of the fruit of his loins he would set one upon his throne
  Ps. 132:11 quoted in Acts 2:30
- The poison of asps in under their lips.
  Ps. 140:3 quoted in Rom. 3:13

Classification of Psalms

Individual Psalms have been classified in various ways, and one psalm sometimes is correctly classified under more than one heading. The following classification of the 150 Psalms puts them under 14 headings.

1. Penitential Psalms
   Asking for God's forgiveness. Psalms 6; 25; 32; 38; 51; 102; 130; 143.
2. Acrostic Psalms
   These have verses or sections beginning with succeeding Hebrew alphabet letters Psalms 25, 119, and 145.
3. Psalms of praise
   Psalms 8; 19; 24; 29; 33; 47; 50; 65; 66; 76; 77; 93; 95; 96; 97; 99; 104; 111; 113; 114;

115; 134; 139; 147; 148; 150.

4. Psalms of thanksgiving
   In general: Psalms 21; 46; 48; 65; 66; 68; 76; 81; 85; 98; 105; 124; 126; 129; 135; 136; 149.
   For God's goodness to good people: Psalms 23; 34; 36; 91; 100; 103; 107; 117; 121; 145; 146.
   For God's mercies to individuals: Psalms 9; 18; 30; 34; 40; 75; 103; 108; 116; 118; 138; 144.
5. Psalms of affliction
   Psalms 4; 5; 7; 11; 13; 17; 22; 26; 28; 35; 41; 42; 43; 44; 57; 59; 60; 63; 64; 69; 70; 74; 77; 79; 80; 83; 84; 86; 89; 94; 102; 109; 120; 123; 129; 137; 140; 141; 142; 143.
6. Psalms of trust when in trouble
   Psalms 3, 16, 27, 31, 54, 56, 57, 61, 62, 71, 86.
7. Didactic Psalms
   God's law: Psalms 19, 119.
   Other teachings: Psalms 1; 5; 7; 9; 10; 11; 12; 14; 15; 17; 24; 25; 32; 34; 36; 37; 39; 49; 50; 52; 53; 58; 73; 75; 82; 84; 90; 91; 92; 94; 101; 112; 121; 125; 127; 128; 131; 133.
8. Intercessory Psalms
   Psalms 20; 67; 122; 132; 144.
9. Imprecatory Psalms
   Asking for God's wrath to fall on one's enemies. Psalm 35, 58, 69, 109, 137.
10. Historical Psalms
   Psalm 78, 105, 114.
11. Prophetic Psalms
   Psalms 2; 16; 40; 45; 68; 72; 87; 97; 110; 118
12. Crucifixion Psalms
   Psalm 22, 69.
13. Coronation Psalms These are sometimes called royal or kingship Psalms.
   Psalm 16, 89, 132.
14. Exaltation Psalm
   Psalm 8

Jesus in the Psalms

In the Psalms Jesus is the promised Messiah.

Types of Jesus in the Psalms

- Jesus is the King, see Psalms 2; 18; 20; 21; 24; 47; 110; 132.
- Jesus is the Servant, see Psalms 17; 22; 41; 69; 109.
- Jesus is the Son of Man, see Psalms 8; 16; 40.
- Jesus is the Son of God, see Psalms 19; 102; 118.

Messianic prophecies

Messianic prophecies about Jesus in the Psalms, and their fulfillment in the New Testament

1. His birth
   - Presented with gifts; Psalm 72:10 fulfilled in Matt 2:1,11
2. His divine nature
   - He will be called Lord; Psalm 110:1 fulfilled in Matt 22:43–45; Luke 2:11
3. His ministry
   - Jesus will be a Priest; Psalm 110:4 fulfilled in Hebrews 3:1; 5:5–6; 7:26–27
   - He will be a King; Ps. 2:6 fulfilled in Matt 27:37; 21:5; John 18:33–38
   - Jesus' zeal for God; Psalm 69:9 fulfilled in John 2:15–17

- Jesus will teach in parables; Ps. 78:2 fulfilled in Matt 13:34–35
- Jesus will be a stumbling block to the Jews; Ps. 118:22 fulfilled in 1 Peter 2:7; Romans 9:32–33

4. Jesus and Good Friday
   - Jesus will be betrayed by a friend; Ps. 41:9; 55:12–14; fulfilled in Matt 10:4; 26:49–50; John 13:21
   - Jesus will be mocked; Psalm 22:7–8; 69:8–13 fulfilled in Matt 27:29–31,39
   - Jesus' hands and his feet will be pierced; Psalm 22:16 fulfilled in Luke 23:33; John 20:25
   - Jesus will be hated for no reason; Psalm 69:4 fulfilled in John 15:25
   - Lots will be thrown for Jesus' clothes; Psalm 22:18 fulfilled in John 19:23–24
   - Jesus will be very thirsty; Psalm 69:21 fulfilled in John 19:28
   - Jesus will utter a cry about being forsaken; Psalm 22:1 fulfilled in Matt 27:46
   - Jesus will commit himself to God; Psalm 31:5 fulfilled in Luke 23:46
   - Jesus' bones will not be broken; Psalm 34:20 fulfilled in John 19:33,36
5. Jesus after Good Friday
   - Jesus will rise from the dead; Ps. 16:10; 30:3; 118:18; fulfilled in Matt 28:6; Luke 24:46; Acts 2:31, 13:35
   - Jesus will ascend into heaven; Psalm 68:18; fulfilled in Acts 1:9; Ephesians 4:8
   - Jesus will sit at the right hand of God; Psalm 110:1 fulfilled in Mark 16:19; Acts 2:34; Hebrews 1:3

Lessons to learn from Psalms

- The Psalms remind us about God's greatness and goodness, and so we see ourselves in his light and fall down in worship before him.
- God cares about our every need.
- While troubles come to everyone, God's followers are to tell God about their troubles and trust him for their deliverance.
- God's rule is over everyone.
- God seeks our obedience and trust.

4. Chapter by chapter: outline of every Psalm

Psalm 1

Matthew Henry's introduction

This psalm shows us,

I. The holiness and happiness of a godly man, vv. 1–3.

II. The sinfulness and misery of a wicked man, vv. 4, 5.

III. The ground and reason of both, v. 6

A detailed analysis of psalm

The holiness and happiness of a godly man. (1–3)

The sinfulness and misery of a wicked man, and the reason for both. (4–6)

Key verse

Verse 3: "And he shall be like a tree planted by the rivers of water."

Key word / key phrase

Verse 1, "blessed."

Key event / key person / key theme

The man who is blessed

Key thought

There are three steps on the evil path in verse 1.

Key thing to look out for

A person blessed by God is like a flourishing tree.

Key Bible cross-reference

Verse 3. See Jeremiah 17:8.

Key "by way of explanation"

Verse 5. When God judges people nobody will be able to stand in his presence.

Key "Quotable Quote"

"The meaning of the psalmist is that it shall be always well with God's devout servants, whose constant endeavor it is to make progress in the study of his law. He teaches us how impossible it is for anyone to apply his mind to meditation upon God's law, who has not first withdrawn and separated himself from the society of the ungodly."

John Calvin

Psalm 2

Matthew Henry's introduction

The Holy Spirit here foretells,

I. The opposition that should be given to the kingdom of the Messiah, vv. 1–3.

II. The baffling and chastising of that opposition, vv. 4, 5.

III. The setting up of the kingdom of Christ, notwithstanding that opposition, v. 6.

IV. The confirmation and establishment of it, v. 7.

V. A promise of the enlargement and success of it, vv. 8, 9.

VI. A call and exhortation to kings and princes to yield themselves the willing subjects of this kingdom,, vv. 10–12.

A detailed analysis of psalm

Warnings against the enemies of Christ's kingdom. (1–6)

Promise to Christ as the Head of this kingdom. (7–9)

Counsel to all, to follow its interests. (10–12)

Key verse

Verse 11: "Serve the LORD with fear, and rejoice with trembling."

Key word / key phrase

Verse 2, "Anointed One."

Key event / key person / key theme

The Lord's Anointed

Key thought

In the New Testament, where this Psalm is often quoted, the Anointed One is applied to Christ.

Key thing to look out for

This Psalm was probably originally written to celebrate the coronation of an heir to David's throne.

Key Bible cross-reference

Verses 1, 2. See Acts 4:25–28.

Key "by way of explanation"

Verse 2. The Hebrew word for "anointed one" is "Messiah." The English word "Christ" comes from the Greek for "anointed one."

Key "Quotable Quote"

"For I believe that the whole of human existence, both the dispositions of the soul and the movements of the thoughts, have been measured out and encompassed in those very words of the Psalter. And nothing beyond these is found among men."

Athanasius the Great

Psalm 3

Matthew Henry's introduction

I. Absalom complains to God of his enemies, vv. 1, 2.

II. Confides in God, and encourages himself in him as his God, notwithstanding, v. 3.

III. Recollects the satisfaction he had in the gracious answers God gave to his prayers, and his experience of his goodness to him, vv. 4, 5.

IV. Triumphs over his fears (v. 6) and over his enemies, whom he prays against, v. 7.

V. Gives God the glory and takes to himself the comfort of the divine blessing and salvation which are sure to all the people of God, v. 8.

A detailed analysis of psalm

David complains to God about his enemies, and confides in God. (1–3)

He triumphs over his fears, and gives God the glory, and is comforted. (4–8)

Key verse

Verse 2: "There is no help for him in God."

Key word / key phrase

Verse 1, "foes."

Key event / key person / key theme

Victory in the face of defeat

Key thought

In the face of many threats the psalmist turns to the Lord in prayer.

Key thing to look out for

All kinds of deliverances belong to the Lord.

Key Bible cross-reference

Verse 7. See Exodus 12:31.

Key "by way of explanation"

Verse 5. The psalmist can sleep in peace knowing that he is being protected by the Lord.

Key "Quotable Quote"

"For whether there was necessity of repentance or confession, or tribulation and trial befell us, or someone was persecuted, or, being plotted against, he was protected . . . or he wants to sing praises and give thanks to the Lord – for any such eventuality he has instruction in the divine Psalms."

Athanasius the Great

Psalm 4

Matthew Henry's introduction

Here

I. David begins with a short prayer (v. 1) and that prayer preaches.

II. He directs his speech to the children of men, and,

A. In God's name reproves them for the dishonor they do to God and the damage they do to their own souls, v. 2.

B. He sets before them the happiness of godly people for their encouragement to be religious, v. 3.

C. He calls on them to consider their ways, v. 4.

III. He exhorts them to serve God and trust in him, v. 5.

IV. He gives an account of his own experiences of the grace of God working in him,

A. Enabling him to choose God's favor for his felicity, v. 6.

B. Filling his heart with joy therein, v. 7.

C. Quieting his spirit in the assurance of the divine protection he was under, night and day, v. 8.

A detailed analysis of psalm

The happiness of godly people. (1–5)

God's favor is happiness. (6–8)

Key verse

Verse 4: "Stand in awe, and sin not."

Key word / key phrase

Verse 8, "lie down and sleep."

Key event / key person / key theme

Evening prayer for deliverance

Key thought

David warns against placing trust in false gods.

Key thing to look out for

David warns against anxiety.

Key Bible cross-reference

Verse 8. See 3:5, 6.

Key "by way of explanation"

Verse 1. God is righteous and always acts faithfully toward his people.

Key "Quotable Quote"

"Thou hast put gladness in my heart, more than in the time that their corn and their wine increased."

Psalm 4:7

Psalm 5

Matthew Henry's introduction

In this psalm,

I. David settles a correspondence between his soul and God, promising to pray, and promising himself that God would certainly hear him, vv. 1–3.

II. He gives to God the glory, and takes to himself the comfort, of God's holiness, vv. 4–6.

III. He declares his resolution to keep close to the public worship of God, v. 7.

IV. He prayed,

A. For himself, that God would guide him, v. 8.

B. Against his enemies, that God would destroy them, vv. 9, 10.
C. For all the people of God, that God would give them joy, and keep them safe, vv. 11, 12. And this is all of great use to direct us in prayer.

A detailed analysis of psalm

God will certainly hear prayer: David gives to God the glory, and is comforted. (1–6)

He prayed for himself, that God would guide him, and for all the Lord's people, that God would give them joy, and keep them safe. (7–12)

Key verse

Verse 2: "Hearken unto the voice of my cry, my King, and my God."

Key word / key phrase

Verse 3, "in the morning."

Key event / key person / key theme

Morning prayer for guidance

Key thought

David warns against trusting what people say.

Key thing to look out for

David pictures the Lord protecting his people with a shield.

Key Bible cross-reference

Verse 8. See 23:3.

Key "by way of explanation"

Verse 10. The curses (or imprecations) in the psalms are cries for justice and the redress of evil.

Key "Quotable Quote"

"For thou, LORD, wilt bless the righteous; with favor wilt thou compass him as with a shield."

Psalm 5:12

Psalm 6

Matthew Henry's introduction

I. David pours out his complaints before God, deprecates his wrath, and begs earnestly for the return of his favor, vv. 1–7.
II. He assures himself of an answer of peace, shortly, to his full satisfaction, vv. 8–10. This psalm is like the book of Job.

A detailed analysis of psalm

The psalmist deprecates God's wrath, and begs for the return of his favor. (1–7)

He assures himself of an answer of peace. (8–10)

Key verse

Verse 3: "My soul is also sore vexed."

Key word / key phrase

Verses 2, "be merciful."

Key event / key person / key theme

Prayer for God's mercy

Key thought

The Lord had sent this illness to discipline David.

Key thing to look out for

David does not attempt to justify himself, but asks for the Lord's mercy.

Key Bible cross-reference

Verse 4. See Deuteronomy 7:9, 12.

Key "by way of explanation"

This psalm, along with psalms 32; 38; 51; 102; 130; 143, was known as one of the seven penitential psalms in early Christian liturgies.

Key "Quotable Quote"

"The LORD hath heard my supplication; the LORD will receive my prayer."

Psalm 6:9

Psalm 7

Matthew Henry's introduction

I. David applies to God for favor, vv. 1, 2.

II. He appeals to God about his innocence as to those things whereof he was accused, vv. 3–5.

III. He prays to God to plead his cause and judge for him against his persecutors, vv. 6–9.

IV. He expresses his confidence in God that he would do so, and would return the mischief on the head of those that designed it against him, vv. 10–16.

V. He promises to give God the glory of his deliverance, v. 17. In this David was a type of Christ, who was himself, and still is in his members, thus injured, but will certainly be righted at last.

A detailed analysis of psalm

The psalmist prays to God to plead his cause, and judge for him. (1–9)

He expresses confidence in God, and will give him the glory for his deliverance. (10–17)

Key verse

Verse 10: "My defense is of God, which saveth the upright in heart."

Key word / key phrase

Verse 6, "decree justice."

Key event / key person / key theme

A prayer asking for justice

Key thought

Because God is just he can be appealed to so that wrongs can be put right.

Key thing to look out for

David states that he is innocent and should never have been attacked.

Key Bible cross-reference

Verse 2. See 1 Samuel 17:34, 35.

Key "by way of explanation"

Verse 11. God does not reserve all his judgments for the future but sends some down every day.

Key "Quotable Quote"

"And this is a genuine and an undoubted proof of our faith, when, being visited with adversity, we, not withstanding, persevere in cherishing and exercising hope in God. From this, we also learn that the gate of mercy is shut against our prayers if the key of faith do not open it for us."

John Calvin, commenting on verses 1, 2

Psalm 8

Matthew Henry's introduction

God is to be glorified,

I. For making known himself and his great name to us, v. 1.

II. For making use of the weakest of the children of men, by them to serve his own purposes, v. 2.

III. For making even the heavenly bodies useful to man, vv. 3, 4.

IV. For making him to have dominion over the creatures in this lower world, and there by placing him but little lower then the angels, vv. 5–8.

A detailed analysis of psalm

God is to be glorified, for making known himself to us. (1, 2)

And for making him only a little lower than the angels. (3–9)

Key verse

Verse 3: "When I consider thy heavens, the work of thy fingers . . ."

Key word / key phrase

Verse 1, "your glory."

Key event / key person / key theme

God's glory and humankind's dominion

Key thought

The greatness of the heavens reflects God's greatness.

Key thing to look out for

Compare the magnificence of God with the temporary nature of human beings.

Key Bible cross-reference

Verse 1. See Genesis 1:26–28.

Key "by way of explanation"

Verses 4–6 are applied to Jesus in Hebrews 2:6–8.

Key "Quotable Quote

"God is not under the necessity of making war with great power to overcome the faithful, who willingly harken to his voice, and manifest a ready obedience, as soon as he gives the smallest intimation of his will. The providence of God, I confess, shines forth principally for the sake of the faithful, because they only have eyes to behold it. But as they show themselves willing to receive instruction, God teaches them with gentleness; while on the other hand, he arms himself against his enemies, who never submit themselves to him but by constraint."

John Calvin, commentating on verse 2

Psalm 9

Matthew Henry's introduction

In this psalm,

I. David praises God for pleading his cause, and giving him victory over his enemies and the enemies of his country (vv. 1–6), and calls on others to join with him in his songs of praise, vv. 11, 12.

II. He prays to God that he might have still further occasion to praise him, for his own deliverances and the confusion of his enemies, vv. 13, 14, 19, 20

III. He triumphs in the assurance he had of God's judging the world (vv. 7, 8), protecting his oppressed people (vv. 9, 10, 18), and bringing his and their implacable enemies to ruin, vv. 15–17.

A detailed analysis of psalm

David praises God for protecting his people. (9:1–10)

And for many reasons to praise him. (9:11–20)

The psalmist complains of the wickedness of the wicked. (10:1–11)

He prays to God to rescue his people. (10:12–18)

Key verse

9:11: "Sing praises to the LORD, which dwelleth in Zion."

Key word / key phrase

9:3, "enemies."

Key event / key person / key theme

Praise for victory over enemies

Key thought

In Psalm 9 David says that those who forget God will come to nothing.

Key thing to look out for

In Psalm 10 the arrogance of those who oppose God is noted but confidence in God's righteous reign is also expressed.

Key Bible cross-reference

9:5. See Numbers 5:23; 2 Kings 14:27.

Key "by way of explanation"

Psalms 10 and 11 were often used together and may even have been one psalm originally.

Key "Quotable Quote"

"I will praise thee, O LORD, with my whole heart; I will show forth all thy marvelous works."

Psalm 9:1

Psalm 10

Matthew Henry's introduction

In this psalm,

I. David complains of the wickedness of the wicked, describes the dreadful pitch of impiety at which they had arrived (to the great dishonor of God and the prejudice of his church and people), and notices the delay of God's appearing against them, vv. 1–11.

II. He prays to God to appear against them for the relief of his people and comforts himself with hopes that he would do so in due time, vv. 12–18.

A detailed analysis of psalm

David praises God for protecting his people. (9:1–10)

And for many reasons to praise him. (9:11–20)

The psalmist complains of the wickedness of the wicked. (10:1–11)

He prays to God to rescue his people. (10:12–18)

Key verse

9:11: "Sing praises to the LORD, which dwelleth in Zion."

Key word / key phrase

9:3, "enemies."

Key event / key person / key theme

Praise for victory over enemies

Key thought

In Psalm 9 David says that those who forget God will come to nothing.

Key thing to look out for

In Psalm 10 the arrogance of those who oppose God is noted but confidence in God's righteous reign is also expressed.

Key Bible cross-reference

9:5. See Numbers 5:23; 2 Kings 14:27.

Key "by way of explanation"

Psalms 10 and 11 were often used together and may even have been one psalm originally.

Key "Quotable Quote"

"I will praise thee, O LORD, with my whole heart; I will show forth all thy marvelous works."

Psalm 9:1

Psalm 11

Matthew Henry's introduction

Observe,

I. How he represents the temptation, and perhaps parleys with it, vv. 1–3.

II. How he answers it, and puts it to silence with the consideration of God's dominion and providence (v. 4), his favor to the righteous, and the wrath which the wicked are reserved for, vv. 5–7.

A detailed analysis of psalm

David's struggle with, and triumph over, a strong temptation to distrust God, and to trust in himself for his own safety, in a time of danger. (1–7)

Key verse

Verse 3: "If the foundations be destroyed, what can the righteous do?"

Key word / key phrase

Verse 5, "examines the righteous."

Key event / key person / key theme

God tests men and women.

Key thought

The fearful are reassured that the Lord still reigns on his heavenly throne.

Key thing to look out for

David encourages the wavering faith of those around him by expressing his rocklike faith in the Lord.

Key Bible cross-reference

Verse 4. This verse is repeated in Habakkuk 2:20.

Key "by way of explanation"

Even though the enemies of God's people appear to be overwhelming this psalm expresses complete trust in the Lord's rule.

Key "Quotable Quote"

"For the righteous LORD loveth righteousness; his countenance doth behold the upright."

Psalm 11:7

Psalm 12

Matthew Henry's introduction

I. David begs help of God, because there were none among men whom he durst trust, vv. 1, 2.

II. He foretells the destruction of his proud and threatening enemies, vv. 3, 4.

III. He assures himself and others that, how ill soever things went now (v. 8), God would preserve and secure to himself his own people (vv. 5, 7), and would certainly make good his promises to them, v. 6.

A detailed analysis of psalm

The psalmist begs help from God, because there is no one he dares to trust. (1–8)

Key verse

Verse 6: "The words of the LORD are pure words."

Key word / key phrase

Verse 6, "the words of the Lord."

Key event / key person / key theme

The pure words of God

Key thought

God's answers the psalmists heartfelt prayer for protection.

Key thing to look out for

Despite the way the wicked strut around David expresses his confidence in the Lord.

Key Bible cross-reference

Verses 1–8. See Micah 7:1–7.

Key "by way of explanation"

Verse 6. The words of the Lord are in total contrast to the boastful words of the arrogant.

Key "Quotable Quote"

"Thou shalt keep them, O LORD, thou shalt preserve them from this generation for ever."

Psalm 12:7

Psalm 13

Matthew Henry's introduction

This psalm is the deserted soul's case and cure. Whether it was penned on any particular occasion does not appear, but in general,

I. David sadly complains that God had long withdrawn from him and delayed to relieve him, vv. 1, 2.

II. He earnestly prays to God to consider his case and comfort him, vv. 3, 4.

III. He assures himself of an answer of peace, and therefore concludes the psalm with joy and triumph, because he concludes his deliverance to be as good as wrought, vv. 5, 6.

A detailed analysis of psalm

The psalmist complains that God's presence has been withdrawn for a long time. He earnestly prays for comfort. (1–6)

Key verse

Verse 1: "How long wilt thou forget me, O LORD?"

Key word / key phrase

Verse 1, "How long, O Lord?"

Key event / key person / key theme

A prayer for God's immediate answer

Key thought

David calls out pleading to know how long his serious illness will last.

Key thing to look out for

David ends this psalm confident of God's salvation.

Key Bible cross-reference

Verse 1. See 30:7; 44:24; 88:14.

Key "by way of explanation"

Verse 3. This serious illness appears to be life-threatening.

Key "Quotable Quote"

"I will sing unto the LORD, because he hath dealt bountifully with me."

Psalm 13:6

Psalm 14

Matthew Henry's introduction

Here is,

I. A charge exhibited against a wicked world, v. 1.

II. The proof of the charge, vv. 2, 3.

III. A serious expostulation with sinners, especially with persecutors, on it, vv. 4–6.

IV. A believing prayer for the salvation of Israel and a joyful expectation of it, v. 7.

A detailed analysis of psalm

A description of the depravity of human nature, and the deplorable corruption of a great part of humankind. (1–7)

Key verse

Verse 1: "The fool hath said in his heart, There is no God."

Key word / key phrase

Verse 4, "evildoers."

Key event / key person / key theme

The characteristics of the godless

Key thought

Two characteristics of the wicked are that they are violent and they do not trust God.

Key thing to look out for

The Lord's people often fall victim to injustice.

Key Bible cross-reference

Verses 1–3. See Romans 3:10–12.

Key "by way of explanation"

Verse 7. "Jacob" and "Israel" are synonymous. See Genesis 32:28.

Key "Quotable Quote"

"Oh that the salvation of Israel were come out of Zion! when the LORD bringeth back the captivity of his people, Jacob shall rejoice, and Israel shall be glad."

Psalm 14:7

Psalm 15

Matthew Henry's introduction

In this psalm,

I. By the question (v. 1) we are directed and excited to enquire for the way.

II. By the answer to that question, in the rest of the psalm, we are directed to walk in that way, vv. 2–5.

III. By the assurance given in the close of the psalm of the safety and happiness of those who answer these characters we are encouraged to walk in that way, v. 5.

A detailed analysis of psalm

The way to heaven, if we want to be happy, is to be holy. We are encouraged to walk in that way. (1–5)

Key verse

Verse 1: "LORD, who shall abide in thy tabernacle?"

Key word / key phrase

Verse 2, "blameless."

Key event / key person / key theme

The characteristics of the godly

Key thought

If people live in awe of the Lord they will live their lives according to his will.

Key thing to look out for

Godly people should not indulge in common evil practices.

Key Bible cross-reference

Verse 1. See 23:6; 27:4–6.

Key "by way of explanation"

Verses 2–5. The importance of moral righteousness is stressed here.

Key "Quotable Quote"

"He that putteth not out his money to usury, nor taketh reward against the innocent. He that doeth these things shall never be moved."

Psalm 15:5

Psalm 16

Matthew Henry's introduction

I. David speaks of himself as a member of Christ, and so he speaks the language of all good Christians, professing his confidence in

God (v. 1), his consent to him (v. 2), his affection to the people of God (v. 3), his adherence to the true worship of God (v. 4), and his entire complacency and satisfaction in God and the interest he had in him, vv. 5–7.

II. He speaks of himself as a type of Christ, and so he speaks the language of Christ himself, to whom all the rest of the psalm is expressly and at large applied (Acts 2:25, etc.). David speaks about him (not about himself), "I foresaw the Lord always before my face," etc. And this he spoke, being a prophet, vv. 30, 31. He spoke,
   A. Of the special presence of God with the Redeemer in his services and sufferings, v. 8.
   B. Of the prospect which the Redeemer had of his own resurrection and the glory that should follow, which carried him cheerfully through his undertaking, vv. 9–11.

A detailed analysis of psalm

This psalm begins with expressions of devotion, which may be applied to Christ; but ends with such confidence in a resurrection, which must be applied to Christ, and to him alone. (1–11)

Key verse

Verse 6: "The lines are fallen unto me in pleasant places."

Key word / key phrase

Verse 2, "You are my Lord."

Key event / key person / key theme

A confident prayer about God's goodness

Key thought

David has chosen the one good thing.

Key thing to look out for

David expresses his joy at being totally secure in the Lord.

Key Bible cross-reference

Verse 8. See 73:23; 121:5.

Key "by way of explanation"

Verse 5. This "cup" is a cup of blessing for the godly, 23:5; but for the wicked it is a cup of wrath, see Jeremiah 25:15.

Key "Quotable Quote"

"Preserve me, O God: for in thee do I put my trust."

Psalm 16:1

Psalm 17

Matthew Henry's introduction

David being in great distress and danger by the malice of his enemies, does, in this psalm, by prayer address himself to God, his tried refuge, and seeks shelter in him.

I. He appeals to God about his integrity, vv. 1–4.

II. He prays to God still to be upheld in his integrity and preserved from the malice of his enemies, vv. 5–8, 13.

III. He gives a character of his enemies, using that as a plea with God for his preservation, vv. 9–12, 14.

IV. He comforts himself with the hopes of his future happiness, v. 15.

A detailed analysis of psalm

David's integrity. (1–7)

The character of his enemies. His hope of happiness. (8–15)

Key verse

Verse 3: "Thou hast proved mine heart."

Key word / key phrase

Verse 8, "the shadow of your wings."

Key event / key person / key theme

God's followers are hidden under God's wings

Key thought

David's plea for vindication.

Key thing to look out for

Note how this psalm is most appropriate for a falsely-accused person to use.

Key Bible cross-reference

Verse 8. See Numbers 6:24; Deuteronomy 32:10.

Key "by way of explanation"

Verse 8. "Wings" may refer to the cherubim over the ark, 1 Kings 8:6, or, to a mother bird, Matthew 23:37.

Key "Quotable Quote"

"Keep me as the apple of the eye, hide me under the shadow of thy wings."

Psalm 17:8

Psalm 18

Matthew Henry's introduction

Holy faith, and love, and joy, and praise, and hope, are here lively, active, and on the wing.

I. He triumphs in God, vv. 1–3.

II. He magnifies the deliverances God had wrought for him, vv. 4–19.

III. He takes the comfort of his integrity, which God had thereby cleared up, vv. 20–28.

IV. He gives to God the glory of all his achievements, vv. 29–42.

V. He encourages himself with the expectation of what God would further do for him and his, vv. 43–50.

(For Psalm 18, see 2 Samuel 22:1–51.)

Psalm 19

Matthew Henry's introduction

There are two excellent books which the great God has published for the instruction and edification of the children of men; this psalm treats of them both, and recommends them both to our diligent study.

I. The book of the creatures, in which we may easily read the power and godhead of the Creator, vv. 1–6.

II. The book of the scriptures, which makes known to us the will of God about our duty. He shows the excellency and use fulness of that book (vv. 7–11) and then teaches us how to improve it, vv. 12–14.

A detailed analysis of psalm

The glory of God's works. (1–6)

His holiness and grace as shown in his word. (7–10)

Prayer to benefit from them. (11–14)

Key verse

Verse 1: "The heavens declare the glory of God."

Key word / key phrase

Verse 1, "The heavens."

Key event / key person / key theme

God's glory in creation

Key thought

The heavenly lights are not divine in themselves but bear witness to the Creator's righteousness.

Key thing to look out for

The Law sets out the path that leads to life.

Key Bible cross-reference

Verse 10. See Amos 5:7; 6:12.

Key "by way of explanation"

Verse 1. The glory of God is seen by looking at the stars, but also in the Law of the Lord.

Key "Quotable Quote"

"The law of the LORD is perfect, converting the soul: the testimony of the LORD is sure, making wise the simple."

Psalm 19:7

Psalm 20

Matthew Henry's introduction

In this psalm we may observe,

I. What it is they beg of God for the king, vv. 1–4.

II. With what assurance they beg it. The people triumph (v. 5), the prince (v. 6), both together (vv. 7, 8), and so he concludes with a prayer to God for audience, v. 9. In this, David may well be looked on as a type of Christ, to whose kingdom and its interests among men the church was, in every age, a hearty well-wisher.

A detailed analysis of psalm

This psalm is a prayer for the kings of Israel, but also refers to Christ. (1–9)

Key verse

Verse 2: "Send thee help from the sanctuary, and strengthen thee out of Zion."

Key word / key phrase

Verse 5, "victorious."

Key event / key person / key theme

A prayer asking for victory

Key thought

It is crucial that the army trusts in the Lord rather than in chariots and horses.

Key thing to look out for

The one thing the army needs is protection and so this is what is prayed for.

Key Bible cross-reference

Verses 7, 8. See 33:16, 17.

Key "by way of explanation"

Verse 5. As the king sets out to engage in a battle this prayer is prayed. See 2 Chronicles 20:1–30.

Key "Quotable Quote"

"Some trust in chariots, and some in horses: but we will remember the name of the LORD our God."

Psalm 20:7

Psalm 21

Matthew Henry's introduction

Those whom we have prayed for we ought to give thanks for, and particularly for kings, in whose prosperity we share. They are here taught,

I. To congratulate him on his victories, and the honor he had achieved, vv. 1–6.

II. To confide in the power of God for the completing of the ruin of the enemies of his kingdom, vv. 7–13. In this there is an eye to Messiah the Prince, and the glory of his kingdom; for to him divers passages in this psalm are more applicable than to David himself.

A detailed analysis of psalm

Thanksgiving for victory. (1–6)

Confidence of further success. (7–13)

Key verse

Verse 5: "His glory is great in thy salvation."

Key word / key phrase

Verse 5, "victories."

Key event / key person / key theme

A prayer of praise after a victory

Key thought

Unlike earthly blessings, God's blessings are eternal.

Key thing to look out for

The psalm begins and ends on a note of praise.

Key Bible cross-reference

Verse 4. See 1 Kings 1:31; Daniel 2:4.

Key "by way of explanation"

Verse 9. This verse states that the king's victories came about as a result of the Lord's wrath.

Key "Quotable Quote"

"Be thou exalted, LORD, in thine own strength: so will we sing and praise thy power."

Psalm 21:13

Psalm 22

Matthew Henry's introduction

In this psalm he speaks,

I. Of the humiliation of Christ (vv. 1–21), where David, as a type of Christ, complains of the very calamitous condition he was in on many accounts.

A. He complains, and mixes comforts with his complaints; he complains (vv. 1, 2), but comforts himself (vv. 3–5), complains again (vv. 6–8), but comforts himself again, vv. 9, 10.

B. He complains, and mixes prayers with his complaints; he complains of the power and rage of his enemies (vv. 12, 13, 16, 18), of his own bodily weakness and decay (vv. 14, 15, 17); but prays that God would not be far from him (vv. 11, 19), that he would save and deliver him, vv. 19–21.

II. Of the exaltation of Christ, that his undertaking should be for the glory of God (vv. 22–25), for the salvation and joy of his people (vv. 26–29), and for the perpetuating of his own kingdom, vv. 30, 31. In singing this psalm we must keep our thoughts fixed on Christ, and be so affected with his sufferings as to experience the fellowship of them, and so affected with his grace as to experience the power and influence of it.

A detailed analysis of psalm

Complaints of discouragement. (1–10)
Prayer for deliverance. (11–21)
Praises for mercies and redemption. (22–31)

Key verse

Verse 1: "My God, my God, why hast thou forsaken me?"

Key word / key phrase

Verse 1, "forsaken me."

Key event / key person / key theme

The psalm of the cross

Key thought

David cries out because of his godly suffering.

Key thing to look out for

Note the links from this psalm to Jesus' death. See Matthew 27:39, 43; John 19:34.

Key Bible cross-reference

Verse 1. See Matthew 27:46; Mark 15:34.

Key "by way of explanation"

Jesus' passion is reflected in the psalm more than any other psalm.

Key "Quotable Quote"

"Be not far from me; for trouble is near; for there is none to help."

Psalm 22:11

Psalm 23

Matthew Henry's introduction

Many of David's psalms are full of complaints, but this is full of comforts, and the expressions of delight in God's great goodness and dependence on him. It is a psalm which has been sung by good Christians, and will be while the world stands, with a great deal of pleasure and satisfaction.

I. The psalmist here claims relation to God, as his shepherd, v. 1.

II. He recounts his experience of the kind things God had done for him as his shepherd, vv. 2, 3, 5.

III. Hence he infers that he should want no good (v. 1), that he needed to fear no evil (v. 4), that God would never leave nor forsake him in a way of mercy; and therefore he resolves never to leave nor forsake God in a way of duty, v. 6. In this he had certainly an eye, not only to the blessings of God's providence, which made his outward condition prosperous, but to the communications of God's grace, received by a lively faith, and returned in a warm devotion, which filled his soul with joy unspeakable. And, as in the previous psalm he represented Christ dying for his sheep, so here he represents Christians receiving the benefit of all the care and tenderness of that great and good shepherd.

A detailed analysis of psalm

Confidence in God's grace and care. (1–6)

Key verse

Verse 1: "The LORD is my shepherd."

Key word / key phrase

Verse 1, "my shepherd."

Key event / key person / key theme

The Shepherd psalm

Key thought

David states that the Lord God is his personal Shepherd.

Key thing to look out for

See how many different ways sheep are cared for in this psalm.

Key Bible cross-reference

Verse 2. See Isaiah 14:30; 17:2; Jeremiah 33:12.

Key "by way of explanation"

Verse 3. "Paths of righteousness." A shepherd leads sheep along safe paths, while the Shepherd–King leads David to eternal security.

Key "Quotable Quote"

"The Lord is my shepherd, that's all I want."

Small child misquoting Psalm 23

Psalm 24

Matthew Henry's introduction

This psalm is about the kingdom of Jesus Christ,

I. His providential kingdom, by which he rules the world, vv. 1, 2.

II. The kingdom of his grace, by which he rules in his church.

A. About the subjects of that kingdom; their character (vv. 4, 6), their charter, v. 5.

B. About the King of that kingdom; and a summons to all to give him admission, vv. 7–10.

A detailed analysis of psalm

The kingdom of Christ, and the subjects of that kingdom. (1–6)

The King of that kingdom. (7–10)

Key verse

Verse 3: "Who shall ascend into the hill of the LORD?"

Key word / key phrase

Verse 8, "The LORD strong and mighty."

Key event / key person / key theme

The psalm of the King of Glory

Key thought

This psalm celebrated the Lord entering Zion.

Key thing to look out for

Those who are allowed to enter God's city.

Key Bible cross-reference

Verse 7. See 3:3; 27:6; 110:7.

Key "by way of explanation"

Verse 4. "Clean hands" speak of pure actions, while a "pure heart" focuses on inner motives. The psalmist emphasizes the need for both.

Key "Quotable Quote"

"This is the generation of them that seek him, that seek thy face, O Jacob."

Psalm 24:6

Psalm 25

Matthew Henry's introduction

This psalm is full of devout affection to God, the out-goings of holy desires towards his favor and grace and of faith in his promises. We may learn out of it,

I. What it is to pray, vv. 1, 15.

II. What we must pray for, the pardon of sin (vv. 6, 7, 18), direction in the way of duty (vv. 4, 5), the favor of God (v. 16), deliverance out of our troubles (vv. 17, 18), preservation from our enemies (vv. 20, 21), and the salvation of the church of God, v. 22.

III. What we may plead in prayer, our confidence in God (vv. 2, 3, 5, 20, 21), our distress and the malice of our enemies (vv. 17, 19), our sincerity, v. 21.

IV. What precious promises we have to encourage us in prayer, of guidance and instruction (vv. 8, 9, 12), the benefit of the covenant (v. 10), and the pleasure of communion with God, vv. 13, 14.

A detailed analysis of psalm

Confidence in prayer. (1–7)

Prayer for remission of sins. (8–14)

For help in affliction. (15–22)

Key verse

Verse 9: "The meek will he guide in judgment."

Key word / key phrase

Verse 4, "teach me your paths."

Key event / key person / key theme

A prayer for guidance and protection

Key thought

David prays to be delivered from his enemies.

Key thing to look out for

David homes in on the blessings of the covenant: God's mercy, grace, and goodness.

Key Bible cross-reference

Verse 10. See 103:7; 138:5.

Key "by way of explanation"

Verse 4. "Your ways," and "your paths" stand for the covenant and its teaching. See verse 10; Deuteronomy 8:6; Joshua 22:5.

Key "Quotable Quote"

"Lead me in thy truth, and teach me: for thou art the God of my salvation; on thee do I wait all the day."

Psalm 25:5

Psalm 26

Matthew Henry's introduction

Holy David is in this psalm putting himself on a solemn trial, not by God and his country, but by God and his own conscience, to both which he appeals touching his integrity (vv. 1, 2), for the proof of which he alleges,

I. His constant regard to God and his grace, v. 3.

II. His rooted antipathy to sin and sinners, vv. 4, 5.

III. His sincere affection to the ordinances of God, and his care about them, vv. 6–8. Having thus proved his integrity,

A. He deprecates the doom of the wicked, vv. 9, 10.

B. He casts himself on the mercy and grace of God, with a resolution to hold fast his integrity, and his hope in God, vv. 11, 12.

A detailed analysis of psalm

David, in this psalm, appeals to God pleading his innocence and integrity. (1–12)

Key verse

Verse 2: "Examine me, O Lord, and prove me."

Key word / key phrase

Verses 1, 11, "a blameless life."

Key event / key person / key theme

The prayer of a person longing to be vindicated by the Lord

Key thought

David refused to settle down with evil people.

Key thing to look out for

This psalm is shot through with praise and reasons for praising the Lord.

Key Bible cross-reference

Verse 4. See Proverbs 6:12–14.

Key "by way of explanation"

"Vindicate," is, in the Hebrew, "judge." The psalm is a call for justice and deliverance.

Key "Quotable Quote"

"But as for me, I will walk in mine integrity: redeem me, and be merciful unto me."

Psalm 26:11

Psalm 27

Matthew Henry's introduction

Here is,

I. The courage and holy bravery of his faith, vv. 1–3.

II. The complacency he took in communion with God and the benefit he experienced by it, vv. 4–6.

III. His desire towards God, and his favor and grace, vv. 7–9, 11, 12.

IV. His expectations from God, and the encouragement he gives to others to hope in him, vv. 10, 13, 14.

A detailed analysis of psalm

The psalmist's faith. (1–6)

His desire for God, and expectation from him. (7–14)

Key verse

Verse 8: "Seek ye my face; my heart said unto thee, Thy face, LORD, will I seek."

Key word / key phrase

Verse 3, "not fear."

Key event / key person / key theme

Trust in the Lord and do not be afraid

Key thought

David prays for deliverance from those who seek his life.

Key thing to look out for

This psalm gives much insight into the nature of David's faith.

Key Bible cross-reference

Verse 4. See 90:17.

Key "by way of explanation"

Verse 1, "light." Light often stands for well-being. See 97:11; Job 18:5, 6; Lamentations 3:2.

Key "Quotable Quote"

"One thing have I desired of the LORD, that will I seek after; that I may dwell in the house of the LORD all the days of my life, to behold the beauty of the LORD, and to inquire in his temple."

Psalm 27:4

Psalm 28

Matthew Henry's introduction

The former part of this psalm is the prayer of a saint now in distress (vv. 1–3), to which is added the doom of God's implacable enemies, vv. 4, 5. The latter part of the psalm is the thanksgiving of a saint triumphant, and delivered out of his distresses (vv. 6–8), to which is added a prophetical prayer for all God's faithful loyal subjects, v. 9.

A detailed analysis of psalm

A prayer in distress. (1–5)

Thanksgiving for deliverance. (6–9)

Key verse

Verse 1: "Unto thee will I cry, O LORD my rock."

Key word / key phrase

Verse 1, "To you I call."

Key event / key person / key theme

A prayer for help

Key thought

David is in danger of being killed by malicious enemies. So he prays.

Key thing to look out for

The psalm includes prayers for all of God's people. David could remember others despite his own pressing trials.

Key Bible cross-reference

Verse 2. See 63:4; 134:2.

Key "by way of explanation"

Verse 5. The "works of the Lord" encompass a great deal, including, the Exodus, the conquest of the promised land, and David becoming king.

Key "Quotable Quote"

"Blessed be the LORD, because he hath heard the voice of my supplications."

Psalm 28:6

Psalm 29

Matthew Henry's introduction

I. He calls on the great ones of the world to give glory to God, vv. 1, 2.

II. To convince them of the goodness of that God whom they were to adore, he takes notice of his power and terror in the thunder, and lightning, and thundershowers (vv. 3–9), his sovereign dominion over the world (v. 10), and his special favor to his church, v. 11.

A detailed analysis of psalm

Exhortation to give glory to God. (1–11)

Key verse

Verse 4: "The voice of the LORD is powerful."

Key word / key phrase

Verse 3, "The voice of the LORD."

Key event / key person / key theme

God's powerful voice

Key thought

David calls all God's people to worship the Lord.

Key thing to look out for

Mighty thunder is likened to the voice of the Lord.

Key Bible cross-reference

Verse 5. See Isaiah 2:13.

Key "by way of explanation"

Verse 10, "enthroned over the flood." See Genesis 1:2, 6–10; 6:17. God is all-powerful, as he showed at creation and during the Flood.

Key "Quotable Quote"

"The LORD will give strength unto his people; the LORD will bless his people with peace."

Psalm 29:11

Psalm 30

Matthew Henry's introduction

I. He here praises God for the deliverances he had wrought for him, vv. 1–3.

II. He calls on others to praise him too, and encourages them to trust in him, vv. 4, 5.

III. He blames himself for his former security, vv. 6, 7.

IV. He recollects the prayers and complaints he had made in his distress, vv. 8–10. With them he stirs up himself to be very thankful to God for the present comfortable change, vv. 11, 12.

A detailed analysis of psalm

Praise to God for deliverance. (1–5)

Valuable lessons learned. (6–12)

Key verse

Verse 2: "O LORD my God, I cried unto thee, and thou hast healed me."

Key word / key phrase

Verse 1, "out of the depths."

Key event / key person / key theme

Thanksgiving for dramatic deliverance

Key thought

David had been saved, probably from an illness, verse 2, and he gives thanks to the Lord for this publicly.

Key thing to look out for

David thanks the Lord for all the situations he transforms.

Key Bible cross-reference

Verse 1. See 69:2; 130:1; Jonah 2:2.

Key "by way of explanation"

Verse 5, "remain for a night." Like a guest who will only stay for one night.

Key "Quotable Quote"

"Hear, O LORD, and have mercy upon me: LORD, be thou my helper."

Psalm 30:10

Psalm 31

Matthew Henry's introduction

I. David professes his cheerful confidence in God, and, in that confidence, prays for deliverance out of his present troubles, vv. 1–8.

II. He complains of the very deplorable condition he was in, and, in the sense of his calamities, still prays that God would graciously appear for him against his persecutors, vv. 9–18.

III. He concludes the psalm with praise and triumph, giving glory to God, and encouraging himself and others to trust in him, vv. 19–24.

A detailed analysis of psalm

Confidence in God. (1–8)

Prayer in trouble. (9–18)

Praise for God's goodness. (19–24)

Key verse

Verse 9: "Have mercy upon me, O LORD, for I am in trouble."

Key word / key phrase

Verse 1, "I have taken refuge."

Key event / key person / key theme

A prayer expressing trust in the Lord

Key thought

David remembers God's wonderful deliverances in the past.

Key thing to look out for

David was able to resist his strong enemies because of his constant trust in the Lord.

Key Bible cross-reference

Verse 5. See Luke 23:46.

Key "by way of explanation"

Verse 5, "commit," literally means to deposit, as in Jeremiah 36:20. So this expression speaks of someone entrusting himself to God's care. See 1 Kings 14:27.

Key "Quotable Quote"

"In thee, O LORD, do I put my trust; let me never be ashamed: deliver me in thy righteousness."

Psalm 31:1

Psalm 32

Matthew Henry's introduction

We have here a summary,

I. Of gospel grace in the pardon of sin (vv. 1, 2), in divine protection (v. 7), and divine guidance, v. 8.

II. Of gospel duty. To confess sin (vv. 3–5), to pray (v. 6), to govern ourselves well (vv. 9, 10), and to rejoice in God, v. 11.

A detailed analysis of psalm

The happiness of a pardoned sinner. (1, 2)

The misery that went before, and the comfort that followed the confession of sins. (3–7)

Sinners instructed, believers encouraged. (8–11)

Key verse

Verse 7: "Thou art my hiding place."

Key word / key phrase

Verse 1, "transgressions are forgiven."

Key event / key person / key theme

The fruit of forgiveness

Key thought

David thanks the Lord for the gift of forgiveness and for the joy this brings.

Key thing to look out for

Note the repetitions in this psalm and what is repeated (for emphasis.) See verses 1, 2, 5.

Key Bible cross-reference

Verse 9. See Isaiah 1:3.

Key "by way of explanation"

Verses 3–5. It appears that David had held on to unacknowledged sin and so had found the Lord's "hand was heavy."

Key "Quotable Quote"

"Scripture gives us the warrant to insist that God's normal way of guiding us is rational, not irrational, namely through the very thought processes which he has created in us. Psalm 32 makes this clear. Verse 8 contains a marvelous threefold promise of divine guidance. If we put together the promise and the prohibition, what God is saying to us is this: 'I promise that I will guide you, and show you the way to go. But do not expect me to guide you as you guide horses and mules.'"

John R.W. Stott

Psalm 33

Matthew Henry's introduction

The psalmist, in this psalm,

I. Calls on the righteous to praise God, vv. 1–3.

II. Furnishes us with matter for praise. We must praise God,

A. For his justice, goodness, and truth, appearing in his word, and in all his works, vv. 4, 5.

B. For his power appearing in the work of creation, vv. 6–9.

C. For the sovereignty of his providence in the government of the world (vv. 10, 11) and again, vv. 13–17.

D. For the peculiar favor which he bears to his own chosen people, which encourages them to trust in him (v. 12) and again, vv. 18–22.

A detailed analysis of psalm

God is to be praised. (1–11)

His people encouraged by his power. (12–22)

Key verse

Verse 12: "Blessed is the nation whose God is the LORD."

Key word / key phrase / key phrase

Verse 1, "Sing joyfully."

Key event / key person / key theme

A song of worship

Key thought

This psalm of praise expresses thanks to Israel's God for national deliverance.

Key thing to look out for

The psalm starts and ends with three verses which contain a call to praise and a response to praise.

Key Bible cross-reference

Verse 4. See 107:20; 147:15, 18.

Key "by way of explanation"

Verse 3. A "new song" was sung to celebrate God's actions which brought about salvation. See 40:3; Isaiah 42:10; Revelation 14:3.

Key "Quotable Quote"

"He loveth righteousness and judgment: the earth is full of the goodness of the LORD."

Psalm 33:5

Psalm 34

Matthew Henry's introduction

I. He praises God for the experience which he and others had had of his goodness, vv. 1–6.

II. He encourages all good people to trust in God and to seek to him, vv. 7–10.

III. He gives good counsel to us all, as unto children, to take heed of sin, and to make conscience of our duty both to God and man, vv. 11–14.

IV. To enforce this good counsel he shows God's favor to the righteous and his displeasure against the wicked, in which he sets before us good and evil, the blessing and the curse, vv. 15–22.

A detailed analysis of psalm

David praises God, and trusts him. (1–10)

Exhortations to reverence God. (11–22)

Key verse

Verse 3: "O magnify the LORD with me."

Key word / key phrase / key phrase

Verse 4, "I sought the LORD."

Key event / key person / key theme

Seeking the Lord

Key thought

This psalm starts with praise, verse 1–7, and then, verses 8–22, turns to instructions for God's followers.

Key thing to look out for

The teaching about the fear of the Lord is contained in a number of commands, such as: "taste," "fear," "come," and "keep."

Key Bible cross-reference

Verse 5. See Isaiah 60:5.

Key "by way of explanation"

Verse 7, "angel of the Lord." God's messenger, or heavenly representative, is sent to earth to convey and carry out the Lord's will. See 35:5, 6.

Key "Quotable Quote"

"The angel of the LORD encampeth round about them that fear him, and delivereth them."

Psalm 34:7

Psalm 35

Matthew Henry's introduction

I. He complains to God of the injuries they did him; they strove with him, fought against him (v. 1), persecuted him (v. 3), sought his ruin (vv. 4, 7), accused him falsely (v. 11), abused him basely (vv. 15, 16), and all his friends (v. 20), and triumphed over him, vv. 21, 25, 26.

II. He pleads his own innocence, that he never gave them any provocation (vv. 7, 19), but, on the contrary, had studied to oblige them, vv. 12–14.

III. He prays to God to protect and deliver him, and appear for him (vv. 1, 2), to comfort him (v. 3), to be nigh to him and rescue him (vv. 17, 22), to plead his cause (vv. 23, 24), to defeat all the designs of his enemies against him (vv. 3, 4), to disappoint their expectations of his fall (vv. 19, 25, 26), and, lastly, to countenance all his friends, and encourage them (v. 27).

IV. He prophesies the destruction of his persecutors, vv. 4–6, 8.

V. He promises himself that he shall yet see better days (vv. 9, 10), and promises God that he will then attend him with his praises, vv. 18, 28.

A detailed analysis of psalm

David prays for safety. (1–10)

He complains about his enemies. (11–16)

And calls upon God to support him. (17–28)

Key verse

Verse 11: "False witnesses did rise up."

Key word / key phrase / key phrase

Verse 2, "come to my aid."

Key event / key person / key theme

Request for God's intervention

Key thought

David appeals to the Lord, his Warrior-King, for help.

Key thing to look out for

After a three verse introduction, the psalm has three sections of petitions, verses 4–10; 11–18, and 19–28, each of which concludes with a resolve to praise God.

Key Bible cross-reference

Verse 13. See 30:11; Genesis 37:34.

Key "by way of explanation"

Verse 15, "stumbled." Here David was brought down, not by immoral actions, but by outside circumstances. See 9:3; 27:2; 37:25; 119:165.

Key "Quotable Quote"

"And my tongue shall speak of thy righteousness and of thy praise all the day long."

Psalm 35:28

Psalm 36

Matthew Henry's introduction

We are here led to consider, and it will do us good to consider seriously,

I. The sinfulness of sin, and how mischievous it is, vv. 1–4.

II. The goodness of God, and how gracious he is,

A. To all his creatures in general, vv. 5, 6.

B. To his own people in a special manner, vv. 7–9. By this the psalmist is encouraged to pray for all the saints (v. 10), for himself in particular and his own preservation (v. 11), and to triumph in the certain fall of his enemies, v. 12.

A detailed analysis of psalm

The bad state of the wicked. (1–4)

The goodness of God. (5–12)

Key verse

Verse 6: "Thy righteousness is like the great mountains."

Key word / key phrase / key phrase

Verse 1, "sinfulness of the wicked."

Key event / key person / key theme

Man's wickedness and God's goodness

Key thought

As David reflects on the godlessness of the wicked and the goodness of God, he asks for God's protection.

Key thing to look out for

In verses 5–9 David's lists some of the wonderful characteristics of the Lord.

Key Bible cross-reference

Verse 3. See 94:8–11; Proverbs 2:9–11.

Key "by way of explanation"

Verse 9. "Fountain," that is the source that never dries up.

Key "Quotable Quote"

"Let not the foot of pride come against me, and let not the hand of the wicked remove me."

Psalm 36:11

Psalm 37

Matthew Henry's introduction

I. He forbids us to fret at the prosperity of the wicked in their wicked ways, vv. 1, 7, 8.

II. He gives very good reasons why we should not fret at it.

A. Because of the scandalous character of the wicked (vv. 12, 14, 21, 32) notwithstanding their prosperity, and the honorable character of the righteous, vv. 21, 26, 30, 31.

B. Because of the destruction and ruin which the wicked are nigh to (vv. 2, 9, 10, 20, 35, 36, 38) and the salvation and protection which the righteous are sure of from all the malicious designs of the wicked, vv. 13, 15, 17, 28, 33, 39, 40.

C. Because of the particular mercy God has in store for all good people and the favor he shows them, vv. 11, 16, 18, 19, 22–25, 28, 29, 37.

III. He prescribes very good remedies against this sin of envying the prosperity of the wicked, and great encouragement to use those remedies, vv. 3–6, 27, 34.

A detailed analysis of psalm

Evil doers. (1–6)

Peace, despite the works of evil. (7–20)

Act justly. (21–33)

We are at God's disposal. (34–40)

Key verse

Verse 7: "Rest in the LORD."

Key word / key phrase / key phrase

Verse 4, "Delight yourself in the Lord."

Key event / key person / key theme

Rest in the Lord

Key thought

This psalm is crammed with teaching about godly wisdom.

Key thing to look out for

This teaching is set out in a series of contrasts between the wicked and the righteous.

Key Bible cross-reference

Verse 13. See 2:4.

Key "by way of explanation"

Verse 10, "A little while." The brevity of time alluded to here underlines the certainty of the event. See 59:9; Job 20:5–11; Haggai 2:6.

Key "Quotable Quote"

"But the salvation of the righteous is of the LORD: he is their strength in the time of trouble."

Psalm 37:39

Psalm 38

Matthew Henry's introduction

He complains,

I. Of God's displeasure, and of his own sin which provoked God against him, vv. 1–5.

II. Of his bodily sickness, vv. 6–10.

III. Of the unkindness of his friends, v. 11.

IV. Of the injuries which his enemies did him, pleading his good conduct towards them, yet confessing his sins against God, vv. 12–20. Lastly, he concludes the psalm with earnest prayers to God for his gracious presence and help, vv. 21, 22.

A detailed analysis of psalm

God's displeasure at sin. (1–11)

The psalmist's sufferings and prayers. (12–22)

Key verse

Verse 1: "O LORD, rebuke me not in thy wrath."

Key word / key phrase / key phrase

Verse 4, "a burden too heavy to bear."

Key event / key person / key theme

Sin's heavy burden

Key thought

David pleads, with great urgency, for relief from his severe illness.

Key thing to look out for

The psalm divides into five four-verse sections with a two-verse conclusion.

Key Bible cross-reference

Verse 18. See 3, 4; Psalm 32.

Key "by way of explanation"

Verse 16, "when my foot slips." These words refer to some setback David experienced, in this instance, to his health. See 66:9; 94:18; 121:3.

Key "Quotable Quote"

"Make haste to help me, O Lord my salvation."

Psalm 38:22

Psalm 39

Matthew Henry's introduction

I. He relates the struggle that was in his breast between grace and corruption, between passion and patience, vv. 1–3.

II. He meditates on the doctrine of man's frailty and mortality, and prays to God to instruct him in it, vv. 4–6.

III. He applies to God for the pardon of his sons, the removal of his afflictions, and the lengthening out of his life till he was ready for death, vv. 7–13.

A detailed analysis of psalm

David meditates on human frailty. (1–6)

He asks for pardon and deliverance. (7–13)

Key verse

Verse 9: "I was dumb, I opened not my mouth."

Key word / key phrase / key phrase

Verse 2, "anguish."

Key event / key person / key theme

The confession of a suffering man

Key thought

David is in the middle of an acute illness, verses 10, 11.

Key thing to look out for

David recalls the fragility of human existence on earth and pours out his soul to the Lord.

Key Bible cross-reference

Verse 5. See 90:4; 144:4.

Key "by way of explanation"

Verse 6 gives a summary of human life, echoing the book of Ecclesiastes.

Key "Quotable Quote"

"And now, Lord, what wait I for? my hope is in thee."

Psalm 39:7

Psalm 40

Matthew Henry's introduction

In this psalm,

I. David records God's favor to him in delivering him out of his deep distress, with thankfulness to his praise, vv. 1–5.

II. Thence he takes occasion to speak of the work of our redemption by Christ, vv. 6–10.

III. That gives him encouragement to pray to God for mercy and grace both for himself and for his friends, vv. 11–17.

A detailed analysis of psalm

Confidence for deliverance. (1–5)

Christ's work of redemption. (6–10)

Prayer for mercy and grace. (11–17)

Key verse

Verse 6: "Sacrifice and offering thou didst not desire."

Key word / key phrase

Verse 8, "I desire to do your will."

Key event / key person / key theme

Delight to do God's will

Key thought

This psalm reflects the fact that David's life was filled with praise to the Lord.

Key thing to look out for

David spends the first five verses of this psalm reflecting on God's mercies.

Key Bible cross-reference

Verse 9. See 68:11; 96:2.

Key "by way of explanation"

Verse 12. David is surrounded by unspecified troubles. But he states that they are caused by "my sins."

Key "Quotable Quote"

"I waited patiently for the LORD; and he inclined unto me, and heard my cry."

Psalm 40:1

Psalm 41

Matthew Henry's introduction

I. He here comforts himself in his communion with God under his sickness, by faith receiving and laying hold of God's promises to him (vv. 1–3) and lifting up his heart in prayer to God, v. 4.

II. He here represents the malice of his enemies against him, their malicious censures of him, their spiteful reflections on him, and their insolent conduct towards him, vv. 5–9.

III. He leaves his case with God, not doubting but that he would own and favor him (vv. 10–12), and so the psalm concludes with a doxology, v. 13.

A detailed analysis of psalm

God's care for his people. (1–4)

The treachery of David's enemies. (5–13)

Key verse

Verse 5: "Mine enemies speak evil of me."

Key word / key phrase

Verse 1, "regard for the weak."

Key event / key person / key theme

Joy in helping the poor

Key thought

David is very ill. He prays.

Key thing to look out for

It is possible to be betrayed by even close friends. See John 13:18.

Key Bible cross-reference

Verse 1. See 72:2, 4, 12–14; Proverbs 29:14.

Key "by way of explanation"

Verse 13 concludes Book I of the psalms and appropriately ends with a doxology. See 72:18, 19; 89:52; 106:48; 150.

Key "Quotable Quote"

"Blessed is he that considereth the poor: the LORD will deliver him in time of trouble."

Psalm 41:1

Psalm 42

Matthew Henry's introduction

I. Faith begins with holy desires towards God and communion with him, vv. 1, 2.

II. Sense complains of the darkness and cloudiness of the present condition, aggravated by the remembrance of the former enjoyments, vv. 3, 4.

III. Faith silences the complaint with the assurance of a good issue at last, v. 5.

IV. Sense renews its complaints of the present dark and melancholy state, vv. 6, 7.

V. Faith holds up the heart, notwithstanding, with hope that the day will dawn, v. 8.

VI. Sense repeats its lamentations (vv. 9, 10) and sighs out the same remonstrance it had before made of its grievances.

VII. Faith gets the last word (v. 11), for the silencing of the complaints of sense, and, though it be almost the same with that (v. 5) yet now it prevails and carries the day.

A detailed analysis of psalms

The conflict in the soul of a believer. (42:1–11) David endeavors to still his spirit, with hope and confidence in God. (43:1–5)

Key verse

42:3: "My tears have been my meat day and night."

Key word / key phrase

42:5, "Why are you downcast?"

Key event / key person / key theme

Why are you depressed?

Key thought

Taking the two psalms together, Psalms 42 and 43 have four four-verse stanzas each of which concludes with the same thought. See 42:5, 11; 43:5.

Key thing to look out for

The psalmist prays for deliverance and for God's presence.

Key Bible cross-reference

42:6. See verses 5,11; 43:5.

Key "by way of explanation"

Psalms 42 and 43 form a single prayer asking for deliverance from an attacking enemy: 42:9; 43:2.

Key "Quotable Quote"

"Why art thou cast down, O my soul? and why art thou disquieted within me? hope thou in God: for I shall yet praise him, who is the health of my countenance, and my God."

Psalm 42:11

Psalm 43

Matthew Henry's introduction

In this psalm.

I. David appeals to God about the injuries that were done him by his enemies, vv. 1, 2.

II. He prays to God to restore to him the free enjoyment of public ordinances again, and promises to make a good improvement of them, vv. 3, 4.

III. He endeavors to still the tumult of his own spirit with a lively hope and confidence in God (v. 5).

A detailed analysis of psalms

The conflict in the soul of a believer. (42:1–11) David endeavors to still his spirit, with hope and confidence in God. (43:1–5)

Key verse

42:3: "My tears have been my meat day and night."

Key word / key phrase

42:5, "Why are you downcast?"

Key event / key person / key theme

Why are you depressed?

Key thought

Taking the two psalms together, Psalms 42 and 43 have four four-verse stanzas each of which concludes with the same thought. See 42:5, 11; 43:5.

Key thing to look out for

The psalmist prays for deliverance and for God's presence.

Key Bible cross-reference

42:6. See verses 5,11; 43:5.

Key "by way of explanation"

Psalms 42 and 43 form a single prayer asking for deliverance from an attacking enemy: 42:9; 43:2.

Key "Quotable Quote"

"Why art thou cast down, O my soul? and why art thou disquieted within me? hope thou in God: for I shall yet praise him, who is the health of my countenance, and my God."

Psalm 42:11

Psalm 44

Matthew Henry's introduction

In this psalm the church is taught,

I. To own with thankfulness, to the glory of God, the great things God has done for their fathers, vv. 1–8.

II. To exhibit a memorial of their present calamitous estate, vv. 9–16.

III. To file a protestation of their integrity and adherence to God notwithstanding, vv. 17–22.

IV. To lodge a petition at the throne of grace for succor and relief, vv. 22–26.

A detailed analysis of psalm

A petition for succor and relief. (1–26)

Key verse

Verse 6: "For I will not trust in my bow, neither shall my sword save me."

Key word / key phrase

Verse 2, "my stronghold."

Key event / key person / key theme

A prayer for protection

Key thought

Israel has just suffered a major defeat.

Key thing to look out for

The whole psalm is a request for God's help.

Key Bible cross-reference

Verse 12. See Deuteronomy 32:30; Judges 2:14.

Key "by way of explanation"

Verse 19, "you crushed us." The psalmist states that this did not happen because they had disobeyed the Lord. He is pleading Israel's innocence.

Key "Quotable Quote"

"In God we boast all the day long, and praise thy name for ever."

Psalm 44:8

Psalm 45

Matthew Henry's introduction

The psalm speaks,

I. Of the royal bridegroom, who is Christ.

A. The transcendent excellency of his person, v. 2.

B. The glory of his victories, vv. 3–5.

C. The righteousness of his government, vv. 6, 7.

D. The splendor of his court, vv. 8, 9.

II. Of the royal bride, which is the church.

A. Her consent gained, vv. 10, 11.

B. The nuptials solemnized, vv. 12–15.

C. The issue of this marriage, vv. 16, 17.

A detailed analysis of psalm

This psalm is a prophecy about the Messiah, the Prince, and points to him as the Bridegroom marrying the Church, and as King. (1–17)

Key verse

Verse 1: " . . . my tongue is the pen of a ready writer."

Key word / key phrase

Title, "A wedding song."

Key event / key person / key theme

A royal wedding song

Key thought

This psalm is a great psalm of praise for a king on his wedding day, verse 1.

Key thing to look out for

Verses 3–9 are addressed to the king, and verses 10–15 are addressed to the bride.

Key Bible cross-reference

Verse 7. See 23:5; Isaiah 61:3.

Key "by way of explanation"

Verse 6, "throne." The everlasting nature of this throne is only ultimately fulfilled in Christ, who was rightly known as the Son of David.

Key "Quotable Quote"

"I will make thy name to be remembered in all generations: therefore shall the people praise thee for ever and ever."

Psalm 45:17

Psalm 46

Matthew Henry's introduction

We are here taught,

I. To take comfort in God when things look very black and threatening, vv. 1–5.

II. To mention, to his praise, the great things he had wrought for his church against its enemies, vv. 6–9.

III. To assure ourselves that God who has glorified his own name will glorify it yet again, and to comfort ourselves with that, vv. 10, 11.

A detailed analysis of psalm

Confidence in God. (1–5)

An exhortation to see the Lord. (6–11)

Key verse

Verse 8: "Come, behold the works of the LORD."

Key word / key phrase

Verse 1, "God is our . . ."

Key event / key person / key theme

God is with us

Key thought

This psalm celebrates the security of God's city, Jerusalem.

Key thing to look out for

Note the numerous reasons why Martin Luther was inspired to write his hymn, "A mighty fortress is our God," which was based on this psalm.

Key Bible cross-reference

Verse 9. See 76:3; 1 Samuel 2:4.

Key "by way of explanation"

Verse 10, "Be still." God's great deeds, done on behalf of his people, will bring global recognition. See 22:27; 99:2, 3; 102:15.

Key "Quotable Quote"

"Be still, and know that I am God: I will be exalted among the heathen, I will be exalted in the earth."

Psalm 46:10

Psalm 47

Matthew Henry's introduction

I. We are directed in what manner to do it, publicly, cheerfully, and intelligently, vv. 1, 6, 7.

II. We are furnished with matter for praise.

A. God's majesty, v. 2.

B. His sovereign and universal dominion, vv. 2, 7–9.

C. The great things he had done, and will do, for his people, vv. 3–5.

A detailed analysis of psalm

The people exhorted to praise God. (1–9)

Key verse

Verse 1: "O clap your hands, all ye people."

Key word / key phrase

Verse 3, "He subdued nations."

Key event / key person / key theme

The Lord will subdue all nations

Key thought

The psalmist celebrates God's rule over every nation in the world.

Key thing to look out for

All the nations are told to praise Israel's God, for he created them.

Key Bible cross-reference

Verse 2. See 89:7; 99:3.

Key "by way of explanation"

Verses 5, 6. The Lord goes to the temple. This is represented by the ark, a symbol of God's throne, going into the temple.

Key "Quotable Quote"

"God is gone up with a shout, the LORD with the sound of a trumpet."

Psalm 47:5

Psalm 48

Matthew Henry's introduction

Jerusalem is here praised,

I. For its relation to God, vv. 1, 2.
II. For God's care of it, v. 3.
III. For the terror it strikes on its enemies, vv. 4–7.
IV. For the pleasure it gives to its friends, who delight to think,
A. Of what God has done, does, and will do for it, v. 3.
B. Of the gracious discoveries he makes of himself in and for that holy city, vv. 9, 10.
C. Of the effectual provision which is made for its safety, vv. 11–13.
D. Of the assurance we have of the perpetuity of God's covenant with the children of Zion, v. 14.

A detailed analysis of psalm

The glories of the Church of Christ. (1–14)

Key verse

Verse 3: "God is known in her palaces for a refuge."

Key word / key phrase

Verse 1, "the city of our God."

Key event / key person / key theme

Zion is God's city

Key thought

This psalm thanks God that his great city gives his people security.

Key thing to look out for

The summary of this psalm is found in its central verse, verse 8.

Key Bible cross-reference

Verse 2. See 1 Kings 10:1–13.

Key "by way of explanation"

Verse 3. The walls of Jerusalem are not Zion's defense. God himself is her defense.

Key "Quotable Quote"

"We have thought of thy loving kindness, O God, in the midst of thy temple."

Psalm 48:9

Psalm 49

Matthew Henry's introduction

I. In the preface he proposes to awaken worldly people out of their security (vv. 1–3) and to comfort himself and other godly people in a day of distress, vv. 4, 5.
II. In the rest of the psalm,
A. He endeavors to convince sinners of their folly in doting on the wealth of this world, by showing them
1. That they cannot, with all their wealth, save their friends from death, vv. 6–9.
2. They cannot save themselves from death, v. 10.
3. They cannot secure to themselves a happiness in this world, vv. 11, 12. Much less,
4. Can they secure to themselves a happiness in the other world, v. 14.
B. He endeavors to comfort himself and other good people,
1. Against the fear of death, v. 15.
2. Against the fear of the prospering power of wicked people, vv. 16–20.

A detailed analysis of psalm

A call for attention. (1–5)

Folly of worldliness. (6–14)

Against fear of death. (15–20)

Key verse

Verse 2: "Both low and high, rich and poor, together."

Key word / key phrase

Verse 12, "riches."

Key event / key person / key theme

Riches cannot redeem

Key thought

This psalm is addressed to the rich who trust in their wealth.

Key thing to look out for

The psalmist points out how foolish it is to be in the grip of riches and offers wisdom to replace wealth.

Key Bible cross-reference

Verse 14. See 96:15; Isaiah 5:14.

Key "by way of explanation"

Verse 15, "redeem from the grave." The psalmist looks forward to being in God's presence in heaven. See Luke 16:22.

Key "Quotable Quote"

"But God will redeem my soul from the power of the grave: for he shall receive me."

Psalm 49:15

Psalm 50

Matthew Henry's introduction

Here is,

I. The glorious appearance of the Prince that gives law and judgment, vv. 1–6.

II. Instruction given to his worshippers, to turn their sacrifices into prayers, vv. 7–15.

III. A rebuke to those that pretend to worship God, but live in disobedience to his commands (vv. 16–20), their doom read (vv. 21, 22), and warning given to all to look to their conversation as well as to their devotions, v. 23.

A detailed analysis of psalm

The glory of God. (1–6)

Sacrifices to be changed for prayers. (7–15)

Sincere obedience required. (16–23)

Key verse

Verse 12: "If I were hungry, I would not tell thee."

Key word / key phrase

Verse 5, "Gather to me."

Key event / key person / key theme

True worship

Key thought

This psalm calls God's faithful people to meet before him in worship.

Key thing to look out for

The psalm calls God's followers to examine their motives and to root out wickedness.

Key Bible cross-reference

Verse 5. See Exodus 24:4–8.

Key "by way of explanation"

In Psalm 50 there are seven names or titles for God. Verse 5, "consecrated one," is a reference to Israel, God's covenant people.

Key "Quotable Quote"

"The mighty God, even the LORD, hath spoken, and called the earth from the rising of the sun unto the going down thereof."

Psalm 50:1

Psalm 51

Matthew Henry's introduction

In this psalm,

I. He confesses his sin, vv. 3–6.

II. He prays earnestly for the pardon of his sin, vv. 1, 2, 7, 9.

III. For peace of conscience, vv. 8, 12.

IV. For grace to go and sin no more, vv. 10, 11, 14.

V. For liberty of access to God, v. 15.

IV. He promises to do what he could for the good of the souls of others (v. 13) and for the glory of God, vv. 16, 17, 19. And, lastly, concludes with a prayer for Zion and Jerusalem, v. 18.

A detailed analysis pslam

Pleas for forgiveness. (1–2)

David's understanding of the nature of sin. (3–5).

David's desire for cleansing and renewal. (6–12)

David's resolve to show his gratitude to God. (13–17)

David's prayer for the rebuilding of Jerusalem. (18–19)

Key verse

Verse 3: "For I acknowledge my transgressions: and my sin is ever before me."

Key word / key phrase

Words expressing heartfelt repentance: "blot out," "wash," and "cleanse," verses 1–2.

Key event / key person / key theme

This is explained by the caption at the beginning of the psalm, "To the chief Musician, A Psalm of David, when Nathan the prophet came unto him, after he had gone in to Bathsheba."

Key thought

The different ways in which David expresses his sincere repentance.

Key thing to look out for

The results that will flow from David's forgiveness by God, healing and restoration.

Key biblical cross-reference

2 Samuel chapters 11–12 record the events in David's life which caused him to pray this psalm.

Key "by way of explanation"

Verse 5, "I was shapen in iniquity; and in sin did my mother conceive me." This is not to suggest that conception or birth are sinful. Rather, "The psalmist confesses his total involvement in human sinfulness, from the very beginning of his existence" A.A. Anderson.

Key "Quotable Quote"

"It is generally agreed that this fifty-first psalm is perhaps the classic statement in the Old Testament on the question of repentance [and] is perhaps the classic statement on this whole matter of repentance in the entire Bible."

Martyn Lloyd-Jones

Psalm 52

Matthew Henry's introduction

I. David arraigns Doeg for what he had done, v. 1.

II. He accuses him, convicts him, and aggravates his crimes, vv. 2–4.

III. He passes sentence on him, v. 5.

IV. He foretells the triumphs of the righteous in the execution of the sentence, vv. 6, 7.

V. He comforts himself in the mercy of God and the assurance he had that he should yet praise him, vv. 8, 9.

A detailed analysis of psalm

The enemies of the truth and the Church described, and their destruction. (1–5)

The righteous rejoice. (6–9)

Key verse

Verse 6: "The righteous also shall see, and fear, and shall laugh at him."

Key word / key phrase

Verse 5, "God will bring you down."

Key event / key person / key theme

God's judgment and grace

Key thought

Even though David is being attacked he expresses his firm confidence in the Lord.

Key thing to look out for

God's enemies will not live forever.

Key Bible cross-reference

Verse 8. See 23:6; 27:4.

Key "by way of explanation"

Verse 5. The wicked will be brought low. This is expressed by three images in this verse: "bring you down," "snatch you up," and "uproot you."

Key "Quotable Quote"

"But I am like a green olive tree in the house of God: I trust in the mercy of God for ever and ever."

Psalm 52:8

Psalm 53

Matthew Henry's introduction

The word, as a convincing word, is compared to a hammer, the strokes whereof must be frequently repeated. God, by the psalmist here,

I. Shows us how bad we are, v. 1.

II. Proves it on us by his own certain knowledge, vv. 2, 3.

III. He speaks terror to persecutors, the worst of sinners, vv. 4, 5.

IV. He speaks encouragement to God's persecuted people, v. 6.

(For Psalm 53, see Psalm 14.)

Psalm 54

Matthew Henry's introduction

Here,

I. David complains to God of the malice of his enemies, and prays for help against them, vv. 1–3.

II. He comforts himself with an assurance of the divine favor and protection, and that, in due time, his enemies should be confounded and be delivered, vv. 4–7.

A detailed analysis of psalm

David complains about the malice of his enemies. (1–3)

Assurance of the divine favor and protection. (4–7)

Key verse

Verse 4: "Behold, God is mine helper."

Key word / key phrase

Verse 1, "Save me."

Key event / key person / key theme

A prayer for protection from enemies

Key thought

As David's life is threatened he turns to the Lord for help.

Key thing to look out for

David is not arrogant in his relationship with the Lord, but he is confident that the Lord will answer his cry for help.

Key Bible cross-reference

Title, "When the Ziphites . . .," see 1 Samuel 23:19.

Key "by way of explanation"

Verse 4. In the psalms the most important verse is often not the first verse, or the last verse, but the central verse. In this case the central verse, verse 4, expresses great confidence in the Lord.

Key "Quotable Quote"

"I will freely sacrifice unto thee: I will praise thy name, O LORD; for it is good."

Psalm 54:6

Psalm 55

Matthew Henry's introduction

I. David prays that God would manifest his favor to him, and pleads his own sorrow and fear, vv. 1–8.

II. He prays that God would manifest his displeasure against his enemies, and pleads their great wickedness and treachery, vv. 9–15 and again vv. 20, 21.

III. He assures himself that God would, in due time, appear for him against his enemies, comforts himself with the hopes of it, and encourages others to trust in God, vv. 16–19 and again vv. 22, 23.

A detailed analysis of psalm

Prayer to God to manifest his favor. (1–8)

The great wickedness and treachery of David's enemies. (9–15)

He is sure that God will in due time appear for him. (16–23)

Key verse

Verse 2: "Attend unto me, and hear me."

Key word / key phrase

Verse 22, "Cast your cares."

Key event / key person / key theme

Cast your burden on the Lord

Key thought

David is under great pressure as he is the object of a conspiracy against him in Jerusalem.

Key thing to look out for

In his longing to escape from his trouble David says that he will cast his worries on the Lord.

Key Bible cross-reference

Verse 22. See 1 Peter 5:7.

Key "by way of explanation"

Verse 18, "ransom." The Lord is said to "ransom," "rescue," and "redeem" his people. See Isaiah 50:2; Jeremiah 31:11.

Key "Quotable Quote"

"Cast thy burden upon the LORD, and he shall sustain thee: he shall never suffer the righteous to be moved."

Psalm 55:22

Psalm 56

Matthew Henry's introduction

I. David complains of the malice of his enemies, and begs mercy for himself and justice against them, vv. 1, 2, 5–7.

II. He confides in God, being assured that he took his part, comforting himself with this, that therefore he was safe and should be victorious, and that while he lived he should praise God, vv. 3, 4, 8–13.

A detailed analysis of psalm

David seeks mercy from God, in the middle of the malice of his enemies. (1–7)

He rests his faith on God's promises, and declares his obligation to praise him for mercies. (8–13)

Key verse

Verse 8: "Thou tellest my wanderings: put thou my tears into thy bottle."

Key word / key phrase

Verse 3, "I will trust in you."

Key event / key person / key theme

Trust in God, despite outward circumstances

Key thought

The title to this psalm supplies its background: "When the Philistines had seized him [David] in Gath."

Key thing to look out for

Because David trusts in God he says he will not be afraid of the most frightening situation.

Key Bible cross-reference

Verse 12. See 66:14.

Key "by way of explanation"

Verse 4, "word." The Lord had often promised

to go to the help of his people if they called on him. See 50:15; 130:5.

Key "Quotable Quote"

"In God will I praise his word: in the LORD will I praise his word."

Psalm 56:10

Psalm 57

Matthew Henry's introduction

I. David begins with prayer and complaint, yet not without some assurance of speeding in his request, vv. 1–6.

II. He concludes with joy and praise, vv. 7–11.

A detailed analysis of psalm

David begins with prayer and complaint. (1–6)
He concludes with joy and praise. (7–11)

Key verse

Verse 8: "Awake up, my glory; awake, psaltery and harp."

Key word / key phrase

Verse 2, "I cry out to God."

Key event / key person / key theme

A prayer for help in trouble

Key thought

David spends a night in acute danger and so pleads for deliverance.

Key thing to look out for

This psalm has a simple structure of two groups of verses, 1–5 and 6–11, both asking for God's help. Both of these sets of verses end with an identical refrain. See verses 5, 11.

Key Bible cross-reference

Verse 5. See Exodus 14:4; Isaiah 59:19.

Key "by way of explanation"

Verse 7. This verse explains why David was no longer in the grip of fear.

Key "Quotable Quote"

"For thy mercy is great unto the heavens, and thy truth unto the clouds."

Psalm 57:10

Psalm 58

Matthew Henry's introduction

I. He describes their sin, and aggravates that, vv. 1–5.

II. He imprecates and foretells their ruin, and the judgments which the righteous God would bring on them for their injustice (vv. 6–9) which would redound,

A. To the comfort of the saints, v. 10.

B. To the glory of God, v. 11.

A detailed analysis of psalm

Wicked judges described and reproved. (1–5)
A prayer that they may fall, and their ruin predicted. (6–11)

Key verse

Verse 6: "Break their teeth, O God, in their mouth."

Key word / key phrase

Verse 2, "injustice."

Key event / key person / key theme

Wicked judges will be punished

Key thought

As God is the supreme Judge, David appeals to him to judge the human judges.

Key thing to look out for

The first and last verses state that God will judge unjust judges.

Key Bible cross-reference

Verse 4. See 140:3; Matthew 23:33.

Key "by way of explanation"

Verses 6–8. The language used here looks rather vicious at first sight. The psalmist was making use of the curses which were commonly used at that time in the ancient Near East.

Key "Quotable Quote"

"So that a man shall say, Verily there is a reward for the righteous: verily he is a God that judgeth in the earth."

Psalm 58:11

Psalm 59

Matthew Henry's introduction

In this psalm,

I. He prays to God to defend and deliver him from his enemies, representing them as very bad men, barbarous, malicious, and atheistic, vv. 1–7.

II. He foresees and foretells the destruction of his enemies, which he would give to God the glory of, vv. 8–17.

A detailed analysis of psalm

David prays for deliverance from his enemies. (1–7)

He foresees their destruction. (8–17)

Key verse

Verse 8: "But thou, O Lord, shalt laugh at them."

Key word / key phrase

Verse 1, "Deliver me."

Key event / key person / key theme

Prayer for deliverance from violent people

Key thought

David is being spied on by Saul's men, and so David turns to the Lord for help.

Key thing to look out for

David often suffered verbal attacks. See verses 3–5.

Key Bible cross-reference

Verse 11. See 78:11; 106:13.

Key "by way of explanation"

Verse 2. The people who maliciously attack the psalmist are often labeled "evildoers" or "bloodthirsty men."

Key "Quotable Quote"

"Unto thee, O my strength, will I sing: for God is my defense, and the God of my mercy."

Psalm 59:17

Psalm 60

Matthew Henry's introduction

In this psalm,

I. He reflects on the bad state of the public interests, for many years, in which God had been contending with them, vv. 1–3.

II. He takes notice of the happy turn lately given to their affairs, v. 4.

III. He prays for the deliverance of God's Israel from their enemies, v. 5.

IV. He triumphs in hope of their victories over their enemies, and begs of God to carry them on and complete them, vv. 6–12.

A detailed analysis of psalm

David prays for the deliverance of Israel from their enemies. (1–5)

He asks God to carry on and complete their victories. (6–12)

Key verse

Verse 6: "God hath spoken in his holiness."

Key word / key phrase

Verse 5, "save us."

Key event / key person / key theme

A heavy defeat from their enemies, probably Edom (verse 9)

Key thought

God's people now seek the Lord's deliverance.

Key thing to look out for

Israel is comforted as they recognize the Lord as their Warrior-King.

Key Bible cross-reference

Title. See 2 Samuel 8:13; 1 Chronicles 18:12.

Key "by way of explanation"

Verse 7. The land that the Israelites conquered and settled in belonged to the Lord and so was under his rule.

Key "Quotable Quote"

"Give us help from trouble: for vain is the help of man."

Psalm 60:11

Psalm 61

Matthew Henry's introduction

I. David will call on God because God had protected him, vv. 1–3.

II. He will call on God because God had provided well for him, vv. 4, 5.

III. He will praise God because he had an assurance of the continuance of God's favor to him, vv. 6–8.

A detailed analysis of psalm

As David seeks God he remembers past deliverance. (1–4)

He vows to serve God. (5–8)

Key verse

Verse 4: "I will abide in thy tabernacle for ever."

Key word / key phrase

Verse 4, "the shelter of your wings."

Key event / key person / key theme

A prayer when overwhelmed

Key thought

This psalm asks for God to be present among his people.

Key thing to look out for

The psalmist knows that he can appeal to the Lord for help, as the Lord has never failed him.

Key Bible cross-reference

Verse 5. See 16:6; 37:18.

Key "by way of explanation"

Verse 2. The psalmist likens security in the Lord to being on a rock.

Key "Quotable Quote"

"So will I sing praise unto thy name for ever, that I may daily perform my vows."

Psalm 61:8

Psalm 62

Matthew Henry's introduction

I. David with a great deal of pleasure professes his own confidence in God and dependence on him, and encourages himself to continue waiting on him, vv. 1–7.

II. With a great deal of earnestness he excites and encourages others to trust in God likewise, and not in any creature, vv. 8–12.

A detailed analysis of psalm

David's confidence in God. (1–7)

No trust is to be put in worldly things. (8–12)

Key verse

Verse 5: "My soul, wait thou only upon God."

Key word / key phrase

Verse 5, "find rest."

Key event / key person / key theme

Wait for God

Key thought

David's trust in God is expressed most wonderfully in this psalm.

Key thing to look out for

David wrote this psalm from a position of weakness and some think it may have been written in his old age.

Key Bible cross-reference

Verse 12. See Jeremiah 17:10; Revelation 2:23.

Key "by way of explanation"

Verse 3. The "leaning wall" and "tottering fence" are expressions of David's fragile state.

Key "Quotable Quote"

"Trust in him at all times; ye people, pour out your heart before him: God is a refuge for us."

Psalm 62:8

Psalm 63

Matthew Henry's introduction

Here we have,

I. His desire towards God, vv. 1, 2.

II. His esteem of God, vv. 3, 4.

III. His satisfaction in God, v. 5.

IV. His secret communion with God, v. 6.

V. His joyful dependence on God, vv. 7, 8.

IV. His holy triumph in God over his enemies

and in the assurance of his own safety, vv. 9–11.

A detailed analysis of psalm

David's desire for God. (1,2)

His satisfaction in God. (3–6)

His dependence upon God, and assurance of safety. (7–11)

Key verse

Verse 3: "Because thy loving kindness is better than life, my lips shall praise thee."

Key word / key phrase

Verse 1, "earnestly I seek you."

Key event / key person / key theme

The psalmist's thirst for God

Key thought

The psalm starts with longing but ends with joy.

Key thing to look out for

The intensity of David's longing for God is seen in his earnestly seeking God, and in his seeking God night and day.

Key Bible cross-reference

Title. See 1 Samuel 13:14.

Key "by way of explanation"

Verse 1 mentions thirst, and verse 5 mentions hunger as ways of expressing David's longing for God.

Key "Quotable Quote"

"Thus will I bless thee while I live: I will lift up my hands in thy name."

Psalm 63:4

Psalm 64

Matthew Henry's introduction

I. David prays to God to preserve him from their malicious designs against him, vv. 1, 2.

II. He gives a very bad character of them, as men marked for ruin by their own wickedness, vv. 3–6.

III. By the spirit of prophecy he foretells their destruction, which would redound to the glory of God and the encouragement of his people, vv. 7–10.

A detailed analysis of psalm

Prayer for deliverance. (1–6)

The destruction of the wicked, and encouragement for the righteous. (7–10)

Key verse

Verse 2: "Hide me from the secret counsel of the wicked."

Key word / key phrase

Verse 1, "protect my life."

Key event / key person / key theme

A prayer for God's protection

Key thought

The main weapon the enemy uses against David in this psalm, as in some others, is his tongue.

Key thing to look out for

David's enemies are full of contempt for him.

Key Bible cross-reference

Verse 3. See 59:7.

Key "by way of explanation"

Verses 9, 10 contrast God's judgments on men and his blessings on them.

Key "Quotable Quote"

"The righteous shall be glad in the LORD, and shall trust in him; and all the upright in heart shall glory."

Psalm 64:10

Psalm 65

Matthew Henry's introduction

In this psalm we are directed to give to God the glory of his power and goodness, which appear,

I. In the kingdom of grace (v. 1), hearing prayer (v. 2), pardoning sin (v. 3), satisfying the souls of the people (v. 4), protecting and supporting them, v. 5.

II. In the kingdom of Providence, fixing the mountains (v. 6), calming the sea (v. 7), preserving the regular succession of day and night (v. 8), and making the earth fruitful, vv. 9–13.

A detailed analysis of psalm

God is to be praised in the kingdom of grace. (1–5)

In the kingdom of providence. (6–13)

Key verse

Verse 11: "Thou crownest the year with thy goodness."

Key word / key phrase

Verse 5, "you answer us."

Key event / key person / key theme

A hymn in praise of God's goodness

Key thought

International events are not beyond the Lord's control.

Key thing to look out for

The beauty and fruitfulness of nature comes from the Lord.

Key Bible cross-reference

Verse 5. See 66:3; Isaiah 64:3.

Key "by way of explanation"

Verse 8. One day everyone will acknowledge God and his salvation.

Key "Quotable Quote"

"The pastures are clothed with flocks; the valleys also are covered over with corn; they shout for joy, they also sing."

Psalm 65:13

Psalm 66

Matthew Henry's introduction

All people are here called on to praise God,

I. For the general instances of his sovereign

dominion and power in the whole creation, vv. 1–7.

II. For the special tokens of his favor to the church, his peculiar people, vv. 8–12. And then,

III. The psalmist praises God for his own experiences of his goodness to him in particular, especially in answering his prayers, vv. 13–20.

A detailed analysis of psalm

Praise for God's sovereign power in the creation. (1–7)

For his favor to his Church. (8–12)

And the psalmist's praise for his experience of God's goodness. (13–20)

Key verse

Verse 8: "O bless our God, ye people, and make the voice of his praise to be heard."

Key word / key phrase

Verse 5, "his works."

Key event / key person / key theme

Remember what God has done

Key thought

All deliverances by God demonstrate his power.

Key thing to look out for

Remembering what God has done leads naturally to praising the Lord.

Key Bible cross-reference

Verse 6. See Exodus 14:21; Joshua 3:14–17.

Key "by way of explanation"

This psalm dovetails in well with the events in 2 Kings 19 where Judah is miraculously delivered from the Assyrians.

Key "Quotable Quote"

"Come and hear, all ye that fear God, and I will declare what he hath done for my soul."

Psalm 66:16

Psalm 67

Matthew Henry's introduction

Here is,

I. A prayer for the prosperity of the church of Israel, v. 1.

II. A prayer for the conversion of the Gentiles and the bringing of them into the church, vv. 2–5.

III. A prospect of happy and glorious times when God shall do this, vv. 6, 7.

A detailed analysis of psalm

A prayer for the enlargement of Christ's kingdom. (1–7)

Key verse

Verse 1: "God be merciful unto us, and bless us."

Key word / key phrase

Verse 4, "guide the nations."

Key event / key person / key theme

God will rule the earth

Key thought

Nobody is the same after being blessed by the Lord.

Key thing to look out for

The fruits of the earth and sea are provided by the Lord.

Key Bible cross-reference

Verse 1. See Numbers 6:24–26.

Key "by way of explanation"

Verse 2. This prayer asks that the whole world may know God's goodness.

Key "Quotable Quote"

"Let the people praise thee, O God; let all the people praise thee."

Psalm 67:3

Psalm 68

Matthew Henry's introduction

I. David begins with prayer, both against God's enemies (vv. 1, 2) and for his people, v. 3.

II. He proceeds to praise, which takes up the rest of the psalm, calling on all to praise God (vv. 4, 26, 32) and suggesting many things as matter for praise.

A. The greatness and goodness of God, vv. 4–6.

B. The wonderful works God had wrought for his people formerly, bringing them through the wilderness (vv. 7, 8), settling them in Canaan (vv. 9, 10), giving them victory over their enemies (vv. 11, 12), and delivering them out of the hands of their oppressors, vv. 13, 14.

C. The special presence of God in his church, vv. 15–17.

D. The ascension of Christ (v. 18) and the salvation of his people by him, vv. 19, 20.

E. The victories which Christ would obtain over his enemies, and the favors he would bestow on his church, vv. 21–28.

F. The enlargement of the church by the accession of the Gentiles to it, vv. 29–31. And so he concludes the psalm with an awful acknowledgment of the glory and grace of God, vv. 32–35.

A detailed analysis of psalm

A prayer: The greatness and goodness of God. (1–6)

The wonderful works God performed for his people. (7–14)

The presence of God in his Church. (15–21)

The victories of Christ. (22–28)

The growth of the Church. (29–31)

The glory and grace of God. (32–35)

Key verse

Verse 8: "The earth shook, the heavens also dropped at the presence of God."

Key word / key phrase

Verse 5, "a father."

Key event / key person / key theme

God is the Father of the fatherless.

Key thought

God's people are meant to be distinct, righteous, and holy.

Key thing to look out for

The Lord promises to bear our burdens, whatever they may be.

Key Bible cross-reference

Verse 18. See Ephesians 4:8.

Key "by way of explanation"

Verse 6. Ruth is a perfect example of the truth of this verse. See Ruth 4:14–17.

Key "Quotable Quote"

"Ascribe ye strength unto God: his excellency is over Israel, and his strength is in the clouds."

Psalm 68:34

Psalm 69

Matthew Henry's introduction

David penned this psalm when he was in affliction; and in it,

I. He complains of the great distress and trouble he was in and earnestly begs of God to relieve and succor him, vv. 1–21.

II. He imprecates the judgments of God on his persecutors, vv. 22–29.

III. He concludes with the voice of joy and praise, in an assurance that God would help and succor him, and would do well for the church, vv. 30–36.

A detailed analysis of psalm

David complains of great distress. (1–12)
And begs for succor. (13–21)
He declares the judgments of God. (22–29)
He concludes with joy and praise. (30–36)

Key verse

Verse 1: "Save me, O God; for the waters are come in unto my soul."

Key word / key phrase

Verse 18, "rescue me."

Key event / key person / key theme

A cry for help

Key thought

After Psalm 22 this psalm is the most quoted psalm in the New Testament because of its foreshadowings of Christ's suffering.

Key thing to look out for

Observe the different reasons given for praising the Lord.

Key Bible cross-reference

Verse 4. See 35:19; John 15:25

Key "by way of explanation"

Verse 9. David's devotion to the temple burnt in him like a fire. But this was even more the case with Jesus, John 2:17.

Key "Quotable Quote"

"Draw nigh unto my soul, and redeem it: deliver me because of mine enemies."

Psalm 69:18

Psalm 70

Matthew Henry's introduction

David here prays that God would send,

I. Help to himself, vv. 1, 5.

II. Shame to his enemies, vv. 2, 3.

III. Joy to his friends, v. 4.

(For Psalm 70, see Psalm 40:13–17.)

Psalm 71

Matthew Henry's introduction

I. David begins the psalm with believing prayers, with prayers that God would deliver him and save him (vv. 2, 4), and not cast him off (v. 9) or be far from him (v. 12), and that his enemies might be put to shame, v. 13. He pleads his confidence in God (vv. 1, 3, 5, 7), the experience he had had of help from God (v. 6), and the malice of his enemies against him, vv. 10, 11.

II. He concludes the psalm with believing praises (vv. 14, etc.). Never was his hope more established, vv. 16, 18, 20, 21. Never were his joys and thanksgivings more enlarged, vv. 15, 19, 22–24.

A detailed analysis of psalm

Prayers that God would deliver and save. (1–13)

Believing praises. (14–24)

Key verse

Verse 3: "Be thou my strong habitation."

Key word / key phrase

Verse 6, "from my birth."

Key event / key person / key theme

Prayer for the poor and needy

Key thought

As the psalmist feels that his strength is fading he turns to the Lord in prayer for help.

Key thing to look out for

Even though he is confronted by so many troubles the psalmist says that he still relies on the Lord.

Key Bible cross-reference

Verse 5. See 22:9.

Key "by way of explanation"

Verses 16,17. The Lord's "mighty acts" which he performed for his people reveal his righteousness and so are also called "righteous acts" in verse 24.

Key "Quotable Quote"

"Let my mouth be filled with thy praise and with thy honor all the day."

Psalm 71:8

Psalm 72

Matthew Henry's introduction

David, in spirit,

I. Begins with a short prayer for his successor, v. 1.

II. He passes immediately into a long prediction of the glories of his reign, vv. 2–17. And,

III. He concludes with praise to the God of Israel, vv. 18–20.

A detailed analysis of psalm

David begins with a prayer for Solomon. (1)

He moves on to a prophecy of the glories of his reign, and of Christ's kingdom. (2–17)

Praise to God. (18–20)

Key verse

Verse 7: "In his days shall the righteous flourish."

Key word / key phrase

Verse 8, "rule from sea to sea."

Key event / key person / key theme

The Messiah's rule

Key thought

Justice and righteousness are the characteristics of the king described in this psalm.

Key thing to look out for

The early Christian Church applied this psalm to Jesus as Messiah.

Key Bible cross-reference

Verse 8. See Zechariah 9:10.

Key "by way of explanation"

Verses 18, 19. As at the end of Book I, these verses are in the form of a doxology and conclude Book II of the five books of the psalms.

Key "Quotable Quote"

"He shall spare the poor and needy, and shall save the souls of the needy."

Psalm 72:13

Psalm 73

Matthew Henry's introduction

He begins his account with a sacred principle, which he held fast, and by the help of which he kept his ground and carried his point, v. 1. He then tells us,

I. How he got into the temptation, vv. 2–14.

II. How he got out of the temptation and gained a victory over it, vv. 15–20.

III. How he got by the temptation and was the better for it, vv. 21–23.

A detailed analysis of psalm

The psalmist's temptation. (1–14)

How he gained a victory over it. (15–20)

How he benefited by it. (21–28)

Key verse

Verse 1: "Truly God is good to Israel."

Key word / key phrase

Verse 24, "into glory."

Key event / key person / key theme

The perspective of eternity

Key thought

The destinies of the godly and wicked are compared.

Key thing to look out for

The righteous can become too absorbed in worrying about the wickedness of the wicked.

Key Bible cross-reference

Verse 14. See Proverbs :12; 23:13, 14.

Key "by way of explanation"

Verse 24. The psalmist expresses his sure hope that the Lord will be with him after this life.

Key "Quotable Quote"

"Thou shalt guide me with thy counsel, and afterward receive me to glory."

Psalm 73:24

Psalm 74

Matthew Henry's introduction

The prophet, in the name of the church

I. Puts in complaining pleas of the miseries they suffered, for the quickening of their desires in prayer, vv. 1–11.

II. He puts in comfortable pleas for the encouraging of their faith in prayer, vv. 12–17.

III. He concludes with divers petitions to God for deliverances, vv. 18–23.

A detailed analysis of psalm

The desolations of the sanctuary. (1–11)
Pleas for encouraging faith. (12–17)
Petitions for deliverance. (18–23)

Key verse

Verse 13: "Thou didst divide the sea by thy strength."

Key word / key phrase

Verse 2, "remember."

Key event / key person / key theme

A prayer asking God to remember his covenant

Key thought

God is the all-powerful King.

Key thing to look out for

The second verse and penultimate verse of this psalm include the key word "remember."

Key Bible cross-reference

Verse 14. See Job 41:1; Isaiah 27:1.

Key "by way of explanation"

Verse 2. The Lord purchased or acquired, or created, or chose, the people of Israel to be his people and always cared for them, as was seen during the Exodus.

Key "Quotable Quote"

"The day is thine, the night also is thine: thou hast prepared the light and the sun."

Psalm 74:16

Psalm 75

Matthew Henry's introduction

In this psalm,

I. David returns God thanks for bringing him to the throne, vv. 1, 9.

II. He promises to lay out himself for the public good, in the use of the power God had given him, vv. 2, 3, 10.

III. He checks the insolence of those that opposed his coming to the throne, vv. 4, 5.

IV. He fetches a reason for all this from God's sovereign dominion in the affairs of the children of men, vv. 6–8.

A detailed analysis of psalm

The psalmist declares his resolution to execute judgment. (1–5)
He rebukes the wicked, and concludes with resolutions to praise God. (6–10)

Key verse

Verse 7: "But God is the judge."

Key word / key phrase

Verse 2, "judge uprightly."

Key event / key person / key theme

God is the Judge.

Key thought

This psalm states that the Lord will judge the wicked and the arrogant.

Key thing to look out for

The psalm starts with thanksgiving and ends with praise.

Key Bible cross-reference

Verse 8. See Proverbs 2, 5; Isaiah 65:11.

Key "by way of explanation"

Verse 4, "Do not lift up your horns." A "horn" often stood for strength in the Bible and to "lift up one's horn" meant to attack or defy someone.

Key "Quotable Quote"

"Unto thee, O God, do we give thanks, unto thee do we give thanks: for that thy name is near thy wondrous works declare."

Psalm 75:1

Psalm 76

Matthew Henry's introduction

To celebrate a victory,

I. The psalmist congratulates the happiness of the church in having God so nigh, vv.1–3.

II. He celebrates the glory of God's power, which this was an illustrious instance of, vv. 4–6.

III. He infers hence what reason all have to fear before him, vv. 7–9. And,

IV. What reason his people have to trust in him and to pay their vows to him, vv. 10–12.

A detailed analysis of psalm

The psalmist speaks of God's power. (1–6)

All have to fear and to trust in him. (7–12)

Key verse

Verse 8: "Thou didst cause judgment to be heard from heaven."

Key word / key phrase

Verse 3, "broke."

Key event / key person / key theme

God's wonderful power

Key thought

The Lord revealed himself through his saving actions among the people of Israel.

Key thing to look out for

God's people are urged to acknowledge all that the Lord has done for them.

Key Bible cross-reference

Verse 6. See Job 26:11; Nahum 1:4.

Key "by way of explanation"

A great victory has just been won at Jerusalem. This psalm may have originally celebrated the capture of Jerusalem by David.

Key "Quotable Quote"

"In Judah is God known: his name is great in Israel."

Psalm 76:1

Psalm 77

Matthew Henry's introduction

I. The psalmist complains here of the deep impressions which his troubles made on his spirits, and the temptation he was in to despair of relief, vv. 1–10.

II. He encourages himself to hope that it would be well at last, by the remembrance of God's former appearances for the help of his people, of which he gives several instances, vv. 11–20.

A detailed analysis of psalm

The psalmist's troubles and temptation. (1–10)
He encourages himself by remembering God's help of his people. (11–20)

Key verse

Verse 2: "In the day of my trouble I sought the Lord."

Key word / key phrase

Verse 2, "distress."

Key event / key person / key theme

An overwhelmed person

Key thought

This psalm is designed to bring comfort in times of distress.

Key thing to look out for

Verse 15 points Christians to the death and resurrection of Christ. See Matthew 28:2; Ephesians 1:18–23.

Key Bible cross-reference

Verse 13. See Exodus 15:11.

Key "by way of explanation"

Verses 1–9. God's people have never found it easy to cope with times when the Lord seems to be doing nothing and they have to wait for him to act.

Key "Quotable Quote"

"I will meditate also of all thy work, and talk of thy doings."

Psalm 77:12

Psalm 78

Matthew Henry's introduction

Here is,

I. The preface to this church history, commanding the attention of the present age to it and recommending it to the study of the generations to come, vv. 1–8.

II. The history itself from Moses to David; it is put into a psalm or song that it might be the better remembered and transmitted to posterity, and that the singing of it might affect them with the things here related, more than they would be with a bare narrative of them. The general scope of this psalm we have (vv. 9–11) where notice is taken of the present rebukes they were under (v. 9), the sin which brought them under those rebukes (v. 10), and the mercies of God to them formerly, which aggravated that sin, v. 11. As to the particulars, we are here told,

A. What wonderful works God had wrought for them in bringing them out of Egypt (vv. 12–16), providing for them in the wilderness (vv. 23–29), plaguing and ruining their enemies (vv. 43–53), and at length putting them in possession of the land of promise, vv. 54, 55.

B. How ungrateful they were to God for his favors to them and how many and great provocations they were guilty of. How they murmured against God and distrusted him (vv. 17–20), and did but counterfeit repentance and submission when he punished them (vv. 34–37), thus grieving and tempting him, vv. 40–42. How they affronted God with their idolatries after they came to Canaan, vv. 56–58.

C. How God had justly punished them for their sins (vv. 21, 22) in the wilderness, making their sin their punishment (vv. 29–33), and now, of late, when the ark was taken by the Philistines, vv. 59–64.

D. How graciously God had spared them and returned in mercy to them, notwithstanding their provocations. He had forgiven them formerly (vv. 38, 39), and now, of late, had removed the judgments they had brought on themselves, and brought them under a happy establishment both in church and state, vv. 65–72.

A detailed analysis of psalm

Attention called for. (1–8)

The history of Israel. (9–39)

Their settlement in Canaan. (40–55)

The mercies of God to Israel contrasted with their ingratitude. (56–72)

Key verse

Verse 1: "Give ear, O my people, to my law."

Key word / key phrase

Verse 2, "parables."

Key event / key person / key theme

God continues to guide, despite unbelief.

Key thought

The psalmist remembers how often Israel has rebelled against the Lord.

Key thing to look out for

God's followers have been chosen by the Lord to follow him, just as he chose the tribe of Judah.

Key Bible cross-reference

Verse 2. See Matthew 13:35.

Key "by way of explanation"

Verse 2, "parables." The Lord taught his people in a wide variety of ways, including riddles, proverbs, and parables.

Key "Quotable Quote"

"He brought streams also out of the rock, and caused waters to run down like rivers."

Psalm 78:16

Psalm 79

Matthew Henry's introduction

We have here,

I. A representation of the very deplorable condition that the people of God were in at this time, vv. 1–5.

II. A petition to God for succor and relief, that their enemies might be reckoned with (vv. 6, 7, 10, 12), that their sins might be pardoned (vv. 8, 9), and that they might be delivered, v. 11.

III. A plea taken from the readiness of his people to praise him, v. 13.

A detailed analysis of psalm

The deplorable condition of the people of God. (1–5)

A prayer for help. (6–13)

Key verse

Verse 5: "How long, LORD? wilt thou be angry for ever?"

Key word / key phrase

Verse 1, "defiled."

Key event / key person / key theme

Jerusalem's defilement will be avenged.

Key thought

God's people ask for the Lord's judgment to fall on their enemies. Some of the evil acts of these people are listed in this psalm.

Key thing to look out for

The psalmist asks for the Lord's forgiveness on Israel's sins and for his help.

Key Bible cross-reference

Verse 1. See 2 Kings 25:8–10; 2 Chronicles 36:17–19.

Key "by way of explanation"

Verse 3. See 2 Kings 21:16.

Key "Quotable Quote"

"Help us, O God of our salvation, for the glory of thy name: and deliver us, and purge away our sins, for thy name's sake."

Psalm 79:9

Psalm 80

Matthew Henry's introduction

The psalmist here,

I. Begs for the tokens of God's presence with them and favor to them, vv. 1–3.

II. He complains of the present rebukes they were under, vv. 4–7.

III. He illustrates the present desolations of the church, by the comparison of a vine and a vineyard, which had flourished, but was now destroyed, vv. 8–16.

IV. He concludes with prayer to God for the preparing of mercy for them and the preparing of them for mercy, vv. 17–19.

A detailed analysis of psalm

The psalmist complains of the miseries endured by God's people. (1–7)

Their former prosperity and present desolation. (8–16)

A prayer for mercy. (17–19)

Key verse

Verse 1: "Give ear, O Shepherd of Israel."

Key word / key phrase

Verse 3, "restore us."

Key event / key person / key theme

Israel pleads for God to restore them.

Key thought

The vine/vineyard metaphor is used to bring comfort to the Lord's people.

Key thing to look out for

Israel has been attacked and defeated by a foreign power. Now she turns to the Lord and asks for his restoration.

Key Bible cross-reference

Verse 1. See Exodus 25:22.

Key "by way of explanation"

Verses 3, 7, 19. These verses each have a similar refrain in them. But their appeal increases in urgency each time: "Lord God," "O God Almighty;" and "O Lord God Almighty."

Key "Quotable Quote"

"Turn us again, O God of hosts, and cause thy face to shine; and we shall be saved."

Psalm 80:7

Psalm 81

Matthew Henry's introduction

The two great intentions of our religious assemblies, and which we ought to have in our eye in our attendance on them, are answered in this psalm, which are, to give glory to God and to receive instruction from God, to "behold the beauty of the Lord and to enquire in his temple;" accordingly by this psalm we are assisted on our solemn feast days,

I. In praising God for what he is to his people (vv. 1–3), and has done for them, vv. 4–7.

II. In teaching and admonishing one another about the obligations we lie under to God (vv. 8–10), the danger of revolting from him (vv. 11, 12), and the happiness we should have if we would but keep close to him, vv. 13–16.

A detailed analysis of psalm

God is praised for what he has done for his people. (1–7)

Their obligations to him. (8–16)

Key verse

Verse 8: "Hear, O my people, and I will testify unto thee."

Key word / key phrase

Verse 8, "if you would but listen to me."

Key event / key person / key theme

God's longing for Israel's obedience

Key thought

The psalm states that the Lord who has always heard and delivered his people seeks their allegiance.

Key thing to look out for

God's people are told off for not listening to the Lord.

Key Bible cross-reference

Verse 7. See Numbers 20:1–13.

Key "by way of explanation"

Verse 3, the "new moon" marks the first day of the month. The "first" is probably the Feast of Tabernacles, a great seven day long autumn festival, beginning on the 15th of the month, when the moon is full.

Key "Quotable Quote"

"Sing aloud unto God our strength: make a joyful noise unto the God of Jacob"

Psalm 81:1

Psalm 82

Matthew Henry's introduction

We have here,

I. The dignity of magistracy and its dependence on God, v. 1.

II. The duty of magistrates, vv. 3, 4.

III. The degeneracy of bad magistrates and the mischief they do, vv. 2, 5.

IV. Their doom read, vv. 6, 7.

V. The desire and prayer of all good people that the kingdom of God may be set up more and more, v. 8.

A detailed analysis of psalm

An exhortation to judges. (1–5)

The doom of evil rulers. (6–8)

Key verse

Verse 1: "God standeth in the congregation of the mighty."

Key word / key phrase

Verse 2, "show partiality."

Key event / key person / key theme

Israel's judges rebuked

Key thought

Many of Israel's judges were unjust. This psalm says that the Lord will call them to account.

Key thing to look out for

The desperate needs of the poor and weak are highlighted in this psalm.

Key Bible cross-reference

Verse 6. See John 10:34.

Key "by way of explanation"

Verse 1, "great assembly." This pictures a Hall of Justice where the Lord presides as the supreme Judge. See 1 Kings 7:7; 22:19.

Key "Quotable Quote"

"Deliver the poor and needy: rid them out of the hand of the wicked."

Psalm 82:4

Psalm 83

Matthew Henry's introduction

The psalmist here makes an appeal and application,

I. To God's knowledge, by a representation of their designs and endeavors to destroy Israel, vv. 1–8.

II. To God's justice and jealousy, both for his church and for his own honor, by an earnest prayer for the defeat of their attempt, that the church might be preserved, the enemies humbled, and God glorified, vv. 9–18.

A detailed analysis of psalm

The purposes of the enemies of Israel. (1–8)

Earnest prayer for their defeat. (9–18)

Key verse

Verse 13: "O my God, make them like a wheel; as the stubble before the wind."

Key word / key phrase

Verse 2, "enemies."

Key event / key person / key theme

Plea for God to destroy Israel's enemies

Key thought

As the whole world seem to be against Israel, God's people ask the Lord to crush their enemies.

Key thing to look out for

The psalm ends with the prayer that even Israel's enemies would turn to the Lord.

Key Bible cross-reference

Verse 11. See Judges 7:25; 8:12.

Key "by way of explanation"

Verse 1, "do not keep silent." This was another way of asking the Lord to act on behalf of his people.

Key "Quotable Quote"

"Keep not thou silence, O God: hold not thy peace, and be not still, O God."

Psalm 83:1

Psalm 84

Matthew Henry's introduction

The psalmist here with great devotion expresses his affection,

I. To the ordinances of God; his value for them (v. 1), his desire towards them (vv. 2, 3), his conviction of the happiness of those that did enjoy them (vv. 4–7), and his placing his own happiness so very much in the enjoyment of them, v. 10.

II. To the God of the ordinances; his desire towards him (vv. 8, 9), his faith in him (v. 11), and his conviction of the happiness of those that put their confidence in him, v. 12.

A detailed analysis of psalm

The pilgrim's longing to be in the temple. (1–3)

The happy pilgrim. (4–7)

A prayer for God's blessing. (8–12)

Key verse

Verse 1: "How amiable are thy tabernacles, O LORD of hosts!"

Key word / key phrase

Verse 4, "Blessed."

Key event / key person / key theme

The joy of living with God

Key thought

The psalmist longs to enter the Lord's temple so he can rest in the Lord's presence.

Key thing to look out for

The psalmist seeks refreshment from the Lord as he travels along on his tough pilgrimage.

Key Bible cross-reference

Verse 7. See Isaiah 40:31.

Key "by way of explanation"

Verse 5, "those whose strength is in you." The Lord gives his strength to those who acknowledge him as their deliverer.

Key "Quotable Quote"

"Blessed are they that dwell in thy house: they will be still praising thee."

Psalm 84:4

Psalm 85

Matthew Henry's introduction

The church is like Noah in the ark, between life and death, between hope and fear; being so,

I. Here is the dove sent forth in prayer. The petitions are against sin and wrath (v. 4) and for mercy and grace, v. 7. The pleas are taken from former favors (vv. 1–3) and present distresses, vv. 5, 6.

II. Here is the dove returning with an olive branch of peace and good tidings; the psalmist expects her return (v. 8) and then recounts the favors to God's Israel which by the spirit of prophecy he gave assurance of to others, and by the spirit of faith he took the assurance of to himself, vv. 9–13.

A detailed analysis of psalm

Prayers for the continuance of former mercies. (1–7)

Trust in God's goodness. (8–13)

Key verse

Verse 4: "Turn us, O God of our salvation, and cause thine anger toward us to cease."

Key word / key phrase

Verse 6, "revive."

Key event / key person / key theme

A prayer for revival

Key thought

God's people, in their distress, express their great desire to be renewed by the Lord.

Key thing to look out for

The psalmist recalls how the Lord has refreshed and restored his people in past times.

Key Bible cross-reference

Verse 9. See Numbers 14:22; Ezekiel 39:21.

Key "by way of explanation"

Verse 10. God's mercy and grace towards his people is expressed in four wonderful personifications: "Love and faithfulness . . . righteousness and peace."

Key "Quotable Quote"

"Show us thy mercy, O LORD, and grant us thy salvation."

Psalm 85:7

Psalm 86

Matthew Henry's introduction

David, in this prayer (according to the nature of that duty),

I. Gives glory to God, vv. 8–10, 12, 13.

II. Seeks for grace and favor from God, that God would hear his prayers (vv. 1, 6, 7), preserve and save him, and be merciful to him (vv. 2, 3, 16), that he would give him joy, and grace, and strength, and put honor on him, vv. 4, 11, 17. He pleads God's goodness (vv. 5, 15) and the malice of his enemies, v. 14.

A detailed analysis of psalm

The psalmist pleads his earnestness, and the mercy of God, as reasons why his prayer should be heard. (1–7)

He renews his requests for help. (8–17)

Key verse

Verse 3: "Be merciful unto me, O Lord: for I cry unto thee daily."

Key word / key phrase

Verse 11, "walk in your truth."

Key event / key person / key theme

Teach my your way, O Lord

Key thought

The psalmist feels battered. He looks to the Lord for mercy and protection.

Key thing to look out for

The psalmist knows that the Lord pours down his love on those to turn to him in prayer.

Key Bible cross-reference

Verse 9. See Revelation 15:4.

Key "by way of explanation"

Verse 11 "teach me." The psalmist recognizes that he must follow the Lord's ways and that it is not enough that his enemies should stop attacking him.

Key "Quotable Quote"

"In the day of my trouble I will call upon thee: for thou wilt answer me."

Psalm 86:7

Psalm 87

Matthew Henry's introduction

Zion, for the temple's sake, is here preferred,

I. Before the rest of the land of Canaan, as being crowned with special tokens of God's favor, vv. 1–3.

II. Before any other place or country whatsoever, as being replenished with more eminent men and with a greater plenty of divine blessings, vv. 4–7.

A detailed analysis of psalm

The glory of Mount Zion, the site of Jerusalem. (1–3)

It is filled with the divine blessing. (4–7)

Key verse

Verse 3: "Glorious things are spoken of thee, O city of God."

Key word / key phrase

Verse 2, "Zion."

Key event / key person / key theme

God's city is glorious

Key thought

This is the only psalm to picture other nations coming in to Jerusalem to be citizens alongside Israel in God's presence (verse 4).

Key thing to look out for

Music and song in praise of God are to be heard in the Lord's city.

Key Bible cross-reference

Verse 1. See Isaiah 14:32.

Key "by way of explanation"

Verse 7, "All my fountains." Everything that refreshes the soul is found in Zion, God's city.

Key "Quotable Quote"

"Glorious things are spoken of thee, O city of God."

Psalm 87:3

Psalm 88

Matthew Henry's introduction

In this psalm we have,

I. The great pressure of spirit that the psalmist was under, vv. 3–6.

II. The wrath of God, which was the cause of that pressure, vv. 7, 15–17.

III. The wickedness of his friends, vv. 8, 18.

IV. The application he made to God by prayer, vv. 1, 2, 9, 13.

V. His humble expostulations and pleadings with God, vv. 10, 12, 14.

A detailed analysis of psalm

The psalmist pours out his soul to God in lamentation. (1–9)

He wrestles by faith, in his prayer to God for comfort. (10–18)

Key verse

Verse 3: "For my soul is full of troubles."

Key word / key phrase

Verse 1, "I cry out."

Key event / key person / key theme

Crying from the depths of affliction

Key thought

The psalmist says he is on the edge of death. He prays to the Lord about his situation.

Key thing to look out for

From the depths of his troubles the psalmist says that he knows salvation is with the Lord.

Key Bible cross-reference

Verse 10. See Isaiah 14:9.

Key "by way of explanation"

This is "the saddest psalm in the whole Psalter" (Kirkpatrick, quoted by L. Allen). Yet in the darkness the psalmist continues to pray.

Key "Quotable Quote"

"Let my prayer come before thee: incline thine ear unto my cry."

Psalm 88:2

Psalm 89

Matthew Henry's introduction

I. The psalmist, in the joyful pleasant part of the psalm, gives glory to God, and takes comfort to himself and his friends. This he does more briefly, mentioning God's mercy and truth (v. 1) and his covenant (vv. 2–4), but more largely in the following verses, in which,

A. He adores the glory and perfection of God, vv. 5–14.

B. He pleases himself in the happiness of those that are admitted into communion with him, vv. 15–18.

C. He builds all his hope on God's covenant with David, as a type of Christ, vv. 19–37.

II. In the melancholy part of the psalm he laments the present calamitous state of the prince and royal family (vv. 38–45), expostulates with God on it (vv. 46–49), and then concludes with prayer for redress, vv. 50, 51.

A detailed analysis of psalm

God's mercy and truth, and his covenant. (1–4)

The glory and perfection of God. (5–14)

The happiness of those in communion with him. (15–18)

God's covenant with David, as a type of Christ. (19–37)

A calamitous state lamented. Prayer for redress. (38–52)

Key verse

Verse 5: "And the heavens shall praise thy wonders, O LORD."

Key word / key phrase

Verse 2. "Your love stands."

Key event / key person / key theme

Claiming God's promises in affliction

Key thought

The psalmist mourns over the fall of David's dynasty, verses 38–45, and feels totally rejected.

Key thing to look out for

The psalmist does, however, also express his trust in the Lord's righteousness and faithfulness.

Key Bible cross-reference

Title. See 1 Samuel 13:14.

Key "by way of explanation"

Verse 10, "Rahab" refers to a mythical monster, supposed to live in the deepest waters, and can be compared with leviathan, 104:26.

Key "Quotable Quote"

"I will sing of the mercies of the LORD for ever:

with my mouth will I make known thy faithfulness to all generations."

Psalm 89:1

Psalm 90

Matthew Henry's introduction

I. Moses comforts himself and his people with the eternity of God and their interest in him, vv. 1, 2.

II. He humbles himself and his people with the consideration of the frailty of man, vv. 3–6.

III. He submits himself and his people to the righteous sentence of God passed on them, vv. 7–11.

IV. He commits himself and his people to God by prayer for divine mercy and grace, and the return of God's favor, vv. 12–17.

A detailed analysis of psalm

The eternity of God, the frailty of humans. (1–6)

Submission to divine chastisements. (7–11)

Prayer for mercy and grace. (12–17)

Key verse

Verse 1: "Lord, thou hast been our dwelling place in all generations."

Key word / key phrase

Verse 12, "Teach us to number our days."

Key event / key person / key theme

Numbering our days

Key thought

The Lord's everlasting nature is compared with transitory human life.

Key thing to look out for

This psalm expresses man's state of hopelessness before the Lord, but does not forget the Lord's unfailing love.

Key Bible cross-reference

Verse 4. See 2 Peter 3:8.

Key "by way of explanation"

Verse 14 "morning." After the dark "night" of God's wrath, the psalmist is confident that God's love will come in the morning.

Key "Quotable Quote"

"For a thousand years in thy sight are but as yesterday when it is past, and as a watch in the night."

Psalm 90:4

Psalm 91

Matthew Henry's introduction

Observe,

I. The psalmist's own resolution to take God for his keeper (v. 2), from which he gives both direction and encouragement to others, v. 9.

II. The promises which are here made, in God's name, to all those that do so in sincerity.

A. They shall be taken under the peculiar care of Heaven, vv. 1, 4.

B. They shall be delivered from the malice of the powers of darkness (vv. 3, 5, 6), and that by a distinguishing preservation, vv. 7, 8.

C. They shall be the charge of the holy angels, vv. 10–12.

D. They shall triumph over their enemies, v. 13.

E. They shall be the special favorites of God himself, vv. 14–16.

A detailed analysis of psalm

The safety of those who have God for their refuge. (1–8)

Their favor with him. (9–16)

Key verse

Verse 11: "For he shall give his angels charge over thee, to keep thee in all thy ways."

Key word / key phrase

Verse 1, "shelter."

Key event / key person / key theme

Living under the shadow of the Almighty

Key thought

This psalm was composed out of a heart that was brimming over with the experience of God's presence.

Key thing to look out for

The psalm states that the godly will be protected from four threats, verses 5, 6, and from four beasts, verse 13.

Key Bible cross-reference

Verse 11. See Matthew 4:6; Luke 4:10.

Key "by way of explanation"

Verse 1, "shelter." It is in the temple that God's followers find the Lord's security and protection.

Key "Quotable Quote"

"He that dwelleth in the secret place of the most High shall abide under the shadow of the Almighty."

Psalm 91:1

Psalm 92

Matthew Henry's introduction

I. Praise, the business of the Sabbath, is here recommended, vv. 1–3.

II. God's works, which gave occasion for the Sabbath, are here celebrated as great and unsearchable in general, vv. 4–6. In particular, with reference to the works both of providence and redemption, the psalmist sings unto God both of mercy and judgment, the ruin of sinners and the joy of saints, three times counterchanged.

A. The wicked shall perish (v. 7), but God is eternal, v. 8.

B. God's enemies shall be cut off, but David shall be exalted, vv. 9, 10.

C. David's enemies shall be confounded (v. 11), but all the righteous shall be fruitful and flourishing, vv. 12–15.

A detailed analysis of psalm

Praise is the business of the Sabbath. (1–6)

The wicked shall perish, but God's people shall be exalted. (7–15)

Key verse

Verse 6: "A brutish man knoweth not; neither doth a fool understand this."

Key word / key phrase

Verse 4, "I sing for joy."

Key event / key person / key theme

It is good to praise the Lord

Key thought

The psalmist looks to God, reflecting on how high he is exalted, and concludes that his enemies will be defeated.

Key thing to look out for

Those who live in God's presence may rest secure.

Key Bible cross-reference

Verse 13. See 2 Kings 21:5; 23:11,12.

Key "by way of explanation"

Verse 6. "Fools" have a completely godless outlook on life.

Key "Quotable Quote"

"It is a good thing to give thanks unto the LORD, and to sing praises unto thy name, O most High."

Psalm 92:1

Psalm 93

Matthew Henry's introduction

About God's kingdom glorious things are here spoken.

I. Have other kings their royal robes? So has he, v. 1.

II. Have they their thrones? So has he, v. 2.

III. Have they their enemies whom they subdue and triumph over? So has he, vv. 3, 4.

IV. Is it their honor to be faithful and holy? So it is his, v. 5.

A detailed analysis of psalm

The majesty, power, and holiness of Christ's kingdom. (1–5)

Key verse

Verse 3: "The floods have lifted up, O LORD."

Key word / key phrase

Verse 1, "majesty."

Key event / key person / key theme

The Lord reigns

Key thought

This psalm, in common with psalms 47, 94–100, praises the Lord for his global reign.

Key thing to look out for

The psalmist longs for the prayer, "thy kingdom come" to be realized.

Key Bible cross-reference

Verse 3. See Job 38:8–11.

Key "by way of explanation"

Verse 5, "statutes." These refer to the Lord's laws which do not change and which need to be followed if people are to live in harmony with God and each other.

Key "Quotable Quote"

"Thy testimonies are very sure: holiness becometh thine house, O LORD, for ever."

Psalm 93:5

Psalm 94

Matthew Henry's introduction

Two things this psalm speaks:

I. Conviction and terror to the persecutors (vv. 1–11), showing them their danger and folly, and arguing with them.

II. Comfort and peace to the persecuted (vv. 12–23), assuring them, both from God's promise and from the psalmist's own experience, that their troubles would end well, and God would, in due time, appear to their joy and the confusion of those who set themselves against them.

A detailed analysis of psalm

The danger and folly of persecutors. (1–11)

Comfort and peace to the persecuted. (12–23)

Key verse

Verse 6: "They slay the widow and the stranger, and murder the fatherless."

Key word / key phrase

Verse 1, "God who avenges."

Key event / key person / key theme

Revenge belongs only to God

Key thought

In the face of blatant injustice and oppression of the poor the psalmist cries out to the Judge of the world.

Key thing to look out for

The psalmist takes comfort in the thought that God knows all about the evil that is being perpetrated in the world.

Key Bible cross-reference

Verse 11. See 1 Corinthians 3:20.

Key "by way of explanation"

Verse 17, "silence of death." If it had not been for the Lord's help the wicked would never have been exposed and the psalmist would lie in silence in his grave.

Key "Quotable Quote"

"The LORD knoweth the thoughts of man, that they are vanity."

Psalm 94:11

Psalm 95

Matthew Henry's introduction

In singing psalms it is intended,

I. That we should "make melody unto the Lord;" this we are here excited to do, and assisted in doing, being called on to praise God (vv. 1, 2) as a great God (vv. 3–5) and as our gracious benefactor, vv. 6, 7.

II. That we should teach and admonish ourselves and one another; and we are here taught and warned to hear God's voice (v. 7), and not to harden our hearts, as the Israelites in the wilderness did (vv. 8, 9), lest we fall under God's wrath and fall short of his rest, as they did, vv. 10, 11.

A detailed analysis of psalm

An exhortation to praise God. (1–7)

A warning not to tempt him. (7–11)

Key verse

Verse 2: "Let us come before his presence with thanksgiving."

Key word / key phrase

Verse 1, "Let us sing . . . to the Lord."

Key event / key person / key theme

A call to worship the Lord

Key thought

The psalmist gives reasons for praising the Lord: he is superior to any other supposed god, and the whole world belongs to him.

Key thing to look out for

Every godly person is called to worship.

Key Bible cross-reference

Verses 8,9. See Exodus 17:1–7; Numbers 20:2–13.

Key "by way of explanation"

Verses 4, 5. God rules everywhere, including all the extremes and corners of the universe, the "depths . . . mountain peaks . . . sea . . . dry land."

Key "Quotable Quote"

"O come, let us worship and bow down: let us kneel before the LORD our maker."

Psalm 95:6

Psalm 96

Matthew Henry's introduction

Here is,

I. A call given to all people to praise God, to worship him, and give glory to him, as a great and glorious God, vv. 1–9.

II. Notice given to all people of God's universal government and judgment, which ought to be the matter of universal joy, vv. 10–13.

(For Psalm 96, see 1 Chronicles 16:23–33.)

Psalm 97

Matthew Henry's introduction

The Lord Jesus reigns, to the joy of all mankind (v. 1); and his government speaks,

I. Terror to his enemies; for he is a prince of inflexible justice and irresistible power, vv. 2–7.

II. Comfort to his friends and loyal subjects, arising from his sovereign dominion, the care he takes of his people, and the provision he makes for them, vv. 8–12.

A detailed analysis of psalm

The Lord reigns in power that cannot be resisted. (1–7)

His care of his people, and his provision for them. (8–12)

Key verse

Verse 11: "Light is sown for the righteous, and gladness for the upright in heart."

Key word / key phrase

Verse 1, "The Lord reigns."

Key event / key person / key theme

The Lord is the supreme ruler

Key thought

The psalmist is filled with joy because God reigns over the universe.

Key thing to look out for

Those who worship idols will be disgraced.

Key Bible cross-reference

Verse 8. See Isaiah 26:9.

Key "by way of explanation"

Verse 6, "proclaim his righteousness." By looking into the night sky people can praise God, for they know that all nature testifies to the Creator.

Key "Quotable Quote"

"Rejoice in the LORD, ye righteous; and give thanks at the remembrance of his holiness."

Psalm 97:12

Psalm 98

Matthew Henry's introduction

I. The glory of the Redeemer, vv. 1–3.

II. The joy of the redeemed, vv. 4–9.

A detailed analysis of psalm

The glory of the Redeemer. (1–3)

The joy of the Redeemer. (4–9)

Key verse

Verse 4: "Make a joyful noise unto the LORD."

Key word / key phrase

Verse 1, "a new song."

Key event / key person / key theme

Israel's God is a glorious King

Key thought

All of God's characteristics, including his rule and his righteousness, are worthy of celebration

Key thing to look out for

The reasons why God is to be praised.

Key Bible cross-reference

Verse 2. See Isaiah 52:10.

Key "by way of explanation"

Verse 2. "Salvation" and "righteousness" are often linked in the psalms, as the Lord's actions which bring about his salvation also demonstrate his righteousness.

Key "Quotable Quote"

"Let the floods clap their hands: let the hills be joyful together."

Psalm 98:8

Psalm 99

Matthew Henry's introduction

The people of Israel are here required to praise and exalt God, and to worship before him, in consideration of these two things:

I. The happy constitution of the government they were under, both in sacred and civil things, vv. 1–5.

II. Some instances of the happy administration of it, vv. 6–9.

A detailed analysis of psalm

God rules the world. (1–3)

God rules over Israel. (4–5)

This holy God is also a merciful God. (6–9)

Key verse

Verse 9: "Exalt the LORD our God, and worship at his holy hill."

Key word / key phrase

Verses 3,5,9. "he is holy."

Key event / key person / key theme

Holiness

Key thought

The psalmist depicts the Lord as the awesome and holy King to whom all nations should bow.

Key thing to look out for

In the middle of worshiping the Lord, the psalmist recalls that he is a forgiving God.

Key Bible cross-reference

Verse 7. See Exodus 33:9.

Key "by way of explanation"

In verse 6, "Moses . . . Aaron . . . Samuel" are selected as they represented the Lord to the Israelites in their moments of special difficulty.

Key "Quotable Quote"

"The LORD reigneth; let the people tremble: he sitteth between the cherubims; let the earth be moved."

Psalm 99:1

Psalm 100

Matthew Henry's introduction

Here,

I. We are called on to praise God and rejoice in him, vv. 1, 2, 4.

II. We are furnished with matter for praise; we must praise him, considering his being and relation to us (v. 3) and his mercy and truth, v. 5.

A detailed analysis of psalm

An exhortation to praise God, and rejoice in him. (1–5)

Key verse

Verse 1: "Make a joyful noise unto the LORD, all ye lands."

Key word / key phrase

Verse 1, "joy."

Key event / key person / key theme

Serve the Lord with gladness

Key thought

The title to this psalm states that it was used as a prayer of thanksgiving.

Key thing to look out for

Reasons for worshiping the Lord with gladness

Key Bible cross-reference

Verse 5. See Ezra 3:11; Jeremiah 33:11.

Key "by way of explanation"

Verse 1, "all the earth." Even though only

God's people have a special relationship with the Lord, everyone on earth is summoned to worship God.

Key "Quotable Quote"

"For the LORD is good; his mercy is everlasting; and his truth endureth to all generations."

Psalm 100:5

Psalm 101

Matthew Henry's introduction

Here is,

I. The general scope of David's vow, vv. 1, 2.

II. The particulars of it, that he would detest and discountenance all manner of wickedness (vv. 3–5, 7, 8) and that he would favor and encourage such as were virtuous, v. 6.

A detailed analysis of psalm

David's vow and profession of godliness. (1–8)

Key verse

Verse 2: "I will behave myself wisely in a perfect way."

Key word / key phrase

Verse 2, "a blameless heart."

Key event / key person / key theme

Commitment to a holy life

Key thought

This psalm is cast in the form of a pledge in which the king promises to rule with justice.

Key thing to look out for

The psalmist determines not to serve the Lord intermittently, but "every morning," verse 8.

Key Bible cross-reference

Verse 2. See 1 Kings 3:7–9.

Key "by way of explanation"

Verse 8. "Every morning," that is, in the daily courts of justice presided over by the king.

Key "Quotable Quote"

"I will sing of mercy and judgment: unto thee, O LORD, will I sing."

Psalm 101:1

Psalm 102

Matthew Henry's introduction

In the psalm we have,

I. A sorrowful complaint which the psalmist makes, either for himself or in the name of the church, of great afflictions, which were very pressing, vv. 1–11.

II. Seasonable comfort fetched in against these grievances,

A. From the eternity of God, vv. 12, 24, 27.

B. From a believing prospect of the deliverance which God would, in due time, work for his afflicted church (vv. 13–22) and the continuance of it in the world, v. 28.

A detailed analysis of psalm

A sorrowful complaint of great afflictions. (1–11)

Future hope. (12–22)

The unchangeableness of God. (23–28)

Key verse

Verse 7: "I watch, and am as a sparrow alone upon the house top."

Key word / key phrase

Verse 1, "my cry for help."

Key event / key person / key theme

The prayer of an overwhelmed believer

Key thought

This psalmist is in great distress. But it is second nature to him to turn to the Lord in prayer.

Key thing to look out for

From the depths of his own situation the psalmist raises his eyes to see the Lord sitting on his throne and ruling the world.

Key Bible cross-reference

Verses 25–27. See Hebrews 1:10–12.

Key "by way of explanation"

Verse 14, "dear to your servants." God's people love Jerusalem. How much more does the Lord love his own city, and thus his people who worship him in it.

Key "Quotable Quote"

"Hear my prayer, O LORD, and let my cry come unto thee."

Psalm 102:1

Psalm 103

Matthew Henry's introduction

The psalmist,

I. Stirs up himself and his own soul to praise God (vv. 1, 2) for his favor to him in particular (vv. 3–5), to the church in general, and to all good men, to whom he is, and will be, just, and kind, and constant (vv. 6–18), and for his government of the world, v. 19.

II. He desires the assistance of the holy angels, and all the works of God, in praising him, vv. 20–22.

A detailed analysis of psalm

An exhortation to bless God for his mercy. (1–5)
And to the Church and to all men. (6–14)
For the constancy of his mercy. (15–18)
For the government of the world. (19–22)

Key verse

Verse 15: "As for man, his days are as grass."

Key word / key phrase

Verse 1, "Praise."

Key event / key person / key theme

Bless the Lord

Key thought

Among many other things, the psalmist thanks the Lord for the personal blessings he has received.

Key thing to look out for

The psalmists many reasons for praising the Lord.

Key Bible cross-reference

Verse 8. See James 5:11.

Key "by way of explanation"

Verses 1, 2, 22, "O my soul." This was a normal way to speak to oneself. See 116:7.

Key "Quotable Quote"

"Bless the LORD, O my soul: and all that is within me, bless his holy name."

Psalm 103:1

Psalm 104

Matthew Henry's introduction

Many great things the psalmist here gives God the glory of

I. The splendor of his majesty in the upper world, vv. 1–4.

II. The creation of the sea and the dry land, vv. 5–9.

III. The provision he makes for the maintenance of all the creatures according to their nature, vv. 10–18, 27, 28.

IV. The regular course of the sun and moon, vv. 19–24.

V. The furniture of the sea, vv. 25, 26.

IV. God's sovereign power over all the creatures, vv. 29–32. And, lastly, he concludes with a pleasant and firm resolution to continue praising God (vv. 33–35), with which we should heartily join in singing this psalm.

A detailed analysis of psalm

God's majesty in the heavens, and the creation of the sea, and the dry land. (1–9)
His provision for all creatures. (10–18)
The regular course of day and night, and God's sovereign power over all the creatures. (19–30)
A resolution to continue praising God. (31–35)

Key verse

Verse 2: "Who coverest thyself with light as with a garment."

Key word / key phrase

Verse 5, "sets the earth."

Key event / key person / key theme

God's creation

Key thought

The Lord God is the Creator and the psalmist therefore worships him.

Key thing to look out for

Many of the psalms follow a particular pattern. This one has stanzas grouped in the following sets of verses: three, five, nine, five, three.

Key Bible cross-reference

Verse 4. See Hebrews 1:7.

Key "by way of explanation"

Verses 1–4 picture the forces of nature being used in God's service. His robe is "light" in verse 2, and his "chariot" is the "clouds" in verse 3.

Key "Quotable Quote"

"The glory of the LORD shall endure for ever: the LORD shall rejoice in his works."

Psalm 104:31

Psalm 105

Matthew Henry's introduction

I. God's covenant with the patriarchs, vv. 8–11.

II. His care of them while they were strangers, vv. 12–15.

III. His raising up Joseph to be the shepherd and stone of Israel, vv. 16–22.
IV. The increase of Israel in Egypt and their deliverance out of Egypt, vv. 23–38.
V. The care he took of them in the wilderness and their settlement in Canaan, vv. 39–45.

A detailed analysis of psalm

A solemn call to praise and serve the Lord. (1–7)

His gracious dealings with Israel. (8–23)

Their deliverance from Egypt, and their settlement in Canaan. (24–45)

Key verse

Verse 5: "Remember his marvelous works that he hath done."

Key word / key phrase

Verse 8, "he remembers."

Key event / key person / key theme

Remember, God keeps his promises

Key thought

The countless ways in which God acted on behalf of his people.

Key thing to look out for

The plagues show that the Lord rules over the hearts of even evil men.

Key Bible cross-reference

Verse 16. See Genesis 41:53–57.

Key "by way of explanation"

Verse 5. "Remember." The Lord has remembered his people, and his people are duty bound to remember him.

Key "Quotable Quote"

"He is the LORD our God: his judgments are in all the earth."

Psalm 105:7

Psalm 106

Matthew Henry's introduction

In this psalm we have,

I. The preface to the narrative, speaking honor to God (vv. 1, 2), comfort to the saints (v. 3), and the desire of the faithful towards God's favor, vv. 4, 5.
II. The narrative itself of the sins of Israel, aggravated by the great things God did for them, an account of which is intermixed. Their provocations at the Red Sea (vv. 6–12), lusting (vv. 13–15), mutinying (vv. 16–18), worshipping the golden calf (vv. 19–23), murmuring (vv. 24–27), joining themselves to Baal-peor (vv. 28–31), quarrelling with Moses (vv. 32, 33), incorporating themselves with the nations of Canaan, vv. 34–39. To this is added an account how God had rebuked them for their sins, and yet saved them from ruin, vv. 40–46.
III. The conclusion of the psalm with prayer and praise, vv. 47, 48.

A detailed analysis of psalm

The happiness of God's people. (1–5)

Israel's sins. (6–12)

Their provocations. (13–33)

Their rebellions in Canaan. (34–46)

Prayer for more complete deliverance. (47,48)

Key verse

Verse 7: "Our fathers understood not thy wonders in Egypt."

Key word / key phrase

Verse 6, "We have sinned."

Key event / key person / key theme

Confessing sin to God

Key thought

The psalmist recalls Israel's unfaithfulness, but nevertheless asks for the Lord's salvation.

Key thing to look out for

The psalmist counts on God's faithfulness, despite the unfaithfulness of his people.

Key Bible cross-reference

Verse 1. See 136:1; Jeremiah 33:11.

Key "by way of explanation"

Verse 31, "This was credited to him as righteousness." This phrase reminds us of Abram's faith in the Lord, Genesis 15:6. But in this verse it is applied to Phinehas' intervention as a result of which the plague was checked.

Key "Quotable Quote"

"Then believed they his words; they sang his praise."

Psalm 106:12

Psalm 107

Matthew Henry's introduction

I. The psalmist specifies some of the most common calamities of human life, and shows how God succors those that labor under them, in answer to their prayers.

A. Banishment and dispersion, vv. 2–9.

B. Captivity and imprisonment, vv. 10–16.

C. Sickness and distemper of body, vv. 17–22.

D. Danger and distress at sea, vv. 23–32. These are put for all similar perils, in which those that cry unto God have ever found him a very present help.

II. He specifies the varieties and vicissitudes of events about nations and families, in all which God's hand is to be eyed by his own people, with joyful acknowledgments of his goodness, vv. 33–43.

A detailed analysis of psalm

God's providential care of the children of men in times of distress, in banishment, and dispersion. (1–9)

In captivity. (10–16)

In sickness. (17–22)

Danger at sea. 23–32)

God's power to be seen by his own people. (33–43)

Key verse

Verse 9: "For he satisfieth the longing soul, and filleth the hungry soul with goodness."

Key word / key phrase

Verse 9, "satisfies."

Key event / key person / key theme

God satisfies the longing soul

Key thought

The psalmist vocalizes his great need of the Lord and looks to him for deliverance.

Key thing to look out for

The psalmist does not skate over the times when the Lord disciplined his followers so that they would be more faithful to him.

Key Bible cross-reference

Verse 1. See 100:5; 106:1.

Key "by way of explanation"

Verse 10. "Darkness" and "gloom" portray the great distress God's people are going through. They are likened to prisoners who live with little hope.

Key "Quotable Quote"

"He maketh the storm a calm, so that the waves thereof are still."

Psalm 107:29

Psalm 108

Matthew Henry's introduction

I. David here gives thanks to God for mercies to himself, vv. 1–5.

II. He prays to God for mercies for the land, pleading the promises of God and putting them in suit, vv. 6–13.

(For Psalm 108: 1–5, see Psalm 57:7–11; Psalm 108: 6–13, see Psalm 60:5–12.)

Psalm 109

Matthew Henry's introduction

I. David complains in the court of heaven of the malice and base ingratitude of his enemies and with it an appeal to the righteous God, vv. 1–5.

II. He prays against his enemies, and devotes them to destruction, vv. 6–20.

III. He prays for himself, that God would help and succor him in his low condition, vv. 21–29.

IV. He concludes with a joyful expectation that God would appear for him, vv. 30, 31.

A detailed analysis of psalm

David complains about his enemies. (1–5)

He prophesies their destruction. (6–20)

Prayers and praises. (21–31)

Key verse

Verse 1: "Hold not thy peace, O God of my praise."

Key word / key phrase

Verse 4, "they accuse."

Key event / key person / key theme

A positive response to slander

Key thought

The psalmist is falsely accused. He asks for the Lord to vindicate him.

Key thing to look out for

The psalmist gives voice to the great afflictions he is enduring.

Key Bible cross-reference

Verse 8. See Acts 1:20.

Key "by way of explanation"

Verse 4. To be "a man of prayer" is to be a person who totally leans on God for help in life.

Key "Quotable Quote"

"I will greatly praise the LORD with my mouth; yea, I will praise him among the multitude."

Psalm 109:30

Psalm 110

Matthew Henry's introduction

Christ, as our Redeemer, carries out the office of a prophet, of a priest, and of a king, with reference both to his humiliation and his exaltation; and of each of these we have here an account.

I. His prophetical office, v. 2.
II. His priestly office, v. 4.
III. His kingly office, vv. 1, 3, 5, 6.
IV. His estates of humiliation and exaltation, v. 7.

A detailed analysis of psalm

Christ's kingdom. (1–7)

Key verse

Verse 2: "The LORD shall send the rod of thy strength out of Zion."

Key word / key phrase

Verse 4, "Melchizedek."

Key event / key person / key theme

The coming of the Priest-King-Judge

Key thought

This psalm was interpreted by Jesus and by New Testament writers as a reference to the coming Messiah.

Key thing to look out for

The psalmist portrays the Priest-King of this psalm as one who has great power to rule over the nations.

Key Bible cross-reference

Verse 4. See Hebrews 5:6; 6:20.

Key "by way of explanation"

Melchizedeh was a priest-king who had ruled over Jerusalem (Genesis 14:18–20). David later conquered Jerusalem, so acquired the rights and position of Jebusite kingship, and was therefore, in title, a priest.

Key "Quotable Quote"

"The LORD hath sworn, and will not repent, Thou art a priest for ever after the order of Melchizedek."

Psalm 110:4

Psalm 111

Matthew Henry's introduction

The psalmist, exhorting to praise God,

I. Sets himself for an example, v. 1.
II. Furnishes us with matter for praise from the works of God.
  A. The greatness of his works and the glory of them.
  B. The righteousness of them.
  C. The goodness of them.

D. The power of them.

E. The conformity of them to his word of promise.

F. The perpetuity of them. These observations are intermixed, vv. 2–9.

III. He recommends the holy fear of God, and conscientious obedience to his commands, as the most acceptable way of praising God, v. 10.

A detailed analysis of psalm

The Lord is to be praised for his works. (1–10)

Key verse

Verse 2: "The works of the LORD are great."

Key word / key phrase

Verse 5, "He provides food."

Key event / key person / key theme

Praise for God's tender care

Key thought

This psalm starts with a note of praise and ends on the theme of wisdom.

Key thing to look out for

God's great deeds performed for his people take center stage in this psalm.

Key Bible cross-reference

Verse 10. See Job 28:28; Proverbs 1:7.

Key "by way of explanation"

Verse 10. This statement about the fear of the Lord being the beginning of wisdom is the foundation of the Old Testament's teaching about wisdom.

Key "Quotable Quote"

"They stand fast for ever and ever, and are done in truth and uprightness."

Psalm 111:8

Psalm 112

Matthew Henry's introduction

We have here,

I. The character of the righteous, v. 1.

II. The blessedness of the righteous.

A. There is a blessing entailed on their posterity, v. 2.

B. There is a blessing conferred on themselves.

1. Prosperity outward and inward, v. 3.
2. Comfort, v. 4.
3. Wisdom, v. 5.
4. Stability, vv. 6–8.
5. Honor, vv. 6, 9.

III. The misery of the wicked, v. 10.

A detailed analysis of psalm

The blessedness of the righteous. (1–10)

Key verse

Verse 7: "He shall not be afraid of evil tidings."

Key word / key phrase

Verse 1, "blessed."

Key event / key person / key theme

The blessings of those who fear God

Key thought

Even bad news need not crush the godly.

Key thing to look out for

A heart that is fixed on God need fear nothing and nobody.

Key Bible cross-reference

Verse 9. See 2 Corinthians 9:9.

Key "by way of explanation"

Verse 4, "darkness" often stands for troubles and serious problems in the Bible.

Key "Quotable Quote"

"Praise ye the LORD. Blessed is the man that feareth the LORD, that delighteth greatly in his commandments."

Psalm 112:1

Psalm 113

Matthew Henry's introduction

I. We are here called on and urged to praise God, vv. 1–3.

II. We are here furnished with matter for praise, and words are put into our mouths, in singing which we must with holy fear and love give to God the glory of,

A. The elevations of his glory and greatness, vv. 4, 5.

B. The condescensions of his grace and goodness (vv. 6–9), which very much illustrate one another, that we may be duly affected with both.

A detailed analysis of psalm

An exhortation to praise God. (1–9)

Key verse

Verse 5: "Who is like unto the LORD our God, who dwelleth on high,"

Key word / key phrase

Verse 7, "raises the poor."

Key event / key person / key theme

God's wonderful grace

Key thought

The psalmist points out how merciful the Lord is, especially to those most in need.

Key thing to look out for

The Lord provides for people who have little or no hope.

Key Bible cross-reference

Verses 7, 8. See 1 Samuel 2:8.

Key "by way of explanation"

This psalm, along with 114–118, was known as the "Egyptian Hallel." These psalms were used at the major Jewish festivals. At the Passover, Psalms 113–114 were said before the meal, and Psalms 115–118 after the meal.

Key "Quotable Quote"

"He maketh the barren woman to keep house, and to be a joyful mother of children. Praise ye the LORD."

Psalm 113:9

Psalm 114

Matthew Henry's introduction

In this psalm it is celebrated in lively strains of praise; it was fitly therefore made a part of the great Hallelujah, or song of praise, which the Jews were wont to sing at the close of the supper-supper. It must never be forgotten,

I. That they were brought out of slavery, v. 1.
II. That God set up his tabernacle among them, v. 2.
III. That the sea and Jordan were divided before them, vv. 3, 5.
IV. That the earth shook at the giving of the law, when God came down on Mount Sinai, vv. 4, 6, 7.
V. That God gave them water out of the rock, v. 8.

A detailed analysis of psalm

An exhortation to fear God. (1–8)

Key verse

Verse 3: "The sea saw it, and fled: Jordan was driven back."

Key word / key phrase

Verse 1, "Egypt."

Key event / key person / key theme

Praise God for the Exodus

Key thought

This psalm was written in order to remind the Israelites to give thanks to the Lord for the Exodus.

Key thing to look out for

The Exodus was the most important miracle in the history of God's people.

Key Bible cross-reference

Verse 3. See Exodus 14:21; Joshua 3:16.

Key "by way of explanation"

Verse 2. "Judah" and "Israel," the northern and southern countries respectively, are here thought of as one people: God's people.

Key "Quotable Quote"

"Judah was his sanctuary, and Israel his dominion."

Psalm 114:2

Psalm 115

Matthew Henry's introduction

In this psalm we are taught to give glory,

I. To God, and not to ourselves, v. 1.
II. To God, and not to idols, vv. 2–8. We must give glory to God,
   A. By trusting in him, and in his promise and blessing, vv. 9–15.
   B. By blessing him, vv. 16–18.

A detailed analysis of psalm

Glory to be ascribed to God. (1–8)
By trusting in him and praising him. (9–18)

Key verse

Verse 1: "Not unto us, O LORD, not unto us, but unto thy name give glory."

Key word / key phrase

Verse 1, "glory."

Key event / key person / key theme

To God alone be the glory

Key thought

Whenever the psalmist remembers the Lord's faithfulness he breaks into praise.

Key thing to look out for

The idea that idols possess power is quite false. No glory should ever be given to them.

Key Bible cross-reference

Verses 4–8. See 135:15–18; Revelation 9:20.

Key "by way of explanation"

Verse 1, "Not to us . . . not to us." Israel is quite sure that they do not deserve any credit for their own existence and that everything is due to God's grace. Therefore, to him alone glory must be given.

Key "Quotable Quote"

"O Israel, trust thou in the LORD: he is their help and their shield."

Psalm 115:9

Psalm 116

Matthew Henry's introduction

Observe,

I. The great distress and danger that the psalmist was in, which almost drove him to despair, vv. 3, 10, 11.

II. The application he made to God in that distress, v. 4.

III. The experience he had of God's goodness to him, in answer to prayer; God heard him (vv. 1, 2), pitied him (vv. 5, 6), delivered him, v. 8.

IV. His care respecting the acknowledgments he should make of the goodness of God to him, v. 12.

A. He will love God, v. 1.

B. He will continue to call on him, vv. 2, 13, 17.

C. He will rest in him, v. 7.

D. He will walk before him, v. 9.

E. He will pay his vows of thanksgiving, in which he will own the tender regard God had to him, and this publicly, vv. 13–15, 17–19. Lastly, He will continue God's faithful servant to his life's end, v. 16.

A detailed analysis of psalm

The psalmist declares his love to the Lord. (1–9)

His desire to be thankful. (10–19)

Key verse

Verse 5: "Gracious is the LORD, and righteous; yea, our God is merciful."

Key word / key phrase

Verse 17, "thank-offering."

Key event / key person / key theme

Remember all that God has done

Key thought

Verses 2,13,17. The psalmist will always call on the Lord in prayer.

Key thing to look out for

The psalmist rejoices because he knows that the Lord listens to him and saves him.

Key Bible cross-reference

Verse 10. See 2 Corinthians 4:13.

Key "by way of explanation"

Verse 15, "precious." None of God's followers die, without the Lord knowing about this and being concerned about it.

Key "Quotable Quote"

"I will take the cup of salvation, and call upon the name of the LORD."

Psalm 116:13

Psalm 117

Matthew Henry's introduction

Here is,

I. A solemn call to all nations to praise God, v. 1.

II. Proper matter for that praise suggested, v. 2.

A detailed analysis of psalm

All people called upon to praise God. (1–2)

Key verse

Verse 1: "O praise the LORD, all ye nations: praise him, all ye people."

Key word / key phrase

Verse 1, "praise."

Key event / key person / key theme

The praise of God's people

Key thought

The shortest psalm, and shortest chapter in the Bible, is like an extended Hallelujah.

Key thing to look out for

This psalm explains that the reason for praising the Lord lies in his love" and faithfulness.

Key Bible cross-reference

Verse 1. See Amos 9:11,12; Micah 5:7–9.

Key "by way of explanation"

Verse 1 shows that it was always the Lord's intention that non-Jews should be saved. This verse is quoted to this effect in Romans 15:11.

Key "Quotable Quote"

"For his merciful kindness is great toward us: and the truth of the LORD endureth for ever. Praise ye the LORD."

Psalm 117:2

Psalm 118

Matthew Henry's introduction

I. David calls on all about him to give to God the glory of his goodness, vv. 1–4.

II. He encourages himself and others to trust in God, from the experience he had had of God's power and pity in the great and kind things he had done for him, vv. 5–18.

III. He gives thanks for his advancement to the throne, as it was a figure of the exaltation of Christ, vv. 19–23.

IV. The people, the priests, and the psalmist himself, triumph in the prospect of the Redeemer's kingdom, vv. 24–29.

A detailed analysis of psalm

It is good to trust in the Lord. (1–18)

The coming of Christ in his kingdom. (19–29)

Key verse

Verse 8: "It is better to trust in the LORD than to put confidence in man."

Key word / key phrase

Verse 8, "refuge."

Key event / key person / key theme

It is better to trust God than any human being

Key thought

The psalmist starts with praising the Lord and then moves on to remembering how oppressed he has been.

Key thing to look out for

The psalmist's many reasons for thanking the Lord.

Key Bible cross-reference

Verse 6. See Hebrews 13:6.

Key "by way of explanation"

Verse 18, "chastened me." The Old Testament teaches that the Lord disciplines his people for their good. Here the psalmist acknowledges that his afflictions were the Lord's severe affliction of him.

Key "Quotable Quote"

"O give thanks unto the LORD; for he is good: because his mercy endureth for ever." *Psalm 118:1*

Psalm 119

Matthew Henry's introduction

This is a psalm by itself, like none of the rest; it excels them all, and shines brightest in this constellation. It is much longer than any of them more than twice as long as any of them. It is not making long prayers that Christ censures, but making them for a pretence, which intimates that they are in themselves good and commendable. It seems to me to be a collection of David's pious and devout ejaculations, the short and sudden breathings and elevations of his soul to God, which he wrote down as they occurred, and, towards the latter end of his time, gathered out of his day-book where they lay scattered, added to them many like words, and digested them into this psalm, in which there is seldom any coherence between the verses, but, like Solomon's proverbs, it is a chest of gold rings, not a chain of gold links. And we may not only learn, by the psalmist's example, to accustom ourselves to such pious ejaculations, which are an excellent means of maintaining constant communion with God, and keeping the heart in frame for the more solemn exercises of religion, but we must make use of the psalmist's words, both for the exciting and for the expressing of our devout affections; what some have said of this psalm is true, "He that shall read it considerately, it will either warm him or shame him." The composition of it is singular and very exact. It is divided into twenty-two parts, according to the number of the letters of the Hebrew alphabet, and each part consists of eight verses, all the verses of the first part beginning with Aleph, all the verses of the second with Beth, and so on, without any flaw throughout the whole psalm. Archbishop Tillotson says, It seems to have more of poetical skill and number in it than we at this distance can easily understand. Some have called it the saints' alphabet; and it were to be wished we had it as ready in our memories as the very letters of our alphabet, as ready as our A B C. Perhaps the penman found it of use to himself to observe this method, as it obliged him to seek for thoughts, and search for them, that he might fill up the quota of every part; and the letter he was to begin with might lead him to a word which might suggest a good sentence; and all little enough to raise any thing that is good in the barren soil of our hearts. However, it would be of use to the learners, a help to them both in committing it to memory and in calling it to mind on occasion; by the letter the first word would be got, and that would bring in the whole verse; thus young people would the more easily learn it by heart and retain it the better even in old age. If any censure it as childish and trifling, because acrostics are now quite out of fashion, let them know that the royal psalmist despises their censure; he is a teacher of babes, and, if this method may be beneficial to them, he can easily stoop to it; if this to be vile, he will be yet more vile.

The general scope and design of it is to magnify the law, and make it honorable; to set forth the excellency and usefulness of divine revelation, and to recommend it to us, not only for the entertainment, but for the government, of ourselves, by the psalmist's own example, who speaks by experience of the benefit of it, and of the good impressions made on him by it, for which he praises God, and earnestly prays, from first to last, for the continuance of God's grace with him, to direct and quicken him in the way of his duty.

There are ten different words by which divine revelation is called in this psalm, and they are synonymous, each of them expressive of the whole compass of it (both that which tells us what God expects from us and that which tells us that we may expect from him) and of the system of religion which is founded on it and guided by it. The things contained in the scripture, and drawn from it, are here called,

1. God's law, because they are enacted by him as our Sovereign.
2. His way, because they are the rule both of his providence and of our obedience.
3. His testimonies, because they are solemnly declared to the world and attested beyond contradiction.
4. His commandments, because given with authority, and (as the word signifies) lodged with us as a trust.
5. His precepts, because prescribed to us and not left indifferent.
6. His word, or saying, because it is the declaration of his mind, and Christ, the essential eternal Word, is all in all in it.
7. His judgments, because framed in infinite wisdom, and because by them we must both judge and be judged.
8. His righteousness, because it is all holy, just, and good, and the rule and standard of righteousness.
9. His statutes, because they are fixed and determined, and of perpetual obligation. His truth, or faithfulness, because the principles on which the divine law is built are eternal truths. And I think there is but one verse (it is v. 122)

in all this long psalm in which there is not one or other of these ten words; only in three or four they are used about God's providence or David's practice (as vv. 75, 84, 121), and v. 132 they are called God's name. The great esteem and affection David had for the word of God is the more admirable considering how little he had of it, in comparison with what we have, no more perhaps in writing than the first books of Moses, which were but the dawning of this day, which may shame us who enjoy the full discoveries of divine revelation and yet are so cold towards it. In singing this psalm there is work for all the devout affections of a sanctified soul, so copious, so various, is the matter of it. We here find that in which we must give glory to God both as our ruler and great benefactor, that in which we are to teach and admonish ourselves and one another (so many are the instructions which we here find about a religious life), and that in which we are to comfort and encourage ourselves and one another, so many are the sweet experiences of one that lived such a life. Here is something or other to suit the case of every Christian. Is any afflicted? Is any merry? Each will find that here which is proper for him. And it is so far from being a tedious repetition of the same thing, as may seem to those who look over it cursorily, that, if we duly meditate on it, we shall find almost every verse has a new thought and something in it very lively. And this, as many other of David's psalms, teaches us to be sententious in our devotions, both alone and when others join with us; for, ordinarily, the affections, especially of weaker Christians, are more likely to be raised and kept by short expressions, the sense of which lies in a little compass, than by long and labored periods.

A detailed analysis of psalm

The psalm consists of twenty-two stanzas, each having eight verses. Each stanza starts with the following letter of the Hebrew Bible. This psalm is an elaborate acrostic. It has twenty-two eight-line stanzas, corresponding to the twenty-two letters of the Hebrew alphabet. Then in each stanzas, every line starts with the letter at the beginning of its stanza.

Key verse

Verse 105: "Thy word is a lamp unto my feet, and a light unto my path."

Key word / key phrase

Verse 2, "statutes."

Key event / key person / key theme

An acrostic psalm in praise of the Scriptures

Key thought

The general scope and design of this psalm is to magnify the divine law, and make it honorable.

Key thing to look out for

The centrality of the word of God.

Key Bible cross-reference

Verse 3. See Genesis 17:1.

Key "by way of explanation"

The psalmist uses eight synonyms for God's

law, each with a slight variation of meaning. In some stanzas he includes all eight synonyms, and he never has fewer than six.

Key "Quotable Quote"

"The law is no do-it-yourself manual which God has handed over to man. It is the written part of a life-long teach-in. With it comes the assurance of his living presence."

Leslie C. Allen

Psalm 120

Matthew Henry's introduction

I. David prays to God to deliver him from the mischief designed him by false and malicious tongues, vv. 1, 2.

II. He threatens the judgments of God against such, vv. 3, 4.

III. He complains of his wicked neighbors that were quarrelsome and vexatious, vv. 5–7.

A detailed analysis of psalm

The psalmist prays to God to deliver him from false and malicious tongues. (1–4)

He complains about wicked neighbors. (5–7)

Key verse

Verse 1: "In my distress I cried unto the LORD, and he heard me."

Key word / key phrase

Verse 1, "in my distress."

Key event / key person / key theme

A cry from the depths of distress

Key thought

The psalmist has been falsely accused and he asks the Lord to deliver him from his accusers.

Key thing to look out for

Verse 4, "sharp arrows." The tongue is said to be a weapon used against the psalmist as he had to cope with endless insults.

Key Bible cross-reference

Verse 3. See 1 Samuel 3:17.

Key "by way of explanation"

Psalm 120 begins a group of fifteen psalms each called "a song of ascents." The word probably refers to a pilgrimage up to the temple in Jerusalem and the psalm would have been sung by pilgrims traveling to the temple. They were not all, however, written as pilgrim songs. Some, like Psalm 120, had a different original purpose.

Key "Quotable Quote"

"Deliver my soul, O LORD, from lying lips, and from a deceitful tongue."

Psalm 120:2

Psalm 121

Matthew Henry's introduction

I. David here assures himself of help from God, vv. 1, 2.

II. He assures others of it, vv. 3–8.

A detailed analysis of psalm

The safety of the godly. (1–8)

Key verse

Verse 1: "I will lift up mine eyes unto the hills, from whence cometh my help."

Key word / key phrase

Verse 1, "my help."

Key event / key person / key theme

God is our Protector

Key thought

The psalmist answers his own opening rhetorical question by expressing his trust in the Lord.

Key thing to look out for

The psalmist expresses his certainty of the Lord's protection.

Key Bible cross-reference

Verse 3. See 1 Kings 18:27.

Key "by way of explanation"

Verse 1, "hills." Jerusalem is surrounded by hills, and is itself set on a hill.

Key "Quotable Quote"

"Behold, he that keepeth Israel shall neither slumber nor sleep."

Psalm 121:4

Psalm 122

Matthew Henry's introduction

Observe,

I. The joy with which they were to go up to Jerusalem, vv. 1, 2.

II. The great esteem they were to have of Jerusalem, vv. 3–5.

III. The great concern they were to have for Jerusalem, and the prayers they were to put up for its welfare, vv. 6–9.

A detailed analysis of psalm

Esteem for Jerusalem. (1–5)

Concern for its welfare. (6–9)

Key verse

Verse 2: "Our feet shall stand within thy gates, O Jerusalem."

Key word / key phrase

Verse 6, "the peace of Jerusalem."

Key event / key person / key theme

Pray for the peace of Jerusalem

Key thought

The pilgrim's joy as he enters Jerusalem.

Key thing to look out for

For God's people Jerusalem was the most significant city in all the world.

Key Bible cross-reference

Verse 1. See 2 Samuel 7:5.

Key "by way of explanation"

Verse 6, "peace." When the psalmist prayed for the peace of Jerusalem, in addition to peace as the absence of war, he would have been praying for the spiritual prosperity of the city.

Key "Quotable Quote"

"Pray for the peace of Jerusalem: they shall prosper that love thee."

Psalm 122:6

Psalm 123

Matthew Henry's introduction

The psalmist begins as if he spoke for himself only (v. 1), but presently speaks in the name of the church. Here is,

I. Their expectation of mercy from God, vv. 1, 2.

II. Their plea for mercy with God,, vv. 3, 4.

A detailed analysis of psalm

Trust in God, in spite of ridicule and contempt from the oppressor. (1–4)

Key verse

Verse 1: "Unto thee lift I up mine eyes, O thou that dwellest in the heavens."

Key word / key phrase

Verse 3, "Have mercy on us."

Key event / key person / key theme

A plea for God's mercy

Key thought

The Lord's throne is both in Jerusalem and in heaven.

Key thing to look out for

Kyrie eleison, long-prayed by the Church.

Key Bible cross-reference

Verse 1. See 122:5; 132:14.

Key "by way of explanation"

Verse 2, "slaves" and "a maid" stand for a powerful image of God's servants who look to their Master in everything.

Key "Quotable Quote"

"Behold, as the eyes of servants look unto the hand of their masters, and as the eyes of a maiden unto the hand of her mistress; so our eyes wait upon the LORD our God, until that he have mercy upon us."

Psalm 123:2

Psalm 124

Matthew Henry's introduction

I. He here magnifies the greatness of the danger they were in, and of the ruin they were at the brink of, vv. 1–5.

II. He gives God the glory of their escape, vv. 6, 7 compared with vv. 1, 2.

III. He takes encouragement thence to trust in God, v. 8.

A detailed analysis of psalm

The deliverance of the Church. (1–5)

Thankfulness for the deliverance. (6–8)

Key verse

Verse 5: "Then the proud waters had gone over our soul."

Key word / key phrase

Verse 2, "on our side."

Key event / key person / key theme

God is on our side

Key thought

Had it not been for the Lord, Israel would have ceased to exist.

Key thing to look out for

The psalmist feels that the Lord's people only escaped by the skin of their teeth.

Key Bible cross-reference

Verse 2. See 123:4.

Key "by way of explanation"

Verses 4,5. The psalmist feels overwhelmed by his attackers, as if they were a "flood," a "torrent" and "raging waters".

Key "Quotable Quote"

"Our help is in the name of the LORD, who made heaven and earth."

Psalm 124:8

Psalm 125

Matthew Henry's introduction

I. It is certainly well with the people of God; for,

A. They have the promises of a good God that they shall be fixed (v. 1), and safe (v. 2), and not always under the hatches, v. 3.

B. They have the prayers of a good man, which shall be heard for them, v. 4.

II. It is certainly ill with the wicked, and particularly with the apostates, v. 5.

A detailed analysis of psalm

The security of the righteous. (1–3)

Prayer for them, and the ruin of the wicked. (4, 5)

Key verse

Verse 1: "They that trust in the LORD shall be as mount Zion."

Key word / key phrase

Verse 1,"trust."

Key event / key person / key theme

Trust in the Lord

Key thought

There is a constant battle between the godly and the ungodly.

Key thing to look out for

The Lord's people are described in a variety of ways throughout this psalm.

Key Bible cross-reference

Verse 5. See Numbers 6:24–26.

Key "by way of explanation"

Verse 2, "surrounds his people." Just as Jerusalem is immovable as she is set in a mountainous area so the Lord will make his people immoveable.

Key "Quotable Quote"

"As the mountains are round about Jerusalem, so the LORD is round about his people from henceforth even for ever."

Psalm 125:2

Psalm 126

Matthew Henry's introduction

I. Those that had returned out of captivity are here called on to be thankful, vv. 1–3.

II. Those that were yet remaining in captivity are here prayed for (v. 4) and encouraged, vv. 5, 6.

A detailed analysis of psalm

Those returned out of captivity are to be thankful. (1–3)

Those still in captivity are encouraged. (4–6)

Key verse

Verse 5: "They that sow in tears shall reap in joy."

Key word / key phrase

Verse 6, "Goes out weeping."

Key event / key person / key theme

Sow in tears, reap in joy

Key thought

Out of sorry God brings great joy.

Key thing to look out for

The good that comes out of suffering.

Key Bible cross-reference

Verses 5, 6. See 20:5.

Key "by way of explanation"

Verse 1, "brought back." This psalm exactly fits the circumstances of God's people returning to Jerusalem after their exile.

Key "Quotable Quote"

"The LORD hath done great things for us; whereof we are glad."

Psalm 126:3

Psalm 127

Matthew Henry's introduction

On God we must depend,

I. For wealth, vv. 1, 2.

II. For heirs to leave it to, vv. 3–5.

A detailed analysis of psalm

The value of the divine blessing. (1–5)

Key verse

Verse 3: "Lo, children are an heritage of the LORD."

Key word / key phrase

Verse 3, "children."

Key event / key person / key theme

Children are God's gift

Key thought

Children are to be greatly valued.

Key thing to look out for

Children should be considered as a sign of God's love.

Key Bible cross-reference

Verse 2. See Matthew 6:25–34; 1 Peter 5:7.

Key "by way of explanation"

Verse 2, "grants sleep." The psalmist teaches that

a good harvest is not to be seen as just the result of hard work, but the result of God's blessing.

Key "Quotable Quote"

"Among the Psalmist's music deep,
Now tell me if that any is,
For gift of grace, surpassing this:
'He giveth his beloved – sleep.'"

Elizabeth Barrett Browning

Psalm 128

Matthew Henry's introduction

In this psalm we are taught that the only way to obtain God's blessing which will benefit our families is to live in the fear of God and in obedience to him. Those that do so, in general, shall be blessed (vv. 1, 2, 4), In particular,

I. They shall be prosperous and successful in their employments, v. 2.
II. Their relations shall be agreeable, v. 3.
III. They shall live to see their families brought up, v. 6.
IV. They shall have the satisfaction of seeing the church of God in a flourishing condition, vv. 5, 6.

A detailed analysis of psalm

The blessings of those who fear God. (1–6)

Key verse

Verse 6: "Yea, thou shalt see thy children's children, and peace upon Israel."

Key word / key phrase

Verse 2, "blessings and prosperity."

Key event / key person / key theme

May God's blessing rest on the God-fearing

Key thought

Verses 1, 4. The secret of blessing.

Key thing to look out for

God's blessing is meant to flow from one generation to the next generation.

Key Bible cross-reference

Verse 6. See 125:5.

Key "by way of explanation"

Verse 3, "vine." A vine was taken to be a symbol of fruitfulness in the Old Testament. See Genesis 49:22.

Key "Quotable Quote"

"Blessed is every one that feareth the LORD; that walketh in his ways."

Psalm 128:1

Psalm 129

Matthew Henry's introduction

I. They look back with thankfulness for the former deliverances God had wrought for them and their fathers out of the many distresses they had been in from time to time, vv. 1–4.
II. They look forward with a believing prayer for and a prospect of the destruction of all the enemies of Zion, vv. 5–8.

A detailed analysis of psalm

Thankfulness for former deliverances. (1–4)
A believing prospect of the destruction of the enemies of Zion. (5–8)

Key verse

Verse 5: "Let them all be confounded and turned back that hate Zion."

Key word / key phrase

Verse 2, "greatly oppressed."

Key event / key person / key theme

A cry of the persecuted

Key thought

The psalmist was all too familiar with persecution. See verse 3.

Key thing to look out for

Those who opposed God's people would be opposed by God.

Key Bible cross-reference

Verse 8. See Ruth 2:4.

Key "by way of explanation"

Verse 6, "like grass on the roof." This refers to one sory houses with flat roofs on which grass might just manage to grow, but as it has no depth of soil to sustain it quickly withers.

Key "Quotable Quote"

"Many a time have they afflicted me from my youth: yet they have not prevailed against me."

Psalm 129:2

Psalm 130

Matthew Henry's introduction

The psalmist here expresses,

I. His desire towards God, vv. 1, 2.

II. His repentance before God, vv. 3, 4.

III. His attendance on God, vv. 5, 6.

IV. His expectations from God, vv. 7, 8.

A detailed analysis of psalm

The psalmist's hope in prayer. (1–4)

His patience in hope. (5–8)

Key verse

Verse 1: "Out of the depths have I cried unto thee, O LORD."

Key word / key phrase

Verse 5, "wait."

Key event / key person / key theme

My soul waits for the Lord

Key thought

The psalmist gives a personal testimony to his trust in the Lord.

Key thing to look out for

The psalmist tells Israel to put their hope for complete redemption in the Lord.

Key Bible cross-reference

Verse 8. See Matthew 1:21; Titus 2:14.

Key "by way of explanation"

Verse 4, "feared." Appropriate synonyms for the word "feared" in this context would be "served," or "worshiped" or "trusted."

Key "Quotable Quote"

"I wait for the LORD, my soul doth wait, and in his word do I hope."

Psalm 130:5

Psalm 131

Matthew Henry's introduction

I. David aimed at nothing high nor great, v. 1.
II. He was very easy in every condition which God allotted him (v. 2); and therefore,
III. He encourages all good people to trust in God as he did, v. 3.

A detailed analysis of psalm

The psalmist's humility. Believers encouraged to trust in God. (1–3)

Key verse

Verse 3: "Let Israel hope in the LORD from henceforth and for ever."

Key word / key phrase

Verse 2, "Like a weaned child."

Key event / key person / key theme

A childlike faith

Key thought

The psalmist knew that the one thing the Lord could not abide was a proud heart.

Key thing to look out for

Israel is encouraged to keep on placing its hope in the Lord, rather than just doing so now and again.

Key Bible cross-reference

Verse 1. See 2 Samuel 6:21,22.

Key "by way of explanation"

Verse 2, "a weaned child" could be a child as old as four or five years old. For in those days children were not weaned as babies, but as toddlers of a few years old.

Key "Quotable Quote"

"Surely I have behaved and quieted myself, as a child that is weaned of his mother: my soul is even as a weaned child."

Psalm 131:2

Psalm 132

Matthew Henry's introduction

I. Solomon had built this house for the honor and service of God; and when he brings the ark into it, the token of God's presence, he desires that God himself would come and take possession of it, vv. 8–10. With these words Solomon concluded his prayer, 2 Chron. 6:41, 42.
II. He had built it in pursuance of the orders he had received from his father, and therefore his pleas to enforce these petitions refer to David.
   A. He pleads David's piety towards God vv. 1–7.
   B. He pleads God's promise to David, vv. 11–18.

A detailed analysis of psalm

David's care for the ark. (1–10)
The promises of God. (11–18)

Key verse

Verse 1: "LORD, remember David, and all his afflictions."

Key word / key phrase

Verse 1, "David."

Key event / key person / key theme

Trust in the God of David

Key thought

The psalmist asks the Lord to treat him mercifully, just as he did David.

Key thing to look out for

The psalmist is constantly expressing his desire to worship the Lord.

Key Bible cross-reference

Verse 17. See 1 Kings 11:36.

Key "by way of explanation"

Verse 12, "statutes." These refer back to the laws which the Lord gave Moses on Mount Sinai.

Key "Quotable Quote"

"I find that the psalms are like a mirror, in which one can see oneself and the movements of one's own heart."

Athanasius

Psalm 133

Matthew Henry's introduction

Here is,

I. The doctrine laid down of the happiness of brotherly love, v. 1.

II. The illustration of that doctrine, in two similitudes, vv. 2, 3.

III. The proof of it, in a good reason given for it (v. 3).

A detailed analysis of psalm

The excellency of brotherly love. (1–3)

Key verse

Verse 1: "Behold, how good and how pleasant it is for brethren to dwell together in unity!"

Key word / key phrase

Verse 1, "live together."

Key event / key person / key theme

Unity

Key thought

God blesses his people when they are united.

Key thing to look out for

What is conveyed by the two similies?

Key Bible cross-reference

Verse 2. See 89:20; Zechariah 4:14.

Key "by way of explanation"

Verse 3, "dew." "Dew" symbolizes the Lord's blessing on his people.

Key "Quotable Quote"

"I'll make David sing like a Christian."

Isaac Watts

Psalm 134

Matthew Henry's introduction

Some make this psalm to be a dialogue.

I. In the first two verses, the priests or Levites who sat up all night to keep the watch of the house of the Lord are called on to spend their time while they were on the guard, not in idle talk, but in the acts of devotion.

II. In the last verse those who were thus called on to praise God pray for him that gave them the exhortation, either the high priest or the captain of the guard.

A detailed analysis of psalm

An exhortation to bless the Lord. (1–3)

Key verse

Verse 2: "Lift up your hands in the sanctuary, and bless the LORD."

Key word / key phrase

Verse 1, "Praise the Lord."

Key event / key person / key theme

A call to praise the Lord

Key thought

There are no exceptions made among God's people about worshiping the Lord.

Key thing to look out for

The psalms are full of short blessings, like the one in verse three of this psalm.

Key Bible cross-reference

Verse 3. See 124:8; 135:6.

Key "by way of explanation"

Verse 1, "night." Services were held in the night during the Feast of Tabernacles.

Key "Quotable Quote"

"The psalms were written as songs and should be read in the spirit of lyric poetry rather than as doctrinal treatises or sermons."

C.S. Lewis

Psalm 135

Matthew Henry's introduction

This is one of the Hallelujah-psalms; that is the title of it, and that is the Amen of it, both its Alpha and its Omega.

I. It begins with a call to praise God, particularly a call to the "servants of the Lord" to praise him, as in the previous psalm, vv. 1–3.

II. It goes on to furnish us with matter for praise. God is to be praised,

A. As the God of Jacob, v. 4.

B. As the God of gods, v. 5.

C. As the God of the whole world, vv. 6, 7.

D. As a terrible God to the enemies of Israel, vv. 8–11.

E. As a gracious God to Israel, both in what he had done for them and what he would do, vv. 12–14.

F. As the only living God, all other gods being vanity and a lie, vv. 15–18.

III. It concludes with another exhortation to all people concerned to praise God, vv. 19–21.

A detailed analysis of psalm

God to be praised for his mercy. (1–4)

For his power and judgments. (5–14)

The vanity of idols. (15–21)

Key verse

Verse 8: "Who smote the firstborn of Egypt, both of man and beast."

Key word / key phrase

Verse 13, "your renown."

Key event / key person / key theme

God has done great things

Key thought

The psalmist gives very important reasons for worshiping the Lord.

Key thing to look out for

Three good reasons to worship the Lord are because the Lord rules over the world of nature, and over the nations, and because he is Israel's Redeemer.

Key Bible cross-reference

Verses 15–18. See Psalm 115:4–8; Revelation 9:20.

Key "by way of explanation"

Verses 15–18. The powerlessness of the false gods is constantly being exposed by the writers of the Old Testament.

Key "Quotable Quote"

"The psalms are the anatomy of all the parts of the soul."

John Calvin

Psalm 136

Matthew Henry's introduction

We must praise God,

I. As great and good in himself, vv. 1–3.

II. As the Creator of the world, vv. 5–9.

III. As Israel's God and Savior, vv. 10–22.

IV. As our Redeemer, vv. 23, 24.

V. As the great benefactor of the whole creation, and God over all, blessed for evermore, vv. 25, 26.

A detailed analysis of psalm

God to be praised as the Creator of the world. (1–9)

As Israel's God and Savior. (10–22)

For his blessings to all. (23–26)

Key verse

Verse 1: "O give thanks unto the LORD; for he is good."

Key word / key phrase

Verse 1, "endures."

Key event / key person / key theme

God's mercy endures forever

Key thought

The psalmist praises the Lord for the critical moments in Israel's history.

Key thing to look out for

This psalm shows how the Lord is Creator, Deliverer, Conqueror and Provider.

Key Bible cross-reference

Verse 20. See Numbers 21:31–35.

Key "by way of explanation"

This psalm is written so worshipers could join in with an easily memorized refrain.

Key "Quotable Quote"

"No part of the Old Testament is more frequently quoted or referred to in the New as the psalms."

Matthew Henry

Psalm 137

Matthew Henry's introduction

Here

I. The melancholy captives cannot enjoy themselves, vv. 1, 2.

II. They cannot humor their proud oppressors, vv. 3, 4.

III. They cannot forget Jerusalem, vv. 5, 6.

IV. They cannot forgive Edom and Babylon, vv. 7–9.

A detailed analysis of psalm

The Jews bewail their captivity. (1–4)

Their affection for Jerusalem. (5–9)

Key verse

Verse 4: "How shall we sing the LORD'S song in a strange land?"

Key word / key phrase

Verse 1, "wept."

Key event / key person / key theme

Tears in exile

Key thought

This psalm reflects the sad times of God's people in exile, where they were cut of from their city and their temple, and so, some thought, from their God.

Key thing to look out for

The Israelites were in no mood to play their harps and sing happy songs.

Key Bible cross-reference

Verse 8. See Revelation 18:6.

Key "by way of explanation"

V. 1. The "rivers" here refer to the River Tigris and the River Euphrates, and their many tributaries.

Key "Quotable Quote"

"The most valuable thing the Psalms do for me is to express that same delight in God which made David dance."

C.S. Lewis

Psalm 138

Matthew Henry's introduction

I. David looks back with thankfulness on the experiences he had had of God's goodness to him, vv. 1–3.

II. He looks forward with comfort, in hopes,

A. That others would go on to praise God like him, vv. 4, 5.

B. That God would go on to do good to him, vv. 6–8.

A detailed analysis of psalm

The psalmist praises God for answering prayer. (1–5)

The Lord's dealing with the humble and the proud. (6–8)

Key verse

Verse 7: "Though I walk in the midst of trouble, thou wilt revive me."

Key word / key phrase

Verse 3, "answered."

Key event / key person / key theme

God answered my prayer

Key thought

Answered prayer is a great spur to keep on praying.

Key thing to look out for

It is clear from this psalm why the Lord looks on some people with favor and looks on other people with disdain.

Key Bible cross-reference

Verse 7. See 124:3; 145:8.

Key "by way of explanation"

Verse 2, "your word." This especially refers to the promises of the Lord that, as his followers discovered, were always kept.

Key "Quotable Quote"

"In the day when I cried thou answeredst me, and strengthenedst me with strength in my soul."

Psalm 138:3

Psalm 139

Matthew Henry's introduction

I. The doctrine of God's omniscience is here asserted, and fully laid down, vv. 1–6.

II. It is confirmed by two arguments:

A. God is every where present; therefore he knows all, vv. 7–12.

B. He made us, therefore he knows us, vv. 13–16.

III. Some inferences are drawn from this doctrine.

A. It may fill us with pleasing admiration of God, vv. 17, 18.

B. With a holy dread and detestation of sin and sinners, vv. 19–22.

C. With a holy satisfaction in our own integrity, about which we may appeal to God, vv. 23, 24.

A detailed analysis of psalm

God knows all things. (1–6)

He is everywhere. (7–16)

The psalmist's hatred of sin, and desire to be led by God. (17–24)

Key verse

Verse 7: "Whither shall I go from thy spirit? or whither shall I flee from thy presence?"

Key word / key phrase

Verse 1, "searched."

Key event / key person / key theme

Search me, O God

Key thought

The psalmist shows his loyalty to the Lord. He is even prepared to be examined by the Lord.

Key thing to look out for

There is nowhere that a godly person can go to hide from the Lord's Spirit.

Key Bible cross-reference

Verse 8. See 63:9; 143:7.

Key "by way of explanation"

Verse 6, "too wonderful." The Lord's knowledge is "too wonderful" in the sense that humans are not able to fully appreciate and understand it.

Key "Quotable Quote"

"Psalms: a 'Little Bible' since it contains, set out in the briefest and most beautiful form, all that is to be found in the whole Bible."

Martin Luther

Psalm 140

Matthew Henry's introduction

In this psalm,

I. David complains of the malice of his enemies, and prays to God to preserve him from them, vv. 1–5.

II. He encourages himself in God as his God, vv. 6, 7.

III. He prays for, and prophesies, the destruction of his persecutors, vv. 8–11.

IV. He assures all God's afflicted people that their troubles would in due time end well (vv. 12, 13).

A detailed analysis of psalm

David encourages himself in God. (1–7)

He prays for, and prophesies the destruction of, his persecutors. (8–13)

Key verse

Verse 1: "Deliver me, O LORD, from the evil man."

Key word / key phrase

Verse 1, "men of violence."

Key event / key person / key theme

Protect me from violent people

Key thought

Evil men with cruel plots surrounded the psalmist. He pleads for the Lord to rescue him.

Key thing to look out for

The poor and the needy are never far from the Lord's care.

Key Bible cross-reference

Verse 3. See Romans 13:3.

Key "by way of explanation"

Verse 13, "will love before you." This promise, given to the righteous, stands in stark contrast to the destiny of the wicked.

Key "Quotable Quote"

"Surely the righteous shall give thanks unto thy name: the upright shall dwell in thy presence."

Psalm 140:13

Psalm 141

Matthew Henry's introduction

I. David prays for God's favorable acceptance, vv. 1, 2.

II. For his powerful assistance, vv. 3, 4.

III. That others might be instrumental of good to his soul, as he hoped to be to the souls of others, vv. 5, 6.

IV. That he and his friends being now brought

to the last extremity God would graciously appear for their relief and rescue, vv. 7–10.

A detailed analysis of psalm

David prays for God's acceptance and assistance. (1–4)

That God would appear for his rescue. (5–10)

Key verse

Verse 3: "Set a watch, O LORD, before my mouth; keep the door of my lips."

Key word / key phrase

Verse 3, "my lips."

Key event / key person / key theme

Deliverance from evil – within the self, and from outside.

Key thought

The psalmist prays that he will never join the ranks of the wicked.

Key thing to look out for

The psalmist makes striking contrasts between the wicked and the righteous.

Key Bible cross-reference

Verse 2. See Revelation 5:8.

Key "by way of explanation"

Verse 4, "their delicacies." The tables of the wealthy were strewn with ill-gotten gains from the poor and oppressed. The psalmist asks to be delivered from even desiring such things.

Key "Quotable Quote"

"But mine eyes are unto thee, O GOD the Lord: in thee is my trust; leave not my soul destitute."

Psalm 141:8

Psalm 142

Matthew Henry's introduction

Here is,

I. The complaint he makes to God (vv. 1, 2) of the subtlety, strength, and malice, of his enemies (vv. 3, 6), and the coldness and indifference of his friends, v. 4.

II. The comfort he takes in God that he knew his case (v. 3) and was his refuge, v. 5.

III. His expectation from God that he would hear and deliver him, vv. 6, 7.

IV. His expectation from the righteous that they would join with him in praises, v. 7.

A detailed analysis of psalm

David's comfort in prayer. (1–7)

Key verse

Verse 7: "Bring my soul out of prison."

Key word / key phrase

Verse 5, "my portion."

Key event / key person / key theme

A prayer for help

Key thought

In the grip of powerful enemies, the psalmist appeals for the Lord to rescue him with his greater power.

Key thing to look out for

When the psalmist was in real need he made a point of bringing that before the Lord in prayer.

Key Bible cross-reference

Title. See 1 Samuel 22:1; 24:3.

Key "by way of explanation"

Verse 7, "prison." The word "prison" is often used in a metaphorical way to indicate being caught up and fettered by some kind of suffering.

Key "Quotable Quote"

"I cried unto the LORD with my voice; with my voice unto the LORD did I make my supplication."

Psalm 142:1

Psalm 143

Matthew Henry's introduction

In this psalm,

I. He complains of his troubles, through the oppression of his enemies (v. 3) and the weakness of his spirit under it, which was ready to sink notwithstanding the likely course he took to support himself, vv. 4, 5.

II. He prays, and prays earnestly (v. 6),

A. That God would hear him, vv. 1–7.

B. That he would not deal with him according to his sins, v. 2.

C. That he would not hide his face from him (v. 7), but manifest his favor to him, v. 8.

D. That he would guide and direct him in the way of his duty (vv. 8, 10) and quicken him in it, v. 11.

5. That he would deliver him out of his troubles, vv. 9, 11.

6. That he would in due time reckon with his persecutors, v. 12.

A detailed analysis of psalm

An appeal for help based on Gold's covenant love. (1–6)

He prays for comfort, guidance, and deliverance. (7–12)

Key verse

Verse 1: "Hear my prayer, O LORD, give ear to my supplications."

Key word / key phrase

Verse 1, "my cry."

Key event / key person / key theme

The psalmist calls on God's grace in his desperate situation.

Key thought

Weakness is not a sin. Rather it is something to pray about.

Key thing to look out for

The psalmist is desperate and asks for immediate help.

Key Bible cross-reference

Verse 2. See Romans 3:20; Galatians 2:16.

Key "by way of explanation"

Verse 6, "spread out my hands." This was one of the ways in which people prayed. See 44:20; Exodus 9:29.

Key "Quotable Quote"

"And enter not into judgment with thy servant: for in thy sight shall no man living be justified."

Psalm 143:2

Psalm 144

Matthew Henry's introduction

In this psalm,

I. He acknowledges, with triumph and thankfulness, the great goodness of God to him in advancing him to the government, vv. 1–4.

II. He prays to God to help him against the enemies who threatened him, vv. 5–8 and again v. 11.

III. He rejoices in the assurance of victory over them, vv. 9, 10.

IV. He prays for the prosperity of his own kingdom, and pleases himself with the hopes of it, vv. 12–15.

A detailed analysis of psalm

David acknowledges the great goodness of God, and prays for help. (1–8)

He prays for the prosperity of his kingdom. (9–15)

Key verse

Verse 4: "Man is like to vanity: his days are as a shadow that passeth away."

Key word / key phrase

Verse 4, "What is man?"

Key event / key person / key theme

Victory comes from God

Key thought

In the face of foreign aggression, the psalmist calls on the Lord.

Key thing to look out for

The Israelites believed that the Lord gave them victory on the battlefield and in all other kinds of conflict.

Key Bible cross-reference

Verse 3. See Job 7:17,18.

Key "by way of explanation"

Verse 12, "daughters . . . like pillars carved." On the Acropolis in Athens, as in other temples, it was not very unusual to find columns carved in the shape of women.

Key "Quotable Quote"

"I will sing a new song unto thee, O God: upon a psaltery and an instrument of ten strings will I sing praises unto thee."

Psalm 144:9

Psalm 145

Matthew Henry's introduction

In this psalm,

I. David engages himself and others to praise God, vv. 1, 2, 4–7, 10–12.

II. He fastens on those things that are proper matter for praise, God's greatness (ver. 3), his goodness (vv. 8, 9), the proofs of both in the administration of his kingdom (v. 13), the kingdom of providence (vv. 14–16), the kingdom of grace (vv. 17–20), and then he concludes with a resolution to continue praising God (v. 21).

A detailed analysis of psalm

David extols the power, goodness, and mercy of the Lord. (1–9)

The glory of God's kingdom, and his care of those that love him. (10–21)

Key verse

Verse 10: "All thy works shall praise thee, O LORD; and thy saints shall bless thee."

Key word / key phrase

Verse 4, "mighty acts."

Key event / key person / key theme

God's kingship

Key thought

Praise

Key thing to look out for

God's followers are meant to speak up about God's goodness and greatness.

Key Bible cross-reference

Verse 11. See 144:7; Proverbs 6:3.

Key "by way of explanation"

Verse 4, "your works." In the psalms the Lord's "works" or "deeds," usually refer to creation, the Exodus, and the conquest of the promised land.

Key "Quotable Quote"

"I will extol thee, my God, O king; and I will bless thy name for ever and ever."

Psalm 145:1

Psalm 146

Matthew Henry's introduction

I. The psalmist engages himself to praise God, vv. 1, 2.

II. He engages others to trust in him, which is one necessary and acceptable way of praising him.

A. He shows why we should not trust in men, vv. 3, 4.

B. Why we should trust in God (v. 5), because of his power in the kingdom of nature (v. 6), his dominion in the kingdom of providence (v. 7), and his grace in the kingdom of the Messiah (vv. 8, 9), that everlasting kingdom (v. 10).

A detailed analysis of psalm

Why we should not trust in men. (1–4)

Why we should trust in God. (5–10)

Key verse

Verse 5: "Happy is he that hath the God of Jacob for his help."

Key word / key phrase

Verse 3, "mortal men."

Key event / key person / key theme

Do not place your trust in princes.

Key thought

Psalm 146 is the first of five psalms of praise which close the whole book of Psalms.

Key thing to look out for

The Lord acts out of love.

Key Bible cross-reference

Verse 6. See Acts 4:24; 14:15.

Key "by way of explanation"

Verse 6, "Maker of heaven and earth." By referring to the Lord as "Maker of heaven and earth" the psalmist is calling attention to the mighty power and infinite goodness of the Lord God Almighty.

Key "Quotable Quote"

"The LORD shall reign for ever, even thy God, O Zion, unto all generations. Praise ye the LORD."

Psalm 146:10

Psalm 147

Matthew Henry's introduction

I. We are called on to praise God, vv. 1, 7, 12.

II. We are furnished with matter for praise, for God is to be glorified,

A. As the God of nature, and so he is very great, vv. 4, 5, 8, 9, 15–18.

B. As the God of grace, comforting his people, vv. 3, 6, 10, 11.

C. As the God of Israel, Jerusalem, and Zion, settling their civil state (vv. 2, 13, 14), and especially settling religion among them, vv. 19, 20.

A detailed analysis of psalm

The people of God are exhorted to praise him for his mercies and care. (1–11)

For the salvation and prosperity that he gives. (12–20)

Key verse

Verse 9: "He giveth to the beast his food, and to the young ravens which cry."

Key word / key phrase

Verse 3, "binds up their wounds."

Key event / key person / key theme

God heals the broken-hearted.

Key thought

The Lord is Lord of all of creation, but he also had a unique relationship with his people, the Israelites.

Key thing to look out for

Peace and prosperity come from the hand of the Lord.

Key Bible cross-reference

Verse 5. See 136:5; Proverbs 1:2.

Key "by way of explanation"

Verse 3, "broken-hearted." There could be no greater example of the "broken-hearted" than the Lord's people in exile from their beloved Jerusalem.

Key "Quotable Quote"

"Great is our Lord, and of great power: his understanding is infinite."

Psalm 147:5

Psalm 148

Matthew Henry's introduction

I. The psalmist calls on the higher house, the creatures that are placed in the upper world, to praise the Lord, both those that are intellectual beings, and are capable of doing it actively (vv. 1, 2), and those that are not, and are therefore capable of doing it only objectively, vv. 3–6.

II. He calls on the lower house, the creatures of this lower world, both those that can only minister matter of praise (vv. 7–10) and those that, being endued with reason, are capable of offering up this sacrifice (vv. 11–13), especially his own people, who have more cause to do it, and are more concerned to do it, than any other, v. 14.

A detailed analysis of psalm

Praise from the heavens. (1–6)

Praise from the earth.. (7–14)

Key verse

Verse 2: "Praise ye him, all his angels: praise ye him, all his hosts."

Key word / key phrase

Verse 2, "all his heavenly hosts."

Key event / key person / key theme

All creation praises the Lord.

Key thought

The whole of the created order is to sing the Lord's praises.

Key thing to look out for

God's people are to join in the praises of creation and worship the Lord alone.

Key Bible cross-reference

Verse 7. See 104:26; Isaiah 27:1.

Key "by way of explanation"

Verse 14, "horn," refers here to the victorious king.

Key "Quotable Quote"

"Let them praise the name of the LORD: for his name alone is excellent; his glory is above the earth and heaven."

Psalm 148:13

Psalm 149

Matthew Henry's introduction

I. Abundance of joy to all the people of God, vv. 1–5.

II. Abundance of terror to the proudest of their enemies, vv. 6–9.

A detailed analysis of psalm

Joy to all the people of God. (1–5)

Terror to their enemies. (6–9)

Key verse

Verse 3: "Let them praise his name in the dance."

Key word / key phrase

Verse 4, "crowns."

Key event / key person / key theme

The Lord takes pleasure in his people.

Key thought

Dancing and music are to accompany the praises of the godly.

Key thing to look out for

The Israelites praised the Lord for being their Maker and for being their Redeemer.

Key Bible cross-reference

Verse 1. See 144:9; Proverbs 19:4.

Key "by way of explanation"

Verse 7, "vengeance." Christians are armed for the spiritual battle with the sword of the Spirit, Ephesians 6:12,17.

Key "Quotable Quote"

"Praise ye the LORD. Sing unto the LORD a new song, and his praise in the congregation of saints."

Psalm 149:1

Psalm 150

Matthew Henry's introduction

The psalmist had been himself full of the praises of God, and here he would fain fill all the world with them: again and again he calls, "Praise the Lord, praise him, praise him," no less than thirteen times in these six short verses. He shows,

I. For what, and on what account, God is to be praised (vv. 1, 2),

II. How, and with what expressions of joy, God is to be praised, vv. 3–5.

III. Who must praise the Lord; it is every one's business, v. 6.

A detailed analysis of psalm

A psalm of praise. (1–6)

Key verse

Verse 6: "Let every thing that hath breath praise the LORD. Praise ye the LORD."

Key word / key phrase

Verse 1, "praise God."

Key event / key person / key theme

Praise the Lord

Key thought

This grand musical hallelujah is a fitting conclusion to Book V of the psalms.

Key thing to look out for

Everyone is to praise the Lord.

Key Bible cross-reference

Verse 2. See 138:2; Daniel 3:26.

Key "by way of explanation"

Verse 4, "flute." The Lord is to be praised with the eight instruments of the full orchestra.

Key "Quotable Quote"

"Praise ye the LORD. Praise God in his sanctuary: praise him in the firmament of his power."

Psalm 150:1

5. Select bibliography for Psalms

Alexander, Joseph A. *Commentary on the Psalms*, Kregel, 1991.

Allen, Leslie C. *Psalms 101–150* (Word), Word Books, 1983.

Calvin, John. *Commentary on the Book of Psalms*. Translated by James Anderson. 3 Vols. Reprint. Grand Rapids: Eerdmans, 1963.

Delitzsch, Franz. *Biblical Commentary on the*

Psalms. KD. Translated by David Eaton. 3 Vols. London: Hodder and Stoughton, 1902.
Goldingay, John. *Songs from a Strange Land. Psalms 42–51*. Downers Grove: InterVarsity, 1978.
Kidner, Derek. *Psalms 1–72* (Tyndale), InterVarsity, 1973.
Kidner, Derek. *Psalms 73–150* (Tyndale), InterVarsity, 1975.
VanGemeren, Willem A. "Psalms" in *Expositor's Bible Commentary*, 5, Zondervan, 1991.
White, R. E. O. *A Christian Handbook to the Psalms*. Grand Rapids: Eerdmans, 1984.

Proverbs

1. Book by book: Introduction to Proverbs

Introduction

Nature and use of proverbs

A proverb is a pithy sentence, concisely expressing some well-established truth susceptible of various illustrations and applications. The word is of Latin derivation, literally meaning for a word, speech, or discourse; that is, one expression for many. The Hebrew word for "proverb" (*mashal*) means a "comparison." Many suppose it was used, because the form or matter of the proverb, or both, involved the idea of comparison. Most of the proverbs are in couplets or triplets, or some modifications of them, the members of which correspond in structure and length, as if arranged to be compared one with another. They illustrate the varieties of parallelism, a distinguishing feature of Hebrew poetry. Many also clearly involve the idea of comparison in the sentiments expressed (compare Prov. 12:1–10; 25:10–15; 26:1–9). Sometimes, however, the designed omission of one member of the comparison, exercising the reader's sagacity or study for its supply, presents the proverb as a "riddle" or "dark saying" (compare Prov. 30:15–33; 1:6; Ps. 49:4). The sententious form of expression, which thus became a marked feature of the proverbial style, was also adopted for continuous discourse, even when not always preserving traces of comparison, either in form or matter (compare Prov. 1:1–9:18). In Ezek. 17:1; 24:3, we find the same word properly translated "parable," to designate an illustrative discourse. Then the Greek translators have used a word, parabola ("parable"), which the gospel writers (except John) employ for our Lord's discourses of the same character, and which also seems to involve the idea of comparison, though that may not be its primary meaning. It might seem, therefore, that the proverbial and parabolic styles of writing were originally and essentially the same. The proverb is a "concentrated parable, and the parable an extension of the proverb by a full illustration." The proverb is thus the moral or theme of a parable, which sometimes precedes it, as in Matt. 19:30 (compare Prov. 20:1); or succeeds it, as in Matt. 22:1–16; Luke 15:1–10. The style being poetical, and adapted to the expression of a high order of poetical sentiment, such as prophecy, we find the same term used to designate such compositions (compare Num. 23:7; Mic. 2:4; Hab. 2:6).

Though the Hebrews used the same term for proverb and parable, the Greek use two, though the sacred writers have not always appeared to recognize a distinction. The term for proverb is, *paroimia*, which the Greek translators employ for the title of this book, evidently with special reference to the later definition of a proverb, as a trite, sententious form of speech, which appears to be the best meaning of the term. John uses the same term to designate our Savior's instructions, in view of their characteristic obscurity (compare Prov. 16:25–29, Greek), and even for his illustrative discourses (Prov. 10:6), whose sense was not at once obvious to all his hearers. This form of instruction was well adapted to aid the learner. The parallel structure of sentences, the repetition, contrast, or comparison of thought, were all calculated to facilitate the efforts of memory; and precepts of practical wisdom which, extended into logical discourses, might have failed to make abiding impressions by reason of their length or complicated character, were thus compressed into pithy, and, for the most part, very plain statements. Such a mode of instruction has distinguished the written or traditional literature of all nations, and was, and still is, peculiarly current in the East.

In this book, however, we are supplied with a proverbial wisdom commended by the seal of divine inspiration. God has condescended to become our teacher on the practical affairs belonging to all the relations of life. He has adapted His instruction to the plain and unlettered, and presented, in this striking and impressive method, the great principles of duty to Him and to our fellow men. To the prime motive of all right conduct, the fear of God, are added all lawful and subordinate incentives, such as honor, interest, love, fear, and natural affection. Besides the terror excited by an apprehension of God's justly provoked judgments, we are warned against evil-doing by the exhibition of the inevitable temporal results of impiety, injustice, profligacy, idleness, laziness, indolence, drunkenness, and debauchery. To the rewards of true piety which follow in eternity, are promised the peace, security, love, and approbation of the good, and the comforts of a clear conscience, which render this life truly happy.

Inspiration and authorship

With no important exception, Jewish and Christian writers have received this book as the inspired production of Solomon. It is the first book of the Bible prefaced by the name of the author. The New Testament abounds with citations from the Proverbs. Its intrinsic excellence commends it to us as the production of a higher authority than the apocryphal writings, such as Wisdom or Ecclesiasticus. Solomon lived five hundred years before the "seven wise men" of Greece, and seven hundred before the age of Socrates, Plato, and Aristotle. It is thus very evident, whatever theory of his sources of knowledge be adopted, that he did not draw on any heathen repositories with which we are acquainted. It is far more probable, that by the various migrations, captivities, and dispersions of the Jews, heathen philosophers drew from this inspired fountain many of those streams which continue to refresh mankind amid the otherwise barren and parched deserts of profane literature.

As, however, the Psalms are ascribed to David, because he was the leading author, so the ascription of this book to Solomon is entirely consistent with the titles of the thirtieth and thirty-first chapters, which assign those chapters to Agur and Lemuel respectively. Of these people we know nothing. This is not the place for discussing the various speculations respecting them. By a slight change of reading some propose to translate Prov. 30:1: "The words of Agur, the son of her who was obeyed Massa," that is, "the queen of Massa"; and Prov. 31:1: "The words of Lemuel, king of Massa"; but to this the earliest versions are contradictory, and nothing other than the strongest exegetical necessity ought to be allowed to justify a departure from a well-established reading and version when nothing useful to our knowledge is gained. It is better to confess ignorance than indulge in useless conjectures.

It is probable that out of the "three thousand proverbs" (1 Kings 4:32) which Solomon spoke, he selected and edited Prov. 1:1–24:34 during his life. Prov. 25:1–29:27 were also of his production, and copied out in the days of Hezekiah, by his "men," perhaps the prophets Isaiah, Hosea, and Micah. Such a work was evidently in the spirit of this pious monarch, who set his heart so fully on a reformation of God's worship. Learned men have endeavored to establish the theory that Solomon himself was only a collector; or that the other parts of the book, as these chapters, were also selections by later hands; but the reasons adduced to maintain these views have never appeared so satisfactory as to change the usual opinions on the subject, which have the sanction of the most ancient and reliable authorities.

Book divisions

Such a work is, of course, not susceptible of any logical analysis. There are, however, some well-defined marks of division, so that very generally the book is divided into five or six parts.

1. The first contains nine chapters, in which are discussed and enforced by illustration, admonition, and encouragement the principles and blessings of wisdom, and the pernicious schemes and practices of sinful people. These chapters are introductory. With few specimens of the proper proverb, they are distinguished by its conciseness and terseness. The sentences follow very strictly the form of parallelism, and generally of the synonymous species, only forty of the synthetic and four (Prov. 3:32–35) of the antithetic appearing. The style is ornate, the figures bolder and fuller, and the illustrations more striking and extended.

2. The antithetic and synthetic parallelism to the exclusion of the synonymous distinguish Prov. 10:1–22:16, and the verses are entirely unconnected, each containing a complete sense in itself.

3. Prov. 22:16–24:34 present a series of admonitions as if addressed to a pupil, and generally each topic occupies two or more verses.

4. Prov. 25:1–29:27 are entitled to be regarded as a distinct portion, for the reason given above as to its origin. The style is very much mixed; of the peculiarities, compare parts two and three.

5. Prov. 30:1–33 is peculiar not only for its authorship, but as a specimen of the kind of proverb which has been described as "dark sayings" or "riddles."

6. To a few concise admonitions, suitable for a king, is added a most inimitable portraiture of female character. In both parts five and six the distinctive peculiarity of the original proverbial style gives

place to the modifications already mentioned as marking a later composition, though both retain the concise and nervous method of stating truth, equally valuable for its deep impression and permanent retention by the memory.

A.R. Faussett

Detailed outline

I. Introduction: 1:1–6

II. Lessons on wisdom: 1:7–9:18

A. The call of wisdom: 1:7–33

B. The rewards of wisdom: 2:1–7:27

C. Praise of divine wisdom: 8:1–9:18

III. Miscellaneous proverbs of Solomon: 10:1–22:16

IV. Collections of proverbs of wise men: 22:17–24:34

V. Proverbs of Solomon: 25:1–29:27

A. Observations about kings; quarrels; relationships with others: 25:1–28

B. Comments on fools, sluggards, and busybodies: 26:1–28

C. Self-love, true love; offenses; thoughts on household care: 27:1–27

D. Contrasts of the wicked and righteous: 28:1–28

E. Proverbs about public government and private affairs: 29:1–27

VI. A proverb of Agur: Confessions and instructions: 30:1–33

VII. A proverb of Lemuel: Praise of a good wife: 31:1–31

2. Helpful summaries of Proverbs

Bird's eye view

The book of Proverbs is a collection of religious and moral maxims giving the reader advice about how to live a good and godly life.

Reading plan

The following reading plan, taking one reading per day, enables you to read through Proverbs in fourteen days.

Proverbs 1–2
Proverbs 3–4
Proverbs 5–6
Proverbs 7–8
Proverbs 9–11
Proverbs 12–13
Proverbs 14–15
Proverbs 16–17
Proverbs 18–19
Proverbs 20–21
Proverbs 22–23
Proverbs 24–25
Proverbs 26–27
Proverbs 28–31

Verses to memorize

Proverbs 2:6

For the Lord giveth wisdom: out of his mouth cometh knowledge and understanding. KJV

Proverbs 3:5

Trust in the Lord with all thine heart; and lean not unto thine own understanding. KJV

Proverbs 3:6

In all thy ways acknowledge him, and he shall direct thy paths. KJV

Proverbs 3:7

Be not wise in thine own eyes: fear the Lord, and depart from evil. KJV

Proverbs 3:9

Honor the Lord with thy substance, and with the first fruits of all thine increase: KJV

Proverbs 4:7

Wisdom is the principal thing; therefore get wisdom: and with all thy getting get understanding.

Proverbs 18:24

A man that hath friends must shew himself friendly: and there is a friend that sticketh closer than a brother. KJV

Proverbs 30:5

God keeps every promise he makes. He is like a shield for all who seek his protection.

Statistics

Twentieth Old Testament book

31 chapters

915 verses

15,043 words

Famous sayings found in Proverbs

- "Soft answer turns away wrath" Proverbs 15:1
- "Pride goes before a fall" Proverbs 16:19
- "Where there is no vision, the people perish" Proverbs 29:18

Names/titles given

Hebrew title: *Mishle Shelomoh:* "Proverbs of Solomon."

Greek title in Septuagint: *Paroimiai Salomontos:* "Proverbs of Solomon."

Latin title in Vulgate: *Liber Proverbiorum:* "Book of Proverbs."

Rabbinical writings: *Sepher Hokhman:* "Book of Wisdom."

3. Helpful keys to turn to in understanding Proverbs

Key words

Wisdom, 104 times

The fear of the Lord

Key verses

Proverbs 1:5–7; 9:10

Themes to study

Wealth and poverty

Work and laziness

Using one's tongue

True friendship

Disciplining and instructing children

- Not sparing the rod, Prov. 13:24
- "Discipline your son," Prov. 19:18
- Train a child in the way he/she should go, Prov. 22:6
- Use of the rod of discipline, Prov. 22:15
- Do not leave your child undisciplined, Prov. 23:13

Proverbs quoted in the New Testament

- For whom the Lord loveth he chasteneth
  Prov. 3:11–12 quoted in Heb. 12:5–6
- God resisteth the proud, but giveth grace to the humble
  Prov. 3:34 quoted in James 4:6 and 1 Pet. 5:5
- And if the righteous is scarcely saved, where

shall the ungodly and sinner appear
Prov. 11:31 quoted in 1 Pet. 4:18

- If thine enemy hunger, feed him
Prov. 25:21–22 quoted in Rom. 12:20
- The dog turning to his own vomit again
Prov. 26:11 quoted in 2 Pet. 2:22

Lessons to learn from Proverbs

- Wisdom, not foolishness, should characterize us.
- We will have to account to God for our every word.
- Faithfulness to one's spouse and family is essential.

4. Chapter by chapter: outline of every chapter of Proverbs

Proverbs 1

Matthew Henry's introduction

In this chapter we have,

I. The title of the book, showing the general scope and design of it, vv. 1–6.

II. The first principle of it recommended to our serious consideration, vv. 7–9.

III. A necessary caution against bad company, vv. 10–19.

IV. A faithful and lively representation of wisdom's reasonings with the children of men, and the certain ruin of those who turn a deaf ear to those reasonings, vv. 20–33.

A detailed analysis of chapter

The use of the proverbs. (1–6)
Exhortations to fear God and obey parents. (7–9)
To avoid sinners. (10–19)
The address of Wisdom to sinners. (20–33)

Key verse

Verse 1: "The proverbs of Solomon the son of David, king of Israel."

Key word / key phrase

Verse 3: "acquiring."

Key event / key person / key theme

The value of proverbs

Key thought

Solomon was renowned for his wisdom.

Key thing to look out for

The importance of gaining wisdom is introduced.

Key Bible cross-reference

Verse 1. See 1 Kings 4:32.

Key "by way of explanation"

Verse 6, "riddles." This word can mean "allegories" as well as "riddles." See Ezekiel 17:2.

Key "Quotable Quote"

"The fear of the Lord is the beginning of knowledge: but fools despise wisdom and instruction."

Proverbs 1:7

Proverbs 2

Matthew Henry's introduction

Solomon, having foretold the destruction of those who are obstinate in their impiety, in this chapter applies himself to those who are willing to be taught; and,

I. He shows them that, if they would diligently use the means of knowledge and grace, they should obtain of God the knowledge and grace which they seek, vv. 1–9.

II. He shows them of what unspeakable advantage it would be to them.

A. It would preserve them from the snares of evil men (vv. 10–15) and of evil women, vv. 16–19.

B. It would direct them into, and keep them in, the way of good men, vv. 20–22. So that in this chapter we are taught both how to get wisdom and how to use it when we have it, that we may neither seek it, nor receive it in vain.

A detailed analysis of chapter

Promises to those who seek wisdom. (1–9)

The advantages of wisdom. (10–22)

Key verse

Verse 1: "My son, if thou wilt receive my words, and hide my commandments with thee."

Key word / key phrase

Verse 2, "applying your heart to understanding."

Key event / key person / key theme

Seek wisdom

Key thought

The many benefits of wisdom.

Key thing to look out for

The danger of leaving the straight and narrow.

Key Bible cross-reference

Verse 7. See Psalm 147:1

Key "by way of explanation"

Verse 13, "dark ways." Jesus warned that ungodly people naturally prefer darkness to light.

Key "Quotable Quote"

"For the LORD giveth wisdom: out of his mouth cometh knowledge and understanding."

Proverbs 2:6

Proverbs 3

Matthew Henry's introduction

I. We must be constant to our duty because that is the way to be happy, vv. 1–4.

II. We must live a life of dependence on God because that is the way to be safe, v. 5.

III. We must keep up the fear of God because that is the way to be healthful, vv. 7, 8.

IV. We must serve God with our estates because that is the way to be rich, vv. 9, 10.

V. We must hear afflictions well because that is the way to get good by them, vv. 11, 12.

VI. We must take pains to obtain wisdom because that is the way to gain her, and to gain by her, vv. 13–20.

VII. We must always govern ourselves by the rules of wisdom, of right reason and religion, because that is the way to be always easy, vv. 21–26.

VIII. We must do all the good we can, and no hurt, to our neighbors, because according as men are just or unjust, charitable or uncharitable, humble or haughty, accordingly they shall receive of God, vv. 27–35.

A detailed analysis of chapter

Exhortations to obedience and faith. (1–6)
To piety, and to improve afflictions. (7–12)
To gain wisdom. (13–20)
Guidance of Wisdom. (21–26)
The wicked and the upright. (27–35)

Key verse

Verse 5: "Trust in the LORD with thine heart; and lean not unto thine own understanding."

Key word / key phrase

God's wisdom. Note each occurrence or reference to the word, or a linked idea (verses 13, 14, 15, 16, 17, 18, 19, 20, 21, 35).

Key event / key person / key theme

The benefits of wisdom

Key thought

The benefits to be derived from divine wisdom are incalculable.

Key thing to look out for

The practical outworking of wisdom in everyday life.

Key Bible cross-reference

God's wisdom revealed in Jesus Christ, 1 Corinthians 1:19–31.

Key "by way of explanation"

Verse 18. Wisdom is described as "a tree of life." This is the source of life and may be linked with the tree in the Garden of Eden, Genesis 2:9.

Key "Quotable Quote"

"The great folly of man in trials is leaning to or on his own understanding and counsels. What is the result of this? Whenever in our trials we consult our own understanding, listen to our own reason, even though they appear to be good, the principle of living by faith is stifled, and we will in this way be let down by our own counsels."

John Owen, commenting on verse 5.

Proverbs 4

Matthew Henry's introduction

Here is,

I. An earnest exhortation to the study of wisdom, that is, of true religion and godliness, borrowed from the good instructions which his father gave him, and enforced with many considerable arguments, vv. 1–13.

II. A necessary caution against bad company and all fellowship with the unfruitful works of darkness, vv. 14–19.

III. Particular directions for the attaining and preserving of wisdom, and bringing forth the fruits of it, vv. 20–27.

A detailed analysis of chapter

Exhortation to the study of wisdom. (1–13)
Warnings against bad company. Exhortation to faith and holiness. (14–27)

Key verse

Verse 14: "Enter not into the path of the wicked, and go not in the way of evil men."

Key word / key phrase

Verse 19, "the road of the wicked."

Key event / key person / key theme

The righteous and the wicked

Key thought

Wisdom is the supreme way of life.

Key thing to look out for

The choice between following wisdom or following evil is always before us.

Key Bible cross-reference

Verse 26. See Hebrews 12:13.

Key "by way of explanation"

Verse 19, "deep darkness." Evil leads on to more and more evil. It eventually leads to destruction.

Key "Quotable Quote"

"Keep thy heart with all diligence; for out of it are the issues of life."

Proverbs 4:23

Proverbs 5

Matthew Henry's introduction

Here is,

I. An exhortation to get acquaintance with and submit to the laws of wisdom in general, v. 2.

II. A particular caution against the sin of whoredom, vv. 3–14.

III. Remedies prescribed against that sin.

A. Conjugal love, vv. 15–20.

B. A regard to God's omniscience, v. 21.

C. A dread of the miserable end of wicked people, vv. 22, 23.

A detailed analysis of chapter

Exhortations to wisdom. The evils of adultery. (1–14)

Remedies against adultery, and the miserable end of the wicked. (15–23)

Key verse

Verse 15: "Drink waters out of thine own cistern, and running waters out of thine own well."

Key word / key phrase

Verse 3, "the lips of an adulteress."

Key event / key person / key theme

Adultery is out, faithfulness is in

Key thought

The book of Proverbs is full of warnings against adultery.

Key thing to look out for

Self-discipline is essential.

Key Bible cross-reference

Verse 4. See Psalm 106:33.

Key "by way of explanation"

Verse 19, "doe . . . deer," are descriptions of a wife, focusing on her beauty.

Key "Quotable Quote"

"He shall die without instruction; and in the greatness of his folly he shall go astray."

Proverbs 5:23

Proverbs 6

Matthew Henry's introduction

In this chapter we have,

I. A caution against rash suretiship, vv. 1–5.

II. A rebuke to slothfulness, vv. 6–11.

III. The character and fate of a malicious mischievous man, vv. 12–15.

IV. An account of seven things which God hates, vv. 16–19.

V. An exhortation to make the word of God familiar to us, vv. 20–23.

VI. A repeated warning of the pernicious consequences of the sin of whoredom, vv. 24–35.

A detailed analysis of chapter

Warnings against rash lending. (1–5)

A rebuke to slothfulness. (6–11)

Seven things God hates. (12–19)

Exhortations to walk according to God's commandments. (20–35)

Key verse

Verse 6: "Go to the ant, thou sluggard; consider her ways, and be wise."

Key word / key phrase

Verse 6, "sluggard."

Key event / key person / key theme

Do not be lazy.

Key thought

How to avoid being foolish.

Key thing to look out for

More warnings against adultery.

Key Bible cross-reference

Verses 10,11. See 24:33,34.

Key "by way of explanation"

Verse 12, "corrupt mouth." The pernicious words of a gossip are spread by a "corrupt mouth."

Key "Quotable Quote"

"A naughty person, a wicked man, walketh with a froward mouth."

Proverbs 6:12

Proverbs 7

Matthew Henry's introduction

In this chapter we have,

I. A general exhortation to get our minds principled and governed by the word of God, as a sovereign antidote against this sin, vv. 1–5.

II. A particular representation of the great danger which unwary young men are in of being inveigled into this snare, vv. 6–23.

III. A serious caution inferred thence, in the close, to take heed of all approaches towards this sin, vv. 24–27.

A detailed analysis of chapter

Invitations to learn wisdom. (1–5)

The ways of seducers, with warnings against them. (6–27)

Key verse

Verse 4: "Say unto wisdom, Thou art my sister."

Key word / key phrase

Verse 10, "dressed like a prostitute."

Key event / key person / key theme

Do not commit adultery.

Key thought

Adultery ends in death.

Key thing to look out for

Being wise can prevent adultery.

Key Bible cross-reference

Verse 22. See Isaiah 14:21.

Key "by way of explanation"

Verse 16, "colored lines from Egypt" were linked with the wealthy as Egyptian linen fetched the top price. See Ezekiel 7:7.

Key "Quotable Quote"

"My son, keep my words, and lay up my commandments with thee."

Proverbs 7:1

Proverbs 8

Matthew Henry's introduction

Now,

I. Divine revelation is the word and wisdom of God, and that pure religion and undefiled which is built on it; and of that Solomon here speaks, recommending it to us as faithful, and well worthy of all acceptation, vv. 1–21. All divine revelation passes through his hand, and centers in him; but of him as the personal Wisdom, the second person in the Godhead, in the judgment of many of the ancients, Solomon here speaks, vv. 22–31. He concludes with a repeated charge to the children of men diligently to attend to the voice of God in his word, vv. 32–36.

A detailed analysis of chapter

Christ, as Wisdom, calls to the sons of men. (1–11)

The nature and riches of Wisdom. (12–21)

Christ one with the Father, in the creation of the world, and rejoicing in his work for the salvation of humankind. (22–31)

Exhortations to hear Christ's word. (32–36)

Key verse

Verse 12: "I wisdom dwell with prudence, and find out knowledge of witty inventions."

Key word / key phrase

Verse 1, "Does not wisdom call out?"

Key event / key person / key theme

In praise of wisdom

Key thought

Wisdom is personified. She longs to be followed.

Key thing to look out for

What wisdom is said to hate, the Lord hates; and what wisdom gives, the Lord gives.

Key Bible cross-reference

Verse 22. See Revelation 3:14.

Key "by way of explanation"

Verse 15, "By me kings reign." At the start of his reign as king, Solomon, in his dream, asked for the wisdom he needed to help him rule.

Key "Quotable Quote"

"Hear instruction, and be wise, and refuse it not."

Proverbs 8:33

Proverbs 9

Matthew Henry's introduction

I. Christ, under the name of Wisdom, invites us to accept of his entertainment, and so to enter into acquaintance and communion with him, vv. 1–6. And having foretold the different success of his invitation (vv. 7–9) he shows, in short, what he requires from us (v. 10) and what he designs for us (v. 11), and then leaves it to our choice what we will do, v. 12.

II. Sin, under the character of a foolish woman, courts us to accept of her entertainment, and (vv. 13–16) pretends it is very charming, v. 17. But Solomon tells us what the reckoning will be, v. 18.

A detailed analysis of chapter

The invitations of Wisdom. (1–12)

The invitations of Folly. (13–18)

Key verse

Verse 1: "Wisdom hath builded her house, she hath hewn out her seven pillars."

Key word / key phrase

Verse 1, "seven pillars."

Key event / key person / key theme

Wisdom and Folly are contrasted

Key thought

The choice between listening to Wisdom and Folly.

Key thing to look out for

The fear of the Lord and wisdom are said to be one.

Key Bible cross-reference

Verse 10. See Job 28:28.

Key "by way of explanation"

Verse 17, "Stolen water." Anything that is stolen may be pleasurable at the time but it is certain to bring disaster in its wake.

Key "Quotable Quote"

"Give instruction to a wise man, and he will be yet wiser: teach a just man, and he will increase in learning."

Proverbs 9:9

Proverbs 10

Matthew Henry's introduction

Hitherto we have been in the porch or preface to the proverbs, here they begin. They are short but weighty sentences; most of them are distichs, two sentences in one verse, illustrating each other; but it is seldom that there is any coherence between the verses, much less any thread of discourse, and therefore in these chapters we need not attempt to reduce the contents to their proper heads, the several sentences will appear best in their own places. The scope of them all is to set before us good and evil, the blessing and the curse. Many of the proverbs in this chapter relate to the good government of the tongue, without which men's religion is vain.

A detailed analysis of chapter

Proverbs of Solomon. (1–32)

Key verse

Verse 1: "A wise son maketh a glad father: but a foolish son is the heaviness of his mother."

Key word / key phrase

Verse 1, "A wise son . . . a foolish son."

Key event / key person / key theme

The godly and the wicked are contrasted

Key thought

Following the paths of wisdom brings happiness and prosperity.

Key thing to look out for

"Through the whole of the Proverbs, we are to look for somewhat beyond the first sense the passage may imply, and this we shall find to be Christ. He is the Wisdom so often spoken of in this book." Matthew Henry

Key Bible cross-reference

Verse 12. See 1 Peter 4:8.

Key "by way of explanation"

Verse 5, "sleeps during harvest." Condemnation of the person who does not work when he should.

Key "Quotable Quote"

"The blessing of the LORD, it maketh rich, and he addeth no sorrow with it."

Proverbs 10:22

Proverbs 11

Weighty sayings.

Also, see comments for chapter 10.

A detailed analysis of chapter

Proverbs of Solomon. (1–31)

Key verse

Verse 1: "A false balance is abomination to the LORD: but a just weight is his delight."

Key word / key phrase

Verse 2, "pride . . . humility."

Key event / key person / key theme

The godly and the wicked are contrasted

Key thought

There is wisdom here for the individual as well as for nations.

Key thing to look out for

Do not give your heart to the love of money.

Key Bible cross-reference

Verse 31. See 1 Peter 4:18

Key "by way of explanation"

Verse 5, "a straight way" enables a traveler to reach his destination.

Key "Quotable Quote"

"As righteousness tendeth to life: so he that pursueth evil pursueth it to his own death."

Proverbs 11:19

Proverbs 12

Advantages of the righteous.

Also, see comments for chapter 10.

A detailed analysis of chapter

Proverbs of Solomon. (1–28)

Key verse

Verse 4: "A virtuous woman is a crown to her husband."

Key word / key phrase

Verse 2, "good man . . . crafty man."

Key event / key person / key theme

The godly and the wicked are contrasted

Key thought

Observe the contrasts in most of the verses.

Key thing to look out for

The way to cope with an insult is given here.

Key Bible cross-reference

Verse 18. See Ecclesiastes 3:3.

Key "by way of explanation"

Verse 4. A wife is a husband's "crown" when she honors him.

Key "Quotable Quote"

"The lip of truth shall be established for ever: but a lying tongue is but for a moment."

Proverbs 12:19

Proverbs 13

Moral maxims.

Also, see comments for chapter 10.

A detailed analysis of chapter

Proverbs of Solomon. (1–25)

Key verse

Verse 5: "A righteous man hateth lying: but a wicked man is loathsome, and cometh to shame."

Key word / key phrase

Verse 3, "guards his lips . . . speaks rashly."

Key event / key person / key theme

The godly and the wicked are contrasted

Key thought

Wisdom is linked to what many in today's society would call "old-fashioned" virtues.

Key thing to look out for

The value of accepting advice, heeding wisdom, and seeking instruction is commended.

Key Bible cross-reference

Verse 9. See Ecclesiastes 2:13.

Key "by way of explanation"

Verse 17, "bring healing." It is possible to pour oil on troubled waters or to inflame a situation.

Key "Quotable Quote"

"Hope deferred maketh the heart sick: but when the desire cometh, it is a tree of life."

Proverbs 13:12

Proverbs 14

Wisdom and folly.

Also, see comments for chapter 10.

A detailed analysis of chapter

Proverbs of Solomon. (1–35)

Key verse

Verse 5: "A faithful witness will not lie: but a false witness will utter lies."

Key word / key phrase

Verse 5, "truthful witness . . . false witness."

Key event / key person / key theme

The godly and the wicked are contrasted

Key thought

The good things which are commended are to be sought after.

Key thing to look out for

The proverbs assume that there is plenty of scope for improvement in our lives.

Key Bible cross-reference

Verse 12. See Proverbs 16:25.

Key "by way of explanation"

Verse 31, "shows contempt for their Maker." The Lord made both the rich and the poor. Both are created in his image. So, for the rich to mistreat the poor is to show contempt for their "Maker."

Key "Quotable Quote"

"The house of the wicked shall be overthrown: but the tabernacle of the upright shall flourish."

Proverbs 14:11

Proverbs 15

The correct use of the tongue.

Also, see comments for chapter 10.

A detailed analysis of chapter

Proverbs of Solomon. (1–33)

Key verse

Verse 1: "A soft answer turneth away wrath: but grievous words stir up anger."

Key word / key phrase

Verse 32, "ignores discipline . . . heeds correction."

Key event / key person / key theme

The godly and the wicked are contrasted

Key thought

Once again the fear of the Lord tops the list.

Key thing to look out for

It is possible for a very proud person to read this list of evil traits and to think that none of them apply to him or her.

Key Bible cross-reference

Verse 27. See Psalm 26:10.

Key "by way of explanation"

Verse 11, "Death" and "Destruction" are where there is no praise given to God and where the dead abide. See Ecclesiastes 9:10; Psalm 88:10.

Key "Quotable Quote"

"The eyes of the LORD are in every place, beholding the evil and the good."

Proverbs 15:3

Proverbs 16

The sovereignty of divine providence.

Also, see comments for chapter 10.

A detailed analysis of chapter

Proverbs of Solomon. (1–33)

Key verse

Verse 8: "Better is a little with righteousness than great revenues without right."

Key word / key phrase

Verse 3, "Commit to the Lord."

Key event / key person / key theme

Encouraging godly living

Key thought

The proverbs are often not linked to each other, but taken together, they give a vast amount of wisdom.

Key thing to look out for

Ways to avoid evil.

Key Bible cross-reference

Verse 25. See 14:12.

Key "by way of explanation"

Verse 15, "his favor is like a rain cloud in spring." For the barley crop to produce a good harvest in the summer, spring rain was essential. It was a sign that the expected good things would indeed follow.

Key "Quotable Quote"

"How much better is it to get wisdom than gold! and to get understanding rather to be chosen than silver!"

Proverbs 16:16

Proverbs 17

False ways and oppression reproved.

Also, see comments for chapter 10.

A detailed analysis of chapter

Proverbs of Solomon. (1–28)

Key verse

Verse 10: "A reproof entereth more into a wise man than an hundred stripes into a fool."

Key word / key phrase

Verse 24, "a discerning man."

Key event / key person / key theme

Encouraging godly lives

Key thought

In Proverbs, many of the good qualities, like discernment, seem to be at a premium.

Key thing to look out for

The proverbs hit out at wrongdoing wherever it is to be found.

Key Bible cross-reference

Verse 21. See Ecclesiastes 7:3.

Key "by way of explanation"

Verse 3, "the crucible for silver and the furnace for gold." Both metals were refined in a fire and came out purified of impurities. In the same way, the Lord disciplines us to refine our characters.

Key "Quotable Quote"

"A friend loveth at all times, and a brother is born for adversity."

Proverbs 17:17

Proverbs 18

Wisdom and folly.

Also, see comments for chapter 10.

A detailed analysis of chapter

Proverbs of Solomon. (1–24)

Key verse

Verse 9: "He also that is slothful in his work is brother to him that is a great waster."

Key word / key phrase

Verse 10, "The name of the Lord."

Key event / key person / key theme

Encouraging godly lives

Key thought

Many of the things we take for granted should become things we take care to thank the Lord for.

Key thing to look out for

The proverbs give warning about taking care over how we speak, since words can kill or give life.

Key Bible cross-reference

Verse 24. See Psalm 119:89.

Key "by way of explanation"

Verse 10, "the name" of a person stood for his personality and character.

Key "Quotable Quote"

"A man that hath friends must show himself friendly: and there is a friend that sticketh closer than a brother."

Proverbs 18:24

Proverbs 19

The disadvantages of poverty.

Also, see comments for chapter 10.

A detailed analysis of chapter

Proverbs of Solomon. (1–29)

Key verse

Verse 4: "Wealth maketh many friends; but the poor is separated from his neighbor."

Key word / key phrase

Verse 8, "He who gets wisdom."

Key event / key person / key theme

Encouraging godly lives

Key thought

These proverbs teach that evil will be punished.

Key thing to look out for

The poor should be looked after.

Key Bible cross-reference

Verse 26. See Job 24:21.

Key "by way of explanation"

Verse 26, "robs his father and drives out his mother." There was no state aid in those days. The children were expected to look after their ill or elderly parents.

Key "Quotable Quote"

"Slothfulness casteth into a deep sleep; and an idle soul shall suffer hunger."

Proverbs 19:15

Proverbs 20

Miscellaneous maxims.

Also, see comments for chapter 10.21

A detailed analysis of chapter

Proverbs of Solomon. (1–30)

Key verse

Verse 15: "There is gold, and a multitude of rubies: but the lips of knowledge are a precious jewel."

Key word / key phrase

Verse 3, "avoid strife."

Key event / key person / key theme

Encouraging godly lives

Key thought

In the early chapters of Proverbs blame for adultery is often attached to the woman. Verse 6 of this chapter appears to find it impossible to find a faithful man.

Key thing to look out for

Many of the proverbs are directly linked to the Lord and his wishes and actions.

Key Bible cross-reference

Verse 27. See Acts 23:1.

Key "by way of explanation"

Verse 9, "without sin." No one in this life can reach sinless perfection. But after our sin is confessed to God and forgiven it may be said that we are "without sin" and so "pure" and "clean."

Key "Quotable Quote"

"Wine is a mocker, strong drink is raging: and whosoever is deceived thereby is not wise."

Proverbs 20:1

Proverbs 21

Miscellaneous maxims.

Also, see comments for chapter 10.

A detailed analysis of chapter

Proverbs of Solomon. (1–31)

Key verse

Verse 21: "To do justice and judgment is more acceptable to the LORD than sacrifice."

Key word / key phrase

Verse 4, "Haughty eyes."

Key event / key person / key theme

Encouraging godly lives

Key thought

The proud, the lazy, and the loud-mouthed come off worst in this chapter.

Key thing to look out for

Wisdom and victory are attributed to the Lord.

Key Bible cross-reference

Verse 20. See Lamentations 4:5.

Key "by way of explanation"

Verse 26, "give without sparing." Generosity should be a characteristic of the righteous. The righteous may also prosper and so find that they are in a better position to help the poor.

Key "Quotable Quote"

"Every way of a man is right in his own eyes: but the LORD pondereth the hearts."

Proverbs 21:2

Proverbs 22

Miscellaneous maxims.

Also, see comments for chapter 10.

A detailed analysis of chapter

Proverbs of Solomon. (1–16)

Sayings of the wise. (17–29)

Key verse

Verse 4: "By humility and the fear of the LORD are riches, and honor, and life."

Key word / key phrase

Verse 17, "the sayings of the wise."

Key event / key person / key theme

Encouraging godly lives

Key thought

The heart is often under scrutiny in these proverbs.

Key thing to look out for

A recurrent theme is the need to choose friends wisely.

Key Bible cross-reference

Verse 28. See Psalm 99:4.

Key "by way of explanation"

Verse 13, "the sluggard." When a lazy person does not want to work he is full of excuses and plausible reasons for not lifting a finger.

Key "Quotable Quote"

"Train up a child in the way he should go: and when he is old, he will not depart from it."

Proverbs 22:6

Proverbs 23

Warnings against luxury and covetousness.
Also, see comments for chapter 10.

A detailed analysis of chapter

Sayings of the wise. (1–35)

Key verse

Verse 10: "Remove not the old landmark; and enter not into the fields of the fatherless."

Key word / key phrase

Verse 5, "riches."

Key event / key person / key theme

Evils bring short-lived pleasures.

Key thought

Envy and fear of the Lord are contrasted in the same verse.

Key thing to look out for

Warnings to drunkards and gluttons, and a vivid description of what it is like to be drunk.

Key Bible cross-reference

Verse 2. See Isaiah 56:11.

Key "by way of explanation"

Verse 4, "Do not wear yourself out to get rich." This warning is phrased in this way because amassing wealth can ruin a person emotionally, physically, and spiritually.

Key "Quotable Quote"

"Labor not to be rich: cease from thine own wisdom."

Proverbs 23:4

Proverbs 24

The excellence of wisdom.
Also, see comments for chapter 10.

A detailed analysis of chapter

Sayings of the wise. (1–22)
More wise sayings. (23–34)

Key verse

Verse 10: "If thou faint in the day of adversity, thy strength is small."

Key word / key phrase

Verse 3, "By wisdom a house is built."

Key event / key person / key theme

What to do in the face of different types of wrongdoing.

Key thought

A godly person should not be envious of evil

people, even if they appear to prosper in their evil ways for a time.

Key thing to look out for

A wise person never seeks or exacts revenge.

Key Bible cross-reference

Verse 14. See Lamentations 1:20.

Key "by way of explanation"

Verse 12, "weighs the heart." The Lord knows everyone's inner motives and can read our minds and thoughts.

Key "Quotable Quote"

"Be not thou envious against evil men, neither desire to be with them."

Proverbs 24:1

Proverbs 25

Pleasures and advantages of wisdom.

Also, see comments for chapter 10.

A detailed analysis of chapter

More of Solomon's proverbs. (1–28)

Key verse

Verse 11: "A word fitly spoken is like apples of gold in pictures of silver."

Key word / key phrase

Verse 17, "your neighbor's house."

Key event / key person / key theme

Proverbs concerning a variety of situations

Key thought

Many proverbs in this chapter are little cameos which are meant to be visualized so that they stay in our memories and we learn from them.

Key thing to look out for

A number of proverbs teach that enough is as good as a feast.

Key Bible cross-reference

Verses 6, 7. See Luke 14:8–10.

Key "by way of explanation"

Verse 14. "Like clouds . . . without rain." In Jude's letter, verse 12, this idea is applied to men who should have been pastors of the flock but are just out to satisfy their own whims.

Key "Quotable Quote"

"He that hath no rule over his own spirit is like a city that is broken down, and without walls."

Proverbs 25:28

Proverbs 26

Correct treatment of fools.

Also, see comments for chapter 10.

A detailed analysis of chapter

More of Solomon's proverbs. (1–28)

Key verse

Verse 3: "A whip for the horse, a bridle for the ass, and a rod for the fool's back."

Key word / key phrase

Verse 13, "The sluggard says."

Key event / key person / key theme

Relationships with fools, the lazy, and gossips

Key thought

Gossips and lazy people are warned against in this chapter.

Key thing to look out for

There are more negative qualities to avoid in this chapter than good ones to emulate.

Key Bible cross-reference

Verse 9. See Ecclesiastes 12:11.

Key "by way of explanation"

Verse 8, "like tying a stone in a sling." If a stone is tied in a sling it will not fly through the air. In the same way, although a fool may have a position of honor, he is unable to act honorably.

Key "Quotable Quote"

"As the door turneth upon his hinges, so doth the slothful upon his bed."

Proverbs 26:14

Proverbs 27

Miscellaneous maxims.

Also, see comments for chapter 10.

A detailed analysis of chapter

More of Solomon's proverbs. (1–27)

Key verse

Verse 2: "Let another man praise thee, and not thine own mouth; a stranger, and not thine own lips."

Key word / key phrase

Verse 1, "tomorrow."

Key event / key person / key theme

Proverbs concerning various activities

Key thought

There are helpful and unhelpful ways to help a friend.

Key thing to look out for

Being prudent is commended.

Key Bible cross-reference

Verse 1. See James 4:13–16.

Key "by way of explanation"

Verse 24, "crown is not secure." Even a king should not think that he is secure in his position.

Key "Quotable Quote"

"Open rebuke is better than secret love."

Proverbs 27:5

Proverbs 28

Miscellaneous maxims.

Also, see comments for chapter 10.

A detailed analysis of chapter

More of Solomon's proverbs. (1–28)

Key verse

Verse 11: "The rich man is wise in his own conceit; but the poor that hath understanding searcheth him out."

Key word / key phrase

Verse 6, "a poor man . . . a rich man."

Key event / key person / key theme

Just and unjust rulers

Key thought

Trusting in the Lord is highlighted.

Key thing to look out for

Good and evil men are compared.

Key Bible cross-reference

Verse 9. See Ecclesiastes 8:5.

Key "by way of explanation"

Verse 3, "driving rain." Different types of rain stand for different things. In Psalm 72:6, 7 gentle rain is linked to the righteous, here driving rain probably refers to the power of the Assyrian army.

Key "Quotable Quote"

"Evil men understand not judgment: but they that seek the LORD understand all things."

Proverbs 28:5

Proverbs 29

Miscellaneous maxims.

Also, see comments for chapter 10.

A detailed analysis of chapter

More of Solomon's proverbs. (1–27)

Key verse

Verse 5: "A man that flattereth his neighbor spreadeth a net for his feet."

Key word / key phrase

Verse 4, "justice."

Key event / key person / key theme

Destruction comes to the wicked.

Key thought

Pride and anger are exposed for what they are.

Key thing to look out for

Unpopular things like justice and discipline are recommended.

Key Bible cross-reference

Verse 11. See Ecclesiastes 7:5.

Key "by way of explanation"

Verse 18, "people cast off restraint." This probably refers to the Israelites making and worshiping the golden calf in Exodus 32:25.

Key "Quotable Quote"

"Where there is no vision, the people perish: but he that keepeth the law, happy is he."

Proverbs 29:18

Proverbs 30

Matthew Henry's introduction

We have here,

I. His confession of faith, vv. 1–6.

II. His prayer, vv. 7–9.

III. A caution against wronging servants, v. 10.
IV. Four wicked generations, vv. 11–14.
V. Four things insatiable (vv. 15, 16), to which is added fair warning to undutiful children, v. 17.
VI. Four things unsearchable, vv. 18–20.
VII. Four things intolerable, vv. 21–23.
VIII. Four things little and wise, vv. 24–28.
IX. Four things stately, v. 29 to the end.

A detailed analysis of chapter

Sayings of Agur. (1–6)
More proverbs. (7–33)

Key verse

Verse 1: "The words of Agur the son of Jakeh."

Key word / key phrase

Verse 8, "daily bread."

Key event / key person / key theme

The proverbs of Agur

Key thought

Size is not everything.

Key thing to look out for

The value of God's word is highlighted.

Key Bible cross-reference

Verse 1. See Psalm 132:11.

Key "by way of explanation"

Verse 14, "teeth . . . jaws." Wicked people are compared to wild animals who tear into their prey with their teeth and jaws.

Key "Quotable Quote"

"Every word of God is pure: he is a shield unto them that put their trust in him."

Proverbs 30:5

Proverbs 31

Matthew Henry's introduction

Here is,

I. An exhortation to Lemuel, a young prince, to take heed of the sins he would be tempted to and to do the duties of the place he was called to, vv. 1–9.
II. The description of a virtuous woman, vv. 10–31.

A detailed analysis of chapter

An exhortation to king Lemuel to take heed of sin, and to carry out his duties. (1–9)
The description of a virtuous woman. (10–31)

Key verse

Verse 1: "The words of king Lemuel."

Key word / key phrase

Verse 10, "a wife."

Key event / key person / key theme

The wise woman

Key thought

All the activities of the good wife stem from her noble character.

Key thing to look out for

The secret of her success is given in verse 30.

Key Bible cross-reference

Verse 2. See Song of Songs 1:16.

Key "by way of explanation"

Verse 25, "laugh at the days to come." This exemplary wife is not burdened by care and worry and does not fear the future. This song of praise is an acrostic.

Key "Quotable Quote"

"Who can find a virtuous woman? for her price is far above rubies."

Proverbs 31:10

5. Select bibliography for Proverbs

Delitzsch, Franz. *Biblical Commentary on the Proverbs of Solomon*. 2 Vols. Reprint. Translated by M. G. Easton. Grand Rapids: Eerdmans, 1970.

Hubbard, David, *Proverbs* (Mastering the Old Testament), Word Books, 1989.

Kidner, Derek. *The Proverbs: An Introduction and Commentary*. (Tyndale Old Testament Commentary) Downers Grove: InterVarsity, 1964.

Ross, Allen P. "Proverbs" in *Expositor's Bible Commentary*, 5, Zondervan, 1991.

Ecclesiastes

1. Book by book: Introduction to Ecclesiastes

Introduction

The Hebrew title is Koheleth, which the speaker in it applies to himself (Eccl. 1:12), "I, Koheleth, was king over Israel." It means an Assembler or Convener of a meeting and a Preacher to such a meeting. The feminine form of the Hebrew noun, and its construction once (Eccl. 7:27) with a feminine verb, show that it not only signifies Solomon, the Preacher to assemblies (in which case it is construed with the verb or noun masculine), but also Divine Wisdom (feminine in Hebrew) speaking by the mouth of the inspired king. In six cases out of seven it is construed with the masculine. Solomon was endowed with inspired wisdom (1 Kings 3:5–14; 6:11, 12; 9:1–9; 11:9–11), specially fitting him for the task. The Orientals delight in such meetings for grave discourse. Thus the Arabs formerly had an assembly yearly, at Ocadh, for hearing and reciting poems. Compare "Masters of assemblies" (see on Eccl. 12:11, also Eccl. 12:9). "The Preacher taught the people knowledge," probably *viva voce* ("orally"); 1 Kings 4:34; 10:2, 8, 24; 2 Chr. 9:1, 7, 23, plainly refer to a somewhat public divan met for literary discussion. So "spake," thrice repeated (1 Kings 4:32, 33), refers not to written compositions, but to addresses spoken in assemblies convened for the purpose. The Holy Spirit, no doubt, signifies also by the term that Solomon's doctrine is intended for the "great congregation," the Church of all places and ages (Ps. 22:25; 49:2–4).

Author

Solomon was plainly the author (Eccl. 1:12, 16; 2:15; 12:9). That the Rabbins attribute it to Isaiah or Hezekiah is explicable by supposing that one or the other inserted it in the canon. The difference of its style, as compared with Proverbs and Song of Solomon, is due to the difference of subjects, and the different period of his life in which each was written; the Song, in the fervor of his first love to God; Proverbs, about the same time, or somewhat later; but Ecclesiastes in late old age, as the seal and testimony of repentance of his apostasy in the intervening period: Ps. 89:30, 33 proves his penitence. The substitution of the title Koheleth for Solomon (that is, peace), may imply that, having troubled Israel, meantime he forfeited his name of peace (1 Kings 11:14, 23); but now, having repented, he wishes to be henceforth a Preacher of righteousness. The alleged foreign expressions in the Hebrew may have been easily imported, through the great intercourse there was with other nations during his long reign. Moreover, supposed Chaldaisms may be fragments preserved from the common tongue of which Hebrew, Syriac, Chaldee, and Arabic were offshoots.

Scope

The scope of Ecclesiastes is to show the vanity of all mere human pursuits, when made the chief end, as contrasted with the real blessedness of true wisdom, that is, religion. The immortality of the soul is dwelt on incidentally, as subsidiary to the main scope. Moses' law took this truth for granted but drew its sanctions of rewards and punishments in accordance with the theocracy, which was under a special providence of God as the temporal King of Israel, from the present life, rather than the future. But after Israel chose an earthly king, God withdrew, in part, His extraordinary providence, so that under Solomon, temporal rewards did not invariably follow virtue, and punishments vice (compare Eccl. 2:16; 3:19; 4:1; 5:8; 7:15; 8:14; 9:2, 11). Hence the need arises to show that these anomalies will be rectified hereafter, and this is the grand "conclusion," therefore, of the "whole" book, that, seeing there is a coming judgment, and seeing that present goods do not satisfy the soul, "man's whole duty is to fear God and keep his commandments" (Eccl. 12:13, 14), and meanwhile, to use, in joyful and serene sobriety, and not abuse, the present life (Eccl. 3:12, 13).

It is objected that sensual epicurism seems to be inculcated (Eccl. 3:12, 13, 22, etc.); but it is a contented, thankful enjoyment of God's present gifts that is taught, as opposed to a murmuring, anxious, avaricious spirit, as is proved by Eccl. 5:18, compare with Eccl. 5:11–15, not making them the chief end of life; not the joy of levity and folly; a misunderstanding which he guards against in Eccl. 7:2–6; 11:9; 12:1. Again, Eccl. 7:16; 9:2–10, might seem to teach fatalism and skepticism. But these are words put in the mouth of an objector; or rather, they were the language of Solomon himself during his apostasy, finding an echo in the heart of every sensualist, who wishes to be an unbeliever, and, who, therefore, sees difficulties enough in the world around wherewith to prop up his willful unbelief. The answer is given (Eccl. 7:17, 18; 9:11, 12; 11:1, 6; 12:13). Even if these passages be taken as words of Solomon, they are to be understood as forbidding a self-made "righteousness," which tries to constrain God to grant salvation to imaginary good works and external strictness with which it wearies itself; also, that speculation which tries to fathom all God's inscrutable counsels (Eccl. 8:17), and that carefulness about the future forbidden in Matt. 6:25.

Purpose

The most important aspect in life is that the possession of that which makes us happy, is to be sought as the end, for its own sake; whereas, all other things are but means towards it. Philosophers, who made it the great subject of inquiry, restricted it to the present life, treating the eternal as unreal, and only useful to awe the multitude with. But Solomon shows the vanity of all human things (so-called philosophy included) to satisfy the soul, and that heavenly wisdom alone is the chief good. He had taught so when young (Prov. 1:20; 8:1); so also; in Song of Solomon, he had spiritualized the subject in an allegory; and now, after having long personally tried the manifold ways in which the worldly seek to reach happiness, he gives the fruit of his experience in old age.

It is divided into two parts: Eccl. 1:1–6:10 showing the vanity of earthly things; Eccl. 6:10–12:14, showing the excellence of heavenly wisdom. Deviations from strict logical methods occur in these divisions, but in the main they are observed. The deviations make it the less stiff and artificial, and the more suited to all capacities. It is in poetry; the hemistichal division is mostly observed, but occasionally not so. The choice of epithets, imagery, inverted order of words, ellipses, parallelism, or, in its absence, similarity of diction, mark versification.

A.R. Faussett

Contents of Ecclesiastes

The book of Ecclesiastes highlights how futile and meaningless life is if it is led without reference to God.

In the preface the speaker lays down the proposition that all things are unreal, and that the results of human effort are illusive Eccl. (1:2,3). Human generations, day and night, the wind, the streams, are alike the repetition of an unending round (1:4–7). The same holds in regard to all human study and thinking (1:8–11). The speaker shows familiarity with the phenomena which we think of as those of natural law, of the persistence of force, but he thinks of them in the main as monotonously limiting human experience. Nothing is new. All effort of Nature or of man is the doing again of something which has already been done.

After the preface the speaker introduces himself, and recounts his experiences. At the outset he had a noble ambition for wisdom and discipline, but all he attained to was unreality and perplexity of mind (Ecclesiastes 1:12–18). This is equally the meaning of the text, whether we translate "vanity and vexation of spirit" or "vanity and a striving after wind," ("emptiness, and struggling for breath"), though the first of these two translations is the better grounded.

Finding no adequate satisfaction in the pursuits of the scholar and thinker, taken by themselves, he seeks to combine these with the pursuit of agreeable sensations—alike those which come from luxury and those which come from activity and enterprise and achievement Eccl. (2:1–12). No one could be in better shape than he for making this experiment, but again he only attains to unreality and perplexity of spirit. He says to himself that at least it is in itself profitable to be a wise man rather than a fool, but his comfort is impaired by the fact that both alike are mortal (2:13–17). He finds little reassurance in the idea of laboring for the benefit of posterity; posterity is often not worthy (2:18–21). One may toil unremittingly, but what is the use (2:22, 23)?

He does not find himself helped by bringing God into the problem. `It is no good for a man that he should eat and drink and make his soul see good in his toil' Eccl. (2:24–26, as most naturally translated), even if he thinks of it as the gift of God; for how can one be sure that the gift of God is anything but luck? He sees, however, that it is not just to dismiss thus lightly the idea of God as a factor in the problem. It is true that there is a time for everything, and that everything is "beautiful in its time." It is also true that ideas of infinity are in men's minds, ideas which they can neither get rid of nor fully comprehend (3:1–18). Here are tokens of God, who has established an infinite order. If we understood His ways better, that might unravel our perplexities. And if God is, immortality may be, and the solution of our problems may lie in that direction. For a moment it looks as if the speaker were coming out into the light, but doubt resumes its hold on him. He asks himself, "Who knoweth?" and he settles back into the darkness. He has previously decided that for a man to "eat and drink, and make his soul enjoy good" is not worth while; and now he reaches the conclusion that, unsatisfactory as this is, there is nothing better (3:19–22).

And so the record of experiences continues, hopeful passages alternating with pessimistic passages. After a while the agnosticism and pessimism recede somewhat, and the hopeful passages become more positive. Even though "the poor man's wisdom is despised," the speaker says, "the words of the wise heard in quiet are better than the cry of him that ruleth among fools" Eccl. (9:17). He says "Surely I know that it shall be well with them that fear God" (8:12), no matter how strongly appearances may indicate the contrary.

The gnomic sections are mostly free from agnosticism and pessimism. The book as a whole sums itself up in the conclusion, "Fear God, and keep his commandments" (Ecclesiastes 12:13).

Of course the agnostic and pessimistic utterances in Eccl. are to be regarded as the presentation of one side of an argument. Disconnect them and they are no part of the moral and religious teaching of the book, except in an indirect way. At no point should we be justified in thinking of the author as really doubting in regard to God or moral obligation. He delineates for us a soul in the toils of mental and spiritual conflict. It is a delineation which may serve for warning, and which is in other ways wholesomely instructive; and in the outcome of it, it is full of encouragement.

In some passages the speaker in Ecclesiastes has in mind the solution of the problems of life which we are accustomed to call Epicurean (e.g. 5:18–20; 7:16, 17; 8:15; but not 2:24)—the solution which consists in avoiding extremes, and in getting from life as many agreeable sensations as possible; but it is not correct to say that he advocates this philosophy. He rather presents it as an alternative.

His conclusion is the important part of his reasoning. All things are vanity. Everything passes away. Yet (he says) it is better to read and use good words than bad words. Therefore because the Great Teacher is wise, he ever teaches the people knowledge, and in so doing he ever seeks good words, acceptable words, upright words, words of truth. "The words of the wise are as goads; and as nails well fastened" ("clinched at the back") (12:11). Such are the words of all the great masters. So (he ends) my son, be warned! There are many books in this world. Choose good ones. And his conclusion is: Reverence the Mighty Spirit. Keep to good principles. That is the whole duty of man. For everything at last becomes clear; and "good" stands out clearly from "evil."

Orr, James, M.A., D.D. General Editor, International Standard Bible Encyclopedia

Detailed outline

I. Searching by personal experimenting: 1:1–2:26
  A. By wisdom: 1:12–18
  B. By pleasure: 2:1–11
  C. A comparison of the two: 2:12–23
  D. The first tentative conclusion: 2:24–26
II. Searching by general observation: 3:1–5:20
  A. Of natural order: 3:1–22
  B. Of human society: 4:1–16
  C. His advice in view of these two: 5:1–17
    1. Regarding religion: 5:1–7
    2. Regarding society: 5:8
    3. Regarding riches: 5:9–17
  D. The third tentative conclusion: 5:18–20
III. Searching by practical morality: 6:1–8:17
  A. Economic level: 6:1–12
  B. Reputation: 7:1–22
  C. Education: 7:23–8:1
  D. Social position: 8:2–14
  E. The third tentative conclusion 8:15–17
IV. The search reviewed: 9:1–12:12
  A. It is utterly futile: 2:11
  B. It is filled with repetition: 3:1–8
  C. It is filled with sorrow: 4:1
  D. It is grievous and frustrating: 2:17
  E. It is uncertain: 9:11–12
  F. It is without purpose: 4:2,3; 8:15
  G. It is incurable: 1:15
  H. It is unjust: 7:15; 8:14; 9:11; 10:6–7
  I. It is on the level of animal existence: 3:19
V. The search concluded; A final conclusion: 12:13–14
  A. What we should do: 12:13
    1. Fear God: 12:13
    2. Keep His commandments: 12:13
  B. Why we should do it: 12:13b-14
    1. It is the whole duty of man: 12:13b
    2. We will someday be judged: 12:14

2. Helpful summaries of Ecclesiastes

Bird's eye view

This book reflects on the problem of meaningless, but assures the reader that God makes a difference in this life.

Reading plan

The following reading plan, taking one reading per day, enables you to read through Ecclesiastes in four days.

Ecclesiastes 1–2

Ecclesiastes 3–4

Ecclesiastes 5–8

Ecclesiastes 9–12

Verses to memorize

Ecclesiastes 5:2

Do not be quick with your mouth, do not be hasty in your heart to utter anything before God.

Ecclesiastes 9:10

Whatever your hand finds to do, do it with all your might, for in the grave, where you are going, there is neither working nor planning nor knowledge nor wisdom.

Ecclesiastes 12:14

For God shall bring every work into judgment, with every secret thing, whether it be good, or whether it be evil. KJV

Statistics

Twenty-first Old Testament book

12 chapters

222 verses

5,584 words

Famous sayings found in Ecclesiastes

"There's nothing new under the sun" Ecclesiastes 1:9

"To everything there is a season" Ecclesiastes 3:1

"Eat, drink, and be merry" Ecclesiastes 8:15

Names/titles given

Hebrew title: Qoheleth: *"Preacher."*

Greek title in Septuagint: *Ekklesiastes:* "Preacher."

Latin title in Vulgate: *Ecclesiastes:* "Preacher."

3. Helpful keys to turn to in understanding Ecclesiastes

Key words

Vanity, 37 times

Under the sun

Key verses

Ecclesiastes 1:2,3; 2:24

Themes to study

True wisdom

Fear of the Lord

The nature of humanity and our mortality

Jesus in Ecclesiastes

In Ecclesiastes Jesus is the purpose for living.

Lessons to learn from Ecclesiastes

- Ecclesiastes asks fundamental questions, such as, "Who am ?" and, "What is life all about?"
- Faced with life's perplexities we see our need of God.

4. Chapter by chapter: outline of every chapter of Ecclesiastes

Ecclesiastes 1

Matthew Henry's introduction

In this chapter we have,

I. The inscription, or title of the book, v. 1.

II. The general doctrine of the vanity of the creature laid down (v. 2) and explained, v. 3.

III. The proof of this doctrine, taken,

A. From the shortness of human life and the multitude of births and burials in this life, v. 4.

B. From the inconstant nature, and constant revolutions, of all the creatures, and the perpetual flux and reflux they are in, the sun, wind, and water, vv. 5–7.

C. From the abundant toil man has about them and the little satisfaction he has in them, v. 8.

D. From the return of the same things again, which shows the end of all perfection, and that the stock is exhausted, vv. 9, 10.

E. From the oblivion to which all things are condemned, v. 11.

IV. The first instance of the vanity of man's knowledge, and all the parts of learning, especially natural philosophy and politics. Observe,

A. The trial Solomon made of these, vv. 12, 13, 16, 17.

B. His judgment of them, that all is vanity, v. 14. For,

1. There is labor in getting knowledge, v. 13.
2. There is little good to be done with it, v. 15.
3. There is no satisfaction in it, v. 18. And, if this is vanity and vexation, all other things in this world, being much inferior to it in dignity and worth, must needs be so too. A great scholar cannot be happy unless he be a true saint.

A detailed analysis of chapter

Without God, all human actions are meaningless and empty. (1–3)

Man's toil and lack of satisfaction. (4–8)

There is nothing new. (9–11)

The pointlessness in pursuing knowledge. (12–18)

Key verse

Verse 1: "The words of the Preacher, the son of David, king in Jerusalem."

Key word / key phrase

Verse 2, "meaningless."

Key event / key person / key theme

Everything seems meaningless

Key thought

Life without God is seen to have no meaning.

Key thing to look out for

Human wisdom has its limits.

Key Bible cross-reference

Verse 16. See 1 Kings 4:29–31.

Key "by way of explanation"

Verse 3, "under the sun." This expression, which comes twenty-nine times in Ecclesiastes, refers to this earthly world and our life in it.

Key "Quotable Quote"

"I believe that nothing that happens to me is meaningless, and that it is good for us all that it should be so, even if it runs counter to our own wishes."

Dietrich Bonhoeffer

Ecclesiastes 2

Matthew Henry's introduction

I. He shows that there is no true happiness and satisfaction to be had in mirth and pleasure, and the delights of sense, vv. 1–11.

II. He reconsiders the pretensions of wisdom, and allows it to be excellent and useful, and yet sees it clogged with such diminutions of its worth that it proves insufficient to make a man happy, vv. 12–16.

III. He enquires how far the business and wealth of this world will go towards making men happy, and concludes, from his own experience, that, to those who set their hearts on it, "it is vanity and vexation of spirit," (vv. 17–23), and that, if there be any good in it, it is only to those that sit loose to it, vv. 24–26.

A detailed analysis of chapter

The vanity of mirth, sensual pleasure, riches, and pomp. (1–11)

Human wisdom is insufficient. (12–17)

This world to be used according to the will of God. (18–26)

Key verse

Verse 2: "I said of laughter, It is mad: and of mirth, What doeth it?"

Key word / key phrase

Verse 20, "toilsome labor."

Key event / key person / key theme

Proof from experience that "All is vanity"

Key thought

Pleasures are meaningless.

Key thing to look out for

Daily work has no meaning.

Key Bible cross-reference

Verses 4–8. See 1 Kings 10:23–27.

Key "by way of explanation"

Verse 17, "meaningless." This is a key word in this book, appearing thirty-five times, and refers to any life lived without God.

Key "Quotable Quote"

"The meaning of earthly existence lies, not as we have grown used to thinking, in prospering, but in the development of the soul."

A. I. Solzhenitsyn

Ecclesiastes 3

Matthew Henry's introduction

We should cheerfully content ourselves with, and make use of, what God has given us, by showing,

I. The mutability of all human affairs, vv. 1–10.

II. The immutability of the divine counsels about them and the unsearchableness of those counsels, vv. 11–15.

III. The vanity of worldly honor and power, which are abused for the support of oppression and persecution if men be not governed by the fear of God in the use of them, v. 16. For a check to proud oppressors, and to show them their vanity, he reminds them,

A. That they will be called to account for it in the other world, v. 17.

B. That their condition, in reference to this world (for of that he speaks), is no better than that of the beasts, vv. 18–21.

A detailed analysis of chapter

The changes of human affairs. (1–10)

The divine counsels are unchangeable. (11–15)

The vanity of worldly power. (16–22)

Key verse

Verse 1: "To every thing there is a season, and a time to every purpose under the heaven."

Key word / key phrase

Verse 1, "a season for every activity."

Key event / key person / key theme

God's plans cannot be changed

Key thought

Everything has been given its time.

Key thing to look out for

As we are creatures of eternity nothing in time is found to be satisfying.

Key Bible cross-reference

Verse 20. See Genesis 3:19.

Key "by way of explanation"

Verse 1, "everything," refers to all activities which are engaged in without reference to God.

Key "Quotable Quote"

"More men fail through lack of purpose than through lack of talent."

Billy Sunday

Ecclesiastes 4

Matthew Henry's introduction

I. The temptation which the oppressed feel to discontent and impatience, vv. 1–3.

II. The temptation which those that love their case feel to take their case and neglect business, for fear of being envied, vv. 4–6.

III. The folly of hoarding up abundance of worldly wealth, vv. 7, 8.

IV. A remedy against that folly, in being made sensible of the benefit of society and mutual assistance, vv. 9–12.

V. The mutability even of royal dignity, not only through the folly of the prince himself (vv. 13, 14), but through the fickleness of the people, let the prince be ever so discreet, vv. 15, 16.

A detailed analysis of chapter

Miseries from oppression. (1–3)

Troubles from envy. (4–6)

The folly of covetousness. (7,8)

The advantages of mutual help. (9–12)

The changes of royalty. (13–16)

Key verse

Verse 7: "Then I returned, and I saw vanity under the sun."

Key word / key phrase

Verse 1, "tears of the oppressed."

Key event / key person / key theme

Inequalities of life

Key thought

Look at all the oppression in the world.

Key thing to look out for

Even advancement is meaningless.

Key Bible cross-reference

Verse 2. See Jeremiah 20:14–18.

Key "by way of explanation"

Verse 4, "a chasing after wind," is a key phrase in this book, coming nine times in the first half. It is a description of any futile activity.

Key "Quotable Quote"

"The whole meaning of the soul is to express the spirit."

Oswald Chambers

Ecclesiastes 5

Matthew Henry's introduction

I. Let us therefore take heed of vanity,
   A. In hearing the word, and offering sacrifice, v. 1.
   B. In prayer, vv. 2, 3.
   C. In making vows, vv. 4–6.
   D. In pretending to divine dreams, v. 7. Now,
      1. For a remedy against those vanities, he prescribes the fear of God, v. 7.
      2. To prevent the offence that might arise from the present sufferings of good people, he directs us to look up to God, v. 8.

II. About the wealth of this world and the vanity and vexation that attend it. The fruits of the earth indeed are necessary to the support of life (v. 9), but as for silver, and gold, and riches,
   A. They are unsatisfying, v. 10.
   B. They are unprofitable, v. 11.
   C. They are disquieting, v. 12.
   D. They often prove hurtful and destroying, v. 13.
   E. They are perishing, v. 14.
   F. They must be left behind when we die, vv. 15, 16.
   G. If we have not a heart to make use of them, they occasion a great deal of uneasiness, v. 17. And therefore he recommends to us the comfortable use of that which God has given us, with an eye to him that is the giver, as the best way both to answer the end of our having it and to obviate the mischiefs that commonly attend great estates, vv. 18–20.

A detailed analysis of chapter

What makes devotion vain. (1–3)
Vows, and oppression. (4–8)
The vanity of riches. (9–7)
The right use of riches. (18–20)

Key verse

Verse 5: "Better is it that thou shouldest not vow, than that thou shouldest vow and not pay."

Key word / key phrase

Verse 10, "Whoever loves money."

Key event / key person / key theme

Insufficiencies of wealth

Key thought

Stand in reverence of God.

Key thing to look out for

Even gaining wealth is meaningless.

Key Bible cross-reference

Verse 4. See Psalm 66:13,14.

Key "by way of explanation"

Verse 4, "fools." "Fools" in the Bible do not usually refer to stupid or uneducated people, but rather to those who refuse to learn.

Key "Quotable Quote"

"Meaninglessness doesn't come from being weary of pain but from being weary of pleasure."

Ravi Zacharias

Ecclesiastes 6

Matthew Henry's introduction

In this chapter,

I. The royal preacher goes on further to show the vanity of worldly wealth, when men place their happiness in it and are eager and inordinate in laying it up. Riches, in the hands of a man that is wise and generous, and good for something, but in the hands of a sordid, sneaking, covetous miser, they are good for nothing.

A. He takes an account of the possessions and enjoyments which such a man may have. He has wealth (v. 2), he has children to inherit it (v. 3), and lives long, vv. 3, 6.

B. He describes his folly in not taking the comfort of it; he has no power to eat of it, lets strangers devour it, is never filled with good, and at last has no burial, vv. 2, 3.

C. He condemns it as an evil, a common evil, vanity, and a disease, vv. 1, 2.

D. He prefers the condition of a still-born child before the condition of such a one, v. 3. The still-born child's infelicity is only negative (vv. 4, 5), but that of the covetous worldling is positive; he lives a great while to see himself miserable, v. 6.

E. He shows the vanity of riches as pertaining only to the body, and giving no satisfaction to the mind (vv. 7, 8), and of those boundless desires with which covetous people vex themselves (v. 9), which, if they be gratified ever so fully, leave a man but a man still, v. 10.

II. He concludes this discourse of the vanity of the creature with this plain inference from the whole, That it is folly to think of making up a happiness for ourselves in the things of this world, vv. 11, 12.

A detailed analysis of chapter

The vanity of riches, long life and flourishing families. (1–6)

The little advantage any one has in outward things. (7–12)

Key verse

Verse 7: "All the labor of man is for his mouth, and yet the appetite is not filled."

Key word / key phrase

Verse 3, "he cannot enjoy."

Key event / key person / key theme

The emptiness of life is inescapable.

Key thought

Nothing seems to bring fulfillment.

Key thing to look out for

Even a good man's life seems meaningless.

Key Bible cross-reference

Verse 12. See 1 Chronicles 29:15.

Key "by way of explanation"

Verse 3, "does not receive a proper burial." Anyone who was not honored in their death or lamented over, see Jeremiah 22:18,19, would not have received "a proper burial."

Key "Quotable Quote"

"Atheism turns out to be too simple. If the whole universe has no meaning, we should never have found out that it has no meaning: just as, if there were no light in the universe and therefore no creatures with eyes, we should never know it was dark."

C.S. Lewis

Ecclesiastes 7

Matthew Henry's introduction

Solomon had given many proofs and instances of the vanity of this world and the things of it; now, in this chapter,

I. He recommends to us some good means proper to be used for the redress of these grievances and the arming of ourselves against the mischief we are in danger of from them, that we may make the best of the bad, as:

A. Care of our reputation, v. 1.

B. Seriousness, vv. 2–6.

C. Calmness of spirit, vv. 7–10.

D. Prudence in the management of all our affairs, vv. 11, 12.

E. Submission to the will of God in all events, accommodating ourselves to every condition, vv. 13–15.

F. A conscientious avoiding of all dangerous extremes, vv. 16–18.

G. Mildness and tenderness towards those that have been injurious to us, vv. 19–22. In short, the best way to save ourselves from the vexation which the vanity of the world creates us is to keep our temper and to maintain a strict government of our passions.

II. He laments his own iniquity, as that which was more vexatious than any of these vanities, that mystery of iniquity, the having of many wives, by which he was drawn away from God and his duty, vv. 23–29.

A detailed analysis of chapter

The benefit of a good name; of death above

life; of sorrow over vain mirth. (1–6)
Oppression, anger, and discontentment. (7–10)
Advantages of wisdom. (11–22)
Experience of the evil of sin. (23–29)

Key verse

Verse 7: "Surely oppression maketh a wise man mad; and a gift destroyeth the heart."

Key word / key phrase

Verse 7, "turns a wise man into a fool."

Key event / key person / key theme

Wisdom and folly contrasted

Key thought

Some wise proverbs to ponder.

Key thing to look out for

Further thoughts about the meaninglessness of life.

Key Bible cross-reference

Verse 9. See James 1:19.

Key "by way of explanation"

Verse 15, "righteous man perishing." Just because someone is righteous that does not mean to say that he or she will not meet an early death.

Key "Quotable Quote"

"The truly wise are those whose souls are in Christ."

Ambrose

Ecclesiastes 8

Matthew Henry's introduction

Solomon, in this chapter, comes to recommend wisdom to us as the most powerful antidote against both the temptations and vexations that arise from the vanity of the world. Here is,

I. The benefit and praise of wisdom, v. 1.
II. Some particular instances of wisdom prescribed to us.
  A. We must keep in due subjection to the government God has set over us, vv. 2–5.
  B. We must get ready for sudden evils, and especially for sudden death, vv. 6–8.
  C. We must arm ourselves against the temptation of an oppressive government and not think it strange, vv. 9, 10. The impunity of oppressors makes them more daring (v. 11), but in the issue it will be well with the righteous and ill with the wicked (vv. 12, 13), and therefore the present prosperity of the wicked and afflictions of the righteous ought not to be a stumbling-block to us, v. 14.
  D. We must cheerfully use the gifts of God's providence, v. 15.
  E. We must with an entire satisfaction acquiesce in the will of God, and, not pretending to find the bottom, we must humbly and silently adore the depth of his unsearchable counsels, being assured they are all wise, just, and good, vv. 16, 17.

A detailed analysis of chapter

Commendations of wisdom. (1–5)
To prepare for sudden evils and death. (6–8)
It will be well with the righteous, but not with

the wicked. (9–13)
Mysteries of providence. (14–17)

Key verse
Verse 11: "Because sentence against an evil work is not executed speedily, therefore the heart of the sons of men is fully set in them to do evil."

Key word / key phrase
Verse 1, "explanation."

Key event / key person / key theme
Inability to understand all of God's actions

Key thought
The wicked and the righteous are contrasted.

Key thing to look out for
The key to the meaning in life is found in reverence for God.

Key Bible cross-reference
Verses 8,9. See 2 Corinthians 5:1–10.

Key "by way of explanation"
Verse 17, "no one can comprehend." God has not revealed everything we would like to know, only what he thinks we need to know. See Deuteronomy 29:29.

Key "Quotable Quote"
"We are ensnared by the wisdom of the serpent; we are set free by the foolishness of God."
Augustine of Hippo

Ecclesiastes 9

Matthew Henry's introduction
Solomon, in this chapter, for a further proof of the vanity of this world, gives us four observations which he had made on a survey of the state of the children of men in it:

I. He observed that commonly as to outward things, good and bad men fare much alike, vv. 1–3.
II. That death puts a final period to all our employments and enjoyments in this world (vv. 4–6), whence he infers that it is our wisdom to enjoy the comforts of life and mind the business of life, while it lasts, vv. 7–10.
III. That God's providence often crosses the fairest and most hopeful probabilities of men's endeavor, and great calamities often surprise men ere they are aware, vv. 11, 12.
IV. That wisdom often makes men very useful, and yet gains them little respect, for that people of great merit are slighted, vv. 13–18.

A detailed analysis of chapter
Good and bad men fare alike as to this world. (1–3)
All men must die. (4–10)
Disappointments are experienced by everyone. (11,12)
Benefits of wisdom. (13–18)

Key verse
Verse 9: "For to him that is joined to all the living there is hope: for a living dog is better than a dead lion."

Key word / key phrase

Verse 2, "a common destiny."

Key event / key person / key theme

Judgment, enjoyment of life, and the value of wisdom

Key thought

Wisdom is superior to folly.

Key thing to look out for

War and sin bring devastating consequences.

Key Bible cross-reference

Verse 10. See Colossians 3:23.

Key "by way of explanation"

Verse 12, "hour." In the Bible an "hour" often refers to the moment of a disaster or the time of a crisis.

Key "Quotable Quote"

"Our wisdom, in so far as it ought to be deemed true and solid wisdom, consists almost entirely of two parts: the knowledge of God and of ourselves."

John Calvin

Ecclesiastes 10

Matthew Henry's introduction

I. He recommends wisdom to private people, who are in an inferior station.

A. It is our wisdom to preserve our reputation, in managing our affairs dexterously, vv. 1–3.

B. To be submissive to our superiors if at any time we have offended them, v. 4.

C. To live quiet and peaceable lives, and not to meddle with those that are factious and seditious, and are endeavoring to disturb the government and the public repose, the folly and danger of which disloyal and turbulent practices he shows, vv. 8–11.

D. To govern our tongues well, vv. 12–15.

E. To be diligent in our business and provide well for our families, vv. 18, 19.

F. Not to speak ill of our rulers, no, not in secret, v. 20.

II. He recommends wisdom to rulers; let them not think that, because their subjects must be quiet under them, therefore they may do what they please; no, but,

A. Let them be careful whom they prefer to places of trust and power, vv. 5–7.

B. Let them manage themselves discreetly, be generous and not childish, temperate and not luxurious, vv. 16, 17.

A detailed analysis of chapter

To preserve a character for wisdom. (1–3)

Subjects and rulers. (4–10)

Foolish talk. (11–15)

Duties of rulers and subjects. (16–20)

Key verse

Verse 6: "Folly is set in great dignity, and the rich sit in low place."

Key word / key phrase

Verse 12, "Words from a wise man's mouth."

Key event / key person / key theme
Wisdom's characteristics

Key thought
Wisdom and foolishness are compared.

Key thing to look out for
The lazy will achieve little.

Key Bible cross-reference
Verse 8. See Proverbs 26:27.

Key "by way of explanation"
Verse 12, "words." "Words" are a frequent theme in all biblical wisdom literature.

Key "Quotable Quote"
"Wisdom and goodness are twin-born, one heart
Must hold both sisters, never seen apart."

William Cowper

Ecclesiastes 11

Matthew Henry's introduction
In this chapter we have,

I. A pressing exhortation to works of charity and bounty to the poor, as the best cure of the vanity which our worldly riches are subject to and the only way of making them turn to a substantial good account, vv. 1–6.

II. A serious admonition to prepare for death and judgment, and to begin betimes, even in the days of our youth, to do so, vv. 7–10.

A detailed analysis of chapter
Exhortation to liberality. (1–6)

An admonition to prepare for death, and to young people to be religious. (7–10)

Key verse
Verse 1: "Cast thy bread upon the waters: for thou shalt find it after many days"

Key word / key phrase
Verse 4, "Whoever watches the wind."

Key event / key person / key theme
Wisdom and business; wisdom and youth

Key thought
The steps of a wise person.

Key thing to look out for
Advice to young people.

Key Bible cross-reference
Verse 1. See Proverbs 11:24.

Key "by way of explanation"
Verse 2, "Give portions of seven," is an instruction to be generous.

Key "Quotable Quote"
"Not until we have become humble and teachable, standing in awe of God's holiness and sovereignty . . . acknowledging our own littleness, distrusting our own thoughts, and willing to have our minds turned upside down, can divine wisdom become ours."

J.I. Packer

Ecclesiastes 12

Matthew Henry's introduction

Here is,

I. An exhortation to young people to begin betimes to be religious and not to put it off to old age (v. 1), enforced with arguments taken from the calamities of old age (vv. 1–5) and the great change that death will make on us, vv. 6, 7.

II. A repetition of the great truth he had undertaken to prove in this discourse, the vanity of the world, v. 8.

III. A confirmation and recommendation of what he had written in this and his other books, as worthy to be duly weighed and considered, v. 9.

IV. The whole matter summed up and concluded, with a charge to all to be truly religious, in consideration of the judgment to come, vv. 13, 14.

A detailed analysis of chapter

A description of the infirmities of age. (1–7)

All is vanity: also a warning of the judgment to come. (8–14)

Key verse

Verse 1: "Remember now thy Creator in the days of thy youth."

Key word / key phrase

Verse 1, "The days of your youth."

Key event / key person / key theme

Remember God in your youth

Key thought

Remember God before decrepitude sets in. Contrast with this the Christian's hope as the body grows frail (2 Corinthians 4:16–18).

Key thing to look out for

Verses 2–4. A poetic and powerful description of old age

Key Bible cross-reference

Verse 14. See Romans 2:16.

Key "by way of explanation"

Verse 13, "Fear God." The basis of all wisdom is a heart full of love and reverence for God.

Key "Quotable Quote"

"I believe that God has made me and all creatures; that he has given and still preserves to me my body and soul, eyes, ears, and all my members, my reason and all my senses; also clothing and shoes, meat and drink, house and home, wife and child, land, cattle and all my goods."

Martin Luther

5. Select bibliography for Ecclesiastes

Bridges, C. *An Exposition of the Book of Ecclesiastes*. London: Banner of Truth Trust, 1960.

Delitzsch, Franz. *Commentary on the Song of Songs and Ecclesiastes*. KD. Grand Rapids: Eerdmans, n.d.

Durham, James. *Song of Solomon*, Banner of Truth, 1982.

Eaton, Michael A. *Ecclesiastes: An Introduction and Commentary*. London: Tyndale, 1983. n.d.

Hubbard, David. *Ecclesiastes, Song of Solomon* (Mastering the Old Testament), Word Books, 1989.

Kidner, Derek. *A Time to Mourn and a Time to Dance*. London: InterVarsity, 1976.

Wright, J. Stafford. "The Interpretation of Ecclesiastes." *Classical Evangelical Essays in Old Testament Interpretation*. Edited by W. C. Kaiser, Jr. Grand Rapids: Baker, 1972.

Song of Songs

1. Book by book: Introduction to Song of Songs

Introduction

The Song of Solomon, called in the Vulgate and Septuagint, "The Song of Songs," from the opening words. This title denotes its superior excellence, according to the Hebrew idiom; so holy of holies, equivalent to "most holy" (Ex. 29:37); the heaven of heavens, equivalent to the highest heavens (Deut. 10:14). It is one of the five volumes (*megilloth*) placed immediately after the Pentateuch in manuscripts of the Jewish Scriptures. It is also fourth of the *Hagiographa* or the third division of the Old Testament, the other two being the Law and the Prophets. The Jewish enumeration of the Cetubim is Psalms, Proverbs, Job, Canticles, Ruth, Lamentations, Ecclesiastes, Esther, Daniel, Ezra (including Nehemiah), and Chronicles. Its canonicity is certain; it is found in all Hebrew manuscripts of Scripture; also in the Greek Septuagint; in the catalogues of Melito, bishop of Sardis, a.d. 170 (Eusebius, *Ecclesiastical History*, 4.26), and of others of the ancient Church.

Origen and Jerome tell us that the Jews forbade it to be read by any until he was thirty years old. It certainly needs a degree of spiritual maturity to enter aright into the holy mystery of love which it allegorically sets forth. To such as have attained this maturity, of whatever age they be, the Song of Songs is one of the most edifying of the sacred writings. Rosenmuller justly says, The sudden transitions of the bride from the court to the grove are inexplicable, on the supposition that it describes merely human love. Had it been the latter, it would have been positively objectionable, and never would have been inserted in the holy canon. The allusion to "Pharaoh's chariots" (Song 1:9) has been made a ground for conjecturing that the love of Solomon and Pharaoh's daughter is the subject of the Song. But this passage alludes to a remarkable event in the history of the Old Testament Church, the deliverance from the hosts and chariots of Pharaoh at the Red Sea. (However, see on Song 1:9). The other allusions are quite opposed to the notion; the bride is represented at times as a shepherdess (Song 1:7), "an abomination to the Egyptians" (Gen. 46:34); so also Song 1:6; 3:4; 4:8; 5:7 are at variance with it.

The Christian fathers, Origen and Theodoret, compared the teachings of Solomon to a ladder with three steps; Ecclesiastes, natural (the nature of sensible things, vain); Proverbs, moral; Canticles, mystical (figuring the union of Christ and the Church). The Jews compared Proverbs to the outer court of Solomon's temple, Ecclesiastes to the holy place, and Canticles to the holy of holies. Understood allegorically, the Song is cleared of all difficulty. "Shulamith" (Song 6:13), the bride, is thus an appropriate name, Daughter of Peace being the feminine of Solomon, equivalent to the Prince of Peace. She by turns is a vinedresser, shepherdess, midnight inquirer, and prince's consort and daughter, and He a suppliant drenched with night dews, and a king in His palace, in harmony with the various relations of the Church and Christ. As Ecclesiastes sets forth the vanity of love of the creature, Canticles sets forth the fullness of the love which joins believers and the Savior. The entire economy of salvation, says Harris, aims at restoring to the world the lost spirit of love. God is love, and Christ is the embodiment of the love of God. As the other books of Scripture present severally their own aspects of divine truth, so Canticles furnishes the believer with language of holy love, wherewith his heart can commune with his Lord; and it portrays the intensity of Christ's love to him; the affection of love was created in man to be a transcript of the divine love, and the Song clothes the latter in words; were it not for this, we should be at a loss for language, having the divine warrant, wherewith to express, without presumption, the fervor of the love between Christ and us.

The image of a bride, a bridegroom, and a marriage, to represent this spiritual union, has the sanction of Scripture throughout; nay, the spiritual union was the original fact in the mind of God, of which marriage is the transcript (Is. 54:5; 62:5; Jer. 3:1, etc.; Ezek. 16:1–63; 23:1–49; Matt. 9:15; 22:2; 25:1, etc.; John 3:29; 2 Cor. 11:2; Eph. 5:23–32, where Paul does not go from the marriage relation to the union of Christ and the Church as if the former were the first; but comes down from the latter as the first and best recognized fact on which the relation of marriage is based; Rev. 19:7; 21:2; 22:17). Above all, the Song seems to correspond to, and form a trilogy with, Psalms 45 and 72, which contain the same imagery; just as Psalm 37 answers to Proverbs, and the Psalms 39 and 73 to Job. Love to Christ is the strongest, as it is the purest, of human passions, and therefore needs the strongest language to express it: to the pure in heart the phraseology, drawn from the rich imagery of Oriental poetry, will not only appear not indelicate or exaggerated, but even below the reality. A single emblem is a type; the actual rites, incidents, and people of the Old Testament were appointed types of truths afterwards to be revealed. But the allegory is a continued metaphor, in which the circumstances are palpably often purely imagery, while the thing signified is altogether real.

The clue to the meaning of the Song is not to be looked for in the allegory itself, but in other parts of Scripture. "It lies in the casket of revelation an exquisite gem, engraved with emblematical characters, with nothing literal thereon to break the consistency of their beauty" (Burrowes). This accounts for the name of God not occurring in it. Whereas in the parable the writer narrates, in the allegory he never does so. The Song throughout consists of immediate addresses either of Christ to the soul, or of the soul to Christ. "The experimental knowledge of Christ's loveliness and the believer's love is the best commentary on the whole of this allegorical Song" (Leighton). Like the curiously wrought Oriental lamps, which do not reveal the beauty of their transparent emblems until lighted up within, so the types and allegories of Scripture, "the lantern to our path" (Ps. 119:105), need the inner light of the Holy Spirit of Jesus to reveal their significance. The details of the allegory are not to be too minutely pressed. In the Song, with an Oriental profusion of imagery, numbers of lovely, sensible objects are aggregated not strictly congruous, but portraying jointly by their very diversity the thousand various and seemingly opposite beauties which meet together in Christ.

Divisions

The unity of subject throughout, and the recurrence of the same expressions (Song 2:6, 7; 3:5; 8:3, 4; 2:16; 6:3; 7:10; 3:6; 6:10; 8:5), prove the unity of the poem, in opposition to those who make it consist of a number of separate erotic songs. The sudden transitions (for example, from the midnight knocking at a humble cottage to a glorious description of the King) accord with the alternations in the believer's experience. However various the divisions assigned be, most commentators have observed four breaks (whatever more they have imagined), followed by four abrupt beginnings (Song 2:7; 3:5; 5:1; 8:4). Thus there result five parts, all alike ending in full repose and refreshment. We read (1 Kings 4:32) that Solomon's songs were "a thousand and five." The odd number five added over the complete thousand makes it not unlikely that the "five" refers to the Song of songs, consisting of five parts.

Interpretations

It answers to the idyllic poetry of other nations. The Jews explain it of the union of Jehovah and ancient Israel; the allusions to the temple and the wilderness accord with this; some Christians of Christ and the Church; others of Christ and the individual believer. All these are true; for the Church is one in all ages, the ancient typifying the modern Church, and its history answering to that of each individual soul in it. Jesus "sees all, as if that all were one, loves one, as if that one were all." "The time suited the manner of this revelation; because types and allegories belonged to the old dispensation, which reached its ripeness under Solomon, when the temple was built" (Moody Stuart). "The daughter of Zion at that time was openly married to Jehovah"; for it is thenceforth that the prophets, in reproving Israel's subsequent sin, speak of it as a breach of her marriage covenant. The songs heretofore sung by her were the preparatory hymns of her childhood; "the last and crowning 'Song of Songs' was prepared for the now mature maiden against the day of her marriage to the King of kings" (Origen). Solomon was peculiarly fitted to clothe this holy mystery with the lovely natural imagery with which the Song abounds; for "he spake of trees, from the cedar in Lebanon, even unto the hyssop that springeth out of the wall" (1 Kings 4:33). A higher qualification was his knowledge of the eternal Wisdom or Word of God (Prov. 8:1–36), the heavenly bridegroom. David, his father, had prepared the way, in Psalms 45 and 72; the son perfected the allegory. It seems to have been written in early life, long before his declension; for after it a song of holy gladness would hardly be appropriate. It was the song of his first love, in the kindness of his youthful espousals to Jehovah. Like other inspired books, its sense is not to be restricted to that local and temporary one in which the writer may have understood it; it extends to all ages, and shadows forth everlasting truth (1 Pet. 1:11, 12; 2 Pet. 1:20, 21).

In this book we may see:

In the individual soul the longing for the manifestation of Christ to it, and the various alternations in its experience (Song 1:2, 4; 2:8; 3:1, 4, 6, 7) of His manifestation;

The abundant enjoyment of His sensible consolations, which is soon withdrawn through the bride's carelessness (Song 5:1–3, etc.), and her longings after Him, and reconciliation (Song 5:8–16; 6:3, etc.; Song 7:1, etc.);

Effects of Christ's manifestation on the believer; namely, assurance, labors of love, anxiety for the salvation of the impenitent, eagerness for the Lord's second coming (Song 7:10, 12; 8:8–10, 14).

A.R. Faussett

History of Interpretation of Song of Songs

The Song of Songs is love poetry written by King Solomon. It records the wooing of a shepherdess by Solomon and their wedding. The book has often been taken as a picture of God's love for humankind.

1. The Allegorical Interpretation

All interpreters of all ages agree in saying that Canticles is a poem of love; but who the lovers are is a subject of keen debate, especially in modern times.

First in point of time and in the number of adherents it has had is theory that the Song of Songs is a pure allegory of the love of Yahweh and His people. The Jewish rabbis, from the latter part of the 1st century a.d. down to our own day, taught that the poem celebrates a spiritual love, Yahweh being the bridegroom and Israel the bride. Canticles was supposed to be a vivid record of the loving intercourse between Israel and her Lord from the exodus on to the glad Messianic time. The Song of Songs is read by the Jews at Passover, which celebrates Yahweh's choice of Israel to be His spouse. The Targum interprets Canticles as an allegory of the marital love of Yahweh and Israel. Origen made the allegorical theory popular in the early church. As a Christian he represented the bride as the church or the soul of the believer. In more recent centuries the Christian allegorical interpreters have favored the idea that the soul of the believer was the bride, though the other type of the allegorical view has all along had its advocates.

Bernard of Clairvaux wrote 86 sermons on the first two chapters of Canticles; and a host of writers in the Roman church and among Protestants have composed similar mystical treatises on the Song. Devout souls have expressed their fervent love to God in the sensuous imagery of Canticles. The imagery could not become too fervid or ecstatic for some of these devout men and women in their highest moments of beatific vision. Whatever may be the final verdict of sane criticism as to the original purpose of the author of the Song, it is a fact that must not be overlooked by the student of

Canticles that some of the noblest religious souls, both Hebrew and Christian, have fed the flame of devotion by interpreting the Song of Songs as an allegory.

What justification is there for theory that Canticles is an allegory of the love between Yahweh and His people, or of the love of Christ and the church, or of the love of the soul of the believer and Christ? It must be frankly confessed that there is not a hint in the Song of Songs itself that it is an allegory. If the modern reader of Canticles had never heard of the allegorical interpretation, nothing in the beginning, middle or end of the poem would be likely to suggest to his mind such a conception of the poet's meaning. How, then, did the early Jewish interpreters come to make this the orthodox interpretation of the Song? The question is not easy to answer. In the forefront of our answer we must recall the fact that the great prophets frequently represent the mutual love of Yahweh and Israel under the symbolism of marriage (Hosea 1–3; Jeremiah 3; Ezekiel 16; 23; Isaiah 50:1; 54:5, 6). The Hebrew interpreter might naturally expect to find some echo of this bold imagery in the poetry of the Kethubhim. In the Torah the frequent command to love Yahweh might suggest the marital relation as well as that of the father and son (Deuteronomy 6:5; 7:7–9, 13; 10:12, 15; 30:16, 20), though it must be said that the language of Deut. suggests the high ethical and religious teaching of Jesus in the matter of love to God, in which the sexual does not appear.

Cheyne suggests (*EB*, I, 683 f) that the Song of Songs was too joyous to be used, in its natural sense, by the Jews after the destruction of Jerusalem, and hence, they consecrated it by allegorical interpretation. The suggestion may contain an element of truth.

It is an interesting fact that the Psalter has so few expressions in which love to Yahweh is expressed (Psalms 31:23; 97:10; 145:20; compare 18:1; 42:1; 63:1). In this manual of devotion one would not be surprised to find the expansion of the image of wedlock as expressive of the soul's relation to God; but we look in vain for such a poem, unless Psalms 45 be capable of allegorical interpretation. Even that beautiful song of love and marriage contains no such highly sensuous imagery as is found in Canticles.

Christian scholars found it easy to follow the Jewish allegorical interpreters; for the figure of wedlock is employed in the New Testament by both Paul and John to represent the intimate and vital union of Christ and His church (2 Corinthians 11:2; Ephesians 5:22–33; Revelation 19:7–9; 21:2, 9).

The entire body of true believers is conceived of as the bride of Christ. Naturally the purity of the church is sullied through the impure conduct of the individuals of whom it is composed. Hence, the appeal to individuals and to local churches to live pure lives (2 Corinthians 11:1). To the unmarried believer the Lord Jesus takes the place of the husband or wife as the person whom one is most eager to please (1 Corinthians 7:32). It is not difficult to understand how the fervid, sensuous imagery of Canticles would appeal to the mind of a man like Origen as a proper vehicle for the expression of his passionate love for Christ.

Sober inquiry discovers no sufficient justification of the allegorical interpretation of the Song of Songs. The pages of the mystical commentators are filled with artificial interpretations and conceits. Many of them practice a familiarity with Christ that is without example in the Biblical devotional literature.

2. The Typical Interpretation

The allegorical interpreters, for the most part, saw in the Song of Songs no historic basis. Solomon and the Shulammite are introduced merely as figures through whom God and His people, or Christ and the soul, can express their mutual love. In modern times interpreters have arisen who regard the Song of Songs as primarily the expression of strong and passionate human love between Solomon and a beautiful maiden, but by virtue of the typical relation of the old dispensation, secondarily, the fitting expression of the love of Christ and the church.

The way for this modern typical interpretation was prepared by Lowth (*Sacred Poetry of the Hebrews*, Lectionaries XXX, XXXI) in his modified allegorical view, which is thus described by Canon Driver: "Bishop Lowth, though not abandoning the allegorical view, sought to free it from its extravagances; and while refusing to press details, held that the poem, while describing the actual nuptials of Solomon with the daughter of Pharaoh, contained also an allegoric reference to Christ espousing a church chosen from among the Gentiles" (Lot, 451). Few interpreters have been found to follow Theodore of Mopsuestia and Lowth in their view that the Song of Songs celebrates the marriage of Solomon and an Egyptian princess; and Lowth's notion of a reference to the espousal of a church chosen from among the Gentiles is one of the curiosities of criticism. Of the typical interpreters Delitzsch is perhaps the ablest (*Commentary on Ecclesiastes and the Song of Songs*).

The typical commentators are superior to the allegorical in their recognition of Canticles as the expression of the mutual love of two human beings. The further application of the language to Yahweh and His people (Keil), or to Christ and the church (Delitzsch), or to God and the soul (M. Stuart) becomes largely a matter of individual taste, interpreters differing widely in details.

3. The Literal Interpretation

Jewish interpreters were deterred from the literal interpretation of Canticles by the anathema in the Mishna on all who should treat the poem as a secular song (Sanhedhrin, 101a). Cheyne says of Ibn Ezra, a great medieval Jewish scholar, he "is so thorough in his literal exegesis that it is doubtful whether he is serious when he proceeds to allegorize." Among Christian scholars Theodore of Mopsuestia interpreted Canticles as a song in celebration of the marriage of Solomon and Pharaoh's daughter. This strictly literal interpretation of the Song of Songs was condemned at the second council of Constantinople (553 a.d.). For the next thousand years the allegorical theory reigned supreme among Christian interpreters. In 1544 Sebastian Castellio revived the literal theory of the Song, though the allegorical view remained dominant until the 19th century.

Herder in 1778 published a remarkable little treatise entitled *Lieder der Liebe, die altesten und schonsten aus dem Morgenlande*, in which he advanced theory that Canticles is a collection of independent erotic songs, about 21 in number, which have been so arranged by a collector as to trace "the gradual growth of true love in its various nuances and stages, till it finds its consummation in wedlock" (Cheyne). But the greatest and most influential advocate of the literal interpretation of Canticles was Heinrich Ewald, who published the 1st edition of his commentary in 1826. It was Ewald who first developed and made popular theory that two suitors compete for the hand of the Shulammite, the one a shepherd and poor, the other a wise and wealthy king. In the Song of Songs he ascribes to Solomon 1:9–11, 15; 2:2; 4:1–7; 6:4–13 (quoting the dialogue between the Shulammite and the ladies of the court in 6:10–13); 7:1–9. To the shepherd lover he assigns few verses, and these are repeated by the Shulammite in her accounts of imaginary or real interviews with her lover. In the following passages the lover described is supposed to be the shepherd to whom the Shulammite had plighted her troth: 1:2–7, 9–14; 1:16–2:1; 2:3–7, 8–17; 3:1–5; 4:8–5:1; 5:2–8; 5:10–16; 6:2; 7:10–8:4; 8:5–14. The shepherd lover is thus supposed to be present in the Shulammite's dreams, and in her waking moments she is ever thinking of him and describing to herself and others his many charms. Not until the closing scene (Song of Solomon 8:5–14) does Ewald introduce the shepherd as an actor in the drama. Ewald had an imperial imagination and a certain strength of mind and innate dignity of character which prevented him from dragging into the mud any section of the Biblical literature. While rejecting entirely the allegorical theory of Canticles, he yet attributed to it an ethical quality which made the Song of Songs worthy of a place in the Old Testament. A drama in praise of fidelity between human lovers may well hold a place beside Ecclesiastes and Proverbs in the Canon. Many of the ablest Old Testament critics have followed Ewald in his general theory that Canticles is a drama celebrating the loyalty of a lowly maiden to her shepherd lover. Not even Solomon in all his glory could persuade her to become his queen.

Within the past quarter of a century the unity of Canticles has been again sharply challenged. An account of the customs of the Syrian peasants in connection with weddings was given by the Prussian consul at Damascus, J. G. Wetzstein, in 1873, in an article in Bastian's *Zeitschrift fur Ethnologie*, 270, on *"Die syrische Dreschtafel,"* in which he illustrated the Old Testament from modern Syrian customs. Driver thus describes the customs that are supposed to throw light on Canticles: "In modern Syria, the first seven days after a wedding are called the `king's week'; the young pair play during this time king and queen; the `threshing-board' is turned into a mock-throne, on which they are seated, while songs are sung before them by the villagers and others, celebrating them on their happiness, among which the *watsf*, or poetical `description' of the physical beauty of the bride and bridegroom, holds a prominent place. The first of these watsfs is sung on the evening of the wedding-day itself: brandishing a naked sword in her right hand, and with a handkerchief in her left, the bride dances in her wedding array, lighted by fires, and surrounded by a circle of guests, half men and half women, accompanying her dance with a watsf in praise of her charms" (Lot, 452). Wetzstein suggested the view that Canticles was composed of the wedding-songs sung during "the king's week." This theory has been most fully elaborated by Budde in an article in the *New World*, March, 1894, and in his commentary (1898). According to Budde, the bridegroom is called King Solomon, and the bride Shulammith. The companions of the bridegroom are the 60 valiant men who form his escort (Song of Solomon 3:7). As a bride, the maiden is called the most beautiful of women (Song of Solomon 1:8; 5:9; 6:1). The pictures of wedded bliss are sung by the men and women present, the words being attributed to the bride and the bridegroom. Thus the festivities continue throughout the week. Budde's theory has some decided advantages over Ewald's view that the poem is a drama; but the loss in moral quality is considerable; the book becomes a collection of wedding-songs in praise of the joys of wedlock.

Orr, James, M.A., D.D. General Editor, International Standard Bible Encyclopedia

Detailed outline

I. Beginning of love: 1:1–5:1
- A. Colloquy of Bride and Friends: 1:1–1:8
- B. Colloquy of Bridegroom, Friends, and Bride: 1:9–2:7
- C. Springtime Rhapsody: 2:8–2:17
- D. Love's Dream: 3:1–3:5
- E. The Groom and His Party Approach: 3:6–3:11
- F. The Bride's Beauty Extolled: 4:1–5:1

II. Broadening of love: 5:2–8:14
- A. Another Dream: 5:2–5:8
- B. Colloquy of Friends and Bride: 5:9–6:3
- C. The Bride's Matchless Beauty: 6:4–6:13
- D. Expressions of Praise: 7:1–8:4
- E. Homecoming: 8:5–8:14

2. Helpful summaries of Song of Songs

Bird's eye view

This oriental poem pictures God's love for humanity.

Reading plan

The following reading plan, taking one reading per day, enables you to read through Song of Songs two days.

Song of Songs 1–4

Song of Songs 5–8

Verse to memorize

Song of Songs 8:7

Many waters cannot quench love; rivers cannot wash it away.

Statistics

Twenty-second Old Testament book

8 chapters

117 verses

2,661 words

Names/titles given

Hebrew title: *Shir Hashirim:* "The Song of Songs." See 1:1.

Greek title in Septuagint: *Asma Asmaton:* "The Song of Songs."

Latin title in Vulgate: *Canticum Canticles:* "Song of Songs/The best song." Hence this book is also called "Canticles."

3. Helpful keys to turn to in understanding Song of Songs

Key word

Beloved, 23 times

Key verses

Song of Songs 6:3; 8:7

Themes to study

Marriage relationships

The strength and joy of love

The value of committed love

Jesus in Song of Songs

In Song of Songs Jesus is Lover of our souls.

Types of Jesus in the Song of Songs

The Song of Songs illustrates that Israel is the bride of the Lord, and it anticipates that the Christian church will be Jesus' bride.

Lessons to learn from Song of Songs

- Human love and sexual love in marriage are God's gifts.
- God's love for us is the greatest thing in the world.

4. Chapter by chapter: outline of every chapter of Song of Songs

Song of Songs 1

Matthew Henry's introduction

In this chapter, after the title of the book (v. 1), we have Christ and his church, Christ and a believer, expressing their esteem for each other.

I. The bride, the church, speaks to the bridegroom (vv. 2–4), to the daughters of Jerusalem (vv. 5, 6), and then to the bridegroom, v. 7.

II. Christ, the bridegroom, speaks in answer to the complaints and requests of his spouse, vv. 8–11.

III. The church expresses the great value she has for Christ, and the delights she takes in communion with him, vv. 12–14.

IV. Christ commends the church's beauty, v. 15.

V. The church returns the commendation, vv. 16, 17.

A detailed analysis of chapter

The title. (1)

The Church confesses her wrong ways. (2–6)

The Church asks Christ to lead her to the resting-place of his people. (7, 8)

Christ's commendation of the Church, her esteem for him. (9–17)

Key verse

Verse 1: "The song of songs, which is Solomon's."

Key word / key phrase

Verse 4, "Take me away with you."

Key event / key person / key theme

The first song

Key thought

The characters are introduced.

Key thing to look out for

The lover uses flattering language.

Key Bible cross-reference

Verse 12. See John 12:3.

Key "by way of explanation"

Verse 1, the phrase "Song of Songs," means the greatest of songs ever composed. The Song of Solomon has often been viewed as an allegory of Christ and the Church.

Key "Quotable Quote"

"The historical books I may compare to the outer courts of the temple; the gospels, the epistles and the psalms bring us into the holy place, or the court of the priests; but the Song of Songs is the most holy place – the holy of holies, before which the veil still hangs to many an untaught believer."

C.H. Spurgeon

Song of Songs 2

Matthew Henry's introduction

In this chapter,

I. Christ speaks both about himself and about his church, vv. 1, 2.

II. The church speaks,

A. Remembering the pleasure and satisfaction she has in communion with Christ, vv. 3, 4.

B. Entertaining herself with the present tokens of his favor and taking care that nothing happen to intercept them, v. 5–7.

C. Triumphing in his approaches towards her, vv. 8, 9.

D. Repeating the gracious calls he had given her to go along with him a walking, invited by the pleasures of the returning spring (vv. 10–13), out of her obscurity (v. 14), and the charge he had given to the servants to destroy that which would be hurtful to his vineyard, v. 15.

E. Rejoicing in her interest in him, v. 16.

F. Longing for his arrival, v. 17.

A detailed analysis of chapter

The mutual love of Christ and his Church. (1–7)
The hope and calling of the Church. (8–13)
Christ's care of the Church, her faith and hope. (14–17)

Key verse

Verse 1: "I am the rose of Sharon, and the lily of the valleys."

Key word / key phrase

Verse 8, "Listen! My lover!"

Key event / key person / key theme

The second song

Key thought

The beloved expresses his love.

Key thing to look out for

The beloved longs to be in the company of the lover.

Key Bible cross-reference

Verse 9. See Isaiah 35:6.

Key "by way of explanation"

Verse 9, "gazelle." The beauty of a gazelle was renowned.

Key "Quotable Quote"

"Most men need patience to die, but a saint who understands what death admits him to should rather need patience to live. I think he should often look out and listen on a deathbed for his Lord's coming; and when he receives the news of his approaching change he should say, 'The voice of my beloved! behold, he cometh leaping over the mountains, skipping upon the hills' 2:8."

John Flavel

Song of Songs 3

Matthew Henry's introduction

In this chapter,

I. The church gives an account of a sore trial wherewith she was exercised through the withdrawing of her beloved from her, the pains she was at before she recovered the comfortable sense of his favor again, and the resolution she took, when she did recover it, not to lose it again, as she had done through her own carelessness, vv. 1–5.

II. The daughters of Jerusalem admire the excellencies of the church, v. 6.

III. The church admires Jesus Christ under the person of Solomon, his bed, and the life-guards about it (vv. 7, 8), his chariot, vv. 9, 10. She calls on the daughters of Zion, who were admiring her, to admire him rather, especially as he appeared on his coronation day and the day of his nuptials, v. 11.

A detailed analysis of chapter

The trials of the Church by the withdrawing of Christ. (1–5)

The excellences of the Church, and the care of Christ for her. (6–11)

Key verse

Verse 3: "The watchmen that go about the city found me."

Key word / key phrase

Verse 6, "coming up from the desert."

Key event / key person / key theme

The third song

Key thought

The woman expresses her love.

Key thing to look out for

Night and day the beloved's mind is filled with thoughts of her lover.

Key Bible cross-reference

Verse 8. See Psalm 91:5.

Key "by way of explanation"

Verse 3, "watchmen." These guards were posted at the gates of a city and kept a look-out for any enemies, especially at night.

Key "Quotable Quote"

"The Song comes to us in this world of sin, where lust and passion are on every hand, where fierce temptation assails us, and try to turn us aside from the God-given standard of marriage."

E.J. Young

Song of Songs 4

Matthew Henry's introduction

In this chapter,

I. Jesus Christ, having espoused his church to himself (3:11), highly commends her beauty in the several expressions of it, concluding her fair, all fair, vv. 1–5 and again, v. 7.

II. He retires himself, and invites her with him, from the mountains of terror to those of delight, vv. 6, 8.

III. He professes his love to her and his delight in her affection to him, vv. 9–14.

IV. She ascribes all she had that was valuable in her to him, and depends on the continued influence of his grace to make her more and more acceptable to him, vv. 15, 16.

A detailed analysis of chapter

Christ sets out the graces of the Church. (1–7)
Christ's love to the Church. (8–15)
The Church desires further influences of divine grace. (16)

Key verse

Verse 1: "Behold, thou art fair, my love; behold, thou art fair; thou hast doves' eyes within thy locks: thy hair is as a flock of goats, that appear from mount Gilead."

Key word / key phrase

Verse 9, "you have stolen my heart."

Key event / key person / key theme

The groom praises the bride

Key thought

The groom is totally attentive to his bride.

Key thing to look out for

The bride is happy to accept the love of the groom.

Key Bible cross-reference

Verse 11. See Proverbs 5:3.

Key "by way of explanation"

Verse 14, "saffron." This flower has beautiful purple flowers and was also used as a spice.

Key "Quotable Quote"

"The Song reminds us, in particularly beautiful fashion, how pure and noble true love is."

E.J. Young

Song of Songs 5

Matthew Henry's introduction

In this chapter we have,

I. Christ's gracious acceptance of the invitation which his church had given him, and the kind visit which he made to her, v. 1.

II. The account which the spouse gives of her own folly, in putting a slight on her beloved, and the distress she was in by reason of his withdrawings, vv. 2–8.

III. The enquiry of the daughters of Jerusalem about the amiable perfections of her beloved (v. 9), and her particular answer to that enquiry, vv. 10–16.

A detailed analysis of chapter

Christ's answer. (1)

The disappointments of the Church from her own folly. (2–8)

The excellences of Christ. (9–16)

Key verse

Verse 8: "I charge you, O daughters of Jerusalem, if ye find my beloved, that ye tell him, that I am sick of love."

Key word / key phrase

Verse 2, "my heart was awake."

Key event / key person / key theme

The fourth song

Key thought

The bride praises the groom.

Key thing to look out for

The bride is not abandoned by her friends.

Key Bible cross-reference

Verse 10. See 1 Samuel 16:12.

Key "by way of explanation"

Verse 15, "choice as its cedars." The cedars of Lebanon were known for their size, beauty and strength. The temple was constructed from them.

Key "Quotable Quote"

"The imagery of The Song is not eidetic; by this is meant it does not, like much modern writing, draw the picture in such realistic detail that the reader imagines himself a participant."

R.W. Orr

Song of Songs 6

Matthew Henry's introduction

In this chapter,

I. The daughters of Jerusalem, moved with the description which the church had given of Christ, enquire after him, v. 1.

II. The church directs them where they may meet with him, vv. 2, 3.

III. Christ is now found of those that sought him, and very highly applauds the beauty of his spouse, as one extremely smitten with it (vv. 4–7), preferring her before all others (vv. 8, 9), recommending her to the love and esteem of all her neighbors (v. 10), and, lastly, acknowledging the impressions which her beauty had made on him and the great delight he took in it, vv. 11–13.

A detailed analysis of chapter

Inquiry where Christ must be sought. (1)

Where Christ may be found. (2, 3)

Christ's commendations of the Church. (4–10)

The work of grace in the believer. (11–13)

Key verse

Verse 3: "I am my beloved's, and my beloved is mine: he feedeth among the lilies."

Key word / key phrase

Verse 4, "You are beautiful."

Key event / key person / key theme

The fifth song, part one

Key thought
The groom praises the bride.

Key thing to look out for
True love is selfless.

Key Bible cross-reference
Verse 9. See Genesis 22:2.

Key "by way of explanation"
Verse 4, "as troops with banners." Soldiers were greatly inspired to march under the banner of their king and country.

Key "Quotable Quote"
"The Song is impressionistic: the symbolic imagery cools the imagination."
E.W. Orr

Song of Songs 7

Matthew Henry's introduction
In this chapter,

I. Christ, the royal bridegroom, goes on to describe the beauties of his spouse, the church, in many instances, and to express his love to her and the delight he has in her conversation, vv. 1–9.

II. The spouse, the church, expresses her great delight in him, and the desire that she had of communion and fellowship with him, vv. 10–13.

A detailed analysis of chapter
The graces of the Church. (1–9)
The delight of the Church in Christ. (10–13)

Key verse
Verse 10: "I am my beloved's, and his desire is toward me."

Key word / key phrase
Verse 6, "how beautiful you are."

Key event / key person / key theme
The fifth song, part two

Key thought
The groom praises the bride again.

Key thing to look out for
The bride responds to her groom's praises.

Key Bible cross-reference
Verse 10. See Genesis 3:16.

Key "by way of explanation"
Verse 5, "royal tapestry," refers to cloth used by royalty which was usually purple in color.

Key "Quotable Quote"
"The community of the Bride and Groom is far above mere sexuality."
E.W. Orr

Song of Songs 8

Matthew Henry's introduction
The affections between Christ and his spouse are as strong and lively here, in this closing chapter of the song, as ever, and rather more so.

I. The spouse continues her importunity for a more intimate communion and fellowship with him, vv. 1–3.

II. She charges the daughters of Jerusalem not to interrupt her communion with her beloved (v. 4); and they, thereon, admire her dependence on him, v. 5.
III. She begs of her beloved, whom she raises up by her prayers (v. 5), that he would by his grace confirm that blessed union with him to which she was admitted, vv. 6, 7.
IV. She makes intercession for others also, that care might be taken of them (vv. 8, 9), and pleases herself with the thoughts of her own interest in Christ and his affection to her, v. 10.
V. She owns herself his tenant for a vineyard she held of him at Baal-hamon, vv. 11, 12.
VI. The song concludes with an interchanging of parting requests. Christ charges his spouse that she should often let him hear from her (v. 13), and she begs of him that he would hasten his return to her, v. 14).

A detailed analysis of chapter

Desire for communion with Christ. (1–4)
The vehemence of this desire. (5–7)
The Church pleads for others. (8–12)
And prays for Christ's coming. (13,14)

Key verse

Verse 14: "Make haste, my beloved, and be thou like to a roe or to a young hart upon the mountains of spices."

Key word / key phrase

Verse 6, "my love is as strong as death."

Key event / key person / key theme

The sixth song

Key thought

The power and value of love is expressed.

Key thing to look out for

True love draws a man and a woman together.

Key Bible cross-reference

Verse 10. See Ezekiel 16:7,8.

Key "by way of explanation"

Verse 6, "seal." Seals were closely guarded and were highly prized as they bore the owner's name on them.

Key "Quotable Quote"

"The Song is charged with psychical energy of nuclear fusion released when two hearts, distanced by the Creator when he made them male and female, approach each other for union in a life-long bond."

E.W. Orr

5. Select bibliography for Song of Songs

Bernard of Clairvaux. *Song of Solomon.* Translated by Samuel J. Eales. Minneapolis: Klock and Klock, 1984.

Bromiley, Geoffrey W. *God and Marriage.* Grand Rapids: Eerdmans, 1980.

Carr, G. Lloyd. *The Song of Solomon.* (Tyndale Old Testament Commentaries) Downer's Grove: InterVarsity, 1984.

Delitzsch, Franz. *Commentary on the Song of*

Songs and Ecclesiastes. Translated from the German by M. G. Easton. Edinburgh: Clark's Foreign Theological Library, LIV, 1885.

Garrett, Duane A. *Proverbs, Ecclesiastes, Song of Songs* (New American Commentary, 14), Zondervan, 1993.

Glickman, S. Craig. *A Song for Lovers.* Downer's Grove: InterVarsity, 1976.

Luther, Martin. *Notes on Ecclesiastes, Lectures on the Song of Solomon, Treatise on the Last Words of David*. Works. Volume 15. Saint Louis: Concordia, 1972.

Isaiah

1. Book by book: Introduction to Isaiah

Introduction

Isaiah, son of Amoz (not Amos); contemporary of Jonah, Amos, Hosea, in Israel, but younger than they; and of Micah, in Judah. His call to a higher degree of the prophetic office (Is. 6:1–13) is assigned to the last year of Uzziah, that is, 754 b.c. The first through fifth chapters belong to the closing years of that reign; not, as some think, to Jotham's reign: in the reign of the latter he seems to have exercised his office only orally, and not to have left any record of his prophecies because they were not intended for all ages. The first through fifth and sixth chapters are all that was designed for the Church universal of the prophecies of the first twenty years of his office. New historical epochs, such as occurred in the reigns of Ahaz and Hezekiah, when the affairs of Israel became interwoven with those of the Asiatic empires, are marked by prophetic writings. The prophets had now to interpret the judgments of the Lord, so as to make the people conscious of His punitive justice, as also of His mercy. Is. 7:1–10:4 belong to the reign of Ahaz. The thirty-sixth through thirty-ninth chapters are historical, reaching to the fifteenth year of Hezekiah; probably the tenth through twelfth chapters and all from the thirteenth through twenty-sixth chapters, inclusive, belong to the same reign; the historical section being appended to facilitate the right understanding of these prophecies; thus we have Isaiah's office extending from about 760 to 713 b.c., forty-seven years. Tradition (Talmud) represents him as having been sawn asunder by Manasseh with a wooden saw, for having said that he had seen Jehovah (Ex. 33:20; 2 Kings 21:16; Heb. 11:37). 2 Chr. 32:32 seems to imply that Isaiah survived Hezekiah; but "first and last" is not added, as in 2 Chr. 26:22, which makes it possible that his history of Hezekiah was only carried up to a certain point. The second part, the fortieth through sixty-sixth chapters, containing complaints of gross idolatry, needs not to be restricted to Manasseh's reign, but is applicable to previous reigns. At the accession of Manasseh, Isaiah would be eighty-four; and if he prophesied for eight years afterwards, he must have endured martyrdom at ninety-two; so Hosea prophesied for sixty years. And Eastern tradition reports that he lived to one hundred and twenty. The conclusive argument against the tradition is that, according to the inscription, all Isaiah's prophecies are included in the time from Uzziah to Hezekiah; and the internal evidence accords with this.

Isaiah's family and clothes

His wife is called the prophetess (Is. 8:3), that is, endowed, as Miriam, with a prophetic gift.

His children were considered by him as not belonging merely to himself; in their names, Shearjashub, "the remnant shall return" (Is. 7:3, Margin), and Maher-shalal-hash-baz, "speeding to the spoil, he hasteth to the prey" (Is. 8:1, Margin), the two chief points of his prophecies are intimated to the people, the judgments of the Lord on the people and the world, and yet His mercy to the elect.

His sackcloth (Is. 20:2), too, was a silent preaching by fact; he appears as the embodiment of that repentance which he taught.

History

History, as written by the prophets, is retroverted prophecy. As the past and future alike proceed from the essence of God, an inspired insight into the past implies an insight into the future, and vice versa. Hence most of the Old Testament histories are written by prophets and are classed with their writings; the Chronicles being not so classed, cannot have been written by them, but are taken from historical monographs of theirs; for example, Isaiah's life of Uzziah, 2 Chr. 26:22; also of Hezekiah, 2 Chr. 32:32; of these latter all that was important for all ages has been preserved to us, while the rest, which was local and temporary, has been lost.

Inscription

The inscription (Is. 1:1) applies to the whole book and implies that Isaiah is the author of the second part (the fortieth through sixty-sixth chapters), as well as of the first. Nor do the words, "about Judah and Jerusalem" (Is. 1:1), oppose the idea that the inscription applies to the whole; for whatever he says against other nations, he says on account of their relation to Judah. So the inscription of Amos, "about Israel" (Amos 1:1), though several prophecies follow against foreign nations. Ewald maintains that the fortieth through sixty-sixth chapters, though spurious, were subjoined to the previous portion, in order to preserve the former. But it is untrue that the first portion is unconnected with those chapters. The former ends with the Babylonian exile (Is. 39:6), the latter begins with the coming redemption from it. The portion, the fortieth through forty-sixth chapters, has no heading of its own, a proof that it is closely connected with what precedes, and falls under the general heading in Is. 1:1. Josephus (*The Antiquities of the Jews*, 11. 1, sec. 1, 2) says that Cyrus was induced by the prophecies of Isaiah (Is. 44:28; 45:1, 13) to aid the Jews in returning and rebuilding the temple Ezra 1:1–11 confirms this; Cyrus in his edict there plainly refers to the prophecies in the second portion, which assign the kingdoms to him from Jehovah, and the duty of rebuilding the temple. Probably he took from them his historical name Cyrus (*Coresh*).

Moreover, subsequent prophets imitate this second portion, which Ewald assigns to later times; for example, compare Jer. 50:1–51:64 with Isaiah's predictions against Babylon (Is. 13:1–14:23). "The Holy One of Israel," occurring but three times elsewhere in the Old Testament (2 Kings 19:22; Ps. 78:41; 89:18; Jer. 50:29; 51:5), is a favorite expression in the second, as in the first portion of Isaiah: it expresses God's covenant faithfulness in fulfilling the promises therein: Jeremiah borrows the expression from him. Also Ecclesiasticus 48:22–25 ("comforted"), quotes Is. 40:1 as Isaiah's. Luke 4:17 quotes Is. 61:1, 2 as Isaiah's, and as read as such by Jesus Christ in the synagogue.

Definite prophecies

The certainty of the prophecies is striking: As in the second portion of Isaiah, so in Mic. 4:8–10, the Babylonian exile, and the deliverance from it, are foretold a hundred fifty years before any hostilities had arisen between Babylon and Judah. On the other hand, all the prophets who foretell the Assyrian invasion coincide in stating, that Judah should be delivered from it, not by Egyptian aid, but directly by the Lord. Again Jeremiah, in the height of the Chaldean prosperity, foretold its conquest by the Medes, who should enter Babylon through the dry bed of the Euphrates on a night of general revelry. No human calculation could have discovered these facts. Eichorn terms these prophecies "veiled historical descriptions," recognizing in spite of himself that they are more than general poetical fancies. The fifty-third chapter of Isaiah was certainly written ages before the Messiah, yet it minutely portrays His sufferings: these cannot be Jewish inventions, for the Jews looked for a reigning, not a suffering, Messiah.

Rationalists are so far right that the prophecies are on a general basis whereby they are distinguished from soothsaying. They rest on the essential idea of God. The prophets, penetrated by this inner knowledge of His character, became conscious of the eternal laws by which the world is governed: that sin is man's ruin, and must be followed by judgment, but that God's covenant mercy to His elect is unchangeable. Without prophetism, the elect remnant would have decreased, and even God's judgments would have missed their end, by not being recognized as such: they would have been unmeaning, isolated facts. Babylon was in Isaiah's days under Assyria; it had tried a revolt unsuccessfully: but the elements of its subsequent success and greatness were then existing. The Holy Spirit enlightened his natural powers to discern this its rise; and his spiritual faculties, to foresee its fall, the sure consequence, in God's eternal law, of the pride which pagan success generates—and also Judah's restoration, as the covenant-people, with whom God, according to His essential character, would not be wroth for ever. True conversion is the prophet's grand remedy against all evils: in this alone consists his politics. Rebuke, threatening, and promise, regularly succeed one another. The idea at the basis of all is in Is. 26:7–9; Lev. 10:3; Amos 3:2.

Tenses used in prophecy

The use of the present and preterite in prophecy is no proof that the author is later than Isaiah. For seers view the future as present, and indicate what is ideally past, not really past; seeing things in the light of God, who "calls the things that are not as though they were." Moreover, as in looking from a height on a landscape, hills seem close together which are really wide apart, so, in events foretold, the order, succession, and grouping are presented, but the intervals of time are overlooked. The time, however, is sometimes marked (Jer. 25:12; Dan. 9:26). Thus the deliverance from Babylon, and that effected by Messiah, are in rapid transition grouped together by the law of prophetic suggestion; yet no prophet so confounds the two as to make Messiah the leader of Israel from Babylon. To the prophet there was probably no double sense; but to his spiritual eye the two events, though distinct, lay so near, and were so analogous, that he could not separate them in description without unfaithfulness to the picture presented before him. The more remote and antitypical event, however, namely, Messiah's coming, is that to which he always hastens, and which he describes with far more minuteness than he does the nearer type; for example, Cyrus (compare Is. 45:1 with Is. 53:1–12). In some cases he takes his stand in the midst of events between, for example, the humiliation of Jesus Christ, which he views as past, and His glorification, as yet to come, using the future tense as to the latter (compare Is. 53:4–9 with 53:10–12). Marks of the time of events are given sparingly in the prophets: yet, as to Messiah, definitely enough to create the general expectation of Him at the time that He was in fact born.

Symbols, visions, and signs

Isaiah's symbols are few and simple, and his poetical images correct; in the prophets, during and after the exile, the reverse holds good; Haggai and Malachi are not exceptions; for, though void of bold images, their style, unlike Isaiah's, rises little above prose: a clear proof that our Isaiah was long before the exile.

As for visions, Isaiah has, strictly speaking, but one, which comes in the sixth chapter; even it is more simple than those in later prophets. But he often gives signs, that is, a present fact as pledge of the more distant future; God condescending to the feebleness of man (Is. 7:14; 37:30; 38:7).

Messiah

The expectation of the Messiah is so strong in Isaiah, that Jerome calls his book not a prophecy, but the gospel: "He is not so much a prophet as an evangelist." The Messiah was already shadowed forth in Gen. 49:10, as the Shiloh, or tranquillizer; also in Psalms 2, 45, 72, 110. Isaiah brings it out more definitely; and, whereas they dwelt on His kingly office, Isaiah develops most His priestly and prophetic office; the hundred tenth Psalm also had set forth His priesthood, but His kingly rather than, as Isaiah, His suffering, priesthood. The latter is especially dwelt on in the second part, addressed to the faithful elect; whereas the first part, addressed to the whole people, dwells on Messiah's glory, the antidote to the fears which then filled the people, and the assurance that the kingdom of God, then represented by Judah, would not be overwhelmed by the surrounding nations.

Judah

Judah, the less apostate people, rather than Israel, was the subject of his prophecies: his residence was mostly at Jerusalem. On his praises, see Ecclesiasticus 48:22–25. Christ and the apostles quote no prophet so frequently.

A.R. Faussett

Contents of Isaiah

The theme of chapters 1–35 is God's judgment.

The theme of chapters 36–39 is the history of King Hezekiah.

The theme of chapters 40–66 is salvation.

There are six general divisions of the book:

(1) Is. 1–12, prophecies about Judah and Jerusalem, closing with promises of restoration and a psalm of thanksgiving;

(2) Is. 13–23, oracles of judgment and salvation, for the most part about those foreign nations whose fortunes affected Judah and Jerusalem;

(3) Is. 24–27, Yahweh's world–judgment in the redemption of Israel;

(4) Is. 28–35, a cycle of prophetic warnings against alliance with Egypt, closing with a prophecy about Edom and a promise of Israel's ransom;

(5) Is. 36–39, history, prophecy and song intermingled; serving both as an appendix to Is. 1–35, and as an introduction to Is. 40–66;

(6) Is. 40–66, prophecies of comfort and salvation, and also of the future glory awaiting Israel.

By examining in detail these several divisions we can trace the prophet's thought.

Chapters 1–12

Thus, Is. 1–12 unfold Judah's social sins (Is. 1–6), and her political entanglements (Is. 7–12); Is. 1 is an introduction, in which the prophet strikes the chief notes of his entire book: namely, thoughtlessness (1:2–9), formalism in worship (1:10–17), pardon (1:18–23) and judgment (1:24–31).

Is. 2–4 contain three distinct pictures of Zion:

her exaltation (2:2–4),

her present idolatry (2:5–4:1), and

her eventual purification (4:2–6).

Is. 5 contains an arraignment of Judah and Jerusalem, composed of three parts:

a parable of Yahweh's vineyard (5:1–7);

a series of six woes pronounced against insatiable greed (5:8–10), dissipation (5:11–17), daring defiance against Yahweh (5:18,19), confusion of moral distinctions (5:20), political self-conceit (5:21), and misdirected heroism (5:22,23); and an announcement of imminent judgment. The Assyrian is on the way and there will be no escape (5:24–30). Is. 6 recounts the prophet's inaugural vision and commission. It is really an apologetic, standing as it does after the prophet's denunciations of his contemporaries. When they tacitly object to his message of threatening and disaster, he is able to reply that, having pronounced "woe" on himself in the year that King Uzziah died, he had the authority to pronounce woe on them (6:5). Plainly Isaiah tells them that Judah's sins are well-nigh hopeless. They are becoming spiritually insensible. They have eyes but they cannot see. Only judgment can, avail: "the righteous judgment of a forgotten God" awaits them. A "holy seed," however, still existed in Israel's stock (6:13).

Coming to Isaiah 7–12, Isaiah appears in the role of a practical statesman. He warns Ahaz against political entanglements with Assyria. The section 7:1–9:7 is a prophecy of Immanuel, history and prediction being intermingled.

They describe the Syro-Ephraimitic uprising in 736 b.c., when Pekah of North Israel and Rezin of Damascus, in attempting to defend themselves against the Assyrians, demanded that Ahaz of Jerusalem should become their ally. But Ahaz preferred the friendship of Assyria, and refused to enter into alliance with them. And in order to defend himself, he applied to Assyria for assistance, sending ambassadors with many precious treasures, both royal and sacred, to bribe Tiglath-pileser. It was at this juncture that Isaiah, at Yahweh's bidding, expostulates with Ahaz about the fatal step he is about to take, and as a practical statesman warns Ahaz, "the king of No-Faith," that the only path of safety lies in loyalty to Yahweh and keeping clear of foreign alliances; that "God is with us" for salvation; and that no "conspiracy" can possibly be successful unless God too is against us. When, however, the prophet's message of promise and salvation finds no welcome, he commits it to his disciples, bound up and sealed for future use; assuring his hearers that unto them a child is born and unto them a son is given, in whose day the empire of David will be established on a basis of justice and righteousness. The Messianic scion is the ground of the prophet's hope; which hope, though unprecedented, he thus early in his ministry commits, written and sealed, to his inner circle of "disciples."

The section Isaiah 9:8–10:4 contains an announcement to North Israel of accumulated wrath and impending ruin, with a refrain (9:12,17,21; 10:4). Here, in an artistic poem composed of four strophes, the prophet describes the great calamities which Yahweh has sent down on North Israel but which have gone unheeded: foreign invasion (9:8–12), defeat in battle (9:13–17), anarchy (9:18–21), and impending captivity (10:1–4). Yet Yahweh's judgments have gone unheeded: "For all this his anger is not turned away, but his hand is stretched out still." Divine discipline has failed; only judgment remains.

In Isaiah 10:5–34, Assyria is declared to be an instrument of Yahweh, the rod of Yahweh's anger. Isaiah 11–12 predict Israel's return from exile, including a vision of the Messiah's reign of ideal peace.

For Isaiah's vision of the nation's future reached far beyond mere exile. To him the downfall of Assyria was the signal for the commencement of a new era in Israel's history. Assyria has no future, her downfall is fatal; Judah has a future, her calamities are only disciplinary. An Ideal Prince will be raised up in whose advent all Nature will rejoice, even dumb animals (11:1–10). A second great exodus will take place, for the Lord will set His hand again "the second time" to recover the remnant of His people "from the four corners of the earth" (11:11,12). In that day, "Ephraim shall not envy Judah, and Judah shall not vex Ephraim" (11:13). On the contrary, the reunited nation, redeemed and occupying their rightful territory (11:14–16), shall sing a hymn of thanksgiving, proclaiming the salvation of Yahweh to all the earth (Is. 12).

Chapters 13–23

Isaiah 13–23 contain oracles of judgment and salvation, for the most part about those foreign nations whose fortunes affected Judah and Jerusalem. They are grouped together by the editor, as similar foreign oracles are in Jer. 46–51 ;wide. First among the foreign prophecies stands the oracle about Babylon (Isaiah 13:1–14:23), in which he predicts the utter destruction of the city (Isaiah 13:2–22), and sings a dirge or taunt-song over her fallen king (Isaiah 14:4–23). The king alluded to is almost beyond doubt an Assyrian (not a Babylonian) monarch of the 8th century; the brief prophecy immediately following in Isaiah 14:24–27 about Assyria tacitly confirms this interpretation. Another brief oracle about Babylon (21:1–10) describes the city's fall as imminent. Both oracles stand or fall together as genuine prophecies of Isaiah. Both seem to have been written in Jerusalem (13:2; 21:9,10). It cannot be said that either is absolutely unrelated in thought and language to Isaiah's age (14:13; 21:2); each foretells the doom to fall on Babylon (13:19; 21:9) at the hands of the Medes (13:17; 21:2); and each describes the Israelites as already in exile—but not necessarily all Israel.

The section Isaiah 14:24–27 tells of the certain destruction of the Assyrian.

The passage Isaiah 14:28–32 is an oracle about Philistia.

Isaiah 15–16 are ancient oracles against Moab, whose dirge like meter resembles that of Isaiah 13–14. It is composed of two separate prophecies belonging to two different periods in Isaiah's ministry (16:13,14). The three points of particular interest in the oracle are:

(1) the prophet's tender sympathy for Moab in her affliction (15:5; 16:11). Isaiah mingles his own tears with those of the Moabites. As Delitzsch says, "There is no prophecy in the Book of Isaiah in which the heart of the prophet is so painfully moved by what his spirit beholds and his mouth must prophecy."

(2) Moab's pathetic appeal for shelter from her foes; particularly the ground on which she urges it, namely, the Messianic hope that the Davidic dynasty shall always stand and be able to repulse its foes (16:5). The prophecy is an echo of 9:5–7.

(3) The promise that a remnant of Moab, though small, shall be saved (16:14). Wearied of prayer to Chemosh in his high places, the prophet predicts that Moab will seek the living God (16:12).

The passage Isaiah 17:1–11 is an oracle about Damascus and North Israel, in which Isaiah predicts the fate of the two allies—Syria and Ephraim—in the Syro-Ephraimitic war of 734 B.C., with a promise that only a scanty remnant will survive (17:6). In 17:12–14, the prophet boldly announces the complete annihilation of Judah's unnamed foes—the Assyrians.

Isaiah 18 describes Ethiopia as in great excitement, sending ambassadors hither and thither—possibly all the way to Jerusalem—ostensibly seeking aid in making preparations for war. Assyria had already taken Damascus (732 B.C.) and Samaria (722 B.C.), and consequently Egypt and Ethiopia were in fear of invasion. Isaiah bids the ambassadors to return home and quietly watch Yahweh thwart Assyria's self-confident attempt to subjugate Judah; and he adds that when the Ethiopians have seen God's hand in the coming deliverance of Judah and Jerusalem (701 B.C.), they will bring a present to Yahweh to His abode in Mount Zion.

Isaiah 19, which is an oracle about Egypt, contains both a threat (19:1–17) and a promise (19:18–25), and is one of Isaiah's most remarkable foreign messages. Egypt is smitten and thereby led to abandon her idols for the worship of Yahweh (19:19–22). Still more remarkable, it is prophesied that in that day Egypt and Assyria will join with Judah in a triple alliance of common worship to Yahweh and of blessing to others (19:23–25). Isaiah's missionary outlook here is wonderful!

Isaiah 20 describes Sargon's march against Egypt and Ethiopia, containing a brief symbolic prediction of Assyria's victory over Egypt and Ethiopia. By donning a captive's garb for three years, Isaiah attempts to teach the citizens of Jerusalem that the siege of Ashdod was but a means to an end in Sargon's plan of campaign, and that it was sheer folly for the Egyptian party in Jerusalem, who were ever urging reliance on Egypt, to look in that direction for help. Isaiah 21:11, 12 is a brief oracle about Seir or Edom, "the only gentle utterance in the Old Testament on Israel's hereditary foe." Edom is in great anxiety. The prophet's answer is disappointing, though its tone is sympathetic. Isaiah 21:13 is a brief oracle about Arabia. It contains a sympathetic appeal to the Temanites to give bread and water to the caravans of Dedan, who have been driven by war from their usual route of travel.

Isaiah 22 is about the foreign temper within theocracy. It is composed of two parts:

(1) an oracle "of the valley of vision," i.e. Jerusalem (22:1–14); and

(2) a philippic against Shebna, the comptroller of the palace. Isaiah pauses, as it were, in his series of warnings to foreign nations to rebuke the foreign temper of the frivolous inhabitants of Jerusalem, and in particular Shebna, a high official in the government.

The reckless and God-ignoring citizens of the capital are pictured as indulging themselves in hilarious eating and drinking, when the enemy is at that very moment standing before the gates of the city. Shebna, on the other hand, seems to have been an ostentatious foreigner, perhaps a Syrian by birth, quite possibly one of the Egyptian party, whose policy was antagonistic to that of Isaiah and the king. Isaiah's prediction of Shebna's fall was evidently fulfilled (36:3; 37:2).

Isaiah 23 is about Tyre. In this oracle Isaiah predicts that Tyre shall be laid waste (23:1), her commercial glory humbled (23:9), her colonies become independent of her (23:10), and she herself forgotten for "seventy years" (23:15); but "after the end of seventy years," her trade will revive, her business prosperity will return, and she will dedicate her gains in merchandise as holy to Yahweh (23:18).

Chapters 24–27

The third great section of the Book of Isaiah embraces Isaiah 24–27, which tell of Yahweh's world-judgment, issuing in the redemption of Israel. These prophecies stand closely related to Isaiah 13–23. They express the same tender emotion as that already observed in 15:5; 16:11, and sum up as in one grand finale the prophet's oracles to Israel's neighbors. For religious importance they stand second to none in the Book of Isaiah, teaching the necessity of Divine discipline and the glorious redemption awaiting the faithful in Israel. They are a spiritual commentary on the great Assyrian crisis of the 8th century; they are messages of salvation intended, not for declamation, but for meditation, and were probably addressed more particularly to the prophet's inner circle of "disciples" (8:16). These chapters partake of the nature of apocalypse. Strictly speaking, however, they are prophecy, not apocalypse. No one ascends into heaven or talks with an angel, as in Daniel 7 and Rev. 4. They are apocalypse only in the sense that certain things are predicted as sure to come to pass. Isaiah was fond of this kind of prophecy. He frequently lifts his reader out of the sphere of mere history to paint pictures of the far-off, distant future (2:2–4; 4:2–6; 11:6–16; 30:27–33).

In Isaiah 24 the prophet announces a general judgment of the earth (i.e. the land of Judah), and of "the city" (collective, for Judah's towns), after which will dawn a better day (24:1–15). The prophet fancies he hears songs of deliverance, but alas! they are premature; more judgment must follow. In Isaiah 25 the prophet transports himself to the period after the Assyrian catastrophe and, identifying himself with the redeemed, puts into their mouths songs of praise and thanksgiving for their deliverance. Isaiah 25:6–8 describe Yahweh's bountiful banquet on Mount Zion to all nations, who, in keeping with 2:2–4, come up to Jerusalem, to celebrate "a feast of fat things," rich and marrowy. While the people are present at the banquet, Yahweh graciously removes their spiritual blindness so that they behold Him as the true dispenser of life and grace. He also abolishes violent death, that is to say, war (compare 2:4) and its sad accompaniment, "tears," so that "the earth" (i.e. the land of Judah) is no longer the battlefield of the nations, but the blessed abode of the redeemed, living in peace and happiness. The prophet's aim is not political but religious.

In Isaiah 26:1–19 Judah sings a song over Jerusalem, the impregnable city of God. The prophet, taking again his stand with the redeemed remnant of the nation, vividly portrays their thankful trust in Yahweh, who has been unto them a veritable "Rock of Ages" (26:4 margin). With hope he joyfully exclaims, Let Yahweh's dead ones live! Let Israel's dead bodies arise! Yahweh will bring life from the dead! (26:19). This is the first clear statement of the resurrection in the Old Testament. But it is national and restricted to Israel (compare 26:14), and is merely Isaiah's method of expressing a hope of the return of Israel's faithful ones from captivity (compare Hosea 6:2; Ezekiel 37:1–14; Daniel 12:2).

In Isaiah 26:20–27:13 the prophet shows that Israel's chastisements are salutary. He begins by exhorting his own people, his disciples, to continue a little longer in the solitude of prayer, till God's wrath has shattered the world-powers (26:20–27:1). He next predicts that the true vineyard of Yahweh will henceforth be safely guarded against the briars and thorns of foreign invasion (27:2–6). And then, after showing that Yahweh's chastisements of Israel were light compared with His judgments on other nations (27:7–11), he promises that if Israel will only repent, Yahweh will spare no pains to gather "one by one" the remnant of His people from Assyria and Egypt (compare 11:11); and together they shall once more worship Yahweh in the holy mountain at Jerusalem (27:12,13).

The prophet's fundamental standpoint in Isaiah 24–27 is the same as that of 2:2–4 and Isaiah 13–23. Yet the prophet not infrequently throws himself forward into the remote future, oscillating backward and forward between his own times and those of Israel's restoration. It is especially noteworthy how he sustains himself in a long and continued transportation of himself to the period of Israel's redemption. He even studies to identify himself with the new Israel which will emerge out of the present chaos of political events. His visions of Israel's redemption carry him in ecstasy far away into the remote future, to a time when the nation's sufferings are all over; so that when he writes down what he saw in vision he describes it as a discipline that is past. For example, in 25:1–8 the prophet, transported to the end of time, celebrates in song what he saw, and describes how the fall of the world-empire is followed by the conversion of the heathen. In 26:8,9 he looks back into the past from the standpoint of the redeemed in the last days, and tells how Israel longingly waited for the manifestation of God's righteousness which has now taken place, while in 27:7–9 he places himself in the midst of the nation's sufferings, in full view of their glorious future, and portrays how Yahweh's dealings with Israel have not been the punishment of wrath, but the discipline of love. This kind of apocalypse, or prophecy, indeed, was to be expected from the very beginning of the group of prophecies, which are introduced with the word "Behold!" Such a manner of introduction is peculiar to Isaiah, and of itself leads us to expect a message which is unique.

The practical religious value of these prophecies to Isaiah's own age would be very great. In a period of war and repeated foreign invasion, when but few men were left in the land (Isaiah 24:6,13; 26:18), and Judah's cities were laid waste and desolate (Isaiah 24:10,12; 25:2; 26:5; 27:10), and music and gladness were wanting (Isaiah 24:8), when the nation still clung to their idols (Isaiah 27:9) and the Assyrians' work of destruction was still incomplete, other calamities being sure to follow (Isaiah 24:16), it would certainly be comforting to know that forgiveness was still possible (Isaiah 27:9), that Yahweh was still the keeper of His vineyard (Isaiah 27:3,4), that His judgments were to last but for a little moment (Isaiah 26:20), and that though His people should be scattered, He would soon carefully gather them "one by one" (Isaiah 27:12,13), and that in company with other nations they would feast together on Mt. Zion as Yahweh's guests (Isaiah 25:6, 7, 10), and that Jerusalem should henceforth become the center of life and religion to all nations (Isaiah 24:23; 25:6; 27:13). Such faith in Yahweh, such exhortations and such songs and confessions of the redeemed, seen in vision, would be a source of rich spiritual comfort to the few suffering saints in Judah and Jerusalem, and a guiding star to the faithful disciples of the prophet's most inner circle.

Chapters 28–35

Isaiah 28–35 contain a cycle of prophetic warnings against alliance with Egypt, closing with a prophecy about Edom and a promise of Israel's ransom. As in 5:8–23, the prophet indulges in a series of six woes:

(1) Woe to drunken, scoffing politicians (Isaiah 28). This is one of the great chapters of Isaiah's book. In the opening section (28:1–6) the prophet points in warning to the proud drunkards of Ephraim whose crown (Samaria) is rapidly fading. He next turns to the scoffing politicians of Jerusalem, rebuking especially the bibulous priests who stumble in judgment, and the staggering prophets who err in vision (28:7–22); closing with a most instructive parable from agriculture, teaching that God's judgments are not arbitrary; that as the husbandman does not plow and harrow his fields the whole year round, so God will not punish His people forever; and as the husbandman does not thresh all kinds of grain with equal severity, no more will God discipline His people beyond their deserts (28:23–29).

(2) Woe to formalists in religion (Isaiah 29:1–14). Isaiah's second woe is pronounced on Ariel, the altar-hearth of God, i.e. Jerusalem, the sacrificial center of Israel's worship. David had first inaugurated the true worship of Yahweh in Zion. But now Zion's worship has become wholly conventional, formal, and therefore insincere; it is learned by rote (29:13; compare 1:10–15; Micah 6:6–8). Therefore, says Isaiah, Yahweh is forced to do an extraordinary work among them, in order to bring them back to a true knowledge of Himself (Isaiah 29:14).

(3) Woe to those who hide their plans from God (Isaiah 29:15–24). What their plans are, which they are devising in secret, the prophet does not yet disclose; but he doubtless alludes to their intrigues with the Egyptians and their purpose to break faith with the Assyrians, to whom they were bound by treaty to pay annual tribute. Isaiah bravely remonstrates with them for supposing that any policy will succeed which excludes the counsel and wisdom of the Holy One. They are but clay; He is the potter. At this point, though somewhat abruptly, Isaiah turns his face toward the Messianic future. In a very little while, he says, Lebanon, which is now overrun by Assyria's army, shall become a fruitful field, and the blind and deaf and spiritually weak shall rejoice in the Holy One of Israel.

(4) Woe to the pro-Egyptian party (Isaiah 30). Isaiah's fourth woe is directed against the rebellious politicians who stubbornly, and now openly, advocate making a league with Egypt. They have at length succeeded apparently in winning over the king to their side, and an embassy is already on its way to Egypt, bearing across the desert of the exodus rich treasures with which to purchase the friendship of their former oppressors. Isaiah now condemns what he can no longer prevent. Egypt is a Rahab "sit-

still," i.e. a mythological sea-monster, menacing in mien but laggard in action. When the crisis comes, she will sit still, causing Israel only shame and confusion.

(5) Woe to those who trust in horses and chariots (Is. 31–32). Isaiah's fifth woe is a still more vehement denunciation of those who trust in Egypt's horses and chariots, and disregard the Holy One of Israel. Those who do so forget that the Egyptians are but men and their horses flesh, and that mere flesh cannot avail in a conflict with spirit. Eventually Yahweh means to deliver Jerusalem, if the children of Israel will but turn from their idolatries to Him; and in that day, Assyria will be vanquished. A new era will dawn on Judah. Society will be regenerated. The renovation will begin at the top. Conscience also will be sharpened, and moral distinctions will no longer be confused (32:1–8). As Delitzsch puts it, "The aristocracy of birth and wealth will be replaced by an aristocracy of character." The careless and indifferent women, too, in that day will no longer menace the social welfare of the state (32:9–14); with the outpouring of Yahweh's spirit an ideal commonwealth will emerge, in which social righteousness, peace, plenty and security will abound (32:15–20).

(6) Woe to the Assyrian destroyer (Isaiah 33). Isaiah's last woe is directed against the treacherous spoiler himself, who has already laid waste the cities of Judah, and is now beginning to lay siege to Jerusalem (701 B.C.). The prophet prays, and while he prays, behold! the mighty hosts of the Assyrians are routed and the long-besieged but now triumphant inhabitants of Jerusalem rush out like locusts on the spoil which the vanishing adversary has been forced to leave behind. The destroyer's plan to reduce Jerusalem has come to naught. The whole earth beholds the spectacle of Assyria's defeat and is filled with awe and amazement at the mighty work of Yahweh. Only the righteous may henceforth dwell in Jerusalem. their eyes shall behold the Messiah-king in his beauty, reigning no longer like Hezekiah over a limited and restricted territory, but over a land unbounded, whose inhabitants enjoy Yahweh's peace and protection, and are free from all sin, and therefore from all sickness (33:17–24). With this beautiful picture of the Messianic future, the prophet's woes find an appropriate conclusion. Isaiah never pronounced a woe without adding a corresponding promise.

In Is. 34–35, the prophet utters a fierce cry for justice against "all the nations," but against Edom in particular. His tone is that of judgment. Edom is guilty of high crimes against Zion (34:8 f), therefore she is doomed to destruction. On the other hand, the scattered ones of Israel shall return from exile and "obtain gladness and joy, and sorrow and sighing shall flee away" (Isaiah 35).

Chapters 36–39

Isaiah 36–39 contain history, prophecy and song intermingled. These chapters serve both as an appendix to Is. 1–35 and as an introduction to Is. 40–66. In them three important historical events are narrated, in which Isaiah was a prominent factor:

(1) the double attempt of Sennacherib to obtain possession of Jerusalem (Is. 36–37);

(2) Hezekiah's sickness and recovery (Is. 38);

(3) the embassy of Merodach-baladan (Is. 39).

With certain important omissions and insertions these chapters are duplicated almost verbatim in 2 Kings 18:13–20:19. They are introduced with the chronological note, "Now it came to pass in the fourteenth year of king Hezekiah." Various attempts have been made to solve the mystery of this date; for, if the author is alluding to the siege of 701 B.C., difficulty arises, because that event occurred not in Hezekiah's "14th" but 26th year, according to the Biblical chronology of his life; or, if with some we date Hezekiah's accession to the throne of Judah as 720 B.C., then the siege of 701 B.C. occurred, as is evident, in Hezekiah's 19th year. It is barely possible of course that "the 14th year of king Hezekiah" was the 14th of the "15 years" which were added to his life, but more probably it alludes to the 14th of his reign. On the whole it is better to take the phrase as a general chronological caption for the entire section, with special reference to Isaiah 38, which tells of Hezekiah's sickness, which actually fell in his 14th year (714 B.C.), and which, coupled with Sargon's expected presence at Ashdod, was the great personal crisis of the king's life.

Sennacherib made two attempts in 701 B.C. to reduce Jerusalem: one from Lachish with an army headed by the Rabshakeh (Isaiah 36:2–37:8), and another from Libnah with a threat conveyed by messengers (Isaiah 37:9). The brief section contained in 2 Kings 18:14–16 is omitted from between verses 1 and 2 of Isaiah 36, because it was not the prophet's aim at this time to recount the nation's humiliation. Isaiah's last "word" about Assyria (Isaiah 37:21–35) is one of the prophet's grandest predictions. It is composed of three parts:

(1) a taunt-song, in elegiac rhythm, on the inevitable humiliation of Sennacherib (Isaiah 37:22–29);

(2) a short poem in different rhythm, directed to Hezekiah, in order to encourage his faith (Isaiah 37:30–32);

(3) a definite prediction, in less elevated style, of the sure deliverance of Jerusalem (Isaiah 37:33–35). Isaiah's prediction was literally fulfilled.

The section Isaiah 38:9–20 contains Hezekiah's So of Thanksgiving, in which he celebrates his recovery from some mortal sickness. It is a beautiful plaintive "writing"; omitted altogether by the author of the Book of Kings (compare 2 Kings 20). Hezekiah was sick in 714 B.C.. Two years later Merodach-baladan, the veteran arch-enemy of Assyria, having heard of his wonderful recovery, sent letters and a present to congratulate him. Doubtless, also, political motives prompted the recalcitrant Babylonian. But be that as it may, Hezekiah was greatly flattered by the visit of Merodach-baladan's envoys, and, in a moment of weakness, showed them all his royal treasures. This was an inexcusable blunder, as the sight of his many precious possessions would naturally excite Babylonian cupidity to possess Jerusalem. Isaiah not only solemnly condemned the king's conduct, but he announced with more than ordinary insight that the days were coming when all the accumulated resources of Jerusalem would be carried away to Babylon (39:3–6; compare Micah 4:10). This final prediction of judgment is the most marvelous of all Isaiah's minatory utterances, because he distinctly asserts that, not the

Assyrians, who were then at the height of their power, but the Babylonians, shall be the instruments of the Divine vengeance in consummating the destruction of Jerusalem. There is absolutely no reason for doubting the genuineness of this prediction. In it, indeed, we have a prophetic basis for Is. 40–66, which follow.

Chapters 40–66

Coming now to Is. 40–66, we have prophecies of comfort, salvation, and of the future glory awaiting Israel. These chapters naturally fall into three sections:

(1) Is. 40–48, announcing deliverance from captivity through Cyrus;

(2) Is. 49–57, describing the sufferings of the "Servant" of Yahweh, this section ending like the former with the refrain, "There is no peace, saith my God, to the wicked" (57:21; compare 48:22);

(3) Is. 58–66, announcing the final abolition of all national distinctions and the future glory of the people of God. Isaiah 60 is the characteristic chapter of this section, as Isaiah 53 is of the second, and Isaiah 40 of the first.

Entering into greater detail, the first section (Is. 40–48) demonstrates the deity of Yahweh through His unique power to predict. The basis of the comfort which the prophet announces is Israel's incomparable God (Isaiah 40). Israel's all-powerful Yahweh in comparison with other gods is incomparable. In the prologue (Isaiah 40:1–11) he hears the four voices:

(1) of grace (Isaiah 40:1,2);

(2) of prophecy (Isaiah 40:3–5);

(3) of faith (Isaiah 40:6–8), and

(4) of evangelism (Isaiah 40:9–11).

Then, after exalting the unique character of Israel's all-but-forgotten God (Isaiah 40:12–26), he exhorts them not to suppose that Yahweh is ignorant of, or indifferent to, Israel's misery. Israel must wait for salvation. They are clamoring for deliverance prematurely. Only wait, he repeats; for with such a God, Israel has no reason to despond (Isaiah 40:27–31).

In Is. 41 he declares that the supreme proof of Yahweh's sole deity is His power to predict. He inquires, "Who hath raised up one from the east?" Though the hero is left unnamed, Cyrus is doubtless in the prophet's mind (compare 44:28; 45:1). He is not, however, already appearing on the horizon of history as some fancy, but rather predicted as sure to come. The verb tenses which express completed action are perfects of certainty, and are used in precisely the same manner as those in 3:8; 5:13; 21:9. The answer to the inquiry is, "I, Yahweh, the first, and with the last, I am he" (41:4). Israel is Yahweh's servant. The dialogue continues; but it is no longer between Yahweh and the nations, as in Isaiah 41:1–7, but between Yahweh and the idols (41:21–29). Addressing the dumb idols, Yahweh is represented as saying, Predict something, if you are real deities. As for myself, I am going to raise up a hero from the north who will subdue all who oppose him. And I announce my purpose now in advance "from the beginning," "beforetime," before there is the slightest ground for thinking that such a hero exists or ever will exist (41:26), in order that the future may verify my prediction, and prove my sole deity. I, Yahweh, alone know the future. In 41:25–29, the prophet even projects himself into the future and speaks from the standpoint of the fulfillment of his prediction. This, as we saw above, was a characteristic of Isaiah in Isaiah 24–27.

In Isaiah 42:1–43:13 the prophet announces also a spiritual agent of redemption, namely, Yahweh's "Servant." Not only a temporal agent (Cyrus) shall be raised up to mediate Israel's redemption, which is the first step in the process of the universal salvation contemplated, but a spiritual factor. Yahweh's "Servant" shall be employed in bringing the good tidings of salvation to the exiles and to the Gentiles also. In 42:1–9 the prophet describes this ideal figure and the work he will carry out. The glorious future evokes a brief hymn of thanksgiving for the redemption which the prophet beholds in prospect (42:10–17). Israel has long been blind and deaf to Yahweh's instructions (41:18,19), but now Yahweh is determined to redeem them even at the cost of the most opulent nations of the world, that they may publish His law to all peoples (42:18–43:13).

In Isaiah 13:14–44:23 forgiveness is made the pledge of deliverance. Yahweh's determination to redeem Israel is all of grace. Salvation is a gift. Yahweh has blotted out their transgressions for His own sake (43:25). "This passage," Dillmann observes, "marks the highest point of grace in the Old Testament." Gods of wood and stone are nonentities. Those who manufacture idols are blind and dull of heart, and are "feeding on ashes." The section 44:9–20 is a most remorseless exposure of the folly of idolatry.

In Isaiah 44:24–45:25 the prophet at length names the hero of Israel's salvation and describes his mission. He is Cyrus. He shall build Jerusalem and lay the foundations of the temple (44:28); he shall also subdue nations and let the exiles go free (45:1,13). He speaks of Cyrus in the most extraordinary, almost extravagant terms. He is Yahweh's "shepherd" (44:28), he is also Yahweh's "anointed," i.e. Messiah (45:1), "the man of my counsel" (46:11), whom Yahweh has called by name, and surnamed without his ever knowing Him (45:3,1); the one "whom Yahweh loveth" (48:14), whose right hand Yahweh upholdeth (45:1), and who will perform all Yahweh's pleasure (44:28); though but "a ravenous bird from the east (46: 11). The vividness with which the prophet speaks of Cyrus leads some to suppose that the latter is already on the horizon. This, however, is a mistake. Scarcely would a contemporary have spoken in such terms of the real Cyrus of 538 B.C.. The prophet regards him (i.e. the Cyrus of his own prediction, not the Cyrus of history) as the fulfillment of predictions spoken long before. That is to say, in one and the same context, Cyrus is both predicted and treated as a proof that prediction is being fulfilled (44:24–28; 45:21). Such a phenomenon in prophecy can best be explained by supposing that the prophet projected himself into the future from an earlier age. Most extraordinary of all, in 45:14–17, the prophet soars in imagination until he sees, as a result of Cyrus' victories, the conquered nations renouncing their idols, and attracted to Yahweh as the Savior of all mankind (45:22). On any theory of origin, the predictive element in these prophecies is written large.

Isaiah 46–47 describe further the distinctive work of Cyrus, though Cyrus himself is but once referred to. Particular emphasis is laid on the complete collapse of the Babylonian religion; the prophet being apparently more concerned with the humiliation of Babylon's idols than with the fall of the city itself. Of course the destruction of the city would imply the defeat of her gods, as also the emancipation of Israel. But here again all is in the future; in fact Yahweh's incomparable superiority and unique deity are proven by His power to predict "the end from the beginning" and bring His prediction to pass (46:10,11).

Isaiah 47 is a dirge over the downfall of the imperial city, strongly resembling the taunt-song over the king of Babylon in 14:4–21.

Isaiah 48 is a hortatory summary and recapitulation of the argument contained in Is. 40–47, the prophet again emphasizing the following points:

(1) Yahweh's unique power to predict;

(2) that salvation is of grace;

(3) that Cyrus' advent will be the crowning proof of Yahweh's abiding presence among His people;

(4) that God's chastisements were only disciplinary; and

(5) that even now there is hope, if they will but accept of Yahweh's proffered salvation. Alas! that there is no peace or salvation for the godless (48:20–22). Thus ends the first division of Isaiah's remarkable "vision" of Israel's deliverance from captivity through Cyrus.

The second section (Is. 49–57) deals with the spiritual agent of salvation, Yahweh's suffering "Servant." With Isaiah 49 the prophet leaves off attempting further to prove the sole deity of Yahweh by means of prediction, and drops entirely his description of Cyrus' victories and the overthrow of Babylon, in order to set forth in greater detail the character and mission of the suffering "Servant" of Yahweh. Already, in Is. 40–48, he had alluded several times to this unique and somewhat enigmatical personage, speaking of him both collectively and as an individual (41:8–10; 42:1–9,18–22; 43:10; 44:1–5, 21–28; 45:4; 48:20–22); but now he defines with greater precision both his prophetic and priestly functions, his equipment for his task, his sufferings and humiliation, and also his final exaltation. Altogether in these prophecies he mentions the "Servant" some 20 t. But there are four distinctively so-called "Servant-Songs" in which the prophet seems to rise above the collective masses of all Israel to at least a personification of the pious within Israel, or better, to a unique Person embodying within himself all that is best in the Israel within Israel. They are the following:

(1) 42:1–9, a poem descriptive of the Servant's gentle manner and world-wide mission;

(2) 49:1–13, describing the Servant's mission and spiritual success;

(3) 50:4–11, the Servant's soliloquy about His perfection through suffering; and

(4) 52:13–53:12, the Servant's vicarious suffering and ultimate exaltation.

In this last of the four "Servant-Songs" we reach the climax of the prophet's inspired symphony, the acme of Hebrew Messianic hope. The profoundest thoughts in the Old Testament revelation are to be found in this section. It is a vindication of the "Servant," so clear and so true, and wrought out with such pathos and potency, that it holds first place among Messianic predictions. Polycarp called it "the golden passional of the Old Testament." It has been realized in Jesus Christ.

Isaiah 58–66 describe the future glory of the people of God. Having described in Is. 40–48 the temporal agent of Israel's salvation, Cyrus, and in Is. 49–57 the spiritual agent of their salvation, the "Servant" of Yahweh, the prophet proceeds in this last section to define the conditions on which salvation may be enjoyed. He begins, as before, with a double imperative, "Cry aloud, spare not" (compare 40:1; 49:1).

In Isaiah 58 he discusses true fasting and faithful Sabbath observance.

In Isaiah 59 he beseeches Israel to forsake their sins. It is their sins, he urges, which have hidden Yahweh's face and retarded the nation's salvation. In 59:9 the prophet identifies himself with the people and leads them in their devotions. Yahweh is grieved over Israel's forlorn condition, and, seeing their helplessness, He arms himself like a warrior to interfere judicially (59:15–19). Israel shall be redeemed. With them as the nucleus of a new nation, Yahweh will enter anew into covenant relation, and put His Spirit on them, which will abide with them henceforth and forever (59:20–21).

Isaiah 60–61 describe the future blessedness of Zion. The long-looked-for "light" (compare 59:9) begins to dawn: "Arise, shine; for thy light is come, and the glory of Yahweh is risen on thee" (60:1). The prophet pauses at this point to paint a picture of the redeemed community. As in 2:3,4, the Gentiles are seen flocking to Zion, which becomes the mistress of the nations. Foreigners build her walls, and her gates are kept open continually without fear of siege. The Gentiles acknowledge that Zion is the spiritual center of the world. Even Israel's oppressors regard her as "the city of Yahweh," as "an eternal excellency," in which Yahweh sits as its everlasting light (60:10–22).

In Isaiah 61, which Drummond has called "the program of Christianity," the "Servant" of Yahweh is again introduced, though anonymously, as the herald of salvation (61:1–3). The gospel monologue of the "Servant" is followed by a promise of the restoration and blessedness of Jerusalem (61:4–11). Thus the prophecy moves steadily forward toward its goal in Jesus Christ (compare Luke 4:18–21).

In Isaiah 62:1–63:6 Zion's salvation is described as drawing near. The nations will be spectators of the great event. A new name which will better symbolize her true character shall be given to Zion, namely, Hephzibah, "My delight is in her"; for Jerusalem shall no more be called desolate. On the other hand, Zion's enemies will all be vanquished. In a brief poem of peculiar dramatic beauty (63:1–6), the prophet portrays Yahweh's vengeance, as a victorious warrior, on all those who retard Israel's deliverance. Edom in particular was Israel's insatiate foe. Hence, the prophet represents Yahweh's judgment of the nations as taking place on Edom's unhallowed soil. Yahweh, whose mighty arm has wrought salvation, returns as victor, having slain all of Israel's foes.

In Isaiah 63:7–64:12, Yahweh's "servants" resort to prayer. They appeal to Yahweh as the Begetter and Father of the nations (63:16; 64:8). With this thought of the fatherhood of God imbedded in his language, Isaiah had opened his very first oracle to Judah and Jerusalem (compare 1:2). As the prayer proceeds, the language becomes increasingly tumultuous. The people are thrown into despair because Yahweh seems to have abandoned them altogether (63:19). They recognize that the condition of Jerusalem is desperate. "Our holy and our beautiful house, where our fathers praised thee, is burned with fire; and all our pleasant places are laid waste" (64:11). Such language, however, is the language of fervent prayer and must not be taken with rigid literalness, as 63:18 and 3:8 plainly show.

Finally, in Is. 65–66, Yahweh answers His people's supplications, distinguishing sharply between His own "servants" and Israel's apostates. Only His chosen "seed" shall be delivered (65:9). Those who have obdurately provoked Yahweh by sacrificing in gardens (65:3; 66:17), offering libations to Fortune and Destiny (65:11), sitting among the graves to obtain oracles from the dead, and, like the Egyptians, eating swine's flesh and broth of abominable things which were supposed to possess magical properties, lodging in vaults or crypts in which heathen mysteries were celebrated (65:4), and at the same time fancying that by celebrating such heathen mysteries they are holier than others and thereby disqualified to discharge the ordinary duties of life (65:5)—such Yahweh designs to punish, measuring their work into their bosom and destroying them utterly with the sword (65:7,12). On the other hand, the "servants" of Yahweh Shall inherit His holy mountains. They shall rejoice and sing for joy of heart, and bless themselves in the God of Amen, i.e. in the God of Truth (65:9,14,16). Yahweh will create new heavens and a new earth, men will live and grow old like the patriarchs; they will possess houses and vineyards and enjoy them; for an era of idyllic peace will be ushered in with the coming of the Messianic age, in which even the natures of wild animals will be changed and the most rapacious of wild animals will live together in harmony (65:17–25). Religion will become spiritual and decentralized, mystic cults will disappear, incredulous scoffers will be silenced. Zion's population will be marvelously multiplied, and the people will be comforted and rejoice (66:1–14). Furthermore, all nations will flock to Zion to behold Yahweh's glory, and from one new moon to another, and from one Sabbath to another, all flesh will come up to worship in Jerusalem (66:15–23).

It is evident that the Book of Isaiah closes, practically as it begins, with a polemic against false worship, and the alternate reward of the righteous and punishment of the wicked. The only essential difference between the prophet's earlier and later oracles is this: Isaiah, in his riper years, on the basis of nearly half a century's experience as a preacher, paints a much brighter eschatological picture than was possible in his early ministry. His picture of the Messianic age not only transcends those of his contemporaries in the 8th century B.C., but he penetrates regions beyond the spiritual horizon of any and all Old Testament seers. Such language as that contained in Isaiah 66:1,2, in particular, anticipates the great principle enunciated by Jesus in John 4:24, namely, that "God is a Spirit: and they that worship him must worship in spirit and truth." To attempt to date such oracles as these on the basis of internal evidence is an absolute impossibility. Humanly speaking, one age could have produced such revelations quite as easily as another. But no age could have produced them apart from the Divine spirit.

Orr, James, M.A., D.D. General Editor, International Standard Bible Encyclopedia

Detailed outline

Part One: Prophecies of condemnation: 1:1–35:10

I. Prophecies about Judah and Jerusalem: 1:1–12:6
- A. General introduction: 1:1–31
- B. Millennial blessing by cleansing: 2:1–4:6
- C. Punishment for Israel's sins: 5:1–30
- D. The prophet's call and commission: 6:1–13
- E. The prophecy of Immanuel: 7:1–25
- F. The prophecy of the Assyrian invasion: 8:1–22
- G. Messianic prediction and warning: 9:1–21
- H. Punishment of Assyria: 10:1–34
- I. Restoration and blessing: 11:1–16
- J. Worship: 12:1–6

II. Prophecies against foreign nations: 13:1–23:18
- A. Babylon: 13:1–14:23
- B. Assyria: 14:24–27
- C. Philistia: 14:28–32
- D. Moab: 15:1–16:14
- E. Damascus: 17:1–14
- F. Land beyond the rivers of Ethiopia: 18:1–7
- G. Egypt: 19:1–25
- H. Egypt and Ethiopia: 20:1–6
- I. Dumah: 21:11–12
- J. Arabia: 21:13–17
- K. Valley of vision: 22:1–25
- L. Tyre: 23:1–18

III. Prophecy of the establishment of the Kingdom: 24:1–27:13
- A. The tribulation: 24:1–23
- B. The character of the kingdom: 25:1–12
- C. The testimony of restored Israel: 26:1–27:13

IV. Prophecy about Judah in relation to Assyria:
- A. The fall of Samaria: 28:1–13
- B. Warning to Judah: 28:14–29
- C. The attack of Zion: 29:1–4
- D. The attacker frustrated: 29:5–8
- E. Reasons for the trial: 29:9–16
- F. Blessings of final deliverance: 29:17–24
- G. Warning against an Egyptian alliance: 30:1–14
- H. Exhortation to rely on God for help: 30:15–31:9
- I. The day of the Lord: 34:1–17
- J. The kingdom blessing: 35:1–10

Part two: An historical connecting link: 36:1–39:8

I. Sennacherib's invasion: 36:1–37:38

II. Hezekiah's sickness and recovery: 38:1–22

III. Arrival of Babylonian envoy and captivity: 39:1–8

Part three: The prophecies of comfort: 40:1–66:24

I. Comfort of the Exiles in the promise of restoration: 40:1–66:24
- A. The promise of restoration: 40:1–11
- B. The basis of comfort: God's character: 40:12–31
- C. The reason for comfort: 41:1–29
- D. The Comforter: 42:1–25
- E. The results of the comfort: 43:1–47:15
  1. The nation restored: 43:1–45:25
  2. The downfall of idols of Babylon: 46:1–13
  3. Downfall of Babylon: 47:1–15

F. Exhortation of comfort for those delivered from captivity: 48:1–22

II. Comfort of the exiles with the prophecy of Jesus the Redeemer: 49:1–57:21

A. Call and work: 49:1–26

B. Obedience and faithfulness: 50:1–11

C. Redemption of Israel: 51:1–52:12

D. Atonement and exaltation: 52:13–53:12

E. Israel's restoration: 54:1–17

F. Worldwide salvation: 55:1–13

G. His warnings and promises: 56:1–57:21

III. Comfort exiles and prophecy of the future glory of Israel: 58:1–66:24

A. Obstacles to the restoration and their removal: 58:1–59:21

B. Glory of Jerusalem in the Messianic age: 60:1–22

C. Blessings of the Messiah for Israel and the world: 61:1–11

D. God's love for Jerusalem and its results: 62:1–12

E. God's vengeance: 63:1–6

F. Prayer of the remnant: 63:7–64:12

G. God's answer: 65:1–16

H. Blessings of the Messianic Kingdom: 65:17–66:24

2. Helpful summaries of Isaiah

Bird's eye view

The book of Isaiah is about God's provision of redemption and salvation for humanity.

Reading plan

The following reading plan, taking one reading per day, enables you to read through Isaiah in twenty days.

Isaiah 1–2
Isaiah 3–6
Isaiah 7–8
Isaiah 9–11
Isaiah 12–15
Isaiah 16–19
Isaiah 20–23
Isaiah 24–26
Isaiah 27–29
Isaiah 30–32
Isaiah 33–36
Isaiah 37–38
Isaiah 39–41
Isaiah 42–43
Isaiah 44–46
Isaiah 47–49
Isaiah 50–53
Isaiah 54–57
Isaiah 58–62
Isaiah 62–66

Verses to memorize

Isaiah 1:18

Though your sins are like scarlet, they shall be white as snow; though they are red as crimson, they shall be like wool.

Isaiah 9:6–7

For unto us a child is born, unto us a son is given: and the government shall be on his shoulder: and his name shall be called Wonderful, Counselor, The mighty God, The everlasting Father, The Prince of Peace.

Of the increase of his government and peace there shall be no end, on the throne of David, and on his kingdom, to order it, and to establish it with judgment and with justice from henceforth even for ever. The zeal of the Lord of hosts will perform this. KJV

Isaiah 40:8

The grass withereth, the flower fadeth: but the word of our God shall stand for ever. KJV

Isaiah 40:28–29

Do you not know?
Have you not heard?
The Lord is the everlasting God, the
Creator of the ends of the earth.
He will not grow tired or weary, and his
understanding no one can fathom.
He gives strength to the weary and increases
the power of the weak.

Isaiah 40:31

but those who hope in the Lord will renew
their strength.
They will soar on wings like eagles;
they will run and not grow weary,
they will walk and not be faint. KJV

Isaiah 41:10

Fear thou not; for I am with thee: be not dismayed; for I am thy God: I will strengthen thee; yea, I will help thee; yea, I will uphold thee with the right hand of my righteousness. KJV

Isaiah 45:22

Look unto me, and be ye saved, all the ends of the earth: for I am God, and there is none else. KJV

Isaiah 53:6

All we like sheep have gone astray; we have turned every one to his own way; and the Lord hath laid on him the iniquity of us all. KJV

Statistics

Twenty-third Old Testament book
66 chapters
1,292 verses
37,044 words

Famous sayings found in Isaiah

"Hammer swords into plowshares" Isaiah 2:4
"Put your house in order" Isaiah 38:1
"Drop in the bucket" Isaiah 40:15
"No peace for the wicked" Isaiah 48:22, Isaiah 57:21

Names/titles given

Hebrew title: *Yesha'yahu:* "The Lord is salvation."
Greek title in Septuagint: *Hesaias:* "The Lord is salvation."
Latin title in Vulgate: *Esaias/Isaias:* "The Lord is salvation."

3. Helpful keys to turn to in understanding Isaiah

Key word

Salvation

Key verses

Isaiah 9:6–7; 53:6

Key sermons in Isaiah

God's case against his People (Is. 1:2–20)
The song of the vineyard (Is. 5:1–7)
The children sermons: Shear-jashub, Immanuel, Maher-shalal-hash-baz (Is. 7–8)

Themes to study

Different aspects of God's character.

Isaiah's perseverance and faithfulness.

The meaning of "The Servant of the Lord."

Isaiah quoted in the New Testament

- Except the Lord of Sabaoth had left us a seed, we should have been as Sodom
  Is. 1:9 quoted in Rom. 9:29
- That seeing they may not see, and hearing they may not understand
  Is. 6:9 quoted in Luke 8:10
- By hearing ye shall hear, and in no wise understand
  Is. 6:9–10 quoted in Matt. 13:14–15 and Mark 4:12
- By hearing ye shall hear, and in no wise understand
  Is. 6:9–10 quoted in Acts 28:26–27
- Lest they should turn, and I should heal them
  Is. 6:10 quoted in John 12:40
- Behold, the virgin shall be with child
  Is. 7:14 quoted in Matt. 1:23
- God with us
  Is. 8:8, 10 quoted in Matt. 1:23
- A stone of stumbling, and a rock of offence
  Is. 8:14 quoted in Rom. 9:33 and 1 Pet. 2:8
- I will put my trust in him
  Is. 8:17 quoted in Heb. 2:13
- Behold, I and the children whom God hath given me
  Is. 8:18 quoted in Heb. 2:13
- The people that sat in darkness saw a great light
  Is. 9:1–2 quoted in Matt. 4:15–16
- It is the remnant that shall be saved
  Is. 10:22–23 quoted in Rom. 9:27–28
- On him shall the Gentiles hope
  Is. 11:10 quoted in Rom. 15:12
- Let us eat and drink, for tomorrow we die
  Is. 22:13 quoted in 1 Cor. 15:32
- Death is swallowed up in victory
  Is. 25:8 quoted in 1 Cor. 15:54
- When I shall take away their sins
  Is. 27:9 quoted in Rom. 11:27
- By men of strange tongues will I speak unto this people
  Is. 28:11–12 quoted in 1 Cor. 14:21
- He that believeth on him shall not be put to shame
  Is. 28:16 quoted in Rom. 9:33, 10:11 and 1 Pet. 2:6
- God gave them a spirit of stupor
  Is. 29:10 quoted in Rom. 11:8
- Teaching as their doctrines the precepts of men
  Is. 29:13 quoted in Matt. 15:8–9 and Mark 7:6–7
- I will destroy the wisdom of the wise
  Is. 29:14 quoted in 1 Cor. 1:19
- All flesh shall see the salvation of God
  Is. 40:3–5 quoted in Luke 3:4–6
- The voice of one crying in the wilderness
  Is. 40:3 quoted in Matt. 3:3, Mark 1:3 and John 1:23
- All flesh is as grass
  Is. 40:6–8 quoted in 1 Pet. 1:24–25
- Who hath known the mind of the Lord?
  Is. 40:13 quoted in Rom. 11:34 and 1 Cor. 2:16
- Behold, my servant whom I have chosen
  Is. 42:1–3 quoted in Matt. 12:18–19

- And in his name shall the Gentiles hope
  Is. 42:4 quoted in Matt. 12:21
- An elect race
  Is. 43:20 quoted in 1 Pet. 2:9
- A people for God's own possession
  Is. 43:21 quoted in 1 Pet. 2:9
- There is none other but he
  Is. 45:21 quoted in Mark 12:32
- To me every knee shall bow
  Is. 45:23 quoted in Rom. 14:11
- A light of the Gentiles
  Is. 49:6 quoted in Acts 13:47
- At an acceptable time I hearkened unto thee
  Is. 49:8 quoted in 2 Cor. 6:2
- As I live, saith the Lord
  Is. 49:18 quoted in Rom. 14:11
- For the name of God is blasphemed among the Gentiles because of you
  Is. 52:5 quoted in Rom. 2:24
- How beautiful are the feet
  Is. 52:7 quoted in Rom. 10:15
- Come out from among them, and be ye separate
  Is. 52:11 quoted in 2 Cor. 6:17
- They shall see, to whom no tidings of him came
  Is. 52:15 quoted in Rom. 15:21
- Who has believed our report?
  Is. 53:1 quoted in John 12:38 and Rom. 10:16
- Himself took our infirmities, and bare our diseases
  Is. 53:4 quoted in Matt. 8:17
- He was led as a sheep to the slaughter
  Is. 53:7–8 quoted in Acts 8:32–33
- Who did no sin, neither was guile found in his mouth
  Is. 53:9 quoted in 1 Pet. 2:22
- And he was reckoned with transgressors
  Is. 53:12 quoted in Luke 22:37
- Rejoice thou barren that bearest not
  Is. 54:1 quoted in Gal. 4:27
- And they shall all be taught of God
  Is. 54:13 quoted in John 6:45
- The sure mercies of David
  Is. 55:3 quoted in Acts 13:34
- My house shall be called a house of prayer
  Is. 56:7 quoted in Matt. 21:13, Mark 11:17 and Luke 19:46
- Their feet are swift to shed blood
  Is. 59:7–8 quoted in Rom. 3:15–17
- He shall turn away ungodliness from Jacob
  Is. 59:20–21 quoted in Rom. 11:26–27
- The Spirit of the Lord is upon me
  Is. 61:1–2 quoted in Luke 4:18–19
- Behold, thy King cometh unto thee
  Is. 62:11 quoted in Matt. 21:5
- Things which eye saw not
  Is. 64:4 quoted in 2 Cor. 2:9
- I was found of them that sought me not
  Is. 65:1 quoted in Rom. 10:20
- A disobedient and gainsaying people
  Is. 65:2 quoted in Rom. 10:21
- The heaven is my throne
  Is. 66:1–2 quoted in Acts 7:49–50

What Jesus is to a Christian in Isaiah

His/Her Sanctuary, 8:14
Wonderful, 9:6
His/Her Counselor, 9:6
His/Her mighty God, 9:6
His/Her everlasting Father, 9:6
His/Her strength, 12:2

His/Her song, 12:2
His/Her salvation, 12:2
Strength to the poor and needy, 25:4
His/Her refuge, 25:4
His/Her shelter from the storm, 25:4
His/Her shade from the heat, 25:4
His/Her cornerstone, 28:16
His/Her sure foundation, 28:16
His/Her hiding place, 32:2
His/Her Judge, 33:22
His/Her Shepherd, 40:11
His/Her bearer of sorrows, 53:4
His/Her Mediator, 53:11
His/Her Interceder, 53:12
His/Her Leader, 55:4
His/Her Redeemer, 59:20
His/Her everlasting Light, 60:20

Seven everlasting things spoken of in Isaiah

Strength, Isaiah 26:4
Judgments, Isaiah 33:14
Joy, Isaiah 35:10
Salvation, Isaiah 45:17
Kindness, Isaiah 54:8
Covenant, Isaiah 55:3
Light, Isaiah 60:19

Unusual events and miracles in Isaiah

- Sennacherib's defeat, in answer to prayer, 36:1–37:38
- Hezekiah's healing and prolonging of his life, 38:1–21

Jesus in Isaiah

In Isaiah Jesus is the Messiah.

Types of Jesus in Isaiah

The book of Isaiah contains numbers messianic promises about Jesus.

- Jesus would be anointed with the Spirit of God: Isaiah 11:2; 61:1; see Matt. 3:16; John 3:34; Acts 10:38.
- Jesus would come from David's family: Isaiah 11:1–5; see Matt. 1:1.
- Jesus would be born of a virgin: Isaiah 7:14; see Matt. 1:18–2:1.
- Jesus would be spat on: Isaiah 50:6; see Matt. 26:67.
- Jesus would be mocked: Isaiah 50:6; see Matt. 26:27–68.
- Jesus would be beaten: Isaiah 50:6; see Matt. 27:26.
- Jesus would die with sinners: Isaiah 53:9–12; see Matt. 27:38.
- Jesus' death would atone for the sins of humankind: Isaiah 53:5–7; see Mark 10:45; John 1:29.
- Jesus would be the cornerstone of the Christian Church: Isaiah 28:16; see Matt. 28:16; Eph. 2:20.
- Jesus would be sought after by Gentiles Isaiah 11:10; see Acts 10:45.

Lessons to learn from Isaiah

- If we reject God we are judged by him, but if we return to God in repentance, we are forgiven.
- God has chosen us to be his witnesses.

4. Chapter by chapter: outline of every chapter of Isaiah

Isaiah 1

Matthew Henry's introduction

The sermon which is contained in this chapter has in it,

I. A high charge exhibited, in God's name, against the Jewish church and nation,
 A. For their ingratitude, vv. 2, 3.
 B. For their incorrigibleness, v. 5.
 C. For the universal corruption and degeneracy of the people, vv. 4, 6, 21, 22.
 D. For the perversion of justice by their rulers, v. 23.

II. A sad complaint of the judgments of God, which they had brought on themselves by their sins, and by which they were brought almost to utter ruin, vv. 7–9.

III. A just rejection of those shows and shadows of religion which they kept up among them, notwithstanding this general defection and apostasy, vv. 10–15.

IV. An earnest call to repentance and reformation, setting before them life and death, life if they compiled with the call and death if they did not, vv. 16–20.

V. A threatening of ruin to those that would not be reformed, vv. 24, 28–31.

VI. A promise of a happy reformation at last, and a return to their primitive purity and prosperity, vv. 25–27.

A detailed analysis of chapter

The corruptions prevailing among the Jews. (1–9)

Severe censures. (10–15)

Exhortations to repentance. (16–20)

The state of Judah is lamented; with gracious promises of the gospel times. (21–31)

Key verse

Verse 1: "The vision of Isaiah the son of Amoz, which he saw concerning Judah and Jerusalem in the days of Uzziah, Jotham, Ahaz, and Hezekiah, kings of Judah."

Key word / key phrase

Verse 4, "sinful nation."

Key event / key person / key theme

God reprimands his people

Key thought

Judah is accused for breaking the covenant.

Key thing to look out for

God's judgment is certain.

Key Bible cross-reference

Verse 9. See Genesis 19:24.

Key "by way of explanation"

Verse 6, "oil," was used to bind up wounds, see Luke 10:34. Verse 1, Isaiah's prophecies were made during the tumultuous reigns of Judah's last kings. Isaiah was a contemporary of Amos, Hosea, and Micah.

Key "Quotable Quote"

"God's mill grinds slow, but sure."

George Herbert

Isaiah 2

Matthew Henry's introduction

The subject of this discourse is Judah and Jerusalem, v. 1. In this chapter the prophet speaks,

I. Of the glory of the Christians, Jerusalem, the gospel-church in the latter days, in the accession of many to it (vv. 2, 3), and the great peace it should introduce into the world (v. 4), whence he infers the duty of the house of Jacob, v. 5.

II. Of the shame of the Jews, Jerusalem, as it then was, and as it would be after its rejection of the gospel and being rejected of God.

A. Their sin was their shame, vv. 6–9.

B. God by his judgments would humble them and put them to shame, vv. 10–17.

C. They should themselves be ashamed of their confidence in their idols and in an arm of flesh, vv. 18–22.

A detailed analysis of chapter

The conversion of the Gentiles. Description of the sinfulness of Israel. (1–9)

The awful punishment of unbelievers. (10–22)

Key verse

Verse 2: "Enter into the rock, and hide thee in the dust, for fear of the LORD, and for the glory of his majesty."

Key word / key phrase

Verse 12, "a day in store."

Key event / key person / key theme

The day of judgment

Key thought

God's people will come to Jerusalem.

Key thing to look out for

"That day" will be a day of judgment.

Key Bible cross-reference

Verse 4. See Joel 3:10.

Key "by way of explanation"

Verse 11, "in that day." This phrase comes seven times in chapters two, three, and four, and refers to God's judgment, or, the Day of the Lord.

Key "Quotable Quote"

"The judgment of all men and women is ultimately going to be in terms of their relationship to the Lord Jesus Christ."

D. Martyn Lloyd-Jones

Isaiah 3

Matthew Henry's introduction

God threatens,

I. To deprive them of all the supports both of their life and of their government, vv. 1–3.

II. To leave them to fall into confusion and disorder, vv. 4, 5, 12.

III. To deny them the blessing of magistracy, vv. 6–8.

IV. To strip the daughters of Zion of their ornaments, vv. 17–24.

V. To lay all waste by the sword of war, vv. 25, 26. The sins that provoked God to deal thus with them were,

A. Their defiance of God, v. 8.

B. Their impudence, v. 9.

C. The abuse of power to oppression and tyranny, vv. 12–15.
D. The pride of the daughters of Zion, v. 16.

In the midst of the chapter the prophet is directed how to address particular people.

1. To assure good people that it should be well with them, notwithstanding those general calamities, v. 10.
2. To assure wicked people that, however God might, in judgment, remember mercy, yet it should go ill with them, v. 11.

A detailed analysis of chapter

The calamities about to come on the land. (1–9)
The wickedness of the people. (10–15)
The distress of the proud, wealthy women of Zion. (16–26)

Key verse

Verse 1: "For, behold, the Lord, the LORD of hosts, doth take away from Jerusalem and from Judah the stay and the staff, the whole stay of bread, and the whole stay of water."

Key word / key phrase

Verse 12, "your guides lead you astray."

Key event / key person / key theme

Society's breakdown

Key thought

Jerusalem will be punished because of her sin.

Key thing to look out for

The women of Jerusalem will be cut down in their pride.

Key Bible cross-reference

Verse 2. See 2 Chronicles 33:6.

Key "by way of explanation"

Verse 14, "vineyard." The vineyard is a picture of Israel, see Isaiah 5:1.

Key "Quotable Quote"

"The passions expelled by grace return to an arrogant soul."

Peter of Damascus

Isaiah 4

Matthew Henry's introduction

In this chapter we have,

I. A threatening of the paucity and scarceness of man (v. 1), which might fitly enough have been added to the close of the previous chapter, to which it has a plain reference.
II. A promise of the restoration of Jerusalem's peace and purity, righteousness and safety, in the days of the Messiah, vv. 2–6.

A detailed analysis of chapter

The havoc caused by war. (1)
The times of the Messiah. (2–6)

Key verse

Verse 2: "In that day shall the branch of the LORD be beautiful and glorious, and the fruit of the earth shall be excellent and comely for them that are escaped of Israel."

Key word / key phrase

Verse 2, "the Branch of the Lord."

Key event / key person / key theme

The Day of the Lord: the branch

Key thought

The Branch of the Lord speaks of God's redemption.

Key thing to look out for

The Lord God shelters and shields his people.

Key Bible cross-reference

Verse 5. See Exodus 13:21.

Key "by way of explanation"

Verse 3, "holy." This means separate in the sense of being totally and exclusively devoted to God.

Key "Quotable Quote"

"Christ is our Redeemer, Savior, peace, atonement and satisfaction, and has made amends or satisfaction toward God for all the sin which they that repent, consenting to the law and believing the promises, do, have done, or shall do."

William Tyndale

Isaiah 5

Matthew Henry's introduction

In this chapter the prophet, in God's name, shows the people of God their transgressions, even the house of Jacob their sins, and the judgments which were likely to be brought on them for their sins,

I. By a parable, under the similitude of an unfruitful vineyard, representing the great favors God had bestowed on them, their disappointing his expectations from them, and the ruin they had thereby deserved, vv. 1–7.

II. By an enumeration of the sins that did abound among them, with a threatening of punishments that should answer to the sins.

A. Covetousness, and greediness of worldly wealth, which shall be punished with famine, vv. 8–10.

B. Rioting, reveling, and drunkenness (vv. 11, 12, 22, 23), which shall be punished with captivity and all the miseries that attend it, vv. 13–17.

C. Presumption in sin, and defying the justice of God, vv. 18, 19.

D. Confounding the distinctions between virtue and vice, and so undermining the principles of religion, v. 20.

E. Self-conceit, v. 21.

F. Perverting justice, for which, and the other instances of reigning wickedness among them, a great and general desolation in threatened, which should lay all waste (vv. 24, 25), and which should be effected by a foreign invasion (vv. 26–30), referring perhaps to the havoc made not long after by Sennacherib's army.

A detailed analysis of chapter

The state and behavior of the Jewish nation. (1–7)

The coming judgments. (8–23)

Those who will carry out these judgments. (24–30)

Key verse

Verse 1: "Now will I sing to my well beloved a song of my beloved touching his vineyard."

Key word / key phrase

Verse 1, "vineyard."

Key event / key person / key theme

The Song of the Vineyard

Key thought

The Lord could have done nothing more for his people.

Key thing to look out for

Rejecting the Lord's love brings the Lord's judgment.

Key Bible cross-reference

Verses 1,2. See Luke 20:9.

Key "by way of explanation"

Verse 10. The tiny crops from this ten-acre site indicate how God punished his people.

Key "Quotable Quote"

"Never before on this earth has there been such a huge number of people who freely and easily, without any shame, without any pangs of conscience 'call evil good, and good evil; that put darkness for light, and light for darkness; that put bitter for sweet, and sweet for bitter!' (Isaiah 5:20)."

Archbishop Averky of Syracuse

Isaiah 6

Matthew Henry's introduction

In this chapter we have,

I. A very awful vision which Isaiah saw of the glory of God (vv. 1–4), the terror it put him into (v. 5), and the relief given him against that terror by an assurance of the pardon of his sins, vv. 6, 7.

II. A very awful commission which Isaiah received to go as a prophet, in God's name (v. 8), by his preaching to harden the impenitent in sin and ripen them for ruin (vv. 9–12) yet with a reservation of mercy for a remnant, (v. 13).

A detailed analysis of chapter

The vision which Isaiah saw in the temple. (1–8)

The Lord declares the blindness to come upon the Jewish nation, and the destruction which would follow. (9–13)

Key verse

Verse 3: "And one cried unto another, and said, Holy, holy, holy, is the LORD of hosts: the whole earth is full of his glory."

Key word / key phrase

Verse 8, "Whom shall I send?"

Key event / key person / key theme

Isaiah's vision and calling

Key thought

Every Christian is called to serve the Lord in some way.

Key thing to look out for

Isaiah needed to have his sin dealt with before he could serve the Lord.

Key Bible cross-reference

Verse 3. See Revelation 4:8.

Key "by way of explanation"

Verse 7, "touched my mouth." This was a purging of the prophet's sin. But it also indicated that Isaiah would speak for the Lord. See Jeremiah 1:9. Uzziah died in 740 BC.

Key "Quotable Quote"

"The Lord called me by the way of simplicity and humility."

Francis of Assisi

Isaiah 7

Matthew Henry's introduction

Here is,

I. The consternation that Ahaz was in on an attempt of the confederate forces of Syria and Israel against Jerusalem, vv. 1, 2.

II. The assurance which God, by the prophet, sent him for his encouragement, that the attempt should be defeated and Jerusalem should be preserved, vv. 3–9.

III. The confirmation of this by a sign which God gave to Ahaz, when he refused to ask one, referring to Christ, and our redemption by him, vv. 10–16.

IV. A threatening of the great desolation that God would bring on Ahaz and his kingdom by the Assyrians, notwithstanding their escape from this present storm, because they went on still in their wickedness, vv. 17–25.

A detailed analysis of chapter

Ahaz threatened by Israel and Syria; and is assured their attack would be in vain. (1–9)

God gives a sure sign by the promise of the long-expected Messiah. (10–16)

The folly and sin of seeking relief from Assyria are reproved. (17–25)

Key verse

Verse 14: "Therefore the Lord himself shall give you a sign; Behold, a virgin shall conceive, and bear a son, and shall call his name Immanuel."

Key word / key phrase

Verse 14, "a sign."

Key event / key person / key theme

The sign of Immanuel

Key thought

Many prophecies were fulfilled in more than one way.

Key thing to look out for

Matthew refers to verse 14 as he applies the name "Immanuel" to Jesus. See Matthew 1:23.

Key Bible cross-reference

Verse 1. See 2 kings 16:5.

Key "by way of explanation"

Verse 20, "Shave . . . heads . . . beards." To have one's beard shaved off was considered a great insult. See 2 Samuel 10:4, 5.

Key "Quotable Quote"

"Immanuel, God with us in our nature, in our sorrow, in our lifework, in our punishment, in our grave, and now with us, or rather we with him, in resurrection, ascension, triumph, and Second Advent splendor."

C.H. Spurgeon

Isaiah 8

Matthew Henry's introduction

In this chapter we have,

I. A prophecy of the destruction of the confederate kingdoms of Syria and Israel by the king of Assyria, vv. 1–4.

II. Of the desolations that should be made by that proud victorious prince in the land of Israel and Judah, vv. 5–8.

III. Great encouragement given to the people of God in the midst of those distractions; they are assured,

A. That the enemies shall not gain their point against them, vv. 9, 10.

B. That if they kept up the fear of God, and kept down the fear of man, they should find God their refuge (vv. 11–14), and while others stumbled, and fell into despair, they should be enabled to wait on God, and should see themselves reserved for better times, vv. 15–18. Lastly, He gives a necessary caution to all, at their peril, not to consult with familiar spirits, for they would thereby throw themselves into despair, but to keep close to the word of God, vv. 19–22.

A detailed analysis of chapter

Exhortations and warnings. (1–8)

Comfort for those who fear God. (9–16)

Afflictions to idolaters. (17–22)

Key verse

Verse 10: "Take counsel together, and it shall come to nought; speak the word, and it shall not stand: for God is with us."

Key word / key phrase

Verse 11, "warning me."

Key event / key person / key theme

Comfort and warning

Key thought

Assyria is to become the Lord's instrument.

Key thing to look out for

Isaiah trusted in the Lord even though he seemed to be hidden from him.

Key Bible cross-reference

Verse 17. See Hebrews 2:13.

Key "by way of explanation"

Verse 12, "conspiracy." When the prophet Isaiah told God's people not to form an alliance with Assyria, as a way of defending themselves against an attack from Israel, it amounted to treason in their eyes.

Key "Quotable Quote"

"To wait upon God is the perfection of activity."

Oswald Chambers

Isaiah 9

Matthew Henry's introduction

Here are,

I. Gracious promises to those that adhere to the law and to the testimony; while those that seek to familiar spirits shall be driven into darkness and dimness, they shall see a great light, relief in the midst of their distresses, typical of gospel grace.

A. In the doctrine of the Messiah, vv. 1–3.

B. His victories, vv. 4, 5.

C. His government and dominion as Immanuel, vv. 6, 7.

II. Dreadful threatenings against the people of Israel, who had revolted from and were enemies to the house of David, that they should be brought to utter ruin, that their pride should bring them down (vv. 8–10), that their neighbors should make a prey of them (vv. 11, 12), that, for their impenitence and hypocrisy, all their ornaments and supports should be cut off (vv. 13–17), and that by the wrath of God against them, and their wrath one against another, they should be brought to utter ruin, vv. 18–21.

A detailed analysis of chapter

The Son that should be born, and his kingdom. (1–7)

The judgments to come upon Israel, and on the enemies of the kingdom of Christ. (8–21)

Key verse

Verse 6: "For unto us a child is born, unto us a son is given: and the government shall be upon his shoulder: and his name shall be called Wonderful, Counselor, The mighty God, The everlasting Father, The Prince of Peace."

Key word / key phrase

Verse 6, "Prince of Peace."

Key event / key person / key theme

The sign of the Prince of Peace

Key thought

See how the titles in verse 6 relate to Jesus.

Key thing to look out for

The Lord will not put up with ungodliness.

Key Bible cross-reference

Verse 7. See Luke 1:32,33.

Key "by way of explanation"

Verse 6, "Mighty God." In the Old Testament the Lord was sometimes pictured as a strong warrior fighting for his people.

Key "Quotable Quote"

"There is no peace without the Prince of Peace."

Augustine of Hippo

Isaiah 10

Matthew Henry's introduction

The prophet, in this chapter, is dealing,

I. With the proud oppressors of his people at home, that abused their power, to pervert justice, whom he would reckon with for their tyranny, vv. 1–4.

II. With a threatening invader of his people from abroad, Sennacherib king of Assyria, about whom observe,
   A. The commission given him to invade Judah, vv. 5, 6.
   B. His pride and insolence in the execution of that commission, vv. 7–11, 13, 14.
   C. A rebuke given to his haughtiness, and a threatening of his fall and ruin, when he had served the purposes for which God raised him up, vv. 12, 15–19.
   D. A promise of grace to the people of God, to enable them to bear up under the affliction, and to get good by it, vv. 20–23.
   E. Great encouragement given to them not to fear this threatening storm, but to hope that, though for the present all the country was put into a great consternation by it, yet it would end well, in the destruction of this formidable enemy, vv. 24–34.

A detailed analysis of chapter

Woes against proud oppressors. (1–4)

The Assyrians are but an instrument in the hand of God for the punishment of his people. (5–19)

The deliverance from the aggressor. (20–34)

Key verse

Verse 5: "O Assyrian, the rod of mine anger, and the staff in their hand is mine indignation."

Key word / key phrase

Verse 20, "the remnant of Israel."

Key event / key person / key theme

A remnant will survive

Key thought

Today, the Christian Church is viewed as God's remnant.

Key thing to look out for

Assyria was but a tool (verse 15), and would be punished for its pride.

Key Bible cross-reference

Verses 5–34. See Isaiah 14:24–27; Nahum 1:1–3:19; Zephaniah 2:13–15.

Key "by way of explanation"

When Isaiah gave this poem, Israel (the northern kingdom) had fallen to Assyria, and now Jerusalem itself was threatened (27–32).

Key "Quotable Quote"

"What is impossible to God? Not that which is difficult to his power, but that which is contrary to his nature."

Ambrose

Isaiah 11

Matthew Henry's introduction

On occasion of the prophecy of the deliverance of Jerusalem from Sennacherib, here comes in a prophecy about Messiah the Prince.

I. His rise out of the house of David, v. 1.

II. His qualifications for his great undertaking, vv. 2, 3.

III. The justice and equity of his government, vv. 3–5.

IV. The peaceableness of his kingdom, vv. 6–9.
V. The accession of the Gentiles to it (v. 10), and with them the remnant of the Jews, that should be united with them in the Messiah's kingdom (vv. 11–16).

A detailed analysis of chapter

The peaceful character of Christ's kingdom and subjects. (1–9)

The conversion of the Gentiles and Jews. (10–16)

Key verse

Verse 2: "And the spirit of the LORD shall rest upon him, the spirit of wisdom and understanding, the spirit of counsel and might, the spirit of knowledge and of the fear of the LORD."

Key word / key phrase

Verse 1, "the stump of Jesse."

Key event / key person / key theme

God's future king

Key thought

Verses from this chapter are read at Christmas time as they speak of the coming of the Messiah.

Key thing to look out for

Note what is said about the stump and the Root of Jesse in verses 1 and 10.

Key Bible cross-reference

Verse 9. See Romans 9:27.

Key "by way of explanation"

Verse 2, "the Spirit." One of the genuine signs of the coming of the Messiah would be that the Spirit would rest on him.

Key "Quotable Quote"

"The great King, immortal, invisible, the divine person called the Holy Ghost, it is he that quickens the soul."

C.H. Spurgeon

Isaiah 12

Matthew Henry's introduction

The salvation promised in the previous chapter was compared to that of Israel "in the day that he came up out of the land of Egypt;" so that chapter ends. Now as Moses and the children of Israel then sang a song of praise to the glory of God (Ex. 15:1) so shall the people of God do in that day when the root of Jesse shall stand for an ensign of the people and shall be the desire and joy of all nations. In that day,

I. Every particular believer shall sing a song of praise for his own interest in that salvation, vv. 1, 3). "Thou shalt say, Lord, I will praise thee." Thanksgiving work shall be closet-work.
II. Many in concert shall join in praising God for the common benefit arising from this salvation (vv. 4–6): "You shall say, Praise you the Lord."

A detailed analysis of chapter

This is a hymn of praise appropriate for the times of the Messiah. (1–6)

Key verse

Verse 5: "Sing unto the LORD; for he hath done excellent things: this is known in all the earth."

Key word / key phrase

Verse 6, "sing for joy."

Key event / key person / key theme

A song of salvation

Key thought

Songs of praise should always be sung to the Savior.

Key thing to look out for

Worship should lead to evangelism. See verse 4.

Key Bible cross-reference

Verse 2. See Exodus 15:2.

Key "by way of explanation"

Verse 3, "wells." Wells of salvation refer to the Lord himself who saves his people as they draw live-giving water from him.

Key "Quotable Quote"

"There is no more urgent and critical question in life than that of your personal relationship with God and your eternal salvation."

Billy Graham

Isaiah 13

Matthew Henry's introduction

In this chapter we have,

I. A general rendezvous of the forces that were to be employed against Babylon, vv. 1–5.

II. The dreadfully bloody work that those forces should make in Babylon, vv. 6–18.

III. The utter ruin and desolation of Babylon, which this should end in, vv. 19–22.

A detailed analysis of chapter

The armies of God's wrath. (1–5)

The conquest of Babylon. (6–18)

Its final desolation. (19–22)

Key verse

Verse 6: "Howl ye; for the day of the LORD is at hand; it shall come as a destruction from the Almighty."

Key word / key phrase

Verse 1, "concerning Babylon."

Key event / key person / key theme

Prophecies against Babylon

Key thought

No matter how powerful great nations appear, God controls their destiny. The beautiful and powerful city of Babylon fell into ruins in the time of Christ, and has never been rebuilt.

Key thing to look out for

Note how God is pictured as a warrior summoning his troops for battle.

Key Bible cross-reference

Verse 21. See Isaiah 34:14.

Key "by way of explanation"

Verse 10, "not show their light." On the Lord's

judgment day darkness fills the land. See Joel 2:10, 31. Chapters 13–27 speak of God's purposes for the nations of the world.

Key "Quotable Quote"

"God hath appointed a day, wherein he will judge the world by Jesus Christ, when everyone shall receive according to his deed; the wicked shall go into everlasting punishment; the righteous, into everlasting life."

James Boyce

Isaiah 14

Matthew Henry's introduction

In this chapter,

I. More weight is added to the burden of Babylon, enough to sink it like a mill-stone;
   A. It is Israel's cause that is to be pleaded in this quarrel with Babylon, vv. 1–3.
   B. The king of Babylon, for the time being, shall be remarkably brought down and triumphed over, vv. 4–20.
   C. The whole race of the Babylonians shall be cut off and extirpated, vv. 21–23.

II. A confirmation of the prophecy of the destruction of Babylon, which was a thing at a distance, is here given in the prophecy of the destruction of the Assyrian army that invaded the land, which happened not long after, vv. 24–27.

III. The success of Hezekiah against the Philistines is here foretold, and the advantages which his people would gain thereby, vv. 28–32.

A detailed analysis of chapter

The destruction of Babylon, and the death of its proud monarch. (1–23)

Assurance of the destruction of Assyria. (24–27)

The destruction of the Philistines. (28–32)

Key verse

Verse 4: "That thou shalt take up this proverb against the king of Babylon, and say, How hath the oppressor ceased! the golden city ceased!"

Key word / key phrase

Verse 24, "as I planned, so it will be."

Key event / key person / key theme

An end of oppression

Key thought

The Lord is full of compassion.

Key thing to look out for

The world's greatest superpower is puny when compared with the Lord.

Key Bible cross-reference

Verse 12. See Revelation 8:10.

Key "by way of explanation"

Verse 8, "pine trees . . . cedars." Isaiah was fond of personifying something from nature.

Key "Quotable Quote"

"A prophet is one who knows his times and what God is trying to say to the people of his times."

A.W. Tozer

Isaiah 15

Matthew Henry's introduction

In this chapter we have,

I. Great lamentation made by the Moabites, and by the prophet himself for them, vv. 1–5.

II. The great calamities which should occasion that lamentation and justify it, vv. 6–9.

A detailed analysis of chapter

The divine judgments about to come upon the Moabites. (1–9)

Key verse

Verse 1: "The burden of Moab."

Key word / key phrase

Verse 1, "concerning Moab."

Key event / key person / key theme

Moab, Israel's constant enemy, will be judged by God.

Key thought

Verse 5. Isaiah feels sympathy for Moab.

Key thing to look out for

God's judgment falls on those who reject him.

Key Bible cross-reference

Verse 2. See 2 Chronicles 32:12.

Key "by way of explanation"

Verse 2, "high places," were pagan shrines.

Key "Quotable Quote"

"It is one thing to fall victim to the flood or to fall prey to cancer; it is another thing to fall into the hands of the living God."

R.C. Sproul

Isaiah 16

Matthew Henry's introduction

This chapter continues and concludes the burden of Moab. In it,

I. The prophet gives good counsel to the Moabites, to reform what was amiss among them, and particularly to be kind to God's people, as the likeliest way to prevent the judgments before threatened, vv. 1–5.

II. Fearing they would not take this counsel (they were so proud), he goes on to foretell the lamentable devastation of their country, and the confusion they should be brought to, and this within three years, vv. 6–14.

A detailed analysis of chapter

Moab is exhorted to obedience. (1–5)

The pride and the judgments of Moab. (6–14)

Key verse

Verse 6: "We have heard of the pride of Moab; he is very proud: even of his haughtiness, and his pride, and his wrath: but his lies shall not be so."

Key word / key phrase

Verse 6, "Moab's pride."

Key event / key person / key theme

Moab's hopeless situation

Key thought

Moab's pride is her downfall.

Key thing to look out for

Note in how many different ways Isaiah focuses on Moab's pride in this chapter.

Key Bible cross-reference

Verse 6. See Jeremiah 48:29.

Key "by way of explanation"

Verse 10, "treads out wine." After grapes had been picked they were trodden on in the winepress, and the juice ran out into a trough.

Key "Quotable Quote"

"Pride is spiritual cancer; it eats the very possibility of love or contentment, or even common sense."

C.S. Lewis

Isaiah 17

Matthew Henry's introduction

I. The destruction of the strong cities both of Syria and Israel is here foretold, vv. 1–5 and vv. 9–11.

II. In the midst of judgment mercy is remembered to Israel, and a gracious promise made that a remnant should be preserved from the calamities and should get good by them, vv. 6–8.

III. The overthrow of the Assyrian army before Jerusalem is pointed at, vv. 12–14.

A detailed analysis of chapter

A prophecy against Damascus.. (1–3)

A prophecy against Israel. (4–14)

Key verse

Verse 1: "The burden of Damascus. Behold, Damascus is taken away from being a city, and it shall be a ruinous heap."

Key word / key phrase

Verse 9, "desolation."

Key event / key person / key theme

The invasion of Judah by the armies of Damascus and Israel in 734 BC.

Key thought

God's enemies will eventually be defeated.

Key thing to look out for

Forgetting the Lord and all he had done was Israel's besetting sin.

Key Bible cross-reference

Verses 1–3. See Zechariah 9:1.

Key "by way of explanation"

Verse 1, "Damascus," the capital of Aram (Syria) had been Israel's great enemy since the time of David.

Key "Quotable Quote"

"I remember two things: that I am a great sinner and that Christ is a great Savior."

John Newton

Isaiah 18

Matthew Henry's introduction

Whatever country it is that is meant here by "the land shadowing with wings," here is a woe denounced against it, for God has, on his people's account, a quarrel with it.

I. They threaten God's people, vv. 1, 2.
II. All the neighbors are hereon called to take notice what will be the issue, v. 3.
III. Though God seem unconcerned in the distress of his people for a time, he will at length appear against their enemies and will remarkable cut them off, vv. 4–6.
IV. This shall redound very much to the glory of God, v. 7.

A detailed analysis of chapter

Prophecy againt Egypt (here called Cush). (1–7)

Key verse

Verse 1: "Woe to the land shadowing with wings, which is beyond the rivers of Ethiopia [Cush]."

Key word / key phrase

Verse 5, "cut down."

Key event / key person / key theme

The king of Egypt had sent envoys to Hezekiah in an attempt to get Hezekiah to join in a coalition against Assyria.

Key thought

All who are against God's people are called "people of the world" and are under God's judgment.

Key thing to look out for

The graphic pictures in the Bible of God's judgment should move us.

Key Bible cross-reference

Verses 18:1–7. See Zephaniah 2:12.

Key "by way of explanation"

Verse 1, "Cush," is the name of a country to the south of Egypt. This country, the ancient Ethiopia, was close to our modern Ethiopia. The prophecy is a description of Egypt, which is addressed as "Cush" because in 715 BC a Cushite dynasty had come to power in Egypt.

Key "Quotable Quote"

"Truly, when the day of judgment comes, we shall not be examined as to what we have read, but what we have done, not how well we have spoken but how we have lived."

Thomas à Kempis

Isaiah 19

Matthew Henry's introduction

Here we have the burden of Egypt, a prophecy about that nation,

I. That it should be greatly weakened and brought low, and should be as contemptible among the nations as now it was considerable, rendered so by a complication of judgments which God would bring on them, vv. 1–17.
II. That at length God's holy religion should be brought into Egypt, and set up there, in part by the Jews that should flee thither for refuge, but more fully by the preachers of the gospel of Christ, through whose ministry churches should be planted in Egypt in the says of the Messiah (vv. 18–25), which would abundantly balance all the calamities here threatened.

A detailed analysis of chapter

Judgments upon Egypt. (1–17)

Its deliverance, and the conversion of the people. (18–25)

Key verse

Verse 1: "The burden of Egypt. Behold, the LORD rideth upon a swift cloud, and shall come into Egypt."

Key word / key phrase

Verse 1, "concerning Egypt."

Key event / key person / key theme

Prophecies against Egypt

Key thought

The repetition of the words "in that day" emphasizes the certainty of God's impending judgment.

Key thing to look out for

The hope offered in verse 25.

Key Bible cross-reference

1–25. See Jeremiah 46:2–26.

Key "by way of explanation"

Verse 15, "head or tail, palm branch or reed." These words refer to Egyptian leaders. See 9:14,15 where they refer to Israel's leaders.

Key "Quotable Quote"

"The death of Jesus means the verdict which God will pronounce over us on the day of judgment has been brought into the present. We therefore do not need to fear the judgment day."

Anthony Hoekema

Isaiah 20

Matthew Henry's introduction

Here is,

I. The sign by which this was foretold, which was the prophet's going for some time barefoot and almost naked, like a poor captive, vv. 1–2.

II. The explication of that sign, with application to Egypt and Ethiopia, vv. 3–5.

III. The good use which the people of God should make of this, which is never to trust in an arm of flesh, because thus it will deceive them, v. 6.

A detailed analysis of chapter

The invasion and conquest of Egypt and its rulers. (1–6)

Key verse

Verse 4: "So shall the king of Assyria lead away the Egyptians prisoners, and the Ethiopians captives, young and old, naked and barefoot, even with their buttocks uncovered, to the shame of Egypt."

Key word / key phrase

Verse 2, "stripped and barefoot."

Key event / key person / key theme

For three years before the fall of Ashdod (in 712/11 BC) Isaiah had walked around Jerusalem stripped and barefoot as a warning to the people of coming disaster.

Key thought

It is fatal to rely on human aid.

Key thing to look out for

The Lord's people are not to ally themselves with the people of this world.

Key Bible cross-reference

Verse 3. See 47:3.

Key "by way of explanation"

Verse 5, "boasted in Egypt." Judah's king, Hezekiah, was advised to make a pact with Egypt, but Isaiah warned him against this. See 30:1–2; 31:1.

Key "Quotable Quote"

"Separation from evil is the necessary first principle of communion with the Lord."

J.N. Darby

Isaiah 21

Matthew Henry's introduction

In this chapter we have a prophecy of sad times coming, and heavy burdens,

I. On Babylon, here called "the desert of the sea," that it should be destroyed by the Medes and Persians with a terrible destruction, which yet God's people should have advantage by, vv. 1–10.

II. On Dumah, or Idumea, vv. 11, 12.

III. On Arabia, or Kedar, the desolation of which country was very near, vv. 13–17.

A detailed analysis of chapter

The taking of Babylon. (1–10)

The Edomites. (11,12)

The Arabs. (13–17)

Key verse

Verse 11: "The burden of Dumah. He calleth to me out of Seir, Watchman, what of the night? Watchman, what of the night?"

Key word / key phrase

Verse 9, "Babylon has fallen."

Key event / key person / key theme

Prophecies against Babylon, Edom, and Arabia

Key thought

No country or evil group of people are strong enough to withstand the Lord's power.

Key thing to look out for

When the Bible says that God has "spoken," as in verse 17, it means that the action is as good as done.

Key Bible cross-reference

Verse 10. See Proverbs 25:25.

Key "by way of explanation"

Verse 9, "its gods lie shattered." When a country was defeated its gods, too, were disgraced.

Key "Quotable Quote"

"Evil is that which God does not will."

Emil Brunner

Isaiah 22

Matthew Henry's introduction

This chapter concerns,

I. The city of Jerusalem itself and the neighborhood depending on it. Here is,

A. A prophecy of the grievous distress they should shortly be brought into by Sennacherib's invasion of the country and laying siege to the city, vv. 1–7.

B. A reproof given them for their misconduct in that distress, in two things:

1. Not having an eye to God in the use of the means of their preservation, vv. 8–11.

2. Not humbling themselves under his mighty hand, vv. 12–14.

II. The court of Hezekiah, and the officers of that court.

A. The displacing of Shebna, a bad man, and turning him out of the treasury, vv. 15–19, 25.

B. The preferring of Eliakim, who should do his country better service, to his place, vv. 20–24.

A detailed analysis of chapter

Jerusalem under siege. (1–11)

Godless revelry condemned. (12–14)

The displacing of the steward Shebna, and the promotion of Eliakim, applied to the Messiah. (15–25)

Key verse

Verse 22: "And the key of the house of David will I lay upon his shoulder; so he shall open, and none shall shut; and he shall shut, and none shall open."

Key word / key phrase

Verse 9, "the city of David."

Key event / key person / key theme

Jerusalem under servere threat

Key thought

When God lifted the danger the people let go of God.

Key thing to look out for

God's people, if they are sinful, will not escape God's judgment.

Key Bible cross-reference

Verse 13. See 1 Corinthians 15:32.

Key "by way of explanation"

Verses 1–14 probably refer to Sennacherib's siege in 701 BC, and the behavior of the citizens when the siege was miraculously ended.

Key "Quotable Quote"

"If God doesn't bring judgment on America soon, he will have to apologize to Sodom and Gomorrah."

Ruth Graham

Isaiah 23

Matthew Henry's introduction

In this chapter is foretold,

I. The lamentable desolation of Tyre, which

was performed by Nebuchadnezzar and the Chaldean army, about the time that they destroyed Jerusalem; and a hard task they had of it, as appears Ezek. 29:18, where they are said to have "served a hard service against Tyre," and yet to have no wages, vv. 1–14.

II. The restoration of Tyre after seventy years, and the return of the Tyrians out of their captivity to their trade again, vv. 15–18.

A detailed analysis of chapter

The overthrow of Tyre. (1–14)

It is established again. (15–18)

Key verse

Verse 1: "The burden of Tyre. Howl, ye ships of Tarshish; for it is laid waste, so that there is no house, no entering in: from the land of Chittim it is revealed to them."

Key word / key phrase

Verse 1, "Tyre is destroyed."

Key event / key person / key theme

Prophecies against Tyre

Key thought

God is the God of the nations and in charge of their rise and fall.

Key thing to look out for

The timing of events in history is in the Lord's hands.

Key Bible cross-reference

Verses 1–18. See Luke 10:13,14.

Key "by way of explanation"

Verse 15, "seventy years." This was also the length of the exile in Babylon, Jeremiah 25:11; 29:10.

Key "Quotable Quote"

"The judgments of God are like thunderclaps. Punishment to one, terror to all."

John Boys

Isaiah 24

Matthew Henry's introduction

In this chapter we have,

I. A threatening of desolating judgments for sin (vv. 1–12), to which is added an assurance that in the midst of them good people should be comforted, vv. 13–15.

II. A further threatening of the like desolations (vv. 16–22), to which is added an assurance that in the midst of all God should be glorified.

A detailed analysis of chapter

The desolation of the land. (1–12)

A few will be preserved. (13–15)

God's kingdom advanced by his judgments. (16–23)

Key verse

Verse 5: "The earth also is defiled under the inhabitants thereof; because they have transgressed the laws, changed the ordinance, broken the everlasting covenant."

Key word / key phrase

Verse 3, "completely laid waste."

Key event / key person / key theme

Warning about coming judgment

Key thought

The images in the Bible about God's judgment all combine to tell us to take it seriously.

Key thing to look out for

Some of the reasons for God's judgments are clearly set out in this chapter.

Key Bible cross-reference

Verse 16. See Jeremiah 9:2.

Key "by way of explanation"

Verse 2. When God's judgment comes all sections of society will be judged.

Key "Quotable Quote"

"Learn from examples in history lest thou be made an example."

John Boys

Isaiah 25

Matthew Henry's introduction

We have here,

I. Thankful praises for what God had done, which the prophet, in the name of the church, offers up to God, and teaches us to offer the like, vv. 1–5.

II. Precious promises of what God would yet further do for his church, especially in the grace of the gospel, vv. 6–8.

III. The church's triumph in God over her enemies thereon, vv. 9–12.

A detailed analysis of chapter

A song of praise. (1–5)

A declaration of the gospel blessings. (6–8)

The destruction of the enemies of God's people. (9–12)

Key verse

Verse 6: "And in this mountain shall the LORD of hosts make unto all people a feast of fat things, a feast of wines on the lees, of fat things full of marrow, of wines on the lees well refined."

Key word / key phrase

Verse 1, "I will exult you."

Key event / key person / key theme

Praise for kingdom blessings

Key thought

A terrifying chapter about God's judgment is followed by an exhilarating chapter in praise of God.

Key thing to look out for

Notice how often it is stated that people are brought down because of their pride.

Key Bible cross-reference

Verse 8. See Revelation 7:17; 21:4.

Key "by way of explanation"

Verse 8, "swallow up death." Paul quotes part of this verse in 1 Corinthians 15:4. Death has now itself been swallowed up, thanks to Jesus' resurrection.

Key "Quotable Quote"

"The Immortal put on mortality in order to die for us, and by his death to slay the death of us all."

Augustine of Hippo

Isaiah 26

Matthew Henry's introduction

The people of God are here taught,

I. To triumph in the safety and holy security both of the church in general and of every particular member of it, under the divine protection, vv. 1–4.

II. To triumph over all opposing powers, vv. 5, 6.

III. To walk with God, and wait for him, in the worst and darkest times, vv. 7–9.

IV. To lament the stupidity of those who regarded not the providence of God, either merciful or afflictive, vv. 10, 11.

V. To encourage themselves, and one another, with hopes that God would still continue to do them good (vv. 12, 14), and engage themselves to continue in his service, v. 13.

VI. To recollect the kind providences of God towards them in their low and distressed condition, and their conduct under those providences, vv. 15–18.

VII. To rejoice in hope of a glorious deliverance, which should be as a resurrection to them (v. 19), and to retire in the expectation of it, vv. 20, 21.

A detailed analysis of chapter

The divine mercies encourage confidence in God. (1–4)

His judgments. (5–11)

His people exhorted to wait on him. (12–19)

Deliverance promised. (20, 21)

Key verse

Verse 4: "Trust ye in the LORD for ever: for in the LORD JEHOVAH is everlasting strength."

Key word / key phrase

Verse 1, "this song will be sung."

Key event / key person / key theme

Israel's song of salvation

Key thought

Only the Lord can establish peace.

Key thing to look out for

The many reasons for praising the Lord

Key Bible cross-reference

Verse 11. See Hebrews 10:27.

Key "by way of explanation"

Verse 19, "your dead will live." This was a reference to the restoration of Israel. For Christians it reminds us about the resurrection of the body.

Key "Quotable Quote"

"If a man does not say in his heart, 'In the world there is only myself and God,' he will not gain peace."

Abba Alonius

Isaiah 27

Matthew Henry's introduction

I. What great things God would do for his church and people, which should now shortly be accomplished in the deliverance of Jerusalem from Sennacherib and the destruction of the Assyrian army; but it is expressed generally, for the encouragement of the church in after ages, with reference to the power and prevalence of her enemies.
   A. That proud oppressors should be reckoned with, v. 1.
   B. That care should be taken of the church, as of God's vineyard, vv. 2, 3.
   C. That God would let fall his controversy with the people, on their return to him, vv. 4, 5.
   D. That he would greatly multiply and increase them, v. 6.
   E. That, as to their afflictions, the property of them should be altered (v. 7), they should be mitigated and moderated (v. 8), and sanctified, v. 9.
   F. That though the church might be laid waste, and made desolate, for a time (vv. 10, 11), yet it should be restored, and the scattered members should be gathered together again, vv. 12, 13.

A detailed analysis of chapter

God's care for his people. (1–5)
Judgment followed by redemption. (6–13)

Key verse

Verse 2: "In that day sing ye unto her, A vineyard of red wine."

Key word / key phrase

Verse 2, "a fruitful vineyard."

Key event / key person / key theme

Probably the destruction of the northern kingdom of Israel

Key thought

God's tender care of his vineyard

Key thing to look out for

Fruitfulness can only be achieved by abiding in the true Vine (John 15:1–16).

Key Bible cross-reference

Verse 1. See Job 41:1.

Key "by way of explanation"

Verse 13, "trumpet will sound." Trumpets were used to call soldiers to fight and often refer to God's judgment.

Key "Quotable Quote"

"We get no deeper into Christ than we allow him to get into us."

J.H. Jowett

Isaiah 28

Matthew Henry's introduction

In this chapter,

I. The Ephraimites are reproved and threatened for their pride and drunkenness, their security and sensuality, vv. 1–8. But, in the midst of this, here is a gracious promise of God's favor to the remnant of his people, vv. 5, 6.

II. They are likewise reproved and threatened for their dullness and stupidity, and inability to profit by the instructions which the prophets gave them in God's name, vv. 9–13.

III. The rulers of Jerusalem are reproved and threatened for their insolent contempt of God's judgments, and setting them at defiance; and, after a gracious promise of Christ and his grace, they are made to know that the vain hopes of escaping the judgments of God with which they flattered themselves would certainly deceive them, vv. 14–22.

IV. All this is confirmed by a comparison borrowed from the method which the husbandman takes with his ground and grain, according to which they must expect God would proceed with his people, whom he had lately called his threshing and the corn of his floor (21:10) vv. 23–29.

A detailed analysis of chapter

The desolations of Samaria, capital of the northern kingdom. (1–13)
Rebuke to the northern kingdom. (14–15)
Christ is pointed out as the sure Foundation for all believers. (16–22)
God's dealings with his people. (23–29)

Key verse

Verse 1: "Woe to the crown of pride, to the drunkards of Ephraim, whose glorious beauty is a fading flower, which are on the head of the fat valleys of them that are overcome with wine!"

Key word / key phrase

Verse 1, "the pride of Ephraim."

Key event / key person / key theme

The folly of refusing to take God seriously

Key thought

A cornerstone for Zion is promised.

Key thing to look out for

Concluding verses containing God's wisdom.

Key Bible cross-reference

Verse 16. See 1 Peter 2:6.

Key "by way of explanation"

Verse 7, "wine . . . beer." The prophets were too drunk to receive God's messages.

Key "Quotable Quote"

"Anything which increases the authority of the body over the mind is an evil thing."

Susannah Wesley, letter to her son John

Isaiah 29

Matthew Henry's introduction

Here is,

I. The event itself foretold, that Jerusalem should be greatly distressed, vv. 1–4, 6), but that their enemies, who distressed them, should be baffled and defeated, vv. 5, 7, 8.

II. A reproof to three sorts of sinners:

A. Those that were stupid, and regardless of the warnings which the prophet gave them, vv. 9–12.

B. Those that were formal and hypocritical in their religious performances, vv. 13, 14.

C. Those politicians that atheistically and profanely despised God's providence, and set up their own projects in competition with it, vv. 15, 16.

III. Precious promises of grace and mercy to a distinguished remnant whom God would sanctify, and in whom he would be sanctified, when their enemies and persecutors should be cut off, vv. 17–24.

A detailed analysis of chapter

Judgments on Jerusalem and on its enemies. (1–8)

The senselessness and hypocrisy of the prophets. (9–12)

God will bring about his plans. (13–24)

Key verse

Verse 9: "Stay yourselves, and wonder; cry ye out, and cry: they are drunken, but not with wine; they stagger, but not with strong drink."

Key word / key phrase

Verse 1, "the city where David settled."

Key event / key person / key theme

Jerusalem is warned

Key thought

The siege of Jerusalem is prophesied.

Key thing to look out for

The Lord hates hypocrisy and exposes it.

Key Bible cross-reference

Verse 10. See Romans 11:8.

Key "by way of explanation"

Verse 13. Jesus quotes from this verse to highlight the hypocrisy of the Pharisees.

Key "Quotable Quote"

"The knowledge of God, and the remembrance of his all-seeing presence, are the most powerful means against hypocrisy."

Richard Baxter

Isaiah 30

Matthew Henry's introduction

Here is,

I. A just reproof to those who, in that distress, trusted to the Egyptians for help, and were all in a hurry to fetch succors from Egypt, vv. 1–7.

II. A terrible threatening against those who slighted the good advice which God by his prophets gave them for the repose of their minds in that distress, assuring them that whatever became of others the judgment would certainly overtake them, vv. 8–17.

III. A gracious promise to those who trusted in God, that they should not only see through the trouble, but should see happy days after it, times of joy and reformation, plenty of the means of grace, and therewith plenty of outward good things and increasing joys and triumphs (vv. 18–26), and many of these promises are very applicable to gospel grace.

IV. A prophecy of the total rout and ruin of the Assyrian army, which should be an occasion of great joy and an introduction to those happy times, vv. 27–33.

A detailed analysis of chapter

The Jews reproved for seeking help from Egypt. (1–7)

Judgments as a result of their contempt of God's word. (8–18)

God's mercies to his people. (19–26)

The ruin of the Assyrian army, and of all God's enemies. (27–33)

Key verse

Verse 8: "Now go, write it before them in a table, and note it in a book, that it may be for the time to come for ever and ever."

Key word / key phrase

Verse 1, "obstinate children."

Key event / key person / key theme

The obstinate are warned

Key thought

God's mercies are highlighted, even though his followers disobey him.

Key thing to look out for

To reject the Lord, verse 15, is to miss out on his wonderful blessings.

Key Bible cross-reference

Verse 6. See Revelation 12:3.

Key "by way of explanation"

Verse 20, "bread of adversity . . . water of affliction." This refers to the bread and water diet of prison. The oracles in this chapter relate to the time when Hezekiah rebelled against Assyria.

Key "Quotable Quote"

"Man calls it an accident, God calls it abomination.
Man calls it a defect, God calls it a disease.
Man calls it an error, God calls it an enmity.
Man calls it a liberty, God calls it lawlessness.
Man calls it a trifle, God calls it a tragedy.
Man calls it a mistake, God calls it a madness.
Man calls it a weakness, God calls it willfulness."

Author unknown

Isaiah 31

Matthew Henry's introduction

Here is,

I. A woe to those who, when the Assyrian army invaded them, trusted to the Egyptians, and not to God, for succor, vv. 1–3.

II. Assurance given of the care God would take of Jerusalem in that time of danger and distress, vv. 4, 5.

III. A call to repentance and reformation, vv. 6, 7.

IV. A prediction of the fall of the Assyrian army, and the fright which the Assyrian king should thereby be put into, vv. 8, 9.

A detailed analysis of chapter

The sin and folly of seeking help from Egypt. (1–5)

God's care for Jerusalem. (6–9)

Key verse

Verse 1: "Woe to them that go down to Egypt for help; and stay on horses, and trust in chariots, because they are many; and in horsemen, because they are very strong; but they look not unto the Holy One of Israel, neither seek the LORD!"

Key word / key phrase
Verse 1, "those who go down to Egypt."

Key event / key person / key theme
Warning against an Egyptian alliance

Key thought
The folly of seeking help from the wrong people.

Key thing to look out for
God's great care for Jerusalem is like a protective shield.

Key Bible cross-reference
Verse 2. See Proverbs 22:23.

Key "by way of explanation"
Verse 9, "fire . . . furnace." God's judgment will be like fire when it falls on people.
Nineveh was destroyed by Babylon in 612 BC.

Key "Quotable Quote"
"Let us not underestimate how hard it is to be compassionate."
Henri Nouwen

Isaiah 32

Matthew Henry's introduction
Here is,

I. A prophecy of that good work of reformation with which he should begin his reign, and the happy influence it should have on the people, who had been wretchedly corrupted and debauched in the reign of his predecessor, vv. 1–8.

II. A prophecy of the great disturbance that would be given to the kingdom in the middle of his reign by the Assyrian invasion, vv. 9–14.

III. A promise of better times afterwards, towards the latter end of his reign, in respect both of piety and peace (vv. 15–20), which promise may be supposed to look as far forward as the days of the Messiah.

A detailed analysis of chapter
Times of peace and happiness. (1–8)
An interval of trouble, yet comfort and blessings in the end. (9–20)

Key verse
Verse 4: "The heart also of the rash shall understand knowledge, and the tongue of the stammerers shall be ready to speak plainly."

Key word / key phrase
Verse 1, "A king will reign."

Key event / key person / key theme
The King is coming

Key thought
Complacency is severely rebuked.

Key thing to look out for
Verses 17–20, the fruit of righteousness

Key Bible cross-reference
Verse 11. See Jeremiah 17:8.

Key "by way of explanation"

Verses 5–8. These verses are similar to the wisdom literature of the Bible where comparisons between the wise and the foolish are constantly made. See Proverbs 9:13–18.

Key "Quotable Quote"

"Complacency is a deadly foe of all spiritual growth."

A.W. Tozer

Isaiah 33

Matthew Henry's introduction

Observe,

I. The great distress that Judah and Jerusalem should then be brought into, vv. 7–9.

II. The particular frights which the sinners in Zion should then be in, vv. 13, 14.

III. The prayers of good people to God in this distress, v. 2.

IV. The holy security which they should enjoy in the midst of this trouble, vv. 15, 16.

V. The destruction of the army of the Assyrians (vv. 1–3), in which God would be greatly glorified, vv. 5, 10–12.

VI. The enriching of the Jews with the spoil the Assyrian camp, vv. 4, 23, 24.

VII. The happy settlement of Jerusalem, and the Jewish state, on this. Religion shall be uppermost (v. 6), and their civil state shall flourish, vv. 17–22.

A detailed analysis of chapter

God's judgments against the enemies of his people. (1–14)

The happiness of his people. (15–24)

Key verse

Verse 2: "O LORD, be gracious unto us; we have waited for thee: be thou their arm every morning, our salvation also in the time of trouble."

Key word / key phrase

Verse 5, "the Lord is exalted."

Key event / key person / key theme

A hymn of thanksgiving

Key thought

The promise for a wonderful future is given.

Key thing to look out for

No matter what circumstances we face, the Lord can be our strength each morning.

Key Bible cross-reference

Verse 18. See Matthew 5:46.

Key "by way of explanation"

Verse 23, "rigging." The picture here is of Jerusalem as a warship.

Key "Quotable Quote"

"To be in Christ is the source of the Christian's life; to be like Christ is the sum of his excellence; to be with Christ is the fullness of his joy."

Charles Hodge

Isaiah 34

Matthew Henry's introduction

Here is,

I. A demand of universal attention, v. 1.

II. A direful scene of blood and confusion presented, vv. 2–7.
III. The reason given for these judgments, v. 8.
IV. The continuance of this desolation, the country being made like the lake of Sodom (vv. 9, 10), and the cities abandoned to wild beasts and melancholy fowls, vv. 11–15.
V. The solemn ratification of all this, vv. 16, 17.

A detailed analysis of chapter

God's vengeance against the enemies of his people. (1–8)

Their desolation. (9–17)

Key verse

Verse 9: "And the streams thereof shall be turned into pitch, and the dust thereof into brimstone, and the land thereof shall become burning pitch."

Key word / key phrase

Verse 1, "pay attention, you peoples!"

Key event / key person / key theme

A warning to the nations: Edom, Israel's long-time enemy, represents all his enemies.

Key thought

God's enemies will never ultimately escape from God's punishment.

Key thing to look out for

Contemplating God's judgment is a terrifying spectacle.

Key Bible cross-reference

Verse 4. See Mark 13:25.

Key "by way of explanation"

Verse 11, "desert owl." These are the birds you would expect to find in deserted cities and among ruins.

Key "Quotable Quote"

"No man is condemned for anything he has done: he is condemned for continuing to do wrong. He is condemned for not coming out of the darkness, for not coming to the light."

George MacDonald

Isaiah 35

Matthew Henry's introduction

I. The Gentiles shall be brought into it, vv. 1, 2, 7.
II. The well-wishers to it, who were weak and timorous, shall be encouraged, vv. 3, 4.
III. Miracles shall be wrought both on the souls and on the bodies of men, vv. 5, 6.
IV. The gospel church shall be conducted in the way of holiness, vv. 8, 9.
V. It shall be brought at last to endless joys, v. 10.

A detailed analysis of chapter

The ultimate joy and peace of the people of God. (1–4)

The privileges of his people. (5–10)

Key verse

Verse 5: "Then the eyes of the blind shall be opened, and the ears of the deaf shall be unstopped."

Key word / key phrase

Verse 2, "burst into bloom."

Key event / key person / key theme

The promise of restoration and transformation

Key thought

Any blossoming flower can remind us that God is victorious.

Key thing to look out for

The joy a Christian experiences is for now and for eternity.

Key Bible cross-reference

Verse 3. See Hebrews 12:12.

Key "by way of explanation"

Verse 9, "ferocious beast." Prowling wild animals, such as lions, made all travel dangerous.

Key "Quotable Quote"

"A joyless life is not a Christian life, for joy is one constant in the recipe for Christian living."

William Barclay

Isaiah 36

Matthew Henry's introduction

In this chapter we have,

I. The descent which the king of Assyria made on Judah, and his success against all the defended cities, v. 1.

II. The conversation he desired to have with Hezekiah, and the managers on both sides, vv. 2, 3.

III. Rabshakeh's railing blasphemous speech, with which he designed to frighten Hezekiah into a submission, and persuade him to surrender at discretion, vv. 4–10.

IV. His appeal to the people, and his attempt to persuade them to desert Hezekiah, and so force him to surrender, vv. 11–20.

V. The report of this made to Hezekiah by his agents, vv. 21, 22.

Isaiah 37

Matthew Henry's introduction

Here we have,

I. Hezekiah's pious reception of Rabshakeh's impious discourse, v. 1.

II. The gracious message he sent to Isaiah to desire his prayers, vv. 2–5.

III. The encouraging answer which Isaiah sent to him from God, assuring him that God would plead his cause against the king of Assyria, vv. 6, 7.

IV. An abusive letter which the king of Assyria sent to Hezekiah, to the same purport with Rabshakeh's speech, vv. 8–13.

V. Hezekiah's humble prayer to God on the receipt of this letter, vv. 14–20.

VI. The further full answer which God sent him by Isaiah, promising him that his affairs should shortly take a happy turn, that the storm should blow over and every thing should appear bright and serene, vv. 21–35.

VII. The immediate accomplishment of this prophecy in the ruin of his army (v. 36) and the murder of himself, vv. 37, 38.

Isaiah 38

Matthew Henry's introduction

This chapter proceeds in the history of Hezekiah. Here is,

I. His sickness, and the sentence of death he received within himself, v. 1.

II. His prayer in his sickness, vv. 2, 3.

III. The answer of peace which God gave to that prayer, assuring him that he should recover, that he should live fifteen years yet, that Jerusalem should be delivered from the king of Assyria, and that, for a sign to confirm his faith herein, the sun should go back ten degrees, vv. 4–8. And this we read and opened before, 2 Kings 20:1, etc. But,

IV. Here is Hezekiah's thanksgiving for his recovery, which we had not before, vv. 9–20. To which are added the means used (v. 21), and the end the good man aimed at in desiring to recover, v. 22.

Isaiah 39

Matthew Henry's introduction

We have here,

I. The pride and folly of Hezekiah, in showing his treasures to the king of Babylon's ambassadors that were sent to congratulate him on his recovery, vv. 1, 2.

II. Isaiah's examination of him about it, in God's name, and his confession of it, vv. 3, 4.

III. The sentence passed on him for it, that all his treasures should, in process of time, be carried to Babylon, vv. 5–7.

IV. Hezekiah's penitent and patient submission to this sentence, v. 8.

(Isaiah chapters 36, 37, 38, 39 are almost identical with 2 Kings 18:13–20:19.)

Isaiah 40

Matthew Henry's introduction

In this chapter we have,

I. Orders given to preach and publish the glad tidings of redemption, vv. 1, 2.

II. These glad tidings introduced by a voice in the wilderness, which gives assurance that all obstructions shall be removed (vv. 3–5), and that, though all creatures fail and fade, the word of God shall be established and accomplished, vv. 5–8.

III. A joyful prospect given to the people of God of the happiness which this redemption should bring along with it, vv. 9–11.

IV. The sovereignty and power of that God magnified who undertakes to work out this redemption, vv. 12–17.

V. Idols therefore triumphed over and idolaters upbraided with their folly, vv. 18–26.

VI. A reproof given to the people of God for their fears and despondencies, and enough said, in a few words, to silence these fears, vv. 27–31.

A detailed analysis of chapter

The preaching of the gospel, and good news of the coming of Christ. (1–11)

The almighty power of God. (12–17)

The folly of idolatry. (18–31)

Key verse

Verse 1: "Comfort ye, comfort ye my people, saith your God."

Key word / key phrase

Verse 2, "speak tenderly."

Key event / key person / key theme

Comfort because of Israel's deliverance

Key thought

This chapter contains some of the most glorious words of hope found in the Bible.

Key thing to look out for

Israel's God cannot be compared with any other so-called "gods."

Key Bible cross-reference

Verse 3. See Matthew 3:3.

Key "by way of explanation"

Verse 3, "voice." Each "voice" mentioned, verses 3, 6, 9, brings a message of comfort.

Key "Quotable Quote"

"If you wish to leave much wealth to your children, leave them in God's care."

John Chrysostom

Isaiah 41

Matthew Henry's introduction

Here,

I. God by the prophet shows the folly of those that worshipped idols, especially that thought their idols able to contest with him and control him, vv. 1–9.

II. He encourages his faithful ones to trust in him, with an assurance that he would take their part against their enemies, make them victorious over them, and bring about a happy change of their affairs, vv. 10–20.

III. He challenges the idols, that were rivals with him for men's adoration, to vie with him either for knowledge or power, either to show things to come or to do good or evil, vv. 21–29.

A detailed analysis of chapter

God's care of his people. (1–9)

They are encouraged not to fear. (10–20)

The vanity and folly of idolatry. (21–29)

Key verse

Verse 1: "Keep silence before me, O islands; and let the people renew their strength: let them come near; then let them speak: let us come near together to judgment."

Key word / key phrase

Verse 4, "with the first of them and with the last."

Key event / key person / key theme

God's supremacy

Key thought

God is in control of world events.

Key thing to look out for

It is God himself who promises to help his followers.

Key Bible cross-reference

Verse 8. See 2 Chronicles 20:7.

Key "by way of explanation"

Verse 14, "worm." This describes the desperate and despised state of the exiles in Babylon.

Key "Quotable Quote"

"God is always present, always available."

Jacques Ellul

Isaiah 42

Matthew Henry's introduction

Here is,

I. A prophecy of the Messiah's coming with meekness, and yet with power, to do the Redeemer's work, vv. 1–4.

II. His commission opened, which he received from the Father, vv. 5–9.

III. The joy and rejoicing with which the glad tidings of this should be received, vv. 10–12.

IV. The wonderful success of the gospel, for the overthrow of the devil's kingdom, vv. 13–17.

V. The rejection and ruin of the Jews for their unbelief, vv. 18–25.

A detailed analysis of chapter

The character and coming of Christ. (1–4)
The blessings of his kingdom. (5–12)
The prevalence of true religion. (13–17)
Unbelief and blindness reproved. (18–25)

Key verse

Verse 1: "Behold my servant, whom I uphold; mine elect, in whom my soul delighteth; I have put my spirit upon him: he shall bring forth judgment to the Gentiles."

Key word / key phrase

Verse 1, "my servant."

Key event / key person / key theme

Comfort because of God's Servant

Key thought

God's promises provide help in a multitude of different ways.

Key thing to look out for

Singing God's praises revitalizes us spiritually.

Key Bible cross-reference

Verse 1. See Matthew 3:17.

Key "by way of explanation"

Verse 14, "for a long time." The seventy-year long exile seemed to be a time when God's people were cut off from him, being away from their city and temple.

Key "Quotable Quote"

"When your heart is full of Christ, you want to sing."

C.H. Spurgeon

Isaiah 43

Matthew Henry's introduction

Here are,

I. Precious promises made to God's people in their affliction, of his presence with them, for their support under it, and their deliverance out of it, vv. 1–7.

II. A challenge to idols to vie with the omniscience and omnipotence of God, vv. 8–13.

III. Encouragement given to the people of God to hope for their deliverance out of Babylon, from the consideration of what God did for their fathers when he brought them out of Egypt, vv. 14–21.

IV. A method taken to prepare the people for their deliverance, by putting them in mind of their sins, by which they had provoked God to send them into captivity and continue them there, that they might repent and seek to God for pardoning mercy, vv. 22–28.

A detailed analysis of chapter

God's unchangeable love for his people. (1–7)
Apostates and idolaters addressed. (8–13)
The deliverance from Babylon, and the conversion of the Gentiles. (14–21)
Admonition to repent of sin. (22–28)

Key verse

Verse 1: "But now thus saith the LORD that created thee, O Jacob, and he that formed thee, O Israel, Fear not: for I have redeemed thee, I have called thee by thy name; thou art mine."

Key word / key phrase

Verse 1, "I have redeemed you."

Key event / key person / key theme

The promise of release

Key thought

Israel never forget the way God had rescued them from Egypt.

Key thing to look out for

The force of the argument is: If God so acted in the past, will you not trust him for the present?

Key Bible cross-reference

Verse 28. See Nehemiah 13:18.

Key "by way of explanation"

Verse 2, "pass through the waters." God's people knew that it was only God's power and presence that had enabled them to cross over the water out of Egypt.

Key "Quotable Quote"

"Jesus saves: indeed, but that means not only saving your soul out of the shipwreck of this world! His saving grace redeems us here and now. He is able to redeem us, really and truly, not just 'spiritually' in a narrow sense."

H.R. Rookmaaker

Isaiah 44

Matthew Henry's introduction

God, by the prophet, goes on in this chapter, as before,

I. To encourage his people with the assurance of great blessings he had in store for them at their return out of captivity, and those typical of much greater which the gospel church, his spiritual Israel, should partake of in the days of the Messiah; and hereby he proves himself to be God alone against all pretenders, vv. 1–8.

II. To expose the sottishness and amazing folly of idol-makers and idolworshippers, vv. 9–20.

III. To ratify and confirm the assurances he had given to his people of those great blessings, and to raise their joyful and believing expectations of them, vv. 21–28.

A detailed analysis of chapter

Here are promises of the influences of the Holy Spirit. (1–8)

An exposure of the folly of idolatry. (9–20)

Also the deliverance of God's people. (21–28)

Key verse

Verse 6: "Thus saith the LORD the King of Israel, and his redeemer the LORD of hosts; I am the first, and I am the last; and beside me there is no God."

Key word / key phrase

Verse 9, "All who make idols."

Key event / key person / key theme

The absurdity of idolatry

Key thought

Jacob was a cheat. But God chose to bless him. From sheer grace every Christian is called by God.

Key thing to look out for

Our God is both the Creator of the world and our personal Savior.

Key Bible cross-reference

Verse 6. See Revelation 22:13.

Key "by way of explanation"

Verse 2, "formed you in the womb," shows how much the Lord cared for us, even before we were born.

Key "Quotable Quote"

"We are a long time in learning that all our strength and salvation is in God."

David Brainerd

Isaiah 45

Matthew Henry's introduction

We have here,

I. The great things which God would do for Cyrus, that he might be put into a capacity to release God's people, vv. 1–4.

II. The proof God would hereby give of his eternal power and godhead, and his universal, incontestable, sovereignty, vv. 5–7.

III. A prayer for the hastening of this deliverance, v. 8.

IV. A check to the unbelieving Jews, who quarreled with God for the lengthening out of their captivity, vv. 9, 10.

V. Encouragement given to the believing Jews, who trusted in God and continued instant in prayer, assuring them that God would in due time accomplish this work by the hand of Cyrus, vv. 11–15.

VI. A challenge given to the worshippers of idols and their doom read, and satisfaction given to the worshippers of the true God and their comfort secured, with an eye to the Mediator, who is made of God to us both righteousness and sanctification, vv. 16–25.

A detailed analysis of chapter

An oracle addressed to Cyrus, God's anointed. (1–7)

God calls for obedience to his almighty power. (8–10)

The settlement of his people. (11–19)

The conversion of the Gentiles. (20–25)

Key verse

Verse 1: "Thus saith the LORD to his anointed, to Cyrus, whose right hand I have holden, to subdue nations before him."

Key word / key phrase

Verse 1, "Cyrus."

Key event / key person / key theme

Cyrus, a pagan emperor, was used to bring about God's plans.

Key thought

The all-powerful God will fulfill his purposes in his way.

Key thing to look out for

The Lord God is our Creator God as well as the Lord of history.

Key Bible cross-reference

Verse 9. See Romans 9:20.

Key "by way of explanation"

Cyrus, the founder of the Persian Empire, captured Babylon in October 539 BC. In the first year of his reign he issued a decree permitting the exiles to return to Jerusalem. He authorized the rebuilding of the temple.

Key "Quotable Quote"

"God has no need of his creatures, but everything created has need of him."

Meister Eckhart

Isaiah 46

Matthew Henry's introduction

I. Let them not be afraid of the idols of Babylon, as if they could in any way obstruct their deliverance, for they should be defaced (vv. 1, 2); but let them trust in that God who had often delivered them to do it still, to do it now, vv. 3, 4.

II. Let them not think to make idols of their own, images of the God of Israel, by them to worship him, as the Babylonians worship their gods, vv. 5–7. Let them not be so sottish (v. 8), but have an eye to God in his word, not in an image; let them depend on that, and on the promises and predictions of it, and God's power to accomplish them all, vv. 9–11. And let them know that the unbelief of man shall not make the word of God of no effect, vv. 12, 13.

A detailed analysis of chapter

The idols could not save themselves, but God saves his people. (1–4)

The folly of worshiping idols. (5–13)

Key verse

Verse 5: "To whom will ye liken me, and make me equal, and compare me, that we may be like?"

Key word / key phrase

Verse 1, "Bel . . . Nebo."

Key event / key person / key theme

Destruction of Babylon's idols

Key thought

God's message to an idol-infested society is: "I alone am God."

Key thing to look out for

The other side of the coin of salvation and forgiveness is judgment and God's wrath.

Key Bible cross-reference

Verse 12. See Proverbs 29:1.

Key "by way of explanation"

Verse 11, "bird of prey." Cyrus, like a bird of prey, was characterized by power and swift action.

Key "Quotable Quote"

"Love can forbear, and Love can forgive but Love can never be reconciled to an unlovely object."

Thomas Traherne

Isaiah 47

Matthew Henry's introduction

In this chapter we have,

I. The greatness of the ruin threatened, that Babylon should be brought down to the dust, and made completely miserable, should fall from the height of prosperity into the depth of adversity, vv. 1–5.

II. The sins that provoked God to bring this ruin on them.

A. Their cruelty to the people of God, v. 6.

B. Their pride and carnal security, vv. 7–9.

C. Their confidence in themselves and contempt of God, v. 10.

D. Their use of magic arts and their dependence on enchantments and sorceries, which should be so far from standing them in any stead that they should but hasten their ruin, vv. 11–15.

A detailed analysis of chapter

God's judgments on Babylon. (1–6)

Carelessness and confidence shall not prevent the evil. (7–15)

Key verse

Verse 4: "As for our redeemer, the Lord of hosts is his name, the Holy One of Israel."

Key word / key phrase

Verse 1, "Sit in the dust."

Key event / key person / key theme

Destruction of Babylon

Key thought

God may stay his hand, but when his judgment does come it is decisive.

Key thing to look out for

The way of darkness and sorcery is certain to lead to death.

Key Bible cross-reference

Verses 8, 9. See Revelation 18:7, 8.

Key "by way of explanation"

Verse 7, "I will continue forever." Many cruel dictators have echoed such words, including Nebuchadnezzar, Daniel 4:30.

Key "Quotable Quote"

"Arrogance has its own built-in misery. The arrogant person may offend others, but he hurts himself more."

Billy Graham

Isaiah 48

Matthew Henry's introduction

I. He charges them with hypocrisy in that which is good and obstinacy in that which is evil, especially in their idolatry, notwithstanding the many convincing proofs God had given them that he is God alone, vv. 1–8.

II. He assures them that their deliverance would be wrought purely for the sake of God's own name and not for any merit of theirs, vv. 9–11.

III. He encourages them to depend purely on God's power and promise for this deliverance, vv. 12–15.

IV. He shows them that, as it was by their own sin that they brought themselves into captivity, so it would be only by the grace of God that they would obtain the necessary preparations for their enlargement, vv. 16–19.

V. He proclaims their release, yet with a proviso that the wicked shall have no benefit by it, vv. 20–22.

A detailed analysis of chapter

The Jews reproved for their idolatry. (1–8)

Yet their deliverance is promised. (9–15)

Solemn warnings of judgment on those who persisted in evil. (16–22)

Key verse

Verse 9: "For my name's sake will I defer mine anger, and for my praise will I refrain for thee, that I cut thee not off."

Key word / key phrase

Verse 4, "stubborn."

Key event / key person / key theme

Israel is stubborn

Key thought

God's love can melt the hardest of hearts.

Key thing to look out for

God's teaching, verse 17, will only be accepted when it is realized that it is all for our own good.

Key Bible cross-reference

Verse 12. See Revelation 1:17.

Key "by way of explanation"

Verse 13, "spread out the heavens" – one of Isaiah's ways of referring to God as the Creator. Isaiah was constantly returning to this theme.

Key "Quotable Quote"

"To see a World in a grain of sand,
And a Heaven in a wild flower,

Hold Infinity in the palm of your hand,
And Eternity in an hour."

William Blake

Isaiah 49

Matthew Henry's introduction

In this chapter we have,

I. The designation of Christ, under the type of Isaiah, to his office as Mediator, vv. 1–3.

II. The assurance given him of the success of his undertaking among the Gentiles, vv. 4–8.

III. The redemption that should be wrought by him, and the progress of that redemption, vv. 9–12.

IV. The encouragement given hence to the afflicted church, vv. 13–17.

V. The addition of many to it, and the setting up of a church among the Gentiles, vv. 18–23.

VI. A ratification of the prophecy of the Jews' release out of Babylon, which was to be the figure and type of all these blessings, vv. 24–26.

A detailed analysis of chapter

The unbelief and rejection of the people. (1–6)
Gracious promise to the Gentiles. (7–12)
God's love for his chosen people. (13–17)
Their increase. (18–23)
And deliverance. (24–26)

Key verse

Verse 1: "Listen, O isles, unto me; and hearken, ye people, from far; The LORD hath called me from the womb."

Key word / key phrase

Verse 6, "to restore."

Key event / key person / key theme

The Messiah's mission

Key thought

Isaiah remained conscious of his pre-natal election.

Key thing to look out for

Nothing and no one is beyond the Lord's restoration.

Key Bible cross-reference

Verse 1. See Jeremiah 1:5.

Key "by way of explanation"

Verse 2l, "polished arrow." Arrows depict God's judgment. See Deuteronomy 32:23,42. A "polished" arrow ensures sure and swift flight.

Key "Quotable Quote"

"He who undertakes anything without a divine call seeks his own glory."

D'Aubigne

Isaiah 50

Matthew Henry's introduction

In this chapter,

I. Those to whom God sends are justly charged with bringing all the troubles they were in on themselves, by their own willfulness and obstinacy, it being made to appear that God was able and ready to help them if they had been fit for deliverance, vv. 1–3.

II. He by whom God sends produces his commission (v. 4), alleges his own readiness to submit to all the services and sufferings he was called to in the execution of it (vv. 5, 6), and assures himself that God, who sent him, would stand by him and bear him out against all opposition, vv. 7–9.

III. The message that is sent is life and death, good and evil, the blessing and the curse, comfort to desponding saints and terror to presuming sinners, vv. 10, 11.

A detailed analysis of chapter

A temporary separation. (1–3)

The sufferings and exaltation of the Messiah. (4–9)

Consolation to the believer, and warning to the unbeliever. (10,11)

Key verse

Verse 4: "The Lord GOD hath given me the tongue of the learned, that I should know how to speak a word in season to him that is weary: he wakeneth morning by morning, he wakeneth mine ear to hear as the learned."

Key word / key phrase

Verse 10, "obeys."

Key event / key person / key theme

The Messiah's obedience

Key thought

Verse 10 gives a picture of abiding in the Lord.

Key thing to look out for

Obedience was one of the key characteristics of God's Servant.

Key Bible cross-reference

Verse 6. See Mark 14:65.

Key "by way of explanation"

Verse 5, "opened my ears." This symbolizes a person who obeys God because he follows what God has enabled him to hear.

Key "Quotable Quote"

"Remember to eat your bread, or your heart will wither away. Fill your soul with richness and strength."

Bernard of Clairvaux

Isaiah 51

Matthew Henry's introduction

Whenever the church of God is in distress her friends and well-wishers may comfort themselves and one another with these words,

I. That God, who raised his church at first out of nothing, will take care that it shall not perish, vv. 1–3.

II. That the righteousness and salvation he designs for his church are sure and near, very near and very sure, vv. 4–6.

III. That the persecutors of the church are weak and dying creatures, vv. 7, 8.

IV. That the same power which did wonders for the church formerly is now engaged and employed for her protection and deliverance, vv. 9–11.

V. That God himself, the Maker of the world, had undertaken both to deliver his people out of their distress and to comfort them under it, and sent his prophet to assure them of it, vv. 12–16.

VI. That, deplorable as the condition of the church now was (vv. 17–20), to the same woeful circumstances her persecutors and oppressors should shortly be reduced, and worse, vv. 21–23.

A detailed analysis of chapter

Exhortations to trust the Messiah. (1–3)

The power of God, and the weakness of man. (4–8)

Christ defends his people. (9–16)

Their afflictions and deliverances. (17–23)

Key verse

Verse 1: "Hearken to me, ye that follow after righteousness, ye that seek the LORD: look unto the rock whence ye are hewn, and to the hole of the pit whence ye are digged."

Key word / key phrase

Verse 3, "comfort Zion."

Key event / key person / key theme

The Messiah's encouragement to Israel

Key thought

All suffering will one day end.

Key thing to look out for

The salvation the Lord offers is everlasting salvation.

Key Bible cross-reference

Verse 17. See Revelation 14:10; 16:19.

Key "by way of explanation"

Verse 1, "rock." "Rock" usually refers to the Lord, especially in the psalms, but here it refers to Abraham, through whose faithfulness God's people were established.

Key "Quotable Quote"

"The Bible declares that the salvation of sinful men is a matter of grace."

Loraine Boettner

Isaiah 52

Matthew Henry's introduction

Observe,

I. The encouragement that is given to the Jews in captivity to hope that God would deliver them in his own way and time, vv. 1–6.

II. The great joy and rejoicing that shall be both with ministers and people on that occasion, vv. 7–10.

III. The call given to those that remained in captivity to shift for their own enlargement when liberty was proclaimed, vv. 11,12.

IV. A short idea given here of the Messiah, which is enlarged on in the next chapter, vv. 13–15.

A detailed analysis of chapter

The welcome news of Christ's kingdom. (1–12)

The humiliation of the Messiah. (13–15)

Key verse

Verse 7: "How beautiful upon the mountains are the feet of him that bringeth good tidings, that publisheth peace; that bringeth good tidings of good, that publisheth salvation; that saith unto Zion, Thy God reigneth!"

Key word / key phrase

Verse 10, "the salvation of our God."

Key event / key person / key theme

The Messiah's atonement

Key thought

God's rescue plan includes physical as well as spiritual blessings.

Key thing to look out for

God's people would have been surprised to learn that God's special Servant whould be a suffering Servant.

Key Bible cross-reference

Verse 5. See Romans 2:24.

Key "by way of explanation"

Verse 7, "the feet of those who bring good news." God's messengers, preachers, teachers, evangelists are not praised for having beautiful feet, but because of the wonderful message they carry.

Key "Quotable Quote"

"If Mark's is the Gospel of Christ the suffering Servant, and Luke's the Gospel of Christ the universal Savior, Matthew's is the Gospel of Christ the ruling King."

John R.W. Stott

Isaiah 53

Matthew Henry's introduction

This chapter is so replenished with the unsearchable riches of Christ that it may be called rather the gospel of the evangelist Isaiah than the pro-phecy of the prophet Isaiah. We may observe here,

I. The reproach of Christ's sufferings: the meanness of his appearance, the greatness of his grief, and the prejudices which many conceived in consequences against his doctrine, vv. 1–3.

II. The rolling away of this reproach, and the stamping of immortal honor on his sufferings, notwithstanding the disgrace and ignominy of them, by four considerations:–

A. That therein he did his Father's will, vv. 4, 6, 10.

B. That thereby he made atonement for the sin of man (vv. 4–6, 8, 11, 12), for it was not for any sin of his own that he suffered, v. 9.

C. That he bore his sufferings with an invincible and exemplary, v. 7.

D. That he should prosper in his undertaking, and his sufferings should end in his immortal honor, vv. 10–12. By mixing faith with the prophecy of this chapter we may improve our acquaintance with Jesus Christ and him crucified, with Jesus Christ and him glorified, dying for our sins and rising again for our justification.

A detailed analysis of chapter

The person. (1–3)

Sufferings. (4–9)

Humiliation, and exaltation of Christ, are described in detail; with the blessings to humankind from his death. (10–12)

Key verse

Verse 6: "All we like sheep have gone astray; we have turned every one to his own way; and the LORD hath laid on him the iniquity of us all."

Key word / key phrase

Verse 6, "laid on him."

Key event / key person / key theme

The Messiah's atonement

Key thought

Verse 6 is one of the clearest pictures of atonement in the Bible.

Key thing to look out for

No other chapter in Isaiah speaks so much about Jesus' crucifixion as this one.

Key Bible cross-reference

Verse 1. See John 12:38.

Key "by way of explanation"

Verse 6, "laid on him the iniquity." This pictures the priest laying his hands on the scapegoat, as God's people thought of their sins being taken away.

Key "Quotable Quote"

"We are also told in Isaiah 53 that Christ's death is to be vicarious."

D. Martyn Lloyd-Jones

Isaiah 54

Matthew Henry's introduction

It is here promised about the Christian church,

I. That, though the beginnings of it were small, it should be greatly enlarged by the accession of many to it among the Gentiles, who had been wholly destitute of church privileges, vv. 1–5.

II. That though sometimes God might seem to withdraw from her, and suspend the tokens of his favor, he would return in mercy and would not return to contend with them any more, vv. 6–10.

III. That, though for a while she was in sorrow and under oppression, she should at length be advanced to greater honor and splendor than ever, vv. 11, 12.

IV. That knowledge, righteousness, and peace, should flourish and prevail, vv. 13, 14.

V. That all attempts against the church should be baffled, and she should be secured from the malice of her enemies, vv. 14–17.

A detailed analysis of chapter

Jerusalem's future prosperity. (1–17)

Key verse

Verse 4: "Fear not; for thou shalt not be ashamed: neither be thou confounded; for thou shalt not be put to shame: for thou shalt forget the shame of thy youth, and shalt not remember the reproach of thy widowhood any more."

Key word / key phrase

Verse 2, "enlarge the place of your tent."

Key event / key person / key theme

The Messiah's promise of Israel's restoration

Key thought

God's love stretches out in front of us and will never end.

Key thing to look out for

Jerusalem is promised a wonderful future, as are God's followers.

Key Bible cross-reference

Verse 1. See Genesis 4:27.

Key "by way of explanation"

Verses 11,12. Jerusalem is pictured in a highly figurative and wonderful way, just as the new Jerusalem is in Revelation 21:10, 18–21.

Key "Quotable Quote"

"Christ is the desire of nations, the joy of angels, the delight of the Father. What solace then must that soul be filled with that hath the possession of him to all eternity!"

John Bunyan

Isaiah 55

Matthew Henry's introduction

Here is,

I. A free and gracious invitation to all to come and take the benefit of gospel grace, v. 1.

II. Pressing arguments to enforce this invitation, vv. 2–4.

III. A promise of the success of this invitation among the Gentiles, v. 5.

IV. An exhortation to repentance and reformation, with great encouragement given to hope for pardon thereon, vv. 6–9.

V. The ratification of all this, with the certain efficacy of the word of God, vv. 10, 11.

A detailed analysis of chapter

An invitation to receive freely the blessings of the Savior. (1–5)

Gracious offers of pardon and peace. (6–13)

Key verse

Verse 1: "Ho, every one that thirsteth, come ye to the waters, and he that hath no money; come ye, buy, and eat; yea, come, buy wine and milk without money and without price."

Key word / key phrase

Verse 1, "all."

Key event / key person / key theme

The Messiah's global invitation

Key thought

Salvation is all of grace. But this should not stop people seeking God.

Key thing to look out for

The Bible is full of descriptions of the joy of salvation, not just of warnings about God's judgment.

Key Bible cross-reference

Verse 1. See Revelation 21:6.

Key "by way of explanation"

Verse 2, "richest of fare." God's blessings are often likened to a feast in the Bible. See Jeremiah 31:14.

Key "Quotable Quote"

"If the pleasures of love can attract a man to a woman, if hunger and loneliness can make a man travel miles in search of food and shelter, how much more will the desire for truth and holiness make a man seek God."

Augustine of Hippo

Isaiah 56

Matthew Henry's introduction

We have here,

I. A solemn charge given to us all to make conscience of our duty, as we hope to have the benefit of those promises, vv. 1, 2.

II. Great encouragement given to strangers that were willing to come under the bonds of the covenant, assuring them of the blessings of the covenant, vv. 3–8.

III. A high charge drawn up against the watchmen of Israel, that were careless and unfaithful in the discharge of their duty (vv. 9–12).

A detailed analysis of chapter

A charge to keep the divine precepts. (1, 2)

Blessings promised. (3–8)

Reproof to the careless watchmen, the teachers and rulers of the Jews. (9–12)

Key verse

Verse 9: "All ye beasts of the field, come to devour, yea, all ye beasts in the forest."

Key word / key phrase

Verse 6, "worship him."

Key event / key person / key theme

The basis of worship

Key thought

God's promise of salvation includes those everyone else would exclude.

Key thing to look out for

Despite all God did his people were unfaithful to him.

Key Bible cross-reference

Verse 7. See Luke 19:46.

Key "by way of explanation"

Verse 4, "eunuchs" were considered to be ceremonially unclean. Yet the Lord promises to give them "an everlasting name."

Key "Quotable Quote"

"Seek not to explore the heights of the divine majesty, but to find salvation in the saving deeds of God our Savior."

William of St Thierry

Isaiah 57

Matthew Henry's introduction

The prophet, in this chapter, makes his observations,

I. On the deaths of good men, comforting those that were taken away in their integrity and reproving those that did not make a due improvement of such providences, vv. 1, 2.

II. On the gross idolatries and spiritual prostitution which the Jews were guilty of, and the destroying judgments they were thereby bringing on themselves, vv. 3–12.

III. On the gracious returns of God to his people to put an end to their captivity and re-establish their prosperity, vv. 13–21.

A detailed analysis of chapter

The blessed death of the righteous. (1,2)

The abominable idolatries of the Jewish nation. (3–12)

Promises to the humble and contrite. (13–21)

Key verse

Verse 2: "He shall enter into peace: they shall rest in their beds, each one walking in his uprightness."

Key word / key phrase

Verse 4, "a brood of rebels."

Key event / key person / key theme

The Messiah rebukes the wicked

Key thought

God's judgments are meant to be pondered in our hearts.

Key thing to look out for

God's many promises of help include healing.

Key Bible cross-reference

Verse 19. See Ephesians 2:17.

Key "by way of explanation"

Verse 9, "Molech," was the chief Ammonite "god."

Key "Quotable Quote"

"I have prayed hundreds, if not thousands, of times for the Lord to heal me – and he finally healed me of the need to be healed."

Tim Hansel

Isaiah 58

Matthew Henry's introduction

Observe,

I. The plausible profession of religion which they made, v. 2.

II. The boasts they made of that profession, and the blame they laid on God for taking no more notice of it, v. 3.

III. The sins they are charged with, which spoiled the acceptableness of their fasts, vv. 4, 5.

IV. Instructions given them how to keep fasts aright, vv. 6, 7.

V. Precious promises made to those who do so keep fasts, vv. 8–12.

VI. The like precious promises made to those that sanctify Sabbaths aright, vv. 13, 14.

A detailed analysis of chapter

Hypocrisy reproved. (1,2)

A counterfeit and a true fast, with promises to real godliness. (3–12)

The keeping of the Sabbath. (13,14)

Key verse

Verse 8: "Then shall thy light break forth as the morning, and thine health shall spring forth speedily: and thy righteousness shall go before thee; the glory of the LORD shall be thy reward."

Key word / key phrase

Verse 7, "share your food."

Key event / key person / key theme

The blessings of true worship

Key thought

If ever Christians need a chapter in the Bible to turn to about social action this is it.

Key thing to look out for

Doing God's will always results in joy.

Key Bible cross-reference

Verse 7. See Matthew 25:25.

Key "by way of explanation"

Verse 7, "provide . . . shelter" – helping the less well off is a sign of behaving in a righteous way.

Key "Quotable Quote"

"The loving service which God sends his people into the world to render includes both evangelism and social action, for each is in itself an authentic expression of love, and neither needs the other to justify it."

John R.W. Stott

Isaiah 59

Matthew Henry's introduction

I. It is here charged on this people that they had themselves stopped the current of God's favors to them, and the particular sins are specified which kept good things from them, vv. 1–8.

II. It is here charged on them that they had themselves procured the judgments of God on them, and they are told both what the judgments were which they had brought on their own heads (vv. 9–11) and what the sins were which provoked God to send those judgments, vv. 12–15.

III. It is here promised that, notwithstanding this, God would work deliverance for them, purely for his own name's sake (vv. 16–19), and would reserve mercy in store for them and entail it on them, vv. 20, 21.

A detailed analysis of chapter

Reproofs of sin and wickedness. (1–8)

Confession of sin, and lamentation for the consequences. (9–15)

Promises of deliverance. (16–21)

Key verse

Verse 1: "Behold, the LORD's hand is not shortened, that it cannot save; neither his ear heavy, that it cannot hear."

Key word / key phrase

Verse 2, "your iniquities."

Key event / key person / key theme

Israel's sins

Key thought

The seriousness of sin is explained in this chapter.

Key thing to look out for

The only way to deal with sin is to confess it to God.

Key Bible cross-reference

Verse 17. See 1 Thessalonians 5:8.

Key "by way of explanation"

Verse 17, "righteousness as his breastplate." We can only be righteous because of God's righteousness.

Key "Quotable Quote"

"The most important ingredient of righteousness is to render to God the service and homage due to him. He is shamefully cheated whenever we do not submit to his authority."

John Calvin

Isaiah 60

Matthew Henry's introduction

It is here promised,

I. That the church shall be enlightened and shone on, vv. 1, 2.

II. That it shall be enlarged and great additions made to it, to join in the service of God, vv. 3–8.

III. That the new converts shall be greatly serviceable to the church and to the interests of it, vv. 9–13.

IV. That the church shall be in great honor and reputation among men, vv. 14–16.

V. That it shall enjoy a profound peace and tranquility, vv. 17, 18.

VI. That, the members of it being all righteous, the glory and joy of it shall be everlasting, vv. 19–22.

A detailed analysis of chapter

The glories of the Church of God, when the fullness of the Gentiles will come in. (1–8)

The Jews will be converted and gathered from their dispersions. (9–14)

The kingdoms of this world will become the kingdom of our Lord, and of his Christ. (15–22)

Key verse

Verse 1: "Arise, shine; for thy light is come, and the glory of the LORD is risen upon thee."

Key word / key phrase

Verse 14, "Zion of the Holy One of Israel."

Key event / key person / key theme

A vision of the new Jerusalem

Key thought

Today nearly all nations ignore God. One day all nations will worship God.

Key thing to look out for

How wonderful to live in a town walled by salvation and guarded with gates of praise.

Key Bible cross-reference

Verse 11. See Revelation 21:25,26.

Key "by way of explanation"

Verse 13, "glory of Lebanon." This refers to the magnificent cedar trees of Lebanon from which the temple was built.

Key "Quotable Quote"

"The whole work of salvation was finished and the whole debit paid, so there is nothing for me to do but to fall down on my knees and accept the Savior."

Hudson Taylor

Isaiah 61

Matthew Henry's introduction

In this chapter,

I. We are sure to find the grace of Christ, published by himself to a lost world in the everlasting gospel, under the type and figure of Isaiah's province, which was to foretell the deliverance of the Jews out of Babylon, vv. 1–3.

II. We think we find the glories of the church of Christ, its spiritual glories, described under the type and figure of the Jews' prosperity after their return out of their captivity.

A. It is promised that they decays of the church shall be repaired, v. 4.

B. That those from without shall be made serviceable to the church, v. 5.

C. That the church shall be a royal priesthood, maintained by the riches of the Gentiles, v. 6.

D. That she shall have honor and joy in lieu of all her shame and sorrow, v. 7.

E. That her affairs shall prosper, v. 8.

F. That prosperity shall enjoy these blessings, v. 9.

G. That righteousness and salvation shall be the eternal matter of the church's rejoicing and thanksgiving, vv. 10, 11.

A detailed analysis of chapter

The Messiah, his character and office. (1–3)
His promises of future blessedness. (4–9)
Praise to God for these mercies. (10,11)

Key verse

Verse 1: "The Spirit of the Lord GOD is upon me; because the LORD hath anointed me to preach good tidings unto the meek; he hath sent me to bind up the brokenhearted, to proclaim liberty to the captives, and the opening of the prison to them that are bound."

Key word / key phrase

Verse 2, "proclaim the year of the Lord's favor."

Key event / key person / key theme

The year of the Lord's favor

Key thought

Without the Spirit of the Lord there is never any spiritual life.

Key thing to look out for

Note how these verses apply to Jesus. See Luke 4:16–21.

Key Bible cross-reference

Verse 1. See Matthew 11:5.

Key "by way of explanation"

Verse 3, "oil of gladness." In times of joy people were anointed with olive oil. The imagery is based on the year of Jubilee (Leviticus 25).

Key "Quotable Quote"

"We who have Christ's eternal life need to throw away our own lives."

George Verwer

Isaiah 62

Matthew Henry's introduction

In this chapter,

I. The prophet determines to apply closely and constantly to this business, v. 1.

II. God appoints him and others of his prophets to continue to do so, for the encouragement of his people during the delays of their deliverance, vv. 6, 7.

III. The promises are here repeated and ratified of the great things God would do for his church, for the Jews after their return out of captivity and for the Christian church when it shall be set up in the world.

A. The church shall be made honorable in the eyes of the world, v. 2.

B. It shall appear to be very dear to God, precious and honorable in his sight, vv. 3–5.

C. It shall enjoy great plenty, vv. 8, 9.

D. It shall be released out of captivity and grow up again into a considerable nation, particularly owned and favored by heaven, vv. 10–12.

A detailed analysis of chapter

God's care of his people. (1–5)

The people urged to a life of prayer. (6–9)

Every hindrance will be removed from the way of salvation. (10–12)

Key verse

Verse 6: "I have set watchmen upon thy walls, O Jerusalem, which shall never hold their peace day nor night."

Key word / key phrase

Verse 4, "your land will be married."

Key event / key person / key theme

Jerusalem's future

Key thought

God's workers need to model themselves on these faithful watchmen.

Key thing to look out for

Note how verse 11 is quoted in Matthew 21:5 to such good effect.

Key Bible cross-reference

Verse 11. See Revelation 22:12.

Key "by way of explanation"

Verse 11, "daughters of Jerusalem," is a personification of Jerusalem and for all its inhabitants.

Key "Quotable Quote"

"I think the first essential mark of the difference between true and false assurance is to be found in the fact that the true brings about humility. There is nothing in the world that works such satanic, profound, God-defiant pride as false assurance; nothing works such utter humility, or brings to such utter self-emptiness, as the child-like spirit of true assurance."

A.A. Hodge

Isaiah 63

Matthew Henry's introduction

In this chapter we have,

I. God coming towards his people in ways of mercy and deliverance, and this is to be joined to the close of the previous chapter, where it was said to Zion, "Behold, thy salvation comes;" for here it is shown how it comes, vv. 1–6.

II. God's people meeting him with their devotions, and addressing themselves to him with suitable affections; and this part of the chapter is carried on to the close of the next. In this we have,

A. A thankful acknowledgment of the great favors God had bestowed on them, v. 7.

B. The magnifying of these favors, from the consideration of God's relation to them (v. 8), his compassionate concern for them (v. 9), their unworthiness (v. 10), and the occasion which it gave both him and them to call to mind former mercies, vv. 11–14.

C. A very humble and earnest prayer to God to appear for them in their present distress, pleading God's mercy (v. 15), their relation to him (v. 16), their desire towards him (v. 17), and the insolence of their enemies, vv. 18, 19.

A detailed analysis of chapter

Christ's victory over his enemies. (1–6)
His mercy toward his people. (7–14)
Prayer for God's deliverance. (15–19)

Key verse

Verse 4: "For the day of vengeance is in mine heart, and the year of my redeemed is come."

Key word / key phrase

Verse 3, "in my wrath."

Key event / key person / key theme

Salvation and judgment

Key thought

The time of redemption and the day of vengeance are spoken of in the same verse, verse 4.

Key thing to look out for

A key part of the prophet's message was to speak about "the kindness of the Lord," verse 7.

Key Bible cross-reference

Verses 1–6. See Amos 1:11,12.

Key "by way of explanation"

Verse 7, "kindness," includes all the ways in which God has been faithful to his covenant promises to his people.

Key "Quotable Quote"

"To me, God and compassion are one and the same. Compassion is the joy of sharing. It's doing small things for the love of each other – just a smile, or carrying a bucket of water, or showing some simple kindness. These are the small things that make up compassion."

Mother Teresa of Calcutta

Isaiah 64

Matthew Henry's introduction

This chapter goes on with that pathetic pleading prayer which the church offered up to God in the latter part of the previous chapter. They had argued from their covenant-relation to God and his interest and concern in them; now here,

I. They pray that God would appear in some remarkable and surprising manner for them against his and their enemies, vv. 1, 2.

II. They plead what God had formerly done, and was always ready to do, for his people, vv. 3–5.

III. They confess themselves to be sinful and unworthy of God's favor, and that they had deserved the judgments they were now under, vv. 6, 7.

IV. They refer themselves to the mercy of God as a Father, and submit themselves to his sovereignty, v. 8.

V. They represent the very deplorable condition they were in, and earnestly pray for the pardon of sin and the turning away of God's anger, vv. 9–12.

A detailed analysis of chapter

Prayer for God's power to be revealed. (1–5)
A confession of sin. (6–12)

Key verse

Verse 1: "Oh that thou wouldest rend the heavens, that thou wouldest come down, that the mountains might flow down at thy presence,"

Key word / key phrase

Verse 4, "acts on behalf of those who wait for him."

Key event / key person / key theme

A prayer for deliverance

Key thought

Godly people would never dream that they could ever outgrow the need to confess their sin to God.

Key thing to look out for

The "awesome things," (verse 3) that must be remembered.

Key Bible cross-reference

Verse 4. See 1 Corinthians 2:9.

Key "by way of explanation"

Verse 7, "No one calls on your name." Just the opposite of this needs to be true, especially in times of trouble.

Key "Quotable Quote"

"We need prayer as much as we need water. All of us need times of quiet before God."

Johann Heinrich Arnold

Isaiah 65

Matthew Henry's introduction

In this chapter we have,

I. The anticipating of the Gentiles with the gospel call, v. 1.

II. The rejection of the Jews for their obstinacy and unbelief, vv. 2–7.

III. The saving of a remnant of them by bringing them into the gospel church, vv. 8–10.
IV. The judgments of God that should pursue the rejected Jews, vv. 11–16.
V. The blessings reserved for the Christian church, which should be its joy and glory, vv. 17–25.

A detailed analysis of chapter

God castigates those who have refused to listen. (1–7)

The Lord will preserve a remnant. (8–10)

Judgments on the wicked. (11–16)

The future happy and flourishing state of God's faithful people. (17–25)

Key verse

Verse 1: "I am sought of them that asked not for me; I am found of them that sought me not."

Key word / key phrase

Verse 9, "my chosen people."

Key event / key person / key theme

The Lord's answer to the remnant

Key thought

From verse 17 this chapter reads like the book of Revelation, see Revelation 21:4.

Key thing to look out for

We cannot think of heaven too often.

Key Bible cross-reference

Verse 1. See Romans 10:20.

Key "by way of explanation"

Verse 7, "burned sacrifices on the mountains" refers to the high places were sacrifices were offered to Baal.

Key "Quotable Quote"

"I saw the heavens opened, and God sitting on his great white throne."

G.F. Handel, explaining how he was inspired during his writing of the Hallelujah chorus.

Isaiah 66

Matthew Henry's introduction

We have here,

I. The contempt God puts on ceremonial services in comparison with moral duties, and an intimation therein of his purpose shortly to put an end to the temple, and sacrifice and reject those that adhered to them, vv. 1–4.
II. The salvation God will in due time work for his people out of the hands of their oppressors (v. 5), speaking terror to the persecutors (v. 6) and comfort to the persecuted, a speedy and complete deliverance (vv. 7–9), a joyful settlement (vv. 10, 11), the accession of the Gentiles to them, and abundance of satisfaction therein, vv. 12–14.
III. The terrible vengeance which God will bring on the enemies of his church and people, vv. 15–18.
IV. The happy establishment of the church on large and sure foundations, its constant attendance on God and triumph over its enemies, vv. 19–24.

A detailed analysis of chapter

God looks at the heart, and vengeance is threatened for guilt. (1–4)

Jew and Gentile will be gathered to the Redeemer. (5–14)

Every enemy will be destroyed, and the final ruin of the ungodly will be seen. (15–24)

Key verse

Verse 1: "Thus saith the LORD, The heaven is my throne, and the earth is my footstool: where is the house that ye build unto me? and where is the place of my rest?"

Key word / key phrase

Verse 1, "heaven is my throne."

Key event / key person / key theme

A new heaven and a new earth

Key thought

Jerusalem's future (and the future of all Christians) is secure and will be glorious.

Key thing to look out for

Verses 12 and 13 picture the loving nature of the Lord God Almighty.

Key Bible cross-reference

Verse 1. See Matthew 5:34,35.

Key "by way of explanation"

Verse 15, "fire," is often linked with God's judgment. See 1:31; 30:27.

Key "Quotable Quote"

"Never can father or mother embrace their child, nor any person embrace another with so much love as God Almighty embraces."

Angela of Foligno

5. Select bibliography for Isaiah

Alexander, J.A. *Isaiah, Translated and Explained*. 2 vols. New York: John Wiley, 1864.

Delitzsch, F. *Biblical Commentary on the Prophecies of Isaiah*. 2 vols. Edinburgh: T. & T. Clark, 1890.

Motyer, Alec *Isaiah* (Tyndale), InterVarsity, 1999.

Smith, G. A. *The Book of Isaiah*. 2 vols. London: Hodder and Stoughton, 1927.

Watts, John D. W. *Isaiah* (Word Biblical Commentary), Word Books, 1987. 2 vols.

Young, E. J. *The Book of Isaiah*. 3 vols. Grand Rapids: Eerdmans, 1965, 1969, 1972.

Youngblood, Joel. *Isaiah*, Wipf & Stock, 1998.

Jeremiah

1. Book by book: Introduction to Jeremiah

Introduction

Jeremiah's life

Jeremiah, son of Hilkiah, one of the ordinary priests, dwelling in Anathoth of Benjamin (Jer. 1:1), not the Hilkiah the high priest who discovered the book of the law (2 Kings 22:8); had he been the same, the designation would have been "the priest", or "the high priest". Besides, his residence at Anathoth shows that he belonged to the line of Abiathar, who was deposed from the high priesthood by Solomon (1 Kings 2:26–35), after which the office remained in Zadok's line. Mention occurs of Jeremiah in 2 Chr. 35:25; 36:12, 21. In 629 b.c. the thirteenth year of King Josiah, while still very young (Jer. 1:5), he received his prophetical call in Anathoth (Jer. 1:2); and along with Hilkiah the high priest, the prophetess Huldah, and the prophet Zephaniah, he helped forward Josiah's reformation of religion (2 Kings 23:1–25). Among the first charges to him was one that he should go and proclaim God's message in Jerusalem (Jer. 2:2). He also took an official tour to announce to the cities of Judah the contents of the book of the law, found in the temple (Jer. 11:6) five years after his call to prophesy. On his return to Anathoth, his countrymen, offended at his reproofs, conspired against his life. To escape their persecutions (Jer. 11:21), as well as those of his own family (Jer. 12:6), he left Anathoth and resided at Jerusalem. During the eighteen years of his ministry in Josiah's reign he was unmolested; also during the three months of Jehoahaz or Shallum's reign (Jer. 22:10–12).

On Jehoiakim's accession it became evident that Josiah's reformation effected nothing more than a forcible repression of idolatry and the establishment of the worship of God outwardly. The priests, prophets, and people then brought Jeremiah before the authorities, urging that he should be put to death for his denunciations of evil against the city (Jer. 26:8–11). The princes, however, especially Ahikam, interposed in his behalf (Jer. 26:16, 24), but he was put under restraint, or at least deemed it prudent not to appear in public. In the fourth year of Jehoiakim (606 B.C.), he was commanded to write the predictions given orally through him, and to read them to the people. Being "shut up", he could not himself go into the house of the Lord (Jer. 36:5); he therefore deputed Baruch, his amanuensis, to read them in public on the fast day. The princes thereon advised Baruch and Jeremiah to hide themselves from the king's displeasure. Meanwhile they read the roll to the king, who was so enraged that he cut it with a knife and threw it into the fire; at the same time giving orders for the apprehension of the prophet and Baruch. They escaped Jehoiakim's violence, which had already killed the prophet Urijah (Jer. 26:20–23). Baruch rewrote the words, with additional prophecies, on another roll (Jer. 36:27–32). In the three months' reign of Jehoiachin or Jeconiah, he prophesied the carrying away of the king and the queen mother (Jer. 13:18; 22:24–30; compare 2 Kings 24:12). In this reign he was imprisoned for a short time by Pashur (Jer. 20:1–18), the chief governor of the Lord's house; but at Zedekiah's accession he was free (Jer. 37:4), for the king sent to him to "inquire of the Lord" when Nebuchadnezzar came up against Jerusalem (Jer. 21:1–3, etc.; Jer. 37:3). The Chaldeans drew off on hearing of the approach of Pharaoh's army (Jer. 37:5); but Jeremiah warned the king that the Egyptians would forsake him, and the Chaldeans return and burn up the city (Jer. 37:7, 8). The princes, irritated at this, made the departure of Jeremiah from the city during the respite a pretext for imprisoning him, on the allegation of his deserting to the Chaldeans (Jer. 38:1–5). He would have been left to perish in the dungeon of Malchiah, but for the intercession of Ebed-melech, the Ethiopian (Jer. 38:6–13).

Zedekiah, though he consulted Jeremiah in secret yet was induced by his princes to leave Jeremiah in prison (Jer. 38:14–28) until Jerusalem was taken.

Nebuchadnezzar directed his captain, Nebuzar-adan, to give him his freedom, so that he might either go to Babylon or stay with the remnant of his people as he chose. As a true patriot, notwithstanding the forty and a half years during which his country had repaid his services with neglect and persecution, he stayed with Gedaliah, the ruler appointed by Nebuchadnezzar over Judea (Jer. 40:6). After the murder of Gedaliah by Ishmael, Johanan, the recognized ruler of the people, in fear of the Chaldeans avenging the murder of Gedaliah, fled with the people to Egypt, and forced Jeremiah and Baruch to accompany him, in spite of the prophet's warning that the people should perish if they went to Egypt, but be preserved by remaining in their land (Jer. 41:1–43:13). At Tahpanhes, a boundary city on the Tanitic or Pelustan branch of the Nile, he prophesied the overthrow of Egypt (Jer. 43:8–13). Tradition says he died in Egypt. According to the Pseudo-Epiphanius, he was stoned at Taphnæ or Tahpanhes. The Jews so venerated him that they believed he would rise from the dead and be the forerunner of Messiah (Matt. 16:14).

Jeremiah's character

Havernick observes that the combination of features in Jeremiah's character proves his divine mission; mild, timid, and susceptible of melancholy, yet intrepid in the discharge of his prophetic functions, not sparing the prince any more than the meanest of his subjects–the Spirit of prophecy controlling his natural temper and qualifying him for his hazardous undertaking, without doing violence to his individuality. Zephaniah, Habakkuk, Daniel, and Ezekiel were his contemporaries. The last forms a good contrast to Jeremiah, the Spirit in his case acting on a temperament as strongly marked by firmness as Jeremiah's was by shrinking and delicate sensitiveness. Ezekiel views the nation's sins as opposed to righteousness–Jeremiah, as productive of misery; the former takes the objective, the latter the subjective, view of the evils of the times. Jeremiah's style corresponds to his character: he is peculiarly marked by pathos, and sympathy with the wretched; his Lamentations illustrate this; the whole series of elegies has but one object–to express sorrow for his fallen country; yet the lights and images in which he presents this are so many, that the reader, so far from feeling it monotonous, is charmed with the variety of the plaintive strains throughout. The language is marked by Aramæisms, which probably was the ground of Jerome's charge that the style is "rustic". Lowth denies the charge and considers him in portions not inferior to Isaiah. His heaping of phrase on phrase, the repetition of stereotyped forms–and these often three times–are due to his affected feelings and to his desire to intensify the expression of them; he is at times more concise, energetic, and sublime, especially against foreign nations, and in the rhythmical parts.

Arrangement of book

The principle of the arrangement of his prophecies is hard to ascertain. The order of kings was–Josiah (under whom he prophesied eighteen years), Jehoahaz (three months), Jehoiakim (eleven years), Jeconiah (three months), Zedekiah (eleven years). But his prophecies under Josiah (the first through twentieth chapters) are immediately followed by a portion under Zedekiah (the twenty-first chapter). Again, Jer. 24:8–10, as to Zedekiah, comes in the midst of the section as to Jehoahaz, Jehoiakim, and Jeconiah (the twenty-second, twenty-third, twenty-fifth chapters, etc.) So the thirty-fifth and thirty-sixth chapters as to Jehoiakim, follow the twenty-seventh, twenty-eighth, twenty-ninth, thirty-third, thirty-fourth chapters, as to Zedekiah; and the forty-fifth chapter, dated the fourth year of Jehoiakim, comes after predictions as to the Jews who fled to Egypt after the overthrow of Jerusalem. Ewald thinks the present arrangement substantially Jeremiah's own; the various portions are prefaced by the same formula, "The word which came to Jeremiah from the Lord " (Jer. 7:1; 11:1; 18:1; 21:1; 25:1; 30:1; 32:1; 34:1, 8; 35:1; 40:1; 44:1; compare Jer. 14:1; 46:1; 47:1; 49:34). Notes of time mark other divisions more or less historical (Jer. 26:1; 27:1; 36:1; 37:1). Two other portions are distinct of themselves (Jer. 29:1; 45:1). The second chapter has the shorter introduction which marks the beginning of a strophe; the third chapter seems imperfect, having as the introduction merely "saying" (Jer. 3:1, Hebrew). Thus in the poetical parts, there are twenty-three sections divided into strophes of from seven to nine verses, marked some way thus, "The Lord said also unto me".

Canonicity

The canonicity of his prophecies is established by quotations of them in the New Testament (see Matt. 2:17; 16:14; Heb. 8:8–12; on Matt. 27:9, see on Introduction to Zechariah); also by the testimony of Ecclesiasticus 49:7, which quotes Jer. 1:10; of Philo, who quotes his word as an "oracle"; and of the list of canonical books in Melito, Origen, Jerome, and the Talmud.

A.R. Faussett

Detailed outline

- I. Introduction: The Prophet's call: 1:1–19
- II. Prophecies against Judah and Jerusalem: 2:1–45:5
  - A. Prophecies during the reigns of Josiah and Jehoiakim: 1:1–20:18
    1. First prophecy: Sin and ingratitude of the nation: 2:1–3:5
    2. Second prophecy: Destruction from the north: 3:6–6:30
    3. Third prophecy: Threat of exile: 7:1–10:25
    4. Fourth prophecy: The broken covenant: 11:1–13:27
    5. Fifth prophecy: 14:1–17:27
       - (a) The drought: 14:1–15:21
       - (b) The unmarried prophet: 16:1–17:18
       - (c) The warning about the Sabbath: 17:19–27

6. The sixth prophecy: The sign the potter's house: 18:1–20:18

B. Prophecies at various times before the fall of Jerusalem: 21:1–39:18

1. Punishment on Zedekiah and the people: 21:1–29:32

2. Future Messianic Kingdom: 30:1–33:26

3. Zedekiah's sin and loyalty of the Rechabites: 34:1–35:19

4. Jehoiakim's opposition: 36:1–32

5. Jeremiah's experiences during the siege: 37:1–39:18

C. Prophecies after the fall of Jerusalem: 40:1–45:5

1. Jeremiah's ministry among the remnant: 40:1–42:22

2. Jeremiah's ministry in Egypt: 43:1–44:30

3. Jeremiah's message to Baruch: 45:1–5

III. Prophecies against the nations: 46:1–51:64

A. Against Egypt: 46:1–28

B. Against Philistia: 47:1–7

C. Against Moab: 48:1–47

D. Against Ammon: 49:1–6

E. Against Edom: 49:7–22

F. Against Damascus: 49:23–27

G. Against Arabia: 49:28–33

H. Against Elam: 49:34–39

I. Against Babylon: 50:1–51:64

IV. Appendix: Fall and liberation: 52:1–52:34

A. The fall and captivity of Judah: 52:1–30

B. The liberation: 52:31–34

2. Helpful summaries of Jeremiah

Bird's eye view

This book contains the biography and messages of Jeremiah, "the weeping prophet."

Reading plan

The following reading plan, taking one reading per day, enables you to read through Jeremiah in twenty-two days.

Jeremiah 1–2
Jeremiah 3–4
Jeremiah 4–5
Jeremiah 6–7
Jeremiah 8–10
Jeremiah 11–13
Jeremiah 14–16
Jeremiah 17–18
Jeremiah 19–22
Jeremiah 23–24
Jeremiah 25–26
Jeremiah 27–29
Jeremiah 30–31
Jeremiah 32–33
Jeremiah 34–35
Jeremiah 36–38
Jeremiah 39–41
Jeremiah 42–45
Jeremiah 46–48
Jeremiah 49
Jeremiah 50
Jeremiah 51–52

Verses to memorize

Jeremiah 1:5

Before I formed you in the womb I knew

you, before you were born, I set you apart.

Jeremiah 29:13

And ye shall seek me, and find me, when ye shall search for me with all your heart. KJV

Jeremiah 32:40

I will make an everlasting covenant with them: I will never stop doing good to them, and I will inspire them to fear me, so that they will never turn away from me. kjv

Statistics

Twenty-fourth Old Testament book
52 chapters
1,364 verses
42,659 words

Famous saying found in Jeremiah

"Can a leopard change his spots?"
Jeremiah 13:23

Names/titles given

Hebrew title: *Yirmeyah:* "The Lord throws" (in the sense of laying a foundation) hence meaning, "The Lord establishes."

Greek title in Septuagint: *Hieremais: Jerehiah.*

Latin title in Vulgate: *Jeremias: Jeremiah*

3. Helpful keys to turn to in understanding Jeremiah

Key word/words

Return, 47 times
Backsliding, 13 times

Key verses

Jeremiah 7:23–24; 31:31–33

Key sermons in Jeremiah

The Temple sermon (Jer. 7 and 26)
The Potter's sermon (Jer. 18)
The Fig sermon (Jer. 24)
The Yoke sermon (Jer. 27–28)

Themes to study

Sin and idolatry
Prophecy and preaching
The hope of the return of the Exiles

Jeremiah quoted in the New Testament

He that glorieth, let him glory in the Lord
Jer. 9:24 quoted in 1 Cor. 1:31 and 2 Cor. 10:17

A voice was heard in Ramah
Jer. 31:15 quoted in Matt. 2:18

Behold, the days come
Jer. 31:31–34 quoted in Heb. 8:8–12

I will put my laws on their heart
Jer. 31:33–34 quoted in Heb. 10:16–17

Jeremiah's Laments

Jer. 11:8–12:6; 15:10–21; 17:14–18; 18:12–22; 19:1–20:18

Jeremiah was rejected by:

- His neighbors, Jeremiah 11:19–21
- His family, Jeremiah 12:6
- Religious leaders, (priests and prophets), Jeremiah 20:1–2
- His friends, Jeremiah 20:10
- His own people, Jeremiah 26:8
- The king, Jeremiah 36:23

Jesus in Jeremiah

In Jeremiah Jesus is the Lord our Righteousness.

Types of Jesus in Jeremiah

- Jesus is pictured as the Shepherd and the righteous Branch in Jeremiah 23:1–8.
- Jesus will bring the new covenant: see Jeremiah 31:31–34.

Lessons to learn from Jeremiah

- Speaking the truth can make us very unpopular.
- Preachers should be full of humility and compassion.
- The trappings of religion are rubbish in God's sight.
- God does not forgive the unrepentant sinner.

4. Chapter by chapter: outline of every chapter of Jeremiah

Jeremiah 1

Matthew Henry's introduction

In this chapter we have,

I. The general inscription or title of this book, with the time of the continuance of Jeremiah's public ministry, vv. 1–3.

II. The call of Jeremiah to the prophetic office, his modest objection against it answered, and an ample commission given him for the execution of it, vv. 4–10.

III. The visions of an almond-rod and a seething-pot, signifying the approaching ruin of Judah and Jerusalem by the Chaldeans, vv. 11–16.

IV. Encouragement given to the prophet to go on undauntedly in his work, in an assurance of God's presence with him, vv. 17–19.

A detailed analysis of chapter

Jeremiah's call to the prophetic office. (1–10)

A vision of an almond tree and a boiling pot, divine protection is promised. (11–19)

Key verse

Verse 1: "The words of Jeremiah the son of Hilkiah, of the priests that were in Anathoth in the land of Benjamin."

Key word / key phrase

Verse 4, "The word of the Lord came to me."

Key event / key person / key theme

Jeremiah's call

Key thought

Jeremiah was called before he was born.

Key thing to look out for

Jeremiah endured a tough prophetic ministry but is told at the start of it not to be afraid.

Key Bible cross-reference

Verse 3. See 2 Chronicles 36:5–8; 11:21.

Key "by way of explanation"

Jeremiah preached from about 620–580 BC. He lived in tumultuous times, witnessing the rise of Babylonian power and the fall of Jerusalem.

Key "Quotable Quote"

"Learn the lesson that, if you are to do the work of a prophet what you need is not a scepter but a hoe."

Bernard of Clairvaux

Jeremiah 2

Matthew Henry's introduction

Now they are told,

I. That this was ungrateful to God, who had been so kind to them, vv. 1–8.

II. That it was without precedent, that a nation should change their god, vv. 9–13.

III. That hereby they had disparaged and ruined themselves, vv. 14–19.

IV. That they had broken their covenants and degenerated from their good beginnings, vv. 20, 21.

V. That their wickedness was too plain to be concealed and too bad to be excused, vv. 22, 23, 35.

VI. That they persisted obstinately in it, and were irreclaimable and indefatigable in their idolatries, vv. 24, 25, 33, 36.

VII. That they shamed themselves by their idolatry and should shortly be made ashamed of it when they should find their idols unable to help them, vv. 26–29, 37.

VIII. That they had not been convinced and reformed by the rebukes of Providence that had been under, v. 30.

IX. That they had put a great contempt on God, vv. 31, 32.

X. That with their idolatries they had mixed the most unnatural murders, shedding the blood of the poor innocents, v. 34.

A detailed analysis of chapter

God expostulates with his people. (1–8)
Their revolt beyond precedent. (9–13)
Guilt the cause of sufferings. (14–19)
The sins of Judah. (20–28)
Their false confidence. (29–37)

Key verse

Verse 9: "Wherefore I will yet plead with you, saith the LORD, and with your children's children will I plead."

Key word / key phrase

Verse 8, "worthless idols."

Key event / key person / key theme

Judah's deliberate sins

Key thought

When repentance is necessary it is essential to confess the relevant sin to God.

Key thing to look out for

Unfaithfulness always ends in punishment.

Key Bible cross-reference

Verse 3. See Deuteronomy 7:6.

Key "by way of explanation"

Verse 24, "wild donkey." The Israelites are likened to the stubborn and untamed nature of such an animal.

Key "Quotable Quote"

"Some men, not content with Christ alone, are borne hither and thither from one hope to another; even if they concern themselves chiefly with him, they nevertheless stray from the right way in turning some part of their thinking in another direction."

John Calvin

Jeremiah 3

Matthew Henry's introduction

Here,

I. It is further shown how bad they had been and how well they deserved to be quite abandoned, and yet how ready God was to receive them into his favor on their repentance, vv. 1–5.

II. The impenitence of Judah, and their persisting in sin, are aggravated from the judgments of God on Israel, which they should have taken warning by, vv. 6–11.

III. Great encouragements are given to these backsliders to return and repent, and promises made of great mercy which God had in store for them, and which he would prepare them for by bringing them home to himself, vv. 12–19.

IV. The charge renewed against them for their apostasy from God, and the invitation repeated to return and repent, to which are here added the words that are put in their mouth, which they should make use of in their return to God, vv. 20–25.

A detailed analysis of chapter

Exhortations to repentance. (1–5)

Judah more guilty than Israel. (6–11)

But pardon is promised. (12–20)

The children of Israel express their sorrow and repentance. (21–25)

Key verse

Verse 6: "The LORD said also unto me in the days of Josiah the king, Hast thou seen that which backsliding Israel hath done?"

Key word / key phrase

Verse 12, "faithless Israel."

Key event / key person / key theme

It is not too late to repent.

Key thought

In the prophet's message to Israel to repent, the Lord is likened to a loving and faithful husband.

Key thing to look out for

No matter how faithless a person has been, the Lord welcomes back the repentant sinner with open arms.

Key Bible cross-reference

Verse 6. See 2 Kings 22:1–23:30

Key "by way of explanation"

"Israel" refers to the northern kingdom of Israel, now destroyed by the Assyrians and her people taken captive. Many were resettled in Assyria's northern province (verse 12).

Key "Quotable Quote"

"I will love you, O Lord, and thank you, and

confess to your name, because you have forgiven me my evil and nefarious deeds."

Augustine of Hippo

Jeremiah 4

Matthew Henry's introduction

It should seem that the first two verses of this chapter might better have been joined to the close of the previous chapter, for they are directed to Israel, the ten tribes, by way of reply to their compliance with God's call, directing and encouraging them to hold their resolution, vv. 1, 2. The rest of the chapter concerns Judah and Jerusalem.

I. They are called to repent and reform, vv. 3, 4.

II. They are warned of the advance of Nebuchadnezzar and his forces against them, and are told that it is for their sins, from which they are again exhorted to wash themselves, vv. 5–18.

III. To affect them the more with the greatness of the desolation that was coming, the prophet does himself bitterly lament it, and sympathize with his people in the calamities it brought on them, and the plunge it brought them to, representing it as a reduction of the world to its first chaos, vv. 19–31.

A detailed analysis of chapter

Exhortations and promises. (1–2)
Judah exhorted to repentance. (3–4)
Judgments denounced. (5–18)
The approaching ruin of Judah. (19–31)

Key verse

Verse 3: "For thus saith the LORD to the men of Judah and Jerusalem, Break up your fallow ground, and sow not among thorns."

Key word / key phrase

Verse 7, "a lion has come."

Key event / key person / key theme

Judah's destruction from the north

Key thought

Jeremiah expresses his sorrow for his people's sins.

Key thing to look out for

People who turn from the Lord do not become stupid, but skilled in evil.

Key Bible cross-reference

Verse 3. See Hosea 10:12.

Key "by way of explanation"

Verse 11, "scorching wind." This dry desert wind, called the *sirocco* wind, brought dust and sand and so caused great aggravation.

Key "Quotable Quote"

"Repentance is a grace, and must have its daily operation, as well as other graces."

Thomas Brooks

Jeremiah 5

Matthew Henry's introduction

I. The sins they are charged with are very great:–Injustice (v. 1), hypocrisy in religion

(v. 2), incorrigibleness (v. 3), the corruption and debauchery of both poor and rich (vv. 4, 5), idolatry and adultery (vv. 7, 8), treacherous departures from God (v. 11), and impudent defiance of him (vv. 12, 13), and, that which is at the bottom of all this, want of the fear of God, notwithstanding the frequent calls given them to fear him, vv. 20–24. In the close of the chapter they are charged with violence and oppression (vv. 26–28), and a combination of those to debauch the nation who should have been active to reform it, vv. 30, 31.

II. The judgments they are threatened with are very terrible. In general, they shall be reckoned with, vv. 9, 29. A foreign enemy shall be brought in on them (vv. 15–17), shall set guards on them (v. 6), shall destroy their fortification (v. 10), shall carry them away into captivity (v. 19), and keep all good things from them, v. 25. Herein the words of God's prophets shall be fulfilled, v. 14. But,

III. Here is an intimation twice given that God would in the midst of wrath remember mercy, and not utterly destroy them, vv. 10, 18.

A detailed analysis of chapter

The people's profession of religion was hypocritical. (1–9)

The destroyer is summoned. (10–18)

Their apostasy and idolatry. (19–31)

Key verse

Verse 1: "Run ye to and fro through the streets of Jerusalem, and see now, and know, and seek in the broad places thereof, if ye can find a man, if there be any that executeth judgment, that seeketh the truth; and I will pardon it."

Key word / key phrase

Verse 7, "forsaken me."

Key event / key person / key theme

Judah's sins

Key thought

The sins of God's people are recorded in some detail so that future generations of God's followers will learn from their unfaithfulness.

Key thing to look out for

Our reaction to the sin of other people gives us a good guide to the state of our own spiritual life.

Key Bible cross-reference

Verse 21. See Ezekiel 12:2.

Key "by way of explanation"

Verse 6, "backslidings." This word indicates that their sin was no passing whim, but a constant apostasy.

Key "Quotable Quote"

"For to sin, indeed is human: but to persevere in sin is not human but altogether satanic."

John Chrysostom

Jeremiah 6

Matthew Henry's introduction

In this chapter, as before, we have,

I. A prophecy of the invading of the land of

Judah and the besieging of Jerusalem by the Chaldean army (vv. 1–6), with the spoils they should make of the country (v. 9) and the terror which all should be seized with on that occasion, vv. 22–26.

II. An account of those sins of Judah and Jerusalem which provoked God to bring this desolating judgment on them. Their oppression (v. 7), their contempt of the word of God (vv. 10–12), their worldliness (v. 13), the treachery of their prophets (v. 14), their impudence in sin (v. 15), their obstinacy against reproofs (vv. 18, 19), which made their sacrifices unacceptable to him (v. 20), and for which he gave them up to ruin (v. 21), but tried them first (v. 27) and then rejected them as irreclaimable, vv. 28–30.

III. Good counsel given them in the midst of all this, but in vain, vv. 8, 16, 17.

A detailed analysis of chapter

No safety in Jerusaelem. (1–8)
The justice of God's judgment. (9–17)
All methods used to change the people of Judah have been unsuccessful. (18–30)

Key verse

Verse 3: "The shepherds with their flocks shall come unto her; they shall pitch their tents against her round about; they shall feed every one in his place."

Key word / key phrase

Verse 1, "Flee from Jerusalem.!"

Key event / key person / key theme

Jerusalem will be destroyed

Key thought

The Lord never punishes his people without giving them ample warning and opportunity to repent.

Key thing to look out for

It often appears that no amount of reasoning can stop some people from choosing to reject the Lord.

Key Bible cross-reference

Verse 14. See Ezekiel 13:10.

Key "by way of explanation"

Verse "peace . . . when there is no peace." This was the cry of a number of unfaithful prophets. "Shepherds," that is, "rulers."

Key "Quotable Quote"

"As heat is opposed to cold, and light to darkness, so grace is opposed to sin."

Thomas Benton Brooks

Jeremiah 7

Matthew Henry's introduction

The prophet having in God's name reproved the people for their sins, and given them warning of the judgments of God that were coming on them, in this chapter prosecutes the same intention for their humiliation and awakening.

I. He shows them the invalidity of the plea they so much relied on, that they had the temple of God among them and constantly attended the service of it, and endeavors to take them off from their confidence in their external privileges and performances, vv. 1–11.

II. He reminds them of the desolations of Shiloh, and foretells that such should be the desolations of Jerusalem, vv. 12–16.

III. He represents to the prophet their abominable idolatries, for which he was thus incensed against them, vv. 17–20.

IV. He sets before the people that fundamental maxim of religion that "to obey is better than sacrifice" (1 Sam. 15:22), and that God would not accept the sacrifices of those that obstinately persisted in disobedience, vv. 21–28.

V. He threatens to lay the land utterly waste for their idolatry and impiety, and to multiply their slain as they had multiplied their sin, vv. 29–34.

A detailed analysis of chapter

Confidence in the temple is vain. (1–16)

The provocation by persisting in idolatry. (17–20)

God justifies his dealings with them. (21–28)

And threatens vengeance. (29–34)

Key verse

Verse 4: "Trust ye not in lying words, saying, The temple of the LORD, The temple of the LORD, The temple of the LORD, are these."

Key word / key phrase

Verse 3, "Reform your ways."

Key event / key person / key theme

The externals of religion

Key thought

God's anger should not make us think negatively about God, but about human sin.

Key thing to look out for

The result of following "the ancient paths" (verse 16).

Key Bible cross-reference

Verse 11. See Matthew 21:13.

Key "by way of explanation"

God had saved Jerusalem in the days of Hezekiah. People believed that the temple was God's dwelling-place, a holy place, and he would never let it be destroyed. Therefore, they were safe.

Key "Quotable Quote"

"I am convinced that the first step toward attaining a higher standard of holiness is to realize more fully the amazing sinfulness of sin."

J.C. Ryle

Jeremiah 8

Matthew Henry's introduction

The prophet proceeds, in this chapter, both to magnify and to justify the destruction that God was bringing on this people, to show how grievous it would be and yet how righteous.

I. He represents the judgments coming as so very terrible that death should appear so as most to be dreaded and yet should be desired, vv. 1–3.

II. He aggravates the wretched stupidity and willfulness of this people as that which brought this ruin on them, vv. 4–12.

III. He describes the great confusion and consternation that the whole land should be in on the alarm of it, vv. 13–17.

IV. The prophet is himself deeply affected with it and lays it very much to heart, vv. 18–22.

A detailed analysis of chapter

The bones of the dead exposed. (1–3)

The stupidity of the people, compared with the instinct of the brute creation. (4–13)

A prophetic description of the devastation that will be caused by the invasion, and a lamentation. (14–22)

Key verse

Verse 5: "Why then is this people of Jerusalem slidden back by a perpetual backsliding?"

Key word / key phrase

Verse 12, "when they are punished."

Key event / key person / key theme

Judgment on Judah is imminent

Key thought

If idolatry is not removed voluntarily God will remove it himself.

Key thing to look out for

In Jeremiah's lament the heart of a true pastor is revealed.

Key Bible cross-reference

Verse 11. See Ezekiel 13:10.

Key "by way of explanation"

Verse 8, "lying pen." This phrase stands for the misuse of God's Law.

Key "Quotable Quote"

"We must feel toward our people as a father toward his children."

Richard Baxter

Jeremiah 9

Matthew Henry's introduction

In this chapter the prophet goes on faithfully to reprove sin and to threaten God's judgments for it, and yet bitterly to lament both, as one that neither rejoiced at iniquity nor was glad at calamities.

I. He here expresses his great grief for the miseries of Judah and Jerusalem, and his detestation of their sins, which brought those miseries on them, vv. 1–11.

II. He justifies God in the greatness of the destruction brought on them, vv. 9–16.

III. He calls on others to bewail the woeful case of Judah and Jerusalem, vv. 17–22.

IV. He shows them the folly and vanity of trusting in their own strength or wisdom, or the privileges of their circumcision, or any thing but God only, vv. 23–26.

A detailed analysis of chapter

A prophecy of the destruction of Jerusalem. (1–11)

The captives will suffer in a foreign land. (12–22)

God's loving-kindness. He threatens the enemies of his people. (23–26)

Key verse

Verse 8: "Their tongue is as an arrow shot out; it speaketh deceit: one speaketh peaceably to his neighbor with his mouth, but in heart he layeth his wait."

Key word / key phrase

Verse 11, "a heap of ruins."

Key event / key person / key theme

Description of Judah's coming judgment

Key thought

Israel's great sin was her idolatry, and this chapter spells out why it was so evil in the Lord's sight.

Key thing to look out for

Even in the middle of these warnings the kindness of the Lord is mentioned.

Key Bible cross-reference

Verse 24. See 1 Corinthians 1:31.

Key "by way of explanation"

Verse 22, "reaper." Death is often personified as the grim reaper. This verse is the background to such an idea.

Key "Quotable Quote"

"Measure not God's love and favor by your own feelings."

Richard Sibbes

Jeremiah 10

Matthew Henry's introduction

We may conjecture that the prophecy of this chapter was delivered after the first captivity, in the time of Jeconiah or Jehoiachin, when many were carried away to Babylon; for it has a double reference:

I. To those that were carried away into the land of the Chaldeans, a country notorious above any other for idolatry and superstition; and they are here cautioned against the infection of the place, not to learn the way of the heathen (vv. 1, 2), for their astrology and idolatry are both foolish things (vv. 3–5), and the worshippers of idols brutish, vv. 8, 9. So it will appear in the day of their visitation, vv. 14, 15. They are likewise exhorted to adhere firmly to the God of Israel, for there is none like him, vv. 6, 7. He is the true God, lives forever, and has the government of the world (vv. 10–13), and his people are happy in him, v. 16.

II. To those that yet remained in their own land. They are cautioned against security, and told to expect distress (vv. 17, 18) and that by a foreign enemy, which God would bring on them for their sin, vv. 20–22. This calamity the prophet laments (v. 19) and prays for the mitigation of it, vv. 23–25.

A detailed analysis of chapter

The absurdity of idolatry. (1–16)

Coming destruction. (17–25)

Key verse

Verse 10: "But the LORD is the true God, he is

the living God, and an everlasting king: at his wrath the earth shall tremble, and the nations shall not be able to abide his indignation."

Key word / key phrase

Verse 12, "God made the earth."

Key event / key person / key theme

The Lord is sovereign

Key thought

The prophets often praised the Lord as they contemplated his power in creation and nature.

Key thing to look out for

Verse 23 is a good verse for anyone seeking guidance.

Key Bible cross-reference

Verse 7. See Revelation 15:4.

Key "by way of explanation"

Verse 18, "hurl out." When David used his sling a stone was "hurled" out with great force. This is what will happen to the people of Jerusalem.

Key "Quotable Quote"

"Self-sacrifice is what the Bible means by love."

John R.W. Stott

Jeremiah 11

Matthew Henry's introduction

In this chapter,

I. God by the prophet puts the people in mind of the covenant he had made with their fathers, and how much he had insisted on it, as the condition of the covenant, that they should be obedient to him, vv. 1–7.

II. He charges it on them that they, in succession to their fathers, and in confederacy among themselves, had obstinately refused to obey him, vv. 8–10.

III. He threatens to punish them with utter ruin for their disobedience, especially for their idolatry (vv. 11, 13), and tells them that their idols should not save them (v. 12), that their prophets should not pray for them (v. 14); he also justifies his proceedings herein, they having brought all this mischief on themselves by their own folly and willfulness, vv. 15–17.

IV. Here is an account of a conspiracy formed against Jeremiah by his fellow-citizens, the men of Anathoth; God's discovery of it to him (vv. 18, 19), his prayer against them (v. 20), and a prediction of God's judgments on them for it, vv. 21–23.

A detailed analysis of chapter

The disobedient Jews reproved for breaking their covenant with God. (1–10)

Their utter ruin. (11–17)

Plots against Jeremiah. (18–23)

Key verse

Verse 9: "And the Lord said unto me, A conspiracy is found among the men of Judah, and among the inhabitants of Jerusalem."

Key word / key phrase

Verse 3, "the man who does not obey."

Key event / key person / key theme

Judah and the broken covenant

Key thought

Disobeying God brings devastating consequences.

Key thing to look out for

It is never safe to be God's representative, as Jeremiah discovered.

Key Bible cross-reference

Verse 12. Deuteronomy 32:28.

Key "by way of explanation"

Verse 10, "refused." The sin here was deliberate and willful. Verse 21, Anathoth was Jeremiah's home-town.

Key "Quotable Quote"

"We sin two kinds of sin. We sin one kind of sin as though we trip off the curb, and it overtakes us by surprise. We sin a second kind of sin when we deliberately set ourselves up to fall."

Francis A. Schaeffer

Jeremiah 12

Matthew Henry's introduction

In this chapter we have,

I. The prophet's humble complaint to God of the success that wicked people had in their wicked practices (vv. 1, 2) and his appeal to God about his own integrity (v. 3), with a prayer that God would, for the sake of the public, bring the wickedness of the wicked to an end, vv. 3, 4.

II. God's rebuke to the prophet for his uneasiness at his present troubles, bidding him prepare for greater, vv. 5, 6.

III. A sad lamentation of the present deplorable state of the Israel of God, vv. 7–13.

IV. An intimation of mercy to God's people, in a denunciation of wrath against their neighbors that helped forward their affliction, that they should be plucked out; but with a promise that if they would at last join themselves with the people of God they should come in sharers with them in their privileges, vv. 14–17.

A detailed analysis of chapter

Jeremiah complains about the prosperity of the wicked. (1–6)

The heavy judgments to come upon the nation. (7–13)

Divine mercy to them, and even to the nations around. (14–17)

Key verse

Verse 7: "I have forsaken mine house, I have left mine heritage; I have given the dearly beloved of my soul into the hand of her enemies."

Key word / key phrase

Verse 1, "a case before you."

Key event / key person / key theme

Jeremiah's complaint, and God's reply

Key thought

Many of the prophets questioned the Lord, as Jeremiah does here.

Key thing to look out for

"God's answer is to brace Jeremiah for yet fiercer, and often subtler, opposition from his family" (D.J. Wiseman).

Key Bible cross-reference

Verse 1. See Ezra 9:15

Key "by way of explanation"

Verse 5: if Jeremiah cannot cope with opposition in his own town, how will he manage in Jerusalem? There were lions and other wild animals in the dense jungle-like vegetation of the Jordan valley.

Key "Quotable Quote"

"Though our Savior's passion is over, his compassion is not."

William Penn

Jeremiah 13

Matthew Henry's introduction

Still the prophet is attempting to awaken this secure and stubborn people to repentance, by the consideration of the judgments of God that were coming on them. He is to tell them,

I. By the sign of a girdle spoiled that their pride should be stained, vv. 1–11.

II. By the sign of bottles filled with wine that their counsels should be blasted, vv. 12–14.

III. In consideration hereof he is to call them to repent and humble themselves, vv. 15–21.

IV. He is to convince them that it is for their obstinacy and incorrigibleness that the judgments of God are so prolonged and brought to extremity, vv. 22–27.

A detailed analysis of chapter

The glory of the Jews was to be marred. (1–11)
All ranks would suffer misery. An earnest exhortation to repentance. (12–17)
An awful message to Jerusalem and its king. (18–27)

Key verse

Verse 12: "Every bottle shall be filled with wine: and they shall say unto thee, Do we not certainly know that every bottle shall be filled with wine?"

Key word / key phrase

Verse 2, "I brought a belt."

Key event / key person / key theme

The close relationship of God and his people (the belt) is now ruined.

Key thought

God's truth can be conveyed in a host of different ways.

Key thing to look out for

The danger of pride and trusting in the self.

Key Bible cross-reference

Verse 22. See Kings 9:9.

Key "by way of explanation"

Verse 6, "Many days later," probably stands for the seventy-year long exile in Babylon.

Key "Quotable Quote"

"Illustrations are just servants."

D. Martyn Lloyd-Jones

Jeremiah 14

Matthew Henry's introduction

Here is,

I. A melancholy description of it, vv. 1–6.

II. A prayer to God to put an end to this calamity and to return in mercy to their land, vv. 7–9.

III. A severe threatening that God would proceed in his controversy, because they proceeded in their iniquity, vv. 10–12.

IV. The prophet's excusing the people, by laying the blame on their false prophets; and the doom passed both on the deceivers and the deceived, vv. 13–16.

V. Directions given to the prophet, instead of interceding for them, to lament them; but his continuing notwithstanding to intercede for them, vv. 17–22.

A detailed analysis of chapter

A drought on the land of Judah. (1–7)

A confession of sin in the name of the people. (8–9)

The divine purpose to punish is declared. (10–16)

The people ask for help. (17–22)

Key verse

Verse 1: "The word of the LORD that came to Jeremiah concerning the dearth."

Key word / key phrase

Verse 3, "no water."

Key event / key person / key theme

Judah's drought is described

Key thought

Even when God's judgments were crystal clear some people would not repent.

Key thing to look out for

The best prophets, like Nehemiah, identified with the sin of God's people and confessed such sin as if it were their own.

Key Bible cross-reference

Verse 11. See Exodus 32:10.

Key "by way of explanation"

Verse 17, "virgin daughter," was a name by which Jerusalem was known.

Key "Quotable Quote"

"I thank God that now when I preach I shall be able to say instead of 'dear brethren,' 'my fellow lepers.'"

Joseph de Veuster

Jeremiah 15

Matthew Henry's introduction

I. Notwithstanding the prophet's prayers, God here ratifies the sentence given against the people, and abandons them to ruin turning a deaf ear to all the intercessions made for them, vv. 1–9.

II. The prophet himself, notwithstanding the satisfaction he had in communion with God, still finds himself uneasy and out of temper.
   A. He complains to God of his continual struggle with his persecutors, v. 10.
   B. God assures him that he shall be taken under special protection, though there was a general desolation coming on the land, vv. 11–14.
   C. He appeals to God about his sincerity in the discharge of his prophetic office and thinks it hard that he should not have more of the comfort of it, vv. 15–18.
   D. Fresh security is given him that, on condition he continue faithful, God will continue his care of him and his favor to him, vv. 19–21.

A detailed analysis of chapter

The destruction of the wicked described. (1–9)
The prophet complains, and is reproved. (10–14)
He asks for pardon, and is promised protection. (15–21)

Key verse

Verse 10: "Woe is me, my mother, that thou hast borne me a man of strife and a man of contention to the whole earth!"

Key word / key phrase

Verse 10, "everyone curses me."

Key event / key person / key theme

God's promise of protection for Jeremiah.

Key thought

It is never right to blame the Lord when things go wrong.

Key thing to look out for

Without being irreverent, it is right to tell the Lord how one is feeling.

Key Bible cross-reference

Verse 2. See Revelation 13:10.

Key "by way of explanation"

Verse 1. In the days of Moses and Samuel the people had listened and repented. But not any longer. Only exile will bring them to their senses.

Key "Quotable Quote"

"Honesty and transparency make you vulnerable. Be honest and transparent anyway."

Mother Teresa of Calcutta

Jeremiah 16

Matthew Henry's introduction

In this chapter,

I. The greatness of the calamity that was coming on the Jewish nation is illustrated by prohibitions given to the prophet neither to set up a house of his own (vv. 1–4) nor to go into the house of mourning (vv. 5–7) nor into the house of feasting, vv. 8, 9.

II. God is justified in these severe proceedings against them by an account of their great wickedness, vv. 10–13.

III. An intimation is given of mercy in reserve, vv. 14, 15.

IV. Some hopes are given that the punishment of the sin should prove the reformation of the sinners, and that they should return to God at length in a way of duty, and so be qualified for his returns to them in a way of favor, vv. 16–21.

A detailed analysis of chapter

Jeremiah's life is to be a sign. (1–9)
The justice of God in these judgments. (10–13)
Future restoration of the Jews, and the conversion of the Gentiles. (14–21)

Key verse

Verse 16: "Behold, I will send for many fishers, saith the LORD, and they shall fish them; and after will I send for many hunters, and they shall hunt them from every mountain, and from every hill, and out of the holes of the rocks."

Key word / key phrase

Verse 10, "a great disaster."

Key event / key person / key theme

When God departs

Key thought

Within this single chapter disaster and restoration are spoken of.

Key thing to look out for

Power and might do not belong to political leaders but to the Lord.

Key Bible cross-reference

Verse 9. See Revelation 18:23.

Key "by way of explanation"

Verse 19, "refuge." The Lord is often pictured in ways that portray his power and strength, especially in the psalms.

Key "Quotable Quote"

"There is no greater joy than the peace and assurance of knowing that, whatever the future may hold, you are secure in the loving arms of the Savior."

Billy Graham

Jeremiah 17

Matthew Henry's introduction

In this chapter,

I. God convicts the Jews of the sin of idolatry by the notorious evidence of the fact, and condemns them to captivity for it, vv. 1–4.

II. He shows them the folly of all their carnal confidences, which should stand them in no stead when God's time came to contend with them, and that this was one of the sins on which his controversy with them was grounded, vv. 5–11.

III. The prophet makes his appeal and address to God on occasion of the malice of his enemies against him, committing himself to the divine protection, and begging of God to appear for him, vv. 12–18.

IV. God, by the prophet, warns the people to keep holy the Sabbath day, assuring them that, if they did, it should be the lengthening out of their tranquility, but that, if not, God would by some desolating judgment assert the honor of his Sabbaths, vv. 19–27.

A detailed analysis of chapter

The fatal consequences of the idolatry of the Jews. (1–4)

The happiness of the people who trust in God; the end of those who do not. (5–11)

The malice of the prophet's enemies. (12–18)

The observance of the Sabbath. (19–27)

Key verse

Verse 1: "The sin of Judah is written with a pen of iron."

Key word / key phrase

Verse 6, "parched places."

Key event / key person / key theme

The results of sin

Key thought

We know how true it is that environmental mismanagement ruins the earth. This principle is just as true in the spiritual realm.

Key thing to look out for

Health, wholeness, and salvation are all linked with each other.

Key Bible cross-reference

Verse 8. See Psalm 1:3.

Key "by way of explanation"

Verse 20, "kings of Judah," refers to all the kings of David's dynasty.

Key "Quotable Quote"

"The Bible deals with heaven and hell, good and bad, God and the devil, right and wrong, salvation and damnation; we like to deal with things in-between."

Oswald Chambers

Jeremiah 18

Matthew Henry's introduction

In this chapter we have,

I. A general declaration of God's ways in dealing with nations and kingdoms, that he can easily do what he will with them, as easily as the potter can with the clay (vv. 1–6), but that he certainly will do what is just and fair with them. If he threaten their ruin, yet on their repentance he will return in mercy to them, and, when he is coming towards them in mercy, nothing but their sin will stop the progress of his favors, vv. 7–10.

II. A particular demonstration of the folly of the men of Judah and Jerusalem in departing from their God to idols, and so bringing ruin on themselves notwithstanding the fair warnings given them and God's kind intentions towards them, vv. 11–17.

III. The prophet's complaint to God of the base ingratitude and unreasonable malice of his enemies, persecutors, and slanderers, and his prayers against them, vv. 18–23.

A detailed analysis of chapter

God's power over his creatures is represented by the potter. (1–10)

The Jews exhorted to repent, and judgments predicted. (11–17)

The prophet appeals to God. (18–23)

Key verse

Verse 6: "O house of Israel, cannot I do with you as this potter?"

Key word

Verse 8, "Repents."

Key event / key person / key theme

Jeremiah receives a message from God as a result of his visit to a potter's workshop.

Key thought

"God is always using everyday objects and the experiences of life to show us truths about himself. Because God is both Creator and Savior it is natural that he should use the created world to develop our spiritual lives."

Stephen Travis

Key thing to look out for

The "if . . . then" sequence in verses 7–10. If the warning of disaster results in turning back to God then God will avert the disaster. But if God's promise of blessing is met with disobedience, then the blessing will end in disaster. Note that the word "if" comes four times in these verses.

Key Bible cross-reference

With verse 15, see Isaiah 17:10–11: both give the results of forgetting God.

Key "by way of explanation"

Verse 3, "Working at the wheel." In Hebrew this is "the two stone-wheels." The lower wheel, which was turned by the potter's feet, made the upper wheel spin round. The potter's hands were thus free to work the clay on the upper wheel.

Key "Quotable Quote"

"Like the New Testament parables, not every part must be pressed for its symbolism for neither nations nor men are lifeless lumps of clay. . . . It is God who molds, breaking down, rebuilds. This power is not exercised arbitrarily and the possibility of renewal by God is conditional on a change of heart."

D.J. Wiseman

Jeremiah 19

Matthew Henry's introduction

The same melancholy theme is the subject of this chapter that was of those foregoing—the approaching ruin of Judah and Jerusalem for their sins. This Jeremiah had often foretold; here he has particularly full orders to foretell it again.

I. He must set their sins in order before them, as he had often done, especially their idolatry, vv. 4, 5.

II. He must describe the particular judgments which were now coming apace on them for these sins, vv. 6–9.

III. He must do this in the valley of Tophet, with great solemnity, and for some particular reasons, vv. 2, 3.

IV. He must summon a company of the elders together to be witnesses of this, v. 1.

V. He must confirm this, and endeavor to affect his hearers with it, by a sign, which was the breaking of an earthen bottle, signifying that they should be dashed to pieces like a potter's vessel, vv. 10–13.

VI. When he had done this in the valley of Tophet he ratified it in the court of the temple, vv. 14, 15.

A detailed analysis of chapter

By the type of breaking an earthen vessel, Jeremiah is to predict the destruction of Judah. (1–15)

Key verse

Verse 15: "Behold, I will bring upon this city and upon all her towns all the evil that I have pronounced against it, because they have hardened their necks, that they might not hear my words."

Key word / key phrase

Verse 10, "break the jar."

Key event / key person / key theme

The sign of the broken flask

Key thought

One of the worst condemnations found in the Bible is that people do not listen to God's words.

Key thing to look out for

Even when Jeremiah knew that the people would not repent he carried out the Lord's commands faithfully.

Key Bible cross-reference

Verse 5. See Leviticus 18:21.

Key "by way of explanation"

Verse 13, "to all the starry hosts." The sun, moon, and stars were worshiped by some of the people of Judah.

Key "Quotable Quote"

"A strong and faithful pulpit is no mean safeguard of a nation's life."

John Hall

Jeremiah 20

Matthew Henry's introduction

Such plain dealing as Jeremiah used in the previous chapter, one might easily foresee, if it did not convince and humble men, would provoke and exasperate them; and so it did; for here we find,

I. Jeremiah persecuted by Pashur for preaching that sermon, vv. 1, 2.

II. Pashur threatened for so doing, and the word which Jeremiah had preached confirmed, vv. 3–6.

III. Jeremiah complaining to God about it, and the other instances of hard measure that he had since he began to be a prophet, and the grievous temptations he had struggled with (vv. 7–10), encouraging himself in God, lodging his appeal with him, not doubting but that he shall yet praise him, by which it appears that he had much grace (vv. 11–13) and yet peevishly cursing the day of his birth (vv. 14–18), by which it appears that he had sad remainders of corruption in him too, and was a man subject to like passions as we are.

A detailed analysis of chapter

The doom of Pashur, who ill-treated the prophet. (1–6)

Jeremiah complains about being persecuted. (7–13)

He regrets ever being born. (14–18)

Key verse

Verse 1: "Now Pashur the son of Immer the priest, who was also chief governor in the house of the LORD, heard that Jeremiah prophesied these things."

Key word / key phrase

Verse 2, "put in the stocks."

Key event / key person / key theme

Jeremiah put in the stocks

Key thought

Most of the leading early disciples of Jesus were martyred or persecuted.

Key thing to look out for

The great, fearless, Jeremiah knew what it was like to wish he was dead.

Key Bible cross-reference

Verses 14–18. See Job 3:1–19.

Key "by way of explanation"

Verse 16, "towns the Lord overthrew." The fate of Sodom and Gomorrah was well known in Jeremiah's day.

Key "Quotable Quote"

"If we only spent more of our time in looking at him we should soon forget ourselves."

D. Martyn Lloyd-Jones

Jeremiah 21

Matthew Henry's introduction

Here is,

I. The message which Zedekiah sent to the prophet, to desire him to enquire of the Lord for them, vv. 1, 2.

II. The answer which Jeremiah, in God's name, sent to that message, in which,

A. He foretells the certain and inevitable ruin of the city, and the fruitlessness of their attempts for its preservation, vv. 3–7.

B. He advises the people to make the best of bad, by going over to the king of Babylon, vv. 8–10.

C. He advises the king and his family to repent and reform (vv. 11, 12), and not to trust to the strength of their city and grow secure, vv. 13, 14.

A detailed analysis of chapter

The only way of deliverance is to surrender to the Babylonians. (1–10)

The wickedness of the king and his household. (11–14)

Key verse

Verse 4: "Thus saith the LORD God of Israel; Behold, I will turn back the weapons of war that are in your hands, wherewith ye fight against the king of Babylon, and against the Chaldeans, which besiege you without the walls, and I will assemble them into the midst of this city."

Key word / key phrase

Verse 4, "I am about to turn against you."

Key event / key person / key theme

Jerusalem's defeat is predicted

Key thought

The choice given in verse 8 is true for each of us every day.

Key thing to look out for

Note why the Lord says he is "against" Jerusalem, verse 13.

Key Bible cross-reference

Verse 2. See 2 Kings 25:1–11.

Key "by way of explanation"

Verse 13, "valley." Jerusalem is set on a high mound, surrounded by valleys.

Key "Quotable Quote"

"Every Christian must refer always and everywhere to the Scriptures for all his choices, becoming like a child before it, seeking in it the most effective remedy against all his various weaknesses, and not daring to take a step without being illuminated by the divine rays of those words."

Pope John Paul II

Jeremiah 22

Matthew Henry's introduction

Here is,

I. A message sent to the royal family, as it should seem in the reign of Jehoiakim, relating partly to Jehoahaz, who was carried away captive into Egypt, and partly to Jehoiakim, who succeeded him and was now on the throne. The king and princes are exhorted to carry out judgment, and are assured that, if they did so, the royal family should flourish, but otherwise it should be ruined, vv. 1–9. Jehoahaz, called here Shallum, is lamented, vv. 10–12. Jehoiakim is reproved and threatened, vv. 13–19.

II. Another message sent them in the reign of Jehoiachin (alias, Jeconiah) the son of Jehoiakim. He is charged with an obstinate refusal to hear, and is threatened with destruction, and it is foretold that in him Solomon's house should fail, vv. 20–30.

A detailed analysis of chapter

Justice is recommended, and destruction threatened in case of disobedience. (1–9)

The captivity of Jehoiakim, and the end of Jeconiah. (10–19)

The doom of the royal family. (20–30)

Key verse

Verse 3: "Execute ye judgment and righteousness, and deliver the spoiled out of the hand of the oppressor: and do no wrong, do no violence to the stranger, the fatherless, nor the widow, neither shed innocent blood in this place."

Key word / key phrase
Verse 13, "woe to him who builds his palace by unrighteousness."

Key event / key person / key theme
Kings condemned

Key thought
The highest power in the land is subject to God's judgment.

Key thing to look out for
The same old sins are repeated again and again.

Key Bible cross-reference
Verse 5. See Matthew 23:38.

Key "by way of explanation"
Verse 9, "forsaken the covenant," that is, by breaking the first and second commandment of the Ten Commandments, they have broken the binding agreement they made with God.

Key "Quotable Quote"
"What destroys faith is that disobedience that hardens into unbelief."
Os Guinness

Jeremiah 23

Matthew Henry's introduction
In this chapter the prophet, in God's name, is dealing his reproofs and threatenings,

I. Among the careless princes, or pastors of the people (vv. 1, 2), yet promising to take care of the flock, which they had been wanting in their duty to, vv. 3–8.

II. Among the wicked prophets and priests, whose bad character is here given at large in divers instances, especially their imposing on the people with their pretended inspirations, at which the prophet is astonished, and for which they must expect to be punished, vv. 9–32.

III. Among the profane people, who ridiculed God's prophets and bantered them, vv. 33–40.

A detailed analysis of chapter
The restoration of the Jews to their own land. (1–8)
The wickedness of the priests and prophets of Judah, and the people exhorted not to listen to false promises. (9–22)
False prophets are warned. (23–32)
Those who scoff at genuine prophecy. (33–40)

Key verse
Verse 6: "In his days Judah shall be saved, and Israel shall dwell safely: and this is his name whereby he shall be called, THE LORD OUR RIGHTEOUSNESS."

Key word / key phrase
Verse 5, "a righteous Branch."

Key event / key person / key theme
The Righteous Branch

Key thought
Faithless shepherds of God's flock are no novelty.

Key thing to look out for

It is possible to lie in God's name as well as to prophecy faithfully in God's name.

Key Bible cross-reference

Verse 14. See Genesis 18:20.

Key "by way of explanation"

Verse 6, "Judah . . . Israel." All of God's people will be united and restored.

Key "Quotable Quote"

"Christ is with those of humble mind, not with those who exalt themselves over his flock."

Clement of Rome

Jeremiah 24

Matthew Henry's introduction

Here is,

I. A vision of two baskets of figs, one very good and the other very bad, vv. 1–3.

II. The explication of this vision, applying the good figs to those that were already sent into captivity for their good (vv. 4–7), the bad figs to those that should hereafter be sent into captivity for their hurt, vv. 8–10.

A detailed analysis of chapter

Good figs (that is the Jews in captivity), and the rotten figs (those left behind). (1–10)

Key verse

Verse 1: "The LORD showed me, and, behold, two baskets of figs were set before the temple of the LORD . . ."

Key word / key phrase

Verse 6, "I will build them up."

Key event / key person / key theme

Two baskets of figs

Key thought

Note the characteristics of those symbolized by the bad figs.

Key thing to look out for

Note the characteristics of those symbolized by the good figs.

Key Bible cross-reference

Verse 1. See 2 Kings 24:12–16.

Key "by way of explanation"

Verse 2, "that ripen early." The figs which ripen in June were noted for being especially succulent. When Jerusalem was captured in March 597 the leaders of the people, and the craftsmen were deported.

Key "Quotable Quote"

"Give us a pure heart
That we may see thee,
A humble heart
That we may hear thee,
A heart of love
That we may serve thee,
A heart of faith
That we may live thee."

Dag Hammarskjöld

Jeremiah 25

Matthew Henry's introduction

Here is,

I. A review of the prophecies that had been delivered to Judah and Jerusalem for many years past, by Jeremiah himself and other prophets, with the little regard given to them and the little success of them, vv. 1–7.

II. A very express threatening of the destruction of Judah and Jerusalem, by the king of Babylon, for their contempt of God, and their continuance in sin (vv. 8–11), to which is annexed a promise of their deliverance out of their captivity in Babylon, after 70 years, vv. 12–14.

III. A prediction of the devastation of divers other nations about, by Nebuchadrezzar, represented by a "cup of fury" put into their hands (vv. 15–28), by a sword sent among them (vv. 29–33), and a desolation made among the shepherds and their flocks and pastures (vv. 34–38); so that we have here judgment beginning at the house of God, but not ending there.

A detailed analysis of chapter

The Jews rebuked for not obeying calls to repentance. (1–7)

Their captivity during seventy years is specifically foretold. (8–14)

Destruction on the nations shown by the cup of wrath. (15–29)

The judgments again declared. (30–38)

Key verse

Verse 1: "The word that came to Jeremiah concerning all the people of Judah in the fourth year of Jehoiakim the son of Josiah king of Judah, that was the first year of Nebuchadrezzar king of Babylon."

Key word / key phrase

Verse 11, "seventy years."

Key event / key person / key theme

The seventy-year captivity

Key thought

God's judgment will fall on everyone.

Key thing to look out for

God's mercy is for those who turn to him.

Key Bible cross-reference

Verse 1. See Daniel 1:1–2.

Key "by way of explanation"

Verse 15, "the wine of my wrath." "Wine" often represents God's wrath and righteous anger.

Key "Quotable Quote"

"A day will come when those who are not born again will wish that they had never been born at all."

J.C. Ryle

Jeremiah 26

Matthew Henry's introduction

As in the history of the Acts of the Apostles that of their preaching and that of their suffering are interwoven, so it is in the account we have of the prophet Jeremiah; witness this chapter, where we are told,

I. How faithfully he preached, vv. 1–6.

II. How spitefully he was persecuted for so doing by the priests and the prophets, vv. 7–11.

III. How bravely he stood to his doctrine, in the face of his persecutors, vv. 12–15.

IV. How wonderfully he was protected and delivered by the prudence of the princes and elders, vv. 16–19. Though Urijah, another prophet, was about the same time put to death by Jehoiakim (vv. 20–23), yet Jeremiah met with those that sheltered him, v. 24.

A detailed analysis of chapter

The destruction of the temple and city foretold. (1–6)

Jeremiah's life is threatened. (7–15)

He is defended by the elders. (16–24)

Key verse

Verse 8: "Now it came to pass, when Jeremiah had made an end of speaking all that the LORD had commanded him to speak unto all the people, that the priests and the prophets and all the people took him, saying, Thou shalt surely die."

Key word / key phrase

Verse 8, "the priests, the prophets and the people seized him."

Key event / key person / key theme

Jeremiah on trial

Key thought

Jeremiah's innocence was clear to all impartial observers.

Key thing to look out for

Jesus was also accused of speaking against the temple.

Key Bible cross-reference

Verse 18. See Micah 3:12.

Key "by way of explanation"

Verse 10, the "officials of Judah" were responsible for dealing with disputes, within the temple area.

Key "Quotable Quote"

"If the biographer gives me credit for being a plodder, he will describe me justly. Anything beyond this will be too much. I can plod. I can persevere in any definite pursuit. To this I owe everything."

William Carey

Jeremiah 27

Matthew Henry's introduction

I. He gives this counsel, in God's name, to the kings of the neighboring nations, that they might make the best of bad, assuring them that there was no remedy, but they must serve the king of Babylon; and yet in time there should be relief, for his dominion should last but 70 years, vv. 1–11.

II. He gives this counsel to Zedekiah king of Judah particularly (vv. 12–15) and to the priests and people, assuring them that the king of Babylon should still proceed against them till things were brought to the last extremity, and a patient submission would be the only way to mitigate the calamity and make it easy, vv. 16–22.

A detailed analysis of chapter

The neighboring nations to be subdued. (1–11)
Zedekiah is warned to give in. (12–18)
The temple treasures to be carried to Babylon, but later would be restored. (19–22)

Key verse

Verse 1: "In the beginning of the reign of Jehoiakim the son of Josiah king of Judah came this word unto Jeremiah from the LORD."

Key word / key phrase

Verse 2, "make a yoke."

Key event / key person / key theme

Jeremiah wears an ox yoke

Key thought

Like Ezekiel Jeremiah acted out what the Lord would do in the future.

Key thing to look out for

Many of the of the chapters in the Bible which focus on God's punishment also contain a message of hope, as this one does. See verse 22.

Key Bible cross-reference

Verse 1. See 2 Chronicles 36:11–13.

Key "by way of explanation"

Jeremiah's messages are not given in chronological order. Chapters 27–29 describe events in about 593 BC.

Key "Quotable Quote"

"Lord, make us instruments of thy peace.
Where there is hatred, let us sow love.
Where there is injury, pardon.
Where there is discord, union.
Where there is doubt, faith.
Where there is despair, hope.
Where there is darkness, light …"

Francis of Assisi

Jeremiah 28

Matthew Henry's introduction

I. Hananiah, a pretender to prophecy, in contradiction to Jeremiah, foretold the sinking of Nebuchadnezzar's power and the return both of the people and of the vessels that were carried away (vv. 1–4), and, as a sing of this, he broke the yoke from the neck of Jeremiah, vv. 10, 11.

II. Jeremiah wished his words might prove true, but appealed to the event whether they were so or no, not doubting but that would disprove them, vv. 5–9.

III. The doom both of the deceived and the deceiver is here read. The people that were deceived should have their yoke of wood turned into a yoke of iron (vv. 12–14), and the prophet that was the deceiver should be shortly cut off by death, and he was so, accordingly, within two months, vv. 15–17.

A detailed analysis of chapter

A false prophet opposes Jeremiah. (1–9)

The false prophet warned of his approaching death. (10–17)

Key verse

Verse 1: "And it came to pass the same year, in the beginning of the reign of Zedekiah king of Judah, in the fourth year, and in the fifth month, that Hananiah the son of Azur the prophet, which was of Gibeon, spake unto me in the house of the LORD."

Key word / key phrase

Verse 1, "the prophet Hananiah."

Key event / key person / key theme

Jeremiah's conflict with the prophet Hananiah

Key thought

Many of the worst enemies facing Christians are found within the ranks of the Church.

Key thing to look out for

The last verse of this chapter reads like God's epitaph on Hananiah.

Key Bible cross-reference

Verse 1. See 2 Kings 24:18–20.

Key "by way of explanation"

Hananiah "thought too much of Israel's privilege and too little of Israel's responsibility." (quoted by D.J. Wiseman)

Key "Quotable Quote"

"Satan labors with all his strength by false teachers, which are his messengers and ambassadors, to deceive, delude and forever destroy the precious souls of men."

Thomas Brooks

Jeremiah 29

Matthew Henry's introduction

Now here is,

I. A letter which Jeremiah wrote to the captives in Babylon, against their prophets that they had there (vv. 1–3), in which letter,

A. He endeavors to reconcile them to their captivity, to be easy under it and to make the best of it, vv. 4–7.

B. He cautions them not to give any credit to their false prophets, who fed them with hopes of a speedy release, vv. 8, 9.

C. He assures them that God would restore them in mercy to their own land again, at the end of 70 years, vv. 10–14.

D. He foretells the destruction of those who yet continued, and that they should be persecuted with one judgment after another, and sent at last into captivity, vv. 15–19.

E. He prophesies the destruction of two of their false prophets that they had in Babylon, that both soothed them up in their sins and set them bad examples (vv. 20–23), and this is the purport of Jeremiah's letter.

II. Here is a letter which Shemaiah, a false prophet in Babylon, wrote to the priests at Jerusalem, to stir them up to persecute

Jeremiah (vv. 24–29), and a denunciation of God's wrath against him for writing such a letter, vv. 30–32. Such struggles as these have there always been between the seed of the woman and the seed of the serpent.

A detailed analysis of chapter

Two letters to the captives in Babylon; in the first, they are recommended to be patient and composed. (1–19)

In the second, judgments are denounced against the false prophets who deceived them. (20–32)

Key verse

Verse 5: "Build ye houses, and dwell in them; and plant gardens, and eat the fruit of them."

Key word / key phrase

Verse 1, "the letter."

Key event / key person / key theme

Jeremiah's letter to the Jews in Babylonia

Key thought

The priority of prayer is apparent in this letter.

Key thing to look out for

God has plans for our lives.

Key Bible cross-reference

Verse 13. See Deuteronomy 4:29.

Key "by way of explanation"

Verse 15, "prophets . . . in Babylon." There were false prophets everywhere, even in Babylon. Jeremiah is writing from Jerusalem to the religious and civil leaders who had been taken to Babylon with Jehoiachin (2 Kings 24:17–20).

Key "Quotable Quote"

"Inconsistent professors injure the gospel more than the sneering critic or the infidel."

C.H. Spurgeon

Jeremiah 30

Matthew Henry's introduction

The sermon which we have in this and the following chapter is of a very different complexion from all those before. The prophet does indeed, by direction from God, change his voice. Most of what he had said hitherto was by way of reproof and threatening; but these two chapters are wholly taken up with precious promises of a return out of captivity, and that typical of the glorious things reserved for the church in the days of the Messiah. The prophet is told not only to preach this, but to write it, because it is intended for the comfort of the generation to come, vv. 1–3. It is here promised,

I. That they should hereafter have a joyful restoration.
   - A. Though they were now in a great deal of pain and terror, vv. 4–7.
   - B. Though their oppressors were very strong, vv. 8–10.
   - C. Though a full end was made of other nations, and they were not restored, v. 11.
   - D. Though all means of their deliverance seemed to fail and be cut off, vv. 12–14.
   - E. Though God himself had sent them into

captivity, and justly, for their sins, vv. 15, 16.

F. Though all about them looked on their case as desperate, v. 17.

II. That after their joyful restoration they should have a happy settlement, that their city should be rebuilt (v. 18), their numbers increased (vv. 19, 20), their government established (v. 21), God's covenant with them renewed (v. 22), and their enemies destroyed and cut off, vv. 23, 24.

A detailed analysis of chapter

Troubles which will occur before the restoration of Israel. (1–11)

Encouragement to trust divine promises. (12–17)

The blessings under Christ, and the wrath on the wicked. (18–24)

Key verse

Verse 10: "Therefore fear thou not, O my servant Jacob, saith the LORD; neither be dismayed, O Israel: for, lo, I will save thee from afar, and thy seed from the land of their captivity; and Jacob shall return, and shall be in rest, and be quiet, and none shall make him afraid."

Key word / key phrase

Verse 3, "back from captivity."

Key event / key person / key theme

Restoration of the land

Key thought

Salvation of every kind is attributed to the Lord.

Key thing to look out for

Salvation includes discipline.

Key Bible cross-reference

Verses 10–11. See 46:27,28.

Key "by way of explanation"

Verse 8, "tear off their bonds." The chains which bind God's people to foreign domination will be broken.

Key "Quotable Quote"

"Discipline is the secret of godliness. You must learn to discipline yourself for the purpose of godliness."

Jay E. Adams

Jeremiah 31

Matthew Henry's introduction

This chapter goes on with the good words and comfortable words which we had in the chapter before, for the encouragement of the captives, assuring them that God would in due time restore them or their children to their own land, and make them a great and happy nation again, especially by sending them the Messiah, in whose kingdom and grace many of these promises were to have their full accomplishment.

I. They shall be restored to peace and honor, and joy and great plenty, vv. 1–14.

II. Their sorrow for the loss of their children shall be at an end, vv. 15–17.

III. They shall repent of their sins, and God will graciously accept them in their repentance, vv. 18–20.

IV. They shall be multiplied and increased, both their children and their cattle, and not be cut off and diminished as they had been, vv. 21–30.

V. God will renew his covenant with them, and enrich it with spiritual blessings, vv. 31–34.

VI. These blessings shall be secured to theirs after them, even to the spiritual seed of Israel for ever, vv. 35–37.

VII. As an earnest of this the city of Jerusalem shall be rebuilt, vv. 38–40.

A detailed analysis of chapter

The restoration of Israel. (1–14)

Promises of guidance and happiness; Rachel lamenting. (15–17)

Ephraim [Israel] laments his errors. (18–20)

The promised Savior. (21–26)

The new covenant. (27–34)

Peace and prosperity in the time of the gospel. (35–40)

Key verse

Verse 31: "Behold, the days come, saith the LORD, that I will make a new covenant with the house of Israel, and with the house of Judah."

Key word / key phrase

Verse 31, "a new covenant."

Key event / key person / key theme

Restoration of both Israel and Judah

Key thought

This is the first mention of the new covenant.

Key thing to look out for

The characteristic of the new covenant is that it will be an internal one to be kept in one's heart.

Key Bible cross-reference

Verse 15. See Matthew 2:18.

Key "by way of explanation"

Verse 15, at Ramah the exiles were chained up before being deported (40:1).

Key "Quotable Quote"

"A covenant cannot be terminated. It can only be violated."

Ross T. Bender

Jeremiah 32

Matthew Henry's introduction

In this chapter we have,

I. Jeremiah imprisoned for foretelling the destruction of Jerusalem and the captivity of king Zedekiah, vv. 1–5.

II. We have him buying land, by divine appointment, as an assurance that in due time a happy end should be put to the present troubles, vv. 6–15.

III. We have his prayer, which he offered up to God on that occasion, vv. 16–25.

IV. We have a message which God thereon entrusted him to deliver to the people.

A. He must foretell the utter destruction of Judah and Jerusalem for their sins, vv. 26–35. But,

B. At the same time he must assure them that, though the destruction was total, it should not be final, but that at length their posterity should recover the peaceable possession of their own land, vv. 36–44.

A detailed analysis of chapter

Jeremiah buys a field. (1–15)

The prophet's prayer. (16–25)

God declares that he will give up his people, but promises to restore them. (26–44)

Key verse

Verse 6: "And Jeremiah said, The word of the LORD came unto me, saying, Behold, Hanameel the son of Shallum thine uncle shall come unto thee, saying, Buy thee my field that is in Anathoth: for the right of redemption is thine to buy it."

Key word / key phrase

Verse 43, "fields will be bought in this land."

Key event / key person / key theme

Jeremiah buys a field: future restoration

Key thought

To buy a field at such a time was a great act of faith and symbol of hope.

Key thing to look out for

Nothing is too hard for the Lord.

Key Bible cross-reference

Verse 28. See 2 Kings 25:1–11.

Key "by way of explanation"

Verse 12, "Baruch," is mentioned here for the first time. He later became very important in preserving Jeremiah's words. Jeremiah bought the field in 588/7 when Jerusalem had been under siege for a year.

Key "Quotable Quote"

"In the midst of worldly employments, there should be some thoughts of sin, death, judgment, and eternity, with at least a word or two of ejaculatory prayer to God."

Samuel Rutherford

Jeremiah 33

Matthew Henry's introduction

It is here promised,

I. That the city shall be rebuilt and re-established "in statu quo—in its former state," vv. 1–6.

II. That the captives, having their sins pardoned, shall be restored, vv. 7, 8.

III. That this shall redound very much to the glory of God, v. 9.

IV. That the country shall have both joy and plenty, vv. 10–14.

V. That way shall be made for the coming of the Messiah, vv. 15, 16.

VI. That the house of David, the house of Levi, and the house of Israel, shall flourish again, and be established, and all three in the kingdom of Christ; a gospel ministry and the gospel church shall continue while the world stands, vv. 17–26.

A detailed analysis of chapter

The restoration of the Jews. (1–13)

The Messiah promised; happiness of his times. (14–26)

Key verse

Verse 3: "Call unto me, and I will answer thee, and show thee great and mighty things, which thou knowest not."

Key word / key phrase

Verse 2, "who made the earth."

Key event / key person / key theme

Reconfirming the covenant

Key thought

These wonderful promises were made to Jeremiah while he was still under arrest.

Key thing to look out for

"The Lord Our Righteousness," verse 16, summarizes the whole point of Jesus' death on the cross.

Key Bible cross-reference

Verse 11. See Psalm 100:5.

Key "by way of explanation"

Verse 8, "forgive all their sins." The covenant was founded on the confession of sin and the forgiveness of sin.

Key "Quotable Quote"

"The greatest of physicians has come to us and forgiven all our sins."

Augustine of Hippo

Jeremiah 34

Matthew Henry's introduction

I. One to foretell the fate of Zedekiah king of Judah, that he should fall into the hands of the king of Babylon, that he should live a captive, but should at last die in peace in his captivity, vv. 1–7.

II. Another to read the doom both of prince and people for their treacherous dealings with God, in bringing back into bondage their servants whom they had released according to the law, and so playing fast and loose with God. They had walked at all adventures with God (vv. 8–11), and therefore God would walk at all adventures with them, in bringing the Chaldean army on them again when they began to hope that they had got clear of them, vv. 12–22.

A detailed analysis of chapter

Zedekiah's death at Babylon foretold. (1–7)

The Jews reproved for compelling their poor brethren, forced by debt to become slaves, to remain in slavery. (8–22)

Key verse

Verse 4: "Yet hear the word of the LORD, O Zedekiah king of Judah; Thus saith the LORD of thee, Thou shalt not die by the sword."

Key word / key phrase

Verse 17, "not obeyed me."

Key event / key person / key theme

A covenant commitment overthrown (verses 10, 11

Key thought

Under the covenant, slaves were set free every seven years. By going back on their promise to keep this covenant commitment, the people had dishonored God.

Key thing to look out for

God's judgment on sin is inevitable as night follows day.

Key Bible cross-reference

Verse 14. See Exodus 21:2.

Key "by way of explanation"

Verse 1, "all the empires and peoples." Nebuchadnezzar's empire was vast. The attack by the Babylonians came in 589 after Zedekiah had rebelled. Though the siege was temporarily lifted (21) Jerusalem was eventually captured.

Key "Quotable Quote"

"There is your brother, naked and crying! And you stand confused over choice of floor covering."

Ambrose

Jeremiah 35

Matthew Henry's introduction

I. He sets before them the obedience of the family of the Rechabites to the commands which were left them by Jonadab their ancestor, and how they persevered in that obedience and would not be tempted from it, vv. 1–11.

II. With this he aggravates the disobedience of the Jews to God and their contempt of his precepts, vv. 12–15.

III. He foretells the judgments of God on the Jews for their impious disobedience to God, vv. 16, 17.

IV. He assures the Rechabites of the blessing of God on them for their pious obedience to their father, vv. 18, 19.

A detailed analysis of chapter

The obedience of the Recabites. (1–11)

The Jews' disobedience to the Lord. (12–19)

Key verse

Verse 3: "Then I took Jaazaniah the son of Jeremiah, the son of Habaziniah, and his brethren, and all his sons, and the whole house of the Rechabites."

Key word / key phrase

Verse 2, "the Recabite family."

Key event / key person / key theme

Message to the Recabites

Key thought

The Recabites are held up as an example of loyalty in the middle of adversity.

Key thing to look out for

Verse 13 asks the pertinent question, "Will you not learn a lesson . . .?"

Key Bible cross-reference

Verse 1. See 2 Chronicles 36:5–7.

Key "by way of explanation"

The Recabites were a nomad clan who were

true worshipers of God, and lived in the desert in protest against the evils of society. They had come into Jerusalem for protection from raiding enemy armies. The events of chapters 35–36 follow chapter 26 (609–598 BC).

Key "Quotable Quote"

"When Christians stand up for righteousness and justice, they evidence the power of the living God."

Charles Colson

Jeremiah 36

Matthew Henry's introduction

Now here we have,

I. The writing of this roll by Baruch, as Jeremiah dictated it, vv. 1–4.

II. The reading of the roll by Baruch to all the people publicly on a fast-day (vv. 5–10), afterwards by Baruch to the princes privately (vv. 11–19), and lastly by Jehudi to the king, vv. 20, 21.

III. The burning of the roll by the king, with orders to prosecute Jeremiah and Baruch, vv. 22–26.

IV. The writing of another roll, with large additions, particularly of Jehoiakim's doom for burning the former, vv. 27–32.

A detailed analysis of chapter

Baruch is to write down the prophecies of Jeremiah. (1–8)

The leaders advise them to hide themselves. (9–19)

The king having heard some of Jeremiah's words, burns the scroll. (20–32)

Key verse

Verse 2: "Take thee a roll of a book, and write therein all the words that I have spoken unto thee against Israel, and against Judah, and against all the nations, from the day I spake unto thee, from the days of Josiah, even unto this day."

Key word / key phrase

Verse 27, "the king burned the scroll."

Key event / key person / key theme

The kings refused to listen to Jeremiah's prophecies.

Key thought

Endless attempts to snuff out God's word have been made by destroying Bibles.

Key thing to look out for

Note how Jeremiah reacted, verse 32, to this scroll burning.

Key Bible cross-reference

Verse 1. See 2 Chronicles 36:5–7.

Key "by way of explanation"

Verse 6, "a day of fasting." God's people fasted in times of crisis.

Key "Quotable Quote"

"Do not let only your mouth fast, but also the eye and the ear and the feet and the hands and all the members of our bodies.

Let the hands fast, by being free of avarice.

Let the feet fast, by ceasing to run after sin.

Let the eyes fast, by disciplining them not to glare at that which is sinful.
Let the ear fast, by not listening to evil talk and gossip.
Let the mouth fast from foul words and unjust criticism."

John Chrysostom

Jeremiah 37

Matthew Henry's introduction

This chapter brings us very near the destruction of Jerusalem by the Chaldeans, for the story of it lies in the latter end of Zedekiah's reign; we have in it,

I. A general idea of the bad character of that reign, vv. 1, 2.
II. The message which Zedekiah, notwithstanding, sent to Jeremiah to desire his prayers, v. 3.
III. The flattering hopes which the people had conceived, that the Chaldeans would quit the siege of Jerusalem, v. 5.
IV. The assurance God gave them by Jeremiah (who was now at liberty, v. 4) that the Chaldean army should renew the siege and take the city, vv. 6–10.
V. The imprisonment of Jeremiah, under pretence that he was a deserter, vv. 11–15.
VI. The kindness which Zedekiah showed him when he was a prisoner, vv. 16–21.

A detailed analysis of chapter

The Babylonian army will return. (1–10)
Jeremiah is imprisoned. (11–21)

Key verse

Verse 5: "Then Pharaoh's army was come forth out of Egypt: and when the Chaldeans that besieged Jerusalem heard tidings of them, they departed from Jerusalem."

Key word / key phrase

Verse 16, "in a dungeon"

Key event / key person / key theme

Jeremiah imprisoned

Key thought

Some of God's servants undergo severe times of persecution in their lives.

Key thing to look out for

Jeremiah was imprisoned for being faithful to the Lord.

Key Bible cross-reference

Verse 1. See 2 Chronicles 36:10.

Key "by way of explanation"

Verse 21, "courtyard of the guard." Jeremiah's imprisonment was made much more bearable. At the end of the Acts Paul had a not dissimilar experience when he was under house-arrest for two years.

Key "Quotable Quote"

"Those persecutions, which we must suffer for the testimony of the Gospel, are remnants of the sufferings of Christ."

John Calvin

Jeremiah 38

Matthew Henry's introduction

Here,

I. Jeremiah for his faithfulness is put into the dungeon by the princes, vv. 1–6.

II. At the intercession of Ebed-melech the Ethiopian, by special order from the king, he is taken up out of the dungeon and confined only to the court of the prison, vv. 7–13.

III. He has a private conversation with the king on the present conjuncture of affairs, vv. 14–22.

IV. Care is taken to keep that conversation private, vv. 24–28.

A detailed analysis of chapter

Jeremiah is thrown into a cistern, from where he is rescued by an Ethiopian. (1–13)
He advises the king to surrender to the Chaldeans. (14–28)

Key verse

Verse 6: "Then took they Jeremiah, and cast him into the dungeon of Malchiah the son of Hammelech, that was in the court of the prison: and they let down Jeremiah with cords."

Key word / key phrase

Verse 6, "into the cistern."

Key event / key person / key theme

Jeremiah dumped in a cistern

Key thought

Without someone to rescue him God's prophet would have died in the cistern.

Key thing to look out for

The faithful action of a few godly people can do an enormous amount of good.

Key Bible cross-reference

Verse 28. See Ezekiel 33:21.

Key "by way of explanation"

Verse 12, "put these old rags . . . under your arms." Ebed-Melech took practical and kind action as he rescued Jeremiah.

Key "Quotable Quote"

"It is impossible to comfort men's hearts with the love of God when their feet are perishing with cold."

William Booth

Jeremiah 39

Matthew Henry's introduction

We are here told,

I. That Jerusalem, after eighteen months' siege, was taken by the Chaldean army, vv. 1–3.

II. That king Zedekiah, attempting to make his escape, was seized and made a miserable captive to the king of Babylon, vv. 4–7.

III. That Jerusalem was burnt to the ground, and the people were carried captive, except the poor, vv. 8–10.

IV. That the Chaldeans were very kind to Jeremiah, and took particular care of him, vv. 11–14.

V. That Ebed-melech too, for his kindness, had a protection from God himself in this day of desolation, vv. 15–18.

A detailed analysis of chapter

The taking of Jerusalem. (1–10)

Jeremiah used well. (11–14)

Promises of safety to Ebed-melech. (15–18)

Key verse

Verse 1: "In the ninth year of Zedekiah king of Judah, in the tenth month, came Nebuchadrezzar king of Babylon and all his army against Jerusalem, and they besieged it."

Key word / key phrase

Verse 1, "Jerusalem was taken."

Key event / key person / key theme

Ebed-Melech rewarded; Jerusalem captured

Key thought

All of God's prophecies will be fulfilled.

Key thing to look out for

Whether in this life or in the next life God's faithful servants are rewarded.

Key Bible cross-reference

Verse 7. See Numbers 16:14.

Key "by way of explanation"

Verse 16, "Go and tell." It is clear that Jeremiah had contact with the outside world, even though he was confined to prison.

Key "Quotable Quote"

"In this life, all things go in pairs: practice and spiritual knowledge, free will and grace, fear and hope, struggle and reward."

Peter of Damascus

Jeremiah 40

Matthew Henry's introduction

In this chapter we have,

I. A more particular account of Jeremiah's discharge and his settlement with Gedaliah, vv. 1–6.

II. The great resort of the Jews that remained scattered in the neighboring countries to Gedaliah, who was made their governor under the king of Babylon; and the good posture they were in for a while under him, vv. 7–12.

III. A treacherous design formed against Gedaliah, by Ishmael, which we shall find carried out in the next chapter, vv. 13–16.

A detailed analysis of chapter

Jeremiah is directed to go to Gedaliah. (1–6)

A conspiracy against Gedaliah. (7–16)

Key verse

Verse 2: "And the captain of the guard took Jeremiah, and said unto him, The LORD thy God hath pronounced this evil upon this place."

Key word / key phrase

Verse 1, "He had found Jeremiah bound in chains."

Key event / key person / key theme

Jeremiah freed

Key thought

Jeremiah knows that the future lay with the exiles in Babylon, yet he decided to stay with the poorest in the land (verse 7).

Key thing to look out for

Jeremiah could have had comfortable old age if he had gone to Babylon (verse 4).

Key Bible cross-reference

Verses 7–9. See 2 Kings 25:22–24.

Key "by way of explanation"

Verses 13–16, the warning was justified (41:1–3). Gedaliah failed to recognize wise counsel. Gedaliah was based at Mizpah.

Key "Quotable Quote"

"Our professed love of freedom is increasingly shown to be a sophistry that replaces wisdom and righteousness with self-gratification."

Carl Henry

Jeremiah 41

Matthew Henry's introduction

I. Gedaliah is barbarously slain by Ishmael, vv. 1, 2.

II. All the Jews that were with him were slain likewise (v. 3) and a pit filled with their dead bodies, v. 9.

III. Some devout men, to the number of fourscore, that were going towards Jerusalem, were drawn in by Ishmael, and murdered likewise, vv. 4–7. Only ten of them escaped, v. 8.

IV. Those that escaped the sword were taken prisoners by Ishmael, and carried off towards the country of the Ammonites, v. 10.

V. By the conduct and courage of Johanan, though the death of the slain is not revenged, yet the prisoners are recovered, and he now becomes their commander-in-chief, vv. 11–16.

VI. His project is to carry them into the land of Egypt (vv. 17, 18), which we shall hear more of in the next chapter.

A detailed analysis of chapter

Ishmael murders Gedaliah at Mizpah. (1–3)

Ishael murders a group of pilgrims and flees with the people of Mizpah as his prisoners. (11–18)

Key verse

Verse 4: "And it came to pass the second day after he had slain Gedaliah, and no man knew it,"

Key word / key phrase

Verse 2, "struck down Gedaliah."

Key event / key person / key theme

Murder and massacre

Key thought

The escalation of evil.

Key thing to look out for

Verse 5, there were still godly people in Israel.

Key Bible cross-reference

Verses 1–3. See 2 Kings 25:25.

Key "by way of explanation"

Verse 7, "cistern." Cisterns were used to dump people in whether they were dead or alive. To murder someone while you were eating together was a gross violation of the laws of hospitality. The other murders were probably to silence witnesses.

Key "Quotable Quote"

"We cannot love good if we do not hate evil."

Jerome

Jeremiah 42

Matthew Henry's introduction

Here is,

I. The fair bargain that was made between Jeremiah and them about consulting God in this matter, vv. 1–6.

II. The message at large which God sent them, in answer to their enquiry, in which,

A. They are commanded and encouraged to continue in the land of Judah, and assured that if they did so it should be well with them, vv. 7–12.

B. They are forbidden to go to Egypt, and are plainly told that if they did it would be their ruin, vv. 13–18.

C. They are charged with dissimulation in their asking what God's will was in this matter and disobedience when they were told what it was; and sentence is accordingly passed on them, vv. 19–22.

A detailed analysis of chapter

Johanan wants Jeremiah to seek God's counsel. (1–6)

God promises them safety in in Judea, but destruction in Egypt. (7–22)

Key verse

Verse 3: "That the LORD thy God may show us the way wherein we may walk, and the thing that we may do."

Key word / key phrase

Verse 19, "Do not go to Egypt."

Key event / key person / key theme

"Don't flee to Egypt."

Key thought

Verse 11, God was with the people, and he was greater than the kings of Babylon, so they must not run away.

Key thing to look out for

Jeremiah could see that their minds were already made up: a sign of arrogance

Key Bible cross-reference

Verse 12. See Exodus 3:21.

Key "by way of explanation"

Verse 6, "we will obey the Lord our God." 43:2 shows how shallow this assertion proved to be.

Key "Quotable Quote"

"I need Thy presence every passing hour:
What but Thy grace can foil the tempter's power?"

Henry Francis Lyte

Jeremiah 43

Matthew Henry's introduction

Here is,

I. The people's contempt of this message; they denied it to be the word of God (vv. 1–3) and then made no difficulty of going directly contrary to it. Into Egypt they went, and took Jeremiah himself along with them, vv. 4–7.

II. God's pursuit of them with another message, foretelling the king of Babylon's pursuit of them into Egypt, vv. 8–13.

A detailed analysis of chapter

The leaders carry the people to Egypt. (1–7)
Jeremiah predicts the conquest of Egypt. (8–13)

Key verse

Verse 7: "So they came into the land of Egypt: for they obeyed not the voice of the LORD: thus came they even to Tahpanhes."

Key word / key phrase

Verse 7, "they entered Egypt."

Key event / key person / key theme

Jeremiah taken to Egypt

Key thought

Verse 8, even in Egypt Jeremiah continued to warn the people. He did not give up.

Key thing to look out for

Safety only lies with following the Lord.

Key Bible cross-reference

Verses 5–7. See 2 Kings 25:26.

Key "by way of explanation"

Verse 10, "my servant Nebuchadnezzar." God can use even pagan leaders to carry out his will.

Key "Quotable Quote"

"One of the outstanding glories of the Gospel is its promise of eternal security to all who truly believe it."

A.W. Pink

Jeremiah 44

Matthew Henry's introduction

In this chapter we have,

I. An awakening sermon which Jeremiah preaches to the Jews in Egypt, to reprove them for their idolatry, notwithstanding the warnings given them both by the word and the rod of God and to threaten the judgments of God against them for it, vv. 1–14.

II. The impudent and impious contempt which the people put on this admonition, and their declared resolution to persist in their idolatries notwithstanding, in despite of God and Jeremiah, vv. 15–19.

III. The sentence passed on them for their obstinacy, that they should all be cut off and perish in Egypt except a very small number; and, as a sign or earnest of it, the king of Egypt should shortly fall into the hands of the king of Babylon and be unable any longer to protect them, vv. 20–30.

A detailed analysis of chapter

The Jews in Egypt persist in idolatry. (1–14)

They refuse to reform. (15–19)

Jeremiah then pronounces destruction on them. (20–30)

Key verse

Verse 10: "They are not humbled even unto this day, neither have they feared, nor walked in my law, nor in my statutes, that I set before you and before your fathers."

Key word / key phrase

Verse 11, "to bring disaster."

Key event / key person / key theme

The Lord's message to the Jews in Egypt

Key thought

Human sinfulness again brings down divine wrath.

Key thing to look out for

The consequences of idolatry are incalculable.

Key Bible cross-reference

Verse 9. See Judges 2:19.

Key "by way of explanation"

Verse 17, "Queen of Heaven," refers to Ishtar, one of the main goddesses among the Babylonian pantheon. Jeremiah's last message to the Jews is dated about 585 BC.

Key "Quotable Quote"

"A man is first startled by sin; then it becomes pleasing, then easy, then delightful, then frequent, then habitual, then confirmed."

Jeremy Taylor

Jeremiah 45

Matthew Henry's introduction

We here find,

I. How Baruch was terrified when he was brought into trouble for writing and reading Jeremiah's roll, vv. 1–3.

II. How his fears were checked with a reproof for his great expectations and silenced with a promise of special preservation, vv. 4, 5.

A detailed analysis of chapter

An encouragement sent to Baruch. (1–5)

Key verse

Verse 1: "The word that Jeremiah the prophet spake unto Baruch the son of Neriah, when he had written these words in a book at the mouth of Jeremiah,"

Key word / key phrase

Verse 1, "Baruch."

Key event / key person / key theme

A message for Baruch, Jeremiah's faithful secretary.

Key thought

Verse 5, "great things." Selfish ambition has no place in the life of the godly person.

Key thing to look out for
All of God's followers need human encouragement.

Key Bible cross-reference
Verse 1. See 2 Kings 24:1,2.

Key "by way of explanation"
This message was written in 605/4 BC (out of chronological order). Baruch's brother held an important office (51:59), and they came from an aristocratic family.

Key "Quotable Quote"
"What brings joy to the heart is not so much the friend's gift as the friend's love."

Aelred of Rievaulx

Jeremiah 46

Matthew Henry's introduction
The prophecy against Egypt is here put first and takes up this whole chapter, in which we have,

I. A prophecy of the defeat of Pharaoh-necho's army by the Chaldean forces at Carchemish, which was accomplished soon after, in the fourth year of Jehoiakim, vv. 1–12.

II. A prophecy of the descent which Nebuchadnezzar should make on the land of Egypt, and his success in it, which was accomplished some years after the destruction of Jerusalem, vv. 13–26.

III. A word of comfort to the Israel of God in the midst of those calamities, vv. 27, 28.

A detailed analysis of chapter
The defeat of the Egyptians. (1–12)
Their overthrow after the siege of Tyre. (13–26)
A promise of comfort to the Jews. (27,28)

Key verse
Verse 2: "Against Egypt, against the army of Pharaohnecho king of Egypt,"

Key word / key phrase
Verse 2, "Concerning Egypt."

Key event / key person / key theme
Prophecies against Egypt

Key thought
The battle belongs to the Lord.

Key thing to look out for
Kingdoms rise and fall but God's kingdom is everlasting.

Key Bible cross-reference
Verse 13. See Jeremiah 43:10–13.

Key "by way of explanation"
Verse 2, "defeated at Carchemish." This reference to Carchemish alludes to one of the most famous battles in the ancient world when Egypt was defeated by the Babylonians. It took place in 605 BC

Key "Quotable Quote"
"Beware of resting in the word of the kingdom, without the spirit and power of the kingdom of that gospel."

John Bunyan

Jeremiah 47

Matthew Henry's introduction

This chapter reads the Philistines their doom, as the former read the Egyptians theirs and by the same hand, that of Nebuchadnezzar. It is short, but terrible; and Tyre and Zidon, though they lay at some distance from them, come in sharers with them in the destruction here threatened.

I. It is foretold that the forces of the northern crowns should come on them, to their great terror, vv. 1–5.

II. That the war should continue long, and their endeavors to put an end to it should be in vain, vv. 6–7.

A detailed analysis of chapter

The calamities of the Philistines. (1–7)

Key verse

Verse 1: "The word of the LORD that came to Jeremiah the prophet against the Philistines, before that Pharaoh smote Gaza."

Key word / key phrase

Verse 1, "Concerning the Philistines."

Key event / key person / key theme

Prophecies against Philistia

Key thought

No country can truly prosper if it defies the living God.

Key thing to look out for

The Philistines were doomed because they loved to attack and crush God's people.

Key Bible cross-reference

Verses 1–47. See Amos 2:1–3; Zephaniah 2:8–11.

Key "by way of explanation"

Verse 3, "hands hang limp." This condition was brought about by fear and terror. Verse 5, "Cut yourself," was a mark of mourning.

Key "Quotable Quote"

"If we desire to live in honor and to be esteemed by our neighbors, then we shall never be solidly rooted in God our Lord, and it will be impossible for us to remain undisturbed when insults come our way."

Ignatius of Loyola

Jeremiah 48

Matthew Henry's introduction

Here is,

I. The destruction foretold, that it should be great and general, should extend itself to all parts of the country (vv. 1–6, 8, and again vv. 21–25, 34), that spoilers should come on them and force some to flee (v. 9), should carry many into captivity (vv. 12, 46), that the enemy should come shortly (v. 16), come swiftly and surprise them (vv. 40, 41), that he should make thorough work (v. 10) and lay the country quite waste, though it was very strong (vv. 14, 15), that there should be no escaping (vv. 42, 45), that this should force them to quit their idols (vv. 13, 35) and put an end to all their joy (vv. 33, 34), that their neighbors shall lament them (vv. 17–19) and the prophet himself does (vv. 31, 36, etc.).

II. The causes of this destruction assigned; it was sin that brought this ruin on them, their pride, and security, and carnal confidence (vv. 7, 11, 14, 29), and their contempt of and enmity to God and his people, vv. 26, 27, 30.

III. A promise of the restoration of Moab, v. 48.

A detailed analysis of chapter

Prophecies against Moab for pride and security. (1–13)

For trust in people and contempt of God. (14–47)

Key verse

Verse 13: "And Moab shall be ashamed of Chemosh, as the house of Israel was ashamed of Bethel their confidence."

Key word / key phrase

Verse 1, "Concerning Moab."

Key event / key person / key theme

Prophecies against Moab

Key thought

Judgment falls on Chemosh and on all who worship him.

Key thing to look out for

The people who despised Israel so much become despicable themselves.

Key Bible cross-reference

Verse 7. See Psalm 49:6.

Key "by way of explanation"

Verse 7, "Chemosh," was worshiped by the Moabites as their national god.

Key "Quotable Quote"

"Christians must seek their delights in a higher sphere than the insipid frivolities of the world!"

C.H. Spurgeon

Jeremiah 49

Matthew Henry's introduction

The cup of trembling still goes round, and the nations must all drink of it, according to the instructions given to Jeremiah, 25:15. This chapter puts it into the hands,

I. Of the Ammonites, vv. 1–6.

II. Of the Edomites, vv. 7–22.

III. Of the Syrians, vv. 23–27.

IV. Of the Kedarenes, and the kingdoms of Hazor, vv. 28–33.

V. Of the Elamites, vv. 34–39. When Israel was scarcely saved where shall all these appear?

A detailed analysis of chapter

Prophecies about the Ammonites. (1–6)

The Edomites. (7–22)

The Syrians. (23–27)

The Kedarenes. (28–33)

The Elamites. (34–39)

Key verse

Verse 1: "Concerning the Ammonites,"

Key word / key phrase

Verses 1,7 "The Lord Almighty says."

Key event / key person / key theme

Prophecies against Ammon, Edom, Damascus, Kedar, and Hazor

Key thought

It is true that the world seems to be in the grip of the evil one.

Key thing to look out for

The deeper truth is that the world is in the loving embrace of its Creator and Sustainer, who is also the God of history.

Key Bible cross-reference

Verse 18. See Genesis 19:24,25.

Key "by way of explanation"

Verse 1, "Molech." He was the leading god among the Ammonites.

Key "Quotable Quote"

"The almighty and everywhere present power of God; whereby, as it were by his hand, he upholds and governs heaven, earth, and all creatures; so that herbs and grass, rain and drought, fruitful and barren years, meat and drink, health and sickness, riches and poverty, yea, and all things come, not by chance, but by his fatherly hand."

Heidelberg Catechism

Jeremiah 50

Matthew Henry's introduction

Here is,

I. The ruin of Babylon, vv. 1–3, 9–16, 21–32, and 35–46.

II. The redemption of God's people, vv. 4–8, 17–20, and 33, 34.

A detailed analysis of chapter

The ruin of Babylon. (1–3, 8–16, 21–32, 35–46)

The redemption of God's people. (4–7, 17–20, 33, 34)

Key verse

Verse 1: "The word that the LORD spake against Babylon and against the land of the Chaldeans [Babylonians] by Jeremiah the prophet."

Key word / key phrase

Verse 1, "concerning Babylon."

Key event / key person / key theme

Babylon's defeat and desolation

Key thought

Babylon, Israel's major enemy, will be punished by God.

Key thing to look out for

The greatest enemies of God's followers should not make godly people quake with fear.

Key Bible cross-reference

Verse 8. See Revelation 18:6.

Key "by way of explanation"

Babylon was the dominant power from 627 to 539 BC when the empire fell to Cyrus (verse 3).

Key "Quotable Quote"

"It is men, not God, who have produced racks,

whips, prisons, slavery, guns, bayonets, and bombs; it is by human avarice or human stupidity, not by the churlishness of nature, that we have poverty and overwork."

C.S. Lewis

Jeremiah 51

Matthew Henry's introduction

Here is,

I. The record of Babylon's doom, with the particulars of it, intermixed with the grounds of God's controversy with her, many aggravations of her fall, and great encouragements given thence to the Israel of God, that suffered such hard things by her, vv. 1–58.

II. The representation and ratification of this by the throwing of a copy of this prophecy into the river Euphrates, vv. 59–64.

A detailed analysis of chapter

Babylon's doom; God's controversy with her; encouragements from this for the Israel of God. (1–58)

This is confirmed. (59–64)

Key verse

Verse 6: "Flee out of the midst of Babylon, and deliver every man his soul: be not cut off in her iniquity; for this is the time of the LORD'S vengeance; he will render unto her a recompense."

Key word / key phrase

Verse 1, "against Babylon."

Key event / key person / key theme

Babylon's destiny

Key thought

Wrongs will be put right.

Key thing to look out for

If we believed that God was totally in control of our world how our worldview would change.

Key Bible cross-reference

Verse 13. See Revelation 17:1.

Key "by way of explanation"

Verse 9, "reaches to the skies." This is clearly a form of poetic speech. However, the truth it conveys remains true and the vivid expression only reinforces the point.

Key "Quotable Quote"

"The teaching of the New Testament is that the whole time the world has been 'lying in the wicked one'."

D. Martyn Lloyd-Jones

Jeremiah 52

Matthew Henry's introduction

In this chapter we have,

I. The bad reign of Zedekiah, very bad in regard both of sin and of punishment, vv. 1–3.

II. The besieging and taking of Jerusalem by the Chaldeans, vv. 4–7.

III. The severe usage which Zedekiah and the princes met with, vv. 8–11.

IV. The destruction of the temple and the city, vv. 12–14.

V. The captivity of the people (vv. 15, 16) and the numbers of those that were carried away into captivity, vv. 28–30.
VI. The carrying off of the plunder of the temple, vv. 17–23.
VII. The slaughter of the priests, and some other great men, in cold blood, vv. 24–27.
VIII. The better days which king Jehoiachin lived to see in the latter end of his time, after the death of Nebuchadnezzar, vv. 31–34.

A detailed analysis of chapter

The fate of Zedekiah. (1–11)
The destruction of Jerusalem. (12–23)
The captivities. (24–30)
The advancement of Jehoiachin. (31–34)

Key verse

Verse 11: "Then he put out the eyes of Zedekiah; and the king of Babylon bound him in chains, and carried him to Babylon, and put him in prison till the day of his death."

Key word / key phrase

Verse 7, "the city wall was broken through."

Key event / key person / key theme

Jerusalem captured, the exile, and signs of hope

Key thought

Verse 27 is one of the saddest verses in the Old Testament.

Key thing to look out for

Jehoiachin's release means that the book of Jeremiah ends on a note of hope with the first step in the restoration being recorded.

Key Bible cross-reference

Verse 4. See Ezekiel 24:2.

Key "by way of explanation"

The last chapter of the book of Jeremiah is an additional historical appendix to the book.

Key "Quotable Quote"

"Hope has two beautiful daughters Their names are anger and courage; anger at the way things are, and courage to see that they do not remain the way they are."

Augustine of Hippo

5. Select bibliography for Jeremiah

Calvin, John. *Commentaries on the Book of the Prophet Jeremiah.* Translated and edited by John Owen. 3 vols. Edinburgh: Calvin Translation Society, 1852.

Cundall, Arthur E. *Jeremiah*. Grand Rapids: Eerdmans, 1969.

Feinberg, Charles. *Jeremiah: A Commentary*, Zondervan, 1982.

Harrison, R. K. *Jeremiah and Lamentations*. Downers Grove, Ill.: InterVarsity, 1973.

Meyer, F. B. *Jeremiah, Priest and Prophet.* London: Morgan & Scott, 1911.

Lamentations

1. Book by book: Introduction to Lamentations

Introduction

In the Hebrew Bible these Elegies of Jeremiah, five in number, are placed among the *Chetuvim,* or "Holy Writings" ("the Psalms," etc., Luke 24:44), between Ruth and Ecclesiastes. But though in classification of compositions it belongs to the *Chetuvim,* it probably followed the prophecies of Jeremiah originally. For thus alone can we account for the prophetical books being enumerated by Josephus (*Against Apion,* 1.1.8) as thirteen: he must have reckoned Jeremiah and Lamentations as one book, as also Judges and Ruth, the two books of Samuel, etc., Ezra and Nehemiah. The Lamentations naturally follow the book which sets forth the circumstances forming the subject of the Elegies. Similar lamentations occur in 2Sa 1:19, etc.; 3:33.

The Jews read it in their synagogues on the ninth of the month Ab, which is a fast for the destruction of their holy city. As in 2 Chr. 35:25, "lamentations" are said to have been "written" by Jeremiah on the death of Josiah, besides it having been made "an ordinance in Israel" that "singing women" should "speak" of that king in lamentations; Josephus (*Antiquities,* 10.5.1), Jerome, etc., thought that they are contained in the present collection. But plainly the subject here is the overthrow of the Jewish city and people, as the Septuagint expressly states in an introductory verse to their version. The probability is that there is embodied in these Lamentations much of the language of Jeremiah's original Elegy on Josiah, as 2 Chr. 35:25 states; but it is now applied to the more universal calamity of the whole state, of which Josiah's sad death was the forerunner. Thus Lam. 4:20, originally applied to Josiah, was "written," in its subsequent reference, not so much of him, as of the throne of Judah in general, the last representative of which, Zedekiah, had just been carried away. The language, which is true of good Josiah, is too strong in favor of Zedekiah, except when viewed as representative of the crown in general. It was natural to embody the language of the Elegy on Josiah in the more general lamentations, as his death was the presage of the last disaster that overthrew the throne and state.

Style

The title more frequently given by the Jews to these Elegies is, "How" (Hebrew, *Eechah*), from the first word, as the Pentateuch is similarly called by the first Hebrew word of Gen. 1:1. The Septuagint calls it "Lamentations," from which we derive the name. It refers not merely to the events which occurred at the capture of the city, but to the sufferings of the citizens (the penalty of national sin) from the very beginning of the siege; and perhaps from before it, under Manasseh and Josiah (2 Chr. 33:11; 35:20–25); under Jehoahaz, Jehoiakim, and Zedekiah (2 Chr. 36:3, 4, 6, 7, 10, 11, etc.). Lowth says, "Every letter is written with a tear, every word the sound of a broken heart." The style is midway between the simple elevation of prophetic writing and the loftier rhythm of Moses, David, and Habakkuk. Terse conciseness marks the Hebrew original, notwithstanding Jeremiah's diffuseness in his other writings. The Elegies are grouped in stanzas as they arose in his mind, without any artificial system of arrangement as to the thoughts. The five Elegies are acrostic: each is divided into twenty-two stanzas or verses.

A.R. Faussett

Detailed outline

I. The condition of Jerusalem: 1:1–22
  Note the following verses of indictment: 1:1, 3, 8, 9, 17

II. Punishment from God: The results described: 2:1–22
  A. God had destroyed every home in Judah: 2:1–2
  B. Every fortress and wall was broken: 2:2
  C. His bow of judgment was bent across the land: 2:4
  D. The Temple had fallen: 2:6
  E. Judah's enemies were given freedom to destroy: 2:15–16
  F. Bodies of the people lined the streets of Jerusalem: 2:21–22

III. The prophet of God: 3:1–66
  A. The affliction of the prophet: 3:1–19
  B. The assurance of the prophet: 3:21–27, 31–33
  C. The advice of the prophet: 3:40–66

IV. Description of conditions continued: 4:1–22
  A. Children are thirsty: 4:4
  B. Youth treated badly: 5:13
  C. Rich were in the streets begging: 4:5
  D. Formerly mighty princes were now thin with blackened faces: 4:7, 8
  E. Women had cooked and eaten their own children: 4:10
  F. False prophets and priests: 4:14
  G. King Zedekiah, captured, blinded, and carried into captivity: 4:20

V. The prayer of the prophet: 5:1–18
  It was a prayer of:
  A. Remembrance: 5:1
  B. Repentance: 5:16
  C. Recognition of God: 5:19
  D. Renewal: 5:21

2. Helpful summaries of Lamentations

Bird's eye view

The book of Lamentations consists of five heart-breaking laments over the fallen and destroyed city of Jerusalem.

Reading plan

The following reading plan, taking one reading per day, enables you to read through Lamentations in three days.

Lamentations 1–2

Lamentations 3

Lamentations 4–5

Verses to memorize

Lamentations 3:22, 23

> Because of the Lord's great love we are not consumed, for his compassions never fail.

They are new every morning; great is your faithfulness.

Lamentations 5:19

You, O Lord, reign forever; your throne endures from generation to generation.

Statistics

Twenty-fifth Old Testament book

5 chapters

154 verses

3,415 words

Names/titles given

Hebrew title: *Ekah:* "And now." (The opening words of chapters 1, 2 and 4.

Hebrew title: *Ginoth:* "Elergies/Lamentations."

Greek title in Septuagint: *Threnoi: "Dirges/Laments."*

Latin title in Vulgate: *Threni:* "Lamentations/Tears."

Sub-title, found in Jerome's Vulgate: *Id est lamentations Jeremiae prophetae:* "The Lamentations of Jeremiah."

"Sequel to the book of Jeremiah."

3. Helpful keys to turn to in understanding Lamentations

Key background reading

The background to the book of Lamentations is set out in 2 Kings 25:8–12.

Key words

Tears

Affliction

Key verses

Lamentation 1:1; 2:5–6

Themes to study

- Hope in disaster
- Jeremiah's identification with the plight of Jerusalem.

Jesus in Lamentations

In Lamentations Jesus is the Man of Sorrows.

Types of Jesus in Lamentations

- The weeping prophet, Jeremiah, is seen as a type of Jesus, see Matt. 23:37–38.
- Jesus is also depicted as the Man of Sorrows in Lamentations: see 1:12; 3:19.

Lessons to learn from Lamentations

- We should never blame God, even in the most appalling of disasters.
- Repentance, and asking for God's help, are the correct ways to face calamities.

4. Chapter by chapter: outline of every chapter of Lamentations

Lamentations 1

Matthew Henry's introduction

We have here the first alphabet of this lamentation, twenty-two stanzas, in which the miseries of Jerusalem are bitterly bewailed and her present deplorable condition is aggravated by comparing it with her former prosperous state; all along, sin is acknowledged and complained of as the procuring cause of all these miseries; and God is appealed to for justice against their enemies and applied to for compassion towards them. The chapter is all of a piece, and the several remonstrances are interwoven; but here is,

I. A complaint made to God of their calamities, and his compassionate consideration desired, vv. 1–11.

II. The same complaint made to their friends, and their compassionate consideration desired, vv. 12–17.

III. An appeal to God and his righteousness about it (vv. 18–22), in which he is justified in their affliction and is humbly solicited to justify himself in their deliverance.

A detailed analysis of chapter

The miserable state of Jerusalem, the just results of its sins. (1–11)

Jerusalem represented as a captive, lamenting, and seeking the mercy of God. (12–22)

Key verse

Verse 1: "How doth the city sit solitary, that was full of people! how is she become as a widow."

Key word / key phrase

Verse 2, "bitterly she weeps."

Key event / key person / key theme

Jerusalem's desolation

Key thought

Mourning is necessary if there is ever to be any recovery.

Key thing to look out for

For the Israelites their city in ruins was tantamount to their God being defeated.

Key Bible cross-reference

Verse 1. See Leviticus 26:43.

Key "by way of explanation"

Verse 1. The opening phrase of the book, "how deserted lies the city", sets the sad and almost desperate atmosphere which pervades every chapter.

Key "Quotable Quote"

"Especially judge not the sons and daughters of sorrow."

C.H. Spurgeon

Lamentations 2

Matthew Henry's introduction

The second alphabetical elegy is set to the same mournful tune with the former, and the substance of it is much the same; it begins with Ecah, as that did, "How sad is our case! Alas for us!"

I. Here is the anger of Zion's God taken notice of as the cause of her calamities, vv. 1–9.

II. Here is the sorrow of Zion's children taken notice of as the effect of her calamities, vv. 10–19.

III. The complaint is made to God, and the matter referred to his compassionate consideration, vv. 20–22.

A detailed analysis of chapter

Lamentation for the misery of Jerusalem. (1–22)

Key verse

Verse 5: "The Lord was as an enemy: he hath swallowed up Israel, he hath swallowed up all her palaces: he hath destroyed his strong holds, and hath increased in the daughter of Judah mourning and lamentation."

Key word / key phrase

Verse 2, "in his wrath."

Key event / key person / key theme

God's anger

Key thought

God's people will not escape God's judgment if they are not faithful.

Key thing to look out for

Jerusalem itself was punished dreadfully.

Key Bible cross-reference

Verse 1. See Jeremiah 12:7.

Key "by way of explanation"

Verse 9, "prophets no longer find visions." One of the signs of God withdrawing from his people was the lack of visions and prophetic messages.

Key "Quotable Quote"

"We are healed of grief only when we express it to the full."

Charles R. Swindoll

Lamentations 3

Matthew Henry's introduction

Here is,

I. A sad complaint of God's displeasure and the fruits of it, vv. 1–20.

II. Words of comfort to God's people when they are in trouble and distress, vv. 21–36.

III. Duty prescribed in this afflicted state, vv. 37–41.

IV. The complaint renewed, vv. 42–54.

V. Encouragement taken to hope in God, and continue waiting for his salvation, with an appeal to his justice against the persecutors of the church, vv. 55–66.

A detailed analysis of chapter

The faithful lament their calamities, and hope in God's mercies. (1–66)

Key verse

Verse 22: "It is of the LORD's mercies that we are not consumed, because his compassions fail not."

Key word / key phrase

Verse 23, "great is your faithfulness."

Key event / key person / key theme

A prayer for mercy

Key thought

To express faith in God when all around speaks of the opposite is faith indeed.

Key thing to look out for

Even in the middle of the greatest tragedy God's love should be remembered.

Key Bible cross-reference

Verse 26. See Isaiah 7:4.

Key "by way of explanation"

Verse 22, "great love." This includes all the promises God made to his people in his covenants.

Key "Quotable Quote"

"Truly, it is in darkness that one finds the light, so when we are in sorrow, then this light is nearest to all of us."

Meister Eckhart

Lamentations 4

Matthew Henry's introduction

This chapter is another single alphabet of Lamentations for the destruction of Jerusalem, like those in the first two chapters.

I. The prophet here laments the injuries and indignities done to those to whom respect used to be shown, vv. 1, 2.

II. He laments the direful effects of the famine to which they were reduced by the siege, vv. 3–10.

III. He laments the taking and sacking of Jerusalem and its amazing desolations, vv. 11, 12.

IV. He acknowledges that the sins of their leaders were the cause of all these calamities, vv. 13–16.

V. He gives up all as doomed to utter ruin, for their enemies were every way too hard for them, vv. 17–20.

VI. He foretells the destruction of the Edomites who triumphed in Jerusalem's fall, v. 21.

VII. He foretells the return of the captivity of Zion at last, v. 22.

A detailed analysis of chapter

The deplorable state of the nation is contrasted with its ancient prosperity. (1–22)

Key verse

Verse 13: "It is of the LORD's mercies that we are not consumed, because his compassions fail not."

Key word / key phrase

Verse 18, "men stalked us at every step."

Key event / key person / key theme

Jerusalem, after its fall

Key thought

The destruction of Jerusalem is open for all to view.

Key thing to look out for

Verse 14 indicates that the sins of Israel's spiritual leaders brought down God's judgment on God's city.

Key Bible cross-reference

Verse 6. See Genesis 19:24.

Key "by way of explanation"

Verse 15, "unclean." The whole of the devastated city of Jerusalem is likened to an unclean leper.

Key "Quotable Quote"

"And no one ever told me about the laziness of grief. Not only writing but even reading a letter is too much. Even shaving. What does it matter now whether my cheek is rough or smooth?"

C.S. Lewis

Lamentations 5

Matthew Henry's introduction

This chapter, though it has the same number of verses with the 1st, 2nd, and 4th, is not alphabetical, as they were, but the scope of it is the same with that of all the previous elegies. We have in it,

I. A representation of the present calamitous state of God's people in their captivity, vv. 1–16.

II. A protestation of their concern for God's sanctuary, as that which lay nearer their heart than any secular interest of their own, vv. 17, 18.

III. A humble supplication to God and expostulation with him, for the returns of mercy (vv. 19–22); for those that lament and do not pray sin in their lamentations. Some ancient versions call this chapter, "The Prayer of Jeremiah."

A detailed analysis of chapter

The Jewish nation asking for divine favor. (1–22)

Key verse

Verse 19: "Thou, O LORD, remainest for ever; thy throne from generation to generation."

Key word / key phrase

Verse 1, "Remember, O Lord."

Key event / key person / key theme

A prayer for restoration

Key thought

A prayer of deep repentance is the only appropriate action on certain occasions.

Key thing to look out for

Not only is there hope for the individual (chapter 3) but hope for the community, because God still reigns (verses 19–22).

Key Bible cross-reference

Verse 20. See Psalm 13:1.

Key "by way of explanation"

Verse 16, "crown." The "crown" refers to the regal nature of God's city and now that it has fallen shows how the city's glory has been lost.

Key "Quotable Quote"

"There is a command to rejoice evermore, but nowhere is it written, mourn continually."

Richard Sibbes

5. Select bibliography for Lamentations

Harrison, R.K. Jeremiah and Lamentations . Downers Grove, III.: InterVarsity, 1973.

Keil, C.F. The Prophecies of Jeremiah . Vol. 2. KD. Grand Rapids Eerdmans, 1949.

Simeon, Charles. Expository Outlines on the Whole Bible . 1847. Reprint. Grand Rapids: Zondervan, 1956.

Waltke, Bruce. "Lamentations." Zondervan Pictorial Encyclopedia of the Bible (ZPEB). 5 vols. Grand Rapids: Zondervan, 1975, 3:862–65.

Ezekiel

1. Book by book: Introduction to Ezekiel

Introduction

Ezekiel the prophet

The name Ezekiel means "(whom) God will strengthen" (Gesenius); or, "God will prevail" (Rosenmuller). His father was Buzi (Ezek. 1:3), a priest, and he probably exercised the priestly office himself at Jerusalem, previous to his captivity, as appears from the matured priestly character to be seen in his prophecies, a circumstance which much increased his influence with his captive fellow countrymen at Babylon. Tradition represents Sarera as the land of his nativity. His call to prophesy was in the fifth year from the date of his being carried away with Jehoiachin (see 2 Kings 24:11–15) by Nebuchadnezzar, 599 B.C. The best portions of the people seem to have been among the first carried away (Ezek. 11:16; Jer. 24:2–7, 8, 10). The ungodly were willing to do anything to remain in their native land; whereas the godly believed the prophets and obeyed the first summons to surrender, as the only path of safety. These latter, as adhering to the theocratic principle, were among the earliest to be removed by the Chaldeans, who believed that, if they were out of the way, the nation would fall to pieces of itself. They were despised by their brethren in the Holy Land not yet captives, as having no share in the temple sacrifices. Thus Ezekiel's sphere of labor was one happier and less impeded by his countrymen than that of Jeremiah at home.

The vicinity of the river Chebar, which flows into the Euphrates near Circeslum, was the first scene of his prophecies (Ezek. 1:1). Tel-Abib there (now Thallaba) was his place of residence (Ezek. 3:15), whither the elders used to come to inquire as to God's messages through him. They were eager to return to Jerusalem, but he taught them that they must first return to their God. He continued to prophesy for at least twenty-two years, that is, to the twenty-seventh year of the captivity (Ezek. 29:17), and probably remained with the captives by the Chebar the rest of his life. A treatise, falsely attributed to Epiphanius, states a tradition that he was killed at Babylon by a prince of his people whom he had reproved for idolatry.

He was contemporary with Jeremiah and Daniel. The former had prophesied for thirty-four years before Ezekiel, and continued to do so for six or seven years after him. The call of Ezekiel followed the very next year after the communication of Jeremiah's predictions to Babylon (Jer. 51:59), and was divinely intended as a sequel to them. Daniel's predictions are mostly later than Ezekiel's but his piety and wisdom had become proverbial in the early part of Ezekiel's ministry (Ezek. 14:14, 16; 28:3). They much resemble one another, especially in the visions and grotesque images. It is a remarkable proof of genuineness that in Ezekiel no prophecies against Babylon occur among those directed against the enemies of the covenant-people. Probably he desired not to give needless offence to the government under which he lived. The effect of his labors is to be seen in the improved character of the people towards the close of the captivity, and their general cessation from idolatry and a return to the law. It was little more than thirty years after the close of his labors when the decree of the Jews' restoration was issued. His leading characteristic is realizing, determined energy; this admirably adapted him for opposing the "rebellious house" "of stubborn front and hard heart," and for maintaining the cause of God's Church among his countrymen in a foreign land, when the external framework had fallen to pieces.

Writing style

His style is plain and simple. His conceptions are definite, and the details even of the symbolical and enigmatical parts are given with lifelike minuteness. The obscurity lies in the substance, not in the form, of his communications. The priestly element predominates in his prophecies, arising from his previous training as a priest. He delights to linger about the temple and to find in its symbolical forms the imagery for conveying his instructions. This was divinely ordered to satisfy the spiritual want felt by the people in the absence of the outward temple and its sacrifices. In his images he is magnificent, though austere and somewhat harsh. He abounds in repetitions, not for ornament, but for force and weight. Poetical parallelism is not found except in a few portions, as in the seventh, twenty-first, twenty-seventh, twenty-eighth, twenty-ninth through thirty-first chapters. His great aim was to stimulate the dormant minds of the Jews. For this end nothing was better suited than the use of mysterious symbols expressed in the plainest words. The superficial, volatile, and willfully unbelieving would thereby be left to judicial blindness (Is. 6:10; Matt. 13:11–13, etc.); whereas the better-disposed would be awakened to a deeper search into the things of God by the very obscurity of the symbols. Inattention to this divine purpose has led the modern Jews so to magnify this obscurity as to ordain that no one shall read this book till he has passed his thirtieth year.

Canonicity

Rabbi Hananias is said to have satisfactorily solved the difficulties (Mischna) which were alleged against its canonicity. Ecclesiasticus 49:8 refers to it, and Josephus *(Antiquities,* 10.5.1). It is mentioned as part of the canon in Melito's catalogue (Eusebius, *Ecclesiastical History,* 4.26); also in Origen, Jerome, and the Talmud. The oneness of tone throughout and the repetition of favorite expressions exclude the suspicion that separate portions are not genuine. The earlier portion, the first through the thirty-second chapters, which mainly treats of sin and judgment, is a key to interpret the latter portion, which is more hopeful and joyous, but remote in date. Thus a unity and an orderly progressive character are imparted to the whole. The destruction of Jerusalem is the central point. Previous to this he calls to repentance and warns against blind confidence in Egypt (Ezek. 17:15–17; compare Jer. 37:7) or other human stay. After it he consoles the captives by promising them future deliverance and restoration. His prophecies against foreign nations stand between these two great divisions, and were uttered in the interval between the intimation that Nebuchadnezzar was besieging Jerusalem and the arrival of the news that he had taken it (Ezek. 33:21).

Havernick marks out nine sections:

(1) Ezekiel's call to prophesy (Ezek. 1:1–3:15).

(2) Symbolical predictions of the destruction of Jerusalem (Ezek. 3:16–7:27).

(3) A year and two months later a vision of the temple polluted by Tammuz or Adonis worship; God's consequent scattering of fire over the city and forsaking of the temple to reveal Himself to an inquiring people in exile; happier and purer times to follow (Ezek. 8:1–11:25).

(4) Exposure of the particular sins prevalent in the several classes–priests, prophets, and princes (Ezek. 12:1–19:14).

(5) A year later the warning of judgment for national guilt repeated with greater distinctness as the time drew nearer (Ezek. 20:1–23:49).

(6) Two years and five months later–the very day on which Ezekiel speaks–is announced as the day of the beginning of the siege; Jerusalem shall be overthrown (Ezek. 24:1–27).

(7) Predictions against foreign nations during the interval of his silence towards his own people; if judgment begins at the house of God, much more will it visit the ungodly world (Ezek. 25:1–32:32). Some of these were uttered much later than others, but they all began to be given after the fall of Jerusalem.

(8) In the twelfth year of the captivity, when the fugitives from Jerusalem (Ezek. 33:21) had appeared in Chaldea, he foretells better times and the re-establishment of Israel and the triumph of God's kingdom on earth over its enemies, Seir, the heathen, and Gog (Ezek. 33:1–39:29).

(9) After an interval of thirteen years the closing vision of the order and beauty of the restored kingdom (Ezek. 40:1–48:35).

The particularity of details as to the temple and its offerings rather discountenances the view of this vision being only symbolical, and not at all literal. The event alone can clear it up. At all events it has not yet been fulfilled; it must be future. Ezekiel was the only prophet (in the strict sense) among the Jews at Babylon. Daniel was rather a seer than a prophet, for the spirit of prophecy was given him to qualify him, not for a spiritual office, but for disclosing future events. His position in a heathen king's palace fitted him for revelations of the outward relations of God's kingdom to the kingdoms of the world, so that his book is ranked by the Jews among the *Hagiographa* or "Sacred Writings," not among the prophetical Scriptures. On the other hand, Ezekiel was distinctively a prophet, and one who had to do with the inward concerns of the divine kingdom. As a priest, when sent into exile, his service was but transferred from the visible temple at Jerusalem to the spiritual temple in Chaldea.

A.R. Faussett

Contents of Ezekiel

The parts of the book are in general very transparent. First of all the book is divided into halves by the announcement of the fall of Jerusalem in Ezekiel 33; of which parts the first predominantly deals with punishments and threats; the other with comfort and encouragement. Possibly it is these two parts of the book that Josephus has in mind when he says (Ant., X) that Ezekiel had written two books. That the introduction of prophecies of redemption after those of threats in other prophetical books also is often a matter of importance, and that the right appreciation of this fact is a significant factor in the struggle against the attacks made on the genuineness of these books.

Down to the time when Jerusalem fell, Ezekiel was compelled to antagonize the hopes, which were supported by false prophets, that God would not suffer this calamity. Over against this, Ezekiel persistently and emphatically points to this fact, that the apostasy had been too great for God not to bring about this catastrophe. There is scarcely a violation of a single command–religious, moral or cultural–which the prophet is not compelled to charge against the people in the three sections, 3:16; 8:1; 20:1, until in 24:1, on the 10th day of the 10th month of the 9th year (589 B.C.) the destruction of Jerusalem was symbolized by the vision of the boiling pot with the piece of meat in it, and the unlamented destruction of the city was prefigured by the unmourned and sudden death of his wife. After the five sections of this subdivision, referring to Israel, there follow as a second subdivision the seven oracles against the Ammonites (25:1); the Moabites (25:8); the Edomites (25:12); the Philistines (25:15); Tyre (26:1); Sidon (28:20); Egypt (29:1), evidently arranged from a geographical point of view.

The most extensive are those against Tyre and the group of oracles against Egypt, both provided with separate dates (compare 26:1–29:1; 30:20; 31:1; 32:1,17). The supplement in reference to Tyre (29:17) is the latest dated oracle of Ezekiel (from the year 571 B.C.), and is found here, at a suitable place, because it is connected with a threat against Egypt (Ezekiel 40; Ezekiel 48 date from the year 573 according to Ezekiel 40:1). The number seven evidently does not occur accidentally, since in other threats of this kind a typical number appears to have been purposely chosen, thus: Isaiah 13–22, i.e. ten; Jeremiah 46; Jeremiah 51, also ten; which fact again under the circumstances is an important argument in repelling attacks on the genuineness of the book.

Probably the five parts of the first subdivision, and the seven of the second, supplement each other, making a total of twelve. The oracles against the foreign countries are not only in point of time to be placed between Ezekiel 24 and 33:21, but also, as concerns contents, help splendidly to solve the difficulty suggested by chapter 24, and in this way satisfactorily fill the gap thus made. The arrival of the news of the fall of Jerusalem, in 586 B.C. (compare 33:21), which had already been foretold in chapter 24, introduced by the mighty watchman's cry to repentance (33:1), and followed by a reproof of the superficial reception of the prophetic word, concludes the first chief part of the book.

The second part also naturally falls into two subdivisions, of which the first contains the development of the nearer and more remote future, as to its inner character and its historical course (Ezek. 34–39):

(1) the true shepherd of Israel (Ezekiel 34);

(2) the future fate of Edom (Ezekiel 35);

(3) Israel's deliverance from the disgrace of the shameful treatment by the heathen, which falls back on the latter again (Ezekiel 36:1–15);

(4) the desecration of the name of Yahweh by Israel and the sanctification by Yahweh (Ezekiel 36:15–38);

(5) the revival of the Israelite nation (Ezekiel 37:1–14);

(6) the reunion of the separated kingdoms, Judah and Israel (Ezekiel 37:15–28);

(7) the overthrow of the terrible Gentile power of the north (Ezekiel 38).

The second subdivision (Ezek. 40–48) contains the reconstruction of the external affairs of the people in a vision, on the birthday of 573, "in the beginning of the year". After the introduction (Ezekiel 40:1–4), there follow five pericopes:

(1) directions with reference to the temple (compare the subscription Ezekiel 43:12) (Ezekiel 40:5–43:12);

(2) the altar (Ezekiel 43:13–46:24);

(3) the wonderful fountain of the temple, on the banks of which the trees bear fruit every month (Ezekiel 47:1–12);

(4) the boundaries of the land and its division among the twelve tribes of Israel (Ezekiel 47:13–48:29);

(5) the size of the holy city and the names of its twelve gates (Ezekiel 48:30–35).

In (3) to (5) the prominence of the number twelve is clear.

The entire second chief part, Ezek. 34–48, contains predictions of deliverance. The people down to 586 were confident, so that Ezekiel was compelled to rebuke them. After the taking of Jerusalem a change took place in both respects. Now the people are despairing, and this is just the time for the prophet to preach deliverance.

The transparent structure of the whole book suggests the idea that the author did not extend the composition over a long period, but wrote it, so to say, at one stretch, which of course does not make it impossible that the separate prophecies were put into written form immediately after their reception, but rather presupposes this. When the prophet wrote they were only woven together into a single uniform book.

Orr, James, M.A., D.D. General Editor, International Standard Bible Encyclopedia

Detailed outline

Part One: Prophecies Before The Siege of Jerusalem–Chapters l–24

I. The prophet's call and commission: 1:1–3:27

A. The vision: 1:1–28

B. The call: 2:1–3:27

II. Prophecies against Judah and Jerusalem: 4:1–24:27

A. Destruction predicted: 4:1–7:27

1. By sign and symbol: 4:1–5:17
2. By prophecies: 6:1–7:27

B. Jerusalem's sin and punishment: 8:1–11:25

1. Vision of sin: 8:1–18
2. Punishment: 9:1–11:25

C. Necessity of punishment: 12:1–19:14

D. Last warning before the fall: 20:1–24:27

Part Two: Prophecies During The Siege Of Jerusalem–Chapters 25–32

These prophecies were directed at Judah's enemies.

I. Prophecies against surrounding nations: 25:1–32:32

A. Against Ammon: 25:1–7
B. Against Moab: 25:8–11
C. Against Edom: 25:12–14
D. Against Philistia: 25:15–17
E. Against Tyre: 26:1–28:19
F. Against Sidon: 28:20–26
G. Against Egypt: 29:1–32:32

Part Three: Prophecies After The Siege Of Jerusalem–Chapters 33–48

These prophecies concerned the restoration of Judah.

I. Events preceding the establishment of the Kingdom: 33:1–39:29

A. The wicked purged: 33:1–33
B. False shepherds give way to the true shepherd: 34:1–31
C. Restoration of the land: 36:1–15
D. Restoration of the people: 36:16–37:28
E. Judgment of Israel's enemies: 38:1–39:24
F. The restored nation: 39:25–29

II. The Millennial Kingdom: 40:1–48:35

A. The temple: 40:1–43:27
B. The worship: 44:1–46:24
C. The land: 47:1–48:35

2. Helpful summaries of Ezekiel

Bird's eye view

Ezekiel records the prophetic ministry of Ezekiel as he spoke God's words to the Israelites during their captivity in Babylon, before and after Jerusalem's destruction.

Reading plan

The following reading plan, taking one reading per day, enables you to read through Ezekiel in eighteen days.

Ezekiel 1–3
Ezekiel 4–7
Ezekiel 8–11
Ezekiel 12–13
Ezekiel 14–16
Ezekiel 17
Ezekiel 18–20
Ezekiel 21
Ezekiel 22–23
Ezekiel 24–26
Ezekiel 27–28
Ezekiel 29–31
Ezekiel 32–33
Ezekiel 34–35
Ezekiel 36–38
Ezekiel 39–41
Ezekiel 42–45
Ezekiel 46–48

Verses to memorize

Ezekiel 34: 11–12

I myself will search for my sheep and look after them. As a shepherd looks after his scattered flock when he is with them, so I will look after my sheep.

Ezekiel 34:23

And I will set up one shepherd over them, and he shall feed them, even my servant David; he shall feed them, and he shall be their shepherd.

Statistics

Twenty-sixth Old Testament book

48 chapters

1,273 verses

39,407 words

Names/titles given

Hebrew title: *yehezke'l:*

"Strengthened by the Lord."

Greek title in Septuagint: *Iezekiel:* "Ezekiel."

Latin title in Vulgate: *Ezechiel:* "Ezekiel."

3. Helpful keys to turn to in understanding Ezekiel

Key word

Vision

Key verses

Ezekiel 1:1; 36:33–35

Key sermons and visions in Ezekiel

Symbolic acts (Ezek. 4–5)

The abandoned baby (Ezek. 16)

Just punishment (Ezek. 18)

Oholah and Oholibah (Ezek. 23)

The shepherds of Israel (Ezek. 34)

The vision of the New Temple (Ezek. 40–48)

Themes to study

- The relationship between human responsibility and divine providence.
- How Ezekiel was God's watchman.

Outstanding events in Ezekiel

- The Lord's glory leaving the temple, 10:16–18; 11:23
- The fall of Jerusalem, 33:21
- Prophecy about the return of the Lord's glory, 44:4

Ezekiel quoted in the New Testament

- I will receive you

  Ezek. 20:34, 41 quoted in 2 Cor. 6:17
- I will be their God

  Ezek. 37:27 quoted in 2 Cor. 6:16

"I wills" found in Ezekiel chapter 34

I will search for them, 11,16

I will deliver them, 12

I will bring them out, 13

I will gather them to myself, 13

I will feed them, 14

I will enable them to lie down/rest, 15

I will bind up the broken, 16

I will strengthen the sick, 16

I will take care of the enemy, 16

I will judge my sheep, 17–22

I will watch over them, 23

I will be their God, 24

I will bless them, 25–26
I will enable them to live in safety, 25
I will make them a blessing, 26
I will abundantly satisfy them, 29–31

Three outstanding events

1. The departure of God's glory from the Temple, 10:16–18; 11:23
2. The fall of Jerusalem, 33:21
3. The prophecy of the return of the Shekinah glory, 44:4

Jesus in Ezekiel

In Ezekiel Jesus is the Son of Man.

Types of Jesus in Ezekiel

Jesus is the tender sprig, 17:22, 53:2
Jesus is the Shepherd, 34:23; 37:24

Lessons to learn from Ezekiel

- People who are renewed by God's Spirit, are happy to embrace God's will, and to be open-hearted towards God, and to look after their neighbors.
- A good Christian leader is dedicated to God's Word, and turns to God for his/her spiritual resources.

4. Chapter by chapter: outline of every chapter of Ezekiel

Ezekiel 1

Matthew Henry's introduction

In this chapter we have,

I. The common circumstances of the prophecy now to be delivered, the time when it was delivered (v. 1), the place where (v. 2), and the person by whom, v. 3.

II. The uncommon introduction to it by a vision of the glory of God,

A. In his attendance and retinue in the upper world, where his throne is surrounded with angels, here called "living creatures," vv. 4–14.

B. In his providences about the lower world, represented by the wheels and their motions, vv. 15–25.

C. In the face of Jesus Christ sitting on the throne, vv. 26–28.

A detailed analysis of chapter

Ezekiel's vision of God, and of the angelic host. (1–14)
Divine providence. (15–25)
A revelation of the Son of man on his heavenly throne. (26–28)

Key verse

Verse 1: "Now it came to pass in the thirtieth year, in the fourth month, in the fifth day of the month, as I was among the captives by the river of Chebar, that the heavens were opened, and I saw visions of God."

Key word / key phrase

Verse 28, "the likeness of the glory of the Lord."

Key event / key person / key theme

Ezekiel sees the glory of God

Key thought

God's glory is beyond human description.

Key thing to look out for

From this vision observe what is said about God's nature.

Key Bible cross-reference

Verse 1. See Revelation 19:11.

Key "by way of explanation"

Ezekiel was one of the Jews deported to Babylon in 597 BC. Here, at Tel Abib (3:15), God calls him to be a prophet.

Key "Quotable Quote"

"Power in the Christian life depends upon our connection with the source of power."

L. Nelson Bell

Ezekiel 2

Matthew Henry's introduction

Now here,

I. He is commissioned to go as a prophet to the house of Israel, now captives in Babylon, and to deliver God's messages to them from time to time, vv. 1–5.

II. He is cautioned not to be afraid of them, v. 6.

III. He is instructed what to say to them, and has words put into his mouth, signified by the vision of a roll, which he was ordered to eat (vv. 7–10), and which, in the next chapter, we find he did eat.

A detailed analysis of chapter

The prophet is told what he is to do. (1–5)

And encouraged to be resolute, faithful, and devoted. (6–10)

Key verse

Verse 6: "And thou, son of man, be not afraid of them, neither be afraid of their words, though briers and thorns be with thee, and thou dost dwell among scorpions."

Key word / key phrase

Verse 3, "I am sending you to the Israelites."

Key event / key person / key theme

Ezekiel is commissioned to give God's message to the exiles in Babylonia.

Key thought

The prophets accepted God's call, even when it meant they would have to suffer.

Key thing to look out for

Ezekiel is warned of danger but told not to fear.

Key Bible cross-reference

Verses 9,10. See Revelation 5:1.

Key "by way of explanation"

Verse 1, "Son of man," that is, "human being." The phrase emphasizes Ezekiel's humanity and his weakness when compared with God.

Key "Quotable Quote"

"We are not made of iron, we are not like rocks, we are mortal men full of fragility."

John Calvin

Ezekiel 3

Matthew Henry's introduction

In this chapter we have the further preparation

of the prophet for the work to which God called him.

I. His eating the roll that was presented to him in the close of the previous chapter, vv. 1–3.
II. Further instructions and encouragements given him to the same purport with those in the previous chapter, vv. 4–11.
III. The mighty impulse he was under, with which he was carried to those that were to be his hearers, vv. 12–15.
IV. A further explication of his office and business as a prophet, under the similitude of a watchman, vv. 16–21.
V. The restraining and restoring of the prophet's liberty of speech, as God pleased, vv. 22–27.

A detailed analysis of chapter

The preparation of the prophet for his work. (1–11)

His office, as a watchman. (12–21)

The restraining and restoring of his speech. (22–27)

Key verse

Verse 5: "For thou art not sent to a people of a strange speech and of an hard language, but to the house of Israel."

Key word / key phrase

Verse 1, "eat this scroll."

Key event / key person / key theme

Ezekiel is instructed about his ministry.

Key thought

Opposition should not be an excuse to stop us witnessing.

Key thing to look out for

The different arguments that are put up against following God.

Key Bible cross-reference

Verses 1–3. See Revelation 10:9,10.

Key "by way of explanation"

Verse 15, "seven days." This was the usual time for mourning and indicates Ezekiel's frame of mind.

Key "Quotable Quote"

"Oh, that there were more crying persons, when there are so many crying sins."

Ralph Venning

Ezekiel 4

Matthew Henry's introduction

Two things are here represented to him in vision:

I. The fortifications that should be raised against the city; this is signified by the prophet's laying siege to the portraiture of Jerusalem (vv. 1–3) and laying first on one side and then on the other side before it, vv. 4–8.
II. The famine that should rage within the city; this is signified by his eating very coarse fare, and confining himself to a little of it, so long as this typical representation lasted, vv. 9–17.

A detailed analysis of chapter

Ezekiel draws a plan of the siege of Jerusalem. (1–3)

The prophet lies on the ground for 430 days by the miniature Jerusalem. (4–8)

Starvation-rations, ceremonially polluted. (9–17)

Key verse

Verse 2: "And lay siege against it, and build a fort against it, and cast a mount against it; set the camp also against it, and set battering rams against it round about."

Key word / key phrase

Verse 1, "Draw the city of Jerusalem."

Key event / key person / key theme

A symbolic acting-out of the siege of Jerusalem

Key thought

Actions speak louder than words.

Key thing to look out for

Verse 4, Ezekiel's complete identification with the sinful people: he *symbolized* the sin; cf. Christ who removed sin (Isaiah 53:11).

Key Bible cross-reference

Verse 16. See Psalm 105:16.

Key "by way of explanation"

Verse 3, "a sign to the house of Israel," is that they should not place their hope in Jerusalem's survival. Ezekiel's rations were 8oz of poor quality bread and two pints of water.

Key "Quotable Quote"

"The Christian hope is hope in the power of God."

William Barclay

Ezekiel 5

Matthew Henry's introduction

This destruction of Judah and Jerusalem is here,

I. Represented by a sign, the cutting, and burning, and scattering of hair, vv. 1–4.

II. That sign is expounded, and applied to Jerusalem.

A. Sin is charged on Jerusalem as the cause of this desolation—contempt of God's law (vv. 5–7) and profanation of his sanctuary, v. 11.

B. Wrath is threatened, great wrath (vv. 8–10), a variety of miseries (vv. 12, 16, 17), such as should be their reproach and ruin, vv. 13–15.

A detailed analysis of chapter

A type of hair, showing the judgments about to come upon the Jews. (1–4)

These awful judgments are declared. (5–17)

Key verse

Verse 1: "And thou, son of man, take thee a sharp knife, take thee a barber's razor, and cause it to pass upon thine head and upon thy beard: then take thee balances to weigh, and divide the hair."

Key word / key phrase

Verse 1, "Shave your head and beard."

Key event / key person / key theme

A fourth symbolic action, and symbolic actions explained

Key thought

Verses 12–17, the destruction will be terrible

Key thing to look out for

These images were not man-made, but given by the Lord.

Key Bible cross-reference

Verse 10. See Lamentations 4:10.

Key "by way of explanation"

Verse 13, the two phrases "they will know" and "I the LORD have spoken," are two themes in Ezekiel.

Key "Quotable Quote"

"Sin is the most expensive thing in the universe, pardoned or unforgiven: pardoned, its cost falls on the atoning sacrifice; unforgiven, it must forever lie upon the impenitent soul."

Charles G. Finney

Ezekiel 6

Matthew Henry's introduction

In this chapter we have,

I. A threatening of the destruction of Israel for their idolatry, and the destruction of their idols with them, vv. 1–7.

II. A promise of the gracious return of a remnant of them to God, by true repentance and reformation, vv. 8–10.

III. Directions given to the prophet and others the Lord's servants, to lament both the iniquities and the calamities of Israel, vv. 11–14.

A detailed analysis of chapter

The divine judgments for idolatry. (1–7)
A remnant shall be saved. (8–10)
The calamities are to be lamented. (11–14)

Key verse

Verse 11: "Smite with thine hand, and stamp with thy foot, and say, Alas for all the evil abominations of the house of Israel!"

Key word / key phrase

Verse 6, "high places demolished."

Key event / key person / key theme

Destruction upon all the land because of idolatry

Key thought

What form does idolatry take today?

Key thing to look out for

The Lord will not put up with certain things.

Key Bible cross-reference

Verse 5. See Leviticus 19:16.

Key "by way of explanation"

Verse 13, "under every spreading tree." Such trees marked the sites of pagan worship.

Key "Quotable Quote"

"The very heart and root of sin is an independent spirit. We erect the idol self, and not only wish others to worship, but worship it ourselves."

Richard Cecil

Ezekiel 7

Matthew Henry's introduction

In this chapter the approaching ruin of the land of Israel is most particularly foretold in affecting expressions often repeated, that if possible they might be awakened by repentance to prevent it. The prophet must tell them,

I. That it will be a final ruin, a complete utter destruction, which would make an end of them, a miserable end, vv. 1–6.

II. That it is an approaching ruin, just at the door, vv. 7–10.

III. That it is an unavoidable ruin, because they had by sin brought it on themselves, vv. 10–15.

IV. That their strength and wealth should be no fence against it, vv. 16–19.

V. That the temple, which they trusted in, should itself be ruined, vv. 20–22.

VI. That it should be a universal ruin, the sin that brought it having been universal, vv. 23–27.

A detailed analysis of chapter

The imminent desolation of the land. (1–15)

The distress of the few who should escape. (16–22)

The captivity. (23–27)

Key verse

Verse 23: "Make a chain: for the land is full of bloody crimes, and the city is full of violence."

Key word / key phrase

Verse 2, "the end has come."

Key event / key person / key theme

The day of destruction described

Key thought

How can the wrong use of money be a stumbling block today?

Key thing to look out for

The catalogue of wrongdoing: spelled out for emphasis

Key Bible cross-reference

Verse 14. See Job 39:24.

Key "by way of explanation"

Verse 22, "my treasured place," refers to the temple, and possibly to the holy of holies in particular. Verse 26, the ultimate horror.

Key "Quotable Quote"

"To live without hope is to cease to live."

Fyodor Dostoevsky

Ezekiel 8

Matthew Henry's introduction

Here God, in vision, brings him to Jerusalem, to show him the sins that were committed there, though God had begun to contend with them (vv. 1–4), and there he sees,

I. The image of jealousy set up at the gate of the altar, vv. 5, 6.

II. The elders of Israel worshipping all manner of images in a secret chamber, vv. 7–12.

III. The women weeping for Tammuz, vv. 13, 14.

IV. The men worshipping the sun, vv. 15, 16.

And then appeals to him whether such a

provoking people should have any pity shown them, vv. 17, 18.

A detailed analysis of chapter

The Spirit transports Ezekiel to Jerusalem. (1–4)
The detestable worship: first Canaanite. (5–6)
Second, Egyptian. (7–13)
Third, Sumerian. (14,15)
Fourth, sun-worship by the priests themselves. 16–18)

Key verse

Verse 3: ". . . the spirit lifted me up between the earth and the heaven, and brought me in the visions of God to Jerusalem, to the door of the inner gate that looketh toward the north; where was the seat of the image of jealousy, which provoketh to jealousy."

Key word / key phrase

Verses 6, 10, 14, 17, "detestable."

Key event / key person / key theme

The glory of the Lord has been driven out of the holy of holies (verse 4), and will soon leave the temple (verse 6).

Key thought

Idolatry is thriving even in God's temple.

Key thing to look out for

What steps can we take to ensure that we avoid the worship of false gods?

Key Bible cross-reference

Verse 4. See 1:28.

Key "by way of explanation"

Verse 3, "took me by the hair of my head." Later, Ezekiel realized that he was describing an ecstatic experience. Verse 1, "the elders of Judah," community life has been re-established.

Key "Quotable Quote"

"The dearest idol I have known,
Whate'er that idol be.
Help me to tear it from the throne,
And worship only thee."

William Cowper

Ezekiel 9

Matthew Henry's introduction

Here is,

I. Preparation made of instruments that were to be employed in the destruction of the city, vv. 1, 2.

II. The removal of the Shechinah from the cherubim to the threshold of the temple, v. 3.

III. Orders given to one of the people employed, who is distinguished from the rest, for the marking of a remnant to be preserved from the common destruction, vv. 3, 4.

IV. The warrant signed for the execution of those that were not marked, and the execution begun accordingly, vv. 5–7.

V. The prophet's intercession for the mitigation of the sentence, and a denial of any mitigation, the decree having now gone forth, vv. 8–10.

VI. The report made by him that was to mark the pious remnant of what he had done in that matter, v. 11. And this shows a usual method of Providence in the government of the world.

A detailed analysis of chapter

A vision denoting the destruction of the inhabitants of Jerusalem, and the departure of the symbol of the divine presence. (1–11)

Key verse

Verse 3: "And the glory of the God of Israel was gone up from the cherub."

Key word / key phrase

Verse 5, "kill."

Key event / key person / key theme

Vision of killing in Jerusalem

Key thought

The severity of the punishment shows the seriousness of the sin.

Key thing to look out for

How does the Lord answer the prophet's question?

Key Bible cross-reference

Verse 4. See Revelation 7:3; 9:4; 14:1.

Key "by way of explanation"

Verse 4, "put a mark." This "mark" was the last letter of the Hebrew alphabet, "taw". It was some kind of protective mark.

Key "Quotable Quote"

"In all our actions, when we come in or go out, when we dress, when we wash, at our meals, before retiring to sleep, we make on our foreheads the sign of the cross. These practices are not committed by a formal law of Scripture, but tradition teaches them, custom confirms them, faith observes them."

Tertullian

Ezekiel 10

Matthew Henry's introduction

The prophet had observed to us (8:4) that when he was in vision at Jerusalem he saw the same appearance of the glory of God there that he had seen by the river Chebar; now, in this chapter, he gives us some account of the appearance there, as far as was requisite for the clearing up of two further indications of the approaching destruction of Jerusalem, which God here gave the prophet:

I. The scattering of the coals of fire on the city, which were taken from between the cherubim, vv. 1–7.

II. The removal of the glory of God from the temple, and its being on the wing to be gone, vv. 8–22. When God goes out from a people all judgments break in on them.

A detailed analysis of chapter

A vision of the burning of the city. (1–7)

The divine glory departing from the temple. (8–22)

Key verse

Verse 8: "And there appeared in the cherubims the form of a man's hand under their wings."

Key word / key phrase

Verse 18, "the glory of the Lord departed."

Key event / key person / key theme

God's glory leaves the temple

Key thought

Can God's presence leave a Christian fellowship?

Key thing to look out for

What was the point of the burning coals?

Key Bible cross-reference

Verse 12. See Revelation 4:8.

Key "by way of explanation"

Verse 4, "The cloud filled." Just as God's glory filled the temple when it was first dedicated.

Key "Quotable Quote"

"The great end of God's work which is variously expressed in Scripture, is indeed but one; and this one end is most properly and comprehensively called, 'the glory of God.'"

Jonathan Edwards

Ezekiel 11

Matthew Henry's introduction

This chapter concludes the vision which Ezekiel saw, and this part of it gave him two messages:

I. A message of wrath against those who continued still at Jerusalem, and were there in the height of presumption, thinking they should never fall, vv. 1–13.

II. A message of comfort to those who were carried captives into Babylon and were there in the depth of despondency, thinking they should never rise. And, as the former are assured that God has judgments in store for them notwithstanding their present security, so the later are assured that God has mercy in store for them notwithstanding their present distress, vv. 14–21. And so the glory of God removes further, vv. 22, 23. The vision disappears (v. 24), and Ezekiel faithfully gives his hearers an account of it, v. 25.

A detailed analysis of chapter

Divine judgments against the wicked at Jerusalem. (1–13)

Divine favor toward those in captivity. (14–21)

The divine presence forsakes the city. (22–25)

Key verse

Verse 6: "Ye have multiplied your slain in this city, and ye have filled the streets thereof with the slain."

Key word / key phrase

Verse 17, "I will gather you from the nations."

Key event / key person / key theme

The promise of restoration

Key thought

Do present-day events in Israel have any bearing on what God promised in the Bible about the land of Israel being given back to the Israelites?

Key thing to look out for

Why were the leaders in Jerusalem wrong to think that they were safe?

Key Bible cross-reference

Verses 19,20. See 36:26–28.

Key "by way of explanation"

Verse 16, "I have been a sanctuary for them." The Lord could live among his people in exile.

Key "Quotable Quote"

"Love divine, all loves excelling,
Joy of heaven, to earth come down,
Fix in us thy humble dwelling,
And thy faithful mercies crown."

Charles Wesley

Ezekiel 12

Matthew Henry's introduction

In this chapter,

I. The prophet, by removing his stuff, and quitting his lodgings, must be a sign to set forth Zedekiah's flight out of Jerusalem in the utmost confusion when the Chaldeans took the city, vv. 1–16.

II. The prophet, by eating his meat with trembling, must be a sign to set forth the famine in the city during the siege, and the consternation that the inhabitants should be in, vv. 17–20.

III. A message is sent from God to the people, to assure them that all these predictions should have their accomplishment very shortly, and not be deferred, as they flattered themselves they would be, vv. 21–28.

A detailed analysis of chapter

The approaching captivity. (1–16)

An emblem of the consternation of the Jews. (17–20)

Answers to the objections of scoffers. (21–28)

Key verse

Verse 5: "Dig thou through the wall in their sight, and carry out thereby."

Key word / key phrase

Verse 3, "pack your belongings."

Key event / key person / key theme

Pictures of the exile

Key thought

Note how people reacted to these warning?

Key thing to look out for

Is there any lesson here to apply to people's attitudes to Jesus' second coming?

Key Bible cross-reference

Verse 2. See Isaiah 6:9–10.

Key "by way of explanation"

Verse 13, "my net . . . my snare," refers to the Lord taking his people into exile.

Key "Quotable Quote"

"I will be a pastor to none that will not be under discipline: That were to be half pastor, and indulge men in an unruliness and contempt of the ordinance of Christ."

Richard Baxter

Ezekiel 13

Matthew Henry's introduction

The prophet here shows the sin and punishment,

I. Of the false prophets, vv. 1–16.

II. Of the false prophetesses, vv. 17–23.

A detailed analysis of chapter

Heavy judgments against lying prophets. (1–9)
The insufficiency of their work. (10–16)
Woes against false prophetesses. (17–23)

Key verse

Verse 4: "O Israel, thy prophets are like the foxes in the deserts."

Key word / key phrase

Verse 1, "prophecy against the prophets."

Key event / key person / key theme

False prophets are condemned

Key thought

What results did these false prophets produce?

Key thing to look out for

In what terms are the false prophets described?

Key Bible cross-reference

Verse 10. See Jeremiah 6:14.

Key "by way of explanation"

Verse 2, "prophesy against the prophets of Israel." False teachers may be accredited by fellow false teachers and hold positions of authority among God's people.

Key "Quotable Quote"

"By entertaining of strange persons, men sometimes entertain angels unawares: but by entertaining of strange doctrines, many have entertained devils unawares."

John Flavel

Ezekiel 14

Matthew Henry's introduction

I. The elders of Israel come to hear the word, and enquire of the prophet, but, because they are not duly qualified, they meet with a rebuke instead of acceptance (vv. 1–5) and are called on to repent of their sins and reform their lives, else it is at their peril to enquire of God, vv. 6–11.

II. Noah, Daniel, and Job, are supposed to pray for this people, and yet, because the decree has gone forth, and the destruction of them is determined by a variety of judgments, their prayers shall not be answered, vv. 12–21. And yet it is promised, in the close, that a remnant shall escape, vv. 22, 23.

A detailed analysis of chapter

Idolatry among the exiles: warnings against hypocrites. (1–11)
God's purpose to punish Jerusaelm, but a few are be saved. (12–23)

Key verse

Verse 6: "Repent, and turn yourselves from your idols; and turn away your faces from all your abominations."

Key word / key phrase

Verse 9, "I will . . . destroy him from among my people."

Key event / key person / key theme

Judgment from God

Key thought

God punishes sin.

Key thing to look out for

What is the point in offering guidance to those who do not sincerely want it?

Key Bible cross-reference

Verse 21. See Revelation 6:8.

Key "by way of explanation"

Verse 8, "I will set my face against that man." Idolatry was such a serious sin that it resulted in this terrible divine punishment.

Key "Quotable Quote"

"If we do not preach about sin and God's judgment on it, we cannot present Christ as Savior from sin and the wrath of God."

J.I. Packer

Ezekiel 15

Matthew Henry's introduction

Here, in this short chapter, he shows him (probably with design that he should tell the people) that it was as requisite Jerusalem should be destroyed as that the dead and withered branches of a vine should be cut off and thrown into the fire.

I. The similitude is very elegant (vv. 1–5), but,

II. The explanation of the similitude is very dreadful, vv. 6–8.

A detailed analysis of chapter

Jerusalem like an unfruitful vine.(1–8)

Key verse

Verse 8: "And I will make the land desolate, because they have committed a trespass, saith the Lord GOD."

Key word / key phrase

Verse 2, "the wood of a vine."

Key event / key person / key theme

Parable of the good-for-nothing vine

Key thought

How did this vine apply to Israel?

Key thing to look out for

How does John 15 apply to us today?

Key Bible cross-reference

Verse 3. See Isaiah 22:23.

Key "by way of explanation"

Verse 7, "although they have come out of the fire." Jerusalem escaped destruction in 597 BC, but there would be no escape next time.

Key "Quotable Quote"

"Sin, in short, is that vast moral disease which affects the whole human race and justly deserves God's wrath and damnation."

J.C. Ryle

Ezekiel 16

Matthew Henry's introduction

In this long discourse are set forth,

I. The despicable and deplorable beginnings of that church and nation, vv. 3–5.

II. The many honors and favors God had bestowed on them, vv. 6–14.

III. Their treacherous and ungrateful departures from him to the services and worship of idols, here represented by the most impudent whoredom, vv. 15–34.

IV. A threatening of terrible destroying judgments, which God would bring on them for this sin, vv. 35–43.

V. An aggravation both of their sin and of their punishment, by comparison with Sodom and Samaria, vv. 44–59.

VI. A promise of mercy in the close, which God would show to a penitent remnant, vv. 60–63.

A detailed analysis of chapter

A parable showing the state of the Jewish nation, its prosperity, idolatries, and punishment. (1–63)

Key verse

Verse 12: "And I put a jewel on thy forehead, and earrings in thine ears, and a beautiful crown upon thine head."

Key word / key phrase

Verse 4, "on the day you were born."

Key event / key person / key theme

God's covenat with Israel pictured as a marriage

Key thought

By worshiping idols, Israel betrayed the marriage, turning herself into a prostitute.

Key thing to look out for

How can we show our gratitude to the Lord who has loved and forgiven us?

Key Bible cross-reference

Verse 22. See Psalm 25:7.

Key "by way of explanation"

Verse 44, "Like mother, like daughter." The present inhabitants of Jerusalem are like the pagan Canaanites who originally lived there. An adulteress was publically shamed and stoned to death.

Key "Quotable Quote"

"Sin is cosmic treason. Sin is treason against a perfectly pure Sovereign."

R.C. Sproul

Ezekiel 17

Matthew Henry's introduction

God was, in the previous chapter, reckoning with the people of Judah, and bringing ruin on them for their treachery in breaking covenant with him; in this chapter he is reckoning with the king of Judah for his treachery in breaking covenant with the king of Babylon; for when God came to contend with them he found many grounds of his controversy. The thing was now in doing: Zedekiah was practicing with the king of Egypt underhand for assistance in a treacherous project he had formed to shake off the yoke of the king of Babylon, and violate the homage and fealty he had sworn to him. For this God by the prophet here,

I. Threatens the ruin of him and his kingdom, by a parable of two eagles and a vine (vv. 1–10), and the explanation of that parable, vv. 11–21. But, in the close,

II. He promises hereafter to raise the royal family of Judah again, the house of David, in the Messiah and his kingdom, vv. 22–24.

A detailed analysis of chapter

An allegory relating to the Jewish nation. (1–10)
An added explanation. (11–21)
A direct promise of the Messiah. (22–24)

Key verse

Verse 5: "He took also of the seed of the land, and planted it in a fruitful field; he placed it by great waters, and set it as a willow tree."

Key word / key phrase

Verse 3, "a great eagle."

Key event / key person / key theme

Zedekiah's attempt to rebel against Babylon

Key thought

God's will can never be thwarted by human action.

Key thing to look out for

With verses 13–16 compare 2 Chronicles 36:13. What sin is attacked?

Key Bible cross-reference

Verses 12–15. See 2 Kings 24:15–20.

Key "by way of explanation"

The last eagle is the king of Babylon; Lebanon is Jerusalem; the topmost branch is Jehoiachin, taken to Babylon; the "seed" is Zedekiah, a vassal king in a lowly position (a low vine). The second eagle is Egypt. The cedar (verse 22) refers to the house of David.

Key "Quotable Quote"

"Where there is no mission, there is no Church, and where there is neither Church nor mission, there is no faith."

Emil Brunner

Ezekiel 18

Matthew Henry's introduction

Here is,

I. The corrupt proverb used by the profane Jews, which gave occasion to the message here sent them, and made it necessary for the justifying of God in his dealings with them, vv. 1–3.

II. The reply given to this proverb, in which God asserts in general his own sovereignty and justice, v. 4. Woe to the wicked; it shall be ill with them, vv. 4, 20. But say to the righteous, It shall be ill with them, vv. 4, 20. But say to the righteous, It shall be well with them, vv. 5–9. In particular, as to the case complained of, he assures us,

A. That it shall be ill with a wicked man, though he had a good father, vv. 10–13.

B. That it shall be well with a good man, though he had a wicked father, vv. 14–18. And therefore in this God is righteous, vv. 19, 20.

C. That it shall be well with penitents, though they began ever so ill, vv. 21–23 and 27, 28.

D. That it shall be ill with apostates, though they began ever so well, vv. 24, 26. And the use of all this is,

1. To justify God and clear the equity of all his proceedings, vv. 25, 29.
2. To engage and encourage us to repent of our sins and turn to God, vv. 30–32.

A detailed analysis of chapter

The soul who sins will die. (1–20)

The divine providence is vindicated. (21–29)

A gracious invitation to repent. (30–32)

Key verse

Verse 2: "What mean ye, that ye use this proverb concerning the land of Israel, saying, The fathers have eaten sour grapes, and the children's teeth are set on edge?"

Key word / key phrase

Verse 4. "The soul who sins is the one who will die."

Key event / key person / key theme

Personal responsibility

Key thought

How does verse 4 answer the question of verse 2?

Key thing to look out for

Verse 32. "I take no pleasure in the death of anyone." Because this is God's nature he extends his hand of mercy out to all.

Key Bible cross-reference

Verse 20. See Deuteronomy 24:16.

Key "by way of explanation"

Ezekiel was here correcting a tendency among the exiles to evade responsibility and to say they were suffering because of the mistakes of previous kings (see 2 Kings 21:10–15). This was only partially true.

Key "Quotable Quote"

"God's mercy is infinite. Everything about it is infinite. It proceeds from infinite Being, flows through the medium of an infinite sacrifice, surmounts obstacles that are infinite, and addresses itself to those that are infinitely unworthy and ill-deserving."

Gardiner Spring

Ezekiel 19

Matthew Henry's introduction

The scope of this chapter is much the same with that of the 17th, to foretell and lament the ruin of the house of David, the royal family of Judah, in the calamitous exit of the four sons and grandsons of Josiah—Jehoahaz, Jehoiakim, Jeconiah, and Zedekiah, in whom that illustrious line of kings was cut off, which the prophet is here ordered to lament, v. 1. And he does it by similitudes.

I. The kingdom of Judah and house of David are here compared to a lioness, and those princes to lions, that were fierce and ravenous, but were hunted down and taken in nets, vv. 2–9.

II. That kingdom and that house are here compared to a vine, and these princes to branches, which had been strong and flourishing, but were now broken off and burnt, vv. 10–14.

A detailed analysis of chapter

A parable lamenting the ruin of Jehoahaz and Jehoiakim. (1–9)

Another describing the desolation of the people. (10–14)

Key verse

Verse 6: "And he went up and down among the lions, he became a young lion, and learned to catch the prey, and devoured men."

Key word / key phrase

Verse 1, "Take up a lament."

Key event / key person / key theme

Lament for three of the kings of Judah

Key thought

What did these kings of Judah do wrong?

Key thing to look out for

How can unfruitfulness in God's service be avoided?

Key Bible cross-reference

Verse 2. See Numbers 23:24.

Key "by way of explanation"

Verse 12, "the east wind made it shrivel." This is a reference to Nebuchadnezzar and his powerful empire. Verse 2, the mother was the tribe of Judah, whose emblem was a lion. Verse 10, here Judah is a vine.

Key "Quotable Quote"

"A man who imagines to arrive at grace by doing all that he is able to do, adds sin to sin, and is doubly guilty."

Martin Luther

Ezekiel 20

Matthew Henry's introduction

In this chapter,

I. The prophet is consulted by some of the elders of Israel, v. 1.

II. He is instructed by his God what answer to give them. He must,

   A. Signify God's displeasure against them, vv. 2, 3. And,

   B. He must show them what just cause he had for that displeasure, by giving them a history of God's grateful dealings with their fathers and their treacherous dealings with God.

      1. In Egypt, vv. 5–9.
      2. In the wilderness, vv. 10–26.
      3. In Canaan, vv. 27–32.

   C. He must denounce the judgments of God against them, vv. 33–36.

   D. He must tell them likewise what mercy

God had in store for them, when he would bring a remnant of them to repentance, re-establish them in their own land, and set up his sanctuary among them again, vv. 37–44.

E. Here is another word dropped towards Jerusalem, which is explained and enlarged on in the next chapter, vv. 45–49.

A detailed analysis of chapter

The elders of Israel are reminded of the idolatry in Egypt. (1–9)

In the desert. (10–26)

In Canaan. (27–32)

God promises to pardon and restore them. (33–44)

Prophecy against Jerusalem. (45–49)

Key verse

Verse 8: "But they rebelled against me, and would not hearken unto me: they did not every man cast away the abominations of their eyes, neither did they forsake the idols of Egypt."

Key word / key phrase

Verse 4, "detestable practices."

Key event / key person / key theme

Looking back on Israel's past rebellion

Key thought

Verses 42–44, note how the Lord says he wants his people to respond to him.

Key thing to look out for

Why does God not just wipe everybody out from the face of the earth?

Key Bible cross-reference

Verse 15. See Numbers 14:26–35.

Key "by way of explanation"

Verse 33, "outstretched arm," is a deliberate reference back to God's spectacular deliverance at the Red Sea.

Key "Quotable Quote"

"No other blessing of the common grace of God is as great as the universal and sincere offer of salvation, nor is any other more obviously a fruit of the atonement."

R.B. Kuiper

Ezekiel 21

Matthew Henry's introduction

In this chapter we have,

I. An explication of the prophecy in the close of the previous chapter about the fire in the forest, which the people complained they could not understand (vv. 1–5), with directions to the prophet to show himself deeply affected with it, vv. 6, 7.

II. A further prediction of the sword that was coming on the land, by which all should be laid waste; and this expressed very emphatically, vv. 8–17.

III. A prospect given of the king of Babylon's approach to Jerusalem, to which he was determined by divination, vv. 18–24.

IV. Sentence passed on Zedekiah king of Judah,

vv. 25–27.

V. The destruction of the Ammonites by the sword foretold, vv. 28–32.

A detailed analysis of chapter

The ruin of Judah under the emblem of a sharp sword. (1–17)

The approach of the king of Babylon described. (18–27)

The destruction of the Ammonites. (28–32)

Key verse

Verse 2: "Son of man, set thy face toward Jerusalem, and drop thy word toward the holy places, and prophesy against the land of Israel."

Key word / key phrase

Verse 3, "I will draw my sword."

Key event / key person / key theme

Jerusalem's great sins

Key thought

God judged his people by means of a pagan king. Is there any lesson to draw from this?

Key thing to look out for

When human leaders fail where should we look for leadership?

Key Bible cross-reference

Verses 28–32. See Amos 1:13–15.

Key "by way of explanation"

Verse 28, "about their insults," refers to their malicious delight in the fall of Jerusalem.

Key "Quotable Quote"

"To ignore evil is to become an accomplice to it."

Martin Luther King, Jr.

Ezekiel 22

Matthew Henry's introduction

Here are three separate messages which God entrusts the prophet to deliver about Judah and Jerusalem, and all to the same purport, to show them their sins and the judgments that were coming on them for those sins.

I. Here is a catalogue of their sins, by which they had exposed themselves to shame and for which God would bring them to ruin, vv. 1–16.

II. They are here compared to dross, and are condemned as dross to the fire, vv. 17–22.

III. All orders and degrees of men among them are here found guilty of the neglect of the duty of their place and of having contributed to the national guilt, which therefore, since none appeared as intercessors, they must all expect to share in the punishment of, vv. 23–31.

A detailed analysis of chapter

The sins of Jerusalem. (1–16)

Israel is condemned as dross. (17–22)

As the corruption is general, so shall be the punishment. (23–31)

Key verse

Verse 3: "The city sheddeth blood in the midst of it, that her time may come, and maketh idols against herself to defile herself."

Key word / key phrase

Verse 3, "brings on herself doom."

Key event / key person / key theme

God's judgment on Jerusalem

Key thought

Verses 17–22, elsewhere in the scriptures the imagery of a furnace is used of purification, here it means destruction.

Key thing to look out for

What are the social and religious sins that are highlighted?

Key Bible cross-reference

Verse 12. See Exodus 22:25; 23:8.

Key "by way of explanation"

Verse 24, "a land that has no rain." Rain was thought of as a blessing coming down from the Lord.

Key "Quotable Quote"

"Grace comes into the soul, as the morning sun into the world; first a dawning, then a light; and at last the sun in his full and excellent brightness."

Thomas Adams

Ezekiel 23

Matthew Henry's introduction

Here is,

I. The apostasy of Israel and Samaria from God (vv. 1–8) and their ruin for it, vv. 9, 10.

II. The apostasy of Judah and Jerusalem from God (vv. 11–21) and sentence passed on them, that they shall in like manner be destroyed for it, vv. 22–35.

III. The joint wickedness of them both together (vv. 36–44) and the joint ruin of them both, vv. 45–49.

A detailed analysis of chapter

A history of the apostasy of God's people from him. (1–49)

Key verse

Verse 2: "Son of man, there were two women, the daughters of one mother."

Key word / key phrase

Verse 3, "prostitutes in Egypt."

Key event / key person / key theme

Parable of two adulterous sisters

Key thought

Jerusalem followed the wicked ways of Samaria.

Key thing to look out for

How can Christians today heed the warning this chapter gives?

Key Bible cross-reference

Verse 2. See Jeremiah 3:7.

Key "by way of explanation"

Verse 25, "They will cut off your noses." Jerusalem will suffer punishment similar to that handed out to some adulterers.

Key "Quotable Quote"

"No life ever grows great until it is focused, dedicated, disciplined."

Harry Emerson Fosdick

Ezekiel 24

Matthew Henry's introduction

I. By the sign of flesh boiling in a pot over the fire are shown the miseries that Jerusalem should suffer during the siege, and justly, for her filthiness, vv. 1–14.

II. By the sign of Ezekiel's not mourning for the death of his wife is shown that the calamities coming on Jerusalem were too great to be lamented, so great that they should sink down under them into a silent despair, vv. 15–27.

A detailed analysis of chapter

The fate of Jerusalem. (1–14)

The extent of the sufferings of the Jews. (15–27)

Key verse

Verse 3: "Set on a pot, set it on, and also pour water into it."

Key word / key phrase

Verse 2, "the king of Babylon has laid siege to Jerusalem."

Key event / key person / key theme

Jerusalem is besieged

Key thought

Note God's estimate of the people of Jerusalem.

Key thing to look out for

Is there anything positive to be gleaned from the death of Ezekiel's wife?

Key Bible cross-reference

Verse 13. See Isaiah 22:14.

Key "by way of explanation"

Verse 6, "empty it piece by piece," refers to the people being deported from Jerusalem.

Key "Quotable Quote"

"God does not discipline us to subdue us, but to condition us for a life of usefulness and blessedness."

Billy Graham

Ezekiel 25

Matthew Henry's introduction

In this chapter we have his prophecy,

I. Against the Ammonites, vv. 1–7.

II. Against the Moabites, vv. 8–11.

III. Against the Edomites, vv. 11–14.

IV. Against the Philistines, vv. 15–17.

A detailed analysis of chapter

Judgments against the Ammonites. (1–7)

Against the Moabites, Edomites, and Philistines. (8–17)

Key verse

Verse 2: "Son of man, set thy face against the Ammonites, and prophesy against them."

Key word / key phrase

Verse 2, "set your face against the Ammonites."

Key event / key person / key theme

Judgment against Ammon, Moab, Edom, and Philistia

Key thought

Note the different ways unbelievers act toward God's people when the latter are brought down.

Key thing to look out for

What are we to think when injustice is not put right?

Key Bible cross-reference

Verses 12–14. See Malachi 1:2–5.

Key "by way of explanation"

Verse 16, "I will cut off the Kerethites." The Kerethites were a synonym for the Philistines.

Key "Quotable Quote"

"God's wounds cure, sin's kisses kill."

William Gurnall

Ezekiel 26

Matthew Henry's introduction

In this chapter we have,

I. The sin charged on Tyre, which was triumphing in the destruction of Jerusalem, v. 2.

II. The destruction of Tyrus itself foretold.

A. The extremity of this destruction: it shall be utterly ruined, vv. 4–6, 12–14.

B. The instruments of this destruction, many nations (v. 3), and the king of Babylon by name with his vast victorious army, vv. 7–11.

C. The great surprise that this should give to the neighboring nations, who would all wonder at the fall of so great a city and be alarmed at it, vv. 15–21.

A detailed analysis of chapter

A prophecy against Tyre.(1–21)

Key verse

Verse 4: "And they shall destroy the walls of Tyrus, and break down her towers: I will also scrape her dust from her, and make her like the top of a rock."

Key word / key phrase

Verse 4, "they will destroy the walls of Tyre."

Key event / key person / key theme

Destruction of Tyre, a city on an island, was the capital of Phoenicia (Lebanon)

Key thought

Note the reason for Tyre's downfall. See verse 2.

Key thing to look out for

In view of what happened in this chapter to mighty Tyre how should we view today's mighty nations?

Key Bible cross-reference

Verse 13. See Revelation 18:22.

Key "by way of explanation"

Verse 2, "the gate to the nations is broken." Once Jerusalem fell the customs barrier between Tyre and the countries in the south was removed.

Key "Quotable Quote"

"God is none other than the Savior of our wretchedness. So we can only know God well by knowing our iniquities."

Blaise Pascal

Ezekiel 27

Matthew Henry's introduction

In this chapter we have,

I. A large account of the dignity, wealth, and splendor of Tyre, while it was in its strength, the vast trade it drove, and the interest it had among the nations (vv. 1–25), which is designed to make its ruin the more lamentable.

II. A prediction of its fall and ruin, and the confusion and consternation which all its neighbors shall thereby be put into, vv. 26–36.

A detailed analysis of chapter

The merchandise of Tyre. (1–25)

Its fall and ruin. (26–36)

Key verse

Verse 7: "Fine linen with broidered work from Egypt was that which thou spreadest forth to be thy sail; blue and purple from the isles of Elishah was that which covered thee."

Key word / key phrase

Verse 2, "take up a lament concerning Tyre."

Key event / key person / key theme

Lament over Tyre

Key thought

Where did Tyre go wrong?

Key thing to look out for

Today, how do nations make shipwreck of their countries?

Key Bible cross-reference

Verses 25–36. See Revelation 18:11–19.

Key "by way of explanation"

Tyre is pictured as a great trading ship, which sinks on the high seas. Ezekiel has a thorough grasp of trade and commerce.

Key "Quotable Quote"

"The corruption [of original sin] is constantly called sin by Paul while the things which spring from it such as adultery, fornication, theft, hatred, murder and revelings, he calls sins. Sins are the fruit of sin."

John Calvin

Ezekiel 28

Matthew Henry's introduction

In this chapter we have,

I. A prediction of the fall and ruin of the king of Tyre, who, in the destruction of that city, is particularly set up as a mark for God's arrows, vv. 1–10.

II. A lamentation for the king of Tyre, when he has thus fallen, though he falls by his own iniquity, vv. 11–19.

III. A prophecy of the destruction of Zidon, which as in the neighborhood of Tyre and had a dependence on it, vv. 20–23.

IV. A promise of the restoration of the Israel of God, though in the day of their calamity they were insulted over by their neighbors, vv. 24–26.

A detailed analysis of chapter

Two oracles against the ruler of Tyre. (1–19)
The fall of Sidon. (20–23)
The restoration of Israel. (24–26)

Key verse

Verse 3: "Behold, thou art wiser than Daniel; there is no secret that they can hide from thee."

Key word / key phrase

Verse 2, "say to the ruler of Tyre."

Key event / key person / key theme

The fall of the ruler of Tyre

Key thought

The downfall of the King of Tyre was caused by pride.

Key thing to look out for

From the prophecy against Sidon, verses 20–26, what do we learn about the purpose of God's judgments, especially in relation to his own followers?

Key Bible cross-reference

Verses 20–26. See Matthew 11:21,22.

Key "by way of explanation"

Verse 18, "desecrated your sanctuaries." They did this by the temple treasury money which had been gained unjustly. In verse 11 Ezekiel draws on a Phoenician version of the Eden story in which the first man is splendidly adorned.

Key "Quotable Quote"

"You will notice that you far oftener meet a man laboring under a sense of sin than one laboring under a sense of mercies."

Andrew Bonar

Ezekiel 29

Matthew Henry's introduction

In this chapter we have,

I. The destruction of Pharaoh foretold, for his dealing deceitfully with Israel, vv. 1–7.
II. The desolation of the land of Egypt foretold, vv. 8–12.
III. A promise of the restoration thereof, in part, after forty years, vv. 13–16.
IV. The possession that should be given to Nebuchadnezzar of the land of Egypt, vv. 17–20.
V. A promise of mercy to Israel, v. 21.

A detailed analysis of chapter

The desolation of Egypt. (1–16)
Also a promise of mercy to Israel. (17–21)

Key verse

Verse 3: "Behold, I am against thee, Pharaoh king of Egypt."

Key word / key phrase

Verse 2, "set your face against Pharaoh king of Egypt."

Key event / key person / key theme

Prophecies against Egypt

Key thought

Pharaoh's downfall is caused by arrogance.

Key thing to look out for

What does this chapter teach about God's treatment of ungodly nations?

Key Bible cross-reference

Verse 6. See Isaiah 36:6.

Key "by way of explanation"

Verse 18, "every shoulder made raw," as a result of carrying heavy loads of military equipment. Verse 1, the date is January 7th, 587 BC.

Key "Quotable Quote"

"Today we need prophetic preachers; not preachers of prophesy merely, but preachers with a gift of prophecy. The word of wisdom is missing."

A.W. Tozer

Ezekiel 30

Matthew Henry's introduction

In this chapter we have,

I. A continuation of the prophecy against Egypt, which we had in the latter part of the previous chapter, just before the desolation of that once flourishing kingdom was completed by Nebuchadnezzar, in which is foretold the destruction of all her allies and confederates, all her interests and concerns, and the several steps which the king of Babylon should take in pushing on this destruction, vv. 1–19.

II. A repetition of a former prophecy against Egypt, just before the desolation of it begun by their own bad conduct, which gradually weakened them and prepared the way for the king of Babylon, vv. 20–26.

A detailed analysis of chapter

A prophecy against Egypt. (1–19)

Another prophecy against Egypt. (20–26)

Key verse

Verse 6: "They also that uphold Egypt shall fall."

Key word / key phrase

Verse 4, "a sword will come against Egypt."

Key event / key person / key theme

Egypt will be destroyed

Key thought

Why will a nation never ultimately prosper that trusts in the power of its own rulers?

Key thing to look out for

How does verse 6 apply to many nations today?

Key Bible cross-reference

Verse 8. See Jeremiah 49:27.

Key "by way of explanation"

Verse 11, "dry up the streams of the Nile." This refers to the Nile delta. If this dried up life in Egypt would at once be threatened.

Key "Quotable Quote"

"Where sin rules and sin reigns sin ruins."

Author unknown

Ezekiel 31

Matthew Henry's introduction

The prophecy of this chapter, as the two chapters before, is against Egypt, and designed for the humbling and mortifying of Pharaoh. In passing sentence on great criminals it is usual to consult precedents, and to see what has been done to others in the like case, which serves both to direct and to justify the proceedings. Pharaoh stands indicted at the bar of divine justice for his pride and haughtiness, and the injuries he had done to God's people; but he thinks himself so high, so great, as not to be accountable to any authority, so strong, and so well guarded, as not to be conquerable by any force. The prophet is therefore directed to make a report to him of the case of the king of Assyria, whose head city was Nineveh.

I. He must show him how great a monarch the king of Assyria had been, what a vast empire he had, what a mighty sway he bore; the king of Egypt, great as he was could not go beyond him, vv. 3–9.

II. He must then show him how like he was to the king of Assyria in pride and carnal security, v. 10.

III. He must next read him the history of the fall and ruin of the king of Assyria, what a noise it made among the nations and what a warning it gave to all potent princes to take heed of pride, vv. 11–17.

IV. He must leave the king of Egypt to apply all this to himself, to see his own face in the looking-glass of the king of Assyria's sin, and to foresee his own fall through the perspective glass of his ruin, v. 18.

A detailed analysis of chapter

The glory of Assyria. (1–9)

Its fall. (10–18)

Key verse

Verse 7: "Thus was he fair in his greatness, in the length of his branches: for his root was by great waters."

Key word / key phrase

Verse 2, "say to Pharaoh king of Egypt."

Key event / key person / key theme

Egypt will fall like a cedar

Key thought

What had happened to Assyria would also happen to Egypt.

Key thing to look out for

What effect should the destruction of the tree have on other nations?

Key Bible cross-reference

Verse 8. See Genesis 2:9.

Key "by way of explanation"

Verse 9, "the garden of God," is a reference to the Garden of Eden in which the opening chapters of Genesis are set.

Key "Quotable Quote"

"Our attitude towards sin is more self-centered than God-centered. We are more concerned about our own 'victory' over sin than we are about the fact that our sin grieves the heart of God."

Jerry Bridges

Ezekiel 32

Matthew Henry's introduction

The destruction of Egypt is here represented under two similitudes:

1. The killing of a lion, or a whale, or some such devouring creature, vv. 1–16.
2. The funeral of a great commander or captain-general, vv. 17–32.

A detailed analysis of chapter

The fall of Egypt. (1–16)

A dirge: Egypt in the land of the dead. (17–32)

Key verse

Verse 2: "Son of man, take up a lamentation for Pharaoh king of Egypt."

Key word / key phrase

Verse 2, "concerning Pharaoh king of Egypt."

Key event / key person / key theme

Egypt, caught up in God's fishing net, is thrown up on the land

Key thought

God's agent in the destruction of Egypt is Babylon (verse 11).

Key thing to look out for

Note how often the personal pronoun "I" is used in this chapter, with reference to the Lord, and how this emphasizes his power in the world.

Key Bible cross-reference

Verse 7. See Isaiah 13:10.

Key "by way of explanation"

Verse 7, "I will cover the heavens." This kind of darkness indicated that great political chaos was about to come.

Key "Quotable Quote"

"There is only one thing to be feared, and that is sin."

John Chrysostom

Ezekiel 33

Matthew Henry's introduction

The prophet has now come off his circuit, which he went as judge, in God's name, to try and pass sentence on the neighboring nations, and, having finished with them, and read them all their doom, in the eight chapters foregoing, he now returns to the children of his people, and receives further instructions what to say to them.

I. He must let them know what office he was in among them as a prophet, that he was a watchman, and had received a charge about them, for which he was accountable, vv. 1–9. The substance of this we had before, 3:17, etc.

II. He must let them know on what terms they stand with God, that they are on their trial, on their good behavior, that if a wicked man repent he shall not perish, but that if a righteous man apostatize he shall perish, vv. 10–20.

III. Here is a particular message sent to those who yet remained in the land of Israel, and (which is very strange) grew secure there, and confident that they should take root there again, to tell them that their hopes would fail them because they persisted in their sins, vv. 21–29.

IV. Here is a rebuke to those who personally attended Ezekiel's ministry, but were not sincere in their professions of devotion, vv. 30–33.

A detailed analysis of chapter

Ezekiel's commission to be a watchman. (1–20)

The desolation of the land. (21–29)

Judgments on the mockers of the prophets. (30–33)

Key verse

Verse 6: "But if the watchman see the sword come, and blow not the trumpet, and the people be not warned; if the sword come, and take any person from among them, he is taken away in his iniquity; but his blood will I require at the watchman's hand."

Key word / key phrase

Verse 2, "their watchman."

Key event / key person / key theme

Ezekiel the watchman

Key thought

In what sense are Christians pastor to be watchmen today?

Key thing to look out for

In what ways are all Christians to be watchmen?

Key Bible cross-reference

Verse 21. See 2 Kings 25:3–10.

Key "by way of explanation"

Verse 2, "When I bring the sword against a land." The prophets often state that a country is plunged into war as a form of divine punishment.

Key "Quotable Quote"

"Sin pays – but it pays in remorse, regret, and failure."

Billy Graham

Ezekiel 34

Matthew Henry's introduction

Here is,

I. A high charge exhibited against them for their negligence, and their unfaithfulness in the management of public affairs, vv. 1–6 and v. 8.

II. Their discharge from their trust, for their insufficiency and treachery, vv. 7–10.

III. A gracious promise that God would take care of his flock, though they did not, and that it should not always suffer as it had done by their maladministrations, vv. 11–16.

IV. Another charge exhibited against those of the flock that were fat and strong, for the injuries they did to those that were weak and feeble, vv. 17–22.

V. Another promise that God would in the fullness of time send the Messiah, to be the great and good Shepherd of the sheep, who should redress all grievances and set every thing to rights with the flock, vv. 23–31.

A detailed analysis of chapter

The rulers reproved. (1–6)

The people are to be restored to their own land. (7–16)

The kingdom of Christ. (17–31)

Key verse

Verse 10: "Behold, I am against the shepherds."

Key word / key phrase

Verse 2, "prophecy against the shepherds of Israel."

Key event / key person / key theme

Message to the shepherds

Key thought

What did the bad shepherds do wrong?

Key thing to look out for

In what ways is Jesus, the Good Shepherd, different from these false shepherds?

Key Bible cross-reference

Verse 5. See Numbers 27:17.

Key "by way of explanation"

Verse 6, "I will search for the lost." This is exactly what the Jesus said the Son of Man would do. See Luke 19:10.

Key "Quotable Quote"

"Do you wish to see God's love? Look at the cross. Do you wish to see God's wrath? Look at the cross."

D.A. Carson

Ezekiel 35

Matthew Henry's introduction

Now here we have,

I. The sin charged on the Edomites, and that was their spite and malice to Israel, vv. 5, 10–13.

II. The ruin threatened, that should come on them for this sin. God will be against them (v. 3) and then their country shall be laid waste (v. 4), depopulated, and made quite desolate (vv. 6–9), and left so when other nations that had been wasted should recover themselves, vv. 14, 15.

A detailed analysis of chapter

A prophecy against Edom. (1–15)

Key verse

Verse 2: "Son of man, set thy face against mount Seir, and prophesy against it."

Key word / key phrase

Verse 2, "set your face against Mount Seir."

Key event / key person / key theme

Judgment on Edom

Key thought

For what sins is Edom condemned?

Key thing to look out for

Note how the punishment Edom will receive matches her sins.

Key Bible cross-reference

Verse 13. See Daniel 7:8.

Key "by way of explanation"

Verse 3, "the Lord was there." The Edomites had no business to take over the land for it belonged to the Lord.

Key "Quotable Quote"

"The pervasive sinfulness of man becomes evident when contrasted with the radiant holiness of God."

Richard J. Foster

Ezekiel 36

Matthew Henry's introduction

I. Here is one that seems chiefly to relate to the temporal estate of the Jews, in which their present deplorable condition is described and the triumphs of their neighbors in it; but it is promised that their grievances shall be all redressed and that in due time they shall be settled again in their own land, in the midst of peace and plenty, vv. 1–15.

II. Here is another that seems chiefly to concern their spiritual estate, in which they are reminded of their former sins and God's judgments on them, to humble them for their sins and under God's mighty hand, vv. 16–20. But it is promised,

A. That God would glorify himself in showing mercy to them, vv. 21–24.

B. That he would sanctify them, by giving them his grace and fitting them for his service; and this for his own name's sake and in answer to their prayers, vv. 25–38.

A detailed analysis of chapter

The land shall be delivered from heathen oppressors. (1–15)

The people are reminded of former sins, and promised deliverance. (16–24)

Also holiness, and gospel blessings. (25–38)

Key verse

Verse 11: "And I will multiply upon you man and beast; and they shall increase and bring fruit: and I will settle you after your old estates, and will do better unto you than at your beginnings: and ye shall know that I am the LORD."

Key word / key phrase

Verse 26, "I will give you a new heart."

Key event / key person / key theme

A new heart and a new spirit

Key thought

God promises a radical cleansing and a new nature, a teachable heart ("heart of flesh") and knowledge of God by his Spirit.

Key thing to look out for

What spiritual blessings that Christians enjoy today are mirrored in these verses?

Key Bible cross-reference

Verses 26–28. See 11:19,20.

Key "by way of explanation"

Verse 26, "new spirit." Once people have this new heart and new spirit, which is nothing other than God's Spirit they will be enabled to keep God's covenant.

Key "Quotable Quote"

"Spirit-filled souls are ablaze for God. They love with a love that glows. They believe with a faith that kindles. They serve with a devotion that consumes. They hate sin with a fierceness that burns. They rejoice with a joy that radiates. Love is perfected in the fire of God."

Samuel Chadwick

Ezekiel 37

Matthew Henry's introduction

I. They were so dispersed among their enemies, so destitute of all helps and advantages which might favor or further their return, and so dispirited likewise in their own minds; on all these accounts they are here, in vision, compared to a valley full of the dry bones of dead men, which should be brought together and raised to life. The vision of this we have (vv. 1–10) and the explication of it, with its application to the present case, vv. 11–14.

II. That they were so divided among themselves, too much of the old enmity between Judah and Ephraim remaining even in their captivity. But, as to this, by a sign of two sticks made one in the hand of the prophet is foreshown the happy coalition that should be, at their return, between the two nations of Israel and Judah, vv. 15–22. In this there was a type of the uniting of Jews and Gentiles, Jews and Samaritans, in Christ and his church. And so the prophet slides into a prediction of the kingdom of Christ, which should be set up in the world with God's tabernacle in it, and of the glories and graces of that kingdom, vv. 23–28.

A detailed analysis of chapter

God restores dried bones to life. (1–14)

The whole house of Israel is represented as enjoying the blessings of Christ's kingdom. (15–28)

Key verse

Verse 1: "The hand of the LORD was upon me, and carried me out in the spirit of the LORD, and set me down in the midst of the valley which was full of bones."

Key word / key phrase

Verse 2, "bones that were very dry."

Key event / key person / key theme

New life for dry bones

Key thought

There is no life at all in the bones: "the most unpromising congregation that any preacher ever addressed" (F.F. Bruce).

Key thing to look out for

What conclusions are we to draw from the dry bones coming to life?

Key Bible cross-reference

Verse 27. See 2 Corinthians 6:16.

Key "by way of explanation"

Verse 10, "breath entered them." This is reminiscent of God the Creator breathing life into the nostrils of the first man. The Hebrew word, *ruah*, means "breath," "wind," and "spirit."

Key "Quotable Quote"

"The Spirit of God is given to the true saints to dwell in them, as his proper lasting abode; and to influence their hearts, as a principle of new nature or as a divine supernatural spring of life and action."

Jonathan Edwards

Ezekiel 38

Matthew Henry's introduction

But, in both, the Old-Testament prophecies had their accomplishment in the Jewish church as the New-Testament prophecies shall have when the time comes in the Christian church. In this chapter we have intermixed,

I. The attempt that Gog and Magog should make on the land of Israel, the vast army they should bring into the field, and their vast preparations (vv. 4–7), their project and design in it (vv. 8–13), God's hand in it, v. 4.

II. The great terror that this should strike on the land of Israel, vv. 15, 16, 18–20.

III. The divine restraint that these enemies should be under, and the divine protection that Israel should be under, vv. 2–4 and v. 14.

IV. The defeat that should be given to those enemies by the immediate hand of God (vv. 21–23), which we shall hear more of in the next chapter.

A detailed analysis of chapter

The army and malice of Gog. (1–13)

God's judgments. (14–23)

Key verse

Verse 2: "Son of man, set thy face against Gog, the land of Magog."

Key word / key phrase

Verse 2, "set your face against Gog."

Key event / key person / key theme

An attack from the north by a mighty coalition of aggresors.

Key thought

Verse 4, God is in control

Key thing to look out for

How will God make himself known to the nations?

Key Bible cross-reference

Verse 2. See Revelation 20:8.

Key "by way of explanation"

Verse 16, "when I show myself holy through you." Israel's God used even these ungodly people to demonstrate his own holiness.

Key "Quotable Quote"

"The first and most important thing we know about God is that we know nothing about him except what he himself makes known."

Emil Brunner

Ezekiel 39

Matthew Henry's introduction

This chapter continues and concludes the prophecy against Gog and Magog, in whose destruction God crowns his favor to his people Israel, which shines very brightly after the scattering of that black cloud in the close of this chapter. Here is,

I. An express prediction of the utter destruction of Gog and Magog, agreeing with what we had before, vv. 1–7.

II. An illustration of the vastness of that destruction, in three consequences of it: the burning of their weapons (vv. 8–10), the burning of their slain (vv. 11–16), and the feasting of the fowls with the dead bodies of those that were unburied, vv. 17–22.

III. A declaration of God's gracious purposes about his people Israel, in this and his other providences about them, and a promise of further mercy that he had yet in store for them, vv. 23–29.

A detailed analysis of chapter

The destruction of Gog. (1–10)
Its extent. (11–22)
Israel again favored. (23–29)

Key verse

Verse 1: "Thus saith the Lord GOD; Behold, I am against thee, O Gog, the chief prince of Meshech and Tubal."

Key word / key phrase

Verse 25, "I will now bring Jacob back from captivity."

Key event / key person / key theme

God's plans for Israel

Key thought

How are God's compassion and holiness linked in verse 25?

Key thing to look out for

How can one benefit from a time during which God "hides" himself from us?

Key Bible cross-reference

Verses 17–20. See Revelation 19:17,18.

Key "by way of explanation"

Verse 7, "the Holy One in Israel." This is a slight variation of the more familiar title given to God, "the Holy One of Israel."

Key "Quotable Quote"

"What men stand most in need of is the knowledge of God."

François Fénelon

Ezekiel 40

Matthew Henry's introduction

In this chapter we have,

I. A general account of this vision of the temple and city, vv. 1–4.

II. A particular account of it entered on; and description given,

A. Of the outside wall, v. 5.

B. Of the east gate, vv. 6–19.
C. Of the north gate, vv. 20–23.
D. Of the south gate (vv. 24–31) and the chambers and other appurtenances belonging to these gates.
E. Of the inner court, both towards the east and towards the south, vv. 32–38.
F. Of the tables, vv. 39–43.
G. Of the lodgings for the singers and the priests, vv. 44–47.
H. Of the porch of the house, vv. 48, 49.

A detailed analysis of chapter

Ezekiel is taken to Jerusalem. (1–4)
The east gate to the outer court. (5–16)
The outer court. (17–19)
The north gate and the south gate. (20–27).
Gates to the inner court. (28–37)
Buildings near the north gate. (38–46)
The inner courtyard and the temple building. (47–49)

Key verse

Verse 2: "In the visions of God brought he me into the land of Israel, and set me upon a very high mountain, by which was as the frame of a city on the south."

Key word / key phrase

Verse 5, "the temple area."

Key event / key person / key theme

The new temple

Key thought

"A purified people implies a purified land . . . the new temple, the holiest place of all – because the divine glory which had abandoned the first temple returns (44:4)" (F.F. Bruce).

Key thing to look out for

In verse 4 what responsibilities are placed on Ezekiel?

Key Bible cross-reference

Verse 2. See Revelation 21:10.

Key "by way of explanation"

Verse 3, "a man whose appearance was like bronze." This is a description of a celestial being, as in Daniel 10:6 in which the "man" had "arms and legs like the gleam of burnished bronze."

Key "Quotable Quote"

"We love the Invisible and know what is beyond understanding."

Richard J. Foster

Ezekiel 41

Matthew Henry's introduction

An account was given of the porch of the house in the close of the previous chapter; this brings us to the temple itself, the description of which here given creates much difficulty to the critical expositors and occasions differences among them. Those must consult them who are nice in their enquiries into the meaning of the particulars of this delineation; it shall suffice us to observe,

I. The dimensions of the house, the posts of it (v. 1), the door (v. 2), the wall and the side-chambers (vv. 5, 6), the foundations and wall of the chambers, their doors (vv. 8–11), and the house itself, v. 13.

II. The dimensions of the oracle, or most holy place, vv. 3, 4.
III. An account of another building over against the separate place, vv. 12–15.
IV. The manner of the building of the house, vv. 7, 16, 17.
V. The ornaments of the house, vv. 18–20.
VI. The altar of incense and the table, v. 22.
VII. The doors between the temple and the oracle, vv. 23–26.

A detailed analysis of chapter

The temple. (1–26)

Key verse

Verse 1: "Afterward he brought me to the temple."

Key word / key phrase

Verse 1, "to the outer sanctuary."

Key event / key person / key theme

The holy place, holy of holies, and interior furniture

Key thought

What privileges do Christians have today which Ezekiel did not have?

Key thing to look out for

Compare verses 3, 4 with Hebrews 9:6–9, 24; 10:19–22.

Key Bible cross-reference

Verse 18. See 1 Kings 6:18.

Key "by way of explanation"

Verse 3, "he went into the inner sanctuary." This corresponds to the holy of holies of Solomon's temple into which only the high priest was allowed to enter once a year.

Key "Quotable Quote"

"Nothing is so easily obtained as the possession and enjoyment of God. He is more present to us than we are to ourselves. He is more desirous of giving himself to us than we are to possess him; we only need to know how to seek him, and the way is easier and more natural to us than breathing."

Jeanne Guyon

Ezekiel 42

Matthew Henry's introduction

This chapter continues and concludes the describing and measuring of this mystical temple, which it is very hard to understand the particular architecture of, and yet more hard to comprehend the mystical meaning of. Here is,

I. A description of the chambers that were about the courts, their situation and structure (vv. 1–13), and the uses for which they were designed, vv. 13, 14.
II. A survey of the whole compass of ground which was taken up with the house, and the courts belonging to it, vv. 15–20.

A detailed analysis of chapter

Two buildings near the temple. (1–14)
Measurements of the temple area. (15–20)

Key verse

Verse 1: "Then he brought me forth into the utter court, the way toward the north: and he brought me into the chamber that was over against the separate place, and which was before the building toward the north."

Key word / key phrase

Verse 1, "the outer court."

Key event / key person / key theme

The priests' rooms and overall dimensions of the temple

Key thought

In what ways is God's holiness underlined in this chapter?

Key thing to look out for

How should this effect our walk with the Holy One of Israel?

Key Bible cross-reference

Verse 13. See Leviticus 6:29.

Key "by way of explanation"

Verse 14, "these are holy." The priests were told to remove the clothes they wore while they ministered, as they were not to mix with people in the outer court in such sanctified garments.

Key "Quotable Quote"

"I want to be open to God, not to what human beings say about God."

Madeleine L'Engle

Ezekiel 43

Matthew Henry's introduction

In this chapter we have,

I. Possession taken of this temple, by the glory of God filling it, vv. 1–6.

II. A promise given of the continuance of God's presence with his people on condition of their return to, and continuance in, the instituted way of worship, and their abandoning idols and idolatry, vv. 7–12.

III. A description of the altar of burnt offerings, vv. 13–17.

IV. Directions given for the consecration of that altar, vv. 18–27.

A detailed analysis of chapter

The Lord returns to the temple. (1–12)

The altar. (13–17)

Consecration of the altar. (18–27)

Key verse

Verse 2: "And, behold, the glory of the God of Israel came from the way of the east: and his voice was like a noise of many waters: and the earth shined with his glory."

Key word / key phrase

Verse 5, "the glory of the Lord filled the temple."

Key event / key person / key theme

God's glory returns to the temple

Key thought

How should God's glory be visible in a Christian today?

Key thing to look out for

In what ways should Christian fellowships display God's glory?

Key Bible cross-reference

Verse 2. See 10:3,4,18,19; 11:22,23.

Key "by way of explanation"

Verse 2, "the glory of God," now returns and fills the new temple as it did in the tabernacle and first temple.

Key "Quotable Quote"

"The person who loves God values knowledge of God more than anything created by God, and pursues such knowledge ardently and ceaselessly."

Maximus the Confessor

Ezekiel 44

Matthew Henry's introduction

In this chapter we have,

I. The appropriating of the east gate of the temple to the prince, vv. 1–3.

II. A reproof sent to the house of Israel for their former profanations of God's sanctuary, with a charge to them to be more strict for the future, vv. 4–9.

III. The degrading of those Levites that had formerly been guilty of idolatry and the establishing of the priesthood in the family of Zadok, which had kept their integrity, vv. 10–16.

IV. Divers laws and ordinances about the priests, vv. 17–31.

A detailed analysis of chapter

Use of east gate. (1–3)

Admission into the temple. (4–9)

Excluded Levites. (10–14)

Priests. (15–31)

Key verse

Verse 9: "Thus saith the Lord GOD; No stranger, uncircumcised in heart, nor uncircumcised in flesh, shall enter into my sanctuary, of any stranger that is among the children of Israel."

Key word / key phrase

Verse 5, "regulations regarding the temple."

Key event / key person / key theme

Laws for the priesthood

Key thought

What place should rules and regulations have in a Christian's life today?

Key thing to look out for

What can we learn from the judgments of God that fell on faithful and unfaithful service in this chapter?

Key Bible cross-reference

Verse 21. See Leviticus 10:9.

Key "by way of explanation"

Verse 9, "uncircumcised in heart and flesh." More important than literal uncircumcision is impiety in the heart. Verse 3, the "prince" is not a messianic figure but a lay ruler/administrator.

Key "Quotable Quote"

"What were we made for? To know God.
What aim should we have in life? To know God.
What is the eternal life that Jesus gives? To know God.
What is the best thing in life? To know God.
What in humans gives God most pleasure? Knowledge of himself."

J.I. Packer

Ezekiel 45

Matthew Henry's introduction

In this chapter is further represented to the prophet, in vision,

I. The division of the holy land, so much for the temple, and the priests that attended the service of it (vv. 1–4), so much for the Levites (v. 5), so much for the city (v. 6), so much for the prince, and the residue to the people, vv. 7, 8.

II. The ordinances of justice that were given both to prince and people, vv. 9–12.

III. The oblations they were to offer, and the prince's part in those oblations, vv. 13–17. Particularly in the beginning of the year (vv. 18–20) and in the Passover, and the feast of tabernacles, vv. 21–25.

A detailed analysis of chapter

Division of the land. (1–12)
Offerings and holy days. (13–25)

Key verse

Verse 1: "Moreover, when ye shall divide by lot the land for inheritance, ye shall offer an oblation unto the LORD."

Key word / key phrase

Verse 1, "When you allot the land."

Key event / key person / key theme

Rules for the prince (the secular ruler); and the festivals

Key thought

Where in this chapter can one deduce that God's holiness should affect our morality?

Key thing to look out for

What does this chapter tell us about God's attitude to injustice and oppression?

Key Bible cross-reference

Verse 10. See Leviticus 19:36.

Key "by way of explanation"

Verse 7, "the prince." The people had to give their offering to the prince as part of his work was to provide the public with their necessary sacrifices. Verses 1–8, an area of land, about 8 miles from north to south was to be set apart. This was where the Levites and priests would live. The temple enclosure was in the center of the land allocated to the priests.

Key "Quotable Quote"

"The right doctrines mentally assented to are not an end in themselves, but should only be the vestibule to a personal and loving communion with God."

Francis A. Schaeffer

Ezekiel 46

Matthew Henry's introduction

In this chapter we have,

I. Some further rules given both to the priests and to the people, relating to their worship, vv. 1–15.

II. A law about the prince's disposal of his inheritance, vv. 16–18.

III. A description of the places provided for the boiling of the sacrifices and the baking of the meat-offerings, vv. 19–24.

A detailed analysis of chapter

The prince and the festivals. (1–12)
Daily offering. (13–15)
The prince and the land. (16–18)
Temple kitchens. (19–24)

Key verse

Verse 3: "Likewise the people of the land shall worship at the door of this gate before the LORD in the Sabbaths and in the new moons."

Key word / key phrase

Verse 1, "the gate of the inner court."

Key event / key person / key theme

Additional princely duties

Key thought

How can we ensure that we worship God "in spirit and in truth" at every Christian worship service?

Key thing to look out for

Does the style of worship service matter to God?

Key Bible cross-reference

Verse 17. See Leviticus 25:10.

Key "by way of explanation"

Verse 16, "his descendants." In Ezekiel's vision some kind of hereditary rulership is in view.

Key "Quotable Quote"

"When we encounter God, the totality of our creatureliness breaks upon us and shatters the myth that we have believed about ourselves, the myth that we are demi-gods, junior-grade deities who will try to live forever."

R.C. Sproul

Ezekiel 47

Matthew Henry's introduction

In this chapter we have,

I. The vision of the holy waters, their rise, extent, depth, and healing virtue, the plenty of fish in them, and an account of the trees growing on the banks of them, vv. 1–12.

II. An appointment of the borders of the land of Canaan, which was to be divided by lot to the tribes of Israel and the strangers that sojourned among them, vv. 13–23.

A detailed analysis of chapter

River flowing from the temple. (1–12)
Boundaries of the land. (13–23)

Key verse

Verse 1: "Afterward he brought me again unto the door of the house; and, behold, waters issued out from under the threshold of the house eastward: for the forefront of the house stood toward the east, and the waters came down from under from the right side of the house, at the south side of the altar."

Key word / key phrase

Verse 1, "I saw water coming out."

Key event / key person / key theme

The river flowing from the temple – a prophecy of the outpoured Spirit of God

Key thought

What does this chapter teach about the principles that should guide us about reforming our society or our Church?

Key thing to look out for

How are the living waters of spiritual life from the Lord Jesus Christ to be increased in the life of individual Christians?

Key Bible cross-reference

Verse 1. See John 7:38.

Key "by way of explanation"

Verse 1, "I saw water." In Ezekiel's vision a river rises in the temple and flows down the Kidron Valley to the Dead Sea. Joel and Zechariah also prophecy that living water will flow from Jerusalem.

Key "Quotable Quote"

"The true knowledge of God will result, not in our being puffed up with conceit at how knowledgeable we are, but in our falling on our faces before God in sheer wonder."

John R.W. Stott

Ezekiel 48

Matthew Henry's introduction

In this chapter we have particular directions given for the distribution of the land, of which we had the metes and bounds assigned in the previous chapter.

I. The portions of the twelve tribes, seven to the north of the sanctuary (vv. 1–7) and five to the south, vv. 23–29.

II. The allotment of land for the sanctuary, and the priests (vv. 8–11), for the Levites (vv. 12–14), for the city (vv. 15–20), and for the prince, vv. 21, 22. Much of this we had before, ch. 45.

III. A plan of the city, its gates, and the new name given to it (vv. 30–35), which seals up, and concludes, the vision and prophecy of this book.

A detailed analysis of chapter

Division of the land. (1–29)

Gates of Jerusalem. (30–35)

Key verse

Verse 11: "It shall be for the priests that are sanctified of the sons of Zadok; which have kept my charge, which went not astray when the children of Israel went astray, as the Levites went astray."

Key word / key phrase

Verse 1, "These are the tribes, listed by name."

Key event / key person / key theme
Division of the land among the tribes

Key thought
Verse 35. What does God's name for the city tell us about God himself?

Key thing to look out for
What abiding lessons are there to draw from the whole book of Ezekiel?

Key Bible cross-reference
Verses 30–34. See Revelation 21:12,13.

Key "by way of explanation"
Verse 35, "the name of the city." The city is called, "The Lord is there." This is the most important reason for calling the city the "holy" city.

Key "Quotable Quote"
"If you keep watch over your hearts, and listen for the voice of God and learn of him, in one short hour you can learn more from him than you could learn from man in a thousand years."
Johann Tauler

5. Select bibliography for Ezekiel

Alexander, Ralph H. *Ezekiel*. Chicago: Moody, 1976.

Allen, Leslie C. *Ezekiel* (Word), Word Books, 1994. (two vols.)

Ellison, Henry L. *Ezekiel: The Man and His Message*. Grand Rapids: Eerdmans, 1956.

Feinberg, Charles Lee. *The Prophecy of Ezekiel: The Glory of the Lord*. Chicago: Moody, 1969.

Hoekema, Anthony. *The Bible and the Future*. Grand Rapids Eerdmans, 1979.

Kaiser, Walter C., Jr. *Toward an Old Testament Theology*. Grand Rapids: Zondervan, 1978.

Keil, Carl F. *Biblical Commentary on the Prophecies of Ezekiel*. KD. 2 vols. Grand Rapids: Eerdmans, 1950.

Taylor, John B. *Ezekiel: An Introduction and Commentary*. Downers Grove, III.: InterVarsity, 1969.

Unger, Merrill F. *Great Neglected Bible Prophecies*. Wheaton, III.: Scripture, 1955.

Daniel

1. Book by book: Introduction to Daniel

Introduction

Daniel the prophet

Daniel, that is, "God is my judge"; probably of the blood royal (compare Dan. 1:3, with 1 Chr. 3:1, where a son of David is named so). Jerusalem may have been his birthplace (though Dan. 9:24, "thy holy city," does not necessarily imply this). He was carried to Babylon among the Hebrew captives brought thither by Nebuchadnezzar at the first deportation in the fourth year of Jehoiakim. As he and his three companions are called (Dan. 1:4) "children," he cannot have been more than about twelve years old when put in training, according to Eastern etiquette, to be a courtier (Dan. 1:3, 6). He then received a new name, by which it was usual to mark a change in one's condition (2 Kings 23:34; 24:17; Ezra 5:14; Esth. 2:7), Belteshazzar, that is, "a prince favored by Bel" (Dan. 1:7).

His piety and wisdom were proverbial among his countrymen at an early period; probably owing to that noble proof he gave of faithfulness, combined with wisdom, in abstaining from the food sent to him from the king's table, as being polluted by the idolatries usual at heathen banquets (Dan. 1:8–16). Hence Ezekiel's reference to him (Ezek. 14:14, 20; 28:3) is precisely of that kind we should expect; a coincidence which must be undesigned. Ezekiel refers to him not as a writer, but as exhibiting a character righteous and wise in discerning secrets, in those circumstances now found in his book, which are earlier than the time when Ezekiel wrote. As Joseph rose in Egypt by interpreting Pharaoh's dreams, so Daniel, by interpreting Nebuchadnezzar's, was promoted to be governor of Babylonia, and president of the Magian priest-caste. Under Evil-merodach, Nebuchadnezzar's successor, as a change of officers often attends the accession of a new king, Daniel seems to have had a lower post, which led him occasionally to be away from Babylon (Dan. 8:2, 27). Again he came into note when he read the mystic writing of Belshazzar's doom on the wall on the night of that monarch's impious feast. Berosus calls the last Babylonian king Nabonidus and says he was not killed, but had an honorable abode in Carmania assigned to him, after having surrendered voluntarily in Borsippa. Rawlinson has cleared up the discrepancy from the Nineveh inscription. Belshazzar was joint king with his father, Evil-merodach or Nabonidus (called Minus in the inscriptions), to whom he was subordinate. He shut himself up in Babylon, while the other king took refuge elsewhere, namely, in Borsippa. Berosus gives the Chaldean account, which suppresses all about Belshazzar, as being to the national dishonor. Had Daniel been a late book, he would no doubt have taken up the later account of Berosus. If he gave a history differing from that current in Babylonia, the Jews of that region would not have received it as true. Darius the Mede, or Cyaxares II, succeeded and reigned two years. The mention of this monarch's reign, almost unknown to profane history (being eclipsed by the splendor of Cyrus) is an incidental proof that Daniel wrote as a contemporary historian of events which he knew, and did not borrow from others.

In the third year of Cyrus he saw the visions (the tenth through twelfth chapters) relating to his people down to the latest days and the coming resurrection. He must have been about eighty-four years old at this time. Tradition represents Daniel as having died and been buried at Shushan. Though his advanced age did not allow him to be among those who returned to Palestine, yet he never ceased to have his people's interests nearest to his heart (Dan. 9:3–19; 10:12).

Genuineness

Dan. 7:1, 28; 8:2; 9:2; 10:1, 2; 12:4, 5, testify that it was composed by Daniel himself. He does not mention himself in the first six chapters, which are historical; for in these it is not the author, but the events which are the prominent point. In the last six, which are prophetical, the author makes himself known, for here it was needed, prophecy being a revelation of words to particular men. It holds a third rank in the Hebrew canon: not among the prophets, but in the *Hagiographa* (*Chetubim*), between Esther and Ezra, books like it relating to the captivity; because he did not strictly belong to those who held exclusively the profession of "prophets" in the theocracy, but was rather a "seer," having the gift, but not the office of prophet. Were the book an interpolated one, it doubtless would have been placed among the prophets.

Its present position is a proof of its genuineness, as it was deliberately put in a position different from that where most would expect to find it. Placed between Esther, and Ezra and Nehemiah, it separated the historical books of the time after the captivity. Thus, Daniel was, as Bengel calls him, the politician, chronologer, and historian among the prophets. The Psalms also, though many are prophetical, are ranked with the *Hagiographa*, not with the prophets; and the Revelation of John is separated from his Epistles, as Daniel is from the Old Testament prophets. Instead of writing in the midst of the covenant people, and making them the foreground of his picture, he writes in a heathen court, the world kingdoms occupying the foreground, and the kingdom of God, though ultimately made the most significant, the background. His peculiar position in the heathen court is reflected in his peculiar position in the canon.

As the "prophets" in the Old Testament, so the epistles of the apostles in the New Testament were written by divinely commissioned people for their contemporaries. But Daniel and John were not in immediate contact with the congregation, but isolated and alone with God, the one in a heathen court, the other on a lonely isle (Rev. 1:9). Porphyry, the assailant of Christianity in the third century, asserted that the Book of Daniel was a forgery of the time of the Maccabees (170–164 B.C.), a time when confessedly there were no prophets, written after the events as to Antiochus Epiphanes, which it professes to foretell; so accurate are the details. A conclusive proof of Daniel's inspiration, if his prophecies can be shown to have been before the events. Now we know, from Josephus (*Antiquities*, 10.11.7), that the Jews in Christ's days recognized Daniel as in the canon. Zechariah, Ezra, and Nehemiah, centuries before Antiochus, refer to it. Jesus refers to it in His characteristic designation, "Son of man," Matt. 24:30 (Dan. 7:13); also expressly by name, and as a "prophet," in Matt. 24:15 (compare Matt. 24:21, with Dan. 12:1, etc.); and in the moment that decided His life (Matt. 26:64) or death, when the high priest adjured him by the living God. Also, in Luke 1:19–26, "Gabriel" is mentioned, whose name occurs nowhere else in Scripture, save in Dan. 8:16; 9:21. Besides the references to it in Revelation, Paul confirms the prophetical part of it, as to the blasphemous king (Dan. 7:8, 25; 11:36), in 1 Cor. 6:2; 2 Thess. 2:3, 4; the narrative part, as to the miraculous deliverances from "the lions" and "the fire," in Heb. 11:33, 34.

Thus the book is expressly attested by the New Testament on the three points made the stumbling-block of neologists—the predictions, the narratives of miracles, and the manifestations of angels. An objection has been stated to the unity of the book, namely, that Jesus quotes no part of the first half of Daniel. But Matt. 21:44 would be an enigma if it were not a reference to the "stone that smote the image" (Dan. 2:34, 35, 44, 45). Thus the New Testament sanctions the second, third, sixth, seventh, and eleventh chapters. The design of the miracles in the heathen courts where Daniel was, as of those of Moses in Egypt, was to lead the world power, which seemed to be victorious over the theocracy, to see the essential inner superiority of the seemingly fallen kingdom of God to itself, and to show prostrate Israel that the power of God was the same as of old in Egypt. The first book of Maccabees (compare 1 Maccabees 1:24; 9:27, 40, with Dan. 12:1; 11:26, of the Septuagint) refers to Daniel as an accredited book, and even refers to the Septuagint Alexandrian version of it. The fact of Daniel having a place in the Septuagint shows it was received by the Jews at large prior to the Maccabean times. The Septuagint version so arbitrarily deviated from the Hebrew Daniel, that Theodotius' version was substituted for it in the early Christian Church. Josephus (*Antiquities*, 11.8.5) mentions that Alexander the Great had designed to punish the Jews for their fidelity to Darius, but that Jaddua (332 B.C.), the high priest, met him at the head of a procession and averted his wrath by showing him Daniel's prophecy that a Grecian monarch should overthrow Persia. Certain it is, Alexander favored the Jews, and Josephus' statement gives an explanation of the fact; at least it shows that the Jews in Josephus' days believed that Daniel was extant in Alexander's days, long before the Maccabees. With Jaddua (high priest from 341–322 b.c.) the Old Testament history ends (Neh. 12:11). (The register of the priests and Levites was not written by Nehemiah, who died about 400 b.c., but was inserted with divine sanction by the collectors of the canon subsequently.)

An objection to Daniel's authenticity has been rested on a few Greek words found in it. But these are mostly names of Greek musical instruments, which were imported by Greece from the East, rather than vice versa. Some of the words are derived from the common Indo-Germanic stock of both Greek and Chaldee: hence their appearance in both tongues. And one or two may have come through the Greeks of Asia Minor to the Chaldee. The fact that from the fourth verse of the second chapter to the end of the seventh, the language is Chaldee, but the rest Hebrew, is not an argument against, but for, its authenticity. So in Ezra the two languages are found. The work, if that of one author, must have been composed by someone in the circumstances of Daniel, that is, by one familiar with both languages. No native-born Hebrew who had not lived in Chaldea would know Chaldee so well as to use it with the same idiomatic ease as his native tongue; the very impurities in Daniel's use of both are just such as were natural to one in his circumstances, but unnatural to one in a later age, or to one not half Hebrew, half Chaldean in residence as Daniel was. Those parts of Daniel which concern the whole world are mostly Chaldee, then the language of the world empire. So Greek was made the language of the New Testament, which was designed for the whole world. Those affecting the Jews, mostly Hebrew; and this not so impure as that of Ezekiel. His Chaldee is a mixture of Hebrew and Aramaic.

Two predictions alone are enough to prove to us that Daniel was a true prophet.

(1) That his prophecies reach beyond Antiochus; namely, he foretells the rise of the four great monarchies, Babylon, Medo-Persia, Greece, and Rome (the last not being in Daniel's time known

beyond the precincts of Italy, or rather of Latium), and that no other earthly kingdom would subvert the fourth, but that it would divide into parts. All this has come to pass. No fifth great earthly monarchy has arisen, though often attempted, as by Charlemagne, Charles V, and Napoleon.

(2) The time of Messiah's advent, as dated from a certain decree, His being cut off, and the destruction of the city. "He who denies Daniel's prophecies," says Sir Isaac Newton, "undermines Christianity, which is founded on Daniel's prophecies about Christ."

The book's characteristics

The vision mode of revelation is the exception in other prophets, the rule in Daniel. In Zechariah (Zech. 1:1–6:15), who lived after Daniel, the same mode appears, but the other form from the seventh chapter to the end. The Revelation of St. John alone is perfectly parallel to Daniel, which may be called the Old Testament Apocalypse. In the contents too there is the difference above noticed, that he views the kingdom of God from the standpoint of the world kingdoms, the development of which is his great subject. This mode of viewing it was appropriate to his own position in a heathen court, and to the relation of subjection in which the covenant-people then stood to the world powers. No longer are single powers of the world incidentally introduced, but the universal monarchies are the chief theme, in which the worldly principle, opposed to the kingdom of God, manifests itself fully. The near and distant are not seen in the same perspective, as by the other prophets, who viewed the whole future from the eschatological point; but in Daniel the historical details are given of that development of the world powers which must precede the advent of the kingdom (Auberlen).

Importance of Babylonian captivity

The exile is the historical basis of Daniel's prophecies, as Daniel implies in the first chapter, which commences with the beginning, and ends with the termination, of the captivity (Dan. 1:1, 21; compare Dan. 9:1, 2). A new stage in the theocracy begins with the captivity. Nebuchadnezzar made three incursions into Judah. The first under Jehoiakim (606 B.C.), in which Daniel was carried away, subjected the theocracy to the Babylonian world power. The second (598 b.c.) was that in which Jehoiachin and Ezekiel were carried away. In the third (588 b.c.), Nebuchadnezzar destroyed Jerusalem and carried away Zedekiah. Originally, Abraham was raised out of the "sea" (Dan. 7:2) of the nations, as an island holy to God, and his seed chosen as God's mediator of His revelations of love to mankind. Under David and Solomon, the theocracy, as opposed to the heathen power, attained its climax in the Old Testament, not only being independent, but lord of the surrounding nations; so that the period of these two kings was henceforth made the type of the Messianic. But when God's people, instead of resting on Him, seek alliance with the world power, that very power is made the instrument of their chastisement. So Ephraim (722 B.C.) fell by Assyria; and Judah also, drawn into the sphere of the world's movements from the time of Ahaz, who sought Assyrian help (740 b.c., Is. 7:1–25) at last fell by

Babylon, and thenceforth has been more or less dependent on the world monarchies, and so, till Messiah, was favored with no revelations from the time of Malachi (four hundred years). Thus, from the beginning of the exile, the theocracy, in the strict sense, ceased on earth; the rule of the world powers superseding it. But God's covenant with Israel remains firm (Rom. 11:29); therefore, a period of blessing under Messiah's kingdom is now foretold as about to follow their long chastisement.

The exile thus is the turning point in the history of the theocracy, which Roos thus divides:

From Adam to the exodus out of Egypt.

From the exodus to the beginning of the Babylonian captivity.

From the captivity to the millennium.

From the millennium to the end of the world.

The position of Daniel in the Babylonian court was in unison with the altered relations of the theocracy and the world power, which new relation was to be the theme of his prophecy. Earlier prophets, from the standpoint of Israel, treated of Israel in its relation to the world powers; Daniel, from Babylon, the center of the then world power, treats of the world powers in their relation to Israel. His seventy years' residence in Babylon, and his high official position there, gave him an insight into the world's politics, fitting him to be the recipient of political revelations; while his spiritual experiences, gained through Nebuchadnezzar's humiliation, Belshazzar's downfall, and the rapid decay of the Babylonian empire itself, as well as the miraculous deliverances of himself and his friends (the third through sixth chapters), all fitted him for regarding things from the spiritual standpoint, from which the world's power appears transient, but the glory of God's kingdom eternal.

As his political position was the body, the school of magicians in which he had studied for three years (Dan. 1:4, 5) was the soul; and his mind strong in faith and nourished by the earlier prophecies (Dan. 9:2), the spirit of his prophecy, which only waited for the spirit of revelation from above to kindle it. So God fits His organs for their work. Auberlen compares Daniel to Joseph: the one at the beginning, the other at the end of the Jewish history of revelation; both representatives of God and His people at heathen courts; both interpreters of the dim presentiments of truth, expressed in God-sent dreams, and therefore raised to honor by the powers of the world: so representing Israel's calling to be a royal priesthood among the nations; and types of Christ, the true Israel, and of Israel's destination to be a light to lighten the whole Gentile world, as Rom. 11:12, 15 foretells. As Achilles at the beginning, and Alexander at the end, of Grecian history are the mirrors of the whole life of the Hellenic people, so Joseph and Daniel of Israel.

A.R. Faussett

John Calvin's introduction to Daniel

We may divide the Book into two parts, and this partition will materially help us. For Daniel relates how he acquired influence over the unbelieving. It was necessary for him to be elevated to the prophetic office in some singular and unusual manner. The condition of the Jews, as is well known, was so confused, that it was difficult for any one to determine whether any Prophet existed. At first Jeremiah was alive, and after him Ezekiel. After their return, the Jews had their own Prophets but Jeremiah and Ezekiel had almost fulfilled their office, when Daniel succeeded them. Others too, as we have already seen, as Haggai, Malachi, and Zechariah, were created Prophets for the purpose of exhorting the people, and hence their duties were partially restricted. But Daniel would scarcely have been considered a Prophet, had not God, as we have said, appointed him in a remarkable way. We shall perceive at the close of the sixth chapter, that he was divinely endued with remarkable signs, so that the Jews might surely ascertain that he had the gift of prophecy, unless they were basely ungrateful to God. His name was known and respected by the inhabitants of Babylon. If the Jews had despised what even the profane Gentiles admired, was not this purposely to suffocate and trample on the grace of God? Daniel, then, had sure and striking marks by which he could by recognized as God's Prophet, and his calling be rendered unquestionable.

A Second Part is afterwards added, in which God predicts by his agency the events which were to occur to his elect people. The Visions, then, from the seventh chapter to the end of the Book, relate peculiarly to the Church of God. There God predicts what should happen hereafter. And that admonition is the more necessary, since the trial was severe, when the Jews had to bear an exile of seventy years; but after their return to their country, instead of seventy years, God protracted their full deliverance till seventy weeks of years. So the delay was increased sevenfold. Their spirits might be broken a thousand times, or even utterly fail; for the Prophets speak so magnificently about their redemption, that the Jews expected their state to be especially happy and prosperous, as soon as they were snatched from the Babylonian Captivity. But since they were oppressed with so many afflictions, and that, too, not for a short period, but for more than four hundred years, their redemption might seem illusory since they were but seventy years in exile. there is no doubt, then, that Satan seduced the minds of many to revolt, as if God were mocking them by bringing them out of Chaldea back again to their own country. For these reasons God shows his servant in a Vision what numerous and severe afflictions awaited his elect people. Besides, Daniel, Se prophesies that he describes almost historically events previously hidden. And this was necessary, since in such turbulent convulsions the people would never have tasted that these had been divinely revealed to Daniel, unless the heavenly testimony had been proved by the event. This holy man ought so to speak and to prophesy about futurity, as if he were relating what had already happened. But we shall see all these things in their own order.

I believe that we may see how useful this Book is to the Church of Christ. First of all, the matter itself shows how Daniel did not speak from his own discretion, but whatever he uttered was dictated by the Holy Spirit for whence could he conceive the things which we shall afterwards behold, if he were only endued with human prudence? for instance, that other Monarchies should arise to blot out that Babylonian Empire which then had the greatest authority in all the world? Then, again, how could he divine about Alexander the Great and his Successors? for long before Alexander was born, Daniel predicted what he should accomplish. Then he shows that his kingdom should not last, since it is directly divided into four horns. Other events also clearly demonstrate that he spoke by the dictation of the Holy Spirit. But our confidence in this is strengthened by other narratives, where he represents the various miseries to which the Church should be subject between two most cruel enemies, the kings of Syria and Egypt. He first recites their treaties, and then their hostile incursions on both sides, and afterwards so many changes, as if he pointed at the things themselves with his finger; and he so follows through their whole progress, that God appears to speak by his mouth. This, then, is a great step, and we shall not repent of taking it, when we acknowledge Daniel to have been only the organ of the Holy Spirit, and never to have brought anything forward by his own private inclination. The authority, too, which he obtained, and which inspired the Jews with perfect confidence in his teaching, extends to us also. Shameful, indeed, and base would be our ingratitude, if we did not embrace him as God's Prophet, whom the Chaldeans were compelled to honor–a people whom we know to have been superstitious and full of pride. These two nations, the Egyptians and Chaldeans, placed themselves before all others; for the Chaldeans thought wisdom's only dwelling-place was with themselves hence they would never have been inclined to receive Daniel's, unless the reality had compelled them, and the confession of his being a true prophet of God had been extorted from them.

Since Daniel's authority is thus established, we must now say a few words about the subjects which he treats. Respecting The Interpretation Of The Dreams, the first of; those of Nebuchadnezzar embraces a matter of great importance, as we shall see, namely, how all the splendor and power of the world vanish away, Christ's kingdom alone remaining stable, and that nothing else is self-enduring. In the Second Dream of Nebuchadnezzar, Daniel's admirable constancy is displayed. Very invidious, indeed, was the office of throwing down the mightiest Monarch of the whole world as he did "Thou excepts thyself from the number of men, and art worshipped like a god; thou shalt hereafter become a beast!" No man of these days would dare thus to address Monarchs; nay, who dares to admonish them even mildly, if they have sinned at all? When, therefore, Daniel intrepidly predicted to King Nebuchadnezzar the disgrace which awaited him, he thus gave a rare and memorable proof of his constancy. And in this way, again, his calling was sealed, since this fortitude sprang from God's Spirit.

But the Second Part is peculiarly worthy of notice, since we there perceive how God cares for his Church. God's providence is, indeed, extended to the whole world. For if a sparrow does not fall to the ground without his permission, he, doubtless, is mindful of the human race! (Matthew 10, and Luke 12.) Nothing, therefore, happens to us by chance, but God in this Book affords us light, while we know His Church to be so governed by him, as to be the object. of His peculiar care. If matters ever were so disturbed in the world, that one could suppose God to be asleep in heaven, and to be forgetful of the human race, surely such were the changes of those times, nay, so multiform, so extensive, and so various were they, that even the most daring must be confounded, since there was no end to the wars.

Egypt prevailed at one time, while at another there were commotion's in Syria. Seeing, then, all things turned up-side (town, what judgment could be passed, except that God neglected the world, and the Jews were miserably deceived in their hope? They thought that as God had been their deliverer, so would he have been the perpetual guardian of their safety. Although all nations were then subject in common to various slaughters, yet if the Syrians were victorious over the Egyptians, they abused their power against the Jews, and Jerusalem lay exposed as their prey, and the reward of their victory if, again, the opposite side were the conquerors, they revenged the injury, or sought compensation against rite Jews. Thus on every side those miserable people were fleeced, and their condition was much worse after their return to their country, than if they had always been exiles or strangers in other regions. When, therefore, they were admonished about the future, this was the best prop on which they could repose. But the use of the same doctrine is at this day applicable to us. We perceive, as in a glass or picture, how God was anxious about his Church, even when he seemed to cast away all regard for it, hence when the Jews were exposed to the injuries of their enemies, it was but, the accomplishment of his designs.

From the Second Part we recognize their wonderful preservation, and that too, by a. greater and more surprising exercise of God's power, than if they had lived in peace, and no one had molested them. We learn this from the seventh to the ninth chapters. Now, when Daniel numbers the years till The Advent Of Christ, how clear and distinct is the testimony which we may oppose against. Satan, and all the taunts of the impious! and how certain it is that the Book of Daniel, was familiarly used by men before this event. But when he enumerates The Seventy Weeks, and says, that Christ should then come, all profane men may come, and boast, and swell with increased swaggering, yet they shall fall down convicted, since Christ is that true Redeemer whom God had promised from the beginning of the world. For He was unwilling to make him known without the most certain demonstration, such as ail the mathematicians can never equal. First of all, it is worthy of observation, that Daniel afterwards discoursed on the various calamities of the Church, and prophesied the time at which God pleased to hew his only-begotten Son to the world. His dissertation on the office of Christ is one of the principal supports of our faith. For he not only describes his Advent, but announces the abolition of the shadows of the Law, since the Messiah would bring with him its complete fulfillment. And when he predicts the Death of Christ, he shows for what purpose he should undergo death, namely, to abolish Sin by his sacrifice, and to bring in Eternal Righteousness. Lastly, this also must be noticed, — as he had instructed the people to bear their cross, so also he warns them that the Church's state would not be tranquil even when the Messiah came. The sons of God should be militant until the end, and not hope for any fruit of their victory until the dead should rise again, and Christ himself should collect us into his own Celestial Kingdom. Now, we comprehend in few words, or rather only taste how useful and fruitful this Book is to us.

John Calvin

Detailed outline

I. Introductory background: The reasons for Daniel's prosperity: 1:1–21

II. Visions and events under Nebuchadnezzar: 2:1–6:28

A. The image and interpretation: 2:1–49

B. The fiery furnace: 3:1–30

1. The king's command: 3:1–7
2. The stand of God's men: 3:8–23
3. Judgment and deliverance: 3:24–30

C. Nebuchadnezzar's tree vision and its meaning: 4:1–37

1. The dream: 4:1–18
2. The interpretation: 4:19–27
3. The fulfillment: 4:28–37

D. Belshazzar's feast: 5:1–31

1. The feast: 5:1–4
2. The judgment: 5:5–9
3. The search for an interpreter: 5:10–16
4. The interpretation: 5:17–29
5. The fulfillment: 5:30–31

E. Daniel's deliverance from the lions' den: 6:1–28

1. An evil plan: 6:1–9
2. Daniel's response: 6:10–20
3. Deliverance from the den: 6:21–28

III. Visions under Belshazzar, Darius, and Cyrus: 7:1–12:13

A. The four beasts and interpretation: 7:1–28

B. The ram and the goat and interpretation: 8:1–27

1. The introduction: 8:1–2
2. The vision: 8:3–14
   (a) The ram is Medo-Persia: 8:3–4
   (b) The goat is Greece: 8:5–14
3. The interpretation of the vision: 8:15–27

C. The seventy weeks: 9:1–27

1. Introduction: 9:1–2
2. The prayer: 9:3–19
3. The seventy weeks: 9:20–27

D. Preparation for the final revelation: 10:1–21

1. Introduction: 10:1–3
2. The man clothed in linen: 10:4–6
3. Daniel's response: 10:10–12
4. Conflict of Gabriel and the Prince of Persia: 10:13
5. Reason for the angel's coming: 10:14–21

E. Vision of events from Darius to the end of time: 11:1–12:13

1. The revelation of events to come: 11:1–12:3
2. The command to seal the book: 12:4
3. A final conversation with the messenger: 12:5–13

2. Helpful summaries of Daniel

Linked New Testament book

Revelation.

Both Daniel and Revelation are full of mysterious signs.

Bird's eye view

The book of Daniel is full of visions about God's plan for the non-Jewish nations and about God's people while the Gentile nations dominate.

Reading plan

The following reading plan, taking one reading per day, enables you to read through Daniel in five days.

Daniel 1–2

Daniel 3–4

Daniel 5–6

Daniel 7–9

Daniel 9–12

Verses to memorize

Daniel 2:20

Praise be to the name of God forever and ever; wisdom and power are his.

Daniel 6:22

My God sent his angel, and he shut the mouths of the lions. They have not hurt me, because I was found innocent in his sight.

Statistics

Twenty-seventh Old Testament book

12 chapters

357 verses

11,606 words

Famous sayings found in Daniel

"Handwriting on the wall" Daniel 5:5

"Weighed in the balances and found wanting" Daniel 5:5

Names/titles given

Hebrew title: *Dani'el:* "God is my Judge."

Greek title in Septuagint:

Greek form of *"Daniel."*

Latin title in Vulgate: Latin form of *"Daniel."*

3. Helpful keys to turn to in understanding Daniel

Key word

Kingdom, 57 times

Key verses

Daniel 2:44; 7:14

Themes to study

Daniel's godly life

The end times

Daniel quoted in the New Testament

- They shall see the Son of man coming on the clouds of heaven

  Dan. 7:13 quoted in Matt. 24:30, 26:64, Mark 13:26, 14:62 and Luke 21:27

Unusual events and miracles in Daniel

- Daniel's interpretation of Nebuchadnezzar's forgotten dream, 2:1–47
- Shadrach, Meshach, and Abednego saved from the burning furnace, 3:19–28
- Nebuchadnezzar becoming like a wild animal, 4:24–28
- Handwriting on the wall, chapter 5
- David rescued from the lion's den, chapter 6

Jesus in Daniel

In Daniel Jesus is the Great Stone who will crush this world's kingdoms, 2:34–35, 44.

Lessons to learn from Daniel

God's presence is with us, even in life's toughest trials.

Christians should not be surprised if they are persecuted.

4. Chapter by chapter: outline of every chapter of Daniel

Daniel 1

Matthew Henry's introduction

This chapter gives us a more particular account of the beginning of Daniel's life, his original and education, than we have of any other of the prophets. Isaiah, Jeremiah, and Ezekiel, began immediately with divine visions; but Daniel began with the study of human learning, and was afterwards honored with divine visions; such variety of methods has God taken in training up men for the service of his church. We have here,

I. Jehoiakim's first captivity (vv. 1, 2), in which Daniel, with others of the seed royal, was carried to Babylon.

II. The choice made of Daniel, and some other young men, to be brought up in the Chaldean literature, that they might be fitted to serve the government, and the provision made for them, vv. 3–7.

III. Their pious refusal to eat the portion of the king's meat, and their determining to live on pulse and water, which, having tried it, the master of the eunuchs allowed them to do, finding that it agreed very well with them, vv. 8–16.

IV. Their wonderful improvement, above all their fellows, in wisdom and knowledge, vv. 17–21.

A detailed analysis of chapter

The captivity of Daniel and his companions. (1–7)

Their refusal to eat the king's meat. (8–16)

Their improvement in wisdom. (17–21)

Key verse

Verse 1: "In the third year of the reign of Jehoiakim king of Judah came Nebuchadnezzar king of Babylon unto Jerusalem, and besieged it."

Key word / key phrase

Verse 6, "Daniel."

Key event / key person / key theme

The personal history of Daniel

Key thought

Daniel could have thought that he would have no life at all as an exile.

Key thing to look out for

The great understanding Daniel had was a gift from God.

Key Bible cross-reference

Verse 1. See 2 Kings 24:1.

Key "by way of explanation"

Verse 5, "assigned them a daily amount." Babylon had a highly organized bureaucracy and the same rations to foreigners were given in many different parts of their empire. The date is probably late 605 BC.

Key "Quotable Quote"

"Go, labor on; spend and be spent –
Thy joy to do the Father's will;
It is the way the Master went;
Should not the servant tread it still?"

Horatius Bonar

Daniel 2

Matthew Henry's introduction

In this chapter we have,

I. The great perplexity that Nebuchadnezzar was put into by a dream which he had forgotten, and his command to the magicians to tell him what it was, which they could not pretend to do, vv. 1–11.

II. Orders given for the destroying of all the wise men of Babylon, and of Daniel among the rest, with his fellows, vv. 12–15.

III. The discovery of this secret to him, in answer to prayer, and the thanksgiving he offered up to God thereon, vv. 16–23.

IV. His admission to the king, and the discovery he made to him both of his dream and of the interpretation of it, vv. 24–45.

V. The great honor which Nebuchadnezzar put on Daniel, in recompense for this service, and the preferment of his companions with him, vv. 46–49.

A detailed analysis of chapter

Nebuchadnezzar's dream. (1–13)
It is revealed to Daniel. (14–23)
He obtains admission to the king. (24–30)
The dream and the interpretation. (31–45)
Honors to Daniel and his friends. (46–49)

Key verse

Verse 1: "And in the second year of the reign of Nebuchadnezzar Nebuchadnezzar dreamed dreams, wherewith his spirit was troubled, and his sleep brake from him."

Key word / key phrase

Verse 28, "There is a God in heaven who reveals mysteries."

Key event / key person / key theme

Nebuchadnezzar's dream of the great image

Key thought

God's timing is perfect.

Key thing to look out for

Daniel's promotion was very similar to Joseph's.

Key Bible cross-reference

Verse 2. See Genesis 41:8.

Key "by way of explanation"

Verse 19, "God of heaven." This description of God, to which "and earth" was sometimes added, focuses on his universal and transcendent reign.

Key "Quotable Quote"

"God in nature is God above us; God in providence is God beyond us; God in law is God against us: but God in Christ is God with us, for us, and in us."

Author unknown

Daniel 3

Matthew Henry's introduction

We have here,

I. Nebuchadnezzar's erecting and dedicating a golden image, and his requiring all his subjects, of what rank or degree soever, to fall down and worship it, and the general compliance of his people with that command, vv. 1–7.

II. Information given against the Jewish princes for refusing to worship this golden image, vv. 8–12.

III. Their constant persisting in that refusal, notwithstanding his rage and menaces, vv. 13–18.

IV. The casting of them into the fiery furnace for their refusal, vv. 19–23.

V. Their miraculous preservation in the fire by the power of God, and their invitation out of the fire by the favor of the king, who was by this miracle convinced of his error in casting them in, vv. 24–27.

VI. The honor which the king gave to God hereon, and the favor he showed to those faithful worthies, vv. 28–30.

A detailed analysis of chapter

Nebuchadnezzar's golden image. (1–7)

Shadrach and his companions refuse to worship it. (8–18)

They are thrown into a furnace, but are miraculously preserved. (19–27)

Nebuchadnezzar gives glory to Jehovah. (28–30)

Key verse

Verse 7: "Therefore at that time, when all the people heard the sound of the cornet, flute, harp, sackbut, psaltery, and all kinds of music, all the people, the nations, and the languages, fell down and worshipped the golden image that Nebuchadnezzar the king had set up."

Key word / key phrase

Verse 1, "Nebuchadnezzar made an image of gold."

Key event / key person / key theme

God deliverance of his loyal servants

Key thought

Promotion of self is a sin none can claim to be free of.

Key thing to look out for

God protected these three faithful men, but some of God's followers become martyrs.

Key Bible cross-reference

Verse 9: See Nehemiah 2:3.

Key "by way of explanation"

Verse 12, "pay no attention to you." This is meant to show how good the king was and how disloyal these three were being to him.

Key "Quotable Quote"

"It is unnatural for Christianity to be popular."

Billy Graham

Daniel 4

Matthew Henry's introduction

Here is,

I. The preface to his narrative, in which he acknowledges God's dominion over him, vv. 1–3.

II. The narrative itself, in which he relates,

A. His dream, which puzzled the magicians, vv. 1–18.

B. The interpretation of his dream by Daniel, who showed him that it was a prognostication of his own fall, advising him therefore to repent and reform, vv. 19–27.

C. The accomplishment of it in his running stark mad for seven years, and then recovering the use of his reason again, vv. 28–36.

D. The conclusion of the narrative, with a humble acknowledgment and adoration of God as Lord of all, v. 37.

A detailed analysis of chapter

Nebuchadnezzar acknowledges the power of Yahweh. (1–18)

Daniel interprets his dream. (19–27)

Its fulfillment. (28–37)

Key verse

Verse 8: "But at the last Daniel came in before me, whose name was Belteshazzar, according to the name of my god, and in whom is the spirit of the holy gods."

Key word / key phrase

Verse 10, "a tree in the middle of the land."

Key event / key person / key theme

Nebuchadnezzar's vision of a great tree

Key thought

Pride comes before a fall.

Key thing to look out for

God's mercy is seen in the restoration of Nebuchadnezzar.

Key Bible cross-reference

Verse 14. See Job 24:20.

Key "by way of explanation"

Verse 26, "Heaven rules." This means that God rules, (cf. Luke 15:18). This is the first time this expression is used in the Bible.

Key "Quotable Quote"

"Jesus shall reign where e'er the sun
Doth his successive journeys run;
His kingdom stretch from shore to shore
Till moons shall wax and wane no more."

Isaac Watts

Daniel 5

Matthew Henry's introduction

We have in this chapter,

I. The riotous, idolatrous, sacrilegious feast which Belshazzar made, in which he filled up the measure of his iniquity, vv. 1–4.

II. The alarm given him in the midst of his jollity by a hand-writing on the wall, which none of his wise men could read or tell him the meaning of, vv. 5–9.

III. The interpretation of the mystical characters by Daniel, who was at length brought in to him, and dealt plainly with him, and showed him his doom written, vv. 10–28.
IV. The immediate accomplishment of the interpretation in the slaying of the king and seizing of the kingdom, vv. 30, 31.

A detailed analysis of chapter

Belshazzar's impious feast; the handwriting on the wall. (1–9)
Daniel is sent for to interpret it. (10–17)
Daniel warns the king of his destruction. (18–31)

Key verse

Verse 30: "In that night was Belshazzar the king of the Chaldeans slain."

Key word / key phrase

Verse 5, "fingers of a human hand appeared."

Key event / key person / key theme

Belshazzar and handwriting on the wall

Key thought

God's judgment can strike at any time.

Key thing to look out for

God does not view people in the way that the world does.

Key Bible cross-reference

Verse 11. See Genesis 41:38.

Key "by way of explanation"

Verse 8, "could not read the writing." Although the words were written in ordinary Aramaic nobody could make head or tail of them. They could read them but not understand them.

Key "Quotable Quote"

"God's actual divine essence and his will, administration and works – are absolutely beyond all human thought, human understanding or wisdom; in short, they are and ever will be incomprehensible, inscrutable, and altogether hidden to human reason."

Martin Luther

Daniel 6

Matthew Henry's introduction

In this chapter we have,

I. Daniel's preferment in the court of Darius, vv. 1–3.
II. The envy and malice of his enemies against him, vv. 4, 5.
III. The decree they obtained against prayer for thirty days, vv. 6–9.
IV. Daniel's continuance and constancy in prayer, notwithstanding that decree, v. 10.
V. Information given against him for it, and the casting of him into the den of lions, vv. 11–17.
VI. His miraculous preservation in the lions' den, and deliverance out of it, vv. 18–23.
VII. The casting of his accusers into the den, and their destruction there, v. 24.
VIII. The decree which Darius made on this occasion, in honor of the God of Daniel, and the prosperity of Daniel afterwards, vv. 25–28.

A detailed analysis of chapter

The malice of Daniel's enemies. (1–5)
His constancy in prayer. (6–10)
He is thrown into the lion's den. (11–17)
His miraculous preservation. (18–24)
The decree of Darius. (25–28)

Key verse

Verse 10: "Now when Daniel knew that the writing was signed, he went into his house; and his windows being open in his chamber toward Jerusalem, he kneeled upon his knees three times a day, and prayed, and gave thanks before his God, as he did aforetime."

Key word / key phrase

Verse 7, "issue an edict."

Key event / key person / key theme

Darius' foolish decree

Key thought

Accepting flattery is a sign of a warped character. The centrality of prayer in Daniel's life.

Key thing to look out for

Even if Daniel had not been unharmed his faith in God would have remained.

Key Bible cross-reference

Verse 15. See Esther 8:8.

Key "by way of explanation"

Verse 16, "the lions' den." Lions were kept in this way so kings could chase them when they were released.

Key "Quotable Quote"

"Let gratitude for the past inspire us with trust for the future."

François Fénelon

Daniel 7

Matthew Henry's introduction

The six previous chapters of this book were historical; we now enter with fear and trembling on the six latter, which are prophetical, in which are many things dark and hard to be understood, which we dare not positively determine the sense of, and yet many things plain and profitable, which I trust God will enable us to make a good use of. In this chapter we have,

I. Daniel's vision of the four beasts, vv. 1–8.
II. His vision of God's throne of government and judgment, vv. 9–14.
III. The interpretation of these visions, given him by an angel that stood by, vv. 15–28. Whether those visions look as far forward as the end of time, or whether they were to have a speedy accomplishment, is hard to say, nor are the most judicious interpreters agreed about it.

A detailed analysis of chapter

Daniel's vision of the four beasts. (1–8)
And of Christ's kingdom. (9–14)
The interpretation. (15–28)

Key verse

Verse 4: "The first was like a lion, and had eagle's wings."

Key word / key phrase

Verse 1, "a dream, and visions."

Key event / key person / key theme

Daniel's vision of four beasts

Key thought

Commentators are not agreed on the identification of the beasts but what is clear is that the future is in God's control, and all evil powers are subservient to him (verse 21).

Key thing to look out for

The description of God's kingdom

Key Bible cross-reference

Verses 4–6. See Revelation 13:2.

Key "by way of explanation"

Verse 18, "the saints" is a phrase rarely found in the Bible. See its equivalent in 8:25; Psalm 16:3; 24:10. It means "the holy ones." The date is about 553 BC, after the death of Nebuchadnezzar but before the supremacy of Persia.

Key "Quotable Quote"

"To attain holiness we must follow the example that Christ gave us, not only in his gentleness, humility, and patience during life, but also in his death."

Basil the Great

Daniel 8

Matthew Henry's introduction

In this chapter we have,

I. The vision itself of the ram, and the he goat, and the little horn that should fight and prevail against the people of God, for a certain limited time, vv. 1–14.

II. The interpretation of this vision by an angel, showing that the ram signified the Persian empire, the he-goat the Grecian, and the little horn a king of the Grecian monarchy, that should set himself against the Jews and religion, which was Antiochus Epiphanes, vv. 15–27.

A detailed analysis of chapter

Daniel's vision of the ram and the he-goat. (1–14)

Its interpretation. (15–27)

Key verse

Verse 3: "Then I lifted up mine eyes, and saw, and, behold, there stood before the river a ram which had two horns: and the two horns were high; but one was higher than the other, and the higher came up last."

Key word / key phrase

Verse 3, "a ram with two horns."

Key event / key person / key theme

Daniel's vision of a ram and a goat – representing Cyrus (Persia), and then Alexander the Great (Greece).

Key thought

Verse 19, "the time of wrath," that is, God's anger against Israel.

Key thing to look out for

Verse 17, "the time of the end." These words indicate that the events in chapter 8, point beyond themselves to future events, of which they are shadows.

Key Bible cross-reference

Verse 16. See Luke 1:19,26.

Key "by way of explanation"

Verse 11. "Daily sacrifice." This refers to the sacrifice prescribed in Exodus 29:38–42 which had to take place every morning and evening. The little lion (9–14 and 23–25) is Antiochus Epiphanes, against whom the Jews rose up. He stopped the daily temple offerings (verse 11). "Rebels" (verse 23) were Jews who forsook God's Law.

Key "Quotable Quote"

"Many souls, to whom visions have never come, are incomparably more advanced in the way of perfection than others to whom many have been given."

John of the Cross

Daniel 9

Matthew Henry's introduction

In this chapter we have,

I. Daniel's prayer for the restoration of the Jews who were in captivity, in which he confesses sin, and acknowledges the justice of God in their calamities, but pleads God's promises of mercy which he had yet in store for them, vv. 1–19.

II. An immediate answer sent him by an angel to his prayer, in which,

A. He is assured of the speedy release of the Jews out of their captivity, vv. 20–23. And,

B. He is informed about the redemption of the world by Jesus Christ (of which that was a type), what should be the nature of it and when it should be accomplished, vv. 24–27. And it is the clearest, brightest, prophecy of the Messiah, in all the Old Testament.

A detailed analysis of chapter

Daniel considers the time of the captivity. (1–3)

His confession of sin, and prayer for national restoration. (4–19)

The revelation about the coming of the Messiah. (20–27)

Key verse

Verse 5: "We have sinned, and have committed iniquity, and have done wickedly, and have rebelled, even by departing from thy precepts and from thy judgment."

Key word / key phrase

Verse 24, "seventy 'sevens'."

Key event / key person / key theme

Daniel's vision of seventy weeks

Key thought

Daniel prays to the Lord, the covenant God (verse 4) – and therefore, with the Sinai covenant in mind, immediately confesses sin.

Key thing to look out for

Daniel's attitude toward God throughout his prayer.

Key Bible cross-reference

Verse 2. See Jeremiah 25:11.

Key "by way of explanation"

Verse 13, "We have not sought the favor of the Lord." The only solution to their sufferings would be found in repentance. Many conflicting attempts have been made to add up the numbers. They may, however, be symbolic. What is certain is that wickedness will end and the Anointed One will bring in everlasting righteousness.

Key "Quotable Quote"

"True repentance is to cease from sin."

Ambrose

Daniel 10

Matthew Henry's introduction

In this chapter we have,

I. Daniel's prayer for the restoration of the Jews who were in captivity, in which he confesses sin, and acknowledges the justice of God in their calamities, but pleads God's promises of mercy which he had yet in store for them, vv. 1–19.

II. An immediate answer sent him by an angel to his prayer, in which,

A. He is assured of the speedy release of the Jews out of their captivity, vv. 20–23. And,

B. He is informed about the redemption of the world by Jesus Christ (of which that was a type), what should be the nature of it and when it should be accomplished, vv. 24–27. And it is the clearest, brightest, prophecy of the Messiah, in all the Old Testament.

A detailed analysis of chapter

Daniel's vision near the river Tigris. (1–9)

He is to expect a discovery of future events. (10–21)

Key verse

Verse 1: "In the third year of Cyrus king of Persia a thing was revealed unto Daniel, whose name was called Belteshazzar; and the thing was true, but the time appointed was long: and he understood the thing, and had understanding of the vision."

Key word / key phrase

Verse 5, "a man dressed in linen."

Key event / key person / key theme

The messenger (since he says he was sent, verse 11, and needed help (verse 13) may be an angel – perhaps Gabriel.

Key thought

All the heavenly powers involved in the great conflict of good against evil

Key thing to look out for

What does verse 15 tell us about Daniel's character?

Key Bible cross-reference

Verses 5,6. See Revelation 1:13–15.

Key "by way of explanation"

The date is 536. A party of Jews, headed by Zerubbabel has returned to Jerusalem, but Daniel has not gone with them. Verse 1, "a revelation was given." Many different words are used of the divine revelation Daniel received. This one is unique.

Key "Quotable Quote"

"The Christian does not begin with what the human intellect has discovered. The Christian begins with what God has revealed."

William Barclay

Daniel 11

Matthew Henry's introduction

Here is,

I. A brief prediction of the setting up of the Grecian monarchy on the ruins of the Persian monarchy, which was now newly begun, vv. 1–4.

II. A prediction of the affairs of the two kingdoms of Egypt and Syria, with reference to each other, vv. 5–20.

III. Of the rise of Antiochus Epiphanes, and his actions and successes, vv. 21–29.

IV. Of the great mischief that he should do to the Jewish nation and religion, and his contempt of all religion, vv. 30–39.

V. Of his fall and ruin at last, when he is in the heat of his pursuit, vv. 40–45.

A detailed analysis of chapter

The kingdoms of Egypt and Syria. (1–20)

The evil king of Syria. (21–45)

Key verse

Verse 5: "And the king of the south shall be strong, and one of his princes; and he shall be strong above him, and have dominion; his dominion shall be a great dominion."

Key word / key phrase

Verse 2, "three more kings."

Key event / key person / key theme

A vision of kings

Key thought

What is the lesson from verse 32?

Key thing to look out for

Verse 36 remains a warning to all rulers.

Key Bible cross-reference

Verse 36. See 2 Thessalonians 2:3, 4.

Key "by way of explanation"

Verse 22, "a prince of the covenant," refers either to Ptolemy V or the high priest Onias III. The identity of some of the people described in Daniel is not certain.

Key "Quotable Quote"

"What is offered to man's apprehension in any specific revelation is not truth concerning God but the living God himself."

William Temple

Daniel 12

Matthew Henry's introduction

We have here,

I. Comforts, and very precious ones, prescribed as cordials for the support of God's people in those times of trouble; and they are such as may indifferently serve both for those former times of trouble under Antiochus and those latter which were prefigured by them, vv. 1–4.

II. A conversation between Christ and an angel about the time of the continuance of these events, designed for Daniel's satisfaction, vv. 5–7.

III. Daniel's enquiry for his own satisfaction, v. 8. And the answer he received to that enquiry, vv. 9–12.

A detailed analysis of chapter

The end times. (1–13)

Key verse

Verse 4: "But thou, O Daniel, shut up the words, and seal the book, even to the time of the end: many shall run to and fro, and knowledge shall be increased."

Key word / key phrase

Verse 12, "a time of distress."

Key event / key person / key theme

The end time

Key thought

Daniel remained faithful to God throughout his long life.

Key thing to look out for

What comfort can be drawn from the concluding verses of this book?

Key Bible cross-reference

Verse 11. See Mark 13:14.

Key "by way of explanation"

Verse 2, "everlasting life." This is a phrase that is well-known to Christians because of Jesus' teaching. This is the first occurrence of it in the Bible.

Key "Quotable Quote"

"Our hope for everlasting life permits no evasion of death's hard reality."

Amy Plantinga Pauw

5. Select bibliography for Daniel

Baldwin, Joyce. *Daniel: An Introduction and Commentary*. Wheaton: InterVarsity, 1978.

Culver, Robert D. *Daniel and the Latter Days*. Chicago: Moody, 1954.

DeHaan, M. R. *Daniel the Prophet*. Grand Rapids: Zondervan, 1947.

Goldingay, John E. *Daniel* (Word Biblical Commentary, 30), Word Books, 1989.

Jerome. *Commentary on Daniel*. Translated by G. L. Archer. Grand Rapids: Baker, 1958.

Wallace, Ronald S. *The Message of Daniel* (The Bible Speaks Today), InterVarsity, 1984.

Wood, Leon. *A Commentary on Daniel*. Grand Rapids: Zondervan, 1973.

Young, E. J. *The Prophecy of Daniel*. Grand Rapids: Eerdmans, 1949.

Hosea

1. Book by book: Introduction to Hosea

Introduction

The minor prophets

The first of the twelve minor prophets in the order of the canon (called "minor," not as less in point of inspired authority, but simply in point of size). The twelve are first mentioned by Jesus, the son of Sirach (Ecclesiasticus 49:10). St. Stephen, in Acts 7:42 (in referring to Amos 5:27), quotes them as forming one collective body of writings, "the book of the prophets." So Jerome and Melito, the first Greek father who has left us a catalogue of these books. The collection of the sacred books is by Jewish tradition attributed to the great synagogue of learned scribes formed by Ezra. Many think Nehemiah completed this collection by adding to the books already in the canon those of his own times. Malachi, the last in the series, probably aided him in determining with infallible authority what books were entitled to be ranked in the inspired canon. The chronological order differs from the canonical. Joel, about 810 B.C.; Jonah, about 810 B.C., or, as others, first, 862 B.C.; Amos, about 790 B.C.; Hosea, about 784 B.C. Hosea, the contemporary of Isaiah, Micah, and Amos, seems to have entered on his prophetical office in the last years of Jeroboam (contemporary in part with Uzziah), and to have ended it in the beginning of Hezekiah's reign, 722 B.C., that is, about sixty years in all, from 784 B.C. to 722 B.C. The prophets, however, were not uninterruptedly engaged in prophesying. Considerable intervals elapsed, though their office as divinely commissioned public teachers was never wholly laid aside.

The book of Hosea

The Book of Hosea which we have constitutes only that portion of his public teachings which the Holy Spirit saw fit to preserve for the benefit of the Church. The cause of his being placed first of the twelve was, probably, the length, the vivid earnestness, and patriotism of his prophecies, as well as their closer resemblance to those of the greater prophets. His style is abrupt, sententious, and unrounded; the connecting particles are few; there are changes of person, and anomalies of gender, number, and construction. His name means Salvation. He was son of Beeri, of the tribe of Issachar, born in Beth-shemesh (Jerome). His mention, in the inscription, of Uzziah, Jotham, Ahaz, and Hezekiah, kings of Judah, is no proof that he belonged to Judah: for the prophets in Israel regarded its separation from Judah, civil as well as religious, as an apostasy from God, who promised the dominion of the theocracy to the line of David. Hence Elijah in Israel took twelve stones to represent Judah, as well as Israel (1 Kings 18:31). Hence Hosea dates from Judah's kings, as well as from Jeroboam of Israel, though he belonged to Israel, with whose sins and fate his book is chiefly occupied. He, however, makes incidental references to Judah. His first prophecy foretells the overthrow of Jehu's house, fulfilled on the death of Jeroboam, Jehu's great-grandson (2 Kings 15:12), in Zachariah, Jeroboam's son, the fourth and last from Jehu, conspired against by Shallum. This first prediction was doubtless in Jeroboam's life, as Zachariah, his son, was only suffered to reign six months; thus the inscription is verified that "the word of the LORD came unto him in the days of Jeroboam" (Hos. 1:1). Again, in Hos. 10:14, Shalmaneser's expedition against Israel is alluded to as past, that is, the first inroad against King Hoshea, who began to reign in the twelfth year of Ahaz; so that as Ahaz' whole reign was sixteen years, the prophecy seems to have been given about the beginning of Hezekiah's reign. Thus the inscription is confirmed that the exercise of his prophetical functions was of such a protracted duration.

Hosea (Hos. 11:1) is quoted in Matt. 2:15; also Hos. 6:6 in Matt. 9:13; 12:7; compare Rom. 9:25, 26, quoting Hos. 1:10; 2:1, 23; 1 Cor. 15:55, quoting Hos. 13:14; 1 Pet. 2:10, quoting Hos. 1:9, 10; 2:23. Messianic references are not frequent; but the predictions of the future conversion of Israel to the Lord their God, and David their king, and of the fulfillment of the promise to Abraham that his spiritual seed should be as the sand of the sea (Hos. 1:10; 3:5), clearly refer to the New Testament dispensation.

The first and third chapters are in prose, the rest of the book is rhythmical.

A.R. Faussett

John Calvin's introduction to Hosea

I have undertaken to expound The Twelve Minor Prophets. The first of them is Hosea, who was specifically destined for the kingdom of Israel: Micah and Isaiah prophesied at the same time among the Jews. But it ought to be noticed, that this Prophet was a teacher in the kingdom of Israel, as Isaiah and Micah were in the kingdom of Judah. The Lord doubtless intended to employ him in that part; for had he prophesied among the Jews, he would not have complimented them; since the state of things was then very corrupt, not only in Judea, but also at Jerusalem, though the palace and sanctuary of God were there. We see how sharply and severely Isaiah and Micah reproved the people; and the style of our Prophet would have been the same had the Lord employed his service among the Jews: but he followed his own call. He knew what the Lord had entrusted to him; he faithfully discharged his own office. The same was the case with the Prophet Amos: for the Prophet Amos sharply inveighs against the Israelites, and seems to spare the Jews; and he taught at the same time with Hosea.

We see, then, in what respect these four differ: Isaiah and Micah address their reproofs to the kingdom of Judah; and Hosea and Amos only assail the kingdom of Israel, and seem to spare the Jews. Each of them undertook what God had committed to his charge; and so each confined himself within the limits of his own call and office. For if we, who are called to instruct the Church, close our eyes to the sins which prevail in it, and neglect those whom the Lord has appointed to be taught by us, we confound all order; since they who are appointed to other places must attend to those to whom they have been sent by the Lord's call.

We now, then, see to whom this whole book of Hosea belongs, – that is, to the kingdom of Israel.

But with regard to the Prophets, this is true of them all, as we have sometimes said, that they are interpreters of the law. And this is the sum of the law, that God designs to rule by his own authority the people whom he has adopted. But the law has two parts, — a promise of salvation and eternal life, and a rule for a godly and holy living. To these is added a third part, — that men, not responding to their call, are to be restored to the fear of God by threatening and reproofs. The Prophets do further teach what the law has commanded respecting the true and pure worship of God, respecting love; in short, they instruct the people in a holy and godly life, and then offer to them the favor of the Lord. And as there is no hope of reconciliation with God except through a Mediator, they ever set forth the Messiah, whom the Lord had long before promised.

As to the third part, which includes threats and reproofs, it was peculiar to the Prophets; for they point out times, and denounce this or that judgment of God: "The Lord will punish you in this way, and will punish you at such a time." The Prophets, then, do not simply call men to God's tribunal, but specify also certain kinds of punishment, and also in the same way they declare prophecies respecting the Lord's grace and his redemption. But on this I only briefly touch; for it will be better to notice each point as we proceed.

I now return to Hosea. I have said that his ministry belonged especially to the kingdom of Israel; for then the whole worship of God was there polluted, nor had corruption lately begun; but they were so obstinate in their superstitions, that there was no hope of repentance. We indeed know, that as soon as Jeroboam withdrew the ten tribes from their allegiance to Rehoboam, the son of Solomon, fictitious worship was set up: and Jeroboam seemed to have wisely contrived that artifice, that the people might not return to the house of David; but at the same time he brought on himself and the whole people the vengeance of God. And those who came after him followed the same impiety. When such perverseness became intolerable, God resolved to put forth his power, and to give some signal proof of his displeasure, that the people might at length repent. Hence Jehu was by God's command anointed King of Israel, that he might destroy all the posterity of Ahab: but he also soon relapsed into the same idolatry. He carried out God's judgment, he pretended great zeal; but his hypocrisy soon came to light, for he embraced false and perverted worship; and his followers were nothing better even down to Jeroboam, under whom Hosea prophesied; but of this we shall speak in considering the inscription of the book.

John Calvin

Detailed outline

I. Introduction: 1:1

II. The symbolic example: 1:1–2:23

A. Israel rejected: Hosea's marriage and birth of children.

1. Charged to take a wife of whoredom: 1:2–3

2. Jezreel symbolizes the overthrow of Jehu's dynasty: 1:4–5

3. Lo-ruhamah: God will no more have

mercy on Israel: 1:6–7
4. Lo-ammi: Utter rejection of Israel: 1:8–9
B. Israel comforted: 1:10–11
C. Israel chastised: 2:1–13
1. Condemnation of sinful conduct: 2:1–7
2. Punishment more fully explained: 2:8–13
D. Israel restored: 2:14–23
1. Promise of conversion: 2:14–17
2. Renewal of covenant: 2:18–23
III. Redemption of an adulterous wife: 3:1–5
A. Hosea's experience: 3:1–3
B. Israel's parallel experience: 3:4–5
IV. The triumph of divine love in the restoration of a repentant nation: 4:1–14:9
A. Israel's guilt: 4:1–19
l. he general charge: 4:1–5
2. Willful ignorance: 4:6–11
3. Idolatry: 4:12–19
B. The divine displeasure: 5:1–15
1. Guilt of priests, people, princes: 5:1–7
2. Judgment will follow: 5:8–15
C. The repentant remnant: 6:1–3
1. Return, but without heartfelt repentance: 6:1–3
D. The response of God: 6:4–13:8
1. God is not deceived: 6:4–11
E. National government corrupt: 7:1–7
F. Foreign policy corrupt: 7:8–16
G. Consequences of national corruption: 8:1–14
H. The apostasy and its punishment: 9:1–9
I. As God found Israel and as they became: 9:10–17
J. Puppet kings and gods: 10:1–3
K. Righteousness becomes poison: 10:4–5
L. Assyria used in judgment: 10:6–7
M. The terror of judgment: 10:8
N. Persistence in rebellion: 10:9–15
O. Ingratitude for God's love: 11:1–7
P. Israel's Canaanitish ways: 11:12–12:14
Q. Idolatry the basis of destruction: 13:1–8
V. The final restoration: 13:9–14:9
1. Distrust in God: 13:9–1.
2. Call to repentance: 14:1–3
3. Promise of healing and Epilogue–Israel repents, God hears: 14:4–9

2. Helpful summaries of Hosea

Bird's eye view

The book of Hosea depicts Hosea's unfaithful and adulterous wife Gomer to illustrate both Israel's unfaithfulness to God and God's constant love for Israel.

Reading plan

The following reading plan, taking one reading per day, enables you to read through Hosea in four days.

Hosea 1–3
Hosea 4–7
Hosea 8–11
Hosea 12–14

Verses to memorize

Hosea 6:3

Let us acknowledge the Lord; let us press on to acknowledge him. As surely as the sun rises, he will appear; he will come to us like the winter rains, like the spring rains that water the earth.

Hosea 14:9

. . . the ways of the Lord are right; the righteous walk in them, but the rebellious stumble in them.

Statistics

Twenty-eighth Old Testament book
14 chapters
197 verses
5,175 words

Names/titles given

Hebrew title: *hoshea:* "Salvation."
Greek title in Septuagint: *Osee:* "Hosea.."
Latin title in Vulgate: *Osee:* "Hosea."

3. Helpful keys to turn to in understanding Hosea

Key word

Return, 15 times

Key verses

Hosea 4:1; 6:3

Themes to study

The need for wisdom
God's love
God's faithfulness
Israel's unfaithfulness

Hosea quoted in the New Testament

- They shall be called sons of the living God
  Hos. 1:10 quoted in Rom. 9:26
- I will call that my people, which was not my people
  Hos. 2:23 quoted in Rom. 9:25
- I desire mercy, and not sacrifice
  Hos. 6:6 quoted in Matt. 9:13 and 12:7
- They shall begin to say to the mountains, Fall on us
  Hos. 10:8 quoted in Luke 23:30
- Out of Egypt did I call my son
  Hos. 11:1 quoted in Matt. 2:15
- O death, where is thy sting?
  Hos. 13:14 quoted in 1 Cor. 15:55

Figurative language linked to evil Israel

"Mixes with the nations" (and not holy and separated to God), Hosea 2:15.
"A flat cake not turned over" (so that they are like dough only baked on one side, that is are half-baked, or, half-hearted), Hosea 7:8.
"Foreigners sap his strength" (and are so weakened by their association with ungodly people), Hosea 7:9.
"His hair is sprinkled with gray" (that is they have become prematurely old), Hosea 7:9.
"Israel is swallowed up" (as their national identity has disappeared), Hosea 8:8.
"A worthless thing", Hosea 8:8.
"Loves to defraud" (as they indulge in dishonest business practice), Hosea 12:7.

Jesus in Hosea

In Hosea Jesus is the Healer of backsliders

Type of Jesus in Hosea

Jesus left Palestine to take refuge in Egypt. See Hosea 11:1 and Matt. 2:15.

Lessons to learn from Hosea

- God sets his face against us if we worship anyone else, or depend on, or serve anyone else.
- God expects his people to be totally faithful to him.
- God may be likened to a husband, father, and shepherd of his people.

4. Chapter by chapter: outline of every chapter of Hosea

Hosea 1

Matthew Henry's introduction

In this chapter we have,

I. The general title of the whole book, v. 1.

II. Some particular instructions which he was ordered to give to the people of God.

A. He must convince them of their sin in going a whoring from God, by marrying a prostitute, vv. 2, 3.

B. He must foretell the ruin coming on them for their sin, in the names of his sons, which signified God's disowning and abandoning them, vv. 4–6, 8, 9.

C. He must speak comfortable to the kingdom of Judah, which still retained the pure worship of God, and assure them of the salvation of the Lord, v. 7.

D. He must give an intimation of the great mercy God had in store both for Israel and Judah, in the latter days (vv. 10, 11), for in this prophecy many precious promises of mercy are mixed with the threatenings of wrath.

A detailed analysis of chapter

The shameful idolatry of the ten tribes. (1–7)

The calling of the Gentiles, and the uniting Israel and Judah under the Messiah. (8–11)

Key verse

Verse 1: "The word of the LORD that came unto Hosea, the son of Beery, in the days of Uzziah, Jotham, Ahaz, and Hezekiah, kings of Judah, and in the days of Jeroboam the son of Joash, king of Israel."

Key word / key phrase

Verse 2, "Take to yourself an adulterous wife."

Key event / key person / key theme

Hosea's marriage

Key thought

Verse 2, "for the land is guilty of the vilest adultery." The purpose of Hosea's book is to expose Israel's unfaithfulness to the Lord and to affirm God's forgiving love. Hosea' own domestic tragedy is a parable of this situation.

Key thing to look out for

The Lord was constantly telling his people to be faithful to him.

Key Bible cross-reference

Verse 10. See Romans 9:26.

Key "by way of explanation"

Hosea married Gomer, who proved to be unfaithful, and left him for another man. He later found her for sale as a slave. In deep love he bought her and eventually took her back as his wife.

Key "Quotable Quote"

"The lukewarmness of our prayers is the source of all our other infidelities."

François Fénelon

Hosea 2

Matthew Henry's introduction

The scope of this chapter seems to be much the same with that of the previous chapter, and to point at the same events, and the causes of them. As there, so here,

I. God, by the prophet, discovers sin to them, and charges it home on them, the sin of their idolatry, their spiritual whoredom, their serving idols and forgetting God and their obligations to him, vv. 1, 2, 5, 8.

II. He threatens to take away from them that plenty of all good things with which they had served their idols, and to abandon them to ruin without remedy, vv. 3, 4, 6, 7, 9–13.

III. Yet he promises at last to return in ways of mercy to them for his own sake (v. 14), to restore them to their former plenty (v. 15), to cure them of their inclination to idolatry (vv. 16, 17), to renew his covenant with them (vv. 18–20), and to bless them with all good things, vv. 21–23.

A detailed analysis of chapter

The idolatry of the people. (1–5)
God's judgments against them. (6–13)
His promises of reconciliation. (14–23)

Key verse

Verse 8: "For she did not know that I gave her corn, and wine, and oil, and multiplied her silver and gold, which they prepared for Baal."

Key word / key phrase

Verse 17, "I will remove the names of the Baals from her lips."

Key event / key person / key theme

Israel's unfaithfulness, God's faithfulness

Key thought

Note the ways in which Israel's unfaithfulness is detailed.

Key thing to look out for

How does God say he will act in this situation?

Key Bible cross-reference

Verse 15. See Joshua 7:24–26.

Key "by way of explanation"

Hosea lived and preached in the northern kingdom during its final years. He probably died before the fall of Samaria. Hosea's ministry overlapped with the ministries of Amos, Micah and Isaiah.

Key "Quotable Quote"

"Incomprehensible and immutable is the love of God."

Augustine of Hippo

Hosea 3

Matthew Henry's introduction

In this chapter we have,

I. The bad character which the people of Israel now had; they were, as is said of the Athenians (Acts 17:16), "wholly given to idolatry," v. 1.

II. The low condition which they should be reduced to by their captivity, and the other instances of God's controversy with them, vv. 2–4.

III. The blessed reformation that should at length be wrought on them in the latter days, v. 5.

A detailed analysis of chapter

Hosea reconciled with his wife. (1–5)

Key verse

Verse 2: "So I bought her to me for fifteen pieces of silver, and for an homer of barley, and an half homer of barley."

Key word / key phrase

Verse 1, "Show your love to your wife again."

Key event / key person / key theme

Hosea buys his wife back

Key thought

God's very great love, shown in his willingness to receive Israel back

Key thing to look out for

How does God "buy us back?"

Key Bible cross-reference

Verse 5. See Isaiah 9:13.

Key "by way of explanation"

Verse 5, "return." This is the key word in the whole book. "Return" or "go back" are repeatedly stated in this book. See 2:7; 5:4; 6:1; 7:10; 11:5; 12:6; 14:1–2.

Key "Quotable Quote"

"God created man because God loves and wanted an object to love. He created man so that he could return his love."

Billy Graham

Hosea 4

Matthew Henry's introduction

Prophets were sent to be reprovers, to tell people of their faults, and to warn them of the judgments of God, to which by sin they exposed themselves; so the prophet is employed in this and the following chapters. He is here, as counsel for the King of kings, opening an indictment against the people of Israel, and laboring to convince them of sin, and of their misery and danger because of sin, that he might prevail with them to repent and reform.

I. He shows them what were the grounds of God's controversy with them, a general prevalence of vice and profaneness (vv. 1, 2), ignorance and forgetfulness of God (vv. 6, 7), the worldly-mindedness of the priests (v. 8), drunkenness and uncleanness (v. 11), using divination and witchcraft (v. 12), offering sacrifice in the high places (v. 13), prostitutes (vv. 14, 18), and bribery among magistrates, v. 18.

II. He shows them what would be the consequences of God's controversy. God would punish them for these things, v. 9. The whole land should be laid waste (v. 3), all sorts of people cut off (v. 5), their honor lost (v. 7), their creature-comforts unsatisfying (v. 10), and themselves made ashamed, v. 19. And, which is several times mentioned here as the sorest judgment of all, they should be let alone in their sins (v. 17), they shall not reprove one another (v. 4), God will not punish them (v. 14), nay, he will let them prosper, v. 16.

III. He gives warning to Judah not to tread in the steps of Israel, because they saw their steps went down to hell, v. 15.

A detailed analysis of chapter

God's judgments against the sins of the people, (1–5)

and of the priests. (6–11)

Idolatry is reproved, and Judah is admonished. (12–19)

Key verse

Verse 6: "My people are destroyed for lack of knowledge."

Key word / key phrase

Verse 1, "the Lord has a charge to bring against you."

Key event / key person / key theme

Israel's sins

Key thought

There is never any point in trying to hide our sins from God.

Key thing to look out for

No matter how many and how bad our sins, they must be owned up to.

Key Bible cross-reference

Verse 16. See Exodus 32:9.

Key "by way of explanation"

Verse 1, "charge." Hosea was the Lord's spokesman and he had charges to bring against his people since they had broken God's covenant.

Key "Quotable Quote"

"Knowledge without repentance will be but a torch to light men to hell."

Thomas Watson

Hosea 5

Matthew Henry's introduction

The scope of this chapter is the same with that of the previous chapter, to discover the sin both of Israel and Judah, and to denounce the judgments of God against them.

I. They are called to hearken to the charge, vv. 1, 8.

II. They are accused of many sins, which are here aggravated.

A. Persecution, vv. 1, 2.

B. Spiritual whoredom, vv. 3, 4.

C. Pride, v. 5.

D. Apostasy from God, v. 7.

E. The tyranny of the princes, and the tameness of the people in submitting to it, vv. 10, 11.

III. They are threatened with God's displeasure for their sins; he knows all their wickedness (v. 3) and makes known his wrath against them for it, v. 9.

A. They shall fall in their iniquity, v. 5.

B. God will forsake them, v. 6.

C. Their portions shall be devoured, v. 7.

D. God will rebuke them, and pour out his wrath on them, vv. 9, 10.

E. They shall be oppressed, v. 11.

F. God will be as a moth to them in secret judgments (v. 12) and as a lion in public judgments, v. 14.

IV. They are blamed for the wrong course they took under their afflictions, v. 13.

V. It is intimated that they shall at length take a right course, v. 15.

A detailed analysis of chapter

The divine judgments against Israel. (1–7)

Approaching desolations threatened. (8–15)

Key verse

Verse 5: "And the pride of Israel doth testify to his face: therefore shall Israel and Ephraim fall in their iniquity; Judah also shall fall with them."

Key word / key phrase

Verse 15, "they will seek my face."

Key event / key person / key theme

Eventual restoration of Israel

Key thought

Why did Israel find it so difficult to admit her guilt? See verse 15.

Key thing to look out for

There is never a time when we should not seek the Lord.

Key Bible cross-reference

Verse 12. See Job 13:28.

Key "by way of explanation"

Verse 6, "seek the Lord." This was to be done in different ways, including through prayer and through offering sacrifices. See 3:5; Amos 5:4, 5.

Key "Quotable Quote"

"Sitting still will lose you heaven, as well as if you run from it."

Richard Baxter

Hosea 6

Matthew Henry's introduction

Observe,

I. Their resolution to return to God, and the comforts wherewith they encourage themselves in their return, vv. 1–3.

II. The instability of many of them in their professions and promises of repentance, and the severe course which God therefore took with them, vv. 4, 5.

III. The covenant God made with them, and his expectations from them (v. 6); their violation of that covenant and frustrating those expectations, vv. 7–11.

A detailed analysis of chapter

A superficial repentance. (1–3)

Israel's instability and breaking of the covenant. (4–11)

Key verse

Verse 2: "After two days will he revive us: in the third day he will raise us up, and we shall live in his sight."

Key word / key phrase

Verse 6, "mercy."

Key event / key person / key theme

God sees through a shallow casual repentance (see verses 1–4 and 7:14).

Key thought

Why can there be no progress if we refuse to repent?

Key thing to look out for

What is verse 6 saying?

Key Bible cross-reference

Verse 6. See Matthew 9:13.

Key "by way of explanation"

Verse 6, "mercy" translates the Hebrew word *hesed*, often used to describe God's covenant love for his people. Here it can refer to being loyal to the Lord or acting in the right way toward people. Here it probably includes both of these meanings.

Key "Quotable Quote"

"There's a wideness in God's mercy,
Like the wideness of the sea;
There's a kindness in his justice,
Which is more than liberty."

F.W. Faber

Hosea 7

Matthew Henry's introduction

In this chapter we have,

I. A general charge drawn up against Israel for those high crimes and misdemeanors by which they had obstructed the course of God's favors to them, vv. 1, 2.

II. A particular accusation,

A. Of the court–the king, princes, and judges, vv. 3–7.

B. Of the country. Ephraim is here charged with conforming to the nations (v. 8), senselessness and stupidity under the judgments of God (vv. 9–11), ingratitude to God for his mercies (v. 13), incorrigibleness under his judgments (v. 14), contempt of God (v. 15), and hypocrisy in their pretences to return to him, v. 16. They are also threatened with a severe chastisement, which shall humble them (v. 12), and, if that prevail not, then with an utter destruction (v. 13), particularly their princes, v. 16.

A detailed analysis of chapter

The many sins of Israel. (1–7)

Their senselessness and hypocrisy. (8–16)

Key verse

Verse 8: "Ephraim [Israel], he hath mixed himself among the people; Ephraim is a cake not turned."

Key word / key phrase

Verse 1, "whenever I would heal Israel."

Key event / key person / key theme

Deliberate refusal to return to the Lord

Key thought

How can such people be helped?

Key thing to look out for

The causes of Israel's many sins and difficulties

Key Bible cross-reference

Verse 2. See Jeremiah 14:10.

Key "by way of explanation"

Verse 2, "I remember." Nothing is hidden from the Lord, and the Lord never forgets anything.

Key "Quotable Quote"

"I am constrained to express my adoration of the Author of my existence for his forgiving mercy revealed to the world through Jesus Christ, through whom I hope for never ending happiness in a future state."

Robert Treat Paine, Signer of the Declaration

Hosea 8

Matthew Henry's introduction

This chapter, as that before, divides itself into the sins and punishments of Israel; every verse almost declares both, and all to bring them to repentance. When they saw the malignant nature of their sin, in the descriptions of that, they could not but be convinced now much it was their duty to repent of what was so bad in itself; and when they saw the mischievous consequences of their sin, in the predictions of them, they could not but see how much it was their interest to repent for the preventing of them.

I. The sin of Israel is here set forth,
  - A. In many general expressions, vv. 1, 3, 12, 14.
  - B. In many particular instances; setting up kings without God (v. 4), setting up idols against God (vv. 4–6, 11), and courting alliances with the neighboring nations, vv. 8–10.
  - C. In this aggravation of it, that they still kept up a profession of religion and relation to God, vv. 2, 13, 14.

II. The punishment of Israel is here set forth as answering to the sin. God would bring an enemy on them, vv. 1, 3. All their projects should be blasted, v. 7. Their confidence both in their idols and in their foreign alliances should disappoint them, vv. 6, 8, 10. Their strength at home should fail them, v. 14. Their sacrifices should have no reckoning made of them, and their sins should have a reckoning made for them, v. 13.

A detailed analysis of chapter

Destruction threatened for the impiety of Israel. (1–4)

For their idolatry. (5–10)

Further warnings for the same sins. (11–14)

Key verse

Verse 3: "Israel hath cast off the thing that is good: the enemy shall pursue him."

Key word / key phrase

Verse 6, "this calf."

Key event / key person / key theme

The state of the nation: deliberate idolatry and unfortunate foreign alliances

Key thought

The cause of their troubles: "Israel has forgotten" verse 14

Key thing to look out for

What instances of God's love are nevertheless found in this chapter?

Key Bible cross-reference

Verse 1. See Numbers 10:2.

Key "by way of explanation"

Verse 5, "calf-idol." Golden calves had been set up in Bethel and Dan by Jeroboam I. See 1 Kings 12:28–33.

Key "Quotable Quote"

"Repentance means that everything must be changed."

Johann Heinrich Arnold

Hosea 9

Matthew Henry's introduction

In this chapter,

I. God threatens to deprive this degenerate seed of Israel of all their worldly enjoyments, because by sin they had forfeited their title to them; so that they should have no comfort either in receiving them themselves or in offering them to God, vv. 1–5.

II. He dooms them to utter ruin, for their own sins and the sins of their prophets, vv. 6–8.

III. He upbraids them with the wickedness of their fathers before them, whose steps they trod in, vv. 9, 10.

IV. He threatens them with the destruction of their children and the rooting out of their posterity, vv. 11–17.

A detailed analysis of chapter

The distress to come upon Israel. (1–6)
The approach of the day of trouble. (7–10)
Judgments on Israel. (11–17)

Key verse

Verse 7: "The days of visitation are come, the days of recompense are come; Israel shall know it: the prophet is a fool, the spiritual man is mad, for the multitude of thine iniquity, and the great hatred."

Key word / key phrase

Verse 17, "My God will reject them."

Key event / key person / key theme

Israel's disobedience

Key thought

Reflect on God's grace to you throughout your life.

Key thing to look out for

God only drives Israel away from him to bring her to her senses.

Key Bible cross-reference

Verse 7. See Luke 21:22.

Key "by way of explanation"

Verse 10, "grapes . . . fruit on the fig-tree." Grapes in the desert and the early figs, refreshing fruit, stand for God's delight in Israel's acceptance of the covenant.

Key "Quotable Quote"

"No powers can separate us from God's love in Christ. Unmasked, revealed in their true nature, they have lost their mighty grip on men. The cross has disarmed them."

Hendrik Berkhof

Hosea 10

Matthew Henry's introduction

In this chapter,

I. The people of Israel are charged with gross corruptions in the worship of God and are threatened with the destruction of their images and altars, vv. 1, 2, 5, 6, 8.

II. They are charged with corruptions in the administration of the civil government and are threatened with the ruin of that, vv. 3, 4, 7.

III. They are charged with imitating the sins of their fathers, and with security in their own sins, and are threatened with smarting humbling judgments, vv. 9–11.

IV. They are earnestly invited to repent and reform, and are threatened with ruin if they did not, vv. 12–15.

A detailed analysis of chapter

The idolatry of Israel. (1–8)

They are exhorted to repent. (9–15)

Key verse

Verse 1: "Israel is an empty vine, he bringeth forth fruit unto himself: according to the multitude of his fruit he hath increased the altars; according to the goodness of his land they have made goodly images."

Key word / key phrase

Verse 15, "the king of Israel will be completely destroyed."

Key event / key person / key theme

God's judgment on Israel

Key thought

Israel's prosperity (verse 1), led her to depend on her own strength (verse 13) and that proved fatal.

Key thing to look out for

Why is sin so appealing?

Key Bible cross-reference

Verse 8. See Luke 23:30.

Key "by way of explanation"

Verse 11, "yoke" is a reference to the law. Steadily doing what is right, showing love and seeking God, will lead to the outpouring of God's blessings.

Key "Quotable Quote"

"All of God's people are ordinary people who have been made extraordinary by the purpose he has given them."

Oswald Chambers

Hosea 11

Matthew Henry's introduction

In this chapter we have,

I. The great goodness of God towards his people Israel, and the great things he had done for them, vv. 1, 3, 4.

II. Their ungrateful conduct towards him, notwithstanding his favors towards them, vv. 2–4, 7, 12.

III. Threatenings of wrath against them for their ingratitude and treachery, vv. 5, 6.

IV. Mercy remembered in the midst of wrath, vv. 8, 9.

V. Promises of what God would yet do for them, vv. 10, 11.

VI. An honorable character given of Judah, v. 12.

A detailed analysis of chapter

God's tender love for Israel; their ingratitude. (1–7)

The divine mercy yet in store. (8–12)

Key verse

Verse 3: "I taught Ephraim also to go, taking them by their arms; but they knew not that I healed them."

Key word / key phrase

Verse 1, "I loved him."

Key event / key person / key theme

God's love for Israel

Key thought

God never stops loving his people.

Key thing to look out for

Life with God is the best life. See verse 11.

Key Bible cross-reference

Verse 1. See Exodus 4:22.

Key "by way of explanation"

Verse 3, "walk." Here the picture depicts a father gently teaching his child to walk – a beautiful picture of God's love for his people.

Key "Quotable Quote"

"The atonement was not the cause but the effect of God's love."

A.W. Pink

Hosea 12

Matthew Henry's introduction

In this chapter we have,

I. A high charge drawn up against both Israel and Judah for their sins, which were the ground of God's controversy with them, vv. 1, 2. Particularly the sin of fraud and injustice, which Ephraim is charged with (v. 7), and justifies himself in, v. 8. And the sin of idolatry (v. 11), by which God is provoked to contend with them, v. 14.

II. The aggravations of the sins they are charged with, taken from the honor God put on their father Jacob (vv. 3–5), the advancement of them into a people from low and mean beginnings (vv. 12, 13), and the provision he had made them of helps for their souls by the prophets he sent them, v. 10.

III. A call to the unconverted to turn to God, v. 6.

IV. An intimation of mercy that God had in store for them, v. 9.

A detailed analysis of chapter

Jacob's deceit. (1–6)

Out of Egypt. (7–14)

Key verse

Verse 6: "Therefore turn thou to thy God: keep mercy and judgment, and wait on thy God continually."

Key word / key phrase

Verse 2, "a change to bring."

Key event / key person / key theme

A look back to the past

Key thought

Like father (Jacob) like son (Israel, cheating at business, cheating on God)

Key thing to look out for

The waywardness of God's people is meant to be a lesson for us.

Key Bible cross-reference

Verse 3. See Genesis 25:26.

Key "by way of explanation"

Verse 8, "I am very rich." One of the downsides of riches is that they tend to make people complacent and self-sufficient.

Key "Quotable Quote"

"No friend of gold ever became a friend of Christ or a friend of people."

John Chrysostom

Hosea 13

Matthew Henry's introduction

The same strings, though generally unpleasing ones, are harped on in this chapter that were in those before. People care not to be told either of their sin or of their danger by sin; and yet it is necessary, and for their good, that they should be told of both, nor can they better hear of either than from the word of God and from their faithful ministers, while the sin may be repented of and the danger prevented. Here,

I. The people of Israel are reproved and threatened for their idolatry, vv. 1–4.

II. They are reproved and threatened for their wantonness, pride, and luxury, and other abuses of their wealth and prosperity, vv. 5–8.

III. The ruin that is coming on them for these and all their other sins is foretold as very terrible, vv. 12, 13, 15, 16.

IV. Those among them that yet retain a respect for their God are here encouraged to hope that he will yet appear for their relief, though their kings and princes, and all their other supports and succors, fail them, vv. 9–11, 14.

A detailed analysis of chapter

The abuse of God's favor leads to punishment. (1–8)

A promise of God's mercy. (9–16)

Key verse

Verse 14: "I will ransom them from the power of the grave; I will redeem them from death."

Key word / key phrase

Verse 4, "no Savior except me."

Key event / key person / key theme

Only God's love can save Israel

Key thought

God insists on being the only God in Israel's life.

Key thing to look out for

Note the sinfulness of sin, in verse 2, for example.

Key Bible cross-reference

Verse 14. See 1 Corinthians 15:55.

Key "by way of explanation"

Verse 14, "I will ransom." This promise states that the Lord will redeem people from death and is echoed in 1 Corinthians 15.

Key "Quotable Quote"

"He that hath one foot in heaven need not fear to put the other into the grave."

John Flavel

Hosea 14

Matthew Henry's introduction

We have here,

I. Directions in repenting, what to do and what to say, vv. 1–3.

II. Encouragements to repent taken from God's readiness to receive returning sinners (vv. 4, 8) and the comforts he has treasured up for them, vv. 5–7.

III. A solemn recommendation of these things to our serious thoughts, v. 9.

A detailed analysis of chapter

An exhortation to repent. (1–3)

Blessings promised, showing the great benefits of the gospel. (4–8)

The just and the wicked. (9)

Key verse

Verse 4: "I will heal their backsliding, I will love them freely: for mine anger is turned away from him."

Key word / key phrase

Verse 1, "Return."

Key event / key person / key theme

God's promise to restore Israel

Key thought

God always extends his forgiving arms to his repentant people.

Key thing to look out for

Note how everything that is good in us comes from God, see verse 8.

Key Bible cross-reference

Verse 1. See Isaiah 19:22.

Key "by way of explanation"

Verse 2, "take words." Sacrifices would not be sufficient. The words that had to be taken needed to be words of repentance.

Key "Quotable Quote"

"Repentance is in every view so desirable, so necessary, so suited to honor God, that I seek that above all. The tender heart, the broken and contrite spirit, are to me far above all the joys that I could ever hope for in this vale of tears."

Charles Simeon

5. Select bibliography for Hosea

Achtemeier, Elizabeth. *Minor Prophets*, Vol. I, Hosea-Micah (NIBC), Hendrickson, 1996.

Hubbard, David A. *Hosea* (Tyndale), InterVarsity Press, 1990.

Kidner, Derek. *Love to the Loveless*. Bible Speaks Truly Today. Downers Grove, Ill.: InterVarsity, 1981.

Pusey, E. B. *The Minor Prophets With a Commentary*. 1885. Reprint. Grand Rapids: Eerdmans, 1949.

Smith, G. A. *The Book of the Twelve Prophets*. Rev. ed. New York: Harper & Brothers, 1928.

Joel

1. Book by book: Introduction to Joel

Introduction

Joel the prophet

Joel (meaning "one to whom Jehovah is God," that is, worshipper of Jehovah) seems to have belonged to Judah, as no reference occurs to Israel; whereas he speaks of Jerusalem, the temple, the priests, and the ceremonies, as if he were intimately familiar with them (compare Joel 1:14; 2:1, 15, 32; 3:1, 2, 6, 16, 17, 20, 21). His predictions were probably delivered in the early days of Joash 870–865 B.C.; for no reference is made in them to the Babylonian, Assyrian, or even the Syrian invasion; and the only enemies mentioned are the Philistines, Phœnicians, Edomites, and Egyptians (Joel 3:4, 19). Had he lived after Joash, he would doubtless have mentioned the Syrians among the enemies whom he numerates since they took Jerusalem and carried off immense spoil to Damascus (2 Chr. 24:23, 24). No idolatry is mentioned; and the temple services, the priesthood, and other institutions of the theocracy, are represented as flourishing. This all answers to the state of things under the high priesthood of Jehoiada, through whom Joash had been placed on the throne and who lived in the early years of Joash (2 Kings 11:17, 18; 12:2–16; 2 Chr. 24:4–14). He was the son of Pethuel.

Joel the book

The first chapter describes the desolation caused by an inroad of locusts–one of the instruments of divine judgment mentioned by Moses (Deut. 28:38, 39) and by Solomon (1 Kings 8:37). The second chapter (Joel 2:1–11): the appearance of them, under images of a hostile army suggesting that the locusts were symbols and forerunners of a more terrible scourge, namely, foreign enemies who would consume all before them. (The absence of mention of personal injury to the inhabitants is not a just objection to the figurative interpretation; for the figure is consistent throughout in attributing to the locusts only injury to vegetation, thereby injuring indirectly man and beast). Joel 2:12–17: exhortation to repentance, the result of which will be: God will deliver His people, the former and latter rains shall return to fertilize their desolated lands, and these shall be the pledge of the spiritual outpouring of grace beginning with Judah, and thence extending to "all flesh." Joel 2:18–3:21: God's judgments on Judah's enemies, whereas Judah shall be established for ever.

Style of book

Joel's style is pre-eminently pure. It is characterized by smoothness and fluency in the rhythms, roundness in the sentences, and regularity in the parallelisms. With the strength of Micah it combines the tenderness of Jeremiah, the vividness of Nahum, and the sublimity of Isaiah. As a specimen of his style take the second chapter in which the terrible aspect of the locusts, their rapidity, irresistible progress, noisy din, and instinct-taught power of marshalling their forces for their career of devastation, are painted with graphic reality.

A.R. Faussett

John Calvin's introduction to Joel

The time in which Joel prophesied is uncertain. Some of the Jews imagine that he exercised his office in the time of Joram, king of Israel, because a dreadful famine then prevailed through the whole land, as it appears evident from sacred history; and as the Prophet record a famine, they suppose that his ministry must be referred to that time. Some think, that he taught under Manasseh, but they bring no reason for this opinion; it is, therefore, a mere conjecture. Others think that he performed his office as a teacher not only under one king, but that he taught, at the same time with Isaiah, under several kings.

But as there is no certainty, it is better to leave the time in which he taught undecided; and, as we shall see, this is of no great importance. Not to know the time of Hosea would be to readers a great loss for there are many parts which could not be explained without a knowledge of history; but as to Joel there is, as I have said, less need of this; for the import of his doctrine is evident, though his time be obscure and uncertain. But we may conclude that he taught at Jerusalem, or at least in the kingdom of Judah. As Hosea was appointed a Prophet to the kingdom of Israel, so Joel had another appointment; for he was to labor especially among the Jews and not among the Ten Tribes: this deserves to be particularly noticed.

Now the sum of the Book is this: At the beginning, he reproves the stupidity of the people, who, when severely smitten by God, did not feel their evils, but on the contrary grew hardened under them:

this is one thing. Then he threatens far more grievous evils; as the people became so insensible under all their punishments, that they were not humbled, the Prophet declares that there were evils at hand much worse than those they had hitherto experienced: this is the second thing. Thirdly, he exhorts the people to repentance, and shows that there was required no common evidence of repentance; for they had not lightly offended God, but by their perverseness provoked him to bring on them utter ruin: since, then, their obstinacy had been so great, he bids them to come as suppliants with tears, with sack-cloth, with mourning, with ashes, that they might obtain mercy; for they were unworthy of being regarded by the Lord, except they thus submissively humbled themselves: this is the third subject. The fourth part of the Book is taken up with promises; for he prophesies of the Kingdom of Christ, and shows, that though now all things seemed full of despair, yet God had not forgotten the covenant he made with the fathers; and that therefore Christ would come to gather the scattered remnants, yea, and to restore to life his people, though they were now lost and dead. This is the sum and substance.

John Calvin

Detailed outline

I. The prophet presented: 1:1

II. A type of the "day of the Lord": 1:2–20

- A. The locust plague: 1:2–7
- B. The people exhorted to repent: 1:8–20
  1. The elders (leaders): 1:2
  2. Old and young: 1:2–3
  3. Drunkards: 1:5–7
  4. Whole nation: 1:8–12
  5. Priests (ministers): 1:9
  6. Husbandmen: Laborers: 1:10–12
- C. Exhortation to repent: 1:13–14
- D. "Day of Jehovah": Prayer for mercy: 1:15–20 Note that we are to . . .
  1. Hear: 1:1
  2. Awake: 1:5
  3. Lament: 1:8
  4. Be ashamed: 1:11
  5. Gird in sackcloth: 1:13
  6. Sanctify a fast: 1:14
  7. Call a solemn assembly of repentance: 1:15
  8. Cry unto the Lord: 1:14, 19

III. The "day of the Lord": 2:1–32

- A. The invading northern army: 2:1–10
- B. God's army at Armageddon: 2:11
- C. The repentant remnant: 2:12–17
  1. Rend the heart, not the garments: 2:12–14
  2. Sincerely repent and fervently pray: 2:15–17
- D. God's response to the remnant: 2:18–29
  1. Repentance: 2:18
  2. Restoration: 2:19–27
  3. Outpouring of Spirit: 2:28–29
  4. Judgment on the wicked: 2:20, 30–31
  5. Escape of the remnant in Zion: 2:32
- E. Signs preceding the "day of the Lord": 2:30–32

IV. The judgment of the nations: 3:1–16

- A. Israel restored: 3:1
- B. The nations judged: 3:2–3
- C. The Phoenicians and Philistines especially condemned:3:4–8

D. The nations challenged to war and judgment: 3:9–16

V. The prophecy of the kingdom blessing: 3:17–21

A. The exaltation of Jerusalem: 3:17

B. Judah's prosperity: 3:18

C. Egypt and Edom's desolation: 3:19

D. Jerusalem's exaltation explained: 3:20–21

2. Helpful summaries of Joel

Bird's eye view

The book of Joel is set against the backdrop of a recent devastating plague of locusts which depicts God's judgment on his people, if they fail to repent.

Reading plan

The following reading plan, taking one reading per day, enables you to read through Joel in one day.

Joel 1–3

Verses to memorize

Joel 2:28

And it shall come to pass afterward, that I will pour out my spirit on all flesh; and your sons and your daughters shall prophesy, your old men shall dream dreams, your young men shall see visions

Joel 2:32

And everyone who calls on the name of the Lord will be saved.

Statistics

Twenty-ninth Old Testament book

3 chapters

73 verses

2,034 words

Names/titles given

Hebrew title: *Yo'el:* "The Lord is God."

Greek title in Septuagint: *Ioel.*

Latin title in Vulgate: *Joel.*

The prophet of the Pentateuch, (as Joel has 25 references to the five books of Moses.)

The prophet of Pentecost, (see Joel 2:28–29.)

3. Helpful keys to turn to in understanding Joel

Key words

Repent

The day of the Lord

Key verses

Joel 2:11, 28,29

Themes to study

God's Spirit, especially when outpoured.

God's judgment

The day of the Lord

Joel quoted in the New Testament

- I will pour forth of my Spirit upon all flesh
  Joel 2:28–32 quoted in Acts 2:17–21
- Whosoever shall call upon the name of the Lord shall be saved
  Joel 2:32 quoted in Rom. 10:13

Jesus in Joel

In Joel Jesus is the Restorer.

Type of Jesus in Joel

Jesus is pictured as the judge of the nations in the Valley of Jehoshaphat, 3:2, 12.

Type of the Holy Spirit in Joel

The Holy Spirit promised in Joel

The coming of the Holy Spirit in Acts 2:16–21 is prophesied in Joel 2:28–32.

Lessons to learn from Joel

Disasters can help us to return to God in deeper repentance.

4. Chapter by chapter: outline of every chapter of Joel

Joel 1

Matthew Henry's introduction

This chapter is the description of a lamentable devastation made of the country of Judah by locusts and caterpillars. Some think that the prophet speaks of it as a thing to come and gives warning of it beforehand, as usually the prophets did of judgments coming. Others think that it was now present, and that his business was to affect the people with it and awaken them by it to repentance.

I. It is spoken of as a judgment which there was no precedent of in former ages, vv. 1–7.

II. All sorts of people sharing in the calamity are called on to lament it, vv. 8–13.

III. They are directed to look up to God in their lamentations, and to humble themselves before him, vv. 14–20.

A detailed analysis of chapter

A plague of locusts. (1–7)

All sorts of people are called to lament it. (8–13)

They are to look to God. (14–20)

Key verse

Verse 12: "The vine is dried up, and the fig tree languisheth; the pomegranate tree, the palm tree also, and the apple tree, even all the trees of the field, are withered: because joy is withered away from the sons of men."

Key word / key phrase

Verse 4, "the locust swarm."

Key event / key person / key theme

The devastating plague of locusts

Key thought

A good question to ask of any disaster is: "What can I learn from God in this situation?"

Key thing to look out for

In God's sight we always need to repent.

Key Bible cross-reference

Verse 28–32. See Acts 2:17–21.

6. See Revelation 9:8.

Key "by way of explanation"

Verse 11, "all the trees of the field." The extent of the damage caused by locusts went beyond the corn and vines to the trees, which included apple trees, fig-trees, and pomegranates. There are no historical details in the book, so the date of Joel is uncertain.

Key "Quotable Quote"

"If God exists, and if He judges good and evil, then we must realize that those who trample on his great gifts will one day know his judgment. The scriptures bear solemn witness to this. Our nation is not immune."

Francis A. Schaeffer

Joel 2

Matthew Henry's introduction

In this chapter we have,

I. A further description of that terrible desolation which should be made in the land of Judah by the locusts and caterpillars, vv. 1–11.

II. A serious call to the people, when they are under this sore judgment, to return and repent, to fast and pray, and to seek unto God for mercy, with directions how to do this aright, vv. 12–17.

III. A promise that, on their repentance, God would remove the judgment, would repair the breaches made on them by it, and restore unto them plenty of all good things, vv. 18–27.

IV. A prediction of the setting up of the kingdom of the Messiah in the world, by the pouring out of the Spirit in the latter days, vv. 28–32.

A detailed analysis of chapter

God's judgments. (1–14)

Exhortations to fasting and prayer; blessings promised. (15–27)

A promise of the Holy Spirit, and of future mercies. (28–32)

Key verse

Verse 1: "Blow ye the trumpet in Zion, and sound an alarm in my holy mountain: let all the inhabitants of the land tremble: for the day of the LORD cometh, for it is nigh at hand."

Key word / key phrase

Verse 1, "the day of the Lord is coming."

Key event / key person / key theme

The Day of the Lord will bring destruction

Key thought

How do you link up the Day of the Lord with the second coming of Jesus?

Key thing to look out for

Note how verse 13 goes to the heart of the matter.

Key Bible cross-reference

Verses 2:28–32. See Acts 2:17–21.

Key "by way of explanation"

Verse 12, "even now." God's judgment had already started. But "even now" it was not too late to escape it if the people repented.

Key "Quotable Quote"

"All true repentance has its root in faith."

Horatius Bonar

Joel 3

Matthew Henry's introduction

Here is a prediction,

I. Of God's reckoning with the enemies of his people for all the injuries and indignities that they had done them, and returning them on their own head, vv. 1–8.

II. Of God's judging all nations when the measure of their iniquity is full, and appearing publicly, to the everlasting confusion of all impenitent sinners and the everlasting comfort of all his faithful servants, vv. 9–17.

III. Of the provision God has made for the refreshment of his people, for their safety and purity, when their enemies shall be made desolate, vv. 18–21.

A detailed analysis of chapter

God's judgments in the latter days. (1–8)

The extent of these judgments. (9–17)

The blessings the messianic age. (18–21)

Key verse

Verse 10: "Beat your plowshares into swords, and your pruninghooks into spears: let the weak say, I am strong."

Key word / key phrase

Verse 4, "what have you against me?"

Key event / key person / key theme

Judgment on the nations

Key thought

Godless nations will be judged by God because of their treatment of God's people

Key thing to look out for

What spiritual blessings are alluded to in verses 17–21?

Key Bible cross-reference

Verses 4–8. See Luke 10:13,14.

Key "by way of explanation"

Verse 18, "valley of acacias," suggests a dry and hot ravine, similar to those that go down to the Dead Sea. "The water flowing from the temple of God will be sufficient for even the most remote and waterless ravine" (Paul E. Leonard). See Ezekiel 47:1–12.

Key "Quotable Quote"

"The Law by which God rules us, is as dear to him as the Gospel by which he saves us."

William Secker

5. Select bibliography for Joel

Allen, Leslie C. *The Books of Joel, Obadiah, Jonah and Micah*. Grand Rapids Eerdmans, 1976.

Achtemeier, Elizabeth. *Minor Prophets*, Vol. I, Hosea-Micah (NIBC), Hendrickson, 1996.

Hubbard, David Allan. *Joel and Amos*, (Tyndale Old Testament Commentaries), InterVarsity, 1989.

Keil, C. F. *The Twelve Minor Prophets*. KD. 2 Vols. Grand Rapids: Eerdmans, 1949.

Pusey, E. B. *The Minor Prophets*. 2 vols. New York: Funk and Wagnalls, 1886.

Dillard, Raymond "Joel" in The Minor Prophets, Vol. I, (ed. T. McComiskey), Baker, 1992.

Amos

1. Book by book: Introduction to Amos

Introduction

Amos the prophet

Amos (meaning in Hebrew "a burden") was (Amos 1:1) a shepherd of Tekoa, a small town of Judah, six miles southeast from Bethlehem, and twelve from Jerusalem, on the borders of the great desert (2 Chr. 20:20; compare 2 Chr. 11:6). The region being sandy was more fit for pastoral than for agricultural purposes. Amos therefore owned and tended flocks, and collected sycamore figs; not that the former was a menial office, kings themselves, as Mesha of Moab (2 Kings 3:4), exercising it. Amos, however (from Amos 7:14, 15), seems to have been of humble rank.

Though belonging to Judah, he was commissioned by God to exercise his prophetical function in Israel; as the latter kingdom abounded in impostors, and the prophets of God generally fled to Judah through fear of the kings of Israel, a true prophet from Judah was the more needed in it. His name is not to be confounded with that of Isaiah's father, Amoz.

Setting

The time of his prophesying was in the reigns of Uzziah king of Judea, and Jeroboam II, son of Joash, king of Israel (Amos 1:1), that is, in part of the time in which the two kings were contemporary; probably in Jeroboam's latter years, after that monarch had recovered from Syria "the coast of Israel from the entering of Hamath to the sea of the plain" (2 Kings 14:25–27); for Amos foretells that these same coasts, "from the entering in of Hamath unto the river of the wilderness," should be the scene of Israel's being afflicted (Amos 6:14); also his references to the state of luxurious security then existing (Amos 6:1, 4, 13), and to the speedy termination of it by the Assyrian foe (Amos 1:5; 3:12, 15; 5:27; 8:2), point to the latter part of Jeroboam's reign, which terminated in 784 B.C., the twenty-seventh year of Uzziah's reign, which continued down to 759 B.C.

He was contemporary with Hosea, only that the latter continued to prophesy in reigns subsequent to Uzziah (Hos. 1:1); whereas Amos ceased to prophesy in the reign of that monarch. The scene of his ministry was Beth-el, where the idol calves were set up (Amos 7:10–13). There his prophecies roused Amaziah, the idol priest, to accuse him of conspiracy and to try to drive him back to Judah.

Style

The first six chapters are without figure; the last three symbolical, but with the explanation subjoined. He first denounces the neighboring peoples, then the Jews, then Israel (from the third chapter to the end), closing with the promise or restoration under Messiah (Amos 9:11–15). His style is thought by

Jerome to betray his humble origin; but though not sublime, it is regular, perspicuous, and energetic; his images are taken from the scenes in nature with which he was familiar; his rhythms are flowing, his parallelisms exact, and his descriptions minute and graphic. Some peculiar expressions occur: "cleanness of teeth," that is, want of bread (Amos 4:6); "the excellency of Jacob" (Amos 6:8; 8:7); "the high places of Isaac" (Amos 7:9); "the house of Isaac" (Amos 7:16); "he that createth the wind" (Amos 4:13).

Canonicity

Philo, Josephus, Melito's catalogue, Jerome, Justin Martyr (*Dialogue with Trypho*, 22, quoting the fifth and six chapters of Amos as "one of the twelve minor prophets"), and the sixtieth canon of the Laodicean council support the canonicity of the book of Amos.

A.R. Faussett

Contents of Amos

The book falls naturally into three parts, recognizable by certain recurring formulas and general literary features.

(1) The first section, which is clearly recognizable, embraces Amos 1 and 2. Here, after the title and designation of the prophet in Amos 1:1, there is a solemn proclamation of Divine authority for the prophet's words. "Yahweh will roar from Zion, and utter his voice from Jerusalem" (verse 2). This is notable in one who throughout the book recognizes God's power as world-wide and His operation as extensive as creation; and it should be a caution in view, on the one hand, of the assertion that the temple at Jerusalem was not more sacred than any of the numerous "high places" throughout the land, and, on the other hand, the superficial manner in which some writers speak of the Hebrew notion of a Deity whose dwelling-place was restricted to one locality beyond which His influence was not felt. For this God, who has His dwelling-place in Zion, now through the mouth of the prophet denounces in succession the surrounding nations, and this mainly not for offenses committed against the chosen people but for moral offenses against one another and for breaches of a law binding on humanity. It will be observed that the nations denounced are not named in geographical order, and the prophet exhibits remarkable rhetorical skill in the order of selection. The interest and sympathy of the hearers is secured by the fixing of the attention on the enormities of guilt in their neighbors, and curiosity is kept awake by the uncertainty as to where the next stroke of the prophetic whip will fall. Beginning with the more distant and alien peoples of Damascus, Gaza and Tyre, he wheels round to the nearer and kindred peoples of Edom, Ammon and Moab, till he rests for a moment on the brother tribe of Judah, and thus, having relentlessly drawn the net around Israel by the enumeration of seven peoples, he swoops down on the Northern Kingdom to which his message is to be particularly addressed.

(2) The second section embraces Amos 3 to 6, and consists apparently of a series of discourses, each introduced by the formula: "Hear this word" (Amos 3:1; 4:1; 5:1), and another introduced by a

comprehensive: "Woe to them that are at ease in Zion, and to them that are secure in the mountain of Samaria" (Amos 6:1). The divisions here are not so clearly marked. It will be observed e. g. that there is another "Woe" at Amos 5:18; and in chapter 4, though the address at the outset is directed to the luxurious women of Samaria, from 4:4 onward the words have a wider reference. Accordingly some would divide this section into a larger number of subsections; and some, indeed, have described the whole book as a collection of ill-arranged fragments. But, while it is not necessary to suppose that the written book is an exact reproduction of the spoken addresses, and while the division into chapters has no authority, yet we must allow for some latitude in the details which an impassioned speaker would introduce into his discourses, and for transitions and connections of thought which may not be apparent on the surface.

(3) The third section has some well-marked characteristics, although it is even less uniform than the preceding. The outstanding feature is the phrase, "Thus the LORD Yahweh showed me" (Amos 7:1,4,7; 8:1) varied at Amos 9:1 by the words, "I saw the Lord standing beside the altar." We have thus a series of "visions" bearing on, and interpreted as applying to, the condition of Israel. It is in the course of one of these, when the prophet comes to the words, "I will rise against the house of Jeroboam with the sword" (Amos 7:9) that the interposition of Amaziah, the priest of Bethel, is recorded, with the prophet's noble reply as to his Divine call, and his rebuke and denunciation of the priest, ending with a prophetic announcement of the downfall and captivity of Israel (Amos 7:14–17).

Orr, James, M.A., D.D. General Editor, International Standard Bible Encyclopedia

Detailed outline

I. Introduction: 1:1–2

II. Judgment on nations neighboring Israel: 1:3–2:3

- A. Damascus 1:3–5
- B. Philistia: 1:6–8
- C. Phoenicia: 1:9–10
- D. Edom: 1:11–12
- E. Ammon: 1:13–15
- F. Moab: 2:1–3

III. Judgment on Judah and Israel: 2:4–16

- A. On Judah: 2:4–5
- B. On Israel: 2:6–16

IV. God's indictment of the family of Jacob: 3:1–9:10

- A. Three addresses of condemnation: 3:1–6:15
  1. Judgment is deserved: 3:1–10
     Judgment is decreed: 3:11–15
  2. Judgment is deserved: 4:1–11
     Judgment is decreed: 4:12–13
  3. Judgment is deserved: 5:1–15
     Judgment is decreed: 5:16–6:14
- B. Five symbolic visions of punishments: 7:1–9:10
  1. The locust: 7:1–3
  2. The drought: 7:4–6
  3. The plumb line with a historical reference: 7:7–17
  4. The fruit basket: 8:1–14
  5. The Lord standing on the altar: 9:1–10

V. The promises of Israel's restoration: 9:11–15

2. Helpful summaries of Amos

Bird's eye view

Basking in the lap of luxury the northern kingdom of Israel receive a wake-up call to return to God through the prophecies of Amos.

Reading plan

The following reading plan, taking one reading per day, enables you to read through Amos in two days.

Amos 1–4

Amos 5–9

Verse to memorize

Amos 5:14

Seek good, not evil, that you may live. Then the Lord God Almighty will be with you just as you say he is.

Statistics

Thirtieth Old Testament book

9 chapters

146 verses

4,217 words

Names/titles given

Hebrew title: *amass:*

"To lift a burden/bur-den-bearer."

Greek title in Septuagint: *Amos.*

Latin title in Vulgate: *Amos.*

3. Helpful keys to turn to in understanding Amos

Key word/words

Plumbline

Key verses

Amos 3:1–2; 7:8

Themes to study

- Listening to God
- Going against God's stated will, compared with doing God's will.
- Punishment God inflicts.

Amos quoted in the New Testament

- Ye took up the tabernacle of Moloch:
  Amos 5:25–27 quoted in Acts 7:42–43
- I will build again the tabernacle of David, which is fallen
  Amos 9:11–12 quoted in Acts 15:16–17

Jesus in Amos

In Amos Jesus is our Judge.

Types of Jesus in Amos

Jesus has authority of judge, 1:1–9:10.

Jesus will restore his people, 9:11–15.

Lessons to learn from Amos

- God cares about injustice in the world.
- God is especially concerned about the poor.
- Luxury should have no place in the lives of God's followers.

4. Chapter by chapter: outline of every chapter of Amos

Amos 1

Matthew Henry's introduction

In this chapter we have,

I. The general title of this prophecy (v. 1), with the general scope of it, v. 2.

II. God's particular controversy with Syria (vv. 3–5), with Palestine (vv. 6–8), with Tyre (vv. 9, 10), with Edom (vv. 11, 12), and with Ammon (vv. 13–15), for their cruelty to his people and the many injuries they had done them. This explains God's pleading with the nations, Joel 3:2.

A detailed analysis of chapter

Introduction. (1–2)

Judgments against Israel's neighbors. (3–15)

Key verse

Verse 1: "The words of Amos, who was among the herdmen of Tekoa, which he saw concerning Israel in the days of Uzziah king of Judah, and in the days of Jeroboam the son of Joash king of Israel, two years before the earthquake."

Key word / key phrase

Verse 3, "three sins of Damascus."

Key event / key person / key theme

The sins of Damascus, Philistia, Phoenicia, Edom, and Ammon

Key thought

Be sure your sin will find you out.

Key thing to look out for

All humans beings are responsible people with consciences.

Key Bible cross-reference

Verse 1. See 2 Kings 15:1–7.

Key "by way of explanation"

Amos, who lived near Bethlehem in Judah, was sent by God to preach at Bethel in Israel, probably about 760–750, during a time of temporary prosperity for both kingdoms. He was not a priest, like Jeremiah and Ezekiel, but a shepherd. He also tended sycamore-fig trees (1:1; 7:14).

Key "Quotable Quote"

"Alas! that prisons should have been peopled, and thousands immolated on the pyre, for the sake of opinions; and that nothing but death could atone for the horrible crime of individual judgment, instead of allowing each to stand or fall to their own Master."

John Foxe

Amos 2

Matthew Henry's introduction

In this chapter,

I. God, by the prophet, proceeds in a like controversy with Moab as before with other nations, vv. 1–3.

II. He shows what quarrel he had with Judah, vv. 4, 5.

III. He at length begins his charge against Israel, to which all that goes before is but an introduction. Observe,

A. The sins they are charged with–injustice, oppression, whoredom, vv. 6–8.
B. The aggravations of those sins–the temporal and spiritual mercies God had bestowed on them, for which they had made him such ungrateful returns, vv. 9–12.
C. God's complaint of them for their sins (v. 13) and his threatenings of their ruin, and their utter inability to prevent it, vv. 14–16.

A detailed analysis of chapter

Judgments against Moab and Judah. (1–8)
The ingratitude and ruin of Israel. (9–16)

Key verse

Verse 4: "Thus saith the LORD."

Key word / key phrase

Verse 6, "For three sins of Israel."

Key event / key person / key theme

The climax: sins of Israel

Key thought

It is easy to sit in judgment on others and to ignore our own sins. Israel will have been shocked when Amos suddenly turned to the sins of Israel.

Key thing to look out for

God's people very often rebel against the Lord God.

Key Bible cross-reference

Verse 9. See Deuteronomy 3:8–11.

Key "by way of explanation"

Verse 8, "garments taken in pledge." This describes the usual way in which a loan was secured. If you wanted to borrow money you would leave your cloak as surety for your debt. Verse 3, "For three . . . even four" a literary device that emphasizes the sin named.

Key "Quotable Quote"

"Original sin is the only rational solution of the undeniable fact of the deep, universal and early manifested sinfulness of men in all ages, of every class, and in every part of the world."

Charles Hodge

Amos 3

Matthew Henry's introduction

A stupid, senseless, heedless people, are, in this chapter, called on to take notice,

I. Of the judgments of God denounced against them and the warnings he gave them of those judgments, and to be here by awakened out of their security, vv. 1–8.
II. Of the sins that were found among them, by which God was provoked thus to threaten, thus to punish, that they might justify God in his controversy with them, and, unless they repented and reformed, might expect no other than that God should proceed in his controversy, vv. 9–15.

A detailed analysis of chapter

Judgments against Israel. (1–8)
Judgments against other nations. (9–15)

Key verse

Verse 10: "For they know not to do right, saith the LORD, who store up violence and robbery in their palaces."

Key word / key phrase

Verse 14, "I punish Israel."

Key event / key person / key theme

God's judgment

Key thought

That fact that God chose his people to follow him in the first place, verse 2, is mentioned here because that alone should have brought Israel back to her senses.

Key thing to look out for

Verse 7 shows how God plans everything and that his plans were often conveyed through his prophets.

Key Bible cross-reference

Verse 14. See 2 Kings 23:15.

Key "by way of explanation"

Verse 15, "houses adorned with ivory." This indicates great wealth obtained at the expense of the poor. Craftsmen were used to inlay the ivory.

Key "Quotable Quote"

"None are true saints except those who have the true character of compassion and concern to relieve the poor, indignant, and afflicted."

Jonathan Edwards

Amos 4

Matthew Henry's introduction

In this chapter,

I. The oppressors in Israel are threatened for their oppression of the poor, vv. 1–3.

II. The idolaters in Israel, being joined to idols, are given up to their own heart's lusts, vv. 4, 5.

III. All the sins of Israel are aggravated from their incorrigibleness in them, and their refusal to return and reform, notwithstanding the various rebukes of Providence which they had been under, vv. 6–11.

IV. They are invited yet at length to humble themselves before God, since it is impossible for them to make their part good against him, vv. 12, 13.

A detailed analysis of chapter

Israel is reproved. (1–5)

Their impenitence shown. (6–13)

Key verse

Verse 4: "Come to Bethel, and transgress."

Key word / key phrase

Verse 1, "women who oppress the poor."

Key event / key person / key theme

The willfulness of Israel's sins

Key thought

The Bible often uses very unflattering language, verse 1, to startle people into paying attention.

Key thing to look out for

Natural justice dictates that the poor should not be trodden under foot. Of all people, God's followers should not have allowed this to happen.

Key Bible cross-reference

Verse 11. See Genesis 19:24.

Key "by way of explanation"

Verse 6, "yet you have not returned to me." This refrain comes at the close of the description of the five natural disasters, verses 6, 8, 9, 10, 11, and parallels Pharaoh's response to the plagues.

Key "Quotable Quote"

"It is human to err; it is devilish to remain willfully in error."

Augustine of Hippo

Amos 5

Matthew Henry's introduction

The scope of this chapter is to prosecute the exhortation given to Israel in the close of the previous chapter to prepare to meet their God; the prophet here tells them,

I. What preparation they must make; they must "seek the Lord," and not seek any more to idols (vv. 4–8); they must seek good, and love it, vv. 14, 15.

II. Why they must make this preparation to meet their God,

A. Because of the present deplorable condition they were in, vv. 1–3.

B. Because it was by sin that they were brought into such a condition, vv. 7, 10–12.

C. Because it would be their happiness to seek God, and he was ready to be found of them, vv. 8, 9, 14.

D. Because he would proceed, in his wrath to their utter ruin, if they did not seek him, vv. 5, 6, 13, 16, 17.

E. Because all their confidences would fail them if they did not seek unto God, and make him their friend.

1. Their profane contempt of God's judgments, and setting them at defiance, would not secure them, vv. 18–20.
2. Their external services in religion, and the shows of devotion, would not avail to turn away the wrath of God, vv. 21–24.
3. Their having been long in possession of church-privileges, and in a course of holy duties, would not be their protection, while all along they had kept up their idolatrous customs, vv. 25–27.

A detailed analysis of chapter

Israel is called to seek the Lord. (1–6)
Earnest exhortations to repent. (7–17)
Warnings about idolatry. (18–27)

Key verse

Verse 24: "But let judgment run down as waters, and righteousness as a mighty stream."

Key word / key phrase

"Hate," verses 10, 15, 21. It is always instructive to see what God and God's prophets "hate."

Key event / key person / key theme

Judgment on Israel is deserved

Key thought

God's assessment of Israel's worship is that it is: "your religious feasts, your assemblies, and your songs," verses 21–23.

Key thing to look out for

The prophetic call for social justice is repeated in the New Testament.

Key biblical cross-reference

Verse 15. See Isaiah 1:17; Romans 12:9.

Key "by way of explanation"

Verse 2 "Fallen is Virgin Israel." The word "Virgin" emphasizes Israel's premature death. Amos says, in effect, "How sad that a whole life of potential love and fruitfulness was cut short."

Key "Quotable Quote"

"Concern for the rights and welfare of all [God's] people flows, like a mighty river, from his own heart. Whoever would truly serve him must go with that flow."

D.A. Hubbard, on verse 24

Amos 6

Matthew Henry's introduction

In this chapter we have,

I. A sinful people studying to put a slight on God's threatenings and to make them appear trivial, confiding in their privileges and pre-eminences above other nations (vv. 2, 3), and their power (v. 13), and wholly addicted to their pleasures, vv. 4–6.

II. A serious prophet studying to put a weight on God's threatenings and to make them appear terrible, by setting forth the severity of those judgments that were coming on these sensualists (v. 7), God's abhorring them, and abandoning them and theirs to death (vv. 8–11), and bringing utter desolation on them, since they would not be wrought on by the methods he had taken for their conviction, vv. 12–14.

A detailed analysis of chapter

The danger of luxury and false security. (1–7)

Punishment of sins. (8–14)

Key verse

Verse 1: "Woe to them that are at ease in Zion."

Key word / key phrase

Verse 14, "I will stir up a nation against you."

Key event / key person / key theme

Israel's end is near

Key thought

Why is luxurious living and feasting picked on as being so sinful?

Key thing to look out for

Complacency, verse 1, heads the list of sins. Why is it so dangerous?

Key Bible cross-reference

Verse 10. See 1 Samuel 31:12.

Key "by way of explanation"

Verse 8, "the Sovereign Lord has sworn." This phrase is used three times in this book. See also 4:2; 8:7. It introduces the Lord's impending judgment.

Key "Quotable Quote"

"Jesus Christ is no longer on trial before men – men are now on trial before him!"

A.W. Tozer

Amos 7

Matthew Henry's introduction

In this chapter we have,

I. God contending with Israel, by the judgments, but are reprieved, and the judgments turned away at the prayer of Amos, vv. 1–6.

II. God's patience is at length worn out by their obstinacy, and they are rejected, and sentenced to utter ruin, vv. 7–9.

III. Israel contending with God, by the opposition given to his prophet.

A. Amaziah informs against Amos (vv. 10, 11) and does what he can to rid the country of him as a public nuisance, vv. 12, 13.

B. Amos justifies himself in what he did as a prophet (vv. 14, 15) and denounces the judgments of God against Amaziah his prosecutor (vv. 16, 17); for, when the contest is between God and man, it is easy to foresee, it is very easy to foretell, who will come off with the worst of it.

A detailed analysis of chapter

Visions of judgments to come upon Israel. (1–9)

Amaziah threatens Amos. (10–17)

Key verse

Verse 7: "Thus he showed me: and, behold, the Lord stood upon a wall made by a plumb line, with a plumb line in his hand."

Key word / key phrase

Verse 4, "judgment by fire."

Key event / key person / key theme

Visions of doom: locusts, fire, and plumb line

Key thought

When we are brought to the end of ourselves, verses 2, what should we do?

Key thing to look out for

Only people with discernment can detect a false prophet.

Key Bible cross-reference

Verse 13. See Joshua 7:2.

Key "by way of explanation"

Verse 6, "the LORD relented." This does not imply that the Lord gave up, regretted or stopped his actions through remorse. Rather it shows that the Lord God himself was personally involved with his people.

Key "Quotable Quote"

"You can't drink your way out of loneliness. Drugs won't take you out of it. God says to you that there is an answer to loneliness. It lies in a personal relationship with the Lord Jesus Christ."

Billy Graham

Amos 8

Matthew Henry's introduction

Sinful times are here attended with sorrowful times, so necessary is the connection between them; it is threatened here again and again that the laughter shall be turned into mourning.

I. By the vision of "basket of summer-fruit" is signified the hastening on of the ruin threatened (vv. 1–3) and that shall change their note.

II. Oppressors are here called to an account for their abusing the poor; and their destruction is foretold, which will set them a mourning, vv. 4–10.

III. A famine of the word of God is here made the punishment of a people that go a whoring after other gods (vv. 11–14); yet for this, which is the most mournful judgment of all, they are not here brought in mourning.

A detailed analysis of chapter

The impending ruin of Israel. (1–3)

Oppression reproved. (4–10)

A famine of the word of God. (11–14)

Key verse

Verse 4: "Hear this, O ye that swallow up the needy, even to make the poor of the land to fail."

Key word / key phrase

Verse 1, "a basket of ripe fruit."

Key event / key person / key theme

Vision of the summer fruit

Key thought

Social injustice is abhorrent in God's sight.

Key thing to look out for

God can send spiritual famines as a judgment.

Key Bible cross-reference

Verse 9. See Job 5:14.

Key "by way of explanation"

Verse 7, "the Pride of Jacob." God's people were very proud of the fact that the Lord God was with them, always went with them, and that he was their God.

Key "Quotable Quote"

"When God measures man, he puts the tape around the heart, not the head."

Author unknown

Amos 9

Matthew Henry's introduction

In this chapter we have,

I. Judgment threatened, which the sinners shall not escape (vv. 1–4), which an almighty power shall inflict (vv. 5, 6), which the people of Israel have deserved as a sinful people (vv. 7, 8); and yet it shall not be the utter ruin of their nation (v. 8), for a remnant of good people shall escape, v. 9. But the wicked ones shall perish, v. 10.

II. Mercy promised, which was to be bestowed in the latter days (vv. 11–15).

A detailed analysis of chapter

The ruin of Israel. (1–10)

The restoration of the Jews and the gospel blessing. (11–15)

Key verse

Verse 8: "Behold, the eyes of the Lord GOD are upon the sinful kingdom, and I will destroy it from off the face of the earth; saving that I will not utterly destroy the house of Jacob, saith the LORD."

Key word / key phrase

Verse 1, "none will escape."

Key event / key person / key theme

God's destruction, but hope for the future

Key thought

Some things have to be torn down before a building can progress.

Key thing to look out for

From verse 11 we observe the Lord's loving heart in his promise of restoration.

Key Bible cross-reference

Verses 11,12. See Acts 15:16–18.

Key "by way of explanation"

Verse 6, "his lofty place." The comparison here is between puny man whose buildings are threatened by the slightest earthquake and God who can build up into the heavens.

Key "Quotable Quote"

"At the end of life, we shall be judged by love."

St John of the Cross

5. Select bibliography for Amos

More recent commentaries

Achtemeier, Elizabeth. *Minor Prophets*, Vol. I, Hosea-Micah (NIBC), Hendrickson, 1996.

Hubbard, David Allan. *Joel and Amos*, (Tyndale Old Testament Commentaries), InterVarsity, 1989.

Motyer, J. *The Day of the Lion*. Downers Grove, Ill.: InterVarsity, 1974.

Stuart, Douglas. *Hosea-Jonah* (Word, 31), Word Books, 1987.

Obadiah

1. Book by book: Introduction to Obadiah

Introduction

This is the shortest book in the Old Testament. The name means "servant of Jehovah." Obadiah stands fourth among the minor prophets according to the Hebrew arrangement of the canon, the fifth according to the Greek.

Some consider him to be the same as the Obadiah who superintended the restoration of the temple under Josiah, 627 B.C. (2 Chr. 34:12). But Obad. 11–16, 20 imply that Jerusalem was by this time overthrown by the Chaldeans, and that he refers to the cruelty of Edom towards the Jews on that occasion, which is referred to also in Lam. 4:21, 22; Ezek. 25:12–14; 35:1–15; Ps. 137:7. From comparing Obad. 5 with Jer. 49:9, Obad. 6 with Jer. 49:10, Obad. 8 with Jer. 49:7, it appears that Jeremiah embodied in his prophecies part of Obadiah's, as he had done in the case of other prophets also (compare Is. 15:1–16:14 with Jer. 48:1–47).

The reason for the present position of Obadiah before other of the minor prophets anterior in date is: Amos at the close of his prophecies foretells the subjugation of Edom hereafter by the Jews; the arranger of the minor prophets in one volume, therefore, placed Obadiah next, as being a fuller statement, and, as it were, a commentary on the previous briefer prophecy of Amos as to Edom (Maurer). (Compare Amos 1:11).

The date of Obadiah's prophecies was probably immediately after the taking of Jerusalem by Nebuchadnezzar, 588 B.C. Five years afterwards (583 B.C.) Edom was conquered by Nebuchadnezzar. Jeremiah must have incorporated part of Obadiah's prophecies with his own immediately after they were uttered, thus stamping his canonicity.

Jerome makes him contemporary with Hosea, Joel, and Amos. It is an argument in favor of this view that Jeremiah would be more likely to insert in his prophecies a portion from a preceding prophet than from a contemporary. If so, the allusion in Obad. 11–14 will be to one of the former captures of Jerusalem: by the Egyptians under Rehoboam (1 Kings 14:25, 26; 2 Chr. 12:2, etc.), or that by the Philistines and Arabians in the reign of Joram (2 Chr. 21:16, 17); or that by Joash, king of Israel, in the reign of Amaziah (2 Chr. 25:22, 23); or that in the reign of Jehoiakim (2 Kings 24:1, etc.); or that in the reign of Jehoiachin (2 Kings 24:8–16). On all occasions the Idumeans were hostile to the Jews; and the terms in which that enmity is characterized are not stronger in Obadiah than in Joel 3:19 (compare Obad. 10); Amos 1:11, 12. The probable capture of Jerusalem alluded to by Obadiah is that by Joash and the Israelites in the reign of Amaziah. For as, a little before, in the reign of the same Amaziah, the Jews had treated harshly the Edomites after conquering them in battle (2 Chr. 25:11–23), it is probable that the Edomites, in revenge, joined the Israelites in the attack on Jerusalem (Jaeger).

Divisions of book

This book may be divided into two parts:

(1) Obad. 1–6 set forth Edom's violence toward his brother Israel in the day of the latter's distress, and his coming destruction with the rest of the foes of Judah;

(2) Obad. 17–21, the coming re-establishment of the Jews in their own possessions, to which shall be added those of the neighboring peoples, and especially those of Edom.

A.R. Faussett

John Calvin's introduction to Obadiah

This Prophecy does not consist of many oracles, nor of many sermons, as other prophecies; but it only denounces on the Idumeans a near destruction, and then promises a restoration to the chosen people of

God. But it threatens the Idumeans for the sake of administering consolation to the chosen people; for it was a grievous and hard trial for the children of Jacob, an elect people, to see the posterity of Esau, who had been rejected by God, flourishing both in wealth and power.

As then the children of Israel were miserable in comparison with their own kindred, the adoption of God might have appeared worthless; and this was in great measure the reason why the Israelites preferred the lot of other is observed by us, our sorrow is enhanced and our weariness is increased. When therefore the Israelites saw the Idumeans living at ease and beyond the reach of danger, and when they also saw them in the enjoyment of every abundance, while they themselves were exposed as a prey to their enemies, and were continually expecting new calamities, it could not have been, but that their faith must have utterly failed, or at least become much weakened. For this reason the Prophet here shows, that though the Idumeans now lived happily, yet in a short time they would be destroyed, for they were hated by God; and he shows that this would be the case, as we shall see from the contents of this Book, for the sake of the chosen people.

We now then perceive the design of the Prophet: as adversity might have weakened the Israelites, and even utterly broken them down, the Prophet here applies comfort and props up their dejected minds, for the Lord would shortly look on them and take due vengeance on their enemies.

And the reason why this prophecy is leveled against the Idumeans only is this, — that they, as we know, raged more cruelly than any others against the Israelites: for it is not said without a cause in Psalm 137:7, “Remember the children of Edom in the day of Jerusalem, who said, Make bare, make bare even to the very foundations.”

Now at what time Obadiah prophesied, it does not appear except that it is probable that this prophecy was announced, when the Idumeans rose up against the Israelites and distressed them by many annoyances: for they seem to be mistaken who think that Obadiah lived before the time of Isaiah. It appears that Jeremiah (Jeremiah 49:7–22) and this Prophet made use of the same thoughts and nearly of the same words, as we shall hereafter see. The Holy Spirit could, no doubt, have expressed the same things in different words; but he was pleased to join together these two testimonies, that they might obtain more credit. I know not whether Obadiah and Jeremiah were contemporaries, and on this subject we need not bestow much labor. It is sufficient for us to know, that this prophecy was added to other prophecies, that the Israelites might feel assured, that though their kindred the Idumeans might prosper for a time, yet they could not escape the hand of God, but would shortly be constrained to give an account of their cruelty, inasmuch as they had without cause been all in a flame against the distressed and afflicted people of God.

Now our Prophet shows at the end that God would become the avenger of this cruelty, which the Idumeans had exercised; for though he chastised his own people, he did not yet forget his gratuitous covenant.

John Calvin

Detailed outline

- I. Edom's destiny prophesied: 1–9
  - A. The message is from the Lord to Obadiah regarding Edom: 1
  - B. Unconquerable Edom will be conquered: 2–4
    1. Edom will be small and despised among the nations: 2
    2. Deceived by pride: 3
    3. Brought down by God: 4
  - C. Edom will be completely plundered and deserted: 5–9
    1. Thieves and robbers: 5
    2. Hidden treasure sought: 6
    3. Edom deceived and trapped: 7.
    4. Wise men destroyed: 8
    5. Mighty men dismayed and Edom cut off: 9
- II. The cause: 10–14
  - A. Violence: 10
  - B. Hostile attitude: 11
  - C. Joy at the calamity of others: 12
  - D. Boasting in times of other's distress: 12
  - E. Spoiling God's people: 13
  - F. Preventing escape of fugitives: 14
  - G. Betrayal: 1:14
- III. The results of the judgment on Edom: 15–18
- IV. Israel's possession of Edom: 19–21

2. Helpful summaries of Obadiah

Bird's eye view

Obadiah predicts the destruction of the nation of Edom on account of their treatment and attitude towards God's people.

Reading plan

The following reading plan, taking one reading per day, enables you to read through Obadiah in one day.

Obadiah 1

Verse to memorize

Obadiah: 15

The day of the Lord is near for all nations. As you have done, it will be done to you; your deeds will return on your own head.

Statistics

Thirty-first Old Testament book

1 chapter

21 verses

670 words

Shortest Old Testament book

Names/titles given

Hebrew title: Obadyah: "Worshipper/Servant of the Lord."

Greek title in Septuagint: Obdiou: "Obadiah."

Latin title in Vulgate: Abdias: "Obadiah."

3. Helpful keys to turn to in understanding Obadiah

Key word/words

Retribution

Key verse

Obadiah, verses 10; 15

Themes to study

God's kingship and rule

Links with Jesus
Jesus in Obadiah
In Obadiah Jesus is our Savior.

Types of Jesus in Obadiah

- Jesus is the Judge of the nations, 15–16.
- Jesus is the Savior of Israel, 17–20.
- Jesus is the One who possesses the kingdom, 21.

Lessons to learn from Obadiah

God is in control of world governments.

4. Verse by verse: outline of Obadiah

Obadiah

Matthew Henry's introduction

This book is wholly about Edom, a nation nearly allied and near adjoining to Israel, and yet an enemy to the seed of Jacob, inheriting the enmity of their father Esau to Jacob. Now here we have, after the preface, v. 1.

I. Threatenings against Edom,
  A. That their pride should be humbled, vv. 2–4.
  B. That their wealth should be plundered, vv. 5–7.
  C. That their wisdom should be infatuated, vv. 8, 9.
  D. That their spiteful behavior towards God's Israel should be avenged, vv. 10–16.
II. Gracious promises to Israel; that they shall be restored and reformed, and shall be victorious over the Edomites, and become masters of their land and the lands of others of their neighbors (vv. 17–20), and that the kingdom of the Messiah shall be set up by the bringing in of the great salvation, v. 21.

A detailed analysis of chapter

Destruction to come on Edom. Their offences against Jacob. (1–16)
The restoration of the Jews, and their flourishing state in the latter times. (17–21)

Key verse

Verse 10: "For thy violence against thy brother Jacob shame shall cover thee, and thou shalt be cut off for ever."

Key word / key phrase

Verse 1, "about Edom."

Key event / key person / key theme

The callous behavior of Edom

Key thought

Some people seem to spend all their lives being openly hostile to God.

Key thing to look out for

Verse 12 is a warning to all people, not just the Edomites.

Key Bible cross-reference

Verses 1–14. See Isaiah 34:5–17; 63:1–6.

Key "by way of explanation"

Verse 10, "your brother Jacob." What made Edom's sins all the worse is that her evil actions were committed against Jacob, her brother nation. The date of this book is uncertain but verses 11–14 seem to indicate the recent destruction of Jerusalem by Babylon in which Edom joined in.

Key "Quotable Quote"

"Jesus will judge us not only for what we did, but also for what we could have done and didn't."

George Otis

5. Select bibliography for Obadiah

Achtemeier, Elizabeth. *Minor Prophets*, Vol. I, Hosea-Micah (NIBC), Hendrickson, 1996.

Allen, Leslie C. *The Books of Joel, Obadiah, Jonah and Micah*. New International Commentary on the Old Testament. Grand Rapids: Eerdmans, 1976.

Baker, D. W., Alexander, T. D. and Waltke, B. K. *Obadiah, Jonah, Micah* (Tyndale), InterVarsity, 1988.

Ellison, H. L. *The Old Testament Prophets*. 1958 Reprint. Grand Rapids: Zondervan, 1966.

Gaebelein, Frank E. *Four Minor Prophets*. Chicago: Moody, 1970.

Henderson, E. *The Twelve Minor Prophets*. Grand Rapids: Baker, 1980.

Keil, Carl F. *The Twelve Minor Prophets*. KD. Grand Rapids: Eerdmans, 1949.

Pusey, E. B. *The Minor Prophets*. Vol. 1. Reprint. Grand Rapids: Baker, 1950.

Jonah

1. Book by book: Introduction to Jonah

Introduction

Jonah was the son of Amittai, of Gath-hepher in Zebulun (called Gittah-hepher in Josh. 19:10–13), so that he belonged to the kingdom of the ten tribes, not to Judah. His date is to be gathered from 2 Kings 14:25–27, "He (Jeroboam II) restored the coast of Israel from the entering of Hamath unto the sea of the plain, according to the word of the Lord God of Israel, which He spake by the hand of His servant Jonah, the son of Amittai, the prophet, which was of Gath-hepher. For the Lord saw the affliction of Israel, that it was very bitter: for there was not any shut up, nor any left, nor any helper for Israel. And the Lord said not that He would blot out the name of Israel from under heaven: but He saved them by the hand of Jeroboam the son of Joash."

Now as this prophecy of Jonah was given at a time when Israel was at the lowest point of depression, when "there was not any shut up or left," that is, confined or left at large, none to act as a helper for Israel, it cannot have been given in Jeroboam's reign, which was marked by prosperity, for in it Syria was worsted in fulfillment of the prophecy, and Israel raised to its former "greatness." It must have been, therefore, in the early part of the reign of Joash, Jeroboam's father, who had found Israel in subjection to Syria, but had raised it by victories which were followed up so successfully by Jeroboam. Thus Jonah was the earliest of the prophets, and close on Elisha, who died in Joash's reign, having just before his death given a token prophetical of the thrice defeat of Syria (2 Kings 13:14–21). Hosea and Amos prophesied also in the reign of Jeroboam II, but towards the closing part of his forty-one years' reign.

The transactions in the Book of Jonah probably occurred in the latter part of his life; if so, the book is not much older than part of the writings of Hosea and Amos. The use of the third person is no argument against Jonah himself being the writer: for the sacred writers in mentioning themselves do so in the third person (compare John 19:26). Nor is the use of the past tense (Jon. 3:3, "Now Nineveh was an exceeding great city") a proof that Nineveh's greatness was past when the Book of Jonah was being written; it is simply used to carry on the negative uniformly,–"the word of the LORD came to Jonah . . . so Jonah arose . . . now Nineveh was," etc. (Jon. 1:1; 3:3). The mention of its greatness proves rather that the book was written at an early date, before the Israelites had that intimate knowledge of it which they must have had soon afterwards through frequent Assyrian inroads.

Jonah and the fish

As early as Julian and Porphyry, pagans ridiculed the credulity of Christians in believing the deliverance of Jonah by a fish. Some infidels have derived it from the heathen fable of the deliverance of Andromeda from a sea monster by Perseus (*Apollodorus*, The Library, 2.4,3); or from that of Arion the musician thrown into the sea by sailors, and carried safe to shore on a dolphin (Herodotus, History, 1.24); or from that of Hercules, who sprang into the jaws of a sea monster, and was three days in its belly, when he undertook to save Hesione (*Diodorus Siculus*, Historical Library, 4.42; Homer, *The Iliad*, 20.145; 21.442). Probably the heathen fables are, vice versa, corruptions of the sacred narrative, if there be any connection. Jerome states that near Joppa lay rocks, pointed out as those to which Andromeda was bound when exposed to the sea monster. This fable implies the likelihood of the story of Jonah having passed through the Phœnicians in a corrupted form to Greece. That the account of Jonah is history, and not parable (as rationalists represent), appears from our Lord's reference to it, in which the personal existence, miraculous fate, and prophetical office of Jonah are explicitly asserted: "No sign shall be given but the sign of the prophet Jonas: for, as Jonas was three days and three nights in the whale's belly, so shall the Son of man be three days and three nights in the heart of the earth" (Matt. 12:39, 40). The Lord recognizes his being in the belly of the fish as a "sign," that is, a real miracle, typical of a similar event in His own history; and assumes the execution of the prophet's commission to Nineveh, "The men of Nineveh . . . repented at the preaching of Jonas; and behold, a greater than Jonas is here" (Matt. 12:41).

It seemed strange to Kimchi, a Jew himself, that the Book of Jonah is among the Scriptures, as the only prophecy in it concerns Nineveh, a heathen city, and makes no mention of Israel, which is referred to by every other prophet. The reason seems to be: a tacit reproof of Israel is intended; a heathen people were ready to repent at the first preaching of the prophet, a stranger to them; but Israel, who boasted of being God's elect, repented not, though warned by their own prophets at all seasons. This was an anticipatory streak of light before the dawn of the full "light to lighten the Gentiles" (Luke 2:32). Jonah is himself a strange paradox: a prophet of God, and yet a runaway from God: a man drowned, and yet alive: a preacher of repentance, yet one that repines at repentance. Yet Jonah, saved from the jaws of death himself on repentance, was the fittest to give a hope to Nineveh, doomed though it was, of a merciful respite on its repentance. The patience and pity of God stand in striking contrast with the selfishness and hard-heartedness of man.

Nineveh

Nineveh in particular was chosen to teach Israel these lessons, on account of its being capital of the then world kingdom, and because it was now beginning to make its power felt by Israel. Our Lord (Matt. 12:41) makes Nineveh's repentance a reproof of the Jews' impenitence in His day, just as Jonah provoked Israel to jealousy (Deut. 32:21) by the same example. Jonah's mission to Nineveh implied that a heathen city afforded as legitimate a field for the prophet's labors as Israel, and with a more successful result (compare Amos 9:7).

Style

The book is prose narrative throughout, except the prayer of thanksgiving in the second chapter (Jon. 2:1–9). The Chaldæisms in the original do not prove spuriousness, or a later age, but were natural in the language of one living in Zebulun on the borders of the north, whence Aramaic peculiarities would readily arise; moreover, his message to Nineveh implies acquaintance with Assyrian. Living as Jonah did in a part of Israel exposed to Assyrian invasions, he probably stood in the same relation to Assyria as Elijah and Elisha had stood to Syria. The purity of the language implies the antiquity of the book, and the likelihood of its being Jonah's own writing. Indeed, none but Jonah could have written or dictated such peculiar details, known only to himself.

Jonah's tomb

The tradition that places the tomb of Jonah opposite to Mosul, and names it "Nebbi Junus" (that is, "prophet Jonah"), originated probably in the spot having been occupied by a Christian church or convent dedicated to him (Layard). A more ancient tradition of Jerome's time placed the tomb in Jonah's native village of Gath-hepher.

A.R. Faussett

John Calvin's introduction to Jonah

At what time Jonah discharged the office of a Teacher, we may in some measure learn from 2 Kings 14:1 for it is certain that he is the person there mentioned in sacred history, as he is expressly called the son of Amittai. It is said there that Jeroboam, the son of Joash, had enlarged the borders of his kingdom, from the entrance into Hamath to the sea of the desert, according to the word of Jonah, the servant of God, the son of Amittai, who came from Gath. It was then at that time, or shortly before, that Jonah prophesied. And it is certain that he was not only sent to the Ninevites, but that he also was counted a Teacher among the people of Israel. And the beginning also of his Book seems to intimate what I have said, – that he was an ordinary Prophet among the people of Israel, for it begins with a copulative, And the Word of the Lord came to Jonah. Though the Holy Spirit does in other places speak sometimes in this manner, yet I doubt not but that Jonah intimates that he was recalled from the discharge of his ordinary office, and had a new charge committed to him, – to denounce on the Ninevites a near destruction.

We must now then understand, that although Jonah taught among the people of Israel, but nevertheless he received a command to go to the Ninevites. It is right that we should know that he was not then only made a Prophet, when he was given as a Teacher to the Ninevites, but that he was sent to the Ninevites after having for some time employed his labors for God and his Church.

This Book is partly historical and partly didactic. For Jonah relates what happened to him after he had attempted to avoid the call of God, and what was the issue of his prophecy: this is one thing. But at the same time he mentions the kind of doctrine which he was commanded to proclaim, and he also writes a Song of Thanksgiving. This last part contains doctrines and is not a mere narrative.

John Calvin

Detailed outline

- I. The first commission: 1:1–2:10
  - A. Divine call: Arise, go, cry: 1:1–2
  - B. Disobedience of Jonah: He arose and fled: 1:3
  - C. Results of disobedience: 1:4–17
    - 1. Caught in a storm: 1:4–6
    - 2. Found guilty: 1:7
    - 3. Thrown overboard: 1:8–16
    - 4. Swallowed by a great fish: 1:17
  - D. Jonah's prayer: 2:1–9
    - 1. Remembers the distress of life: 2:3, 5–6
    - 2. Realizes the direction of God's hand: 2:3
    - 3. Recognizes it is the desire of the Lord to answer prayer: 2:2,7
    - 4. Requires rededication and repentance: 2:9
    - 5. Results in deliverance: 2:10
  - E. Jonah's deliverance: 2:10
- II. The second commission: Arise, go, proclaim: 3:1–10
  - A. Obedience: He arose, went, cried: 3:1–4
  - B. Results of obedience: 3:5–10
    - 1. The people believed: 3:5
    - 2. The people repented: 3:5–9
    - 3. The city was preserved: 3:10
- III. The prophet's problem: 4:1–11
  - A. Jonah's prayer: 4:1–3
  - B. God rebukes Jonah: 4:4–11

2. Helpful summaries of Jonah

Bird's eye view

God's prophet, Jonah, is sent on a mission to preach a message of repentance to Nineveh, the capital city of the cruel Assyrians.

Reading plan

The following reading plan, taking one reading per day, enables you to read through Jonah in two days.

Jonah 1–2

Jonah 3–4

Verse to memorize

Jonah 2:9

But I, with song of thanksgiving, will sacrifice to you. What I have vowed, I will make good. Salvation comes from the Lord.

Statistics

Thirty-second Old Testament book

4 chapters

48 verses

1,321 words

The book of Jonah contains more biographical information about the prophet than any other Old Testament prophetic book.

Names/titles given

Hebrew title: *Yonah:* "Dove."

Greek title in Septuagint: *Ionas:* "Jonah."

Latin title in Vulgate: *Jonas:* "Jonah."

3. Helpful keys to turn to in understanding Jonah

Key words

Preach

Arise and go

Key verses

Jonah 3:2; 4:2

Themes to study

- How can God bless the wicked?
- The link between Jonah and Jesus.
- Disobedience and obedience to God.

Jonah quoted in the New Testament

- For as Jonah was three days and three nights in the belly of a huge fish

  Jon. 1:17 quoted in Matt. 12:40

Jesus in Jonah

In Jonah Jesus is the Resurrection and Life.

Types of Jesus in Jonah

- Jesus likened himself to only one prophet: to Jonah, see Matt. 12:39–41.
- Jonah's experiences portray Jesus' burial, death, and resurrection.

Lessons to learn from Jonah

- Second, and successive changes are possible with God.
- People matter more than things.

4. Chapter by chapter: outline of every chapter of Jonah

Jonah 1

Matthew Henry's introduction

In this chapter we have,

I. A command given to Jonah to preach at Nineveh, vv. 1, 2.
II. Jonah's disobedience to that command, v. 3.
III. The pursuit and arrest of him for that disobedience by a storm, in which he was asleep, vv. 4–6.
IV. The discovery of him, and his disobedience, to be the cause of the storm, vv. 7–10.
V. The casting of him into the sea, for the stilling of the storm, vv. 11–16.
VI. The miraculous preservation of his life there in the belly of a fish (v. 17), which was his reservation for further services.

A detailed analysis of chapter

Jonah, sent to Nineveh, flees to Tarshish. (1–3)
He is caught in a storm at sea. (4–7)
His conversation with the sailors. (8–12)
He is thrown into the sea, and miraculously preserved. (13–17)

Key verse

Verse 1: "Now the word of the LORD came unto Jonah the son of Amittai."

Key word / key phrase

Verse 3, "Jonah ran away."

Key event / key person / key theme

Jonah is thrown overboard

Key thought

It is possible to run away from God's wishes, but not to evade them forever.

Key thing to look out for

God's plan B is always better than our own disobedience.

Key Bible cross-reference

Verse 17. See Matthew 12:40.

Key "by way of explanation"

Joppa (and Tarsish) are in the opposite direction to Nineveh. A probable date for the book of Jonah is after the ministries of Amos and Hosea, and before the fall of Israel and Samaria to Assyria in 722–721 BC.

Key "Quotable Quote"

"It will not do to say that you have no special call to go to China. With these facts before you and with the command of the Lord Jesus to go and preach the gospel to every creature, you need rather to ascertain whether you have a special call to stay at home."

James Hudson Taylor

Jonah 2

Matthew Henry's introduction

In this chapter God hears from him, for we find him praying; in the next Nineveh hears from him, for we find him preaching. In his prayer we have,

I. The great distress and danger he was in, vv. 2, 3, 5, 6.
II. The despair he was thereby almost reduced to, v. 4.

III. The encouragement he took to himself, in this deplorable condition, vv. 4, 7.

IV. The assurance he had of God's favor to him, vv. 6, 7.

V. The warning and instruction he gives to others, v. 8.

VI. The praise and glory of all given to God, v. 9. In the last verse we have Jonah's deliverance out of the belly of the fish, and his coming safe and sound on dry land again.

A detailed analysis of chapter

The prayer of Jonah. (1–9)

He is delivered from the fish. (10)

Key verse

Verse 10: "And the LORD spake unto the fish, and it vomited out Jonah upon the dry land."

Key word / key phrase

Verse 1, "From inside the fish Jonah prayed."

Key event / key person / key theme

Jonah prays from inside the great fish

Key thought

In desperate trouble, Jonah turned to the Lord in sincere prayer.

Key thing to look out for

Verse 2, "I called . . . he answered." This is thus Jonah's second prayer: a prayer of thanksgiving for answered prayer.

Key Bible cross-reference

Verse 3. See Psalm 88:6.

Key "by way of explanation"

Verse 3, "all your waves and breakers swept over me." The four Hebrew words which make up this sentence are also found in Psalm 42:7. Either Jonah was quoting the psalmist or the psalmist was quoting Jonah.

Key "Quotable Quote"

"I am convinced that the really great issues before us will be settled on our knees."

D.A. Carson

Jonah 3

Matthew Henry's introduction

In this chapter we have,

I. Jonah's mission renewed, and the command a second time given him to go preach at Nineveh, vv. 1, 2.

II. Jonah's message to Nineveh faithfully delivered, by which its speedy overthrow was threatened, vv. 3, 4.

III. The repentance, humiliation, and reformation of the Ninevites hereon, vv. 5–9.

IV. God's gracious revocation of the sentence passed on them, and the preventing of the ruin threatened, v. 10.

A detailed analysis of chapter

Jonah sent again to Nineveh, preaches there. (1–4)

Nineveh is spared as the inhabitants repent. (5–10)

Key verse

Verse 5: "So the people of Nineveh believed God, and proclaimed a fast, and put on sackcloth, from the greatest of them even to the least of them."

Key word / key phrase

Verse 2, "the great city of Nineveh."

Key event / key person / key theme

Jonah goes to Nineveh

Key thought

Witnessing should not be governed by the reaction that is expected.

Key thing to look out for

God always has compassion on people who repent.

Key Bible cross-reference

Verses 3, 4. See Matthew 12:41.

Key "by way of explanation"

Verse 10. "God had compassion," but previously had threatened his judgment on Nineveh. When people repent the Bible is never worried about saying that God shows mercy, and in this sense "changed his mind."

Key "Quotable Quote"

"Prayer is the midwife of mercy, that helps to bring it forth."

Matthew Henry

Jonah 4

Matthew Henry's introduction

Here is,

I. Jonah's repining at God's mercy to Nineveh, and the fret he was in about it, vv. 1–3.

II. The gentle reproof God gave him for it, v. 4.

III. Jonah's discontent at the withering of the gourd, and his justifying himself in that discontent, vv. 5–9.

IV. God's improving it for his conviction, that he ought not to be angry at the sparing of Nineveh, vv. 10–11. Man's badness and God's goodness serve here for a foil to each other, that the former may appear the more exceedingly sinful and the latter the more exceedingly gracious.

A detailed analysis of chapter

Jonah sulks because of God's mercy to Nineveh, and is reproved. (1–4)

He is taught by the withering of a gourd that he did wrong. (5–11)

Key verse

Verse 1: "But it displeased Jonah exceedingly, and he was very angry..

Key word / key phrase

Verse 11, "should I not be concerned?"

Key event / key person / key theme

God's pity for the people of Nineveh

Key thought

Some of the Lord's most faithful followers have also made Jonah's request: "take away my life," verse 3.

Key thing to look out for

God's provision takes many forms, some of them most unexpected.

Key Bible cross-reference

Verse 2. See Exodus 34:6.

Key "by way of explanation"

Verse 8, "a scorching east wind." This wind, known as the *sirocco*, was a particularly dry and hot wind which blew off the desert. It would have certainly increased Jonah's discomfort.

Key "Quotable Quote"

"Repentance must not be mistaken for remorse. It does not consist in feeling terribly sorry that things went wrong in the past; it is an active, positive attitude which consists in moving in the right direction."

Metropolitan Anthony of Sourozh

5. Select bibliography for Jonah

Achtemeier, Elizabeth. *Minor Prophets*, Vol. I, Hosea-Micah (NIBC), Hendrickson, 1996.

Aalders, G. *The Problem of the Book of Jonah*. London: Tyndale, 1948.

Allen, L. C. *The Books of Joel, Obadiah, Jonah and Micah*. Grand Rapids: Eerdmans, 1976, pp. 175–235.

Baker, D. W., Alexander, T. D. and Waltke, B. K. *Obadiah, Jonah, Micah* (Tyndale), InterVarsity, 1988.

Baldwin, Joyce. "Jonah" in The Minor Prophets, Vol. II (ed. T. McComiskey), Baker, 1993.

Ellison, H. L. *The Prophets of Israel*. Grand Rapids: Eerdmans, 1969.

Ellul, J. *The Judgment of Jonah*. Translated by G. W. Bromiley. Grand Rapids Eerdmans, 1971.

Gaebelein, F. E. *Four Minor Prophets*. Chicago: Moody, 1970.

Hugh, Martin. *Jonah* (Geneva), Banner of Truth, 1982.

Smith, G. A. *The Book of the Twelve Prophets*. 2 Vols. London Hodder & Stoughton, 1898.

Micah

1. Book by book: Introduction to Micah

Introduction

Micah was born in Moresheth, not the same as Mareshah in Mic. 1:15, but the town called Moresheth-gath (Mic. 1:14), which lay near Eleutheropolis, west of Jerusalem, on the border of the Philistine country; so called to distinguish it from Moresheth of Judah. His full name is Micaiah (not the Micaiah mentioned 1 Kings 22:8, the son of Imlah), signifying, Who is like Jehovah?

Date

The time of his prophesying is stated in the introduction to be in the reigns of Jotham, Ahaz, and Hezekiah, that is, between 757 and 699 B.C. Jeremiah (Jer. 26:18) quotes Mic. 3:12, as delivered in the reign of Hezekiah. He was thus a contemporary of Isaiah and Hosea. The idolatries practiced in the reign of Ahaz accord with Micah's denunciations of such gross evils, and confirm the truth of the time assigned Mic. 1:1. His prophecies are partly against Israel (Samaria), partly against Judah. As Samaria, Israel's metropolis, was taken first, and Jerusalem, the capital of Judah subsequently, in the introductory heading, Mic. 1:1, Samaria is put first, then Jerusalem. He prophesies the capture of both; the Jews' captivity and restoration; and the coming and reign of Messiah.

Style

His style is full, round, and perspicuous; his diction pure, and his parallelisms regular. His description of Jehovah (Mic. 7:18, 19) is not surpassed by any elsewhere in Scripture.

Isaiah and Micah

The similarity between Isaiah and Micah in some passages (compare Mic. 4:1–3, with Is. 2:2–4) is to be accounted for by their being contemporaries, acquainted with each other's inspired writings, and having the same subjects for their theme. Hengstenberg maintains that the passage in Micah is the original. Isaiah was somewhat the older, being a prophet in the reign of Uzziah, Jotham's predecessor, whereas Micah began his prophecies under Jotham.

Breakdown

The book consists of two parts:

(1) the first through fifth chapters;

(2) the sixth and seventh chapters, a dialogue or contestation between Jehovah and His people, in which He reproaches them with their unnatural and ungrateful conduct, and threatens judgment for their corruptions, but consoles them with the promise of restoration from captivity.

A.R. Faussett

Contents of Micah

Micah combats in his discourses, as does Isaiah, the heathenish abuses which had found their way into the cult, not only in Samaria, but also in Judah and Jerusalem, and which the reformation of Hezekiah could counteract only in part and not at all permanently (compare Micah 1:5–7; 5:11–13; 6:7, 16). Further, he rebukes them for the social injustice, of which particularly the powerful and the great in the land were guilty (Micah 2:1; 3:2–10); and the dishonesty and unfaithfulness in business and in conduct in general (compare Micah 6:10; 7:2). At all times Micah, in doing this, was compelled to defend himself against false prophets, who slighted these charges as of little importance, and threatened and antagonized the prophet in his announcements of impending evil (compare 2:5, 11). In pronounced opposition to these babblers and their predictions of good things, Micah announces the judgment through the enemies that are approaching, and he even goes beyond Isaiah in the open declaration that Jerusalem and the temple are to be destroyed (Micah 3:12; 4:10; 5:1). The first- mentioned passage is also confirmed by the event reported in Jeremiah 26:17. The passage Micah 4:10, where in a surprising way Babylon is mentioned as the place of the exile, is for this reason regarded as unauthentic by the critics, but not justly. Micah predicts also the deliverance from Babylon and the reestablishment of Israel in Jerusalem, and declares that this is to take place through a King who shall come forth from the deepest humiliation of the house of David and shall be born in Bethlehem, and who, like David, originally a simple shepherd boy, shall later become the shepherd of the people, and shall make his people happy in peace and prosperity. Against this King the last great onslaught of the Gentiles will avail nothing (4:11–13; 5:4). As a matter of course, he will purify the country of all heathen abuses (5:9). In the description of this ruler, Micah again agrees with Isaiah, but without taking the details from that prophet.

Orr, James, M.A., D.D. General Editor, International Standard Bible Encyclopedia

Detailed outline

- I. Introduction: 1:1
- II. General prophecy of judgment: 1:2–2:13
  - A. Judgment against Samaria: 1:2–8
    - 1. Announcement of judgment: 1:2–4
    - 2. Destruction of Samaria: 1:2–8
  - B. Judgment against Judah: 1:9–16
  - C. Judgment on oppressors: 2:1–11
    - 1. Arrogance and violence of the nobles: 2:1–5
    - 2. False prophets who would silence the true prophets: 2:6–11
  - D. Mercy on a remnant: 2:12–13
- III. The establishment of the Messianic Kingdom: 3:1–5:15
  - A. Judgment on wicked rulers, false prophets, and the nations: 3:1–12
    - 1. ins of the civil rulers: 3:1–4
    - 2. Sins of the false prophets: 3:5–8
    - 3. Rulers, prophets, and priests: 3:9–11
  - B. Character of the Kingdom: 4:1–5
  - C. Setting up the Kingdom: 4:6–13
    - 1. Restoration of the former dominion: 4:6–8
    - 2. Into Babylon before restoration: 4:9–10
    - 3. Deliverance of Zion and destruction of the enemy: 4:11–5:1
  - D. The first advent and rejection of the King: 5:1–2
  - E. The interval between the King's rejection and return: 5:3
  - F. Events on His return: 5:4–15
    - 1. He will provide food for the flock: 5:4
    - 2. He will be peace of His people: 5:5–6
    - 3. He will provide power to His people: 5:7–9
      - (a) The remnant as dew: 5:7
      - (b) The remnant as a lion: 5:8
      - (c) The remnant triumphant: 5:9–15
- IV. The Lord's problem with His people and His final mercy: 6:1–7:20
  - A. The people's ingratitude and wickedness: 6:1–7:6

1. Ingratitude for blessings: 6:1–5
2. Righteous conduct, not outward sacrifice: 6:6–8
3. God's threat of judgment: 6:9–14

B. The promise of final salvation: 7:7–20

2. Helpful summaries of Micah

Bird's eye view

The prophet Micah directs his prophecies against the prevailing corruption in society and among the religious leaders of both Israel and Judah.

Reading plan

The following reading plan, taking one reading per day, enables you to read through Micah in two days.

Micah 1–4

Micah 5–7

Verses to memorize

Micah 6:8

And what does the Lord require of you? To act justly and to love mercy and to walk humbly with God.

Micah 7:7

Therefore I will look unto the Lord; I will wait for the God of my salvation: my God will hear me. KJV

Micah 7:19

He will turn again, he will have compassion on us; he will subdue our iniquities; and thou wilt cast all their sins into the depths of the sea. KJV

Statistics

Thirty-third Old Testament book

7 chapters

105 verses

3,153 words

Names/titles given

Hebrew title: *Michayahu/Michaia:* "Who is like God?"

Greek title in Septuagint: *Michaias:* "Micah."

Latin title in Vulgate: *Micha:* "Micah."

3. Helpful keys to turn to in understanding Micah

Key word

Hear

Key verses

Micah 1:2; 6:8

Themes to study

Hope and justice

The necessity of social justice.

Micah quoted in the Old Testament

The elders quoted Micah 3:12, in Jeremiah 26:16–19, and so saved Jeremiah's life.

Micah quoted in the New Testament

And thou Bethlehem, land of Judah,
Art in no wise least among the princes of Judah

Mic. 5:2 was quoted by the Sanhedrin to Herod the Great, about the time of Jesus' birth, in Matt. 2:6.

For I came to set a man at variance against his father

Mic. 7:6 quoted in Matt. 10:35–36

Jesus in Micah

In Micah Jesus is the promised Messiah.

Types of Jesus in Micah

- Jesus' birthplace is prophesied, 5:2; see Matt. 2:5–6.
- Jesus will usher in a reign of righteousness, 2:12–13; 4:1–8; 5:4–5.

Lessons to learn from Micah

- God hates shallow religion.
- God loves justice and kindness in every walk of life, including business life.

4. Chapter by chapter: outline of every chapter of Micah

Micah 1

Matthew Henry's introduction

In this chapter we have,

I. The title of the book (v. 1) and a preface demanding attention, v. 2.

II. Warning given of desolating judgments hastening on the kingdoms of Israel and Judah (vv. 3, 4), and all for sin, v. 5.

III. The particulars of the destruction specified, vv. 6, 7.

IV. The greatness of the destruction illustrated,

A. By the prophet's sorrow for it, vv. 8, 9.

B. By the general sorrow that should be for it, in the several places that must expect to share in it, vv. 10–16. These prophecies of Micah might well be called his lamentations.

A detailed analysis of chapter

The wrath of God against Israel. (1–7)

Also against Jerusalem and other cities, and the precautions they take in vain. (8–16)

Key verse

Verse 1: "The word of the LORD that came to Micah the Morasthite in the days of Jotham, Ahaz, and Hezekiah, kings of Judah, which he saw concerning Samaria and Jerusalem."

Key word / key phrase

Verse 1, "vision."

Key event / key person / key theme

Samaria will be destroyed; the enemy approaches Jerusalem

Key thought

Idolatry is again mentioned. It kept on leading people away from God.

Key thing to look out for

Repentance and mourning is the order of the day.

Key Bible cross-reference

Verse 1. See 2 Kings 15:32–16:20.

Key "by way of explanation"

Verse 13 "Lachish," a border town and one of Judah's largest towns. It received its chariots and horses from Egypt. Micah was a contemporary of Isaiah and Hosea. He preached to the northern kingdom.

Key "Quotable Quote"

"All sin is against God, and for that reason he who truly grieves for his own sin will grieve for other men's too."

Ralph Venning

Micah 2

Matthew Henry's introduction

In this chapter we have,

I. The sins with which the people of Israel are charged–covetousness and oppression, fraudulent and violent practices (vv. 1, 2), dealing barbarously, even with women and children, and other harmless people, vv. 8, 9. Opposition of God's prophets and silencing them (vv. 6, 7), and delighting in false prophets, v. 11.

II. The judgments with which they are threatened for those sins, that they should be humbled, and impoverished (vv. 3–5), and banished, v. 10.

III. Gracious promises of comfort, reserved for the good people among them, in the Messiah, vv. 12, 13. And this is the sum and scope of most of the chapters of this and other prophecies.

A detailed analysis of chapter

The sins and desolations of Israel. (1–5)

Their evil practices. (6–11)

A promise of restoration. (12,13)

Key verse

Verse 6: "Prophesy ye not, say they to them that prophesy: they shall not prophesy to them, that they shall not take shame."

Key word / key phrase

Verse 2, "defraud a man of his home."

Key event / key person / key theme

The corruption and greed of the rich

Key thought

Note the timelessness of Micah's message. These conditions still prevail in the world today.

Key thing to look out for

The message of false prophets and false teachers often sounds very plausible.

Key Bible cross-reference

Verse 1. See Isaiah 29:20.

Key "by way of explanation"

Verse 2, "They covet fields and seize them." They not only buy up land which came on the open market but they stole fields that belonged to poor families who could not stop them.

Key "Quotable Quote"

"Any religion that professes to be concerned with the souls of men and is not concerned with the slums that damn them, the economic conditions that strangle them, and the social conditions that cripple them, is a dry-as-dust religion."

Martin Luther King, Jr.

Micah 3

Matthew Henry's introduction

Magistracy and ministry are two great ordinances of God, for good to his church, but these were both corrupted and the intentions of them perverted; and on those that abused them, and so abused the church with them, the prophet is very severe, and justly so.

I. He gives them their lesson severally, reproving and threatening princes (vv. 1–4) and false flattering prophets, vv. 5–7.

II. He gives them their lesson jointly, putting them together, as acting in conjunction for the ruin of the kingdom, which they should see the ruins of, vv. 9–12.

A detailed analysis of chapter

The cruelty of the princes. The false prophets. (1–8)

Their false security. (9–12)

Key verse

Verse 8: "But truly I am full of power by the spirit of the LORD, and of judgment, and of might, to declare unto Jacob his transgression, and to Israel his sin."

Key word / key phrase

Verse 3, "Listen, you leaders of Jacob."

Key event / key person / key theme

The leaders are judged.

Key thought

Verse 8, a description of a genuine spiritual leader

Key thing to look out for

Verse 4. Jesus also warned that some people may cry out to the Lord and be turned away (Matthew 7:21).

Key Bible cross-reference

Verse 12. See Jeremiah 26:18.

Key "by way of explanation"

Verse 3, "who eat my people's flesh." These leaders live in such an evil way that they are no better than cannibals. This is not meant to be taken literally but as a description of their dreadful behavior.

Key "Quotable Quote"

"True greatness, true leadership, is achieved not by reducing men to one's service but in giving oneself in selfless service to them."

Oswald Sanders

Micah 4

Matthew Henry's introduction

Comparing this chapter with the close of the previous chapter, the comfortable promises here with the terrible threatenings there, we may, with the apostle, "behold the goodness and severity of God," (Rom. 11:22), towards the Jewish church which fell, severity when Zion was ploughed as a field, but towards the Christian church, which was built on the ruins of it, goodness, great goodness; for it is here promised,

I. That it shall be advanced and enlarged by the accession of the nations to it, vv. 1, 2.

II. That it shall be protected in tranquility and peace, vv. 3, 4.

III. That it shall be kept close, and constant, and faithful to God, v. 5.
IV. That under Christ's government, all its grievances shall be redressed, vv. 6, 7.
V. That it shall have an ample and flourishing dominion, v. 8.
VI. That its troubles shall be brought to a happy issue at length, vv. 9, 10.
VII. That its enemies shall be disquieted, nay, that they shall be destroyed in and by their attempts against it, vv. 11–13.

A detailed analysis of chapter

The peace of the kingdom of Christ. (1–8)
The judgments to come on Jerusalem, but the final triumph of God's people. (9–13)

Key verse

Verse 5: "For all people will walk every one in the name of his god, and we will walk in the name of the LORD our God for ever and ever."

Key word / key phrase

Verse 6, "I will assemble the exiles."

Key event / key person / key theme

The Lord's future reign, and the return from exile

Key thought

God always has a positive plan, no matter how desperate the situation.

Key thing to look out for

God always wants to bless his people.

Key Bible cross-reference

Verse 3. See Joel 3:10.

Key "by way of explanation"

Verses 1,2, "let us go up to the mountain of the Lord. . . . He will teach us." Jerusalem would become the pre-eminent place where people would be taught about God's revelation.

Key "Quotable Quote"

"I was more convinced than ever that preaching like an Apostle, without joining together those that are awakened and training them up in the ways of God, is only begetting children for the murderer."

John Wesley

Micah 5

Matthew Henry's introduction

In this chapter we have,

I. A prediction of the troubles and distresses of the Jewish nation, v. 1.
II. A promise of the Messiah, and of his kingdom, to support the people of God in the day of these troubles.
  A. Of the birth of the Messiah, vv. 2, 3.
  B. Of his advancement, v. 4.
  C. Of his protection of his people, and his victory over his and their enemies, vv. 5, 6.
  D. Of the great world by it, v. 7.
  E. Of the destruction of the enemies of the church, both those without, that attack it, and those within, that expose it, vv. 8–15.

A detailed analysis of chapter

The birth of Christ and conversion of the Gentiles. (1–6)

Deliverance of the remnant and destruction of idolatry. (7–15)

Key verse

Verse 2: "But thou, Bethlehem Ephratah, though thou be little among the thousands of Judah, yet out of thee shall he come forth unto me that is to be ruler in Israel; whose goings forth have been from of old, from everlasting."

Key word / key phrase

Verse 5, "he will be their peace."

Key event / key person / key theme

The promise about the coming King

Key thought

Bethlehem was only a small town, but important because it was chosen by God.

Key thing to look out for

Deliverance and destruction are both attributed to God's power.

Key Bible cross-reference

Verse 2. See Matthew 2:6.

Key "by way of explanation"

Verse 3, "abandoned until . . . she . . . gives birth." Israel will be handed over to her enemies, but only temporarily. When the Messiah is born; God's family will be reunited.

Key "Quotable Quote"

"Bethlehem and Golgotha, the Manger and the Cross, the birth and the death, must always be seen together, if the real Christmas is to survive."

J. Sidlow Baxter

Micah 6

Matthew Henry's introduction

Here,

I. God enters an action against his people for their base ingratitude, and the bad returns they had made him for his favors, vv. 1–5.

II. He shows the wrong course they should have taken, vv. 6–8.

III. He calls on them to hear the voice of his judgments, and sets the sins in order before them for which he still proceeded in his controversy with them (v. 9), their injustice (vv. 10–15), and their idolatry (v. 16), for both which ruin was coming on them.

A detailed analysis of chapter

God's controversy with Israel. (1–5)

The duties God requires. (6–8)

The wickedness of Israel. (9–16)

Key verse

Verse 8: "He hath showed thee, O man, what is good; and what doth the LORD require of thee, but to do justly, and to love mercy, and to walk humbly with thy God?"

Key word / key phrase

Verse 8, "what does the Lord require of you?"

Key event / key person / key theme

The Lord pleads for repentance

Key thought

Verse 8 sums up how all God's followers should live.

Key thing to look out for

Being unfaithful to God is a most fearful prospect.

Key Bible cross-reference

Verse 4. See Exodus 4:10–16.

Key "by way of explanation"

Verse 5, "Balaam," had been asked to curse Balak's enemies but he blessed them three times.

Key "Quotable Quote"

"You will never make yourself feel that you are a sinner, because there is a mechanism in you as a result of sin which will always be defending you against every accusation. We are all on very good terms with ourselves, and we can always put up a good case for ourselves even if we try to make ourselves feel that we are sinners; we will never do it. There is only one way to know that we are sinners, and that is to have some dim, glimmering conception of God."

D. Martyn Lloyd-Jones

Micah 7

Matthew Henry's introduction

In this chapter,

I. The prophet, in the name of the church, sadly laments the woeful decay of religion in the age in which he lived, and the deluge of impiety and immorality which overwhelmed the nation, which leveled the differences, and bore down the fences, of all that is just and sacred, vv. 1–6.

II. The prophet, for the sake of the church, prescribes comforts, which may be of use at such a time, and gives counsel what to do.

A. They must have an eye to God, v. 7.

B. They must courageously bear up against the insolences of the enemy, vv. 8–10.

C. They must patiently lie down under the rebukes of their God, v. 9.

D. They must expect no other than that the trouble would continue long, and must endeavor to make the best of it, vv. 11–13.

E. They must encourage themselves with God's promises, in answer to the prophet's prayers, vv. 14, 15.

F. They must foresee the fall of their enemies, that now triumphed over them, vv. 16, 17.

G. They must themselves triumph in the mercy and grace of God, and his faithfulness to his covenant (vv. 18–20), and with that comfortable word the prophecy concludes.

A detailed analysis of chapter

The general prevalence of wickedness. (1–7)

Reliance on God, and triumph over enemies. (8–13)

Promises and encouragements for Israel. (14–20)

Key verse

Verse 7: "Therefore I will look unto the LORD; I will wait for the God of my salvation: my God will hear me."

Key word / key phrase

Verse 18, "who pardons sin."

Key event / key person / key theme

The promise of final salvation

Key thought

Micah thanked God for his past mercies.

Key thing to look out for

Micah's prayer shows how much he appreciated all that God had done.

Key Bible cross-reference

Verse 6. See Luke 12:53.

Key "by way of explanation"

Verse 8, "Though I have fallen." This is Micah looking forward to the future even though he writes as if the event, the destruction of Jerusalem in 586 BC, had already taken place.

Key "Quotable Quote"

"If any one would tell you the shortest, surest way to all happiness and all perfection, he must tell you to make it a rule to yourself to thank and praise God for everything that happens to you."

William Law

5. Select bibliography for Micah

Achtemeier, Elizabeth. *Minor Prophets*, Vol. I, Hosea-Micah (NIBC), Hendrickson, 1996.

Allen, Leslie. *The Books of Joel, Obadiah, Jonah, and Micah* (NICOT), Eerdmans, 1994.

Baker, D. W., Alexander, T. D. and Waltke, B. K. *Obadiah, Jonah, Micah* (Tyndale), InterVarsity, 1988.

Hailey, H. *A Commentary on the Minor Prophets*. Grand Rapids: Baker, 1972.

Kaiser, Walter. *Micah, Nahum, Habakkuk, Zephaniah, Haggai, Zechariah, Malachi* (Mastering the Old Testament), Word Books, 1992.

Keil, C. F. *The Twelve Minor Prophets*. KD. Vol. 1. Grand Rapids: Eerdmans, 1949.

Smith, Ralph L. *Micah-Malachi*, (Word Biblical Commentary, 32), Word Books, 1984.

Nahum

1. Book by book: Introduction to Nahum

Introduction

Nahum means "consolation" and "vengeance"; symbolizing the "consolation" in the book for God's people, and the "vengeance" coming on their enemies. In the first chapter the two themes alternate; but as the prophet advances, vengeance on the capital of the Assyrian foe is the predominant topic. He is called "the Elkoshite" (Nah. 1:1), from Elkosh, or Elkesi, a village of Galilee, pointed out to Jerome as a place of note among the Jews, having traces of ancient buildings. The name Capernaum, that is, "village of Nahum," seems to take its name from Nahum having resided in it, though born in Elkosh in the neighborhood. There is another Elkosh east of the Tigris, and north of Mosul, believed by Jewish pilgrims to be the birthplace and burial place of the prophet. But the book of Nahum in its allusions shows a particularity of acquaintance with Palestine (Nah. 1:4), and only a more general knowledge as to Nineveh (Nah. 2:4–6; 3:2, 3).

His graphic description of Sennacherib and his army (Nah. 1:9–12) makes it not unlikely that he was in or near Jerusalem at the time: hence the number of phrases corresponding to those of Isaiah (compare Nah. 1:8, 9, with Is. 8:8; 10:23; Nah. 2:10, with Is. 24:1; 21:3; Nah. 1:15, with Is. 52:7). The prophecy in Nah. 1:14 probably refers to the murder of Sennacherib twenty years after his return from Palestine (Is. 37:38). The date of his prophecies, thus, seems to be about the former years of Hezekiah. So Jerome thinks. He plainly writes while the Assyrian power was yet unbroken (Nah. 1:12; 2:11–13 Nah. 3:15–17).

Nahum and Isaiah and Hezekiah

The similarity between the sentiments of Nahum and those of Isaiah and Hezekiah, as recorded in Second Kings and Isaiah, proves the likelihood of Nahum's prophecies belonging to the time when Sennacherib was demanding the surrender of Jerusalem, and had not yet raised the siege (compare Nah. 1:2, etc., with 2 Kings 19:14, 15; Nah. 1:7, with 2 Kings 18:22; 19:19, 31; 2 Chr. 32:7, 8; Nah. 1:9, 11, with 2 Kings 19:22, 27, 28; Nah. 1:14, with 2 Kings 19:6, 7; Nah. 1:15; 2:1, 2, with 2 Kings 19:32, 33; Nah. 2:13, with 2 Kings 19:22, 23).

Historical background

The historical data in the book itself are the humiliation of Israel and Judah by Assyria (Nah. 2:2); the invasion of Judah (Nah. 1:9, 11); and the conquest of No-ammon, or Thebes, in Upper Egypt (Nah. 3:8–10). Tiglath-pileser and Shalmaneser had carried away Israel. The Jews were harassed by the Syrians, and impoverished by Ahaz' payments to Tiglath-pileser (2 Chr. 28:1–27; Is. 7:9). Sargon, Shalmaneser's successor, after the reduction of Phœnicia by the latter, fearing lest Egypt should join Palestine against him, undertook an expedition to Africa (Is. 20:1–6), and took Thebes; the latter fact we know only from Nahum, but the success of the expedition in general is corroborated in Is. 20:1–6. Sennacherib, Sargon's successor, made the last Assyrian attempt against Judea, ending in the destruction of his army in the fourteenth year of Hezekiah (713–710 B.C.). As Nahum refers to this in part prophetically, in part as matter of history (Nah. 1:9–13; 2:13), he must have lived about 720–714 B.C., that is, almost a hundred years before the event foretold, namely, the overthrow of Nineveh by the joint forces of Cyaxares and Nabopolassar in the reign of Chyniladanus, 625 or 603 B.C.

Purpose of prophecy

The prophecy is remarkable for its unity of aim. Nahum's object was to inspire his countrymen, the Jews, with the assurance that, however alarming their position might seem, exposed to the attacks of the mighty Assyrian, who had already carried away the ten tribes, yet that not only should the Assyrian (Sennacherib) fail in his attack on Jerusalem, but Nineveh, his own capital, be taken and his empire overthrown; and this, not by an arbitrary exercise of Jehovah's power, but for the iniquities of the city and its people.

Canon

His position in the canon is seventh of the minor prophets in both the Hebrew and Greek arrangement. He is seventh in point of date.

Style

His style is clear, elegant, and forcible. Its most striking characteristic is the power of representing several phases of an idea in the briefest sentences, as in the majestic description of God in the commencement, the conquest of Nineveh, and the destruction of No-ammon (Eichorn). De Wette calls attention to his variety of manner in presenting ideas, as marking great poetic talent. "Here there is something sonorous in his language there something murmuring; with both these alternates something that is soft, delicate, and melting, as the subject demands." Excepting two alleged Assyrian words (Nah. 3:17), English Version, "crowned," or princes, and English Version, "captains," or satraps (used by Jer. 51:27), the language is pure. These two, doubtless, came to be known in Judea from the links with Assyria in the eighth and seventh centuries B.C.

A.R. Faussett

Contents of Nahum

Nahum is the prophet of Nineveh's doom. Nahum 1 (plus 2:2) contains the decree of Nineveh's destruction. Yahweh is a God of vengeance and of mercy (1:2,3); though He may at times appear slack in punishing iniquity, He will surely punish the sinner. No one can stand before Him in the day of judgment (1:4–6). Yahweh, faithful to those who rely upon Him (1:7), will be terrible toward His enemies and toward the enemies of His people (1:8). Judah need not fear: the present enemy is doomed (1:9–14), which will mean the exaltation of Judah (1:15; 2:2). The army appointed to carry out the decree is approaching, ready for battle (2:1–4). All efforts to save the city are in vain; it falls (2:5,6), the queen and her attendants are captured (2:7), the inhabitants flee (2:8), the city is sacked and left a desolation (2:9–13). The destruction of the bloody city is imminent (3:1–3); the fate is well deserved and no one will bemoan her (3:4–7); natural strength and resources will avail nothing (3:8–11); the soldiers turn cowards and the city will be utterly cut off (3:12–18); the whole earth will rejoice over the downfall of the cruel oppressor (3:19).

Orr, James, M.A., D.D. General Editor, International Standard Bible Encyclopedia

Detailed outline

I. Prophecy of destruction, part one: 1:1–14
  A. Introduction: 1:1
  B. Source of destruction: God Himself: 1:2–9
    1. Vengeance and God's mercy: 1:2–3
    2. His terrible anger against sin: 1:4–6
    3. The greatness of His mercy: 1:7
    4. The pursuer of His enemies: 1:8
  C. Reason for destruction: Sin: 1:9–14
    1. God's faithfulness in the present crisis: 1:9–11
    2. Destruction of Assyria: 1:12–14
    3. Rejoicing in Zion: 1:15
II. Promise to Judah: They no longer need fear this cruel nation: 1:15
III. Prophecy of destruction, part two: 2:1–3:19
  A. The siege and destruction of the city: 2:3–13
    1. Assault on Ninevah: Doom of the city: 2:1–7
      (a) Furious preparation for battle: 2:1–4
      (b) Hopelessness of resistance: 2:5–6
      (c) The city as a queen is captured: 2:7
    2. Flight of the people and spoiling of the city: 2:8–13
      (a) The inhabitants flee: 2:8–10
      (b) The destruction is complete: 2:11–13
  B. Reasons for Ninevah's fall: 3:1–9
    1. Description of the battle: 3:1–3
    2. The cause: Her sins: 3:1–6,16,19
    3. The uncovering of her shame is of God: 3:5–7
  C. Comparison of Nineveh to No Amon: 3:8–11
  D. Inability of Ninevah to save the city: 3:12–19
    1. Fall of outlying strongholds: 3:12–13
    2. Siege and destructions of the city: 3:14–19a
    3. Universal joy over the fall of Ninevah: 3:19b

2. Helpful summaries of Nahum

Bird's eye view

To a casual observer Nineveh appeared to be indestructible. But Nahum warms the city that it will be brought low by God's judgment.

Reading plan

The following reading plan, taking one reading per day, enables you to read through Nahum in one day.

Nahum 1–3

Verse to memorize

Nahum 1:7

The Lord is good, a refuge in times of trouble. He cares for those who trust in him.

Statistics

Thirty-fourth Old Testament book
3 chapters
47 verses
1,285 words

Names/titles given

Hebrew title: *nahum:* "Comfort/consoltion."

Greek title in Septuagint: *Naoum:* "Nahum."
Latin title in Vulgate: *Nahum.*

3. Helpful keys to turn to in understanding Nahum

Key word/words
Jealous

Key verse/verses
Nahum 1:2; 3:5–7

Themes to study
The Lord's jealousy
God's judgment
God's care for everyone

Jesus in Nahum
In Nahum is our Fortress in the day of disaster.

Lessons to learn from Nahum
Everyone is answerable to God.

4. Chapter by chapter: outline of every chapter of Nahum

Nahum 1

Matthew Henry's introduction
In this chapter we have,

I. The inscription of the book, v. 1.

II. A magnificent display of the glory of God, in a mixture of wrath and justice against the wicked, and mercy and grace towards his people, and the discovery of his majesty and power in both, vv. 2–8.

III. A particular application of this (as most interpreters think) to the destruction of Sennacherib and the Assyrian army, when they besieged Jerusalem, which was a very memorable and illustrious instance of the power both of God's justice and of his mercy, and spoke abundance of terror to his enemies and encouragement to his faithful servants, vv. 9–16.

A detailed analysis of chapter
The justice and power of the Lord. (1–8)
The overthrow of the Assyrians. (9–15)

Key verse
Verse 2: "God is jealous, and the LORD revengeth; the LORD revengeth, and is furious; the LORD will take vengeance on his adversaries, and he reserveth wrath for his enemies."

Key word / key phrase
Verse 2, "The Lord is jealous."

Key event / key person / key theme
A portrait of God

Key thought
If we did not sin we would not have to be confronted with God's righteous reaction to it.

Key thing to look out for
Verse 7 deserves to be meditated upon.

Key Bible cross-reference
Verse 15. See Isaiah 52:7.

Key "by way of explanation"

Verse 13, "I will break their yoke." Judah was ruled by Assyria. But this is a promise that in the future the Assyrian yoke around Judah's neck will be broken and Judah will be free. Nineveh fell to Babylon in 612 BC. Thebes, described as already conquered (3:10) was taken in 663. Therefore, it is probable that Nahum gave his prophecy between these two dates.

Key "Quotable Quote"

"It is only the doctrine of the wrath of God, of his irreconcilable hostility to all evil, which makes human life tolerable in such a world as ours."

Stephen Neill

Nahum 2

Matthew Henry's introduction

Here is foretold,

I. The approach of the enemy that should destroy Nineveh, and the terror of his military preparations, vv. 1–5.

II. The taking of the city, v. 6.

III. The captivity of the queen, the flight of the inhabitants, the seizing of all its wealth, and the great consternation it should be in, vv. 7–10.

IV. All this is traced up to its true causes–their sinning against God and God's appearing against them, vv. 11–13.

A detailed analysis of chapter

Nineveh's destruction foretold. (1–10)

The real reason, their sinning against God, and his appearing against them. (11–13)

Key verse

Verse 6: "The gates of the rivers shall be opened, and the palace shall be dissolved."

Key word / key phrase

Verse 1, "An attacker advances against you, Nineveh."

Key event / key person / key theme

Nineveh's destruction described

Key thought

God's enemies are no match for God's power.

Key thing to look out for

Spiritual renewal is a gift from God.

Key Bible cross-reference

Verse 1. See Jeremiah 51:20.

Key "by way of explanation"

Verse 13, "I will burn up." The prophecy states that Nineveh's fall will not simply be due to weapons of war but because the Lord God himself has stepped in.

Key "Quotable Quote"

"I believe, that, being fallen in Adam, my first father, I am by nature a child of wrath, under the condemnation of God and corrupted in body and soul, prone to evil and liable to eternal death."

Benjamin B. Warfield

Nahum 3

Matthew Henry's introduction

This chapter goes on with the burden of Nineveh, and concludes it.

I. The sins of that great city are charged on it, murder (v. 1), whoredom and witchcraft (v. 4), and a general extent of wickedness, v. 19.

II. Judgments are here threatened against it, blood for blood (vv. 2, 3), and shame for shameful sins, vv. 5–7.

III. Instances are given of the like desolations brought on other places for the like sins, vv. 8–11.

IV. The overthrow of all those things which they depended on, and put confidence in, is foretold, vv. 12–19.

A detailed analysis of chapter

The sins and judgments of Nineveh. (1–7)

Its utter destruction. (8–19)

Key verse

Verse 1: "Woe to the bloody city! it is all full of lies and robbery; the prey departeth not."

Key word / key phrase

Verse 5, "I am against you."

Key event / key person / key theme

Nineveh's destruction is deserved

Key thought

God makes no mistakes in his judgments.

Key thing to look out for

Evil will not win.

Key Bible cross-reference

Verse 1. See Ezekiel 22:2.

Key "by way of explanation"

Verse 19, "your injury is fatal." Nineveh will be so overrun that she could not be rebuilt. A few centuries after this prophecy, all that was left of Nineveh was under wind-blown sand.

Key "Quotable Quote"

"No sin, but the sin of final impenitence, can prove a man reprobate."

John Bunyan

5. Select bibliography for Nahum

Kaiser, Walter. *Micah, Nahum, Habakkuk, Zephaniah, Haggai, Zechariah, Malachi* (Mastering the Old Testament), Word Books, 1992.

Keil, C. F. *The Twelve Minor Prophets*. KD. Vol. 1. Grand Rapids: Eerdmans, 1949.

Elizabeth Achtemeier, Nahum-Malachi (Interpretation), Westminster John Knox, 1986.

Baker, Nahum, David W. *Habakkuk, Zephaniah* (Tyndale), Inter-Varsity, 1988.

F. F. Bruce "Habakkuk" in The Minor Prophets, Vol. II, (ed. T. McComisky), Baker, 1993.

Kaiser, Walter. *Micah, Nahum, Habakkuk, Zephaniah, Haggai, Zechariah, Malachi* (Mastering the Old Testament), Word Books, 1992.

Smith, Ralph L. *Micah-Malachi*, (Word Biblical Commentary, 32), Word Books, 1984.

Habakkuk

1. Book by book: Introduction to Habakkuk

Introduction

Habakkuk, from a Hebrew root meaning to "embrace," denoting a "favorite" (namely, of God) and a "struggler" (for his country's good). Some ancient authors represent him as belonging to the tribe of Levi; others (*Pseudo Epiphanius*), to that of Simeon. The inscription to Bel and the dragon in the Septuagint asserts the former; and Hab. 3:19 perhaps favors this. Eusebius (*Ecclesiastical History,* 7.29) states that in his time Habakkuk's tomb was shown at Celia in Palestine.

Date

The time seems to have been about 610 b.c. For the Chaldeans attacked Jerusalem in the ninth month of the fifth year of Jehoiakim, 605 B.C. (2 Kings 24:1; 2 Chr. 36:6; Jer. 46:2; 36:9). And Habakkuk (Hab. 1:5, 6, etc.) speaks of the Chaldeans as about to invade Judah, but not as having actually done so. In the second chapter he proceeds to comfort his people by foretelling the humiliation of their conquerors, and that the vision will soon have its fulfillment. In the third chapter the prophet in a sublime ode celebrates the deliverances wrought by Jehovah for His people in times past, as the ground of assurance, notwithstanding all their existing calamities, that He will deliver them again. Hab. 3:16 shows that the invader is still coming, and not yet arrived; so that the whole refers to the invasion in Jehoiakim's times, not those under Jehoiachin and Zedekiah. The Apocryphal appendix to Daniel states that he lived to see the Babylonian exile (588 B.C.), which accords with his prophesying early in Jehoiakim's reign, about 610 B.C.

Position in Old Testament

The position of the book immediately after Nahum is appropriate; as Nahum treated of the judgments of the Lord on Assyria, for its violence against Israel, so Habakkuk, those inflicted by, and on, the Chaldeans for the same reason.

Style

The style is poetical and sublime. The parallelisms are generally regular. Borrowed ideas occur (compare Hab. 3:19, with Ps. 18:33; Hab. 2:6, with Is. 14:4; Hab. 2:14, with Is. 11:9).

Habakkuk and the New Testament

The ancient catalogues imply that his book is part of the canon of Scripture. In the New Testament,

Rom. 1:17 quotes Hab. 2:4 (though not naming him); compare also Gal. 3:11; Heb. 10:38. Acts 13:40, 41 quotes Hab. 1:5. One or two Hebrew words peculiar to Habakkuk occur (Hab. 1:9; 2:6, 16).

A.R. Faussett

John Calvin's introduction to Habakkuk

The substance of the Book may be thus stated: – In the First chapter he complains of the rebellious obstinacy of the people, and deplores the corruptions which then prevailed; he then appears as the herald of God, and warns the Jews of their approaching ruin; he afterwards applies consolation, as God would punish the Chaldeans when their pride became intolerable. In the second chapter he exhorts the godly to patience by his own example, and speaks at large of the near ruin of Babylon; and in the third chapter he turns to supplication and prayer.

John Calvin

Detailed outline

I. Topic sentence: 1:1
II. Habakkuk's first complaint: 1:2–4
 A. The prophet's questions: 1:2–3a
 B. The moral and civil conditions of Judah: 1:3b
 C. The prophet's conclusions: 1:4
III. The Lord's reply: 1:5–11
 A. The marvelous work announced: 1:5
 B. The Chaldeans and their might: 1:6–11
IV. Habakkuk's confidence in the Lord: 1:12
V. Habakkuk's second complaint: 1:13–17
VI. The waiting prophet: 2:1
VII. The Lord's answer: 2:2–4
 A. The vision to be written plainly: 2:2
 B. The vision surely to come: 2:3
 C. The vision: 2:4
VIII. The five woes: 2:5–19
 A. Introduction: 2:5–6a
 B. The five woes on the Chaldeans: 2:6b-19
  1. The first woe: 2:6b-8
  2. The second woe: 2:9–11
  3. The third woe: 2:12–13 (Earth filled with the knowledge of the Lord: 2:14)
  4. The fourth woe: 2:15–18
  5. The fifth woe: 2:19
IX. Habakkuk's psalm: 3:1–19
 A. The title: 2:1
 B. The plea: 3:2
 C. The Lord's answer: 3:3–15
 D. Habakkuk's response: 3:16–19a
 E. The musical ascription: 3:19b

2. Helpful summaries of Habakkuk

Bird's eye view

The prophet Habakkuk voices a number of questions that trouble him, about the wicked prospering while the righteous are afflicted.

Reading plan

The following reading plan, taking one reading per day, enables you to read through Habakkuk in one day.

Habakkuk 1–3

Verses to memorize

Habakkuk 2:4

. . . the righteous will live by his faith.

Habakkuk 3:19

The sovereign Lord is my strength; he makes my feet like the feet of a deer, he enables me to go on the heights.

Statistics

Thirty-fifth Old Testament book

3 chapters

56 verses

1,476 words

Names/titles given

Hebrew title: *Habaqquq:* "One who embraces."

Greek title in Septuagint: *Ambabouk:* "Habakkuk."

Latin title in Vulgate: *Habacuc:* "Habakkuk."

3. Helpful keys to turn to in understanding Habakkuk

Key word

Faith

Key verses

Habakkuk 2:4; 3:17–18

Themes to study

God's characteristics mentioned.

What "justification by faith" means.

Habakkuk quoted in the New Testament

- For I work a work in your days, which ye shall in no wise believe
Hab. 1:5 quoted in Acts 13:41
- But my righteous one shall live by faith
Hab. 2:3–4 quoted in Heb. 10:37–38
- But my righteous one shall live by faith
Hab. 2:4 quoted in Rom. 1:17 and Gal. 3:11

Jesus in Habakkuk

In Habakkuk Jesus is the God of our salvation.

Lessons to learn from Habakkuk

- We live in a fallen world.
- There is nothing wrong in asking questions about our faith when we are puzzled. But this need not stop us from trusting God.

4. Chapter by chapter: outline of every chapter of Habakkuk

Habakkuk 1

Matthew Henry's introduction

In this chapter,

I. The prophet complains to God of the violence done by the abuse of the sword of justice among his own people and the hardships thereby put on many good people, vv. 1–4.

II. God by him foretells the punishment of that abuse of power by the sword of war, and the desolations which the army of the Chaldeans should make on them, vv. 5–11.

III. Then the prophet complains of that too, and is grieved that the Chaldeans prevail so far (vv. 12–17).

A detailed analysis of chapter

Habakkuk's first problem: why does God allow injustice? (1–4)

God's reply: punishment will come at the hand of the Babylonians. (5–11)

Habakkuk's response: How can a holy God possibly use Babylon? (12–2:1)

Key verse

Verse 1: "The burden which Habakkuk the prophet did see."

Key word / key phrase

Verse 2, "How long, O Lord, must I call for help?"

Key event / key person / key theme

God's apparent inaction in the face of wrongdoing

What

Key thought

Whatever the problem or difficulty the way through is to keep on telling God exactly and truthfully how we feel.

Key thing to look out for

Why did Habakkuk feel that God was not listening to him? See verse 2.

Key Bible cross-reference

Verse 5. See Acts 13:41.

Key "by way of explanation"

Habakkuk was a contemporary of Jeremiah. He lived and preached in Judah. His book takes the form of a dialogue between God and his prophet.

Key "Quotable Quote"

"Though Satan instills his poison, and fans the flames of our corrupt desires within us, we are yet not carried by any external force to the commission of sin, but our own flesh entices us, and we willingly yield to its allurements."

John Calvin

Habakkuk 2

Matthew Henry's introduction

In this chapter we have an answer expected by the prophet (v. 1), and returned by the Spirit of God, to the complaints which the prophet made of the violence and victories of the Chaldeans in the close of the previous chapter. The answer is,

I. That after God has served his own purposes by the prevailing power of the Chaldeans, has tried the faith and patience of his people, and distinguished between the hypocrites and the sincere among them, he will reckon with the Chaldeans, will humble and bring down, not only that proud monarch Nebuchadnezzar, but that proud monarchy, for their boundless and insatiable thirst after dominion and wealth, for which they themselves should at length be made a prey, vv. 2–8.

II. That not they only, but all other sinners like them, should perish under a divine woe.

A. Those that are covetous, are greedy of wealth and honors, vv. 9, 11.

B. Those that are injurious and oppressive, and raise estates by wrong and rapine, vv. 12–14.

C. Those that promote drunkenness that they may expose their neighbors to

shame, vv. 15–17.
D. Those that worship idols, vv. 18–20.

A detailed analysis of chapter

God's second answer, judgment will come on the Babylonians. (2–20)

Key verse

Verse 4: "Behold, his soul which is lifted up is not upright in him: but the just shall live by his faith."

Key word / key phrase

Verse 9, "unjust gain."

Key event / key person / key theme

God's hatred of injustice

Key thought

Verse 4, "Faith," that is faithfulness. In contrast to the works of the wicked, the righteous exercise trust in their great God.

Key thing to look out for

Note the importance of silent worship, verse 20.

Key Bible cross-reference

Verses 3,4. See Hebrews 10:37,38. See also Romans 1:17; Galatians 3:11.

Key "by way of explanation"

Verse 9, "nest on high." The Babylonians thought that their military power was as mighty as the swooping eagle who built her nest where no one could reach.

Key "Quotable Quote"

"God's spiritual 'law of gravity' humbles the high and exalts the low."

Anne Graham Lotz

Habakkuk 3

Matthew Henry's introduction

I. Habakkuk earnestly begs of God to relieve and succor his people in affliction, to hasten their deliverance, and to comfort them in the mean time, v. 2.
II. He calls to mind the experiences which the church formerly had of God's glorious and gracious appearances on her behalf, when he brought Israel out of Egypt through the wilderness to Canaan, and there many a time wrought wonderful deliverances for them, vv. 3–15.
III. He affects himself with a holy concern for the present troubles of the church, but encourages himself and others to hope that the issue will be comfortable and glorious at last, though all visible means fail, vv. 16–19.

A detailed analysis of chapter

The prophet beseeches God for his people. (1, 2)
He calls to mind previous deliverances. (3–15)
His firm trust in God's mercy. (16–19)

Key verse

Verse 4: "And his brightness was as the light; he had horns coming out of his hand: and there was the hiding of his power."

Key word / key phrase

Verse 2, "I stand in awe of your deeds."

Key event / key person / key theme

Habakkuk's prayer

Key thought

The world around us reflects the glory of God.

Key thing to look out for

After all his complaints Habakkuk ends up by praising God for his power and righteous judgments, and affirming his trust in God, come what may.

Key Bible cross-reference

Verse 19. See 2 Samuel 22:34.

Key "by way of explanation"

Verse 5, "plague went before him." God often used plagues and pestilence as a form of punishment on those who rejected him.

Key "Quotable Quote"

"When my attitudes and actions become marked by pride, it's usually been much too long since I've repented and experienced the key discipline of mourning."

Gary Thomas

5. Select bibliography for Habakkuk

Baker, David W. *Nahum, Habakkuk, Zephaniah* (Tyndale), InterVarsity, 1988.

Calvin, John. *Commentaries on the Twelve Minor Prophets*. Grand Rapids: Eerdmans, n.d.

Ellison, H. L. *The Old Testament Prophets*. Grand Rapids: Zondervan, 1966.

Feinberg, Charles L. *The Minor Prophets*. Chicago: Moody, 1976.

Gaebelein, Frank E. *Four Minor Prophets*. Chicago: Moody, 1970.

Henderson, E. *The Twelve Minor Prophets*. Grand Rapids: Baker, 1980.

Kaiser, Walter. *Micah, Nahum, Habakkuk, Zephaniah, Haggai, Zechariah, Malachi* (Mastering the Old Testament), Word Books, 1992.

Keil, Carl F. *The Twelve Minor Prophets*. Vol. 2. Grand Rapids: Eerdmans, 1949.

Lloyd-Jones, M. *From Fear to Faith*. London Inter-Varsity, 1953.

Pusey, E.B. *The Minor Prophets*. Vol. 2. Grand Rapids: Baker, 1950.

Smith, George A. *The Book of the Twelve Prophets*. Vol. 2. ExB. London: Hodder & Stoughton, 1898.

Zephaniah

1. Book by book: Introduction to Zephaniah

Introduction

Zephaniah, ninth in order of the minor prophets, prophesied "in the days of Josiah" (Zeph. 1:1), that is, between 642 and 611 B.C. The name means "Jehovah hath guarded," literally, "hidden" (Ps. 27:5; 83:3). The specification in the introductory heading, of not only his father, but also his grandfather, and great-grandfather, and great-great-grandfather, implies that the latter were people of note, or else the design was to distinguish him from another Zephaniah of note at the time of the captivity. The Jews' supposition, that people recorded as a prophet's ancestors were themselves endowed with the prophetic spirit, seems groundless. There is no impossibility of the Hezekiah, who was Zephaniah's great-great-grandfather, being King Hezekiah as to the number of generations; for Hezekiah's reign of twenty-nine years, and his successor's reign of fifty-five years, admit of four generations interposing between. Yet the omission of the designation, "king of Judah," is fatal to the theory (compare Prov. 25:1; Is. 38:9).

Date

He must have flourished in the earlier part of Josiah's reign. In Zeph. 2:13–15 he foretells the doom of Nineveh, which happened in 625 B.C.; and in Zeph. 1:4 he denounces various forms of idolatry, and specially that of Baal. Now Josiah's reformation began in the twelfth and was completed in the eighteenth year of his reign. Zephaniah, therefore, in denouncing Baal worship, co-operated with that good king in his efforts, and so must have prophesied somewhere between the twelfth and eighteenth years of his reign. The silence of the historical books is no argument against this, as it would equally apply against Jeremiah's prophetical existence at the same time. Jewish tradition says that Zephaniah had for his colleagues Jeremiah, whose sphere of labor was the thoroughfares and market places, and Huldah the prophetess, who exercised her vocation in the college in Jerusalem.

Themes

The prophecy begins with the nation's sin and the fearful retribution coming at the hands of the Chaldeans. These are not mentioned by name, as in Jeremiah; for the prophecies of the latter, being nearer the fulfillment, become more explicit than those of an earlier date. The second chapter dooms the persecuting states in the neighborhood as well as Judea itself. The third chapter denounces Jerusalem, but concludes with the promise of her joyful re-establishment in the theocracy.

Style

The style, though not generally sublime, is graphic and vivid in details (compare Zeph. 1:4–12). The language is pure, and free from Aramaisms. There are occasional coincidences with former prophets (compare Zeph. 2:14, with Is. 34:11; Zeph. 2:15, with Is. 47:8; Zeph. 3:10, with Is. 18:1; Zeph. 2:8, with Is. 16:6; also Zeph. 1:5, with Jer. 8:2; Zeph. 1:12, with Jer. 48:11). Such coincidences in part arise from the phraseology of Hebrew prophetic poetry being the common language of the inspired brotherhood. The New Testament, at Rom. 15:6, seems to refer to Zeph. 3:9.

A.R. Faussett

John Calvin's introduction to Zephaniah

Zephaniah is placed the last of the Minor Prophets who performed their office before the Babylonian Captivity; and the inscription shows that he exercised his office of teaching at the same time with Jeremiah, about thirty years before the city was destroyed, the Temple pulled down, and the people led into exile. Jeremiah, it is true, followed his vocation even after the death of Josiah, while Zephaniah prophesied only during his reign.

The substance of his Book is this: He first denounces utter destruction on a people who were so perverse, that there was no hope of their repentance; – he then moderates his threatening, by denouncing God's judgments on their enemies, the Assyrians, as well as others, who had treated with cruelty the Church of God; for it was no small consolation, when the Jews heard that they were so regarded by God, that he would undertake their cause and avenge their wrongs. He afterwards repeats again his reproofs, and shortly mentions the sins which then prevailed among the elect people of God; and, at the same time, he turns his discourse to the faithful, and exhorts them to patience, setting before them the hope of favor, provided they ever looked to the Lord; and provided they relied on the gratuitous covenant which he made with Abraham, and doubted not but that he would be a Father to them, and also looked, with a tranquil mind, for that redemption which had been promised to them. This is the sum of the whole Book.

John Calvin

Detailed outline

I. Introduction: 1:1–3
- A. The messenger: 1:1
- B. Summary of the message: 1:2–3

II. A look within: 1:4–2:3
- A. The fact of judgment: 1:4–14
  1. Judgment on four kinds of worshipers: 1:4–7
  2. Judgment on sinners of every rank: 1:8–13
- B. The nature and results of judgment: 1:14–18
  1. It is at hand: 1:14
  2. Even the mighty are brought low: 1:14
  3. Dark day of distress, waste, desolation: 1:15–16
  4. Distress, blood, flesh as dung: 1:17
  5. No deliverance: 1:18
  6. Day of the Lord's anger: 1:2–3
- C. The name of judgment: Day of the Lord: 2:1–3
- D. Hope in judgment: 2:3

III. A look around: Judgment coming on all nations: 2:4–3:7
- A. Philistine cities: 2:4–7
- B. Moab and Ammon: 2:8–11
- C. Ethiopia: 2:12
- D. Assyria and its capitol, Nineveh: 2:13–15
- E. Judgment on Jerusalem: 3:1–7
  1. Note the condition of Jerusalem:
     (a) Filthy, oppressing, polluted: 3:1
     (b) Disobedient: 3:2
     (c) Evil secular leaders: 3:3
     (d) Evil spiritual leaders: 3:4

2. Note the mercies of God: 3:5–7

IV. A look beyond: After judgment, healing will come: 3:8–20

A. God's purpose accomplished: 3:8

B. From among the heathen, God's remnant will come: 3:9–10, 12–13

C. Judgment on those who were once enemies of God: 3:9–13

D. Israel's Messiah manifested as King: 3:14–20

2. Helpful summaries of Zephaniah

Bird's eye view

Zephaniah warns Judah about God's impending judgment on them because of their constant refusal to turn back to God.

Reading plan

The following reading plan, taking one reading per day, enables you to read through Zephaniah in one day.

Zephaniah 1–3

Verse to memorize

Zephaniah 3:17

The Lord your God is with you, he is mighty to save. He will take great delight in you, he will quiet you with his love, he will rejoice over you with singing.

Statistics

Thirty-sixth Old Testament book

3 chapters

53 verses

1,617 words

Names/titles given

Hebrew title: *Tsephan-yah:* "The Lord has hidden."

Greek title in Septuagint: *Sophonias:* "Zephaniah."

Latin title in Vulgate: *Sophonias:* "Zephaniah."

3. Helpful keys to turn to in understanding Zephaniah

Key words

Search

The day of the Lord

Key verses

Zephaniah 1:12; 2:3

Themes to study

The day of the Lord

The Lord as ruler over all.

Jesus in Zephaniah

In Zephaniah Jesus is the Lord who fulfils his promises.

Lessons to learn from Zephaniah

- We are meant to take notice of God's warnings and to change our ways.
- No one is excluded from seeking God.

4. Chapter by chapter: outline of every chapter of Zephaniah

Zephaniah 1

Matthew Henry's introduction

After the title of the book (v. 1) here is,

I. A threatening of the destruction of Judah and Jerusalem, an utter destruction, by the Chaldeans, vv. 2–4.

II. A charge against them for their gross sin, which provoked God to bring that destruction on them (vv. 5, 6); and so he goes on in the rest of the chapter, setting both the judgments before them, that they might prevent them or prepare for them, and the sins that destroy them, that they might judge themselves, and justify God in what was brought on them.

A. They must hold their peace because they had greatly sinned, vv. 7–9. But,

B. They shall howl because the trouble will be great. The day of the Lord is near, and it will be a terrible day, vv. 10–18. Such fair and timely warning as this did God give to the Jews of the approaching captivity; but they hardened their neck, which made their destruction remediless.

A detailed analysis of chapter

Warnings against sinners. (1–6)

More warnings. (7–13)

Fear of the approaching judgments. (14–18)

Key verse

Verse 1: "The word of the LORD which came unto Zephaniah the son of Cushi, the son of Gedaliah, the son of Amariah, the son of Hizkiah, in the days of Josiah the son of Amon, king of Judah."

Key word / key phrase

Verse 4, "I will stretch out my hand against Judah."

Key event / key person / key theme

Judah is judged

Key thought

Beware of complacency, see verse 12.

Key thing to look out for

God visits, either to judge or to bless.

Key Bible cross-reference

Verse 1. See 2 Kings 22:1–23:30.

Key "by way of explanation"

Zephaniah was a contemporary of Jeremiah, Nahum, and Habbakuk. He lived in Jerusalem and his prophecy was probably given early in Josiah's reign, before Josiah's reforms.

Key "Quotable Quote"

"If a man is called to be a street sweeper, he should sweep streets even as Michelangelo painted, or Beethoven played music, or Shakespeare wrote poetry."

Martin Luther King, Jr.

Zephaniah 2

Matthew Henry's introduction

In this chapter we have,

I. An earnest exhortation to the nation of the Jews to repent and make their peace with God, and so to prevent the judgments threatened before it was too late (vv. 1–3), and this inferred from the revelation of God's wrath against them in the previous chapter.

II. A denunciation of the judgments of God against several of the neighboring nations that had assisted, or rejoiced in, the calamity of Israel.
   A. The Philistines, vv. 4–7.
   B. The Moabites and Ammonites, vv. 8–11.
   C. The Ethiopians and Assyrians, vv. 12–15. All these shall drink of the same cup of trembling that is put into the hands of God's people, as was also foretold by other prophets before and after.

A detailed analysis of chapter

An exhortation to repent. (1–3)
Judgments on other nations. (4–15)

Key verse

Verse 3: "Seek ye the LORD, all ye meek of the earth, which have wrought his judgment; seek righteousness, seek meekness: it may be ye shall be hid in the day of the LORD'S anger."

Key word / key phrase

Verse 8, "the insults of Moab."

Key event / key person / key theme

Oracles against the nations

Key thought

If people will not listen to God he will eliminate them.

Key thing to look out for

God always tells people how they should serve him, see verse 3.

Key Bible cross-reference

Verses 4–7. See Isaiah 14:29–31.

Key "by way of explanation"

Verse 9, "like Sodom . . . Gomorrah." The destruction of the cities of Sodom and Gomorrah was also remembered as an instance of the way God dealt with evil people.

Key "Quotable Quote"

"Before God can deliver us we must undeceive ourselves."

Augustine of Hippo

Zephaniah 3

Matthew Henry's introduction

We now return to Jerusalem, and must again hear what God has to say to her,

I. By way of reproof and threatening, for the abundance of wickedness that was found in her, of which divers instances are given, with the aggravations of them, vv. 1–7.

II. By way of promise of mercy and grace, which God had yet in reserve for them. Two general heads of promises here are:
   A. That God would bring in a glorious work of reformation among them, cleanse them from their sins, and bring them home to himself; many promises of this kind here are, vv. 8–13.
   B. That he would bring about a glorious work of salvation for them, when he had thus prepared them for it, vv. 14–20. Thus the "Redeemer shall come to Zion," and to clear his own way, shall "turn away ungodliness from Jacob." These promises

were to have their full accomplishment in gospel-times and gospel-graces.

A detailed analysis of chapter

Further reproofs for sin. (1–7)

Encouragement to look for mercy. (8–13)

Promises of future favor and prosperity. (14–20)

Key verse

Verse 6: "I have cut off the nations: their towers are desolate; I made their streets waste, that none passeth by: their cities are destroyed, so that there is no man, that there is none inhabitant."

Key word / key phrase

Verse 14, "Sing, O Daughter of Zion."

Key event / key person / key theme

Salvation on the Day of the Lord

Key thought

Blessed are the meek. See verse 12.

Key thing to look out for

God promises to restore his people.

Key Bible cross-reference

Verse 13. See Revelation 14:5.

Key "by way of explanation"

Verse 14, "Sing . . . with all your heart." In Hebrew thinking the "heart" was the center of a person, especially his intellect. Unlike the unthinking worshipers of Baal, God's followers were to use their minds as they worshiped.

Key "Quotable Quote"

"God hears no more than the heart speaks; and if the heart be dumb, God will certainly be deaf."

Thomas Brooks

5. Select bibliography for Zephaniah

More recent commentaries

Baker, David W. *Nahum, Habakkuk, Zephaniah* (Tyndale), Inter-Varsity, 1988.

Kaiser, Walter. *Micah, Nahum, Habakkuk, Zephaniah, Haggai, Zechariah, Malachi* (Mastering the Old Testament), Word Books, 1992.

Calvin, John. *The Minor Prophets*. Vol. 6. Calvin's Commentaries. Grand Rapids: Associated Publishers and Authors, n d.

Keil, C. F. *The Twelve Minor Prophets*. Vol. 2. Biblical Commentary on the Old Testament. KD. Grand Rapids: Eerdmans, 1949.

Motyer, J. Alec. "Zephaniah" in *The Minor Prophets*, Vol. III, (ed. T. McComiskey), Baker, 1998.

Smith, George Adam. *The Twelve Prophets*. New York: A.C. Armstrong and Son, 1901.

Haggai

1. Book by book: Introduction to Haggai

Introduction

The name Haggai means "my feast"; given, according to Cocceius, in anticipation of the joyous return from exile. He probably was one of the Jewish exiles (of the tribes Judah, Benjamin, and Levi) who returned under Zerubbabel, the civil head of the people, and Joshua, the high priest, 536 B.C., when Cyrus (actuated by the striking prophecies as to himself, Is. 44:28; 45:1) granted them their liberty, and furnished them with the necessaries for restoring the temple (2 Chr. 36:23; Ezra 1:1; 2:2). The work of rebuilding went on under Cyrus and his successor Cambyses (called Ahasuerus in Ezra 4:6) in spite of opposition from the Samaritans, who, when their offers of help were declined, began to try to hinder it. These at last obtained an interdict from the usurper Smerdis the Magian (called Artaxerxes in Ezra 4:7–23), whose suspicions were easy to rouse. The Jews thereon became so indifferent to the work that when Darius came to the throne (521 B.C.), virtually setting aside the prohibitions of the usurper, instead of recommencing their labors, they pretended that as the prophecy of the seventy years applied to the temple as well as to the captivity in Babylon (Hag. 1:2), they were only in the sixty-eighth year of it (Henderson); so that, the proper time not having yet arrived, they might devote themselves to building splendid mansions for themselves. Haggai and Zechariah were commissioned by Jehovah (Hag. 1:1) in the second year of Darius (Hystaspes), 520 B.C., sixteen years after the return under Zerubbabel, to rouse them from their selfishness to resume the work which for fourteen years had been suspended. Haggai preceded Zechariah in the work by two months.

Date

The dates of his four distinct prophecies are accurately given:

(1) The first (Hag. 1:1–15), on the first day of the sixth month of the second year of Darius, 520 b.c., reproved the people for their apathy in allowing the temple to lie in ruins and reminded them of their ill success in everything because of their not honoring God as to His house. The result was that twenty-four days afterwards they commenced building under Zerubbabel (Hag. 1:12–15).

(2) The second, on the twenty-first day of the seventh month (Hag. 2:1–9), predicts that the glory of the new temple would be greater than that of Solomon's, so that the people need not be discouraged by the inferiority in outward splendor of the new, as compared with the old temple, which had so moved to tears the elders who had remembered the old (Ezra 3:12, 13). Isaiah, Jeremiah, and Ezekiel had implied the same prediction, whence some had doubted whether they ought to proceed with a building so inferior to the former one; but Haggai shows where the superior glory lay, namely, in the presence of Him who is the "desire of all nations" (Hag. 2:7).

(3) The third, on the twenty-fourth day of the ninth month (Hag. 2:10–19), refers to a period when building materials had been collected, and the workmen had begun to put them together, from which time forth God promises His blessing; it begins with removing their past error as to the efficacy of mere outward observances to cleanse from the taint of disobedience as to the temple building.

(4) The fourth (Hag. 2:20–23), on the same day as the preceding, was addressed to Zerubbabel, as the representative of the theocratic people, and as having asked as to the national revolutions spoken of in the second prophecy (Hag. 2:7).

The prophecies are all so brief as to suggest the supposition that they are only a summary of the original discourses. The space occupied is but three months from the first to the last.

The Jews' adversaries, on the resumption of the work under Zerubbabel, Haggai, and Zechariah, tried to set Darius against it; but that monarch confirmed Cyrus' decree and ordered all help to be given to the building of the temple (Ezra 5:3, etc.; Ezra 6:1, etc.). So the temple was completed in the sixth year of Darius' reign 516–515 B.C. (Ezra 6:14).

Style

The style of Haggai is consonant with his messages: pathetic in exhortation, vehement in reproofs, elevated in contemplating the glorious future. The repetition of the same phrases (for example, "saith the Lord," or "the Lord of hosts," Hag. 1:2, 5, 7; and thrice in one verse, Hag. 2:4; so "the spirit," thrice in one verse, Hag. 1:14) gives a simple earnestness to his style, calculated to awaken the solemn attention of the people, and to awaken them from their apathy, to which also the interrogatory form, often adopted, especially tends. Chaldaisms occur (Hag. 2:3; 2:6; 2:16), as might have been expected in a writer who was so long in Chaldea. Parts are purely prose history; the rest is somewhat rhythmical, and observant of poetic parallelism.

Haggai is referred to in Ezra 5:1; 6:14; and in the New Testament (Heb. 12:26; compare Hag. 2:6, 7, 22).

A.R. Faussett

John Calvin's introduction to Haggai

After the return of the people, they were favored, we know, especially with three Prophets, who roused their fainting hearts, and finished all predictions, until at length the Redeemer came in his appointed time. During the time of The Babylonian Exile the office of teaching was discharged among the captives by Ezekiel, and also by Daniel; and there were others less celebrated; for we find that some of the Psalms were then composed, either by the Levites, or by some other teachers. But these two, Ezekiel and Daniel, were above all others eminent. Then Ezra and Nehemiah followed them, the authority of whom was great among the people; but we do not read that they were endued with the Prophetic gift.

It then appears certain that three only were divinely inspired to proclaim the future condition of the people.

Daniel had before them foretold whatever was to happen till the coming of Christ, and his Book is a remarkable mirror of God's Providence; for he paints, as on a tablet, three things which were to be fulfilled after his death, and of which no man could have formed any conjecture. He has given even the number of years from the return of the people to the building of the Temple, and also to the death of Christ. But we must come to the other witnesses, who confirmed the predictions of Daniel. The Lord raised up three witnesses — Haggai, Zechariah, and Malachi.

The first condemned the sloth of the people; for, being intent on their own advantages, they all neglected the building of the Temple; and he shows that they were deservedly suffering punishment for their ingratitude; for they despised God their Deliverer, or at least honored him less than they ought to have done, and deprived him of the worship due to him. He then encouraged them to hope for a complete restoration, and showed that there was no reason for them to be disheartened by difficulties, and that though they were surrounded by enemies, and had to bear many evils, and were terrified by threatening edicts, they ought yet to have entertained hope; for the Lord would perform the work which he had begun — to restore their ancient dignity to his people, and Christ also would at length come to secure the perfect happiness and glory of the Church.

John Calvin

Detailed outline

I. First message: A summons to rebuild the temple: 1:1–15
- A. The date: 1:1
- B. The message: 1:2–11
  - 1. The people's procrastination: 1:2–4
  - 2. It's consequences: 1:5–11
- C. The people's response: 1:12–15
  - 1. Obedience and fear of the Lord: 1:12
  - 2. The work of encouragement: 1:13
  - 3. The work begun: 1:14
  - 4. The date: 1:15

II. Second message: The glory of the latter temple: 2:1–9
- A. The date: 2:1
- B. The message: 2:2–9
  - 1. The temples compared: 2:2–3
  - 2. The answer to discouragement: 2:4–5
  - 3. The universal shaking and later glory of the temple: 2:6–9

III. Third message: The present blessings of obedience: 2:10–19
- A. The date: 2:10
- B. The message: Sin is contagious: 2:11–19
  - 1. The priests questioned: 2:11–13
  - 2. The application: 2:14–19

IV. Fourth message: The promise of future blessings: 2:20–23
- A. The date: 2:20
- B. The message: 2:21–23
  - 1. Overthrow of earthly power: 2:21–22
  - 2. Zerubbabel the signet: 2:23

2. Helpful summaries of Haggai

Bird's eye view

Haggai urges the Jews who had returned to Jerusalem after the Babylonian exile to finish rebuilding the temple.

Reading plan

The following reading plan, taking one reading per day, enables you to read through Haggai in one day.

Haggai 1–2

Verse to memorize

Haggai 2:7

"I will shake all nations, and the desired of all nations will come, and I will fill this house with glory," says the Lord Almighty.

Statistics

Thirty-seventh Old Testament book

2 chapters

38 verses

1,131 words

Famous sayings found in Haggai

"The people feared the Lord." 1:12, NIV

"Be strong . . . and work." 2:4, NIV

"'The silver is mine and the gold is mine,' declares the Lord Almighty.' 2:8, NIV

"The glory of this present house will be greater than the glory of the former house." 2:9, NIV

Names/titles given

Hebrew title: *haggiah:* "Festival of the Lord."

Greek title in Septuagint: *Aggaios:* "Haggai."

Latin title in Vulgate: *Aggaios:* "Haggai."

3. Helpful keys to turn to in understanding Haggai

Key word

Build

Key verses

Haggai 1:8; 2:7–9

Themes to study

The importance of the Temple in the Old Testament.

Haggai quoted in the New Testament

Yet once more I will shake the earth

Hag. 2:6 quoted in Heb. 12:26

Jesus in Haggai

In Haggai Jesus is the One desired by all nations.

Type of Jesus in Haggai

Zerubbabel portrays of the future Messiah, 2:23.

Lessons to learn from Haggai

We should not delay in doing God's work.

God and his work should be our overriding priority.

4. Chapter by chapter: outline of every chapter of Haggai

Haggai 1

Matthew Henry's introduction

In this chapter, after the preamble of the prophecy, we have,

I. A reproof of the people of the Jews for their dilatoriness and slothfulness in building the temple, which had provoked God to contend with them by the judgment of famine and scarcity, with an exhortation to them to resume that good work and to prosecute it in good earnest, vv. 1–11.

II. The good success of this sermon, appearing in the people's return and close application to that work, in which the prophet, in God's name, animated and encouraged them, assuring them that God was with them, vv. 12–15.

A detailed analysis of chapter

Haggai's first message: he reproves the Jews for neglecting the temple. (1–11)

He promises them God's assistance. (12–15)

Key verse

Verse 1: "In the second year of Darius the king, in the sixth month, in the first day of the month, came the word of the LORD by Haggai the prophet unto Zerubbabel the son of Shealtiel, governor of Judah, and to Joshua the son of Josedech, the high priest."

Key word / key phrase

Verse 8, "build the house."

Key event / key person / key theme

A call to build the house of the Lord

Key thought

What personal activities do we substitute for getting on with the Lord's work?

Key thing to look out for

God's presence is promised to all who serve him.

Key Bible cross-reference

Verse 1. See Ezra 4:24–5:2.

Key "by way of explanation"

Haggai's four messages were given over a four-month period in 520 BC, seventeen years after the first group of exiles, led by Zerubbabel, had returned to Jerusalem, and started rebuilding the temple. After two years, in the face of severe opposition the work had stopped but when Darius the Great became Emperor in 522, he encouraged the rebuilding and gave generous financial support. Ezra 4:5; 4:24–5:2; 6:14 give this historical background.

Key "Quotable Quote"

"The false and the genuine prophet will be known by their ways. If a prophet teaches the truth but does not practice what he teaches, he is a false prophet."

Didache

Haggai 2

Matthew Henry's introduction

In this chapter we have three sermons preached by the prophet Haggai for the encouragement of those that are forward to build the temple.

In the first he assures the builders that the glory of the house they were now building should, in spiritual respects, though not in outward, exceed that of Solomon's temple, in which he has an eye to the coming of Christ, vv. 1–9.

In the second he assures them that though their sin, in delaying to build the temple, had retarded the prosperous progress of all their other affairs, yet now that they had set about it in good earnest he would bless them, and give them success, vv. 10–19.

In the third he assures Zerubbabel that, as a reward of his pious zeal and activity herein, he should be a favorite of Heaven, and one of the ancestors of Messiah the Prince, whose kingdom should be set up on the ruins of all opposing powers, vv. 20–23.

A detailed analysis of chapter

Second message: an encouragement to work. (1–5)

Greater glory promised for the second temple than for the first. (6–9)

Third message: sins hindered the work. (10–19)

Fourth message: promise to Zerubbabel. (20–23)

Key verse

Verse 9: "The glory of this latter house shall be greater than of the former, saith the LORD of hosts: and in this place will I give peace, saith the LORD of hosts."

Key word / key phrase

Verse 23, "On that day."

Key event / key person / key theme

The kingdom of Christ foretold (20–23)

Key thought

God's Spirit is meant to be always with God's people.

Key thing to look out for

God's glory is meant to be the abiding concern of God's people.

Key Bible cross-reference

Verse 6. See Hebrews 12:26.

Key "by way of explanation"

Verse 8, "The silver is mine and the gold is mine." All the silver and gold used in the construction of the temple belonged to the Lord.

Key "Quotable Quote"

"Numerous passages of Scripture assert that the manifestation of the glory of God is the great end of creation, that he has himself chiefly in view in all his works and dispensations, and that it is a purpose in which he requires that all his intelligent creatures should acquiesce, and seek and promote it as their first and paramount duty."

Robert Haldane

5. Select bibliography for Haggai

Baker, David W. *Nahum, Habakkuk, Zephaniah* (Tyndale), Inter-Varsity, 1988.

Baldwin, Joyce G. *Haggai, Zechariah and*

Malachi. Downers Grove, Ill.: InterVarsity, 1972.

Calvin, John. *Minor Prophets IV*. Grand Rapids: Eerdmans, 1950.

Freeman, Hobart E. *An Introduction to the Old Testament Prophets*. Chicago: Moody, 1968.

Gaebelein, Frank E. *Four Minor Prophets*. Chicago: Moody, 1970.

Kaiser, Walter. *Micah, Nahum, Habakkuk, Zephaniah, Haggai, Zechariah, Malachi* (Mastering the Old Testament), Word Books, 1992.

Keil, C. F. *The Twelve Minor Prophets*. KD. 2 Vols. Grand Rapids: Eerdmans, 1949.

Moore, T. V. *The Prophets of the Restoration: Haggai, Zechariah, Malachi*. 1856. Reprint. London: Banner of Truth Trust, 1960.

Taylor, John B. *The Minor Prophets*. Grand Rapids: Eerdmans, 1970.

Zechariah

1. Book by book: Introduction to Zechariah

Introduction

The name Zechariah means one whom Jehovah remembers: a common name, four others of the same name occurring in the Old Testament. Like Jeremiah and Ezekiel, he was a priest as well as a prophet, which adapts him for the sacerdotal character of some of his prophecies (Zech. 6:13). He is called "the son of Berechiah the son of Iddo" (Zech. 1:1); but simply "the son of Iddo" in Ezra 5:1; 6:14. Probably his father died when he was young; and hence, as sometimes occurs in Jewish genealogies, he is called "the son of Iddo," his grandfather. Iddo was one of the priests who returned to Zerubbabel and Joshua from Babylon (Neh. 12:4).

Zechariah started early on his prophetic functions (Zech. 2:4); only two months later than Haggai, in the second year of Darius' reign, 520 B.C. The design of both prophets was to encourage the people and their religious and civil leaders, Joshua and Zerubbabel, in their work of rebuilding the temple, after the interruption caused by the Samaritans (see Introduction to Haggai). Zechariah does so especially by unfolding in detail the glorious future in connection with the present depressed appearance of the theocracy, and its visible symbol, the temple. He must have been very young in leaving Babylonia, where he was born.

The Zechariah, son of Barachias, mentioned by our Lord (Matt. 23:35) as slain between the porch and the altar, must have been the one called the son of Jehoiada in 2 Chr. 24:21, who so perished: the same person often had two names; and our Lord, in referring to the Hebrew Bible, of which Second Chronicles is the last book, would naturally mention the last martyr in the Hebrew order of the canon, as He had instanced Abel as the first. Owing to Matt. 27:9 quoting Zech. 11:12, 13 as the words of Jeremiah, Mede doubts the authenticity of the ninth through the fourteenth chapters, and ascribes them to Jeremiah: he thinks that these chapters were not found till after the return from the captivity, and being approved by Zechariah, were added to his prophecies, as Agur's Proverbs were added to those of Solomon. All the oldest authorities, except two manuscripts of the old Italian or Pre-Vulgate version, read Jeremiah in Matt. 27:9. The quotation there is not to the letter copied from Zechariah, Jer. 18:1, 2; 32:6–12, may also have been in the mind of Matthew, and perhaps in the mind of Zechariah, whence the former mentions Jeremiah. Hengstenberg similarly thinks that Matthew names Jeremiah, rather than Zechariah, to turn attention to the fact that Zechariah's prophecy is but a reiteration of the fearful oracle in Jer. 18:1–19:15, to be fulfilled in the destruction of the Jewish nation. Jeremiah had already, by the image of a potter's vessel, portrayed their ruin in Nebuchadnezzar's invasion; and as Zechariah virtually repeats this threat, to be inflicted again under Messiah for the nation's rejection of Him, Matthew, virtually, by mentioning Jeremiah, implies that the "field of blood" (Matt. 27:8, 9), now bought by "the reward of iniquity" (Acts 1:18) in the valley of Hinnom, was long ago a scene of prophetic doom in which awful disaster had been symbolically predicted: that the present purchase of that field with the traitor's price renewed the prophecy and revived the curse—a curse pronounced of old by Jeremiah, and once fulfilled in the Babylonian siege—a curse reiterated by Zechariah, and again to be verified in the Roman desolation.

The mention of "Ephraim" and "Israel" in these chapters as distinct from Judah, does not prove that the prophecy was written while the ten tribes existed as a separate kingdom. It rather implies that hereafter not only Judah, but the ten tribes also, shall be restored, the earnest of which was given in the numbers out of the ten tribes who returned with their brethren the Jews from captivity under Cyrus. There is nothing in these characters to imply that a king reigned in Judah at that time. The editor of the Hebrew canon joined these chapters to Zechariah, not to Jeremiah; the Septuagint, three hundred years B.C., confirms this.

Contents

The prophecy consists of four parts:

(1) Introductory, Zech. 1:1–6.

(2) Symbolical, Zech. 1:7, to the end of the sixth chapter, containing nine visions; all these were vouchsafed in one night, and are of a symbolical character.

(3) Didactic, the seventh and eighth chapters containing an answer to a query of the Beth-elites about a certain feast. And

(4) Prophetic, the ninth chapter to the end.

These six last chapters predict Alexander's expedition along the west coast of Palestine to Egypt; God's protection of the Jews, both at that time and under the Maccabees; the advent, sufferings, and reign of Messiah; the destruction of Jerusalem by Rome, and dissolution of the Jews' polity; their conversion and restoration; the overthrow of the wicked confederacy which assailed them in Canaan; and the Gentiles' joining in their holy worship (Henderson).

The difference in style between the former and the latter chapters is due to the difference of subject; the first six chapters being of a symbolical and peculiar character, while the poetical style of the concluding chapters is adapted admirably to the subjects treated. The titles (Zech. 9:1; 12:1) accord with the prophetic matter which follows; nor is it necessary for unity of authorship that the introductory formulas occurring in the first eight chapters should occur in the last six. The non-reference in the last six chapters to the completion of the temple and the Jews' restoration after the captivity is just what we should expect, if, as seems likely, these chapters were written long after the completion of the temple and the restoration of the Jews' polity after the captivity, in circumstances different from those which engaged the prophet when he wrote the earlier chapters.

Style

The style varies with the subject: at one time conversational, at another poetical. His symbols are enigmatical and are therefore accompanied with explanations. His prose is like that of Ezekiel–diffuse, uniform, and repetitious. The rhythm is somewhat unequal, and the parallelisms are not altogether symmetrical. Still, there is found often much of the elevation met with in the earlier prophets, and a general congruity between the style and the subjects. Graphic vividness is his peculiar merit. Chaldæisms occur occasionally. Another special characteristic of Zechariah is his introduction of spiritual beings into his prophetic scenes.

A.R. Faussett

John Calvin's introduction to Zechariah

Zechariah was a fellow-helper and colleague of Haggai, and also of Malachi. These three, then, were sent by God nearly at the same time, that they might assist one another, and that they might thus by one consent and one mouth confirm what God had committed to them. It was indeed of great service that several bore their testimony: their prophecies gained thus greater authority; and this was needful, for the people had to contend with various and most grievous trials. Satan had already raised up great opposition to them; but there were still greater evils at hand. Hence, to prevent them from despairing, it was necessary to encourage them; by many testimonies.

But what our Prophet had especially in view was, to remind the Jews why it was that God dealt so severely with their fathers, and also to animate them with hope, provided they really repented, and elevated their minds to the hope of true and complete deliverance. He at the same time severely reproves them; for there was need of much cleansing, as they still continued in their filth. For though the recollection of their exile ought to have restrained them, and to have made them careful to fear and obey God, yet it seemed to have been otherwise; and it will appear more fully as we proceed, that being not conscious of having been punished for their sins, they were so secure, that there was among them hardly and fear of God, or hardly any religion. It was therefore needful to blend strong and sharp reproofs with promises of favor, that they might thus be prepared to receive Christ. This is the substance of the whole.

John Calvin

Detailed outline

I. Introductory call to repentance: 1:1–6
II. Prophecies by vision: 1:7–6:8
  A. The man among the myrtle trees: 1:7–17
  B. The four horns: 1:18–21
  C. The man with the measuring rod: 2:1–13
  D. Joshua the high priest: 3:1–10
  E. The candlestick and the two trees: 4:1–14
    1. The first question and explanation: 4:1–10
    2. The second question and explanation: 4:11–14
  F. The flying roll: 5:1–4
  G. The woman in the ephah: 5:5–11
  H. The four chariots: 6:1–8
II. Illustrative prophecies: 6:9–8:23
  A. The returning Jews: 6:9–15
  B. Vanities of the people: 7:1–8:23
    1. Fast days of Israel and obedience to the Word: 7:1–17
      (a) Occasion of the prophecy: 7:1–3
      (b) Fasting not essential, but hearing is: 7:4–7
    2. First half of the Lord's answer to the question of fasting: 7:8–14
      (a) What God requires of the fathers: 7:8–10
      (b) Refusal of the fathers to hearken: 7:11–14
    3. The second half of the Lord's answer: 8:1–23
      (a) The time of redemption: 8:1–8
      (b) Message of encouragement: 8:9–17
      (c) Fasting to be changed to rejoicing: 8:18–23
IV. Direct prophecies: 9:1–14:21
  A. The first prophecy: The rejection of the Messiah: 9:1–11:17
    1. Fall of the heathen world and deliverance of Zion: 9–10
    2. Good and foolish shepherds: 11:1–17
      (a) The humiliated land: 11:1–3
      (b) The good shepherd: 11:4–14
      (c) The foolish shepherd: 11:15–17
  B. The second prophecy: Deliverance: 12:1–14:21
    1. Future deliverance and conversion of Israel: 12:1–13:9
      (a) Deliverance of Judah and Jerusalem: 12:1–9
      (b) Spirit of grace and lamentation: 12:10–14
      (c) A fountain of grace for salvation: 13:1–6
    2. The Messiah's reign: 14:1–21
      (a) Judgment and deliverance: 14:1–5
      (b) Complete salvation: 14:6–11
      (c) Destruction of enemy nations: 14:12–15
      (d) Conversion of heathen nations: 14:16–19
      (e) Everything unholy removed: 14:20–21

2. Helpful summaries of Zechariah

Bird's eye view

Zechariah, who prophesied at the same time as Haggai, urges the Jews to complete the rebuilding of the temple.

Reading plan

The following reading plan, taking one reading per day, enables you to read through Zechariah in four days.

Zechariah 1–5
Zechariah 6–8
Zechariah 9–11
Zechariah 12–14

Verse to memorize

Rejoice greatly, O Daughter of Zion!
Shout, Daughter of Jerusalem!
See, your king comes to you, righteous and having salvation, gentle and riding on a donkey, on a colt, the foal of a donkey.
Zechariah 9:9

Statistics

Thirty-eighth Old Testament book
14 chapters
211 verses
6,444 words

Famous saying found in Zechariah

"Apple of my eye" Zechariah 2:8

Names/titles given

Hebrew title: *Zekar-yah:* "God remembers."
Greek title in Septuagint: *Zacharias:* "Zechariah."
Latin title in Vulgate: *Zacharias:* "Zechariah."

3. Helpful keys to turn to in understanding Zechariah

Key word

Turn

Key verses

Zechariah 1:3; 8:3

Themes to study

Zechariah as a shepherd.
Joashua as the High Priest.
Zerubbabel as the king.

Zechariah quoted in the New Testament

- Speak ye truth each one with his neighbor
  Zech. 8:16 quoted in Eph. 4:25
- Tell ye the daughter of Zion, Behold, thy King cometh unto thee
  Zech. 9:9 quoted in Matt. 21:5, John 12:15
- And they took the thirty pieces of silver
  Zech. 11:12–13 quoted in Matt. 27:9–10
- They shall look on him whom they pierced
  Zech. 12:10 quoted in John 19:37
- I will smite the shepherd, and the sheep of the flock shall be scattered abroad
  Zech. 13:7 quoted in Matt. 26:31 and Mark 14:27

Jesus in Zechariah

In Zechariah Jesus is the Righteous Branch.

Types of Jesus in Zechariah

- Jesus is the Righteous Branch, 3:8.
- Jesus is the King-Priest, 6:13.
- Jesus is the humble King, 9:9–10.
- Jesus is the good Shepherd, sold for thirty shekels, 11:4–13.
- Jesus is the pierced One, 12:10.
- Jesus is the Judge and King who will come, chapter 14.

Lessons to learn from Zechariah

One of Satan's tricks is to make accusations against us in order to bring us down.

4. Chapter by chapter: outline of every chapter of Zechariah

Zechariah 1

Matthew Henry's introduction

In this chapter, after the introduction (v. 1), we have,

I. An awakening call to a sinful people to repent of their sins and return to God, vv. 2–6.

II. Great encouragement given to hope for mercy.

A. By the vision of the horses, vv. 7–11.

B. By the prayer of the angel for Jerusalem, and the answer to that prayer, vv. 12–17.

C. By the vision of the four carpenters that were employed to cut off the four horns with which Judah and Jerusalem were scattered, vv. 18–21.

A detailed analysis of chapter

An exhortation to repent. (1–6)

First vision: horseman among the myrtle trees. (7–17)

Second vision: the four horns and four craftsmen. (18–21)

Key verse

Verse 1: "In the eighth month, in the second year of Darius, came the word of the LORD unto Zechariah, the son of Berechiah, the son of Iddo the prophet."

Key word / key phrase

Verse 8, "During the night I had a vision."

Key event / key person / key theme

The ministry of angels, who act as interpreters (first vision); the defeat of Judah's enemies (second vision)

Key thought

Note the results of repentance. See verse 6.

Key thing to look out for

The prophet is happy to show his total dependence on the Lord.

Key Bible cross-reference

Verse 8. See Revelation 6:2–8.

Key "by way of explanation"

Verse 8, "red, brown and white horses." Horses were also seen in John's vision, see Revelation 6:1–8. Horses symbolized power and dominance. Zechariah was a priest and a contemporary of Haggai (Ezra 5:1). He continued his ministry after Haggai, perhaps because he was younger

(2:4). He was born in Babylonia, and returned with the first group of exils led by Zerubbabel.

Key "Quotable Quote"

"Repentance ranges from regretting obvious sins like murder, adultery, abuse, swearing, and stealing to the realization that not loving (loving your brother as yourself) is a murder, and that an evil look is adultery and the love of praise is stealing God's glory."

John Chrysostom

Zechariah 2

Matthew Henry's introduction

In this chapter we have,

I. Another vision which the prophet saw, not for his own entertainment, but for his satisfaction and the edification of those to whom he was sent, vv. 1, 2.

II. A sermon on it, in the rest of the chapter.

A. By way of explication of the vision, showing it to be a prediction of the replenishing of Jerusalem and of its safety and honor, vv. 3–5.

B. By way of application. Here is,

1. A use of exhortation to the Jews that were yet in Babylon, pressing them to hasten their return to their own land, vv. 6–9.
2. A use of consolation to those that were returned, in reference to the many difficulties they had to struggle with, vv. 10–12.
3. A use of caution to all not to prescribe to God, or limit him, but patiently to wait for him, v. 13.

A detailed analysis of chapter

Third vision: man with a measuring line.

The prosperity of Jerusalem. (1–5)

The Jews called to return to their own land. (6–9)

A promise of God's presence. (10–13)

Key verse

Verse 6: "Ho, ho, come forth, and flee from the land of the north."

Key word / key phrase

Verse 10, "Shout and be glad, O Daughter of Zion."

Key event / key person / key theme

Full restoration for people, temple, and city

Key thought

There is nothing that God does not know about us.

Key thing to look out for

Verse 13 commends stillness in God's presence.

Key Bible cross-reference

Verse 5. See Isaiah 26:1.

Key "by way of explanation"

Verse 12, "the holy land." This is the only place where this phrase comes in the Bible. But also see Psalm 2:6; 15:1; 99:9. This land was the national home for God's people and given over to God.

Key "Quotable Quote"

"Jewish infidelity shall be overthrown. The Jews in all their dispersions shall cast away their old infidelity, and shall have their hearts wonderfully changed, and abhor themselves for their past unbelief and obstinacy."

Jonathan Edwards

Zechariah 3

Matthew Henry's introduction

Here is,

I. A vision relating to Joshua, as the representative of the church in his time, representing the disadvantages he labored under, and the people in him, with the redress of the grievances of both.

A. He is accused by Satan, but is brought off by Christ, vv. 1, 2.

B. He appears in filthy garments, but has them changed, vv. 3–5.

C. He is assured of being established in his office if he conduct himself well, vv. 6, 7.

II. A sermon relating to Christ, who is here called "The branch," who should be endued with all perfections for his undertaking, should be carried triumphantly through it, and by whom we should have pardon and peace, vv. 8–10.

A detailed analysis of chapter

Fourth vision: clean clothes for the high priest

Restoration. (1–5)

A promise about the Messiah. (6–10)

Key verse

Verse 7: "I will give thee places to walk among these that stand by."

Key word / key phrase

Verse 1, "to accuse him."

Key event / key person / key theme

Joshua the priest is accused and acquitted

Key thought

Verse 4 should fill us with wonder and gratitude.

Key thing to look out for

God requires us to serve him in certain specific ways.

Key Bible cross-reference

Verse 2. See Jude 9.

Key "by way of explanation"

Verse 3, "filthy clothes." Joshua's clothes were like those someone wore who had escaped from a fire. The clothes symbolized the sins of the people and so needed to be exchanged for "rich garments."

Key "Quotable Quote"

"Purity is 'that which is undiluted by other substances.' Now, join that to the place Jesus pointed at, to the heart of a man: that's where God seeks undiluted commitment."

Jack Hayford

Zechariah 4

Matthew Henry's introduction

Here is,

I. The awakening of the prophet to observe the vision, v. 1.

II. The vision itself, of a candlestick with seven lamps, which were supplied with oil, and kept burning, immediately from two olive-trees that grew by it, one on either side, vv. 2, 3.

III. The general encouragement hereby intended to be given to the builders of the temple to go on in that good work, assuring them that it should be brought to perfection at last, vv. 4–10.

IV. The particular explication of the vision, for the illustration of these assurances, vv. 11–14.

A detailed analysis of chapter

Fifth vision: gold lampstand, with two olive trees. (1–7)

Further encouragement. (8–10)

An explanation about the olive trees. (11–14)

Key verse

Verse 2: "And said unto me, What seest thou? And I said, I have looked, and behold a candlestick all of gold."

Key word / key phrase

Verse 2, "a solid gold lampstand."

Key event / key person / key theme

The temple would not be built through shear labor, or by human power and ability, but by the Spirit.

Key thought

There is no light without oil. There is not spiritual light without God's Spirit.

Key thing to look out for

The only way to serve the Lord successfully is summarized in verse 6.

Key Bible cross-reference

Verse 3. See Revelation 11:4.

Key "by way of explanation"

Verse 2, the bowl will have contained oil for the lamps; seven symbolizes perfection of light. The two olive trees are the two lines of leadership, the priestly line and the royal line. The lampstand represents the testimony of the people of God. The oil is God's power and God's anointing.

Key "Quotable Quote"

"All of us who have received one and the same Spirit, that is, the Holy Spirit, are in a sense blended together with one another and with God."

Cyril of Alexandria

Zechariah 5

Matthew Henry's introduction

I. God will reckon severely with those particular people among them that are wicked and profane, and that hated to be reformed in these times of reformation; while God is showing kindness to the body of the nation, and loading that with his blessings, they and their families shall, notwithstanding that, lie under the curse, which the prophet sees in a flying roll, vv. 1–4.

II. If the body of the nation hereafter degenerate, and wickedness prevail among them, it shall be carried off and hurried away with a swift destruction, under the pressing weight of divine wrath, represented by a talent of lead on the mouth of an ephah, carried on the wing I know not where, vv. 5–11.

A detailed analysis of chapter

Sixth vision: the flying scroll. (1–4)

Seventh vision: a woman in a basket. (5–11)

Key verse

Verse 1: "Then I turned, and lifted up mine eyes, and looked, and behold a flying roll."

Key word / key phrase

Verse 1, "a flying scroll."

Key event / key person / key theme

Three evils which need to be dealt with: theft, false witness, unrighteousness

Key thought

God is constantly giving us warnings to heed.

Key thing to look out for

When we clearly see what we must do we still need to rely on God for his help.

Key Bible cross-reference

Verse 11. See Genesis 10:10.

Key "by way of explanation"

Verse 1, "a flying scroll." This could be read by everyone and depicts the renewed interest in the law in the days after the Exile.

Key "Quotable Quote"

"God's truth judges created things out of love, and Satan's truth judges them out of envy and hatred."

Dietrich Bonhoeffer

Zechariah 6

Matthew Henry's introduction

Here is,

I. God, as King of nations, ruling the world by the ministry of angels, in the vision of the four chariots, vv. 1–8.

II. God, as King of saints, ruling the church by the mediation of Christ, in the figure of Joshua the high priest crowned, the ceremony performed, and then explained about Christ, vv. 9–15.

A detailed analysis of chapter

Eighth vision: the four chariots. (1–8)

Joshua, the high priest, crowned as a type of Christ. (9–15)

Key verse

Verse 1: "And I turned, and lifted up mine eyes, and looked, and, behold, there came four chariots out from between two mountains; and the mountains were mountains of brass."

Key word / key phrase

Verse 1, "four chariots."

Key event / key person / key theme

The angelic spirits are the symbols and agents of God's judgment

Key thought

God's presence among his people is symbolized by the temple.

Key thing to look out for

God longs to rule in our hearts.

Key Bible cross-reference

Verse 5. See Revelation 7:1.

Key "by way of explanation"

Verse 11, "crown." This special crowning of the high priest looks forward to the time when all prophecy will be consummated in the rule of the messianic Priest-King.

Key "Quotable Quote"

"That book [Bible], sir, is the rock on which our republic rests."

Andrew Jackson

Zechariah 7

Matthew Henry's introduction

In this chapter we have,

I. A case of conscience proposed to the prophet by the children of the captivity about fasting, whether they should continue their solemn fasts which they had religiously observed during the seventy years of their captivity, vv. 1–3.

II. The answer to this question, which is given in this and the next chapter; and this answer was given not all at once, but by piecemeal, and, it should seem, at several times, for here are four distinct discourses which have all of them reference to this case, each of them prefaced with "the word of the Lord came," vv. 4–8 and 8:1, 18. The method of them is very observable. In this chapter,

A. The prophet sharply reproves them for the mismanagements of their fasts, vv. 4–7.

B. He exhorts them to reform their lives, which would be the best way of fasting, and to take heed of those sins which brought those judgments on them which they kept these fasts in memory of, vv. 8–14.

A detailed analysis of chapter

The captives' inquiry about fasting. (1–7)

Sin is the reason for their captivity. (8–14)

Key verse

Verse 9: "Execute true judgment, and show mercy and compassions every man to his brother."

Key word / key phrase

Verse 13, "When I called."

Key event / key person / key theme

A call to repentance

Key thought

Verse 13 is a picture of the basis of all sin.

Key thing to look out for

Over and over again the prophets emphasize the need for social justice. See verses 9, 10.

Key Bible cross-reference

Verse 1. See Ezra 5:1.

Key "by way of explanation"

Verse 9, "justice." This is proper ordering of every society. See 8:16; Isaiah 42:1,4; Micah 6:8.

Key "Quotable Quote"

"The Christian's goal is not power but justice. We are to seek to make the institutions of power just, without being corrupted by the process necessary to do this."

Charles Colson

Zechariah 8

Matthew Henry's introduction

Here are two words from the Lord of hosts, and they are both good words and comfortable words. In the former of these messages (v. 1) God promises that Jerusalem shall be restored, reformed, replenished (vv. 2–8), that the country shall be rich, and the affairs of the nation shall be successful, their reputation retrieved, and their state in all respects the reverse of what it had been for many years past (vv. 9–15); he then exhorts them to reform what was amiss among them, that they might be ready for these favors designed them (vv. 16, 17). In the latter of these messages (v. 18) he promises that their fasts should be superseded by the return of mercy (v. 19), and that thereon they should be replenished, enriched, and strengthened, by the accession of foreigners to them, vv. 20–23.

A detailed analysis of chapter

The restoration of Jerusalem. (1–8)

The people encouraged by promises of God's favor, and exhorted to holiness. (9–17)

The Jews in the latter days. (18–23)

Key verse

Verse 8: "And I will bring them, and they shall dwell in the midst of Jerusalem: and they shall be my people, and I will be their God, in truth and in righteousness."

Key word / key phrase

Verse 3, "I will . . . dwell in Jerusalem."

Key event / key person / key theme

Jerusalem's wonderful future

Key thought

The greatest blessing we can receive from the Lord is his presence.

Key thing to look out for

This chapter has ten promises, each beginning, "The LORD Almighty says."

Key Bible cross-reference

Verse 16. See Ephesians 4:25.

Key "by way of explanation"

Verse 2, "jealous." The Hebrew word indicates very strong feelings. An alternative translation might be, "with great zeal."

Key "Quotable Quote"

"The main hinge on which faith turns is this: we must not imagine that the Lord's promises are true objectively but not in our experience. We must make them ours by embracing them in our hearts."

John Calvin

Zechariah 9

Matthew Henry's introduction

Here is,

I. A prophecy against the Jews' unrighteous neighbors–the Syrians, Tyrians, Philistines, and others (vv. 1–6), with an intimation of mercy to some of them, in their conversion (v. 7), and a promise of mercy to God's people, in their protection, v. 8.

II. A prophecy of their righteous King, the Messiah, and his coming, with a description of him (v. 9) and of his kingdom, the nature and extent of it, v. 10.

III. An account of the obligation the Jews lay under to Christ for their deliverance out of their captivity in Babylon, vv. 11, 12.

IV. A prophecy of the victories and successes God would grant to the Jews over their enemies, as typical of our great deliverance by Christ, vv. 13–15.

V. A promise of great plenty, and joy, and honor, which God had in reserve for his people (vv. 16, 17), which was written for their encouragement.

A detailed analysis of chapter

God's defense of his people. (1–8)

Christ's coming and his kingdom. (9–11)

Promises to God's people. (12–17)

Key verse

Verse 9: "Rejoice greatly, O daughter of Zion; shout, O daughter of Jerusalem: behold, thy King cometh unto thee: he is just, and having salvation; lowly, and riding upon an ass, and upon a colt the foal of an ass."

Key word / key phrase

Verse 5, "Gaza will lose her king."

Key event / key person / key theme

Judgment on the surrounding nations, and the Messiah-King

Key thought

It is not up to us to take revenge on people, God will punish them in due course.

Key thing to look out for

God is majestic. God is humble. See verse 9.

Key Bible cross-reference

Verse 10. See Psalm 72:8.

Key "by way of explanation"

Verse 9, "gentle and riding on a donkey." This verse is quoted in the New Testament, Matthew 21:5; John 12:15, to refer to the Messiah entering his city, that is, to Jesus entering Jerusalem on Palm Sunday. Chapters 9 to 14 consist of a series of prophecies about the end times.

Key "Quotable Quote"

"Our personal afflictions involve the living God; the only way in which Satan can persecute or afflict God is through attacking the people of God. The only way we can have personal victory in the midst of these flying arrows raining down on us is to call upon the Lord for help. It is his strength, supplied to us in our weakness, that makes victory after victory possible."

Edith Schaeffer

Zechariah 10

Matthew Henry's introduction

Now,

I. They are here directed to eye the great God in all events that concerned them, and, both in the evils they suffered and in the comforts they desired, to acknowledge his hand, vv. 1–4.

II. They are encouraged to expect strength and success from him in all their struggles with the enemies of their church and state, and to hope that the issue would be glorious at last, vv. 5–12.

A detailed analysis of chapter

Blessings to be sought from the Lord. (1–5)
God will restore his people. (6–12)

Key verse

Verse 6: "And I will strengthen the house of Judah, and I will save the house of Joseph, and I will bring them again to place them; for I have mercy upon them: and they shall be as though I had not cast them off: for I am the LORD their God, and will hear them."

Key word / key phrase

Verse 6, "I will strengthen the house of Judah."

Key event / key person / key theme

The Lord promises deliverance

Key thought

Jesus echoed verse 2 in Mark 6:34 where also showed his compassion for people needing spiritual care.

Key thing to look out for

Only God can redeem people. See verse 8.

Key Bible cross-reference

Verse 1. See Leviticus 26:4.

Key "by way of explanation"

Verse 8, "redeem." This Hebrew word refers to rescuing people from slavery or leading them out of captivity. See Isaiah 35:10; 1 Peter 1:18, 19.

Key "Quotable Quote"

"When a man undergoes treatment from a doctor, he does not need to know the way in which the drug works on his body in order to be cured. There is a sense in which Christianity is like that. At the heart of Christianity there is a mystery, but it is not the mystery of intellectual appreciation; it the mystery of redemption."

William Barclay

Zechariah 11

Matthew Henry's introduction 11

Here is,

I. A prediction of the destruction itself that

should come on the Jewish nation, vv.1–3.

II. The putting of it into the hands of the Messiah.

A. He is charged with the custody of that flock, vv. 4–6.

B. He undertakes it, and bears rule in it, vv. 7, 8.

C. Finding it perverse, he gives it up (v. 9), breaks his shepherd's staff (vv. 10, 11), resents the indignities done him and the contempt put on him (vv. 12, 13), and then breaks his other staff, v. 14.

D. He turns them over into the hands of foolish shepherds, who, instead of preventing, shall complete their ruin, and both the blind leaders and the blind followers shall fall together into the ditch, vv. 15–17. This is foretold to the poor of the flock before it comes to pass, that, when it does come to pass, they may not be offended.

A detailed analysis of chapter

Destruction to come on the Jews. (1–3)

The Lord's dealing with the Jews. (4–14)

The emblem and curse of a foolish shepherd. (15–17)

Key verse

Verse 10: "And I took my staff, even Beauty, and cut it asunder, that I might break my covenant which I had made with all the people."

Key word / key phrase

Verse 4, "Pasture the flock."

Key event / key person / key theme

The good shepherd and the bad shepherds

Key thought

We are all pastors to the people with whom we live and work.

Key thing to look out for

Which shepherd do we resemble?

Key Bible cross-reference

Verse 12. See Matthew 26:15.

Key "by way of explanation"

Verse 9, "eat one another's flesh." The siege of Jerusalem in AD 70 was so severe that the historian Josephus claims that cannibalism took place.

Key "Quotable Quote"

"It takes some of us a lifetime to learn that Christ, our Good Shepherd, knows exactly what he is doing with us. He understands us perfectly."

Phillip Keller

Zechariah 12

Matthew Henry's introduction

Now, in this chapter, we have the blessings of the latter, many precious promises made to the gospel-Jerusalem by him who (v. 1) declares his power to make them good. It is promised,

I. That the attempts of the church's enemies against her shall be to their own ruin, and they shall find that it is at their peril if they do her any hurt, vv. 2–4, 6.

II. That the endeavors of the church's friends and patrons for her good shall be pious, regular, and successful, v. 5.

III. That God will protect and strengthen the meanest and weakest that belong to his church, and work salvation for them, vv. 7, 8.

IV. That as a preparative for all this mercy, and a pledge of it, he will pour on them a spirit of prayer and repentance, the effect of which shall be universal and very particular, vv. 9–14.

A detailed analysis of chapter

Punishment of the enemies of Judah. (1–8)
Repentance and sorrow of the Jews. (9–14)

Key verse

Verse 3: "And in that day will I make Jerusalem a burdensome stone for all people: all that burden themselves with it shall be cut in pieces, though all the people of the earth be gathered together against it."

Key word / key phrase

Verse 2, "I am going to make Jerusalem a cup."

Key event / key person / key theme

Jerusalem is saved, and the way of salvation

Key thought

Verse 8 is a good verse for when we feel feeble.

Key thing to look out for

Verse 10 speaks of God pouring out his Spirit of grace. How can we receive this today?

Key Bible cross-reference

Verse 10. See John 19:37.

Key "by way of explanation"

Verse 4, "panic . . . madness . . . blind." In Deuteronomy 28:28 these are said to be the afflictions God will bring down on his people. Now they will rest on Israel's enemies. "Cup," that is Jerusalem will be the agent of God's judgment (drinking strong wine is often a metaphor for the experience of God's judgment, e.g. Isaiah 51:17).

Key "Quotable Quote"

"The true way to mourn the dead is to take care of the living who belong to them."

Edmund Burke

Zechariah 13

Matthew Henry's introduction

In this chapter we have,

I. Some further promises relating to gospel times. Here is a promise of the remission of sins (v. 1), of the reformation of manners (v. 2), and particularly of the convicting and silencing of false prophets, vv. 2–6.

II. A clear prediction of the sufferings of Christ and the dispersion of his disciples thereon (v. 7), of the destruction of the greater part of the Jewish nation not long after (v. 8), and of the purifying of a remnant of them, a peculiar people to God, v. 9.

A detailed analysis of chapter

The fountain for the remission of sins, and the conviction of the false prophets. (1–6)
The death of Christ, and the saving of a remnant of the people. (7–9)

Key verse

Verse 1: "In that day there shall be a fountain opened to the house of David and to the inhabitants of Jerusalem for sin and for uncleanness."

Key word / key phrase

Verse 1, "cleanse them from sin and impurity."

Key event / key person / key theme

Impurity abolished, and the remnant refined

Key thought

If God disciplines us it is to make us more godly.

Key thing to look out for

Nobody can any longer strike and scatter the Good Shepherd's flock.

Key Bible cross-reference

Verse 7. See Mark 14:27.

Key "by way of explanation"

Verse 7, "my shepherd." This refers to the Good Shepherd, see 11:4–14, and contrasts with the faithless shepherds, see 11:15–17.

Key "Quotable Quote"

"Our speech, our thoughts, our actions, our reactions, our relationships, our goals, our values – all are transformed if only we live in the self-conscious enjoyment of the love of Christ."

D.A. Carson

Zechariah 14

Matthew Henry's introduction

I. The gates of hell are here threatening the church (vv. 1, 2) and yet not prevailing.

II. The power of Heaven appears here for the church and against the enemies of it, vv. 3, 5.

III. The events about the church are here represented as mixed (vv. 6, 7), but issuing well at last.

IV. The spreading of the means of knowledge is here foretold, and the setting up of the gospel-kingdom in the world (vv. 8, 9), which shall be the enlargement and establishment of another Jerusalem, vv. 10, 11.

V. Those shall be reckoned with that fought against Jerusalem (vv. 12–15) and those that neglect his worship there, vv. 17–19.

VI. It is promised that there shall be great resort to the church, and great purity and piety in it, vv. 16, 20, 21.

A detailed analysis of chapter

The sufferings of Jerusalem. (1–7)

Encouraging prospects, and the destruction of her enemies. (8–15)

The holiness of the latter days. (16–21)

Key verse

Verse 3: "Then shall the LORD go forth, and fight against those nations, as when he fought in the day of battle."

Key word / key phrase

Verse 10, "Jerusalem will be raised up and remain in its place."

Key event / key person / key theme

The Messiah's reign

Key thought

Every day should be a holy day.

Key thing to look out for

Everything we do should be done to the glory of our holy God.

Key Bible cross-reference

Verse 8. See John 7:38.

Key "by way of explanation"

Verse 20, "HOLY TO THE LORD." This inscription was engraved on a gold plate and worn on the turban of the high priest, see Exodus 28:36–38.

Key "Quotable Quote"

"Sever me from myself
that I may be grateful to you;
may I perish to myself
that I may be safe in you;
may I die to myself
that I may live in you;
may I wither to myself
that I may blossom in you;
may I be emptied of myself
that I may abound in you;
may I be nothing to myself
that I may be all in you."

Desiderius Erasmus

5. Select bibliography for Zechariah

Baker, David W. *Nahum, Habakkuk, Zephaniah* (Tyndale), Inter-Varsity, 1988.

Baldwin, Joyce C. *Haggai, Zechariah, Malachi: An Introduction and Commentary*. Downers Grove, Ill.: InterVarsity, 1972.

Kaiser, Walter. *Micah, Nahum, Habakkuk, Zephaniah, Haggai, Zechariah, Malachi* (Mastering the Old Testament), Word Books, 1992.

Pusey, E. B. *The Minor Prophets*. 2 Vols. Reprint edition. Grand Rapids: Baker, 1950.

Smith, George Adam. *The Book of the Twelve Prophets*. 2 Vols. New York: Harper & Brothers, n.d.

Unger, Merrill F. *Zechariah*. Grand Rapids: Zondervan, 1962.

Malachi

1. Book by book: Introduction to Malachi

Introduction

Malachi forms the transition link between the two dispensations, the Old and the New, "the skirt and boundary of Christianity" (Tertullian), to which perhaps is due the abrupt earnestness which characterizes his prophecies. His very name is somewhat uncertain. Malachi is the name of an office, rather than a person, "My messenger," and as such is found in Mal. 3:1. The Septuagint favors this view in Mal. 1:1; translate, not "by Malachi," but "by the hand of His messenger" (compare Hag. 1:13). Malachi is the last inspired messenger of the Old Testament, announcing the advent of the Great Messenger of the

New Testament. The Chaldee paraphrase identifies him with Ezra wrongly, as Ezra is never called a prophet but a scribe, and Malachi never a scribe but a prophet. Still it hence appears that Malachi was by some old authorities not regarded as a proper name.

The analogy of the headings of other prophets, however, favors the common view that Malachi is a proper name. As Haggai and Zechariah, the contemporary prophets, supported Joshua and Zerubbabel in the building of the temple, so he at a subsequent period supported the priest Ezra and the governor Nehemiah. Like that ruler, he presupposes the temple to have been already built (Mal. 1:10; 3:1–10). Both alike censure the abuses still unreformed (Neh. 13:5, 15–22, 23–30), the profane and mercenary character of the priests, the people's marriages contracted with foreigners, the non-payment of the tithes, and want of sympathy towards the poor on the part of the rich (Neh. 6:7) implies that Nehemiah was supported by prophets in his work of reformation. The date thus will be about 420 B.C., or later. Both the periods after the captivity (that of Haggai and Zechariah, and that of Malachi) were marked by royal, priestly, and prophetic men at the head of God's people. The former period was that of the building of the temple; the latter, that of the restoration of the people and rebuilding of the city. It is characteristic of the people of God that the first period after the restoration was exclusively devoted to the rebuilding of the temple; the political restoration came secondarily. Only a colony of fifty thousand settled with Joshua and Zerubbabel in Palestine (Ezra 2:64). Even these became intermingled with the heathen around during the sixty years passed over by Ezra in silence (Ezra 9:6–15; Neh. 1:3). Hence a second restoration was needed which should mould the national life into a Jewish form, re-establishing the holy law and the holy city—a work effected by Ezra and Nehemiah, with the aid of Malachi, in a period of about half a century, ending with the deaths of Malachi and Nehemiah in the last ten years of the fifth century B.C.; that is, the "seven weeks" (Dan. 9:25) put in the beginning of the "seventy" by themselves, to mark the fundamental difference between them, the last period of Old Testament revelation, and the period which followed without any revelation (the sixty-two weeks), preceding the final week standing out in unrivalled dignity by itself as the time of Messiah's appearing. The seventy weeks thus begin with the seventh year of Artaxerxes who allowed Ezra to go to Jerusalem, 457 B.C., in accordance with the commandment which then went forth from God. Ezra the priest performed the inner work of purifying the nation from heathenish elements and reintroducing the law; while Nehemiah did the outer work of rebuilding the city and restoring the national polity (Auberlen). Vitringa makes the date of Malachi's prophecies to be about the second return of Nehemiah from Persia, not later than 424 B.C., the date of Artaxerxes' death (Neh. 13:6). About this time Socrates was teaching the only approach to a pure morality which corrupt Athens ever knew.

Moore distinguishes six portions:

(1) Charge against Israel for insensibility to God's love, which so distinguished Israel above Edom (Mal. 1:1–5).

(2) The priests are reproved for neglect and profanation (Mal. 1:6–2:9).

(3) Mixed marriages, and the wrongs done to Jewish wives, are reproved (Mal. 2:10–16).

(4) Coming of Messiah and His forerunners (Mal. 2:17–3:6).

(5) Reproof for tithes withheld (Mal. 3:7–12).

(6) Contrast between the godly and the ungodly at the present time, and in the future judgment; exhortation, therefore, to return to the law (Mal. 3:13–4:6).

Style

The style is animated, but less grand, and the rhythm less marked, than in some of the older prophets.

Canonicity

The canonicity of the book is established by the references to it in the New Testament (Matt. 11:10; 17:12; Mark 1:2; 9:11, 12; Luke 1:17; Rom. 9:13).

A.R. Faussett

John Calvin's introduction to Malachi

Malachi was no doubt one of the Prophets, and, as it appears, the last; for at the end of his Book he exhorts the people to continue in their adherence to the pure doctrine of the Law: and this he did, because God was not afterwards to send Prophets in succession as before; for it was his purpose that the Jews should have a stronger desire for Christ, they having been for a time without any Prophets. It was indeed either a token of God's wrath, or a presage of Christ's coming, when they were deprived of that benefit which Moses mentions in Deuteronomy 18; for God had then promised to send Prophets, that the Jews might know that he cared for their safety. When therefore God left his people without Prophets, it was either to show his great displeasure, as during the Babylonian exile, or to hold them in suspense, that they might with stronger desire look forward to the coming of Christ.

However we may regard this, I have no doubt but he was the last of the Prophets; for he bids the people to adhere to the doctrine of the Law until Christ should be revealed.

The sum and substance of the Book is, — that though the Jews had but lately returned to their own country, they yet soon returned to their own nature, became unmindful of God's favor, and so gave themselves up to many corruptions; that their state was nothing better than that of their fathers before them, so that God had as it were lost all his labor in chastising them. As then the Jews had again relapsed into many vices, our Prophet severely reproves them, and upbraids them with ingratitude, because they rendered to God their deliverer so shameful a recompense. He also mentions some of their sins, that he might prove the people to be guilty, for he saw that they were full of evasions. And he addresses the priests, who had by bad examples corrupted the morals of the people, when yet their office required a very different course of life; for the Lord had set them over the people to be teachers of religion and of uprightness; but from them did emanate a great portion of the vices of the age; and hence our Prophet the more severely condemns them.

He shows at the same time that God would remember his gratuitous covenant, which he had made with their fathers, so that the Redeemer would at length come. This is the substance of the whole.

John Calvin

Detailed outline

- I. Introduction: 1:1–5
  - A. The messenger: 1:1
  - B. The message: 1:1
  - C. The recipient of the message: Israel: 1:1
  - D. God's love for Israel: 1:2–5
    - 1. Esau and Jacob: 1:2–3
    - 2. God and Edom: 1:4–5
- II. A message to the priests: 1:6–2:9
  - A. Their neglect in religious duties: 1:6–2:9
    - 1. The priests despise the name of the Lord: 1:6–14
    - 2. The Lord curses the priests: 2:1–9
- III. The sin of the people of Israel: 2:10–3:15
  - A. Idolatry: 2:10–13
  - B. The people engage in divorce: 2:14–16
  - C. The Lord will judge when he comes: 2:17–3:5
  - D. The people rob God: 3:6–12
  - E. The people doubt God's character: 3:13–15
- IV. Promises to the nation: 3:16–4–6
  - A. The Book of Remembrance: 3:16–18
  - B. Rewards from the coming Messiah: 4:1–3
  - C. The prophecy of the coming Elijah: 4:4–6

2. Helpful summaries of Malachi

Bird's eye view

Malachi's message is directed at the Jews who had returned from exile in Babylon but who now lived in Jerusalem with cold and indifferent hearts towards God. Malachi warns these backsliders about God's judgment on them.

Reading plan

The following reading plan, taking one reading per day, enables you to read through Malachi in two days.

Malachi 1–2

Malachi 3–4

Verse to memorize

Malachi 3:1

"See, I will send my messenger, who will prepare the way before me. Then suddenly the Lord you are seeking will come to his temple; the messenger of the covenant, whom you desire, will come," says the Lord Almighty.

Statistics

Thirty-ninth Old Testament book

4 chapters

55 verses

1,782 words

After Malachi's prophecy there was a four hundred year silence, during which no biblical prophet spoke or wrote.

Names/titles given

Hebrew title: *Mal'aki:* "my messenger."

Greek title in Septuagint: *Malachias:* "by the hand of the messenger."

Latin title in Vulgate: *Maleachi:* "Malachi."

3. Helpful keys to turn to in understanding Malachi

Key words

The day of the Lord

Key verses

Malachi 4:2, 5–6

Themes to study

God's promises

God's love

What makes God unhappy.

Malachi quoted in the New Testament

- Jacob I loved, but Esau I hated
  Mal. 1:2–3 quoted in Rom. 9:13
- Behold, I send my messenger before thy face
  Mal. 3:1 quoted in Matt. 11:10, Mark 1:2, and Luke 7:27

Jesus in Malachi

In Malachi Jesus is the Sun of Righteousness.

Type of John the Baptist

Malachi predicted the coming of the messenger to prepare the way of the Lord, who came in the person of John the Baptist, 3:1, see Matthew 3:3.

Lessons to learn from Malachi

- We are to constantly recall that God is a God of love.
- Formal religion cuts no ice with God.

4. Chapter by chapter: outline of every chapter of Malachi

Malachi 1

Matthew Henry's introduction

This prophet is sent first to convince and then to comfort. God had provided (and one would think effectually) for the engaging of Israel to himself by providences and ordinances; but it seems, by the complaints here made of them, that they received the grace of God in both these in vain.

I. They were very ungrateful to God for his favors to them, and rendered not again according to the benefit they received, vv. 1–5.

II. They were very careless and remiss in the observance of his institutions; the priests especially were so, who were in a particular manner charged with them, vv. 6–14.

A detailed analysis of chapter

The ingratitude of Israel. (1–5)

They are careless about God's institutions. (6–14)

Key verse

Verse 1: "The burden of the word of the LORD to Israel by Malachi."

Key word / key phrase

Verse 2, "I have loved you."

Key event / key person / key theme

God loves Israel, but indicts the priests

Key thought

So often, God's leaders seem to be unfaithful to God.

Key thing to look out for

The existence of God's people is founded on God's love.

Key Bible cross-reference

Verses 2–3. See Romans 9:13.

Key "by way of explanation"

Verse 3, "Esau I have hated." This does not mean that God literally "hated" Esau. Rather it contrasts God's great love for Jacob, in comparison with which it might be said that he hated Esau. Malachi was probably a contemporary of Nehemiah. The book may have been written about 433 BC when Nehemiah returned to Persia, after the city walls has been rebuilt.

Key "Quotable Quote"

"The love which brought the Son of God's love from heaven to earth, from earth to the cross, from the cross to the grave, from the grave to glory – that love which was weary, hungry, tempted, scorned, scourged, buffeted, spat upon, crucified, pierced – which fasted, prayed, taught, healed, wept, sweated, bled, died, that love will eternally embrace you."

Richard Baxter

Malachi 2

Matthew Henry's introduction

There are two great ordinances which divine wisdom has instituted, the wretched profanation of both of which is complained of and sharply reproved in this chapter.

I. The ordinance of the ministry, which is peculiar to the church, and is designed for the maintaining and keeping up of that; this was profaned by those who were themselves dignified with the honor of it and entrusted with the business of it. The priests profaned the holy things of God; this they are here charged with; their sin is aggravated, and they are severely threatened for it, vv. 1–9.

II. The ordinance of marriage, which is common to the world of mankind, and was instituted for the maintaining and keeping up of that; this was profaned both by the priests and by the people, in marrying strangers (vv. 11, 12), treating their wives unkindly (v. 13), putting them away (v. 16), and herein dealing treacherously, vv. 10, 14, 15. And that which was at the bottom of this and other instances of profaneness and downright atheism, thinking God altogether such a one as themselves, which was, in effect, to say, There is no God, v. 17.

A detailed analysis of chapter

The priests reproved for neglecting the covenant. (1–9)

The people reproved for their evil practices. (10–17)

Key verse

Verse 6: "The law of truth was in his mouth, and iniquity was not found in his lips: he walked with me in peace and equity, and did turn many away from iniquity."

Key word / key phrase

Verse 1, "this abomination is for you, O priests."

Key event / key person / key theme

Israel's (that is, all the Jews who had returned from exile) faithlessness in worship and marriage

Key thought

Not listening to God seems to be the first step we take in falling away from God.

Key thing to look out for

There can be no excuse for deliberately breaking God's laws.

Key Bible cross-reference

Verse 4. See Numbers 3:11–13.

Key "by way of explanation"

Verse 5, "a covenant of life and peace." This is the only occurrence of this phrase in the Bible. To enter into a covenant relationship with God is the beginning of spiritual life and this leads to peace and health and salvation.

Key "Quotable Quote"

"When everything we receive from him is received and prized as a pledge of his covenant love, then his bounties, instead of being set up as rivals and idols to draw our heart from him, awaken us to fresh exercises of gratitude and furnish us with fresh motives of cheerful obedience every hour."

John Newton

Malachi 3

Matthew Henry's introduction

In this chapter we have,

I. A promise of the coming of the Messiah, and of his forerunner; and the errand he comes on is here particularly described, both the comfort which his coming brings to his church and people and the terror which it will bring to the wicked, vv. 1–6.

II. A reproof of the Jews for their corrupting God's ordinances and sacrilegiously robbing him of his dues, with a charge to them to amend this matter, and a promise that, if they did, God would return in mercy to them, vv. 7–12.

III. A description of the wickedness of the wicked that speak against God (vv. 13–15), and of the righteousness of the righteous that speak for him, with the precious promises made to them, vv. 16–18.

A detailed analysis of chapter

The coming of God's messenger. (1–5)
The Jews reproved for their corruptions. (6–12)
God's care of his people. The distinction between the righteous and the wicked. (13–18)

Key verse

Verse 1: "Behold, I will send my messenger, and he shall prepare the way before me: and the Lord, whom ye seek, shall suddenly come to his temple, even the messenger of the covenant, whom ye delight in: behold, he shall come, saith the LORD of hosts."

Key word / key phrase

Verse 8, "Will a man rob God?"

Key event / key person / key theme

Robbing God, tithing and God's blessing

Key thought

Everything belongs to God. We own nothing. At best, we are tenants.

Key thing to look out for

Trusting our finances to the Lord seems to be about the last thing we ever do.

Key Bible cross-reference

Verse 1. See Matthew 11:10.

Key "by way of explanation"

Verses 1–5, the messenger is a future prophet who will make the people ready for the Day of the Lord. This prophecy was fulfilled when John the Baptist started preaching (see also 4:5–6).

Key "Quotable Quote"

"May I be patient! It is so difficult to make real what one believes, and to make these trials, as they are intended, real blessings."

John Henry Newman

Malachi 4

Matthew Henry's introduction

We have here proper instructions given us (very proper to close the canon of the Old Testament with),

I. About the state of recompense and retribution that is before us, the misery of the wicked and the happiness of the righteous in that state, vv. 1–3. And this is represented to us under a prophecy of the destruction of Jerusalem, and the unbelieving Jews with it, and of the comforts and triumphs of those among them that received the gospel.

II. About the state of trial and preparation we are now in, in which we are directed to have an eye to divine revelation, and to follow that; they then must keep to the law of Moses (v. 4) and expect a further discovery of God's will by Elijah the prophet, that is, by John Baptist, the harbinger of the Messiah, vv. 5, 6. The last chapter of the New Testament is much to the same purport, setting before us heaven and hell in the other world, and obliging us to adhere to the word of God in this world.

A detailed analysis of chapter

The judgments on the wicked, and the happiness of the righteous. (1–3)

Regard for the Law. John the Baptist promised as the Messiah's forerunner. (4–6)

Key verse

Verse 5: "Behold, I will send you Elijah the prophet before the coming of the great and dreadful day of the LORD."

Key word / key phrase

Verse 5, "I will send you the prophet Elijah."

Key event / key person / key theme

The Day of the Lord, and the coming of Elijah

Key thought

Any visitation from the Lord is characterized by joy.

Key thing to look out for

We seek no new message, but just follow the old one of repentance.

Key Bible cross-reference

Verse 5. See Matthew 11:14; 17:10–13.

Key "by way of explanation"

Verse 5, "Elijah." Malachi concludes his prophecy by looking forward to a future prophet who will have a ministry similar to the prophet Elijah and call people back to God in repentance.

Key "Quotable Quote"

"He shows himself worthy, in that he confesses himself unworthy."

Augustine of Hippo

5. Select bibliography for Malachi

Baldwin, Joyce G. *Haggai, Zechariah, Malachi*. Downers Grove, Ill: InterVarsity, 1972.

Calvin, John. *Minor Prophets IV*. Grand Rapids: Eerdmans, 1950.

Keil, C. F. *The Minor Prophets*. KD. 2 Vols. Grand Rapids: Eerdmans, 1949.

Moore, T. V. *The Prophets of the Restoration: Haggai, Zechariah, Malachi*. 1856. Reprint. London: Banner of Truth Trust, 1968.

Smith, Ralph L. *Micah-Malachi*, (Word Biblical Commentary, 32), Word Books, 1984.

Taylor, John B. *The Minor Prophets*. Grand Rapids: Eerdmans, 1970.

Wolf, Herbert. *Haggai/Malachi: Rededication and Renewal*. Chicago: Moody, 1976.

Part Two
New Testament Books

Matthew

1. Book by book: Introduction to Matthew

Introduction

Author

The author of this Gospel was a publican or tax gatherer, residing at Capernaum, on the western shore of the Sea of Galilee.

In Mark and Luke he is called Levi, which seems to have been his family name. In their lists of the twelve apostles, however, Mark and Luke give him the name of Matthew, which seems to have been the name by which he was known as a disciple. While he himself sinks his family name, he is careful not to sink his occupation, the obnoxious associations with which he would place over against the grace that called him from it, and made him an apostle. Mark alone tells us (Mark 2:14) that he was "the son of Alphæus"–the same, probably, with the father of James the Less. From this and other considerations it is pretty certain that he must at least have heard of our Lord before this meeting.

Hardly anything is known of his apostolic labors. That, after preaching to his countrymen in Palestine, he went to the East, is the general testimony of antiquity; but the precise scene or scenes of his ministry cannot be determined. That he died a natural death may be concluded from the belief of the best-informed of the Fathers–that of the apostles only three, James the Greater, Peter, and Paul, suffered martyrdom. That the first Gospel was written by this apostle is the testimony of all antiquity.

Date

For the date of this Gospel we have only internal evidence, and that far from decisive. Accordingly, opinion is much divided. That it was the first of all the Gospels was universally believed. Hence, although in the order of the Gospels, those by the two apostles were placed first in the oldest manuscripts of the Old Latin version, while in all the Greek manuscripts, with scarcely an exception, the order is the same as in our Bibles, the Gospel according to Matthew is in every case placed first. And as this Gospel is of all the four the one which bears the most evident marks of having been prepared and constructed with a special view to the Jews–who certainly first required a written Gospel, and would be the first to make use of it–there can be no doubt that it was issued before any of the others. That it was written before the destruction of Jerusalem is equally certain. For when he reports our Lord's prophecy of that awful event, on coming to the warning about "the abomination of desolation" which they should "see standing in the holy place," he interposes (contrary to his invariable practice, which is to relate without remark) a call to his readers to read intelligently–"Whoso readeth, let him understand" (Matt. 24:15) –a call to attend to the divine signal for flight which could be intended only for those who lived before the event.

But how long before that event this Gospel was written is not so clear. Some internal evidences seem to imply a very early date. Since the Jewish Christians were, for five or six years, exposed to persecution from their own countrymen–until the Jews, being persecuted by the Romans, had to look to themselves–it is not likely (it is argued) that they should be left so long without some written Gospel to reassure and sustain them, and Matthew's Gospel was eminently fitted for that purpose. But the digests to which Luke refers in his introduction would be sufficient for a time, especially as the living voice of the "eye-witnesses and ministers of the Word" was yet sounding abroad. Other considerations in favor of a very early date–such as the tender way in which the author seems studiously to speak of Herod Antipas, as if still reigning, and his writing of Pilate apparently as if still in power–seem to have no foundation in fact, and cannot therefore be made the ground of reasoning as to the date of this Gospel. Its Hebraic structure and hue, though they prove, as we think, that this Gospel must have been published at a period considerably before to the destruction of Jerusalem, are no evidence in favor of so early a date as A.D. 37 or 38–according to some of the Fathers.

On the other hand, the date suggested by the statement of Irenaeus (*Against Heresies,* 3.1), that Matthew put forth his Gospel while Peter and Paul were at Rome preaching and founding the Church–or after A.D. 60–though probably the majority of critics are in favor of it, would seem rather too late, especially as the second and third Gospels, which were doubtless published, as well as this one, before the destruction of Jerusalem, had still to be issued. Certainly, such statements as the following, "Wherefore that field is called the field of blood unto this day" (Matt. 27:8); "And this saying is commonly reported among the Jews until this day" (Matt. 28:15), indicate a date considerably later than the events recorded.

We incline, therefore, to a date intermediate between the earlier and the later dates assigned to this Gospel, without pretending to greater precision.

Readers

We have alluded to the strikingly Jewish character and coloring of this Gospel. The facts which it selects, the points to which it gives prominence, the cast of thought and phraseology, all underline the Jewish point of view from which it was written and to which it was directed. This has been noticed from the beginning, and is universally acknowledged. It is of the greatest consequence to the right interpretation of it; but the tendency among some even of the best of the Germans to infer, from this special design of the first Gospel, a certain laxity on the part of the Evangelist in the treatment of his facts, must be guarded against.

Relationship to Mark and Luke

On the relationship of Matthew to Mark and Luke–whether one or more of the Evangelists made use of the materials of the other Gospels, and, if so, which of the Evangelists drew from which–the opinions are just as numerous as the possibilities of the case, every conceivable way of it having one or more who plead for it. The most popular opinion until recently—and perhaps the most popular still—is that the second Evangelist availed himself more or less of the materials of the first Gospel, and the third of the materials of both the first and second Gospels. Here we can but state our own belief, that each of the first three Evangelists wrote independently of both the others; while the fourth, familiar with the first three, wrote to supplement them, and, even where he travels along the same line, wrote quite independently of them. This judgment we express, with all deference for those who think otherwise, as the result of a close study of each of the Gospels in immediate juxtaposition and comparison with the others.

David Brown

Dr. Philip Schaff on the resurrection of Jesus

The resurrection of Christ from the dead is reported by the four Gospels, taught in the Epistles, believed throughout Christendom, and celebrated on every "Lord's Day," as an historical fact, as the crowning miracle and divine seal of his whole work, as the foundation of the hopes of believers, as the pledge of their own future resurrection. It is represented in the New Testament both as an act of the Almighty Father who raised his Son from the dead, and as an act of Christ himself, who had the power to lay down his life and to take it again. The ascension was the proper conclusion of the resurrection: the risen life of our Lord, who is "the Resurrection and the Life," could not end in another death on earth, but must continue in eternal glory in heaven. Hence, St. Paul says, "Christ being raised from the dead dieth no more; death hath no more dominion over him. For the death that he died he died unto sin once; but the life that he liveth, he liveth unto God."

The Christian church rests on the resurrection of its Founder. Without this fact the church could never have been born, or if born, it would soon have died a natural death. The miracle of the resurrection and the existence of Christianity are so closely connected that they must stand or fall together. If Christ was raised from the dead, then all his other miracles are sure, and our faith is impregnable; if he was not raised, he died in vain, and our faith is vain. It was only his resurrection that made his death available for our atonement, justification and salvation; without the resurrection, his death would be the grave of our hopes; we should be still unredeemed and under the power of our sins. A gospel of a dead Savior would be a contradiction and wretched delusion. This is the reasoning of St. Paul, and its force is irresistible.

The resurrection of Christ is therefore emphatically a test question on which depends the truth or falsehood of the Christian religion. It is either the greatest miracle or the greatest delusion which history records.

Christ had predicted both his crucifixion and his resurrection, but the former was a stumbling-block to the disciples, the latter a mystery which they could not understand till after the event. They no doubt expected that he would soon establish his Messianic kingdom on earth, Hence their utter disappointment and downheartedness after the crucifixion. The treason of one of their own number, the triumph of hierarchy, the fickleness of the people, the death and burial of the beloved Master, had in a few hours rudely blasted their Messianic hopes and exposed them to the contempt and ridicule of their enemies. For two days they were trembling on the brink of despair. But on the third day, behold, the same disciples underwent a complete revolution from despondency to hope, from timidity to courage, from doubt to faith, and began to proclaim the gospel of the resurrection in the face of an unbelieving world and at the peril of their lives. This revolution was not isolated, but general among them; it was not the result of an easy credulity, but brought about in spite of doubt and hesitation; it was not superficial and momentary, but radical and lasting; it affected not only the apostles, but the whole history of the world. It reached even the leader of the persecution, Saul of Tarsus, one of the clearest and strongest intellects, and converted him into the most devoted and faithful champion of this very gospel to the hour of his martyrdom.

This is a fact patent to every reader of the closing chapters of the Gospels, and is freely admitted even by the most advanced skeptics.

The question now rises whether this inner revolution in the life of the disciples, with its incalculable effect on the fortunes of mankind, can be rationally explained without a corresponding outward revolution in the history of Christ; in other words, whether the professed faith of the disciples in the risen Christ was true and real, or a hypocritical lie, or an honest self-delusion.

Four theories

There are four possible theories which have been tried again and again, and defended with as much learning and ingenuity as can be summoned to their aid. Historical questions are not like mathematical problems. No argument in favor of the resurrection will avail with those critics who start with the philosophical assumption that miracles are impossible, and still less with those who deny not only the resurrection of the body, but even the immortality of the soul. But facts are stubborn, and if a critical hypothesis can be proven to be psychologically and historically impossible and unreasonable, the result is fatal to the philosophy which underlies the critical hypothesis. It is not the business of the historian to construct a history from preconceived notions and to adjust it to his own liking, but to reproduce it from the best evidence and to let it speak for itself.

1. The historical view

The historical view, presented by the Gospels and believed in the Christian church of every denomination and sect. The resurrection of Christ was an actual though miraculous event, in harmony with his previous history and character, and in fulfillment of his own prediction. It was a re-animation of the dead body of Jesus by a return of his soul from the spirit-world, and a rising of body and soul from the grave to a new life, which, after repeated manifestations to believers during a short period of forty days, entered into glory by the ascension to heaven. The object of the manifestations was not only to convince the apostles personally of the resurrection, but to make them witnesses of the resurrection and heralds of salvation to all the world.

Truth compels us to admit that there are serious difficulties in harmonizing the accounts of the evangelists, and in forming a consistent conception of the nature of Christ's resurrection-body, hovering as it were between heaven and earth, and oscillating for forty days between a natural and a supernatural state, of a body clothed with flesh and blood and bearing the wound-prints, and yet so spiritual as to appear and disappear through closed doors and to ascend visibly to heaven. But these difficulties are not so great as those which are created by a denial of the fact itself. The former can be measurably solved, the latter cannot. We do not know all the details and circumstances which might enable us to clearly trace the order of events, But among all the variations the great central fact of the resurrection itself and its principal features "stand out all the more sure." The period or forty days in the nature of the case the most mysterious in the life of Christ, and transcends all ordinary Christian experience. The Christophanies resemble in some respects the Theophanies of the Old Testament, which were granted only to few believers, yet for the general benefit. At all events the fact of the resurrection furnishes the only key for the solution of the psychological problem of the sudden, radical and permanent change in the mind and conduct of the disciples; it is the necessary link in the chain which connects their history before and after that event. Their faith in the resurrection was too clear, too strong, too steady, too effective to be explained in any other way. They showed the strength and boldness of their conviction by soon returning to Jerusalem, the post of danger, and founding there, in the very face of the hostile Sanhedrim, the mother-church of Christendom.

2. The theory of fraud

The theory of fraud claims that the apostles stole and hid the body of Jesus, and deceived the world.

This infamous lie carries its refutation on its face: for if the Roman soldiers who watched the grave at the express request of the priests and Pharisees, were asleep, they could not see the thieves, nor would they have proclaimed their military crime; if they, or only some of them, were awake, they would have prevented the theft. As to the disciples, they were too timid and desponding at the time to venture on such a daring act, and too honest to cheat the world. And finally a self-invented falsehood could not give them the courage and constancy of faith for the proclamation of the resurrection at the peril of their lives. The whole theory is a wicked absurdity, and insult to the common sense and honor to mankind.

3. The swoon theory

The swoon theory states that the physical life of Jesus was not extinct, but only exhausted, and was restored by the tender care of his friends and disciples, or (as some absurdly add) by his own medical skill; and after a brief period he quietly died a natural death.

Josephus, Valerius Maximus, psychological and medical authorities have been searched and appealed to for examples of such apparent resurrections from a trance or asphyxy, especially on the third day, which is supposed to be a turning-point for life or putrefaction.

But besides insuperable physical difficulties–as the wounds and loss of blood from the very heart pierced by the spear of the Roman soldier–this theory utterly fails to account for the moral effect. A brief sickly existence of Jesus in need of medical care, and terminating in his natural death and final burial, without even the glory of martyrdom which attended the crucifixion, far from restoring the faith of the apostles, would have only in the end deepened their gloom and driven them to utter despair.

4. The imagination theory

The imagination theory claims that Christ rose merely in the imagination of his friends, who mistook a subjective vision or dream for actual reality, and were thereby encouraged to proclaim their faith in the resurrection at the risk of death. Their wish was father to the belief, their belief was father to the fact, and the belief, once started, spread with the power of a religious epidemic from person to person and from place to place. The Christian society wrought the miracle by its intense love for Christ. Accordingly the resurrection does not belong to the history of Christ at all, but to the inner life of his disciples. It is merely the embodiment of their reviving faith.

This hypothesis was invented by a heathen adversary in the second century and soon buried out of sight, but rose to new life in the nineteenth, and spread with epidemical rapidity among skeptical critics in Germany, France, Holland and England.

The advocates of this hypothesis appeal first and chiefly to the vision of St. Paul on the way to Damascus, which occurred several years later, and is nevertheless put on a level with the former appearances to the older apostles (1 Cor. 15:8); next to supposed analogies in the history of religious enthusiasm and mysticism, such as the individual visions of St. Francis of Assisi, the Maid of Orleans, St. Theresa (who believed that she had seen Jesus in person with the eyes of the soul more distinctly than she could have seen him with the eyes of the body), Swedenborg, even Mohammed, and the collective visions of the Montanists in Asia Minor, the Camisards in France, the spectral resurrections of the martyred Thomas a Becket of Canterbury and Savonarola of Florence in the excited imagination of their admirers, and the apparition of the Immaculate Virgin at Lourdes.

Nobody will deny that the subjective fancies and impressions are often mistaken for objective realities. But, with the exception of the case of St. Paul which we shall consider in its proper place, and which turns out to be, even according to the admission of the leaders of skeptical criticism, a powerful argument against the mythical or visionary theory–these supposed analogies are entirely irrelevant; for, not to speak of other differences, they were isolated and passing phenomena which left no mark on history; while the faith in the resurrection of Christ has revolutionized the whole world. It must therefore be treated on its own merits as an altogether unique case.

(a) The first insuperable argument against the visionary nature, and in favor of the objective reality, of the resurrection is the empty tomb of Christ. If he did not rise, his body must either have been removed, or remained in the tomb. If removed by the disciples, they were guilty of a deliberate falsehood in preaching the resurrection, and then the vision-hypothesis gives way to the exploded theory of fraud. If removed by the enemies, then these enemies had the best evidence against the resurrection, and would not have failed to produce it and thus to expose the baselessness of the vision. The same is true, of course, if the body had remained in the tomb. The murderers of Christ would certainly not have missed such an opportunity to destroy the very foundation of the hated sect.

To escape this difficulty, Strauss removes the origin of the illusion away off to Galilee, whither the disciples fled; but this does not help the matter, for they returned in a few weeks to Jerusalem, where they were all assembled on the day of Pentecost.

This argument is fatal even to the highest form of the vision hypothesis, which admits a spiritual manifestation of Christ from heaven, but denies the resurrection of the body.

(b) If Christ did not really rise, then the words which he spake to Mary Magdalene, to the disciples of Emmaus, to doubting Thomas, to Peter on the lake of Tiberias, to all the disciples on Mount Olivet, were likewise pious fictions. But who can believe that words of such dignity and majesty, so befitting the solemn moment of the departure to the throne of glory, as the commandment to preach the gospel to every creature, to baptize the nations in the name of the Father, the Son, and the Holy Spirit, and the promise to be with his disciples always to the end of the world–a promise abundantly verified in the daily experience of the church–could proceed from dreamy and self-deluded enthusiasts or crazy fanatics any more than the Sermon on the Mount or the Sacerdotal Prayer! And who, with any spark of historical sense, can suppose that Jesus never instituted baptism, which has been performed in his name ever since the day of Pentecost, and which, like the celebration of the Lord's Supper, bears testimony to him every day as the sunlight does to the sun!'

(c) If the visions of the resurrection were the product of an excited imagination, it is unaccountable that they should suddenly have ceased on the fortieth day (Acts 1:15), and not have occurred to any of the disciples afterwards, with the single exception of Paul, who expressly represents his vision of Christ as "the last." Even on the day of Pentecost Christ did not appear to them, but, according to his promise, "the other Paraclete" descended on them; and Stephen, saw Christ in heaven, not on earth.

(d) The chief objection to the vision-hypothesis is its intrinsic impossibility. It makes the most exorbitant claim on our credulity. It requires us to believe that many people, singly and collectively, at different times, and in different places, from Jerusalem to Damascus, had the same vision and dreamed the same dream; that the women at the open sepulcher early in the morning, Peter and John soon afterwards, the two disciples journeying to Emmaus on the afternoon of the resurrection day, the assembled apostles on the evening in the absence of Thomas, and again on the next Lord's day in the presence of the skeptical Thomas, seven apostles at the lake of Tiberias, on one occasion five hundred brethren at once, most of whom were still alive when Paul reported the fact, then James, the brother of the Lord, who formerly did not believe in him, again all the apostles on Mount Olivet at the ascension, and at last the clear-headed, strong-minded persecutor on the way to Damascus–that all these men and women on these different occasions vainly imagined they saw and heard the self-same Jesus in bodily shape and form; and that they were by this baseless vision raised all at once from the deepest gloom in which the crucifixion of their Lord had left them, to the boldest faith and strongest hope which impelled them to proclaim the gospel of the resurrection from Jerusalem to Rome to the end of their lives! And this illusion of the early disciples created the greatest revolution not only in their own views and conduct, but among Jews and Gentiles and in the subsequent history of mankind! This illusion we are expected to believe, by the unbelievers, gave birth to the most real and most mighty of all facts, the Christian Church which has lasted these eighteen hundred years and is now spread all over the civilized world, embracing more members than ever and exercising more moral power than all the kingdoms and all other religions combined!

The vision-hypothesis, instead of getting rid of the miracle, only shifts it from fact to fiction; it makes an empty delusion more powerful than the truth, or turns all history itself at last into a delusion. Before we can reason the resurrection of Christ out of history we must reason the apostles, and Christianity itself out of existence. We must either admit the miracle, or frankly confess that we stand here before an inexplicable mystery.

Dr. Philip Schaff, History of the Christian Church

Detailed outline

Part One: The Genealogy Of The King 1:1–17

- I. Introduction: 1:1
- II. People in the genealogy: 1:2–16
- III. The plan of the genealogy: 1:17

Part Two: The Birth Of The King 1:18–2:23

- I. The conception: 1:18–23
- II. The birth: 1:24–25
- III. Events related to the birth: 2:1–23
  - A. Visit of the wise men and Herod's plot: 2:1–12
  - B. The flight to Egypt: 2:13–15
  - C. Herod's revenge: 2:16–18
  - D. Return to the Nazareth home: 2:19–23

Part Three: Preparation 3:1–4:11

- I. Preparation for the King's coming: 3:1–17
  - A. The ministry and message of John the Baptist: 3:1–12
  - B. The baptism of the King: 3:13–17
- II. Preparation of the King: 4:1–11
  - A. His humanity attacked by Satan: 4:1–4
  - B. His divinity attacked by Satan: 4:5–7
  - C. His Lordship attacked by Satan: 4:8–11

Part Four: Ministry Of The King In Galilee 4:12–13:58

- I. A call to repentance: 4:12–17
- II. Four fishermen called to discipleship: 4:18–22
- III. Early success: 4:23–25
- IV. Principles of conduct for Kingdom citizens: 5:1–7:28
  - A. Attitudes that should characterize Kingdom citizens: 5:1–12
  - B. The witness of Kingdom citizens: Light and salt: 5:13–16
  - C. Kingdom principles in relation to the law and the prophets: 5:17–48
    - 1. God's law in general: 15:17–20
    - 2. The new law: 15:21–48
      - (a) Killing: 15:21–26
      - (b) Adultery: 15:27–30
      - (c) Divorce: 15:31–32
      - (d) Oaths: 15:33–37
      - (e) Treatment of others: 15:38–48
  - D. Three attitudes of worship in the Kingdom: 6:1–18
    - 1. Giving: 6:1–4
    - 2. Praying: 6:5–15
    - 3. Fasting: 6:16–18
  - E. Priorities for Kingdom citizens: 6:19–33
    - 1. In relation to values: 6:19–21
    - 2. In relation to service: 6:22–24
    - 3. In relation to material needs: 6:25–34
    - 4. The proper priority: The Kingdom: 6:33
  - F. Proper conduct for Kingdom citizens: 7:1–29
    - 1. Judging: 7:1–5
    - 2. Care for what is holy: 7:6
    - 3. Prayer: 7:7–12
      - (a) Three kinds of prayer: Asking, seeking, knocking: 7:7–8
      - (b) Natural fathers and the Heavenly Father compared: 7:9–11
  - G. Special warnings to Kingdom citizens: 7:13–29
    - 1. Two gates: 7:13–14
    - 2. False prophets: 7:15–20
    - 3. Doing God's will: 7:21–23
    - 4. A comparison of wise and foolish men: 7:24–27
  - H. Surprise at Jesus' teaching: 7:28–29
- V. The authority of the King: 8:1–9:38
  - A. Authority over disease: 8:1–17
    - 1. Healing of a leper: 8:1–4
    - 2. Healing of the Centurion's servant: 8:5–13
    - 3. Healing of Peter's mother-in-law: 8:14–15
    - 4. Healing of all types of diseases: 8:16–17
  - B. Authority over His disciples: 8:18–22
  - C. Authority over natural elements: 8:23–27
  - D. Authority over demons: 8:28–34
  - E. Authority over sin: 9:1–8
  - F. Authority over men: 9:9–17
    - 1. The calling of Matthew: 9:9
    - 2. Eating with sinners: 9:10–13
    - 3. Answering a challenge: 9:14–17
  - G. Authority over death: The ruler's daughter: 9:18–19, 23–26
  - H. Authority over physical conditions: 9:20–38
    - 1. Woman with bleeding: 9:20–22
    - 2. Blindness: 9:27–31

3. Deafness and demon possession: 9:32–34
4. The compassion of Jesus: 9:35–38

VI. Commissioned by the King: 10:1–42
A. The twelve missionaries and their authority: 10:1–4
B. Instructions for the journey: 10:5–42
1. Where to go: 10:5–6
2. The ministry: 10:7–8
3. Material instructions: 10:9–15
4. Spiritual instructions: 10:16–42

VII. Attitudes towards the Kingdom: 11:1–30
A. The Kingdom misunderstood: 11:1–11
B. The Kingdom perverted: 11:12–19
C. The Kingdom rejected: 11:20–24
D. The Kingdom accepted: 11:25–30

VIII. Controversies with the Pharisees: 12:1–14
A. Harvesting on the Sabbath: 12:1–8
B. Healing on the Sabbath: 12:9–13
C. The results: 12:14–21

IX. The unpardonable sin: 12:22–37

X. Christ's reply to the Pharisees: 12:38–45

XI. The priority of spiritual over physical relationships in the Kingdom: 12:46–50

XII. Parables of the Kingdom: 13:1–53
A. Parable of the sower: 13:1–9
B. The reason for speaking in parables: 13:10–17
C. Interpretation of the parable of the sower: 13:18–23
D. Parable of the tares: 13:24–30
E. Parable of the mustard seed: 13:31–32
F. Parable of the leaven: 13:33
G. A summary about parables: 13:34–35
H. Interpretation of the parable of the tares: 13:36–43
I. Parable of the treasure hidden in a field: 13:44
J. Parable of the pearl of great value: 13:45–46
K. Parable of the net: 13:47–50
L. Concluding remarks about parables: 13:51–52

XIII. The King's reception in His home town: 13:53–58

Part Five: Ministry In Regions Near Galilee 14:1–18:35

I. The death of John the Baptist: 14:1–12

II. Jesus' withdrawal beyond the sea: 14:13–15:20
A. Feeding the 5,000: 14:13–21
B. Following for loaves and fishes: 14:22–23
C. Walking on the sea: 14:24–33
D. Ministry in Gennesaraet: 14:34–36
E. Controversy with the Pharisees and Scribes: 15:1–20

III. Jesus' withdrawal to the region of Tyre and Sidon: 15:21–28
A. The women of Tyre and Sidon: 15:21–28

IV. Jesus' withdrawal to the vicinity of Decapolis: 15:29–38
A. Healing ministry near the Sea of Galilee: 15:29–31
B. Feeding the 4,000: 15:32–38

V. Ministry in the regions of Magadan: 15:39–16:4

VI. Warning the disciples about the Pharisees and the Sadducees: 16:5–12
A. Seeking for a sign: 16:1–4
B. Warning about their doctrine: 16:5–12

- VII. Withdrawal to Caesarea-Philippi: 16:13–17:21
  - A. Testing the disciples: 16:13–20
  - B. Announcement of His death, resurrection, and return: 16:21–28
  - C. The transfiguration: 17:1–13
  - D. Healing a boy with a demon: 17:14–20
- VIII. A brief visit to Galilee: 17:22–18:35
  - A. A reminder of His death and resurrection: 17:22–23
  - B. Paying the temple tax: 17:24–27
  - C. A lesson in greatness: 18:1–6
  - D. Warnings about offenses: 18:7–9
  - E. Parable of the lost sheep: 18:10–14
  - F. Settling disputes among Kingdom citizens: 18:15–35
    - 1. How to settle disputes: 18:15–17
    - 2. The responsibilities and privileges of Kingdom citizens: 18:18–20
    - 3. A question on forgiveness: 18:21–22
    - 4. The King and his debtors: 18:23–35

Part Six: Ministry Of The King In Perea 19:1–20:34

- I. Healing multitudes in Judea: 19:1–2
- II. The question about divorce: 19:3–12
- III. Children blessed by Jesus: 19:13–15
- IV. Conversation with the rich young ruler: 19:16–22
- V. The peril of riches: 19:23–30
- VI. Parable of the workers in the vineyard: 20:1–16
- VII. Impending death and resurrection of Jesus: 20:17–19
- VIII. A mother's selfish request: 20:20–28
- IX. Two blind men healed near Jericho: 20:29–34

Part Seven: The King's Last Week 21:1–27:31

- I. The royal entry into Jerusalem: 21:1–11
- II. Cleansing the temple: 21:12–17
- III. The fig tree cursed: 21:18–22
- IV. The authority of Jesus challenged: 21:23–32
- V. Parable of the tenants: 21:33–46
- VI. Parable of the marriage feast: 22:1–14
- VII. Attempts to discredit Jesus: 22:15–45
  - A. Question of paying taxes to Caesar: 22:15–22
  - B. Question about the resurrection: 22:23–33
  - C. Question of the great commandment: 22:34–40
  - D. Questions by Jesus: 22:41–46
- VIII. Discussion about the Scribes and Pharisees: 23:1–39
  - A. They assume to have religious authority: 23:1–3
  - B. They impose burdens: 23:4
  - C. They covet praise: 23:5–7
  - D. Advice to His disciples: 23:8–12
  - E. Woes to the Scribes and Pharisees: 23:13–36
  - F. A cry for Jerusalem: 23:37–39
- IX. The future of the Kingdom: 24:1–25:46
  - A. The destruction of the temple: 24:1–2
  - B. Signs of the end: 24:3–14
  - C. The tribulation period: 24:15–22
  - D. The return of Jesus: 24:23–31
  - E. Parable of the fig tree: 24:32–35
  - F. The day of the Lord: 24:36–41
  - G. The command to watch: 24:42–51
  - H. Parables about the end times: 25:1–46
    - 1. The ten virgins: 25:1–13

2. The talents: 25:14–30
3. The sheep and goats: 25:31–46

X. Events before to the crucifixion: 26:1–27:31
A. Announcement of approaching death: 26:1–2
B. The plot to kill Jesus: 26:3–5
C. Anointed for burial: 26:6–13
D. Judas agrees to betray Jesus: 26:14–16
E. The Last Supper: 26:17–29
1. Preparations for the Passover: 26:17–19
2. The Last Supper: 26:20–29
3. Jesus' warning and Peter's boast: 26:30–35
F. Gethsemane: 26:36–46
G. Betrayal and arrest: 26:47–56
H. The trials of Jesus: 26:57–27:26

Part Eight: The King's Death And Triumph 27:27–28:20

I. The crucifixion and burial: 27:27–66
A. The soldiers mock Jesus: 27:27–31
B. The road to and death on Calvary: 27:32–54
C. The faithful women, the burial, and tomb guard: 27:55–66

II. The resurrection: 28:1–15
III. The Great Commission: 28:16–20

2. Helpful summaries of Matthew's Gospel

Bird's eye view

Jesus the Son of God and Lord according to the promises in the Old Testament.

Outline

Offer of the King 1:1–11:1
Rejection of the King 11:2–28:20

Reading plan

The following reading plan, taking one reading per day, enables you to read through Matthew's Gospel in forty-nine days.

Matthew 1:1–1:25
Matthew 2:1–2:23
Matthew 3:1–3:17
Matthew 4:1–4:25
Matthew 5:1–5:20
Matthew 5:21–5:48
Matthew 6:1–6:15
Matthew 6:16–6:34
Matthew 7:1–7:29
Matthew 8:1–8:27
Matthew 8:28–9:8
Matthew 9:9–9:38
Matthew 10:1–10:15
Matthew 10:16–10:42
Matthew 11:1–11:19
Matthew 11:20–12:8
Matthew 12:9–12:32
Matthew 12:33–12:50
Matthew 13:1–13:23
Matthew 13:24–13:46
Matthew 13:47–14:12
Matthew 14:13–14:36
Matthew 15:1–15:20
Matthew 15:21–15:39
Matthew 16:1–16:28
Matthew 17:1–17:27
Matthew 18:1–18:14
Matthew 18:15–18:35
Matthew 19:1–19:15
Matthew 19:16–20:16

Matthew 20:17–20:34
Matthew 21:1–21:27
Matthew 21:28–21:46
Matthew 22:1–22:22
Matthew 22:23–22:46
Matthew 23:1–23:22
Matthew 23:23–23:39
Matthew 24:1–24:28
Matthew 24:29–24:51
Matthew 25:1–25:13
Matthew 25:14–25:46
Matthew 26:1–26:13
Matthew 26:14–26:35
Matthew 26:36–26:56
Matthew 26:57–26:75
Matthew 27:1–27:26
Matthew 27:27–27:56
Matthew 27:57–27:66
Matthew 28:1–28:20

Verses to memorize

Matthew 1:21

"She [Mary] will give birth to a son, and you are to give him the name Jesus, because he will save his people from their sins."

Matthew 5:3

"Blessed are the poor in spirit, for theirs is the kingdom of heaven."

Matthew 5:16

Let your light so shine before men, that they may see your good works, and glorify your Father which is in heaven. kjv

Matthew 6:33

But seek ye first the kingdom of God, and his righteousness; and all these things shall be added unto you. kjv

Matthew 6:14–15

"If you forgive men when they sin against you, your heavenly Father will also forgive you. But if you do not forgive men their sins, your Father will not forgive your sins."

Matthew 16:24

"If anyone would come after me, he must deny himself and take up his cross and follow me."

Matthew 24:13

"He who stands firm to the end will be saved."

Matthew 28:19–20

"Therefore go and make disciples of all nations, baptizing them in the name of the Father and of the Son and of the Holy Spirit, and teaching them to obey everything I have commanded you. And surely I am with you always, to the very end of the age."

Statistics

First New Testament book
First Gospel
28 chapters
1,071 verses
23,684 words
Number of Old Testament quotations and allusions in Matthew: 96.

Events and sayings found only in Matthew's Gospel

The Magi visiting Jesus, 2:1.
Mary, Joseph and Jesus fleeing to Egypt, 2:13–14.
Herod's killing of the male toddlers, 2:16.
Mary, Joseph and Jesus return to Nazareth, 2:19–23.

The Pharisees and Sadducees going to John the Baptist, 3:7.
The complete Sermon on the Mount, 5–7.
"Come to me, all you who are weary." 11:28
Peter walking on the water, 14:28–31.
The denunciation of the Pharisees, chapter 23.
Judas accepting thirty silver coins, 26:15.
Judas returning the thirty silver coins, 27:3–10.
The dream Pilate's wife had, 27:19.
Resurrection saints appearing, 27:52.
The watch set at the tomb, 27:64–66.
The earthquake, 28:2.
The soldiers bribed, 28:12–13.
The great commission, 28:19–20.

Miracles found only in Matthew
Two blind men healed, 9:28–36.
Sick healed in Jerusalem, 14:14
Peter walking on water, 14:29
Jesus supplying the temple tax, 17:24–27.

Parables found only in Matthew
The weeds, 13:24
The hidden treasure, 13:44.
The fine pearl, 13:45.
The net, 13:47.
The unmerciful servant, 18:23.
The workers in the vineyard, 20:1–16.
The two sons, 21:28–32.
The marriage of the king's son, 22:1–14.
The ten virgins, 25:1–13.
The talents, 25:14–30.
The sheep and the goats, 25:31–46.

Names/titles given
Kata Matthaion: "According to Matthew."

Symbol for
Man: Matthew's emblem is the man, emphasizing the kingly and human characteristics of Jesus.

3. Helpful keys to turn to in understanding Matthew's Gospel

Key words/phrase
King, 5 occurrences
Kingdom, 50 occurrences
That it might be fulfilled: 1:22.

Key verses
Matthew 1:1; 16:16–19

Themes to study
- The Old Testament quotations in Matthew.
- God as our heavenly Father.
- The kingdom of heaven.
- The various ways in which Jesus described in Matthew.

Unusual events and other miracles in Mathew
- The virgin birth of Jesus, 1:18–25
- Star leading wise men to Jesus, 2:1–12
- Herod killing innocent children, 2:13–18
- Jesus' baptism, 3:13–16
- God's voice from heaven, 3:16–17
- Jesus' transfiguration, 17:1–9
- Moses and Elijah appearing during Jesus' transfiguration, 17:3
- Darkness during Jesus' crucifixion, 27:45

- Curtain of the Temple torn in two, 27:51
- Earthquake as Jesus died, 27:51
- Resurrection of saints, 27:52–53
- Earthquake on resurrection morning, 28:2
- Jesus' resurrection, 28:1–6

Jesus in Matthew

In Matthew Jesus is the promised Messiah.

Lessons to learn from Matthew's Gospel

- The Gospels are the best place to find out about Jesus' life and work.
- The Old Testament sheds light on Jesus as the world's Messiah.
- For a follower of Jesus, being involved in some kind of Christian mission is no optional extra.

4. Chapter by chapter: outline of every chapter of Matthew

Matthew 1

Matthew Henry's introduction

This evangelist begins with the account of Christ's parents and birth, the ancestors from whom he descended, and the way he entered the world. In this way they demonstrate that he was indeed the promised Messiah promised, for it was foretold that he would be the son of David, and would be born of a virgin; and that he was so is clearly shown here.

Dr. Adam Clarke's analysis of chapter

The genealogy of Christ divided into three groups of fourteen generations each:

The first fourteen, from Abraham to David, 2–6.

The second fourteen, from Solomon to Jechonias, 7–10.

The third fourteen, from Jechonias to Christ, 11–16.

The sum of these generations, 17.

Christ is conceived by the Holy Spirit, and born of the Virgin Mary, when she was engaged to Joseph, 18.

Joseph's anxiety and doubts are removed by the ministry of an Angel, 19, 20; by whom the child is named JESUS, 21.

The fulfillment of Isaiah's prophecy, 22, 23.

Joseph takes home his wife, Mary, and Christ is born, 24, 25.

A detailed analysis of chapter

The genealogy of Jesus. (1–17)

An angel appears to Joseph. (18–25)

Key verse

Verse 1: "A record of the genealogy of Jesus Christ the son of David, the son of Abraham."

Key word / key phrase

Verse 1, "the genealogy of Jesus Christ."

Key event / key person / key theme

Jesus' family tree

Key thought

God planned our salvation a long time ago.

Key thing to look out for

Jesus' birth was natural and supernatural.

Key Bible cross-reference

Verse 23. See Isaiah 7:14.

Key "by way of explanation"

Verse 18, "pledged to be married." Betrothal was much more binding than our modern engagements and if broken required a legal divorce settlement.

Key "Quotable Quote"

"Immanuel, God with us in our nature, in our sorrow, in our lifework, in our punishment, in our grave, and now with us, or rather we with him, in resurrection, ascension, triumph, and second Advent splendor."

C.H. Spurgeon

Matthew 2

Matthew Henry's introduction

In this chapter, we have the history of our Savior's infancy, where we find how early he began to suffer, and that in him the word of righteousness was fulfilled, before he himself began to fulfill all righteousness.

Dr. Adam Clarke's analysis of chapter

Wise men come from the east to worship Christ, 1, 2.

Herod, hearing of the birth of our Lord, is greatly troubled, 3; and asks the chief priests and scribes, where the Christ should be born, 4.

They inform him of the prophecy relative to Bethlehem, 5, 6.

The wise men, going to Bethlehem, are asked by Herod to bring him word when they have found the child, pretending that he wished to pay him homage, 7, 8.

The wise men are directed by a star to the place where the young child lay, adore him, and offer him gifts, 9–11.

Being warned by God not to return to Herod, they return to their own country another way, 12.

Joseph and Mary are divinely warned to escape into Egypt, because Herod sought to destroy Jesus, 13, 14.

They obey, and continue in Egypt till the death of Herod, 15.

Herod, finding that the wise men did not return, is enraged, and orders all the young children in Bethlehem, under two years of age, to be massacred, 16–18.

Herod dies, and Joseph is divinely warned to return to the land of Israel, 19–21.

Finding that Archelaus reigned in Judea in place of his father Herod, he goes to Galilee, and takes up his residence at Nazareth, 22, 23.

A detailed analysis of chapter

The wise men's search for Christ. (1–8)

The wise men worship Jesus. (9–12)

Jesus taken to Egypt. (13–15)

Herod's massacre of the infants of Bethlehem. (16–18)

Death of Herod, Jesus taken to Nazareth. (19–23)

Key verse

Verse 3: "When King Herod heard this he was disturbed, and all Jerusalem with him."

Key word / key phrase

Verse 1: "Jesus was born."

Key event / key person / key theme

Jesus' infancy

Key thought

King Herod epitomizes the evil people who have always been seeking to destroy Christianity.

Key thing to look out for

The number of times Matthew refers to the fulfillment of prophesy.

Key Bible cross-reference

Verse 6. See Micah 5:2.

Key "by way of explanation"

Verse 11, "house." By the time the Magi visited Jesus, Mary and Joseph had managed for find better accommodation.

Key "Quotable Quote"

"The Word was made man in order that we might be made divine."

Athanasius

Matthew 3

Matthew Henry's introduction

At the beginning of this chapter, with the baptism of John, begins the gospel (Mark 1:1); what went before is but preface or introduction; this is "the beginning of the gospel of Jesus Christ." And Peter observes the same date, Acts 1:22, beginning from the baptism of John, for then Christ began first to appear in him, and then to appear to him, and through him to the world.

Dr. Adam Clarke's analysis of chapter

John the Baptist begins to preach, 1.
The subject of his preaching, 2, 3.
Description of his clothing and food, 4.
The success of his ministry, 5, 6.
His exhortation to the Pharisees, 7–9.
He denounces the judgments of God against the impenitent, 10.
The design of his baptism, and that of Christ, 11, 12.
He baptizes Christ in Jordan, 13–15; who is attested to be the Messiah by the Holy Spirit, and a voice from heaven, 16, 17.

A detailed analysis of chapter

John the Baptist, his preaching, lifestyle, and baptism. (1–6)
John reproves the Pharisees and Sadducees. (7–12)
The baptism of Jesus. (13–17)

Key verse

Verse 11: "I baptize you with water for repentance. But after me will come one who is more powerful than I, whose sandals I am not fit to carry. He will baptize you with the Holy Spirit and with fire."

Key word / key phrase

Verse 1, "John the Baptist."

Key event / key person / key theme

John the Baptist and the baptism of Jesus

Key thought

John the Baptist shows courage as he challenges people to repent.

Key thing to look out for

John the Baptist shows humility in the way he relates to Jesus.

Key Bible cross-reference

Verse 3. See Isaiah 40:3.

Key "by way of explanation"

Verse 3. This verse quotes Isaiah 40:3. Matthew, Mark, and Luke all apply this verse to John the Baptist.

Key "Quotable Quote"

"The beginning of repentance proceeds from fear of God."

Boniface

Matthew 4

Matthew Henry's introduction

John Baptist said about Christ, He must increase, but I must decrease; and so it proved. For, after John had baptized Christ, and borne his testimony to him, we hear little more of his ministry; he had done what he came to do, and thenceforward there is as much talk of Jesus as ever there had been of John. As the rising Sun advances, the morning star disappears.

Dr. Adam Clarke's analysis of chapter

Jesus, in the wilderness, is tempted by Satan, 1–11.

He goes into Galilee, 12; and Capernaum, 13.

The prophecy which was thus fulfilled, 14–16.

He begins to preach publicly, 17.

Calls Simon Peter, and his brother Andrew, 18–20.

Calls also James and John, the sons of Zebedee, 21, 22.

Preaches and works miracles throughout Galilee, 23.

Becomes famous in Syria, and is followed by multitudes from various quarters, among whom he works a great variety of miracles, 24, 25.

A detailed analysis of chapter

The temptation of Christ. (1–11)

The start of Christ's ministry in Galilee. (12–17)

Call of Simon and others. (18–22)

Jesus teaches and performs miracles. (23–25)

Key verse

Verse 8: "Again, the devil took him to a very high mountain and showed him all the kingdoms of the world and their splendor."

Key word / key phrase

Verse 17, "Repent, for the kingdom of heaven is near."

Key event / key person / key theme

The temptation of Jesus

Key thought

If Jesus was tempted we should hardly be surprised that we are.

Key thing to look out for

Jesus resisted temptation by quoting from the Old Testament.

Key Bible cross-reference

Verse 7. See Deuteronomy 6:16.

Key "by way of explanation"

Verse 3, "If you are the Son of God." The devil is not saying that Jesus was not the Son of God, but rather, was trying to make him use his powers in a selfish way.

Key "Quotable Quote"

"The devil tempts that he may ruin; God tests that he may crown."

St Ambrose

Matthew 5

Matthew Henry's introduction

This chapter, and the two that follow it, are a sermon; a famous sermon; the sermon on the mount. It is the longest and fullest continued discourse of our Savior that we have on record in all the gospels. It is a practical discourse; there is not much of the credenda of Christianity in it–the things to be believed, but it is wholly taken up with the agenda–the things to be done; these Christ began with in his preaching; for if any man will do his will, he shall know of the doctrine, whether it be of God.

The circumstances of the sermon being accounted for (vv. 1, 2), the sermon itself follows, the scope of which is, not to fill our heads with notions, but to guide and regulate our practice.

I. He proposes blessedness as the end, and gives us the character of those who are entitled to blessedness (very different from the sentiments of a vain world), in eight beatitudes, which may justly be called paradoxes, vv. 3–12.

II. He prescribes duty as the way, and gives us standing rules of that duty. He directs his disciples,

A. To understand what they are–the salt of the earth, and the lights of the world, vv. 13–16.

B. To understand what they have to do–they are to be governed by the moral law. Here is,

1. A general ratification of the law, and a recommendation of it to us, as our rule, vv. 17–20.

2. A particular rectification of divers mistakes; or, rather, a reformation of divers willful, gross corruptions, which the scribes and Pharisees had introduced in their exposition of the law; and an authentic explication of divers branches which most needed to be explained and vindicated, v. 20. Particularly, here is an explication,

a. Of the sixth commandment, which forbids murder, vv. 21–26.

b. Of the seventh commandment, against adultery, vv. 27–32.

c. Of the third commandment, vv. 33–37.

d. Of the law of retaliation, vv. 38–42.

e. Of the law of brotherly love, vv. 43–48. And the scope of the whole is, to show that the law is spiritual.

Dr. Adam Clarke's analysis of chapter

Christ begins his sermon on the mount, 1, 2.

The beatitudes, 3–12.

The disciples the salt of the earth, and light of the world, 13–16.

Christ is not come to destroy, but confirm and fulfill, the Law and the Prophets, 17–19.

Of the righteousness of the scribes and Pharisees, 20.

Interpretation of the precepts relative to murder, anger, and injurious speaking, 21, 22.

Of reconciliation, 23–26.

Of impure acts and propensities, and the necessity of mortification, 27–30.

Of divorce, 31, 32.

Of oaths and profane swearing, 33–37.

Of bearing injuries and persecution, 38–41.

Of borrowing and lending, 42

Of love and hatred, 43– 46.

Of civil respect, 47.

Christ's disciples must resemble their heavenly Father, 48.

A detailed analysis of chapter

Christ's Sermon on the Mount. (1,2)

Who are blessed. (3–12)

Exhortations and warnings. (13–16)

Christ came to confirm the Law. (17–20)

The sixth commandment. (21–26)

The seventh commandment. (27–32)

The third commandment. (33–37)

The law of retaliation. (38–42)

The law of love explained. (43–48)

Key verse

Verse 5: "Blessed are the meek, for they will inherit the earth."

Key word / key phrase

Verse 2, "He began to teach."

Key event / key person / key theme

The Beatitudes

Key thought

The Sermon on the Mount describes the way of life of those who belong to Christ's kingdom.

Key thing to look out for

Ways in which Jesus brought out the true meaning (fulfilled) of the law.

Key Bible cross-reference

Verse 8. See Psalm 24:3,4.

Key "by way of explanation"

Verse 22, "Raca." This word involves speaking to someone as if you think that person is contemptible.

Key "Quotable Quote"

"Good morning, theologians! You wake and sing. But I, old fool, know less than you and worry over everything, instead of simply trusting in the heavenly Father's care."

Martin Luther, talking to birds

Matthew 6

Matthew Henry's introduction

Christ having, in the previous chapter, armed his disciples against the corrupt doctrines and opinions of the scribes and Pharisees, especially in their expositions of the law (that was called their leaven, 16:12), comes in this chapter to warn them against their corrupt practices, against the two sins which, though in their doctrine they did not justify, yet in their conversation they were notoriously guilty of, and so as even to recommend them to their admirers: these were hypocrisy and worldly-mindedness, sins which, of all others, the professors of religion need most to guard against, as sins that most easily beset those who have escaped the grosser pollutions that are in the world through lust, and which are therefore highly dangerous. We are here cautioned against hypocrisy, and being worldly.

Dr. Adam Clarke's analysis of chapter

Of alms-giving, 1–5.
Of prayer, 6–8.
The Lord's prayer, or model according to which Christians should pray, 9–13.
Of forgiveness, 14, 15.
Of fasting, 16, 17.
Of laying up treasures, 18–21.
Of the single eye, 22, 23.
The impossibility of serving two masters, 24.
Of contentment and confidence in the Divine providence, 25–32.
Directions about seeking the kingdom of God, 33, 34.

A detailed analysis of chapter

Against hypocrisy in giving money. (1–4)
Against hypocrisy in prayer. (5–8)
How to pray. (9–15)
About fasting. (16–18)
The evil of being worldly-minded. (19–24)
Trust in God commended. (25–34)

Key verse

Verse 8: "Do not be like them, for your Father knows what you need before you ask him."

Key word / key phrase

Verse 16, "hypocrites."

Key event / key person / key theme

Right motives

Key thought

A right way and a wrong way to give.

Key thing to look out for

There is no better model prayer than the Lord's Prayer.

Key Bible cross-reference

Verse 29. See 1 Kings 10:4–7.

Key "by way of explanation"

Verse 48, "be perfect." This side of heaven no one will reach perfection. But Jesus said we should still aim for perfection.

Key "Quotable Quote"

"If you say, 'It is enough. I have reached perfection,' all is lost, since it is the function of perfection to make one know one's imperfections."

Augustine of Hippo

Matthew 7

Matthew Henry's introduction

This chapter continues and concludes Christ's sermon on the mount, which is purely practical, directing us to order our conversation aright, both toward God and man; for the design of the Christian religion is to make men good, every way good.

Dr. Adam Clarke's analysis of chapter

Our Lord warns men against rash judgment and uncharitable censures, 1–5.

Shows that holy things must not be profaned, 6; gives encouragement to fervent persevering prayer, 7–11.

Shows how men should deal with each other, 12.

Exhorts the people to enter in at the strait gate, 13, 14; to beware of false teachers, who are to be known by their fruits, 15–20.

Shows that no man shall be saved by his mere profession of Christianity, 22, 23.

The parable of the wise man who built his house on a rock, 24, 25.

Of the foolish man who built his house, without a foundation, on the sand, 26, 27.

Christ concludes his sermon, and the people are astonished at his doctrine, 28, 29.

A detailed analysis of chapter

Christ reproves rash judgment. (1–6)

Encouragements to prayer. (7–11)

The broad and narrow way. (12–14)

Against false prophets. (15–20)

To be doers of the word, not hearers only. (21–29)

Key verse

Verse 12: "So in everything, do to others what you would have them do to you, for this sums up the Law and the Prophets."

Key word / key phrase

Verse 15, "false prophets."

Key event / key person / key theme

The road that leads to life.

Key thought

There is no room in the Christian life for judging other people.

Key thing to look out for

While it is true that God searches us out this should never stop us seeking God with all our hearts.

Key Bible cross-reference

Verse 23. See Psalm 6:8.

Key "by way of explanation"

Verse 12. This verse is known as "the Golden Rule." While a negative version of it is found in Judaism, Hinduism, Buddhism and Confucianism, only Jesus said it in this positive way.

Key "Quotable Quote"

"We cannot be truly Christian people so long as we flaunt the central teachings of Jesus: brotherly love and the Golden Rule."

Martin Luther King, Jr.

Matthew 8

Matthew Henry's introduction

The evangelist having, in the previous chapters, given us a specimen of our Lord's preaching, proceeds now to give some instances of the miracles he wrought, which prove him a Teacher come from God, and the great Healer of a diseased world.

Dr. Adam Clarke's analysis of chapter

Great multitudes follow Christ, 1.

He heals a leper, 2–4.

Heals the centurion's servant, 5–13.

Heals Peter's wife's mother, 14, 15; and several other ill people, 16, 17.

Departs from that place, 18.

Two people offer to be his disciples, 19–22.

He and his disciples are overtaken with a tempest, which he miraculously stills, 23–27.

He cures demoniacs, and the demons which went out enter into a herd of swine, which, rushing into the sea, perish, 28–32.

The swine- herds announce the miracle to the Gergesenes, who request Christ to depart from their country, 33, 34.

A detailed analysis of chapter

Crowds follow Christ. (1)

He heals a leper. (2–4)

A centurion's servant healed. (5–13)

Peter's wife's mother healed. (14–17)

The scribe's zealous proposal. (18–22)

Christ in a storm. (23–27)

He heals two possessed with devils. (28–34)

Key verse

Verse 1: "When he came down from the mountainside, large crowds followed him."

Key word / key phrase

Verse 3, "he was cured."

Key event / key person / key theme

Healing miracles

Key thought

Jesus demonstrated his love for people and he healed them.

Key thing to look out for

Jesus showed his power over many kinds of evil.

Key Bible cross-reference

Verse 17. See Isaiah 53:4.

Key "by way of explanation"

Verse 22, "let the dead bury their dead." Jews thought it most important that children should look after the funeral arrangements of their parents. Jesus says there is a higher loyalty than family loyalty.

Key "Quotable Quote"

"Christ does not want to win numbers but dedicated hearts."

Johann Heinrich Arnold

Matthew 9

Matthew Henry's introduction

We have in this chapter remarkable instances of the power and pity of the Lord Jesus, sufficient to convince us that he is both able to save to the uttermost all that come to God by him, and as willing as he is able. His power and pity appear here in the good offices he did.

Dr. Adam Clarke's analysis of chapter

Christ heals a paralytic person at Capernaum, 1–8.

Calls Matthew, 9–10.

Eats with publicans and sinners, at which the Pharisees are offended, and he vindicates his conduct, 11, 12.

The disciples of John come to him and inquire about fasting, 14–17.

A ruler requests him to heal his daughter, 18, 19.

On his road to the ruler's house, he heals a diseased woman, 20–22.

Arriving at the ruler's house, he restores the young woman to life, 23–26.

Heals two blind men, 27–31.

Casts out a dumb demon, 32–34.

Preaches and works miracles in all the cities and villages, 35.

Is greatly affected at the desolate and dark state of the Jewish people, 36.

Exhorts his disciples to pray to God to send them proper instructors, 37, 38.

A detailed analysis of chapter

Jesus returns to Capernaum, and heals a paralytic. (1–8)

Matthew called. (9)

Matthew's feast. (10–13)

Objections of John's disciples. (14–17)

Christ raises the daughter of Jairus. He heals a woman with bleeding. (18–26)

He heals two blind men. (27–31)

Christ expels a dumb spirit. (32–34)

He sends out the apostles. (35–38)

Key verse

Verse 9: "Matthew got up and followed him."

Key word / key phrase

Verse 9, "Follow me."

Key event / key person / key theme

What God desires

Key thought

Matthew shows his delight in following Jesus but throwing a party.

Key thing to look out for

Verses 36–38, Jesus' response to the crowds.

Key Bible cross-reference

Verse 13. See Hosea 6:6.

Key "by way of explanation"

Verse 23, "flute players," were used in bereavement rituals. People were also hired to lament and cry out, forming a "noisy crowd."

Key "Quotable Quote"

"A Pharisee is a righteous man whose righteousness is nourished by the blood of sinners."

Thomas Merton

Matthew 10

Matthew Henry's introduction

This chapter is an ordination sermon, which our

Lord Jesus preached, when he advanced his twelve disciples to the degree and dignity of apostles. In the close of the previous chapter, he had stirred up them and others to pray that God would send forth laborers, and here we have an immediate answer to that prayer: while they are yet speaking he hears and performs. What we pray for, according to Christ's direction, shall be given.

Dr. Adam Clarke's analysis of chapter

Jesus calls, commissions, and names his twelve disciples, 1–4.

Gives them particular instructions relative to the objects of their ministry, 5, 6.

Mode of preaching, etc., 7–15.

Foretells the afflictions and persecutions they would have to endure, and the support they should receive, 16–25.

Cautions them against betraying his cause, in order to procure their personal safety, 26–39.

And gives especial promises to those who should assist his faithful servants in the execution of their work, 40–42.

A detailed analysis of chapter

The apostles called. (1–4)

The apostles instructed and sent out. (5–15)

Directions to the apostles. (16–42)

Key verse

Verse 1: "He called his twelve disciples to him and gave them authority to drive out evil spirits and to heal every disease and sickness."

Key word / key phrase

Verse 10, "He called his twelve."

Key event / key person / key theme

Fearless into danger and difficulty

Key thought

"If the love of ourselves hinders us from following Christ, we must resist it courageously."
John Calvin

Key thing to look out for

Jesus chose disciples for mission.

Key Bible cross-reference

Verse 15. See Genesis 19:24–28.

Key "by way of explanation"

Verse 38, "take his cross." This is the first time Matthew mentions the cross, a Roman instrument for torture and execution. When Jesus spoke of it he was challenging people to follow him unreservedly.

Key "Quotable Quote"

"Those who are excessively desirous of an earthly life, take pains to guard themselves with unfounded confidence, as if they were looking well to themselves, but their life, though defended by such powerful safeguards, will pass away; for they will bring to them everlasting ruin. On the other hand, when believers surrender themselves to die, their soul, which appears to vanish in a moment, passes into a better life."
John Calvin, commentating on Matthew 10:37

Matthew 11

Matthew Henry's introduction

In this chapter we have,

I. The constant and unwearied diligence of our Lord Jesus in his great work of preaching the gospel, v. 1.

II. His discourse with the disciples of John about his being the Messiah, vv. 2–6.

III. The honorable testimony that Christ bore to John Baptist, vv. 7–15.

IV. The sad account he gives of that generation in general, and of some particular places with reference to the success, both of John's ministry and of his own, vv. 16–24.

V. His thanksgiving to his Father for the wise and gracious method he had taken in revealing the great mysteries of the gospel, vv. 25, 26.

VI. His gracious call and invitation of poor sinners to come to him, and to be ruled, and taught, and saved by him, vv. 27–30. No Where have we more of the terror of gospel woes for warning to us, or of the sweetness of gospel grace for encouragement to us, than in this chapter, which sets before us life and death, the blessing and the curse.

Dr. Adam Clarke's analysis of chapter

Christ, having finished his instructions to his disciples, departs to preach in different cities, 1.

John sends two of his disciples to him to inquire whether he were the Christ, 2–6.

Christ's testimony about John, 7–15.

He upbraids the Jews with their capriciousness, 16–19.

The condemnation of Chorazin, and Bethsaida, and Capernaum, for their unbelief and impenitence, 20–24.

Praises the Divine wisdom for revealing the Gospel to the simple-hearted, 25, 26.

Shows that none can know God but by the revelation of his Son, 27.

Invites the distressed to come unto him, and gives them the promise of rest for their souls, 29–30.

A detailed analysis of chapter

Christ's preaching. (1)

Christ's answer to John's disciples. (2–6)

Christ's testimony to John the Baptist. (7–15)

The perverseness of the Jews. (16–24)

The gospel revealed to the simple. The heavy-laden invited. (25–30)

Key verse

Verse 11: "I tell you the truth: Among those born of women there has not risen anyone greater than John the Baptist; yet he who is least in the kingdom of heaven is greater than he."

Key word / key phrase

Verse 4, "report to John what you hear and see."

Key event / key person / key theme

Jesus fulfilled the Old Testament prophecies about the Messiah.

Key thought

Why did people comment about John the Baptist in the way that is recorded in verse 18?

Key thing to look out for

The kind of rest Jesus offered his followers was much greater than absence from work.

Key Bible cross-reference

Verse 5. See Isaiah 35:5,6.

Key "by way of explanation"

Verse 12, "forceful men laid hold of it." This does not mean that you have to be violent to become a Christian but that this may require great effort and concentrated attention.

Key "Quotable Quote"

"Our Lord's words are not, 'Do this, or don't do that,' but – 'Come to me.'"

Oswald Chambers

Matthew 12

Matthew Henry's introduction

In this chapter, we have,

I. Christ's clearing of the law of the fourth commandment about the Sabbath-day, and vindicating it from some superstitious notions advanced by the Jewish teachers; showing that works of necessity and mercy are to be done on that day, vv. 1–13.

II. The prudence, humility, and self-denial of our Lord Jesus in working his miracles, vv. 14–21.

III. Christ's answer to the blasphemous cavils and calumnies of the scribes and Pharisees, who imputed his casting out devils to a compact with the devil, vv. 22–37.

IV. Christ's reply to a tempting demand of the scribes and Pharisees, challenging him to show them a sign from heaven, vv. 38–45.

V. Christ's judgment about his kindred and relations, vv. 46–50.

Dr. Adam Clarke's analysis of chapter

Jesus and his disciples go through the corn fields on the Sabbath, and the latter pluck and eat some of the ears, at which the Pharisees take offense, 1, 2.

Our Lord vindicates them, 3–8.

The man with the withered hand cured, 9–13.

The Pharisees seek his destruction, 14.

He heals the multitudes, and fulfils certain prophecies, 15–21.

Heals the blind and dumb demoniac, 22, 23.

The malice of the Pharisees reproved by our Lord, 24–30.

The sin against the Holy Spirit, 31, 32.

Good and bad trees known by their fruits-evil and good men by their conduct, 33–37.

Jonah, a sign of Christ's death and resurrection, 38–40.

The men of Nineveh and the queen of the south shall rise up in the judgment against the Jews, 41, 42.

Of the unclean spirit, 43–45.

Christ's mother and brethren seek him, 46–50.

A detailed analysis of chapter

Jesus defends his disciples for picking corn on the Sabbath day. (1–8)

Jesus heals a man with a withered hand on the Sabbath. (9–13)

The malice of the Pharisees. (14–21)

Jesus heals a demoniac. (22–30)

Blasphemy of the Pharisees. (31, 32)

Evil words come from an evil heart. (33–37)
The scribes and Pharisees told off for seeking a sign. (38–45)
The disciples of Christ are his closest relations. (46–50)

Key verse
Verse 12: "How much more valuable is a man than a sheep! Therefore it is lawful to do good on the Sabbath."

Key word / key phrase
Verse 2, "When the Pharisees."

Key event / key person / key theme
The opposition of the Pharisees

Key thought
Clear teaching is given here about the perplexing topic of "blasphemy against the Spirit."

Key thing to look out for
The importance of the mission of Jonah is underlined by Jesus himself.

Key Bible cross-reference
Verses 18–21. See Isaiah 42:1–4.

Key "by way of explanation"
Verse 31, "blasphemy against the Spirit" will not be forgiven because such a person is attributing Jesus' miracles to Satan. Such a person has written off the work of God's Spirit, yet the Spirit which is the only way to find salvation.

Key "Quotable Quote"
"The disciple who is in the condition of abiding in Jesus is in the will of God, and his apparent free choices are God's foreordained decrees. Mysterious? Logically absurd? But a glorious truth to a saint."

Oswald Chambers

Matthew 13

Matthew Henry's introduction
In this chapter, we have,

I. The favor which Christ did to his countrymen in preaching the kingdom of heaven to them, vv. 1–2. He preached to them in parables, and here gives the reason why he chose that way of instructing, vv. 10–17. And the evangelist gives another reason, vv. 34, 35. There are eight parables recorded in this chapter, which are designed to represent the kingdom of heaven, the method of planting the gospel kingdom in the world, and of its growth and success. The great truths and laws of that kingdom are in other scriptures laid down plainly, and without parables: but some circumstances of its beginning and progress are here laid open in parables.

A. Here is one parable to show what are the great hindrances of people's profiting by the word of the gospel, and in how many it comes short of its end, through their own folly, and that is the parable of the four sorts of ground, delivered, vv. 3–9, and expounded, vv. 18–23.

B. Here are two parables intended to show that there would be a mixture of good and bad in the gospel church, which would continue till the great separation between them in the judgment day: the parable of the tares put forth (vv. 24–30), and expounded at the request of the disciples (vv. 36–43); and that of the net cast into the sea, vv. 47–50.

C. Here are two parables intended to show that the gospel church should be very small at first, but that in process of time it should become a considerable body: that of the grain of mustard seed (vv. 31, 32), and that of the leaven, v. 33.

D. Here are two parables intended to show that those who expect salvation by the gospel must be willing to venture all, and quit all, in the prospect of it, and that they shall be no losers by the bargain; that of the treasure hid in the field (v. 44), and that of the pearl of great price, vv. 45, 46.

E. Here is one parable intended for direction to the disciples, to make use of the instructions he had given them for the benefit of others; and that is the parable of the good householder, vv. 51, 52.

II. The contempt which his countrymen put on him on account of the meanness of his parentage, vv. 53–58.

Dr. Adam Clarke's analysis of chapter

Christ teaches the multitudes out of a ship, they standing on the shore, 1, 2.

The parable of the sower, 3–9.

He gives his reasons for speaking in parables, 10–17.

Explains the parable of the sower, 18–23.

Parable of the tares and the wheat, 24– 30.

Of the grain of mustard seed, 31, 32.

Of the leaven, 33.

The prophecy fulfilled by this mode of teaching, 34, 35.

He explains the parable of the tares and the wheat, 36–43.

Parable of the treasure hid in a field, 44. Of the pearl-merchant, 45, 46.

Of the dragnet, 47–50.

His application of the whole, 51, 52.

He teaches in his own country, and his neighbors take offense, 53–56.

Our Lord's observations on this, 57.

He works no miracle among them because of their unbelief, 58.

A detailed analysis of chapter

The parable of the sower. (1–23)

The parable of the weeds. (24–30; 36–43)

The parables of the mustard seed and the leaven. (31–35)

The parables of the hidden treasure, the pearl of great price, the net thrown into the sea, and the owner of a house. (44–52)

Jesus is again rejected at Nazareth. (53–58)

Key verse

Verse 3: "A farmer went out to sow his seed."

Key word / key phrase

Verse 3, "in parables."

Key event / key person / key theme

The parables of the kingdom

Key thought

The amazing increase produced by each fruitful seed is sometimes missed here.

Key thing to look out for

What are the weeds?

Key Bible cross-reference

Verse 35. See Psalm 78:2.

Key "by way of explanation"

Verse 33. Teaching about "the kingdom of heaven," God's present rule and God's forthcoming rule, is the main plank of Jesus' teaching. Matthew mentions it over fifty times.

Key "Quotable Quote"

"Each of us ought to endeavor to tear the thorns out of his heart, if we do not choose that the word of God should be choked; for there is not one of us whose heart is not filled with a vast quantity, and, I may say, a thick forest, of thorns. And, indeed, we perceive how few there are that reach maturity; for there is scarcely one individual out of ten that labors, I do not say to root out, but even to cut down the thorns."

John Calvin

Matthew 14

Matthew Henry's introduction

John the Baptist had said about Christ, He must increase, but I must decrease, John 3:30. The morning-star is here disappearing, and the Sun of righteousness rising to its meridian luster.

Dr. Adam Clarke's analysis of chapter

Herod, having heard the fame of Christ, supposes him to be John the Baptist, risen from the dead, 1, 2.

A circumstantial account of the beheading of John the Baptist, 3–12.

Five thousand men, besides women and children, fed with five loaves and two fishes, 13–21.

The disciples take ship, and Jesus stays behind, and goes privately into a mountain to pray, 22, 23.

A violent storm arises, by which the lives of the disciples are endangered, 24.

In their extremity, Jesus appears to them, walking on the water, 25–27.

Peter, at the command of his Master, leaves the ship, and walks on the water to meet Christ, 28–31.

They both enter the ship, and the storm ceases, 32, 33.

They come into the land of Gennesaret, and he heals many diseased people, 34–36.

A detailed analysis of chapter

Death of John the Baptist. (1–12)

Five thousand people miraculously fed. (13–21)

Jesus walks on the water. (22–33)

Jesus heals the sick. (34–36)

Key verse

Verse 14: "When Jesus landed and saw a large crowd, he had compassion on them and healed their sick."

Key word / key phrase

Verse 10, "John beheaded."

Key event / key person / key theme

Execution of John the Baptist

Key thought

John's outspoken faithfulness caused him to lose his head.

Key thing to look out for

Jesus shows that he is the bread of life in a most unforgettable way.

Key Bible cross-reference

Verse 4. See Leviticus 18:16.

Key "by way of explanation"

Verse 6. The Gospels do not tell us the name of the dancing "daughter of Herodias." But Josephus (*Ant.* XVIII. v. 4) records that she was called Salome.

Key "Quotable Quote"

"Why, they ask, do not those miracles, which you preach as of past events, happen nowadays? I might reply that they were necessary before the world believed, to bring the world to believe; but whoever is still looking for prodigies to make him believe is himself a great prodigy for refusing to believe where the world believes."

Augustine of Hippo

Matthew 15

Matthew Henry's introduction

In this chapter, we have our Lord Jesus, as the great Prophet teaching, as the great Physician healing, and as the great Shepherd of the sheep feeding; as the Father of spirits instructing them; as the Conqueror of Satan dispossessing him; and as concerned for the bodies of his people, providing for them.

Dr. Adam Clarke's analysis of chapter

The Pharisees accuse the disciples of eating with unwashed hands, 1, 2.

Our Lord answers, and convicts them of gross hypocrisy, 3–9.

Teaches the people and the disciples what it is that renders men unclean, 10–20.

Heals the daughter of a Canaanitish woman, 21–28.

Heals many diseased people on a mountain of Galilee, 29–31.

With seven loaves, and a few little fishes, he feeds 4,000 men, besides women and children, 32–38.

Having dismissed the multitudes, he comes to the coast of Magdala, 39.

A detailed analysis of chapter

Jesus speaks about human traditions. (1–9)

He warns about things which really defile. (10–20)

He heals the daughter of a Canaanite woman. (21–28)

Jesus heals the sick, and miraculously feeds four thousand. (29–39)

Key verse

Verse 2: "Why do your disciples break the tradition of the elders? They don't wash their hands before they eat!"

Key word / key phrase

Verse 1, "Pharisees and teachers of the law."

Key event / key person / key theme

Rejection by scribes and Pharisees

Key thought

In some of the recorded conversations people had with Jesus, Jesus appears to be almost harsh. But all he did was to draw out people's faith in him.

Key thing to look out for

It is all too easy to honor God with our lips in a Sunday worship service and to dishonor him a little later.

Key Bible cross-reference

Verse 4. See Exodus 20:12.

Key "by way of explanation"

Verse 26, "their dogs." Jesus is referring to a pet dog here. Even though Jesus is saying the gospel was for the Jews first of all, the woman would not be put off, and persists and reveals the depth of her faith in Jesus.

Key "Quotable Quote"

"Some people think that having reasons for faith is an insult to God. But verification itself depends on the unchanging authority and stability of the Word of God. We are not insulting God but bringing glory to him by taking his Word as the stable, authoritative truth it is."

Os Guinness

Matthew 16

Matthew Henry's introduction

None of Christ's miracles are recorded in this chapter, but four of his discourses. Here is,

I. A conversation with the Pharisees, who challenged him to show them a sign from heaven, vv. 1–4.

II. Another with his disciples about the leaven of the Pharisees, vv. 5–12.

III. Another with them about himself, as the Christ, and about his church built on him, vv. 13–20.

IV. Another about his sufferings for them, and theirs for him, vv. 21–28. And all these are written for our learning.

Dr. Adam Clarke's analysis of chapter

The Pharisees insidiously require our Lord to give them a sign, 1.

They are severely rebuked for their hypocrisy and wickedness, 2–5.

The disciples are cautioned to beware of them and their destructive doctrine, 6–12.

The different opinions formed by the people of Christ, 13, 14.

Peter's confession, and our Lord's discourse on it, 15–20.

He foretells his sufferings, and reproves Peter, 21–23.

Teaches the necessity of self-denial, and shows the reasons on which it is founded, 24–26.

Speaks of a future judgment, 27.

And promises the speedy opening of the glory of his own kingdom on earth, 28.

A detailed analysis of chapter

The Pharisees and Sadducees ask a sign. (1–4)

Jesus warns against the teaching of the Pharisees. (5–12)

Peter's testimony that Jesus is the Christ. (13–20)

Christ predicts his sufferings, and rebukes Peter. (21–23)

The necessity of self-denial. (24–28)

Key verse

Verse 1: "The Pharisees and Sadducees came to Jesus and tested him by asking him to show them a sign from heaven."

Key word / key phrase

Verse 16, "You are the Christ."

Key event / key person / key theme

Peter's confession

Key thought

A miracle in itself is by no means guaranteed to elicit faith.

Key thing to look out for

Peter had divine insight to see who Jesus really was.

Key Bible cross-reference

Verse 27. See Psalm 62:12.

Key "by way of explanation"

Verse 19 "bind . . . loose." What is conferred on Peter here is not the authority to determine who is guilty and who is innocent, but just the responsibility to announce this.

Key "Quotable Quote"

"He is no fool who gives what he cannot keep to gain what he cannot lose."

Jim Elliot, the young American missionary killed by Auca Indians in Ecuador in 1956, reflecting on Jesus' words in verses 24–26.

Matthew 17

Matthew Henry's introduction

In this chapter we have,

I. Christ in his pomp and glory transfigured, vv. 1–13.

II. Christ in his power and grace, casting the devil out of a child, vv. 14–21. And,

III. Christ in his poverty and great humiliation,

A. Foretelling his own sufferings, vv. 22, 23.

B. Paying tribute, vv. 24–27. So that here is Christ, the Brightness of his Father's glory, by himself purging our sins, paying our debts, and destroying for us him that had the power of death, that is, the devil. Thus were the several indications of Christ's gracious intentions admirable interwoven.

Dr. Adam Clarke's analysis of chapter

The transfiguration of Christ, 1–8.

Christ's discourse with his disciples on the subject, 9–13.

He heals a lunatic, 14–18.

His discourse with his disciples on this subject also, 19–21.

He foretells his own sufferings and death, 22, 23.

He is required to pay tribute at Capernaum, 24–26; and provides the money by a miracle, 27.

A detailed analysis of chapter

The transfiguration of Christ. (1–13)

Jesus expels a dumb and deaf spirit. (14–21)

He again predicts his sufferings. (22,23)

He performs a miracle to pay the temple tax. (24–27)

Key verse

Verses 20,21: "Because you have so little faith. I tell you the truth, if you have faith as small as a mustard seed, you can say to this mountain, 'Move from here to there' and it will move. Nothing will be impossible for you."

Key word / key phrase

Verse 2, "he was transfigured."

Key event / key person / key theme

Jesus' transfiguration

Key thought

For a brief moment part of the glory is made visible to the human eye.

Key thing to look out for

Peter shows his obedience and faith in Jesus in verses 24–27.

Key Bible cross-reference

Verse 16. See Deuteronomy 19:15.

Key "by way of explanation"

Verse 24. The "two-drachma tax" was the annual temple tax. Every male over the age of twenty had to pay it.

Key "Quotable Quote"

"As Moses and Elijah stood with Jesus on the Mount of Transfiguration, the Law, with its requirement and its sacrifices, and prophecy, with its forward-looking gaze, stood there in their representatives and bore witness that their converging lines meet in Jesus. Their presence and their speech were the acknowledgment that this was he whom they had seen from afar."

Alexander MacLaren

Matthew 18

Matthew Henry's introduction

The gospels are, in short, a record of what Jesus began both to do and to teach. In the previous chapter, we had an account of his doings, in this, of his teachings; probably, not all at the same time, in a continued discourse, but at several times, on divers occasions, here put together, as near akin. We have here,

I. Instructions about humility, vv. 1–6.

II. About offences in general (v. 7), particularly offences given,

A. By us to ourselves, vv. 8, 9.

B. By us to others, vv. 10–14.

C. By others to us; which are of two sorts,

1. Scandalous sins, which are to be reproved, vv. 15–20.

2. Personal wrongs, which are to be forgiven, vv. 21–35.

See how practical Christ's preaching was; he could have revealed mysteries, but he pressed plain duties, especially those that are most displeasing to flesh and blood.

Dr. Adam Clarke's analysis of chapter

The disciples inquiring who should be greatest in Christ's kingdom, 1.

He takes occasion to recommend humility, simplicity, and disinterestedness, 2–6.

Warns them against offenses, 7.

Recommends mortification and self-denial. 8, 9.

Charges them to avoid giving offense. 10, 11.

Parable of him who had lost one sheep out of his flock consisting of one hundred, 12–14.

How to deal with an offending brother, 15–18.

A gracious promise to social prayer, 19, 20.

How often an offending brother who expresses sorrow, and promises amendment, is to be forgiven, 21, 22.

The parable of the king, who calls his servants to account, and finds one who owed him ten thousand talents, who, being unable to pay, and imploring mercy, is forgiven, 23–27.

Of the same person, who treated his fellow servant unmercifully, who owed him but a small sum, 28–30.

Of the punishment inflicted on this unmerciful servant, 31–35.

A detailed analysis of chapter

The importance of humility. (1–6)

Warning about causing people to sin. (7–9)

The parable of the lost sheep. (10–14)

The brother who sins against you. (15–20)

Forgiving your brother, and the parable of the unmerciful servant. (21–35)

Key verse

Verse 4: "Therefore, whoever humbles himself like this child is the greatest in the kingdom of heaven."

Key word / key phrase

Verse 1, "Who is the greatest?"

Key event / key person / key theme

The Church's lifestyle

Key thought

The greatest in the kingdom is in stark contrast to greatness in the world.

Key thing to look out for

Jesus' great love is illustrated wonderfully in the short parable in verses 12–14.

Key Bible cross-reference

Verse 4. See Genesis 1:27; 5:2.

Key "by way of explanation"

Verse 9, "fire of hell." In 5:22,29,30 this is called Gehenna, after the "Valley of Hinnom" which was a rubbish dump outside Jerusalem. It was always on fire.

Key "Quotable Quote"

"God forgives talents; we cannot forgive pence. God forgives a hundred thousand; we cannot forgive a hundred (Matthew 18). We look that God should forgive us, and we will not forgive others."

Thomas Manton

Matthew 19

Matthew Henry's introduction

In this chapter, we have,

I. Christ changing his quarters, leaving Galilee, and coming into the coasts of Judea, vv. 1, 2.

II. His dispute with the Pharisees about divorce, and his discourse with his disciples on occasion of it, vv. 3–12.

III. The kind entertainment he gave to some little children which were brought to him, vv. 13–15.

IV. An account of what passed between Christ and a hopeful young gentleman that applied himself to him, vv. 16–22.

V. His discourse with his disciples on that occasion, about the difficulty of the salvation of those that have much in the world, and the certain recompense of those that leave all for Christ, vv. 23–30.

Dr. Adam Clarke's analysis of chapter

Jesus leaves Galilee, and comes into the coasts of Judea, and is followed by great multitudes, whom he heals, 1, 2.

The question of the Pharisees about divorce answered, and the doctrine of marriage explained, 3–9.

The inquiry of the disciples on this subject, 10.

Our Lord's answer, explaining the case of eunuchs, 11, 12.

Little children brought to Christ for his blessing, 13–15.

The case of the young man who wished to obtain eternal life, 16–22.

Our Lord's reflections on this case, in which he shows the difficulty of a rich man's salvation, 23–26.

What they shall possess who have left all for Christ's sake and the Gospel. 27–29.

How many of the first shall be last, and the last first, 30.

A detailed analysis of chapter

Jesus enters Judea. (1,2)

The Pharisees' question about divorce. (3–12)

Young children brought to Jesus. (13–15)

The rich young man's question. (16–22)

The reward for Christ's followers. (23–30)

Key verse

Verse 3: "Is it lawful for a man to divorce his wife for any and every reason?"

Key word / key phrase

Verse 22, "he had great wealth."

Key event / key person / key theme

A rich young man

Key thought

Jesus reveals much about his attitude to children in verses 13–15.

Key thing to look out for

This man was in the grip of his riches.

Key Bible cross-reference

Verse 18. See Exodus 20:13–16.

Key "by way of explanation"

Verse 16, "what good thing must I do?" The rich man thought that he could enter heaven by doing some great deed. Jesus pointed out that he needed to give his most treasured possessions to God and that the rich man was not prepared to do.

Key "Quotable Quote"

"It is the one exception that gives prominence to the illegitimacy of every other reason. Preoccupation with the one exception should never be permitted to obscure the force of the negation of all others."

John Murray, commentating on Matthew 5:32 and 19:9

Matthew 20

Matthew Henry's introduction

We have four things in this chapter.

I. The parable of the laborers in the vineyard, vv. 1–16.

II. A prediction of Christ's approaching sufferings, vv. 17–19.

III. The petition of two of the disciples, by their mother, reproved, vv. 20–28.

IV. The petition of the two blind men granted, and their eyes opened, vv. 29–34.

Dr. Adam Clarke's analysis of chapter

The similitude of the householder hiring laborers into his vineyard, to show that the Gentiles should be preferred to the Jews, according to what was hinted at the close of the last chapter, 1–16.

On the way going up to Jerusalem he predicts his sufferings and death, 17–19.

The mother of Zebedee's children requests dignities for her sons, 20, 21.

Christ, by his answer, shows that sufferings, not worldly honors, are to be the lot of his most faithful followers, and that seats in glory can be given only to those who are prepared for them, 22, 23.

From this our Lord takes occasion to teach the necessity of humility, and to show that those who wished to be chief must be servants of all, 24–28.

On his coming to Jericho, he restores sight to two blind men, who, being restored, follow him, 29–34.

A detailed analysis of chapter

The parable of the workers in the vineyard. (1–16)

Jesus again predicts his sufferings. (17–19)

The ambition of James and John. (20–28)

Jesus heals two blind men near Jericho. (29–34)

Key verse

Verse 28: "just as the Son of Man did not come to be served, but to serve, and to give his life as a ransom for many."

Key word / key phrase

Verse 16, "the first will be last."

Key event / key person / key theme

Parable of the workers in the vineyard

Key thought

To claim that Jesus was taken unawares and crucified flies in the face of the most cursory reading of the Gospels.

Key thing to look out for

Verses 21 and 32. A question that Jesus still asks.

Key Bible cross-reference

Verse 8. See Leviticus 19:13.

Key "by way of explanation"

Verse 22, "drink the cup." This meant to experience something and in this instance refers to Jesus' suffering. See Jeremiah 25:15; Ezekiel 23:32.

Key "Quotable Quote"

"We must first make up our minds about Christ before coming to conclusions about the miracles attributed to him."

F.F. Bruce

Matthew 21

Matthew Henry's introduction

The death and resurrection of Jesus Christ are the two main hinges on which the door of salvation turns. He came into the world on purpose to give his life a ransom; so he had lately said, 20:28. And therefore the history of his sufferings, even unto death, and his rising again, is more particularly recorded by all the evangelists than any other part of his story; and to that this evangelist now hastens apace. For at this chapter begins that which is called the passion-week. He had said to his disciples more than once, Behold, we go up to Jerusalem, and there the Son of man must be betrayed. A great deal of good work he did by the way, and now at length he is come up to Jerusalem.

Dr. Adam Clarke's analysis of chapter

Christ rides into Jerusalem on an ass, and the multitude receive him joyfully, 1–11.

He enters the temple, and expels the money changers, etc. 12, 13.

The blind and the lame come to him and are healed, 14.

The chief priests and scribes are offended, 15.

Our Lord confounds them, and goes to Bethany, 16, 17.

The barren fig-tree blasted, 18–22.

While teaching in the temple, the chief priests and elders question his authority; he answers and confutes them, 23–27.

The parable of the man and his two sons, 28–32.

The parable of a vineyard let out to husbandmen, 33–42; applied to the priests and Pharisees, 43–45; who wish to kill him, but are restrained by the fear of the people, who acknowledge Christ for a prophet, 46.

A detailed analysis of chapter

Christ enters Jerusalem. (1–11)

He drives out those who profaned the temple. (12–17)

The barren fig tree cursed. (18–22)

Jesus' teaching in the temple. (23–27)

The parable of the two sons. (28–32)

The parable of the wicked landowner. (33–46)

Key verse

Verse 8: "A very large crowd spread their cloaks on the road, while others cut branches from the trees and spread them on the road."

Key word / key phrase

Verse 22, "If you believe."

Key event / key person / key theme

Jesus enters Jerusalem

Key thought

One minute a crowd welcome Jesus, later in the week they call for his blood.

Key thing to look out for

The chief priests knew where Jesus' authority came from, but they just did not care to bow before God.

Key Bible cross-reference

Verse 5. See Zechariah 9:9.

Key "by way of explanation"

Verse 33, "watchtower." The watchtower was for shelter and for a lookout post for any enemies.

Key "Quotable Quote"

"Jesus promised his disciples three things – that they would be completely fearless, absurdly happy and in constant trouble."

G.K. Chesterton

Matthew 22

Matthew Henry's introduction

This chapter is a continuation of Christ's discourses in the temple, two or three days before he died. His discourses then are largely recorded, as being of special weight and consequence.

Dr. Adam Clarke's analysis of chapter

The parable of the marriage of a king's son, 1–14.

The Pharisees and Herodians question him about the lawfulness of paying tribute to Caesar, 15–22.

The Sadducees question him about the resurrection, 23–33.

A lawyer questions him about the greatest commandment in the law, 34–40.

He asks them their opinion of the Christ, and confounds them, 41–46.

A detailed analysis of chapter

The parable of the marriage feast. (1–14)

The Pharisees question Jesus about paying taxes to Caesar. (15–22)

The Sadducees and the resurrection. (23–33)

The greatest commandment. (34–40)

Jesus questions the Pharisees. (41–46)

Key verse

Verse 37: "'Love the Lord your God with all your heart and with all your soul and with all your mind.'"

Key word / key phrase

Verse 22, "in parables."

Key event / key person / key theme

Parables and questions

Key thought

Verse 35 was a much-debated question among the rabbis. Until Jesus came, no one had ever put the two separate commandments together to from one whole.

Key thing to look out for

In the Old Testament, "Love your neighbor" meant your fellow-Jew. Jesus gave it a new meaning: "Love your fellow human being."

Key Bible cross-reference

Verse 24. See Deuteronomy 25:5.

Key "by way of explanation"

Verse 11, "not wearing wedding clothes." Some of the people at the banquet had been hauled in from the streets. They would have had to avail themselves of a wedding garment from the host. If they were not wearing one it shows that they had deliberately refused to put one on.

Key "Quotable Quote"

"Only our refusal to trust him . . . can hinder his purposes in our lives."

Joni Eareckson Tada

Matthew 23

Matthew Henry's introduction

In the previous chapter, we had our Savior's discourses with the scribes and Pharisees; here we have his discourse about them, or rather against them.

Dr. Adam Clarke's analysis of chapter

The character of the scribes and Pharisees, and directions to the people and the disciples to receive the law from them, but not to follow their bad example, 1–7.

The disciples exhorted to humility, 8–12.

Different woes pronounced against the scribes and Pharisees for their intolerance, 13;

rapacity, 14;

false zeal, 15;

superstition in oaths and tithes, 16–23;

hypocrisy, 24–28.

Their cruelty, 29–32.

Their persecution of the apostles, etc. Their destruction foretold, 33–36.

Christ's lamentation over Jerusalem, 37–39.

A detailed analysis of chapter

Jesus reproves the scribes and Pharisees. (1–12)

Evil actions of the Pharisees. (13–33)

The guilt of Jerusalem. (34–39)

Key verse

Verse 12: "For whoever exalts himself will be humbled, and whoever humbles himself will be exalted."

Key word / key phrase

Verse 13, "Woe to you."

Key event / key person / key theme

Jesus denounces the Pharisees

Key thought

Jesus called some Pharisees, "you snakes," verse 33, to help them face the reality of their vile selves.

Key thing to look out for

Serious times call for serious talking.

Key Bible cross-reference

Verse 29. See Isaiah 13:10.

Key "by way of explanation"

Verse 35, "Abel to . . . Zechariah." This was Jesus' summary of the people who had been martyred in the Old Testament. Zechariah is "Zechariah son of Jehoiada" who comes in 2 Chronicles 24:20–22. According to the Hebrew arrangement of the book of the Old Testament, 2 Chronicles came last.

Key "Quotable Quote"

"Jesus offered us, not an excursion, but an execution."

Billy Graham

Matthew 24

Matthew Henry's introduction

Christ's preaching was mostly practical; but, in this chapter, we have a prophetical discourse, a prediction of things to come; such however as had a practical tendency, and was intended, not to gratify the curiosity of his disciples, but to guide their consciences and conversations, and it is therefore concluded with a practical application. The church has always had particular prophecies, besides general promises, both for direction and for encouragement to believers; but it is observable, Christ preached this prophetical sermon in the close of his ministry, as the Apocalypse is the last book of the New Testament, and the prophetical books of the Old Testament are placed last, to intimate to us, that we must be well grounded in plain truths and duties, and those must first be well digested, before we dive into those things that are dark and difficult; many run themselves into confusion by beginning their Bible at the wrong end.

Dr. Adam Clarke's analysis of chapter

Christ foretells the destruction of the temple, 1, 2.

His disciples inquire when and what shall be the sign of this destruction, 3.

Our Lord answers, and enumerates them-false Christs, 5.

Wars, famines, pestilences, and earthquakes, 6–8.

Persecution of his followers, 9.

Apostasy from the truth, 10–13.

General spread of the Gospel, 14.

He foretells the investment of the city by the Romans, 15–18.

The calamities of those times, 19–22.

Warns them against seduction by false prophets, 23–26.

The suddenness of these calamities, 27, 28.

Total destruction of the Jewish polity, 29–31.

The whole illustrated by the parable of the fig-tree, 32, 33.

The certainty of the event, though the time is concealed, 34–36.

Careless state of the people, 37–41.

The necessity of watchfulness and fidelity, illustrated by the parable of the two servants, one faithful, the other wicked, 42–51.

A detailed analysis of chapter

Christ predicts the destruction of the temple. (1–3)

The troubles before the destruction of Jerusalem. (4–28)

Christ predicts other signs. The end of the world. (29–41)

Exhortations to be watchful. (42–51)

Key verse

Verse 4: "Watch out that no one deceives you."

Key word / key phrase

Verse 3, "the end of the age."

Key event / key person / key theme

Jesus teaches about the end of the age

Key thought

When someone says he knows when the world will end we know he must be wrong.

Key thing to look out for

The end of the world is certain and Jesus warns people to be alert and ready for it.

Key Bible cross-reference

Verse 29. See Isaiah 13:10; 34:4.

Key "by way of explanation"

Verse 28, "vultures." When Jesus does come again it will be clear for all to see, as obvious as vultures circling over some dead body.

Key "Quotable Quote"

"He who loves the coming of the Lord is not he who affirms it is far off, nor is it he who says it is near. It is he who, whether it be far or near, awaits it with sincere faith, steadfast hope, and fervent love."

Augustine of Hippo

Matthew 25

Matthew Henry's introduction

This chapter continues and concludes our Savior's discourse, which began in the previous chapter, about his second coming and the end of the world. This was his farewell sermon of caution, as that, John 14:15, 16, was of comfort to his disciples; and they had need of both in a world of so much temptation and trouble as this is. The application of that discourse, was, Watch therefore, and be ye also ready. Now, in prosecution of these serious awakening cautions, in this chapter we have three parables, the scope of which is the same–to quicken us all with the utmost care and diligence to get ready for Christ's second coming, which, in all his farewells to his church, mention was made of, as in that before he died (John 14:2), in that at his ascension (Acts 1:11), and in that at the shutting up of the canon of the scriptures, Rev. 22:20. Now it concerns us to prepare for Christ's coming.

Dr. Adam Clarke's analysis of chapter

The parable of the ten virgins, five of whom were wise, and five foolish, 1–12.

The necessity of being constantly prepared to appear before God, 13.

The parable of the talents, 14–30.

The manner in which God shall deal with the

righteous and the wicked in the judgment of the great day, 31–46.

A detailed analysis of chapter

The parable of the ten virgins. (1–13)

The parable of the talents. (14–30)

The judgment. (31–46)

Key verse

Verse 14: "Again, it will be like a man going on a journey, who called his servants and entrusted his property to them."

Key word / key phrase

Verse 30, "into the darkness."

Key event / key person / key theme

Jesus predicts judgment at his coming

Key thought

Talents are to be used, not hidden away.

Key thing to look out for

God's day of judgment will certainly come.

Key Bible cross-reference

Verse 46. See Daniel 12:2.

Key "by way of explanation"

Verses 34–40. The "rewards" given to the faithful are not given because they "merit" them. Everyone is saved by grace, but everyone should also serve Jesus and his kingdom, "seeking for no reward."

Key "Quotable Quote"

"The kingdom of heaven" is the great theme of Matthew's Gospel.

John R.W. Stott

Matthew 26

Matthew Henry's introduction

The narrative of the death and sufferings of Christ is more particularly and fully recorded by all the four evangelists than any part of his history; for what should be determine, and desire to know, but Christ, and him crucified? And this chapter begins that memorable narrative. The year of the redeemed was now come, the seventy weeks determined were now accomplished, when transgression must be finished, reconciliation made, and an everlasting righteousness brought in, by the cutting off of Messiah the Prince, Dan. 9:24, 26. That awful scene is here introduced, to be read with reverence and holy fear.

Dr. Adam Clarke's analysis of chapter

Christ predicts his being betrayed and crucified, 1, 2.

The chief priests, scribes, and elders consult about his death, 3–5.

A woman anoints his head at Bethany, at which the disciples are offended, but Christ vindicates her conduct, 6– 13.

Judas, for thirty pieces of silver, engages with the chief priests to betray him, 14–16.

He eats a Passover with his disciples, and assures them of his approaching death, and that one of them would betray him, 17–21.

On each asking, Is it I? Christ asserts that Judas

is the traitor, 22–25.

Having eaten his last supper, he institutes the eucharist, to be observed in his Church as a memorial of his sacrificial death, 26–29.

They sing a hymn, go to the mount of Olives, and he again announces his approaching death and resurrection, 30–32.

Peter asserts his resolution to be faithful to his Master, and Christ foretells his denial and apostasy, 33–35.

He goes to Gethsemane; the transactions there, 36–46.

Judas comes with the high priest's mob and betrays him with a kiss, 47–50.

Peter cuts off the ear of the high priest's servant; Christ discourses with the multitude, 51–55.

The disciples flee, and he is led to Caiaphas, 56, 57.

Peter follows at a distance, 58.

They seek false witnesses, and question our Lord, who declares himself to be the Christ, 59–64.

They accuse him of blasphemy, and abuse him, 65–68.

Peter's denial and repentance, 69–75.

A detailed analysis of chapter

The rulers plot against Christ. (1–5)

Christ anointed at Bethany. (6–13)

Judas agrees to betray Christ. (14–16)

The Passover. (17–25)

Christ institutes his holy supper. (26–30)

He warns his disciples. (31–35)

His agony in the garden. (36–46)

He is betrayed. (47–56)

Christ before Caiaphas. (57–68)

Peter denies him. (69–75)

Key verse

Verse 4: ". . . they plotted to arrest Jesus in some sly way and kill him."

Key word / key phrase

Verse 17, "to eat the Passover."

Key event / key person / key theme

The Last Supper

Key thought

God's covenant with the Jews was a refrain that runs throughout the Old Testament. That covenant was based on God's Law. Jesus here inaugurates a new covenant. By his death people enter into a covenant of grace and love.

Key thing to look out for

Jesus' command in verse 41.

Key Bible cross-reference

Verse 2. See Exodus 12:1–27.

Key "by way of explanation"

Verse 63, "I charge you under oath." This meant that Jesus was legally bound to answer the question.

Key "Quotable Quote"

"He said to Judas when he betrayed him: 'Friend, wherefore art thou come?' Just as if he had said: 'Thou hatest me, and art mine enemy, yet I love thee, and am thy friend.'"

Theologia Germanica

Matthew 27

Matthew Henry's introduction

It is a very affecting story which is recorded in this chapter about the sufferings and death of our Lord Jesus. Considering the thing itself, there cannot be a more tragic story told us; common humanity would melt the heart, to find an innocent and excellent person thus misused. But considering the design and fruit of Christ's sufferings, it is gospel, it is good news, that Jesus Christ was thus delivered for our offences; and there is nothing we have more reason to glory in than the cross of Christ.

Dr. Adam Clarke's analysis of chapter

In the morning, Christ is bound and delivered to Pontius Pilate, 1, 2.

Judas, seeing his Master condemned, repents, acknowledges his transgression to the chief priests, attests Christ's innocence, throws down the money, and goes and hangs himself, 3–5.

They buy the potter's field with the money, 6–10.

Christ, questioned by Pilate, refuses to answer, 11–14.

Pilate, while inquiring of the Jews whether they would have Jesus or Barabbas released, receives a message from his wife to have nothing to do in this wicked business, 15–19.

The multitude, influenced by the chief priests and elders, desire Barabbas to be released, and Jesus to be crucified, 20–23.

Pilate attests his innocence, and the people make themselves and their posterity responsible for his blood, 24, 25.

Barabbas is released, and Christ is scourged, 26.

The soldiers strip him, clothe him with a scarlet robe, crown him with thorns, mock, and variously insult him, 27–31.

Simon compelled to bear his cross, 32.

They bring him to Golgotha, give him vinegar mingled with gall to drink, crucify him, and cast lots for his raiment, 33–36.

His accusation, 37.

Two thieves are crucified with him, 38.

He is mocked and insulted while hanging on the cross, 39–44.

The awful darkness, 45.

Jesus calls on God, is offered vinegar to drink, expires, 46–50.

Prodigies that accompanied and followed his death, 51–53.

He is acknowledged by the centurion, 54.

Several women behold the crucifixion, 55, 56.

Joseph of Arimathea begs the body of Pilate, and deposits it in his own new tomb, 57–60.

The women watch the sepulcher, 61.

The Jews consult with Pilate how they may prevent the resurrection of Christ, 62– 64.

He grants them a guard for the sepulcher, and they seal the stone that stopped the mouth of the tomb where he was laid, 65, 66.

A detailed analysis of chapter

Christ handed over to Pilate, and the despair of Judas. (1–10)

Christ before Pilate. (11–25)

Barabbas freed, Christ mocked. (26–30)

Christ led to be crucified. (31–34)

He is crucified. (35–44)

The death of Christ. (45–50)

Events at the crucifixion. (51–56)
The burial of Christ. (57–61)
The sepulcher secured. (62–66)

Key verse

Verse 45: "From the sixth hour until the ninth hour darkness came over all the land."

Key word / key phrase

Verse 35, "when they had crucified him."

Key event / key person / key theme

Jesus is crucified

Key thought

Verse 46. See 2 Corinthians 5:21: "God made him who had no sin to be sin for us." The major characteristic of sin is that it separates the sinners from God.

Key thing to look out for

Note the first thing Matthew records after Jesus' death, verse 51.

Key Bible cross-reference

Verses 9,10. See Zechariah 11:12,13.

Key "by way of explanation"

Verse 51, "curtain." This separated the Holy Place from the innermost Most Holy Place in the temple. Now it was torn in half and the way to God was open. Verse 46: the words are in Aramaic, one of the languages spoken in Palestine.

Key "Quotable Quote"

"No other death has aroused one hundredth part of the interest, or been remembered with one hundredth part of the intensity and concern."

Malcolm Muggeridge

Matthew 28

Matthew Henry's introduction

In the previous chapters, we saw the Captain of our salvation engaged with the powers of darkness, attacked by them, and vigorously attacking them; victory seemed to hover between the combatants; nay, at length, it inclined to the enemies' side, and our Champion fell before them; behold, God has delivered his strength into captivity, and his glory into the enemies' hand. Christ in the grave is like the ark in Dagon's temple; the powers of darkness seemed to ride masters, but then the Lord awaked as one out of sleep, and like a mighty man that shouteth by reason of wine, Ps. 78:61, 65. The prince of our peace is in this chapter rallying again, coming out of the grave, a Conqueror, yea, more than a conqueror, leading captivity captive; though the ark be a prisoner, Dagon falls before it, and it proves that none is able to stand before the holy Lord God. Now the resurrection of Christ being one of the main foundations of our religion, it is requisite that we should have infallible proofs of it; four of which proofs we have in this chapter, which are but a few of many, for Luke and John give a larger account of the proofs of Christ's resurrection than Matthew and Mark do.

Dr. Adam Clarke's analysis of chapter

The resurrection of Christ declared by an angel to the two Marys at the sepulcher, 1–6.

They are commissioned to announce this to the disciples, 7.

They go, and are met by Christ himself who promises to meet the disciples in Galilee, 8–10.

The watch go into the city, and report to the chief priests what had taken place, 11.

They give them money, to say that his disciples had stolen the body by night, while they slept, 12–15.

Christ meets the eleven disciples in a mountain of Galilee, 16, 17.

He gives them a commission to preach the Gospel throughout the earth; to baptize in the name of the Father, and of the Son, and of the Holy Spirit; and promises to be with them to the end of the world, 18–20.

A detailed analysis of chapter

Christ's resurrection. (1–8)

He appears to the women. (9,10)

The guards' report. (11–15)

Christ's commission to his disciples. (16–20)

Key verse

Verse 20: "And surely I am with you always, to the very end of the age."

Key word / key phrase

Verse 6, "he has risen."

Key event / key person / key theme

Jesus' resurrection

Key thought

The resurrection is the proof of Jesus' deity (Romans 1:4) and the guarantee of our resurrection and salvation.

Key thing to look out for

Note Jesus' last recorded words, verses 18–20.

Key Bible cross-reference

Verse 19. See Acts 1:8.

Key "by way of explanation"

Verse 20, "with you." Matthew, in his opening chapter, announced that God was "with us," 1:23, now he writes that Jesus will be "with you" forever.

Key "Quotable Quote"

"Of all the things in the world that can set the heart burning, there is none like the presence of Jesus."

C.H. Spurgeon

5. Select bibliography for Matthew's Gospel

Bruce, F. F. *Matthew.* Grand Rapids: Eerdmans, 1970.

Calvin, John. *Calvin's New Testament Commentaries: Matthew, Mark, and Luke.* 3 Vols. Translated by A.W. Morrison and T. H. L. Parker. Edited by D.W. Torrance and T. F. Torrance. Grand Rapids, 1972.

France, R. T. Matthew. Tyndale New Testament Commentaries. Leicester and Grand Rapids: Inter-Varsity and Eerdmans, 1985.

Hendriksen, William. *The Gospel of Matthew.* Grand Rapids: Baker, 1973.

Morgan, G. Campbell. *The Gospel According to Matthew.* Old Tappan: Revell, 1929.

Plumptre, E. H. *The Gospel According to Matthew.* Reprint. Grand Rapids: Zondervan, 1957.

Tasker, R. V. G. *The Gospel According to St. Matthew: An Introduction and Commentary.* London: IVP, 1961.

Mark

1. Book by book: Introduction to Mark

Introduction

Writer

That the second Gospel was written by Mark is universally agreed, though by what Mark, not so. The great majority of critics take the writer to be "John whose surname was Mark," of whom we read in the Acts, and who was "sister's son to Barnabas" (Col. 4:10). But no reason whatever is assigned for this opinion, for which the tradition, though ancient, is not uniform; and one cannot but wonder how it is so easily taken for granted by Wetstein, Hug, Meyer, Ebrard, Lange, Ellicott, Davidson, Tregelles, etc. Alford goes the length of saying it "has been universally believed that he was the same person with the John Mark of the Gospels." But Grotius thought differently, and so did Schleiermacher, Campbell, Burton, and Da Costa; and the grounds on which it is concluded that they were two different people appear to us quite unanswerable. "Of John, surnamed Mark," says Campbell, in his Preface to this Gospel, "one of the first things we learn is, that he attended Paul and Barnabas in their apostolic journeys, when these two traveled together (Acts 12:25; 13:5). And when afterwards there arose a dispute between them about him, insomuch that they separated, Mark accompanied his uncle Barnabas, and Silas attended Paul. When Paul was reconciled to Mark, which was probably soon after, we find Paul again employing Mark's assistance, recommending him, and giving him a very honorable testimony (Col. 4:10; 2 Tim. 4:11; Phile. 24). But we hear not a syllable of his attending Peter as his minister, or assisting him in any capacity." And yet, as we shall presently see, no tradition is more ancient, more uniform, and better sustained by internal evidence, than that Mark, in his Gospel, was but "the interpreter of Peter," who, at the close of his first Epistle speaks of him as "Marcus my son" (1 Pet. 5:13), that is, without doubt, his son in the Gospel–converted to Christ through his instrumentality. And when we consider how little the Apostles Peter and Paul were together–how seldom they even met–how different were their tendencies, and how separate their spheres of labor, is there not, in the absence of all evidence of the fact, something approaching to violence in the supposition that the same Mark was the intimate associate of both? "In brief," adds Campbell, "the accounts given of Paul's attendant, and those of Peter's interpreter, concur in nothing but the name, Mark or Marcus; too slight a circumstance to conclude the sameness of the person from, especially when we consider how common the name was at Rome, and how customary it was for the Jews in that age to assume some Roman name when they went thither."

The evangelist Mark

Regarding the Evangelist Mark, then, as another person from Paul's companion in travel, all we know of his personal history is that he was a convert, as we have seen, of the Apostle Peter. But as to his Gospel, the tradition regarding Peter's hand in it is so ancient, so uniform, and so remarkably confirmed by internal evidence, that we must regard it as an established fact. "Mark," says Papias (according to the testimony of Eusebius, [Ecclesiastical History, 3.39]), "becoming the interpreter of Peter, wrote accurately, though not in order, whatever he remembered of what was either said or done by Christ; for he was neither a hearer of the Lord nor a follower of Him, but afterwards, as I said, (he was a follower) of Peter, who arranged the discourses for use, but not according to the order in which they were uttered by the Lord." To the same effect Irenaeus (Against Heresies, 3. 1): "Matthew published a Gospel while Peter and Paul were preaching and founding the Church at Rome; and after their departure (or decease), Mark, the disciple and interpreter of Peter, he also gave forth to us in writing the things which were preached by Peter." And Clement of Alexandria is still more specific, in a passage preserved to us by Eusebius (Ecclesiastical History, 6.14): "Peter having publicly preached the word at Rome, and spoken forth the Gospel by the Spirit, many of those present exhorted Mark, as having long been a follower of his, and remembering what he had said, to write what had been spoken; and that having prepared the Gospel, he delivered it to those who had asked him for it; which, when Peter came to the knowledge of, he neither decidedly forbade nor encouraged him." Eusebius' own testimony, however, from other accounts, is rather different: that Peter's hearers were so penetrated by his preaching that they gave Mark, as being a follower of Peter, no rest till he consented to write his Gospel, as a memorial of his oral teaching; and "that the apostle, when he knew by the revelation of the Spirit what had been done, was delighted with the zeal of those men, and sanctioned the reading of the writing (that is, of this Gospel of Mark) in the churches" (Ecclesiastical History, 2.15). And giving in another of his works a similar statement, he says that "Peter, from excess of humility, did not think himself qualified to write the Gospel; but Mark, his acquaintance and pupil, is said to have recorded his relations of the deeds of Jesus. And Peter testifies these things of himself; for all things that are recorded by Mark are said to be memoirs of Peter's discourses." It is needless to go farther–to Origen, who says Mark composed his Gospel "as Peter guided" or "directed him, who, in his Catholic Epistle, calls him his son," etc.; and to Jerome, who but echoes Eusebius.

Readers

It remains only to advert, in a word or two, to the readers for whom this Gospel was, in the first instance, designed, and the date of it. That it was not for Jews but Gentiles, is evident from the great number of explanations of Jewish usages, opinions, and places, which to a Jew would at that time have been superfluous, but were highly needful to a Gentile. We can here but refer to Mark 2:18; 7:3, 4; 12:18; 13:3; 14:12; 15:42, for examples of these.

Date

Regarding the date of this Gospel–about which nothing certain is known–if the tradition reported by Irenaeus can be relied on, that it was written at Rome, "after the departure of Peter and Paul," and if by that word "departure" we are to understand their death, we may date it somewhere between the years 64 and 68; but in all likelihood this is too late. It is probably nearer the truth to date it eight or ten years earlier.

David Brown

Detailed outline

I. The period of preparation: 1:1–13
- A. The beginning of the Gospel: 1:1–3
- B. The ministry of John the Baptist: 1:4–8
- C. The baptism of Jesus: 1:9–11
- D. The temptation of Jesus: 1:12–13

II. The Galilean Ministry: 1:14–6:30
- A. The beginning of Jesus' ministry: 1:14–15
- B. The call of four fisherman: 1:16–20
- C. Healing of a demon possessed man: 1:21–28
- D. Healing of Peter's mother-in-law: 1:29–31
- E. Growing popularity: 1:32–34
- F. The quiet time: 1:35–37
- G. The first tour of Galilee: 1:38–39
- H. Healing a leper: 1:40–45
- I. Healing a paralyzed man: 2:1–12
- J. The call of Matthew: 2:13–14
- K. A celebration, criticism, and reply: 2:15–22
- L. The Sabbath controversy: 2:23–3:6
- M. Ministry by the sea: 3:7–12
- N. The commissioning of the twelve disciples: 3:13–19
- O. Jesus' zeal: 3:20–21
- P. The unpardonable sin: 3:22–30
- Q. True relationship with Jesus: 3:31–35
- R. A series of parables: 4:1–34
  - 1. The parable of the soils: 4:1–20
  - 2. The parable of the lamp: 4:21–25
  - 3. The parable of gradual growth: 4:26–29
  - 4. The parable of the mustard seed: 4:30–34
- S. A storm at sea: 4:35–41
- T. The healing of a demon-possessed man: 5:1–20
- U. Jarius' daughter and a woman who was subject to bleeding: 5:21–43
- V. Rejection at Nazareth: 6:1–6
- W. The mission of the twelve disciples: 6:7–13
- X. The death of John the Baptist: 6:14–29
- Y. The report of the twelve: 6:30

III. The period of withdrawal: 6:31–9:50
- A. The feeding of the 5,000: 6:31–46
- B. Walking on water: 6:47–52
- C. The ministry at Gennesaret: 6:53–56

D. The rebuking of the Pharisees: 7:1–23
E. The Syrophoenician woman: 7:24–30
F. Healing of a deaf mute: 7:31–37
G. Feeding of the 4,000: 8:1–9
H. A demand for a sign: 8:10–13
I. A warning about leaven: 8:14–21
J. Healing the blind man: 8:22–26
K. A lesson at Caesarea Philippi: 8:27–9:1
L. The transfiguration of Jesus: 9:2–10
M. The problem of Elijah: 9:11–13
N. The healing of a demon possessed boy: 9:14–29
O. Final teaching in Galilee: 9:30–50

IV. The ministry in Perea and Judea: 10:1–52
A. A lesson about divorce: 10:1–12
B. Children blessed: 10:13–16
C. The rich young ruler: 10:17–22
D. A warning about the danger of riches: 10:23–27
E. A discussion about rewards: 10:28–31
F. The prediction of Jesus's death: 10:32–34
G. A request for prominence: 10:35–45
H. The healing of Bartimaeus: 10:46–52

V. Events of the final week: 11:1–15:47
A. The royal entry to Jerusalem: 11:1–11
B. Cursing the barren fig tree: 11:12–14
C. Cleansing of the temple: 11:15–19
D. A lesson about faith: 11:20–26
E. A challenge to Christ's authority: 11:27–33
F. The parable of the husbandmen: 12:1–12
G. A question about paying taxes to Caesar: 12:13–17
H. The problem of the resurrection: 12:18–27
I. A question about the Great Commandment: 12:28–34
J. A question about the Christ: 12:35–37
K. A warning against Scribes: 12:38–40
L. The widow's mite: 12:41–44
M. Faith for the future: 13:1–37
N. The Sanhedrin's plot: 14:1–2
O. Dinner in Bethany: 14:3–9
P. Judas' plot: 14:10–11
Q. The Passover: 14:12–21
R. The Last Supper: 14:22–26
S. Peter's denial foretold: 14:27–31
T. Prayer in Gethsemane: 14:32–42
U. The betrayal and arrest: 14:43–52
V. The Jewish trial: 14:53–65
W. The denials of Peter: 14:66–72
X. The Roman trial: 15:1–21
Y. The crucifixion of Jesus: 15:22–41
Z. The burial of Jesus: 15:42–47

VI. The resurrection of Jesus: 16:1–8
A. First at the tomb: 16:1–3
B. The empty tomb: 16:4–6
C. The commission to preach the resurrection message: 16:7–8

VII. The appearances of Jesus: 16:9–14
A. To Mary Magdalene: 16:9–11
B. To two disciples: 16:12–13
C. To the eleven disciples: 16:14

VIII. The Great Commission: 16:15–18

IX. The ascension of Jesus: 16:19

X. Fulfilling the Commission: 16:20

2. Helpful summaries of Mark's Gospel

Bird's eye view

Mark, the shortest and most pity of the four Gospels, makes the essentials of the message about Jesus Christ immediately available to his readers.

Reading plan

The following reading plan, taking one reading per day, enables you to read through Mark's Gospel in twenty-nine days.

Mark 1:1–1:28
Mark 1:29–1:45
Mark 2:1–2:28
Mark 3:1–3:19
Mark 3:20–3:35
Mark 4:1–4:25
Mark 4:26–4:41
Mark 5:1–5:20
Mark 6:30–6:56
Mark 7:1–7:23
Mark 7:24–7:37
Mark 8:1–8:21
Mark 8:22–8:38
Mark 9:1–9:29
Mark 9:30–9:50
Mark 10:1–10:31
Mark 10:32–10:52
Mark 11:1–11:14
Mark 11:15–11:33
Mark 12:1–12:27
Mark 12:28–12:44
Mark 13:1–13:23
Mark 13:24–13:37
Mark 14:1–14:21
Mark 14:22–14:52
Mark 14:53–14:72
Mark 15:1–15:20
Mark 15:21–15:47
Mark 16:1–16:20

Verses to memorize

Mark 1:35

And in the morning, rising up a great while before day, he went out, and departed into a solitary place, and there prayed. KJV

Mark 8:36

For what shall it profit a man, if he shall gain the whole world, and lose his own soul? KJV

Mark 10:44

And whosoever of you will be the chiefest, shall be servant of all. KJV

Mark 10:45

For even the Son of man came not to be ministered unto, but to minister, and to give his life a ransom for many. KJV

Mark 11:22

Have faith in God. KJV

Mark 11:23

For verily I say unto you, That whosoever shall say unto this mountain, Be thou removed, and be thou cast into the sea; and shall not doubt in his heart, but shall believe that those things which he saith shall come to pass; he shall have whatsoever he saith. KJV

Statistics

Second New Testament book
Second Gospel
16 chapters
678 verses
15,171 words
Number of Old Testament quotations and allusions in Mark: 34.

Parables found only in Mark's Gospel

The growing seed, 4:26–29.

The householder, 13:34.

Miracles found only in Mark's Gospel

Deaf and dumb healed, 7:33.

Blind man healed, 8:23.

Famous sayings found in Mark

"Wars and rumors of wars" Mark 13:7

"False prophets, which come to you in sheep's clothing" Mark 13:22

Names/titles given

Kata Markon: "According to Mark."

Symbol for

Lion: Mark's emblem is the lion, underlining Jesus' courage, strength, and dignity.

3. Helpful keys to turn to in understanding Mark's Gospel

Key word

At once/straightway/immediately, 42 times

Key verses

Mark 8:34–37; 10:45

Themes to study

Jesus, the Savior, who meets our deepest spiritual needs.

The various ways in which Jesus described in Mark.

The authority Jesus displays.

Unusual events and other miracles in Mark

- Jesus' baptism, 1:9
- God's voice from heaven, 1:10–11
- Jesus' transfiguration, 9:1–9
- Appearance of Moses and Elijah at Jesus' transfiguration, 9:4–5
- Darkness at Jesus crucifixion, 15:32–33
- Temple's curtain torn in two, 15:37–38
- Jesus' resurrection, 16:1–6

Jesus in Mark

In Mark Jesus is God's Servant.

Lessons to learn from Mark's Gospel

Christians should not be surprised if religious people oppose them.

Genuine miracles should fill us with awe and wonder.

Jesus' teachings should govern our way of thinking and everything we do.

4. Chapter by chapter: outline of every chapter of Mark

Mark 1

Matthew Henry's introduction

Mark's narrative does not take rise so early as those of Matthew and Luke do, from the birth of our Savior, but from John's baptism, from which he soon passes to Christ's public ministry.

Dr. Adam Clarke's analysis of chapter

The mission, preaching, and success of John Baptist, 1–5.

His manner of life, 6.

Proclaims Christ, and baptizes him in Jordan, 7–11.

The temptation of Christ, 12, 13.

John being put in prison, Christ begins to preach, 14, 15.

He calls Andrew and Simon, 16–18.

James and John, 19, 20.

Teaches in Capernaum, 21, 22.

Casts out a demon, 23–28.

Goes into the house of Simon, and heals his mother-in-law, 29–31.

Heals many diseased people, 32–34.

Goes to the desert, and is followed by his disciples, 35–37.

Preaches in different towns and synagogues of Galilee, and casts cut devils, 38, 39.

Cleanses a leper, who publishes abroad his miraculous cure, 40–45.

A detailed analysis of chapter

John the Baptist is introduced. (1–8)

The baptism and temptation of Christ. (9–13)

Christ preaches and calls disciples. (14–22)

He expels an unclean spirit. (23–28)

He heals many ill people. (29–39)

He heals a leper. (40–45)

Key verse

Verse 1: "The beginning of the gospel about Jesus Christ, the Son of God."

Key word / key phrase

Verse 32, "the people brought to Jesus all the sick."

Key event / key person / key theme

The gospel of Jesus in action

Key thought

The reality of Satan

Key thing to look out for

The basis for Jesus' healing ministry is found in verse 41.

Key Bible cross-reference

Verse 2. See Malachi 3:1.

Key "by way of explanation"

Verse 41, "touched the man." According to Mosaic law you became ceremonially unclean if you touched a leper. By his actions Jesus showed his great care for this man.

Key "Quotable Quote"

"Humility consists, not in condemning our conscience, but in recognizing God's grace and compassion."

St. Mark the Ascetic

Mark 2

Matthew Henry's introduction

In this chapter, we have,

I. Christ's healing a man that was sick of a palsy, vv. 1–12.

II. His calling of Matthew from the receipt of custom, and his eating, on that occasion, with publicans and sinners, and justifying himself in so doing, vv. 13–17.

III. His justifying his disciples in not fasting so much as those plucking the ears of corn on the Sabbath day, vv. 23–28.All which passages we had before, Matt. 9 and 12.

Dr. Adam Clarke's analysis of chapter

Christ preaches in Capernaum, 1, 2.

A paralytic person is brought to him, whose sins are pronounced forgiven, 3–5.

The scribes accuse him of blasphemy, 6, 7.

He vindicates himself, and proves his power to forgive sins, by healing the man's disease, 8–11.

The people are astonished and edified, 12. He calls Levi from the receipt of custom, 13, 14.

Eats in his house with publicans and sinners, at which the Pharisees murmur, 15, 16.

He vindicates his conduct, 17.

Vindicates his disciples, who are accused of not fasting, 18–22; and for plucking the ears of corn on the Sabbath day, 23–26; and teaches the right use of the Sabbath, 27, 28.

A detailed analysis of chapter

Christ heals a paralytic. (1–12)

Levi's call, and the dinner given to Jesus. (13–17)

Why Christ's disciples did not fast. (18–22)

He justifies his disciples for picking corn on the Sabbath. (23–28)

Key verse

Verse 8: "Immediately Jesus knew in his spirit that this was what they were thinking in their hearts."

Key word / key phrase

Verse 9, "Get up."

Key event / key person / key theme

Jesus heals

Key thought

Jesus knows everything. We can hide nothing about our motives or anything else from him, verse 8.

Key thing to look out for

Jesus' purpose in coming.

Key Bible cross-reference

Verse 23. See Deuteronomy 23:25.

Key "by way of explanation"

Verse 17, "I have not come to call the righteous." The person who thinks he does not need God will not go to God for help.

Key "Quotable Quote"

"Unless you humble yourself before God in the dust, and confess before him your iniquities and sins, the gate of heaven, which is open only for sinners, saved by grace, must be shut against you forever."

D.L. Moody

Mark 3

Matthew Henry's introduction

In this chapter, we have,

I. Christ's healing a man that had a withered hand, on the Sabbath day, and the combination of his enemies against him for it, vv. 1–6.

II. The universal resort of people to him from all parts, to be healed, and the relief they all found with him, vv. 7–12.

III. His ordaining his twelve apostles to be attendants on him, and the preachers of his gospel, vv. 13–21.

IV. His answer to the blasphemous cavils of the scribes, who imputed his power to cast out devils to a confederacy with the prince of the devils, vv. 22–30.

V. His owning his disciples for his nearest and dearest relations, vv. 31–35.

Dr. Adam Clarke's analysis of chapter

The man with the withered hand healed, 1–5.

The Pharisees plot our Lord's destruction, 6.

Christ withdraws, and is followed by a great multitude, 7–9.

He heals many, and goes to a mountain to pray, 10–13.

He ordains twelve disciples, and, gives them power to preach and work miracles, 14, 15.

Their names, 16–19.

The multitudes throng him, and the scribes attribute his miracles to Beelzebub, 20–22.

He vindicates himself by a parable, 23–27.

Of the blasphemy against the Holy Spirit, 28–30.

His mother and brethren send for him, 31, 32.

And he takes occasion from this to show, that they who do the will of God are to him as his brother, sister, and mother, 33–35.

A detailed analysis of chapter

Christ heals a man with a shriveled hand. (1–5)

Crowds follow Christ. (6–12)

The apostles called. (13–21)

The blasphemy of the scribes. (22–30)

Christ's relatives. (31–35)

Key verse

Verse 7: "Jesus withdrew with his disciples to the lake, and a large crowd from Galilee followed."

Key word / key phrase

Verse 14, "He appointed twelve."

Key event / key person / key theme

Jesus appoints the Twelve

Key thought

The spirit world was all too aware of who Jesus was and of his great power.

Key thing to look out for

The Jesus family is united by spiritual factors, not by ordinary family ties.

Key Bible cross-reference

Verse 21. See Acts 26:24.

Key "by way of explanation"

Verse 14, "appointed twelve." The word "disciple" means "pupil" or "student." Moses, Gamaliel, and John the Baptist all had disciples. Those who followed Jesus as a result of the ministry of the Twelve were also called disciples, Matthew 28:19; Acts 11:26.

Key "Quotable Quote"

"Now do I begin to be a disciple of my Master, Christ."

Ignatius of Antioch, traveling cheerfully to the place where he was to be thrown to the lions.

Mark 4

Matthew Henry's introduction

In this chapter, we have,

I. The parable of the seed, and the four sorts of ground (vv. 1–9), with the exposition of it (vv. 10–20), and the application of it, vv. 21–25.

II. The parable of the seed growing gradually, but insensibly, vv. 26–29.

III. The parable of the grain of mustard seed, and a general account of Christ's parables, vv. 30–34.

IV. The miracle of Christ's sudden stilling a storm at sea, vv. 35–41.

Dr. Adam Clarke's analysis of chapter

The parable of the sower, 1–9.

Its interpretation, 10–20.

The use we should make of the instructions we receive, 21–26.

The parable of the progressively growing seed, 26–29.

Of the mustard seed, 30–34.

Christ and his disciples are overtaken by a storm, 35–38.

He rebukes the wind and the sea, and produces fair weather, 39–41.

A detailed analysis of chapter

The parable of the sower. (1–20)

Other parables. (21–34)

Christ stills a storm. (35–41)

Key verse

Verse 11: "The secret of the kingdom of God has been given to you."

Key word / key phrase

Verse 3, "A farmer went out to sow."

Key event / key person / key theme

Four parables

Key thought

What conclusions should be drawn from these parables?

Key thing to look out for

Jesus' power extended over the natural order.

Key Bible cross-reference

Verse 12. See Isaiah 6:9,10.

Key "by way of explanation"

Verses 26–29. This parable is only recorded by Mark. It stresses the great and mysterious power of the seed. The gospel has unique spiritual power.

Key "Quotable Quote"

"We must meditate on what we read in the Gospels. This even the most unlearned person can do, and will do, if he has a will to do it."

John Henry Newman

Mark 5

Matthew Henry's introduction

In this chapter, we have,

I. Christ's casting the legion of devils out of the man possessed, and suffering them to enter into the swine, vv. 1–20.

II. Christ's healing the woman with the bloody issue, in the way as he was going to raise

Jairus's daughter to life, vv. 21–43.

These three miracles we had the story of before (Matt. 8:28, etc. and Matt. 9:18, etc.) but more fully related here.

Dr. Adam Clarke's analysis of chapter

The man possessed with a legion of demons cured, 1–20.

He raises Jairus's daughter to life, and cures the woman who had an issue of blood, 21–43.

For Mark chapter 5:1–20, see Luke 8:26–39; for Mark 5:22–43, see Luke8:41–56.

Mark 6

Matthew Henry's introduction

A great variety of observable passages we have, in this chapter, about our Lord Jesus, the substance of all which we had before in Matthew, but divers circumstances we have, which we did not there meet with.

Dr. Adam Clarke's analysis of chapter

Our Lord's countrymen are astonished at his wisdom and mighty works, and are offended at him, 1–4.

He works few miracles there, because of their unbelief, 5, 6.

He sends forth his disciples by two and two to preach, etc., 7–11.

They depart, preach, and work miracles, 12, 13.

Different opinions of Christ, 14–16.

Account of the beheading of John Baptist, 17–29.

The disciples return, and give an account of their mission, 30.

He departs with them to a place of privacy, but the people follow him, 31–33.

He has compassion on them, and miraculously feeds five thousand with five loaves and two fishes, 34–44.

He sends the disciples by sea to Bethsaida, and himself goes into a mountain to pray, 45, 46.

The disciples meet with a storm, and he comes to them walking on the water, and appeases the winds and the sea, 47–52.

They come into the land of Gennesaret, and he works many miracles, 53–56.

For Mark chapter 6:1–6, see Matthew 13:54–58; for Mark 6:7–11, see Matthew 10:1,9–14; for Mark 6:14–29, see Matthew 14:1–12; for Mark 6:32–44, see John 6:5–13.

Mark 7

Matthew Henry's introduction

In this chapter we have,

I. Christ's dispute with the scribes and Pharisees about eating meat with unwashed hands (vv. 1–13); and the needful instructions he gave to the people on that occasion, and further explained to his disciples, vv. 14–23.

II. His curing of the woman Canaan's daughter that was possessed, vv. 24–30.

III. The relief of a man that was deaf, and had an impediment in his speech, vv. 31–37.

Dr. Adam Clarke's analysis of chapter

The Pharisees find fault with the disciples for eating with unwashed hands, 1–5.

Christ exposes their hypocrisy, and shows that

they had made the word of God of no effect by their traditions, 6–13.

He shows what things defile men, 14– 16; and teaches his disciples in private, that the sin of the heart alone, leading to vicious practices, defiles the man, 17–23.

The account of the Syrophoenician woman, 24–30.

He heals a man who was dumb, and had an impediment in his speech, 31–37.

For Mark chapter 7:1–23, see Matthew 15:1–20; for Mark 7:24–30, see Matthew 15:21–28; for Mark 7:31–37, see Matthew 15:29–31.

Mark 8

Matthew Henry's introduction

In this chapter, we have,

I. Christ's miraculous feeding of four thousand with seven loaves and a few small fishes, vv. 1–9.

II. His refusing to give the Pharisees a sign from heaven, vv. 10–13.

III. His cautioning his disciples to take heed of the leaven of Pharisaism and Herodianism, vv. 14–21.

IV. His giving of sight to a blind man at Bethsaida, vv. 22–26.

V. Peter's confession of him, vv. 27–30.

VI. The notice he gave his disciples of his own approaching sufferings (vv. 31–33), and the warning he gave them to prepare for sufferings likewise, vv. 34–38.

Dr. Adam Clarke's analysis of chapter

Four thousand people fed with seven loaves and a few small fishes, 1–8.

Christ refuses to give any farther sign to the impertinent Pharisees, 10–12.

Warns his disciples against the corrupt doctrine of the Pharisees and of Herod, 13–21.

He restores sight to a blind man, 22–26.

Asks his disciples what the public thought of him, 27–30.

Acknowledges himself to be the Christ, and that he must suffer, 31–33.

And shows that all his genuine disciples must take up their cross, suffer in his cause, and confess him before men, 34–38.

A detailed analysis of chapter

Four thousand people miraculously fed. (1–10)

Christ warns against the Pharisees and Herodians. (11–21)

A blind man healed. (22–26)

Peter's testimony to Christ. (27–33)

Christ must be followed. (34–38)

Key verse

Verse 6: "He told the crowd to sit down on the ground. When he had taken the seven loaves and given thanks, he broke them and gave them to his disciples to set before the people, and they did so."

Key word / key phrase

Verse 34, "take up his cross."

Key event / key person / key theme

Four thousand are fed

Key thought

What is Jesus warning his hearers against in verses 14–21?

Key thing to look out for

As soon as Peter says who Jesus is, Jesus speaks of his death. Peter shows how little he understands, so that Jesus even has to call him "Satan."

Key Bible cross-reference

Verse 18. See Jeremiah 5:21.

Key "by way of explanation"

Verse 15, "Yeast" often stands for corruption and evil.

Key "Quotable Quote"

"To take up the cross means that you take your stand for the Lord Jesus no matter what it costs."

Billy Graham

Mark 9

Matthew Henry's introduction

In this chapter, we have,

I. Christ's transfiguration on the mount, vv. 1–13.

II. His casting the devil out of a child, when the disciples could not do it, vv. 14–29.

III. His prediction of his own sufferings and death, vv. 30–32.

IV. The check he gave to his disciples for disputing who should be greatest (vv. 33–37); and to John for rebuking one who cast out devils in Christ's name, and did not follow with them, vv. 38–41.

V. Christ's discourse with his disciples of the danger of offending one of his little ones (v. 42), and of indulging that in ourselves, which is an offence and an occasion of sin to us (vv. 43–50), most of which passages we had before, Matt. 17. and 18.

Dr. Adam Clarke's analysis of chapter

The transfiguration of Christ, and the discourse occasioned by it, 1–13.

He casts out a dumb spirit which his disciples could not, 14–29.

He foretells his death, 30–32.

The disciples dispute about supremacy, and Christ corrects them, 33–37.

Of the person who cast out demons in Christ's name, but did not follow him, 38–40.

Every kind of office done to the disciples of Christ shall be rewarded by him, and all injuries done to them shall be punished, 41, 42.

The necessity of mortification and self-denial, 43–48.

Of the salting of sacrifices, 49; and the necessity of having union among the disciples of Christ, 50.

A detailed analysis of chapter

The transfiguration. (1–13)

An evil spirit expelled. (14–29)

The apostles reproved. (30–40)

Pain to be preferred to sin. (41–50)

Key verse

Verse 3: "His clothes became dazzling white, whiter than anyone in the world could bleach them."

Key word / key phrase

Verse 2, "he was transfigured."

Key event / key person / key theme

Jesus' transfiguration

Key thought

The vital importance of prayer is stressed by Jesus, verse 29.

Key thing to look out for

God's command.

Key Bible cross-reference

Verses 2–7. See 2 Peter 1:17,18.

Key "by way of explanation"

Verse 7, "a voice came from the cloud." Clouds stood for God's presence and his ability to protect people and to guide them.

Key "Quotable Quote"

"The key to missions is not work, but prayer. Too often work is used as a substitute for, or a by-pass to, fervent prayer."

Oswald Chambers

Mark 10

Matthew Henry's introduction

In this chapter, we have,

I. Christ's dispute with the Pharisees about divorce, vv. 1–12.

II. The kind entertainment he gave to the little children that were brought to him to be blessed, vv. 13–16.

III. His trial of the rich man that enquired what he must do to get to heaven, vv. 17–22.

IV. His discourse with his disciples, on that occasion, about the peril of riches (vv. 23–27), and the advantage of being impoverished for his sake, vv. 28–31.

V. The repeated notice he gave his disciples of his sufferings and death approaching, vv. 32–34.

VI. The counsel he gave to James and John, to think of suffering with him, rather than of reigning with him, vv. 15–45.

VII. The cure of Bartimaeus, a poor blind man, vv. 46–52.

All which passages of story we had the substance of before, Matt. 19 and 20.

Dr. Adam Clarke's analysis of chapter

The Pharisees question our Lord about divorce, 1–12.

Little children are brought to him, 13–16.

The person who inquired how he might inherit eternal life, 17–22.

How difficult it is for a rich man to be saved, 23–27.

What they shall receive who have left all for Christ and his Gospel, 28–31.

He foretells his death, 32–34.

James and John desire places of pre-eminence in Christ's kingdom, 35–41.

Christ shows them the necessity of humility, 42–46.

Blind Bartimaeus healed, 46–52.

For Mark chapter 10:1–12, see Matthew 19:1–9; for Mark 10:13–16, see Matthew 19:13–15;

10:17–31, see Matthew 19:16–30, for Mark 10:32–52, see Matthew 20:17–34

Mark 11

Matthew Henry's introduction

We are now come to the Passion Week, the week in which Christ died, and the great occurrences of that week.

I. Christ's riding in triumph into Jerusalem, vv. 1–11.

II. His cursing the barren fig-tree, vv. 12–14.

III. His driving those out of the temple that turned it into an exchange, vv. 15–19.

IV. His discourse with his disciples about the power of faith and the efficacy of prayer, on occasion of the withering of the fig tree he cursed, vv. 20–26.

V. His reply to those who questioned his authority, vv. 27–33.

Dr. Adam Clarke's analysis of chapter

Christ rides triumphantly into Jerusalem, 1–11.
The barren fig tree cursed, 12–14.
He cleanses the temple, 15–17.
The scribes and chief priests are enraged, 18.
Reflections on the withered fig tree, 19–23.
Directions about prayer and forgiveness, 24–26.
The chief priests, etc., question him by what authority he did his works, 27, 28.
He answers, and confounds them, 29–33.

A detailed analysis of chapter

Christ's triumphant entry into Jerusalem. (1–11)
The barren fig tree cursed, and the temple cleansed. (12–18)
Prayer in faith. (19–26)
The priests and elders questioned about John the Baptist. (27–33)

Key verse

Verse 8: "Many people spread their cloaks on the road, while others spread branches they had cut in the fields."

Key word / key phrase

Verse 22, "Have faith in God."

Key event / key person / key theme

Jesus enters Jerusalem

Key thought

The Gospel writers were deeply conscious of the way Jesus fulfilled Old Testament prophecy.

Key thing to look out for

Jesus' cursing of the fig tree was an enacted parable (c.f. Ezekiel's symbolic actions). What was he condemning?

Key Bible cross-reference

Verse 9. See Psalm 118:25,26.

Key "by way of explanation"

Verse 17, "a house of prayer for all nations." Non-Jews could take comfort in the fact that Isaiah had given this name to the temple (Isaiah 56:7). But the Jews allowed the Court of the Gentiles to be taken over by a noisy market.

Key "Quotable Quote"

"What is needed desperately today is prophetic insight. Scholars can interpret the past; it takes prophets to interpret the present."

A.W. Tozer

Mark 12

Matthew Henry's introduction

In this chapter, we have,

I. The parable of the vineyard let out to unthankful husbandmen, representing the sin and ruin of the Jewish church, vv. 1–12.

II. Christ's silencing those who thought to ensnare him with a question about paying tribute Cæsar, vv. 13–17.

III. His silencing the Sadducees, who attempted to perplex the doctrine of the resurrection, vv. 18–27.

IV. His conversation with a scribe about the first and great command of the law, vv. 28–34.

V. His puzzling the scribes with a question about Christ's being the Son of David, vv. 35–37.

VI. The caution he gave the people, to take heed of the scribes, vv. 38–40.

VII. His commendation of the poor widow that cast her two mites into the treasury, vv. 41–44.

Dr. Adam Clarke's analysis of chapter

The parable of the vineyard let out to wicked husbandmen, 1–12.

The Pharisees and Herodians question him about paying tribute to Caesar, 13–17.

The Sadducees question him about the resurrection, 18–27.

A scribe questions him about the chief commandment of the law, 28–34.

Christ asks the scribes why the Messiah is called David's son, 35–37.

He warns his disciples against the scribes, 38–40.

Of the widow that cast two mites into the treasury, 41–44.

For Mark chapter 12:1–27, see Luke 20:9–38; 12:28–37, see Matthew 22:34–46; 12:38–40, see Luke 20:45–47; 12:41–44, see Luke 21:1–4.

Mark 13

Matthew Henry's introduction

We have here the substance of that prophetical sermon which our Lord Jesus preached, pointing at the destruction of Jerusalem, and the consummation of all things; it was one of the last of his sermons, and not *ad populum*–to the people, but *ad clerum*–to the clergy; it was private, preached only to four of his disciples, with whom his secret was.

Dr. Adam Clarke's analysis of chapter

Jesus predicts the destruction of the temple, 1, 2.

His disciples inquire when this shall be, and what previous sign there shall be of this calamity, 3, 4;

which questions he answers very solemnly and minutely, 5–27;

illustrates the whole by a parable, 28, 29;

asserts the absolute certainty of the events, 30, 31;

shows that the precise minute cannot be known by man, 32;

and inculcates the necessity of watchfulness and prayer, 33–37.

A detailed analysis of chapter

The destruction of the temple predicted. (1–4)

Christ's prophetic declaration. (5–13)

Christ's prophesy. (14–23)

More prophetic declarations. (24–27)

Watchfulness urged. (28–37)

Key verse

Verse 9: "You must be on your guard. You will be handed over to the local councils and flogged in the synagogues."

Key word / key phrase

Verse 4, "what will be the sign?"

Key event / key person / key theme

Jesus teaches about the future

Key thought

Jesus mentioned specific signs which would usher in the end of the age.

Key thing to look out for

The last word in this chapter gives the Christian response to the teaching it contains.

Key Bible cross-reference

Verse 24. See Joel 2:10,31.

Key "by way of explanation"

Verse 32. "No one knows" the timing of Jesus' return. If we did it might hinder our life of faith.

Key "Quotable Quote"

"I hope that when Christ comes He will find me either praying or preaching."

Augustine of Hippo

Mark 14

Matthew Henry's introduction

In this chapter begins the account which this evangelist gives of the death and sufferings of our Lord Jesus, which we are all concerned to be acquainted, not only with the history of, but with the mystery of.

Dr. Adam Clarke's analysis of chapter

The Jews conspire against Christ, 1, 2.

He is anointed in the house of Simon the Leper, 3–9.

Judas Iscariot sells him to the chief priests for thirty pieces of money, 10, 11.

He orders his disciples to prepare the Passover, 12–16.

Predicts his approaching death, 17–21.

Institutes the holy eucharist, 22–26.

Foretells the unfaithfulness of his disciples in general, 27, 28, and Peter's denial, 29–31.

His agony in the garden, 32–36.

The disciples overcome by sleep, 37–42.

Judas comes with a mob from the chief priests, and betrays him with a kiss; they seize him, 43–49.

The disciples flee, 50.

A young man following, and about to be apprehended, makes his escape, 51, 52.

Jesus is brought before the chief priests, and Peter follows at a distance, 53, 54.

He is examined, insulted, and abused, and condemned on false evidence, 55–65.

Peter thrice denies him, reflects on his wickedness, and repents of his sin, 66–72.

A detailed analysis of chapter

Christ anointed at Bethany. (1–11)
The Passover, Jesus declares that Judas will betray him. (12–21)
The Lord's Supper instituted. (22–31)
Christ's agony in the garden. (32–42)
He is betrayed and arrested. (43–52)
Christ before the high priest. (53–65)
Peter denies Christ. (66–72)

Key verse

Verse 3: "While he was in Bethany, reclining at the table in the home of a man known as Simon the Leper, a woman came with an alabaster jar of very expensive perfume, made of pure nard. She broke the jar and poured the perfume on his head."

Key word / key phrase

Verse 34, "Keep watch."

Key event / key person / key theme

Gethsemane

Key thought

Jesus had a betrayer among his disciples.

Key thing to look out for

Peter did not heed Jesus' warning.

Key Bible cross-reference

Verse 18. See Psalm 41:9.

Key "by way of explanation"

Verse 51, "young man." This unidentified person may have been the author of this Gospel, John Mark.

Key "Quotable Quote"

"The saddest road to hell is that which runs under the pulpit, past the Bible and through the midst of warnings and invitations."

J.C. Ryle

Mark 15

Matthew Henry's introduction

What we read of the sufferings of Christ, in the previous chapter, was but the prologue or introduction; here we have the completing of them. We left him condemned by the chief priests; but they could only show their teeth, they could not bite.

Dr. Adam Clarke's analysis of chapter

Jesus is brought before Pilate, examined, and accused, but makes no answer, 1–5.
The multitude clamor for the release of Barabbas, and the crucifixion of Christ, 6–14.
Pilate consents, and he is led away, mocked, insulted, and nailed to the cross, 15–26.
Two thieves are crucified with him, 27, 28.
While hanging on the cross, he is mocked and insulted, 29–32.
The miraculous darkness and our Lord's death, 33–37.
The rending of the veil, and the confession of the centurion, 38, 39.
Several women attend and behold his death, 40, 41.

Joseph of Arimathea begs the body from Pilate, and buries it, 42–46.

Mary Magdalene, and Mary the mother of Joses, note the place of his burial, 47.

A detailed analysis of chapter

Christ before Pilate. (1–14)

Christ led out to be crucified. (15–21)

The crucifixion. (22–32)

The death of Christ. (33–41)

His body buried. (42–47)

Key verse

Verse 3: "The chief priests accused him of many things."

Key word / key phrase

Verse 39, "saw how he died."

Key event / key person / key theme

Jesus' death and burial

Key thought

Few people come out well in the trials and death of Jesus.

Key thing to look out for

Jesus' physical pain is certainly not the central focus in the description of his death. What is?

Key Bible cross-reference

Verse 21. See Romans 16:13.

Key "by way of explanation"

Verse 37, "with a loud cry." Most crucified people endured agony which led to exhaustion and then unconsciousness before death. Jesus' great cry indicates that he did not die an ordinary death.

Key "Quotable Quote"

"Those who belong to Christ have 'crucified' their flesh or sinful nature. It is an astonishing metaphor. For crucifixion was a horrible, brutal form of execution. Yet it illustrates graphically what our attitude to our fallen nature is to be. We are not to coddle or cuddle it, not to pamper or spoil it, not to give it any encouragement or even toleration."

John R.W. Stott

Mark 16

Matthew Henry's introduction

In this chapter, we have a short account of the resurrection and ascension of the Lord Jesus: and the joys and triumphs which it furnished all believers with, will be very acceptable to those who sympathized and suffered with Christ in the previous chapters.

Dr. Adam Clarke's analysis of chapter

Early in the morning after the Sabbath, the three Marys come to the sepulcher, bringing sweet spices to embalm the body, 1–4.

They see an angel who announces the resurrection of our Lord, 5–8.

Jesus appears to Mary Magdalene, who goes and tells the disciples, 9–11.

He appears also to the two disciples who were going into the country, who also tell it to the rest, 12, 13.

Afterwards he appears unto the eleven, and

commissions them to preach the Gospel to all humankind, 14–16.

And promises to endue them with power to work miracles, 17, 18.

He is received up into heaven, 19.

And they go forth to preach and work miracles, 20.

A detailed analysis of chapter

Christ's resurrection made known to the women. (1–8)

Christ appears to Mary Magdalene and other disciples. (9–13)

His commission to the apostles. (14–18)

Christ's ascension. (19,20)

Key verse

Verse 8: "Trembling and bewildered, the women went out and fled from the tomb. They said nothing to anyone, because they were afraid."

Key word / key phrase

Verse 6, "He has risen!"

Key event / key person / key theme

Jesus' resurrection

Key thought

Verse 6. How could Jesus' resurrection cause anyone to be alarmed?

Key thing to look out for

Verse 14. Lack of faith was rebuked by Jesus.

Key Bible cross-reference

Verse 15. See Acts 1:8.

Key "by way of explanation"

Verse 3, "who will roll the stone away?" The stone rolled in front of a tomb fell into a hollow. It could not possibly have been rolled back by a group of women.

Key "Quotable Quote"

"Worship…is the most appropriate response that can be made to resurrection."

Eugene H. Peterson

5. Select bibliography for Mark's Gospel

Calvin, John. *Commentary on a Harmony of the Evangelists*. 3 Vols. Grand Rapids: Baker, 1979.

Cole, A. *The Gospel According to Mark*. TNTC. Grand Rapids: Eerdmans, 1961.

Cranfield, C. E. B. *The Gospel According to St. Mark*. New York: Cambridge University Press, 1959.

Earle, Ralph. *The Gospel According to Mark*. The Evangelical Commentary on the Bible. Grand Rapids: Zondervan, 1957.

Martin, R. P. *Mark: Evangelist and Theologian*. Grand Rapids: Zondervan, 1972.

Moule, C. F. D. *The Gospel According to Mark*. The Cambridge Bible Commentary. Cambridge: Cambridge University Press, 1965.

Nineham, D. E. *Saint Mark*. Pelican Gospel Commentary. Baltimore: Penguin, 1963.

Stonehouse, N. B. *The Witness of Matthew and Mark to Christ*. Grand Rapids: Eerdmans, 1958.

Swete, H. B. *The Gospel According to St. Mark*. Macmillan New Testament Commentaries. London: Macmillan, 1927.

Luke

1. Book by book: Introduction to Luke

Introduction

Author

The writer of this Gospel is universally thought to have been Lucas (an abbreviated form of Lucanus, as Silas of Silvanus), though he is not expressly named either in the Gospel or in the Acts. From Col. 4:14 we learn that he was a "physician"; and by comparing that verse with Col. 4:10, 11 –in which the apostle enumerates all those of the circumcision who were then with him, but does not mention Luke, though he immediately afterwards sends a salutation from him–we gather that Luke was not a born Jew. Some have thought he was a freed-man (libertinus), as the Romans devolved the healing art on people of this class and on their slaves, as an occupation beneath themselves. His intimate acquaintance with Jewish customs, and his facility in Hebraic Greek, seem to show that he was an early convert to the Jewish faith; and this is curiously confirmed by Acts 21:27–29, where we find the Jews enraged at Paul's supposed introduction of Greeks into the temple, because they had seen "Trophimus the Ephesian" with him; and as we know that Luke was with Paul on that occasion, it would seem that they had taken him for a Jew, as they made no mention of him. On the other hand, his fluency in classical Greek confirms his Gentile origin. The time when he joined Paul's company is clearly indicated in the Acts by his changing (at Acts 16:10) from the third person singular ("he") to the first person plural ("we"). From that time he hardly ever left the apostle till near the period of his martyrdom (2 Tim. 4:11). Eusebius says he was from Antioch. If so, he would have every advantage for cultivating the literature of Greece and such medical knowledge as they then possessed. That he died a natural death is generally agreed among the ancients; Gregory of Nazianzen alone affirming that he died a martyr.

Date

The time and place of the publication of his Gospel are alike uncertain. But we can approximate to it. It must at any rate have been issued before the Acts, for there the 'Gospel' is expressly referred to as the same author's "former treatise" (Acts 1:1). Now the Book of the Acts was not published for two whole years after Paul's arrival as a prisoner at Rome, for it concludes with a reference to this period; but probably it was published soon after that, which would appear to have been early in the year 63. Before that time, then, we have reason to believe that the Gospel of Luke was in circulation, though the majority of critics make it later. If we date it somewhere between a.d. 50 and 60, we shall probably be near the truth; but nearer than that we cannot say with any certainty. Conjectures as to the place of publication are too uncertain to be mentioned here.

Readers

That it was addressed, in the first instance, to Gentile readers, is beyond doubt. This is no more, as Davidson remarks than was to have been expected from the companion of an "apostle of the Gentiles," who had witnessed marvelous changes in the condition of many heathens by the reception of the Gospel. But the explanations in his Gospel of things known to every Jew, and which could only be intended for Gentile readers, make this quite plain–see Luke 1:26; 4:31; 8:26; 21:37; 22:1; 24:13. A number of other minute particulars, both of things inserted and of things omitted, confirm the conclusion that it was Gentiles whom this Evangelist had in the first instance in view.

Luke and Paul

We have already noted the classical style of Greek with which this Evangelist writes–just what might have been expected from an educated Greek and traveled physician. But we have also observed that along with this he shows a wonderful flexibility of style, so much so, that when he comes to relate transactions wholly Jewish, where the speakers and actors and incidents are all Jewish, he writes in such Jewish Greek as one would do who had never been out of Palestine or mixed with any but Jews. In Da Costa's Four Witnesses will be found some traces of "the beloved physician" in this Gospel. But far more striking and important are the traces in it of his intimate connection with the apostle of the Gentiles. That one who was so long and so constantly in the society of that master mind has in such a work as this shown no traces of that connection, no stamp of that mind, is hardly to be believed. Writers of Introductions seem not to see it, and take no notice of it. But those who look into the interior of it will soon discover evidences enough in it of a Pauline cast of mind. Referring for a number of details to Da Costa, we notice here only two examples: In 1 Cor. 11:23, Paul ascribes to an express revelation from Christ Himself the account of the Institution of the Lord's Supper which he there gives. Now, if we find this account differing in small yet striking particulars from the accounts given by Matthew and Mark, but agreeing to the letter with Luke's account, it can hardly admit of a doubt that the one had it from the other; and in that case, of course, it was Luke that had it from Paul. Now Matthew and Mark both say of the Cup, "This is my blood of the New Testament"; while Paul and Luke say, in identical terms, "This cup is the New Testament in My blood" (1 Cor. 11:25; Luke 22:20). Further, Luke says, "Likewise also the cup after supper, saying," etc.; while Paul says, "After the same manner He took the cup when He had supped, saying," etc.; whereas neither Matthew nor Mark mention that this was after supper.

But still more striking is another point of coincidence in this case. Matthew and Mark both say of the Bread merely this: "Take, eat; this is My body" (Matt. 26:26; Mark 14:22); whereas Paul says, "Take, eat, this is My body, which is broken for you" (1 Cor. 11:24), and Luke, "This is My body, which is given for you" (Luke 22:19). And while Paul adds the precious clause, "This do in remembrance of Me," Luke does the same, in identical terms. How can one who reflects on this resist the conviction of a Pauline stamp in this Gospel? The other proof of this to which we ask the reader's attention is in the fact that Paul, in enumerating the parties by whom Christ was seen after His resurrection, begins, singularly enough, with Peter–"And that He rose again the third day according to the Scriptures and that He was seen of Cephas, then of the Twelve" (1 Cor. 15:4, 5) –coupled with the remarkable fact, that Luke is the only one of the Evangelists who mentions that Christ appeared to Peter at all. When the disciples had returned from Emmaus to tell their brethren how the Lord had appeared to them in the way, and how He had made Himself known to them in the breaking of bread, they were met, as Luke relates, ere they had time to utter a word, with this wonderful piece of news, "The Lord is risen indeed, and hath appeared to Simon" (Luke 24:34).

David Brown

Detailed outline

Part One: Preparation 1:1–2:52

I. Introduction:
- A. The note to Theophilus: 1:1–4
- B. The vision of Zechariah: 1:5–25
- C. The vision of Mary: 1:26–38
- D. The visit of Mary to Elizabeth: 1:39–56
- E. The birth of John the Baptist: 1:57–80

II. Birth and childhood of Jesus:
- A. The birth of Jesus: 2:1–7
- B. The visit of the shepherds: 2:8–20
- C. The circumcision and naming of Jesus: 2:21
- D. The presentation of Jesus: 2:22–40
- E. The visit of Jesus to the Temple: 2:41–52

Part Two: The Beginning Of Christ's Ministry 3:1–4:3

I. The ministry of John the Baptist: 3:1–20

II. The baptism of Jesus: 3:21–22

III. The genealogy of Jesus: 3:23–38

IV. The temptation of Jesus: 4:1–13

Part Three: Jesus In Galilee 4:14–9:62

I. The rejection of Jesus in Nazareth: 4:14–30

II. The demon-possessed man in the synagogue at Capernaum: 4:31–37

III. The healing of Peter's mother-in-law: 4:38–39

IV. Further miracles and preaching: 4:40–44

V. Miraculous catch of fish and the call of Simon Peter, James, and John: 5:1–11

VI. Healing a leper: 5:12–16

VII. Forgiving and healing a paralyzed man: 5:17–26

VIII. Matthew's call: 5:27–28

IX. The feast with publicans: 5:29–32

X. Teaching about fasting: 5:33–39

XI. Plucking and eating grain on the Sabbath: 6:1–5

XII. Healing of a man with a crippled hand: 6:6–11

XIII. Choosing the twelve disciples: 6:12–16

XIV. The sermon on the Mount: 6:17–49

XV. Healing a centurion's servant: 7:1–10
XVI. Raising a widow's son from the dead: 7:11–17
XVII. The question about John the Baptist: 7:18–35
XVIII. Anointing by and forgiveness of the sinful woman: 7:36–50
XIX. Preaching with support from some women: 8:1–3
XX. The parable of the Sower: 8:4–15
XXI. Parable of the lamp on a stand: 8:16–18
XXII. True spiritual relationship: 8:19–21
XXIII. Stilling the storm: 8:22–25
XXIV. Healing the demoniac: 8:26–40
XXV. Healing a woman who suffered from bleeding and raising Jarius' daughter: 8:40–56
XXVI. The mission of the twelve disciples: 9:1–6
XXVII. The death of John the Baptist: 9:7–9
XXVIII. Feeding of the 5,000: 9:10–17
XXIX. Peter's confession: 9:18–21
XXX. Prediction of Christ's death: 9:22
XXXI. A call to discipleship: 9:23–27
XXXII. The transfiguration: 9:28–36
XXXIII. The deliverance of a demon possessed boy: 9:37–45
XXXIV. A lesson about greatness: 9:46–48
XXXV. Teaching about tolerance: 9:49–50

Part Four: Jesus On The Way To Jerusalem 10:1–19:48

I. Resolve to go to Jerusalem and the rejection by a Samaritan village: 9:51–56
II.Remarks on discipleship: 9:57–62
III. The mission of the seventy: 10:1–24
IV. The parable of the Good Samaritan: 10:25–37
V. Dinner with Mary and Martha: 10:38–42
VI. Teaching on prayer: 11:1–13
VII. Defense against the accusation about Satanic power: 11:14–26
VIII. The importance of keeping God's Word: 11:27–28
IX. Seeking a sign: 11:29–36
X. Exposing the Pharisees and Scribes: 11:37–54
XI. Warnings: 12:1–59
  A. Against hypocrisy: 12:1–12
  B. Against covetousness: 12:13–21
  C. Against anxiety: 12:22–34
  D. About servants waiting for masters: 12:35–48
  E. About understanding Christ's mission: 12:49–59
XII. A call to repentance: 13:1–9
XIII. The healing of the woman who had been crippled by a spirit: 13:10–17
XIV. Parables: 13:18–30
  A. The mustard seed: 13:18–19
  B. The leaven: 13:20–21
  C. The narrow door: 13:22–30
XV. A message from and to Herod: 13:31–33
XVI. A lament over Jerusalem: 13:34–35
XVII. Healing of a man with dropsy: 14:1–6
XVIII. Parables: 14:7–16:31
  A. The marriage feast: 14:7–14
  B. The great banquet: 14:15–24
  C. The builder: 14:25–30

D. The king who goes to war: 14:31–35
E. The lost sheep: 15:1–7
F. The lost coin: 15:8–10
G. The prodigal son: 15:11–32
H. The unjust steward and further comments on the Pharisees: 16:1–18
I. The rich man and Lazarus: 16:19–31

XIX. Offenses: 17:1–4
XX. Increasing faith: 17:5–10
XXI. Healing the lepers: 17:11–19
XXII. The future of the Kingdom of God: 17:20–37
XXIII. Parable about the widow and the unjust judge: 18:1–8
XXIV. Parable about the Pharisee and the publican: 18:9–14
XXV. Welcoming little children: 18:15–17
XXVI. The rich young ruler: 18:18–30
XXVII. Prediction of Jesus' death and resurrection: 18:31–34
XXVIII. Healing the blind man near Jericho: 18:35–43
XXIX. The conversion of Zacchaeus: 19:1–10
XXX. The parable of the ten minas: 19:11–27

Part Five: Jesus In Jerusalem 19:28–24:53

I. Events prior to the death of Jesus: 19:28–23:25
  A. The triumphal entry: 19:28–48
  B. Temple disputes: 20:1–47
    1. The question of authority: 20:1–8
    2. The parable of the faithless tenants: 20:9–18
    3. The question of paying taxes to Caesar: 20:19–26
    4. The question of the resurrection: 20:27–40
    5. A question and a warning: 20:41–47
  C. Temple teachings: 21:1–38
    1. The widow's offering: 21:1–4
    2. The future: 21:5–28
    3. The warning to watch: 21:29–38
  D. Passover and the final night: 22:1–71
    1. The plot against Jesus: 22:1–6
    2. The preparation for the Passover: 22:7–13
    3. The Last Supper: 22:14–23
    4. True greatness: 22:24–30
    5. The warning given to Peter: 22:31–34
    6. Warning given to the disciples: 22:35–38
    7. Prayer in the garden: 22:39–46
    8. The arrest of Jesus: 22:47–53
    9. Peter's denials: 22:54–62
    10. The trial of Jesus: 22:63–71
      (a) Abuse by the soldiers: 22:63–65
      (b) Condemnation by the Sanhedrin: 22:66–71
      (c) The hearing before Herod: 23:1–12
      (d) The hearing before Pilate: 23:13–25

II. The death of Jesus: 23:26–56
  A. The crucifixion: 23:26–49
    1. On the way to Golgotha: 23:26–31
    2. The crucifixion and mocking of Jesus: 23:32–38
    3. The repentant criminal 23:39–43
    4. The death of Jesus: 23:44–49
    5. The burial of Jesus: 23:50–56

III. The resurrection of Jesus: 24:1–12

IV. The post-resurrection ministry: 24:13–49

A. The walk to Emmaus: 24:13–35

B. The appearance in Jerusalem: 24:36–49

C. A final charge: 24:44–49

D. The ascension of Jesus: 24:50–53

2. Helpful summaries of Luke's Gospel

Bird's eye view

Luke writes a well-ordered account of the birth, ministry, death, and resurrection of Jesus, which he states he received from reliable eyewitnesses.

Reading plan

The following reading plan, taking one reading per day, enables you to read through Luke's Gospel in fifty-two days.

Luke 1:1–1:25
Luke 1:26–1:56
Luke 1:57–1:80
Luke 2:1–2:24
Luke 2:25–2:52
Luke 3:1–3:18
Luke 3:19–3:38
Luke 4:1–4:15
Luke 4:16–4:44
Luke 5:1–5:16
Luke 5:17–5:39
Luke 6:1–6:26
Luke 6:27–6:49
Luke 7:1–7:17
Luke 7:18–7:50
Luke 8:1–8:18
Luke 8:19–8:39
Luke 8:40–8:56
Luke 9:1–9:27
Luke 9:28–9:45
Luke 9:46–9:62
Luke 10:1–10:20
Luke 10:21–10:42
Luke 11:1–11:28
Luke 11:29–11:54
Luke 12:1–12:21
Luke 12:22–12:40
Luke 12:41–12:59
Luke 13:1–13:17
Luke 13:18–13:35
Luke 14:1–14:14
Luke 14:15–14:35
Luke 15:1–15:32
Luke 16:1–16:31
Luke 17:1–17:19
Luke 17:20–17:37
Luke 18:1–18:17
Luke 18:18–18:43
Luke 19:1–19:27
Luke 19:28–19:48
Luke 20:1–20:26
Luke 20:27–20:47
Luke 21:1–21:24
Luke 21:25–21:38
Luke 22:1–22:23
Luke 22:24–22:53
Luke 22:54–22:71
Luke 23:1–23:25
Luke 23:26–23:56
Luke 24:1–24:12

Luke 24:13–24:35

Luke 24:36–24:53

Verses to memorize

Luke 1:37

"For with God nothing shall be impossible." KJV

Luke 4.18

"The Spirit of the Lord is on me, because he hath anointed me to preach the gospel to the poor; he hath sent me to heal the broken hearted, to preach deliverance to the captives, and recovering of sight to the blind, to set at liberty them that are bruised," KJV

Luke 12:48

"For unto whomsoever much is given, of him shall be much required: and to whom men have committed much, of him they will ask the more." KJV

Luke 14:11

"For whosoever exalteth himself shall be abased; and he that humbleth himself shall be exalted." KJV

Luke 15:20

"And he arose, and came to his father. But when he was yet a great way off, his father saw him, and had compassion, and ran, and fell on his neck, and kissed him."

Luke 17:3–4

"Take heed to yourselves: If thy brother trespass against thee, rebuke him; and if he repent, forgive him. And if he trespass against thee seven times in a day, and seven times in a day turn again to thee, saying, I repent; thou shalt forgive him." KJV

Luke 19:10

"For the Son of man is come to seek and to save that which was lost." KJV

Statistics

Third New Testament book

Third Gospel

24 chapters

1,151 verses

25,944 words

Number of Old Testament quotations and allusions in Luke: 58.

Parables found only in Luke's Gospel

The two debtors, 7:41–43

The Good Samaritan, 10:30–36.

The friend at midnight, 11:5–8.

The rich fool, 12:16–21.

The wedding banquet, 12:35–40.

The faithful and wise manager, 12:42–48.

The barren fig tree, 13:6–9.

The great banquet, 14:16–24.

The lost coin, 15:8–10.

The lost son, 15:11–32.

The shrewd manager, 16:1–9.

The rich man and Lazarus, 16:19–31

The unworthy servants, 17:7–10

The persistent widow, 18:1–8

The Pharisee and the tax-collector, 18:9–14

The ten minas, 19:11–27

Miracles found only in Luke's Gospel

Catch of fishes, 5:6.

Raising of widow of Cain's son, 7:11.

Ten lepers healed, 17:12.

Woman with spirit of infirmity healed, 13:11.

Man with dropsy, 14:2.

Malchus' ear healed, 22:51.

Luke's emphasis on prayer

Luke has three parables about prayer:

1. The friend at midnight, 11:5–8;
2. The unjust judge, 18:1–8;
3. The Pharisee and the tax-collector, 18:9–14.

Luke records the following prayers of Jesus:

- At Jesus' baptism, 3:21;
- In the desert, 5:16;
- Before he chose his disciples, 6:12;
- During his transfiguration, 9:29;
- Before he gave the Lord's Prayer, 11:1;
- Jesus' prayer for Peter, 22:32;
- His prayer in the Garden of Gethsemane, 22:44;
- Jesus' prayer on the cross, 23:46.

Famous sayings found in Luke

"Blind leading the blind" Luke 6:39

"Good Samaritan" Luke 10:25–37

"A house divided" Luke 11:17

"He gave up the ghost" Luke 23:46

Names/titles given

Kata Loukon: "According to Luke."

Renan viewed Luke's gospel as "the most beautiful book that has ever been written."

3. Helpful keys to turn to in understanding Luke's Gospel

Key words

Seek

Save

Key verses

Luke 1:3–4; 19:10

Themes to study

- The Son of Man and his service among us.
- Jesus, the world's Savior.
- The various ways in which Jesus described in Luke.
- Prayer
- The Holy Spirit
- Women described in Luke's Gospel
- Children described in Luke's Gospel

Unusual events and other miracles in Luke

- Jesus' virgin birth, 2:5–7
- Angel's announcement of Jesus' birth, 2:9–14
- Jesus' baptism, 3:21–22
- God's voice from heaven, 9:34–36
- Jesus' transfiguration, 9:28–36
- Appearance of Moses and Elijah at Jesus' transfiguration, 9:30–31
- Darkness at Jesus' crucifixion, 23:44–45
- Curtain in Temple torn in two, 23:45
- Jesus' resurrection, 24:1–12

Jesus in Luke

In Luke Jesus is the Son of Man.

Symbol for

Ox: the ox is used as the symbol for Luke's Gospel as it indicated Jesus' power and sacrifice.

Lessons to learn from Luke

- We can derive great benefit from all of Luke's teaching about prayer in his Gospel.

- Putting our selfish nature to death should be our daily activity.

4. Chapter by chapter: outline of every chapter of Luke

Luke 1

Matthew Henry's introduction

The narrative which this evangelist gives us (or rather God by him) of the life of Christ begins earlier than either Matthew or Mark. We have reason to thank God for them all, as we have for all the gifts and graces of Christ's ministers, which in one make up what is wanting in the other, while all put together make a harmony.

Dr. Adam Clarke's analysis of chapter

The preface, or St. Luke's private epistle to Theophilus, 1– 4.

The conception and birth of John Baptist fore told by the angel Gabriel, 5–17.

Zacharias doubts, 18.

And the angel declares he shall be dumb, till the accomplishment of the prediction, 19–25.

Six months after the angel Gabriel appears to the virgin Mary, and predicts the miraculous conception and birth of Christ, 26–38.

Mary visits her cousin Elisabeth, 39–45.

Mary's song of exultation and praise, 46–56.

John the Baptist is born, 57–66.

The prophetic song of his father Zacharias, 67–79.

John is educated in the desert, 80.

A detailed analysis of chapter

The preface. (1–4)

Zechariah and Elizabeth. (5–25)

Christ's birth announced. (26–38)

Mary visits Elizabeth. (39–56)

The birth of John the Baptist. (57–66)

The Song of Zechariah. (67–80)

Key verse

Verse 3: "Therefore, since I myself have carefully investigated everything from the beginning, it seemed good also to me to write an orderly account for you, most excellent Theophilus."

Key word / key phrase

Verse 31, "you will be with child."

Key event / key person / key theme

Jesus' birth is foretold

Key thought

Luke gives his reasons for writing his "orderly account" verses 1–4.

Key thing to look out for

Note the links between two expectant mothers.

Key Bible cross-reference

Verse 37. See Genesis 18:14.

Key "by way of explanation"

Verse 25, "taken away my disgrace." In Jewish society in those days childlessness was thought to be a sign of God's disfavor.

Key "Quotable Quote"

"Earth grows into heaven, as we come to live

and breathe in the atmosphere of the incarnation. Jesus makes heaven wherever he is."

F.W. Faber

Luke 2

Matthew Henry's introduction

In this chapter, we have an account of the birth and infancy of our Lord Jesus: having had notice of his conception, and of the birth and infancy of his forerunner, in the previous chapter. The First-begotten is here brought into the world; let us go meet him with our hosannas, blessed is he that cometh.

Dr. Adam Clarke's analysis of chapter

The decree of Augustus to enroll all the Roman empire, 1, 2.
Joseph and Mary go to their own city to be enrolled, 3–5.
Christ is born, 6, 7.
His birth is announced to the shepherds, 8–14.
They go to Bethlehem, and find Joseph, Mary, and Christ, 15–20.
Christ is circumcised, 21.
His parents go to present him in the temple, 22–24.
Simeon receives him: his song, 25–35.
Anna the prophetess, 36–38.
The holy family return to Nazareth, 39, 40.
They go to Jerusalem at the feast of the Passover, and leave Jesus behind in Jerusalem, 41–44.
They return seeking him, and find him in the midst of the doctors, 45–47.
His mother chides him, 48.
His defense of his conduct, 49, 50.
They all return to Nazareth, 51, 52.

A detailed analysis of chapter

The birth of Christ. (1–7)
It is made known to the shepherds. (8–20)
Christ presented in the temple. (21–24)
Simeon prophesies about Jesus. (25–35)
Anna prophesies about him. (36–40)
Christ with the teachers in the temple. (41–52)

Key verse

Verse 7: ". . . she gave birth to her firstborn, a son. She wrapped him in cloths and placed him in a manger, because there was no room for them in the inn."

Key word / key phrase

Verse 7, "she gave birth to her firstborn."

Key event / key person / key theme

Jesus' birth and childhood

Key thought

Shepherd's work made it impossible for him to keep all the demands of the ceremonial law. He was therefore despised by religious people. Yet shepherds were God's first witness of the birth of the baby.

Key thing to look out for

See how the different people who met Jesus react to him.

Key Bible cross-reference

Verse 32. See Isaiah 42:6.

Key "by way of explanation"

Verse 14, "Glory to God in the highest." From

the Latin translation of these words in the *Vulgate* translation of the Bible this angelic prayer is now known as the *Gloria in Excelsis Deo*."

Key "Quotable Quote"

"Thirty years of our Lord's life are hidden in the words, 'He was subject unto them.'"

Jacques Benigne Bossuet

Luke 3

Matthew Henry's introduction

Nothing is related about our Lord Jesus from his twelfth year to his entrance on his thirtieth year. We often think it would have been a pleasure and advantage to us if we had journals, or at least annuls, of occurrences about him; but we have as much as Infinite Wisdom thought fit to communicate to us, and, if we improve not that, neither should we have improved more if we had had it. The great intention of the evangelists was to give us an account of the gospel of Christ, which we are to believe, and by which we hope for salvation: now that began in the ministry and baptism of John, and therefore they hasten to give us an account of that. We could wish, perhaps, that Luke had wholly passed by what was related by Matthew and Mark, and had written only what was new, as he has done in his two first chapters. But it was the will of the Spirit that some things should be established out of the mouth, not only of two, but of three witnesses; and we must not reckon it a needless repetition, nor shall we do so if we renew out meditations on these things, with suitable affections.

Dr. Adam Clarke's analysis of chapter

The time in which John the Baptist began to preach, 1–3.

The prophecies which were fulfilled in him, 4–6.

The matter and success of his preaching, 7–9;

among the people, 10, 11;

among the publicans, 12, 13;

among the soldiers, 14.

His testimony about Christ, 15–18.

The reason why Herod put him afterwards in prison, 19, 20.

He baptizes Christ, on whom the Spirit of God descends, 21, 22.

Our Lord's genealogy, 23–38.

A detailed analysis of chapter

John the Baptist's ministry. (1–14)

John the Baptist testifies about Christ. (15–20)

The baptism of Christ. (21,22)

The genealogy of Christ. (23–38)

Key verse

Verses 3,4: "He went into all the country around the Jordan, preaching a baptism of repentance for the forgiveness of sins. As is written in the book of the words of Isaiah the prophet."

Key word / key phrase

Verse 3, "preaching a baptism of repentance."

Key event / key person / key theme

John the Baptist's ministry

Key thought

In his baptism Jesus was saying yes to John's

work as forerunner and identifying with all those who were coming to be baptized by John.

Key thing to look out for

Verses 10–14: what does repentance involve?

Key Bible cross-reference

Verse 22. See Genesis 22:2.

Key "by way of explanation"

Verse 4, "prepare the way." Just as roads and highways were repaired good before a king set out on a journey, so John the Baptist was sent ahead of Jesus to prepare people's hearts for his coming and his message. It was a slave's job to take off a man's sandals.

Key "Quotable Quote"

"God gets down on his knees among us; gets on our level and shares himself with us. He does not reside afar off and send diplomatic messages."

Eugene H. Peterson

Luke 4

Matthew Henry's introduction

We left Christ newly baptized, and owned by a voice from heaven and the descent of the Holy Spirit on him. Now, in this chapter, we have,

I. A further preparation of him for his public ministry by his being tempted in the wilderness, of which we had the same account before in Matthew as we have here, vv. 1–13.

II. His entrance on his public work in Galilee (vv. 14, 15), particularly,

A. At Nazareth, the city where he had been bred up (vv. 16–30), which we had no account of before in Matthew.

B. At Capernaum, where, having preached to admiration (vv. 31–32), he cast the devil out of a man that was possessed (vv. 33–37), cured Peter's mother-in-law of a fever (vv. 38, 39), and many others that were sick and possessed (vv. 40, 41), and then went and did the same in other cities of Galilee, vv. 42–44.

Dr. Adam Clarke's analysis of chapter

Christ's temptation, 1–13.

Teaches in the synagogues of Galilee, 14, 15.

He preaches in a synagogue at Nazareth, 16– 28.

They attempt to kill him, 29, 30.

He preaches in Capernaum, 31, 32,

and casts out a demon, 33–37.

Heals Peter's mother-in-law, and various others, 38–41.

He goes to the desert, and preaches afterwards in the synagogues of Galilee, 42–44.

A detailed analysis of chapter

The temptation of Christ. (1–13)

Christ in the synagogue of Nazareth. (14–30)

He expels an unclean spirit and heals the sick. (31–44)

Key verse

Verse 1: "Jesus, full of the Holy Spirit, returned from the Jordan and was led by the Spirit in the desert."

Key word / key phrase

Verse 2, "he was tempted by the devil."

Key event / key person / key theme

Jesus' temptation

Key thought

"The question facing Jesus was, 'What does it mean to live as the obedient Son of God?'" (Stephen Travis)

Key thing to look out for

Jesus came to minister to people. Luke records the opening scenes of Jesus' compassionate work here.

Key Bible cross-reference

Verse 12. See Deuteronomy 6:16.

Key "by way of explanation"

Verse 23, "this proverb." The Greek word used here for "proverb" is *parabole.* It is taken from a verb which means to set things side by side next to each other so that they may be compared with each other. This word is used in the New Testament for both a short descriptive story, and for a proverb.

Key "Quotable Quote"

"Let him who would indeed be a Christian learn from the lives of eminent Christians the best ways to overcome temptation and to grow in every aspect of holiness."

William Wilberforce

Luke 5

Matthew Henry's introduction

In this chapter, we have,

I. Christ preaching to the people out of Peter's ship, for want of a better pulpit, vv. 1–3.

II. The recompense he made to Peter for the loan of his boat, in a miraculous draught of fishes, by which he intimated to him and his partners his design to make them, as apostles, fishers of men, vv. 4–11.

III. His cleansing the leper, vv. 12–15.

IV. A short account of his private devotion and public ministry, vv. 16, 17.

V. His cure of the man sick of the palsy, vv. 18–26.

VI. His calling Levi the publican, and conversing with publicans on that occasion, vv. 27–32.

VII. His justifying his disciples in not fasting so frequently as the disciples of John and the Pharisees did, vv. 33–39.

Dr. Adam Clarke's analysis of chapter

The miraculous draught of fishes at the lake of Gennesaret, 1–11.

Christ heals a leper, 12–14.

His fame being published abroad, he withdraws to the desert, 15, 16.

He heals a paralytic person, at which the scribes and Pharisees murmur, but the people glorify God, 17–26.

He calls the publican Levi, who makes a feast for Christ, to which he invites a great number of publicans and others, at which the scribes and Pharisees murmur, and our Lord vindicates his conduct, 27–32.

The question about fasting answered, 33–35.

The parable of the new piece of cloth put on the old garment, and the new wine in old bottles, 36–39.

A detailed analysis of chapter

The miraculous catch of fish. Peter, James, and John called. (1–11)

A leper healed. (12–16)

A paralytic cured. (17–26)

Levi called. Christ's answer to the Pharisees. (27–39)

Key verse

Verse 5: "Master, we've worked hard all night and haven't caught anything. But because you say so, I will let down the nets."

Key word / key phrase

Verse 17, "to heal the sick."

Key event / key person / key theme

Miracles

Key thought

The startling newness of the Christian life.

Key thing to look out for

Jesus was constantly being questioned by people who had no sympathy with him.

Key Bible cross-reference

Verse 14. See Leviticus 14:1–32.

Key "by way of explanation"

Verse 17, "Pharisees." The name "Pharisee" refers to a religious party and means "Separated One." In order, as they thought, to please God, Pharisees sought to keep every minute requirement of the Law – not only the law of Moses, but the extensive elaborations of it. The "scribes" were men whose full-time job it was to interpret, teach and apply the Law. Most scribes came from the party of the Pharisees. Scribes and Pharisees were held in great respect by ordinary people.

Key "Quotable Quote"

"God is in the hypocrite's mouth, but the world is in his heart."

William Gurnall

Luke 6

Matthew Henry's introduction

In this chapter we have Christ's exposition of the moral law, which he came not to destroy, but to fulfill, and to fill up, by his gospel.

I. Here is a proof of the lawfulness of works of necessity and mercy on the Sabbath day, the former in vindication of his disciples' plucking the ears of corn, the latter in vindication of himself healing the withered hand on that day, vv. 1–11.

II. His retirement for secret prayer, v. 12.

III. His calling his twelve apostles, vv. 13–16.

IV. His curing the multitudes of those under various diseases who made their application to him, vv. 17–19.

V. The sermon that he preached to his disciples and the multitude, instructing them in their duty both to God and man, vv. 20–49.

Dr. Adam Clarke's analysis of chapter

The disciples pluck and eat the ears of corn on the Sabbath day, and the Pharisees find fault, 1, 2.

Our Lord shows the true use of the Sabbath, 3–5.

He heals the man with the withered hand, 6–11.

He goes into a mountain to pray, and calls twelve disciples, 12–16.

Multitudes are instructed and healed, 17–19.

Pronounces four blessings, 20–23,

and four woes, 24–26.

Gives various instructions about loving our enemies, being patient, gentle, kind, grateful, and merciful, 27–36.

Harsh judgments censured, and charity recommended, 37, 38.

The parable of the blind leading the blind, 39.

Of the mote in a brother's eye, 40–42.

Of the good and corrupt tree, 43, 44.

The good and evil treasure of the heart, 45.

The parable of the two houses, one built on the rock, and the other on the sand, 46–49.

A detailed analysis of chapter

The disciples pick corn on the Sabbath. (1–5)

Works of mercy allowed on the Sabbath day. (6–11)

The apostles chosen. (12–19)

Blessings and woes declared. (20–26)

Christ teaches about mercy. (27–36)

And justice and sincerity. (37–49)

Key verse

Verse 7: "The Pharisees and the teachers of the law were looking for a reason to accuse Jesus, so they watched him closely to see if he would heal on the Sabbath."

Key word / key phrase

Verse 13, "chose twelve."

Key event / key person / key theme

Jesus chooses the Twelve

Key thought

"Love your enemies" must have always seemed to be an impossible command to carry out.

Key thing to look out for

The more we appreciate God's mercy the more merciful we should be.

Key Bible cross-reference

Verse 4. See Leviticus 24:9.

Key "by way of explanation"

Verse 37, "do not judge." Jesus forbade his followers from indulging in hypocritical judging of other people. This is not the same as exercising discernment between right and wrong, which Jesus did encourage.

Key "Quotable Quote"

"If we had no faults ourselves, we should not take so much delight in noticing those of others."

François duc de La Rochefoucauld

Luke 7

Matthew Henry's introduction

In this chapter we have,

I. Christ confirming the doctrine he had preached in the previous chapter, with two glorious miracles–the curing of one at a distance, and that was the centurion's servant (vv. 1–10), and the raising of one to life that was dead, the widow's son at Nain, vv. 11–18.

II. Christ confirming the faith of John who was now in prison, and of some of his disciples, by sending him a short account of the miracles he wrought, in answer to a question he received from him (vv. 19–23), to which he adds an honorable testimony about John, and a just reproof to the men of that generation for the contempt they put on him and his doctrine, vv. 24–35.

III. Christ comforting a poor penitent that applied herself to him, all in tears of godly sorrow for sin, assuring her that her sins were pardoned, and justifying himself in the favor he showed her against the cavils of a proud Pharisee, vv. 36–50.

Dr. Adam Clarke's analysis of chapter

Christ heals the servant of a centurion, who is commended for his faith, 1–10.

Raises a widow's son to life at Nain, 11–17.

John Baptist hears of his fame, and sends two of his disciples to inquire whether he was the Christ, 18–23.

Christ's character of John, 24–30.

The obstinate blindness and capriciousness of the Jews, 31–35.

A Pharisee invites him to his house, where a woman anoints his head with oil, and washes his feet with her tears, 36–38.

The Pharisee is offended 39.

Our Lord reproves him by a parable, and vindicates the woman, 40–46;

and pronounces her sins forgiven, 47–50.

A detailed analysis of chapter

The centurion's servant healed. (1–10)

The widow's son raised. (11–18)

John the Baptist's question about Jesus. (19–35)

Christ anointed in the house of the Pharisee and the parable of the two debtors. (36–50)

Key verse

Verse 12: "As he approached the town gate, a dead person was being carried out – the only son of his mother, and she was a widow."

Key word / key phrase

Verse 50, "your faith has saved you."

Key event / key person / key theme

Jesus brings back to life the son of the widow of Nain

Key thought

This chapter is full of people with remarkable faith.

Key thing to look out for

Note how the four people demonstrated their faith in Jesus.

Key Bible cross-reference

Verse 22. See Isaiah 61:1.

Key "by way of explanation"

Verse 14, "coffin." When Jesus spoke to the dead man he told him to sit up. This indicates that he was carried in an open coffin which was common Jewish practice.

Key "Quotable Quote"

"She sat and wept, and with her untressed hair
She wiped the feet she was blest to touch;
And he wiped off the soiling despair
From her sweet soul – because she loved so much."

Dante Gabriel Rossetti

Luke 8

Matthew Henry's introduction

Most of this chapter is a repetition of divers passages of Christ's preaching and miracles which we had before in Matthew and Mark; they are all of such weight, that they are worth repeating, and therefore they are repeated, that out of the mouth not only of two, but of three, witnesses every word may be established.

Dr. Adam Clarke's analysis of chapter

Jesus preaches through every city and village, 1.
Women minister to him, 2, 3.
Instructs the multitudes by the parable of the sower, 4–8.
Explains it at large to his disciples, 9–15.
Directions how to improve by hearing the Gospel, 16–18.
His mother and brethren seek him, 19–21.
He and his disciples go on the lake, and are taken in a storm, 22–25.
They arrive among the Gadarenes, 26,
where he cures a demoniac, 27–39.
He returns from the Gadarenes, and is requested by Jairus to heal his daughter, 40–42.
On the way he cures a diseased woman, 43–48.
Receives information that the daughter of Jairus is dead, 49.
Exhorts the father to believe; arrives at the house, and raises the dead child to life, 60–66.

A detailed analysis of chapter

The ministry of Christ. (1–3)
The parable of the sower. (4–21)
Christ calms the storm and heals a demon-possessed man. (22–40)
The daughter of Jairus restored to life. (41–56)

Key verse

Verse 21: "My mother and brothers are those who hear God's word and put it into practice."

Key word / key phrase

Verse 25, "Who is this?"

Key event / key person / key theme

Parable of the sower

Key thought

Note the different things that prevent spiritual growth according to the parable of the sower.

Key thing to look out for

Verse 18 places a heavy responsibility on the shoulders of those who have been blessed with special talents and opportunities.

Key Bible cross-reference

Verse 10. See Isaiah 6:9,10.

Key "by way of explanation"

Verse 18, "consider carefully how you listen." This was especially important for these first disciples since what they heard they taught to others. See also Luke 19:26.

Key "Quotable Quote"

"Whatever you have received more than others in health, talents, abilities, success, a pleasant childhood, or in harmonious conditions of home life, all this you must not take to yourself as a matter of course. In gratitude for your good fortune, render some sacrifice of your own life for another life."

Albert Schweitzer

Luke 9

Matthew Henry's introduction

In this chapter we have,

I. The commission Christ gave to his twelve apostles to go out for some time to preach the gospel, and confirm it by miracles, vv. 1–6.

II. Herod's terror at the growing greatness of our Lord Jesus, vv. 7–9.

III. The apostles' return to Christ, his retirement with them into a place of solitude, the great resort of people to them notwithstanding, and his feeding five thousand men with five loaves and two fishes, vv. 10–17.

IV. His discourse with his disciples about himself and his own sufferings for them, and their for him, vv. 18–27.

V. Christ's transfiguration, vv. 28–36.

VI. The cure of a lunatic child, vv. 37–42.

VII. The repeated notice Christ gave his disciples of his approaching sufferings, vv. 43–45.

VIII. His check to the ambition of his disciples (vv. 46–48), and to their monopolizing the power over devils to themselves, vv. 49, 50.

IX. The rebuke he gave them for an over-due resentment of an affront given him by a village of the Samaritans, vv. 51–56.

X. The answers he gave to several that were inclined to follow him, but not considerately, or not zealously and heartily, so inclined, vv. 57–62.

Dr. Adam Clarke's analysis of chapter

Christ sends his apostles to preach and work miracles, 1–6.

Herod, hearing of the fame of Jesus, is perplexed; some suppose that John Baptist is risen from the dead; others, that Elijah or one of the old prophets was come to life, 7–9.

The apostles return and relate the success of their mission. He goes to a retired place, and the people follow him, 10, 11.

He feeds five thousand men with five loaves and two fishes, 12–17.

He asks his disciples what the public think of him, 18–21.

Foretells his passion, 22.

Shows the necessity of self-denial, and the importance of salvation, 23–25.

Threatens those who deny him before men, 26.

The transfiguration, 27–36.

Cures a demoniac, 37–43.

Again foretells his passion, 44, 45.

The disciples contend who shall be greatest, 46–48.

Of the person who cast out devils in Christ's name, but did not associate with the disciples, 49, 50.

Of the Samaritans who would not receive him, 51–56.

Of the man who wished to follow Jesus, 57, 58.
He calls another disciple who asks permission first to bury his father, 59.
Our Lord's answer 60–62.

A detailed analysis of chapter

The apostles sent out. (1–9)
The multitude miraculously fed. (10–17)
Peter's testimony to Christ. Self-denial commanded. (18–27)
The transfiguration. (28–36)
An evil spirit expelled. (37–42)
Christ checks the ambition of his disciples. (43–50)
He reproves their mistaken zeal. (51–56)
Everything to be given up for Christ. (57–62)

Key verse

Verse 23: "If anyone would come after me, he must deny himself and take up his cross daily and follow me."

Key word / key phrase

Verse 29, "as bright as a flash of lightning."

Key event / key person / key theme

Jesus' transfiguration

Key thought

Here is the truth about being a disciple of Jesus.

Key thing to look out for

The frequent references made to Jesus' impending death. When Jesus set out "resolutely" (verse 51) for Jerusalem, he had the cross in view.

Key Bible cross-reference

Verses 3–5. See Acts 13:51.

Key "by way of explanation"

Verse 30: "departure." When Jesus was transfigured Moses and Elijah spoke of his "departure." In Greek, the word is "exodus." Jesus' death is linked to God's rescue of his people from Egypt.

Key "Quotable Quote"

Verse 22: "The Son of Man must suffer." "The 'must' is not of resignation to fate but of self-giving to God's plan of salvation."

J.C. Ryle

Luke 10

Matthew Henry's introduction

In this chapter we have,

I. The ample commission which Christ gave to the seventy disciples to preach the gospel, and to confirm it by miracles; and the full instructions he gave them how to manage themselves in the execution of their commissions, and great encouragements therein, vv. 1–16.

II. The report which the seventy disciples made to their Master of the success of their negotiation, and his discourse thereon, vv. 17–24.

III. Christ's discourse with a lawyer about the way to heaven, and the instructions Christ gave him by a parable to look on every one as his neighbor whom he had occasion to show kindness to, or receive kindness from, vv. 25–37.

IV. Christ's entertainment at Martha's house, the reproof he gave to her for her care about the world, and his commendation of Mary for her care about her soul, vv. 38–42.

Dr. Adam Clarke's analysis of chapter

Christ appoints seventy disciples to go before him, two by two, to preach, heal, etc., 1–12.

Pronounces woes on Chorazin and Capernaum, 13–16.

The seventy return, and give account of their mission, 17–20.

Christ rejoices that the things which were hidden from the wise and prudent had been revealed unto babes, and shows the great privileges of the Gospel, 21–24.

A lawyer inquires how he shall inherit eternal life, and is answered, 25–29.

The story of the good Samaritan, 30–37.

The account of Martha and Mary, 38–42.

A detailed analysis of chapter

Seventy-two disciples sent out. (1–16)

The joy of Christ's disciples. (17–24)

The good Samaritan. (25–37)

Jesus at the home of Martha and Mary. (38–42)

Key verse

Verse 1: "After this the Lord appointed seventy-two others and sent them two by two ahead of him to every town and place where he was about to go."

Key word / key phrase

Verse 37, "Go and do likewise."

Key event / key person / key theme

The good Samaritan

Key thought

As the harvest is still plentiful what should happen?

Key thing to look out for

Note, verse 21, what made Jesus full of joy.

Key Bible cross-reference

Verse 7. See 1 Corinthians 9:14.

Key "by way of explanation"

Verse 27, "Love . . . God . . . Love your neighbor." When Jesus said this he was linking together Deuteronomy 6:5 and Leviticus 19:18. Jesus demanded nothing short of total devotion to God and dedication to helping people. Verse 1: some early manuscripts have seventy-two, and others have seventy here.

Key "Quotable Quote"

"Attitudes displayed in the parable of the good Samaritan

1. The Robbers: What's yours is mine if I can get it.
2. The Priest: What's mine is mine if I can keep it.
3. The Innkeeper: What's mine is yours if you can pay for it.
4. The Samaritan: What's mine is yours if you need it."

Tear Fund

Luke 11

Matthew Henry's introduction

In this chapter,

I. Christ teaches his disciples to pray, and quickens and encourages them to be frequent, instant, and importunate in prayer, vv. 1–13.

II. He fully answers the blasphemous imputation of the Pharisees, who charged him with casting out devils by virtue of a compact and confederacy with Beelzebub, the prince of the devils, and shows the absurdity and wickedness of it, vv. 14–26.

III. He shows the honor of obedient disciples to be greater than that of his own mother, vv. 27, 28.

IV. He upbraids the men of that generation for their infidelity and obstinacy, notwithstanding all the means of conviction offered to them, vv. 29–36.

V. He severely reproves the Pharisees and consciences of those that submitted to them, and their hating and persecuting those that witnessed against their wickedness, vv. 37–54.

Dr. Adam Clarke's analysis of chapter

Christ teaches his disciples to pray, 1–4.

Shows the necessity of importunity in prayer, 5–13.

Casts out a dumb demon, 14.

The Jews ascribe this to the power of Beelzebub; our Lord vindicates his conduct, 15–23.

Miserable state of the Jews, 24–26.

Who they are that are truly blessed, 27, 28.

He preaches to the people, 29–36.

A Pharisee invites him to dine with him, who takes offense because he washed not his hands, 37, 38.

Our Lord exposes their hypocrisy, 39–44. He denounces woes against the lawyers, 45–52.

The scribes and Pharisees are greatly offended, and strive to entangle him in his words, 53, 54.

A detailed analysis of chapter

The disciples taught to pray. (1–4)

Christ encourages believing prayer. (5–13)

Christ expels a devil, and the blasphemy of the Pharisees. (14–26)

True happiness. (27,28)

Christ reproves the Jews. (29–36)

He reproves the Pharisees. (37–54)

Key verse

Verse 1: "Lord, teach us to pray, just as John taught his disciples."

Key word / key phrase

Verse 2, "when you pray."

Key event / key person / key theme

The Lord's Prayer

Key thought

"Your kingdom come." The word "kingdom" does not refer to a place but to a "situation in which God is King." "Wherever God is in control, his sovereignty accepted and his will obeyed, there is God's kingship." (R.T. France)

Key thing to look out for

How to avoid three terrible states: the empty soul (verse 25), the soul full of darkness (verse 34), the soul full of greed and wickedness (verse 39).

Key Bible cross-reference

Verse 42. See Leviticus 27:30.

Key "by way of explanation"

Verse 46, "load people down." Experts in the Law knew ways round the Law but made existing laws sit even more heavily on the shoulders of ordinary people by adding to them and by not helping anyone to keep them.

Key "Quotable Quote"

"True religion disposes persons to be much alone in solitary places for holy meditation and prayer."

Jonathan Edwards

Luke 12

Matthew Henry's introduction

In this chapter we have divers excellent discourses of our Savior's on various occasions, many of which are to the same purport with what we had in Matthew on other the like occasions; for we may suppose that our Lord Jesus preached the same doctrines, and pressed the same duties, at several times, in several companies, and that one of the evangelists took them as he delivered them at one time and another at another time; and we need thus to have precept on precept, line on line.

Dr. Adam Clarke's analysis of chapter

Christ preaches to his disciples against hypocrisy; and against timidity in publishing the Gospel, 1–5.

Excites them to have confidence in Divine providence, 6, 7.

Warns them against denying him, or betraying his cause, 8, 9.

Of the blasphemy against the Holy Spirit, 10.

Promises direction and support in persecution, 11, 12.

Warns the people against covetousness, 13–15.

Parable of the rich man who pulled down his granaries to build greater, 16–21.

Cautions against carking cares and anxieties, 22–32.

The necessity of living to God, and in reference to eternity, 33–40.

At the request of Peter, he farther explains the preceding discourse, 41–48.

The effects that should be produced by the preaching of the Gospel, 49–53.

The signs of the times, 54–57.

The necessity of being prepared to appear before the judgment seat of God, 58, 59.

A detailed analysis of chapter

Christ reproves the interpreters of the Law. (1–12)

A caution against greed. The parable of the rich man. (13–21)

Worldly care reproved. (22–40)

Watchfulness commanded. (41–53)

A warning to be reconciled to God. (54–59)

Key verse

Verse 13: "Teacher, tell my brother to divide the inheritance with me."

Key word / key phrase

Verse 1, "a crowd of many thousands."

Key event / key person / key theme

Jesus teaches a large crowd

Key thought

Called to be watchful and fearless.

Key thing to look out for

What can be learned from the warnings in this chapter?

Key Bible cross-reference

Verse 53. See Micah 7:6.

Key "by way of explanation"

Verse 29, "worry." This word in the Greek describes a storm-tossed ship which is literally raised between heaven and earth. Worry achieves nothing. Jesus points out that it is irrational to worry.

Key "Quotable Quote"

"There is no Christian solution of the problems presented by self-will; but there is a Christian cure and if that is effective, the problem is abolished. So when a man wanted Jesus to divide an inheritance, that is to arbitrate between two self-centered claims, he refused. He did not settle the dispute; but he did tell them how to avoid continuing the dispute. 'Take heed and keep yourselves from covetousness.'"

William Temple

Luke 13

Matthew Henry's introduction

In this chapter we have,

I. The good improvement Christ made of a piece of news that was brought him about some Galileans, that were lately massacred by Pilate, as they were sacrificing in the temple at Jerusalem, vv. 1–5.

II. The parable of the fruitless fig-tree, by which we are warned to bring forth fruits meet for that repentance to which he had in the previous passage called us, vv. 6–9.

III. Christ's healing a poor infirm woman on the Sabbath day, and justifying himself in it, vv. 11–17.

IV. A repetition of the parables of the grain of mustard-seed and the leaven, vv. 18–22.

V. His answer to the question about the number of the saved, vv. 23–30.

VI. The slight he put on Herod's malice and menaces, and the doom of Jerusalem read, vv. 31–35.

Dr. Adam Clarke's analysis of chapter

Christ preaches the necessity of repentance, from the punishment of the Galileans massacred by Pilate, 1–3.

And by the death of those on whom the tower in Siloam fell, 4, 5.

The parable of the barren fig tree, 6–29.

Christ cures a woman who had been afflicted eighteen years, 10–13.

The ruler of the synagogue is incensed and is reproved by our Lord, 14– 17.

The parable of the mustard seed, 18, 19;

of the leaven, 20–21.

He journeys towards Jerusalem, and preaches, 22.

The question, Are there few saved? and our Lord's answer, with the discourse thereon, 23–30.

He is informed that Herod purposes to kill him, 31, 32.

Predicts his own death at Jerusalem, and denounces judgments on that impenitent city, 33–35.

A detailed analysis of chapter

Christ exhorts people to repent, using the example of the Galileans and others. (1–5)

Parable of the barren fig tree. (6–9)

A crippled woman healed. (10–17)

The parables of the mustard seed, and yeast. (18–22)

Command to enter through the narrow gate. (23–30)

Christ's reproof to Herod, and to the people of Jerusalem. (31–35)

Key verse

Verse 14: "There are six days for work. So come and be healed on those days, not on the Sabbath."

Key word / key phrase

Verse 34, "O Jerusalem, Jerusalem."

Key event / key person / key theme

Jesus weeps over Jerusalem

Key thought

Jesus never minced his words.

Key thing to look out for

Note the fate of those who refuse to repent.

Key Bible cross-reference

Verse 27. See Psalm 6:8.

Key "by way of explanation"

Verse 15, "untie his ox." Leading Jews had many clever ways of circumventing the law. They could justify assisting their own ox on the Sabbath, but this did not stop them from accusing Jesus of breaking the Sabbath for working on it, and healing someone.

Key "Quotable Quote"

"Superstition, idolatry, and hypocrisy have ample wages, but truth goes a begging."

Martin Luther

Luke 14

Matthew Henry's introduction

In this chapter we have,

I. The cure which our Lord Jesus wrought on a man that had the dropsy, on the Sabbath day, and his justifying himself therein against those who were offended at his doing it on that day, vv. 1–6.

II. A lesson of humility gives to those who were ambitious of the highest rooms, vv. 7–11.

III. A lesson of charity to those who feasted the rich, and did not feed the poor, vv. 12–14.

IV. The success of the gospel not foretold in the parable of the guests invited to a feast, signifying the rejection of the Jews and all others that set their hearts on this world, and the entertainment of the Gentiles and all others that come to be filled with Christ, vv. 15–24.

V. The great law of discipleship laid down, with a caution to all that will be Christ's disciples to undertake it deliberately and with consideration, and particularly to ministers, to retain their savor, vv. 25–35.

Dr. Adam Clarke's analysis of chapter

Christ heals a man ill of the dropsy, on a Sabbath day, 1–6.

He inculcates humility by a parable, 7–11.

The poor to be fed, and not the rich, 12–14.

The parable of the great supper, 15–24.

How men must become disciples of Christ, 25–27.

The parable of the prudent builder, who estimates the cost before he commences his work, 28–30.

And of the provident king, 31, 32.

The use of these parables, 33.

The utility of salt while in its strength and perfection; and its total uselessness when it has lost its savor; 34, 35.

A detailed analysis of chapter

Christ heals a man on the Sabbath. (1–6)

He teaches humility. (7–14)

Parable of the great supper. (15–24)

The necessity for consideration and self-denial. (25–35)

Key verse

Verse 7: "When he noticed how the guests picked the places of honor at the table, he told them this parable."

Key word / key phrase

Verse 1, "a prominent Pharisee."

Key event / key person / key theme

Jesus teaches the Pharisees

Key thought

Jesus insists on humility.

Key thing to look out for

Jesus never underestimated the cost involved in following him.

Key Bible cross-reference

Verse 35. See Jeremiah 22:5.

Key "by way of explanation"

Verse 26, "hate his father." Jesus is clearly exaggerating to make a point here. As he had told people to love their neighbors he would not now tell them to hate their fathers. The expression sets out absolute priorities. Loyalty to Jesus always comes first.

Key "Quotable Quote"

"Luke 14:33 shows what is meant by the calculation of expenses, with which Christ enjoins his followers to begin: it is to lead them to consider that they must forsake all. In vain do persons who are delighted with an easy, indolent life, and with exemption from the cross, undertake a profession of Christianity."

John Calvin

Luke 15

Matthew Henry's introduction

Evil manners, we say, beget good laws; so, in this chapter, the murmuring of the scribes and Pharisees at the grace of Christ, and the favor he showed to publicans and sinners, gave occasion for a more full discovery of that grace than perhaps otherwise we should have had in these three parables which we have in this chapter, the scope of all of which is the same, to show, not only what God had said and sworn in the Old Testament, that he had no pleasure in the death and ruin of sinners, but that he had great pleasure in their return and repentance, and rejoices in the gracious entertainment he gives them thereon.

Dr. Adam Clarke's analysis of chapter

Publicans and sinners draw near to hear our Lord, at which the Pharisees are offended, 1, 2.

Christ vindicates his conduct in receiving them by the parable of the lost sheep, 3–7.

The parable of the lost piece of money, 8–10; and the affecting parable of the prodigal son, 11–32.

A detailed analysis of chapter

Parables of the lost sheep, and the piece of silver. (1–10)

The prodigal son, his wickedness and distress. (11–16)

His repentance and pardon. (17–24)

The elder brother is offended. (25–32)

Key verse

Verse 11: "There was a man who had two sons."

Key word / key phrase

Verses 4,9,32, "lost."

Key event / key person / key theme

Three "lost" parables

Key thought

Jesus welcomes sinners (verse 2).

Key thing to look out for

Where did the elder son go wrong?

Key Bible cross-reference

Verse 20. See Genesis 45:14,15.

Key "by way of explanation"

Verse 15, "to feed pigs." That was the last thing a Jew would dream of doing, as pigs were regarded as "unclean" animals.

Key "Quotable Quote"

"His father saw him – there were eyes of mercy;
he ran to meet him – there were legs of mercy;
he put his arms round his neck – there were arms of mercy;
he kissed him – there were kisses of mercy;
he said to him – there were words of mercy;
Bring here the best robe – there were deeds of mercy;
Wonders of mercy – all mercy!
Oh, what a God of mercy he is!"

Matthew Henry

Luke 16

Matthew Henry's introduction

The scope of Christ's discourse in this chapter is to awaken and quicken us all so to use this world as not to abuse it, so to manage all our possessions and enjoyments here as that they may make for us, and may not make against us in the other world; for they will do either the one or the other, according as we use them now.

Dr. Adam Clarke's analysis of chapter

The parable of the unjust steward, 1–8.
Christ applies this to his hearers, 9–13.
The Pharisees take offense, 14.
Our Lord reproves them, and shows the immutability of the law, 15–17.
Counsels against divorce, 18.
The story of the rich man and the beggar, commonly called Dives and Lazarus, 10–31.

A detailed analysis of chapter

The parable of the unjust steward. (1–12)
Christ reproves the hypocrisy of the covetous Pharisees. (13–18)
The rich man and Lazarus. (19–31)

Key verse

Verse 8: "For the people of this world are more shrewd in dealing with their own kind than are the people of the light."

Key word / key phrase

Verse 1, "there was a rich man."

Key event / key person / key theme

Jesus teaches about money

Key thought

Note the point commended in the parable about the manager.

Key thing to look out for

Where did the rich man go wrong in the parable of the rich man and Lazarus?

Key Bible cross-reference

Verse 18. See 1 Corinthians 7:10,11.

Key "by way of explanation"

Verse 9, "use worldly wealth." There are many warnings about the dangers of riches in the Bible. But this verse teaches that wealth can be thought of as talent which should be fully employed in God's service.

Key "Quotable Quote"

"The fulfillment of the Lord's mercy does not depend upon believers' works, but . . . in those who are directed to the good by his Spirit he recognizes the only genuine insignia of his children."

John Calvin

Luke 17

Matthew Henry's introduction

In this chapter we have,

I. Some particular discourses which Christ had with his disciples, in which he teaches them to take heed of giving offence, and to forgive the injuries done them (vv. 1–4), encourages them to pray for the increase of their faith (vv. 5, 6), and then teaches them humility, whatever service they had done for God, vv. 7–10.

II. His cleansing ten lepers, and the thanks he had from one of them only, and he a Samaritan, vv. 11–19.

III. His discourse with his disciples, on occasion of an enquiry of the Pharisees, when the kingdom of God should appear, vv. 20–37.

Dr. Adam Clarke's analysis of chapter

Christ teaches the necessity of avoiding offenses, 1, 2.

How to treat an offending brother, 3, 4.

The efficacy of faith, 5, 6.

No man by his services or obedience can profit his Maker, 7–10.

He cleanses ten lepers, 11–19.

The Pharisees inquire when the kingdom of God shall commence; Christ answers them, and corrects their improper views of the subject, 20–37.

A detailed analysis of chapter

Sin, faith, duty. (1–10)

Ten lepers cleansed. (11–19)

Christ's kingdom. (20–37)

Key verse

Verse 6: "If you have faith as small as a mustard seed, you can say to this mulberry tree, 'Be uprooted and planted in the sea,' and it will obey you."

Key word / key phrase

Verse 12, "ten men who had leprosy."

Key event / key person / key theme

Gratitude

Key thought

What does ingratitude indicate?

Key thing to look out for

The point about faith is not its size but in whom it is placed.

Key Bible cross-reference

Verse 27. See Genesis 7:6–24.

Key "by way of explanation"

Verse 2, "millstone." The point about the very heavy stones used for grinding is that it conjures up a terrible picture of punishment: death by drowning.

Key "Quotable Quote"

"The first element in faith is what we can only call receptivity. Faith is the response of trust of a man's total personality to the love of God as shown to us in the life and death of Jesus Christ."

William Barclay

Luke 18

Matthew Henry's introduction

In this chapter we have,

I. The parable of the importunate widow, designed to teach us fervency in prayer, vv. 1–8.

II. The parable of the Pharisee and publican, designed to teach us humility, and humiliation for sin, in prayer, vv. 9–14.

III. Christ's favor to little children that were brought to him, vv. 15–17.

IV. The trial of a rich man that had a mind to follow Christ, whether he loved better Christ or his riches; his coming short on that trial; and Christ's discourse with his disciples on that occasion, vv. 18–30.

V. Christ's foretelling his own death and sufferings, vv. 31–34.

VI. His restoring sight to a blind man, vv. 35–43.

And these four passages we had before in Matthew and Mark.

Dr. Adam Clarke's analysis of chapter

The parable of the importunate widow, 1–8.

Of the Pharisee and the publican, 9–14.

Infants brought to Christ, 15–17.

The ruler who wished to know how he might inherit eternal life, 18–23.

Our Lord's reflections on his case, 24–27.

What they shall receive who follow Christ, 28–30.

He foretells his approaching passion and death, 31–34.

He restores a blind man to sight at Jericho, 35–43.

A detailed analysis of chapter

The parable of the persistent widow. (1–8)

The Pharisee and the tax-collector. (9–14)

Children brought to Christ. (15–17)

The ruler hindered by his riches. (18–30)

Christ talks of his death. (31–34)

A blind man restored to sight. (35–43)

Key verse

Verse 27: "What is impossible with men is possible with God."

Key word / key phrase

Verse 16, "Jesus called the children to him."

Key event / key person / key theme

Jesus and prayer

Key thought

The only way to enter the kingdom of heaven is as a little child.

Key thing to look out for

What do the stories and conversations in this chapter have to say about prayer?

Key Bible cross-reference

Verse 32. See Genesis 19:26.

Key "by way of explanation"

Verse 31, "everything that is written by the prophets." The death of the Messiah is prophesied in a number of places in the Old Testament, such as Psalm 22, Isaiah 53, and Zechariah 13:7.

Key "Quotable Quote"

"What the Church needs today is not more or better machinery, not new organizations, or more novel methods; but men whom the Holy Spirit can use – men of prayer, men mighty in prayer."

E.M. Bounds

Luke 19

Matthew Henry's introduction

In this chapter we have,

I. The conversion of Zaccheus the publican at Jericho, vv. 1–10.

II. The parable of the pounds which the king entrusted with his servants, and of his rebellious citizens, vv. 11–27.

III. Christ's riding in triumph (such triumph as it was) into Jerusalem; and his lamentation in prospect of the ruin of that city, vv. 28–44.

IV. His teaching in the temple, and casting the buyers and sellers out of it, vv. 45–48.

Dr. Adam Clarke's analysis of chapter

The conversion of Zaccheus, 1–10.

The parable of the nobleman, his ten servants, and the ten pounds, 11–27.

Christ sends his disciples for a colt on which he rides into Jerusalem, 28–40.

He weeps over the city, and foretells its destruction, 41–44.

Goes into the temple, and casts out the buyers and sellers, 45, 46.

The chief priests and the scribes seek to destroy him, but are afraid of the people, who hear him attentively. 47, 48.

A detailed analysis of chapter

The conversion of Zacchaeus. (1–10)

The parable of the nobleman and his servants. (11–27)

Christ enters Jerusalem. (28–40)

Christ weeps over Jerusalem. (41–48)

Key verse

Verse 2: "A man was there by the name of Zacchaeus; he was a chief tax collector and was wealthy"

Key word / key phrase

Verse 10, "to seek and to save what was lost."

Key event / key person / key theme

Entering Jerusalem

Key thought

In the parable about the ten minas Jesus praises faithfulness.

Key thing to look out for

The many different responses to Jesus

Key Bible cross-reference

Verse 38. See Psalm 118:26.

Key "by way of explanation"

Verse 30, "colt." Jesus entered Jerusalem in the most humble way imaginable. He was also doing so in a most public way. He was the son of David entering his city as King.

Key "Quotable Quote"

"Humility is the secret of blessing, our salvation, true heavenly-mindedness, the primacy in the Church, the only ladder to honor in God's kingdom, the most essential element of discipleship."

Andrew Murray

Luke 20

Matthew Henry's introduction

In this chapter we have,

I. Christ's answer to the chief priests' question about his authority, vv. 1–8.

II. The parable of the vineyard let out to the unjust and rebellious husbandmen, vv. 9–19.

III. Christ's answer to the question proposed to him about the lawfulness of paying tribute to Cæsar, vv. 20–26.

IV. His vindication of that great fundamental doctrine of the Jewish and Christian institutes–the resurrection of the dead and the future state, from the foolish cavils of the Sadducees, vv. 27–38.

V. His puzzling the scribes with a question about the Messiah's being the Son of David, vv. 39–44.

VI. The caution he gave his disciples to take heed of the scribes, vv. 45–47.

All which passages we had before in Matthew and Mark, and therefore need not enlarge on them here, unless on those particulars which we had not there.

Dr. Adam Clarke's analysis of chapter

The question about the authority of Christ, and the baptism of John, 1–8.

The parable of the vine-yard let out to wicked husbandmen, 9–18.

The chief priests and scribes are offended, and lay snares for him, 19, 20.

The question about tribute, 21–26.

The question about the resurrection of the dead, and our Lord's answer, 27–40.

How Christ is the son of David, 41–44.

He warns his disciples against the hypocrisy of the scribes, whose condemnation he points out, 45–47.

Luke chapter 20:1–8, see Matthew 21:23–27; 20:9–19, see Matthew 21:33–46; 20–47, see Matthew 22:15–23:7.

Luke 21

Matthew Henry's introduction

In this chapter we have,

I. The notice Christ took, and the approbation he gave, of a poor widow that cast two mites into the treasury, vv. 1–4.

II. A prediction of future events, in answer to his disciples' enquiries about them, vv. 5–7.

A. Of what should happen between that and the destruction of Jerusalem–false Christs arising, bloody wars and persecutions of Christ's followers, vv. 8–19.

B. Of that destruction itself, vv. 20–24.

C. Of the second coming of Jesus Christ to judge the world, under the type and figure of that, vv. 25–33.

III. A practical application of this, by way of caution and counsel (vv. 34–36), and an account of Christ's preaching and the people's attendance on it, vv. 37, 38.

Dr. Adam Clarke's analysis of chapter

The poor widow casting two mites into the treasury, 1–4.

The destruction of the temple foretold, 5, 6.

The signs of this desolation, 7.

False Christs, 8.

Wars, 9, 10.

Earthquakes and fearful sights, 11.

Persecutions against the godly, 12–19.

Directions how to escape, 20–22.

The tribulation of those times, 23–28.

The parable of the fig tree, illustrative of the time when they may expect these calamities, 29–33.

The necessity of sobriety and watchfulness, 34–36.

He teaches by day in the temple, and lodges by night in the mount of Olives, and the people come early to hear him, 37, 38.

A detailed analysis of chapter

Christ commends a poor widow. (1–4)

His prophecy. (5–28)

Christ commands watchfulness. (29–38)

Key verse

Verse 2: "He also saw a poor widow put in two very small copper coins."

Key word / key phrase

Verse 8, "Watch out that you are not deceived."

Key event / key person / key theme

Jesus teaches about the future

Key thought

At every point of our lives Jesus responds to our motives.

Key thing to look out for

What do dissipation, drunkenness and anxiety have in common?

Key Bible cross-reference

Verse 25. See Ezekiel 32:7.

Key "by way of explanation"

Verse 1, "the temple treasury" consisted of thirteen boxes in the court of women into which people put their gifts for the temple.

Key "Quotable Quote"

"A sacrifice without a heart, without salt, without fire, of what value is it?"

John Owen

Luke 22

Matthew Henry's introduction

All the evangelists, whatever they omit, give us a particular account of the death and resurrection of Christ, because he died for our sins and rose for our justification, this evangelist as fully as any, and with many circumstances and passages added which we had not before.

Dr. Adam Clarke's analysis of chapter

The chief priests and scribes plot our Lord's destruction, 1, 2.

Judas, at the instigation of the devil, betrays him, 3–6.

He eats his last supper with his disciples, 7–18.

Institutes the eucharist, 19, 20.

Announces one of his disciples as the traitor, 21–23:

The contention which should be greatest, 24–30.

Warns Peter against Satan's devices, 31, 32.

Peter's resolution, 33.

His denial foretold, 34.

Tells his disciples to make prudent provision for their own support, 35–37.

The two swords, 38.

He goes to the Mount of Olives, and has his agony in the garden, 39–46.

Judas comes with a mob, 47, 48.

Peter cuts off the ear of the high priest's servant, which Christ heals by a touch, 49–51.

He addresses the chief priests and captains of the temple, 52, 53.

They lead him to the high priest's house, and Peter follows and denies his Master, 54–60.

Christ looks on him, he is stung with remorse, and weeps bitterly, 61, 62.

Jesus is mocked, and variously insulted, 63–65.

The next morning he is questioned before the council, 66, 67.

He acknowledges himself to be the Son of God, 68–70.

They condemn him, 71.

A detailed analysis of chapter

The treachery of Judas. (1–6)

The Passover. (7–18)

The Lord's Supper instituted. (19,20)

Christ admonishes the disciples. (21–38)

Christ's agony in the garden. (39–46)

Christ betrayed. (47–53)

The fall of Peter. (54–62)

Christ declares himself to be the Son of God. (63–71)

Key verse

Verse 8: "Go and make preparations for us to eat the Passover."

Key word / key phrase

Verse 54, "Peter followed at a distance."

Key event / key person / key theme

The last supper; Jesus arrested

Key thought

Nobody forced Judas to betray Jesus.

Key thing to look out for

Even at the last supper the disciples were quarrelling about who was the most important.

Key Bible cross-reference

Verse 20. See Jeremiah 31:31–34.

Key "by way of explanation"

Verse 44, "drops of blood," could have been a mingling of sweat and blood, known as haematidrosis, or just a description of perspiration. Either way, these words highlight Jesus' anguish. There was an interrogation in the middle of the night followed by a formal trial at daybreak before a full session of the Sanhedrin.

Key "Quotable Quote"

"The death of Jesus was not the death of a martyr, it was the revelation of the eternal heart of God."

Oswald Chambers

Luke 23

Matthew Henry's introduction

This chapter carries on and concludes the history of Christ's sufferings and death.

Dr. Adam Clarke's analysis of chapter

Christ is led to Pilate, and accused by the Jews, 1, 2.

Pilate examines, and pronounces him innocent, 3, 4.

The Jews virulently accuse him, 5.

Pilate, understanding that he was of Galilee, sends him to Herod, by whom he is examined, 6–9.

The chief priests and scribes vehemently accuse him, and Herod and his soldiers mock him, 10, 11.

Pilate and Herod become friends, 12.

Pilate, before the chief priests, rulers, and people, pronounces Christ to be innocent, and offers to release him, 13–20.

The Jews clamor for his condemnation, and Pilate gives him up to their will, 21–25.

Simon bears his cross, 26.

The people bewail him, and he foretells the destruction of the Jewish state, 27–31.

He and two malefactors are brought to Calvary, and are crucified, 32, 33.

He prays for his crucifiers, 34.

He is derided, mocked, and insulted by the rulers, and by the soldiers, 35–37.

The superscription on the cross, 38.

The conduct of the two malefactors, to one of whom he promises paradise, 39–43.

The great darkness, 44, 45.

He gives up the ghost, 46.

The centurion and many others are greatly affected at his death, 47–49.

Joseph of Arimathea begs the body, and puts it in his own new tomb, 50–53.

The women prepare spices and ointments to embalm him, 54–56.

A detailed analysis of chapter

Christ before Pilate. (1–5)

Christ before Herod. (6–12)

Barabbas preferred to Christ. (13–25)

Christ speaks about the destruction of Jerusalem. (26–31)

The crucifixion, and the repentant criminal. (32–43)

The death of Christ. (44–49)

The burial of Christ. (50–56)

Key verse

Verse 7: "When he learned that Jesus was under Herod's jurisdiction, he sent him to Herod, who was also in Jerusalem at that time."

Key word / key phrase

Verse 33, "they crucified him."

Key event / key person / key theme

The death of Jesus

Key thought

Even there in the mess and horror and torture of the cross, we see Jesus' deep compassion for others and communion with the Father (verse 46).

Key thing to look out for

The differing responses of the people: at the foot of the cross, including those who ignored Jesus. Where do we place ourselves?

Key Bible cross-reference

Verse 30. See Hosea 10:8.

Key "by way of explanation"

Under Roman law the Sanhedrin did not have authority to pass a death sentence on Jesus. He therefore had to be taken to Pilate. Verse 38, "written notice." Above the head of the dying criminal a notice was placed on which was written his crime. Pilate's notice would have greatly annoyed the Jews.

Key "Quotable Quote"

"It costs God nothing, so far as we know, to create nice things: but to convert rebellious wills cost him crucifixion."

C.S. Lewis

Luke 24

Matthew Henry's introduction

Our Lord Jesus went gloriously down to death, in spite of the malice of his enemies, who did all they could to make his death ignominious; but he rose again more gloriously, of which we have an account in this chapter; and the proofs and evidences of Christ's resurrection are more fully related by this evangelist than they were by Matthew and Mark.

Dr. Adam Clarke's analysis of chapter

The women coming early to the sepulcher on the first day of the week, bringing their spices, find the stone rolled away, and the tomb empty, 1–3.

They see a vision of angels, who announce Christ's resurrection, 4–8.

The women return and tell this to the eleven, 9, 10.

They believe not, but Peter goes and examines the tomb, 11, 12.

Christ, unknown, appears to two of the disciples who were going to Emmaus, and converses with them, 13–29.

While they are eating together, he makes him self known, and immediately disappears, 30, 31.

They return to Jerusalem, and announce his resurrection to the rest of the disciples, 32–35.

Jesus himself appears to them, and gives them the fullest proof of the reality of his resurrection, 36–43.

He preaches to them, and gives them the promise of the Holy Spirit, 44–49.

He takes them to Bethany, and ascends to heaven in their sight, 50, 51.

They worship him, and return to Jerusalem, 52, 53.

5. Select bibliography for Luke

Ellis, E. E. *The Gospel of Luke*. NCB. New York: Nelson, 1966.

Geldenhuys, Johannes Norval. *Commentary on the Gospel of Luke*. NIC. Grand Rapids: Eerdmans, 1951.

Godet, Frederic. *A Commentary on the Gospel of St. Luke*. Translated by E. W. Marshall, I. H. The Gospel of Luke: A Commentary on the Greek Text. Grand Rapids: Eerdmans, 1978.

Morris, L. *The Gospel According to St. Luke: An Introduction and Commentary*. Grand Rapids: Eerdmans, 1974.

Shalders and M. D. Cusin. Edinburgh: T. & T. Clark, 1893.

Hendriksen, William. *Exposition of the Gospel According to Luke*. Grand Rapids: Baker, 1978.

Wilcock, Michael. *Savior of the World. The Message of Luke's Gospel*. Downers Grove, Ill.: InterVarsity, 1979.

John

1. Book by book: Introduction to John

Author

The author of the Fourth Gospel was the younger of the two sons of Zebedee, a fisherman on the Sea of Galilee, who lived in Bethsaida, where Peter and Andrew his brother, were born, as was Philip.

His mother's name was Salome, who, though not without her imperfections (Matt. 20:20–28), was one of those dear and honored women who accompanied the Lord on one of His preaching circuits through Galilee, ministering to His physical needs; who followed Him to the cross, and bought sweet spices to anoint Him after His burial, but, on bringing them to the grave, on the morning of the First Day of the week, found their loving services gloriously superseded by His resurrection before they arrived.

His father, Zebedee, appears to have been well-off, owning a boat of his own and having hired servants (Mark 1:20).

Our Evangelist, who was a fisherman with his father, was beyond doubt a disciple of John the Baptist, and one of the two who had the first conversation with Jesus. He was called while engaged at his secular occupation (Matt. 4:21, 22), and again on a memorable occasion (Luke 5:1–11), and finally chosen as one of the Twelve Apostles (Matt. 10:2).

He was the youngest of the Twelve–the "Benjamin," as Dan. Costa calls him–and he and James his brother were called, "Boanerges," which the Evangelist Mark (Mark 3:17) explains to mean "Sons of thunder"; no doubt from their natural vehement character.

They and Peter constituted that select triumvirate of Peter, James, and John. These three had been partners before in secular business; now they were the only witnesses of the resurrection of Jairus' daughter (Mark 5:37), the transfiguration, and the agony in the garden (Mark 14:33).

But the highest honor bestowed on this disciple was being allowed to sit at the special place with his Lord at the table, as "the disciple whom Jesus loved" (John 13:23; 20:2; 21:7, 20:24), and to have committed to him by the dying Redeemer the care of His mother (John 19:26, 27). There can be no reasonable doubt that this distinction was due to a sympathy with His own spirit and mind on the part of John which the all-penetrating eye of their common Master observed in none of the other disciples. Although this was probably never seen either in his life or in his ministry by his fellow apostles, it is brought out wonderfully in his writings, which, in Christ-like spirituality, heavenliness, and love, surpass, we may freely say, all the other inspired writings.

After the effusion of the Spirit on the day of Pentecost, we find him in constant but silent company with Peter, the great spokesman in the infant Church until the accession of Paul. While his love to the Lord Jesus drew him spontaneously to the side of His eminent servant, and his chastened vehemence made him ready to stand courageously by him, and suffer with him, in all that his testimony to Jesus might cost him, his modest humility, as the youngest of all the apostles, made him an admiring listener and faithful supporter of his brother apostle rather than a speaker or separate actor. *Ecclesiastical History* is uniform in testifying that John went to Asia Minor; but it is next to certain that this could not have been till after the death both of Peter and Paul; that he lived in Ephesus, from where, as from a center, he looked after the churches of that region, paying them occasional visits; and that he long survived the other apostles. Whether the mother of Jesus died before this, or went with John to Ephesus, where she died and was buried, is not agreed.

In the reign of Domitian (A.D. 81–96) he was banished to "the isle that is called Patmos" (a small rocky and then almost uninhabited island in the Ægean Sea), "for the word of God and for the testimony of Jesus Christ" (Rev. 1:9). Irenaeus and Eusebius say that this took place about the end of Domitian's reign. That he was thrown into a cauldron of boiling oil, and miraculously delivered, is one of those legends which, though reported by Tertullian and Jerome, is entitled to no credit. His return from exile took place during the brief but tolerant reign of Nerva; he died at Ephesus in the reign of Trajan (Eusebius, *Ecclesiastical History,* 3.23), more than ninety years old, according to some; according to others, one hundred; and even one hundred twenty, according to others still. The intermediate number is generally regarded as probably the nearest to the truth.

Date

As to the date of this Gospel, the arguments for its having been composed before the destruction of Jerusalem (though relied on by some superior critics) are of the slenderest nature; such as the expression in John 5:2, "there is at Jerusalem, by the sheep-gate, a pool," etc.; there being no allusion to Peter's martyrdom as having occurred according to the prediction in John 21:18–a thing too well known to require mention. That it was composed long after the destruction of Jerusalem, and after the death of all the other apostles, is most probable, though the precise time cannot be determined. Probably it was before his exile, however; and if we date it between the years 90 and 94, we shall probably be close to the truth.

Readers

As to the readers for whom it was first written, that they were Gentiles we might naturally presume from the lateness of the date; but the numerous explanations of things familiar to every Jew puts this beyond all question.

No doubt was ever thrown on the genuineness and authenticity of this Gospel until the end of the eighteenth century; nor were these embodied in any formal attack on it until Bretschneider, in 1820, issued his famous treatise, *Probabilia*, the conclusions of which he afterwards was candid enough to admit had been satisfactorily disproved. To detail his arguments would be as painful as unnecessary; consisting as they mostly do of assertions regarding the discourses of our Lord recorded in this Gospel which are at odds with every spiritual mind.

The Tubingen school did their best, in their peculiar way of reasoning, to galvanize into fresh life this theory of the post-Johanine date of the Fourth Gospel; and some Unitarian critics still cling to it. But to use the striking language of Van Oosterzee regarding similar speculations on the Third Gospel, "Behold, the feet of them that shall carry it out dead are already at the door" (Acts 5:9). Is there one mind of the least elevation of spiritual discernment that does not see in this Gospel marks of historical truth and a surpassing glory such as none of the other Gospels possess, brightly as they too attest their own verity; and who will not be ready to say that if not historically true, and true *just as it stands*, it never could have been by mortal man composed or conceived?

Special features

Of the peculiarities of this Gospel, we note here only two.

The one is its *reflective* character. While the others are purely *narrative*, the Fourth Evangelist, "pauses, as it were, at every turn," as Dan. Costa says, "at one time to give a reason, at another to fix the attention, to deduce consequences, or make applications, or to give utterance to the language of praise." See John 2:20, 21, 23–25; 4:1, 2; 7:37–39; 11:12, 13, 49–52; 21:18, 19, 22, 23.

The other peculiarity of this Gospel is its *supplementary* character. By this, in the present instance, we mean something more than the studiousness with which he omits many most important particulars in our Lord's history, for no conceivable reason but that they were already familiar as household words to all his readers, through the three preceding Gospels, and his substituting in place of these an immense quantity of the richest matter not found in the other Gospels.

We refer here more particularly to the *nature* of the additions which distinguish this Gospel; particularly the notices of the different Passovers which occurred during our Lord's public ministry, and the record of His teaching at Jerusalem, without which it is not too much to say that we could have had but a most imperfect conception either of the duration of His ministry or of the plan of it. But another feature of these additions is quite as noticeable and not less important. "We find," to use again the words of Dan. Costa "only six of our Lord's miracles recorded in this Gospel, but these are all of the most remarkable kind, and surpass the rest in depth, specialty of application, and fullness of meaning. Of these six we find only one in the other three Gospels—the multiplication of the loaves. That miracle chiefly, it would seem, on account of the important instructions of which it furnished the occasion (John 6:1–71), is here recorded anew. The five other tokens of divine power are distinguished from among the many recorded in the three other Gospels by their furnishing a still higher display of power and command over the ordinary laws and course of nature. Thus we find recorded here the first of all the miracles that Jesus wrought—the changing of water into wine (John 2:1–11), the cure of the nobleman's son *at a distance* (John 4:43–54); of the numerous cures of the lame and the paralytic by the word of Jesus, only one—of the man impotent for *thirty and eight years* (John 5:1–9); of the many cures of the blind, one only—of the man *born blind* (John 9:1–12); the restoration of Lazarus, not from a deathbed, like Jairus' daughter, nor from a bier, like the widow of Nain's son, but *from the grave*, and after lying there four days, and there sinking into corruption (John 11:1–44); and lastly, after His resurrection, the miraculous draught of fishes on the Sea of Tiberias (John 21:5–11). But these are all recorded chiefly to give occasion for the record of those astonishing discourses and conversations, alike with friends and with foes, with His disciples and with the multitude which they drew forth."

David Brown

Detailed outline

Part One: Introduction 1:1–51

I. Introducing Jesus, the Christ: 1:1–18
- A. Jesus, the Word: 1:1–3
- B. Jesus, the life and light: 1:4–13
- C. Jesus in the flesh: 1:14–18
- D. Jesus, the fullness of God's grace: 1:16–18

II. The witness of John: 1:19–34
- A. To Jesus the Messiah: 1:19–28
- B. To Jesus the Lamb and the Son: 1:29–36
  1. The baptism: 1:29–34
  2. The confession: 1:35–36

III. The first disciples: 1:35–51
- A. Andrew: 1:34–40
- B. Simon: 1:40–42
- C. Philip: 1:43–44
- D. Nathaniel: 1:45–51

Part Two: Public Ministry 2:1–12:50

I. Turning water into wine: 2:1–10

II. Authority over the temple: 2:12–25
- A. Going to Jerusalem: 2:12–13
- B. The cleansing of the temple: 2:14–22
- C. Reaction to the cleansing: 2:23–25

III. Conversation with Nicodemus: 3:1–21

IV. Verification of Jesus by John the Baptist: 3:22–36

V. A mission among the Samaritans: 4:1–42

VI. A miracle in Galilee: 4:43–54
- A. Going to Galilee: 4:43–45
- B. Healing of a nobleman's son: 4:46–54

VII. Sickness to health on the Sabbath: 5:1–47
- A. Healing on the Sabbath: 5:1–9
- B. The Jews and the man who was healed: 5:10–13
- C. Jesus and the man who was healed: 5:14
- D. The Jews and the man who was healed: 5:15–18
- E. A sermon following the healing: 5:19–47
  1. Jesus claims equality with God: 5:19–29
  2. Witnesses to the divine claims of Jesus: 5:30–40
  3. Condemnation of unbelief: 5:40–47

VIII. Christ the Bread of Life: 6:1–15
- A. The setting: 6:1–4
- B. The problem: 6:5–7
- C. The feeding of the five thousand: 6:8–13
- D. Disappointing results: 6:14–15

IX. Fear into faith in the midst of a storm:

6:16–21

X. The sequel to the feeding of the 5,000: 6:22–71
  A. The "five thousand" reassembled: 6:22–24
  B. Teaching about the Bread of Life: 6:25–71
    1. The bread of Moses compared to that of Jesus: 6:25–34
    2. The bread that nourishes eternal life: 6:35–40
    3. The living bread from Heaven: 6:41–51
    4. The bread of Christ's death: 6:52–59
  C. Results of the dialogue: 6:60–71
    1. Many turned back: 6:60–66
    2. Twelve were left: 6:67–71

XI. Jesus at the Jerusalem feast: 7:1–53
  A. Journey to Jerusalem: 7:1–10
  B. Jesus in Jerusalem: A controversial figure: 7:11–13
  C. Inconsistency of Jesus' critics: 7:14–24
  D. Jesus: The object of speculation: 7:25–36
  E. The proclamation of Jesus: 7:37–39
  F. The divided crowd: 7:40–44
  G. The divided council: 7:45–53

XII. Teaching in the temple: 8:1–59
  A. The woman caught in the act of adultery: 8:1–11
  B. Jesus the light of the world: 8:12–20
  C. Preview of the cross and reaction of the crowd: 8:21–30
  D. The Jews and discipleship: 8:31–59
    1. Freedom through knowledge of truth: 8:31–36
    2. Sons of Abraham: 8:37–40
    3. Sons of Satan: 8:41–47
    4. An accusation about being demon possessed: 8:48–52
  E. Reaction to the teaching: Jesus versus Abraham: 8:52–59

XIII. Jesus heals a blind man: 9:1–41
  A. Man blind from birth is healed: 9:1–7
  B. Reaction of the blind man's neighbors: 9:8–12
  C. Reaction of the Pharisees: 9:13–34
    1. Interview with the blind man: 9:13–17
    2. Interview with his parents: 9:18–23
    3. Another interview with the blind man: 9:24–34
  D. The conclusion: Jesus, the blind man, and the Pharisees: 9:35–41

XIV. The pastoral dialogue: 10:1–42
  A. The True Shepherd of the sheep: 10:1–6
  B. The Door to the sheepfold: 10:7–10
  C. The Good Shepherd of the flock: 10:11–18

XV. Mounting hostility towards Jesus: 10:19–42
  A. Division over demon-possession: 10:19–21
  B. A demand for plain speaking: 10:22–24
  C. Jesus' response: 10:25–30
  D. Jesus escapes being stoned: 10:31–39
  E. Refuge beyond Jordan: 10:40–42

XVI. Death turned into life: 11:1–44
  A. The setting: 11:1–6
  B. The plan: 11:7–16
  C. Dialogue on the significance of the following event: 11:17–27
  D. The hopelessness of death: 11:28–39
  E. The raising of Lazarus: 11:40–44
  F. Results of the miracle: 11:45–12:11

1. Reaction of some who believed: 11:45
2. Reaction of the council: 11:46–53
3. Implications for the security of Jesus: 11:54–57
4. Anointed for death: 12:1–8
5. Various reactions: 12:9–11

XVII. King Jesus: 12:12–50
A. Increasing popularity of the King: 12:12–19
B. The visit of the Greeks to the King: 12:20–22
C. The death of the King: 12:23–50
1. Prediction of the King's death: 12:23–27
2. Assurance from the Father to the King: 12:28–30
3. Witness by the King: 12:30–36
4. Unbelief in the King: 12:37–43
5. Belief in the King: 12:44–50

Part Three: Private Ministry 13:1–17:26

I. The Last Supper: 13:1–38
A. An object lesson: Foot washing: 13:1–11
1. The occasion: 13:1–3
2. The act: 13:4–5
3. The interpretation of the act: 13:6–17
B. Exposure of Judas: 13:18–30
C. Prediction of Jesus' departure: 13:31–35
D. Prediction of Peter's denials: 13:36–38

II. A message of preparation and comfort: 14:1–27
A. The preparation: 14:1–4
B. The way: 14:5–15
C. The Comforter: 14:16–21,26
D. Manifestation to His own: 14:22–31

III. Union with Jesus: 15:1–27
A. Union with the vine: 15:1–8
B. Union in love: 15:9–17
C. Separation from the world: 15:18–25
D. Union with the Comforter: 15:26–27

IV. Preview of the future: 16:1–33
A. Coming persecution foretold: 16:1–6
B. The Comforter to come: 16:7–16
C. Prophecy of Christ's return to Heaven: 16:16
D. The perplexed disciples: 16:17–19
E. Turning sorrow to joy: 16:20–30
F. Faith for the future: 16:31–33

V. The prayer of Jesus: 17:1–26
A. For Himself: 17:1–8
B. For His present disciples: 17:9–19
C. For His future followers: 17:20–26

Part Four: The Final Days 18:1–19:42

I. The capture: 18:1–14
A. Meeting in the Garden: 18:1
B. Betrayal of Judas: 18:2–3
C. The non-resistance of Jesus: 18:4–9
D. Violence rejected by Jesus: 18:10–11
E. Jesus taken to Annas: 18:12–14

II. Peter's first denial: 18:15–18

III. The hearing before Annas: 18:19–24
A. Testimony of defense: 18:19–21
B. Judgment by Annas: 18:22–24

IV. The second denial by Peter: 18:25–26

V. The third denial by Peter: 18:26–27

VI. The hearing before Pilate: 18:28–19:16
A. Public hearing: 18:28–32
B. Private hearing: 18:33–38
C. Barabbas: 18:38–40
D. Abuse by the Romans: 19:1–3
E. Death demanded: 19:4–8
F. Pardon rejected: 19:9–16

VII. The death of Jesus: 19:17–30
- A. The crucifixion: 19:17–18
- B. The obituary title: 19:19–22
- C. A show of unconcern: 19:23–24
- D. The bereaved: 19:25–27
- E. The death of Jesus: 19:28–30

VIII. The burial: 19:31–42
- A. Inspection of the body: 19:31–37
- B. The burial: 19:38–42

Part Five: Resurrection And Appearances 20:1–21:23

I. The resurrection of Jesus: 20:1–31
- A. The open tomb: 20:1–10
- B. The testimony of two angels: 20:11–13
- C. The witness of the risen Lord: 20:14–29
  1. To Mary Magdalene: 20:14–18
  2. To the disciples without Thomas: 20:19–25
  3. To the disciples and Thomas: 20:26–29
- D. A summary conclusion: 20:30–31

II. A meeting by the sea: 21:1–23
- A. An unsuccessful night of fishing: 21:1–3
- B. Jesus' solution: 21:4–6
- C. Breakfast with Jesus: 21:7–14
- D. Peter reinstated: 21:15–19
- E. Origin of a legend: that the disciple John would never die: 21:20–23

Conclusion 21:24–25

I. John is the disciple testifying and writing: 21:24

II. There are many other things Jesus did which are not recorded by John: 21:25

2. Helpful summaries of John's Gospel

Bird's eye view 1

John's Gospel has a very different feel about it from the first three Gospels of Matthew, Mark, and Luke. It sometimes reads like a Gospel tract as the author wants to bring his readers to belief in Jesus.

Bird's eye view 2

Light 1–12
Love 13–17
Live 18–21

Reading plan

The following reading plan, taking one reading per day, enables you to read through John's Gospel in forty days.

John 1:1–1:34
John 1:35–1:51
John 2:1–2:25
John 3:1–3:21
John 3:22–3:26
John 4:1–4:26
John 4:27–4:54
John 5:1–5:18
John 5:19–5:47
John 6:1–6:24
John 6:25–6:51
John 6:52–6:71
John 7:1–7:24
John 7:25–7:39
John 7:40–7:53
John 8:1–8:20
John 8:21–8:47

John 8:48–8:59
John 9:1–9:12
John 9:13–9:41
John 10:1–10:21
John 10:22–10:42
John 11:1–11:27
John 11:28–11:57
John 12:1–12:26
John 12:27–12:50
John 13:1–13:20
John 13:21–13:38
John 14:1–14:14
John 14:15–14:31
John 15:1–15:27
John 16:1–16:33
John 17:1–17:26
John 18:1–18:24
John 18:25–18:40
John 19:1–19:16
John 19:17–19:42
John 20:1–20:18
John 20:19–21:31
John 21:1–21:25

Verses to memorize

John 3:30

He must increase, but I must decrease. KJV

John 4:24

God is a Spirit: and they that worship him must worship him in spirit and in truth. KJV

John 7:38

He that believeth on me, as the scripture hath said, out of his belly shall flow rivers of living water. KJV

John 8:36

If the Son therefore shall make you free, ye shall be free indeed. KJV

John 10:10

The thief cometh not, but for to steal, and to kill, and to destroy: I am come that they might have life, and that they might have it more abundantly. KJV

John 11:25

Jesus said unto her, I am the resurrection, and the life: he that believeth in me, though he were dead, yet shall he live: KJV

John 13:35

By this shall all men know that ye are my disciples, if ye have love one to another. KJV

John 15:7

If ye abide in me, and my words abide in you, ye shall ask what ye will, and it shall be done unto you. KJV

John 16:33

These things I have spoken unto you, that in me ye might have peace. In the world ye shall have tribulation: but be of good cheer; I have overcome the world. KJV

John 20:21

Then said Jesus to them again, Peace be unto you: as my Father hath sent me, even so send I you. KJV

Statistics

Fourth New Testament book
Fourth Gospel
21 chapters
878 verses
19,099 words
Number of Old Testament quotations and allusions in John: 40.

Names/titles given, and quotes about

Kata Ioannen, "According to John."

Fourth Gospel.

"A spiritual Gospel," Clement of Alexandria.

God's last word to humankind.

"The Gospel of John, one of the twelve apostles, which was spoken in the city of Ephesus, in the Greek Roman tongue." Persic version

"The heart of Christ."

"The bosom of Christ."

"Crown of the Gospels."

Symbol for

Eagle: the symbol for John's Gospel is the eagle, a winged creature that is able to soar to great heights and whose keen vision is able to penetrate to the depths.

3. Helpful keys to turn to in understanding John's Gospel

Key words/phrases

God as Father, more than 100 times
Jew, more than 60 times
Believe, nearly 100 times
Eternal life, 35 times
Light, 25 times
Judgment/Judge, 24 times
Water, 24 times
Bread, 23 times
Witness, 21 times
Love 20 times
He that believeth, 3:36.
Faith
Life
Spirit
Truth

Key verses

John 3:16; 20:31

Themes to study

Summary

The life of Christ, including important conversations not recorded in the other Gospels.

John portrays Jesus' deity. He is depicted as God's Son in order to ignite faith in his readers.

John's Gospel revolves around seven miraculous signs and seven "I am" sayings.

Other important themes are:

The Holy Spirit
Jesus' death for sinners
Jesus and the Father
Eternal life

Details of themes

The seven witnesses

John presents seven witness who give their testimony that Jesus is the Son of God. The seven witnesses and what they said are listed below:

1. John 1:34 (1:19–36)
2. John 1:49 (43–51)
3. John 6:69 (66–69)
4. John 11:27
5. John 20:28
6. John 20:31
7. John 10:36 (31–47).

All the "I ams" of Jesus

Jesus used the same expression "I am" to refer to himself, as the Lord God did of himself when he spoke to Moses in the burning bush. It is clear from John 8:58–59 that the Jews realized that Jesus was claiming to have existed before his human life on earth, that he was divine, for they took up stones to stone him.

- I am the Messiah
  John 4:26
- I am the bread of life
  John 6:35
- I am from above
  John 8:23
- I am the eternal one
  John 8:58
- I am the light of the world
  John 9:5
- I am the door
  John 10:7
- I am God's Son
  John 10:36
- I am the resurrection and the life
  John 11:25
- I am your Teacher and Lord
  John 13:13
- I am the way and the truth and the life
  John 14:6
- I am the true vine
  John 15:1

Also, see Revelation 1:8 for Jesus as the Alpha and Omega, the first and the last, Revelation 1:17.

The seven "I ams"

From the total list of the "I am" sayings of Jesus, the following seven have been selected, and have become known as the "seven 'I am' sayings of Jesus."

Each one sheds light on Jesus' divine nature.

1. Bread
   "I am the bread of life; he who comes to Me shall not hunger." John 6:35
2. Light
   "I am the light of the world; he who fallows Me shall not walk in the darkness, but shall have the light of life." John 8:12
3. Gate
   "I am the gate; if anyone enters through Me, he shall be saved, and shall go in and out, and find pasture." John 10:9
4. Good Shepherd
   "I am the good shepherd; the good shepherd lays down His life for His sheep."
   John 10:11
5. Resurrection and life
   "I am the resurrection and the life; he who believes in Me shall live even if he dies."
   John 11:25
6. Way, truth, life
   "I am the way, and the truth, and the life; no one comes to the Father, but through Me." John 14:6
7. True vine
   "I am the true vine, and My Father is the vinedresser." John 15:1

"Verily, verily" and the Christian's new spiritual life

In John's Gospel the expression, "verily, verily," ("I tell you the truth" NIV) is used to introduce an especially important saying of Jesus.

The necessity of this new life

John 3:3

How to obtain this new life

John 5:24

How to keep this new life

John 6:53

How to spend this new life

John 12:24

How to live out this new life John 14:12

Eternal life

Matthew, Mark, and Luke describe eternal life as "the kingdom of God." John uses the words "life" and "eternal life" instead of the "the kingdom of God." This eternal life is linked with the second birth, or the new birth.

See John 1:4, 12–13;
3:3–7, 16, 36;
4:14, 36;
5:21, 24–29;
6:27, 40, 47, 54, 57–58, 68;
10:28;
11:25;
12:25, 50;
17:2–3.

Lack of parables

There are no parables in John's Gospel. The word "parable" occurs only once, in John 10:6, but even there it is not the usual Greek word parabole but paroimia. The way John speaks about the Good Shepherd is in the style of a discourse, than in the form of a parable.

(Compare Luke's parable about the lost sheep in Luke 15 to see the difference).

Jesus and God the Father

The word "Father" occurs 140 times in this Gospel. John's Gospel continuously teaches that Jesus is God's Son.

See John 1:1–18;
3:13, 31, 35;
5:17–23, 26–27, 30;
6:38, 46, 57;
7:16–17, 29;
8:28–29, 38, 42;
12:44–45, 49–50;
13:3, 31–32;
14:7–11; 20, 28, 31;
15:23–24;
16:15, 28, 32;
17:1–2, 4–5, 10–11, 21–23;
20:17.

The name Jesus

John uses the name "Jesus" almost invariably, in preference to the name "Christ."

The name "Jesus" comes 242 times in John, compared with 143 times in Matthew, and 84 times in Luke.

Other names John uses for Jesus are:
"the Son" 19 times,
"the Son of God" 9 times,
"the Son of man" 13 times,
"the Life" 22 times, and
"the Light" 25 times.

John also calls Jesus:
"the Holy One of God"
"the Lamb of God" and
"the King of Israel."

John refers to Jesus 333 times in his Gospel.

Jesus in every chapter of John's Gospel

Chapter 1 Jesus the Son of God
Chapter 2 Jesus the Son of Man
Chapter 3 Jesus the divine Teacher
Chapter 4 Jesus the Soul-winner world
Chapter 5 Jesus the great Healer
Chapter 6 Jesus the bread of life
Chapter 7 Jesus the water of life
Chapter 8 Jesus the Defender of the weak
Chapter 9 Jesus the Light of the world
Chapter 10 Jesus the Good Shepherd
Chapter 11 Jesus the Prince of life
Chapter 12 Jesus the King
Chapter 13 Jesus the Servant
Chapter 14 Jesus the Consoler
Chapter 15 Jesus the true Vine
Chapter 16 Jesus Giver of the Holy Spirit
Chapter 17 Jesus the Intercessor
Chapter 18 Jesus the Model Sufferer
Chapter 19 Jesus the Savior
Chapter 20 Jesus the Conqueror of Death
Chapter 21 Jesus the Restorer of the penitent

Unique features in John's Gospel

There are many conversations, people, and incidents in the life of Jesus that are unique to John's Gospel. The following list details parts of Jesus' life that are not mentioned in Matthew, Mark, or Luke.

- Identified as "the Lamb of God" by John the Baptist (1:29,36).
- Calls His first disciples (1:35–51).
- Turns water into wine at a wedding in Cana (2:1–11).
- Drives the moneychangers out of the temple near the beginning of his ministry (2:13–22).
- Teaches Nicodemus about being born again (3:1–21).
- Remains in Judea with his disciples where they baptize disciples. John the Baptist says who Jesus is (3:22–36).
- Encounters the Samaritan woman (4:5–42).
- Heals a nobleman's son (4:46–54).
- Heals a lame man at Bethesda pool (5:1–15).
- Preaches to the crowd who had been miraculously fed and refers to himself as "the bread of life" (6:22–71).
- Teaches in the temple during the Feast of Booths where the crowd is divided over his claim to be the Christ (7:1–53).
- Forgives a woman caught in adultery (8: 1–11).
- Refers to himself as "the light of the world" (8:12).
- Calls the Pharisees children of the devil and claims to be the I AM of Abraham's day (8:21–59).
- Gives sight to a beggar born blind (9:1–41).
- Declares himself to be the good shepherd and the door to the sheepfold (10:1–21).
- Claims to be one with the Father–prompting the Jews, for a third time, to try to stone him (10:22–41).
- Raises Lazarus from the dead (11:1–44).
- Withdraws from the public after the Jewish leaders plan to capture and to kill him (11:45–57).
- Prays to the Father, who answers him with a voice from heaven that was heard by those around him (12:27–30).
- Washes the disciples' feet (13:1–20).
- Gives parting words of exhortation and

encouragement to His disciples (14–16).

- Prays for his disciples and for all future Christians (17:1–26).
- Put on trial before Annas (18:12–14,19–23).
- Entrusts his mother into John's care (19:26,27).
- His side pierced by a Roman soldier (19:31–37).
- Appears to disciples and dispels Thomas' doubt that he had risen from the dead (20:26–29).
- Appears to seven disciples by the Sea of Galilee (21:1–14)
- Restores Peter, instructs him to care for his followers, and predicts how he will die (21:15–22).

Jesus' divinity

Jesus' divinity is acknowledged by numerous people in John's Gospel:

By Nathanael
John 1:49

By the Samaritans
John 4:42

By Martha
John 11:27

By Thomas
John 20:28

Truth misunderstood

In the first eight chapters of John's Gospel there are the following examples of truth being misunderstood.

- Christ's body is confused with the earthly temple, John 2:20
- The new birth is confused with the physical birth, John 3:4
- The water of life is confused with physica water, John 4:15
- Spiritual nourishment is confused with food, John 4:33
- Feeding spiritually on Christ's Spirit is confused with eating his body and drinking his blood, John 6:52
- Christ's departure is confused with suicide, John 8:22
- Spiritual bondage is confused with physical slavery, John 8:33; 11:12

The Holy Spirit in John's Gospel: in summary

- The person and work of the Holy Spirit is a major theme in John's Gospel:
- He is the ever-present Counselor, John 14:16
- He is the Teacher who reminds us about Jesus' teaching, John 14:26
- He is the Spirit of truth who gives testimony about Jesus, 15:26
- He convicts the world about sin and righteousness, 16:7,8
- He guides Christians into the truth, 16:13
- He brings glory to Jesus, 16:14
- He makes known to Christians what belongs to Jesus, 16:15

The Holy Spirit in John's Gospel: in detail

John wrote more about the Holy Spirit than the other gospel writers. The Spirit is the gift of the Son of God to us. Some information about the Spirit is given in the early chapters of John, but most of the teaching appears Jesus' private conversation with his disciples in the upper room.

- Jesus' public ministry (1–12)
- John the Baptist testified that he saw the

Holy Spirit descend on Jesus (1:29–34). John saw this as a sign that Jesus was the Son of God (v.34). He announced that Jesus would baptize with the Holy Spirit (v.33).

- From other passages in the first twelve chapters of John's Gospel we learn:
- We are born again by water and by the Holy Spirit (3:5–8).
- The Holy Spirit is not limited (3:34).
- The Holy Spirit leads us in true worship (4:24).
- The Holy Spirit gives spiritual life (6:63).
- Jesus gives the Holy Spirit to believers (7:38, 39).
- Jesus' private ministry (13–16)
- Jesus gives a great deal of important teaching about the Holy Spirit in the upper room.

1. Titles given to the Holy Spirit

a. Helper: 14:16, 26; 15:26; 16:7.

The Greek word means "one called alongside," and this idea is conveyed by the words "Helper, Counselor, and Comforter."

Jesus promised to send the Spirit to do for the disciples what He had been doing.

b. Spirit of truth: 14:17; 15:26; 16:13

Jesus promised that the Holy Spirit would reveal truth to the disciples.

2. The work of the Holy Spirit

He would guide the disciples into truth (16:13).

He would glorify Christ (16:14).

He would give believers the power to witness (15:26, 27).

He would help the disciples to remember the truths Jesus taught (14:26).

He would convict people about their sin (16:1–8).

3. The Holy Spirit is a gift

The Spirit is said to be the gift of the Father in John 14:16, 26, and the gift of the Son in John 15:26; 16:7, which emphasizes the unity of the Father and the Son.

4. When the Holy Spirit will be given

Jesus taught that the Holy Spirit would not be sent until after he had left his disciples (16:7, see 7:39).

5. The limits of the Holy Spirit

The Holy Spirit is "limited" in the sense that he only lives in believers (14:17).

John foreshadows Pentecost

Pentecost was foreshadowed when the risen Jesus breathed on the disciples and they received the Holy Spirit (20:22,23). On the Day of Pentecost the Spirit came in fulfillment of Christ's promise (Acts 2:1–12).

Prophetic warnings and promises of Jesus found in John's Gospel

- Jesus foretells his resurrection to be within three days of his burial, John 2:19–21
- His crucifixion, and its result, John 3:14–16
- The substitution of the new for the old dispensation, John 4:21–24
- The general resurrection of the dead, John 5:25–29
- His flesh to be food for his people, with the promise of resurrection and eternal life, John 6:39, 40, 54–58
- One of the Twelve has a devil, John 6:70, 71
- His Ascension, John 7:34

- The gift of the Holy Spirit, John 7:37–39
- The way he would die and its result, John 12:32, 33
- Peter's denial, John 13:38
- Several prophecies about the Holy Spirit, John 14:16, 17, 26; 15:26, 27; 16:7–14
- His ascension, John 16:28
- His disciples to forsake him, John 16:32
- His ascension, John 20:17
- Peter's crucifixion, John 21:18, 19

Jesus in John

In John Jesus is the Son of God.

Lessons to learn from John's Gospel

Jesus is the only way to God.

Jesus asks us to respond to him and his love.

Eternal life starts now.

With the help of the Holy Spirit we are to witness to Jesus.

4. Chapter by chapter: outline of every chapter of John

John 1

Matthew Henry's introduction

The scope and design of this chapter is to confirm our faith in Christ as the eternal Son of God, and the true Messiah and Savior of the world, that we may be brought to receive him, and rely on him, as our Prophet, Priest, and King, and to give up ourselves to be ruled, and taught, and saved by him.

Dr. Adam Clarke's analysis of chapter

The eternity of the Divine Logos, or Word of God, the dispenser of light and life, 1–5.

The mission of John the Baptist, 6–13.

The incarnation of the Logos or Word of God, 14.

John's testimony about the Logos, 15–18.

The priests and Levites question him about his mission and his baptism, 19–22.

His answer, 23–28.

His additional testimony on seeing Christ, 29–34.

He points out Jesus to two of his disciples, who then follow Jesus, 35–37.

Christ's speaks to them, 38, 39.

Andrew invites his brother, Simon Peter; Jesus speaks to him, 40–42. Christ calls Philip, and Philip invites Nathanael, 43–46.

Christ's estimate of Nathanael, 47.

A remarkable conversation between him and this disciple, 48–61.

A detailed analysis of chapter

The divinity of Christ. (1–5)

His divine and human nature. (6–14)

John the Baptist's testimony to Christ. (15–18)

John's public testimony about Christ. (19–28)

Other testimonies of John about Christ. (29–36)

Andrew and Simon Peter follow Jesus. (37–42)

Philip and Nathanael are called to follow Jesus. (43–51)

Key verse

Verse 1: "In the beginning was the Word, and the Word was with God, and the Word was God."

Key word / key phrase

Verse 17, "grace and truth came through Jesus Christ."

Key event / key person / key theme

The Word becomes flesh

Key thought

Note how John opens his Gospel is a totally different way from the other three Gospels.

Key thing to look out for

How does someone become a child of God?

Key Bible cross-reference

Verse 51. See Genesis 28:12.

Key "by way of explanation"

Verse 29, "Lamb of God." This verse and verse 36 are the only places where this expression is found in the Bible. But under the Old Testament law, lambs were sacrificed regularly for the sins of the people. See Isaiah 53:7; Jeremiah 11:19.

Key "Quotable Quote"

"The four Gospels all had the same purpose: to point out Christ. The first three Gospels show his body, so to speak, but John shows his soul. For this reason I usually say that this Gospel is a key to understanding the rest; for whoever understands the power of Christ strikingly pictured here will then profit by reading what the others tell about the Redeemer who appeared."

John Calvin

John 2

Matthew Henry's introduction

In this chapter, we have the account of Jesus' first miracle, the account of the first Passover he kept at Jerusalem after he began his public ministry; his driving the buyers and sellers out of the temple; and the sign he gave to those who argued with him about this; with an account of some who almost believed in him, for some time, but he knew them too well to put any confidence in them.

Dr. Adam Clarke's analysis of chapter

The miracle at Cana in Galilee, where Jesus changed water into wine, 1–11.

He goes to Capernaum, 12.

He cleanses the temple at the feast of the Passover, 13–17.

The Jews require a miracle, as a proof that he had authority to do these things, 18.

In answer he refers to his own death and resurrection, 19–22.

Many believe on him while at the feast of the Passover, to whom Jesus would not trust himself, 23– 25.

A detailed analysis of chapter

The miracle at Cana. (1–11)

Christ throw the traders out of the temple. (12–22)

Many believe in Christ. (23–25)

Key verse

Verse 11: "This, the first of his miraculous signs, Jesus performed at Cana in Galilee. He thus revealed his glory, and his disciples put their faith in him."

Key word / key phrase

Verse 1, "a wedding . . . at Cana."

Key event / key person / key theme

The wedding at Cana

Key thought

John always refers to Jesus' miracles as "signs," verse 11. In this way he highlights the fact that the purpose of the miracles was to point to the identity of Jesus and stimulate faith.

Key thing to look out for

The fine wine was a symbol of the new covenant inaugurated by Jesus. What was the effect of this first sign?

Key Bible cross-reference

Verse 17. See Psalm 69:9.

Key "by way of explanation"

Verse 1, "a wedding." Celebrations after a wedding often went on for up to a week. To run out of wine would have been more than a slight embarrassment. It would have been thought of as a major sign of inhospitality.

Key "Quotable Quote"

"I prefer you to make mistakes in kindness than work miracles in unkindness."

Mother Teresa of Calcutta

John 3

Matthew Henry's introduction

In this chapter we have, Christ's discourse with Nicodemus, a Pharisee, about the great mysteries of the gospel, in which he here privately instructs him and John the Baptist's discourse with his disciples about Christ.

Dr. Adam Clarke's analysis of chapter

The conversation between Nicodemus and Jesus, about the new birth and faith, 1–15.

The love of God, the source of human salvation, 16.

Who are condemned, and who are approved of, 17–21.

Jesus and his disciples come to Judea, and baptize, 22.

John baptizes in Aenon, 23, 24.

The disciples of John and the Pharisees argue about purification, 25.

The conversation between John and his disciples about Christ, in which the excellence, perfection, and privileges, of the Christian dispensation are pointed out, 26–36.

A detailed analysis of chapter

Christ's conversation with Nicodemus. (1–21)

John the Baptist's testimony about Christ. (22–36)

Key verse

Verse 16: "For God so loved the world that he gave his one and only Son, that whoever believes in him shall not perish but have eternal life."

Key word / key phrase

Verse 1, "a member of the Jewish ruling council."

Key event / key person / key theme

Jesus and Nicodemus

Key thought

Note the context of the most famous verse in the Bible, verse 16.

Key thing to look out for

Jesus insists on the necessity of the new birth.

Key Bible cross-reference

Verse 14. See Numbers 21:9.

Key "by way of explanation"

Verse 2, "at night." Nicodemus came to Jesus at night. Maybe he wanted to speak with Jesus when others would not see him, or maybe he wanted an unhurried time with Jesus, which the bustle of Jesus' day would have prevented.

Key "Quotable Quote"

"The Church is largely wasting her time in talking politics, and in imagining that, if you give people the Christian ethic and urge them to practice it, the problems of the world will be solved. It cannot be done: regeneration is essential."

D. Martyn Lloyd-Jones

John 4

Matthew Henry's introduction

It was, more than any thing else, the glory of the land of Israel, that it was Emmanuel's land (Is. 8:8), not only the place of his birth, but the scene of his preaching and miracles. This land in our Savior's time was divided into three parts: Judea in the south, Galilee in the north, and Samaria lying between them. Now, in this chapter, we have Christ in each of these three parts of that land.

I. Leaving Judea.
II. Passing through Samaria.
III. We find him staying for some time in Galilee where he healed a nobleman's son.

Dr. Adam Clarke's analysis of chapter

Jesus, because the Pharisees are upset that he made many disciples, leaves Judea to go to Galilee, 1–3.

Passing through Samaria Jesus comes to Sychar, and rests at Jacob's well, 4–6.

While his disciples were gone to the city to buy meat, a woman from Samaria comes to draw water. Jesus has a long conversation with her about the spiritual nature of his teaching, the perfection of the Divine nature, and the purity of his worship, 7–24.

On learning that he was the Messiah, she leaves her water jug, and goes to inform the people of Samaria, 25–30.

Jesus' conversation with his disciples in her absence, 31–38.

Many of the Samaritans believe on him, 39–42

He stays two days with them, and goes into Galilee, 43–45.

He comes to Cana, and heals a royal official's son, who then believes in him, with all his family, 46–54.

A detailed analysis of chapter

Christ goes to Galilee. (1–3)

His conversation with the Samaritan woman. (4–26)

The effects of Christ's conversation with the woman of Samaria. (27–42)

Christ heals the nobleman's son. (43–54)

Key verse

Verse 42: "We no longer believe just because of what you said; now we have heard for ourselves, and we know that this man really is the Savior of the world."

Key word / key phrase

Verse 14, "a spring of water welling up to eternal life."

Key event / key person / key theme

Jesus and the woman of Samaria

Key thought

This woman witnessed immediately and many Samaritans believed in Jesus.

Key thing to look out for

Note how Jesus turns the conversation to spiritual matters.

Key Bible cross-reference

Verse 9. See Ezra 4:1–5.

Key "by way of explanation"

Verse 42, "the Savior of the world." Only John, in 1 John 4:14 and here in this verse, uses this expression. It points to Jesus as the Savior, and to his global significance. John gives only seven "signs" (miracles) in his Gospel. The healing of the nobleman's son is the second.

Key "Quotable Quote"

"He who in his preaching neglects to lead men to a fuller knowledge of God and to the way of eternal salvation may be called an idle declaimer, but not a preacher of the Gospel."

Pope Benedict XV

John 5

Matthew Henry's introduction

We have in the gospels a faithful record of all that Jesus began both to do and to teach, Acts 1:1. These two are interwoven, because what he taught explained what he did, and what he did confirmed what he taught. Accordingly, we have in this chapter a miracle and a sermon.

I. The miracle was the cure of a man who had been ill for thirty-eight years.

II. The sermon was Christ's vindication of himself before the Sanhedrim, when he was prosecuted as a criminal for healing the man on the Sabbath day.

Dr. Adam Clarke's analysis of chapter

A man who had been ill for thirty-eight years is healed on the Sabbath, 1–9.

The Jews object to this, persecute Jesus, and seek to kill him, because he had healed on the Sabbath, 10–16.

Our Lord vindicates his conduct, and shows, from the testimony of the Father, the Scriptures, John the Baptist, and his own deeds, that he came from God, to be the light and salvation of the world, 17–39.

He reproves the Jews for their obstinacy, 40;
hatred to God, 41, 42;
pride, 43, 44;
and disbelief of their own law, 45–47.

A detailed analysis of chapter

The healing at the pool of Bethesda. (1–9)
The Jews' displeasure. (10–16)
Christ reproves the Jews. (17–23)
Christ's teaching. (24–47)

Key verse

Verse 14: "See, you are well again. Stop sinning or something worse may happen to you."

Key word / key phrase

Verse 16, "the Jews persecuted him."

Key event / key person / key theme

Jesus faces opposition

Key thought

Verse 24 must rank as one of the clearest verses about eternal life to be found in the Gospels.

Key thing to look out for

What Jesus looked for in people was the love of God in their hearts, verse 42.

Key Bible cross-reference

Verse 29. See Daniel 12:2.

Key "by way of explanation"

Verse 30, "By myself I can do nothing." Jesus often explained that without his heavenly Father he was unable to achieve anything.

Key "Quotable Quote"

"It is a destructive addition to add anything to Christ."

Richard Sibbes

John 6

Matthew Henry's introduction

In this chapter we have,

I. The miracle of the loaves.

II. Christ's walking on the water.

III. The people's flocking after him to Capernaum.

IV. His words to them, caused by the miracle of the loaves, in which he reproves them for seeking human food, and directs them to spiritual food, showing them how they must labor for spiritual food, and what that spiritual food is.

V. Their objection to what he said, and the reproof he gave them for this.

VI. The apostasy of many from him, and his discourse with his disciples who stayed with him.

Dr. Adam Clarke's analysis of chapter

Jesus passes the sea of Tiberias, and a large crowd follow him, 1–4.

He feeds five thousand with five loaves, and two fishes, 5–13.

They acknowledge him to be the prophet who would come into the world, 14.

They try to make him their king; and he withdraws from the crowd, 15.

The disciples take a boat towards Capernaum, and are caught up in a storm, 16–18.

Christ comes to them, walking on the water, 19–21.

The people get into boats and follow him, 22–24.

He reproves their unspiritual motives, 25–27.

They profess a desire to be instructed, 28.

Christ preaches to them, and shows them that he is the bread of life, and that those who reject him are without excuse, 29–40.

They are offended, and complain, 41, 42.

He asserts and illustrates his previous discourse, 43–51.

They again complain, and Christ gives farther explanations, 52–59.

Several of the disciples are do not accept his assertion, that unless they ate his flesh and drank his blood they could not have life, 60.

He shows them that his words are to be spiritually understood, 61–65.

Several of them withdraw from him, 66.

He questions the twelve, whether they will also forsake him, and Peter answers for them all, 67–69.

Christ exposes the treachery of Judas, 70, 71.

A detailed analysis of chapter

Five thousand miraculously fed. (1–14)

Jesus walks on the sea. (15–21)

He teaches about spiritual food. (22–27)

His teaching to the crowds. (28–65)

Many disciples turned back from following Christ. (66–71)

Key verse

Verse 15: "Jesus, knowing that they intended to come and make him king by force, withdrew again to a mountain by himself."

Key word / key phrase

Verse 35, "I am the bread of life."

Key event / key person / key theme

Jesus is the bread of life

Key thought

Jesus' actions, verses 1–15, always shed light on who he is, verse 35.

Key thing to look out for

Grumbling has no place among those who seek God, verse 43.

Key Bible cross-reference

Verse 45. See Isaiah 54:13.

Key "by way of explanation"

Verse 35, "I am." Jesus' use of this phrase was deliberate. This is the first of seven times that it is recorded by John. The words are emphatic in the Greek and echo Exodus 3:14.

Key "Quotable Quote"

"I don't preach a social gospel; I preach the Gospel, period. The gospel of our Lord Jesus Christ is concerned for the whole person. When people were hungry, Jesus didn't say, 'Now is that political or social?' He said, 'I feed you.' Because the good news to a hungry person is bread."

Desmond Tutu

John 7

Matthew Henry's introduction

In this chapter we have,

I. Christ's refusal for some time to appear publicly in Judea.

II. His intention to go up to Jerusalem at the feast of tabernacles, and his discourse in Galilee about his going up to this feast.

III. His preaching publicly in the temple at that feast.

Dr. Adam Clarke's analysis of chapter

Jesus continues in Galilee, 1.

His brothers ask him to go to the feast of tabernacles, 2–5.

His answer, 6–9.

He goes up, and the Jews seek him at the feast, 10–13.

He teaches in the temple, 14–24.

The Jews are confounded by his preaching, 25– 27.

He continues to teach; they wish to kill him, 28–30.

Many of the people believe in him, 31.

The Pharisees murmur, and our Lord reasons with them, 32–36.

His preaching on the last day of the feast, 37–39.

The people are divided in their opinions over him, 40–44.

The officers, who were sent by the Pharisees to take him, return, and because they did not bring him, their employers are offended, 45–49.

Nicodemus reasons with them, 50–53.

A detailed analysis of chapter

Christ goes to the Feast of Tabernacles. (1–13)

His teaching at the Feast. (14–39)

The people argue about Christ. (40–53)

Key verse

Verse 16: "My teaching is not my own. It comes from him who sent me."

Key word / key phrase

Verse 37, "come to me and drink."

Key event / key person / key theme

Jesus is the water of life

Key thought

Wherever Jesus went he caused a division among his hearers.

Key thing to look out for

The religious leaders were Jesus' fiercest enemies.

Key Bible cross-reference

Verse 2. See Leviticus 23:34.

Key "by way of explanation"

Verse 39, "glorified," refers to Jesus' death, resurrection, and ascension. The Feast of Tabernacles was the Harvest Festival, and the time when the Jews remembered God's care for them in the wilderness.

Key "Quotable Quote"

"Spirituality really means 'Holy Spirit at work.'"

Leon Joseph Suenens

John 8

Matthew Henry's introduction

In this chapter we have,

I. Christ's evading the trap which the Jews laid for him, in bringing to him a woman taken in adultery.

II. Various conversations of his with the Jews who complained and argued with him.

Dr. Adam Clarke's analysis of chapter

The story of the woman taken in adultery, 1–11.

Jesus declares himself the light of the world, 12.

The Pharisees complain, 13.

Jesus answers, and shows his authority, 14–20.

He delivers a second discourse, in which he convicts them of sin, and foretells their dying in it, because of their unbelief, 21–24.

They question him; he answers, and foretells his own death, 25–29.

Many believe in him 30.

He gives them advice, 31, 32.

The Jews again complain, and plead the advantages of their birth, 33.

Jesus shows the vanity of their pretensions, and the wickedness of their hearts, 34–47.

They blaspheme, and Christ convicts and reproves them, and asserts his divine nature, 48–58.

They attempt to stone him, 59.

A detailed analysis of chapter

The Pharisees and the adulteress. (1–11)

Christ's teaching with the Pharisees. (12–59)

Key verse

Verse 12: "I am the light of the world. Whoever follows me will never walk in darkness, but will have the light of life."

Key word / key phrase

Verse 12, "I am the light of the world."

Key event / key person / key theme

Jesus the Light of the world

Key thought

Jesus is the one who takes away our darkness.

Key thing to look out for

Considering how genuinely humble Jesus was, is it not remarkable that he was so outspoken about who he was?

Key Bible cross-reference

Verse 5. See Leviticus 20:10.

Key "by way of explanation"

Verse 12, "I am." This is the second of Jesus' "I ams." See also John 6:35; 9:5; 10:7, 9; 10:11, 14; 11:25; 14:6; 15:1, 5.

Key "Quotable Quote"

"We live in a world full of people struggling to be, or at least to appear strong, in order not to be weak; and we follow a gospel which says that when I am weak, then I am strong. And this gospel is the only thing that brings healing."

N.T. Wright

John 9

Matthew Henry's introduction

In this chapter we have,

I. The miraculous cure of a man who was born blind.

II. The discourses which followed this.

Dr. Adam Clarke's analysis of chapter

Account of the man who was born blind, 1–5.

Christ heals him, 6, 7.

The man is questioned by his neighbors, 8–12.

He is brought to the Pharisees, who question

him, 13–17,

and then his parents, 18–23.

They again interrogate the man, who, vindicating the conduct of Christ, is excommunicated by them, 24–34.

Jesus, hearing how the Pharisees behaved, finds the man, and reveals himself to him, 35–38.

He passes judgment on the obduracy and blindness of the Pharisees, 39–41.

A detailed analysis of chapter

Christ heals a man born blind. (1–7)

The account given by the blind man. (8–12)

The Pharisees question the man who had been blind. (13–17)

They ask about him. (18–23)

They throw him out. (24–34)

Christ's words to the man that had been blind. (35–38)

He reproves the Pharisees. (39–41)

Key verse

Verse 2: "Rabbi, who sinned, this man or his parents, that he was born blind?"

Key word / key phrase

Verse 7, "came home seeing."

Key event / key person / key theme

Jesus heals a blind man.

Key thought

Note the links between physical and spiritual sight in this chapter.

Key thing to look out for

Verse 38 puts belief in Jesus and worship of Jesus side by side.

Key Bible cross-reference

Verse 31. See Genesis 18:23–32.

Key "by way of explanation"

Verse 18, "the Jews" were among Jesus' most strident opponents. Instead of seeing Jesus' actions as miraculous they tried to undermine his every step and every statement.

Key "Quotable Quote"

"There is no strength in unbelief."

George MacDonald

John 10

Matthew Henry's introduction

In this chapter we have,

I. Christ's parabolic discourse about himself as the door of the sheepfold, and the shepherd of the sheep.

II. Other people commenting on this.

III. The dispute Christ had with the Jews in the temple at the feast of dedication.

IV. Christ leaving for the country.

Dr. Adam Clarke's analysis of chapter

Christ gives the parable of the sheepfold, 1–6.

Proclaims himself the door of the sheepfold, 7–10

and the good shepherd who lays down his life for the sheep, 11–18.

The Jews are again divided, and some revile and some vindicate our Lord, 19–21.

His discourse with the Jews at the temple, on the feast of dedication, 22–29.

Having asserted that he was one with the Father, the Jews attempt to stone him, 30, 31.

He vindicates his conduct, and appeals to his deeds, 32– 38.

They strive to apprehend him; he escapes, and goes back beyond Jordan, 39, 40.

Many follow him and believe on him there, 41, 42.

A detailed analysis of chapter

The parable of the good shepherd. (1–5)
Christ the Door. (6–9)
Christ the good shepherd. (10–18)
The Jews' opinion about Jesus. (19–21)
His teaching at the Feast of Dedication. (22–30)
The Jews attempt to stone Jesus. (31–38)
He leaves Jerusalem. (39–42)

Key verse

Verse 11: "I am the good shepherd. The good shepherd lays down his life for the sheep."

Key word / key phrase

Verse 11, "I am the good shepherd."

Key event / key person / key theme

Jesus is the Good Shepherd

Key thought

Verse 15, "I lay down my life." This is the gospel of Jesus in a nutshell. It shows that his death was voluntary and purposeful and for others.

Key thing to look out for

This chapter indicates how often Jesus' opponents longed to get their hands on him.

Key Bible cross-reference

Verse 33. See Leviticus 24:16.

Key "by way of explanation"

In the Old Testament God was called the Shepherd. "The gate" or "door." The sheepfolds on the hillsides that shepherds build in the summer did not have doors. The shepherd himself would lie across the opening.

Key "Quotable Quote"

"To Christ all the types and shadows point! Of Christ all the prophecies give witness! While all the glory of the Scriptures, from Genesis to Revelation, culminates at the cross of Christ."

Octavius Winslow

John 11

Matthew Henry's introduction

In this chapter we have the record of Christ's miracle which he did shortly his death – the raising of Lazarus to life. This is recorded only by this evangelist; for the other three confine themselves to what Christ did in Galilee, where he stayed most of the time, and hardly ever recount Christ's activities in Jerusalem until the passion-week: whereas John concentrates mainly on what occurred in Jerusalem; this passage therefore was reserved for his pen.

This miracle is recorded in more detail than any other of Christ's miracles, not only because there are many aspects about it that are very instructive and because the miracle of itself is such good evidence about Christ's mission, but because it was a foreshadowing of Christ's own resurrection.

Dr. Adam Clarke's analysis of chapter

Account of the sickness of Lazarus, 1.

His sisters Martha and Mary send for Christ, 2.

Our Lord's discourse with his disciples on this sickness and consequent death, 3–16.

He arrives at Bethany four days after Lazarus has been buried, 17, 18.

Martha meets Christ–their conversation, 19–27.

She returns and Mary goes out to meet him, in great distress, 28– 33.

Christ comes to the grave–his conversation there, 34–42.

He raises Lazarus from the dead, 43–46.

The priests and Pharisees, hearing of this, hold a council, and plan to kill him, 47, 48.

Caiaphas' remarkable prophecy, and the consequent proceedings of the Jews, 49–53.

Jesus withdraws into a city called Ephraim, 54.

They lay wait for him at the Passover, 55–67.

A detailed analysis of chapter

Lazarus' illness. (1–6)

Christ returns to Judea. (7–10)

The death of Lazarus. (11–16)

Christ arrives at Bethany. (17–32)

He raises Lazarus. (33–46)

The Pharisees call a meeting about Jesus. (47–53)

The Jews look for him. (54–57)

Key verse

Verse 25: "I am the resurrection and the life. He who believes in me will live, even though he dies."

Key word / key phrase

Verse 43, "Lazarus, come out!"

Key event / key person / key theme

Jesus brings Lazarus back to life

Key thought

Note the link between the "I am" of Jesus, verse 25, and Jesus bringing Lazarus back to life.

Key thing to look out for

The purpose of the raising of Lazarus. Note also John 20:31.

Key Bible cross-reference

Verse 24. See Daniel 12:2.

Key "by way of explanation"

Verse 35, "Jesus wept." This is the shortest verse in the Bible. It refers to shedding tears rather than loud wailing.

Key "Quotable Quote"

"Jesus Christ's claim of divinity is the most serious claim anyone ever made. Everything about Christianity hinges on his incarnation, crucifixion, and resurrection. That's what Christmas, Good Friday, and Easter are all about."

Luis Palau

John 12

Matthew Henry's introduction

In contrast with the end of the previous chapter where the scribes and Pharisees asserted that Christ was a traitor to their church, this chapter has people heaping honor on the head of the Lord Jesus, even in the depths of his humiliation.

I. Mary honored him by anointing his feet at the supper in Bethany.

II. The ordinary people honored him, with their acclamations of joy, when he rode in triumph into Jerusalem.

III. The Greeks honored him, by asking to see him.

IV. God the Father honored him, by a voice from heaven, bearing testimony to him.

V. The Old Testament prophets honored him, as they foretold the unfaithfulness of those who heard about him.

VI. Some of the chief rulers honored him, as their consciences witnessed for him.

VII. He claimed honor for himself, by asserting his divine mission.

Dr. Adam Clarke's analysis of chapter

Jesus eats at Lazarus' home, and Mary anoints his feet, 1–3.

Judas Iscariot complains, and reproves her, 4–6.

Jesus vindicates Mary and reproves Judas, 7, 8.

The chief priests plan to put Lazarus to death, because through him many believed in Jesus, 9–11.

He enters Jerusalem in triumph; the people meet him, and the Pharisees are up set, 12–19.

Greeks inquire after Jesus, 20–22.

Our Lord's discourse this, 23–26.

Speaks of his passion, and is answered by a voice from heaven, 27, 28.

The people are amazed at the voice, and Jesus explains it to them, and foretells his death, 29–33.

They question him about the eternity of the Messiah, and he instructs them, 34–36.

Many do not believe; and in them the saying of Isaiah is fulfilled, 37–41.

Some of the chief rulers believe, but are afraid to confess him, 42, 43.

He proclaims himself the light of the world, and shows the danger of rejecting his words, 44–50.

A detailed analysis of chapter

Christ anointed by Mary. (1–11)

He enters Jerusalem. (12–19)

Greeks ask to see Jesus. (20–26)

A voice from heaven bears testimony to Christ. (27–33)

His teaching the people. (34–36)

Unbelief of the Jews. (37–43)

Christ speaks to them. (44–50)

Key verse

Verse 32: "But I, when I am lifted up from the earth, will draw all men to myself."

Key word / key phrase

Verse 23, "the hour has come."

Key event / key person / key theme

Jesus teaches about his death

Key thought

Bringing Lazarus back to life did have an effect on some people, verses 17,18.

Key thing to look out for

Sheer jealousy seems to have held sway in the hearts of the Pharisees, verse 19.

Key Bible cross-reference

Verse 15. See Zechariah 9:9.

Key "by way of explanation"

Verse 12, "great crowd." This large number of people would have been in Jerusalem at this time for the Passover Feast. It was one of the three annual festivals that Jewish men had to attend.

Key "Quotable Quote"

"No more energy must be wasted in the wrangling and jealousy that can only lead to death."

Clement of Rome

John 13

Matthew Henry's introduction

Our Savior, having finished his public discourses, in which he "endured the contradiction of sinners," now applies himself to a private conversation with his friends. Here we have an account of what passed between him and his disciples, and the instructions and comfort he gave them. His hour is at hand, so he sets his house in order.

Dr. Adam Clarke's analysis of chapter

Christ washes his disciples' feet, and gives them instructions about humility and love, 1–17.

He tells them that one of them will betray him, 18–20.

The disciples do not know who he is speaking about; Peter wants John to ask Jesus, 21–25.

Jesus indicates that it is Judas Iscariot, 26.

Satan enters into Judas, and he leaves the company, 27–30.

Christ speaks about his approaching death, and commands his disciples to love one another, 31–35.

Peter, professing strong attachment to Christ, is informed of his denial. 36–38.

A detailed analysis of chapter

Christ washes the disciples' feet. (1–17)

The treachery of Judas foretold. (18–30)

Christ commands the disciples to love one another. (31–38)

Key verse

Verse 5: "After that, he poured water into a basin and began to wash his disciples' feet, drying them with the towel that was wrapped around him."

Key word / key phrase

Verse 14, "you also should wash one another's feet."

Key event / key person / key theme

Jesus washes his disciples' feet

Key thought

Verse 34, "A new command." It may be asked in what sense this command, which was really an old one, see Leviticus 19:18, could be called a "new" one. It was new in the sense that it showed the quality of the love followers of Jesus should have, as a result of Jesus' love for them.

Key thing to look out for

Note that Jesus is in control of all the events of the last few days of his life.

Key Bible cross-reference

Verse 18. See Psalm 41:9.

Key "by way of explanation"

At a meal a host would frequently offer a special tit-bit to one of the diners. It was a token of special friendship.

Key "Quotable Quote"

"Jesus said love one another. He didn't say love the whole world."

Mother Teresa of Calcutta

John 14

Matthew Henry's introduction

This chapter is a continuation of Christ's discourse with his disciples after supper. When he had convicted and discarded Judas, he set about comforting the rest, who were full of sorrow about what he had said about leaving them. The discourse is interspersed with some comments from this disciples; as Peter in the previous chapter, so Thomas, and Philip, and Judas (not Iscariot), in this interposed their thoughts about what he said. The general scope of this chapter is in the first verse; it is designed to keep trouble from their hearts.

Dr. Adam Clarke's analysis of chapter

Christ comforts his disciples by telling them that he is going to prepare a place for them in heaven, 1–4.

Thomas questions him about the way to the Father, and is answered, 5–7.

Philip raises a difficulty, and Christ shows that he and the Father are one; that he is Mediator between God and humankind; and that what ever is asked in his name will be given, 8–14.

He promises them the Holy Spirit as the Comforter and Spirit of truth, 15–18.

Shows them that he will soon leave them, and that those who love him will be loved by the Father, 19–21.

Judas (not Iscariot) asks a question about how Christ is to manifest himself to the disciples, and not to the Jews? 22.

Christ answers, and shows that the manifestation is to be made to those who love God, and to them the Holy Spirit will be an infallible teacher, 23–26.

He bestows his peace to them, and strengthen them to face discouragements, 27–29.

Foretells his approaching death, 30, 31.

A detailed analysis of chapter

Christ comforts his disciples. (1–4)

Seeing the Father. (5–11)

The purpose of faith. (12–14)

The Holy Spirit (15–31)

Key verse

Verse 3: "And if I go and prepare a place for you, I will come back and take you to be with me that you also may be where I am."

Key word / key phrase

Verse 26, "the Counselor, the Holy Spirit."

Key event / key person / key theme

Jesus teaches about the promised Holy Spirit

Key thought

Verse 1. Trusting in Jesus is the same as trusting in the Father.

Key thing to look out for

What did Jesus promise about the Holy Spirit?

Key Bible cross-reference

Verse 1. See Psalm 4:5.

Key "by way of explanation"

Verse 17, "the Spirit of truth." Everything about the Holy Spirit is linked to and characterized by truth. The Holy Spirit leads people to the truth about God and to God himself, who is the truth.

Key "Quotable Quote"

"Christianity is not a system of philosophy, nor a ritual, nor a code of laws; it is the impartation of a divine vitality. Without the way there is no going, without the truth there is no knowing, without life there is no living."

Merrill Tenney

John 15

Matthew Henry's introduction

It is generally agreed that Christ's discourse in this and the next chapter was at the close of the last supper, the night in which he was betrayed. What he chooses to speak about is very pertinent to the present sad occasion of a farewell sermon. Now that he was about to leave them,

I. They would be tempted to leave him, and return to Moses again; and therefore he tells them how necessary it was that they should by faith adhere to him and abide in him.

II. They would be tempted to grow apart from each other, and so he urges them to love one another.

III. They would be tempted to shrink from their apostleship when they met with hardships; and therefore he prepared them to bear the shock of the world's ill will. There are four words to which his conversation in this chapter may be reduced;

A. Fruit, 1–8.

B. Love, 9–17.

C. Hatred, 18–25.

D. The Comforter, 26, 27.

Dr. Adam Clarke's analysis of chapter

The union of Jesus Christ with his followers, as seen in the parable of a vine and its branches, 1–11.

He exhorts them to mutual love, 12.

Calls them his friends, and promises to lay down his life for them, 13–15.

Appoints them their work, and promises them success in it, 16.

Renews the exhortation to mutual love, 17, and foretells the opposition they will find from the world, 18–21.

The sin of the Jews in rejecting Christ, 22–25.

The Holy Spirit is promised as a witness for

Christ, and the Comforter of the disciples, 26, 27.

A detailed analysis of chapter

Christ the true vine. (1–8)
His love for his disciples. (9–17)
Persecution predicted. (18–25)
The Comforter promised. (26,27)

Key verse

Verse 5: "I am the vine; you are the branches. If a man remains in me and I in him, he will bear much fruit; apart from me you can do nothing."

Key word / key phrase

Verse 3, "Remain in me."

Key event / key person / key theme

Jesus is the true vine

Key thought

If we wish to know what "abiding" means, there is no better chapter in the Bible than this.

Key thing to look out for

Verse 9 explains, as no other Bible verse does, how much we are loved, and by whom we are loved.

Key Bible cross-reference

Verse 25. See Psalm 35:19.

Key "by way of explanation"

Verse 15, "servants . . . friends." To be a servant of Jesus is a great enough privilege. To be his friend blows the mind. But that is what is stated here.

Key "Quotable Quote"

"The true, the genuine worship is when man, through his spirit, attains to friendship and intimacy with God."

William Barclay

John 16

Matthew Henry's introduction

God spoke of himself as, I wound, and I heal, Deut. 32:39. Christ's words in this chapter, which continues and concludes his farewell sermon to his disciples, does so.

I. Here are wounding words about the troubles that are ahead of them.

II. Here are healing words in the comforts he gives them. There are five of these:

A. That he would send them the Comforter, 7–15.

B. That he would visit them again at his resurrection, 16–22.

C. That he would give them an answer of peace to all their prayers, 23–27.

D. That he was now but returning to his Father, 28–32.

E. That, whatever troubles they might meet with in this world, because of his victory over it they should find peace in him, 33.

Dr. Adam Clarke's analysis of chapter

Christ warns his disciples, and foretells the persecutions they will receive from the Jews, 1–4.

Foretells his death, and promises them the Comforter, 5–7.

Points out his work among the Jews, and in the world, 8–11.

His special influences on the souls of the disciples, 12–15.

Speaks figuratively about his death and resurrection, at which his disciples are puzzled, 16–18.

He explains and illustrates, 19–22.

Shows himself to be the Mediator between God and humankind, and that all prayers must be made in his name, 23–28.

The disciples grasp his meaning and express their strong faith in him, 29, 30.

He again foretells their persecution, and promises them his peace and support, 31–33.

A detailed analysis of chapter

Persecution predicted. (1–6)

The promise of the Holy Spirit, and his ministry. (7–15)

Christ's departure and return. (16–22)

Encouragement to pray. (23–27)

Christ and the Father. (28–33)

Key verse

Verse 16: "In a little while you will see me no more, and then after a little while you will see me."

Key word / key phrase

Verse 28, "I am leaving the world."

Key event / key person / key theme

Jesus predicts his own death and resurrection

Key thought

Jesus explains the work of the Holy Spirit in salvation.

Key thing to look out for

Verse 33. Jesus offers peace in a turbulent world. Rather, Jesus offers himself. This brings peace.

Key Bible cross-reference

Verse 2. See Revelation 6:9.

Key "by way of explanation"

Verse 23, "you will no longer ask me anything." This does not mean that the disciples should cease to ask for things in prayer. Rather they will not have any need for information. After the Resurrection and Pentecost they will understand what has hitherto baffled them.

Key "Quotable Quote"

"Oh, if thou knewest what peace to thyself thy holy life should bring . . . and what joy to others, me thinketh thou wouldst be more zealous for spiritual profit."

Thomas à Kempis

John 17

Matthew Henry's introduction

This chapter is a prayer, it is the Lord's prayer, the Lord Christ's prayer. There was one Lord's prayer which he taught us to pray, and did not pray himself, for he needed not to pray for the forgiveness of sin; but this was properly and peculiarly his, and suited him only as a Mediator, and is a sample of his intercession, and yet is of use to us both for instruction and encouragement in prayer.

Dr. Adam Clarke's analysis of chapter

Jesus prays to the Father to glorify him, 1.

What eternal life consists of, 2–3.

Jesus that he has glorified his Father, by fulfilling his will on earth, and revealing him to the disciples, 4–8.

Jesus prays for them, for their unity, and to be kept from evil, 9–16.

Prays for their sanctification, 17–19.

Prays also for those who will believe in him through their preaching, that they may be united, and finally brought to eternal glory, 20–26.

A detailed analysis of chapter

Christ's prayer for himself. (1–5)

His prayer for his disciples. (6–20)

His prayer for all believers. (21–26)

Key verse

Verse 4: "I have brought you glory on earth by completing the work you gave me to do."

Key word / key phrase

Verse 21, "that all of them may be one."

Key event / key person / key theme

Jesus prays to his Father

Key thought

Verse 4 explains what bringing glory to God involves.

Key thing to look out for

Jesus never outgrew his need for prayer.

Key Bible cross-reference

Verse 12. See Psalm 41:9.

Key "by way of explanation"

Verse 12, "I protected them." In his own prayer Jesus shows that he has power to keep his followers safe. In that sense people have said that Christians are under God's special protection.

Key "Quotable Quote"

"We stand at better advantage to find truth, and keep it also, when devoutly praying for it, than fiercely wrangling and contending about it."

William Gurnall

John 18

Matthew Henry's introduction

Up until now this evangelist has recorded little of the history of Christ. But now that Jesus must die he gives details about the circumstances of his sufferings, especially his sayings. This chapter relates,

I. How Christ was arrested in the garden and surrendered himself a prisoner.

II. How he was abused in the high priest's court, and how Peter.

III. How he was prosecuted before Pilate, and examined by him, and how Barabbas was released and not him.

Dr. Adam Clarke's analysis of chapter

Jesus goes to the garden of Gethsemane, 1.

Judas, having betrayed him, comes to the place with soldiers to take him, 2, 3.

Jesus speaks to them, and they fall to the ground, 4–6.

He speaks to them again, and Peter strikes Malchus, 7–11.

They seize Jesus and lead him away to Caiaphas, 12–14.

Peter follows to the palace of the high priest, 15–18.

The high priest questions Christ about his doctrine, and Jesus answers, and is hit, 19–23.

Peter denies his Lord twice, 24–27.

Jesus is led to the judgment hall, and Pilate and the Jews speak about him, 28–32.

Pilate speaks with Jesus, who informs him of the spiritual nature of his kingdom, 33–37.

Pilate returns to the Jews, and declares Christ to be innocent, 38.

He tries to release him, and the Jews clamor for his condemnation, 39. 40.

A detailed analysis of chapter

Christ arrested in the garden. (1–12)

Christ before Annas and Caiaphas. (13–27)

Christ before Pilate. (28–40)

Key verse

Verse 3: "So Judas came to the grove, guiding a detachment of soldiers and some officials from the chief priests and Pharisees."

Key word / key phrase

Verse 12, "arrested Jesus."

Key event / key person / key theme

Jesus' arrest

Key thought

Jesus only went to the cross because he was following his Father's will.

Key thing to look out for

Peter, the rock, reveals his feet of clay.

Key Bible cross-reference

Verse 1. See 2 Samuel 15:23.

Key "by way of explanation"

Verse 17, "the girl at the door." It is remarkable that all four Gospels pick up this detail that the first person to suggest to Peter that he knew Jesus was a slave girl. Such a person would have been totally despised in society in those days.

Key "Quotable Quote"

"When we are right with God, he gives us our desires and aspirations. Our Lord had only one desire, and that was to do the will of his Father, and to have this desire is characteristic of a disciple."

Oswald Chambers

John 19

Matthew Henry's introduction

In the story of this chapter we have,

I. The rest of Christ's trial before Pilate.

II. Sentence given.

III. The title over his head.

IV. The soldiers taking his clothes

V. The provision he make for his mother.

VI. Vinegar being given to him to drink.

VII. His dying word.

VIII. His side pierced.

IX. The burial of his body.

O that in meditating on these things we may experimentally know the power of Christ's death, and the fellowship of his sufferings!

Dr. Adam Clarke's analysis of chapter

Jesus is scourged, crowned with thorns, and mocked by the soldiers, 1–3.

He is paraded by Pilate, wearing the purple robe; and the Jews clamor for his death, 4–8.

Conversation between our Lord and Pilate, 9–11.

Pilate expostulates with the Jews on their barbarous demands; but they become more hardened, and he delivers Christ into their hands, 12–16.

He, bearing his cross, is led to Golgotha, and crucified, 17–22.

The soldiers cast lots for his clothes, 23, 24.

Jesus commends his mother to the care of John, 25–27.

Jesus thirsts, receives vinegar, and dies, 28–30.

The Jews request that the legs of those who were crucified should be broken; the soldiers break those of the two thieves, and pierce the side of Christ; the Scriptures fulfilled in these acts, 31–37.

Joseph of Arimathea asks for the body of Christ; and Nicodemus brings spices to embalm it, 38–40.

He is laid in a new sepulcher, 41, 42.

The trials of Jesus

By a comparison of the four accounts of this momentous trial it is easy to trace its successive stages.

1. We have an account of the informal examination before Annas, recorded only by John (18:13–24), which terminates with the statement that Annas sent him bound to Caiaphas.
2. Next is the preliminary examination conducted by Caiaphas assisted by a section of the Sanhedrim, of which accounts are given in Matt. 26:57–68 and Mark 14:55–65.
3. Luke gives an account of the formal meeting of the great Sanhedrim after the dawn of day (22:66–71).
4. Next comes the formal accusation before Pilate, recorded in all the Gospels.
5. The first conversation between Christ and Pilate is recorded in John 18:33–38.
6. Pilate's first acquittal; further charges; Christ's silence (Matt. 27:12–14; Mark 15:3–5; Luke 23:4, 5).
7. Case sent to Herod (Luke 23:6–12).
8. Before Pilate again; second formal acquittal (Luke 23:13–16).
9. Jesus or Barabbas (Matt. 27:15–18; Mark 15:6–10).
10. Message of warning from Pilate's wife (while people are deciding) (Matt. 27:19).
11. Barabbas chosen. Cries of "Crucify him!" (Matt. 27:20–22; Mark 15:11–13.)
12. Pilate tries to save Jesus (Matt. 27:23; Mark 15:12–14).
13. Pilate washes his hands; declaration of Christ's innocence (Matt. 27:24, 25).

14. Sentence of crucifixion (Mark 15:15; Luke 23:24, 25).
15. Scourging and mockery (Matt. 27:26–30; Mark 15:16–19; John 19:1–3).
16. Further efforts of Pilate to save Jesus (John 19:4–16).
17. Led away to be crucified (Matt. 27:31; Mark 15:20).

B.W. Johnson

A detailed analysis of chapter

Christ condemned and crucified. (1–18)
Christ on the cross. (19–30)
His side pierced. (31–37)
The burial of Jesus. (38–42)

Key verse

Verse 7: "We have a law, and according to that law he must die, because he claimed to be the Son of God."

Key word / key phrase

Verse 30, "It is finished."

Key event / key person / key theme

Jesus' death

Key thought

"Our Lord's death on the cross is the supreme manifestation of the love of God."

D. Martyn Lloyd-Jones

Key thing to look out for

Even on the cross Jesus shows his care for others.

Key Bible cross-reference

Verse 24. See Psalm 22:18.

Key "by way of explanation"

Verse 20, "this sign." The wording on the sign was in three languages so everyone who passed by would be able to read it. It was in one of the Jewish languages, Aramaic, in the official language of the Romans, Latin, and the everyday language used throughout the Empire, Greek.

Key "Quotable Quote"

"There is only one answer to the question as to why Christ had to die – the holiness of God!"

D. Martyn Lloyd-Jones

John 20

Matthew Henry's introduction

This evangelist, although he did not start his gospel as the rest did, yet concludes it as they did, with the history of Christ's resurrection; not of the thing itself, for none of them describe how he rose, but of the proofs and evidences of it, which demonstrated that he was risen. The proofs of Christ's resurrection, which we have in this chapter, are:

I. Such as occurred immediately at the sepulcher. The sepulcher found empty, and the grave clothes in good order. Two angels appearing to Mary Magdalene at the sepulcher. Christ himself appearing to her.

II. The events that occurred later with the meetings of the apostles. The evening of that Christ rose, when Thomas was absent. Eight days later when Thomas was with them. What is related here is mostly omitted by the other evangelists.

Dr. Adam Clarke's analysis of chapter

Mary Magdalene, coming early to the sepulcher, finds it empty, and runs and tells Peter, 1, 2.

Peter and John run to the tomb, and find everything as Mary had reported, 3–10.

Mary sees a vision of angels in the tomb, 11–13.

Jesus himself appears to her, and sends her with a message to the disciples, 14–18.

He appears to the disciples, gives the fullest proof of the reality of his resurrection, and gives them a foretaste of the Holy Spirit, 19–23.

The determined incredulity of Thomas, 24, 25.

Eight days after, Jesus appears again to the disciples, Thomas being present, to whom he gives the proofs he had asked for, 26, 27.

Thomas is convinced, and makes a confession of faith, 28.

Our Lord's reflections on his case, 29.

Various signs done by Christ, not recorded here, 30.

Why others are recorded, 31.

The risen Lord Jesus seen by the apostles

After the Savior's first recorded appearance, to Mary Magdalene, he revealed himself at some time during this eventful day, the first Lord's day in the history of the world, to Simon Peter, and late in the evening appeared to the disciples on the way to Emmaus. They hurried back to Jerusalem with this wonderful news, and found the eleven gathered, with others, discussing the account told by the women and by Peter. They added their testimony, but still there was such skepticism about the resurrection that many refused to believe. Then, while the followers were eating, with the doors closed for fear of the Jews, suddenly the Lord appeared to them, with the greeting, "Peace be unto you."

The following are the recorded appearances of the Savior after his crucifixion. There were ten or eleven in all.

1. To Mary Magdalene alone (Mark 16:9; John 20:11–18), near Jerusalem.
2. To the women returning from the sepulcher (Matt. 28:9, 10), near Jerusalem. I suspect this is another version of the appearance to Mary Magdalene.
3. To Simon Peter alone (Luke 24:34), near Jerusalem.
4. To the two disciples going to Emmaus (Luke 24:13).
5. To the apostles at Jerusalem, except for Thomas, who was absent (John 20:19).
6. To the apostles at Jerusalem a second time, when Thomas was present (John 20:26, 29).
7. At the Sea of Tiberias, when seven disciples were fishing (John 21:1).
8. To the eleven disciples on a mountain in Galilee (Matt. 28:16).
9. To more than 500 brethren at once (1 Cor. 15:6).
10. To James by himself (1 Cor. 15:7).
11. To all the apostles on Mount Olivet at his ascension (Luke 24:51).

B.W. Johnson

A detailed analysis of chapter

The sepulcher is found to be empty. (1–10)
Christ appears to Mary. (11–18)
He appears to the disciples. (19–25)
The unbelief of Thomas. (26–29)
Conclusion. (30,31)

Key verse

Verse 2: "They have taken the Lord out of the tomb, and we don't know where they have put him!"

Key word / key phrase

Verse 8, "he saw and believed."

Key event / key person / key theme

Jesus' resurrection

Key thought

Without the resurrection appearances the disciples would have understood little.

Key thing to look out for

What encouragement is there from the experience of Thomas?

Key Bible cross-reference

Verse 22. See Galatians 3:2.

Key "by way of explanation"

Verse 22, "Receive the Holy Spirit." This foreshadowed what would take place on the Day of Pentecost. A disciple might receive God's commission but would never be able to carry it out without the Spirit's help.

Key "Quotable Quote"

"Christ's call is to save the lost, not the stiff-necked; He came not to call scoffers but sinners to repentance; not to build and furnish comfortable chapels, churches, and cathedrals at home in which to rock Christian professors to sleep by means of clever essays, stereotyped prayers, and artistic musical performances, but to capture men from the devil's clutches and the very jaws of Hell. This can be accomplished only by a red-hot devotion, in the power of the Holy Spirit, to the Lord Jesus Christ."

C.T. Studd

John 21

Matthew Henry's introduction

The evangelist had said that there were many other signs that Jesus did as proof of his resurrection. And in this chapter he mentions one of them. This was Christ's appearance to some of his disciples at the sea of Tiberias. In this account we have:

I. How he made himself known to them as they were fishing.
II. The conversation he had with Peter.
III. The solemn conclusion of this gospel, vv. 24, 25.

Dr. Adam Clarke's analysis of chapter

Jesus shows himself to the disciples at the sea of Tiberias, 1–5.
The miraculous net full of fish, 6–11.
He eats with his disciples, 12–14.
Questions Peter about his love for him, and commissions him to feed his sheep, 15–17.
Foretells how Peter will die, 18, 19.

Peter inquires about John, and receives an answer that was later misunderstood, 20–23.

John's concluding testimony about the authenticity of his Gospel, and the purpose for which it was written, 24, 25.

A detailed analysis of chapter

Christ appears to his disciples. (1–14)

His teaching with Peter. (15–19)

Christ's declaration about John. (20–24)

The conclusion. (25)

Key verse

Verse 25: "Jesus did many other things as well. If every one of them were written down, I suppose that even the whole world would not have room for the books that would be written."

Key word / key phrase

Verse 15, "Feed my lambs."

Key event / key person / key theme

Resurrection appearances of Jesus.

Key thought

From Peter we learn that failure need never be the end of the story.

Key thing to look out for

John 21:19, "Follow me." (Cf the same words in Mark 1:17). What do these words now mean to Peter?

Key Bible cross-reference

Verse 16. See Ezekiel 34:2.

Key "by way of explanation"

Verse 19, "the kind of death." This verse indicates that Peter would be killed against his will. According to tradition Peter was martyred, upside-down, on a cross.

Key "Quotable Quote"

"Fear had denied Christ three times. Three times love confessed him. A threefold negation, the desertion of truth; a threefold confession, the witness of love."

John Calvin

5. Select bibliography for John's Gospel

Barrett, C. K. *The Gospel According to John.* London: SPCK, 1958.

Beasley-Murray, G. R. *John*. Waco: Word, 1987.

Bruce, F. F. *The Gospel of John*. Grand Rapids: Eerdmans, 1984.

Hendriksen, William. *Exposition of the Gospel According to John*. New Testament Commentary. 2 vols. Grand Rapids: Baker, 1953–54.

Ellis, E. E. *The World of St. John*. Grand Rapids: Eerdmans, 1984.

Hunter, A. M. *According to John: The New Look on the Fourth Gospel*. Philadelphia: Westminster, 1968.

Kruse, Colin G. *John* (Tyndale New Testament Commentaries) Leicester, IVP, 2005.

Lightfoot, R. H. *St. John's Gospel: A Commentary*. Edited by C.F. Evans. London: Oxford University, 1969.

Linda's, Barnabas. *The Gospel of John*. NCB. London: Olyphants, 1972.

D. E. Nineham. Hammondsworth, Middlesex, England: Penguin Books, 1972.

Milne, Bruce. *The Message of John, The Bible Speaks Today*, Leicester: IVP, 1993

Morgan, G. Campbell. *The Gospel of John*. Old Tappan, N.J.: Revell, n.d.

Morris, Leon. *The Gospel According to St. John*. NIC. Grand Rapids: Eerdmans, 1971.

Smalley, S. S. *John: Evangelist and Interpreter*. New York: Thomas Nelson, 1978.

Turner, George A., and Mantey, J. R. *The Gospel According to St. John*. Evangelical Commentary. Grand Rapids: Eerdmans, 1964.

Westcott, B. F. *The Gospel According to St. John*. 2 Vols. London: John Murray, 1908.

Acts

1. Book by book: Introduction to Acts

Introduction

A sequel and an introduction

This book is to the Gospels what the fruit is to the tree that bears it. In the Gospels we see the corn of wheat falling into the ground and dying: in the Acts we see it bringing forth much fruit (John 12:24). There we see Christ purchasing the Church with His own blood: here we see the Church, so purchased, rising into actual existence; first among the Jews of Palestine, and next among the surrounding Gentiles, until it gains a footing in the great capital of the ancient world–sweeping majestically from Jerusalem to Rome. Nor is this book of less value as an Introduction to the Epistles which follow it, than as a Sequel to the Gospels which precede it. For without this history the Epistles of the New Testament–presupposing, as they do, the historical circumstances of the parties addressed, and deriving from these so much of their freshness, point, and force–would in no respect be what they now are, and would in a number of places be scarcely intelligible.

Inclusion in canon

The genuineness, authenticity, and canonical authority of this book were never called in question within the ancient Church. It stands immediately after the Gospels, in the catalogues of the *Homologoumena,* or universally acknowledged books of the New Testament. It was rejected, indeed, by certain heretical sects in the second and third centuries–by the Ebionites, the Severians (see Eusebius, *Ecclesiastical History*, 4.29), the Marcionites, and the Manicheans: but the totally uncritical character of their objections not only deprives them of all weight, but indirectly shows on what solid grounds the Christian Church had all along proceeded in recognizing this book.

In our day, however, its authenticity has, like that of all the leading books of the New Testament, been made the subject of keen and protracted controversy. De Wette, while admitting Luke to be the author of the entire work, pronounces the earlier portion of it to have been drawn up from unreliable sources. But the Tubingen school, with Baur at their head, have gone much farther. As their fantastic theory of the post-Joannean date of the Gospels could not pretend even to a hearing so long as the authenticity of the Acts of the Apostles remained unshaken, they contend that the earlier portion of this work can be shown to be unworthy of credit, while the latter portion is in flat contradiction to the Epistle to the Galatians–which this school regard as unassailable–and bears internal evidence of being a designed distortion of facts for the purpose of setting up the catholic form which Paul gave to Christianity in opposition to the narrow Judaic but original form of it which Peter preached, and which after the death of the apostles was held exclusively by the sect of the Ebionites. It is painful to think that anyone should have spent so many years, and, aided by learned and acute disciples in different parts of the argument, should have expended so much learning, research, and ingenuity in attempting to build up a hypothesis regarding the origination of the leading books of the New Testament which breaks all the principles of sober criticism and legitimate evidence. As a school, this party at length broke up: its head, after living to find himself the sole defender of the theory as a whole, left this earthly scene complaining of desertion.

Author

The manifest connection between this book and the third Gospel–of which it professes to be simply the continuation by the same author–and the striking similarity which marks the style of both productions, leave no room to doubt that the early Church was right in ascribing it with one consent to Luke. The difficulty which some fastidious critics have made about the sources of the earlier portion of the history has no solid ground. That the historian himself was an eye-witness of the earliest scenes–as Hug concludes from the circumstantiality of the narrative–is altogether improbable: but there were hundreds of eye-witnesses of some of the scenes, and enough of all the rest, to give to the historian, partly by oral, partly by written testimony, all the details which he has embodied so graphically in his history; and it will appear, we trust, from the commentary, that De Wette's complaints of confusion, contradiction, and error in this portion are without foundation. The same critic, and one or two others, would ascribe to Timothy those later portions of the book in which the historian speaks in the first person plural–"we"; supposing him to have taken notes of all that passed under his own eye, which Luke embodied in his history just as they stood. It is impossible here to refute this gratuitous hypothesis in detail; but the reader will find it done by Ebrard and by Davidson.

Purpose

Much has been written about the object of this history. Certainly "the Acts of the Apostles" are but very partially recorded. But for this title the historian is not responsible. Between the two extremes–of supposing that the work has no plan at all, and that it is constructed on an elaborate and complex plan, we shall probably be as near the truth as is necessary if we take the design to be to record the diffusion of Christianity and the rise of the Christian Church, first among the Jews of Palestine, the seat of the ancient Faith, and next among the surrounding Gentiles, with Antioch for its headquarters, until, finally, it is seen waving over imperial Rome, as a token of its universal triumph. In this view of it, there is no difficulty in accounting for the almost exclusive place which it gives to the labors of Peter in the first instance, and the all but entire disappearance from the history both of him and of the rest of the Twelve after the great apostle of the Gentiles came on the stage–like the lesser lights on the rise of the great luminary.

David Brown

Detailed outline

Introduction Acts 1:1–11

I. Introduction: 1:1–2
- A. To: Theophilus: 1:1
- B. What Jesus continued to do and teach after His ascension: 1:1–2

II. The ministry of Jesus after the resurrection: 1:3

III. The final meeting of Jesus with His disciples: 1:4–8

IV. The ascension of Jesus into Heaven: 1:9–11
- A. Description of the ascension: 1:9
- B. Declaration of His second coming: 1:10–11

Part One: Forming The Witness In Jerusalem Acts 1:12–7

I. The forming of the witness: 1:12–2:4
- A. Christ's disciples waiting in Jerusalem: 1:12–26
  1. The gathering of the disciples: 1:12–15
     (a) Their meeting place: 1:12–13
     (b) Their number and names: 1:13–15
     (c) Their purpose: 1:14
  2. The exhortation given to the disciples: 1:15–22
  3. The response of the disciples: 1:23–26
     (a) The nomination: 1:23
     (b)The prayer: 1:24–25
     (c) The election: 1:26
- B. The baptism in the Holy Spirit: 2:1–4
  1. The occasion: 2:1
  2. The people: 2:1
  3. The place: 2:1
  4. The event: 2:2–4
     (a) The wind: 2:2
     (b) The tongues as of fire: 2:3
     (c) Speaking in tongues: 2:4

Part Two: Functioning Of The Witness In Jerusalem Acts 2:5–7

I. The first witness: 2:4–40
- A. The way in which the witness was given: 2:4–6
- B. The reaction to the witness: 2:7–13
- C. The sermon by Peter: 2:14–36
  1. Prophecy about the time: 2:17
  2. Prophecy about the spirit: 2: 17–18
  3. Prophecy about the event: 2:19–20
  4. Prophecy about salvation: 2:21
  5. The work of Jesus: 2:22–36
- D. Response to the message: 2:37–40
  1. Conviction: 2:37
  2. Inquiry: 2:37

3. Instruction: 2:38
4. Promises: 2:38–39
5. Exhortation: 2:40

II. The first local church: 2:41–47
A. Membership of the first church: 2:41
B. Spiritual practices of the first church: 2:42
C. The living pattern of the first church: 2:44–46
1. Voluntary communal system: 2:44–45
2. Daily worship and testimony: 2:46
3. Fellowship in the homes: 2:46
4. Unity: 2:46
D. The witness of the local church: 2:46–47

III. The first miracle: 3:1–26
A. The miracle described: 3:1–11
B. The miracle explained: 3:12–18
C. The message of Peter: 3:19–26
1. The promise made by Peter: 3:19–21
2. The prophecy of the prophets: 3:22–26

IV. The first opposition: 4:1–31
A. The arrest: 4:1–4
B. The trial: 4:5–14
1. The court: 4:5–6
2. Questions of the court: 4:7
3. Statement by Peter: 4:8–12
4. The evidence considered by the court: 4:13–14
5. The decision: 4:15–22
6. The reaction: 4:21–31
(a) The prayer of the church: 4:23–30
(b) The activity of the church: 4:31

V. Sin in the church fellowship: 4:32–5:16
A. Organization of the church: 4:32–37
B. The first sin disrupting the fellowship: 5:1–10
1. The sin: 5:1–2
2. Exposure of the sin: 5:3–4
3. Disciplining of the sin: 5:5–10
C. The results of discipline: Fruitful witness of the fellowship: 5:11–16
1. Reverent attitude of the members: 5:11
2. Unity: 5:12
3. Miraculous signs: 5:12, 15–16
4. Community response: 5:12–14

VI. The first persecution: 5:17–43
A. Source of opposition: 5:17
B. Action of the opposition: 5:18
C. Deliverance by God: 5:19–26
D. Trial: 5:27–40
1. Indictment by the Sanhedrin: 5:27–28
2. Defense made by Peter: 5:29–32
3. Investigation by the Sanhedrin: 5:33–39
4. Injustice of the Sanhedrin's: 5:40
E. Response to persecution: 5:41–42

VII. The first organization: 6:1–7
A. The need for the organization: 6:1
B. The organization suggested: 6:2–4
C. The organization set up: 6:5–6
D. The results of the organization: 6:7

VIII. The first martyr: 6:8–8:1
A. The description of Stephen: 6:3–15
1. One of the seven: 6:3,5
2. Filled with the Holy Spirit: 6:5
3. A man of good reputation: 6:3
4. A man of faith: 6:5
5. A man of wisdom: 6:3, 10
6. A man with special power: 6:8
7. An effective witness: 6:9–10
B. The persecution of Stephen: 6:11–15

C. The message of Stephen: 7:1–53
1. Abraham: 7:1–8
2. The patriarchs: 7:9–16
3. Moses: 7:17–43
(a) In Egypt: 7:17–28
(b) In the wilderness: 7:29–43
4. The tabernacle: 7:44–50
(a) Of Moses: 7:44
(b) Of Joshua: 7:45
(c) Of David: 7:45–46
(d) Of Solomon: 7:47–50
(e) Of God: 7:48–50
5. The prophets: 7:51–53
D. The witness of Stephen: 7:54–8:1
1. The attitude of the council: 7:54
2. The announcement by Stephen: 7:55–56
3. The action of the council: 7:57–59
4. The death of Stephen: 7:59–8:1

Part Three: The Witness In Judaea and Samaria Acts 8–12

I. Transition: Results of the death of Stephen: 8:1–4
A. The persecution: 8:1,3
B. The burial of Stephen: 8:2
C. The expanded witness of the church: 8:4
II. The witness of Philip: 8:5–40
A. Ministry in Samaria: 8:5–25
1. The witness of Philip: 8:5–13
(a) The work of Philip: 8:5–7, 12
(b) The response of the Samaritans: 8:6–12
(c)Simon the Sorcerer: 8:9–13
2. The work Peter and John: 8:14–17
(a) The coming of Peter and John: 8:14
(b) The coming of the Holy Spirit: 8:15–17
(c) The response of Simon: 8:18–19
(d) The warning of Simon: 8:20–24
B. Ministry to the Ethiopian: 8:26–40
1. Preparation: 8:26–28
2. The witness: 8:29–35
3. The response: 8:36–38
C. Azotus: 8:39–40
III. The witness of Saul: 9:1–31
A. The conversion of Saul: 9:1–9
1. His purpose: 9:1–2
2. His vision: 9:3–9
3. The voice: 9:4–7
4. The blindness: 9:8–9
B. The commissioning of Saul through Ananias: 9:10–19
1. The call: 9:10–16
2. The commission: 9:17–19
C. The mission of Saul: 9:20–31
1. Saul at Damascus: 9:20–25
(a) His witness: 9:20–22
(b) The response: 9:21–23
(c) His escape: 9:23–25
2. Saul at Jerusalem: 9:26–30
(a) His reception: 9:26–28
(b) His activity: 9:28–29
(c) His departure: 9:29–30
D. Transition: Rest in the church: 9:31
IV. The witness of Peter: 9:32–12:35
A. At Lydda: 9:32–35
1. The believers: 9:32
2. The sick man: 9:33
3. Healing of the sick man: 9:34
4. The response: 9:35
B. At Joppa: 9:36–43

1. The death of Dorcus: 9:36–37
2. The call of Peter: 9:38–39
3. The ministry of Peter: 9:40–41
4. Response to the ministry: 9:42–43

C. At Caesarea: 10:1–48

1. Cornelius' vision: 10:1–8
   (a) The man Cornelius: 10:1–2
   (b) The vision of Cornelius: 10:3–6
   (c) The response of Cornelius: 10:7–8
2. Peter's vision: 10:9–22
   (a) The vision: 10:9–12
   (b) The voice: 10:13–16
3. The arrival of the messengers: 10:17–22
4. The visit to Cornelius' house: 10:23–48
   (a) The journey: 10:23
   (b) The reception: 10:24–27
   (c) The explanation: 10:27–28
   (d) The question: 10:29
   (e) The answer: 10:30–33
   (f) The unfinished sermon: 10:34–43
   (g) Cornelius' response: 8:44–48

D. At Jerusalem: 11:1–12:25

1. The problem of Gentile conversion: 11:1–18
   (a) The problem: 11:1–3
   (b) Explaining God's work among the Gentiles: 11:4–17
   (c) The decision: 4:18

V. The church in Antioch of Syria: 11:19–30

A. Evangelization of Antioch: 11:19–21
B. Visit by Barnabus: 11:22–24
C. Saul chosen as pastor-teacher: 11:25–26
D. Information revealed by Agabus: 11:27–30

VI. Persecution led by Herod: 12:1–25

A. The murder of James: 12:1–2
B. The arrest of Peter: 12:3–4
C. The deliverance of Peter 12:5–19
D. The death of Herod: 12:20–23

VII. The declaration of the Word: 12:24–25

Part Four: Witness To The Known World Acts 13–28

I. The first missionary journey: 13:1–14:28

A. The call to ministry: Acts 13:1–3
B. Ministry in Paphos in Cyprus: 13:4–12
C. Ministry in Antioch in Pisidia: 13:13–50

1. Pisidia: 13:13–16
2. The message: 13:17–37
   (a) The exodus deliverance: 13:17
   (b) The wilderness wanderings: 13:18
   (c) The conquest of Canaan: 13:19
   (d) The rule of Saul and David: 13:20–23
   (e) The ministry of John the Baptist: 13:24–25
   (f) Crucifixion and resurrection of Jesus: 13:26–37
   (g) The invitation: 13:38–41
3. The response: 13:42–50

D. Ministry in Iconium: 13:51–14:5
E. Ministry in Lystra: 14:6–25
F. Ministry in Syria: 14:26–28

II. The Jerusalem council: 15:1–35

A. The problem: 15:1–3
B. The meetings: 15:4–21

1. First public session: 15:4–5
2. Private session of the apostles and elders: 15:6
3. Second public session: 15:7–21
   (a) Peter's report: 15:7–11
   (b) Paul and Barnabas' report: 15:12

(c) James' report: 15:13–21
C. The decision: 15:19–21
D. The letters: 15:22–35
III. Second missionary journey: 15:36–18:22
A. Disagreement between Paul and Barnabas: 15:36–41
B. Ministry in Lystra: 16:1–5
C. Ministry in Troas: 16:6–10
D. Ministry in Philippi: 16:11–40
E. Ministry in Thessalonica: 17:1–9
F. Ministry in Berea: 17:10–14
G. Ministry in Athens: 17:15–34
H. Ministry in Corinth: 18:1–18
I. Ministry in Ephesus: 18:19–21
J. Jerusalem and Antioch: 18:22
IV. Third missionary journey: 18:23–21:14
A. Asia Minor: 18:23
B. Ministry in Ephesus: 18:24–19:41
1. Apollos: 18:24–28
2. Disciples of John: 19:1–7
3. School of Tyranus: 19:8–12
4. The sons of Sceva: 19:13–17
5. Dedication of the converts: 19:18–20
6. The decision: 19:21
7. Defenders of Diana: 19:23–41
C. Ministry in Macedonia and Greece: 20:1–5
D. Ministry in Troas: 20:6–12
E. Ministry in Miletus: 20:13–38
1. The journey: 20:13–16
2. Meeting with the elders from Ephesus: 20:17–35
(a) Review of his ministry: 20:17–21
(b) Facing the future: 20:22–24
(c) Paul's conscience: 20:25–27
(d) he warning 20:28–31
(e) Commended to God: 20:32
(f) Paul's example of hard work: 20:33–35
3. The farewell: 20:36–38
F. Ministry in Tyre: 21:1–6
G. Ministry in Ptolemias: 21:7
H. Ministry in Caesarea: 21:8–14
V. The final visit to Jerusalem and the trip to Rome: 21:15–28:31
A. Jerusalem: 21:15–23:32
1. Journey to Jerusalem: 21:15–17
2. Rumors against Paul: 21:18–30
(a) That he had degraded the law of Moses: 21:18–26
(b) That he had desecrated the Temple: 21:27–30
3. The reaction of Paul: 21:23–26
4. The rescue of Paul: 21:30–32
5. Replies by Paul: 21:33–23:10
(a) The Jewish crowd: 22:1–23
(b) The Roman centurion: 22:24–26
(c) Chief captain: 22:26–30
(d) The Sanhedrin: 23:1–10
(l) Paul's defense: 23:1
(2) Encounter with the high priest: 23:2–5
(3) A divided court: 23:6–10
6. Paul's revelation: 23:11
7. Revenge against Paul: 23:12–15
8. Rescue of Paul: 23:16–32
(a) The plot revealed: 23:16–22
(b) The letter: 23:25–30
(b) The escape: 23–32
B. Caesarea: 23:33–26:32
1. Before Felix: 23:33–24:27
(a) The accusations of Tertulius: 24:1–9

(b) The answer of Paul: 24:10–21
(c) The response of Felix: 24:22–27
2. Before Festus: 25:1–12
3. Festus and Agrippa: 25:13–27
4. Before Agrippa: 26:1–32
(a) Paul speaks for himself: 26:1–23
(a) Agrippa challenged by Paul: 26:24–29
(c) The verdict: 26:30–32

C. Enroute to Rome: 27:17–28:31
1. The storm: 27:1–44
2. The viper: 28:1–6
3. The healing: 28:7–10
4. The journey continues: 28:11–15

D. Rome: 28:16–31
1. Meeting with the Jews: 28:16–29
2. Ministry: 28:30–31

2. Helpful summaries of Acts

Bird's eye view

Acts is Luke the historian's account of the spread of Christianity from Jerusalem to the Rome, the capital of the known world, in the days after Jesus' death and resurrection.

Reading plan

The following reading plan, taking one reading per day, enables you to read through Acts in forty-six days.

Acts 1:1–26
Acts 2:1–2:21
Acts 2:22–2:47
Acts 3:1–3:26
Acts 4:1–4:22
Acts 4:23–4:37
Acts 5:1–5:16
Acts 5:17–5:42
Acts 6:1–6:15
Acts 7:1–7:19
Acts 7:20–7:45
Acts 7:46–7:60
Acts 8:1–8:25
Acts 8:26–8:40
Acts 9:1–9:22
Acts 9:23–9:43
Acts 10:1–10:23
Acts 10:24–10:48
Acts 11:1–11:30
Acts 12:1–12:25
Acts 13:1–13:31
Acts 13:32–13:52
Acts 14:1–14:28
Acts 15:1–15:21
Acts 15:22–15:41
Acts 16:1–16:15
Acts 16:16–16:40
Acts 17:1–17:15
Acts 17:16–17:34
Acts 18:1–18:28
Acts 19:1–19:20
Acts 19:21–19:41
Acts 20:1–20:16
Acts 20:17–20:38
Acts 21:1–21:16
Acts 21:17–21:40
Acts 22:1–22:30
Acts 23:1–23:22
Acts 23:23–23:35
Acts 24:1–24:27
Acts 25:1–25:27
Acts 26:1–26:32
Acts 27:1–27:12

Acts 27:13–27:44

Acts 28:1–28:15

Acts 28:16–28:31

Verses to memorize

Acts 1:8

But ye shall receive power, after that the Holy Spirit is come on you: and ye shall be witnesses unto me both in Jerusalem, and in all Judaea, and in Samaria, and unto the uttermost part of the earth. KJV

Acts 4:12

Neither is there salvation in any other: for there is none other name under heaven given among men, whereby we must be saved. KJV

Acts 5:42

And daily in the temple, and in every house, they ceased not to teach and preach Jesus Christ. KJV

Acts 10:43

To him give all the prophets witness, that through his name whosoever believeth in him shall receive remission of sins. KJV

Statistics

Fifth New Testament book

28 chapters

1,007 verses

24,250 words

Number of Old Testament quotations and allusions in Acts: 57.

Famous saying found in Acts

"More blessed to give than to receive" Acts 20:35

Names/titles given

Praxeis: "Acts." (That is a summary of the achievements of certain men.)

The Acts of the Apostles

The Acts of the Holy Spirit

3. Helpful keys to turn to in understanding Acts

Key word/phrase

Witness

The promise of the Father, 1:4.

Key verse/verses

Acts 1:8; 2:42

Themes to study

What Jesus continued to do and to teach through his Spirit in the apostles.

Conversions in Acts

Acts as a blueprint for evangelism

Spirit-filled people in Acts

"All of them were filled with the Holy Spirit and began to speak in other tongues." Acts 2:4

Peter, Acts 4:8

Peter and John, Acts 4:31

Stephen, Acts 7.55

Barnabas, Acts 11:24

Paul, Acts 13:9

The disciples, Acts 13:52

Miracles performed by Peter

Cures a lame man, Acts 3:7

Ananias and Sapphira are struck down dead, Acts 5:5, 10

Heals the sick, Acts 5:15

Heals the paralytic, Aeneas, Acts 9:34

Brings Dorcas back to life, Acts 9:40

Jesus is proclaimed as the central truth of the Gospel

Acts 2:23–24

Acts 3:14–15

Acts 10:39–41

Acts 17:3

Jesus in Acts

In Acts Jesus is the resurrected Savior.

Lessons to learn from Acts

- Christian meetings should include:
- Christian teaching
- Fellowship
- Breaking of bread
- Praying
- Christian fellowships should be known for their loving care of people.
- The book of Acts shows us how Christian mission should be carried out.

4. Chapter by chapter: outline of every chapter of Acts

Acts 1

Matthew Henry's introduction

The inspired historian begins his narrative of the Acts of the Apostles,

I. With a reference to, and a brief recapitulation of, his gospel, or history of the life of Christ, inscribing this, as he had done that, to his friend Theophilus, vv. 1, 2.

II. With a summary of the proofs of Christ's resurrection, his conversation with his disciples, and the instructions he gave them during the forty days, of his continuance on earth, vv. 3–5.

III. With a particular narrative of Christ's ascension into heaven, his disciples' discourse with him before he ascended, and the angels' discourse with them after he ascended, vv. 6–11.

IV. With a general idea of the embryo of the Christian church, and its state from Christ's ascension to the pouring out of the Spirit, vv. 12–14.

V. With a particular account of the filling up of the vacancy that was made in the sacred college by the death of Judas, by the electing of Matthias in his room, vv. 15–26.

Dr. Adam Clarke's analysis of chapter

St. Luke's prologue, containing a repetition of Christ's history from his passion till his ascension, 1–9.

Remarkable circumstances in the ascension, 10, 11.

The return of the disciples to Jerusalem, and their employment there, 12–14.

Peter's discourse about the death of Judas Iscariot, 15– 20, and the necessity of choosing another apostle in his place, 21, 22.

Barnabas and Matthias being set apart by prayer, the apostles having given their votes, Matthias is chosen to succeed Judas, 23–26.

A detailed analysis of chapter

Proofs of Christ's resurrection. (1–5)

Christ's ascension. (6–11)
The apostles unite in prayer. (12–14)
Matthias chosen in the place of Judas. (15–26)

Key verse

Verse 3: "After his suffering, he showed himself to these men and gave many convincing proofs that he was alive. He appeared to them over a period of forty days and spoke about the kingdom of God."

Key word / key phrase

Verse 9, "he was taken up."

Key event / key person / key theme

The ascension of Jesus

Key thought

The beginning of the chapter makes a helpful link between the life of the early Church and the Gospels.

Key thing to look out for

Verse 8 states that "witnessing" was to be the job of Jesus' followers.

Key Bible cross-reference

Verse 20. See Psalm 69:25.

Key "by way of explanation"

Verse 3. "In Acts 1, Luke tells us that Jesus showed himself alive by many infallible proofs (*en pollois tekmeriois*), an expression indicating the strongest type of legal evidence." Bernard Ramm

Key "Quotable Quote"

"When Jesus ascended, he changed his presence for his omnipresence."

F.P. Wood

Acts 2

Matthew Henry's introduction

Between the promise of the Messiah (even the latest of those promises) and his coming many ages intervened; but between the promise of the Spirit and his coming there were but a few days; and during those days the apostles, though they had received orders to preach the gospel to every creature, and to begin at Jerusalem, yet lay perfectly wind-bound, incognito–concealed, and not offering to preach. But in this chapter the north wind and the south wind awake, and then they awake, and we have them in the pulpit presently.

Dr. Adam Clarke's analysis of chapter

The day of Pentecost being arrived, and the disciples assembled, the Holy Spirit descended as a mighty rushing wind, and in the likeness of fiery tongues sat on them; in consequence of which, they were all enabled to speak different languages, which they had never learned, 1–4.

An account of people from various countries who there present, and were astonished to hear the apostles declare the wonderful works of God in their respective languages, 5–12.

Some cavil, 13, and are confounded by Peter, who asserts that this work is of God; and that thereby a most important prophecy was fulfilled, 14–21.

He takes occasion from this to preach Jesus to them, as the true Lord and only Messiah, 22–36.

The people are alarmed and convinced, and inquire what they shall do, 37.

He exhorts them to repent and be baptized in the name of Jesus, that they may receive remission of sins and the gift of the Holy Spirit, 38–40.

They gladly receive his word, about three thousand are baptized and added to the Church in one day; they continue steadfast in the apostles' doctrine and fellowship, 41, 42.

The apostles work many miracles; and the disciples have all things in common, and live in a state of great happiness and Christian fellowship, 43–47.

A detailed analysis of chapter

The arrival of the Holy Spirit on the Day of Pentecost. (1–4)

The apostles speak in different languages. (5–13)

Peter's sermon to the Jews. (14–36)

Three thousand people converted. (37–41)

The fellowship of the believers. (42–47)

Key verse

Verse 3: "They saw what seemed to be tongues of fire that separated and came to rest on each of them."

Key word / key phrase

Verse 4, "filled with the Holy Spirit."

Key event / key person / key theme

The coming of the Holy Spirit

Key thought

No wonder Pentecost has been called the birthday of the Christian Church.

Key thing to look out for

Peter assumes the role of leader among the Christians.

Key Bible cross-reference

Verses 17–21. See Joel 2:28–32.

Key "by way of explanation"

Verse 22, "accredited . . . by miracles, wonders, and signs." Jesus' miracles demonstrated that the expected Messiah had indeed arrived.

Key "Quotable Quote"

"No man is excluded from calling upon God, the gate of salvation is set open unto all men: neither is there any other thing which keepeth us back from entering in, save only our own unbelief."

John Calvin, commentating on Acts 2:21

Acts 3

Matthew Henry's introduction

In this chapter we have a miracle and a sermon: the miracle wrought to make way for the sermon, to confirm the doctrine that was to be preached, and to make way for it into the minds of the people; and then the sermon to explain the miracle, and to sow the ground which by it was broken up.

Dr. Adam Clarke's analysis of chapter

Peter and John go to the temple at the hour of prayer, and heal a man who had been lame from his mother's womb, 1–8.

The people are astonished, and the apostles inform them that it was not by their own power they had healed the man, but through the power of Jesus of Nazareth, whom they had crucified, 9–16.

Peter both excuses and reproves them, and exhorts them to repentance, 17–21.

Shows that in Jesus Christ the prophecy of Moses was fulfilled; and that all the prophets testified of Jesus and his salvation, 22–24; and that, in him, the covenant made with Abraham is fulfilled; and that Christ came to bless them by turning them away from their iniquities, 25, 26.

A detailed analysis of chapter

A lame man healed by Peter and John. (1–11)

Peter's sermon to the Jews. (12–26)

Key verse

Verse 6: "Silver or gold I do not have, but what I have I give you. In the name of Jesus Christ of Nazareth, walk."

Key word / key phrase

Verse 6, "in the name of Jesus Christ of Nazareth, walk."

Key event / key person / key theme

Peter heals and preaches

Key thought

It is repentance that brings God's gift of forgiveness (verse 19), refreshment (verse 19) knowledge of Jesus (verse 20), and restoration (verse 21), but repentance involves a change of lifestyle (verse 26).

Key thing to look out for

Peter used every available opportunity to preach the gospel.

Key Bible cross-reference

Verse 13. See Exodus 3:15.

Key "by way of explanation"

Verse 24, "all the prophets from Samuel on." The prophecies of all the prophets from the time of Samuel all contained some important strand about the Messiah.

Key "Quotable Quote"

"If you are feeling tired and therefore in need of a spiritual tonic, go to the book of Acts."

D. Martyn Lloyd-Jones

Acts 4

Matthew Henry's introduction

In going over the last two chapters, where we met with so many good things that the apostles did, I wondered what was become of the scribes and Pharisees, and chief priests, that they did not appear to contradict and oppose them, as they had used to treat Christ himself; surely they were so confounded at first with the pouring out of the Spirit that they were for a time struck dumb! But I find we have not lost them; their forces rally again, and here we have an encounter between them and the apostles; for from the beginning the gospel met with opposition.

Dr. Adam Clarke's analysis of chapter

The priests And Sadducees are incensed at the apostles' teaching, and put them in prison, 1–3.

The number of those who believed, 4.

The rulers, elders, and scribes call the apostles before them, and question them about their authority to teach, 5–7.

Peter, filled with the Holy Spirit, answers, and proclaims Jesus, 8–12.

They are confounded at his discourse and the miracle wrought on the lame man, yet command them not to preach in the name of Jesus, 13–18.

Peter and John refuse to obey, 19, 20.

They are farther threatened and dismissed, 21, 22.

They return to their own company, who all join in praise and prayer to God, 23–30.

God answers, and fills them with the Holy Spirit, 31.

The blessed state of the primitive disciples, 32–35.

The case of Joses, who sells his estate, and brought the money to the common stock. 36. 37.

A detailed analysis of chapter

Peter and John imprisoned. (1–4)

The apostles boldly testify to Christ. (5–14)

Peter and John refuse to be silenced. (15–22)

The believers unite in prayer and praise. (23–31)

The believers share their possessions. (32–37)

Key verse

Verse 13: "When they saw the courage of Peter and John and realized that they were unschooled, ordinary men, they were astonished and they took note that these men had been with Jesus."

Key word / key phrase

Verse 12, "salvation is found in no one else."

Key event / key person / key theme

Peter before the Sanhedrin

Key thought

In the face of threats of punishments, the believers praised God and asked, not for release from danger, but for courage. See also 5:41.

Key thing to look out for

The characteristics of the early church.

Key Bible cross-reference

Verse 11. See Psalm 118:22.

Key "by way of explanation"

Verse 13, "courage." This is one of the characteristics of the first Christians. See 2:29; 4:29, 31; 28:31.

Key "Quotable Quote"

"To witness to the gospel by word and life is the

great calling of the ministry of the layperson."

Robert C. Jones, former National Director, Church Army, USA

Acts 5

Matthew Henry's introduction

In this chapter we have,

I. The sin and punishment of Ananias and Sapphira, who, for lying to the Holy Spirit, were struck dead at the word of Peter, vv. 1–11.

II. The flourishing state of the church, in the power that went along with the preaching of the gospel, vv. 12–16.

III. The imprisonment of the apostles, and their miraculous discharge out of prison, with fresh orders to go on to preach the gospel, which they did, to the great vexation of their persecutors, vv. 17–26.

IV. Their arraignment before the great Sanhedrim, and their justification of themselves in what they did, vv. 27–33.

V. Gamaliel's counsel about them, that they should not persecute them, but let them alone, and see what would come of it, and their concurrence, for the present, with this advice, in the dismissing of the apostles with no more than a scourging, vv. 34–40.

VI. The apostles' cheerful progress in their work notwithstanding the prohibition laid on them and the indignity done them, vv. 41, 42.

Dr. Adam Clarke's analysis of chapter

The hypocrisy of Ananias and his wife Sapphira, and their awful death, 1–11.

The apostles work many miracles, and the Church of God is increased, 12–16.

The high priest and the Sadducees, being incensed against the apostles, seize and put them in prison, 17, 18.

The angel of God delivers them, and commands them to go to the temple, and proclaim the Gospel, 19, 20.

The high priest, having gathered the council together in the morning, sends to the prison to have the apostles brought before him, 21.

The offers return, and report that they found the prison shut, and the watch set, but that the men had got out, 22, 23.

A messenger arrives in the meanwhile, and says that the apostles are preaching in the temple, 24, 25.

The captain and officers go and bring than before the council, who expostulate with them, 26–28.

The apostles defend themselves, and charge the council with the murder of Christ; and assert his resurrection from the dead and ascension to the right hand of God, 29–32.

The council are confounded, and purpose to slay the apostles, 33.

Gamaliel gives them seasonable and prudent advice, 34–39.

The council agree to it, but, before they discharge the apostles, beat them, and command them not to teach in the name of Jesus, 40.

They depart rejoicing in their persecution, and continue to preach Jesus Christ, 41, 42.

A detailed analysis of chapter

The death of Ananias and Sapphira. (1–11)

The power which accompanied the preaching

of the gospel. (12–16)

The apostles imprisoned, but freed by an angel. (17–25)

The apostles witness to Christ before the council. (26–33)

The advice of Gamaliel, and the council let the apostles go. (34–42)

Key verse

Verse 12: "The apostles performed many miraculous signs and wonders among the people."

Key word / key phrase

Verse 3, "lied to the Holy Spirit."

Key event / key person / key theme

Ananias and Sapphira

Key thought

God's judgment comes to the early Christian fellowship.

Key thing to look out for

Verse 42, for a summary of the message of the apostles.

Key Bible cross-reference

Verse 19. See Genesis 16:7.

Key "by way of explanation"

Verse 40, "flogged." This refers to the Jewish punishment of thirty-nine lashes. See 2 Corinthians 11:24.

Key "Quotable Quote"

"After I have been wearied almost to death in preaching, writing and conversation, and going from place to place, God imparted new life to my soul, and enabled me to intercede with him for an hour and a half and two hours together."

George Whitefield

Acts 6

Matthew Henry's introduction

In this chapter we have,

I. The discontent that was among the disciples about the distribution of the public charity, v. 1.

II. The election and ordination of seven men, who should take care of that matter, and ease the apostles of the burden, vv. 2–6.

III. The increase of the church, by the addition of many to it, v. 7.

IV. A particular account of Stephen, one of the seven.

- A. His great activity for Christ, v. 8.
- B. The opposition he met with from the enemies of Christianity, and his disputes with them, vv. 9, 10.
- C. The convening of him before the great Sanhedrim, and the crimes laid to his charge, vv. 11–14.
- D. God's owning him on his trial, v. 15.

Dr. Adam Clarke's analysis of chapter

The Hellenistic Jews complain against the Hebrews, that their widows were neglected in the daily ministration, 1.

To remedy the evil complained of, the apostles appoint seven deacons to superintend the temporal affairs of the Church, 2–6.

The progress of the word of God in Jerusalem, 7.

Stephen, one of the deacons, becomes very eminent, and confounds various Jews of the synagogues of the Libertines, etc., 8–10.

They suborn false witnesses against him, to get him put to death, 11–14.

He appears before the council with an angelic countenance, 15.

A detailed analysis of chapter

The appointment of deacons. (1–7)

Stephen falsely accused of blasphemy. (8–15)

Key verse

Verse 11: "We have heard Stephen speak words of blasphemy against Moses and against God."

Key word / key phrase

Verse 7, "so the word of God spread."

Key event / key person / key theme

Deacons appointed

Key thought

Verses 13,14. There is a striking similarity between the changes brought against Jesus, and those brought against Stephen. He seems to have grasped the revolutionary newness of the Christian faith.

Key thing to look out for

The qualities needed for these "servants."

Key Bible cross-reference

Verse 3. See Exodus 18:21.

Key "by way of explanation"

Verse 6, "prayed and laid their hands on them." In the Old Testament people were commissioned for special tasks and had hands laid on them as a sign of God's blessing, Numbers 27:23. Prayer is seen to be vital here.

Key "Quotable Quote"

"Jesus Christ didn't commit the gospel to an advertising agency; he commissioned disciples."

Joseph Bayly

Acts 7

Matthew Henry's introduction

When our Lord Jesus called his apostles out to be employed in services and sufferings for him, he told them that yet the last should be first, and the first last, which was remarkably fulfilled in St. Stephen and St. Paul, who were both of them late converts, in comparison of the apostles, and yet got the start of them both in services and sufferings; for God, in conferring honors and favors, often crosses hands. In this chapter we have the martyrdom of Stephen, the first martyr of the Christian church, who led the van in the noble army. And therefore his sufferings and death are more largely related than those of any other, for direction and encouragement to all those who are called out to resist unto blood, as he did. Here is,

I. His defense of himself before the council, in answer to the matters and things he stood charged with, the scope of which is to show that it was no blasphemy against God, nor any injury at all to the glory of his name, to say that the temple should be destroyed and the customs of the ceremonial law changed. And,

A. He shows this by going over the history of the Old Testament, and observing that God never intended to confine his favors to that place, or that ceremonial law; and that they had no reason to expect he should, for the people of the Jews had always been a provoking people, and had forfeited the privileges of their peculiarity: nay, that that holy place and that law were but figures of good things to come, and it was no disparagement at all to them to say that they must give place to better things, vv. 1–50. And then,

B. He applies this to those that prosecuted him, and sat in judgment on him, sharply reproving them for their wickedness, by which they had brought on themselves the ruin of their place and nation, and then could not bear to hear of it, vv. 51–53.

II. The putting of him to death by stoning him, and his patient, cheerful, pious submission to it, vv. 54–60.

Dr. Adam Clarke's analysis of chapter

Stephen, being permitted to answer for himself relative to the charge of blasphemy brought against him by his accusers, gives a circumstantial relation of the call of Abraham, when he dwelt in Mesopotamia, in Charran, The history of Jacob and Joseph, 1–17.

The persecution of their fathers in Egypt, 18,19.

The history of Moses and his acts till the exodus from Egypt, 20–37.

The rebellion and idolatry of the Israelites in the wilderness, 38–43.

The erection of the tabernacle of witness, which continued till the time of David, 44–46.

Of the temple built by Solomon for that God who cannot be confined to temples built by hands, 47–50.

Being probably interrupted in the prosecution of his discourse, he urges home the charge of rebellion against God, persecution of his prophets, the murder of Christ, and neglect of their own law against them, 51–53.

They are filled with indignation, and proceed to violence, 54.

He sees the glory of God, and Christ at the right hand of the Father; and declares the glorious vision, 55,56.

They rush on him, drag him out of the city, and stone him, 57,58.

He involves the Lord Jesus, prays for his murderers, and expires, 59,60.

A detailed analysis of chapter

Stephen's defense. (1–50)

Stephen reproves the Jews for the death of Christ. (51–53)

The martyrdom of Stephen. (54–60)

Key verse

Verse 58: "Meanwhile, the witnesses laid their clothes at the feet of a young man named Saul."

Key word / key phrase

Verse 58, "began to stone him."

Key event / key person / key theme

Stephen's sermon and martyrdom

Key thought

Stephen's speech/sermon is a great summary of Old Testament salvation history.

Key thing to look out for

The first we hear of Saul (Paul) is in connection with the first Christian martyrdom.

Key Bible cross-reference

Verses 2–3. See Genesis 12:1.

Key "by way of explanation"

Verse 51, "uncircumcised hearts and ears." Stephen's hearers were all physically circumcised and proud to be Jews. But when Stephen pointed to the evil in their hearts they could not allow him to go on living.

Key "Quotable Quote"

"Solemn prayers, rapturous devotions, are but repeated hypocrisies unless the heart and mind be conformable to them."

William Law

Acts 8

Matthew Henry's introduction

In this chapter we have an account of the persecutions of the Christians, and the propagating of Christianity thereby. It was strange, but very true, that the disciples of Christ the more they were afflicted the more they multiplied.

Dr. Adam Clarke's analysis of chapter

A general persecution is raised against the Church, 1.

Stephen's burial, 2.

Saul greatly oppresses the followers of Christ, 3, 4.

Philip the deacon goes to Samaria, preaches, works many miracles, converts many people, and baptizes Simon the sorcerer, 5–13.

Peter and John are sent by the apostles to Samaria; they confirm the disciples, and by prayer and imposition of hands they confer the Holy Spirit, 14–17.

Simon the sorcerer, seeing this, offers them money, to enable him to confer the Holy Spirit, 18, 19.

He is sharply reproved by Peter, and exhorted to repent, 20–23.

He appears to be convinced of his sin, and implores an interest in the apostle's prayers, 24.

Peter and John, having preached the Gospel in the villages of Samaria, return to Jerusalem, 25.

An angel of the Lord commands Philip to go towards Gaza, to meet an Ethiopian eunuch, 26.

He goes, meets, and converses with the eunuch, preaches the Gospel to him, and baptizes him, 27–38.

The Spirit of God carries Philip to Azotus, passing through which, he preaches in all the cities till he comes to Caesarea, 39, 40.

A detailed analysis of chapter

Saul persecutes the Church. (1–4)

Philip's success at Samaria. Simon the sorcerer baptized. (5–13)
The hypocrisy of Simon detected. (14–25)
Philip and the Ethiopian. (26–40)

Key verse

Verse 4: "Those who had been scattered preached the word wherever they went."

Key word / key phrase

Verses 15,17,19, "received the Holy Spirit."

Key event / key person / key theme

The expansion of the Church

Key thought

The spread of the Christian message was one positive result of persecution.

Key thing to look out for

Philip's openness to the Holy Spirit was such that he could be led from a busy city mission to minister to one person on an inter-city highway.

Key Bible cross-reference

Verses 32–33. See Isaiah 53:7,8.

Key "by way of explanation"

Verse 30, "heard the man reading." In those days it was quite normal to read aloud, rather than read silently.

Key "Quotable Quote"

"Assent to the truth of the Word is but an act of the understanding, which reprobates and devils may exercise. But justifying faith is a compounded habit, and hath its seat both in the understanding and will: and, therefore, called a believing 'with the heart' (Romans 10:10), yea, a believing 'with all the heart' (Acts 8:37)."

William Gurnall

Acts 9

Matthew Henry's introduction

In this chapter we have,

I. The famous story of St. Paul's conversion from being an outrageous persecutor of the gospel of Christ to be an illustrious professor and preacher of it.

A. How he was first awakened and wrought on by an appearance of Christ himself to him as he was going on an errand of persecution to Damascus: and what a condition he was in while he lay under the power of those convictions and terrors, vv. 1–9.

B. How he was baptized by Ananias, by immediate directions from heaven, vv. 10–19.

C. How he immediately commenced doctor, and preached the faith of Christ, and proved what he preached, vv. 20–22.

D. How he was persecuted, and narrowly escaped with his life, vv. 23–25.

E. How he was admitted among the brethren at Jerusalem: how he preached, and was persecuted there, vv. 26–30.

F. The rest and quietness which the churches enjoyed for some time after this, v. 31.

II. The cure wrought by Peter on Eneas, who had long been laid up with a palsy, vv. 32–35.

III. The raising of Tabitha from death to life, at the prayer of Peter, vv. 36–43.

Dr. Adam Clarke's analysis of chapter

Saul, bent on the destruction of the Christians, obtains letters from the high priest, authorizing him to seize those whom he should find at Damascus, and bring them bound to Jerusalem, 1, 2.

On his way to Damascus, he has a Divine vision, is convinced of his sin and folly, is struck blind, and remains three days without sight, and neither eats nor drinks, 3–9.

Ananias, a disciple, is commanded in a vision to go and speak to Saul, and restore his sight, 10–16.

Ananias goes and lays his hands on him, and he receives his sight, and is baptized, 17–19.

Saul, having spent a few days with the Christians at Damascus, goes to the synagogues, pro claims Christ, and confounds the Jews, 20–22.

The Jews lay wait to kill him, but the disciples let him down over the walls of the city in a basket, by night, and he escapes to Jerusalem, 23–25.

Having wished to associate with the disciples there, they avoid him; but Barnabas takes and brings him to the apostles, and declares his conversion, 26, 27.

He continues in Jerusalem preaching Christ, and arguing with the Hellenistic Jews, who endeavor to slay him; but the disciples take him to Caesarea, and send him thence to his own city Tarsus, 28–30.

About this time, the Churches, being freed from persecution, are edified and multiplied, 31.

Peter heals Eneas at Lydda, who had been afflicted with the palsy eight years: in consequence of which miracle, all the people of Lydda and Saron are converted, 32–35.

Account of the sickness and death of a Christian woman named Tabitha, who dwelt at Joppa; and her miraculous restoration to life by the ministry of Peter, 36–41.

Gracious effects produced among the inhabitants of Lydda by this miracle, 42, 43.

A detailed analysis of chapter

The conversion of Saul. (1–22)

Saul is persecuted at Damascus, and goes to Jerusalem. (23–31)

Aeneas is healed. (32–35)

Dorcas is raised to life. (36–43)

Key verse

Verse 3: "As he neared Damascus on his journey, suddenly a light from heaven flashed around him."

Key word / key phrase

Verse 3, "a light from heaven flashed."

Key event / key person / key theme

Saul's conversion

Key thought

Saul's conversion is so pivotal that Luke records it three times. See also 22:3–16; 26:9–18.

Key thing to look out for

Paul's conversion illustrates perfectly that salvation is all due to God's grace.

Key Bible cross-reference

Verse 2. See Isaiah 17:1.

Key "by way of explanation"

Verse 10, "Ananias." He is only mentioned here and in 22:12. Like so many of God's faithful servants, his service for God went largely unrecorded.

Key "Quotable Quote"

"Entrance into heaven is not at the hour of death, but at the moment of conversion."

Benjamin Whichcote

Acts 10

Matthew Henry's introduction

It is a turn very new and remarkable which the story of this chapter gives to the Acts of the apostles; hitherto, both at Jerusalem and every where else where the ministers of Christ came, they preached the gospel only to the Jews, or those Greeks that were circumcised and proselyted to the Jews' religion; but now, "Lo, we turn to the Gentiles;" and to them the door of faith is here opened: good news indeed to us sinners of the Gentiles. The apostle Peter is the man that is first employed to admit uncircumcised Gentiles into the Christian church; and Cornelius, a Roman centurion or colonel, is the first that with his family and friends is so admitted.

Dr. Adam Clarke's analysis of chapter

An angel appears to Cornelius, a centurion, and directs him to send to Joppa, for Peter, to instruct him in the way of salvation, 1–6.

He sends accordingly, 7, 8.

While the messengers are on their way to Joppa, Peter has a remarkable vision, by which he is taught how he should treat the Gentiles, 9–16.

The messengers arrive at the house of Simon the tanner, and deliver their message, 17–22.

They lodge there that night, and on the morrow Peter accompanies them to Caesarea, where they find Cornelius and his friends assembled, waiting the coming of Peter, 23, 24.

Peter makes an apology for his coming, and inquires for what purpose Cornelius had sent for him, 25–29.

Cornelius answers, 30–33.

And Peter preaches unto him Jesus, as the Savior of the world, and the Judge of quick and dead, 34–43.

While he speaks the Holy Spirit descends on Cornelius and his company; and they speak with new tongues, and magnify God, 44–46.

Peter commands them to be baptized in the name of the Lord, 47, 48.

A detailed analysis of chapter

Cornelius is told to send for Peter. (1–8)

Peter's vision. (9–18)

He goes to Cornelius. (19–33)

His teaching given to Cornelius. (34–43)

The gifts of the Holy Spirit poured out. (44–48)

Key verse

Verse 42: "He commanded us to preach to the people and to testify that he is the one whom God appointed as judge of the living and the dead."

Key word / key phrase

Verse 45, "even on the Gentiles."

Key event / key person / key theme

Peter and Cornelius

Key thought

The early Christians begin to learn that the gospel is not only for Jews.

Key thing to look out for

It is possible for the most dedicated Christian to be full of prejudice.

Key Bible cross-reference

Verse 34. See Deuteronomy 10:17.

Key "by way of explanation"

Verse 28, "God has shown me." Peter needed a vision to get his thinking in line with God's thinking about non-Jews. Now he saw that Jews and non-Jews were equal in God's sight.

Key "Quotable Quote"

"One filled with joy preaches without preaching."

Mother Teresa of Calcutta

Acts 11

Matthew Henry's introduction

In this chapter we have,

I. Peter's necessary vindication of what he did in receiving Cornelius and his friends into the church, from the censure he lay under for it among the brethren, and their acquiescence in it, vv. 1–18.

II. The good success of the gospel at Antioch, and the parts adjacent, vv. 19–21.

III. The carrying on of the good work that was begun at Antioch, by the ministry of Barnabas first, and afterwards of Paul in conjunction with him, and the lasting name of Christian first given to the disciples there, vv. 22–26.

IV. A prediction of an approaching famine, and the contribution that was made among the Gentile converts for the relief of the poor saints in Judea, on that occasion, vv. 27–30.

Dr. Adam Clarke's analysis of chapter

Peter returns to Jerusalem, and is accused of having associated with the Gentiles, 1–3.

He defends himself by relating at large the whole business about Cornelius, 4–17.

His defense is accepted, and the whole Church glorifies God for having granted unto the Gentiles repentance unto life, 18.

An account of the proceedings of those who were scattered abroad by the persecution that was raised about Stephen; and how they had spread the Gospel among the circumcision, in Phoenice, Cyprus, and Antioch, 19–21.

The Church at Jerusalem, hearing of this, sends Barnabas to confirm them in the faith, 22, 23.

His character, 24.

He goes to Tarsus to seek Saul, whom he brings to Antioch, where the disciples are first called CHRISTIANS, 25, 26.

Certain prophets foretell the dearth which afterwards took place in the reign of the Emperor Claudias, 27, 28.

The disciples send relief to their poor brethren to Judea, by the hands of Barnabas and Saul, 29. 30.

A detailed analysis of chapter

Peter's defense. (1–18)

The success of the gospel at Antioch. (19–24)

The disciples called Christians. Relief sent to Judea. (25–30)

Key verse

Verse 15: "As I began to speak, the Holy Spirit came on them as he had come on us at the beginning."

Key word / key phrase

Verse 4, "Peter . . . explained everything."

Key event / key person / key theme

Peter defends his ministry

Key thought

Verse 18 makes a convenient summary of the important step the early Christians had now taken about preaching the gospel.

Key thing to look out for

Verse 29 shows how Christians should set about using their resources to help fellow-Christians.

Key Bible cross-reference

Verse 1. See Hebrews 4:12.

Key "by way of explanation"

Verse 18, "repentance unto life." All too often repentance is pictured as a negative turning away from sin without its integral second part being included: turning to Jesus for life.

Key "Quotable Quote"

"It is a quality of the Kingdom of Christ that in it the repentance of sinners must always be preached."

Martin Bucer

Acts 12

Matthew Henry's introduction

In this chapter we have the story,

I. Of the martyrdom of James the apostle, and the imprisonment of Peter by Herod Agrippa, who now reigned as king in Judea, vv. 1–4.

II. The miraculous deliverance of Peter out of prison by the ministry of an angel, in answer to the prayers of the church for him, vv. 6–19.

III. The cutting off of Herod in the height of his pride by the stroke of an angel, the minister of God's justice (vv. 20–23); and this was done while Barnabas and Saul were at Jerusalem, on the errand that the church of Antioch sent them on, to carry their charity; and therefore in the close we have an account of their return to Antioch, vv. 24, 25.

Dr. Adam Clarke's analysis of chapter

Herod persecutes the Christians, 1.

Kills James, 2.

And casts Peter into prison, 3, 4.

The Church makes incessant prayer for his deliverance, 5.

An angel of God opens the prison doors and leads him out, 6–10.

Peter rejoices, and comes to the house of Mary, where many were praying, and declares how he was delivered, 11–17.

The soldiers who kept the prison are examined by Herod, and he commands them to be put to death, 18, 19.

Herod is enraged against the people of Tyre, but is appeased by their submission, 20.

He makes an oration to the people, receives idolatrous praises, and an angel of the Lord smites him, and he dies a miserable death, 21–23.

The word of God increases, 24.

Barnabas and Saul, having fulfilled their ministry, return from Jerusalem accompanied by John Mark, 25.

A detailed analysis of chapter

The martyrdom of James, and the imprisonment of Peter. (1–5)

He is delivered from prison by an angel. (6–11)

Peter departs, Herod's rage. (12–19)

The death of Herod. (20–25)

Key verse

Verse 11: "Now I know without a doubt that the Lord sent his angel and rescued me from Herod's clutches and from everything the Jewish people were anticipating."

Key word / key phrase

Verse 1, "King Herod arrested."

Key event / key person / key theme

Herod's persecution

Key thought

Miracles and prayer (verse 12) go together.

Key thing to look out for

It is hard not to laugh at the scene so graphically described by Luke.

Key Bible cross-reference

Verse 4. See Exodus 12:1–27.

Key "by way of explanation"

Verse 17, James, the Lord's brother, was now the leader of the church in Jerusalem.

Key "Quotable Quote"

"One can believe intellectually in the efficacy of prayer and never do any praying."

Catherine Marshall

Acts 13

Matthew Henry's introduction

We have not yet met with things about the spreading of the gospel to the Gentiles which bears any proportion to the largeness of that commission, "Go, and disciple all nations." The door was opened in the baptizing of Cornelius; but since then we had the gospel preached to the Jews only, 11:19. It should seem as if the light which began to shine on the Gentile world had withdrawn itself. But here in this chapter that work, that great good work, is revived in the midst of the years; and though the Jews shall still have the first offer of the gospel made to them, yet, on their refusal, the Gentiles shall have their share of the offer of it.

Dr. Adam Clarke's analysis of chapter

Of the prophets and teachers in the Church of Antioch, 1.

By command of the Holy Spirit the Church appoints Saul and Barnabas to a particular work, 2, 3.

They depart, and travel to Seleucia, Cyprus, and Salamis, preaching in the Jewish synagogues, 4, 5.

At Paphos they meet with Bar-Jesus or Elymas, a Jewish sorcerer, who endeavored to prevent the deputy of the island from receiving the Christian faith, 6–8.

Saul, for the first time called Paul, denounces the judgments of God on him, and he is struck blind, 9–11.

The deputy, seeing this, is confirmed in the faith, 12.

Paul and his company leave Paphos, and come to Pamphylia, where John Mark leaves them, and returns to Jerusalem, 13.

Paul and Barnabas proceed to Antioch; and, coming into a synagogue of the Jews, are requested by the rulers of it to preach to the people, 14, 15.

Paul preaches, and proves that Jesus is the Christ, 16–41.

The Gentiles desire the sermon to be preached to them the next Sabbath, and many of the Jews and proselytes receive the Christian faith, 42, 43.

The next Sabbath the whole city attend; and the Jews, filled with envy, contradict and blaspheme, 44, 45.

Paul and Barnabas with great boldness show that, by the order of God, the Gospel was to be preached first to them; but, seeing they had rejected it, it should now be taken from them, and sent to the Gentiles, 46, 47.

The Gentiles rejoice and receive the truth, 48, 49.

The Jews raise a persecution against the apostles, and expel them, 50. They come to Iconium, full of joy and the Holy Spirit, 51, 52.

A detailed analysis of chapter

The mission of Paul and Barnabas. (1–3)

Elymas the sorcerer. (4–13)

Paul's teaching at Antioch. (14–41)

He preaches to the Gentiles, and is persecuted by the Jews. (42–52)

Key verse

Verse 12: "When the proconsul saw what had happened, he believed, for he was amazed at the teaching about the Lord."

Key word / key phrase

Verse 4, "sent on their way by the Holy Spirit."

Key event / key person / key theme

First part of Paul's first missionary journey

Key thought

Verses 29, 30. The death and resurrection of Jesus formed the basis of early preaching.

Key thing to look out for

Verse 49. A wonderful portrait of the result of preaching the gospel. It is immediately followed by persecution from the Jews.

Key Bible cross-reference

Verse 17. See Exodus 1:7.

Key "by way of explanation"

Verse 46, "had to speak . . . to you first." Paul thought that he should preach to Jews first of all, as the gospel came from Jews and was first preached to them, and because he was a Jew himself. However, the Lord himself had commissioned Paul to go to the Gentiles (Acts 22:21).

Key "Quotable Quote"

"It is possible for the most obscure person in a church, with a heart right toward God, to exercise as much power for the evangelization of the world, as it is for those who stand in the most prominent positions."

John R. Mott

Acts 14

Matthew Henry's introduction

We have, in this chapter, a further account of the progress of the gospel, by the ministry of Paul and Barnabas among the Gentiles; it goes on conquering and to conquer, yet meeting with opposition, as before, among the unbelieving Jews. Here is,

I. Their successful preaching of the gospel for some time at Iconium, and their being driven thence by the violence of their persecutors, both Jews and Gentiles, and forced into the neighboring countries, vv. 1–7.

II. Their healing a lame man at Lystra, and the profound veneration which the people conceived of them thereon, which they had much ado to keep from running into an extreme, vv. 8–18.

III. The outrage of the people against Paul, at the instigation of the Jews, the effect of which was that they stoned him, as they thought, to death; but he was wonderfully restored to life, vv. 19, 20.

IV. The visit which Paul and Barnabas made to the churches which they had planted, to confirm them, and put them into order, vv. 21–23.

V. They return to Antioch, whence they were sent forth; the good they did by the way, and the report they made to the church of Antioch of their expedition, and, if I may so say, of the campaign they had made, vv. 24–28.

Dr. Adam Clarke's analysis of chapter

Paul and Barnabas, having preached at Iconium with great success, are persecuted, and obliged to flee to Lystra and Derbe, 1–6.

Here they preach, and heal a cripple; on which, the people, supposing them to be gods, are about to offer them sacrifices, and are with difficulty prevented by these apostles, 7–18.

Certain Jews from Antioch and Iconium, coming thither, induce the people to stone Paul; who, being dragged out of the city as dead, while the disciples stand around him, rises up suddenly, and returns to the city, and the next day departs to Derbe, 19, 20.

Having preached here, he and Barnabas return to Lystra, Iconium, and Antioch, confirming the disciples, and ordaining elders in every Church, 21–23.

They pass through Pisidia and Pamphylia, 24.

Through Perga and Attalia, 25;

and sail to Antioch in Syria, 26.

When, having called the disciples together, they inform them of the door of faith opened to the Gentiles, and there abode a long time with the Church, 27, 28.

A detailed analysis of chapter

Paul and Barnabas at Iconium. (1–7)

A cripple healed at Lystra, and the attempt to sacrifice to Paul and Barnabas. (8–18)

Paul stoned at Lystra, and the churches visited again. (19–28)

Key verse

Verse 11: "The gods have come down to us in human form!"

Key word / key phrase

Verse 22, "many hardships."

Key event / key person / key theme

Second part of Paul's first missionary journey

Key thought

In their report to their home church, at the end of this first missionary journey, Paul and Barnabas emphasized that God was in control.

Key thing to look out for

Verse 22, Paul's honesty. In what way were his words strengthening?

Key Bible cross-reference

Verse 15. See Exodus 20:11.

Key "by way of explanation"

Verse 5, "stone them." Under the law this was the Jewish punishment for blasphemy.

Key "Quotable Quote"

"Lo, persecution and adversity for the truth's sake is God's scourge and God's rod and pertaineth unto all his children indifferently."

William Tyndale

Acts 15

Matthew Henry's introduction

Hitherto we have, with a great deal of pleasure, attended the apostles in their glorious travels for the propagating of the gospel in foreign parts, have seen the bounds of the church enlarged by the accession both of Jews and Gentiles to it; and thanks be to that God who always caused them to triumph. We left them, in the close of the previous chapter, reposing themselves at Antioch, and edifying the church there with the rehearsal of their experiences, and it is a pity they should ever be otherwise employed; but in this chapter we find other work (not so pleasant) cut out for them. The Christians and ministers are engaged in controversy, and those that should have been now busied in enlarging the dominions of the church have as much as they can do to compose the divisions of it; when they should have been making war on the devil's kingdom they have much ado to keep the peace in Christ's kingdom. Yet this occurrence and the record of it are of great use to the church, both for warning to us to expect such unhappy discords among Christians, and direction to us what method to take for accommodating them.

Dr. Adam Clarke's analysis of chapter

Certain teachers from Judea insist on the necessity of the converted Gentiles being circumcised, 1.

Paul and Barnabas are sent to Jerusalem to consult the apostles on this subject, 2.

They come to Jerusalem, and inform the apostles of the conversion of the Gentiles; and of the trouble which certain Pharisees had occasioned about circumcision, 3–5.

The apostles having assembled to consider the question, Peter delivers his opinion, 6–11.

Barnabas and Paul relate their success among the Gentiles, 12.

James delivers his judgment, 13–21.

The apostles and elders agree to what he proposes, and send Judas and Silas with Paul and Barnabas to the converted Gentiles, 22;

and send an epistle containing their decree to the Churches of Antioch, Syria, and Cilicia, 23–29.

Paul and his company return, and read the epistle to the brethren at Antioch, which produces great joy; and Judas and Silas preach to them, 30–32.

Judas returns to Jerusalem, but Silas continues with Paul and Barnabas, teaching and preaching, 33–35.

Paul proposes to Barnabas to visit the Churches where they had preached; and, on the latter determining to take John Mark with them, Paul refuses, 36–38.

They disagree; and Barnabas, taking John Mark, sails to Cyprus, 39.

And Paul, taking Silas, goes through Syria and Cilicia, confirming the Churches, 40, 41.

A detailed analysis of chapter

The dispute caused by false teachers. (1–6)

The council at Jerusalem. (7–21)

The letter from the council. (22–35)

Paul and Barnabas separate. (36–41)

Key verse

Verse 12: "The whole assembly became silent as they listened to Barnabas and Paul telling about the miraculous signs and wonders God had done among the Gentiles through them."

Key word / key phrase

Verse 6, "the apostles and elders met."

Key event / key person / key theme

The Jerusalem Council

Key thought

There is no difference between Jew and Gentile.

Key thing to look out for

Sharp differences arose between even the most missionary-minded of Christians. See verses 36–40.

Key Bible cross-reference

Verses 16–18. See Amos 9:11, 12.

Key "by way of explanation"

The Council of Jerusalem was called to solve an urgent and serious disagreement: Did Gentile Christians have to become Jews, that is, be circumcised and obey the Jewish Law? Jews who held this view wanted to turn Christianity into a Jewish sect. The Council decided in favor of Paul and Peter.

Key "Quotable Quote"

"There is great force hidden in a gentle command."

George Herbert

Acts 16

Matthew Henry's introduction

It is some rebuke to Barnabas that after he left Paul we hear no more of him, of what he did or suffered for Christ. But Paul, as he was recommended by the brethren to the grace of God, so his services for Christ after this are largely recorded; we are to attend him in this chapter from place to place, wherever he came doing good, either watering or planting, beginning new work or improving what was done.

Dr. Adam Clarke's analysis of chapter

Paul, coming to Derbe and Lystra, meets with Timothy, the son of a Jewess by a Greek father, whom he circumcises and takes with him into his work, 1–3.

As they pass through the different cities, they deliver the apostles' decrees to the Churches; and they are established in the faith, and daily increase in numbers, 4, 5.

They travel through Phrygia, Galatia, Mysia, and to Troas, 6–8.

Where Paul has a vision, relative to his preaching in Macedonia, 9, 10.

Leaving Troas, he sails to Samothracia and Neapolis, and comes to Philippi in Macedonia, 11, 12.

Lydia, a seller of purple, receives the apostles teaching; and she and her family are baptized, 13–16.

A young woman, with a spirit of divination, dispossessed by St. Paul, 16–18.

Her masters, finding their gain by her sooth saying gone, make an attack on Paul and Silas, drag them before the magistrates, who command them to be beaten, thrust into the closest prison, and their feet made fast in the stocks, 19–24.

Paul and Silas singing praises at midnight, the prison doors are miraculously opened, and all the bonds of the prisoners loosed, 25, 26.

The keeper being alarmed, supposing that the prisoners were fled, is about to kill himself, but is prevented by Paul, 27–28.

He inquires the way of salvation, believes, and he and his whole family are baptized, 29–34.

The next morning the magistrates order the apostles to be dismissed, 35, 36.

Paul pleads his privilege as a Roman, and accuses the magistrates of injustice, who, being alarmed, come themselves to the prison, deliver them, and beg them to depart from the city, 37–39.

They leave the prison, enter into the house of Lydia, comfort the brethren, and depart, 40.

A detailed analysis of chapter

Paul takes Timothy to be his assistant. (1–5)

Paul proceeds to Macedonia, and the conversion of Lydia. (6–15)

An evil spirit expelled, Paul and Silas scourged and imprisoned. (16–24)

The conversion of the jailer at Philippi. (25–34)

Paul and Silas released. (35–40)

Key verse

Verse 14: "One of those listening was a woman named Lydia, a dealer in purple cloth from the city of Thyatira, who was a worshiper of God. The Lord opened her heart to respond to Paul's message."

Key word / key phrase

Verse 1, "He came to Derbe."

Key event / key person / key theme

First part of Paul's second missionary journey: from Asia Minor to Europe.

Key thought

It is the Holy Spirit who is directing Paul.

Key thing to look out for

Paul's and Silas' response to severe flogging, and unjust imprisonment.

Key Bible cross-reference

Verse 14. See Revelation 1:11.

Key "by way of explanation"

Verse 37, "without a trial." A Roman citizen could not be beaten in public. What is worse here is that the trial of Paul and Silas was also clearly contrary to Roman law. Verse 10: here for the first time, the story is told in the first person: "we". Luke has joined Paul, and is giving his own eyewitness account of events.

Key "Quotable Quote"

"No human birth can compare to the supernatural birth of a child of God."

J.M. Boice

Acts 17

Matthew Henry's introduction

We have here a further account of the travels of Paul, and his services and sufferings for Christ. He was not like a candle on a table, that gives light only to one room, but like the sun that goes its circuit to give light to many.

Dr. Adam Clarke's analysis of chapter

Paul and his company, passing through Amphipolis and Apollonia, come to Thessalonica, were they preach the Gospel to the Jews, several of whom believe, 1–4.

Others raise a mob, and bring Jason, who had received the apostles, before the magistrates, who, having taken bail of him and his companions, dismiss them, 5–9.

Paul and Silas are sent away by night unto Berea, where they preach to the Jews, who gladly receive the Gospel, 10–12.

Certain Jews from Thessalonica, hearing that the Bereans had received the Gospel, come thither and raise up a persecution, 13.

Paul is sent away by the brethren to Athens, where he preaches to the Jews, 14–17.

He is encountered by the Epicureans and Stoics,

who bring him to the Areopagus, and desire him to give a full explanation of his doctrine, 18–20.

The character of the Athenians, 21.

Paul preaches to them, and gives a general view of the essential principles of theology, 22–31.

Some mock, some hesitate, and some believe, and, among the latter, Dionysias and Damaris, 32–34.

A detailed analysis of chapter

Paul at Thessalonica. (1–9)

The noble behavior of the Bereans. (10–15)

Paul at Athens. (16–21)

He preaches there. (22–31)

The scornful behavior of the Athenians. (32–34)

Key verse

Verse 5: "But the Jews were jealous; so they rounded up some bad characters from the marketplace, formed a mob and started a riot in the city."

Key word / key phrase

Verse 16, "Paul was greatly distressed."

Key event / key person / key theme

Second part of Paul's second missionary journey

Key thought

Verse 31, the proof of the truth of Christ is in the resurrection.

Key thing to look out for

Verse 11. The good characteristic displayed by the Bereans in this verse is a model for all time.

Key Bible cross-reference

Verses 24, 25. See 1 Kings 8:27.

Key "by way of explanation"

In the time of Paul the Areopagus was a court which dealt with problems concerning religion and morals.

Key "Quotable Quote"

"Were you but as willing to get the knowledge of God and heavenly things as you are to know how to work in your trade, you would have set yourself to it before this day, and you would have spared no cost or pains till you had got it. But you account seven years little enough to learn your trade, and will not bestow one day in seven in diligent learning the matters of your salvation."

Richard Baxter

Acts 18

Matthew Henry's introduction

In this chapter we have,

I. Paul's coming to Corinth, his private converse with Aquila and Priscilla, and his public reasonings with the Jews, from whom, when they rejected him, he turned to the Gentiles, vv. 1–6.

II. The great success of his ministry there, and the encouragement Christ gave him in a vision to continue his labors there, in hopes of further success, vv. 7–11.

III. The molestations which after some time he met with there from the Jews, which he got pretty well through by the coldness of Gallio, the Roman governor, in the cause, vv. 12–17.

IV. The progress Paul made through many countries, after he had continued long at Corinth, for the edifying and watering of the churches which he had founded and planted, in which circuit he made a short visit to Jerusalem, vv. 18–23.

V. An account of Apollo's improvement in knowledge, and of his usefulness in the church, vv. 24–28.

Dr. Adam Clarke's analysis of chapter

Paul, leaving Athens, comes to Corinth, meets with Aquila and Priscilla, and labors with them at tent-making, 1–3.

He preaches, and proves that Jesus was the Christ, 4, 5.

The Jews oppose and blaspheme; and he purposes to go to the Gentiles, 6.

Justus, Crispus, and several of the Corinthians believe, 7, 8.

Paul has a vision, by which he is greatly comforted, 9, 10.

He continues there a year and six months, 11.

Gallio being deputy of Achaia, the Jews make insurrection against Paul, and bring him before the deputy, who dismisses the cause; whereon the Jews commit a variety of outrages, 12–17.

Paul sails to Syria, and from thence to Ephesus, where he preaches, 18–20.

He leaves Ephesus-goes to Caesarea, visits Antioch, Galatia, and Phrygia, 21–23.

Account of Apollos and his preaching, 24–28.

A detailed analysis of chapter

Paul at Corinth, with Aquila and Priscilla. (1–6)

He continues to preach at Corinth. (7–11)

Paul before Gallio. (12–17)

He visits Jerusalem. (18–23)

Apollos teaches at Ephesus and in Achaia. (24–28)

Key verse

Verse 11: "So Paul stayed for a year and a half, teaching them the word of God."

Key word / key phrase

Verse 26, "they invited him to their home."

Key event / key person / key theme

Paul's ministry in Corinth

Key thought

Verses 5–7. It was not for lack of trying that Paul tried to convert the Jews.

Key thing to look out for

How encouraging Paul's vision must have been in the middle of all the persecution he received. See verse 9.

Key Bible cross-reference

Verse 18. See Numbers 6:18.

Key "by way of explanation"

Verse 11, "a year and a half." Paul stayed varying lengths of time in different places on his missionary travels. His year and a half stay in Corinth was one of the longer times he spent in one town.

Key "Quotable Quote"

"Christianity is a missionary religion, converting, advancing, aggressive, encompassing the world; a non-missionary Church is in the bands of death."

Friedrich Max Müller

Acts 19

Matthew Henry's introduction

We left Paul in his circuit visiting the churches (18:23), but we have not forgotten, nor has he, the promise he made to his friends at Ephesus, to return to them, and make some stay there; now this chapter shows us his performance of that promise, his coming to Ephesus, and his continuance there two years.

Dr. Adam Clarke's analysis of chapter

Paul, coming to Ephesus, finds certain disciples who had not received the gift of the Holy Spirit, knowing only the baptism of John, but receive it through the imposition of his hands, 1–7.

He preaches for three months in the synagogues, 8.

Many being hardened, he leaves the synagogues, and teaches daily in the school of Tyrannus for two years, 9, 10.

He works many miracles, 11, 12.

Account of the vagabond exorcist Jews, and the seven sons of Sceva, 13–17.

Many are converted, and burn their magical books, 18–20.

Paul purposes to pass through Macedonia and Achaia, to go to Jerusalem, and afterwards to Rome; but, having sent Timotheus and Erastus to Macedonia, continues a little longer in Asia, 21, 22.

Demetrius, a silversmith of Ephesus, raises an uproar against Paul, which, after some tumultuous proceedings, is appeased by the town clerk, 23–41.

A detailed analysis of chapter

Paul instructs the disciples of John at Ephesus. (1–7)

He teaches there. (8–12)

The Jewish exorcists disgraced. Some Ephesians burn their evil books. (13–20)

The storm of protest at Ephesus. (21–31)

The assembly appeased. (32–41)

Key verse

Verse 8: "Paul entered the synagogue and spoke boldly there for three months, arguing persuasively about the kingdom of God."

Key word / key phrase

Verse 23, "the Way."

Key event / key person / key theme

Paul's ministry in Ephesus

Key thought

Repentance is not enough. Christianity is made complete when the Holy Spirit is received following faith in Christ and his forgiveness.

Key thing to look out for

Demetrius the silversmith has not been the last person to viciously oppose Christianity in order to protect his commercial interests.

Key Bible cross-reference

Verse 4. See John 1:26, 27.

Key "by way of explanation"

Ephesus was a wealthy and powerful city, "the treasure house of Asia." Paul's missionary strategy was to choose important centers with influence and links over a wide area.

Key "Quotable Quote"

"The Church is: a conspiracy of love for a dying world, a spy mission into enemy occupied territory ruled by the powers of evil, a prophet from God with the greatest news the world has ever heard, the most life changing and most revolutionary institution that has existed on earth."

Peter Kreeft

Acts 20

Matthew Henry's introduction

In this chapter we have,

I. Paul's travels up and down about Macedonia, Greece, and Asia, and his coming at length to Troas, vv. 1–6.

II. A particular account of his spending one Lord's day at Troas, and his raising Eutychus to life there, vv. 7–12.

III. His progress, or circuit, for the visiting of the churches he had planted, in his way towards Jerusalem, where he designed to be by the next feast of Pentecost, vv. 13–16.

IV. The farewell sermon he preached to the presbyters at Ephesus, now that he was leaving that country, vv. 17–35.

V. The very sorrowful parting between him and them, vv. 36–38. And in all these we find Paul very busy to serve Christ, and to do good to the souls of men, not only in the conversion of heathen, but in the edification of Christians.

Dr. Adam Clarke's analysis of chapter

Paul retires to Macedonia, 1.

He goes into Greece, where he tarries three months and, purposing to sail to Syria, he returns through Macedonia, 2,3.

Several people accompany him into Asia, and then go before and tarry for him at Troas, 4,5.

Paul and Luke sail from Philippi, and in five days reach Troas, where they meet their brethren from Asia, and abide there seven days, 6.

On the first day of the week, the disciples coming together to break bread, Paul preaching to them, and continuing his speech till mid night, a young man of the name of Eutychus, being in a deep sleep, fell from the third loft and was killed, 7–9.

Paul restores him to life, resumes his discourse, and continuing it till daybreak, then departs, 10–12.

Luke and his companions come to Assos, whither Paul comes by land, 13.

He embarks with them at Assos, comes to Mitylene, 14.

Sails thence, and passes by Chios, arrives at Samos, tarries at Trogyllium, and comes to Miletus, 15.

Purposing to get as soon as possible to Jerusalem,

he sends from Miletus, and calls the elders of the Church of Ephesus, to whom he preaches a most directing sermon, gives them the most solemn exhortations, kneels down and prays with them, takes a very affecting leave of them, and sets sail for Caesarea, in order to go to Jerusalem, 16–38.

A detailed analysis of chapter

Paul's journeys. (1–6)
Eutychus restored to life. (7–12)
Paul travels toward Jerusalem. (13–16)
Paul's teaching to the elders of Ephesus. (17–27)
Their farewell. (28–38)

Key verse

Verse 7: "On the first day of the week we came together to break bread. Paul spoke to the people and, because he intended to leave the next day, kept on talking until midnight."

Key word / key phrase

Verse 28, "keep watch."

Key event / key person / key theme

Second part of Paul's third missionary journey

Key thought

Paul did not believe in ten-minute-long sermons.

Key thing to look out for

By God's grace Paul was able to turn Eutychus' tragic death into a triumph.

Key Bible cross-reference

Verse 24. See 2 Timothy 4:7.

Key "by way of explanation"

Verse 3, "a plot against him." This time the Jews thought that they would be able to finish Paul off. But God saved him through his last minute change of route.

Key "Quotable Quote"

"Wherever the missionary character of the doctrine of election is forgotten then God's people have betrayed their trust."

Leslie Newbigin

Acts 21

Matthew Henry's introduction

We have, with a great deal of pleasure, attended the apostle in his travels throughout the Gentile nations to preach the gospel, and have seen a great harvest of souls gathered in to Christ; there we have seen likewise what persecutions he endured; yet still out of them all the Lord presently delivered him, 2 Tim. 3:11. But now we are to attend him to Jerusalem, and there into lasting bonds; the days of his service now seem to be over, and nothing to remain but days of suffering, days of darkness, for they are many. It is a thousand pities that such a workman should be laid aside; yet so it is, and we must not only acquiesce, as his friends then did, saying, "The will of the Lord be done;" but we must believe, and shall find reason to do so, that Paul in the prison, and at the bar, is as truly glorifying God, and serving Christ's interest, as Paul in the pulpit was.

Dr. Adam Clarke's analysis of chapter

Paul and his company sail from Miletus, and come to Coos, Rhodes, and Patara, 1.

Finding a Phoenician ship at Patara, they go on board, sail past Cyprus, and land at Tyre, 2, 3.

Here they find disciples, and stay seven days, and are kindly entertained, 4, 5.

Having bade the disciples farewell, they take ship and sail to Ptolemais, salute the brethren, stay with them one day, come to Caesarea, and lodge with Philip, one of the seven deacons, 6–9.

Here they tarry a considerable time, and Agabus the prophet foretells Paul's persecution at Jerusalem, 10, 11.

The disciples endeavor to dissuade him from going; but he is resolute, and he and his company depart, 12–16.

They are kindly received by James and the elders, who advise Paul, because of the Jews, to show his respect for the law of Moses, by purifying himself, with certain others that were under a vow; with which advice he complies, 17–26.

Some of the Asiatic Jews, finding him in the temple, raise an insurrection against him, and would have killed him had he not been rescued by the chief captain, who orders him to be bound and carried into the castle, 27–36.

Paul requests liberty to address the people, and is permitted, 37–40.

A detailed analysis of chapter

Paul's journey toward Jerusalem. (1–7)

Paul at Caesarea. The prophecy of Agabus, Paul at Jerusalem. (8–18)

He is persuaded to join in ceremonial observances. (19–26)

Being in danger from the Jews, he is rescued by the Romans. (27–40)

Key verse

Verse 12: "When we heard this, we and the people there pleaded with Paul not to go up to Jerusalem."

Key word / key phrase

Verse 33, "and arrested him."

Key event / key person / key theme

Paul is arrested

Key thought

The importance of discernment. Here, the Spirit warned of coming trials; the addition, "not to go," did not come from the Spirit. Paul was going under the compulsion of the Spirit (8:22).

Key thing to look out for

Paul's life was saved by Roman soldiers, stationed in the Fortress of Antonia at the northern end of the temple. Notice what the commander wanted (verse 34).

Key Bible cross-reference

Verses 23, 24. See Numbers 6:13–21.

Key "by way of explanation"

Verse 18, "James." This James was Jesus' brother, the author of the New Testament letter bearing his name, and the leader of the Christians in Jerusalem.

Key "Quotable Quote"

"The Great Commission is far more than evangelism. The Great Commission is to make disciples."

Chuck Colson

Acts 22

Matthew Henry's introduction

In the close of the previous chapter we had Paul bound, according to Agabus's prophecy of the hard usage he should receive from the Jews at Jerusalem, yet he had his tongue set at liberty, by the permission the chief captain gave him to speak for himself; and so intent he is on using that liberty of speech which is allowed him, to the honor of Christ and the service of his interest, that he forgets the bonds he is in, makes no mention of them, but speaks of the great things Christ had done for him with as much ease and cheerfulness as if nothing had been done to ruffle him or put him into disorder.

Dr. Adam Clarke's analysis of chapter

Paul, in his address to the people, gives an account of his birth and education, 1–3.

His prejudices against Christianity, 4, 5.

And of his miraculous conversion, and call to the apostleship, 6–21.

The Jews, hearing him say that God had sent him to preach the Gospel to the Gentiles, become exceedingly outrageous, and clamor for his life, 22, 23.

The chief captain orders him to be examined by scourging; but he, pleading his privilege as a Roman citizen, escapes the torture, 24–29.

The next day the chief captain brings Paul before the chief priests and their council, 30.

A detailed analysis of chapter

Paul's account of his conversion. (1–11)

Paul directed to preach to the Gentiles. (12–21)

The anger of the Jews. Paul appeals to his Roman citizenship. (22–30)

Key verse

Verse 21: "Go; I will send you far away to the Gentiles."

Key word / key phrase

Verse 3, "I am a Jew."

Key event / key person / key theme

Paul's defense before the mob

Key thought

Verse 25. Paul used his God-given wits and his Roman citizenship to good effect.

Key thing to look out for

It seems that Paul never tired of telling his personal conversion story. His defense was to tell his story.

Key Bible cross-reference

Verse 2. See John 5:2.

Key "by way of explanation"

Verse 3, "brought up in this city." Although Paul was born in Tarsus, he was educated in Jerusalem and had the privilege of sitting at the feet of Gamaliel, the leading rabbi of the day.

Key "Quotable Quote"

"If my testimony makes anyone wish to emulate me, it is a mistaken testimony; it is not a witness to Jesus."

Oswald Chambers

Acts 23

Matthew Henry's introduction

The close of the previous chapter left Paul in the high priest's court, into which the chief captain (whether to his advantage or no I know not) had removed his cause from the mob; and, if his enemies act there against him with less noise, yet it is with more subtlety. Now here we have,

I. Paul's protestation of his own integrity, and of a civil respect to the high priest, however he had on a sudden spoken warmly to him, and justly, vv. 1–5.

II. Paul's prudent contrivance to get himself clear of them, by setting the Pharisees and Sadducees at variance one with another, vv. 6–9.

III. The governor's seasonable interposal to rescue him out of their hands likewise, v. 10.

IV. Christ's more comfortable appearing to him, to animate him against those difficulties that lay before him, and to tell him what he must expect, v. 11.

V. A bloody conspiracy of some desperate Jews to kill Paul, and their drawing in the chief priests and the elders to be aiders and abettors with them in it, vv. 12–15.

VI. The discovery of this conspiracy to Paul, and by him to the chief captain, who perceived so much of their inveterate malice against Paul that he had reason enough to believe the truth of it, vv. 16–22.

VII. The chief captain's care of Paul's safety, by which he prevented the execution of the design; he sent him away immediately under a strong guard from Jerusalem to Cæsarea, which was now the residence of Felix, the Roman governor, and there he safely arrived, vv. 23–35.

Dr. Adam Clarke's analysis of chapter

Paul defending himself before the high priest, he commands him to be smitten on the mouth, 1, 2.

Paul sharply reproves him, and, being reproved for this by one of the attendants, accounts for his conduct, 3–5.

Seeing that the assembly was composed of Pharisees and Sadducees, and that he could expect no justice from his judges, he asserts that it was for his belief in the resurrection that he was called in question, on which the Pharisees declare in his favor, 6–9.

A great dissension arises, and the chief captain, fearing lest Paul should be pulled to pieces, brings him into the castle, 10. He is comforted by a dream, 11.

More than forty people conspire his death, 12–15. Paul's sister's son, hearing of it, informs the captain of the guard, 16–22.

He sends Paul by night, under a strong escort of horse and foot, to Caesarea, to Felix, and with him a letter, stating the circumstances of the case, 23–33.

They arrive at Caesarea, and Felix promises him a hearing when his accusers shall come down, 34, 35.

A detailed analysis of chapter

Paul's defense before the council of the Jews. (1–5)

Paul's defense. He receives a divine assurance that he will go to Rome. (6–11)

The Jews plot to kill Paul, Lysias sends him to Caesarea. (12–24)

Lysias's letter to Felix. (25–35)

Key verse

Verse 11: "Take courage! As you have testified about me in Jerusalem, so you must also testify in Rome."

Key word / key phrase

Verse 14, "until we have killed Paul."

Key event / key person / key theme

Plot to kill Paul

Key thought

The plot to kill Paul this time involved a solemn oath taken by those who wanted him dead.

Key thing to look out for

Had it not been for the quick thinking and courageous action of Paul's unnamed nephew Paul would have been killed.

Key Bible cross-reference

Verse 5. See Philippians 3:5.

Key "by way of explanation"

Verse 3, "whitewashed wall!" Paul was not paying any compliment here. Inside the well-painted tomb there were rotting corpses. Paul is calling the high priest Ananias a hypocrite to his face.

Key "Quotable Quote"

"The greatest mission field we face is not in some faraway land. It's barely across the street. The culture most lost to the gospel is our own–our children and neighbors."

Dwight Ozard

Acts 24

Matthew Henry's introduction

We left Paul a prisoner at Cæsarea, in Herod's judgment-hall, expecting his trial to come on quickly; for in the beginning of his imprisonment his affairs moved very quickly, but afterwards very slowly. In this chapter we have his arraignment and trial before Felix the governor at Cæsarea.

Dr. Adam Clarke's analysis of chapter

After five days, Ananias the high priest, the elders, and one Tertullus, an orator, come to Caesarea to accuse Paul, 1.

The oration of Tertullus, 2–9.

Paul's defense, 10–21.

Felix, having heard his defense, proposes to leave the final determination of it till Claudius Lysias should come down; and, in the mean time, orders Paul to be treated with humanity and respect, 22, 23.

Felix, and Drusilla his wife, hear Paul about the faith of Christ; and Felix it greatly affected, 24, 25.

On the expectation of obtaining money for his liberation, Felix keeps Paul in prison, 26,

and being superseded in the government of Judea by Porcius Festus, in order to please the Jews, he leaves Paul bound, 27.

A detailed analysis of chapter

The Tertullus' speech against Paul. (1–9)

Paul's defense before Felix. (10–21)

Felix trembles at Paul's arguments. (22–27)

Key verse

Verse 14: "I admit that I worship the God of our fathers as a follower of the Way, which they call a sect."

Key word / key phrase

Verse 27, "he left Paul in prison."

Key event / key person / key theme

Paul before Felix

Key thought

Verse 16. One of the sources of Paul's strength came from the fact that he had a clear conscience.

Key thing to look out for

What made Felix afraid?

Key Bible cross-reference

Verse 9. See 1 Thessalonians 2:16.

Key "by way of explanation"

Verse 5, "ringleader of a Nazarene sect." If this could be proved to be the case then Paul had broken the law. It was illegal to be the leader of a religious group, without the prior approval of the Romans.

Key "Quotable Quote"

"It is a crime against lost humanity to go in the name of Christ and missions just to do the social work and yet neglect calling men to repent and follow Christ with all their hearts."

K.P. Yohannan

Acts 25

Matthew Henry's introduction

Some think that Felix was turned out, and Festus succeeded him, quickly after Paul's imprisonment, and that the two years mentioned in the close of the previous chapter are to be reckoned from the beginning of Nero's reign; but it seems more natural to compute them from Paul's being delivered into the hands of Felix. However, we have here much the same management of Paul's case as we had in the previous chapter.

Dr. Adam Clarke's analysis of chapter

Porcius Festus being appointed governor of Judea, instead of Felix, the Jews beseech him to have Paul brought up to Jerusalem, that he might be tried there; they lying in wait to kill him on the way, 1–3.

Festus refuses, and desires those who could prove any thing against him, to go with him to Caesarea, 4, 5.

Festus, having tarried at Jerusalem about ten days, returns to Caesarea, and the next day Paul is brought to his trial, and the Jews of Jerusalem bring many groundless charges against him, against which he defends himself, 6–8.

In order to please the Jews, Festus asks Paul if he be willing to go up to Jerusalem, and be tried there, 9.

Paul refuses, and appeals to Caesar, and Festus admits the appeal, 10–13.

King Agrippa, and Bernice his wife, come to Cesarea to visit Festus, and are informed by him of the accusations against Paul, his late trial, and his appeal from them to Caesar, 14–21.

Agrippa desires to hear Paul; and a hearing is appointed for the following day, 22.

Agrippa, Bernice, the principal officers and chief men of the city being assembled, Paul is brought forth, 23.

Festus opens the business with generally stating the accusations against Paul, his trial on these accusations, the groundless and frivolous nature of the charges, his own conviction of his innocence, and his desire that the matter might be heard by the king himself, that he might have something specifically to write to the emperor, to whom he was about to send Paul, agreeably to his appeal, 24–27.

A detailed analysis of chapter

Paul before Festus, he appeals to Caesar. (1–12)

Festus confers with Agrippa about Paul. (13–27)

Key verse

Verse 10: "I am now standing before Caesar's court, where I ought to be tried. I have not done any wrong to the Jews, as you yourself know very well."

Key word / key phrase

Verse 12, "To Caesar you will go!"

Key event / key person / key theme

Paul appeals to the Emperor

Key thought

Verse 9. From this we can see that Paul was maliciously and falsely charged with heresy, sacrilege, and sedition. It is no wonder that he knew there would be no justice in Jerusalem.

Key thing to look out for

Verses 19,26. If it were not so tragic, Festus' bewilderment would be amusing.

Key Bible cross-reference

Verse 23. See 26:30.

Key "by way of explanation"

Verse 11, "I appeal to Caesar!" This meant appealing to Nero. As a Roman citizen Paul was claiming his rights. To appear before Caesar was to appear before the highest court in the empire.

Key "Quotable Quote"

"I hope no missionary will ever be as lonely as I have been."

Lottie Moon

Acts 26

Matthew Henry's introduction

We left Paul at the bar, and Festus, and Agrippa, and Bernice, and all the great men of the city of Cæsarea, on the bench, or about it, waiting to hear what he had to say for himself. Now in this chapter we have,

I. The account he gives of himself, in answer to the calumnies of the Jews. And in this,

A. His humble address to king Agrippa, and the compliment he passed on him, vv. 1–3.

B. His account of his origin, and education, his profession as a Pharisee, and his adherence still to that which was then the main article of his creed, in distinction from the Sadducees, the "resurrection of the dead," however in rituals he had since departed from it, vv. 3–8.

C. Of his zeal against the Christian religion, and the professors of it, in the beginning of his time, vv. 9–11.

D. Of his miraculous conversion to the faith of Christ, vv. 12–16.

E. Of the commission he received from heaven to preach the gospel to the Gentiles, vv. 17, 18.

F. Of his proceedings pursuant to that commission, which had given this mighty offence to the Jews, vv. 19–21.

G. Of the doctrine which he had made it his business to preach to the Gentiles, which was so far from destroying the law and the prophets that it showed the fulfilling of both, vv. 22, 23.

II. The remarks that were made on his apology.

A. Festus thought he never heard a man talk so madly, and slighted him as crazed, v. 24. In answer to him, he denies the charge, and appeals to king Agrippa, vv. 25–27.

B. King Agrippa, being more closely and particularly dealt with, thinks he never heard a man talk more rationally and convincingly, and owns himself almost his convert (v. 28), and Paul heartily wishes him so, v. 29.

C. They all agreed that he was an innocent man, that he ought to be set at liberty, and that it was a pity he was provoked to put a bar in his own door by appealing to Cæsar, vv. 30–32.

Dr. Adam Clarke's analysis of chapter

Paul answers for himself before Agrippa, to whom he pays a true compliment, in order to secure a favorable hearing, 1–3;

gives an account of his education from his youth up, 4, 5;

shows that the Jews persecuted him for his maintaining the hope of the resurrection, 6–8;

states his persecution of the Christians, 9–11;

gives an account of his miraculous conversion, 12–16;

and of his call to the ministry, 16–18.

His obedience to that call, and his success in preaching the doctrine of Christ crucified, 19–23.

While he is thus speaking, Festus interrupts him, and declares him to be mad through his abundant learning, 24;

which charge he modestly refutes with inimitable address, and appeals to King Agrippa for the truth and correctness of his speech, 25–27.

On which, Agrippa confesses himself almost converted to Christianity, 28.

Paul's affectionate and elegant address to him on this declaration, 29.

The council breaks up, and they all pronounce him innocent, 30–32.

A detailed analysis of chapter

Paul's defense before Agrippa. (1–11)

His conversion and preaching to the Gentiles. (12–23)

Festus and Agrippa convinced of Paul's innocence. (24–32)

Key verse

Verse 13: "About noon, O king, as I was on the road, I saw a light from heaven, brighter than the sun, blazing around me and my companions."

Key word / key phrase

Verse 19, "not disobedient."

Key event / key person / key theme

Paul is tried before Agrippa

Key thought

Paul was accused of everything under the sun, including going mad.

Key thing to look out for

King Agrippa is put on the spot by Paul.

Key Bible cross-reference

Verse 23. See Isaiah 49:6.

Key "by way of explanation"

Verse 11, "I tried to force them to blaspheme." Paul, by his own admission here, in his pre-Christian days had tried to make Christians guilty of blasphemy so that they would be guilty of a capital offence.

Key "Quotable Quote"

"The missionary work of the non-professional missionary is essentially to live his daily life in Christ."

Roland Allen

Acts 27

Matthew Henry's introduction

This whole chapter is taken up with an account of Paul's voyage towards Rome, when he was sent thither a prisoner by Festus the governor, on his appeal to Cæsar.

Dr. Adam Clarke's analysis of chapter

It being determined that Paul should be sent to Rome, he is delivered to Julius, a centurion, 1.

They embark in a ship of Adramyttium, and come the next day to Sidon, 2, 3.

They sail thence, and pass Cyprus, Cilicia, and Pamphylia, and come to Myra, 4, 5.

They are transferred there to a ship of Alexandria going to Italy; sail past Cnidus, Crete, Salmone, and come to the Fair Havens, 6–8. Paul predicts a disastrous voyage, 9–11.

They sail from the Fair Havens, in order to reach Crete, and winter there; but, having a comparatively favorable wind, they sail past Crete, and meet with a tempest, and are brought into extreme peril and distress, 12–20.

Paul's exhortation and prediction of the loss of the ship, 21–26.

After having been tossed about in the Adriatic Sea, for many days, they are at last ship wrecked on the island of Melita; and the whole crew, consisting of two hundred and seventy-six people, escape safe to land, on broken fragments of the ship, 27–44.

A detailed analysis of chapter

Paul's travels toward Rome. (1–11)

Paul and his companions endangered by a tempest. (12–20)

He receives God's assurance of safety. (21–29)

Paul encourages those with him. (30–38)

They are shipwrecked. (39–44)

Key verse

Verse 37: "Altogether there were 276 of us on board."

Key word / key phrase

Verse 41, "the ship struck a sandbar."

Key event / key person / key theme

Paul sails for Rome and is shipwrecked

Key thought

Paul showed that the more heavenly minded you are, the more earthly use you are.

Key thing to look out for

Had it not been for Paul, all the prisoners on the ship would have been killed.

Key Bible cross-reference

Verse 3. See Matthew 11:21.

Key "by way of explanation"

Verse 43, "the centurion wanted to spare Paul's life." The centurion ordered his soldiers not to kill any of the prisoners. Out of respect for Paul the centurion followed Paul's advice and not the instincts of his own soldiers. Paul was probably the most experienced traveler on the ship.

Key "Quotable Quote"

"There are no closed doors to the gospel, provided that, once you go through the door, you don't care whether or not you come back out."

Brother Andrew

Acts 28

Matthew Henry's introduction

We are the more concerned to take notice of and to improve what is here recorded about blessed Paul because, after the story of this chapter, we hear no more of him in the sacred history, though we have a great deal of him yet before us in his epistles. We have attended him through several chapters from one judgment-seat to another, and could at last have taken leave of him with the more pleasure if we had left him at liberty; but in this chapter we are to condole with him, and yet congratulate him.

I. We condole with him as a poor ship wrecked passenger, stripped of all; and yet congratulate him,

A. As singularly owned by his God in his distress, preserved himself from receiving hurt by a viper that fastened on his hand (vv. 1–6), and being made an instrument of much good in the island on which they were cast, in healing many that were sick, and particularly the father of Publius, the chief man of the island, vv. 7–9.

B. As much respected by the people there, v. 10.

II. We condole with him as a poor confined prisoner, carried to Rome under the notion of a criminal removed by "habeas corpus" (vv. 11–16), and yet we congratulate him,

A. On the respect shown him by the Christians at Rome, who came a great way to meet him, v. 15.

B. On the favor he found with the captain of the guard, into whose custody he was delivered, who suffered him to dwell by himself, and did not put him in the common prison, v. 16.

C. On the free conversation he had with the Jews at Rome, both about his own affair (vv. 17–22) and on the subject of the Christian religion in general (v. 23), the issue of which was that God was glorified, many were edified, the rest left inexcusable, and the apostles justified in preaching the gospel to the Gentiles, vv. 24–29.

D. On the undisturbed liberty he had to preach the gospel to all comers in his own house for two years together, vv. 30–31.

Dr. Adam Clarke's analysis of chapter

St. Paul, and the rest of the crew, getting safely ashore, find that the island on which they were shipwrecked is called Melita, 1.

They are received with great hospitality by the inhabitants, 2.

A viper comes out of the bundle of sticks, laid on the fire, and seizes on Paul's hand, 3.

The people, seeing this, suppose him to be a murderer, and thus pursued by Divine vengeance, 4.

Having shook it off his hand, without receiving any damage, they change their minds, and suppose him to be a god, 5, 6.

Publius, the governor of the island, receives them courteously, and Paul miraculously heals his father, who was ill of a fever, He heals several others also, who honor them much, and give them presents, 9, 10.

After three months' stay, they embark in a ship of Alexandria, land at Syracuse, stay there three days, sail thence, pass the straits of Rhegium, and land at Puteoli; find some Christians there, tarry seven days, and set forward for Rome, 11–14.

They are met at Appii Forum by some Christians, and Paul is greatly encouraged, 15.

They come to Rome, and Julius delivers his prisoners to the captain of the guard, who permits Paul to dwell by himself only attended by the soldier that kept him, 16.

Paul calls the chief Jews together, and states his case to them, 17–20. They desire to hear him about the faith of Christ, 21, 22;

and, having appointed unto him a day, he expounds to them the kingdom of Christ, 23.

Some believe, and some disbelieve; and Paul informs them that, because of their unbelief and disobedience, the salvation of God is sent to the Gentiles, 24–29.

Paul dwells two years in his own hired house, preaching the kingdom of God, 30, 31.

A detailed analysis of chapter

Paul welcomed at Malta. (1–10)

He arrives at Rome. (11–16)

His meeting with the Jews. (17–22)

Paul preaches to the Jews, and lives in Rome as a prisoner. (23–31)

Key verse

Verse 31: "Boldly and without hindrance he preached the kingdom of God and taught about the Lord Jesus Christ."

Key word / key phrase

Verse 30, "for two whole years."

Key event / key person / key theme

Paul arrives in Rome to a two-year house arrest

Key thought

The gospel is now being proclaimed in the heart of the empire.

Key thing to look out for

Verse 3. The man who had taken command of the ship, now collects wood.

Key Bible cross-reference

Verses 26,27. See Isaiah 6:9,10.

Key "by way of explanation"

Verse 30, "two whole years." On reaching Rome Paul wasted no time in summoning the leading Jews in order to explain the kingdom of God to them.

Key "Quotable Quote"

"Young man, if I thought I could win one more soul for Christ by standing on my head and beating a tambourine with my feet I would learn how to do it."

William Booth, to Rudyard Kipling, after the latter had said how much he disliked tambourines.

5. Select bibliography for Acts

Blaiklock, E. M. *The Acts of the Apostles: An Historical Commentary.* Grand Rapids: Eerdmans, 1959.

Bruce, F. F. *Commentary on the Book of Acts.* Rev. ed. Grand Rapids: Eerdmans, 1988.

Bruce, F. F. *The Acts of the Apostles: The Greek Text with Introduction and Commentary.* Grand Rapids: Eerdmans, 1951.

Calvin, John. *Commentary On the Acts of the Apostles*. 2 vols. Edited by H. Beveridge. Grand Rapids: Eerdmans, 1949.

Harrison, E. F. *Acts: The Expanding Church.* Chicago: Moody, 1976.

Marshall, I. Howard. *Luke: Historian and Theologian*. Grand Rapids: Zondervan, 1970.

Ramsay, W. M. *St. Paul the Traveller and Roman Citizen*. Reprint. Grand Rapids: Baker, 1951.

Ramsay, William M. *The Historical Geography of Asia Minor*. London: J. Murray, 1890.

Romans

1. Book by book: Introduction to Romans

Introduction

Its genuineness

The genuineness of the Epistle to the Romans has never been questioned. It has the unbroken testimony of all antiquity, up to Clement of Rome, the apostle's "fellow laborer in the Gospel, whose name was in the Book of Life" (Phil. 4:3), and who quotes from it in his undoubted Epistle to the Corinthians, written before the close of the first century. The most searching investigations of modern criticism have left it untouched.

Date and place of writing

When and where this Epistle was written we have the means of determining with great precision, from the Epistle itself compared with the Acts of the Apostles. Up to the date when it was written the apostle had never been to Rome (Rom. 1:11, 13, 15). He was then on the eve of visiting Jerusalem with a pecuniary contribution for its Christian poor from the churches of Macedonia and Achaia, after which his purpose was to pay a visit to Rome on his way to Spain (Rom. 15:23–28). Now this contribution we know that he carried with him from Corinth, at the close of his third visit to that city, which lasted three months (Acts 20:2, 3; 24:17). On this occasion there accompanied him from Corinth certain people whose names are given by the historian of the Acts (Acts 20:4), and four of these are expressly mentioned in our Epistle as being with the apostle when he wrote it–Timotheus, Sosipater, Gaius, and Erastus (Rom. 16:21, 23). Of these four, the third, Gaius, lived in Corinth (1 Cor. 1:14), and the fourth, Erastus, was "the city's director of public works " (Rom. 16:23), which can hardly be supposed to be other than Corinth. Finally, Phœbebe, the bearer, as appears, of this Epistle, was a deaconess of the Church at Cenchrea, the eastern port of Corinth (Rom. 16:1). Putting these facts together, it is impossible to resist the conviction, in which all critics agree, that Corinth was the place from which the Epistle was written, and that it was dispatched about the close of the visit above mentioned, probably in the early spring of the year 58.

Founder of the church at Rome

The founder of this celebrated church is unknown. That it owed its origin to the apostle Peter, and that he was its first bishop, though an ancient tradition and taught in the Church of Rome as a fact not to be doubted, is refuted by the clearest evidence, and is given up even by candid Romanists. On that supposition, how are we to account for so important a circumstance being passed by in silence by the historian of the Acts, not only in the narrative of Peter's labors, but in that of Paul's approach to the metropolis, of the deputations of Roman "brethren" that came as far as Appii Forum and the Three Taverns to meet him, and of his two years' labors there (Acts 28:15, 30)? And how, consistently with his declared principle–not to build on another man's foundation (Rom. 15:20) –could he express his desire to come to them that he might have some fruit among them also, even as among other Gentiles (Rom. 1:13), if all the while he knew that they had the apostle of the circumcision for their spiritual father? And how, if so, is there no greeting to Peter among the many in this Epistle? Or, if it may be thought that he was known to be elsewhere at that particular time, how does there occur in all the Epistles which our apostle afterwards wrote from Rome not one allusion to such an origin of the church at Rome? The same considerations would seem to prove that this church owed its origin to no prominent Christian laborer; and this brings us to the much-litigated question.

Readers

Why group of Christians was this Epistle principally designed–Jewish or Gentile? That a large number of Jews and Jewish proselytes resided at this time at Rome is known to all who are familiar with the classical and Jewish writers of that and the immediately subsequent periods; and that some of them who were at Jerusalem on the day of Pentecost (Acts 2:10), and formed probably part of the three thousand converts of that day, would on their return to Rome carry the glad tidings with them, there can be no doubt. Nor are indications wanting that some of those embraced in the greetings of this Epistle were Christians already of long standing, if not among the earliest converts to the Christian faith. Others of them who had made the apostle's acquaintance elsewhere, and who, if not indebted to him for their first knowledge of Christ, probably owed much to his ministrations, seemed to have charged themselves with the duty of cherishing and consolidating the work of the Lord in the capital. And thus it is not improbable that up to the time of the apostle's arrival the Christian community at Rome had been dependent on subordinate agency for the increase of its numbers, aided by occasional visits of stated preachers from the provinces; and perhaps it may be gathered from the greetings of the last chapter that it was up to that time in a less organized, though far from less flourishing state, than some other churches to whom the apostle had already addressed Epistles. Certain it is, that the apostle writes to them expressly as a Gentile Church (Rom. 1:13, 15; 15:15, 16); and though it is plain that there were Jewish Christians among them, and the whole argument presupposes an intimate acquaintance on the part of his readers with the leading principles of the Old Testament, this will be sufficiently explained by supposing that the bulk of them, having before they knew the Lord been Gentile proselytes to the Jewish faith, had entered the pale of the Christian Church through the gate of the ancient economy.

Contents

It remains only to speak briefly of the plan and character of this Epistle. Of all the undoubted Epistles of our apostle, this is the most elaborate, and at the same time the most glowing. It has just as much in common with a theological treatise as is consistent with the freedom and warmth of a real letter. We here merely note that its first great topic is what may be termed the legal relation of man to God as a violator of His holy law, whether as merely written on the heart, as in the case of the heathen, or, as in the case of the Chosen People, as further known by external revelation; that it next treats of that legal relation as wholly reversed through believing connection with the Lord Jesus Christ; and that its third and last great topic is the new life which accompanies this change of relation, embracing at once a blessedness and a consecration to God which, rudimentally complete already, will open, in the future world, into the bliss of immediate and stainless fellowship with God.

The bearing of these wonderful truths on the condition and destiny of the Chosen People, to which the apostle next comes, though it seem but the practical application of them to his kinsmen according to the flesh, is in some respects the deepest and most difficult part of the whole Epistle, carrying us directly to the eternal springs of Grace to the guilty in the sovereign love and inscrutable purposes of God; after which, however, we are brought back to the historical platform of the visible Church, in the calling of the Gentiles, the preservation of a faithful Israeli remnant amidst the general unbelief and fall of the nation, and the ultimate recovery of all Israel to constitute, with the Gentiles in the latter day, one catholic Church of God on earth.

The remainder of the Epistle is devoted to sundry practical topics, winding up with greetings and outpourings of heart delightfully suggestive.

David Brown

Martin Luther's Preface to Romans

This letter is truly the most important piece in the New Testament. It is purest Gospel. It is well worth a Christian's while not only to memorize it word for word but also to occupy himself with it daily, as though it were the daily bread of the soul. It is impossible to read or to meditate on this letter too much or too well. The more one deals with it, the more precious it becomes and the better it tastes. Therefore I want to carry out my service and, with this preface, provide an introduction to the letter, insofar as God gives me the ability, so that every one can gain the fullest possible understanding of it. Up to now it has been darkened by glosses (explanatory notes and comments which accompany a text) and by many a useless comment, but it is in itself a bright light, almost bright enough to illumine the entire Scripture.

To begin with, we have to become familiar with the vocabulary of the letter and know what St. Paul means by the words law, sin, grace, faith, justice, flesh, spirit, etc. Otherwise there is no use in reading it.

You must not understand the word law here in human fashion, i.e., a regulation about what sort of works must be done or must not be done.

That's the way it is with human laws: you satisfy the demands of the law with works, whether your heart is in it or not. God judges what is in the depths of the heart. Therefore his law also makes demands on the depths of the heart and doesn't let the heart rest content in works; rather it punishes as hypocrisy and lies all works done apart from the depths of the heart. All human beings are called liars (Psalm 116), since none of them keeps or can keep God's law from the depths of the heart. Everyone finds inside himself an aversion to good and a craving for evil. Where there is no free desire for good, there the heart has not set itself on God's law. There also sin is surely to be found and the deserved wrath of God, whether a lot of good works and an honorable life appear outwardly or not.

Therefore in chapter 2, St. Paul adds that the Jews are all sinners and says that only the doers of the law are justified in the sight of God. What he is saying is that no one is a doer of the law by works. On the contrary, he says to them, "You teach that one should not commit adultery, and you commit adultery. You judge another in a certain matter and condemn yourselves in that same matter, because you do the very same thing that you judged in another." It is as if he were saying, "Outwardly you live quite properly in the works of the law and judge those who do not live the same way; you know how to teach everybody. You see the speck in another's eye but do not notice the beam in your own."

Outwardly you keep the law with works out of fear of punishment or love of gain. Likewise you do everything without free desire and love of the law; you act out of aversion and force. You'd rather act otherwise if the law didn't exist. It follows, then, that you, in the depths of your heart, are an enemy of the law. What do you mean, therefore, by teaching another not to steal, when you, in the depths of your heart, are a thief and would be one outwardly too, if you dared. (Of course, outward work doesn't last long with such hypocrites.) So then, you teach others but not yourself; you don't even know what you are teaching. You've never understood the law rightly. Furthermore, the law increases sin, as St. Paul says in chapter 5. That is because a person becomes more and more an enemy of the law the more it demands of him what he can't possibly do.

In chapter 7, St. Paul says, "The law is spiritual." What does that mean?

If the law were physical, then it could be satisfied by works, but since it is spiritual, no one can satisfy it unless everything he does springs from the depths of the heart. But no one can give such a heart except the Spirit of God, who makes the person be like the law, so that he actually conceives a heartfelt longing for the law and henceforward does everything, not through fear or coercion, but from a free heart. Such a law is spiritual since it can only be loved and fulfilled by such a heart and such a spirit. If the Spirit is not in the heart, then there remain sin, aversion and enmity against the law, which in itself is good, just and holy.

You must get used to the idea that it is one thing to do the works of the law and quite another to fulfill it. The works of the law are every thing that a person does or can do of his own free will and by his own powers to obey the law. But because in doing such works the heart abhors the law and yet is forced to obey it, the works are a total loss and are completely useless. That is what St. Paul means in chapter 3 when he says, "No human being is justified before God through the works of the law." From this you can see that the schoolmasters (i.e., the scholastic theologians) and sophists are seducers when they teach that you can prepare yourself for grace by means of works. How can anybody prepare himself for good by means of works if he does no good work except with aversion and constraint in his heart? How can such a work please God, if it proceeds from an averse and unwilling heart?

But to fulfill the law means to do its work eagerly, lovingly and freely, without the constraint of the law; it means to live well and in a manner pleasing to God, as though there were no law or punishment. It is the Holy Spirit, however, who puts such eagerness of unconstrained love into the heart, as Paul says in chapter 5. But the Spirit is given only in, with, and through faith in Jesus Christ, as Paul says in his introduction. So, too, faith comes only through the word of God, the Gospel, that preaches Christ: how he is both Son of God and man, how he died and rose for our sake. Paul says all this in chapters 3, 4 and 10.

That is why faith alone makes someone just and fulfills the law; faith it is that brings the Holy Spirit through the merits of Christ. The Spirit, in turn, renders the heart glad and free, as the law demands. Then good works proceed from faith itself. That is what Paul means in chapter 3 when, after he has thrown out the works of the law, he sounds as though the wants to abolish the law by faith. No, he says, we uphold the law through faith, i.e. we fulfill it through faith. "Sin" in the Scriptures means not only external works of the body but also all those movements within us which bestir themselves and move us to do the external works, namely, the depth of the heart with all its powers.

Therefore the word "do" should refer to a person's completely falling into sin. No external work of sin happens, after all, unless a person commit himself to it completely, body and soul. In particular, the Scriptures see into the heart, to the root and main source of al sin: unbelief in the depth of the heart. Thus, even as faith alone makes just and brings the Spirit and the desire to do good external works, so it is only unbelief which sins and exalts the flesh and brings desire to do evil external works. That's what happened to Adam and Eve in Paradise (cf. Genesis 3).

That is why only unbelief is called sin by Christ, as he says in John, chapter 16, "The Spirit will punish the world because of sin, because it does not believe in me." Furthermore, before good or bad works happen, which are the good or bad fruits of the heart, there has to be present in the heart either faith or unbelief, the root, sap and chief power of all sin. That is why, in the Scriptures, unbelief is called the head of the serpent and of the ancient dragon which the offspring of the woman, i.e. Christ, must crush, as was promised to Adam (cf. Genesis 3). "Grace" and "gift" differ in that grace actually denotes God's kindness or favor which he has toward us and by which he is disposed to pour Christ and the Spirit with his gifts into us, as becomes clear from chapter 5, where Paul says, "Grace and gift are in Christ, etc." The gifts and the Spirit increase daily in us, yet they are not complete, since evil desires and sins remain in us which war against the Spirit, as Paul says in chapter 7, and in Galatians, chapter 5. And Genesis, chapter 3, proclaims the enmity between the offspring of the woman and that of the serpent. But grace does do this much: that we are accounted completely just before God.

God's grace is not divided into bits and pieces, as are the gifts, but grace takes us up completely into God's favor for the sake of Christ, our intercessor and mediator, so that the gifts may begin their work in us.

In this way, then, you should understand chapter 7, where St. Paul portrays himself as still a sinner, while in chapter 8 he says that, because of the incomplete gifts and because of the Spirit, there is nothing damnable in those who are in Christ. Because our flesh has not been killed, we are still sinners, but because we believe in Christ and have the beginnings of the Spirit, God so shows us his favor and mercy, that he neither notices nor judges such sins. Rather he deals with us according to our belief in Christ until sin is killed.

Faith is not that human illusion and dream that some people think it is.

When they hear and talk a lot about faith and yet see that no moral improvement and no good works result from it, they fall into error and say, "Faith is not enough. You must do works if you want to be virtuous and get to heaven." The result is that, when they hear the Gospel, they stumble and make for themselves with their own powers a concept in their hearts which says, "I believe." This concept they hold to be true faith. But since it is a human fabrication and thought and not an experience of the heart, it accomplishes nothing, and there follows no improvement.

Faith is a work of God in us, which changes us and brings us to birth anew from God (cf. John 1). It kills the old Adam, makes us completely different people in heart, mind, senses, and all our powers, and brings the Holy Spirit with it. What a living, creative, active powerful thing is faith!

It is impossible that faith ever stop doing good. Faith doesn't ask whether good works are to be done, but, before it is asked, it has done them. It is always active. Whoever doesn't do such works is without faith; he gropes and searches about him for faith and good works but doesn't know what faith or good works are. Even so, he chatters on with a great many words about faith and good works.

Faith is a living, unshakeable confidence in God's grace; it is so certain, that someone would die a thousand times for it. This kind of trust in and knowledge of God's grace makes a person joyful, confident, and happy with regard to God and all creatures. This is what the Holy Spirit does by faith. Through faith, a person will do good to everyone without coercion, willingly and happily; he will serve everyone, suffer everything for the love and praise of God, who has shown him such grace. It is as impossible to separate works from faith as burning and shining from fire. Therefore be on guard against your own false ideas and against the chatterers who think they are clever enough to make judgments about faith and good works but who are in reality the biggest fools. Ask God to work faith in you; otherwise you will remain eternally without faith, no matter what you try to do or fabricate.

Now "justice" is just such a faith. It is called God's justice or that justice which is valid in God's sight, because it is God who gives it and reckons it as justice for the sake of Christ our Mediator. It influences a person to give to everyone what he owes him. Through faith a person becomes sinless and eager for God's commands. Thus he gives God the honor due him and pays him what he owes him.

He serves people willingly with the means available to him. In this way he pays everyone his due. Neither nature nor free will nor our own powers can bring about such a justice, for even as no one can give himself faith, so too he cannot remove unbelief. How can he then take away even the smallest sin? Therefore everything which takes place outside faith or in unbelief is lie, hypocrisy and sin (Romans 14), no matter how smoothly it may seem to go.

You must not understand flesh here as denoting only unchastity or spirit as denoting only the inner heart. Here St. Paul calls flesh (as does Christ in John 3) everything born of flesh, i.e. the whole human being with body and soul, reason and senses, since everything in him tends toward the flesh. That is why you should know enough to call that per son "fleshly" who, without grace, fabricates, teaches and chatters about high spiritual matters. You can learn the same thing from Galatians, chapter 5, where St. Paul calls heresy and hatred works of the flesh. And in Romans, chapter 8, he says that, through the flesh, the law is weakened. He says this, not of unchastity, but of all sins, most of all of unbelief, which is the most spiritual of vices.

On the other hand, you should know enough to call that person "spiritual" who is occupied with the most outward of works as was Christ, when he washed the feet of the disciples, and Peter, when he steered his boat and fished. So then, a person is "flesh" who, inwardly and outwardly, lives only to do those things which are of use to the flesh and to temporal existence. A person is "spirit" who, inwardly and outwardly, lives only to do those things which are of use to the spirit and to the life to come.

Unless you understand these words in this way, you will never understand either this letter of St. Paul or any book of the Scriptures. Be on guard, therefore against any teacher who uses these words differently, no matter who he be, whether Jerome, Augustine, Ambrose, Origen or anyone else as great as or greater than they. Now let us turn to the letter itself.

The first duty of a preacher of the Gospel is, through his revealing of the law and of sin, to rebuke and to turn into sin everything in life that does not have the Spirit and faith in Christ as its base. Thereby he will lead people to a recognition of their miserable condition, and thus they will become humble and yearn for help.

This is what St Paul does. He begins in chapter 1 by rebuking the gross sins and unbelief which are in plain view, as were (and still are) the sins of the pagans, who live without God's grace. He says that, through the Gospel, God is revealing his wrath from heaven on all mankind because of the godless and unjust lives they live. For, although they know and recognize day by day that there is a God, yet human nature in itself, without grace, is so evil that it neither thanks not honors God. This nature blinds itself and continually falls into wickedness, even going so far as to commit idolatry and other horrible sins and vices. It is unashamed of itself and leaves such things unpunished in others.

In chapter 2, St. Paul extends his rebuke to those who appear outwardly pious or who sin secretly. Such were the Jews, and such are all hypocrites still, who live virtuous lives but without eagerness and love; in their heart they are enemies of God's law and like to judge other people. That's the way with hypocrites: they think that they are pure but are actually full of greed, hate, pride and all sorts of filth (cf. Matthew 23). These are they who despise God's goodness and, by their hardness of heart, heap wrath on themselves. Thus Paul explains the law rightly when he lets no one remain without sin but proclaims the wrath of God to all who want to live virtuously by nature or by free will. He makes them out to be no better than public sinners; he says they are hard of heart and unrepentant.

In chapter 3, Paul lumps both secret and public sinners together: the one, he says, is like the other; all are sinners in the sight of God. Besides, the Jews had God's word, even though many did not believe in it. But still God's truth and faith in him are not thereby rendered use less. St. Paul introduces, as an aside, the saying from Psalm 51, that God remains true to his words. Then he returns to his topic and proves from Scripture that they are all sinners and that no one becomes just through the works of the law but that God gave the law only so that sin might be perceived.

Next St. Paul teaches the right way to be virtuous and to be saved; he says that they are all sinners, unable to glory in God. They must, however, be justified through faith in Christ, who has merited this for us by his blood and has become for us a mercy seat (cf. Exodus 25:17, Leviticus 16:14 ff, and John 2:2) in the presence of God, who forgives us all our previous sins. In so doing, God proves that it is his justice alone, which he gives through faith, that helps us, the justice which was at the appointed time revealed through the Gospel and, previous to that, was witnessed to by the Law and the Prophets. Therefore the law is set up by faith, but the works of the law, along with the glory taken in them, are knocked down by faith. (As with the term "spirit," the word "law" seems to have for Luther, and for St. Paul, two meanings. Sometimes it means "regulation about what must be done or not done," as in the third paragraph of this preface; sometimes it means "the Torah," as in the previous sentence. And sometimes it seems to have both meanings, as in what follows.) In chapters 1 to 3, St. Paul has revealed sin for what it is and has taught the way of faith which leads to justice. Now in chapter 4 he deals with some objections and criticisms. He takes up first the one that people raise who, on hearing that faith make just without works, say, "What?

Shouldn't we do any good works?" Here St. Paul holds up Abraham as an example. He says, "What did Abraham accomplish with his good works?

Were they all good for nothing and useless?" He concludes that Abraham was made righteous apart from all his works by faith alone. Even before the "work" of his circumcision, Scripture praises him as being just on account of faith alone (cf. Genesis 15). Now if the work of his circumcision did nothing to make him just, a work that God had commanded him to do and hence a work of obedience, then surely no other good work can do anything to make a person just. Even as Abraham's circumcision was an outward sign with which he proved his justice based on faith, so too all good works are only outward signs which flow from faith and are the fruits of faith; they prove that the person is already inwardly just in the sight of God.

St. Paul verifies his teaching on faith in chapter 3 with a powerful example from Scripture. He calls as witness David, who says in Psalm 32 that a person becomes just without works but doesn't remain with out works once he has become just. Then Paul extends this example and applies it against all other works of the law. He concludes that the Jews cannot be Abraham's heirs just because of their blood relationship to him and still less because of the works of the law. Rather, they have to inherit Abrahams's faith if they want to be his real heirs, since it was prior to the Law of Moses and the law of circumcision that Abraham became just through faith and was called a father of all believers. St. Paul adds that the law brings about more wrath than grace, because no one obeys it with love and eagerness. More disgrace than grace come from the works of the law.

Therefore faith alone can obtain the grace promised to Abraham. Examples like these are written for our sake, that we also should have faith.

In chapter 5, St. Paul comes to the fruits and works of faith, namely: joy, peace, love for God and for all people; in addition: assurance, steadfastness, confidence, courage, and hope in sorrow and suffering. All of these follow where faith is genuine, because of the overflowing good will that God has shown in Christ: he had him die for us before we could ask him for it, yes, even while we were still his enemies. Thus we have established that faith, without any good works, makes just. It does not follow from that, however, that we should not do good works; rather it means that morally upright works do not remain lacking. About such works the "works-holy" people know nothing; they invent for themselves their own works in which are neither peace nor joy nor assurance nor love nor hope nor steadfastness nor any kind of genuine Christian works or faith.

Next St. Paul makes a digression, a pleasant little side-trip, and relates where both sin and justice, death and life come from. He opposes these two: Adam and Christ. What he wants to say is that Christ, a second Adam, had to come in order to make us heirs of his justice through a new spiritual birth in faith, just as the old Adam made us heirs of sin through the old fleshy birth.

St. Paul proves, by this reasoning, that a person cannot help himself by his works to get from sin to justice any more than he can prevent his own physical birth. St. Paul also proves that the divine law, which should have been well-suited, if anything was, for helping people to obtain justice, not only was no help at all when it did come, but it even increased sin. Evil human nature, consequently, becomes more hostile to it; the more the law forbids it to indulge its own desires, the more it wants to. Thus the law makes Christ all the more necessary and demands more grace to help human nature.

In chapter 6, St. Paul takes up the special work of faith, the struggle which the spirit wages against the flesh to kill off those sins and desires that remain after a person has been made just. He teaches us that faith doesn't so free us from sin that we can be idle, lazy and self-assured, as though there were no more sin in us. Sin "is" there, but, because of faith that struggles against it, God does not reckon sin as deserving damnation.

Therefore we have in our own selves a lifetime of work cut out for us; we have to tame our body, kill its lusts, force its members to obey the spirit and not the lusts. We must do this so that we may conform to the death and resurrection of Christ and complete our Baptism, which signifies a death to sin and a new life of grace. Our aim is to be completely clean from sin and then to rise bodily with Christ and live forever St. Paul says that we can accomplish all this because we are in grace and not in the law. He explains that to be "outside the law" is not the same as having no law and being able to do what you please. No, being "under the law" means living without grace, surrounded by the works of the law.

Then surely sin reigns by means of the law, since no one is naturally well disposed toward the law. That very condition, however, is the greatest sin.

But grace makes the law lovable to us, so there is then no sin any more, and the law is no longer against us but one with us.

This is true freedom from sin and from the law; St. Paul writes about this for the rest of the chapter. He says it is a freedom only to do good with eagerness and to live a good life without the coercion of the law. This freedom is, therefore, a spiritual freedom which does not suspend the law but which supplies what the law demands, namely eagerness and love.

These silence the law so that it has no further cause to drive people on and make demands of them. It's as though you owed something to a moneylender and couldn't pay him. You could be rid of him in one of two ways: either he would take nothing from you and would tear up his account book, or a pious man would pay for you and give you what you needed to satisfy your debt. That's exactly how Christ freed us from the law. Therefore our freedom is not a wild, fleshy freedom that has no obligation to do anything. On the contrary, it is a freedom that does a great deal, indeed everything, yet is free of the law's demands and debts.

In chapter 7, St. Paul confirms the previous by an analogy drawn from married life. When a man dies, the wife is free; the one is free and clear of the other. It is not the case that the woman may not or should not marry another man; rather she is now for the first time free to marry someone else. She could not do this before she was free of her first husband. In the same way, our conscience is bound to the law so long as our condition is that of the sinful old man. But when the old man is killed by the spirit, then the conscience is free, and conscience and law are quit of each other.

Not that conscience should now do nothing; rather, it should now for the first time truly cling to its second husband, Christ, and bring forth the fruit of life.

Next St. Paul sketches further the nature of sin and the law. It is the law that makes sin really active and powerful, because the old man gets more and more hostile to the law since he can't pay the debt demanded by the law. Sin is his very nature; of himself he can't do otherwise. And so the law is his death and torture. Now the law is not itself evil; it is our evil nature that cannot tolerate that the good law should demand good from it.

It's like the case of a sick person, who cannot tolerate that you demand that he run and jump around and do other things that a healthy person does.

St. Paul concludes here that, if we understand the law properly and comprehend it in the best possible way, then we will see that its sole function is to remind us of our sins, to kill us by our sins, and to make us deserving of eternal wrath. Conscience learns and experiences all this in detail when it comes face to face with the law. It follows, then, that we must have something else, over and above the law, which can make a person virtuous and cause him to be saved. Those, however, who do not understand the law rightly are blind; they go their way boldly and think they are satisfying the law with works. They don't know how much the law demands, namely, a free, willing, eager heart. That is the reason that they don't see Moses rightly before their eyes. (In both Jewish and Christian teaching, Moses was commonly held to be the author of the Pentateuch, the first five books of the bible. Cf. the involved imagery of Moses' face and the veil over it in 2 Corinthians 3:7–18.) For them he is covered and concealed by the veil.

Then St. Paul shows how spirit and flesh struggle with each other in one person. He gives himself as an example, so that we may learn how to kill sin in ourselves. He gives both spirit and flesh the name "law," so that, just as it is in the nature of divine law to drive a person on and make demands of him, so too the flesh drives and demands and rages against the spirit and wants to have its own way. Likewise the spirit drives and demands against the flesh and wants to have its own way. This feud lasts in us for as long as we live, in one person more, in another less, depending on whether spirit or flesh is stronger. Yet the whole human being is both: spirit and flesh. The human being fights with himself until he becomes completely spiritual.

In chapter 8, St. Paul comforts fighters such as these and tells them that this flesh will not bring them condemnation. He goes on to show what the nature of flesh and spirit are. Spirit, he says, comes from Christ, who has given us his Holy Spirit; the Holy Spirit makes us spiritual and restrains the flesh. The Holy Spirit assures us that we are God's children no matter how furiously sin may rage within us, so long as we follow the Spirit and struggle against sin in order to kill it. Because nothing is so effective in deadening the flesh as the cross and suffering, Paul comforts us in our suffering. He says that the Spirit, (cf. previous note about the meaning of "spirit.") love and all creatures will stand by us; the Spirit in us groans and all creatures long with us that we be freed from the flesh and from sin.

Thus we see that these three chapters, 6, 7 and 8, all deal with the one work of faith, which is to kill the old Adam and to constrain the flesh.

In chapters 9, 10 and 11, St. Paul teaches us about the eternal providence of God. It is the original source which determines who would believe and who wouldn't, who can be set free from sin and who cannot.

Such matters have been taken out of our hands and are put into God's hands so that we might become virtuous. It is absolutely necessary that it be so, for we are so weak and unsure of ourselves that, if it depended on us, no human being would be saved. The devil would overpower all of us.

But God is steadfast; his providence will not fail, and no one can prevent its realization. Therefore we have hope against sin.

But here we must shut the mouths of those sacrilegious and arrogant spirits who, mere beginners that they are, bring their reason to bear on this matter and commence, from their exalted position, to probe the abyss of divine providence and uselessly trouble themselves about whether they are predestined or not. These people must surely plunge to their ruin, since they will either despair or abandon them selves to a life of chance.

You, however, follow the reasoning of this letter in the order in which it is presented. Fix your attention first of all on Christ and the Gospel, so that you may recognize your sin and his grace. Then struggle against sin, as chapters 1–8 have taught you to. Finally, when you have come, in chapter 8, under the shadow of the cross and suffering, they will teach you, in chapters 9–11, about providence and what a comfort it is. (The context here and in St. Paul's letter makes it clear that this is the cross and passion, not only of Christ, but of each Christian.) Apart from suffering, the cross and the pangs of death, you cannot come to grips with providence without harm to yourself and secret anger against God. The old Adam must be quite dead before you can endure this matter and drink this strong wine.

Therefore make sure you don't drink wine while you are still a babe at the breast. There is a proper measure, time and age for understanding every doctrine.

In chapter 12, St. Paul teaches the true liturgy and makes all Christians priests, so that they may offer, not money or cattle, as priests do in the Law, but their own bodies, by putting their desires to death. Next he describes the outward conduct of Christians whose lives are governed by the Spirit; he tells how they teach, preach, rule, serve, give, suffer, love, live and act toward friend, foe and everyone. These are the works that a Christian does, for, as I have said, faith is not idle.

In chapter 13, St. Paul teaches that one should honor and obey the secular authorities. He includes this, not because it makes people virtuous in the sight of God, but because it does insure that the virtuous have outward peace and protection and that the wicked cannot do evil without fear and in undisturbed peace. Therefore it is the duty of virtuous people to honor secular authority, even though they do not, strictly speaking, need it. Finally, St. Paul sums up everything in love and gathers it all into the example of Christ: what he has done for us, we must also do and follow after him.

In chapter 14, St. Paul teaches that one should carefully guide those with weak conscience and spare them. One shouldn't use Christian freedom to harm but rather to help the weak. Where that isn't done, there follow dissention and despising of the Gospel, on which every thing else depends. It is better to give way a little to the weak in faith until they become stronger than to have the teaching of the Gospel perish completely. This work is a particularly necessary work of love especially now when people, by eating meat and by other freedoms, are brashly, boldly and unnecessarily shaking weak consciences which have not yet come to know the truth.

In chapter 15, St. Paul cites Christ as an example to show that we must also have patience with the weak, even those who fail by sinning publicly or by their disgusting morals. We must not cast them aside but must bear with them until they become better. That is the way Christ treated us and still treats us every day; he puts up with our vices, our wicked morals and all our imperfection, and he helps us ceaselessly. Finally Paul prays for the Christians at Rome; he praises them and commends them to God. He points out his own office and the message that he preaches. He makes an unobtrusive plea for a contribution for the poor in Jerusalem. Unalloyed love is the basis of all he says and does.

The last chapter consists of greetings. But Paul also includes a salutary warning against human doctrines which are preached alongside the Gospel and which do a great deal of harm. It's as though he had clearly seen that out of Rome and through the Romans would come the deceitful, harmful Canons and Decretals along with the entire brood and swarm of human laws and commands that is now drowning the whole world and has blotted out this letter and the whole of the Scriptures, along with the Spirit and faith. Nothing remains but the idol Belly, and St. Paul depicts those people here as its servants. God deliver us from them. Amen.

We find in this letter, then, the richest possible teaching about what a Christian should know: the meaning of law, Gospel, sin, punishment, grace, faith, justice, Christ, God, good works, love, hope and the cross. We learn how we are to act toward everyone, toward the virtuous and sinful, toward the strong and the weak, friend and foe, and toward our selves.

Paul bases everything firmly on Scripture and proves his points with examples from his own experience and from the Prophets, so that nothing more could be desired. Therefore it seems that St. Paul, in writing this letter, wanted to compose a summary of the whole of Christian and evangelical teaching which would also be an introduction to the whole Old Testament. Without doubt, whoever takes this letter to heart possesses the light and power of the Old Testament. Therefore each and every Christian should make this letter the habitual and constant object of his study. God grant us his grace to do so. Amen

Martin Luther

Detailed outline

- I. Introduction: 1:1–7
  - A. The messenger: Paul: 1:1–6
    1. Servant of Jesus Christ.
    2. Called as an apostle.
    3. Separated for the Gospel of God.
  - B. The readers: 1:7
    1. Believers in Rome.
    2. The beloved of God.
    3. Those called to be saints.
  - C. The greeting: Grace and peace from God and Jesus: 1:7
- II. Paul's relationship to the Romans: 1:8–16
  - A. His thanksgiving for them: 1:8
  - B. His prayer for them: 1:9–10
  - C. His desire to visit them: 1:11–16
- III. The Gospel of power reveals the righteouness of God: 1:16–17

Part One: Doctrinal The Righteousness of God as revealed in the Gospel 1:18–8:39

I. The need for righteousness because of universal sin: 1:18–3:20

A. A condemnation of the Gentile world: 1:18–32

1. The wrath of God against sin: 1:18

2. Reasons for the wrath of God: 1:19–23

(a) They have no excuse: 1:19–20.

(b) Their corruption of the knowledge of God: 1:21–23

3. The wrath of God: 1:24–32

(a) They are given up to uncleanness: 1:24–25

(b) They are given up to evil passions: 1:26–27

(c) They are given up to a depraved mind: 1:28–32

B. The condemnation of the Jew: 2:1–3:8

1. The principle of divine judgment: 2:1–16

(a) The judgment of God according to truth: 2:1–5

(1) The guilt of the one judging others: 2:1

(2) The principle of judgment: 2:2

(3) An appeal to the guilty: 2:3–5

(b) The judgment of God according to deeds: 2:6–15

(1) The principle of judgment: 2:6

(2) The two classes in the judgment: 2:7–12

(3) Obedience to light as the test in judgment: 2:13–15

(c) The judgment in relation to Paul's Gospel: 2:16

2. The Jew's moral failure: 2:17–29

(a) Claims of the Jew: 2:17–20

(b) Refutation of the claims of the Jew: 2:21–24

(c) Failure to live up to responsibilities: 2:25–29

(l) Circumcision: 2:25

(2) Obedience: 2:26–27

(3) A true and false view of a Jew: 2:28–29

3. The Jew's objections: 3:1–8

(a) The question of the Jews: 3:1–8

(1) The question: 3:1

(2) The answer: 3:2–4

(3) The objection: 3:5

(4) Denial of the objection: 3:6–8

C. Condemnation of the whole world: 3:9–20

1. The charge that all have sinned: 3:9

2. The proof of universal sin from Scripture: 3:10–18

(a) The character of sin: 3:10–12

(b) The practice of sin: 3:13–17

(1) In speech: 3:13–14

(2) In conduct: 3:15–17

(c) The reason for sin: 3:18

3. The application to the Jew who has the law: 3:19–20

II. The righteousness of God in justification: 3:21–5:21

A. Justification by faith: 3:21–26

1. It is the manifestation of the righteousness of God: 3:21

2. The description of justification by faith: 3:21–26

(a) Its relation to the Old Testament: 3:21

(b) Availability through faith: 3:22–23
(c) Its basis in Christ's redemption: 3:24–25
(d) The demonstration of God's justice: 3:25–26

B. Summary of the doctrine of justification: 3:27–31
1. The exclusion of personal merit: 3:27–28
2. The presentation of God's character: 3:29–30
3. The establishment of the law: 3:31

C. The proof of justification by faith from Scripture: 4:1–25
1. Abraham's justification: 4:1–12
(a) The question about Abraham's experience: 4:1
(b) The means of his justification: 4:2–3
(c) The comparison of the two ways of justification: 4:4–5
(d) The confirmation from David's testimony: 4:6–8
2. Justification by faith apart from circumcision: 4:9–12
(a) The question about circumcision: 4:9–10
(b) The answers from Abraham's condition: 4:10
(c) Abraham's circumcision: 4:11–12
3. The promise achieved by faith: 4:13–17
(a) The means of attaining the inheritance: 4:13
(b) The reason for faith: 4:14–15
(c) The recipients of the promise: 4:16
(d) The harmony with Scripture: 4:17
4. The example of the faith of Abraham: 4:17–25

D. The permanency of justification: 5:1–11
1. The present results of justification: 5:1–2
2. The inability of trials to destroy this hope: 5:3–5
3. The love of God in Christ confirms this hope: 5:6–11
(a) God's love: 5:6–10
(l) The demonstration of His love for the lost: 5:6–8
(2) The assurance of salvation: 5:9–10
(b) The experience of reconciliation: 5:11

E. The foundation of righteousness: 5:12–21
1. Two representative men: 5:12–14
(a) The result of Adam's act: 5:12–14
(b) The headship of Adam as a type of Christ: 5:14
2. The differences between Adam and Christ: 5:15–17
3. The similarities of Adam and Christ: 5:18–21

III. The righteousness of God in sanctification: 6:1–8:39

A. The believer's relationship to sin: 6:1–23
1. Death to the principle of sin: 6:1–14
(a) The question of remaining in sin: 6:1
(b) Rejection of the suggestion: 6:2
(c) Our position in baptism: 6:3–11
(l) The question of ignorance about baptism: 6:3

(2) The importance of baptism: 6:4
(3) The application to believers: 6:5–10
(4) The call to this position: 6:11
2. The believer's death to the practice of sin: 6:15–23
(a) The question of continued sin: 6:15
(b) Rejection of the suggestion: 6:15
(c) An answer from the illustration of slavery: 5:16–23
B. The believer's relationship to the law: 7:1–25
1. Dead to the law but alive to God: 7:1–6
(a) The dominion of the law: 7:1
(b) An illustration from the law of marriage: 7:2–3
(c) The application of the principle to the believer: 7:4–6
2. The inability of the law to deliver from sin: 7:7–25
(a) The relation of the law to sin: 7:7–13
(1) The nature of the law is not sinful: 7:7
(2) The revelation of sin through the law: 7:7–13
(3) The work of sin through the law: 7:8–11
(4) The sinfulness of sin: 7:12–13
(b) The law's inability to give victory over sin: 7:14–25
(l) Defeat by sin: 7:14–17
(2) Indwelling sin: 7:18–20
(3) The way of victory: 7:21–25
C. The believer's victory through the Spirit: 8:1–39
1. Deliverance from the power of the flesh by the Spirit: 8:1–11
(a) The believer's freedom from condemnation: 8:1–2
(b) The basis for the deliverance: 8:3
(c) The purpose of the deliverance: 8:4
(d) The method of the deliverance: 8:5–10
(1) The two classes of men: 8:5
(2) The two minds: 8:6–7
(3) The two spheres: Flesh and spirit: 8:8–10
(e) The deliverance from physical death: 8:11
2. The life of son ship through the Spirit: 8:12–17
(a) The obligation to live in the Spirit: 8:12–13
(b) Evidence of life in the Spirit: 8:14–17
(1) The leading of the Spirit: 8:14
(2) The nature of the Spirit: 8:15
(3) The witness of the Spirit: 8:16
(4) The heir ship of the believer: 8:17
3. Glorification in present suffering: 8:18–30
(a) The evaluation of present suffering: 8:18
(b) Assurances of glorification: 8:19–30
(1) Assurance from creation: 8:19–22
(2) Assurance from the present hope: 8:23–25

(3) Assurance by the Spirit: 8:26–27
(4) Assurance in life's circumstances: 8:28
(5) God's continued working in us: 8:29–30
4. The assurance of the believer's victory: 8:31–39
(a) The believer's relation to God: 8:31–33
(b) The believer's relation to Christ: 8:34
(c) The believer's relation to circumstances of evil: 8:35–39

Part Two: Historical. The righteousness of God in His dealings with Israel and all humankind 9:1–11:36

I. The sorrow of Paul because of Israel's rejection: 9:1–5
II. The rejection of Israel and God's sovereignty: 9:6–29
A. The rejection of Israel and God's promise: 9:6–13
1. The denial of the failure of God's Word: 9:6
2. The promise is not based on physical descent: 9:6–13
(a) Proof from the family of Abraham: 9:6–9
(b) Proof from the family of Isaac: 9:10–13
B. The rejection of Israel and God's justice: 9:14–29
1. The justice of God in the manifestation of His will: 9:14–18
(a) The question of God's justice: 9:14
(b) The revelation of God's will: 9:15–17
(1) His mercy revealed according to His will: 9:15–16
(2) His judgment is according to His will: 9:17
(c) God's action according to His will: 9:18
2. The sovereign power of God: 9:19–29
(a) The question and the rebuke: 9:19–20
(b) The right of God to act: 9:20–21
(c) The exercise of God's power: 9:22–24
(1) His patience with the wicked: 9:22
(2) His revelation of glory: 9:22–24
(d) Anticipation of the call of Jew and Gentile: 9:25–29
(1) The call of the Gentile: 9:25–26
(2) Announcement of the fate of Israel: 9:27–29
III. The rejection of Israel: 9:30–10:21
A. The failure of Israel to achieve righteousness: 9:30–33
B. The refusal by Israel to accept God's righteousness: 10:1–11
1. The cause for Israel's rejection: 10:1–4
2. The nature of righteousness by faith: 10:5–11
(a) The comparison of two methods for righteousness: 10:5–8
(1) Righteousness through keeping the law: 10:5
(2) Righteousness through faith: 10:6–8

(b) The realization of righteousness through faith: 10:9–10
(c) Scriptural assurance of righteousness by faith: 10:11

C. The neglect by Israel of the universal Gospel: 10:12–21
1. The fact of a universal Gospel: 10:12–13
2. The proclamation of the universal Gospel: 10:14–15
3. The reaction of Israel to this universal Gospel: 10:16–21
(a) Disregarded: 10:16–17
(b) Rejected: 10:18–21

IV. The rejection of Israel and God's purpose for their future: 11:1–32
A. The rejection of Israel left a remnant: 11:1–10
1. The denial that God has cut off His people: 11:1–2
2. The proof of a remaining remnant: 11:2–6
(a) The proof from Scripture: 11:2–4
(b) The proof from the existence of the remnant: 11:5–6
3. The contrast of the remnant with the nation: 11:7–10
B. The rejection of Israel is not permanent: 11:11–32
1. Israel's condition: 11:11–16
(a) The fall of Israel is not permanent: 11:11
(b) The fall of Israel is overruled for Gentile salvation: 11:11
(c) The restoration of Israel will bring universal blessing: 11:12–15
(d) The indication of Israel's future from the past: 11:16
2. The warning to the Gentiles: 11:17–24
(a) Against boastfulness: 11:17–18
(b) Against pride: 11:19–21
(c) Against presumption: 11:22–24
3. The argument for the restoration of Israel: 11:23–24
4. The prophecy about Israel's future restoration: 11:25–32
(a) The revelation about Israel's restoration: 11:25–26
(b) Harmony of the restoration with prophecy: 11:26–27.
(c) Harmony with the divine call of Israel: 11:28–29
(d) Harmony with God's purposes: 11:30–32

V. The benediction in praise of God: 11:33–36
A. The declaration about God: 11:33
B. The questions about God: 11:34–35
C. Praise to God: 11:36

Part Three: Practical. The righteousness of God applied to the life of the believer 12:1–15:13

I. The believer in relation to God: 12:1–2
A. Self-presentation to God: 12:1
B. Continued experience of transformation: 12:2

II. The believer in relation to the church: 12:3–13
A. The use of spiritual gifts with humility: 12:3–8
1. The need for humility: 12:3
2. The relation of the members to each other in the Body: 12:4–5

3. The expression of humility in service: 12:6–8
   - (a) The diversity of the gifts given: 12:6
   - (b) The ministering gifts: 12:6–8

B. The practice of love to members in the church: 12:9–13
1. The nature of this love: 12:9
2. The manifestations of such love: 12:9–13
   - (a) Without dissimulation: 12:9
   - (b) Abhor what is evil: 12:9
   - (c) Cling to that which is good: 12:9
   - (d) Be devoted to each other: 12:10
   - (e) Show brotherly love: 12:10
   - (f) Honor one another above yourselves: 12:10
   - (g) Do not lack zeal: 12:11
   - (h) Be fervent in spirit: 12:11
   - (i) Serve the Lord: 12:11
   - (j) Rejoice in hope: 12:12
   - (k) Be patient in affliction: 12:12
   - (l) Be faithful in prayer: 12:12
   - (m) Share with needy people: 12:13
   - (n) Be given to hospitality: 12:13
   - (o) Bless those who persecute you: 12:14
   - (p) Rejoice with those who rejoice: 12:15
   - (q) Weep with those who weep: 12:15
   - (r) Live in harmony with one to another: 12:16
   - (s) Do not be proud: 12:16
   - (t) Do not be conceited: 12:16
   - (u) Do not repay anyone with evil: 12:17
   - (v) Do what is right in the sight of men: 12:17
   - (w) Live at peace: 12:18
   - (x) Do not take revenge: 12:19
   - (y) Respond in love and care to your enemy: 12:20
   - (z) Do not be overcome with evil but overcome evil: 12:21

III. The believer in relation to the state: 13:1–14

A. The believer's duties to the government: 13:1–7
1. The duty of obedience to the government: 13:1
2. The reason for obedience to the government: 13:1
3. Refusing obedience to the government: 13:2
4. The motives for obedience to the state: 13:3–5
   - (a) From the function of the government: 13:3–4
   - (b) From Christian conscience: 13:5
5. An illustration of obedience to government: 13:6
6. The call for obedience to the government: 13:7

B. The believer's duties to fellow citizens: 13:8–10

C. The believer's motivation in the hope of the return of Jesus: 13:11–14
1. An appeal to alertness: 13:11
2. The reason for alertness: 13:11–12
3. An exhortation for alertness: 13:12–13

4. The provision for alertness: 13:14

IV. The believer in relation to a weaker brother: 14:1–15:13

A. The warning against judging a brother: 14:1–12

1. The proper attitude toward the weaker brother: 14:1

2. The areas of difficulty: 14:2–5

(a) The first problem and how to act: 14:2–4

(b) The second problem and how to act: 14:5

3. Making the adjustment: 14:6

4. The motivation: 14:7–9

5. The rebuke for judging a brother: 14:10–12

(a) The questions of rebuke: 14:10

(b) The basis for the rebuke: 14:10–12

(b) Do not violate a brother's conscience: 14:13–23

(1) Exhortation not to judge one another: 14:13

(2) The apostle's conviction about foods: 14:14

(3) The application of this conviction: 14:15–20

(4) The guiding principle for a strong brother: 14:21

(5) An appeal to both strong and weak: 14:22–23

B. The effort toward unity by following Christ's example: 15:1–13

1. The obligation of a strong brother: 15:1

2. The appeal for unity from Christ's example: 15:2–4

(a) The statement of the appeal: 15:2

(b) Arguments for the appeal: 15:3–4

(1) The example of Christ: 15:3

(2) The purpose of the Scriptures: 15:4

3. The request of the Apostle: 15:5–6

4. The command to receive one another: 15:7

5. The illustration from Christ's relation to Jew and Gentile: 15:8–12

(a) The ministry of Christ: 15:8–9

(b) Scriptural proof: 15:9–12

6. The Apostolic prayer: 15:13

The Conclusion 15:14–16:20

I. Personal matters: 15:14–33

A. Paul's explanation for writing: 15:14–21

1. His attitude in writing: 15:14–16

(a) His recognition of them: 15:14

(b) His boldness in writing them: 15:15

(c) The statement of his commission: 15:16

2. His authorization for writing: 15:17–21

(a) His personal boasting: 15:17

(b) His humility in speaking of his work: 15:18

(c) His ministry to the Gentiles: 15:18–19

(d) His aim in selecting a field of labor: 15:20–21

B. His personal plans at the time of writing: 15:22–29

1. Unfulfilled plans: 15:22–24

(a) His plans to visit Rome: 15:22–23

(b) His plans for Spain: 15:24

2. His immediate plans: 15:25–27
   (a) His present plans: 15:25
   (b) Significance of his present plans: 15:26–27
3. His plans for the future: 15:28–29

C. His request for their prayers: 15:30–33
1. The request for prayer: 15:30–32
2. The benediction: 15:33

II. Friendship matters: 16:1–23
A. A commendation of Phoebe: 16:1–2
B. The greeting to friends at Rome: 16:3–16
1. Greetings to individuals at Rome: 16:3–15
2. Greetings among believers at Rome: 16:16
3. Greeting from the churches to the Roman believers: 16:16

C. The warning to believers at Rome: 16:17–20
1. Contents of the warning: 16:17
2. Description of the men of whom he is warning: 16:18
3. The reason for the warning: 6:19
4. The promise of victory: 16:20
5. The benediction: 16:20

D. Greetings from his companions: 16:21–24

III. The concluding benediction: 16:25–27

2. Helpful summaries of Romans

Bird's eye view

Paul plans to make his first visit to Rome. He sends this letter to the Christians there. It contains the fullest explanation of the gospel about Jesus found in the New Testament letters.

Reading plan

The following reading plan, taking one reading per day, enables you to read through Romans in nineteen days.

Romans 1:18–1:32
Romans 2:1–2:29
Romans 3:1–3:31
Romans 4:1–4:25
Romans 5:1–5:21
Romans 6:1–6:23
Romans 7:1–7:25
Romans 8:1–8:17
Romans 8:18–8:39
Romans 9:1–9:33
Romans 10:1–10:21
Romans 11:1–11:21
Romans 11:22–11:36
Romans 12:1–12:21
Romans 13:1–13:14
Romans 14:1–14:23
Romans 15:1–15:21
Romans 15:22–15:33
Romans 16:1–16:27

Verses to memorize

Romans 3:23

For all have sinned, and come short of the glory of God; KJV

Romans 5:1

Therefore being justified by faith, we have peace with God through our Lord Jesus Christ: KJV

Romans 5:8

But God commendeth his love toward us, in that, while we were yet sinners, Christ died for us. KJV

Romans 6:23

For the wages of sin is death; but the gift of God is eternal life through Jesus Christ our Lord. KJV

Romans 8:28

And we know that all things work together for good to them that love God, to them who are the called according to his purpose. KJV

Romans 10:17

So then faith cometh by hearing, and hearing by the word of God. KJV

Romans 12:1

I beseech you therefore, brethren, by the mercies of God, that ye present your bodies a living sacrifice, holy, acceptable unto God, which is your reasonable service. KJV

Romans 12:21

Be not overcome of evil, but overcome evil with good. KJV

Statistics

Sixth New Testament book

First letter by the apostle Paul

16 chapters

433 verses

9,447 words

Number of Old Testament quotations and allusions in Romans: 74.

Famous saying found in Romans

"A law unto themselves" Romans 2:14

Names/titles given

Pros Romaious: "To the Romans."

The "constitution" of Christianity.

3. Helpful keys to turn to in understanding Romans

Key words/phrase

Law, 78 times

Righteousness, over 60 times

Faith, 62 times

Sin, 60 times

Death, 42 times

Justify/justification, 17 times

In Christ, 33 times

Key verse/verses

1:16–17; 3:21–25

Themes to study

How we can be justified before God.

The meaning of "faith".

The meaning of "grace".

Key terms for understanding Romans

Knowing the meaning of the following words are a help in studying Romans.

- *Adoption*: God's action in which he made us a member of his family as his sons and daughters and joint-heirs with Christ.
- *Conversion*: the act by which a person, through the power of the Holy Spirit, turns in faith to Jesus Christ.
- *Death*: separation from God (spiritual); separation of body and soul (physical); separation from God in hell (eternal).
- *Faith*: believing and trusting in what God has revealed about himself, especially concerning sin and salvation.

- *Glorification*: the goal of our salvation; God's action by which we are transformed into his likeness.
- *Gospel*: literally "good news."
- *Grace*: the undeserved favor of God towards sinners.
- *Imputation*: God's action by which the righteousness Jesus earned for us by his sinless life and atoning death is legally given to us.
- *Justification*: God's action by which he judicially declares a believing sinner to be righteous and acceptable before him.
- *Mercy*: the undeserved kindness of God towards humankind.
- *Reconciliation*: the removal of the hostility between us and God by means of Christ's saving work on the cross.
- *Redemption*: God's action in Christ by which we are bought from the marketplace of sin and given spiritual freedom.
- *Regeneration*: the Holy Spirit's work by which the person who believes in Christ is given new life, that is born again.
- *Righteousness*: a quality in God's character that comes from his intrinsic holiness; a quality that he gives to those who believe on Jesus Christ.
- *Salvation*: God's grace by which he rescues us from the eternal consequences of our sin.
- *Sanctification*: the setting apart of the believer by God for a life of holiness and service and growth in godliness.
- *Sin*: the violation of God's moral law. It often carries the idea of missing the mark, lawlessness, unrighteousness, transgression.
- *Wrath of God*: God's righteous anger against sin.

Jesus in Romans

In Romans Jesus is our Righteousness.

Lessons to learn from Romans

- Salvation starts and ends with God's grace.
- We should treasure our times of fellowship with fellow Christians.
- The needed power to live a holy life comes from the Holy Spirit.

4. Chapter by chapter: outline of every chapter of Romans

Romans 1

Matthew Henry's introduction

In this chapter we may observe,

I. The preface and introduction to the whole epistle, to v. 16.

II. A description of the deplorable condition of the Gentile world, which begins the proof of the doctrine of justification by faith, here laid down at v. 17.

The first is according to the then usual formality of a letter, but intermixed with excellent expressions.

Dr. Adam Clarke's analysis of chapter

St. Paul shows the Romans his Divine call to the apostleship, and for what end he was thus called, 1–6.

His salutation to the Church at Rome, and his commendation of their faith, 7,8.

His earnest desire to see them, that he might

impart to them some spiritual gifts, 9–15.
His description of the Gospel of Christ, 16,17.
The crimes and profligacy of the Gentile world, which called aloud for the judgments of God, 18–32.

A detailed analysis of chapter

The apostle's commission. (1–7)

Paul prays for the saints at Rome, and expresses his desire to see them. (8–15)

The gospel way of justification by faith, for Jews and Gentiles. (16,17)

The sins of the Gentiles. (18–32)

Key verse

Verse 16: "I am not ashamed of the gospel, because it is the power of God for the salvation of everyone who believes: first for the Jew, then for the Gentile."

Key word / key phrase

Verse 17, "a gospel of righteousness."

Key event / key person / key theme

Paul states his gospel

Key thought

Paul longed to meet up with the Christians in Rome.

Key thing to look out for

Paul's definition of the gospel.

Key Bible cross-reference

Verse 17. See Habakkuk 2:4.

Key "by way of explanation"

Verse 9, "gospel of his Son." For Paul this was identical with the gospel of God, see verse 1. The word "gospel" translates the Greek word *euangelian*, literally "good news."

Key "Quotable Quote"

"Romans 1:18 stands in its insistence that even in the most excellent men, however endowed with law, righteousness, wisdom, and all virtues, free will, their most excellent part, is nonetheless ungodly, and unrighteous, and merits God's wrath."

Martin Luther

Romans 2

Matthew Henry's introduction

The scope of the first two chapters of this epistle may be gathered from 3:9, "We have before proved both Jews and Gentiles that they are all under sin." This we have proved on the Gentiles (ch. 1.), now in this chapter he proves it on the Jews, as appears by v. 17, "thou art called a Jew."

I. He proves in general that Jews and Gentiles stand on the same level before the justice of God, to v. 11.

II. He shows more particularly what sins the Jews were guilty of, notwithstanding their profession and vain pretensions (v. 17 to the end).

Dr. Adam Clarke's analysis of chapter

The apostle shows that the Jew, who condemns the Gentiles, and considers them utterly unworthy of the blessings of the Gospel, is inexcusable, because he is guilty of the same crimes; and therefore shalt not escape the righteous judgment of God, 1–3.

It is an awful thing to despise the goodness and long-suffering of God, which lead to repentance, 4, 5.

God, the impartial judge, will render to every man according to his works, 6–11.

The Jews and the Gentiles will be judged according to their respective advantages and disadvantages, 12, 13.

In some cases, the Gentiles, who had no law, have shown a better disposition than the Jews, 14–16.

The Jews, by their unfaithfulness, have been a stumbling-block to the Gentiles, 17–24.

Jewish rites and ceremonies of no advantage, unless productive of change of heart and conduct, 25.

The Gentiles, who attend to the small light which they have received from God, are in a better state than the unfaithful Jews, with all their superior privileges, 26, 27.

What constitutes a real Jew in the sight of God, 28, 29.

A detailed analysis of chapter

The Jews could not be justified by the Law of Moses, any more than the Gentiles by the law of nature. (1–16)

The sins of the Jews and all their vain confidence in their outward privileges. (17–29)

Key verse

Verse 12: "All who sin apart from the law will also perish apart from the law, and all who sin under the law will be judged by the law."

Key word / key phrase

Verse 2, "God's judgment."

Key event / key person / key theme

God will be our judge

Key thought

Verse 28. Paul's teaching about Jews who are not really Jews would have been hard for most Jews to swallow.

Key thing to look out for

What mattered for Paul was not the opinions of men, but to be praised by God.

Key Bible cross-reference

Verse 6. See Psalm 62:12.

Key "by way of explanation"

Verse 1, "no excuse." Like Jesus, Paul is saying that nobody has the right to pass judgment on anyone else. The Jews were especially guilty of despising anyone who did not keep the Law.

Key "Quotable Quote"

"For we account a man to be justified by faith alone, without the works of the law."

Martin Luther

Romans 3

Matthew Henry's introduction

The apostle, in this chapter, carries on his discourse about justification. He had already proved the guilt both of Gentiles and Jews.

Now in this chapter,

I. He answers some objections that might be made against what he had said about the Jews, vv. 1–8.

II. He asserts the guilt and corruption of mankind in common, both Jews and Gentiles, vv. 9–18.

III. He argues thence that justification must needs be by faith, and not by the law, which he gives several reasons for (v. 19 to the end). The many digressions in his writings render his discourse sometimes a little difficult, but his scope is evident.

Dr. Adam Clarke's analysis of chapter

The apostle points out the peculiar privileges of the Jews, 1–8.

But shows that they, also, as well as the Gentiles, had sinned, and forfeited all right and title to God's especial favor, 9.

The corrupt state of all mankind, 10–18.

All the world is guilty before God, and none can be justified by the works of the law, 19, 20.

God's MERCY in providing redemption for a lost world, by Jesus Christ, 21–26.

This excludes boasting on the part both of Jew and Gentile; provides salvation through faith for both; and does not set aside, but establishes the law, 27–31.

A detailed analysis of chapter

Objections answered. (1–8)

All humankind are sinners. (9–18)

Both Jews and Gentiles cannot be justified by their own deeds. (19, 20)

The free grace of God through faith in the righteousness of Christ, yet the law is not done away. (21–31)

Key verse

Verse 25: "God presented him as a sacrifice of atonement, through faith in his blood."

Key word / key phrase

Verse 22, "righteousness from God."

Key event / key person / key theme

Why the Jews did not believe, and righteousness described

Key thought

The thought that nobody in God's sight is righteous is new to many people.

Key thing to look out for

The idea that righteousness comes through faith, and is a gift, goes against the grain.

Key Bible cross-reference

Verse 14. See Psalm 10:7.

Key "by way of explanation"

Verse 18, "fear of God." This is reverence for God. It does not mean being afraid of God, but standing in awe of God. Without such "fear of God" godliness is impossible.

Key "Quotable Quote"

"The works of faith involve doing all that is commanded in Scripture. That is why the Mosaic law is a "law of faith" (Romans 3:27; cf. 9:31f.). Every command in the Bible should be understood as specifying an obedience which is inspired from knowing that God has promised to be one's God."

Daniel Fuller

Romans 4

Matthew Henry's introduction

The great gospel doctrine of justification by faith without the works of the law was so very contrary to the notions the Jews had learnt from those that sat in Moses' chair, that it would hardly go down with them; and therefore the apostle insists very largely on it, and labors much in the confirmation and illustration of it. He had before proved it by reason and argument, now in this chapter he proves it by example, which in some places serves for confirmation as well as illustration. The example he pitches on is that of Abraham, whom he chooses to mention because the Jews gloried much in their relation to Abraham, put it in the first rank of their external privileges that they were Abraham's seed, and truly they had Abraham for their father. Therefore this instance was likely to be more taking and convincing to the Jews than any other. His argument stands thus: "All that are saved are justified in the same way as Abraham was; but Abraham was justified by faith, and not by works; therefore all that are saved are so justified;" for it would easily be acknowledged that Abraham was the father of the faithful. Now this is an argument, not only à pari–from an equal case, as they say, but à fortiori–from a stronger case. If Abraham, a man so famous for works, so eminent in holiness and obedience, was nevertheless justified by faith only, and not by those works, how much less can any other, especially any of those that spring from him, and come so far short of him in works, set up for a justification by their own works? And it proves likewise, ex abundanti–the more abundantly, as some observe, that we are not justified, no not by those good works which flow from faith, as the matter of our righteousness; for such were Abraham's works, and are we better than he? The whole chapter is taken up with his discourse on this instance, and there is this in it, which hath a particular reference to the close of the previous chapter, where he has asserted that, in the business of justification, Jews and Gentiles stand on the same level.

Dr. Adam Clarke's analysis of chapter

Abraham was justified by faith, and not by the works of the law; for his faith was imputed to him for righteousness, 1–5.

David also bears testimony to the same doctrine, 6–8.

Abraham, the father of the Jewish race, was justified by faith, even before he was circumcised; therefore salvation must be of the Gentiles as well as the Jews, 9–12.

And the promise that all the nations of the earth should be blessed in him, was made to him while he was in an uncircumcised state; and, therefore, if salvation were of the Jews alone, the law, that was given after the promise, would make the promise of no effect, 13–17.

Description of Abraham's faith, and its effects, 18–22.

This account is left on record for our salvation, that we might believe on Christ, who was delivered for our offences, and raised again for our justification, 23–25.

A detailed analysis of chapter

The doctrine of justification by faith is shown by the case of Abraham. (1–12)

He received the promise through the righteousness of faith. (13–22)

And we are justified in the same way. (23–25)

Key verse

Verse 18: "Against all hope, Abraham in hope believed and so became the father of many nations."

Key word / key phrase

Verse 3, "it was credited to him as righteousness."

Key event / key person / key theme

Righteousness illustrated

Key thought

In verse 18, Abraham is said to have believed against all hope.

Key thing to look out for

Paul summarizes the point of Jesus' death and resurrection in verse 25.

Key Bible cross-reference

Verse 11. See Genesis 17:10.

Key "by way of explanation"

Verse 1, "Abraham, our forefather." Paul introduces Abraham, the patriarch of the Jewish nation, as all Jews looked up to him. But Paul uses him as the great example of somebody who was justified by faith.

Key "Quotable Quote"

"Justification by faith is the very heart of the gospel."

C.H. Spurgeon

Romans 5

Matthew Henry's introduction

The apostle, having made good his point, and fully proved justification by faith, in this chapter proceeds in the explication, illustration, and application of that truth.

I. He shows the fruits of justification, vv. 1–5.

II. He shows the fountain and foundation of justification in the death of Jesus Christ, which he discourses of at large in 6–23.

Dr. Adam Clarke's analysis of chapter

The effects of justification by faith, peace with God, 1.

The joyous hope of eternal glory, 2.

Glorying in tribulations, 3.

And gaining thereby patience, experience, and hope, 4.

And having the love of God shed abroad in the heart by the Holy Spirit, 5.

The state of the world when Christ died for it, 6–10.

Jesus Christ is an atonement, 11.

Sin and death entered into the world by Adam's

transgression, and all became guilty before God, 12–14.

God's grace in sending Christ into the world to save fallen man, 15–19.

The law is brought in to show the exceeding sinfulness of sin, 20.

The grace of Christ is to be as extensive in its influences and reign, as sin has been in its enslaving and destructive nature, 21.

A detailed analysis of chapter

The results of justification through faith in the righteousness of Christ. (1–5)

That we are reconciled by his blood. (6–11)

The fall of Adam brought all humankind into sin and death. (12–14)

The grace of God, through the righteousness of Christ, has more power to bring salvation, than Adam's sin had to bring misery, (15–19)

as grace increased all the more. (20, 21)

Key verse

Verse 1: "Therefore, since we have been justified through faith, we have peace with God through our Lord Jesus Christ."

Key word / key phrase

Verse 1, "we have peace with God."

Key event / key person / key theme

Peace with God, and salvation from God's wrath

Key thought

The whole point of Paul's teaching is to have peace with God, verse 1.

Key thing to look out for

Note how Paul contrasts Adam with Jesus from verse 12.

Key Bible cross-reference

Verse 12. See Genesis 3:6.

Key "by way of explanation"

Verse 14, "pattern." Through Adam sin spread to every person who is born. Adam is said to be a "pattern" in the sense that his actions can be seen as foreshadowing what Christ would do in reverse. That is, Jesus' one act brought universal blessing, in place of Adam's universal sin.

Key "Quotable Quote"

"If we have peace with God and the peace of God, we will become peacemakers."

Billy Graham

Romans 6

Matthew Henry's introduction

The apostle having at large asserted, opened, and proved, the great doctrine of justification by faith, for fear lest any should suck poison out of that sweet flower, and turn that grace of God into wantonness and licentiousness, he, with a like zeal, copiousness of expression, and cogency of argument, presses the absolute necessity of sanctification and a holy life, as the inseparable fruit and companion of justification; for, wherever Jesus Christ is made of God unto any soul righteousness, he is made of God unto that soul sanctification, 1 Cor. 1:30. The water and the blood came streaming together out of the pierced side of the dying Jesus. And what God hath thus joined together let not us dare to put asunder.

Dr. Adam Clarke's analysis of chapter

We must not abuse the boundless goodness of God by continuing in sin, under the wicked persuasion that the more we sin the more the grace of God will abound, 1.

For, having been baptized into Christ, we have professed thereby to be dead to sin, 2–4.

And to be planted in the likeness of his resurrection, 5.

For we profess to be crucified with him, to die and rise again from the dead, 6–11.

We should not, therefore, let sin reign in our bodies, but live to the glory of God, 12–14.

The Gospel makes no provision for living in sin, any more than the law did; and those who commit sin are the slaves of sin, 15–19.

The degrading and afflictive service of sin, and its wages eternal death; the blessed effects of the grace of God in the heart, of which eternal life is the fruit, 20–23.

A detailed analysis of chapter

Believers must die to sin, and live for God. (1, 2)

This is urged by their Christian baptism and union with Christ. (3–10)

They are made alive to God. (11–15)

And are freed from the dominion of sin. (16–20)

The end of sin is death. (21–23)

Key verse

Verse 5: "If we have been united with him like this in his death, we will certainly also be united with him in his resurrection."

Key word / key phrase

Verse 23, "the wages of sin is death."

Key event / key person / key theme

Sanctification and sin

Key thought

"As soon as we are incorporated in Christ, we have the certitude that in the end we shall achieve victory in the fight." John Calvin, commentating on Romans 6:6.

Key thing to look out for

Paul says we are to count ourselves dead to sin.

Key Bible cross-reference

Verse 4. See Colossians 2:12.

Key "by way of explanation"

Verse 11, "count yourselves." The first step on the path of sanctification is to "count yourselves" dead to sin. Then do not let sin dominate your life, verse 12; and then offer yourself to God, verse 13.

Key "Quotable Quote"

"We are free from sin – yet we must battle against it."

Anders Nygren

Romans 7

Matthew Henry's introduction

We may observe in this chapter,

I. Our freedom from the law further urged as an argument to press on us sanctification, vv. 1–6.

II. The excellency and usefulness of the law asserted and proved from the apostle's own experience, notwithstanding, vv. 7–14.

III. A description of the conflict between grace and corruption in the heart, vv. 15–25.

Dr. Adam Clarke's analysis of chapter

The law has power over a man as long as he lives, 1.

And a wife is bound to her husband only as long as he lives, 2,3.

Christian believers are delivered from the Mosaic law by Christ Jesus, and united to God, 5–7.

By the law is the knowledge of sin, 8. But it gives no power over it, 9–11.

Yet it is holy, just, and good, 12.

How it convinces of sin, and brings into bondage, 13–24.

No deliverance from its curse but by Jesus Christ, 25.

A detailed analysis of chapter

Believers are united to Christ, that they may be fruitful. (1–6)

The use and excellence of the Law. (7–13)

The spiritual conflicts between corruption and grace in a believer. (14–25)

Key verse

Verse 7: "What shall we say, then? Is the law sin? Certainly not! Indeed I would not have known what sin was except through the law."

Key word / key phrase

Verse 7, "Is the law sin?"

Key event / key person / key theme

Sanctification and the Law

Key thought

Paul states that Christians need to struggle against sin.

Key thing to look out for

In his own great battle with sin Paul is jubilant because he was rescued by Jesus Christ.

Key Bible cross-reference

Verse 7. See Exodus 20:17.

Key "by way of explanation"

Verse 23, "another law." Paul states that there remains in a Christian "another law" which is always trying to tempt him away from Christ and from obeying God.

Key "Quotable Quote"

"The Law is a kind of mirror. When we look in the mirror we notice any dirty marks on our faces, so in the Law we are made aware first of our helplessness, then of our sin and finally the judgment."

John Calvin

Romans 8

Matthew Henry's introduction

The apostle, having fully explained the doctrine of justification, and pressed the necessity of sanctification, in this chapter applies himself to the consolation of the Lord's people. Ministers are helpers of the joy of the saints. "Comfort ye, comfort ye my people," so runs our commission, Is. 40:1. It is the will of God that his people should be a comforted people. And we have here such a draught of the gospel charter, such a display of the unspeakable privileges of true believers, as may furnish us with abundant matter for joy and peace in believing, that by all these immutable things, in which it is impossible for God to lie, we might have strong consolation. Many of the people of God have, accordingly, found this chapter a well-spring of comfort to their souls, living and dying, and have sucked and been satisfied from these breasts of consolation, and with joy drawn water out of these wells of salvation. There are three things in this chapter:

I. The particular instances of Christians' privileges, vv. 1–28.
II. The ground thereof laid in predestination, vv. 29, 30.
III. The apostle's triumph herein, in the name of all the saints, v. 31 to the end.

Dr. Adam Clarke's analysis of chapter

The happy state of those who believe in Christ, and walk under the influence of his Spirit, 1, 2.

The design of God in sending his Son into the world was to redeem men from sin, 3, 4.

The miserable state of the carnally minded, 6–8.

How Christ lives and works in his followers; their blessedness here, and their happiness hereafter, 9–17.

Sufferings are the common lot of all men; and from which Gentiles and Jews have the hope of being finally delivered, 18–23.

The use and importance of hope, 24, 25.

The Spirit makes intercession for the followers of Christ, 26, 27.

All things work together for good to them that love God, and who act according to his gracious purpose in calling them, 28.

The means used to bring men to eternal glory, 29, 30.

The great blessedness, confidence, and security of all genuine Christians, whom, while they hold fast faith and a good conscience, nothing can separate from the love of God, 31–39.

A detailed analysis of chapter

The freedom of believers from condemnation. (1–9)

Their privileges as children of God. (10–17)

Their hope despite trials. (18–25)

Their assistance from the Spirit in prayer. (26, 27)

Their interest in the love of God. (28–31)

Their final triumph, through Christ. (32–39)

Key verse

Verse 8: "Therefore, there is now no condemnation for those who are in Christ Jesus."

Key word / key phrase

Verse 1, "No condemnation."

Key event / key person / key theme

Sanctification and the Holy Spirit

Key thought

"We are free from death – yet we long for the redemption of our bodies."

Anders Nygren

Key thing to look out for

Note how the statement that Christians are no longer condemned by God is explained in detail in verses 2–17.

Key Bible cross-reference

Verse 36. See Psalm 44:22.

Key "by way of explanation"

Verse 2, "the law of the Spirit of life." In this phrase the word "law" means a controlling power. Paul uses it to refer to the power of the Holy Spirit. This is the power that deals with sin and death for the Christian.

Key "Quotable Quote"

"The essential contrast which Paul paints is between the weakness of the law and the power of the Spirit. For over against indwelling sin, which is the reason the law is unable to help us in our moral struggle (7:17, 20), Paul now sets the indwelling Spirit, who is both our liberator now from 'the law of sin and death' (8:2) and the guarantee of resurrection and eternal glory in the end (8:11, 17, 23)."

John R.W. Stott

Romans 9

Matthew Henry's introduction

The apostle, having plainly asserted and largely proved that justification and salvation are to had by faith only, and not by the works of the law, by Christ and not by Moses, comes in this and the following chapters to anticipate an objection which might be made against this. If this be so, then what becomes of the Jews, of them all as a complex body, especially those of them that do not embrace Christ, nor believe the gospel? By this rule they must needs come short of happiness; and then what becomes of the promise made to the fathers, which entailed salvation on the Jews? Is not that promise nullified and made of none effect? Which is not a thing to be imagined about any word of God. That doctrine therefore, might they say, is not to be embraced, from which flows such a consequence as this. That the consequence of the rejection of the unbelieving Jews follows from Paul's doctrine he grants, but endeavors to soften and mollify, vv. 1–5. But that from this it follows that the word of God takes no effect he denies (v. 6), and proves the denial in the rest of the chapter, which serves likewise to illustrate the great doctrine of predestination, which he had spoken of (8:28) as the first wheel which in the business of salvation sets all the other wheels a-going.

Dr. Adam Clarke's analysis of chapter

Paul expresses his great sorrow for the unbelief and obstinacy of the Jews, 1–3.

Whose high privileges he enumerates, 4, 5.

Points out the manner in which God has chosen to communicate the knowledge of his name to both Jews and Gentiles; and how he deals, whether in judgment or mercy, with individuals; and produces the cases of Abraham, Isaac, Jacob, Esau, and Pharaoh, 6–17.

God shows mercy and judgment as he thinks proper, and none have a right to find fault with his proceedings, 18–20.

He has the same power over the human race as the potter has over the clay, 21–23.

The prophets predicted the calling of the Gentiles, and the rejection of the Jews, 24–29.

The Gentiles have attained to the knowledge of God's method of saving sinners; while the Jews have not attained this knowledge, 30, 31.

The reason why the Jews have not attained the salvation provided for them in the Gospel, 32, 33.

A detailed analysis of chapter

The apostle's concern that his countrymen were strangers to the gospel. (1–5)

The promises are made good to the spiritual seed of Abraham. (6–13)

Answers to objections against God's sovereignty in exercising mercy and justice. (14–24)

This sovereignty is in God's dealing both with Jews and Gentiles. (25–29)

The Jews seek justification, not by faith, but by the works of the law. (30–33)

Key verse

Verse 18: "Therefore God has mercy on whom he wants to have mercy, and he hardens whom he wants to harden."

Key word / key phrase

Verse 4, "the people of Israel."

Key event / key person / key theme

What about the Jews?

Key thought

Chapters 9–11 are a digression about the Jews.

Key thing to look out for

Everything about salvation depends on God's mercy.

Key Bible cross-reference

Verse 9. See Genesis 18:10.

Key "by way of explanation"

Verse 32, "not by faith." Paul is pointing out where Israel went wrong. She relied on her own "works" (deeds) rather than faith as she attempted to win God's favor.

Key "Quotable Quote"

"You cannot say that Luther invented the idea of justification by faith alone. Long before Luther it was taught by Augustine and Paul and Jesus and Moses. . . . Luther merely restated what true Christians have understood for centuries, that justification is by faith alone."

John MacArthur, Jr.

Romans 10

Matthew Henry's introduction

The dissolving of the peculiar church-state of the Jews, and the rejection of that polity by the repealing of their ceremonial law, the vacating of all the institutions of it, the abolishing of their priesthood, the burning of their temple, and the taking away of their place and nation, and in their room the substituting and erecting of a catholic church-state among the Gentile nations, though to us, now that these things have long since been done and completed, they may seem no great matter, yet to those who lived when they were doing, who knew how high the Jews had stood in God's favor, and how deplorable the condition of the Gentile world had been for many ages, it appeared very great and marvelous, and a mystery hard to be understood. The apostle, in this chapter, as in the previous and that which follows, is explaining and proving it; but with several very useful digressions, which a little interrupt the thread of his discourse. To two great truths I would reduce this chapter:

I. That there is a great difference between the righteousness of the law, which the unbelieving Jews were wedded to, and the righteousness of faith offered in the gospel, vv. 1–11.

II. That there is no difference between Jews and Gentiles; but, in point of justification and acceptance with God, the gospel sets them both on the same level, v. 12 to the end.

Dr. Adam Clarke's analysis of chapter

The apostle expresses his earnest desire for the salvation of the Jews, 1.

Having a zeal for God, but not according to knowledge, they sought salvation by works, and not by faith in Christ, 2–4.

The righteousness which is of the law described, 5.

That which is by faith described also, 6–10. He that believes and calls on the name of the Lord shall be saved, 11–13.

What is necessary to salvation, believing, hearing, preaching, a Divine mission, the Gospel, and obedience to its precepts, 14–16.

Faith comes by hearing, 17.

The universal spread of the Gospel predicted by the prophets, 18–20.

The ingratitude and disobedience of the Israelites, 21.

A detailed analysis of chapter

The apostle's earnest desire for the salvation of the Jews. (1–4)

The difference between the righteousness of the Law, and the righteousness of faith. (5–11)

The Gentiles stand on the same ground as the Jews, in justification and salvation. (12–17)

The Jews know this from Old Testament prophecies. (18–21)

Key verse

Verse 1: "Brothers, my heart's desire and prayer to God for the Israelites is that they may be saved."

Key word / key phrase

Verse 9, "Jesus is Lord."

Key event / key person / key theme

Israel rejected Jesus and the prophets

Key thought

Paul reveals his deep concern for the Jews.

Key thing to look out for

Note Paul's use of Old Testament quotations to back up his arguments.

Key Bible cross-reference

Verse 5. See Leviticus 18:5.

Key "by way of explanation"

Verse 15, "How beautiful are the feet of those

who bring good news!" This quotation from Isaiah 52:7 refers to the people who told the exiles that they were about to be released from Babylon. Paul applies this to Christian preachers who bring good news about release from sin.

Key "Quotable Quote"

"The good news is that sin has been dealt with; that Jesus has suffered its penalty for us as our representative, so that we might never have to suffer it; and that therefore all who believe in him can look forward to heaven."

J.M. Boice

Romans 11

Matthew Henry's introduction

The apostle, having reconciled that great truth of the rejection of the Jews with the promise made unto the fathers, is, in this chapter, further laboring to mollify the harshness of it, and to reconcile it to the divine goodness in general. It might be said, "Hath God then cast away his people?" The apostles therefore sets himself, in this chapter, to make a reply to this objection, and that two ways:

I. He shows at large what the mercy is that is mixed with this wrath, vv. 1–32.

II. He infers thence the infinite wisdom and sovereignty of God, with the adoration of which he concludes this chapter and subject, vv. 33–36.

Dr. Adam Clarke's analysis of chapter

God has not universally nor finally rejected Israel; nor are they all at present rejecters of the Gospel, for there is a remnant of true believers now, as there was in the days of the Prophet Elijah, 1–5.

These have embraced the Gospel, and are saved by grace, and not by the works of the law, 6.

The body of the Israelites, having rejected this, are blinded, according to the prophetic declaration of David, 7–10.

But they have not stumbled, so as to be finally rejected; but through their fall, salvation is come to the Gentiles, 11–14.

There is hope of their restoration, and that the nation shall yet become a holy people, 15, 16.

The converted Gentiles must not exult over the fallen Jews; the latter having fallen by unbelief, the former stand by faith, 17–20.

The Jews, the natural branches, were broken off from the true olive, and the Gentiles having been grafted in, in their place, must walk uprightly, else they also shall be cut off, 21, 22.

The Jews, if they abide not in unbelief, shall be again grafted in; and when the fullness of the Gentiles is come in, the great Deliverer shall turn away ungodliness from Jacob, according to the covenant of God, 23–27.

For the sake of their forefathers God loves them, and will again call them, and communicate His gifts to them, 28, 29.

The Gospel shall he again sent to them, as it has now been sent to the Gentiles, 30–32.

This procedure is according to the immensity of the wisdom, knowledge, and unsearchable judgments of God, who is the Creator, Preserver, and Governor of all things, and to whom all adoration is due, 33–36.

A detailed analysis of chapter

The rejection of the Jews is not universal. (1–10)

God overruled their unbelief and made the Gentiles take part in the gospel privileges. (11–21)

Key verse

Verse 6: "And if by grace, then it is no longer by works; if it were, grace would no longer be grace."

Key word / key phrase

Verse 1, "Does God reject his people?"

Key event / key person / key theme

Israel's future and her restoration

Key thought

This chapter revolves around the kindness and severity of God, verse 22.

Key thing to look out for

One day Israel will return to the Lord.

Key Bible cross-reference

Verse 8. See Isaiah 29:10.

Key "by way of explanation"

Verse 22, "kindness and sternness of God." Paul taught about both aspects of God's nature. Without his kindness he might appear to be a tyrant. Without his sternness he might appear to be an indulgent father.

Key "Quotable Quote"

"It was not human beings who accomplished anything here [on the cross]; no, God alone did it. He came to human beings in infinite love. He judged what is human. And he granted grace beyond any merit."

Dietrich Bonhoeffer

Romans 12

Matthew Henry's introduction

The apostle, having at large cleared and confirmed the prime fundamental doctrines of Christianity, comes in the next place to press the principal duties. We mistake our religion if we look on it only as a system of notions and a guide to speculation. No, it is a practical religion, that tends to the right ordering of the conversation. It is designed not only to inform our judgments, but to reform our hearts and lives. From the method of the apostle's writing in this, as in some other of the epistles (as from the management of the principal ministers of state in Christ's kingdom) the stewards of the mysteries of God may take direction how to divide the word of truth: not to press duty abstracted from privilege, nor privilege abstracted from duty; but let both go together, with a complicated design, they will greatly promote and befriend each other. The duties are drawn from the privileges, by way of inference. The foundation of Christian practice must be laid in Christian knowledge and faith. We must first understand how we receive Christ Jesus the Lord, and then we shall know the better how to walk in him. There is a great deal of duty prescribed in this chapter. The exhortations are short and pithy, briefly summing up what is good, and what the Lord our God in Christ requires of us. It is an abridgment of the Christian directory, an excellent collection of rules for the right ordering of the conversation, as becomes the gospel. It is joined to the previous discourse by the word "therefore." It is the practical application of doctrinal truths that is the life of preaching. He had been discoursing at large of justification by faith, and of the riches of free grace, and the pledges and assurances we have of the glory that is to be revealed. Hence carnal libertines would be apt to infer. "Therefore we may live as we list, and walk in the way of our hearts and the sight of our eyes." Now this does not follow; the faith that justifies is a faith that "works by love." And there is no other way to heaven but the way of holiness and obedience. Therefore what God hath joined together let no man put asunder. The particular exhortations of this chapter are reducible to the three principal heads of Christian duty: our duty to God t ourselves, and to our brother. The grace of God teaches us, in general, to live "godly, soberly, and righteously;" and to deny all that which is contrary hereunto. Now this chapter will give us to understand what godliness, sobriety, and righteousness, are though somewhat intermixed.

Dr. Adam Clarke's analysis of chapter

Such displays of God's mercy as Jews and Gentiles have received should induce them to consecrate themselves to Him; and not be conformed to the world, 1, 2.

Christians are exhorted to think meanly of themselves, 3.

And each to behave himself properly in the office which he has received from God, 4–8;

Various important moral duties recommended, 9–18.

We must not avenge ourselves, but overcome evil with good, 19–21.

A detailed analysis of chapter

Believers are to dedicate themselves to God. (1, 2)

To be humble, and faithfully to use their spiritual gifts. (3–8)

Exhortations about various duties. (9–16)

And to peaceful behavior toward all people. (17–21)

Key verse

Verse 2: "Do not conform any longer to the pattern of this world, but be transformed by the renewing of your mind."

Key word / key phrase

Verse 9, "cling to what is good."

Key event / key person / key theme

Christian behavior in the Church and in the world

Key thought

Christians are to be living sacrifices.

Key thing to look out for

Note that Christian behavior should be governed by love.

Key Bible cross-reference

Verse 16. See Proverbs 3:7.

Key "by way of explanation"

Verse 1, "living sacrifices." All Paul's readers were familiar with the Old Testament sacrificial system. Paul says Christians, in stark contrast to dead animal sacrifices, are to be "living sacrifices."

Key "Quotable Quote"

"All the fruits of the Spirit which we have are signs of grace, are summed up in charity, or Christian love; because this is the sum of all grace."

Jonathan Edwards

Romans 13

Matthew Henry's introduction

There are three good lessons taught us in this chapter, where the apostle enlarges more on his precepts than he had done in the previous chapter, finding them more needful to be fully pressed.

I. A lesson of subjection to lawful authority, vv. 1–6.

II. A lesson of justice and love to our brethren, vv. 7–10.

III. A lesson of sobriety and godliness in ourselves, v. 11 to the end.

Dr. Adam Clarke's analysis of chapter

Subjection to civil governors inculcated, from the consideration that civil government is according to the ordinance of God; and that those who resist the lawfully constituted authorities shall receive condemnation, 1, 2.

And those who are obedient shall receive praise, 3.

The character of a lawful civil governor, 4.

The necessity of subjection, 5.

The propriety of paying lawful tribute, 6, 7.

Christians should love one another, 8–10.

The necessity of immediate conversion to God proved from the shortness and uncertainty of time, 11, 12.

How the Gentiles should walk so as to please God, and put on Christ Jesus in order to their salvation, 13, 14.

A detailed analysis of chapter

The duty of subjection to the governing authorities. (1–7)

Exhortations to mutual love. (8–10)

To decent behavior and sobriety. (11–14)

Key verse

Verse 7: "Give everyone what you owe him: If you owe taxes, pay taxes; if revenue, then revenue; if respect, then respect; if honor, then honor."

Key word / key phrase

Verse 1, "the governing authorities."

Key event / key person / key theme

Christians, the authorities, and neighbors

Key thought

Paul teaches that the state authorities have been put in place by God.

Key thing to look out for

Evil practices have no place in the Christian life.

Key Bible cross-reference

Verse 9. See Exodus 20:13–15.

Key "by way of explanation"

Verse 1, "governing authorities." Some Christians thought that they need not submit to pagan authorities since they only acknowledged Christ's authority. Paul teaches otherwise.

Key "Quotable Quote"

"If the correction of unbridled despotism is the Lord's to avenge, let us not at once think that it is entrusted to us, to whom no command has been given except to obey and suffer."

John Calvin

Romans 14

Matthew Henry's introduction

The apostle having, in the previous chapter, directed our conduct one towards another in civil things, and prescribed the sacred laws of justice, peaceableness, and order, to be observed by us as members of the commonwealth, comes in this and part of the following chapter in like manner to direct our demeanor one towards another in sacred things, which pertain more immediately to conscience and religion, and which we observe as members of the church. Particularly, he gives rules how to manage our different apprehensions about indifferent things, in the management of which, it seems, there was something amiss among the Roman Christians, to whom he wrote, which he here labors to redress. But the rules are general, and of standing use in the church, for the preservation of that Christian love which he had so earnestly pressed in the previous chapter as the fulfilling of the law. It is certain that nothing is more threatening, nor more often fatal, to Christian societies, than the contentions and divisions of their members. By these wounds the life and soul of religion expire. Now in this chapter we are furnished with the sovereign balm of Gilead; the blessed apostle prescribes like a wise physician. "Why then is not the hurt of the daughter of my people recovered," but because his directions are not followed? This chapter, rightly understood, made use of, and lived up to, would set things to rights, and heal us all.

Dr. Adam Clarke's analysis of chapter

In things indifferent, Christians should not condemn each other, 1.

Particularly with respect to different kinds of food, 2–4.

And the observation of certain days, 5, 6.

None of us should live unto himself, but unto Christ, who lived and died for us, 7–9.

We must not judge each other; for all judgment belongs to God, 10–13.

We should not do any thing by which a weak brother may be stumbled or grieved; lest we destroy him for whom Christ died, 14–16.

The kingdom of God does not consist in outward things, 17, 18.

Christians should endeavor to cultivate peace and brotherly affection, and rather deny themselves of certain privileges than be the means of stumbling a weak brother, 19–21.

The necessity of doing all in the spirit of faith, 22, 23.

A detailed analysis of chapter

The Jewish converts cautioned against judging, and Gentile believers against despising Jews. (1–13)

And the Gentiles told to take care not to give offense unnecessarily. (14–23)

Key verse

Verse 1: "Accept him whose faith is weak, without passing judgment on disputable matters."

Key word / key phrase

Verse 10, "what leads to peace."

Key event / key person / key theme

The principles of Christian freedom

Key thought

Look after the weaker brother.

Key thing to look out for

Behave like a member of God's kingdom.

Key Bible cross-reference

Verse 11. See Isaiah 45:23.

Key "by way of explanation"

Verse 15. "your brother for whom Christ died." Christ died for those who are weak. If this is born in mind the strong Christian should not mind putting up with the weaker brothers and sisters.

Key "Quotable Quote"

"To be a Christian is primarily to live in union with Jesus Christ, as a result of which baptism, belief and behavior slot naturally into place."

John R.W. Stott

Romans 15

Matthew Henry's introduction

The apostle, in this chapter, continues the discourse of the former, about mutual forbearance in indifferent things; and so draws towards a conclusion of the epistle. Where such differences of apprehension, and consequently distances of affection, are among Christians, there is need of precept on precept, line on line, to allay the heat, and to beget a better temper. The apostle, being desirous to drive the nail home, as a nail in a sure place, follows his blow, unwilling to leave the subject till he has some hopes of prevailing, to which end he orders the cause before them and fills his mouth with the most pressing arguments. We may observe, in this chapter,

I. His precepts to them.
II. His prayers for them.
III. His apology for writing to them.
IV. His account of himself and his own affairs.
V. His declaration of his purpose to come and see them.
VI. His desire of a share in their prayers.

Dr. Adam Clarke's analysis of chapter

The strong should bear the infirmities of the weak, and each strive to please, not himself, but his neighbor, after the example of Christ, 1–3.

Whatsoever was written in old times was written for our learning, 4.

We should be of one mind, that we might with one mouth glorify God, 5, 6.

We should accept each other as Christ has accepted us, 7.

Scriptural proofs that Jesus Christ was not only the minister of the circumcision, but came also for the salvation of the Gentiles, 8–12.

The God of hope can fill us with all peace and joy in believing, 13.

Character of the Church of Rome, 14.

The reason why the apostle wrote so boldly to the Church in that city-what God had wrought by him, and what he purposed to do, 15–24.

He tells them of his intended journey to Jerusalem, with a contribution to the poor saints-a sketch of this journey, 25–29.

He commends himself to their prayers, 30–33.

A detailed analysis of chapter

How to behave toward the weak. (1–7)

Receive one another as brethren. (8–13)

The writing and preaching of the apostle. (14–21)

His intended journey. (22–29)

He requests their prayers. (30–33)

Key verse

Verse 7: "Accept one another, then, just as Christ accepted you, in order to bring praise to God."

Key word / key phrase

Verse 24, "when I go to Spain."

Key event / key person / key theme

Paul's missionary plans

Key thought

Be like Christ in the way you accept people.

Key thing to look out for

I hope to visit you soon.

Key Bible cross-reference

Verse 10. See Deuteronomy 32:43.

Key "by way of explanation"

Verse 17, "I glory." When Paul used this expression he was not attempting to boast about himself but rather about what Christ had achieved through him.

Key "Quotable Quote"

"Among the attributes of God, although they are all equal, mercy shines with even more brilliance than justice."

Miguel de Cervantes

Romans 16

Matthew Henry's introduction

Paul is now concluding this long and excellent epistle, and he does it with a great deal of affection. As in the main body of the epistle he appears to have been a very knowing man, so in these appurtenances of it he appears to have been a very loving man. So much knowledge and so much love are a very rare, but (where they exist) a very excellent and amiable–composition; for what is heaven but knowledge and love made perfect? It is observable how often Paul speaks as if he were concluding, and yet takes fresh hold again. One would have thought that solemn benediction which closed the previous chapter should have ended the epistle; and yet here he begins again, and in this chapter he repeats the blessing (v. 20), "The grace of our Lord Jesus Christ be with you, Amen." And yet he has something more to say; nay, again he repeats the blessing (v. 24), and yet has not done; an expression of his tender love. These repeated benedictions, which stand for valedictions, show how loathed Paul was to part. Now, in this closing chapter, we may observe,

I. His recommendation of one friend to the Roman Christians, and his particular salutation of several among them, vv. 1–16.

II. A caution to take heed of those who caused divisions, vv. 17–20.

III. Greetings added from some who were with Paul, vv. 21–24.

IV. He concludes with a solemn celebration of the glory of God, vv. 25–27.

Dr. Adam Clarke's analysis of chapter

The apostle commends to the Christians at Rome Phoebe, a deaconess of the Church at Cenchrea, 1, 2.

Sends greetings to Aquila and Priscilla, of whom he gives a high character; and greets also the Church at their house, 3–5.

Mentions several others by name, both men and women, who were members of the Church of Christ at Rome, 6–16.

Warns them to beware of those who cause dissensions and divisions, of whom he gives an awful character, 17, 18.

Extols the obedience of the Roman Christians, and promises them a complete victory over Satan, 19, 20.

Several people send their greetings, 21–23.

To whose good wishes he subjoins the apostolic blessing; commends them to God; gives own abstract of the doctrines of the Gospel: and concludes with ascribing glory to the only wise God, through Christ Jesus, 24–27.

A detailed analysis of chapter

The apostle recommends Phoebe to the Church at Rome, and greets several friends there. (1–16)

Warns the Church against those who cause divisions. (17–20)

Christian greetings. (21–24)

The letter concludes by giving glory to God. (25–27)

Key verse

Verse 3 "Greet Priscilla and Aquila, my fellow workers in Christ Jesus."

Key word / key phrase

Verse 3, "Greet."

Key event / key person / key theme

Paul greets his many friends in Rome

Key thought

Note how many people Paul knew in Rome.

Key thing to look out for

Verses 25–27. Paul's reasons for praising God.

Key Bible cross-reference

Verse 23. See 2 Timothy 4:20.

Key "by way of explanation"

Verse 25, "my gospel." Paul is not saying that he has a gospel that is different from the gospel every other Christian has. Rather Paul calls it "my" gospel as he received it by direct revelation. See Galatians 1:12.

Key "Quotable Quote"

"The gospel is so simple that small children can understand it, and it is so profound that studies by the wisest theologians will never exhaust its riches."

Charles Hodge

5. Select bibliography for Romans

Barrett, C. K. *A Commentary on the Epistle to the Romans*. New York: Harper and Brothers, 1957.

Bruce, F. F. *The Epistle of Paul to the Romans*. TNTC. Grand Rapids: Eerdmans, 1963.

Calvin, John. *Commentary on the Epistle of Paul the Apostle to the Romans*. Grand Rapids: Eerdmans, 1947.

Denney, James. *St. Paul's Epistle to the Romans*. EGT (vol. II). London: Hodder and Stoughton, 1917.

Godet, F. *Commentary on St. Paul's Epistle to the Romans*. Edinburgh: T. & T. Clark, 2 Vols. E.T. 1883–84.

Godet, F. *Commentary on the Epistle to the Romans*. Grand Rapids: Kregel, 1977.

Haldane, Robert. *Exposition of the Epistle to the Romans*. New York: Robert Carter and Bros., 1860.

Hodge, Charles. *A Commentary on the Epistle to the Romans*. New York: Armstrong, 1896.

Luther, Martin. *Commentary on the Epistle to the Romans*. Grand Rapids: Zondervan, E.T. 1954.

Moule, Handley C. G. *Epistle of St. Paul to the Romans*. 5th ed. New York: Armstrong, 1902.

Murray, John. *The Epistle to the Romans*. NIC. Grand Rapids: Eerdmans, 1968.

Nygren, Anders. *Commentary on Romans*. Philadelphia: Muhlenberg Press, E.T. 1949.

1 Corinthians

1. Book by book: Introduction to 1 Corinthians

Introduction

Authenticity of letter

The authenticity of this Epistle is attested by Clement of Rome (*First Epistle to the Corinthians*, 47), Polycarp (*Epistle to the Philippians*, 11), and Irenaeus (*Against Heresies*, 4.27.3).

Corinth

The city to which it was sent was famed for its wealth and commerce, which were chiefly due to its situation between the Ionian and Ægean Seas on the isthmus connecting the Peloponese with Greece. In Paul's time it was the capital of the province Achaia and the seat of the Roman proconsul (Acts 18:12).

The state of morals in it was notorious for debauchery, even in the profligate heathen world; so much so that "to Corinthianize" was a proverbial phrase for "to play the wanton"; hence arose dangers to the purity of the Christian Church at Corinth. That Church was founded by Paul on his first visit (Acts 18:1–17).

Corinthian Church

Paul had been the instrument of converting many Gentiles (1 Cor. 12:2), and some Jews (Acts 18:8), notwithstanding the vehement opposition of the countrymen of the latter (Acts 18:5), during the year and a half in which he sojourned there. The converts were chiefly of the humbler classes (1 Cor. 1:26, etc.). Crispus (1 Cor. 1:14; Acts 18:8), Erastus, and Gaius (Caius) were, however, men of rank (Rom. 16:23). A variety of classes is also implied in 1 Cor. 11:22. The risk of contamination by contact with the surrounding corruptions, and the temptation to a craving for Greek philosophy and rhetoric (which Apollos' eloquent style rather tended to foster, Acts 18:24, etc.) in contrast to Paul's simple preaching of Christ crucified (1 Cor. 2:1, etc.), as well as the opposition of certain teachers to him, naturally caused him anxiety. Emissaries from the Judaizers of Palestine boasted of "letters of commendation" from Jerusalem, the metropolis of the faith. They did not, it is true, insist on circumcision in refined Corinth, where the attempt would have been hopeless, as they did among the simpler people of Galatia; but they attacked the apostolic authority of Paul (1 Cor. 9:1, 2; 2 Cor. 10:1, 7, 8), some of them declaring themselves followers of Cephas, the chief apostle, others boasting that they belonged to Christ Himself (1 Cor. 1:12; 2 Cor. 10:7), while they haughtily repudiated all subordinate teaching. Those people gave out themselves for apostles (2 Cor. 11:5, 13). The ground taken by them was that Paul was not one of the Twelve, and not an eye-witness of the Gospel facts, and durst not prove his apostleship by claiming sustenance from the Christian Church. Another section avowed themselves followers of Paul himself, but did so in a party spirit, exalting the minister rather than Christ. The followers of Apollos, again, unduly prized his Alexandrian learning and eloquence, to the disparagement of the apostle, who studiously avoided any deviation from Christian simplicity (1 Cor. 2:1–5). In some of this last philosophizing party there may have arisen the Antinomian tendency which tried to defend theoretically their own practical immorality: hence their denial of the future resurrection, and their adoption of the Epicurean motto, prevalent in heathen Corinth, "Let us eat and drink, for to-morrow we die" (1 Cor. 15:32). Hence, perhaps, arose their connivance at the incestuous intercourse kept up by one of the so-called Christian body with his stepmother during his father's life. The household of Chloe informed Paul of many other evils: such as contentions, divisions, and lawsuits brought against brethren in heathen law courts by professing Christians; the abuse of their spiritual gifts into occasions of display and fanaticism; the interruption of public worship by simultaneous and disorderly ministrations, and decorum violated by women speaking unveiled (contrary to Oriental practice), and so usurping the office of men, and even the holy communion desecrated by greediness and reveling on the part of the communicants.

Other messengers, also, came from Corinth, consulting him on the subject of:

(1) the controversy about meats offered to idols;

(2) the disputes about celibacy and marriage;

(3) the due exercise of spiritual gifts in public worship;

(4) the best way to make the collection which he had requested for the saints at Jerusalem (1 Cor. 16:1, etc.). Such were the circumstances which called forth the *First Epistle to the Corinthians*, the most varied in its topics of all the Epistles.

A previous letter

In 1 Cor. 5:9, "I wrote unto you in an Epistle not to company with fornicators," it is implied that Paul had written a previous letter to the Corinthians (now lost). Probably in it he had also asked them to make a contribution for the poor saints at Jerusalem, whereon they seem to have asked directions about this, to which he now replies (1 Cor. 16:2). It also probably announced his intention of visiting them on way to Macedonia, and again on his return from Macedonia (2 Cor. 1:15, 16), which purpose he changed hearing the unfavorable report from Chloe's household (1 Cor. 16:5–7), for which he was charged with (2 Cor. 1:17). In the first Epistle which we have, the subject of fornication is alluded to only in a way, as if he were rather replying to an excuse set up after rebuke in the matter, than introducing for the first time (Alford). Preceding this former letter, he seems to have paid a second visit to Corinth. For in 2 Cor. 12:4; 13:1, he speaks of his intention of paying them a third visit, implying he had already twice visited them. See on 2 Cor. 2:1; 2 Cor. 13:2; also see on 2 Cor. 1:15; 2 Cor. 1:16. It is hardly likely that during his three years' stay at Ephesus he would have failed to revisit his Corinthian converts, which he could so readily do by sea, there being constant maritime intercourse between the two cities. This second visit was probably a short one (compare 1 Cor. 16:7); and attended with pain and humiliation (2 Cor. 2:1; 12:21), occasioned by the scandalous conduct of so many of his own converts. His milder censures having then failed to produce reformation, he wrote briefly directing them "not to company with fornicators." On their misapprehending this injunction, he explained it more fully in the Epistle, the first of the two extant (1 Cor. 5:9, 12). That the second visit is not mentioned in Acts is no objection to its having really taken place, as that book is fragmentary and omits other leading incidents in Paul's life; for example, his visit to Arabia, Syria, and Cilicia (Gal. 1:17–21).

Place and date of writing

The place of writing is fixed to be Ephesus (1 Cor. 16:8). The subscription in English Version, "From Philippi," has no authority whatever, and probably arose from a mistaken translation of 1 Cor. 16:5, "For I am passing through Macedonia." At the time of writing Paul implies (1 Cor. 16:8) that he intended to leave Ephesus after Pentecost of that year. He really did leave it about Pentecost (A.D. 57). Compare Acts 19:20. The allusion to Passover imagery in connection with our Christian Passover, Easter (1 Cor. 5:7), makes it likely that the season was about Easter. Thus the date of the Epistle is fixed with tolerable accuracy, about Easter, certainly before Pentecost, in the third year of his residence at Ephesus, A.D. 57.

Sosthenes

The Epistle is written in the name of Sosthenes "[our] brother." Birks supposes he is the same as the Sosthenes, Acts 18:17, who, he thinks, was converted subsequently to that occurrence. He bears no part in the Epistle itself, the apostle in the very next verses (1 Cor. 1:4, etc.) using the first person: so Timothy is introduced, 2 Cor. 1:1. The bearers of the Epistle were probably Stephanas, Fortunatus, and Achaicus (see the subscription, 1 Cor. 16:24), whom he mentions (1 Cor. 16:17, 18) as with him then, but who he implies are about to return back to Corinth; and therefore he commends them to the regard of the Corinthians.

A. R. Faussett

Detailed outline

- I. Introduction: 1:1–9
  - A. The writers: Paul and Sosthenes: 1:1
  - B. The readers: 1:2
  - C. The greeting: Grace and peace from God and Jesus: 1:3
  - D. The thanksgiving: 1:4–8
    - 1. The nature of the thanksgiving: 1:4
    - 2. The basis for the thanksgiving: 1:4
    - 3. The thanksgiving for their past enrichment: 1:5–6
    - 4. Thanksgiving for their present condition: 1:7–8
  - E. The affirmation of faith: 1:9
- II. Church divisions: 1:10–4:21
  - A. Reaction to the report of their divisions: 1:10–17
    - 1. An appeal for unity: 1:10
    - 2. The source of his information about their divisions: 1:11
    - 3. The nature of their divisions: 1:12
    - 4. Questioning the divisions: 1:13
    - 5. Their divisions not due to his ministry: 1:14–17
  - B. Arguments against church divisions: 1:18–4:5
    - 1. Division is inconsistent with the Gospel: 1:18–3:4
      - (a) The Gospel is not worldly wisdom: 1:18–2:5
        - (1) The proof from reactions to the Gospel: 1:18–25
        - (2) The proof from the composition of the church: 1:26–31
        - (3) The proof from Paul's work: 2:1–5
      - (b) The Gospel is heavenly wisdom: 2:6–3:4

(1) The recipients of this wisdom: 2:6
(2) The nature of the wisdom: 2:6–12
(3) The acquisition of this wisdom: 2:13–3:4

2. Description of true ministers: 3:5–4:5
 (a) The ministers are laborers in God's field: 3:5–9
  (1) The function of ministers: 3:5
  (2) The work and reward of ministers: 3:6–8
  (3) Summary of the teaching: 3:9
 (b) Ministers are builders of God's sanctuary: 3:10–23
  (1) The work of the builder will be tested: 3:10–15
  (2) The destruction of God's sanctuary is punished: 3:16–17
  (3) An exhortation about their view of ministers: 3:18–23
 (c) The ministers are stewards of the mysteries of God: 4:1–5
  (1) The view to be taken of ministers: 4:1
  (2) The demand for faithfulness in the steward: 4:2
  (3) The Lord as judge of stewards: 4:3–4
  (4) The appeal to withhold judgment until the Lord comes: 4:5

C. The appeal to the Corinthians: 4:6–21
1. Application of the argument to their divisions: 4:6–21
 (a) The purpose of the application: 4:6
 (b) The failure to recognize talents as gifts: 4:7
 (c) The results: 4:8
 (d) The experience of the apostles: 4:9–13
  (l) The low position of the apostles: 4:9
  (2) The contrast between them and the Corinthians: 4:10
  (3) The description of their experiences: 4:11–13
2. The appeal to follow his example: 4:14–17
 (a) His aim in writing: 4:14
 (b) His relation as their spiritual father: 4:15–16
 (c) His reason for sending Timothy to them: 4:17
3. The warning that their attitude will determine his actions: 4:18–21
 (a) The puffed-up attitude of some believers: 4:18
 (b) The coming of Paul to Corinth: 4:19–21

III. Moral problems in the church: 5:1–6:20
A. Immorality: 5:1–13
1. Discipline of the incestuous person: 5:1–8
 (a) The nature of the sin: 5:1
 (b) Failure of the church to act: 5:2
 (c) udgment of the guilty person: 5:3–5
 (d) Appeal to the church to act: 5:6–8
2. The general principle in handling such cases: 5:9–13
 (a) His former instructions: 5:9–11

(b) The call to act on this principle: 5:12–13

B. The evil of litigation before worldly courts: 6:1–11

1. The question of such litigations: 6:1
2. The reasons for settling problems in the church: 6:2–6
   (a) Because of the church's future work of judging: 6:2–3
   (b) Because their lawsuits set up unqualified judges: 6:4–5
   (c) It shows the church's failure to exercise judgment: 6:5–6
3. The results: 6:7–8
4. The warning against unrighteousness: 6:9–11

C. Holiness of the body: 6:12–20

1. The limitation on Christian liberty: 6:12
2. The application of the principle in two areas: 6:13–14
   (a) To foods: 6:13
   (b) To sex: 6:13–14
3. The nature of the believer's body forbids fornication: 6:15
4. A contrast between two unions: 6:16–17
5. Warning to flee from sexual immorality: 6:18
6. The nature of the sin of sexual immorality: 6:18
7. The proper use of the body: 6:19–20

IV. Marriage: 7:1–40

A. The problem of marriage and celibacy: 7:1–9

1. The approval of the celibate life: 7:1
2. Instructions about married life: 7:2–6
   (a) The reason for preferring marriage: 7:2
   (b) The nature of marriage relations: 7:2
   (c) Duties in marriage: 7:3–4
   (d) Regulation of sex relationships: 7:5–6
3. The recognition of both marriage and celibacy as proper: 7:7
4. Advice to the unmarried: 7:8–9

B. The problem of marriage and separation: 7:10–16

1. A charge to Christian couples: 7:10–11
   (a) Authority for the charge: 7:10
   (b) Contents of the charge: 7:10–11
2. A charge to those of mixed marriages: 7:12–16
   (a) Nature of the charge: 7:12
   (b) Contents of the charge: 7:12–16
      (1) Separation not to be caused by the believer: 7:12–14
      (2) Separation when caused by the unbeliever: 7:15–16

C. The believer's life and earthly position: 7:17–24

1. The basic principle of life for the believer: 7:17
2. The application of the principle to life: 7:18–24
   (a) Applied to form religious distinctions: 7:18–20
   (b) Applied to the social status of believers: 7:21–24

D. Advice about the unmarried: 7:25–40

1. Advice about virgins: 7:25–35

(a) The nature of the advice: 7:25–27
(b) The reason for the advice: 7:28–31
(c) Freedom resulting from his advice: 7:33–35
2. Advice to parents of marriageable daughters: 7:36–38
(a) When marriage should be permitted: 7:36
(b) When permission to marry should be denied: 7:37
(c) Both are proper: 7:38
3. Advice to widows: 7:39–40
V. Food offered to idols: 8:1–11:1
A. The relationship of love to knowledge: 8:1–13
1. The need for love with knowledge: 8:1–3
2. The claim to liberty through knowledge: 8:4–8
(a) Liberty to eat: 8:4–6
(b) Danger to a weaker brother: 8:7
(c) Food does not determine relationship to God: 8:8
3. Warning against causing a weaker brother to sin: 8:9–12
(a) The warning to those with knowledge: 8:9
(b) The effect of this knowledge: 8:10
(c) Consequences of acting on knowledge: 8:11–12
(d) The voluntary restriction of liberty: 8:13
B. Paul's example of voluntary restriction of liberties: 9:1–27
1. His authority as an apostle: 9:1–3
2. His rights as an apostle: 9:4–12
(a) The rights claimed: 9:4–7
(b) Justification of his claim: 9:8–12
3. His reasons for waiving these rights: 9:12–23
(b) He would not hinder the Gospel: 9:12–14
(b) It gives him ground for boasting: 9:15–18
(c) It enables him to win more to Christ: 9:19–23
4. An appeal for them to follow his example: 9:24–27
C. The history of Israel as a warning against abuse of liberty: 10:1–13
1. The reminder of Israel's history: 10:1–5
(a) Privileges of Israel: 10:1–4
(b) The fate of Israel: 10:5
2. Warnings from the history of Israel: 10:6–10
(a) Lessons in Israel's history: 10:6–10
(1) The general warning against evil: 10:6
(2) Specific examples: 10:7–10
(b) The significance of Israel's experiences: 10:11
3. The resulting admonition to those under testing: 10:12–13
(a) Realize the danger of falling: 10:12
(b) Encouragement to those being tempted: 10:13
4. The appeal to avoid idolatry: 10:14–22
(a) Flee from idolatry: 10:14

(b) The argument against participation: 10:15–22
(l) Recipient of the argument: 10:15
(2) The significance of participation: 10:16–22
D. Summary of general principles governing conduct: 10:23–11:1
1. Limitations on Christian liberty: 10:23
2. Proper consideration for others: 10:24
3. Instructions about meats sold for food: 10:25–30
(a) Instructions to those eating at home: 10:25–26
(b) Instructions to those eating with unbelievers: 10:27–30
E. Concluding instructions: 10:31–11:1
1. Do all to God's glory: 10:31
2. Maintain proper relations with all men: 10:32–33
3. Follow the apostolic example: 11:1
VI. Public worship: 11:2–14:40
A. The covering of women: 11:2–16
1. Praise for their obedience: 11:2
2. The principle of subordination: 11:3–6
3. Establishing the principle of subordin ation: 11:7–15
(a) From the creative relation: 11:7–12
(b) From the spiritual relationship: 11:13–15
(c) Conclusion of the discussion: 11:16
B. Disorders connected with the Lord's Supper: 11:17–34
1. Corinthian disorders at the Lord's Supper: 11:17–22
(a) The nature of their disorders: 11:18–21
(1) The report of their divisions: 11:18–19
(2) The description of disorders: 11:20–21
(b) The rebuke for disorders: 11:22
2. The Lord's Supper: 11:23–28
(a) Revelation about the Lord's Supper: 11:23
(b) The order of the Lord's Supper: 11:23–25
(c) The meaning of the Lord's Supper: 11:26
(d) Participation in an unworthy manner: 11:27
(e) Participation in a worthy manner: 11:28
3. Consequences of disorderly participation: 11:27–34
C. The problem about spiritual gifts in the Church: 12:1–14:40
1. The endowment of the gifts: 12:1–31
(a) The test of the Spirit: 12:1–3
(1) The desire for them to be informed: 12:1
(2) The reminder of their past condition: 12:2
(3) The test for one speaking in the Spirit: 12:3
(b) The diversity of gifts: 12:4–11
(1) The common source: 12:4–6
(2) The purpose of the gifts: 12:7
(3) The gifts: 12:8–10
(4) The source of all gifts: 12:11

(c) The nature of the Body of Christ: 12:12–31
(1) Unity of the Body: 12:12
(2) Entrance into the Body: 12:13
(3) Harmony in the Body: 12:14–26
(4) Identification of the Body: 12:27
(5) Differing functions of the members: 12:28–31
2. Using the gifts: 13:1–13
(a) The necessity for love in the use of gifts: 13:1–3
(1) The need for love with the gifts of tongues: 13:1
(2) Love and superior gifts: 13:2
(3) Love and giving: 13:3
(b) Characteristics of love: 13:4–7
(1) Negative characteristics of love: 13:4–6
(2) Positive characteristics of love: 13:6–7
(c) The superiority of love: 13:8–13
(l) Love and passing things: 13:8–12
(2) The superiority of love: 13:13
3. The proper use of spiritual gifts: 14:1–40
(a) Tongues and prophecy compared: 14:1–25
(1) Their value in the church: 14:1–19
(2) Their function to unbelievers: 14:20–25
(b) The orderly use of tongues and prophecy: 14:26–36
(1) Order in worship: 14:26
(2) Instructions for worship services: 14:27–36
(c) Concluding statements: 14:37–40

VII. The resurrection: 15:1–58
A. The Gospel of Christ's resurrection: 15:1–11
1. The proclamation and reception of the Gospel: 15:1–2
2. The nature of the Gospel: 15:3–4
3. Witnesses to the resurrection of Christ: 15:5–10
4. Summary statement: 15:11
B. The necessity of Christ's resurrection: 15:12–34
1. The necessity of His resurrection for salvation: 15:12–19
(a) The denial of the resurrection by some: 15:12
(b) Consequences of their denial: 15:13–19
2. Historic necessity of the resurrection: 15:20–28
(a) Historic necessity: 15:20
(b) The divine provision: 15:21–22
(c) The divine order in the program: 15:23–28
(1) Jesus' resurrection as the first fruits: 15:23
(2) The resurrection of those in Christ: 15:23
(3) The end of God's program: 15:24–28
3. Christ's resurrection and present Christian conduct: 15:29–34
(a) The question about baptism for the dead: 15:29
(b) The question of jeopardizing our lives: 15:30–34

(l) The foolishness of such conduct: 15:30–32
(2) The rebuke: 15:33–34
4. The prospect of the Christian's resurrection: 15:35–58
(a) The nature of the resurrected body: 15:35–49
(l) Questions about the resurrected body: 15:35
(2) Answers about the resurrected body: 15:36–49
(b) he change that produces the resurrected body: 15:50–58
(1) The condition requiring the change: 15:50
(2) The nature of the change: 15:51–52
(3) The requirement for the change: 15:53
(4) The triumph of the change: 15:54–57
(5) The concluding appeal for steadfastness: 15:58

VIII. Practical and personal matters: 16:1–24
A. Instructions for raising the collection: 16:1–4
1. Instructions also to be given to the Galatians churches: 16:1
2. The method to be used in collecting money: 16:2
3. The transmission of the collection: 16:3–4
B. Planned visits to Corinth: 16:5–12
1. Paul's visit: 16:5–9
2. The visit of Timothy: 16:10–11
3. The visit of Apollos: 16:12
C. Concluding admonitions to the Corinthians: 16:13–14
D. Acknowledgment of the representatives from Corinth: 16:15–18
1. An appeal about the house of Stephanas: 16:15–16
2. The coming of the three representatives: 16:17–18
E. Concluding greetings: 16:19–24
1. Greetings from others: 16:19–20
2. Salutation from Paul himself: 16:21–24
(a) His signature: 16:21
(b) A final warning: 16:22
(c) The benediction: 16:23
(d) The expression of affection: 16:24

2. Helpful summaries of 1 Corinthians

Bird's eye view

1 Corinthians is like listening to one end of a telephone conversation. Paul answers questions from the newly established Christian church in Corinth and sends firm instructions to correct their non-Christian ways.

Reading plan

The following reading plan, taking one reading per day, enables you to read through 1 Corinthians in twenty-three days.

1 Corinthians 1:1–1:31
1 Corinthians 2:1–2:16
1 Corinthians 3:1–3:23
1 Corinthians 4:1–4:21
1 Corinthians 5:1–5:13
1 Corinthians 6:1–6:20

1 Corinthians 7:1–7:24
1 Corinthians 7:25–7:40
1 Corinthians 8:1–8:13
1 Corinthians 9:1–9:27
1 Corinthians 10:1–10:33
1 Corinthians 11:1–11:16
1 Corinthians 11:17–11:34
1 Corinthians 12:1–12:31
1 Corinthians 13:1–13:13
1 Corinthians 14:1–14:25
1 Corinthians 14:26–14:40
1 Corinthians 15:1–15:34
1 Corinthians 15:35–15:58
1 Corinthians 16:1–16:24
1 Corinthians 15:1–15:34
1 Corinthians 15:35–15:58
1 Corinthians 16:1–16:24

Verses to memorize

1 Corinthians 1:18

For the preaching of the cross is to them that perish foolishness; but unto us which are saved it is the power of God. KJV

1 Corinthians 3:11

For other foundation can no man lay than that is laid, which is Jesus Christ. KJV

1 Corinthians 6:19–20

What? know ye not that your body is the temple of the Holy Spirit which is in you, which ye have of God, and ye are not your own? For ye are bought with a price: therefore glorify God in your body, and in your spirit, which are God's. KJV

1 Corinthians 10:12

Wherefore let him that thinketh he standeth take heed lest he fall. KJV

1 Corinthians 10:13

There hath no temptation taken you but such as is common to man: but God is faithful, who will not suffer you to be tempted above that ye are able; but will with the temptation also make a way to escape, that ye may be able to bear it. KJV

1 Corinthians 10:31

Whether therefore ye eat, or drink, or whatsoever ye do, do all to the glory of God. KJV

Statistics

Seventh New Testament book
Second letter by the apostle Paul
16 chapters
437 verses
9,489 words
Number of Old Testament quotations and allusions in 1 Corinthians: 41.

Famous saying found in 1 Corinthians

"Twinkling of an eye" 1 Corinthians 15:52

Names/titles given

Pros Korinthious A: "First to the Corinthians."

3. Helpful keys to turn to in understanding 1 Corinthians

Key word/phrase

Wisdom

Let all things be done decently and in order, 14:40.

Key verses

1 Corinthians 2:7, 8; 10:12–13

Themes to study

- Church order and discipline.
- Our relations to one another in the Christian fellowship.

Jesus in 1 Corinthians

In 1 Corinthians Jesus is our Lord.

Lessons to learn from 1 Corinthians

- God's wisdom is superior to human thinking.
- Jesus' resurrection should be central to our Christian belief.
- Church discipline is sometimes a necessity.

4. Chapter by chapter: outline of every chapter of 1 Corinthians

1 Corinthians 1

Matthew Henry's introduction

In this chapter we have,

I. The preface or introduction to the whole epistle, vv. 1–9.

II. One principal occasion of writing it hinted, namely, their divisions and the origin of them, vv. 10–13.

III. An account of Paul's ministry among them, which was principally preaching the gospel, vv. 14–17.

IV. The manner in which he preached the gospel, and the different success of it, with an account how admirably it was fitted to bring glory to God and beat down the pride and vanity of men, v. 17 to the end.

Dr. Adam Clarke's analysis of chapter

The salutation of Paul and Sosthenes, 1, 2.

The apostolic benediction, 3.

Thanksgiving for the prosperity of the Church at Corinth, 4.

In what that prosperity consisted, 5–9.

The apostle reproves their dissensions, and vindicates himself from being any cause of them, 10–17.

States the simple means which God uses to convert sinners and confound the wisdom of the wise, 18–21.

Why the Jews and Greeks did not believe, 22.

The matter of the apostle's preaching, and the reasons why that preaching was effectual to the salvation of men, 23–29.

All should glory in God, because all blessings are dispensed by Him through Christ Jesus, 30, 31.

A detailed analysis of chapter

A greeting and thanksgiving. (1–9)

Exhortation to brotherly love, and reproof for divisions. (10–16)

The teaching of a crucified Savior, which promotes the glory of God, (17–25)

and humbles all people before him. (26–31)

Key verse

Verse 25: "For the foolishness of God is wiser than man's wisdom, and the weakness of God is stronger than man's strength."

Key word

Verse 18, "cross."

Key event / key person / key theme

The disunity in the Church at Corinth

Key thought

Christ is preeminent and must be so in any fellowship if its abuses are to be corrected.

Key thing to look out for

The links and contrasts between wisdom and power.

Key Bible cross-reference

Verse 21. See Luke 10:21.

Key "by way of explanation"

Verse 23. Christ crucified was a "stumbling-block" to the Jews because they were not expecting a crucified Messiah, but a politically triumphant Messiah. Paul wrote this letter when we was coming to the end of his three years at Ephesus (16:5–9; Acts 20:31).

Key "Quotable Quote"

"Forbid it, Lord, that I should boast,
Save in the death of Christ my God.
All the vain things that charm me most
I sacrifice them to his blood."

Isaac Watts

1 Corinthians 2

Matthew Henry's introduction

The apostle proceeds with his argument in this chapter, and,

I. Reminds the Corinthians of the plain manner in which he delivered the gospel to them, vv. 1–5. But yet,

II. Shows them that he had communicated to them a treasure of the truest and highest wisdom, such as exceeded all the attainments of learned men, such as could never have entered into the heart of man if it had not been revealed, nor can be received and improved to salvation but by the light and influence of that Spirit who revealed it, v. 6 to the end.

Dr. Adam Clarke's analysis of chapter

The apostle makes an apology for his manner of preaching, 1.

And gives the reason why he adopted that manner, 2–5.

He shows that this preaching, notwithstanding it was not with excellence of human speech or wisdom, yet was the mysterious wisdom of God, which the princes of this world did not know, and which the Spirit of God alone could reveal, 6–10.

It is the Spirit of God only that can reveal the things of God, 11.

The apostles of Christ know the things of God by the Spirit of God, and teach them, not in the words of man's wisdom, but in the words of that Spirit, 12, 13.

The natural man cannot discern the things of the Spirit, 14.

But the spiritual man can discern and teach them, because he has the mind of Christ, 15, 16.

A detailed analysis of chapter

The simple way in which the apostle preached Christ crucified. (1–5)

The wisdom contained in this teaching. (6–9)

It cannot be known but by the Holy Spirit. (10–16)

Key verse

Verse 10: "The Spirit searches all things, even the deep things of God."

Key word / key phrase

Verse 13, "words taught by the Spirit."

Key event / key person / key theme

True wisdom and the Spirit

Key thought

God's wisdom comes from the Holy Spirit.

Key thing to look out for

Paul defines the spiritual person.

Key Bible cross-reference

Verse 9. See Isaiah 64:4.

Key "by way of explanation"

Verse 10, "Spirit searches all things." Because the Spirit understands the depths of God and his wonderful grace, he is able to reveal this to believers.

Key "Quotable Quote"

"For the message of the cross is the doctrine of salvation through the crucifixion of the Son of God as a sacrifice for human sins."

Charles Hodge

1 Corinthians 3

Matthew Henry's introduction

In this chapter the apostle,

I. Blames the Corinthians for their carnality and divisions, vv. 1–4.

II. He instructs them how what was amiss among them might be rectified, by remembering,

A. That their ministers were no more than ministers, v. 5.

B. That they were unanimous, and carried on the same design, vv. 6–10.

C. That they built on one and the same foundation, vv. 11–15.

III. He exhorts them to give due honor to their bodies, by keeping them pure (vv. 16, 17), and to humility and self-diffidence, vv. 18–21.

IV. And forbids them from glorying in particular ministers, because of the equal interest they had in all, v. 22 to the end.

Dr. Adam Clarke's analysis of chapter

Because of the carnal, divided state of the people at Corinth, the apostle was obliged to treat them as children in the knowledge of sacred things, 1–3.

Some were for setting up Paul, others Apollos, as their sole teachers, 4.

The apostle shows that himself and fellow apostles were only instruments which God used to bring them to the knowledge of the truth; and even their sowing, and watering the seed was of no use unless God gave the increase, 5–8.

The Church represented as God's husbandry, and as God's building, the foundation of which is Christ Jesus, 9–11.

Ministers must beware how and what they build on this foundation, 12–15.

The Church of God is his temple, and he that

defiles it shall be destroyed, 16, 17.

No man should depend on his own wisdom; for the wisdom of the world is foolishness with God, 18–20.

None should glory in man as his teacher; God gives his followers every good, both for time and eternity, 21–23.

A detailed analysis of chapter

The Corinthians reproved for their divisions. (1–4)

The true servants of Christ can do nothing without him. (5–9)

He is the only foundation, and every one should take care how he builds on this. (10–15)

The churches of Christ should be pure and humble. (16, 17)

And they should not boast because all they have comes from Christ. (18–23)

Key verse

Verse 11: "For no one can lay any foundation other than the one already laid, which is Jesus Christ."

Key word / key phrase

Verse 10, "an expert builder."

Key event / key person / key theme

The nature of ministers

Key thought

Paul hated Christian disunity.

Key thing to look out for

Only spiritual foundations will survive.

Key Bible cross-reference

Verse 20. See Hebrews 5:12, 13.

Key "by way of explanation"

Verse 10, "I laid a foundation." Paul did this by preaching about Christ and his death.

Key "Quotable Quote"

"Next to the wicked lives of men, nothing is so great a disparagement and weakening to religion as the divisions of Christians."

John Tillotson

1 Corinthians 4

Matthew Henry's introduction

In this chapter the apostle,

I. Directs them how to account of him and his fellow ministers, and therein, tacitly at least, reproves them for their unworthy carriage towards him, vv. 1–6.

II. He cautions them against pride and selfelation, and hints at the many temptations they had to conceive too highly of themselves, and despise him and other apostles, because of the great diversity in their circumstances and condition, vv. 7–13.

III. He challenges their regard to him as their father in Christ, vv. 14–16.

IV. He tells them of his having sent Timothy to them, and of his own purpose to come to them shortly, however some among them had pleased themselves, and grown vain, on the quite contrary expectation, v. 17 to the end.

Dr. Adam Clarke's analysis of chapter

Ministers should be esteemed by their flocks as

the stewards of God, whose duty and interest it is to be faithful, 1, 2. Precipitate and premature judgments condemned, 3–5.

The apostle's caution to give the Corinthians no offence, 6.

We have no good but what we receive from God, 7.

The worldly mindedness of the Corinthians, 8.

The enumeration of the hardships, trials, and sufferings of the apostles, 9–13.

For what purpose St. Paul mentions these things, 14–16.

He promises to send Timothy to them, 17.

And to come himself shortly, to examine and correct the abuses that had crept in among them, 18–21.

A detailed analysis of chapter

The true character of gospel ministers. (1–6)

Warns against despising the apostle. (7–13)

He tells them to view him as their spiritual father in Christ, and shows his concern for them. (14–21)

Key verse

Verse 4: "My conscience is clear, but that does not make me innocent. It is the Lord who judges me."

Key word / key phrase

Verse 4, "my conscience is clear."

Key event / key person / key theme

Paul's ministry is misunderstood

Key thought

Paul writes about his special relationship with the Corinthian Christians.

Key thing to look out for

When Christians had gone astray Paul never pulled his punches.

Key Bible cross-reference

Verse 12. See Acts 18:3.

Key "by way of explanation"

Verse 12, "we work hard with our own hands." By trade, Paul was a tentmaker. Acts 18:3.

Key "Quotable Quote"

"Set your own will entirely aside and strive to keep before your eyes your one and only goal, that is, the greater service and glory of God."

Ignatius of Loyola

1 Corinthians 5

Matthew Henry's introduction

In this chapter the apostle,

I. Blames them for their indulgence in the case of the incestuous person, and orders him to be excommunicated, and delivered to Satan, vv. 1–6.

II. He exhorts them to Christian purity, by purging out the old leaven, vv. 7, 8. And,

III. Directs them to shun even the common conversation of Christians who were guilty of any notorious and flagitious wickedness, v. 9 to the end.

Dr. Adam Clarke's analysis of chapter

Account of the incestuous person, or of him who had married his father's wife, 1.

The apostle reproves the Corinthians for their carelessness in this matter, and orders them to excommunicate the transgressor, 2–5.

They are reprehended for their glorying, while such scandals were among them, 6.

They must purge out the old leaven, that they may properly celebrate the Christian Passover, 7–9.

They must not associate with any who, professing the Christian religion, were guilty of any scandalous vice, and must put away from them every evil person, 10–13.

A detailed analysis of chapter

The apostle blames the Corinthians for tolerating sexual immorality in their fellowship (1–8); and tells them how to deal with this scandalous situation. (9–13)

Key verse

Verse 2: "And you are proud!"

Key word / key phrase

Verse 1, "a man has his father's wife."

Key event / key person / key theme

Sexual immorality among Christians

Key thought

"Your immorality knows no bounds."

Key thing to look out for

"Do not put up with wickedness in your fellowship."

Key Bible cross-reference

Verse 13. See Deuteronomy 13:5.

Key "by way of explanation"

Verse 1, "not . . . even among pagans." Paul was hitting out against incest among Christians. He points out that even pagans did not go in for this practice. Cicero said that incest was hardly ever found in Roman society.

Key "Quotable Quote"

"Satan fails to speak of the remorse, the futility, the loneliness, and the spiritual devastation which go hand in hand with immorality."

Billy Graham

1 Corinthians 6

Matthew Henry's introduction

In this chapter the apostle,

I. Reproves them for going to law with one another about small matters, and bringing the cause before heathen judges, vv. 1–8.

II. He takes occasion hence to warn them against many gross sins, to which they had been formerly addicted, vv. 9–11.

III. And, having cautioned them against the abuse of their liberty, he vehemently tells them not to indulge in fornication, by various arguments, v. 12 to the end.

Dr. Adam Clarke's analysis of chapter

The Corinthians are reproved for their litigious disposition; brother going to law with brother, and that before the heathen, 1–6.

They should suffer wrong rather than do any, 7, 8.

No unrighteous person can enter into the glory of God, 9, 10.

Some of the Corinthians had been grievous sinners, but God had saved them, 11.

Many things may be lawful which are not at all times expedient, 12.

Meats are for the belly, and the belly for meats; but the body is not for uncleanness, 13.

Christ's resurrection a pledge of ours, 14.

The bodies of Christians are members of Christ, and must not be defiled, 15–17.

He that commits fornication sins against his own body, 18.

Strong arguments from it, 19, 20.

A detailed analysis of chapter

Warns against going to law before non-Christians. (1–8)

Sins which exclude one from the kingdom of God. (9–11)

Our bodies, which are the members of Christ, and temples of the Holy Spirit, must not be defiled. (12–20)

Key verse

Verse 11: "And that is what some of you were. But you were washed, you were sanctified, you were justified in the name of the Lord Jesus Christ and by the Spirit of our God."

Key word / key phrase

Verse 9, "Do not be deceived."

Key event / key person / key theme

Taking a fellow-Christian to court, and sexual immorality

Key thought

The whole person, spirit and body, belongs to Christ. The Christians are not to be under the control of any passion – emotional, or physical. Christ is their master.

Key thing to look out for

The reason why Christians must shun sexual immorality.

Key Bible cross-reference

Verse 16. See Genesis 2:24.

Key "by way of explanation"

Verse 19, "your body is a temple of the Holy Spirit." Christians should view their bodies as if they were sacred, lived in by God's Spirit. So their bodies should not indulge in sexual immorality."

Key "Quotable Quote"

"The monstrosity of sexual intercourse outside marriage is that those who indulge in it are trying to isolate one kind of union (the sexual) from all other kinds of union which were intended to go along with it and make up the total union."

C.S. Lewis

1 Corinthians 7

Matthew Henry's introduction

In this chapter the apostle answers some cases proposed to him by the Corinthians about marriage. He,

I. Shows them that marriage was appointed as a remedy against fornication, and therefore that people had better marry than burn, vv. 1–9.

II. He gives direction to those who are married to continue together, though they might have an unbelieving relative, unless the unbeliever would part, in which case a Christian would not be in bondage, vv. 10–16.

III. He shows them that becoming Christians does not change their external state; and therefore advises every one to continue, in the general, in that state in which he was called, vv. 17–24.

IV. He advises them, by reason of the present distress, to keep themselves unmarried; hints the shortness of time, and how they should improve it, so as to grow dead and indifferent to the comforts of the world; and shows them how worldly cares hinder their devotions, and distract them in the service of God, vv. 25–35.

V. He directs them in the disposal of their virgins, vv. 36–38.

VI. And closes the chapter with advice to widows how to dispose of themselves in that state, vv. 39, 40.

Dr. Adam Clarke's analysis of chapter

A solution of several difficult cases about marriage and married people, 1–6.

God has given every man his proper gift, 7.

Directions to the unmarried and widows, 8, 9.

Directions to the married, 10, 11.

Directions to men married to heathen women, and to women married to heathen men, 12–16.

Every man should abide in his vocation, 17–24.

Directions about virgins, and single people in general, 25–28.

How all should behave themselves in the things of this life, in reference to eternity, 29–31.

The trials of the married state, 39–35.

Directions about the state of virginity or celibacy, 36–38.

How the wife is bound to her husband during his life, and her liberty to marry another after his death, 39, 40.

A detailed analysis of chapter

The apostle answers several questions about marriage. (1–9)

Married Christians should not seek to part from their unbelieving partners. (10–16)

Stay in the place you were in when the Lord called you. (17–24)

It is most desirable, because of the present crisis, for people to sit loose to this world. (25–35)

Great prudence should be used in marriage; it should be only in the Lord. (36–40)

Key verse

Verse 29: "What I mean, brothers, is that the time is short."

Key word / key phrase

Verse 3, "marital duty."

Key event / key person / key theme

Counsel about marriage

Key thought

Paul highlights the advantages of remaining single.

Key thing to look out for

Verse 35, Paul's underlying and controlling principle.

Key Bible cross-reference

Verses 10,11. See Luke 16:18.

Key "by way of explanation"

Verse 26, "present crisis." Paul's teaching is here colored by the "present crisis" which may refer to the evil society in which Christians are living. It is only because of this "present crisis" that Paul gives this teaching.

Key "Quotable Quote"

"Whenever anybody asks me a question about divorce, I refuse to answer it until I have first talked about two other subjects, namely, marriage and reconciliation."

John R.W. Stott

1 Corinthians 8

Matthew Henry's introduction

The apostle, in this chapter, answers another case proposed to him by some of the Corinthians, about eating things that had been sacrificed to idols.

I. He hints at the occasion of this case, and gives a caution against too high an esteem of their knowledge, vv. 1–3.

II. He asserts the vanity of idols, the unity of the Godhead, and the sole mediation of Christ between God and man, vv. 4–6.

III. He tells them that on supposition that it were lawful in itself to eat of things offered to idols (for that they themselves are nothing), yet regard must be had to the weakness of Christian brethren, and nothing done that would lay a stumbling block before them, and occasion their sin and destruction, v. 7 to the end.

Dr. Adam Clarke's analysis of chapter

The question of the Corinthians about meats offered to idols, and the apostle's preface to his instructions on that head, 1–3.

The nature of idolatry, 4, 5.

Of genuine worship, 6.

Some ate of the animals that had been offered to idols knowingly, and so defiled their conscience, 7.

Neither eating nor abstinence in themselves recommend us to God, 8.

But no man should use his Christian liberty so as to put a stumbling block before a brother, 9, 10.

If he act otherwise, he may be the means of a brother's destruction, 11.

Those who act so as to wound the tender con science of a brother, sin against Christ, 12.

The apostle's resolution on this head, 13.

A detailed analysis of chapter

The danger of having a wrong view of knowledge. (1–6)

Take care not to upset weak Christians. (7–13)

Key verse

Verse 1: "Knowledge puffs up, but love builds up."

Key word / key phrase

Verse 9, "a stumbling block."

Key event / key person / key theme

Christian freedom, and the weaker brother

Key thought

When you sin against a fellow Christian you sin against Christ (verse 12).

Key thing to look out for

The underlying principle to apply here comes in verse 1.

Key Bible cross-reference

Verse 1. See 1 Corinthians 1:1.

Key "by way of explanation"

Verse 1, "knowledge puffs up, but love builds up." Knowledge puffs up because it flatters our pride. Love builds up because it has the greatest good of the fellow Christian as the top priority.

Key "Quotable Quote"

"Brotherly love is still the distinguishing badge of every true Christian."

Matthew Henry

1 Corinthians 9

Matthew Henry's introduction

In this chapter the apostle seems to answer some cavils against himself.

I. He asserts his apostolic mission and authority, and gives in his success among them as a testimony to it, vv. 1, 2.

II. He claims a right to subsist by his ministry, and defends it by several arguments from natural reason and the Mosaic law, and asserts it also to be a constitution of Christ, vv. 3–14.

III. He shows that he had willingly waived this privilege and power for their benefit, vv. 15–18.

IV. He specifies several other things, in which he had denied himself for the sake of other men's spiritual interest and salvation, vv. 19–23. And,

V. Concludes his argument by showing what animated him to this course, even the prospect of an incorruptible crown, v. 24, to the end.

Dr. Adam Clarke's analysis of chapter

St. Paul vindicates his apostleship, and shows that he has equal rights and privileges with Peter and the brethren of our Lord; and that he is not bound, while doing the work of an apostle, to labor with his hands for his own support, 1–6.

He who labors should live by the fruit of his own industry, 7.

For the law will not allow even the ox to be muzzled which treads out the corn, 8–10.

Those who minister in spiritual things have a right to a secular support for their work, 11–14.

He shows the disinterested manner in which he has preached the Gospel, 15–18.

Now he accommodated himself to the prejudices of men, in order to bring about their salvation, 19–23.

The way to heaven compared to a race, 24.

The qualifications of those who may expect success in the games celebrated at Corinth, and what that success implies, 25.

The apostle applies these things spiritually to himself; and states the necessity of keeping his body in subjection, lest, after having proclaimed salvation to others, he should become a castaway, 26, 27.

A detailed analysis of chapter

The apostle shows his authority, and asserts his right to be provided for. (1–14)

For the good of others he never insisted on this. (15–23)

He did all this, with care and diligence, to gain a crown that never fades. (24–27)

Key verse

Verse 14: "In the same way, the Lord has commanded that those who preach the gospel should receive their living from the gospel."

Key word / key phrase

Verse 1, "Am I not free?"

Key event / key person / key theme

Paul's Christian freedom

Key thought

Paul is forced to defend his own apostleship.

Key thing to look out for

Verse 22 summarizes Paul's policy toward fellow-Christians.

Key Bible cross-reference

Verse 9. See Deuteronomy 25:4.

Key "by way of explanation"

Verse 22, does not refer to letting go of principles, but shows Paul's deep sympathy, and intention always to come alongside people and feel with them where they are.

Key "Quotable Quote"

"The only right a Christian has is the right to give up his rights"

Oswald Chambers

1 Corinthians 10

Matthew Henry's introduction

In this chapter the apostle prosecutes the argument at the close of the last, and,

I. Warns the Corinthians against security, by the example of the Jews, who, notwithstanding their profession and privileges, were terribly punished of God for their many sins, their history being left on record for the admonition of Christians, vv. 1–14.

II. He resumes his former argument (ch. 8.), about eating things offered to idols; and shows that it was utterly inconsistent with true Christianity, that it was downright gross idolatry, to eat them as things offered to idols; it is having fellowship with devils, which cannot consist with having fellowship with God, vv. 15–22.

III. He lets them yet know that though they must not eat of things sacrificed to idols as such, and out of any regard to the idol, yet they might buy such flesh in the markets, or eat it at the table of heathen acquaintances, without asking any questions; for that the heathens' abuse of them did not render the creatures of God unfit to be the food of his servants. Yet liberty of this kind must be used with a due regard to weak consciences, and no offence given by it t Jew nor Gentile, nor to the church of God, v. 23, to the end.

Dr. Adam Clarke's analysis of chapter

Peculiar circumstances in the Jewish history were typical of the greatest mysteries of the Gospel; particularly their passing through the Red Sea, and being overshadowed with the miraculous cloud, 1, 2.

The manna with which they were fed, 3.

And rock out of which they drank, 4.

The punishments inflicted on them for their disobedience are warnings to us, 5.

We should not lust as they did, 6.

Nor commit idolatry, 7.

Nor fornication as they did; in consequence of which twenty-three thousand of them were destroyed, 8.

Nor tempt Christ as they did, 9.

Nor murmur, 10.

All these transgressions and their punishments are recorded as warnings to us, that we may not fall away from the grace of God, 11, 12.

God never suffers any to be tempted above their strength, 13.

Idolatry must be detested, 14.

And the sacrament of the Lord's Supper properly considered and taken, that God may not be provoked to punish us, 15–22.

There are some things which may be legally done which are not expedient; and we should endeavor so to act as to edify each other, 23, 24.

The question about eating things offered to idols considered, and finally settled, 25–30.

We should do all things to the glory of God, avoid whatsoever might be the means of stumbling another, and seek the profit of others in spiritual matters rather than our own gratification, 31–33.

A detailed analysis of chapter

Learn from the mistakes of the Israelites in the desert. (1–5)

Warns against all idolatrous, and other sinful practices. (6–14)

Taking part in idolatry cannot exist side by side with having fellowship with Christ. (15–22)

Everything we do is to be to the glory of God, and should not offend other peoples' consciences. (23–33)

Key verse

Verse 14: "Therefore, my dear friends, flee from idolatry."

Key word / key phrase

Verse 23, "not everything is beneficial."

Key event / key person / key theme

The correct use of Christian freedom

Key thought

An idol is anything that I instinctively turn to, to hold my life together and keep me going.

Key thing to look out for

By looking at the example of the Israelites, what do we learn not to do?

Key Bible cross-reference

Verse 26. See Psalm 24:1.

Key "by way of explanation"

Verse 31, "all for the glory of God." In chapters 8–10 Paul answers questions raised by the Corinthians. The basic principle in all these matters is that everything should be done for the glory of God, not for self-indulgence.

Key "Quotable Quote"

"Your days at the most cannot be very long, so use them to the best of your ability for the glory of God and the benefit of your generation."

William Booth

1 Corinthians 11

Matthew Henry's introduction

In this chapter the apostle blames, and endeavors to rectify, some great indecencies and manifest disorders in the church of Corinth; as,

I. The misconduct of their women (some of whom seem to have been inspired) in the public assembly, who laid by their veils, the common token of subjection to their husbands in that part of the world. This behavior he reprehends, requires them to keep veiled, asserts the superiority of the husband, yet so as to remind the husband that both were made for mutual help and comfort, vv. 1–16.

II. He blames them for their discord and neglect and contempt of the poor, at the Lord's supper, vv. 17–22.

III. To rectify these scandalous disorders, he sets before them the nature and intentions of this holy institution, directs them how they should attend on it, and warns them of the danger of a conduct to indecent as theirs, and of all unworthy receiving, v. 23, to the end.

Dr. Adam Clarke's analysis of chapter

The apostle reprehends the Corinthians for several irregularities in their manner of conducting public worship; the men praying or prophesying with their heads covered, and the women with their heads uncovered, contrary to custom, propriety, and decency, 1–6.

Reasons why they should act differently, 7–16.

They are also reproved for their divisions and heresies, 17–19.

And for the irregular manner in which they celebrated the Lord's Supper, 20–22.

The proper manner of celebrating this holy rite laid down by the apostle, 23–26.

Directions for a profitable receiving of the Lord's Supper, and avoiding the dangerous consequences of communicating unworthily, 27–34.

A detailed analysis of chapter

The apostle, after an exhortation to follow him (1),

corrects some abuses. (2–16)

Also he rebukes their divisions, and disorderly celebrations of the Lord's Supper. (17–22)

He reminds them of the nature and purpose of its institution. (23–26)

And tells them the correct way to take part in this. (27–34)

Key verse

Verse 1: "Follow my example, as I follow the example of Christ."

Key word / key phrase

Verse 20, "when you come together."

Key event / key person / key theme

Public prayer and disorder at the Lord's Supper

Key thought

Verse 11, "In the Lord," men and women are partners, mutually dependant, and each must behave out of respect for the other in submission to God.

Key thing to look out for

Why were so many feeble and ill?

Key Bible cross-reference

Verse 7. See Genesis 1:26, 27.

Key "by way of explanation"

Verse 20, "not the Lord's Supper you eat." Their gluttony made a mockery of the Lord's Supper. For a woman to take off her head-covering was, in those days, a sign of sexual promiscuity. A shaved head was a sign of public disgrace.

Key "Quotable Quote"

"The Lord's Supper (re)-presents the death of Christ and proclaims that death in and through the shared celebration."

James D.G. Dunn

1 Corinthians 12

Matthew Henry's introduction

In this chapter the apostle,

I. Considers the case of spiritual gifts, which were very plentifully poured out on the Corinthian church. He considers their original, that they are from God; their variety and use, that they were all intended for one and the same general end, the advancement of Christianity and the church's edification, vv. 1–11.

II. He illustrates this by an allusion to a human body, in which all the members have a mutual relation, and each has its proper place and use, vv. 12–26.

III. He tells us that the church is the body of Christ, and the members are variously gifted for the benefit of the whole body, and each particular member, vv. 27–30. And them,

IV. Closes with an exhortation to seek some what more beneficial than these gifts, v. 31.

Dr. Adam Clarke's analysis of chapter

The apostle proceeds to the question of the Corinthians about spiritual gifts, 1.

He calls to their remembrance their former state, and how they were brought out of it, 2, 3.
Shows that there are diversities of gifts which proceed from the Spirit, 4.
Diversities of administrations which proceed from the Lord Jesus, 5.
And diversities of operations which proceed from God, 6.
What these gifts are, and how they are dispensed, 7–11.
Christ is the Head, and the Church his members; and this is pointed out under the similitude of the human body, 12, 13.
The relation which the members of the body have to each other; and how necessary their mutual support, 14–26.
The members in the Church, or spiritual body, and their respective offices, 27–30.
We should earnestly covet the best gifts, 31.

A detailed analysis of chapter

The different uses of spiritual gifts are given. (1–11)
In the human body every part has its place and use. (12–26)
This is applied to the Church of Christ. (27–30)
There is something more excellent than spiritual gifts. (31)

Key verse

Verse 4: "There are different kinds of gifts, but the same Spirit."

Key word / key phrase

Verse 1, "about spiritual gifts."

Key event / key person / key theme

The importance and correct use of spiritual gifts

Key thought

Verse 27. Each Christian is a part of Christ's spiritual body. This is not a metaphor but is literally true.

Key thing to look out for

I am an organic part of Christ's body – what are the implications for me?

Key Bible cross-reference

Verse 28. See Ephesians 4:11

Key "by way of explanation"

Verse 7, "given for the common good." Some of the Corinthians had managed to misuse their God-given spiritual gifts. Paul corrects them by saying that all such gifts are not for personal indulgence, but for the "common good" of the Christian fellowship.

Key "Quotable Quote"

"What was special about the new dispensation was that, first of all, these gifts were not confined to any one group of people but extended to all – male and female, young and old. Secondly, these supernatural endowments were wonderfully diverse."

Charles Hodge

1 Corinthians 13

Matthew Henry's introduction

In this chapter the apostle goes on to show more particularly what that more excellent way was of which he had just before been speaking. He recommends it,

I. By showing the necessity and importance of it, vv. 1–3.

II. By giving a description of its properties and fruits, vv. 4–7.

III. By showing how much it excels the best of gifts and other graces, by its continuance, when they shall be no longer in being, or of any use, v. 8, to the end.

Dr. Adam Clarke's analysis of chapter

Charity, or love to God and man, the sum and substance of all true religion; so that without it, the most splendid eloquence, the gift of prophecy, the most profound knowledge, faith by which the most stupendous miracles might be wrought, benevolence the most unbounded, and zeal for the truth, even to martyrdom, would all be unavailing to salvation, 1–3.

The description and praise of this grace, 4–7.

Its durableness; though tongues, prophecies, and knowledge shall cease, yet this shall never fail, 8–10.

Description of the present imperfect state of man, 11, 12.

Of all the graces of God in man, charity, or love, is the greatest, 13.

A detailed analysis of chapter

The necessity and advantage of the grace of love. (1–3)

Its excellency is seen in its nature and in its effects (4–7);

and by its enduring characteristic. (8–13)

Key verse

Verse 13: "And now these three remain: faith, hope and love. But the greatest of these is love."

Key word / key phrase

Verse 13, "the greatest of these is love."

Key event / key person / key theme

Paul's hymn on love

Key thought

"All you need is love."

Key thing to look out for

Christian love is the antidote to all wrong thinking and wrong behavior.

Key Bible cross-reference

Verse 13. See Galatians 5:6.

Key "by way of explanation"

Verse 13, "the greatest of these is love." Love is even more important than spiritual gifts. For God is love, God gives us his love, and Christians are to show love to each other.

Key "Quotable Quote"

"Love seeketh not itself to please
Nor for itself hath any care,
But for another gives its ease
And builds a heaven in hell's despair."

William Blake

1 Corinthians 14

Matthew Henry's introduction

In this chapter the apostle directs them about the use of their spiritual gifts, preferring those that are best and fitted to do the greatest good.

I. He begins with advising them of all spiritual gifts to prefer prophesying, and shows that this is much better than speaking with tongues, vv. 1–5.

II. He goes on to show them how unprofitable the speaking of foreign languages is, and useless to the church; it is like piping in one tone, like sounding a trumpet without any certain note, like talking gibberish; whereas gifts should be used for the good of the church, vv. 6–14.

III. He advises that worship should be celebrated so that the most ignorant might understand, and join in prayer and praise, and presses the advice by his own example, vv. 15–20.

IV. He informs them that tongues were a sign for unbelievers rather than those that believe; and represents the advantage of prophecy above speaking with tongues, from the different suggestions they would give to the mind of an unbeliever coming into their assemblies, vv. 21–25.

V. He blames them for the disorder and confusion they had brought into the assembly, by their vanity and ostentation of their gifts; and directs them in using the gifts both of tongues and prophecy, vv. 26–33.

VI. He forbids women speaking in the church; and closes this subject by requiring them to perform every thing in the public worship with order and decency, v. 34, to the end.

Dr. Adam Clarke's analysis of chapter

We should earnestly desire spiritual gifts; but prophesying is to be preferred, because it is superior to the gift of tongues, 1, 2.

Prophesying defined, 3.

How to regulate this supernatural gift of tongues, in teaching for the edification of the Church, 4–13.

In praying and giving thanks, 14–17.

Those who speak with tongues should interpret that others may be edified, 18–22.

What benefit may accrue from this in the public assemblies, 23–28.

How the prophets or teachers should act in the Church, 29–33.

Women should keep silence in the church, 34, 35.

All should be humble, and every thing should be done in love, 36–40.

A detailed analysis of chapter

Prophecy preferred to the gift of tongues. (1–5)

The uselessness of speaking in unknown languages. (6–14)

Exhortations to worship in a way that can be understood. (15–25)

The selfish display of gifts (26–33);

and women speaking in the Church. (34–40)

Key verse

Verse 12: "Since you are eager to have spiritual gifts, try to excel in gifts that build up the church."

Key word / key phrase

Verse 1, "eagerly desire spiritual gifts."

Key event / key person / key theme

Prophecy, tongues, and public worship

Key thought

Verse 1 gives the principle. The Greek verb translated "follow" means "pursue" – it suggests endeavor.

Key thing to look out for

Verse 12, "excel in gifts that build up the church." This is Paul's overriding consideration in connection with spiritual gifts. When you seek spiritual gifts seek those which will help the Christian fellowship.

Key Bible cross-reference

Verse 21. See Isaiah 28:11, 12.

Key "by way of explanation"

"Prophecy" may be a prediction of future events. It also means seeing the will of God for specific needs in the immediate situation, and making that clear.

Key "Quotable Quote"

"The Spirit gives different Christians different gifts . . . but he works to produce the same fruit in all."

John R.W. Stott

1 Corinthians 15

Matthew Henry's introduction

In this chapter the apostle treats of that great article of Christianity–the resurrection of the dead.

I. He establishes the certainty of our Savior's resurrection, vv. 1–11.

II. He, from this truth, sets himself to refute those who said, There is no resurrection of the dead, vv. 12–19.

III. From our Savior's resurrection he establishes the resurrection of the dead and confirms the Corinthians in the belief of it by some other considerations, vv. 20–34.

IV. He answers an objection against this truth, and takes occasion thence to show what a vast change will be made in the bodies of believers at the resurrection, vv. 35–50.

V. He informs us what a change will be made in those who shall be living at the sound of the last trumpet, and the complete conquest the just shall then obtain over death and the grave, vv. 51–57. And,

VI. He sums up the argument with a very serious exhortation to Christians, to be resolved and diligent in their Lord's service, because they know they shall be so gloriously rewarded by him, v. 58.

Dr. Adam Clarke's analysis of chapter

The Gospel which the apostle preached to the Corinthians; viz. that Christ died for our sins, and rose again the third day, 1–4.

The witnesses of his resurrection, Peter, James, and more than five hundred brethren, 5–7.

Lastly, Paul himself saw him, and was called by him to the apostleship, 8–11.

Objections against the resurrection of the dead answered, 12–34.

The manner in which this great work shall be performed, 35–49.

The astonishing events that shall take place in the last day, 50–57.

The use we should make of this doctrine, 58.

A detailed analysis of chapter

The apostle testifies to the resurrection of Christ from the dead. (1–11)

He replies to those who deny the resurrection of the body. (12–19)

The resurrection of believers to eternal life. (20–34)

Objections against it answered. (35–50)

The mystery of the change that will occur to those living at Christ's second coming. (51–54)

The believer's triumph over death and the grave. An exhortation to be diligent. (55–58)

Key verse

Verse 58: "Therefore, my dear brothers, stand firm. Let nothing move you. Always give yourselves fully to the work of the Lord, because you know that your labor in the Lord is not in vain."

Key word / key phrase

Verse 4, "he was raised."

Key event / key person / key theme

Teaching about the resurrection

Key thought

Verse 56. Because Christ is raised the poison is taken out of death and Christians are made victorious.

Key thing to look out for

Paul gives pictures about the nature of the resurrection body.

Key Bible cross-reference

Verse 27. See Psalm 8:6.

Key "by way of explanation"

Verse 12, "Christ has been raised." Paul uses this verb "has been raised" seven times here to emphasize the certainty of Christ's bodily resurrection. See verses 4, 12–14, 16, 17, 20.

Key "Quotable Quote"

"Many Christians entirely disbelieve the resurrection; many fortify themselves with the horoscope; many adhere to superstitious observances, and to omens, and auguries."

John Chrysostom

1 Corinthians 16

Matthew Henry's introduction

In this chapter the apostle,

I. Gives directions about some charitable collection to be made in this church, for the afflicted and impoverished churches in Judea, vv. 1–4.

II. He talks of paying them a visit, vv. 5–9.

III. He recommends Timothy to them, and tells them Apollos intended to come to them, vv. 10–12.

IV. He presses them to watchfulness, constancy, charity, and to pay a due regard to all who helped him and his fellow-laborers in their work, vv. 13–19.

V. After greetings from others, and his own, he closes the epistle with a solemn admonition to them, and his good wishes for them, v. 20, to the end.

Dr. Adam Clarke's analysis of chapter

The apostle exhorts the Corinthians to make a contribution for the relief of the poor Christians at Jerusalem; and directs to the best mode of doing it, 1–4.

Promises to pay them a visit after Pentecost, 5–9.

Gives directions about the treatment of Timothy and Apollos, 10–12.

And about watchfulness, 13, 14.

Commends the house of Stephanas, and expresses his satisfaction at the visit paid him by Stephanas, Fortunatus and Achaicus, 15–18.

Sends the greetings of different people, 19, 21.

Shows the awful state of those who were enemies to Christ, 22.

And concludes the epistle with the apostolic benediction, 23, 24.

A detailed analysis of chapter

A collection for the poor at Jerusalem. (1–9)

Timothy and Apollos commended. (10–12)

Exhortation to be alert in faith and love. (13–18)

Christian greetings. (19–24)

Key verse

Verse 14: "Do everything in love."

Key word / key phrase

Verse 2, "set aside a sum of money."

Key event / key person / key theme

Collecting for Jerusalem, and greetings

Key thought

Paul cannot trust the Corinthians even to welcome visiting Christian leaders.

Key thing to look out for

Paul reiterates that they must do everything in love.

Key Bible cross-reference

Verse 19. See Acts 18:2.

Key "by way of explanation"

Verse 2, "set aside a sum of money in keeping with his income." This is to be done "on the first day of the week." The amount should be in proportion to one's means, that is, one's income. This money was to be used exclusively for the Lord's work.

Key "Quotable Quote"

"The tithe can be a beginning way to acknowledge God as the owner of all things, but it is only a beginning and not an ending."

Richard J. Foster

5. Select bibliography for 1 and 2 Corinthians

Barrett, C. K. *The First Epistle to Corinthians* in "Black's New Testament Commentary." New York: Harper, 1968.

Bruce, F. F. *I & II Corinthians*. Grand Rapids: Eerdmans, 1971.

Calvin, John. *New Testament Commentaries*. Philadelphia: Westminster Press, 1958.

Godet, F. *Commentary on St. Paul's First Epistle to the Corinthians*. n.d. Reprint, tr. Hodge,

Charles. 1 Corinthians . New York: A.C. Armstrong, 1891.

Morris, Leon. *The First Epistle of Paul to the Corinthians* in "The Tyndale New Testament Commentary." Grand Rapids: Eerdmans, 1958.

2 Corinthians

1. Book by book: Introduction to 2 Corinthians

Introduction

Reasons for letter

The following reasons seem to have induced Paul to write this Second Epistle to the Corinthians:

That he might explain the reasons for his having deferred to pay them his promised visit, by taking Corinth as his way to Macedonia (1 Cor. 4:19; 2 Cor. 1:15, 16; compare 1 Cor. 16:5); and so that he might set forth to them his apostolic walk in general (2 Cor. 1:12, 24; 6:3–13; 7:2).

That he might commend their obedience in reference to the directions in his First Epistle, and at the same time direct them now to forgive the offender, as having been punished sufficiently (2 Cor. 2:1–11; 7:6–16).

That he might urge them to collect for the poor saints at Jerusalem (2 Cor. 8:1–9, 15).

That he might maintain his apostolic authority and reprove his opponents.

Genuineness

The external testimonies for its genuineness are Irenaeus (*Against Heresies,* 3, 7, 1); Athenagoras (*Of the Resurrection of the Dead*); Clement of Alexandria (*Miscellanies,* 3, p. 94; 4, p. 101); Tertullian (*On Modesty,* 13).

Date

The time of writing was after Pentecost, A.D. 57, when Paul left Ephesus for Troas. Having stayed in the latter place for some time preaching the Gospel with effect (2 Cor. 2:12), he went on to Macedonia, being eager to meet Titus there, having been disappointed in his not coming to Troas, as had been agreed on between them. Having heard from him the news he so much desired of the good effect produced on the Corinthians by his First Epistle, and after having tested the liberality of the Macedonian churches (2 Cor. 8:1), he wrote this Second Epistle, and then went on to Greece, where he stayed for three months; and then, after traveling by land, reached Philippi on his return at Passover or Easter, A.D. 58 (Acts 20:1–6). So that this Epistle must have been written about autumn, A.D. 57.

Place of writing

Macedonia was the place from which it was written (2 Cor. 9:2, where the present tense, "I boast," or "am boasting," implies his presence then in Macedonia). In Asia (Lydian Asia) he had undergone some great danger to his life (2 Cor. 1:8, 9), whether the reference be (Paley) to the opposition at Ephesus (Acts 19:23–41), or, as Alford thinks, to a dangerous illness in which he despaired of life. From there he went via Troas to Philippi, the first city which he would come to on entering Macedonia. The importance of the Philippian Church would induce him to stay there some time; as also his desire to collect contributions from the Macedonian churches for the poor saints at Jerusalem. His anxious state of mind is recorded (2 Cor. 7:5) as occurring when he came into Macedonia, and therefore must have been at Philippi, which was the first city of Macedonia in coming from Troas; and here, too, from 2 Cor. 7:6, compared with 2 Cor. 7:5, must have been the scene of his receiving the comforting tidings from Titus. "Macedonia" is used for Philippi in 2 Cor. 11:9, as is proved by comparison with Phil. 4:15, 16. So it is probably used here (2 Cor. 7:5). Alford argues from 2 Cor. 8:1, where he speaks of the "grace bestowed on the churches (plural) of Macedonia," that Paul must have visited other churches in Macedonia, besides Philippi, when he wrote, for example, Thessalonica, Berea, etc., and that Philippi, the first on his route, is less likely to have been the scene of his writing than the last on his route, whichever it was, perhaps Thessalonica. But Philippi, as being the chief town of the province, was probably the place to which all the collections of the churches were sent. Ancient tradition, too (as appears from the subscription to this Epistle), favors the view that Philippi was the place from which this Epistle was sent by the hands of Titus who received, besides, a charge to prosecute at Corinth the collection which he had begun at his first visit (2 Cor. 8:6).

Style

The style is most varied, and passes rapidly from one kind of feeling to another; now joyous and consolatory, again severe and full of reproof; at one time gentle and affectionate, at another, sternly rebuking opponents and upholding his dignity as an apostle. This variety of style accords with the warm and earnest character of the apostle, which nowhere is manifested more beautifully than in this Epistle. His bodily frailty, and his chronic illness, and which is often alluded to (2 Cor. 4:7; 5:1–4; 12:7–9; compare Note, see on 2 Cor. 1:8), must have been especially trying to one of his ardent temperament. But besides this, was the more pressing anxiety of the "care of all the churches." At Corinth, as elsewhere, Judaizing emissaries wished to bind legal fetters of letter and form (compare 2 Cor. 3:3–18) on the freedom and universality of the Church.

On the other hand, there were free thinkers who defended their immorality of practice by godless theories (1 Cor. 15:12, 32–36). These were the "fightings without," and "fears within" (2 Cor. 7:5, 6) which troubled the apostle's mind until Titus brought him comforting news from Corinth. Even then, while the majority at Corinth had testified their repentance, and, as Paul had desired, excommunicated the incestuous person, and contributed for the poor Christians of Judea, there was still a minority who, more contemptuously than ever, resisted the apostle. These accused him of crafty and mercenary motives, as if he had personal gain in view in the collection being made; and this, notwithstanding his scrupulous care to be above the possibility of reasonable suspicion, by having others besides himself to take charge of the money. This insinuation was palpably inconsistent with their other charge, that he could be no true apostle, as he did not claim maintenance from the churches which he founded. Another accusation they brought of cowardly weakness; that he was always threatening severe measures without daring to execute them (2 Cor. 10:8–16; 13:2); and that he was vacillating in his teaching and practice, circumcising Timothy, and yet withholding circumcision from Titus; a Jew among the Jews, and a Greek among the Greeks. That most of these opponents were of the Judaizing party in the Church, appears from 2 Cor. 11:22. They seem to have been headed by an emissary from Judea ("he that cometh," 2 Cor. 11:4), who had brought "letters of commendation" (2 Cor. 3:1) from members of the Church at Jerusalem, and who boasted of his purity of Hebrew descent, and his close connection with Christ Himself (2 Cor. 11:13, 23). His partisans contrasted his high pretensions with the timid humility of Paul (1 Cor. 2:3); and his rhetoric with the apostle's plain and unadorned style (2 Cor. 11:6; 10:10, 13). It was this state of affairs at Corinth, reported by Titus, that caused Paul to send him back at once with this Second Epistle, which is addressed, not to Corinth only (1 Cor. 1:2), but to all the churches also in Achaia (2 Cor. 1:1), which had in some degree been affected by the same causes as affected the Corinthian Church.

The widely different tone in different parts of the Epistle is due to the diversity which existed at Corinth between the penitent majority and the refractory minority. The former he addresses with the warmest affection; the latter with menace and warning. Two deputies, chosen by the churches to take charge of the contribution to be collected at Corinth, accompanied Titus (2 Cor. 8:18, 19, 22).

A. R. Faussett

Detailed outline

I. Introduction: 1:1–11
- A. Greeting: 1:1–2
  - 1. From: Paul and Timothy: 1:1
  - 2. To: The Church of God at Corinth and all saints in Achaia: 1:1
  - 3. Grace and peace from God and Jesus: 1:2
- B. Suffering: 1:3–11
  - 1. Praise to God for suffering: 1:3
    - (a) The father of Jesus Christ.
    - (b) Father of mercies.
    - (c) God of all comfort.
  - 2. Value of suffering: 1:4–7
    - (a) Comforting others: 1:4
    - (b) Personal consolation in Christ: 1:5
    - (c) Consolation and salvation for others: 1:6–7
  - 3. An example of suffering: Paul in Asia: 1:8–11

Part One: Exhortation Regarding The Ministry 1:12–7:16

I. Paul's conduct: 1:12–14
   A. His testimony: 1:12
      1. Simplicity.
      2. Godly sincerity.
      3. Not with fleshly wisdom.
      4. By the grace of God.
   B. His letters: 1:13
   C. His relationship: 1:14
   D. His plans: 1:15–2:4
      1. Original plan: 1:15–16
      2. The change of plans: 1:17–22
      3. Reason for the change: 1:22–2:4
   E. Instructions regarding the repentant offender: 2:5–11
      1. The offense: 2:5
      2. Action advised: 2:6–8
      3. Motive for the action: 2:9–11

II. The nature of the ministry: 2:12–6:10
   A. Triumph of the ministry: 2:12–17
      1. Anxiety at Troas: 2:12–13
      2. Triumph in Christ: 2:14–17
   B. Authorization of the ministry: 3:1–3
      1. Questions about their authorization: 3:1
      2. Basis of the authority: 3:2–3
   C. The glory of the ministry: 3:4–18
      1. It is empowered by God: 3:4–6
      2. It is a glorious ministry: 3:7–11
      3. It is a simple ministry: 3:12
      4. It is an open, revealed ministry: 3:13–16
      5. It is a ministry of freedom: 3:17
      6. It is a ministry which changes lives: 3:18
   D. The perseverance of the ministry: 4:1–5:10
      1. Perseverance in spite of blindness to the Gospel message: 4:1–7
         (a) Sincerity of the ministers: 4:1–2
         (b) Spiritual blindness of the lost: 4:3–4
         (c) Satanic opposition to the ministry: 4:4
         (d) Light of the Gospel penetrates darkness: 4:5–6
         (e) The treasure of this ministry in earthen vessels: 4:7
      2. Perseverance in suffering: 4:7–15
         (a) Description of suffering: 4:8–9
         (b) Purpose of suffering: 4:10–12
         (c) Victory in suffering: 4:13–15
      3. Perseverance inspired by hope: 4:16–5:10
         (a) Hope in this life: 4:16–18
         (b) Hope in the future life: 5:1–10
      4. The present attitude because of this hope: 5:6–8
         (a) Confidence: 5:6
         (b) Faith: 5:7
         (c) Fearlessness of death: 5:8
         (d) Acceptable living: 5:9
      5. The end of this hope: 5:10
   E. The motivation for the ministry: 5:11–17
      1. Motives of fear of the Lord: 5:11
      2. Motive of concern for others: 5:12–13
      3. Motive of the love of Christ: 5:14–15
      4. Motive of new life in Christ: 5:16–17
   F. The message of the ministry: 5:18–21
      1. The position of the ministers: Reconciled 5:18
      2. The ministry of the ministers: Reconciliation: 5:18–19

3. The plea of the ministers: Reconciliation: 5:20
4. The basis for the message: 5:21

III. A summary of the ministry: 6:1–10
- A. Position of the minister: Workers together with Him: 6:1
- B. Plea of the ministers: 6:1–2
- C. Conduct of the ministers: 6:3–10
  1. Negative: Giving no offense in anything: 6:3
  2. Positive: Approving themselves as ministers of God: 6:4–10

IV. Consequent appeals in view of this ministry: 6:11–7:4
- A. A fatherly appeal: 6:11–13
- B. Appeal for separation: 6:14–7:1
  1. The command for separation: 6:14
  2. Arguments for separation: 6:14–16
  3. The results of separation: 6:17–6:18
     (a) Removal: 6:17
     (b) Reception: 6:17
     (c) Relationship: 6:18
- C. Appeal for holiness: 7:1
- D. Appeal for affection: 7:2–4

V. Recognition of the ministry: 7:5–16
- A. Afflictions in Macedonia: 7:5
- B. The coming of Titus: 7:6–7
  1. Comfort through Titus: 7:6
  2. His message: 7:7
- C. Paul's former letter: 7:8–12
  1. The letter: 7:8
  2. Results of the letter: 7:8–11
  3. Purpose of the former letter: 7:12
- D. Comfort from the joy of Titus: 7:13–15
- E. Confidence expressed in the Corinthian believers: 7:16

Part Two: A Plea About The Collection 8:1–9:15

I. Example: The giving of the Macedonians: 8:1–6
- A. The explanation about their giving: 8:1
- B. The circumstances of their giving: 8:2
- C. The manner of their giving: 8:3–5
- D. The result their giving: 8:6

II. Exhortation: The appeal for Christian giving: 8:7–15
- A. The appeal: 8:7
- B. The motives of such giving: 8:8–12
  1. Love: 8:8
  2. Example of Jesus Christ: 8:9
  3. Willingness: 8:19–12
- C. Principles of equality in giving: 8:13–15

III. The messengers to Corinth: 8:16–9:5
- A. Approval of the messengers: 8:16–24
  1. The coming of Titus to Corinth: 8:16–17
  2. Brethren accompanying Titus to Corinth: 8:18–22
  3. Recommendation of the messengers: 8:23
  4. Request to receive them properly: 8:24
- B. Explanation for sending the messengers: 9:1–5
  1. The situation in Achaia about the collection: 9:1–2
  2. Purposes for sending the brethren about the collection: 9:3–4
  3. Commission of the brethren about the collection: 9:5

IV. The blessings of generous giving: 9:6–15
- A. The basic principle of giving: 9:6
- B. The right spirit for giving: 9:7
- C. The results of generous giving: 9:8–14

1. All grace from God: 9:8
2. Sufficiency in all things: 9:8
3. Abounding in every good work: 9:8
4. Blessings on the poor: 9:9
5. Material blessings: 9:10
6. Spiritual blessings: 9:10
7. Increase in fruits of righteousness: 9:10
8. Enriched in all things: 9:11

D. Reaction of those receiving the gift: 9:11–14
1. Thankfulness to God: 9:11–13
2. Regard for the givers; 9:14

E. The basis of the blessings of giving: 9:15

V. Vindication: Paul's defense of his ministry: 10:1–13:10

A. Power: The apostle's authority: 10:1–18
1. His appeal to the church: 10:1–6
(a) The basis for his appeal: 10:1
(b) The contents of his appeal: 10:2
(c) A description of his warfare: 10:3–6
(1) The spiritual nature of his warfare: 10:3
(2) The spiritual weapons of his warfare: 10:4
(3) The battle in the warfare: 10:5–6

B. The answer to a misled member: 10:7–11
1. An appeal to consider reality: 10:7
2. The verification of his authority: 10:8–9
3. The criticism: 10:10
4. The warning to "such a one": 10:11

C. The claims of false teachers: 10:12–18
1. The boasting of false teachers: 10:12
2. Justified boasting: 10:13–18
(a) The standard of measurement: 10:13
(b) The achievement to be measured: 10:14–18

VI. Apostleship: Paul's boasting: 11:1–12:13

A. His request to be permitted to boast: 11:1–4
1. Statement of the request: 11:1
2. Reasons for the request: 11:2–4
(a) His personal concern for them: 11:2
(b) His anxiety about them: 11:3–4

B. Refuting personal inferiority: 11:5–15
1. His position: 11:5
2. His preaching: 11:6
3. His service: 11:7–15

C. Paul's reasons for boasting: 11:16–12:10
1. The preparation for boasting: 11:16–21
(a) The reluctance to boast: 11:16–17
(b) The need for the boasting: 11:18
(c) The consolation in his boasting: 11:19–21
2. The first boasting: 11:22–33
(a) Boasting as to the flesh: 11:22
(b) Boasting about service: 11:23–29
(c) Boasting in infirmities: 11:30–33
3. The second boasting: 12:1–10
(a) His feeling about boasting: 12:1
(b) Boasting about visions: 12:2–5
(c) Boasting in weakness: 12:6–10

D. A review of his boasting: 12:11–13
1. The feeling about the boasting: 12:11
2. The cause for the boasting: 12:11–13
(a) Their failure to commend him: 12:11

(b) Their obligation to commend him: 12:11–13

VII. The apostle's proposed visit to Corinth: 12:14–13:10

A. His service to them: 12:14–18

1. His free service on arrival: 12:14
2. The reasons for his attitude: 12:14
3. His willingness to be spent for them: 12:15
4. Refutation of slander against him: 12:16–18

B. His concern about conditions on his arrival: 12:19–21

1. Correction of false impressions: 12:19
2. His concerns about them: 12:20–21

C. His plan on arrival: 13:1–4

1. The investigation he will make: 13:1–2
2. The proof that will be given them: 13:3–4

D. A final appeal to the Corinthian believers: 13:5–10

1. An appeal for self-testing: 13:5–10
2. A prayer for them: 13:7–9
3. The purpose of his letter: 13:10

Conclusion 13:11–14

I. An exhortation: 13:11

A. The command: 13:11

1. Be perfect.
2. Be of good comfort.
3. Be of one mind.
4. Live in peace.

B. The result: 13:11

II. The closing greetings: 13:12–13

III. The benediction: 13:14

A. Grace of the Lord Jesus Christ.

B. Love of God.

2. Helpful summaries of 2 Corinthians

Bird's eye view

Paul writes 2 Corinthians to defend his call and apostolic ministry against those who sought to discredit him and his message.

Reading plan

The following reading plan, taking one reading per day, enables you to read through 2 Corinthians in thirteen days.

2 Corinthians 1:1–1:24
2 Corinthians 2:1–2:17
2 Corinthians 3:1–3:18
2 Corinthians 4:1–4:18
2 Corinthians 5:1–5:21
2 Corinthians 6:1–6:18
2 Corinthians 7:1–7:16
2 Corinthians 8:1–8:24
2 Corinthians 9:1–9:15
2 Corinthians 10:1–10:18
2 Corinthians 11:1–11:33
2 Corinthians 12:1–12:21
2 Corinthians 13:1–13:14

Verses to memorize

2 Corinthians 1:3–4

Blessed be God, even the Father of our Lord Jesus Christ, the Father of mercies, and the God of all comfort; Who comforteth us in all our tribulation, that we may be able to comfort them which are in any trouble, by the comfort wherewith we ourselves are comforted of God. KJV

2 Corinthians 5:17

Therefore if any man be in Christ, he is a new

creature: old things are passed away; behold, all things are become new. KJV

2 Corinthians 5:20

Now then we are ambassadors for Christ, as though God did beseech you by us: we pray you in Christ's stead, be ye reconciled to God. KJV

2 Corinthians 5:21

For he hath made him to be sin for us, who knew no sin; that we might be made the righteousness of God in him. KJV

2 Corinthians 12:10

Therefore I take pleasure in infirmities, in reproaches, in necessities, in persecutions, in distresses for Christ's sake: for when I am weak, then am I strong. KJV

Statistics

Eighth New Testament book

Third letter by the apostle Paul

13 chapters

257 verses

6,092 words

Number of Old Testament quotations and allusions in 2 Corinthians: 13.

Famous sayings found in 2 Corinthians

"Letter of the law" 2 Corinthians 3:6

"Suffer fools gladly" 2 Corinthians 11:19

"Thorn in the flesh" 2 Corinthians 12:7

Names/titles given

Pros Korinthious B: "Second to the Corinthians."

3. Helpful keys to turn to in understanding 2 Corinthians

Key word/phrase

Boast/glory

The signs of an apostle, 12:12.

Key verses

2 Corinthians 4:5; 5:17–19

Themes to study

- The Christian ministry.
- Our relationship to the world and to people in the world.

Jesus in 2 Corinthians

In 2 Corinthians Jesus is our Substitute.

Lessons to learn from 2 Corinthians

- Christians should not be fearful at the prospect of death.
- Being a faithful Christian leader is often a painful task.

4. Chapter by chapter: outline of every chapter of 2 Corinthians

2 Corinthians 1

Matthew Henry's introduction

After the introduction (vv. 1, 2) the apostle begins with the narrative of his troubles and God's goodness, which he had met with in Asia, by way of thanksgiving to God (vv. 3–6), and for the edification of the Corinthians, vv. 7–11. Then he attests his and his fellow-laborers' integrity (vv. 12–14), and afterwards vindicates himself from the imputation of levity and inconstancy, vv. 15–24.

Dr. Adam Clarke's analysis of chapter

St. Paul encourages them to trust in God in all adversities, from a consideration of the support which he had granted them already in times of afflictions; and expresses his strong confidence of their fidelity, 1–7.

Mentions the heavy tribulation which he had passed through in Asia; as also his deliverance, 8–11.

Shows in what the exultation of a genuine Christian consists, 12.

Appeals to their own knowledge of the truth of the things which he wrote to them, 13, 14.

Mentions his purpose of visiting them; and how sincere he was in forming it; and the reason why he did not come, as he had purposed, 15–24.

A detailed analysis of chapter

The apostle blesses God for comfort in, and deliverance from troubles. (1–11)

He states his own and his fellow-laborers' integrity. (12–14)

He tells them why he was not able to visit them. (15–24)

Key verse

Verse 7: "And our hope for you is firm, because we know that just as you share in our sufferings, so also you share in our comfort."

Key word / key phrase

Verse 4, "who comforts us."

Key event / key person / key theme

The God of all comfort

Key thought

It is in catastrophes and crises that we discover the mighty power of God.

Key thing to look out for

"My actions stem from God's grace, not worldly considerations."

Key Bible cross-reference

Verse 1. See Acts 18:1.

Key "by way of explanation"

Verse 3, "the God of all comfort." When Christians are going through a time of suffering they are to remember to turn to God for comfort. When they comfort others they should do so with the comfort that they were comforted with.

Key "Quotable Quote"

"The letters to the Corinthians reveal to us more of the personal character of the apostle than any of his other letters. They show him to us as a man, as a pastor, as a counselor, as in conflict not only with heretics, but with personal enemies. They reveal his wisdom, his zeal, his forbearance, his liberality of principle and practice in all matters not affecting salvation, his strictness in all matters of right and wrong, his humility, and perhaps above all, his unwearied activity and wonderful endurance."

Charles Hodge

2 Corinthians 2

Matthew Henry's introduction

In this chapter the apostle proceeds in the account of the reasons why he did not come to Corinth, vv. 1–4. Then he writes about the incestuous person who lay under censure; and gives direction for restoring him, together with the reasons for their so doing (vv. 5–11), and afterwards informs them of his labors and success in preaching the gospel in several places, vv. 12–17.

Dr. Adam Clarke's analysis of chapter

The apostle farther explains the reasons why he did not pay his intended visit to the Corinthians, 1.

And why he wrote to them in the manner he did, 2–5.

He exhorts them also to forgive the incestuous person, who had become a true penitent; and therefore he had forgiven him in the name of Christ, 6–11.

He mentions the disappointment he felt when he came to Troas in not meeting with Titus, from whom he expected to have heard an account of the state of the Corinthian Church, 12, 13.

Gives thanks to God for the great success he had in preaching the Gospel, so that the influence of the name of Christ was felt in every place, 14.

Shows that the Gospel is a savor of life to them that believe, and of death to them that believe not, 15, 16.

And that he and his brethren preached the pure, unadulterated doctrine of God among the people, 17.

A detailed analysis of chapter

Reasons why the apostle did not come to Corinth. (1–4)

Instructions about restoring a repentant Christian. (5–11)

An account of his work and success in spreading the gospel of Christ. (12–17)

Key verse

Verse 14: "But thanks be to God, who always leads us in triumphal procession in Christ and through us spreads everywhere the fragrance of the knowledge of him"

Key word / key phrase

Verse 4, "great distress and anguish."

Key event / key person / key theme

Punishment and forgiveness

Key thought

Dealing with the Corinthians caused Paul pain.

Key thing to look out for

Paul emphasizes that he has been sent by God.

Key Bible cross-reference

Verses 12, 13. See Acts 20:1.

Key "by way of explanation"

Verse 17, "we do not peddle the word of God for profit." Paul is attacking those false teachers who have wormed their way into the Corinthian Church and have taken the gullible for a ride.

Key "Quotable Quote"

"The Church authorities have excommunicated me for heresy, I excommunicate them in the name of the sacred truth of God. Christ will judge whose excommunication will stand."

Martin Luther

2 Corinthians 3

Matthew Henry's introduction

The apostle makes an apology for his seeming to commend himself, and is careful not to assume too much to himself, but to ascribe all praise unto God, vv. 1–5. He then draws a comparison between the Old Testament and the New, and shows the excellency of the later above the former (vv. 6–11), whence he infers what is the duty of gospel ministers, and the advantage of those who live under the gospel above those who lived under the law, v. 12, to the end.

Dr. Adam Clarke's analysis of chapter

The apostle shows, in opposition to his detractors, that the faith and salvation of the Corinthians were sufficient testimony of his Divine mission; that he needed no letters of recommendation, the Christian converts at Corinth being a manifest proof that he was an apostle of Christ, 1–3.

He extols the Christian ministry, as being infinitely more excellent than that of Moses, 4–12.

Compares the different modes of announcing the truth under the law and under the Gospel: in the former it was obscurely delivered; and the veil of darkness, typified by the veil which Moses wore, is still on the hearts of the Jews; but when they turn to Christ this veil shall be taken away, 13–16.

On the contrary, the Gospel dispensation is spiritual; leads to the nearest views of heavenly things; and those who receive it are changed into the glorious likeness of God by the agency of his Spirit, 17, 18.

A detailed analysis of chapter

The preference of the gospel over the Law given by Moses. (1–11)

The preaching of the apostle and the power of the Holy Spirit. (12–18)

Key verse

Verse 15: "Even to this day when Moses is read, a veil covers their hearts."

Key word / key phrase

Verse 6, "he has made us competent."

Key event / key person / key theme

All ability is from God, and the superiority of the new covenant

Key thought

Paul claims that his capacity to serve God is God-given.

Key thing to look out for

Christians are to be increasingly transformed into Christ's likeness.

Key Bible cross-reference

Verse 6. See Jeremiah 31:31.

Key "by way of explanation"

Verse 3, "Are we beginning to commend ourselves again?" Paul is always having to justify himself before the accusing Corinthian Christians and the evil intentions of the false teachers in Corinth.

Key "Quotable Quote"

"The first service that one owes to others in the fellowship consists in listening to them."

Dietrich Bonhoeffer

2 Corinthians 4

Matthew Henry's introduction

In this chapter we have an account,

I. Of the constancy of the apostle and his fellow-laborers in their work. Their constancy in declared (v. 1), their sincerity is vouched (v. 2), an objection is obviated (vv. 3, 4), and their integrity proved, vv. 5–7.

II. Of their courage and patience under their sufferings. Where see what their sufferings were, together with their allays (vv. 8–12), and what it was that kept them from sinking and fainting under them, v. 13, to the end.

Dr. Adam Clarke's analysis of chapter

St. Paul shows the integrity with which he had preached the Gospel of Christ, 1, 2.

And that, if it was unprofitable to any who had heard it, it was because their unbelieving hearts were blinded, 3, 4.

How he preached, and how he was qualified for the work, 5–7.

The troubles and difficulties he met with in his labors, and the hope and consolations by which he was supported, 8–15.

And the prospect he had of eternal blessedness, 16–18.

A detailed analysis of chapter

The apostles worked with great diligence, sincerity, and faithfulness. (1–7)

They suffered a great deal on account of the gospel, but were also well-supported. (8–12)

Prospects of eternal glory keep believers from collapsing under troubles. (13–18)

Key verse

Verse 8: "We are hard pressed on every side, but not crushed; perplexed, but not in despair."

Key word / key phrase

Verse 1, "we have this ministry."

Key event / key person / key theme

Paul's ministry, a most unlikely apostle, and Christian hope

Key thought

People do not believe because they are blinded by Satan. The result of this darkness is tragic: they do not see the glory of Christ (verse 4).

Key thing to look out for

Paul explains why he does not lose heart.

Key Bible cross-reference

Verse 6. See Genesis 1:3.

Key "by way of explanation"

Verse 7, "we have this treasure in jars of clay."

Treasures were kept is very ordinary looking jars. The gospel is the treasure. Paul is but a frail, unattractive jar of clay, keeping safe a great treasure.

Key "Quotable Quote"

"We cannot be content with an evangelism which does not lead to the drawing of converts into the Church, nor with a church order whose principle of cohesion is a superficial social camaraderie instead of a spiritual fellowship with the Father and with his Son, Jesus Christ."

John R.W. Stott

2 Corinthians 5

Matthew Henry's introduction

The apostle proceeds in showing the reasons why they did not faint under their afflictions, namely, their expectation, desire, and assurance of happiness after death (vv. 1–5), and deduces an inference for the comfort of believers in their present state (vv. 6–8), and another to quicken them in their duty, vv. 9–11. Then he makes an apology for seeming to commend himself, and gives a good reason for his zeal and diligence (vv. 12–15), and mentions two things that are necessary in order to our living to Christ, regeneration and reconciliation, v. 16, to the end.

Dr. Adam Clarke's analysis of chapter

The apostle's strong hope of eternal glory, and earnest longings after that state of blessedness, 1–4.

The assurance that he had of it from the Holy Spirit, and his carefulness to be always found pleasing to the Lord, 5–9.

All must appear before the judgment seat of Christ, 10.

Knowing that this awful event must take place, he labored to convince men of the necessity of being prepared to meet the Lord, being influenced to this work by his love of Christ, 11–13.

Jesus Christ having died for all, is a proof that all were dead, 14.

Those for whom he died should live to him, 15.

We should know no man after the flesh, 16.

They who are in Christ are new creatures, 17.

The glorious ministry of reconciliation, 18–21.

A detailed analysis of chapter

The apostle's hope and desire for heavenly glory. (1–8)

Why Paul had such concern for the Corinthians. (9–15)

The necessity of regeneration, and of reconciliation with God through Christ. (16–21)

Key verse

Verse 7: "We live by faith, not by sight."

Key word / key phrase

Verse 5, "what is to come."

Key event / key person / key theme

Death and future glory

Key thought

All Christians have two homes.

Key thing to look out for

"This is how you should look at people."

Key Bible cross-reference

Verse 10. See Romans 14:10.

Key "by way of explanation"

Verse 10, "appear before the judgment seat of Christ." This does not refer to a person being judged about whether he or she is a Christian. This is a different judgment when the value of what a Christian has done is on trial.

Key "Quotable Quote"

"Do something good for someone you like least, today."

Saint Anthony

2 Corinthians 6

Matthew Henry's introduction

In this chapter the apostle gives an account of his general errand to all to whom he preached; with the several arguments and methods he used, vv. 1–10. Then he addresses himself particularly to the Corinthians, giving them good cautions with great affection and strong arguments, vv. 11–18.

Dr. Adam Clarke's analysis of chapter

We should not receive the grace of God in vain, having such promises of support from him, 1, 2.

We should act so as to bring no disgrace on the Gospel, 3.

How the apostles behaved themselves, preached, suffered, and rejoiced, 4–10.

St. Paul's affectionate concern for the Corinthians, 11–13.

He counsels them not to be yoked with unbelievers, and advances several arguments why they should avoid them, 14–16.

Exhorts them to avoid evil companions and evil practices, on the promise that God will be their Father and that they shall be his sons and his daughters, 17, 18.

A detailed analysis of chapter

The apostle, with others, showed themselves to be faithful ministers of Christ, by their blameless life and behavior. (1–10)

On account of their affection for them they did not want them to have any fellowship with unbelievers and idolaters. (11–18)

Key verse

Verse 14: "Do not be yoked together with unbelievers."

Key word / key phrase

Verse 13, "open wide your hearts."

Key event / key person / key theme

Reconciliation among Christians, and separation from unbelievers

Key thought

"Do not become inextricably linked up with non-believers."

Key thing to look out for

The results of Paul's hardships.

Key Bible cross-reference

Verse 5. See Acts 16:23.

Key "by way of explanation"

Verse 14, "Do not be yoked together with unbelievers." Today, this verse is often applied to a Christian contemplating marriage with a non-Christian. In Paul's day it referred to the danger of aligning oneself with false teachers and their cancerous teaching.

Key "Quotable Quote"

"Whoever sheds a fervent tear for the hardships of his fellow man, heals his own wounds."

Basil the Great

2 Corinthians 7

Matthew Henry's introduction

This chapter begins with an exhortation to progressive holiness and a due regard to the ministers of the gospel, vv. 1–4. Then the apostle returns from a long digression to speak further of the affair about the incestuous person, and tells them what comfort he received in his distress about that matter, on his meeting with Titus (vv. 5–7), and how re rejoiced in their repentance, with the evidences thereof, vv. 8–11. And, lastly, he concludes with endeavoring to comfort the Corinthians, on whom his admonitions had had so good an effect, vv. 12–16.

Dr. Adam Clarke's analysis of chapter

The apostle's inference from the preceding exhortation, 1.

He presses them to receive him with affection, because of his great love towards them, 2–4.

He tells them what distress he felt on their account in Macedonia, till he had met with Titus, and heard of their prosperity, 6–7.

He rejoices that his first epistle was made the means of their reformation, 8, 9.

States how they were affected by his letter, and the process of their reformation, 10, 11.

Shows why he had written to them, 12.

Rejoices that his boasting of them to Titus is found to be a truth; and takes occasion to mention the great affection of Titus for them, and his own confidence in them, 13–16.

A detailed analysis of chapter

An exhortation to be holy. (1–4)

He rejoiced that their sorrow over their sins led to repentance. (5–11)

And he rejoiced in the comfort they and Titus shared. (12–16)

Key verse

Verse 6: "But God, who comforts the downcast, comforted us by the coming of Titus."

Key word / key phrase

Verse 14, "Titus has proved to be true."

Key event / key person / key theme

Meeting Titus, and response to Paul's letter

Key thought

"Welcome us in your hearts."

Key thing to look out for

God's promises should lead to a pure life.

Key Bible cross-reference

Verse 5. See 2 Corinthians 2:13.

Key "by way of explanation"

Verse 10, "godly sorrow . . . worldly sorrow." Paul points out that there is more than one kind of sorrow. Worldly sorrow after the consequences of sin leads only to death, but godly sorrow, which involves repentances, leads to life.

Key "Quotable Quote"

"Earth has no sorrow that heaven cannot heal."
Thomas Moore

2 Corinthians 8

Matthew Henry's introduction

In this and the following chapter Paul is exhorting and directing the Corinthians about a particular work of charity–to relieve the necessities of the poor saints at Jerusalem and in Judea, according to the good example of the churches in Macedonia, Rom. 15:26. The Christians at Jerusalem, through war, famine, and persecution, had become poor, many of them had fallen into decay, and perhaps most of them were but poor when they first embraced Christianity; for Christ said, "The poor receive the gospel." Now Paul, though he was the apostle of the Gentiles, had a fonder regard, and kind concern, for those among the Jews who were converted to the Christian faith; and, though many of them had not so much affection to the Gentile converts as they ought to have had, yet the apostle would have the Gentiles to be kind to them, and stirred them up to contribute liberally for their relief. On this subject he is very copious, and writes very affectingly. In this eighth chapter he acquaints the Corinthians with, and commends, the good example of the Macedonians in this work of charity, and that Titus was sent to Corinth to collect their bounty, vv. 1–6. He the proceeds to urge this duty with several cogent arguments (vv. 7–15), and commends the people who were employed in this affair, vv. 16–24.

Dr. Adam Clarke's analysis of chapter

The apostle stirs them up to make a collection for the poor Christians at Jerusalem, by the very liberal contributions of the people of Macedonia for the same purpose, who were comparatively a poor people, 1–5.

He tells them that he had desired Titus to finish this good work among them which he had begun; hoping that as they abounded in many excellent gifts and graces, they would abound in this also, 6–8.

He exhorts them to this by the example of Jesus Christ, who, though rich, subjected himself to voluntary poverty, that they might be enriched, 9.

He shows them that this contribution, which had been long ago begun, should have been long since finished, 10.

And that they should do every thing with a ready and willing mind, according to the ability which God had given them; that abundance should not prevail on one hand, while pinching poverty ruled on the other; but that there should be an equality, 11–14.

He shows from the distribution of the manna in the wilderness, that the design of God was, that every member of his spiritual household should have the necessaries of life, 15.

He tells them that he had now sent Titus, and another with him, to Corinth, to complete this great work, 16–22.

The character which he gives of Titus and the others employed in this business, 23, 24.

A detailed analysis of chapter

The apostle urges them to be generous toward the poor saints. (1–6)

He underlines this by referring to their gifts, and by the love and grace of Christ. (7–9)

And by the willingness they had shown to do this good work. (10–15)

He commends Titus to them. (16–24)

Key verse

Verse 2: "Out of the most severe trial, their overflowing joy and their extreme poverty welled up in rich generosity."

Key word / key phrase

Verse 7, "grace of giving."

Key event / key person / key theme

Will you follow Macedonia's example in giving money?

Key thought

"Service is a great privilege."

Key thing to look out for

Verses 13–15 express an important principle

Key Bible cross-reference

Verses 1–4. See Romans 15:26.

Key "by way of explanation"

Verse 21, "For we are taking pains to do what is right." Paul had a clear conscience before God. He had not acted in a wrong way. But he was constantly being maligned. So he had to explain that he was always taking great care to do what was right, no matter what other people might accuse him of.

Key "Quotable Quote"

"Joy can be real only if people look upon their life as a service, and have a definite object in life outside themselves and their personal happiness."

Leo Tolstoy

2 Corinthians 9

Matthew Henry's introduction

In this chapter the apostle seems to excuse his earnestness in pressing the Corinthians to the duty of charity (vv. 1–5), and proceeds to give directions about the acceptable way and manner of performing it, namely, bountifully, deliberately, and freely; and gives good encouragement for so doing, v. 6, to the end.

Dr. Adam Clarke's analysis of chapter

St. Paul intimates that so ready were the Corinthians to make this charitable contribution, that it was scarcely necessary for him to write, 1, 2.

But lest they should not be ready when he came, he had sent the brethren, Titus, lest, if any of the Macedonians should come with him, they should find them not prepared, though he had boasted so much of their ready mind, 3–5.

He gives them directions how they shall contribute; and the advantage to be gained by it, in the fulfillment of the promises of God, 6–11.

He shows them that by this means the poor shall be relieved, God glorified, their Christian temper manifested, and the prayers of many engaged in their behalf, 12–14.

And concludes with giving thanks to God for his unspeakable gift, 15.

A detailed analysis of chapter

The reason for sending Titus to collect their gifts of money. (1–5)

The Corinthians should be cheerful in their giving. The apostle thanks God for his indescribable gift. (6–15)

Key verse

Verse 6: "Whoever sows sparingly will also reap sparingly, and whoever sows generously will also reap generously."

Key word / key phrase

Verse 6, "whoever sows generously."

Key event / key person / key theme

Giving money is a spiritual act

Key thought

"God is the greatest giver."

Key thing to look out for

"How to be a great giver."

Key Bible cross-reference

Verse 9. See Psalm 112:9.

Key "by way of explanation"

Verse 14, "the surpassing grace God has given you." Paul is trying to encourage the Corinthians to live with a generous spirit. Here he says that their concern for their fellow-Christians has not gone unnoticed, and that it is in itself a gift from God.

Key "Quotable Quote"

"Wesley's famous formula, 'Get all you can; save all you can; give all you can,' must be supplemented. It should read: get all you can; save all you can; freely use all you can within a properly disciplined spiritual life; and control all you can for the good of humankind and God's glory. Giving all you can would then naturally be a part of an overall wise stewardship."

Dallas Willard

2 Corinthians 10

Matthew Henry's introduction

There was no place in which the apostle Paul met with more opposition from false apostles than at Corinth; he had many enemies there. Let not any of the ministers of Christ think it strange if they meet with perils, not only from enemies, but from false brethren; for blessed Paul himself did so. Though he was so blameless and inoffensive in all his carriage, so condescending and useful to all, yet there were those who bore him ill-will, who envied him, and did all they could to undermine him, and lesson his interest and reputation. Therefore he vindicates himself from their imputation, and arms the Corinthians against their insinuations. In this chapter the apostle, in a mild and humble manner, asserts the power of his preaching, and to punish offenders, vv. 1–6. He then proceeds to reason the case with the Corinthians, asserting his relation to Christ, and his authority as an apostle of Christ (vv. 7–11), and refuses to justify himself, or to act by such rules as the false teachers did, but according to the better rules he had fixed for himself, v. 12, to the end.

Dr. Adam Clarke's analysis of chapter

The apostle vindicates himself against the aspersions cast on his person by the false apostle; and takes occasion to mention his spiritual might and authority, 1–6.

He shows them the impropriety of judging after the outward appearance, 7.

Again refers to his apostolic authority, and informs them that when he again comes among them he will show himself in his deeds as powerful as his letters intimated, 8–11.

He shows that these false teachers sat down in other men's labors, having neither authority nor influence from God to break up new ground, while he and the apostles in general had the regions assigned to them through which they were to sow the seed of life; and that he never entered into any place where the work was made ready to his hand by others, 12–16.

He concludes with intimating that the glorying of those false apostles was bad; that they had nothing but self-commendation; and that they who glory should glory in the Lord, 17, 18.

A detailed analysis of chapter

The apostle states his authority with meekness and humility. (1–6)

The apostle reasons with the Corinthians. (7–11)

The apostle seeks the glory of God, and to be approved by him. (12–18)

Key verse

Verse 4: "The weapons we fight with are not the weapons of the world. On the contrary, they have divine power to demolish strongholds."

Key word / key phrase

Verse 6, "every act of disobedience."

Key event / key person / key theme

Discipline

Key thought

If the great apostle Paul was so misunderstood in his own day it is hardly surprising that he continues to be maligned today.

Key thing to look out for

Paul's ministry is a war. How is victory to be won?

Key Bible cross-reference

Verse 17. See Jeremiah 9:24.

Key "by way of explanation"

Verse 5, "every thought . . . obedient to Christ." If this is accomplished then everything else in the Christian life will be better. For Christ needs to be Lord of our thinking.

Key "Quotable Quote"

"Christ is either Lord of all, or he is not Lord at all."

James Hudson Taylor

2 Corinthians 11

Matthew Henry's introduction

In this chapter the apostle goes on with his discourse, in opposition to the false apostles, who were very industrious to lessen his interest and reputation among the Corinthians, and had prevailed too much by their insinuations.

I. He apologizes for going about to commend himself, and gives the reason for what he did, vv. 1–4.

II. He mentions, in his own necessary vindication, his equality with the other apostles, and with the false apostles in this particular of preaching the gospel to the Corinthians freely, without wages, vv. 5–15.

III. He makes another preface to what he was about further to say in his own justification, vv. 16–21. And,

IV. He gives a large account of his qualifications, labors, and sufferings, in which he exceeded the false apostles, v. 22, to the end.

Dr. Adam Clarke's analysis of chapter

The apostle apologizes for expressing his jealousy relative to the true state of the Corinthians; still fearing lest their minds should have been drawn aside from the simplicity of the Gospel, 1–3.

From this he takes occasion to extol his own ministry, which had been without charge to them, having been supported by the Churches of Macedonia while he preached the Gospel at Corinth, 4–11.

Gives the character of the false apostles, 12–16.

Shows what reasons he has to boast of secular advantages of birth, education, Divine call to the ministry, labors in that ministry, grievous persecutions, great sufferings, and extraordinary hazards, 16–33.

A detailed analysis of chapter

The apostle explains why he speaks about commending himself. (1–14)

He shows that he had freely preached the gospel. (5–15)

He explains what he was going to add in order to defend his own character. (16–21)

He gives an account of his work, concerns, sufferings, dangers, and deliverances. (22–33)

Key verse

Verse 14: "Satan himself masquerades as an angel of light."

Key word / key phrase

Verse 25, "three times I was shipwrecked."

Key event / key person / key theme

The apostle and his sufferings

Key thought

Love wants God's best for people. Therefore, as Paul does here, it exposes false claims.

Key thing to look out for

"Consider how I have been suffering for Christ."

Key Bible cross-reference

Verse 3. See Genesis 3:1–5.

Key "by way of explanation"

Verse 13, "masquerading as apostles of Christ." Those who claimed to be "super-apostles," verse 5, Paul now unmasks as being in the grip of "Satan." These false apostles were Jewish Christians (11:22), visitors to Corinth, who also spoke eloquently and criticized Paul. There is no clear indication of their teaching, but their behavior is certainly unchristian (e.g. 11:20).

Key "Quotable Quote"

"Suffering is one of the marks of the true Church."

Martin Luther

2 Corinthians 12

Matthew Henry's introduction

In this chapter the apostle proceeds in maintaining the honor of his apostleship. He magnified his office when there were those who vilified it. What he says in his own praise was only in his own justification and the necessary defense of the honor of his ministry, the preservation of which was necessary to its success. First, He makes mention of the favor God had shown him, the honor done him, the methods God took to keep him humble, and the use he made of this dispensation, vv. 1–10. Then he addresses himself to the Corinthians, blaming them for what was faulty among them, and giving a large account of his behavior and kind intentions towards them, v. 11, to the end.

Dr. Adam Clarke's analysis of chapter

St. Paul mentions some wonderful revelations which he had received from the Lord, 1–5.

He speaks of his suffering in connection with these extraordinary revelations, that his character might be duly estimated, 6.

That he might not be too much exalted, a messenger of Satan is sent to buffet him; his prayer for deliverance, and the Divine answer, 7–9.

He exults in sufferings and reproaches, and vindicates his apostleship, 10–13.

Promises to come and visit them, 14, 15.

Answers some objections, 16–18.

And expresses his apprehensions that when he visits them he shall find many evils and disorders among them, 19–21.

A detailed analysis of chapter

The apostle's revelations. (1–6)

They were to his spiritual advantage. (7–10)

Key verse

Verse 9: "Therefore I will boast all the more gladly about my weaknesses, so that Christ's power may rest on me."

Key word / key phrase

Verse 9, "my grace is sufficient."

Key event / key person / key theme

Boast about your weakness, and Paul's proposed third visit

Key thought

Paul has been deeply wronged.

Key thing to look out for

How does Paul show his love for the Corinthian Christians?

Key Bible cross-reference

Verse 2. See Romans 16:3.

Key "by way of explanation"

Verse 13, "I was never a burden to you." The Corinthians could not accuse Paul of sponging off them. He lived at his own expense. He did not accept any payment from the Corinthians. (See Acts 18:3.)

Key "Quotable Quote"

"This life is not righteousness, but growth in righteousness, not health but healing, not being but becoming, not rest but exercise. We are not yet what we shall be, but we are growing toward it; the process is not yet finished but it is going on. This is not the end of the road; all does not yet gleam in glory but all is being purified."

Martin Luther

2 Corinthians 13

Matthew Henry's introduction

In this chapter the apostle threatens to be severe against obstinate sinners, and assigns the reason thereof (vv. 1–6); then he makes a suitable prayer to God on the behalf of the Corinthians, with the reasons inducing him thereto (vv. 7–10), and concludes his epistle with a valediction and a benediction, vv. 11–14.

Dr. Adam Clarke's analysis of chapter

The apostle again says that this is the third time he has purposed to come and see them; and threatens that he will, by the power of Christ, punish every incorrigible sinner, 1–4.

Exhorts them to examine themselves, whether they be in the faith, 5, 6.

Prays that they may do no evil, 7.

And shows how ardently he wished their complete restoration to unity and purity, 8, 9.

Tells them for what reason he writes to them, 10.

Bids them farewell, 11.

Gives them some directions, and concludes with his apostolic benediction, 12–14.

A detailed analysis of chapter

The apostle threatens obstinate offenders. (1–6)
He prays for them to reform their ways. (7–10)
He ends the letter with a greeting and blessing. (11–14)

Key verse

Verse 11: "Aim for perfection."

Key word / key phrase

Verse 5, "examine yourselves."

Key event / key person / key theme

Examine yourselves, and greetings

Key thought

"Give yourself a good spiritual check up."

Key thing to look out for

"We are your servants."

Key Bible cross-reference

Verse 1. See Deuteronomy 17:6.

Key "by way of explanation"

Verse "Examine yourselves." The false teachers were always on the attack, falsely accusing Paul. Paul tells the Corinthian Christians that they should rather look into their own hearts and take their spiritual pulse.

Key "Quotable Quote"

"We have fallen into the temptation of separating ministry from spirituality, service from prayer."

Henri Nouwen

5. Select bibliography for 2 Corinthians

Barrett, C. K. *A Commentary on the Second Epistle to the Corinthians*. London: A. and C. Black, 1973.

Bruce, F. F. *1 and 2 Corinthians*. London: Olyphant's, 1971.

Denney, J. *The Second Epistle to the Corinthians*. London: Hodder and Stoughton, 1894.

Hodge, C. *A Commentary on the Second Epistle to the Corinthians*. London: Banner of Truth, 1959 reprint of 1857 work.

Hughes, P. E. *Paul's Second Epistle to the Corinthians*. Grand Rapids: Eerdmans, 1962.

Martin, R. P. *2 Corinthians*. Waco: Word, 1985.

Tasker, R. V. G. *The Second Epistle of Paul to the Corinthians*. Grand Rapids: Eerdmans, 1958.

Galatians

1. Book by book: Introduction to Galatians

Introduction

Author

The internal and external evidence for Paul's authorship is conclusive. The style is characteristically Pauline. The superscription, and allusions to the apostle of the Gentiles in the first person, throughout the Epistle, establish the same truth (Gal. 1:1, 13–24; 2:1–14). His authorship is also upheld by the unanimous testimony of the ancient Church: compare Irenaeus (*Against Heresies,* 3, 7, 2) (Gal. 3:19); Polycarp (*Epistle to the Philippians,* 3) quotes Gal. 4:26; 6:7; Justin Martyr, or whoever wrote the Discourse to the Greeks, alludes to Gal. 4:12; 5:20.

Readers

The Epistle was written "To the churches of Galatia" (Gal. 1:2), a district of Asia Minor, bordering on Phrygia, Pontus, Bithynia, Cappadocia, and Paphlagonia. The inhabitants (Gallo-græci, contracted into Galati, another form of the name Celts) were Gauls in origin, the latter having overrun Asia Minor after they had pillaged Delphi, about 280 b.c. and at last permanently settled in the central parts, thence called Gallo-græcia or Galatia. Their character, as shown in this Epistle, is in entire consonance with that ascribed to the Gallic race by all writers. Cæsar (*Commentaries on the Gallic War,* 4, 5), "The infirmity of the Gauls is that they are fickle in their resolves and fond of change, and not to be trusted." So Thierry (quoted by Alford), "Frank, impetuous, impressible, eminently intelligent, but at the same time extremely changeable, inconstant, fond of show, perpetually quarrelling, the fruit of excessive vanity."

They received Paul at first with all joy and kindness; but soon wavered in their allegiance to the Gospel and to him, and listened as eagerly now to Judaizing teachers as they had before to him (Gal. 4:14–16). The apostle himself had been the first preacher among them (Acts 16:6; Gal. 1:8; 4:13; see on Gal. 4:13; "on account of infirmity of flesh I preached unto you at the first": implying that sickness detained him among them); and had then probably founded churches, which at his subsequent visit he "strengthened" in the faith (Acts 18:23). His first visit was about A.D. 51, during his second missionary journey.

Josephus (*Antiquities*, 16.62) testifies that many Jews resided in Ancyra in Galatia. Among these and their brethren, doubtless, as elsewhere, he began his preaching. And though subsequently the majority in the Galatian churches were Gentiles (Gal. 4:8, 9), yet these were soon infected by Judaizing teachers, and almost suffered themselves to be persuaded to undergo circumcision (Gal. 1:6; 3:1, 3; 5:2, 3; 6:12, 13).

Accustomed as the Galatians had been, when heathen, to the mystic worship of Cybele (prevalent in the neighboring region of Phrygia), and the theosophistic doctrines connected with that worship, they were the more readily led to believe that the full privileges of Christianity could only be attained through an elaborate system of ceremonial symbolism (Gal. 4:9–11; 5:7–12). They even gave ear to the insinuation that Paul himself observed the law among the Jews, though he persuaded the Gentiles to renounce it, and that his motive was to keep his converts in a subordinate state, excluded from the full privileges of Christianity, which were enjoyed by the circumcised alone (Gal. 5:11, Gal. 4:16, compare with Gal. 2:17); and that in "becoming all things to all men," he was an interested flatterer (Gal. 1:10), aiming at forming a party for himself: moreover, that he falsely represented himself as an apostle divinely commissioned by Christ, whereas he was but a messenger sent by the Twelve and the Church at Jerusalem, and that his teaching was now at variance with that of Peter and James, "pillars" of the Church, and therefore ought not to be accepted.

Purpose of letter

Paul's purpose, then, in writing this Epistle was:

to defend his apostolic authority (Gal. 1:11–19; 2:1–14);

to counteract the evil influence of the Judaizers in Galatia (Gal. 3:1–4:31), and to show that their doctrine destroyed the very essence of Christianity, by lowering its spirituality to an outward ceremonial system;

to give exhortation for the strengthening of Galatian believers in faith towards Christ, and in the fruits of the Spirit (Gal. 5:1–6:18). He had already, face to face, testified against the Judaizing teachers (Gal. 1:9; 4:16; Acts 18:23); and now that he has heard of the continued and increasing prevalence of the evil, he writes with his own hand (Gal. 6:11: a labor which he usually delegated to an amanuensis) this Epistle to oppose it. The sketch he gives in it of his apostolic career confirms and expands the account in Acts and shows his independence of human authority, however exalted. His protest against Peter in Gal. 2:14–21, disproves the figment, not merely of papal, but even of that apostle's supremacy; and shows that Peter, save when specially inspired, was fallible like other men.

There is much in common between this Epistle and that to the Romans on the subject of justification by faith only, and not by the law. But the Epistle to the Romans handles the subject in a didactic and logical mode, without any special reference; this Epistle, in a controversial manner, and with special reference to the Judaizers in Galatia.

Style

The style combines the two extremes, sternness. (Gal. 1:1–24; 3:1–5) and tenderness (Gal. 4:19, 20), the characteristics of a man of strong emotions, and both alike well suited for acting on an impressible people such as the Galatians were. The beginning is abrupt, as was suited to the urgency of the question and the greatness of the danger. A tone of sadness, too, is apparent, such as might be expected in the letter of a warm-hearted teacher who had just learned that those whom he loved were forsaking his teachings for those of perverters of the truth, as well as giving ear to calumnies against himself.

Date

The time of writing was after the visit to Jerusalem recorded in Acts 15:1, etc.; that is, a.d. 50, if that visit be, as seems probable, identical with that in Gal. 2:1. Further, as Gal. 1:9 ("as we said before"), and Gal. 4:16 ("Have [Alford] I become your enemy?" namely, at my second visit, whereas I was welcomed by you at my first visit), refer to his second visit (Acts 18:23), this Epistle must have been written after the date of that visit (the autumn of A.D. 54). Gal. 4:13, "Ye know how . . . I preached . . . at the first" (Greek, "at the former time"), implies that Paul, at the time of writing, had been twice in Galatia; and Gal. 1:6, "I marvel that ye are so soon removed," implies that he wrote not long after having left Galatia for the second time; probably in the early part of his residence at Ephesus (Acts

18:23; 19:1, etc., from A.D. 54, the autumn, to A.D. 57, Pentecost) (Alford). Conybeare and Howson, from the similarity between this Epistle and that to the Romans, the same line of argument in both occupying the writer's mind, think it was not written till his stay at Corinth (Acts 20:2, 3), during the winter of 57–58, whence he wrote his Epistle to the Romans; and certainly, in the theory of the earlier writing of it from Ephesus, it does seem unlikely that the two Epistles to the Corinthians, so dissimilar, should intervene between those so similar as the Epistles to the Galatians and Romans; or that the Epistle to the Galatians should intervene between the second to the Thessalonians and the first to the Corinthians. The decision between the two theories rests on the words, "so soon." If these be not considered inconsistent with little more than three years having elapsed since his second visit to Galatia, the argument, from the similarity to the Epistle to the Romans, seems to me conclusive. This to the Galatians seems written on the urgency of the occasion, tidings having reached him at Corinth from Ephesus of the Judaizing of many of his Galatian converts, in an admonitory and controversial tone, to maintain the great principles of Christian liberty and justification by faith only; that to the Romans is a more deliberate and systematic exposition of the same central truths of theology, subsequently drawn up in writing to a Church with which he was personally unacquainted. Paley (*Horæ Paulinæ*) well remarks how perfectly adapted the conduct of the argument is to the historical circumstances under which the Epistle was written! Thus, that to the Galatians, a Church which Paul had founded, he puts mainly on authority; that to the Romans, to whom he was not personally known, entirely on argument.

A. R. Faussett

Detailed .outline

- I. Introduction: 1:1–5
  - A. From: Paul: 1:1
  - B. To: The churches of Galatia: 1:2
  - C. Grace and peace from Jesus: 1:3–5
    - 1. Who gave Himself for our sins: 1:4
    - 2. Who delivered us from the present evil world: 1:4
    - 3. According to the will of God the Father: 1:4
    - 4. To whom be glory for ever: 1:5
- II. The rebuke: 1:6–10
  - A. Astonishment at the departure from the Gospel: 1:6
  - B. Statement of the departure to "another gospel" which is false: 1:6–7
  - C. No matter who preaches another gospel, they are accursed: 1:8–9
  - D. Paul's attitude towards the matter: 1:10

Part One: The Liberty Of The Gospel A Personal Argument 1:11–2:21

- I. How Paul received the Gospel: 1:11–24
  - A. The origin through revelation: 1:11–12
  - B. His conduct previous to receiving the Gospel: 1:13–14
    - 1. Taught the Jewish religion: 1:13
    - 2. Persecuted the Church of God: 1:13
    - 3. Profited in the Jewish religion above his equals: 1:14

4. Was zealous of the Jewish tradition: 1:14

C. Description the revelation received: 1:15–17

D. Paul's independence of the Jerusalem apostles: 1:18–20

1. His first visit to Jerusalem: 1:18–20
   (a) The time of the visit: 1:18
   (b) The purpose of the visit: 1:18
   (c) The duration of the visit: 1:18
   (d) Contacts during the visit: 1:19–20

E. Paul's subsequent absence from Jerusalem: 1:21–24

1. The place of his withdrawal: 1:21
2. The lack of acquaintance with the churches in Judea: 1:22
3. The response of the churches to reports about him: 1:23–24

II. How the Gospel received by Paul was confirmed by the apostles: 2:1–10

A. The circumstances of its presentation to them: 2:1–2

1. The journey to Jerusalem: 2:2
2. The presentation made by Paul at Jerusalem: 2:2

B. The result of Paul's presentation of the Gospel o them: 2:3–10

1. His position as reflected in Titus: 2:3
2. His conflict with false brethren: 2:4–5
   (a) Their presence: 2:4
   (b) Paul's refusal to yield to their demands: 2:5
3. Approval by Jerusalem leaders of Paul's Gospel: 2:6–10
   (a) Their failure to add anything to his Gospel: 2:6
   (b) Their approval of his Gospel: 2:7–10
   (c) The basis of their approval: 2:7–9
   (d) The expression of their approval: 2:9
   (e) The one request made in their approval: 2:10

III. Paul's rebuke of Peter for giving way to legalistic pressure in Antioch: 2:11–21

A. Reason for the rebuke: 2:12

B. Effect of the inconsistent conduct of Peter: 2:13

C. Justification for giving the rebuke: 2:14–21

1. Paul's question to Peter: 2:14
2. Paul's explanation of his doctrinal position: 2:15–21
   (a) Insufficiency of the law: 2:15–18
   (b) The new life in Christ: 2:19–21

Part Two: The Liberty Of The Gospel A Doctrinal Argument 3:1–4:31

I. The doctrine of justification by faith: 3:1–4:7

A. Justification by faith: 3:1–14

1. Inconsistency of their conduct: 3:1–5
   (a) Turning from Christ: 3:1
   (b) Question about the start of their Christian life: 3:2
   (c) A question about their method of perfection: 3:3
   (d) The question about their sufferings as believers: 3:4
   (e) The question about the basis of God's work in them: 3:5

B. The example of Abraham's justification: 3:6–9

1. The means of Abraham's justification: 3:6
2. The identity of the sons of Abraham: 3:7
3. Abraham's justification through faith: 3:8
4. The heirs of the blessings of Abraham: 3:9

C. Deliverance from law and works through Jesus Christ: 3:10–14
1. The curse on those under law and works: 3:10
2. The inability of law and works to justify: 3:11–12
3. Deliverance from the curse through Jesus: 3:13–14
(a) The means of deliverance from the curse: 3:13
(b) The purpose in deliverance from the curse: 3:14

D. The limitations of the law and its relation to faith: 3:15–4:7
1. The covenant of faith with Abraham: 3:15–18
(a) The covenant was binding: 3:15
(b) It was to Abraham and his descendants: 3:16
(c) The promise was not altered by the law: 3:17
(d) The inheritance is by promise: 3:18
2. The true place and purpose of the law: 3:19–29
(a) The temporary nature of the law: 3:19–20
(b) The inability of the law to produce life: 3:21–22
(c) The law was a means to bring us to Christ: 3:23–29

E. The contrasts of law and faith: 4:1–7
1. The illustration of the position of an heir as a minor: 4:1–2
2. Application of the illustration to believers: 4:3–6
(a) Bondage as minors: 4:3
(b) Free as sons: 4:4–6
3. The conclusion for the believer: 4:7

II. An appeal to the Galatian believers to drop their legalism: 4:8–31

A. Accepting Jewish legalism is a return to slavery: 4:8–11
1. Their past condition of slavery: 4:8
2. Their deliverance from slavery: 4:9
3. Legalism is returning to slavery: 4:9–10
4. Their actions cause concern to Paul: 4:11

B. The appeal from his relation to them: 4:12–20
1. An appeal for them to adopt Paul's position: 4:12
2. A reminder of his past relation to them: 4:12–14
3. The change in their relation to him: 4:15–18
4. The pain he is experiencing for them: 4:19–20

C. The appeal from the two contrasted covenants, law and grace: 4:21–31
1. A question to those desiring to be under the law: 4:21
2. The story of Abraham's two sons: 4:22–23

3. The interpretation of the story: 4:24–23
   - (a) The two methods represent two covenants: 4:24
   - (b) The description of the two covenants: 4:24–28
     - (l) One represents slavery: 4:24–25
     - (2) The other represents freedom: 4:26–28
   - (c) The expulsion of the son of slavery: 4:29–30
   - (d) Conclusion of the story: 4:31

Part Three: The Liberty Of The Gospel Practical Application 5:1–6:18

I. The call to maintain Christian liberty: 5:1–12

A. The danger of circumcision: 5:2–6
1. It makes Christ useless to them: 5:2
2. It makes them subject to the whole law: 5:3
3. It severs them from Christ: 5:4
4. It is a fall from grace: 5:4
5. The proper Christian attitude: 5:5–6

B. The condemnation of the false teacher: 5:7–12
1. Their error: 5:7–8
2. Example of their teaching: 5:9
3. Condemnation of the one troubling them: 5:10–12

II. The life of Christian liberty: 5:13–6:10

A. The life is directed by love: 5:13–15
1. The believer is called to liberty: 5:13
2. The proper use of Christian liberty: 5:13
3. The fulfillment of the law through love: 5:14
4. The results of a lack of love: 5:15

B. It is a walk in the Spirit, not in the flesh: 5:16–25
1. The command to walk in the Spirit: 5:16
2. The conflict between the Spirit and the flesh: 5:17–18
3. The contrast between the flesh and the Spirit: 5:19–23
   - (a) The works of the flesh: 5:19–21
   - (b) The fruit of the Spirit: 5:22–23
4. The people living by the Spirit: 5:24–25
   - (a) They have crucified the flesh: 5:24
   - (b) They live and walk in the Spirit: 5:25

C. It is a life of mutual burden bearing: 5:26–6:10
1. Bearing faults: 5:26–6:5
   - (a) The warning against wrong attitudes toward others: 5:26
   - (b) The attitude of humility in restoring the fallen: 6:1
   - (c) The duty of mutual burden-bearing: 6:2
   - (d) The proper attitude towards self: 6:3–5

D. It is a life governed by basic principles: 6:6–10
1. The principle of communication: 6:6
2. The principle of spiritual harvest: 6:7–8
3. The principle of well doing: 6:9–10

III. The conclusion:

A. Reference to his large letters: 6:11

B. Rebuke of his adversaries: 6:12–13

C. His confidence in the cross: 6:14–16

1. Glorying in the cross: 6:14
2. Crucifixion through the cross: 6:15
3. Blessings on those accepting this principle: 6:16
4. He bears the marks of the Lord in his own body: 6:17

IV. The benediction: 6:18

2. Helpful summaries of Galatians

Bird's eye view

Paul cannot stand by when he hears about Galatians Christians who came to Jesus by grace but who are now returning to rely on the law. Paul writes a blunt and firm letter to address this situation.

Reading plan

The following reading plan, taking one reading per day, enables you to read through Galatians in six days.

Galatians 1:1–1:24
Galatians 2:1–2:21
Galatians 3:1–3:29
Galatians 4:1–4:31
Galatians 5:1–5:26
Galatians 6:1–6:18

Verses to memorize

Galatians 2:20

I am crucified with Christ: nevertheless I live; yet not I, but Christ liveth in me: and the life which I now live in the flesh I live by the faith of the Son of God, who loved me, and gave himself for me. KJV

Galatians 5:1

Stand fast therefore in the liberty wherewith Christ hath made us free, and be not entangled again with the yoke of bondage. KJV

Galatians 5:22–23

But the fruit of the Spirit is love, joy, peace, longsuffering, gentleness, goodness, faith, Meekness, temperance: against such there is no law. KJV

Galatians 6:9

And let us not be weary in well doing: for in due season we shall reap, if we faint not. KJV

Statistics

Ninth New Testament book
Fourth letter by the apostle Paul
6 chapters
149 verses
3,098 words
Number of Old Testament quotations and allusions in Galatians: 16.

Names/titles given

Pros Galatas: "To the Galatians."
"Magna Charta of Christian liberty."
"Magna Charta of the Church."
"Christian's Declaration of Independence."

3. Helpful keys to turn to in understanding Galatians

Key word

Freedom

Key verses

Galatians 2:16; 5:1

Themes to study

- Christian freedom contrasted with the Law.
- How to stand firm in the freedom which Jesus has given us.

Jesus in Galatians

In Galatians Jesus is our Freedom.

Lessons to learn from Galatians

- Our salvation comes from Jesus' freely given grace. We could never do enough to earn our way into heaven.
- Christian truth should never be diluted or ignored.

4. Chapter by chapter: outline of every chapter of Galatians

Galatians 1

Matthew Henry's introduction

In this chapter, after the preface or introduction (vv. 1–5), the apostle severely reproves these churches for their defection from the faith (vv. 6–9), and then proves his own apostleship, which his enemies had brought them to question,

I. From his end and design in preaching the gospel, v. 10.

II. From his having received it by immediate revelation, vv. 11, 12. For the proof of which he acquaints them,

A. What his former conversation was, vv. 13, 14.

B. How he was converted, and called to the apostleship, vv. 15, 16.

C. How he behaved himself afterwards, v. 16, to the end.

Dr. Adam Clarke's analysis of chapter

St. Paul shows that he was especially called of God to be an apostle, 1.

Directs his epistle to the Churches through the regions of Galatia, 2.

Commends them to the grace of Christ, who gave himself for their sins, 3–5.

Marvels that they had so soon turned away from the grace of the Gospel of Christ, to what falsely pretended to be another gospel, 6, 7.

Pronounces him accursed who shall preach any other doctrine than that which he had delivered to them, 8,9.

Shows his own uprightness, and that he received his doctrine from God, 10–12.

Gives an account of his conversion and call to the apostleship, 13–17.

How three years after his conversion he went up to Jerusalem, and afterwards went through the regions of Syria and Cilicia, preaching the faith of Christ to the great joy of the Christian Churches in Judea, 18–24.

A detailed analysis of chapter

The apostle Paul asserts his apostolic authority. (1–5)

He reproves the Galatians for moving away from the gospel of Christ under the influence of evil teachers. (6–9)

Key verse

Verse 6: "I am astonished that you are so quickly deserting the one who called you by the grace of Christ and are turning to a different gospel."

Key word / key phrase

Verse 12, "by revelation from Jesus Christ."

Key event / key person / key theme

Paul's credentials

Key thought

The Christians in Galatia were turning away from the true gospel.

Key thing to look out for

How does Paul show that his gospel is genuine?

Key Bible cross-reference

Verse 13. See Acts 8:3.

Key "by way of explanation"

Verse 8, "eternally condemned." Paul believes that it is so serious a sin to preach any gospel other than the true one that such people will be, and deserve to be, condemned by God forever.

Key "Quotable Quote"

"We have no cause to be ashamed of the gospel of Christ; but the gospel of Christ may justly be ashamed of us."

John Tillotson

Galatians 2

Matthew Henry's introduction

The apostle, in this chapter, continues the relation of his past life and conduct, which he had begun in the former; and, by some further instances of what had passed between him and the other apostles, makes it appear that he was not beholden to them either for his knowledge of the gospel or his authority as an apostle, as his adversaries would insinuate; but, on the contrary, that he was owned and approved even by them, as having an equal commission with them to this office.

I. He particularly informs them of another journey which he took to Jerusalem many years after the former, and how he behaved himself at that time, vv. 1–10. And,

II. Gives them an account of another interview he had with the apostle Peter at Antioch, and how he was obliged to behave himself towards him there. From the subject-matter of that conversation, he proceeds to discourse on the great doctrine of justification by faith in Christ, without the works of the law, which it was the main design of this epistle to establish, and which he enlarges more on in the two following chapters.

Dr. Adam Clarke's analysis of chapter

The apostle mentions his journey to Jerusalem with Barnabas and Titus, 1.

Shows that he went thither by revelation; and what he did while there, and the people with whom he had intercourse, 2–8.

How the apostles gave him the right hand of fellowship, 9, 10.

Here he opposes Peter at Antioch, and the reason why, 11–14.

Shows that the Jews as well as the Gentiles must be justified by faith, 15, 16.

They who seek this justification should act with consistency, 17, 18.

Gives his own religious experience, and shows, that through the law he was dead to the law, and crucified with Christ, 19, 20.

Justification is not of the law, but by the faith of Christ, 21.

A detailed analysis of chapter

The apostle declares he is an apostle of the Gentiles. (1–10)

He had publicly opposed Peter for telling Christians to adopt Jewish practices. (11–14)

Key verse

Verse 16: "[we . . .] know that a man is not justified by observing the law, but by faith in Jesus Christ. So we, too, have put our faith in Christ Jesus that we may be justified by faith in Christ and not by observing the law, because by observing the law no one will be justified."

Key word

Verse 16: "justified."

Key event / key person / key theme

The arrival of "the men from James" leading to Peter's distancing himself from Paul, and Paul's confrontation of Peter.

Key thought

Paul's complaint against Peter is summed up in verse 14. Peter's conduct in no longer eating with the Gentiles belied the truth of the gospel.

Key thing to look out for

What led Peter to act as he did?

Key Bible cross-reference

Verse 14. See Acts 15:10.

Key "by way of explanation"

Verse 12, "Circumcision group." These are the "false brothers" of verse 4, Judaizers, who insisted that non-Jews who became followers of Jesus had to be circumcised and keep the Law of Moses. In other words, faith in Jesus was not enough to obtain salvation.

Key "Quotable Quote"

"Paul taught that the Gentiles were justified by faith alone, without works of the law."

Martin Luther

Galatians 3

Matthew Henry's introduction

The apostle in this chapter,

I. Reproves the Galatians for their folly, in suffering themselves to be drawn away from the faith of the gospel, and endeavors, from several considerations, to impress them with a sense of it.

II. He proves the doctrine which he had reproved them for departing from–that of justification by faith without the works of the law,

A. From the example of Abraham's justification.
B. From the nature and tenor of the law.
C. From the express testimony of the Old Testament; and,
D. From the stability of the covenant of God with Abraham. Lest any should hereon say, "Wherefore then serveth the law?" he answers,
   1. It was added because of transgressions.
   2. It was given to convince the world of the necessity of a Savior.
   3. It was designed as a schoolmaster, to bring us to Christ. And then he concludes the chapter by acquainting us with the privilege of Christians under the gospel state.

Dr. Adam Clarke's analysis of chapter

The apostle inquires how they could be so foolish as to renounce the Gospel of Christ and turn back to the law, after having heard, received, and suffered so much for the Gospel, 1–5.

Asserts the doctrine of justification by faith, on the example of Abraham, 6–9.

Shows that all who are under the law are under the curse, from which Christ alone redeems us; and the promise made to Abraham comes to the Gentiles who believe, 10–14.

For the covenant is not by the works of the law, but by promise, 15–18.

The law was given to show the sinfulness of sin, and to act as a schoolmaster till Christ should come, 19–25.

It is by faith only that any become children of God, 26.

And under the Gospel, all those distinctions which subsisted under the law are done away; and genuine believers, whether Jews or Gentiles, bond or free, are one in Christ Jesus, and accounted the genuine children of Abraham, 27–29.

A detailed analysis of chapter

The Galatians reproved for moving away from the great doctrine of justification alone, through faith in Christ. (1–5)

This doctrine is seen in the example of Abraham (6–9);

from the tenor of the Law and the severity of its curse (10–14);

from the covenant of promises, which the Law could not disannul. (15–18)

The law was a schoolmaster to lead them to Christ. (19–25)

Under the gospel true believers are all one in Christ. (26–29)

Key verse

Verse 6: "He believed God, and it was credited to him as righteousness."

Key word / key phrase

Verse 22, "through faith in Jesus Christ."

Key event / key person / key theme

Paul gives the content of the gospel

Key thought

"You have been taken for a ride."

Key thing to look out for

Verses 10–14 – the two gifts that come from faith in Christ.

Key Bible cross-reference

Verse 6. See Genesis 15:6.

Key "by way of explanation"

Verse 13, "hung on a tree." This was the pole on which criminals were crucified. Here it refers to the cross on which Jesus was crucified.

Key "Quotable Quote"

"Christ took away the curse of the law and the right which it had, so that even though you have sinned, even though you now have sin (for we must use the language of Scripture), yet you are saved. Our Samson has shattered the power of death, the power of sin, the gates of hell. This is what Paul means in Galatians 3:13. 'Christ redeemed us from the curse of the law, having become a curse for us.'"

Philip Melanchthon

Galatians 4

Matthew Henry's introduction

The apostle, in this chapter, is still carrying on the same general design as in the former–to recover these Christians from the impressions made on them by the judaizing teachers, and to represent their weakness and folly in suffering themselves to be drawn away from the gospel doctrine of justification, and to be deprived of their freedom from the bondage of the law of Moses. For this purpose he makes use of various considerations; such as,

I. The great excellence of the gospel state above the legal, vv. 1–7.
II. The happy change that was made in them at their conversion, vv. 8–11.
III. The affection they had had for him and his ministry, vv. 12–16.
IV. The character of the false teachers by whom they had been perverted, vv. 17, 18.
V. The very tender affection he had for them, vv. 19, 20.
VI. The history of Isaac and Ishmael, by a comparison taken from which he illustrates the difference between such as rested in Christ and such as trusted in the law. And in all these, as he uses great plainness and faithfulness with them, so he expresses the tenderest concern for them.

Dr. Adam Clarke's analysis of chapter

The apostle shows that, as an heir in nonage is under tutors and guardians, so were the Galatians while under the law; and, as the heir when he comes of age is no longer under guardians, so they, when the Gospel came, arrived at full maturity, and were redeemed from the law, 1–3.

He shows, farther, that when the fullness of the time came God sent forth his Son, that we might obtain the adoption of sons, and have the strongest evidence of that adoption, 4–6.

Those who are children of God are heirs of heaven, 7.

He compares their former and latter state, and

shows the reason he had to fear that his labor on their behalf was in vain, 8–11.

He mentions his trials among them, and their kindness to him, 12–16.

Shows his tender affection for them, and exhorts them to return to the Gospel, 17–20.

Shows the excellence of the Gospel beyond that of the law, by the allegory of Mount Sinai and Jerusalem, 21–27.

Shows also that the believing Gentiles are children of the promise, as Isaac was; and have been elected in the place of the Jews, who have been cast out according to the Scriptures, 28–31.

A detailed analysis of chapter

The folly of returning to legal observances for justification. (1–7)

The glad transformation made in the Gentile believers. (8–11)

The apostle argues against following false teachers. (12–18)

He expresses his earnest concern for them. (19, 20)

And then explains the difference between what is to be expected from the Law, and from the gospel. (21–31)

Key verse

Verse 11: "I fear for you, that somehow I have wasted my efforts on you."

Key word / key phrase

Verse 7, "no longer a slave."

Key event / key person / key theme

Salvation is through faith, not through works of the Law

Key thought

"Do you want to become slaves again?"

Key thing to look out for

"Learn from Hagar and Sarah."

Key Bible cross-reference

Verse 27. See Isaiah 54:1.

Key "by way of explanation"

Verse 11, "wasted my efforts." If the Galatian Christians go back to keeping the Law, Paul feels that he will have wasted his breath teaching them about the gospel of grace which Jesus brought.

Key "Quotable Quote"

"It is one thing to have sin alarmed only by convictions, and another to have it crucified by converting grace. Many, because they have been troubled in conscience for their sins, think well of their case, miserably mistaking conviction for conversion."

Joseph Alliene

Galatians 5

Matthew Henry's introduction

In this chapter the apostle comes to make application of his previous discourse. He begins it with a general caution, or exhortation (v. 1), which he afterwards enforces by several considerations, vv. 2–12. He then presses them to serious practical godliness, which would be the best antidote against the snares of their false teachers; particularly,

I. That they should not strive with one another, vv. 13–15.

II. That they would strive against sin, where he shows,

A. That there is in every one a struggle between flesh and spirit, v. 17.

B. That it is our duty and interest, in this struggle, to side with the better part, vv. 16, 18.

C. He specifies the works of the flesh, which must be watched against and mortified, and the fruits of the Spirit, which must be brought forth and cherished, and shows of what importance it is that they be so, vv. 19–24. And then concludes the chapter with a caution against pride and envy.

Dr. Adam Clarke's analysis of chapter

The apostle exhorts the Galatians to stand fast in the liberty of the Gospel, and not by receiving circumcision bring themselves into a yoke of bondage, 1–4.

Shows the superior excellence of Christianity, 5, 6.

Mentions their former steadiness, and warns them against the bad doctrine which was then preached among them, 7–9.

Expresses his confidence that they will yet return; and shows that he who perverted them shall bear his own punishment, 10–12.

States that they are called to liberty, and that love is the fulfilling of the law, 13, 14.

Warns them against dissensions, and enumerates the fruits of the flesh, which exclude those who bear them from the kingdom of God, 15–21.

Enumerates also the fruits of the Spirit, which characterize the disciples of Christ, 22–24.

Exhorts them to live in the Spirit, and not provoke each other, 25, 26.

A detailed analysis of chapter

An earnest exhortation to stand firm in the freedom of the gospel. (1–12)

To beware of indulging a sinful temper. (13–15)

And to walk in the Spirit, and not to fulfill the evil desires of the flesh: the deeds of both are described. (16–26)

Key verse

Verse 7: "You were running a good race. Who cut in on you and kept you from obeying the truth?"

Key word / key phrase

Verse 16, "live by the Spirit."

Key event / key person / key theme

Paul's description of Christian freedom

Key thought

Christians are freed people. Note that Galatians 5:22, 23 is a portrait of Christ.

Key thing to look out for

The fruit of sin is contrasted with the fruit of the Spirit.

Key Bible cross-reference

Verse 14. See Leviticus 19:18.

Key "by way of explanation"

Verse 22, "the fruit of the Spirit." This is not produced by keeping the Law. Discipline does help. But without the work of the Holy Spirit in a believer's life there will be no spiritual fruit.

Key "Quotable Quote"

"There are two freedoms – the false, where a man is free to do what he likes; the true, where a man is free to do what he ought."

Charles Kingsley

Galatians 6

Matthew Henry's introduction

This chapter chiefly consists of two parts. In the former the apostle gives us several plain and practical directions, which more especially tend to instruct Christians in their duty to one another, and to promote the communion of saints in love, vv. 1–10. In the latter he revives the main design of the epistle, which was to fortify the Galatians against the arts of their judaizing teachers, and confirm them in the truth and liberty of the gospel, for which purpose he,

I. Gives them the true character of these teachers, and shows them from what motives, and with what views, they acted, vv. 11–14. And,

II. On the other hand he acquaints them with his own temper and behavior. From both these they might easily see how little reason they had to slight him, and to fall in with them. And then he concludes the epistle with a solemn benediction.

Dr. Adam Clarke's analysis of chapter

The apostle teaches them to be tender and affectionate towards any who, through surprise and the violence of temptation, had fallen into sin; and to bear each other's burdens, 1, 2.

To think humbly of themselves, and to conclude about their own character rather from the evidence of their works than from any thing else, 3–5.

To minister to the support of those who instruct them in righteousness, 6.

He warns them against self-deception, because whatever a man soweth that he shall reap, 7, 8.

Exhorts them not to be weary in well doing, and to embrace every opportunity to do good, 9, 10.

Intimates that his love to them led him to write this whole epistle with his own hand, 11.

Points out the object that those had in view who wished them to be circumcised, 12, 13.

He exults in the cross of Christ, and asserts that a new creation of the soul is essential to its salvation; and wishes peace to them who act on this plan, 14–16.

States that he bears in his body the marks of the Lord Jesus, 17.

And concludes with his apostolic benediction, 18.

A detailed analysis of chapter

Exhortations to be meek, gentle, and humble. (1–5)

To be kind toward all people, especially to believers. (6–11)

The Galatians warned against the judaizing

teachers. (12–15)

A solemn blessing. (16–18)

Key verse

Verse 7: "Do not be deceived: God cannot be mocked. A man reaps what he sows."

Key word / key phrase

Verse 2, "fulfill the law of Christ."

Key event / key person / key theme

The gospel and service and separation from the world

Key thought

"Be a burden-bearer."

Key thing to look out for

"I only want to boast in Jesus' death."

Key Bible cross-reference

Verse 15. See 1 Corinthians 7:19.

Key "by way of explanation"

Verse 12, "compel you to be circumcised." The "Judizers" thought that if Gentile converts to Christianity were circumcised in obedience to the Law, the Jews who wanted to persecute the Christians would be appeased. So they strongly advocated circumcision.

Key "Quotable Quote"

"It is not fitting, when one is in God's service, to have a gloomy face or a chilling look."

Francis of Assisi

5. Select bibliography for Galatians

Boice, J. M. "Galatians," in the *Expositor's Bible Commentary*. Grand Rapids: Zondervan, 1976.

Bruce, F. F. *The Epistle to the Galatians*. Grand Rapids: Eerdmans, 1982.

Guthrie, D. *Galatians*. Greenwood, S.C.: Attic, 1977.

Calvin, John. *The Epistles of Paul the Apostle to the Galatians, Philippians and Colossians*. Grand Rapids: Eerdmans, 1965. Original edition, 1548.

Cole, R. A. *The Epistle of Paul to the Galatians*, TNTC. London: Tyndale, 1965.

Guthrie, Donald. *Galatians*. NCB. Camden, N.J.: Nelson, 1969.

Lightfoot, J. B. *The Epistle of St. Paul to the Galatians*. Grand Rapids: Zondervan, 1957. Original edition, 1865.

Luther, Martin. *A Commentary on St Paul's Epistle to the Galatians*. Westwood, N.J.: Revell, 1953. Original edition, 1535.

Stott, John R. W. *The Message of Galatians*, "The Bible Speaks Today." Downers Grove, Ill.: Inter-Varsity Press, 1968.

Tenney, Merrill C. *Galatians: The Charter of Christian Liberty*. Grand Rapids: Eerdmans, 1950.

Ephesians

1. Book by book: Introduction to Ephesians

Introduction

Author

The headings (Eph. 1:1, and Eph. 3:1, show that this Epistle claims to be that of Paul. This claim is confirmed by the testimonies of Irenaeus, (*Against Heresies*, 5.2, 3; 1.8,5); Clement of Alexandria, (*Miscellanies*, 4, P. 65, and The Instructor, 1.8); Origen, (*Against Celsus*, 4, 211). It is quoted by Valentinus, A.D. 120, namely, Eph. 3:14–18, as we know from Hippolytus (*The Refutation of All Heresies*, p. 193). Polycarp (*Epistle to the Philippians*, 12), testifies to its canonicity. So Tertullian (*Against Marcion*, 5, 17). Ignatius (*Epistle to the Ephesians,* 12), which alludes to the frequent and affectionate mention made by Paul of the Christian state, privileges, and people of the Ephesians in his Epistle.

Readers

Two theories, besides the ordinary one, have been held on the question, to whom the Epistle is addressed.

Grotius, after the heretic Marcion, maintains that it was addressed to the Church at Laodicea, and that it is the Epistle to which Paul refers in Col. 4:16. But the Epistle to the Colossians was probably written before that to the Ephesians, as appears from the parallel passages in Ephesians bearing marks of being expanded from those in Colossians; and Marcion seems to have drawn his notion, as to our Epistle, from Paul's allusion (Col. 4:16) to an Epistle addressed by him to the Laodiceans. Origen and Clement of Alexandria, and even Tertullian, who refers to Marcion, give no sanction to his notion. No single manuscript contains the heading, "to the saints that are at Laodicea." The very resemblance of the Epistle to the Ephesians, to that to the Colossians, is against the theory; for if the former were really the one addressed to Laodicea (Col. 4:16), Paul would not have deemed it necessary that the churches of Colosse and Laodicea should interchange Epistles. The greetings, moreover (Col. 4:15), which he sends through the Colossians to the Laodiceans, are quite incompatible with the idea that Paul wrote an Epistle to the Laodiceans at the same time, and by the same bearer, Tychicus (the bearer of our Epistle to the Ephesians, as well as of that to Colosse, Eph. 6:21; Col. 4:7); for who, under such circumstances, would not send the greetings directly in the letter to the party saluted? The letter to Laodicea was evidently written some time before that to Colosse.

Archbishop Ussher has advanced the second theory: That it was an encyclical letter headed, as in Manuscript B., "to the saints that are . . . and to the faithful," the name of each Church being inserted in the copy sent to it; and that its being sent to Ephesus first, occasioned its being entitled, as now, the

Epistle to the Ephesians. Alford makes the following objections to this theory:

It is at variance with the spirit of the Epistle, which is clearly addressed to one set of people throughout, co-existing in one place, and as one body, and under the same circumstances.

The improbability that the apostle, who in two of his Epistles (Second Corinthians and Galatians) has so plainly specified their encyclical character, should have here omitted such specification.

The still greater improbability that he should have, as on this hypothesis must be assumed, written a circular Epistle to a district, of which Ephesus was the commercial capital, addressed to various churches within that district, yet from its very contents (as by the opponents' hypothesis) not admitting of application to the Church of that metropolis, in which he had spent so long a time, and to which he was so affectionately bound.

The inconsistency of this hypothesis with the address of the Epistle, and the universal testimony of the ancient Church. The absence of personal greetings is not an argument for either of the two theories; for similarly there are none in Galatians, Philippians, First and Second Thessalonians, First Timothy. The better he knows the parties addressed, and the more general and solemn the subject, the less he seems to give of these individual notices. Writing, as he does in this Epistle, on the constitution and prospects of Christ's universal Church, he refers the Ephesians, as to personal matters, to the bearer of the Epistle, Tychicus (Eph. 6:21, 22). As to the omission of "which are at Ephesus" (Eph. 1:1), in Manuscript B., so "in Rome" (Rom. 1:7) is omitted in some old manuscripts: it was probably done by churches among whom it was read, in order to generalize the reference of its contents, and especially where the subject of the Epistle is catholic. The words are found in the margin of Manuscript B, from a first hand; and are found in all the oldest manuscripts and versions.

Paul and Ephesus

Paul's first visit to Ephesus (on the seacoast of Lydia, near the river Cayster) is related in Acts 18:19–21. The work, begun by his disputations with the Jews in his short visit, was carried on by Apollos (Acts 18:24–26), and Aquila and Priscilla (Acts 18:26). At his second visit, after his journey to Jerusalem, and from there to the east regions of Asia Minor, he remained at Ephesus "three years" (Acts 19:10, the "two years" in which verse are only part of the time, and Acts 20:31); so that the founding and rearing of this Church occupied an unusually large portion of the apostle's time and .care; hence his language in this Epistle shows a warmth of feeling, and a free outpouring of thought, and a union in spiritual privileges and hope between him and them (Eph. 1:3, etc.), such as are natural from one so long and so intimately associated with those whom he addresses. On his last journey to Jerusalem, he sailed by Ephesus and summoned the elders of the Ephesian Church to meet him at Miletus, where he delivered his remarkable farewell charge (Acts 20:18–35).

Date

This Epistle was addressed to the Ephesians during the early part of his imprisonment at Rome, immediately after that to the Colossians, to which it bears a close resemblance in many passages, the apostle having in his mind generally the same great truths in writing both. It is an undesigned proof of genuineness that the two Epistles, written about the same date, and under the same circumstances, bear a closer mutual resemblance than those written at distant dates and on different occasions.

Compare Eph. 1:7 with Col. 1:14; Eph. 1:10 with Col. 1:20; Eph. 3:2 with Col. 1:25; Eph. 5:19 with Col. 3:16; Eph. 6:22 with Col. 4:8; Eph. 1:19; 2:5 with Col. 2:12, 13; Eph. 4:2–4 with Col. 3:12–15; Eph. 4:16 with Col. 2:19; Eph. 4:32 with Col. 3:13; Eph. 4:22–24 with Col. 3:9, 10; Eph. 5:6–8 with Col. 3:6–8; Eph. 5:15, 16 with Col. 4:5; Eph. 6:19, 20 with Col. 4:3, 4; Eph. 5:22–33; 6:1–9 with Col. 3:18; Eph. 4:24, 25 with Col. 3:9; Eph. 5:20–22 with Col. 3:17, 18.

Tychicus and Onesimus were being sent to Colosse, the former bearing the two Epistles to the two churches respectively, the latter furnished with a letter of recommendation to Philemon, his former master, residing at Colosse. The date was probably about four years after his parting with the Ephesian elders at Miletus (Acts 20:6–38), about A.D. 62, before his imprisonment had become of the more severe kind, which appears in his Epistle to the Philippians. From Eph. 6:19, 20 it is plain he had at the time, though a prisoner, some degree of freedom in preaching, which accords with Acts 28:23, 30, 31, where he is represented as receiving at his lodgings all inquirers. His imprisonment began in February A.D. 61 and lasted "two whole years" (Acts 28:30) at least, and perhaps longer.

The Ephesian church

The Church of Ephesus was made up of converts partly from the Jews and partly from the Gentiles (Acts 19:8–10). Accordingly, the Epistle so addresses a Church constituted (Eph. 2:14–22). Ephesus was famed for its idol temple of Artemis or Diana, which, after its having been burnt down by Herostratus on the night that Alexander the Great was born (355 B.C.), was rebuilt at enormous cost and was one of the wonders of the world. Hence, perhaps, have arisen his images in this Epistle drawn from a beautiful temple: the Church being in true inner beauty that which the temple of the idol tried to realize in outward show (Eph. 2:19–22). The Epistle (Eph. 4:17; 5:1–13) implies the profligacy for which the Ephesian heathen were notorious. Many of the same expressions occur in the Epistle as in Paul's address to the Ephesian elders. Compare Eph. 1:6, 7; 2:7, as to "grace," with Acts 20:24, 32: this may well be called "the Epistle of the grace of God" (Alford). Also, as to his "bonds," Eph. 3:1, and 4:1 with Acts 20:22, 23. Also Eph. 1:11, as to "the counsel of God," with Acts 20:27. Also Eph. 1:14, as to "the redemption of the purchased possession," with Acts 20:28. Also Eph. 1:14, 18; 2:20; 5:5, as to "building up" the "inheritance," with Acts 20:32.

Purpose of letter

The object of the Epistle is "to set forth the ground, the course, and the aim and end of the church of the faithful in Christ. He speaks to the Ephesians as a type or sample of the Church universal" (Alford). Hence, "the Church" throughout the Epistle is spoken of in the singular, not in the plural, "churches." The Church's foundation, its course, and its end, are his theme alike in the larger and smaller divisions of the whole Epistle. "Everywhere the foundation of the Church is in the will of the Father; the course of the Church is by the satisfaction of the Son; the end of the Church is the life in the Holy Spirit" (Alford). Compare respectively Eph. 1:11; 2:5; 3:16. This having been laid down as a matter of doctrine (this part closing with a sublime doxology, Eph. 3:14–21), is then made the ground of practical exhortations. In these latter also (from Eph. 4:1, onward), the same threefold division prevails, for the Church is represented as founded on the counsel of "God the Father, who is above all, through all, and in all," reared by the "one Lord," Jesus Christ, through the "one Spirit" (Eph. 4:4–6, etc.), who give their respective graces to the several members. These last are therefore to exercise all these graces in the several relations of life, as husbands, wives, servants, children, etc. The conclusion is that we must put on "the whole armor of God" (Eph. 6:13).

Style

The sublimity of the style and language corresponds to the sublimity of the subjects and exceeds almost that of any part of his Epistles. It is appropriate that those to whom he so wrote were Christians long grounded in the faith. The very sublimity is the cause of the difficulty of the style, and of the presence of peculiar expressions occurring, not found elsewhere.

A. R. Faussett

Detailed outline

Part One: Our Wealth In Christ 1:1–3:21

I. Introduction: 1:1–2
- A. From Paul: 1:1
- B. To the saints at Ephesus: 1:1
- C. Grace and peace from God and Jesus: 1:2

II. Praise for spiritual possession: 1:3–14
- A. He has chosen us: 1:4
- B. He has predestined us: 1:5–6
- C. We have redemption in Him: 1:7
- D. He shows wisdom towards us: 1:8
- E. He reveals the mystery of His will: 1:9–10
- F. In Him we have obtained an inheritance: 1:11–12
- G. We have been sealed by the Spirit: 1:13–14

III. Prayer for spiritual perception through Christ: 1:15–23
- A. The basis of the prayer: 1:15
- B. The nature of the prayer: 1:16
- C. The God addressed by the prayer: 1:17
- D. The gifts requested in the prayer: 1:17
  1. Wisdom.
  2. Revelation in the knowledge of Him.
- E. The purpose of the prayer: 1:18–23

1. That they may realize the hope of His calling: 1:18
2. That they may receive the riches of His inheritance: 1:18
3. That they may know His power: 1:19–23
   (a) The nature of His power: 1:19
   (b) The manifestation of His power in Christ: 1:20–23

IV. Our condition in Christ: 2:1–10
  A. Before Christ: 2:1–3
  B. Our new condition in Christ: 2:4–10
  C. The reason for the new condition: 2:8–10
    1. Salvation which is: 2:8
      (a) By faith: 2:8
      (b) A gift of God: 2:8
    2. Salvation which is not: 2:8–9
      (a) Of ourselves: 2:8
      (b) Of works: 2:9
    3. The continual working of Christ Jesus in our lives: 2:10

V. Our old relationship: 2:11–12

VI. The new relationship: 2:19–22

VII. How the change happened: 2:13–18

VIII. Revealing the divine mystery: 3:1–13
  A. Paul as a messenger of the mystery: 3:1–13
    1. His relation to the mystery: 3:1–5
      (a) His position as prisoner on behalf of the Gentiles: 3:1
      (b) His stewardship of God's grace towards the Gentiles: 3:2
      (c) His knowledge of the mystery by revelation: 3:3–5
    2. Statement of the mystery: 3:6
    3. Paul's ministry in connection with this mystery: 3:7–12
      (a) The source of his ministry: 3:7
      (b) The attitude of one given this ministry: 3:8
      (c) The contents of the ministry: 3:8–9
      (d) The purpose of the ministry: 3:10–11
      (e) The blessings of the ministry: 3:12
      (f) The sufferings of the ministry: 3:13

IX. Possessing the divine mystery: 3:14–21
  A. Introduction to the prayer for possession: 3:14–15
  B. The request: 3:16–17
    1. That they might be strengthened by the Spirit: 3:16
    2. That they might experience the presence of Christ: 3:17
    3. That they will be rooted and grounded in love: 3:17
    4. That they will know about the love of Christ: 3:18–19
      (a) Its boundaries: 3:18
      (b) Its divine nature: 3:19
    5. That they might be filled with the fullness of God: 3:19
  C. Conclusion of the prayer: 3:20–21
    1. The ability of the One addressed: 3:20
    2. Praise to the One addressed: 3:21

Part Two: Our Walk In Christ 4:1–6:24

I. The corporate walk of the church: Walk worthy: 4:1–16
  A. Through proper attitude: 4:2

B. Through unity: 4:3–6
1. In peace: 4:3
2. In one body: 4:4
3. In one spirit: 4:4
4. In one hope of your calling: 4:4
5. In one Lord: 4:5
6. In one faith: 4:5
7. In one baptism: 4:5
8. In one God: 4:6
C. By following the example of Christ: 4:7–10
D. Through proper structure: 4:11–13
1. Spiritual gifts: 4:11
(a) Apostles.
(b) Prophets.
(c) Evangelists.
(d) Pastors.
(e) Teachers.
2. Their purposes: 4:12–16
E. By becoming part of the Body: 4:16
1. Joined together.
2. Each part of the body functioning in its place.
3. Increasing through the edification of love.
II. The individual walk of believers: 4:17–5:2
A. How not to walk: 4:17–25
B. How to walk: 4:20–5:2
III. Our walk in relation to the world: 5:2–21
A. Walk in love following Christ's example: 5:2
B. Walk in holiness: 5:3–5
C. Walk with eternity in mind: 5:5
D. Do not be deceived with vain words: 5:6
E. Do not form evil alliances: 5:7
F. Walk in the light: 5:8
G. Develop the fruit of the Spirit: 5:9
H. Prove what is acceptable unto the Lord: 5:10
I. Do not walk in darkness: 5:11–14
J. Walk as the wise, not as fools: 5:15
K. Redeem the time: 5:16
L. Understand God's will: 5:17
M. Do not be drunk with wine: 5:18
N. Be filled with the Spirit: 5:18
1. Speak in psalms, hymns, and spiritual songs: 5:19
2. Make music in your heart: 5:19
3. Giving thanks for all things to God in the name of Jesus: 5:20
IV. Our walk in regards to special relationships: 5:21–6:9
A. Other believers: Submit yourselves in the fear of God: 5:21
B. Wives: 5:22–24
1. Submit yourselves unto your own husband as unto the Lord: 5:22
2. Recognize the husband is the head of the wife: 5:23
3. Be subject to husbands as the Church is subject to Christ: 5:24
C. Husbands: 5:25–33
1. Love your wives as Christ loved the church: 5:25–29
2. Be joined to your wife as the Church is joined to Christ: 5:30–33
(a) One body: 5:30
(b) Forsaking all others: 5:31–32
D. To both husband and wife: 5:33
1. Husband love your wife as yourself: 5:33
2. Wife reverence your husband: 5:33

E. Children: Honor your parents: 6:1–3

F. Fathers: 6:4

1. Do not provoke your children to wrath.
2. Bring them up in the instruction of the Lord.

G. Servants: 6:5–8

1. Be obedient to your masters: 6:5
2. Have an attitude of respect: 6:5
3. Be loyal: 6:5
4. Serve them as you are serving Christ: 6:6–7
5. Recognize your reward comes from the Lord: 6:8

H. Masters: 6:9

V. Our walk as it regards Satanic powers: 6:10–20

A. Be strong in the Lord and the power of His might: 6:10

B. Put on the whole armor of God: 6:11–20

1. The purpose: That you are able to stand against Satan: 6:11, 13
2. The enemy: 6:12
   (a) Principalities.
   (b) Powers.
   (c) Rulers of the darkness of this world.
   (d) Spiritual wickedness in high places.
3. The armor: 6:14–20
   (a) Belt of truth: 6:14
   (b) Breastplate of righteousness: 6:14
   (c) Feet fitted with the Gospel of peace: 6:15
   (d) The shield of faith: 6:16
   (e) The helmet of salvation: 6:16
   (f) The sword of the Spirit: 6:17
   (g) Prayer: 6:18–20

VI. Conclusion: 6:21–24

A. Personal matters: 6:21–22

1. Commissioning of Tychicus as messenger: 6:21
2. The purpose of sending Tychicus to them: 6:21–22
   (a) To make known the message: 6:21–22
   (b) To inform of Paul's affairs: 6:22
   (c) To comfort them: 6:22

B. The conclusion: 6:23–24

1. Paul's prayer for the brethren: 6:23
   (a) Peace.
   (b) Love.
   (c) Faith.
2. The blessing on those loving Christ: 6:24

2. Helpful summaries of Ephesians

Bird's eye view

Paul states that God's instrument in the world is the Christian church and reminds his readers that they are to exult the name of Jesus.

Reading plan

The following reading plan, taking one reading per day, enables you to read through Ephesians in six days.

Ephesians 1:1–1:23
Ephesians 2:1–2:22
Ephesians 3:1–3:21
Ephesians 4:1–4:32
Ephesians 5:1–5:33
Ephesians 6:1–6:24

Verses to memorize

Ephesians 2:8

For by grace are ye saved through faith; and that not of yourselves: it is the gift of God: KJV

Ephesians 4:1–3

I therefore, the prisoner of the Lord, beseech you that ye walk worthy of the vocation wherewith ye are called, With all lowliness and meekness, with longsuffering, forbearing one another in love; Endeavoring to keep the unity of the Spirit in the bond of peace. KJV

Ephesians 4:32

And be ye kind one to another, tenderhearted, forgiving one another, even as God for Christ's sake hath forgiven you. KJV

Ephesians 6:10–11

Finally, my brethren, be strong in the Lord, and in the power of his might.

Put on the whole armor of God, that ye may be able to stand against the wiles of the devil. KJV

Statistics

Tenth New Testament book

Fifth letter by the apostle Paul

6 chapters

155 verses

3,039 words

Number of Old Testament quotations and allusions in Ephesians: 11.

Names/titles given

Pros Ephesious: "To the Ephesians."

3. Helpful keys to turn to in understanding Ephesians

Key word

Fullness

Key verse/verses

Ephesians 1:3; 4:1–3

Themes to study

Grace

Conflict and spiritual warfare

Unity and relationships

Jesus in Ephesians

In Ephesians Jesus raises us and seats us with him.

Lessons to learn from Ephesians

Satan is alive and well, and all his activities should be resisted.

As we are members of God's family we should behave so that we bring credit to our heavenly Father.

4. Chapter by chapter: outline of every chapter of Ephesians

Ephesians 1

Matthew Henry's introduction

In this chapter we have,

I. The introduction to the whole epistle, which is much the same as in others, vv. 1, 2.

II. The apostle's thanksgivings and praises to God for his inestimable blessings bestowed on the believing Ephesians, vv. 3–14.

III. His earnest prayers to God in their behalf, vv. 15–23. This great apostle was wont to abound in prayers and in thanksgivings to almighty God, which he generally so disposes and orders that at the same time they carry with them and convey the great and important doctrines of the Christian religion, and the most weighty instructions to all those who seriously peruse them.

Dr. Adam Clarke's analysis of chapter

The apostle's salutation to the Church, 1, 2.

He blesses God for calling the Gentiles to the adoption of children by Jesus Christ, by whose sacrificial death both they and the Jews find redemption, 3–7.

He shows that it was through the great abundance of God's wisdom and goodness that the Gentiles were called into a state of salvation, and that they should receive the Holy Spirit as the earnest of their inheritance, 8–15.

He praises God for their conversion, and prays that they may be farther enlightened, that they may see the glory of Christ, and partake of the blessings procured by his passion and exaltation, 16–23.

A detailed analysis of chapter

A greeting, and an account of saving blessings, prepared in God's eternal election, and bought by Christ's blood. (1–8)

Open to Jews and Gentiles. (9–14)

Prayer for spiritual enlightenment. (15–23)

Key verse

Verse 4: "For he chose us in him before the creation of the world to be holy and blameless in his sight."

Key word / key phrase

Verse 3, "every spiritual blessing."

Key event / key person / key theme

Spiritual blessings in Christ

Key thought

"This is your wonderful spiritual inheritance."

Key thing to look out for

Nobody knows Jesus fully. Paul stresses the need to press on and know him more and more.

Key Bible cross-reference

Verse 1. See Acts 18:19–21.

Key "by way of explanation"

Verse 7, "In him we have redemption." The idea of redemption was not unfamiliar to the Ephesians who knew all about a ransom being paid as the price for redeeming a slave. Sinners were to be freed now that Christ had paid the ransom price for sin by his death on the cross.

Key "Quotable Quote"

"The riches of the glory of his inheritance in the saints. Besides the heavenly inheritance prepared for the saints, there is a present inheritance in the saints; for grace is glory begun, and holiness is happiness in the bud. There is a glory in this inheritance, riches of glory, rendering the Christian more excellent and more truly honorable than all about him: and it is desirable to know this experimentally, to be acquainted with the principles, pleasures, and powers, of the spiritual and divine life."

Matthew Henry

Ephesians 2

Matthew Henry's introduction

This chapter contains an account,

I. Of the miserable condition of these Ephesians by nature (vv. 1–3) and again, vv. 11, 12.

II. Of the glorious change that was wrought in them by converting grace (vv. 4–10) and again, v. 13.

III. Of the great and mighty privileges that both converted Jews and Gentiles receive from Christ, vv. 14–22. The apostle endeavors to affect them with a due sense of the wonderful change which divine grace had wrought in them; and this is very applicable to that great change which the same grace works in all those who are brought into a state of grace. So that we have here a lively picture both of the misery of unregenerate men and of the happy condition of converted souls, enough to awaken and alarm those who are yet in their sins and to put them on hastening out of that state, and to comfort and delight those whom God hath quickened, with a consideration of the mighty privileges with which they are invested.

Dr. Adam Clarke's analysis of chapter

The character of the Ephesians previously to their conversion to Christianity, 1–3.

By what virtue they were changed, and for what purpose, 4–7.

They were saved by faith, 8,9.

And created unto good works, 10.

The apostle enters into the particulars of their former miserable state, 11,12.

And those of their present happy state, 13.

Christ has broken down the middle wall of partition between the Jews and Gentiles, and proclaims reconciliation to both, 14–17.

The glorious privileges of genuine believers, 18–22.

A detailed analysis of chapter

The riches of God's grace toward men and women. This is seen in the dreadful state that they are naturally in, and by the happy change divine grace makes in them. (1–10)

The Ephesians called to reflect on their pre-Christian state. (11–13)

And the privileges and blessings of the gospel. (14–22)

Key verse

Verse 10: "For we are God's workmanship, created in Christ Jesus to do good works, which God prepared in advance for us to do."

Key word / key phrase

Verse 6, "God raised us up."

Key event / key person / key theme

The resurrection life and unity

Key thought

The fact that salvation is a gift, and is not dependent on who I am, or what I have achieved. This is utterly liberating.

Key thing to look out for

Verse 4, the reason why God saved us.

Key Bible cross-reference

Verse 17. See Isaiah 57:19.

Key "by way of explanation"

Verse 21, "joined together." Christians belong to Jesus. They are also linked up with all other followers of Jesus, and in this sense, are "joined together." Paul spells out the consequences of this.

Key "Quotable Quote"

"The work of redemption, including its purpose, method and result, could hardly be stated in clearer language than this."

Paton A. Gloag

Ephesians 3

Matthew Henry's introduction

This chapter consists of two parts.

I. Of the account which Paul gives the Ephesians about himself, as he was appointed by God to be the apostle of the Gentiles, vv. 1–13.

II. Of his devout and affectionate prayer to God for the Ephesians, vv. 14–21. We may observe it to have been very much the practice of this apostle to intermix, with his instructions and counsels, intercessions and prayers to God for those to whom he wrote, as knowing that all his instructions and teachings would be useless and vain, except God did co-operate with them, and render them effectual. This is an example that all the ministers of Christ should copy after, praying earnestly that the efficacious operations of the divine Spirit may attend their ministrations, and crown them with success.

Dr. Adam Clarke's analysis of chapter

Paul, a prisoner for the testimony of Jesus, declares his knowledge of what had been a mystery from all ages, that the Gentiles should be fellow heirs and of the same body with the Jews, 1–6.

Which doctrine he was made a minister, that he might declare the unsearchable riches of Christ, and make known to principalities and powers this eternal purpose of God, 7–12.

He desires them not to be discouraged on account of his tribulations, 13.

His prayer that they might be filled with all the fullness of God, 14–19.

His doxology, 20, 21.

A detailed analysis of chapter

The apostle states the scope of his ministry, and his qualifications and call for this. (1–7)

God's wisdom has been made known. (8–13)

He prays for the Ephesians. (14–19)

And adds a thanksgiving. (20,21)

Key verse

Verse 12: "In him and through faith in him we may approach God with freedom and confidence."

Key word / key phrase

Verse 4, "insight into the mystery of Christ."

Key event / key person / key theme

A revealed mystery

Key thought

Paul never tires of calling himself a servant.

Key thing to look out for

Paul tells the Ephesians what he prays for them.

Key Bible cross-reference

Verses 4–6. See Colossians 1:26,27.

Key "by way of explanation"

Verse 19, "surpasses knowledge." Paul is not saying that it is impossible to know anything about the Christian faith. But he is saying that it is so profound that nobody fully comprehends it.

Key "Quotable Quote"

"Everything a theologian does in the Church contributes to the spread of the knowledge of God and the salvation of men."

Martin Luther

Ephesians 4

Matthew Henry's introduction

We have gone through the former part of this epistle, which consists of several important doctrinal truths, contained in the three preceding chapters. We enter now on the latter part of it, in which we have the most weighty and serious exhortations that can be given. We may observe that in this, as in most others of Paul's epistles, the former part is doctrinal, and fitted to inform the minds of men in the great truths and doctrines of the gospel, the latter is practical, and designed for the direction of their lives and manners, all Christians being bound to endeavor after soundness in the faith, and regularity in life and practice. In what has gone before we have heard of Christian privileges, which are the matter of our comfort. In what follows we shall hear of Christian duties, and what the Lord our God requires of us in consideration of such privileges vouchsafed to us. The best way to understand the mysteries and partake of the privileges of which we have read before is conscientiously to practice the duties prescribed to us in what follows: as, on the other hand, a serious consideration and belief of the doctrines that have been taught us in the previous chapters will be a good foundation on which to build the practice of the duties prescribed in those which are yet before us. Christian faith and Christian practice mutually befriend each other. In this chapter we have divers exhortations to important duties.

I. One that is more general, v. 1.

II. An exhortation to mutual love, unity, and concord, with the proper means and motives to promote them, vv. 2–16.

III. An exhortation to Christian purity and holiness of life; and that both more general (vv. 17–24) and in several particular instances, v. 25, to the end.

Dr. Adam Clarke's analysis of chapter

The apostle exhorts them to walk worthy of their vocation, and to live in peace and unity, 1–6.

Shows that God has distributed a variety of

gifts, and instituted a variety of offices in his Church, for the building up and perfecting of the body of Christ, 7–13.

Teaches them the necessity of being well instructed and steady in Divine things, 14.

Teaches how the body or Church of Christ is constituted, 15, 16.

Warns them against acting like the Gentiles, of whose conduct he gives a lamentable description, 17–19.

Points out how they had been changed, in consequence of their conversion to Christianity, 20, 21.

Gives various exhortations relative to the purification of their minds, their conduct to each other, and to the poor, 22–28.

Shows them that their conversation should be chaste and holy, that they might not grieve the Spirit of God; that they should avoid all bad tempers, be kindly affectioned one to another, and be of a forgiving spirit, 29–32.

A detailed analysis of chapter

Exhortations to be loving and united. (1–6)

To an awareness and use of spiritual gifts and graces. (7–16)

To purity and holiness. (17–24)

And to beware of the sins practiced by the heathen. (25–32)

Key verse

Verse 14: "Then we will no longer be infants, tossed back and forth by the waves, and blown here and there by every wind of teaching and by the cunning and craftiness of men in their deceitful scheming."

Key word / key phrase

Verse 16, "joined and held together."

Key event / key person / key theme

The nature of the Christian Church

Key thought

The gifts bestowed on us by the ascended Christ.

Key thing to look out for

What we are to put on and put off.

Key Bible cross-reference

Verse 8. See Psalm 68:18.

Key "by way of explanation"

Verse 17, "futility of their thinking." Non-Christians, no matter how clever they are, possess unenlightened minds. In this sense they will die in the "futility of their thinking." For any life without God is ultimately meaningless and far from being intellectually satisfying.

Key "Quotable Quote"

"No one can get anything out of life without God."

Meister Eckhart

Ephesians 5

Matthew Henry's introduction

We had several important exhortations in the close of the previous chapter, and they are continued in this: particularly,

I. We have here an exhortation to mutual love and charity, vv. 1, 2.

II. Against all manner of uncleanness, with proper arguments and remedies proposed against such sins: and some further cautions are added, and other duties recommended, vv. 3–20.

III. The apostle directs to the conscientious discharge of relative duties, from v. 21, throughout this, and in the beginning of the next chapter.

Dr. Adam Clarke's analysis of chapter

Christians should imitate their heavenly Father, and walk in love, after the example of Christ, 1, 2.

They should avoid all uncleanness, impurity, covetousness, and foolish jesting, and idolatry, because these things exclude from the kingdom of God, 3–7.

The Ephesians were once in darkness, but being now light in the Lord, they are exhorted to walk in that light, and bring forth the fruits of the Spirit; and to have no fellowship with the workers of iniquity, whose evil deeds are manifested by the light, 8–13.

All are exhorted to awake; to walk circum spectly; to redeem the time; and to learn what the will of the Lord is, 14–17.

The apostle gives particular directions relative to avoiding excess of wine, 18.

To singing and giving thanks, 19, 20.

Submission to each other, 21.

To husbands that they should love their wives, as Christ loved the Church; for by the marriage union, the union between Christ and the Church is pointed out; and wives are exhorted to reverence their husbands, 22–33.

A detailed analysis of chapter

Exhortation to brotherly love. (1, 2)

Warns against several sins. (3–14)

Instructions about living in a different way. (15–21)

The duties of wives and husbands are underlined by reference to the spiritual relationship between Christ and the Church. (22–33)

Key verse

Verse 11: "Have nothing to do with the fruitless deeds of darkness, but rather expose them."

Key word / key phrase

Verse 14, "wake up."

Key event / key person / key theme

Challenging evil; wives and husbands

Key thought

Christians are God's dearly loved children.

Key thing to look out for

Paul unpacks what it means to live as children of light.

Key Bible cross-reference

Verse 2. See Exodus 29:18.

Key "by way of explanation"

Verse 8, "darkness . . . light." Paul frequently uses such contrasts in his letters. Christians are to be full of light because God is light.

Key "Quotable Quote"

"Give light, and the darkness will disappear of itself."

Desiderius Erasmus

Ephesians 6

Matthew Henry's introduction

In this chapter,

I. The apostle proceeds in the exhortation to relative duties which he began in the former, particularly he insists on the duties of children and parents, and of servants and masters, vv. 1–9.

II. He exhorts and directs Christians how to behave themselves in the spiritual warfare with the enemies of their souls; and to the exercise of several Christian graces, which he proposes to them as so many pieces of spiritual armor, to preserve and defend them in the conflict, vv. 10–18.

III. We have here the conclusion of the epistle, in which he takes his leave of them, recommending himself to the prayers of the believing Ephesians, and praying for them, vv. 19–24.

Dr. Adam Clarke's analysis of chapter

Children should obey their parents, that they may live long and be happy, 1–3.

Parents should be tender towards their children, 4.

Servants should show all obedience and fidelity to their masters, 5–8.

And masters should treat their servants with humanity, 9.

All should be strong in the Lord, and be armed with his armor, because of their wily, powerful, and numerous foes, 10–13.

The different parts of the Christian armor enumerated, 14–17.

The necessity of all kinds of prayer and watchfulness, 18–20.

Tychicus is commissioned to inform the Ephesians of the apostle's affairs, 21, 22.

The apostolic benediction and farewell, 23, 24.

A detailed analysis of chapter

The duties of children and parents. (1–4)

The duties of servants and masters. (5–9)

All Christians are to put on spiritual armor against the enemy of their souls. (10–18)

The apostle seeks their prayers, and ends with his apostolic blessing. (19–24)

Key verse

Verse 11: "Put on the full armor of God so that you can take your stand against the devil's schemes."

Key word / key phrase

Verse 11, "Put on the full armor of God."

Key event / key person / key theme

Fighting the spiritual battle

Key thought

The Christian is able to obey, fight and win because of God's mighty power (verse 10).

Key thing to look out for

Note the power of God's armor.

Key Bible cross-reference

Verse 17. See Isaiah 59:17.

Key "by way of explanation"

Verse 12, "not against flesh and blood." Sometimes it must have seemed to Paul that he spent all his life fending off those who attacked him. But here Paul points to the source of such attacks and all evil. So he warns not so much about "flesh and blood" but about "the powers of the dark world."

Key "Quotable Quote"

"To remove warfare from a spiritual life is to render it unspiritual."

Watchman Nee

5. Select bibliography for Ephesians

Bruce, F. F. *The Epistles to the Colossians, to Philemon, and to the Ephesians*. Grand Rapids: Eerdmans, 1984.

Hendriksen, William. *Ephesians*. Grand Rapids: Baker, 1967.

Moule, H. C. G. *The Epistle to the Ephesians*. Cambridge: University Press, 1887.

Robinson, J. Armitage. *St. Paul's Epistle to the Ephesians*. London: Macmillan, 1903.

Simpson, E. K. and Bruce, F. F. *Commentary on the Epistles to the Ephesians and the Colossians*. London: Marshall, Morgan and Scott, 1957.

Stott, J. R. W. *The Message of Ephesians: God's New Society*. Downers Grove: Inter-Varsity, 1979.

Philippians

1. Book by book: Introduction to Philippians

Introduction

Author

The internal evidence for the authenticity of this Epistle is strong. The style, manner of thought, and doctrine, accord with Paul's. The incidental allusions also establish his authorship. Paley (*Horæ Paulinæ,* ch. 7) instances the mention of the object of Epaphroditus' journey to Rome, the Philippian contribution to Paul's wants, Epaphroditus' sickness (Phil. 1:7; 2:25–30; 4:10–18), the fact that Timothy had been long with Paul at Philippi (Phil. 1:1; 2:19), the reference to his being a prisoner at Rome now for a long time (Phil. 1:12–14; 2:17–28), his willingness to die (compare Phil. 1:23, with 2 Cor. 5:8), the reference to the Philippians having seen his maltreatment at Philippi (Phil. 1:29, 30; 2:1, 2).

The external evidence is equally decisive: Polycarp (*Epistle to the Philippians*, 3; 11); Irenaeus (*Against Heresies,* 4.18.4); Clement of Alexandria (*The Instructor,* 1.1, p. 107); Eusebius (The Epistle of the Churches of Lyons and Vienne, in *Ecclesiastical History,* 5. 2); Tertullian (*On the Resurrection of the Flesh,* 23); Origen (*Against Celsus,* 1.3, p. 122); Cyprian (*Testimonies against the Jews,* 3.39).

Philippi

Philippi was the first (that is, the farthest from Rome, and first which met Paul in entering Macedonia) Macedonian city of the district, called Macedonia Prima (so called as lying farthest eastward). The Greek (Acts 16:12) should not be translated "the chief city," as English Version, but as above (Alford). Not it, but Thessalonica, was the chief city of the province, and Amphipolis, of the district called Macedonia Prima. It was a Roman "colony" (Acts 16:12), made so by Augustus, to commemorate his famous victory over Brutus and Cassius. A colony was in fact a portion of Rome itself transplanted to the provinces, an offshoot from Rome, and as it were a portrait of the mother city on a small scale. Its inhabitants were Roman citizens, having the right of voting in the Roman tribes, governed by their own senate and magistrates, and not by the governor of the province, with the Roman law and Latin language.

Paul and Pilippi

Paul, with Silas and Timothy, planted the Gospel there (Acts 16:12, etc.), in his second missionary journey, A.D. 51. Doubtless he visited it again on his journey from Ephesus into Macedonia (Acts 20:1); and Acts 20:3, 6, expressly mentions his third visit on his return from Greece (Corinth) to Syria by way of Macedonia. His sufferings at Philippi (Acts 16:19, etc.) strengthened the Christian bond between him and his Philippian converts, who also, like him, were exposed to trials for the Gospel's sake (1 Thess. 2:2). They alone sent supplies for his temporal needs, twice shortly after he had left them (Phil. 4:15, 16), and again a third time shortly before writing this Epistle (Phil. 4:10, 18; 2 Cor. 11:9). This fervent attachment on their part was, perhaps, also in part due to the fact that few Jews were in Philippi, as in other scenes of his labors, to sow the seeds of distrust and suspicion. There was no synagogue, but merely a Jewish Proseucha, or oratory, by the riverside. So that there only do we read of his meeting no opposition from Jews, but only from the masters of the divining damsel, whose gains had been put an end to by her being dispossessed.

The Philippian Church

Though the Philippian Church was as yet free from Judaizing influence, yet it needed to be forewarned of that danger which might at any time assail it from without (Phil. 3:2); even as such evil influences had crept into the Galatian churches. In Phil. 4:2, 3 we find a trace of the fact recorded in the history (Acts 16:13, 14), that female converts were among the first to receive the Gospel at Philippi.

As to the state of the Church, we gather from 2 Cor. 8:1, 2 that its members were poor, yet most liberal; and from Phil. 1:28–30, that they were undergoing persecution. The only blemish referred to in their character was, on the part of some members, a tendency to dissension. Hence arise his admonitions against disputings (Phil. 1:27; 2:1–4, 12, 14; 4:2).

Purpose of letter

The object of the Epistle is general: not only to thank the Philippians for their contribution sent by Epaphroditus, who was now in returning to take back the apostle's letter, but to express his Christian love and sympathy, and to exhort them to a life consonant with that of Christ, and to warn them against existing dissensions and future possible assaults of Judaizers from without. It is remarkable in this Epistle alone, as compared with the others, that, among many commendations, there are no express censures of those to whom it is addressed. No doctrinal error, or schism, has as yet sprung up; the only blemish hinted at is, that some of the Philippian Church were somewhat lacking humility which resulted in an argument. Two women, Euodias and Syntyche, are mentioned in this respect (Phil. 4:2, 3).

Contents

The Epistle may be divided into three parts:

Affectionate address to the Philippians; reference to his own state as a prisoner at Rome, and to theirs, and to his mission of Epaphroditus to them (the first and second chapters). Epaphroditus probably held a leading office in the Philippian Church, perhaps as a presbyter. After Tychicus and Onesimus had departed (A.D. 62), carrying the Epistles to the Ephesians, Colossians, and Philemon, Paul was cheered in his imprisonment by the arrival of Epaphroditus with the Philippian contribution. That faithful "brother, companion in labor, and fellow soldier" (Phil. 2:25), had brought on himself by the fatigues of the journey a dangerous sickness (Phil. 2:26, 30). But now that he was recovered, he "longed" (Phil. 2:26) to return to his Philippian flock, and in person to relieve their anxiety on his behalf, in respect to his sickness; and the apostle gladly availed himself of the opportunity of writing to them a letter of grateful acknowledgments and Christian exhortations.

Caution against Judaizing teachers, supported by reference to his own former and present feeling towards Jewish legalism (Phil. 3:1–21).

Admonitions to individuals, and to the Church in general, thanks for their seasonable aid, and concluding benedictions and greetings (Phil. 4:1–23).

Place of writing

This Epistle was written from Rome during the imprisonment, the beginning of which is related in Acts 28:16, 20, 30, 31. The reference to "Cæsar's household" (Phil. 4:22), and to the "palace" (Phil. 1:13, Greek, "Prætorium," probably, the barrack of the Prætorian bodyguard, attached to the palace of Nero) confirms this. It must have been during his first imprisonment at Rome, for the mention of the Prætorium agrees with the fact that it was during his first imprisonment he was in the custody of the Prætorian Prefect, and his situation, described in Phil. 1:12–14, agrees with his situation in the first two years of his imprisonment (Acts 28:30, 31).

The following reasons show, moreover, that it was written towards the close of that imprisonment: He, in it, expresses his expectation of the immediate decision of his cause (Phil. 2:23).

Enough time had elapsed for the Philippians to hear of his imprisonment, to send Epaphroditus to him, to hear of Epaphroditus' arrival and sickness, and send back word to Rome of their distress (Phil. 2:26).

It must have been written after the three other Epistles sent from Rome, namely, Colossians, Ephesians, and Philemon; for Luke is no longer with him (Phil. 2:20); otherwise he would have been specified as saluting them, having formerly labored among them, whereas he is mentioned as with him, Col. 4:14; Phile. 24. Again, in Eph. 6:19, 20, his freedom to preach is implied: but in Phil. 1:13–18, his bondage is dwelt on, and it is implied that, not himself, but others, preached, and made his imprisonment known. Again, in Phile. 22, he confidently anticipates his release, which contrasts with the more depressed anticipations of this Epistle.

A considerable time had elapsed since the beginning of his imprisonment, for "his bonds" to have become so widely known, and to have produced such good effects for the Gospel (Phil. 1:13).

There is evidently an increase in the rigor of his imprisonment implied now, as compared with the early stage of it, as described in Acts 28:1–31; compare Phil. 1:29, 30; 2:27. History furnishes a probable clue to account for this increase of vigor. In the second year of Paul's imprisonment (A.D. 62), Burrus, the Prætorian Prefect, to whose custody he had been committed (Acts 28:16, "the captain of the guard"), died; and Nero the emperor having divorced Octavia, and married Poppoea, a Jewish proselytess (who then caused her rival, Octavia, to be murdered, and gloated over the head of her victim), exalted Tigellinus, the chief promoter of the marriage, a monster of wickedness, to the Prætorian Prefecture. It was then he seems to have been removed from his own house into the Prætorium, or barrack of the Prætorian guards, attached to the palace, for stricter custody; and hence he writes with less hopeful anticipations as to the result of his trial (Phil. 2:17; 3:11). Some of the Prætorian guards who had the custody of him before, would then naturally make known his "bonds," in accordance with Phil. 1:13; from the smaller Prætorian bodyguard at the palace the report would spread to the general permanent Prætorian camp, which Tiberius had established north of the city, outside of the walls. He had arrived in Rome, February, 61; the "two whole years (Acts 20:30) in his own hired house" ended February, 63, so that the date of this Epistle, written shortly after, evidently while the danger was imminent, would be about spring or summer, 63. The providence of God averted the danger. He probably was thought beneath the notice of Tigellinus, who was more intent on court intrigues. The death of Nero's favorite, Pallas, the brother of Felix, this same year, also took out of the way another source of danger.

Style

The style is abrupt and discontinuous, his fervor of affection leading him to pass rapidly from one theme to another (Phil. 2:18, 19–24, 25–30; 3:1, 2, 3, 4–14, 15). In no Epistle does he use so warm expressions of love. In Phil. 4:1 he seems at a loss for words sufficient to express all the extent and ardor of his affection for the Philippians: "My brethren dearly beloved and longed for, my joy and crown, so stand fast in the Lord, my dearly beloved." The mention of bishops and deacons in Phil. 1:1 is due to the late date of the Epistle, at a time when the Church had begun to assume that order which is laid down in the Pastoral Epistles, and which continued the prevalent one in the first and purest age of the Church.

A. R. Faussett

Detailed outline

I. Introduction: 1:1–26
  A. Greeting: 1:1–2
    1. From Paul and Timotheus: 1:1
    2. To: Saints in Christ Jesus, overseers, and deacons at Philippi: 1:1
    3. Grace and peace: 1:2
  B. Prayer for Philippians: 1:3–11
    1. His thanksgiving for them: 1:3–5
      (a) Motivation for thanksgiving: 1:3
      (b) Expression of thanksgiving: 1:4
      (c) Cause for thanksgiving: 1:5
    2. His confidence in them: 1:6–7
      (a) The nature of the confidence: 1:6
      (b) The justification for this confidence: 1:7
    3. His longing: 1:8
    4. His prayer for them: 1:9–11
      (a) That love may abound in knowledge and judgment: 1:9
      (b) That you have discernment: 1:10
      (c) That you may be blameless: 1:10
      (d) Filled with the fruit of righteousness: 1:11
  C. Personal matters: 1:12–26
    1. Events which have served to spread the Gospel: 1:12–18
      (a) Imprisonment: 1:12–14
      (b) Preaching: 1:15–18
      (c) Prayer: 1:19
    2. Questioning about whether it is best to live or die: 1:19–26
      (a) The contrast of life and death: 1:20–21
      (b) The appeal of life: 1:22
      (c) The competing desire for death: 1:23–24
      (d) Assurance for a longer life: 1:25–26

II. Exhortations for unity 1:27–2:18
  A. Appeal for unity in suffering: 1:27–30
  B. Unity in Christ: 2:1–11
    1. Through correct behavior: 2:1–4
    2. Christ's humiliation: 2:6–8
      (a) Made himself nothing: 2:7
      (b) Form of servant: 2:7
      (c) Likeness of men: 2:7
      (d) Humbled self: 2:8
      (e) Obedient to death of cross: 2:8
    3. Christ's exaltation: 2:9–11
      (a) Highly exalted: 2:9
      (b) A name above all others: 2:9
      (c) Every knee shall bow: 2:10
      (d) Every tongue will confess: 2:11
  C. Spiritual growth brings unity: 2:12–18
    1. Work out your salvation in fear: It is

God: 2:12–13
2. Do everything without complaining: 2:14–15
3. Hold out the word of life: 2:16–18

III. Paul's plans: 2:19–30
A. His plans for Timothy: 2:19–23
1. The plan: 2:19
2. The motive for the plan: 2:19
3. Reasons for choosing Timothy: 2:20–21
4. The relation of Timothy and Paul: 2:22
5. The timing of Timothy's trip: 2:23
B. Plans for himself: 2:24
C. Plans for Epaphroditus: 2:25–30
1. Statement of the plan: 2:25
2. Testimony of Epaphroditus: 2:25
3. The reason for sending Epaphroditus: 2:26–27
4. The welcome to be given: 2:28–30

IV. Warnings 3:1–4:1
A. Against Judaizing teachers: 3:1–16
1. The joy of the Lord as a defense against them: 3:1
2. Admonition to watch them: 3:2
3. Identification of true Israelites: 3:3
4. Paul's experiences in relation to this matter: 3:4–11
(a) His grounds for legalistic pride: 3:4–6
(b) His change of valu/es: 3:7–11
(1) Nature of the change: 3:7
(2) Reasons for the change: 3:8
(3) Motives for the change: 3:8–11
5. Perfection as a defense against legalism: 3:12–16
(a) Attitude towards perfection: 3:12
(b) Efforts to reach the goal: 13–14
(c) Exhortation to perfection: 3:15–16
B. Against false teachers: 3:17–21
1. Their character: 3:18
2. Their fate: 3:19
3. The response of the believer: 3:20–21

V. Exhortations: 4:1–9
A. Unity between Euodias and Syntyce: 4:1–3
B. Unity in joy: 4:4
C. Unity in moderation: 4:5
D. Unity in prayer: 4:6
E. Unity in peace: 4:7
F. Unity in mind: Proper thought process: 4:8
G. Unity between knowledge and actions: 4:9

VI. Thanks for their gift: 4:10–20
A. The secret of contentment: 4:10–13
1. His thanks for their gift: 4:10
2. His independence of material need: 4:11
3. Explanation of his secret: 4:11–12
4. His source of strength: 4:13
B. The secret of provision: 4:14–20
1. His appreciation of the gift: 4:14
2. His reminder of their past record: 4:15–16
3. His attitude towards their gift: 4:17
4. His receipt of the gift: 4:18
5. The secret of provision: 4:19–20

VII. Benediction 4:21–23
A. Salute the saints in Christ Jesus: 4:21
B. The brethren with Paul send greetings: 4:21

C. The saints and those of Caesar's household send greetings: 2:22

D. Grace be with you: 2:23

2. Helpful summaries of Philippians

Bird's eye view

From his prison Paul thanks the Christians at Philippi for their special love towards him and constantly speaks of his joy in the Lord in this letter.

Reading plan

The following reading plan, taking one reading per day, enables you to read through Philippians in four days.

Philippians 1:1–1:30

Philippians 2:1–2:30

Philippians 3:1–3:21

Philippians 4:1–4:23

Verses to memorize

Philippians 1:6

Being confident of this very thing, that he which hath begun a good work in you will perform it until the day of Jesus Christ: KJV

Philippians 2:5–11

[5] Let this mind be in you, which was also in Christ Jesus:

[6] Who, being in the form of God, thought it not robbery to be equal with God:

[7] But made himself of no reputation, and took on him the form of a servant, and was made in the likeness of men:

[8] And being found in fashion as a man, he humbled himself, and became obedient unto death, even the death of the cross.

[9] Wherefore God also hath highly exalted him, and given him a name which is above every name:

[10] That at the name of Jesus every knee should bow, of things in heaven, and things in earth, and things under the earth;

[11] And that every tongue should confess that Jesus Christ is Lord, to the glory of God the Father. KJV

Philippians 4:8

Finally, brethren, whatsoever things are true, whatsoever things are honest, whatsoever things are just, whatsoever things are pure, whatsoever things are lovely, whatsoever things are of good report; if there be any virtue, and if there be any praise, think on these things. KJV

Philippians 4:13

I can do all things through Christ which strengtheneth me. KJV

Statistics

Eleventh New Testament book

Sixth letter by the apostle Paul

4 chapters

104 verses

2,002 word

Number of Old Testament quotations and allusions in Philippians: 3.

Names/titles given

Pros Philippesious "To the Philippians."

3. Helpful keys to turn to in understanding Philippians

Key words/phrase

Joy/rejoice

Rejoice in the Lord, 4:4.

Key verses

Philippians 1:21; 2:5

Themes to study

Joy and contentment

Christlikeness and Christian values

Jesus in Philippians

In Philippians Jesus is our joy.

Lessons to learn from Philippians

- There are numerous qualities in this letter that should characterize all Christians.
- We should try to reconcile Christians who are at each other's throats.

4. Studying Philippians chapter by chapter

Philippians 1

Matthew Henry's introduction

He begins with the inscription and benediction, vv. 1, 2. He gives thanks for the saints at Philippi, vv. 3–6. He speaks of his great affection and concern for their spiritual welfare (vv. 7, 8), his prayers for them (vv. 9–11), his care to prevent their offence at his sufferings (vv. 12–20), his readiness to glorify Christ by life or death (vv. 21–26), and then concludes with a double exhortation to strictness and constancy, vv. 27–30.

Dr. Adam Clarke's analysis of chapter

Paul, in conjunction with Timothy, addresses himself to the saints at Philippi, and gives them his apostolic benediction, 1, 2.

Thanks God for their conversion and union, and expresses his persuasion that God will continue his work among them, 3–6.

Tells them of his strong affection for them, and prays that they may be filed with the salvation of God, 7–11.

Shows them how much his persecution had contributed to the success of the Gospel, 12–14.

Informs that there were some at Rome who preached the Gospel from unworthy motives; yet he was convinced that this, which was designed to injure him, should turn to his advantage, 15–19.

Mentions his uncertainty whether he should be liberated or martyred, and his perfect readiness to meet either; yet, on the whole, expresses a hope that he should again visit them, 20–26.

Exhorts them to a holy life, and comforts them under their tribulations, 27–30.

A detailed analysis of chapter

The apostle offers up thanksgivings and prayers, for the good work of grace in the Philippians. (1–7)

He expresses his affection for them, and prays for them. (8–11)

He tells them not to be upset at his sufferings. (12–20)

He is prepared to glorify Christ by life, or death. (21–26)

Instructions to live in a way which is worthy of the gospel. (27–30)

Key verse

Verse 12: "Now I want you to know, brothers, that what has happened to me has really served to advance the gospel."

Key word / key phrase

Verse 13, "I am in chains."

Key event / key person / key theme

Paul writes from prison to thank God for the Philippians' partnership in the gospel.

Key thought

Paul says that he may be in chains but the gospel is not.

Key thing to look out for

What will be the result, for the Philippians, of conducting themselves in a manner worthy of the gospel (verse 27)?

Key Bible cross-reference

Verse 1. See Acts 16:12.

Key "by way of explanation"

Verse 17, "the former preach Christ out of selfish ambition." You might be forgiven for thinking that all who preach in Christ's name are good Christian preachers. But, no. Far from it, says Paul. Some preachers preach from jealousy and others from warped motives.

Key "Quotable Quote"

"The whole point of the letter to the Philippians is: I do rejoice – do you rejoice?"

J.A. Bengel

Philippians 2

Matthew Henry's introduction

The apostle proceeds to further exhortations to several duties, to be like-minded, and lowly-minded, which he presses from the example of Christ (vv. 1–11), to be diligent and serious in the Christian course (vv. 12, 13), and to adorn their Christian profession by several suitable graces, vv. 14–18. He then concludes with particular notice and commendation of two good ministers, Timothy and Epaphroditus, whom he designed to send to them, vv. 19–30.

Dr. Adam Clarke's analysis of chapter

The apostle beseeches them by various consid erations, to live in unity and in the spirit of the Gospel, loving each other; and each to prefer his brother to himself, 1–4.

He exhorts them to be like-minded with Christ, who, though in the form of God, and equal with God, made himself of no reputation, and humbled himself to the death of the cross for the salvation of man; in consequence of which he was highly exalted, and had a name above every name; to whose authority every knee should bow, and whose glory every tongue should acknowledge, 5–11.

They are exhorted to work out their own salva tion through his power who works in them, that they may be blameless, and that the apostle's labor may not be in vain, 12–16.

He expresses his readiness to offer his life for the Gospel, 17, 18.

Intends to send Timothy to them, of whom he gives a very high character; yet hopes to see them himself shortly, 19–24.

In the meantime sends Epaphroditus, who had been near death, and whom he begs them to receive with especial tenderness, 25–30.

A detailed analysis of chapter

Exhortations to a kind, humble spirit. (1–4)

The example of Christ. (5–11)

Diligence in the affairs of salvation, and to be examples to the world. (12–18)

The apostle's purpose in visiting Philippi. (19–30)

Key verse

Verse 3: "Do nothing out of selfish ambition or vain conceit, but in humility consider others better than yourselves."

Key word / key phrase

Verse 5, "your attitude."

Key event / key person / key theme

The attitude of Christ

Key thought

Paul sets out the example that all Christians should always follow.

Key thing to look out for

Verses 1–4 give four reasons for Christian love. Verses 5–11 give a further crowning reason.

Key Bible cross-reference

Verses 10, 11. See Isaiah 45:23.

Key "by way of explanation"

Verse 7, "but made himself nothing." Literally this reads, "emptied himself." When Jesus came to this earth in human form he was still God and the only thing he emptied himself of was God's glory, which was only occasionally glimpsed in his life, during his transfiguration, for example. Verses 5–11 were probably an early Christian hymn.

Key "Quotable Quote"

"It's not great talents that God blesses, but great likeness to Jesus."

Robert Murray M'Cheyne

Philippians 3

Matthew Henry's introduction

He cautions them against judaizing seducers (vv. 1–3) and proposes his own example: and here he enumerates the privileges of his Jewish state which he rejected (vv. 4–8), describes the matter of his own choice (vv. 9–16), and closes with an exhortation to beware of wicked men, and to follow his example, vv. 17–21.

Dr. Adam Clarke's analysis of chapter

The apostle exhorts the Philippians to rejoice in the Lord, 1.

And to beware of false teachers, 2.

Shows that Christians are the true circumcision, who worship God in the Spirit, 3.

And that himself had more reason to trust in the flesh than any of the Jews, 4–6.

But that he counted all things loss for Christ, 7–11.

He longs after a conformity to Christ in his death, and presses onward to the attainment of his high calling, 12–14.

Exhorts them to be like-minded, 15–17.

Warns them against certain people who were enemies to the cross of Christ, 18, 19.

Shows the nature of their heavenly privileges, and the resurrection and glorification of the human body, 20, 21.

A detailed analysis of chapter

The apostle warns the Philippians against judaizing false teachers, and renounces his own former privileges. (1–11)

Expresses earnest desire to be found in Christ; also his pressing on toward perfection. (12–21)

Key verse

Verse 14: "I press on toward the goal to win the prize for which God has called me heavenward in Christ Jesus."

Key word / key phrase

Verse 10, "I rejoice greatly."

Key event / key person / key theme

Knowing Christ

Key thought

Note how Paul shows that he lived his life under the power of Jesus' resurrection.

Key thing to look out for

Even though Paul was at the end of his life he still pressed on to know Jesus better.

Key Bible cross-reference

Verse 5. See Acts 23:6.

Key "by way of explanation"

Verse 8, "knowing Christ Jesus my Lord." This was Paul's aim in his Christian life. This knowledge was more than an accumulation of facts, it was a daily experience.

Key "Quotable Quote"

"This is clear: He who does not know Christ does not know God hidden in suffering. Therefore he prefers works to suffering, glory to the cross, strength to weakness, wisdom to folly. These are the people whom the apostle calls 'enemies of the cross of Christ' (Philippians. 3:18) for they hate the cross and suffering and love works and the glory of works. Thus they call the good of the cross evil and the evil of a deed good. God can be found only in suffering and the cross."

Martin Luther

Philippians 4

Matthew Henry's introduction

Exhortations to several Christian duties, as steadfastness, unanimity, joy, etc., vv. 1–9. The apostle's grateful acknowledgments of the Philippians' kindness to him, with expressions of his own content, and desire of their good, vv. 10–19. He concludes the epistle with praise, greetings, and blessing, vv. 20–23.

Dr. Adam Clarke's analysis of chapter

The apostle exhorts them to stand fast in the Lord, 1.

And beseeches Euodias and Syntyche to be of one mind in Divine things, 2.

And requests his true yokefellow to help them to a good understanding, 3.

Gives them directions about their temper and frame of mind, 4–7.

And how to act in all respects as becomes the purity and excellence of the Gospel, as they had heard from and seen in him, 8, 9.

Thanks them for their attention to him in his captivity, in sending him what was necessary for his support, though he had learned to be contented in all situations in life, 10–14.

Mentions particular cases in which they had ministered to him; promises them, through the riches of glory in Christ, a supply of all their spiritual wants; and renders thanks to God, 15–20.

Salutes all the saints, and those particularly of the emperor's household, 21,22.

And concludes with his usual apostolic benediction, 23.

A detailed analysis of chapter

The apostle exhorts the Philippians to stand firm in the Lord. (1)

Gives directions to some particular people, and to all in general. (2–9)

States that he is content no matter what happens to him. (10–19)

He concludes with prayer to God the Father, and his usual blessing. (20–23)

Key verse

Verse 4: "Rejoice in the Lord always. I will say it again: Rejoice!"

Key word / key phrase

Verse 4, "Rejoice in the Lord always."

Key event / key person / key theme

Joy in contentment

Key thought

Note how the theme of joy runs through this letter.

Key thing to look out for

In verse 13 Paul gives us the secret of his spiritual strength.

Key Bible cross-reference

Verse 18. See Exodus 29:18.

Key "by way of explanation"

Verse 13, "who gives me strength." As Paul lived his life in union with Jesus so he was given the necessary strength to cope with the constant pressures which assaulted him.

Key "Quotable Quote"

"A child of God should be a visible beatitude for joy and happiness, and a living doxology for gratitude and adoration."

C.H. Spurgeon

5. Select bibliography for Philippians

Davidson, F. "The Epistle to the Philippians." NBC1. Edited by F. Davidson, A. M. Stibbs, and E. F. Kevan. Grand Rapids: Eerdmans, 1954.

Hendriksen, William. *Exposition of Philippians.* Grand Rapids: Baker, 1962.

Lightfoot, J. B. *Saint Paul's Epistle to the Philippians.* Grand Rapids: Zondervan, repr. of 1913 edition.

Martin, Ralph P. *Carmen Christi: Philippians 25–11 in Recent Interpretation and in the Setting of Early Christian Worship.* Cambridge: Cambridge University Press, 1967.

Motyer, J. A. *Philippian Studies: The Richness of Christ.* Chicago: Inter-Varsity Press, 1966.

Moule, H. C. G. *The Epistle to the Philippians.* Cambridge: Cambridge University Press, 1873.

Colossians

1. Book by book: Introduction to Colossians

Introduction

Genuineness

The genuineness of this Epistle is attested by Justin Martyr (*Dialogue with Trypho*, p. 311, B.), who quotes "the first-born of every creature," in reference to Christ, from Col. 1:15. Theophilus of Antioch (*To Autolychus*, 2, p. 100). Irenaeus (*Against Heresies*, 3.14.1), quotes expressly from this "Epistle to the Colossians" (Col. 4:14). Clement of Alexandria (*Miscellanies*, 1. p. 325), quotes Col. 1:28; also elsewhere he quotes Col. 1:9–11, 28; 2:2, etc.; Col. 2:8; 3:12, 14; 4:2, 3, etc. Tertullian (*The Prescription against Heretics*, 7), quotes Col. 2:8; (*On the Resurrection of the Flesh*, 23), and quotes Col. 2:12, 20; 3:1, 2. Origen (*Against Celsus*, 5.8), quotes Col. 2:18, 19.

Colosse

Colosse (or, as it is spelt in the best manuscripts, "Colassæ") was a city of Phrygia, on the river Lycus, a branch of the Meander. The Church there was mainly composed of Gentiles (compare Col. 2:13). Alford infers from Col. 2:1, that Paul had not seen its members, and therefore could not have been its founder, as Theodoret thought. Col. 1:7, 8 suggests the probability that Epaphras was the first founder of the Church there. The date of its foundation must have been subsequent to Paul's visitation, "strengthening in order" all the churches of Galatia and Phrygia (Acts 18:24); for otherwise he must have visited the Colossians, which Col. 2:1 implies he had not. Had Paul been their father in the faith, he would doubtless have alluded to the fact, as in 1 Cor. 3:6, 10; 4:15; 1 Thess. 1:5; 2:1. It is only in the Epistles, Romans and Ephesians, and this Epistle, such allusions are lacking; in that to the Romans, because, as in this Church of Colosse, he had not been the instrument of their conversion; in that to the Ephesians, owing to the general nature of the Epistle. Probably during the "two years" of Paul's stay at Ephesus, when "all which dwelt in Asia heard the word of the Lord Jesus" (Acts 19:10, 26), Epaphras, Philemon, Archippus, Apphia and those born at Colosse, becoming converted at Ephesus, were subsequently the first sowers of the Gospel seed in their own city. This will account for their personal acquaintance with, and attachment to, Paul and his fellow ministers, and for his loving language as to them, and their greetings to him. So also with respect to "them at Laodicea," (Col. 2:1).

Purpose

The Object of the Epistle is to counteract Jewish false teaching, by setting before the Colossians their true standing in Christ alone (exclusive of all other heavenly beings), the majesty of His person, and the completeness of the redemption brought about by Him; hence they ought to be conformed to their risen Lord, and to show that conformity in all the relations of ordinary life Col. 2:16. "New moon, Sabbath days," shows that the false teaching opposed in this Epistle is that of Judaizing Christians. These mixed up with pure Christianity Oriental theosophy and angel-worship, and the asceticism of certain sections of the Jews, especially the Essenes. Compare Josephus (*Wars of the Jews*, 2.8, 13). These theosophists promised to their followers a deeper insight into the world of spirits, and a closer proximity to heavenly purity and intelligence, than the simple Gospel affords. Conybeare and Howson think that some Alexandrian Jew had appeared at Colosse, imbued with the Greek philosophy of Philo's school, combining with it the Rabbinical theosophy and angelology which afterwards was embodied in the Cabbala. Compare Josephus (*Antiquities,* 12.3, 4), from which we know that Alexander the Great had garrisoned the towns of Lydia and Phrygia with two thousand Mesopotamian and Babylonian Jews in the time of a threatened revolt. The Phrygians themselves had a mystic tendency in their worship of Cybele, which inclined them to receive the more readily the incipient Gnosticism of Judaizers, which afterward developed itself into the strangest heresies. In the Pastoral Epistles, the evil is spoken of as having reached a more deadly phase (1 Tim. 4:1–3; 6:5), whereas he brings no charge of immorality in this Epistle: a proof of its being much earlier in date.

Place of writing

The place from which it was written seems to have been Rome, during his first imprisonment there (Acts 28:17–31). In my Introduction to the Epistle to the Ephesians, it was shown that the three Epistles, Ephesians, Colossians, and Philemon, were sent at the same time, namely, during the freer portion of his imprisonment, before the death of Burrus. Col. 4:3, 4; Eph. 6:19, 20, imply greater freedom than he had while writing to the Philippians, after the promotion of Tigellinus to be Prætorian Prefect. See Introduction to Philippians.

This Epistle, though carried by the same bearer, Tychicus, who bore that to the Ephesians, was written previously to that Epistle; for many phrases similar in both appear in the more expanded form in the Epistle to the Ephesians (compare also Note, see on Eph. 6:21). The Epistle to the Laodiceans (Col. 4:16) was written before that to the Colossians, but probably was sent by him to Laodicea at the same time with that to the Church at Colosse.

Style

The style is peculiar: many Greek phrases occur here, found nowhere else. Compare Col. 2:8, "spoil you"; "making a show of them openly" (Col. 2:15); "beguile of your reward," and "intruding" (Col. 2:18); "will-worship"; "satisfying" (Col. 2:23); "filthy communication" (Col. 3:8); "rule" (Col. 3:15); "comfort" (Col. 4:11).

The loftiness and artificial elaboration of style correspond to the majestic nature of his theme, the majesty of Christ's person and office, in contrast to the beggarly system of the Judaizers, the discussion of which was forced on him by the controversy. Hence arises his use of unusual phraseology. On the other hand, in the Epistle of the Ephesians, subsequently written, in which he was not so hampered by the exigencies of controversy, he dilates on the same glorious truths, so congenial to him, more at large, freely and uncontroversially, in the fuller outpouring of his spirit, with less of the elaborate and antithetical language of system, such as was needed in cautioning the Colossians against the particular errors threatening them. Hence arises the striking similarity of many of the phrases in the two Epistles written about the same time, and generally in the same vein of spiritual thought; while the peculiar phrases of the Epistle to the Colossians are such as are natural, considering the controversial purpose of that Epistle.

A. R. Faussett

Detailed outline

- I. Introduction: 1:1–14
  - A. Greetings: 1:1–2
    - 1. From: Paul and Timothy: 1:1
    - 2. To: The saints and faithful brethren in Christ at Colosse: 1:2
    - 3. Grace and peace from God and Jesus: 1:2
  - B. Thanksgiving: 1:3–8
  - C. Paul's prayer for Christians at Colosse: 1:9–14
- II. The person and work of Jesus: 1:15–23
  - A. Lord of creation: 1:15–17
    - 1. In relation to its origin: 1:15–16
    - 2. In relation to its continuity: 1:17
  - B. Lord of the church: 1:18–19
  - C. Reconciler: 1:20–23
    - 1. He has made peace through the blood of His cross: 1:20
    - 2. He has reconciled all things to Himself: 1:20
    - 3. Those alienated by wicked works He has reconciled: 1:21
    - 4. Through His death, we can be presented: 1:22
    - 5. We are to continue in the faith: 1:23
- III. Paul: God's minister of reconciliation: 1:24–2:7
  - A. Sufferings: 1:24
  - B. Minister of the mystery of Christ: 1:25–29

1. The circumstances of his ministry: 1:25
2. The message of his ministry: 1:26–27
   (a) Mystery of God: 1:26–27
   (b) Jesus Himself: 1:27
3. The methods of his ministry: 1:28
4. Presenting everyone perfect in Jesus: l:28
5. The power behind his ministry: 1:29

C. Desire for unity and stability in Christ: 2:1–7
1. His striving for the believers: 2:1
2. He strives for God the Father and Christ: 2:2
3. The purpose of the striving: 2:2–7

IV. Christ's Lordship over false teaching: 2:8–3:4

A. Lord of every power: 2:8–10

B. The new life: 2:11–14
1. Circumcision of the heart: 2:11
2. Buried with Him in baptism: 2:12
3. Risen with Him through faith: 2:12
4. Made alive with Him: 2:13
5. All sins forgiven: 2:13
6. Cancelled the written code against us: 2:14

C. Conqueror of principalities and power: 2:15

D. Practices denying Christ's lordship: 2:16–3:4
1. Ritual: 2:16–17
   (a) Meat: 2:16
   (b) Drink: 2:16
   (c) Holy days: 2:16
   (d) New moon: 2:16
   (e) Sabbath days: 2:16
2. Angel worship: A person who practices this is: 2:18–19
3. Died to the basic principles of this world: 2:20–23
   (a) We are not to be subject to them: 2:20
   (b) What they concern: 2:21
   (c) The commandments and doctrines of men: 2:22
   (d) They are an outward shew: 2:23
4. Worldly, temporal affections: 3:1–4
   (a) Seek those things above: 3:1
   (b) Set your affections on things above, not on this earth: 3:2
   (c) This is possible because of your union with Jesus: 3:3–4

V. Christ's lordship and the Christian life: 3:5–4:6

A. We are responsible to put to death our earthly nature: 3:5

B. The wrath of God comes on those who disobey: 3:6

C. In times past, we walked in these sinful ways: 3:7–8

D. Old life to put off: 3:5–9

E. New life to put on: 3:10–17

F. Special situations: 3:18–4:6
1. Home: 3:18–21
   (a) Wives: 3:18
   (b) Husbands: 3:19
   (c) Children: 3:20
   (d) Fathers: 3:21
2. Work relationships: 3:22; 4:1
   (a) Obey your masters: 3:22
   (b) Serve as unto Christ: 3:22
   (c) Masters act fairly: 4:1

3. General guidelines: 3:23–25
   (a) Do all as to the Lord and not to men: 3:23
   (b) Recognize that you serve the Lord: 3:24
   (c) Wrongdoers will receive justice from God: 3:25

VI. Final instructions: 4:2–6
- A. Duty of prayer: 4:2–4
  1. Responsibility to continue in prayer: 4:2
  2. To watch with thanksgiving: 4:2
  3. To pray for open doors for those spreading the Gospel: 4:3–4
- B. Duty of witness: 4:5–6
  1. Proper walk in wisdom: 4:5
  2. Proper use of time: 4:5
  3. Proper speech: 4:6

VII. Closing: 4:7–18
- A. Personal greetings: 4:7–17
  1. The bearers of the letter: 4:7–9
     (a) Tychicus: 4:7–8
     (b) Onesimus: 4:9
  2. Greetings from his companions: 4:10–14
  3. Greetings to the Laodiceans: 4:15–16
  4. A special message to Arcippus: 4:17
- B. Greeting: 4:18
  1. By the hand of Paul.
  2. Request to remember his chains.
  3. Grace be with you.

2. Helpful summaries of Colossians

Bird's eye view

Paul stresses the important of the preeminance of Jesus and warns his readers not to be taken in by false teachers.

Reading plan

The following reading plan, taking one reading per day, enables you to read through Colossians in four days.

Colossians 1:1–1:29
Colossians 2:1–2:23
Colossians 3:1–3:25
Colossians 4:1–4:18

Verses to memorize

Colossians 2:9

For in him [Christ] dwelleth all the fullness of the Godhead bodily. KJV

Colossians 3:1–2

[1] If ye then be risen with Christ, seek those things which are above, where Christ sitteth on the right hand of God.

[2] Set your affection on things above, not on things on the earth. KJV

Statistics

Twelfth New Testament book
Seventh letter by the apostle Paul
4 chapters
95 verses
1,988 words
Number of Old Testament quotations and allusions in Colossians: 3.

Names/titles given

Pros Kolossaeis: To the Colossians.

3. Helpful keys to turn to in understanding Colossians

Key word/phrase

Fullness

With Christ

Key verses

Colossians 2:9, 10; 3:1–2

Themes to study

Christian maturity

Jesus' part in our salvation

Jesus in Colossians

In Colossians Jesus is our life.

Lessons to learn from Colossians

- Christian maturity should be the goal of every Christian.
- Jesus is our example, *par excellance.*

4. Studying Colossians chapter by chapter

Colossians 1

Matthew Henry's introduction

We have here,

I. The inscription, as usual, vv. 1, 2.

II. His thanksgiving to God for what he had heard about them–their faith, love, and hope, vv. 3–8.

III. His prayer for their knowledge, fruitfulness, and strength, vv. 9–11.

IV. An admirable summary of the Christian doctrine about the operation of the Spirit, the person of the Redeemer, the work of redemption, and the preaching of it in the gospel, vv. 12–29.

Dr. Adam Clarke's analysis of chapter

The salutation of Paul and Timothy to the Church at Colosse, 1, 2.

They give thanks to God for the good estate of that Church, and the wonderful progress of the Gospel in every place, 3–6;

having received particulars of their state from Epaphroditus, which not only excited their gratitude, but led them to pray to God that they might walk worthy of the Gospel; and they give thanks to Him who had made them meet for an inheritance among the saints in light, 7–12.

This state is described as a deliverance from the power of darkness, and being brought into the kingdom of God's dear Son, 13, 14.

The glorious character of Jesus Christ, and what He has done for mankind, 15–20.

The salvation which the Colossians had received, and of which the apostle had been the minister and dispenser, 21–26.

The sum and substance of the apostle's preach ing, and the manner in which he carried out his ministry, 27–29.

A detailed analysis of chapter

The apostle Paul greets the Colossians, and blesses God for their faith, love, and hope. (1–8)

Prays for their fruitfulness in spiritual knowledge. (9–14)

Emphasizes the supremacy of Christ. (15–23)
And shows how he is the apostle of the Gentiles. (24–29)

Key verse
Verse 10: "And we pray this in order that you may live a life worthy of the Lord and may please him in every way."

Key word / key phrase
Verse 18, "he might have the supremacy."

Key event / key person / key theme
The supremacy of Christ

Key thought
Paul links redemption with forgiveness of sins very clearly in verse 14.

Key thing to look out for
For Paul, Christ was supreme over everything and everyone because he alone was God.

Key Bible cross-reference
Verse 14. See Ephesians 1:7.

Key "by way of explanation"
Verse 14, "In whom we have redemption." From verses like this the doctrine of substitutionary atonement flows.

Key "Quotable Quote"
"When Christ is called the image of the invisible God (Colossians 1: 15), the expression is designed to remind us that we can have no knowledge of our salvation, until we behold God in Christ."

John Calvin

Colossians 2

Matthew Henry's introduction

I. The apostle expresses concern for the Colossians, vv. 1–3.
II. He repeats it again, v. 5.
III. He cautions them against false teachers among the Jews (vv. 4, 6, 7), and against the Gentile philosophy, vv. 8–12.
IV. He represents the privileges of Christians, vv. 13–15. And,
V. Concludes with a caution against the judaizing teachers, and those who would introduce the worship of angels, vv. 16–23.

Dr. Adam Clarke's analysis of chapter

The apostle shows his great concern for the Church at Colosse and at Laodicea; and exhorts them to steadfastness in the faith, and to beware of being seduced by specious and enticing words, 1–5.

And to walk in Christ, as they had been taught, and to abound in faith and holiness, 6, 7.

To beware of false teachers, who strove to pervert the Gospel, and to lead their minds from him in whom the fullness of the Godhead dwells; with whom they were filled; by whom they had received spiritual circumcision; and into whom they were bap tized and were quickened, and raised from a death of sin to a life of righteousness, 8–12.

He points out their former state, and the great things which Christ had done for them, 13–15.

Warns them against particular tenets of the

Judaizing teachers relative to meats, drinks, holydays, festivals, and the specious pre tences of deceivers, 16–19.

And shows that all the things taught by these, though they had a show of wisdom, yet per ished in the using, and were the command ments and doctrines of men, 20–23.

A detailed analysis of chapter

The apostle expresses his love toward, and joy in the believers. (1–7)

He warns against the errors of heathen philosophy; also against Jewish traditions, and rites which had been fulfilled in Christ. (8–17)

Against worshiping angels; and against legal ordinances. (18–23)

Key verse

Verse 9: "For in Christ all the fullness of the Deity lives in bodily form."

Key word / key phrase

Verse 15, "disarmed the powers."

Key event / key person / key theme

Freedom in Jesus

Key thought

Paul stresses that for Christians all power comes as a result of the resurrection of Christ.

Key thing to look out for

Human regulations have no place for a person living his or her life in the Spirit.

Key Bible cross-reference

Verse 16. See Romans 14:1–6.

Key "by way of explanation"

Verse 9, "fullness of the Deity." This is one of the most important statements about the deity of Jesus made in the New Testament.

Key "Quotable Quote"

"God is best known in Christ; the sun is not seen but by the light of the sun."

William Bridge

Colossians 3

Matthew Henry's introduction

I. The apostle exhorts us to set our hearts on heaven and take them off from this world, vv. 1–4.

II. He exhorts to the mortification of sin, in the various instances of it, vv. 5–11.

III. He earnestly presses to mutual love and compassion, vv. 12–17. And concludes with exhortations to relative duties, of wives and husbands, parents and children, masters and servants, vv. 18–25.

Dr. Adam Clarke's analysis of chapter

The apostle exhorts the Colossians to heavenly-mindedness after the example of Christ, that they may be prepared to appear with him in glory, 1–4.

Exhorts them also to mortify their members, and calls to their remembrance their former state, 5–7.

Shows how completely they were changed from that state, and gives them various direc tions relative to truth, compassion, meekness, long-suffering, forgiveness, charity, 8–14.

Shows that they are called to unity and holi ness; and commands them to have the doc trine of Christ dwelling richly in them; and how they should teach and admonish each other, and do every thing, in the name of the Lord Jesus, 15–17.

The relative duties of wives, 18.

Of husbands, 19.

Of children, 20.

Of fathers, 21.

Of servants, 22.

He concludes by showing that he that does wrong shall be treated accordingly, for God is no respecter of people, 23–25.

A detailed analysis of chapter

The Colossians are told to be heavenly-minded (1–4);

to put to death all corrupt desires (5–11);

to live in mutual love, forbearance, and forgiveness (12–17);

and as wives and husbands, children, parents, and servants, to live as servants of Christ. (18–25)

Key verse

Verse 12: "Therefore, as God's chosen people, holy and dearly loved, clothe yourselves with compassion, kindness, humility, gentleness and patience."

Key word / key phrase

Verse 1, "raised with Christ."

Key event / key person / key theme

Living the risen life with Christ

Key thought

For Paul, there was definitely a right way and a wrong way to live.

Key thing to look out for

Paul gives guidelines for Christian families.

Key Bible cross-reference

Verse 19. See 1 Peter 3:7.

Key "by way of explanation"

Verse 15, "peace of Christ." Christians are meant to be characterized, not by fighting and arguing, but by the peace that only Jesus can give. It is meant to rule them, in the sense that it governs all of their lives.

Key "Quotable Quote"

"There is only one permanent way to have the peace of soul that wells up in joy, contentment and happiness, and that is by repentance for sin and by personal faith in Jesus Christ as Savior."

Billy Graham

Colossians 4

Matthew Henry's introduction

I. He continues his account of the duty of masters, from the close of the previous chapter, v. 1.

II. He exhorts to the duty of prayer (vv. 2–4), and to a prudent and decent conduct towards those with whom we converse, vv. 5, 6.

III. He closes the epistle with the mention of several of his friends, of whom he gives an honorable testimony, vv. 7–18.

Dr. Adam Clarke's analysis of chapter

The duty of masters to their servants, 1.

Continuance in prayer recommended, to which watchfulness and thanksgiving should be joined, 2.

And to pray particularly for the success of the Gospel, 3, 4.

Directions about walking wisely, redeeming of time, and godly conversation, 5, 6.

He refers them to Tychius and Onesimus, whom he sends to them for particulars rela tive to his present circumstances, 7–9.

Mentions the greetings of several then at Rome, of whom he gives some interesting particu lars, 10–14.

Sends his own greetings to the brethren in Laodicea, and to Nymphas and the Church at his house, 15.

Directs this epistle to be read in the Church of the Laodiceans, and that to them to be read at Colosse, 16.

Directions to Archippus relative to his ministry, 17.

Concludes with greetings to the people at Colosse, to whom he sends his apostolic benediction, 18.

A detailed analysis of chapter

Masters should act in a right and fair way toward their servants. (1)

Christian people from every walk of life should persevere in prayer, and Christian prudence. (2–6)

The apostle refers to others for an account of his affairs. (7–9)

Sends greetings; and concludes with a blessing. (10–18)

Key verse

Verse 14: "Our dear friend Luke, the doctor, and Demas send greetings."

Key word / key phrase

Verses 3, 4, "pray."

Key event / key person / key theme

Prayer and wisdom, and personal greetings

Key thought

Paul wanted to ensure that the Colossians did not think that prayer was an optional extra.

Key thing to look out for

Verses 3 and 10 reveal that Paul is writing from his prison cell, but not with an imprisoned spirit.

Key Bible cross-reference

Verse 12. See Colossians 1:7.

Key "by way of explanation"

Verse 18, "I, Paul, write this greeting." As was quite usual in those days, Paul dictated his letters. But he often added a personal greeting at the end, in own hand, as here.

Key "Quotable Quote"

"We must not talk about prayer, we must pray."

Andrew Bonar

5. Select bibliography for Colossians

Bruce, F. F. *The Epistles to the Colossians, to Philemon, and to the Ephesians*. Grand Rapids: Eerdmans, 1984.

Calvin, John. *The Epistles of Paul the Apostle to the Galatians, Ephesians, Philippians and Colossians*. Translated by T. H. L. Parker. Edited by David W. and Thomas F. Torrence. Grand Rapids: Eerdmans, 1965.

Carson, H. M. *The Epistles of Paul to the Colossians and Philemon*. TNTC. Edited by R. V. G. Tasker. Grand Rapids: Eerdmans.

Martin, Ralph P. *Colossians: The Church's Lord and the Christian's Liberty*. Grand Rapids: Zondervan, 1973.

Moule, C. F. D. *The Epistles Of Paul the Apostle to the Colossians and to Philemon*. CGT. Edited by C. F. D. Moule, Cambridge: Cambridge University Press, 1957.

Moule, Handley C. G. *Colossian Studies*. New York: Hodder and Stoughton, 1898.

Simpson, E. K., and Bruce, F. F. *Commentary on the Epistles to the Ephesians and the Colossians*. NIC. Grand Rapids Eerdmans, 1957.

1 Thessalonians

1. Book by book: Introduction to 1 Thessalonians

Introduction

Authenticity

The authenticity of this Epistle is attested by Irenaeus (*Against Heresies,* 5.6.1), quoting 1 Thess. 5:23; Clement of Alexandria (*The Instructor,* 1.88), quoting 1 Thess. 2:7; Tertullian (*On the Resurrection of the Flesh*, 24), quoting 1 Thess. 5:1; Caius in Eusebius' *Ecclesiastical History* (6.20); Origen (*Against Celsus*, 3).

Purpose

The object of the epistle. Thessalonica was at this time capital of the Roman second district of Macedonia (Livy, *Histories*, 45.29). It lay on the bay of Therme, and has always been, and still is, under its modern name Saloniki, a place of considerable commerce. After his imprisonment and scourging at Philippi, Paul (1 Thess. 2:2) passed on to Thessalonica; and with Silas (Acts 17:1–9) and Timotheus (Acts 16:3; 17:14, compare with 1 Thess. 1:1; 3:1–6; 2 Thess. 1:1) founded the Church there. The Jews, as a body, rejected the Gospel when Paul preached for three successive Sabbaths (Acts 17:2); but some few "believed and consorted with Paul and Silas, and of the devout (that is, proselytes to Judaism) Greeks a great multitude, and of the chief women not a few."

The believers received the word joyfully, notwithstanding trials and persecutions (1 Thess. 1:6; 2:13) from their own countrymen and from the Jews (1 Thess. 2:14–16). His stay at Thessalonica was doubtless not limited to the three weeks in which were the three Sabbaths specified in Acts 17:2; for his laboring there with his hands for his support (1 Thess. 2:9; 2 Thess. 3:8), his receiving supplies there more than once from Philippi (Phil. 4:16), his making many converts from the Gentiles (1 Thess. 1:9; and as two oldest manuscripts read, Acts 17:4, "of the devout and of the Greeks a great multitude," Acts 17:4), and his appointing ministers–all imply a longer stay. Probably as at Pisidian Antioch (Acts 13:46), at Corinth (Acts 18:6, 7), and at Ephesus (Acts 19:8, 9), having preached the Gospel to the Jews, when they rejected it, he turned to the Gentiles. He probably then held the Christian meetings in the house of Jason (Acts 17:5), perhaps "the kinsman" of Paul mentioned in Rom. 16:21.

His great subject of teaching to them seems to have been the coming and kingdom of Christ, as we may infer from 1 Thess. 1:10; 2:12, 19; 3:13; 4:13–18; 5:1–11, 23, 24; and that they should walk worthy of it (1 Thess. 2:12; 4:1). And it is an undesigned coincidence between the two Epistles and Acts 17:5, 9, that the very charge which the assailants of Jason's house brought against him and other brethren was, "These do contrary to the decrees of Cæsar, saying that there is another king, one Jesus." As in the case of the Lord Jesus Himself (John 18:33–37; 19:12; compare Matt. 26:64), they perverted the doctrine of the coming kingdom of Christ into a ground for the charge of treason against Cæsar. The result was, Paul and Silas were obliged to flee under the cover of night to Berea; Timothy had probably preceded him (Acts 17:10, 14). But the Church had been planted, and ministers appointed. They virtually became missionaries themselves for which they possessed facilities in the extensive commerce of their city, and both by word and example were extending the Gospel in Macedonia, Achaia, and elsewhere (1 Thess. 1:7, 8).

From Berea, also, Paul, after having planted a Scripture-loving Church, was obliged to flee by the Thessalonian Jews who followed him thither. Timothy (who seems to have come to Berea separately from Paul and Silas, compare Acts 17:10, with Acts 17:14) and Silas remained there, when Paul went by sea to Athens. While there he more than once longed to visit the Thessalonians again, and see personally their spiritual state, and "perfect that which was lacking in their faith" (1 Thess. 3:10); but (probably using the Thessalonian Jews as his instruments, John 13:27) "Satan hindered" him (1 Thess. 2:18; compare Acts 17:13). He therefore sent Timotheus, who seems to have followed him to Athens from Berea (Acts 17:15), immediately on his arrival to Thessalonica (1 Thess. 3:1); glad as he would have been of Timothy's help in the midst of the cavils of Athenian opponents, he felt he must forego that help for the sake of the Thessalonian Church. Silas does not seem to have come to Paul at Athens at all, though Paul had desired him and Timothy to "come to him with all speed" (Acts 17:15); but seems with Timothy (who from Thessalonica called for him at Berea) to have joined Paul at Corinth first; compare Acts 18:1, 5, "When Silas and Timothy were come from Macedonia." The Epistle makes no mention of Silas at Athens, as it does of Timothy (1 Thess. 3:1).

Timothy's account of the Thessalonian Church was highly favorable. They abounded in faith and charity and reciprocated his desire to see them (1 Thess. 3:6–10). Still, as nothing human on earth is perfect, there were some defects. Some had too exclusively dwelt on the doctrine of Christ's coming kingdom, so as to neglect the sober-minded discharge of present duties (1 Thess. 4:11, 12). Some who had lost relatives by death, needed comfort and instruction in their doubts as to whether they who died before Christ's coming would have a share with those found alive in His kingdom then to be revealed. Moreover, also, there had been committed among them sins against chastity and sobriety (1 Thess. 5:5–7), as also against charity (1 Thess. 4:3–10; 5:13, 15). There were, too, symptoms in some of a lack of respectful love and subordination to their ministers; others dismissed the manifestations of the Spirit in those possessing His gifts (1 Thess. 5:19). To give spiritual admonition on these subjects, and at the same time commend what deserved commendation, and to testify his love to them, was the object of the Epistle.

Place of writing

It was doubtless Corinth, where Timothy and Silas rejoined him (Acts 18:5) soon after he arrived there (compare 1 Thess. 2:17) in the autumn of A.D. 52.

Date of writing

The time of writing was evidently immediately after having received from Timothy the tidings of their state (1 Thess. 3:6) in the winter of a.d. 52, or early in 53. For it was written not long after the conversion of the Thessalonians (1 Thess. 1:8, 9), while Paul could speak of himself as only taken from them for a short season (1 Thess. 2:17). Thus this Epistle was first in date of all Paul's extant Epistles. The Epistle is written in the joint names of Paul, Silas, and Timothy, the three founders of the Thessalonian Church. The plural first person "we," is used everywhere, except in 1 Thess. 2:18; 3:5; 5:27. "We" is the true reading, 1 Thess. 4:13. The English Version "I," in 1 Thess. 4:9 1 Thess. 5:1, 23, is not supported by the original (Edmunds).

Style

The style is calm and equable, in accordance with the subject matter, which deals only with Christian duties in general, taking for granted the great doctrinal truths which were not as yet disputed. There was no deadly error as yet to call forth his more vehement bursts of feeling and impassioned argument. The earlier Epistles, as we should expect, are moral and practical. It was not until Judaistic and legalizing errors arose at a later period that he wrote those Epistles (for example, Romans and Galatians) which unfold the cardinal doctrines of grace and justification by faith. Still, later the Epistles from his Roman prison confirm the same truths. And last of all, the Pastoral Epistles are suited to the more developed ecclesiastical constitution of the Church, and give directions as to bishops and deacons, and correct abuses and errors of later growth.

The prevalence of the Gentile element in this Church is shown by the fact that these two Epistles are among the very few of Paul's writings in which no quotation occurs from the Old Testament.

A. R. Faussett

Detailed outline

- I. Introduction: 1:1
  - A. From: Paul, Silvanus, and Timotheus.
  - B. To: Believers at Thessalonica.
  - C. Grace and peace from God and Jesus: 1:1
- II. Looking back: 1:2–3:13
  - A. Exemplary conversion to Christ: 1:2–10
    - 1. Power of the Gospel: 1:2–5
    - 2. Examples of the Gospel: 1:5–6
      - (a) Following the example of Paul: 1:5–6
      - (b) They became examples to other believers: 1:7
    - 3. Witnesses of the Gospel: 1:8–10
      - (a) The faith of the Thessalonian believers spread: 1:8
      - (b) Witness to the truth of the Gospel: 1:9–10
  - B. Exemplary evangelism: 2:1–20
    - 1. In motive: 2:1–6
      - (a) Not in vanity: 2:1
      - (b) In boldness: 2:2
      - (c) Not in deceit, uncleanness, or guile: 2:3
      - (d) To please God rather than men: 2:4
      - (e) Without flattering words: 2:5
      - (f) Without covetousness: 2:5
      - (g) Not to seek glory of men: 2:6
    - 2. In conduct: 2:7–11
      - (a) Gentleness: 2:7
      - (b) Dealing as a nurse with children: 2:7
      - (c) In affection: 2:8
      - (d) In labor and travail: 2:9
      - (e) With proper behavior: 2:10
      - (f) As a father with children: 2:11
    - 3. In message: 2:12–13
      - (a) That you walk worthy of God: 2:12
      - (b) It was based on the Word of God: 2:13
    - 4. In reception: 2:13–16
      - (a) The nature of their reception of the Word: 2:13
      - (a) The result of their reception of the Word: 2:14–16
        - (l) They imitated the Judean churches: 2:14
        - (2) Fellowship of suffering for the Word: 2:14–16
  - C. Exemplary follow up care of converts: 3:1–13
    - 1. Their concern: 3:1–5
      - (a) Their motive: 3:1
      - (b) The sending of Timothy: 3:2
      - (c) Description of the one sent: 3:2
        - (1) Our brother.
        - (2) Minister.
        - (3) Fellow-laborer in the Gospel.
      - (d) The purpose in sending Timothy: 3:2–4
        - (1) To establish you: 3:2
        - (2) To comfort you: 3:2
        - (3) To encourage stability despite

afflictions: 3:3–4

(4) To guard from the tempter: 3:5

(5) To protect their labor: 3:5

2. The follow up process: 3:6–8

(a) The contents of Timothy's report: 3:6

(b) The reaction to Timothy's report: 3:7–10

(1) Comfort and encouragement: 3:7–8

(2) Thanksgiving and prayer: 3:9–13

III. Looking ahead: Conduct in light of the return of the Lord: 4:1–5:24

A. God-pleasing conduct: 4:1–2

B. Sanctification: 4:3–8

1. The basis for sanctification: It is God's will: 4:3

2. The application of sanctification: 4:3–8

(a) To abstain from fornication: 4:3–5

(b) To abstain from defrauding a brother: 4:6

C. Reasons for proper conduct: 4:6–8

1. Sin brings God's vengeance: 4:6

2. Proper conduct is in accord with the call of God: 4:7

3. Rejection of proper conduct is rejection of God: 4:8

D. Brotherly love: 4:9–10

1. Commendation of their love: 4:9

2. Exhortation to further love: 4:10

E. Exhortations to be industrious: 4:11–12

1. Study to be quiet: 4:11

2. Do your own business: 4:11

3. Work with your own hands: 4:11

4. Walk honestly toward unbelievers: 4:12

F. Instructions about the dead in Christ: 4:12–18

1. The need for proper instruction: 4:12–13

2. The relation of the dead to the returning Christ: 4:14–15

(a) The dead in Christ will be brought with Him: 4:14

(b) The living will not precede the dead in Christ: 4:15

3. The manner and results of Christ's coming: 4:16–17

(a) The manner of His coming: 4:16

(b) The results of His coming: 4:16–17

(1) The dead raised first: 4:16

(2) The living caught up: 4:17

(3) Believers forever with the Lord: 4:17

4. The comfort in these words to be utilized by believers: 4:18

G. Watchfulness in view of the Lord's coming: 5:1–11

1. Uncertainty in the time of His coming: 5:1–2

(a) Their lack of need for instruction: 5:1

(b) Their knowledge about how he will come: 5:2

2. The result of this uncertainty for those who are unprepared: 5:3

3. The effect of this uncertainty on believers: 5:4–11

(a) Be prepared: 5:4

(b) Walk in the light: 5:5

(c) Do not sleep spiritually: 5:6

(d) Watch: 5:6
(e) Be sober: 5:6–8
(f) Put on the breastplate of faith and love: 5:8
4. The assurance of the believer: 5:9–11
(a) Appointed to salvation, not to wrath: 5:9–10
(b) Comfort and edification because of this hope: 5:11

H. Church relationships: 5:12–15
1. Know those who labor among you and are over you: 5:12
2. Hold them in high regard: 5:13
3. Warn the unruly: 5:14
4. Comfort the feebleminded: 5:14
5. Support the weak: 5:14
6. Be patient towards all: 5:14
7. Do not return evil for evil: 5:15
8. Follow that which is good: 5:15

I. Personal conduct: 5:16–22
1. Rejoice evermore: 5:16
2. Pray without ceasing: 5:17
3. In every thing give thanks: 5:18
4. Quench not the Spirit: 5:19
5. Despise not prophesying: 5:20
6. Prove all things: 5:21
7. Hold fast that which is good: 5:21
8. Abstain from the appearance of evil: 5:22

IV. Conclusion: 5:23–28
A. A blessing on them: 5:23–24
B. Request for prayer: 5:25
C. Greetings: 5:26
D. The charge: 5:27
E. The wish for grace of the Lord: 5:28

2. Helpful summaries of 1 Thessalonians

Bird's eye view

Paul summarizes his ministry among the newly founded Christian church at Thessalonica and then urges his readers to lead a pure life and look forward to Jesus' return.

Reading plan

The following reading plan, taking one reading per day, enables you to read through 1 Thessalonians five days.

1 Thessalonians 1:1–1:10
1 Thessalonians 2:1–2:20
1 Thessalonians 3:1–3:13
1 Thessalonians 4:1–4:18
1 Thessalonians 5:1–5:28

Verses to memorize

1 Thessalonians 3:12–13

And the Lord make you to increase and abound in love one toward another, and toward all men, even as we do toward you: To the end he may stablish your hearts unblameable in holiness before God, even our Father, at the coming of our Lord Jesus Christ with all his saints. KJV

1 Thessalonians 5:16–22

[16] Rejoice evermore.
[17] Pray without ceasing.
[18] In every thing give thanks: for this is the will of God in Christ Jesus about you.
[19] Quench not the Spirit.
[20] Despise not prophesyings.

[21] Prove all things; hold fast that which is good.

[22] Abstain from all appearance of evil. KJV

Statistics

Thirteenth New Testament book

Eighth letter by the apostle Paul

5 chapters

89 verses

1,857 words

Number of Old Testament quotations and allusions in 1 Thessalonians: 2.

Famous saying found in 1 Thessalonians

"Labor of love" 1 Thessalonians 1:3

Names/titles given

Pros Thessalonikeis A: "First to the Thessalonians."

3. Helpful keys to turn to in understanding 1 Thessalonians

Key word/phrase

Coming

In Christ

Key verses

1 Thessalonians 1:9,10; 3:12,13

Themes to study

The Gospel and conversion

The Word of God

Christian service

Jesus in 1 Thessalonians

In 1 Thessalonians Jesus is our hope of salvation.

Lessons to learn from 1 Thessalonians

- Our prayer lives would be enhanced by following the advice in 1 Thessalonians 1:2,3; 3:11–13; 5:23,24.
- The new Christian church at Thessalonica is in many ways an excellent example for us to follow.

4. Studying 1 Thessalonians chapter by chapter

1 Thessalonians 1

Matthew Henry's introduction

After the introduction (v. 1) the apostle begins with a thanksgiving to God for the saving benefits bestowed on them, vv. 2–5. And then mentions the sure evidences of the good success of the gospel among them, which was notorious and famous in several other places, vv. 6–10.

Dr. Adam Clarke's analysis of chapter

The apostle sets forth how the Gospel was brought and preached to the Thessalonians, in consequence of his being persecuted at Philippi, 1, 2.

The manner in which the apostles preached, the matter of their doctrine, and the tenor of their lives, 3–11.

He exhorts them to walk worthy of God, 12.

And commends them for the manner in which they received the Gospel, 13.

How they suffered from their own countrymen, as the first believers did from the Jews, who endeavored to prevent the apostles from preaching the Gospel to the Gentiles, 14–16.

St. Paul's apology for his absence from them; and his earnest desire to see them, founded on his great affection for them, 17–20.

A detailed analysis of chapter

The faith, love, and patience of the Thessalonians, are evident tokens of their election which was manifested in power when the gospel came to them. (1–5)

Its powerful effects on their hearts and lives. (6–10)

Key verse

Verse 3: "We continually remember before our God and Father your work produced by faith, your labor prompted by love, and your endurance inspired by hope in our Lord Jesus Christ."

Key word / key phrase

Verse 7, "you became a model."

Key event / key person / key theme

Thanksgiving for the faith of the Thessalonians

Key thought

Paul links the Holy Spirit to conviction and power.

Key thing to look out for

The Thessalonians are waiting for Jesus' return.

Key Bible cross-reference

Verse 1. See Acts 17:1.

Key "by way of explanation"

Verse 3, "faith . . . love . . . hope." Paul often linked these three Christian graces. See 5:8; Romans 5:2–5; 1 Corinthians 13:13; Galatians 5:5, 6; Colossians 1:4,5. Paul's visit to Thessalonica is described in Acts 17:1–9. This was probably in the winter of AD 49/50.

Key "Quotable Quote"

"The Christian hope is the hope which has seen everything and endured everything, and has still not despaired, because it believes in God."

William Barclay

1 Thessalonians 2

Matthew Henry's introduction

In this chapter the apostle puts the Thessalonians in mind of the manner of his preaching among them, vv. 1–6. Then of the manner of his conversation among them, vv. 7–12. Afterwards of the success of his ministry, with the effects both on himself and on them (vv. 13–16), and then apologizes for his absence, vv. 17–20.

Dr. Adam Clarke's analysis of chapter

The inscription by Paul, Silvanus, and Timotheus, to the Church of the Thessalonians, 1.

St. Paul gives thanks to God for their good estate, and prays for their continuance in the faith, 2–4.

Shows how the Gospel came to them, and the blessed effects it produced in their life and conversation, 5–7.

How it became published from them through Macedonia and Achaia, and how their faith was everywhere celebrated, 8.

He shows farther, that the Thessalonians had turned from idolatry, become worshippers of the true God, and were waiting for the reve lation of Christ, 9, 10.

A detailed analysis of chapter

The apostle reminds the Thessalonians of his preaching and behavior. (1–12)

He reminds them of how they received the gospel as the word of God. (13–16)

His joy on their account. (17–20)

Key verse

Verse 10: "You are witnesses, and so is God, of how holy, righteous and blameless we were among you who believed."

Key word / key phrase

Verse 2, "in spite of strong opposition."

Key event / key person / key theme

Paul's foundation of the Church, and Satan's attack

Key thought

The apostles' blameless conduct, sincerity and love in Thessalonica.

Key thing to look out for

What do you find most challenging about the ministry of the apostles in Thessalonica?

Key Bible cross-reference

Verse 14. See Acts 17:5.

Key "by way of explanation"

Verse 9, "toil and hardship." Paul was never frightened of rolling up his sleeves and getting stuck in, unlike the Greeks, who looked down on manual labor.

Key "Quotable Quote"

"Christian leadership . . . appears to break down into five main ingredients – clear vision, hard work, dogged perseverance, humble service and iron discipline."

John R.W. Stott

1 Thessalonians 3

Matthew Henry's introduction

In this chapter the apostle gives further evidence of his love to the Thessalonians, reminding them of his sending Timothy to them, with the mention of his design therein and his inducements so to do, vv. 1–5. He acquaints them also with his great satisfaction at the return of Timothy, with good tidings about them, vv. 6–10. And concludes with fervent prayer for them, v. 11, to the end.

Dr. Adam Clarke's analysis of chapter

St Paul informs them how, being hindered him self from visiting them, he had sent Timothy to comfort them, of whom he gives a high character, 1, 2.

Shows that trials and difficulties are unavoidable in the present state, 3, 4.

Mentions the joy he had on hearing by Timothy

of their steadiness in the faith, for which he returns thanks to God; and prays earnestly for their increase, 5–10.

Prays also that God may afford him an oppor tunity of seeing them, 11.

And that they may abound in love to God and one another, and be unblamable in holiness at the coming of Christ, 12, 13.

A detailed analysis of chapter

The apostle sent Timothy to strengthen and comfort the Thessalonians (1–5)

He rejoiced at the good news about their faith and love. (6–10)

And for their increase in grace. (11–13)

Key verse

Verse 13: "May he strengthen your hearts so that you will be blameless and holy in the presence of our God and Father when our Lord Jesus comes with all his holy ones."

Key word / key phrase

Verse 12 "God's fellow-worker."

Key event / key person / key theme

Paul's intense love and care for his spiritual children.

Key thought

Verse 5, the power of the devil to tempt and harm young Christians.

Key thing to look out for

What does Paul specially pray for these persecuted Christians?

Key Bible cross-reference

Verse 3. See 2 Timothy 2:12.

Key "by way of explanation"

It is clear from these verses that Timothy met Paul in Athens, then returned to Thessalonica, joining Paul again in Corinth. This is a fuller account than the narrative in Acts 17:14–15 and 18:1–5.

Key "Quotable Quote"

"True patience grows with the growth of love."

Gregory the Great

1 Thessalonians 4

Matthew Henry's introduction

In this chapter the apostle gives earnest exhortations to abound in holiness, with a caution against uncleanness, enforced with several arguments, vv. 1–8. He then mentions the great duties of brotherly love, and, quietness with industry in our callings, vv. 9–12. And concludes with comforting those who mourned for their relations and friends that died in the Lord, vv. 13–18.

Dr. Adam Clarke's analysis of chapter

The apostle exhorts them to attend to the direc tions which he had already given them, that they might know how to walk and please God, 1, 2.

Gives them exhortations about continence, chastity, and matrimonial fidelity, 3–8.

Speaks about their love to each other, and love to the Churches of Christ; and exhorts them to continue and increase in it, 9, 10.

Counsels them to observe an inoffensive con duct, to mind their own affairs, to do their own business, and to live honestly, 11, 12.

Not to sorrow for the dead, as people who have no hope of a resurrection; because to Christians the resurrection of Christ is a proof of the resurrection of his followers, 13, 14.

Gives a short but awful description of the appearing of Christ to judge the world, 15.

A detailed analysis of chapter

Exhortations to purity and holiness. (1–8)

To brotherly love, peaceful behavior, and diligence. (9–12)

Key verse

Verse 9: "Now about brotherly love we do not need to write to you, for you yourselves have been taught by God to love each other."

Key word / key phrase

Verse 16, "the dead in Christ will rise first."

Key event / key person / key theme

Sexual morality, earning a living, and the dead

Key thought

Christians please God by living holy, loving, peaceful, and productive lives.

Key thing to look out for

Verse 18. In what way are verses 13–17 an encouragement?

Key Bible cross-reference

Verses 15–17. See 1 Corinthians 15:51, 52.

Key "by way of explanation"

Verses 13–18. Christians in Thessalonica seem to have been afraid that dead Christians would not experience the glory of the Second Coming. Paul corrects this view. "Clouds" are often a reference to the presence of the diving glory.

Key "Quotable Quote"

"Faith in Jesus without the expectation of Christ's *parousia* is a check that is never cashed, a promise that is not made in earnest."

Peter Lewis

1 Thessalonians 5

Matthew Henry's introduction

The apostle, having spoken in the end of the previous chapter about the resurrection, and the second coming of Christ, proceeds to speak about the uselessness of enquiring after the particular time of Christ's coming, which would be sudden and terrible to the wicked, but comfortable to the saints, vv. 1–5. He then exhorts them to the duties of watchfulness, sobriety, and the exercise of faith, love, and hope, as being suitable to their state, vv. 6–10. In the next words he exhorts them to several duties they owed to others, or to one another (vv. 11–15), afterwards to several other Christian duties of great importance (vv. 16–22), and then concludes this epistle, vv. 23–28.

Dr. Adam Clarke's analysis of chapter

The apostle continues to speak of Christ's com ing to judgment, and the uncertainty of the time in which it shall take place, and the careless state of sinners, 1–3.

Shows the Thessalonians that they are children of the light; that they should watch and pray, and put on the armor of God, being called to obtain salvation by Christ, who died for them; that whether dead or alive, when the day of judgment comes, they may live for ever with him; and that they should comfort and edify each other with these considerations, 4–11.

He exhorts them to remember those who labor among them, and are over them in the Lord; and to esteem such highly for their work's sake, 12, 13.

He charges them to warn, comfort, and support those who stood in need of such assistance, and to be patient and beneficent towards all, 14, 15.

He points out their high spiritual privileges; warns them against neglecting or misusing the gifts of the Spirit, and the means of grace, 16–20.

They are also exhorted to prove all things; to abstain from all evil; and to expect to be sanctified, through spirit, soul, and body, by him who has promised this, and who is faithful to his promises, 21–24.

Recommends himself and brethren to their prayers; shows them how they are to greet each other; charges them to read this epistle to all the brethren; and concludes with the usual apostolic benediction, 25–28.

A detailed analysis of chapter

The apostle tells the Christians to be ready for the coming of Christ which will come suddenly. (1–11)

He gives instructions about several particular duties. (12–22)

And concludes with prayer, greetings, and a blessing. (23–28)

Key verse

Verse 17: "Pray continually."

Key word / key phrase

Verse 2, "will come like a thief in the night."

Key event / key person / key theme

The Day of the Lord, and holy living

Key thought

Note how Paul contrasts light and darkness in this chapter.

Key thing to look out for

Paul insists that evil must be avoided.

Key Bible cross-reference

Verse 8. See Isaiah 59:17.

Key "by way of explanation"

Verse 21, "Test everything." If the Christians Paul wrote to had not been so gullible he would not have had to issue so many warnings to them. All teaching had to be in line with the gospel of Jesus. That was the supreme test.

Key "Quotable Quote"

"I do not think that in the last forty years I have lived one conscious hour that was not influenced by the thought of our Lord's return."

Lord Shaftesbury

5. Select bibliography for 1 Thessalonians

Bruce, F. F. *I and II Thessalonians*. Waco: Word, 1982.

Guthrie, Donald. *New Testament Introduction*. Downers Grove, Ill.: InterVarsity, 1970.

Hendriksen, William. *I and II Thessalonians* (New Testament Commentary). Grand Rapids: Baker Book House, 1955.

Lightfoot, J. B. *Notes on the Epistles of St. Paul*. Grand Rapids: Zondervan (1957 reprint), 1895.

Marshall, I. H. *I and II Thessalonians*. Grand Rapids: Eerdmans, 1983.

Morris, Leon. *The First and Second Epistles to the Thessalonians* (NIC). Grand Rapids: Eerdmans, 1959.

2 Thessalonians

1. Book by book: Introduction to 2 Thessalonians

Introduction

Introduction

Genuineness

Its genuineness is attested by Polycarp (*Epistle to the Philippians*, 11), who alludes to 2 Thess. 3:15. Justin Martyr *(Dialogue with Trypho*, p. 193.32), alludes to 2 Thess. 2:3. Irenaeus (*Against Heresies,* 7.2) quotes 2 Thess. 2:8. Clement of Alexandria (*Miscellanies*, 1.5, p. 554; *The Instructor*, 1.17), quotes 2 Thess. 3:2, as Paul's words. Tertullian (*On the Resurrection of the Flesh*, 24) quotes 2 Thess. 2:1, 2, as part of Paul's Epistle.

Purpose

The accounts from Thessalonica, after sending of the first Epistle, represented the faith and love of the Christians there as on the increase; and their constancy in the middle of persecutions unshaken. One error of doctrine, however, resulting in practical evil, had sprung up among them. The apostle's description of Christ's sudden second coming (1 Thess. 4:13, etc., and 1 Thess. 5:2), and the possibility of its being at any time, led them to believe it was actually at hand. Some professed to know by "the Spirit" (2 Thess. 2:2) that it was so; and others alleged that Paul had said so when with them. A letter, too, purporting to be from the apostle to that effect, seems to have been circulated among them. (That 2 Thess. 2:2 refers to such a spurious letter, rather than to Paul's first Epistle, appears likely from the statement, 2 Thess. 3:17, as to his autograph salutation being the mark whereby his genuine letters might be known). Hence some neglected their daily business and threw themselves on the charity of others, as if their sole duty was to wait for the coming of the Lord.

This error, therefore, needed rectifying, and forms a leading topic of the second Epistle. He in it tells them (2 Thess. 2:1–17), that before the Lord comes, there must first be a great apostasy, and the Man of Sin must be revealed; and that the Lord's sudden coming is no ground for neglecting daily business; that to do so would only bring scandal on the Church, and was contrary to his own practice among them (2 Thess. 3:7–9), and that the faithful must withdraw themselves from such disorderly professors (2 Thess. 3:6, 10–15).

Thus, there are three divisions of the Epistle:

2 Thess. 1:1–12. Commendations of the Thessalonians' faith, love, and patience, amidst persecutions.

2 Thess. 2:1–17. The error as to the immediate coming of Christ corrected, and the previous rise and downfall of the Man of Sin foretold.

2 Thess. 3:1–16. Exhortations to orderly conduct in their whole walk, with prayers for them to the God of peace, followed by his autograph salutation and benediction.

Date

As the Epistle is written in the joint names of Timothy and Silas, as well as Paul's own, and as these were with Paul while at Corinth, and not with him for a long time subsequently to his having left that city (compare Acts 18:18, with Acts 19:22; indeed, as to Silas, it is doubtful whether he was ever subsequently with Paul), it follows, the place of writing must have been Corinth, and the date, during the one "year and six months" of his stay there, Acts 18:11 (namely, beginning with the autumn of A.D. 52, and ending with the spring of A.D. 54), say about six months after his first Epistle, early in A.D. 53.

Style

The style is not different from that of most of Paul's other writings, except in the prophetic portion of it (2 Thess. 2:1–12), which is distinguished from them in subject matter. As is usual in his more solemn passages (for instance, in the denunciatory and prophetic portions of his Epistles, for example, compare Col. 2:8, 16, with 2 Thess. 2:3; 1 Cor. 15:24–28, with 2 Thess. 2:8, 9; Rom. 1:18, with 2 Thess. 2:8, 10), his diction here is more lofty, abrupt, and elliptical. As the former Epistle dwells mostly on the second Advent in its aspect of glory to the sleeping and the living saints (1 Thess. 4:1–5:28), so this Epistle dwells mostly on it in its aspect of everlasting destruction to the wicked and him who shall be the final consummation of wickedness, the Man of Sin. So far was Paul from laboring under an erroneous impression as to Christ's speedy coming, when he wrote his first Epistle (which rationalists impute to him), that he had distinctly told them, when he was with them, the same truths as to the apostasy being about first to arise, which he now insists on in this second Epistle (2 Thess. 2:5). Several points of coincidence occur between the two Epistles, confirming the genuineness of the latter. Thus, compare 2 Thess. 3:2, with 1 Thess. 2:15, 16; again, 2 Thess. 2:9, the Man of Sin "coming after the working of Satan," with 1 Thess. 2:18; 3:5, where Satan's incipient work as the hinderer of the Gospel, and the tempter, appears; again, mild warning is enjoined, 1 Thess. 5:14; but, in this second Epistle, when the evil had grown worse, stricter discipline (2 Thess. 3:6, 14): "withdraw from" the "company" of such.

Paul and Thessalonica

Paul probably visited Thessalonica on his way to Asia subsequently (Acts 20:4), and took with him thence Aristarchus and Secundus: the former became his "companion in travel" and shared with him his perils at Ephesus, also those of his shipwreck, and was his "fellow prisoner" at Rome (Acts 27:2; Col. 4:10; Phile. 24). According to tradition he became bishop of Apamea.

A. R. Faussett

Detailed outline

- I. Introduction: 1:1–2
  - A. From Paul, Silvanus, and Timotheus: 1:1
  - B. To the church of the Thessalonians: 1:1
  - C. Grace and peace from God and Jesus: 1:2
- II. Comfort in the hope of Christ's return: 1:3–12
  - A. Thanksgiving for their Christian example: 1:3–4
  - B. Comfort in the righteous judgment of God: 1:5–10
    1. The indication of God's righteous judgment: 1:5
    2. The revelation of God's righteous judgment: 1:6–8
    3. The consequences of God's righteous judgment: 1:9–10
       - (a) Eternal punishment of the lost: 1:9
       - (b) Glorification of the saints: 1:10
  - C. Prayer for the believers: 1:11–12
    1. The content of the prayer: 1:11
    2. The purpose of the prayer: 1:12
- III. Caution regarding the time of Christ's return: 2:1–17
  - A. Paul's concern: 2:1–2
    1. His concern is about the coming of the day of the Lord: 2:1
    2. Attitudes prohibited: 2:2
  - B. Signs of the end: 2:3–12
    1. A great falling away: 2:3
    2. The man of sin (antichrist) is revealed: 2:3–6
       - (a) He opposes God: 2:4
       - (b) He will sit as God in the temple: 2:4
       - (c) He will claim to be God: 2:4
       - (d) He will be revealed in his time: 2:5–6
    3. He already is at work in the world: 2:7–8
    4. His destiny: 2:8
    5. Signs which show the antichrist: 2:9–12
  - C. A prayer for the Thessalonian believers: 2:13–17
    1. Thanksgiving because of God's choice of them: 2:13–14
    2. Exhortation to be steadfast: 2:15

3. A prayer for their comfort and stability: 2:16–17

IV. Commands in the light of Christ's return: 3:1–15

A. A command to pray: 3:1–2

1. For freedom to spread the Gospel: 3:1
2. For safety of the messengers: 3:2

B. A command to grow spiritually: 3:3–5

C. Commands regarding conduct and relationships: 3:6–12

1. Keep away from idle brothers: 3:6
2. Follow right examples of spiritual leadership: 3:7–10
3. Each believer is to be productive: 3:10–12
4. Do not be weary in well-doing: 3:13
5. Have no company with those who do not obey the Word: 3:14
6. Do not think of them as enemies: 3:15

V. Conclusion: 3:16–18

A. The supplication: 3:16

B. Paul's signature: 3:17

C. The benediction: 3:18

2. Helpful summaries of 2 Thessalonians

Bird's eye view

Some Christians at Thessalonica had some warped ideas about Jesus' return and had even stopped working. Paul corrects their wrong thinking in this matter.

Reading plan

The following reading plan, taking one reading per day, enables you to read through 2 Thessalonians in three days.

2 Thessalonians 1:1–1:12
2 Thessalonians 2:1–2:17
2 Thessalonians 3:1–3:18

Verse to memorize

2 Thessalonians 3:5

And the Lord direct your hearts into the love of God, and into the patient waiting for Christ. KJV

Statistics

Fourteenth New Testament book
Ninth letter by the apostle Paul
3 chapters
47 verses
1,042 words
Number of Old Testament quotations and allusions in 2 Thessalonians: 2.

Names/titles given

Pros Thessalonikeis B: "Second to the Thessalonians."

3. Helpful keys to turn to in understanding 2 Thessalonians

Key word

Waiting

Key verses

2 Thessalonians 2:2,3; 2:13,14

Themes to study

Jesus' return and judgment
Satan

Jesus in 2 Thessalonians

In 2 Thessalonians Jesus is our returning Lord.

Lessons to learn from 2 Thessalonians

- Christians should not be work shy.
- "Difficult" people are not to be shunned or ignored.

4. Studying 2 Thessalonians chapter by chapter

2 Thessalonians 1

Matthew Henry's introduction

After the introduction (vv. 1, 2) the apostle begins this epistle with an account of his high esteem for these Thessalonians, vv. 3, 4. He then comforts them under their afflictions and persecutions (vv. 5–10) and tells them what his prayers were to God for them, vv. 11, 12.

Dr. Adam Clarke's analysis of chapter

The salutation of St. Paul and his companions, 1, 2.

The apostle gives thanks to God for their faith, love, and union; and for their patience under persecutions, 3, 4.

Speaks of the coming of our Lord Jesus Christ, the punishment of the ungodly, and the glori fication of the righteous, 5–10.

Prays that God may count them worthy of their calling, that the name of Jesus may be glori fied in them, 11, 12.

A detailed analysis of chapter

The apostle blesses God for the growing state of the love and patience of the Thessalonians. (1–4)

And encourages them to persevere despite all their sufferings for Christ. They are to keep his Second Coming again in mind. (5–12)

Key verse

Verse 8: "He will punish those who do not know God and do not obey the gospel of our Lord Jesus."

Key word / key phrase

Verse 3, "we ought always to thank God for you."

Key event / key person / key theme

Thanksgiving and prayer

Key thought

When Paul taught some aspect of the Christian faith he most often linked it to God's own nature.

Key thing to look out for

Here in verse 6 Paul says God is just and then he goes on to teach what flows from this.

Key Bible cross-reference

Verse 1. See Acts 17:1.

Key "by way of explanation"

Verse 6, "God is just." Because of God's justice he cannot ignore or wink at sin. God punishes sin, especially unrepentant sinners.

Key "Quotable Quote"

"The Lord is not only tender and merciful and full of compassion, but he is also the God of justice, holiness, and wrath."

Billy Graham

2 Thessalonians 2

Matthew Henry's introduction

The apostle is very careful to hinder the spreading of an error into which some among them had fallen about the coming of Christ, as being very near, vv. 1–3. Then he proceeds to confute the error he cautioned them against, by telling them of two great events that were antecedent to the coming of Christ–a general apostasy, and the revelation of antichrist, about whom the apostle tells them many remarkable things, about his name, his character, his rise, his fall, his reign, and the sin and ruin of his subjects, vv. 4–12. He then comforts them against the terror of this apostasy, and exhorts them to steadfastness, vv. 13–15. And concludes with a prayer for them, vv. 16, 17.

Dr. Adam Clarke's analysis of chapter

He exhorts the Thessalonians to stand fast in the faith, and not to be alarmed at the rumors they heard about the sudden coming of Christ, 1, 2.

Because, previously to this coming, there would be a great apostasy from the true faith, and a manifestation of a son of perdition, of whose unparalleled presumption he gives an awful description; as well as of his pernicious success among men, and the means which he would use to deceive and pervert the world; and particularly those who do not receive the love of the truth, but have pleasure in unrighteousness, 3–12.

He thanks God for their steadfastness; shows the great privileges to which they were called; and prays that they may be comforted and established in every good word and work, 13–17.

A detailed analysis of chapter

Warns against the erroneous view that the time of Christ's coming is at hand. There will first be a widespread rebellion against God from the faith, and a revealing of the antichristian man of sin. (1–4)

His destruction, and the destruction of those who obey him. (5–12)

Encouragement that the Thessalonians will be kept safe from apostasy; an exhortation to steadfastness, and prayer for them. (13–17)

Key verse

Verse 14: "He called you to this through our gospel, that you might share in the glory of our Lord Jesus Christ."

Key word / key phrase

Verse 1, "Concerning the coming of our Lord."

Key event / key person / key theme

Explanation about the Day of the Lord

Key thought

Christians must stand firm.

Key thing to look out for

Verse 10. The lovers of evil have freely chosen their course of action.

Key Bible cross-reference

Verse 4. See Daniel 11:36.

Key "by way of explanation"

Verse 8, "the lawless one will be revealed, whom the Lord Jesus will overthrow." The lawless one may seem to be mighty and strong but he will be defeated by a mere "breath" from the mouth of Jesus. The "lawless one", possibly the worst of the antichrists (1 John 2:18) will lead the rebellion against God.

Key "Quotable Quote"

"When we fail to wait prayerfully for God's guidance and strength, we are saying with our actions, if not our lips, that we do not need him."

Charles Hummel

2 Thessalonians 3

Matthew Henry's introduction

In the close of the previous chapter, the apostle had prayed earnestly for the Thessalonians, and now he desires their prayers, encouraging them to trust in God, to which he subjoins another petition for them, vv. 1–5. He then proceeds to give them commands and directions for correcting some things he was informed were amiss among them (vv. 6–15) and concludes with benedictions and prayers, vv. 16–18.

Dr. Adam Clarke's analysis of chapter

The apostle recommends himself and his brethren to the prayers of the Church, that their preaching might be successful, and that they might be delivered from wicked men, 1, 2.

Expresses his confidence in God and them, and prays that they may patiently wait for the coming of Christ, 3–5.

Gives them directions about strict discipline in the Church; and shows how he and his fellow laborers had behaved among them, not avail ing themselves of their own power and authority, 6–9.

Shows them how to treat disorderly and idle people, and not to get weary in well doing, 10–13.

Directs them not to associate with those who obey not the orders contained in this epistle, 14, 15.

Prays that they may have increasing peace, 16,

And concludes with his salutation and benedic tion, 17, 18.

A detailed analysis of chapter

The apostle expresses confidence in the Thessalonians, and prays for them. (1–5)

He urges them to steer clear of the lazy and of busybodies. (6–15)

And concludes with a prayer for them, and a greeting. (16–18)

Key verse

Verse 11: "We hear that some among you are idle. They are not busy; they are busybodies."

Key word / key phrase

Verse 6, "every brother who is idle."

Key event / key person / key theme

Pray for us, God is faithful, don't be idle

Key thought

It was never beneath Paul to ask other Christians to pray for him.

Key thing to look out for

Paul did not believe that idleness should have any place in the life of a Christian.

Key Bible cross-reference

Verse 16. See Ruth 2:4.

Key "by way of explanation"

Verse 11, "busybodies." One worse, in Paul's book, than the idle, were the busybodies. Perhaps because they had so much time on their hands they interfered with other people's lives.

Key "Quotable Quote"

"Thou wilt never be spiritually minded and godly unless thou art silent concerning other men's matters and take full heed to thyself."

Thomas à Kempis

5. Select bibliography for 2 Thessalonians

See Select bibliography for 1 Thessalonians.

1 Timothy

1. Book by book: Introduction to 1 Timothy

Introduction

Genuineness

The ancient Church never doubted of their being canonical and written by Paul. They are in the Peschito Syriac version of the second century. Muratori's Fragment on the Canon of Scripture, at the close of the second century, acknowledges them as such. Irenaeus (*Against Heresies*, 1; 3.3.3; 4.16.3; 2.14.8; 3.11.1; 1.16.3), quotes 1 Tim. 1:4, 9; 6:20; 2 Tim. 4:9–11; Titus 3:10. Clement of Alexandria (*Miscellanies*, 2, p. 457; 3, pp. 534, 536; 1, p. 350), quotes 1 Tim. 6:1, 20; Second Timothy, as to deaconesses; Titus 1:12. Tertullian (*The Prescription against Heretics*, 25; 6), quotes 1 Tim. 6:20; 2 Tim. 1:14; 1 Tim. 1:18; 6:13, etc.; 2 Tim. 2:2; Titus 3:10, 11. Eusebius includes the three in the "universally acknowledged" Scriptures. Also Theophilus of Antioch (*To Autolychus*, 3.14), quotes 1 Tim. 2:1, 2; Titus 3:1, and Caius (in Eusebius [*Ecclesiastical History*, 6.20]) recognizes their authenticity. Clement of Rome, in the end of the first century, in his *First Epistle to the Corinthians,* quotes 1 Tim. 2:8. Ignatius, in the beginning of the second century, in Epistle to Polycarp, alludes to 2 Tim. 2:4. Polycarp, in the beginning of the second century (*Epistle to the Philippians*, 4), alludes to 2 Tim. 2:4; and in the ninth chapter to 2 Tim. 4:10. Hegisippus, in the end of the second century, in Eusebius (*Ecclesiastical*

History, 3.32), alludes to 1 Tim. 6:3, 20. Athenagoras, in the end of the second century, alludes to 1 Tim. 6:16. Justin Martyr, in the middle of the second century (*Dialogue with Trypho*, 47), alludes to Titus 3:4. The Gnostic Marcion alone rejected these Epistles.

Heresies

The heresies opposed in them form the transition stage from Judaism, in its ascetic form, to Gnosticism, as subsequently developed. The references to Judaism and legalism are clear (1 Tim. 1:7; 4:3; Titus 1:10, 14; 3:9). Traces of beginning Gnosticism are also unequivocal (1 Tim. 1:4). The Gnostic theory of a twofold principle from the beginning, evil as well as good, appears in germ in 1 Tim. 4:3, etc. In 1 Tim. 6:20 the term Gnosis ("science") itself occurs.

Another Gnostic error, namely, that "the resurrection is past," is alluded to in 2 Tim. 2:17, 18. The Judaism herein opposed is not that of the earlier Epistles, which upheld the law and tried to join it with faith in Christ for justification. It first passed into that phase of it which appears in the Epistle to the Colossians, whereby will-worship and angel-worship were superadded to Judaizing opinions. Then a further stage of the same evil appears in the Epistle to the Philippians (Phil. 3:2, 18, 19), whereby immoral practice accompanied false doctrine as to the resurrection (compare 2 Tim. 2:18, with 1 Cor. 15:12, 32, 33). This descent from legality to superstition, and from superstition to godlessness, appears more matured in the references to it in these Pastoral Epistles.

The false teachers now know not the true use of the law (1 Tim. 1:7, 8), and further, have put away good conscience as well as the faith (1 Tim. 1:19; 4:2); speak lies in hypocrisy, are corrupt in mind, and regard godliness as a means of earthly gain (1 Tim. 6:5 Titus 1:11); overthrow the faith by heresies eating as a canker, saying the resurrection is past (2 Tim. 2:17, 18), leading captive silly women, ever learning yet never knowing the truth, reprobate as Jannes and Jambres (2 Tim. 3:6, 8), defiled, unbelieving, professing to know God, but in works denying Him, abominable, disobedient, reprobate (Titus 1:15, 16). This description accords with that in the Catholic Epistles of St. John and St. Peter, and, in the Epistle to the Hebrews. This fact proves the later date of these Pastoral Epistles as compared with Paul's earlier Epistles. The Judaism reprobated herein is not that of an earlier date, so scrupulous as to the law; it was now tending to immortality of practice. On the other hand, the Gnosticism opposed in these Epistles is not the anti-Judaic Gnosticism of a later date, which arose as a consequence of the overthrow of Judaism by the destruction of Jerusalem and the temple, but it was the intermediate phase between Judaism and Gnosticism, in which the Oriental and Greek elements of the latter were in a kind of amalgam with Judaism, just prior to the overthrow of Jerusalem.

Instructions to church leaders

The instructions to church leaders and ministers, "bishop-elders, and deacons," are such as were natural for the apostle, in prospect of his own impending departure, to give to Timothy, the president of the Church at Ephesus, and to Titus, holding the same office in Crete, for securing the due administration of the Church when he should be no more, and at a time when heresies were rapidly springing up. Compare his similar anxiety in his address to the Ephesian elders (Acts 20:21–30). The Presbyterate (elders; priest is a contraction from presbyter) and Diaconate had existed from the earliest times in the Church (Acts 6:3; 11:30; 14:23). Timothy and Titus, as superintendents or overseers (so bishop subsequently meant), were to exercise the same power in ordaining elders at Ephesus which the apostle had exercised in his general supervision of all the Gentile churches.

Special expressions and ways of thinking

The special ways of thinking and special expressions are suited to the different subject and circumstances of those addressed and those spoken of in these Epistles. Some of these peculiar phrases occur also in Galatians, in which, as in the Pastoral Epistles, he, with his characteristic fervor, attacks the false teachers. Compare 1 Tim. 2:6; Titus 2:14, "gave Himself for us," with Gal. 1:4; 1 Tim. 1:17; 2 Tim. 4:18, "for ever and ever," with Gal. 1:5: "before God," 1 Tim. 5:21; 6:13; 2 Tim. 2:14; 4:1, with Gal. 1:20: "a pillar," 1 Tim. 3:15, with Gal. 2:9: "mediator," 1 Tim. 2:5, with Gal. 3:20: "in due season," 1 Tim. 2:6; 6:15; Titus 1:3 with Gal. 6:9.

Date and place of writing

The First Epistle to Timothy was written not long after Paul had left Ephesus for Macedon (1 Tim. 1:3). Now, as Timothy was in Macedon with Paul (2 Cor. 1:1) on the occasion of Paul's having passed from Ephesus into that country, as recorded, Acts 19:22; 20:1, whereas the First Epistle to Timothy contemplates a longer stay of Timothy in Ephesus, Mosheim supposes that Paul was nine months of the "three years" stay mostly at Ephesus (Acts 20:31) in Macedonia, and elsewhere (perhaps Crete), (the mention of only "three months" and "two years," Acts 19:8, 10, favors this, the remaining nine months being spent elsewhere); and that during these nine months Timothy, in Paul's absence, looked after the Church of Ephesus. It is not likely that Ephesus and the neighboring churches should have been left long without church officers and church organization, rules about which are given in this Epistle. Moreover, Timothy was still "a youth" (1 Tim. 4:12), which he could hardly be called after Paul's first imprisonment, when he must have been at least thirty-four years of age. Lastly, in Acts 20:25, Paul asserts his knowledge that the Ephesians would not all see his face again, so that 1 Tim. 1:3 will thus refer to his stay in Ephesus, recorded in Acts 19:10, from where he went on into Macedonia. But the difficulty is to account for the false teachers having sprung up almost immediately (according to this theory) after the foundation of the Church. However, his visit recorded in Acts 19:1–41 was not his first visit. The beginning of the Church at Ephesus was probably made at his visit a year before (Acts 18:19–21). Apollos, Aquila and Priscilla, carried on the work (Acts 18:24–26). Thus, as to the sudden growth of false teachers, there was time enough for their springing up, especially considering that the first converts at Ephesus were under Apollos' imperfect Christian teachings at first, imbued as he was likely to be with the tenets of Philo of Alexandria, Apollos' home town, combined with John the Baptist's Old Testament teachings (Acts 18:24–26). Besides Ephesus, from its position in Asia, its notorious voluptuousness and sorcery (Acts 19:18, 19), and its lewd worship of Diana (similar to the Phœnician Ashtoreth), was likely from the first to tinge Christianity in some of its converts with Oriental speculations and Asiatic licentiousness of practices. Thus the phenomenon of the phase of error presented in this Epistle, being between Judaism and later Gnosticism, might occur at an early period in the Ephesian Church, as well as later, when we know it had open "apostles" of error (Rev. 2:2, 6), and Nicolaitans infamous in practice.

As to the close connection between this First Epistle and the Second Epistle (which must have been written at the close of Paul's life), on which Alford relies for his theory of making the First Epistle also written at the close of Paul's life, the similarity of circumstances, the person addressed being one and the same, and either in Ephesus at the time, or at least connected with Ephesus as its church overseer, and having heretics to contend with of the same stamp as in the First Epistle, would account for the connection. There is not so great identity of tone as to compel us to adopt the theory that some years could not have elapsed between the two Epistles.

However, all these arguments against the later date may be answered. This First Epistle may refer not to the first organization of the Church under its bishops, or elders and deacons, but to the moral qualifications laid down at a later period for those officers when scandals rendered such directions needful. Indeed, the object for which he left Timothy at Ephesus he states (1 Tim. 1:3) to be, not to organize the Church for the first time, but to restrain the false teachers. The directions about the choice of suitable elders and deacons refer to the filling of vacancies, not to their first appointment. The fact that there existed an institution for Church widows implies an established organization.

As to Timothy's "youth," it may be spoken of in comparison with Paul, now "the aged" (Phile. 9), and with some of the Ephesian elders, senior to Timothy their overseer. As to Acts 20:25, we know not but that "all" of the elders of Ephesus called to Miletus "never saw Paul's face" afterwards, as he "knew" (doubtless by inspiration) would be the case, which obviates the need of Alford's lax view, that Paul was wrong in this his positive inspired anticipation (for such it was, not a mere boding surmise as to the future). Thus he probably visited Ephesus again (1 Tim. 1:3; 2 Tim. 1:18; 4:20, he would hardly have been at Miletum, so near Ephesus, without visiting Ephesus) after his first imprisonment in Rome, though all the Ephesian elders whom he had addressed formerly at Miletus did not again see him.

The general similarity of subject and style, and of the state of the Church between the two Epistles, favors the view that they were written fairly close together. Also, against the theory of the early date is the difficulty of defining, when, during Paul's two or three years' stay at Ephesus, we can insert an absence of Paul from Ephesus long enough for the requirements of the case, which imply a lengthened stay and superintendence of Timothy at Ephesus (see, however, 1 Tim. 3:14, on the other side) after having been "left" by Paul there. Timothy did not stay there when Paul left Ephesus (Acts 19:22; 20:1;

2 Cor. 1:1). In 1 Tim. 3:14, Paul says, "I write, hoping to come unto thee shortly," but on the earlier occasion of his passing from Ephesus to Macedon he had no such expectation, but had planned to spend the summer in Macedon, and the winter in Corinth, (1 Cor. 16:6). The expression "Till I come" (1 Tim. 4:13), implies that Timothy was not to leave his post till Paul should arrive; this and the former objection, however, do not hold good against Mosheim's theory. Moreover, Paul in his farewell address to the Ephesian elders prophetically anticipates the rise of false teachers hereafter of their own selves; therefore this First Epistle, which speaks of their actual presence at Ephesus, would naturally seem to be not prior, but subsequent, to the address, that is, will belong to the later date assigned. In the Epistle to the Ephesians no notice is taken of the Judaeo-Gnostic errors, which would have been noticed had they been really in existence; however, they are alluded to in the contemporaneous sister Epistle to Colossians (Col. 2:1–23).

Whatever doubt must always remain as to the date of the First Epistle, there can be hardly any as to that of the Second Epistle. In 2 Tim. 4:13, Paul directs Timothy to bring the books and cloak which the apostle had left at Troas. Assuming that the visit to Troas referred to is the one mentioned in Acts 20:5–7, it will follow that the cloak and parchments lay for about seven years at Troas, that being the time that elapsed between the visit and Paul's first imprisonment at Rome: a very unlikely supposition, that he should have left either unused for so long. Again, when, during his first Roman imprisonment, he wrote to the Colossians (Col. 4:14) and Philemon (Phile. 24), Demas was with him; but when he was writing 2 Tim. 4:10, Demas had forsaken him from love of this world, and gone to Thessalonica. Again, when he wrote to the Ephesians, Colossians, Philippians, and Philemon, he had good hopes of a speedy liberation; but here in 2 Tim. 4:6–8, he anticipates immediate death, having been at least once already tried (2 Tim. 4:16). Again, he is in this Epistle seen in closer confinement than he was when writing those former Epistles in his first imprisonment (even in the Philippians, which represent him in greater uncertainty as to his life, he cherished the hope of soon being delivered, Phil. 2:24; 2 Tim. 1:16–18; 2:9; 4:6–8, 16). Again (2 Tim. 4:20), he speaks of having left Trophimus sick at Miletum. This could not have been on the occasion, Acts 20:15. For Trophimus was with Paul at Jerusalem shortly afterwards (Acts 21:29). Besides, he would thus be made to speak of an event six or seven years after its occurrence, as a recent event: moreover, Timothy was, on that occasion of the apostle being at Miletum, with Paul, and therefore needed not to be informed of Trophimus' sickness there (Acts 20:4–17). Also, the statement (2 Tim. 4:20), "Erastus abode at Corinth," implies that Paul had shortly before been at Corinth, and left Erastus there; but Paul had not been at Corinth for several years before his first imprisonment, and in the interval Timothy had been with him, so that he did not need to write subsequently about that visit. He must therefore have been liberated after his first imprisonment (indeed, Heb. 13:23, 24, expressly proves that the writer was in Italy and at liberty), and resumed his apostolic journeyings, and been imprisoned at Rome again, whence shortly before his death he wrote Second Timothy.

Eusebius (*Chronicles,* Anno 2083) (beginning October, a.d. 67), says, “Nero, to his other crimes, added the persecution of Christians: under him the apostles Peter and Paul consummated their martyrdom at Rome.” So Jerome (*On Illustrious Men*), “In the fourteenth year of Nero, Paul was beheaded at Rome for Christ’s sake, on the same day as Peter, and was buried on the Ostian Road, in the thirty-seventh year after the death of our Lord.” Alford reasonably conjectures the Pastoral Epistles were written near this date. The interval was possibly filled up (so Clement of Rome states that Paul preached as far as “to the extremity of the west”) by a journey to Spain (Rom. 15:24, 28), according to his own original intention. Muratori’s Fragment on the Canon of Scripture (about a.d. 170) also alleges Paul’s journey into Spain. So Eusebius, Chrysostom, and Jerome. Be that as it may, he seems shortly before his second imprisonment to have visited Ephesus, where a new body of elders governed the Church (Acts 20:25), say in the latter end of a.d. 66, or beginning of 67. Supposing him thirty at his conversion, he would now be upwards of sixty, and older in constitution than in years, through continual hardship. Even four years before he called himself “Paul the aged” (Phile. 9).

From Ephesus he went into Macedonia (1 Tim. 1:3). He may have written the First Epistle to Timothy from that country. But his use of “went,” not “came,” in 1 Tim. 1:3, “When I went into Macedonia,” implies he was not there when writing. Wherever he was, he writes uncertain how long he may be detained from coming to Timothy (1 Tim. 3:14, 15). Birks shows the probability that he wrote from Corinth, between which city and Ephesus the communication was rapid and easy. His course, as on both former occasions, was from Macedon to Corinth. He finds a coincidence between 1 Tim. 2:11–14, and 1 Cor. 14:34, as to women being silent in Church; and 1 Tim. 5:17, 18, and 1 Cor. 9:8–10, as to the maintenance of ministers, on the same principle as the Mosaic law, that the ox should not be muzzled that treadeth out the corn; and 1 Tim. 5:19, 20, and 2 Cor. 13:1–4, as to charges against elders. It would be natural for the apostle in the very place where these directions had been enforced, to reproduce them in his letter.

The date of the Epistle to Titus must depend on that assigned to First Timothy, with which it is connected in subject, phraseology, and tone. There is no difficulty in the Epistle to Titus, viewed by itself, in assigning it to the earlier date, namely, before Paul’s first imprisonment. In Acts 18:18, 19, Paul, in journeying from Corinth to Palestine, for some cause or other landed at Ephesus. Now we find (Titus 3:13) that Apollos in going from Ephesus to Corinth was to touch at Crete (which seems to coincide with Apollos’ journey from Ephesus to Corinth, recorded in Acts 18:24, 27; 19:1); therefore it is not unlikely that Paul may have taken Crete similarly on his way between Corinth and Ephesus; or, perhaps been driven out of his course to it in one of his three shipwrecks spoken of in 2 Cor. 11:25, 26; this will account for his taking Ephesus on his way from Corinth to Palestine, though out of his regular course. At Ephesus Paul may have written the Epistle to Titus (Hug); there he probably met Apollos and gave the Epistle to Titus to his charge, before his departure for Corinth by way of Crete, and before the apostle’s departure for Jerusalem (Acts 18:19–21, 24). Moreover, on Paul’s way back from

Jerusalem and Antioch, he traveled some time in Upper Asia (Acts 19:1); and it was then, probably, that his intention to "winter at Nicopolis" was realized, there being a town of that name between Antioch and Tarsus, lying on Paul's route to Galatia (Titus 3:12). Thus, First Timothy will, in this theory, be placed two and a half years later (Acts 20:1; compare 1 Tim. 1:3).

Alford's argument for classing the Epistle to Titus with First Timothy, as written after Paul's first Roman imprisonment, stands or falls with his argument for assigning First Timothy to that date. Indeed, Hug's unobjectionable argument for the earlier date of the Epistle to Titus, favors the early date assigned to First Timothy, which is so much akin to it, if other arguments be not thought to counterbalance this. The Church of Crete had been just founded (Titus 1:5), and yet the same heresies are censured in it as in Ephesus, which shows that no argument, such as Alford alleges against the earlier date of First Timothy, can be drawn from them (Titus 1:10, 11, 15, 16; 3:9, 11). But vice versa, if, as seems likely from the arguments adduced, the First Epistle to Timothy be assigned to the later date, the Epistle to Titus must, from similarity of style, belong to the same period. Alford traces Paul's last journey before his second imprisonment thus: To Crete (Titus 1:5), Miletus (2 Tim. 4:20), Colosse (fulfilling his intention, Phile. 22), Ephesus (1 Tim. 1:3; 2 Tim. 1:18), from which neighborhood he wrote the Epistle to Titus; Troas, Macedonia, Corinth (2 Tim. 4:20), Nicopolis (Titus 3:12) in Epirus, where he had intended to winter; a place in which, as being a Roman colony, he would be free from violence, and yet would be more open to a direct attack from foes in the metropolis, Rome. Being known in Rome as the leader of the Christians, he was probably (Alford) arrested as implicated in causing the fire in a.d. 64, attributed by Nero to the Christians, and was sent to Rome by the Duumvirs of Nicopolis. There he was imprisoned as a common malefactor (2 Tim. 2:9); his Asiatic friends deserted him, except Onesiphorus (2 Tim. 1:16). Demas, Crescens, and Titus, left him. Tychicus he had sent to Ephesus. Luke alone remained with him (2 Tim. 4:10–12). Under the circumstances he writes the Second Epistle to Timothy, most likely while Timothy was at Ephesus (2 Tim. 2:17; compare 1 Tim. 1:20; 2 Tim. 4:13), begging him to come to him before winter (2 Tim. 4:21), and anticipating his own execution soon (2 Tim. 4:6). Tychicus was perhaps the bearer of the Second Epistle (2 Tim. 4:12). His defense was not made before the emperor, for the latter was then in Greece (2 Tim. 4:16, 17). Tradition represents that he died by the sword, which accords with the fact that his Roman citizenship would exempt him from torture; probably late in A.D. 67 or A.D. 68, the last year of Nero.

Timothy is first mentioned, Acts 16:1, as dwelling in Lystra (not Derbe, compare Acts 20:4). His mother was a Jewess named Eunice (2 Tim. 1:5); his father, "a Greek" (that is, a Gentile). As Timothy is mentioned as "a disciple" in Acts 16:1, he must have been converted before, and this by Paul (1 Tim. 1:2), probably at his former visit to Lystra (Acts 14:6); at the same time, probably, that his Scripture-loving mother, Eunice, and grandmother, Lois, were converted to Christ from Judaism (2 Tim. 3:14, 15). Not only the good report given as to him by the brethren of Lystra, but also his origin, partly Jewish, partly Gentile, adapted him specially for being Paul's assistant in missionary work, laboring as the apostle did in each place, firstly among the Jews, and then among the Gentiles. In order to obviate Jewish prejudices, he first circumcised him. He seems to have accompanied Paul in his tour through Macedonia; but when the apostle went forward to Athens, Timothy and Silas remained in Berea. Having been sent back by Paul to visit the Thessalonian Church (1 Thess. 3:2), he brought his report of it to the apostle at Corinth (1 Thess. 3:6). Hence we find his name joined with Paul's in the addresses of both the Epistles to Thessalonians, which were written at Corinth. We again find him "ministering to" Paul during the lengthened stay at Ephesus (Acts 19:22). Thence he was sent before Paul into Macedonia and to Corinth (1 Cor. 4:17; 16:10). He was with Paul when he wrote the Second Epistle to Corinthians (2 Cor. 1:1); and the following winter in Corinth, when Paul sent from thence his Epistle to the Romans (Rom. 16:21). On Paul's return to Asia through Macedonia, he went forward and waited for the apostle at Troas (Acts 20:3–5). Next we find him with Paul during his imprisonment at Rome, when the apostle wrote the Epistles to Colossians (Col. 1:1), Philemon (Phile. 1), and Philippians (Phil. 1:1). He was imprisoned and set at liberty about the same time as the writer of the Hebrews (Heb. 13:23). In the Pastoral Epistles, we find him mentioned as left by the apostle at Ephesus to superintend the Church there (1 Tim. 1:3). The last notice of him is in the request which Paul makes to him (2 Tim. 4:21) to "come before winter," that is about A.D. 67 (Alford). Eusebius (*Ecclesiastical History*, 3.42), reports that he was first bishop of Ephesus; and (Nicophorus, *Ecclesiastical History*, 3.11), represents that he died by martyrdom. If then, St. John, as tradition represents, resided and died in that city, it must have been at a later period. Paul himself ordained or consecrated him with laying on of his own hands, and those of the presbytery, in accordance with prophetic intimations given respecting him by those possessing the prophetic gift (1 Tim. 1:18; 4:14 2 Tim. 1:6). His self-denying character is shown by his leaving home at once to accompany the apostle, and submitting to circumcision for the Gospel's sake; and also by his abstemiousness (noted in 1 Tim. 5:23) notwithstanding his bodily infirmities, which would have warranted a more generous diet. Timidity and a want of self-confidence and boldness in dealing with the difficulties of his position, seem to have been a defect in his otherwise beautiful character as a Christian minister (1 Cor. 16:10; 1 Tim. 4:12; 2 Tim. 1:7).

Purpose

The purpose of the First Epistle was:

to direct Timothy to charge the false teachers against continuing to teach other doctrine than that of the Gospel (1 Tim. 1:3–20; compare Rev. 2:1–6);

to give him instructions as to the orderly conducting of worship, the qualifications of bishops and deacons, and the selection of widows who should, in return for Church charity, do appointed service (1 Tim. 2:1–6:2);

to warn against covetousness, a sin prevalent at Ephesus, and to urge to good works (1 Tim. 6:3–19).

A. R. Faussett

Detailed outline

I. Introduction: 1:1–3

A. From: Paul: 1:1

B. To: Timothy, a son in the faith: 1:2

C. Grace, mercy, and peace from God and Jesus: 1:2

D. Personal instructions to stay in Ephesus: 1:3

Part One: A Charge To Timothy Preserve Sound Doctrine 1:3–20

I. Preserve the purity of the Gospel: 1:3–11

A. The charge: 1:3–4

B. The aim of the charge: Charity: 1:5

C. The reason for the charge: 1:6–11

II. Paul's relation to the Gospel: 1:12–17

A. Thanksgiving for his call into God's service: 1:12

B. The description of the one called: 1:13

C. The explanation for his appointment: 1:13–26

1. Due to God's grace: 1:13–14

2. To make him an example to others: 1:15–16

D. Paul's praise for his relationship to the Gospel: 1:17

III. Review of the charge of Timothy: 1:18–20

A. The committing of the charge: 1:18

B. The work of Timothy: 1:18–19

1. Fight the good fight: 1:18

2. Hold the faith: 1:19

3. Have a good conscience: 1:19–20

(a) Warning about people who have lost faith: 1:29

(b) Hymenaeus and Alexander: 1:20

Part Two: Organization And Administration Of The Church 2:1–3:13

I. Prayer: 2:1–8

A. The duty of prayer: 2:1

B. The nature of prayer: 2:1

C. The scope of prayer: 2:1–2

1. For all men: 2:1

2. For kings: 2:2

3. For all in authority: 2:2

D. The results of prayer: 2:2–3

1. A quiet, peaceable life in godliness and honesty: 2:2

2. Approval in God's sight: 2:3

E. The mediator of prayer: 2:5–7

1. Jesus Christ the Savior: 2:5–6

2. Paul is ordained as a preacher, apostle, and teacher: 2:7

F. The universality of prayer: 2:8

II. Women in the church: 2:9–15

A. Their appearance: 2:9–10

1. Modest clothes: 2:9

2. Good deeds rather than appearance: 2:9–10

B. Their worship: 2:11–12

C. Their salvation: 2:13–15

III. Qualifications of overseers: 3:1–7

IV. Qualifications of deacons: 3:8–13

V. Paul's reason for writing: Correct behavior in the church: 3:14–16

Part Three: The Minister And His Conduct 4:1–6:21

I. The minister and false teaching: 4:1–5

A. Some will depart from the faith in the last days: 4:1

B. Their errors: 4:1–5

II. Miscellaneous instructions on being a good minister: 4:6–16

III. The minister and his conduct towards various groups in the church: 5:1–6:10

A. Older and younger: 5:1–2

1. Treat an elder as a father: 5:1
2. Treat younger men as brothers: 5:1
3. Treat elderly women as mothers: 5:2
4. Treat younger women as sisters with purity: 5:2

B. Widows: 5:3–16

1. Honor those who are widows indeed: 5:3
2. Responsibilities of relatives of widows: 5:4
3. Definition of a "widow indeed": 5:5–6
4. Responsibilities of relatives of widows continued: 5:7–8
5. Qualifications for "widows indeed": 5:9–13
6. Those not qualified: Younger widows: 5:11–15
7. Instructions to younger widows: 5:16–17
   (a) Marry: 5:16
   (b) Bear children: 5:16
   (c) Guide the house: 5:16
   (d) Live beyond reproach: 5:16
   (e) Warning that some have turned aside after Satan: 5:17

C. Elders: 5:17–25

1. Honor those who rule well: 5:17
2. Provide for those who labor full time in this position: 5:17–18
3. Those who have not ruled well: 5:19–20
   (a) Accusation must be by more than one witness: 5:19
   (b) They are to be rebuked before the assembly: 5:20

D. Miscellaneous: 5:21–25

E. Servants: 6:1–8

1. Honor masters: 6:1
2. Do not take advantage of masters who are believers: 6:2

F. All men:

1. If they teach contrary to sound doctrine of Jesus they are (3):
   (a) Proud: 6:4.
   (b) Know nothing: 6:4
   (c) Engage in controversies and quarrels about words: 6:4–5
2. Withdraw yourself from these type of men: 6:5
3. Godliness with contentment is great gain: 6:6–7
   (a) We came into the world without anything: 6:7
   (b) We can take nothing out of the world: 6:7
   (c) We should be content to have our basic needs met: 6:8

G. Rich: 6:9–19

1. The problems of the rich: 6:9
2. The wrong motive of the rich: 6:10
3. Response of the minister towards riches: 6:11–19
   (a) Flee these things: 6:11
   (b) Follow after: 6:11
      (1) Righteousness.
      (2) Godliness.
      (3) Faith.
      (4) Love.
      (5) Patience.

(6) Meekness.

(c) Fight the good fight of faith: 6:12

(d) Take hold of eternal life: 6:12

(e) Keep this commandment: 6:13–16

(f) Instructions to the rich: 6:17–19

IV. Conclusion: 6:20–21

A. Keep what is entrusted to your care: 6:20

B. Avoid godless talk: 6:20

C. Avoid so-called knowledge: 6:20

D. Grace be with you: 6:21

2. Helpful summaries of 1 Timothy

Bird's eye view

Paul's encouragement to the young pastor Timothy, advising him how to behave and work as a minister.

Reading plan

The following reading plan, taking one reading per day, enables you to read through 1 Timothy in six days.

1 Timothy 1:1–1:20

1 Timothy 2:1–2:15

1 Timothy 3:1–3:16

1 Timothy 4:1–4:16

1 Timothy 5:1–5:25

1 Timothy 6:1–6:21

Verses to memorize

1 Timothy 1:15

This is a faithful saying, and worthy of all acceptation, that Christ Jesus came into the world to save sinners; of whom I am chief. KJV

1 Timothy 2:5

For there is one God, and one mediator between God and men, the man Christ Jesus; KJV

1 Timothy 6:11

But thou, O man of God, flee these things; and follow after righteousness, godliness, faith, love, patience, meekness. KJV

1 Timothy 6:12

Fight the good fight of faith, lay hold on eternal life, whereunto thou art also called, and hast professed a good profession before many witnesses. KJV

Statistics

Fifteenth New Testament book

Tenth letter by the apostle Paul

6 chapters

113 verses

2,269 words

Number of Old Testament quotations and allusions in 1 Timothy: 6.

Famous sayings found in 1 Timothy

"Fight the good faith" 1 Timothy 6:12

"The love of money is the root of all evil" 1 Timothy 6:10

Names/titles given

Pros Timotheon A: "First to Timothy."

3. Helpful keys to turn to in understanding 1 Timothy

Key word/phrase

Charge

In Christ

Key verses

1 Timothy 3:14–16

Themes to study

Christian leadership

Prayer

False teachers

Jesus in 1 Timothy

In 1 Timothy Jesus is our Teacher.

Lessons to learn from 1 Timothy

- Christians must be vigilant against false teaching.
- A Christian minister should be a godly example to his flock.

4. Studying 1 Timothy chapter by chapter

1 Timothy 1

Matthew Henry's introduction

After the inscription (vv. 1, 2) we have,

I. The charge given to Timothy, vv. 3, 4.

II. The true end of the law (vv. 5–11), where he shows that it is entirely agreeable to the gospel.

III. He mentions his own call to be an apostle, for which he expresses his thankfulness, vv. 12–16.

IV. His doxology, v. 17.

V. A renewal of the charge to Timothy, v. 18. And of Hymenæus and Alexander, vv. 19, 20.

Dr. Adam Clarke's analysis of chapter

Paul's salutation to Timothy, 1, 2.

For what purpose he had left him at Ephesus, 3.

What the false apostles taught in opposition to the truth, 4–7.

The true use of the law, 8–11.

He thanks God for his own conversion, and describes his former state, 12–17.

Exhorts Timothy to hold fast faith and a good conscience, and speaks of Hymeneus and Alexander who had made shipwreck of their faith, 18–20.

A detailed analysis of chapter

The apostle greets Timothy. (1–4)

The purpose of the Law given by Moses. (5–11)

Paul's own conversion and call to be an apostle. (12–17)

The obligation to maintain faith and a good conscience. (18–20)

Key verse

Verse 6: "Some have wandered away from these and turned to meaningless talk."

Key word / key phrase

Verse 7, "they do not know what they are talking about."

Key event / key person / key theme

Beware of false teachers

Key thought

Verse 4, "myths and endless genealogies." There are some things that are just best avoided. There is no need to delve into every heresy.

Key thing to look out for

Verse 20, "handed over to Satan," possibly means excommunication – that is, put out of the church, into the world, where Satan rules.

Key Bible cross-reference

Verse 2. See Acts 16:1.

Key "by way of explanation"

Paul writes this letter to Timothy when Timothy has been left in charge of the church at Ephesus (1:3). His purpose is to advise and encourage "his true son in the faith" (1:2; 3:14, 15).

Key "Quotable Quote"

"For all the vigor of his polemic, St. Paul does not content himself with the denunciation of error, but finds the best defense against its insidious approaches in a closer adherence to the love of God and faith in Christ."

F.F. Bruce

1 Timothy 2

Matthew Henry's introduction

In this chapter Paul treats,

I. Of prayer, with many reasons for it, vv. 1–8.

II. Of women's apparel, vv. 9, 10.

III. Of their subjection, with the reasons of it, vv. 11–14.

IV. A promise given for their encouragement in child-bearing, v. 15.

Dr. Adam Clarke's analysis of chapter

Prayer, supplication, and thanksgiving, must be made for all men; because God wills that all should be saved, 1–4.

There is but one God and one Mediator, 5–7.

How men should pray, 8.

How women should adorn themselves, 9, 10.

They are not suffered to teach, nor to nor to usurp authority over men, 11–14.

How they may expect to be saved in child bearing, 15.

A detailed analysis of chapter

Pray for all people. (1–7)

How men and women ought to behave. (8–15)

Key verse

Verse 5: "For there is one God and one mediator between God and men, the man Christ Jesus."

Key word / key phrase

Verse 1, "thanksgiving be made for everyone."

Key event / key person / key theme

Praying in public, and women in public worship

Key thought

God's purpose is that all people should lead peaceful, quiet and holy lives.

Key thing to look out for

Verses 4–5 give the reason why it is very important to pray for everyone, without distinction.

Key Bible cross-reference

Verse 7. See 2 Timothy 1:11.

Key "by way of explanation"

Verses 11–14. Some say that Paul is expressing a ruling for all time, others that the underlying principles (humility, quietness, submission, obedience) may be expressed differently at different times in different cultures. Women are undeniably called to bear children and in doing this experience God's saving grace if they continue in the faith.

Key "Quotable Quote"

"The marks of the Spirit's presence are biblical teaching, loving fellowship, living worship, and an ongoing, outgoing evangelism."

John R.W. Stott

1 Timothy 3

Matthew Henry's introduction

In this chapter our apostle treats of church-officers. He specifies,

I. The qualifications of a person to be admitted to the office of a bishop, vv. 1–7.

II. The qualifications of deacons (vv. 8–10), and of their wives (v. 11), again of the deacons, vv. 12, 13.

III. The reasons of his writing to Timothy, whereon he speaks of the church and the foundation-truth professed therein, v. 14, to the end.

Dr. Adam Clarke's analysis of chapter

About bishops, their qualifications and work, 1–7.

Of deacons, and how they should be proved, 8–10.

Of their wives and children, and how they should be governed, 11–13.

How Timothy should behave himself in the Church, 14, 15.

The great mystery of godliness, 16.

A detailed analysis of chapter

The qualifications and behavior of gospel bishops. (1–7)

And of deacons and their wives. (8–13)

The reason for writing about these, and other church affairs. (14–16)

Key verse

Verse 1: "Here is a trustworthy saying: If anyone sets his heart on being an overseer, he desires a noble task."

Key word / key phrase

Verse 8, "deacons."

Key event / key person / key theme

Qualifications for Christian leadership

Key thought

Paul set high standards for anyone who aspires to be a deacon.

Key thing to look out for

In verse 15 Paul gives two descriptions of the Church.

Key Bible cross-reference

Verses 2–7. See Titus 1:6–9.

Key "by way of explanation"

Verse 8, "Deacons." "Deacon" means someone who serves. A deacon's job, according to Acts 6:1–6, included setting the elders free for their work of prayer and preaching. Apart from "overseers", who are also called elders, the job of a deacon is the only local Church office mentioned in the New Testament.

Key "Quotable Quote"

"According to the Scriptures the Spirit is the first and principal Leader."

Robert Barclay

1 Timothy 4

Matthew Henry's introduction

Paul here foretells,

I. A dreadful apostasy, vv. 1–3.

II. He treats of Christian liberty, vv. 4, 5.

III. He gives Timothy divers directions with respect to himself, his doctrine, and the people under his care, v. 6, to the end.

Dr. Adam Clarke's analysis of chapter

Apostasy from the true faith predicted, and in what that apostasy should consist, 1–5.

Exhortations to Timothy to teach the truth, 6.

To avoid old wives' fables; to exercise himself to godliness, 7, 8.

To labor, command, and teach, 9, 10, 11.

To act so that none might despise his youth, 12.

To give attendance to reading and preaching, 13, 14.

To give up himself wholly to the Divine work, 15.

And so doing he should both save himself and them that heard him, 16.

A detailed analysis of chapter

Departures from the faith that have begun to appear. (1–5)

Several instructions, with reasons for carrying out various duties. (6–16)

Key verse

Verse 7: "Have nothing to do with godless myths and old wives' tales; rather, train yourself to be godly."

Key word / key phrase

Verse 2, "hypocritical liars."

Key event / key person / key theme

False teachers

Key thought

Verse 8, Godliness comes with practice.

Key thing to look out for

The error that has crept into the church is false asceticism. What is Paul's answer? (Note – food is not changed – the spirit of the person eating is changed.)

Key Bible cross-reference

Verse 1. See Acts 8:29.

Key "by way of explanation"

Verse 10, "Savior of all." Clearly it would be quite contrary to many other parts of biblical teaching to try to claim that this verse supports the idea of universalism. But what it does definitely say is that God is the Savior of all who go to him.

Key "Quotable Quote"

"You must not lose confidence in God because you lost confidence in your pastor. If our confidence in God had to depend upon our confidence in any human person, we would be on shifting sand."

Francis A. Schaeffer

1 Timothy 5

Matthew Henry's introduction

Here the apostle,

I. Directs Timothy how to reprove, vv. 1, 2.

II. Adverts to widows, both elder and younger, vv. 3–16.

III. To elders, vv. 17–19.

IV. Treats of public reproof, v. 20.

V. Gives a solemn charge about ordination, vv. 21, 22.

VI. Refers to his health (v. 23), and states men's sins to be very different in their effects, vv. 24, 25.

Dr. Adam Clarke's analysis of chapter

Rules to be observed in giving reproofs to the old and to the young, 1, 2.

Directions about widows, 3–16.

Of elders that rule well, 17, 18.

How to proceed against elders when accused, and against notorious offenders, 10–21.

Directions about imposition of hands, 22.

About Timothy's health, 23.

Reasons why no person should be hastily appointed to sacred offices, 24, 25.

A detailed analysis of chapter

Instructions for older and younger men and women. (1, 2)

Instructions to poor widows. (3–8)

Instructions about widows. (9–16)

The churches responsibility toward its overseers; Timothy's own health. (17–25)

Key verse

Verse 8: "If anyone does not provide for his relatives, and especially for his immediate family, he has denied the faith and is worse than an unbeliever."

Key word / key phrase

Verse 21, "keep these instructions."

Key event / key person / key theme

Church discipline

Key thought

Wisdom is needed when helping people.

Key thing to look out for

Which of these instructions are of particular relevance in your life?

Key Bible cross-reference

Verse 18. See Deuteronomy 25:4.

Key "by way of explanation"

Verse 23, "stop drinking water only." Paul's advice here should be thought of in connection with Paul's great concern for the physical and spiritual well-being of Timothy, rather than in connection with teaching about drinking or nor drinking alcohol.

Key "Quotable Quote"

"If your theology doesn't change your behavior, it will never change your destiny."

C.H. Spurgeon

1 Timothy 6

Matthew Henry's introduction

I. He treats of the duty of servants, vv. 1, 2.
II. Of false teachers, vv. 3–5.
III. Of godliness and covetousness, vv. 6–10.
IV. What Timothy was to flee, and what to follow, vv. 11, 12.
V. A solemn charge, vv. 13–16.
VI. A charge for the rich, vv. 17–19.
VII. And lastly, a charge to Timothy, vv. 20, 21.

Dr. Adam Clarke's analysis of chapter

Of the duty of servants, 1, 2.
Of false teachers, who suppose gain to be god liness, 3–5.
Of true godliness, and contentment, 6–8.
Of those, and their dangerous state, who deter mine to be rich; and of the love of money, 9, 10.
Timothy is exhorted to fight the good fight of faith, and to keep the charge delivered to him, 11–14.
A sublime description of the majesty of God, 15, 16.
How the rich should behave themselves; and the use they should make of their property, 17–19.
Timothy is once more exhorted to keep what was committed to his trust; and to avoid pro fane babblings, through which some have erred from the faith, 20, 21.

A detailed analysis of chapter

The duty of Christians toward believing, and other masters. (1–5)
The advantage of godliness with contentment. (6–10)
A solemn charge to Timothy to be faithful. (11–16)
The apostle repeats his warning to the rich, and closes with a blessing. (17–21)

Key verse

Verse 6: "But godliness with contentment is great gain."

Key word / key phrase

Verse 11, "pursue righteousness."

Key event / key person / key theme

Having the correct attitude

Key thought

Verse 10 is among the most misquoted verses in the Bible.

Key thing to look out for

What the rich are commanded to do.

Key Bible cross-reference

Verse 13. See John 18:37.

Key "by way of explanation"

Verse 20, "what has been entrusted to your care." Paul was very keen for Timothy to appreciate the very great responsibility God had given him in calling him to be a pastor.

Key "Quotable Quote"

"The pastoral charge consists in feeding the hungry, giving drink to the thirsty, covering the naked, receiving guests, visiting the sick and those in prison."

Robert Grosseteste, Letter, 1250

5. Select bibliography for 1 Timothy

Alford, Henry. *The Greek Testament* 4 Vols. Revised by E. F. Harrison. Chicago: Moody, 1958 (1861).

Barrett, C. K. *The Pastoral Epistles*. Oxford: Clarendon, 1963.

Guthrie, Donald. *The Pastoral Epistles*. Grand Rapids: Eerdmans, 1957.

Hendriksen, William. *New Testament Commentary: Pastoral Epistles*. Grand Rapids: Baker, 1957.

Kelly, J. N. D. *A Commentary on the Pastoral Epistles*. New York: Harper & Row, 1963.

Stott, J. R. W. *Guard the Gospel*. Downers Grove: InterVarsity, 1973.

2 Timothy

1. Book by book: Introduction to 2 Timothy

Introduction

Place of writing

Paul, in the interval between his first and second imprisonment, after having written First Timothy from Macedonia or Corinth (Birks) (if we are to adopt the opinion that First Timothy was written after his first imprisonment), returned to Ephesus, as he intended, by way of Troas, where he left the books, etc. (mentioned in 2 Tim. 4:13), with Carpus. From Ephesus he went to Crete for a short visit and returned, and then wrote to Titus. Next he went by Miletus to Corinth (2 Tim. 4:20), and thence to Nicopolis (Titus 3:12), whence he proceeded to Rome. From his prison there he wrote the Second Epistle to Timothy, shortly before his martyrdom. It is not certain where Timothy was at this time. Some of the internal evidences favor the view of his having been then at Ephesus; thus the salutation of Priscilla and Aquila, who generally resided there (2 Tim. 4:19); also that of the household of Onesiphorus, who is stated in 2 Tim. 1:16–18 to have ministered to Paul at Ephesus, a circumstance implying his residence there. Also, the Hymenæus of 2 Tim. 2:17 seems to be the same as the Hymenæus at Ephesus (1 Tim. 1:20); and probably "Alexander the coppersmith" (2 Tim. 4:14) is the same as the Alexander joined with Hymenæus (1 Tim. 1:20), and possibly the same as the Alexander put forward by the Jews to clear themselves, not to befriend Paul, at the riot in Ephesus (Acts 19:33, 34). The difficulty is, on this supposition, how to account for 2 Tim. 4:12, 20: if Timothy was at Ephesus, why did he need to be told that Paul had sent Tychicus to Ephesus? or that Paul had left Trophimus, himself an Ephesian (Acts 21:29), sick at Miletus, which was only thirty miles from Ephesus? However, see on 2 Tim. 4:12; 2 Tim. 4:20. Troas lay on the road to Rome from either Ephesus or Pontus, so that 2 Tim. 4:13 will accord with the theory of either Ephesus or any other place in the northwest of Asia Minor, being Timothy's place of sojourn at the time. Probably, he had the general superintendence of the Pauline churches in Asia Minor, in accordance with his mission combining the office of evangelist, or itinerant missionary, with that of presiding overseer. Ephesus was probably his headquarters.

Date

(1) Paul's first imprisonment, described in Acts 28:17–31, was much milder than that in which he was when writing Second Timothy. In the former, he had liberty to live in his own hired house, and to receive all comers, guarded only by a single soldier; in the latter, he was so closely confined that Onesiphorus with difficulty found him; he was chained, his friends had forsaken him, and he had narrowly escaped sentence of execution from the Roman emperor. Medieval legends represent the Mamertine prison, or Tullianum, as the scene of his incarceration with Peter. But this is irreconcilable with the fact of Onesiphorus, Linus, Pudens, etc., having access to him. He was probably under military custody, as in his former imprisonment, though of a severer kind (2 Tim. 1:16–18; 2:9; 4:6–8, 16, 17).

(2) The visit to Troas (2 Tim. 4:13) can hardly have been that mentioned in Acts 20:5–7, the last before his first imprisonment; for, if it were, the interval between that visit and the first imprisonment would be seven or eight years, a period most unlikely for him to have allowed to pass without sending for his cloak and parchments, when they might have been of service to him in the interim.

(3) Paul's leaving Trophimus sick at Miletus (2 Tim. 4:20), could not have been on the occasion mentioned in Acts 20:15; for, subsequent to that, Trophimus was with Paul in Jerusalem (Acts 21:29).

(4) The words (2 Tim. 4:20), "Erastus abode at Corinth," imply that Paul had shortly before been at Corinth, where he left Erastus. But before his first imprisonment, Paul had not been at Corinth for several years; and in the interval Timothy had been with him, so that Timothy did not need at a later period to be told about that visit (Acts 20:2, 4). For all these reasons the imprisonment, during which he wrote Second Timothy, is shown to be his second imprisonment. Moreover, Heb. 13:23, 24, represents the writer (who was probably Paul) as in Italy, and at liberty. So Clement of Rome (*First Epistle to the Corinthians*, 1.5), the disciple of Paul, explicitly states, "In the east and west, Paul as a preacher instructed the whole world (that is, the Roman empire) in righteousness, and having gone to the extremity of the west, and having borne witness before the rulers (of Rome), he so was removed from the world." This plainly implies that he fulfilled his design (Rom. 15:24–28) of a missionary journey

into Spain. The canon of the New Testament, compiled about A.D. 170 (called *Muratori's Canon*), also mentions "the journey of Paul from Rome to Spain."

His martyrdom is universally said to have occurred in Nero's reign (Eusebius, *Ecclesiastical History*, 2.22; Jerome, *On Illustrious Men*). Five years thus seem to have elapsed between the first imprisonment, a.d. 63 (Acts 28:17–31), and his martyrdom, June a.d. 68, the last year of Nero's reign. He was probably arrested by the magistrates in Nicopolis (Titus 3:12) in Epirus, in the winter, on a double charge, first, of being one of the Christians who had conspired, it was alleged by Nero's partisans, to set fire to Rome, a.d. 64; secondly, of introducing a novel and unlawful religion. His friends all left him, except Luke: Demas from "love of this present world": the others from various causes (2 Tim. 4:10, 11). On the first charge he seems to have been acquitted. His liberation from his first imprisonment took place in a.d. 63, the year before the great fire at Rome, which Nero made the pretext for his persecution of the Christians. Every cruelty was heaped on them; some were crucified; some were arrayed in the skins of wild beasts and hunted to death by dogs; some were wrapped in pitch-robes and set on fire by night to illuminate the circus of the Vatican and gardens of Nero, while that monster mixed among the spectators in the garb of a charioteer. But now (a.d. 67 or 68) some years had elapsed since the first excitement which followed the fire. Hence, Paul, being a Roman citizen, was treated in his trial with a greater respect for the forms of the law, and hence was acquitted (2 Tim. 4:17) on the first charge of having instigated the Christians to their supposed acts of incendiarism before his last departure from Rome. Alexander the coppersmith seems to have been a witness against him (2 Tim. 4:14). Had he been condemned on the first charge, he would probably have been burnt alive, as the preceding martyrs were, for arson. His judge was the city Præfect. Clement of Rome specifies that his trial was (not before the emperor, but) "before the rulers." No advocate ventured to plead his cause, no patron appeared for him, such as under ordinary circumstances might have aided him; for instance, one of the powerful Æmilian house, under which his family possibly enjoyed clientship (2 Tim. 4:16, 17), whence he may have taken his name Paul. The place of trial was, probably, one of the great basilicas in the Forum, two of which were called the Pauline Basilicas, from L. Æmilius Paulus, who had built one and restored the other. He was remanded for the second stage of his trial. He did not expect this to come on until the following "winter" (2 Tim. 4:21), whereas it took place about midsummer; if in Nero's reign, not later than June. In the interim Luke was his only constant companion; but one friend from Asia, Onesiphorus, had diligently sought him and visited him in prison, undeterred by the danger. Linus, too, the future bishop of Rome, Pudens, the son of a senator, and Claudia, his bride, perhaps the daughter of a British king (see on 2 Tim. 4:21), were among his visitors; and Tychicus, before he was sent by Paul to Ephesus (2 Tim. 4:12; perhaps bearing with him this Epistle).

Purpose

Paul was anxious to see his disciple Timothy, before his death, and that Timothy should bring Mark with him (2 Tim. 1:4; 4:9, 11, 21). But feeling how uncertain it was whether Timothy should arrive in time, he felt it necessary, also, to give him by letter a last warning as to the heresies, the germs of which were then being scattered in the Churches. Hence he writes a series of exhortations to faithfulness, and zeal for sound doctrine, and patience amidst trials: a charge which Timothy seems to have needed, if we are to judge from the apostle's earnestness in urging him to boldness in Christ's cause, as though Paul thought he saw in him some signs of constitutional timidity (2 Tim. 2:2–8; 4:1–5; 1 Tim. 5:22, 23).

Paul's death

Dioysius, bishop of Corinth (quoted in Eusebius [*Ecclesiastical History*, 2.25]) about A.D. 170, is the earliest authority for the tradition that Peter suffered martyrdom at Rome "about the same time" as Paul, after having labored for some time there. He calls Peter and Paul "the founders of the Corinthian and Roman Churches." The Roman presbyter, Caius (about A.D. 200), mentions the tradition that Peter suffered martyrdom in the Vatican.

But (1) Peter's work was among the Jews (Gal. 2:9), whereas Rome was a Gentile Church (Rom. 1:13. Moreover, (2) the First Epistle of Peter (1 Pet. 1:1; 5:13) represents him as laboring in Babylon in Mesopotamia. (3) The silence about Peter of Paul's Epistles written in Rome, negatives the tradition of his having founded, or labored long at Rome; though it is possible he may have endured martyrdom there.

His martyrdom, certainly, was not, as Jerome says, "on the same day" with that of Paul, else Paul would have mentioned Peter's being at Rome in 2 Tim. 4:11. The legend says that Peter, through fear, was fleeing from Rome at early dawn by the Appian Way, when he met our Lord, and falling at His feet, asked, Lord, whither goest thou? to which the Lord replied, I go again to be crucified. The disciple returned penitent and ashamed, and was martyred. The Church of Domine quo vadis, on the Appian Way, commemorates the supposed fact. Paul, according to Caius (quoted in Eusebius [*Ecclesiastical History*, 2.25]), suffered martyrdom on the Ostian Way. So also Jerome, who gives the date, the fourteenth year of Nero. It was common to send prisoners, whose death might attract too much notice at Rome, to some distance from the city, under a military escort, for execution; hence the soldier's sword, not the executioner's axe, was the instrument of his decapitation (Orosius, *The Seven Books of History against the Pagans*, 7.7). Paul appears, from Phil. 1:12–30, to have had his partisans even in the palace, and certainly must have exercised such an influence as would excite sympathy in his behalf, to avoid which the execution was ordered outside the city. Compare Tacitus (*Histories,* 4.11). The Basilica of St. Paul, first built by Constantine, now stands outside Rome on the road to Ostia: before the Reformation it was under the protection of the kings of England, and the emblem of the order of the Garter is still to be seen among its decorations. The traditional spot of the martyrdom is the Tre Fontane, not far from the Basilica (Conybeare and Howson).

A. R. Faussett

Detailed outline

I. Introduction: 1:1–2
- A. From: Paul: 1:1
- B. To: Timothy: 1:2

II. Thanksgiving: 1:3–5
- A. Gratitude to God: 1:3
- B. Reasons for his gratitude: 1:3–5
  1. His memory of Timothy: 1:3
  2. His longing for Timothy: 1:4
  3. His memory of Timothy's steadfast faith: 1:5

III. Exhortation to faithful ministry: 1:6–2:13
- A. Use your spiritual gifts: 1:6
- B. Have a courageous attitude: 1:7–8
  1. Do not be fearful: 1:7
  2. Have a spirit of power, love, and a sound mind: 1:7
  3. Do not be ashamed of your testimony: 1:8
- C. Recognize your calling: 1:9–12
  1. It is from God: 1:9
  2. It is through salvation, not deeds: 1:9
  3. It is to accomplish God's purpose: 1:9
  4. It is through the grace of God: 1:9
  5. It is based on Jesus Christ: 1:10–11
  6. It will bring suffering: 1:12
  7. It is based on eternal values: 1:12

IV. Exhortation to sound doctrine: 2:13–26
- A. Guard it: 1:13–14
- B. The reason for the exhortation: 1:15–18
  1. Phygellus and Hermogenes: 1:15
  2. The mercy of Onesiphrous: 1:16–18
- C. The commission of sound doctrine to others: 2:1–2
  1. To faithful men: 2:2
  2. Who will be able to teach others: 2:2
- D. The guarding of sound doctrine like a soldier: 2:3–4
  1. Endure hardness: 2:3
  2. Do not get entangled with the affairs of this life: 2:4
- E. Striving for sound doctrine like an athlete: 2:5
- F. Laboring for sound doctrine like a farmer: 2:6
- G. The duty regarding sound doctrine: 2:7
- H. Suffering for sound doctrine: 2:8–13
  1. Based on the example of Jesus: 2:8
  2. Suffering does not stop sound doctrine: 2:9
  3. If we are dead with him, we will live with him: 2:10
  4. If we suffer, we will reign: 2:12
  5. If we deny Him, He will deny us: 2:12
  6. If we are unfaithful, he remains faithful to us: 2:13
- I. Do not strive over unimportant issues: 2:14
- J. Study sound doctrine in order to: 2:15
  1. Be approved by God.
  2. Not be ashamed.
  3. Rightly divide the word of truth.
- K. Avoid godless chatter: 2:16–18
  1. They lead to more ungodliness: 2:16
  2. Hymenaeus and Philetus are examples of this: 2:17–18
- L. Establish yourself on the true foundation: 2:19
- M. Be an article used for a noble purpose: 2:20–21
- N. Flee evil youthful desires: 2:22

O. Follow after: 2:22
P. Avoid stupid arguments: 2:23–26
V. Exhortation for the last days: 3:1–4:8
A. Announcement of terrible times: 3:1
B. Description of evil men of last days: 3:2–7
C. Jannes and Jambres as an example of such evil men: 3:8
D. The limitation on such evil men: 3:9
E. Persecution in the last days: 3:10–12
1. Paul as an example of one who has borne persecution: 3:10–11
2. All who live godly will suffer persecution: 3:12
F. Deteriorating conditions of the last days: 3:13
G. The response of the minister to the conditions of the last days: 3:14–4:5
1. Continue in sound doctrine: 3:14–15
2. Be established in the Scriptures: 3:15–17
(a) They will make you wise unto salvation: 3:15
(b) They were given by inspiration of God: 3:16
(c) They are profitable: 3:16
(l) For doctrine.
(2) For reproof.
(3) For correction.
(4) For instruction in righteousness.
(d) The Word results in perfection: 3:17
(e) The Word results in equipping for good deeds: 3:17
H. Keep the sacred charge: 4:1
I. Preach the Word: 4:2
J. Preach in season and out: 4:2
K. Reprove, rebuke, exhort with long suffering and doctrine: 4:2–4
L. Watch in all things: 4:5
M. Endure affliction: 4:5
N. Do the work of an evangelist: 4:5
O. Carry out the duties of your ministry: 4:5
VI. Conclusion: 4:6–22
A. Paul's testimony: 4:6–8
B. A request for Timothy to come: 4:9–13
1. The request to come: 4:9
2. The reason: 4:10–12
3. Instructions about what to bring: 4:13
VII. Paul's trials: 4:14–18
A. The evil done by Alexander: 4:14–15
B. Paul had to stand alone at first: 4:16
C. But God stood with him through the trial: 4:17
D. God will stand with him in future trials: 4:18
VIII. Conclusion: 4:19–22
A. Greetings to Prisca, Aquila, and the household of Onesiphrous: 4:19
B. News about Paul's companions: 4:20
C. A final appeal for Timothy to come: 4:21
D. Special greetings: 4:21
E. Benediction: 4:22

2. Helpful summaries of 2 Timothy

Bird's eye view

Paul's further encouragement and instructions to the young pastor Timothy in his work as a minister.

Reading plan

The following reading plan, taking one reading per day, enables you to read through 2 Timothy in four days.

2 Timothy 1:1–1:18
2 Timothy 2:1–2:26
2 Timothy 3:1–3:17
2 Timothy 4:1–4:22

Verses to memorize

2 Timothy 2:15

Study to shew thyself approved unto God, a workman that needeth not to be ashamed, rightly dividing the word of truth. KJV

2 Timothy 3:12

Yea, and all that will live godly in Christ Jesus shall suffer persecution. KJV

2 Timothy 3:15–17

[15] And that from a child thou hast known the holy scriptures, which are able to make thee wise unto salvation through faith which is in Christ Jesus.

[16] All scripture is given by inspiration of God, and is profitable for doctrine, for reproof, for correction, for instruction in righteousness:

[17] That the man of God may be perfect, throughly furnished unto all good works. KJV

Statistics

Sixteenth New Testament book
Eleventh letter by the apostle Paul
4 chapters
83 verses
1,703 words
Number of Old Testament quotations and allusions in 2 Timothy: 2.

Names/titles given

Pros Timotheon B: "Second to Timothy."

3. Helpful keys to turn to in understanding 2 Timothy

Key word

Charge

Key verses

2 Timothy 2:3–4, 15

Themes to study

Christian service
Scripture
Suffering
Being unfaithful to Jesus

Jesus in 2 Timothy

In 2 Timothy Jesus is our Example.

Lessons to learn from 2 Timothy

- Pointless theological arguments are to be avoided.
- One of Paul's mottos was, "Remember Jesus Christ."

4. Studying 2 Timothy chapter by chapter

2 Timothy 1

Matthew Henry's introduction

After the introduction (vv. 1, 2) we have,

I. Paul's sincere love to Timothy, vv. 3–5.
II. Divers exhortations given to him, vv. 6–14.
III. He speaks of Phygellus and Hermogenes, with others, and closes with Onesiphorus, v. 15, to the end.

Dr. Adam Clarke's analysis of chapter

Paul's address to Timothy, and declaration of his affection for him, 1–4.

His account of the piety of Timothy's mother and grandmother, and the religious education they had given their son, 5.

He exhorts him to stir up the gift of God that is in him, and not to be ashamed of the testimony of the Lord, 6–8.

How God has saved them that believe; and how Christ has brought life and immortality to light by the Gospel, 9, 10.

The apostle's call to preach it, and the persecu tions which he had been obliged in conse quence to endure, 11, 12.

Timothy is exhorted to hold fast the form of sound words, 13, 14.

And is informed of the apostasy of several in Asia: and particularly of Phygellus and Hermogenes, 15.

And of the great kindness of Onesiphorus to the apostle in his imprisonment, 16–18.

A detailed analysis of chapter

Paul expresses great affection for Timothy. (1–5)

Exhorts him to improve his spiritual gifts. (6–14)

Tells him of many who deserted him; but speaks with affection of Onesiphorus. (15–18)

Key verse

Verse 7: "For God did not give us a spirit of timidity, but a spirit of power, of love and of self-discipline."

Key word / key phrase

Verse 8, "do not be ashamed."

Key event / key person / key theme

Be faithful to God

Key thought

The Christian life starts and finishes with grace.

Key thing to look out for

The instructions given to Timothy.

Key Bible cross-reference

Verse 2. See Acts 16:1.

Key "by way of explanation"

Verse 5, "your grandmother Lois." Paul reminds Timothy of the privilege he had to be born into a family that had a god-fearing grandmother, and mother who was a Christian. Verse 14, "the good deposit" is the gospel.

Key "Quotable Quote"

"Every Christian family ought to be, as it were, a little church consecrated to Christ, and wholly influenced and governed by his rules."

Jonathan Edwards

2 Timothy 2

Matthew Henry's introduction

In this chapter our apostle gives Timothy many

exhortations and directions, which may be of great use to other, both ministers and Christians, for whom they were designed as well as for him.

I. He encourages him in his work, showing him whence he must fetch help, v. 1.
II. He must take care of a succession in the ministry, that the office might not die with him, v. 2.
III. He exhorts him to constancy and perseverance in this work, as a soldier and as a husbandman, considering what would be the end of all his sufferings, etc., vv. 3–15.
IV. He must shun profane and vain babblings (vv. 16–18), for they will be pernicious and mischievous.
V. He speaks of the foundation of God, which standeth sure, vv. 19–21.
VI. What he is to avoid–youthful lusts, and foolish and unlearned questions; and what to do, v. 22, to the end.

Dr. Adam Clarke's analysis of chapter

He exhorts Timothy to constancy, fidelity, and courage; and to acquit himself as a true soldier of Jesus Christ; and patiently expect the fruit of his labors, 1–7.

What the apostle's doctrine was relative to Christ, 8.

He mentions his own sufferings and consola tions, 9–13.

What Timothy is to preach, how he is to acquit himself, and what he is to shun, 14–16.

Of Hymeneus and Philetus, and their errors, 17, 18.

Of the foundation of God, and its security, 19.

The simile of a great house and its utensils, 20, 21.

Timothy is to avoid youthful lusts, and foolish and unlearned questions, 22, 23.

How he is to act in reference to false teachers, 24–26.

A detailed analysis of chapter

The apostle exhorts Timothy to persevere with diligence, like a soldier, an athlete, and a farmer. (1–7)

Encouraging him by assurances of a happy result of his faithfulness. (8–13)

Warnings to shun quarrels and dangerous errors. (14–21)

Instructions to flee evil desires of youth, and to be zealous against error. Be kind to everyone. (22–26)

Key verse

Verse 10: "Therefore I endure everything for the sake of the elect, that they too may obtain the salvation that is in Christ Jesus, with eternal glory."

Key word / key phrase

Verse 16, "avoid godless chatter."

Key event / key person / key theme

Characteristics of a faithful minister

Key thought

In serving Christ, Timothy should use every ounce of energy he has.

Key thing to look out for

Paul knew the negative effect of quarrelling among Christians.

Key Bible cross-reference

Verse 19. See Numbers 16:5.

Key "by way of explanation"

Verse 10, "I endure everything for the sake of the elect." As far as Paul was concerned no suffering could be too great if it was going to help people to find salvation in Jesus.

Key "Quotable Quote"

"The leader should immerse himself in books that will further equip him for a higher quality of service and leadership in the kingdom of God."

J. Oswald Sanders

2 Timothy 3

Matthew Henry's introduction

I. The apostle forewarns Timothy what the last days would be, with the reasons thereof, vv. 1–9.

II. Prescribes various remedies against them (v. 10, to the end), particularly his own example ("But thou hast fully known my doctrine," etc.) and the knowledge of the holy scriptures, which are able to make us wise unto salvation, and will be the best antidote against the corruptions of the times we live in.

In this chapter Paul tells Timothy how bad others would be, and therefore how good he should be; and this use we should make of the badness of others, thereby to engage us to hold our own integrity so much the firmer.

Dr. Adam Clarke's analysis of chapter

Dangerous times in the latter days, from the apostasy and wickedness of men, of whom an affecting description is given, 1–7.

It shall happen to them as to Jannes and Jambres, who withstood Moses, 8, 9.

The apostle speaks of his persecutions and suf ferings, and shows that all those who will live a godly life must suffer persecution, 10–12, because evil men and seducers will wax worse and worse, 13.

Timothy is exhorted to continue in the truths he had received, having known the Scriptures from a child, 14, 15.

All Scripture is given by Divine inspiration, 16, 17.

A detailed analysis of chapter

The apostle predicts the rise of dangerous enemies to the gospel. (1–9)

States how he is an example to Timothy. (10–13)

And exhorts him to continue in the teaching he had learned from the Scriptures. (14–17)

Key verse

Verse 16: "All Scripture is God-breathed and is useful for teaching, rebuking, correcting and training in righteousness."

Key word / key phrase

Verse 1, "terrible times in the last days."

Key event / key person / key theme

A snapshot of the last days

Key thought

"Do not be put off by godlessness."

Key thing to look out for

Paul warns that Christians are bound to face persecution for the name of Jesus.

Key Bible cross-reference

Verse 8. See Exodus 7:11.

Key "by way of explanation"

Verse 16, "All Scripture is God-breathed." As not all of the New Testament had been written at this stage, when Paul wrote these words he had the Old Testament especially in mind. This is the part of the Bible which is so often treated as irrelevant today.

Key "Quotable Quote"

"The Scriptures of the Old and New Testaments were given by inspiration of God, and are the only sufficient, certain and authoritative rule of all saving knowledge, faith, and obedience."

James Boyce

2 Timothy 4

Matthew Henry's introduction

In this chapter,

I. Paul with great solemnity and earnestness presses Timothy to the diligent and conscientious discharge of his work and office as an evangelist; and the charge given to him all gospel ministers are to take to themselves, vv. 1–5.

II. The reason of his concern in this case, Why must Timothy now be instant in season, etc., in a particular manner? Because the church was likely to be deprived of the apostle's labors, for his departure was at hand, vv. 6–8.

III. Divers particular matters, with a hint and caution, about Alexander the coppersmith, vv. 9–15.

IV. He informs him of what befell him at his first answer; though men forsook him, the Lord stood by him, and this encouraged him to hope for future deliverance (vv. 16–18) And then he concludes with greetings and a benediction, v. 19, to the end.

Dr. Adam Clarke's analysis of chapter

The apostle charges Timothy to be diligent, incessant, and faithful in his preaching; to watch, suffer patiently, and give full proof of his ministry, 1–5.

He predicts his own approaching death, and expresses the strongest confidence of being eternally happy, 6–8.

Desires Timothy to come and see him; shows that several had forsaken him, that others were gone to different districts, and that he had only Luke with him, 9–12.

Desires him to bring the cloak, book, and parchments, which he had left at Troas, 13.

Of Alexander the coppersmith's opposition, 14, 15.

Tells Timothy how he was deserted by all when obliged to make his first defense before

Nero; how God supported him, and the con fidence with which he was inspired, 16–18.

Greetings to different people at Ephesus, and from different people at Rome, 19–21.

The apostolic benediction, 22.

A detailed analysis of chapter

The apostle solemnly charges Timothy to be diligent, even though many will not listen to sound teaching. (1–5)

Reinforces this by mentioning his own impending martyrdom. (6–8)

Asks him to visit him soon. (9–13)

He mentions those who have deserted him; and expresses his faith about his own safe arrival in the heavenly kingdom. (14–18)

Friendly greetings and his usual blessing. (19–22)

Key verse

Verse 9: "Do your best to come to me quickly."

Key word / key phrase

Verse 6, "poured out like a drink offering."

Key event / key person / key theme

Paul's impending martyrdom

Key thought

Verse 6. This is Paul's last will and testament to his beloved Timothy.

Key thing to look out for

Verse 9. Christian friendship meant a great deal to Paul.

Key Bible cross-reference

Verse 19. See Acts 18:2.

Key "by way of explanation"

Verse 6, "I am already being poured out like a drink offering." Paul was expecting to be martyred at any time. Paul wrote this letter after his fourth missionary journey (not described in Acts). He was probably imprisoned in the Mamertine dungeon in Rome. The date was about 66/67 and Nero was the emperor.

Key "Quotable Quote"

"It is not the pain but the purpose that makes the martyr."

Augustine of Hippo

5. Select bibliography for 2 Timothy

See Select bibliography for 1 Timothy.

Titus

1. Book by book: Introduction to Titus

Introduction

Genuineness

Clement of Rome quotes it (*Epistle to the Corinthians*, 2); Irenaeus (*Against Heresies*, 3.3.4) refers to it as Paul's; Theophilus of Antioch (*To Autolychus*, 3.14), quotes it as Scripture. Compare Clement of

Alexandria (*Miscellanies*, 1, p. 299); Tertullian (*The Prescription against Heretics*, 6).

Time and place of writing

This Epistle seems to have been written from Corinth (Birks), subsequently to his first imprisonment, when Paul was on his way to Nicopolis (Titus 3:12) in Epirus, where he planned to spend the winter, shortly before his martyrdom, a.d. 67. Birks thinks, from the similarity of the Epistle to Titus and First Timothy, that both were written from the same place, Corinth, and at dates not far apart; First Timothy shortly after coming to Corinth, before he had planned a journey to Epirus, the Epistle to Titus afterwards.

The journey to Crete and Ephesus for those who delivered his letters would be easy from Corinth, and he could himself from there easily go into Epirus. He had shortly before visited Crete, where a Church existed (though without much organization), the first foundation of which he may have partly laid at his former visit (Acts 27:7, etc.), when on his way to his first imprisonment at Rome. That he returned to the East after his first imprisonment appears most probable from Phil. 2:24; Phile. 22. However, there may have been seeds of Christianity sown in Crete, even before his first visit, by the Cretans who heard Peter's preaching on Pentecost (Acts 2:11).

Reason for letter

Corrupt elements soon showed themselves in the Cretan Church, similar to those noted in the Epistles to Timothy, as existing in the Ephesian Church, Judaism, false pretensions to science, and practical ungodliness. Paul, on his recent visit, had left Titus in Crete to establish Church government, and ordain presbyters (deacons are not mentioned). Titus had been several times used by Paul on a mission to the Corinthian Churches, and had probably visited Crete from there, which was within easy reach of Corinth. Hence he was an ideal person to be selected by the apostle to be in charge of the Cretan Church. Paul now follows up with instructions by letter those he had already given to Titus in person on the qualifications of elders, and the graces becoming the old, the young, and females, and warns him against the unprofitable speculations so rife in Crete.

The national character of the Cretans was low in the extreme, as Epimenides, quoted in Titus 1:12, paints it. Livy (*History,* 44.45), stigmatizes their avarice; Polybius (*Histories*, 6.46.9), their ferocity and fraud; and (*Histories*, 6.47.5), their mendacity, so much so, that "to Cretanize" is another name for to lie: they were included in the proverbial three infamous initials "K" or "C," "Cappadocia, Crete, Cilicia."

Titus the person

It is strange that he is never mentioned by this name in Acts, and there seems no one mentioned in that book who exactly fits a description of him. He was a Greek, and therefore a Gentile (Gal. 2:1, 3), and converted by Paul (Titus 1:4). He accompanied the apostle on the deputation sent from the Church of Antioch to Jerusalem, to consult the apostles about the circumcision of Gentile converts (Acts 15:2); and, agreeably to the decree of the council there, was not circumcised. He was with Paul at Ephesus, from where he was sent to Corinth to begin the collection for the Jerusalem saints, and to ascertain the effect of the First Epistle on the Corinthians (2 Cor. 7:6–9; 8:6; 12:18). He next went to Macedon, where he joined Paul, who had been already eagerly expecting him at Troas (2 Cor. 2:12, 13, "Titus my brother," 2 Cor. 7:6). He was then used by the apostle in preparing the collection for the poor saints in Judea, and became the bearer of the Second Epistle to the Corinthians (2 Cor. 8:16, 17, 23). Paul in it calls him "my partner and fellow helper about you."

Being located in Crete (Titus 1:5) was subsequent to Paul's first imprisonment, and shortly before the second, about A.D. 67, ten years subsequent to the last mention of him in Second Corinthians (2 Cor. 12:18), A.D. 57. He probably met Paul, as the apostle wished, at Nicopolis; for his subsequent journey into Dalmatia, from there, (or else from Rome, to where he may have accompanied Paul) would be more likely, than from the distant Crete (2 Tim. 4:10, written subsequently to the Epistle to Titus). In the unsettled state of things then, Titus' episcopal commission in Crete was to be but temporary, Paul requiring the presence of Titus with himself, whenever Artemas or Tychicus should arrive in Crete and set him free from his duties there.

Tradition represents him to have died peaceably in Crete, as archbishop of Gortyna, at an advanced age.

A. R. Faussett

Detailed outline

I. Introduction: 1:1–4
- A. From Paul: 1:1–3
  - 1. Servant of God: 1:1
  - 2. Apostle of Jesus Christ: 1:1–2
  - 3. Entrusted with preaching: 1:3
- B. To Titus: 1:4

II. Purpose: "For this reason left I you in Crete": 1:5
- A. To set things in order.
- B. To establish church structure under Paul's direction.

III. Leaders in the church: 1:6–16
- A. Their qualifications: 1:6–9:
- B. The necessity for their qualifications: 1:9–16
  - 1. To be able to reprove erring believers by sound doctrine: 1:9,13
  - 2. These erring believers described: 1:10–16

IV. Different groups in the church: 2:1–3:2
- A. Older men should be: 2:2
- B. Older women should be: 2:3–4
- C. Young women should be: 2:4–8
- D. Young men: 2:6
- E. All believers: 2:7–8
- F. Slaves: 2:9–10
- G. All believers: 2:11–3:2

V. Additional instructions for church order: 3:3–11

A. Deal with members on the basis of how God dealt with you: 3:3–7
1. In times past you were: 3:3
2. But God loved you despite this and: 3:4–7
B. Devote yourselves to what is good: 3:8, 14
C. Things to avoid: 3:9
D. After the first and second admonition of a heretic: 3:10–11
1. Reject him: 3:10
2. Recognize that he is warped: 3:11
3. Recognize his sin: 3:11
4. Know that he is self-condemned: 3:11
VI. Conclusion: Personal instructions and greetings: 3:12–15

2. Helpful summaries of Titus

Bird's eye view

Instructions for ministers about their ministerial duties and what they should teach.

Reading plan

The following reading plan, taking one reading per day, enables you to read through Titus in three days.

Titus 1:1–1:16
Titus 2:1–2:15
Titus 3:1–3:15

Verse to memorize

Titus 3:5

Not by works of righteousness which we have done, but according to his mercy he saved us, by the washing of regeneration, and renewing of the Holy Ghost; KJV

Statistics

Seventeenth New Testament book
Twelfth letter by the apostle Paul
3 chapters
46 verses
921 words

Names/titles given

Pros Titon: "To Titus."

3. Helpful keys to turn to in understanding Titus

Key phrases

New birth
In Christ

Key verse

Titus 3:5

Themes to study

- Living at home
- How vital faithful teaching and correct Christian behavior are.

Jesus in Titus

In Titus Jesus is our Redeemer.

Lessons to learn from Titus

- Christian leadership should always be spiritual.
- The thought of Jesus' return should inspire us to live holy lives.

4. Studying Titus chapter by chapter

Titus 1

Matthew Henry's introduction

In this chapter we have,

I. The preface or introduction to the epistle, showing from and to whom it was written, with the apostle's salutation and prayer for Titus, wishing all blessings to him, vv. 1–4.

II. Entrance into the matter, by signifying the end of Titus's being left at Crete, v. 5.

III. And how the same should be pursued in reference both to good and bad ministers, v. 6, to the end.

Dr. Adam Clarke's analysis of chapter

The apostle's statement of his character, his hope, and his function, 1–3.

His address to Titus, and the end for which he left him in Crete, 4, 5.

The qualifications requisite in those who should be appointed elders and bishops in the Church of God, 6–9.

Of false teachers, 10, 11.

The character of the Cretans, and how they were to be dealt with, 12–14.

Of the pure, the impure, and false professors of religion, 15, 16.

A detailed analysis of chapter

The apostle greets Titus. (1–4)

The qualifications of a faithful pastor. (5–9)

The evil spirit and practices of false teachers. (10–16)

Key verse

Verse 11: "They must be silenced, because they are ruining whole households by teaching things they ought not to teach – and that for the sake of dishonest gain."

Key word / key phrase

Verse 5, "I left you in Crete."

Key event / key person / key theme

Titus' work on the island of Crete

Key thought

Paul gives a check-list for all elders.

Key thing to look out for

Christians are not to be naïve, but to discern deceiving spirits (see also 1 Timothy 4:1).

Key Bible cross-reference

Verse 4. See 2 Timothy 4:10.

Key "by way of explanation"

Verse 12, "their own prophets." Paul is here referring to the poet Epimenides who was born in Knossos, a town in Crete. In Greek literature to "Cretanise" meant to tell a lie.

Key "Quotable Quote"

"The five tasks of pastoral care are:
to seek and to find all the lost;
to bring back those that are scattered;
to heal the wounded;
to strengthen the sickly;
to protect the healthy and to put them to pasture."

Martin Bucer

Titus 2

Matthew Henry's introduction

The apostle here directs Titus about the faithful discharge of his own office generally (v. 1), and particularly as to several sorts of people (vv. 2–10) and gives the grounds of these and of other following directions (vv. 11–14), with a summary direction in the close, v. 15.

Dr. Adam Clarke's analysis of chapter

Sundry directions to aged men, 1, 2.

To aged women, 3.

To young women, 4, 5.

To young men, 6.

Directions to Titus, relative to his own conduct, 7, 8.

Directions to servants, 9, 10.

What the Gospel of the grace of God teaches all men, 11, 12.

The glorious prospect held out by it; salvation from all sin, and final glory, 13–15.

A detailed analysis of chapter

The duties which go hand in hand with sound teaching. (1–8)

Believing servants must be obedient. (9,10)

The grace of God. (11–15)

Key verse

Verses 1,2,3,9, "Teach."

Key word / key phrase

Verse 2, "teach."

Key event / key person / key theme

Sound teaching

Key thought

Different aspects of Christian teaching are relevant to different groups of people.

Key thing to look out for

Verse 12, the teacher is himself taught.

Key Bible cross-reference

Verse 14. See Psalm 130:8.

Key "by way of explanation"

Verse 11, "grace of God." Paul could hardly put pen to paper without writing about the grace of God. This refers to God's love toward us shown in the death of Christ on the cross, so that those who believe in him might be forgiven.

Key "Quotable Quote"

"Our office is a ministry of grace and salvation."

Martin Luther

Titus 3

Matthew Henry's introduction

Of duties which concern Christians more in common, and the reasons of them, vv. 1–8. What Titus in teaching should avoid, and how he should deal with a heretic, with some other directions (vv. 9–14), and greetings in the close, v. 15.

Dr. Adam Clarke's analysis of chapter

The necessity of obedience to the civil powers, and of meek and gentle deportment towards all men, is to be diligently enforced, 1, 2.

The wretched state of man, previously to the advent of Christ, 3.

The wonderful change which the grace of God

makes, and the means which it uses to bring men to glory, 4–7.

The necessity of a holy life, and of avoiding things which produce strifes and contentions, and are unprofitable and vain, 8, 9.

How to deal with those who are heretics, 10, 11.

St. Paul directs Titus to meet him at Nicopolis, and to bring Zenas and Apollos with him, 12; 13.

Concluding directions and greetings, 14, 15.

A detailed analysis of chapter

Be obedient to rulers and authorities. (1–7)

Good deeds must be carried out, and useless disputes avoided. (8–11)

Instructions and exhortations. (12–15)

Key verse

Verse 9: "But avoid foolish controversies and genealogies and arguments and quarrels about the law, because these are unprofitable and useless."

Key word / key phrase

Verse 8, "devote themselves to doing what is good."

Key event / key person / key theme

Keep up the good deeds

Key thought

Rebirth is the work of the Holy Spirit.

Key thing to look out for

What must Titus avoid?

Key Bible cross-reference

Verse 13. See Acts 18:24.

Key "by way of explanation"

Verse 5, "saved us . . . because of his mercy." Paul stressed that personal salvation was a free gift from God and could never be earned. Thus he links "mercy" and "salvation" in this verse.

Key "Quotable Quote"

"As judgment is God's justice confronting moral iniquity, so mercy is the goodness of God confronting human suffering and guilt."

A.W. Tozer

5. Select bibliography for Titus

See Select Bibliography for 1 Timothy.

Philemon

1. Book by book: Introduction to Philemon

Introduction

Authenticity

The testimonies to its authenticity are: Origen (*Homily 19, on Jeremiah*, vol. 1., p. 185, Edition Huetius), cites it as the letter of Paul to Philemon about Onesimus; Tertullian (*Against Marcion*, 5.21): "The brevity of this Epistle is the sole cause of its escaping the falsifying hands of Marcion." Eusebius

(*Ecclesiastical History*, 3.25), mentions it among "the universally acknowledged Epistles of the canon"; Jerome (*Commentary on Philemon*, vol.4, p. 442), argues for it against those who objected to its canonicity on the ground of its subject being beneath an apostle to write about. Ignatius (*Epistle to the Ephesians, 2; Epistle to the Magnesians,* 12), seems to allude to Phile. 20. Compare Epistle to Polycarp (1 and 6). Its brevity is the cause of its not being often quoted by the Fathers. Paley (*Horæ Paulinæ*), has shown striking proofs of its authenticity in the undesigned coincidences between it and the Epistle to the Colossians.

Place and date of writing

This Epistle is closely linked with the Epistle to the Colossians. Both were carried by the same bearer, Onesimus (with whom, however, Tychicus is joined in the Epistle to the Colossians), Col. 4:9. The people sending greetings are the same, except one, Jesus called Justus (Col. 4:11). In both Archippus is addressed (Phile. 2; Col. 4:17). Paul and Timothy are in the headings of both. And in both Paul appears as a prisoner (Phile. 9; Col. 4:18). Hence it follows, it was written at the same time and place as the Epistle to the Colossians (which was about the same time as the *Epistle to the Ephesians*), namely, at Rome, during Paul's first imprisonment, A.D. 61 or 62.

Purpose

Onesimus, of Colosse ("one of you," Col. 4:9), slave of Philemon, had fled from his master to Rome, after having probably defrauded him (Phile. 18). He there was converted to Christianity by Paul, and being induced by him to return to his master, he was given this Epistle, recommending him to Philemon's favorable reception. For he was now no longer a mere servant, but also a brother in Christ. Paul ends by requesting Philemon to prepare a guest room for him, as he intended to visit him, as he hoped to be set free and visit Colosse soon.

This Epistle is addressed also to Apphia, thought to have been Philemon's wife, and Archippus (a minister of the Colossian Church, Col. 4:17), thought to be a close relative.

Onesimus

Onesimus in the *Apostolical Canons*, is said to have been emancipated by his master. The A*postolical Constitutions* (7.46) state that he was consecrated by Paul, bishop of Berea, in Macedonia, and that he was martyred at Rome. Ignatius (*Epistle to the Ephesians*, 1), speaks of him as bishop of the Ephesians.

Style

It has been happily termed, from its graceful and delicate urbanity, "the polite Epistle." Yet it is not an insincere compliment. It is manly and straightforward, without misrepresentation or suppression of facts; at the same time it is most captivatingly persuasive. Alford quotes Luther's eloquent description,

"This Epistle showeth a right, noble, lovely example of Christian love. Here we see how St. Paul layeth himself out for the poor Onesimus, and with all his means pleadeth his cause with his master, and so setteth himself as if he were Onesimus, and had himself done wrong to Philemon. Yet all this doeth he, not with force, as if he had right thereto, but he stripped himself of his right, and thus enforceth Philemon to forego his right also. Even as Christ did for us with God the Father, thus also doth St. Paul for Onesimus with Philemon: for Christ also stripped Himself of His right, and by love and humility the Father set aside His wrath and power, and to take us to His grace for the sake of Christ, who lovingly pleadeth our cause, and with all His heart layeth Himself out for us; for we are all His Onesimi, to my thinking."

A. R. Faussett

Detailed outline

I. Introduction: 1–7
- A. Greetings of grace and peace: 1–3
  - 1. From Paul and Timothy: 1
- B. To: 1–2
  - 1. Philemon: 1
  - 2. Apphia: 2
  - 3. Archippus: 2
  - 4. Church in Philemon's home: 2
- C. Thanksgiving for: 4–7
  - 1. Love: 5
  - 2. Faith: 5
  - 3. Fellowship of faith: 6
  - 4. Refreshing of saints: 7

II. The request: 8–21
- A. Paul's personal interest in Onesimus: 8–14
  - 1. He was an unprofitable servant: 11
  - 2. He is now a profitable believer: 11, 13
- B. Paul's plea for Onesimus: 15–18
  - 1. Forgive him for your sake: 15
  - 2. Forgive him for his sake: 16
  - 3. Forgive him for my sake: 17–18
- C. The basis of his request: 19–20
- D. Confidence in an answer: 21

III. Conclusion: 22–25
- A. Paul's proposed visit: 22
- B. Greetings: 23–25

2. Helpful summaries of Philemon

Bird's eye view

Paul asks Philemon to have his runaway slave back.

Reading plan

The following reading plan, taking one reading per day, enables you to read through Philemon in one day.

Philemon:1–1:25

Statistics

Eighteenth New Testament book
Thirteenth letter by the apostle Paul
1 chapter
25 verses
445 words

Names/titles given

Pros Philemona: "To Philemon."
"The polite epistle."

3. Helpful keys to turn to in understanding Philemon

Key word

Receive

Key verse

Philemon verse 16

Themes to study

The necessity of a forgiving spirit

The role of an advocate

Jesus in Philemon

In Philemon Jesus our Lord and Master.

Lessons to learn from Philemon

Forgiving others is a Christian imperative.

4. Studying Philemon chapter by chapter

Philemon

Matthew Henry's introduction

In this epistle we have,

I. The preface, vv. 1–7.

II. The substance and body of it, vv. 8–21. And then the conclusion, v. 22, to the end.

Dr. Adam Clarke's analysis of chapter

Paul's salutation to Philemon, and the Church at his house, 1–3.

He extols his faith, love, and Christian charity, 4–7.

Entreats forgiveness for his servant Onesimus, 8–14.

Urges motives to induce Philemon to forgive him, 15–17.

Promises to repair any wrong he had done to his master, 18, 19.

Expresses his confidence that Philemon will comply with his request, 20, 21.

Directs Philemon to prepare him a lodging, 22.

Greetings and apostolic benediction, 23–25.

A detailed analysis of chapter

The apostle's joy and praise for Philemon's steady faith in the Lord Jesus, and love for all the saints. (1–7)

He presents Onesimus as a transformed person. The apostle promises to repay the value of whatever Onesimus has stolen. (8–22)

Greetings and a blessing. (23–25)

Key verse

Verse 14: "But I did not want to do anything without your consent, so that any favor you do will be spontaneous and not forced."

Key word / key phrase

Verse 10, "I appeal to you."

Key event / key person / key theme

Paul is pleading with Philemon to receive back his runaway slave.

Key thought

Love (verse 8) and gratitude (verse 19) are to be Philemon's motives.

Key thing to look out for

The reasons why Paul always thanks God for Philemon.

Key Bible cross-reference

Verse 9. See Colossians 4:9.

Key "by way of explanation"

Verse 11, "useless . . . useful." This is a play on the word "Onesimus" which means useful. He was useless. But now he, Onesimus, is living up to his name and is indeed useful. Onesimus and Tychicus are taking this letter to Colosse, along with Paul's letter to the Colossians (Colossians 4:16). Under Roman law the punishment for Onesimus, a runaway slave and a thief, was death.

Key "Quotable Quote"

"Storm the throne of grace and persevere therein, and mercy will come down."

John Wesley

5. Select bibliography for Philemon

Calvin, John. *The Second Epistle of Paul the Apostle to the Corinthians and the Epistles to Timothy, Titus, and Philemon*. Translated by T. A. Smail. Edited by D. W. Torrance and T. F. Torrance. Grand Rapids: Eerdmans, 1964.

Hendriksen, W. *Exposition of Colossians and Philemon*. Grand Rapids: Baker, 1964.

Lightfoot, J. B. *St. Paul's Epistles to the Colossians and Philemon*. 1879. Reprint. Grand Rapids: Zondervan, 1957.

Luther, Martin. "Preface to the Epistle of Saint Paul to Philemon, 1546 (1522)," in *Luther's Works*, American edition, vol. 35, ed. E. Theodore Bachmann. Philadelphia: Fortress, 1960.

Moule, C. F. D. "The Epistles of Paul the Apostle to the Colossians and to Philemon" in the *Cambridge Greek Commentary*. Cambridge: Cambridge University Press, 1957.

Hebrews

1. Book by book: Introduction to Hebrews

Introduction

Canonicity and authorship

Clement of Rome, at the end of the first century (A.D), copiously uses it, adopting its words just as he does those of the other books of the New Testament; not indeed giving to either the term "Scripture," which he reserves for the Old Testament (the canon of the New Testament not yet having been formally established), but certainly not ranking it below the other New Testament acknowledged Epistles. As our Epistle claims authority on the part of the writer, Clement's adoption of extracts from it is virtually sanctioning its authority, and this in the apostolic age.

Justin Martyr quotes it as divinely authoritative, to establish the titles "apostle," as well as "angel," as applied to the Son of God. Clement of Alexandria attributes it to Paul, on the authority of Pantænus, chief of the Catechetical school in Alexandria, in the middle of the second century, saying, that as Jesus is termed in it the "apostle" sent to the Hebrews, Paul, through humility, does not in it call himself apostle of the Hebrews, being apostle to the Gentiles. Clement also says that Paul, as the Hebrews were prejudiced against him, prudently omitted to put forward his name in the beginning; also, that it was originally written in Hebrew for the Hebrews, and that Luke translated it into Greek for the Greeks, so that the style is similar to that of Acts. He, however, quotes frequently the words of the existing Greek Epistle as Paul's words. Origen similarly quotes it as Paul's Epistle. However, in his Homilies, he regards the style as distinct from that of Paul, and as "more Grecian," but the thoughts as the apostle's; adding that the "ancients who have handed down the tradition of its Pauline authorship, must have had good reason for doing so, though God alone knows the certainty who was the actual writer" (that is, probably "transcriber" of the apostle's thoughts).

In the African Church, in the beginning of the third century, Tertullian ascribes it to Barnabas. Irenaeus, bishop of Lyons, is mentioned in Eusebius, as quoting from this Epistle, though without attributing it to Paul. About the same time, Caius, the presbyter, in the Church of Rome, mentions only thirteen Epistles of Paul, whereas, if the Epistle to the Hebrews were included, there would be fourteen. So the canon fragment of the end of the second century, or beginning of the third, published by Muratori, apparently omits mentioning it. And so the Latin Church did not recognize it as Paul's till a considerable time after the beginning of the third century. Thus, also, Novatian of Rome, Cyprian of Carthage, and Victorinus, also of the Latin Church. But in the fourth century, Hilary of Poitiers (A.D. 368), Lucifer of Cagliari (A.D. 371), Ambrose of Milan (A.D. 397) and other Latins, quote it as Paul's; and the fifth Council of Carthage (A.D. 419) formally reckons it among his fourteen Epistles.

As to the similarity of its style to that of Luke's writings, this is due to him having been Paul's companion for so long. Chrysostom, comparing Luke and Mark, says, "Each imitated his teacher: Luke imitated Paul flowing along with more than river fullness; but Mark imitated Peter, who studied brevity of style." Besides, there is a greater predominance of Jewish feeling and familiarity with the peculiarities of the Jewish schools apparent in this Epistle than in Luke's writings. There is no clear evidence for attributing the authorship to him, or to Apollos, whom Alford upholds as the author.

It plainly was written before the destruction of Jerusalem, which would have been mentioned in the Epistle had that event gone before, compare Heb. 13:10; and probably to churches in which the Jewish members were the more numerous, as those in Judea, and perhaps Alexandria. In the latter city were the greatest number of resident Jews next to Jerusalem. In Leontopolis, in Egypt, was another temple, with the arrangements of which, Wieseler thinks the notices in this Epistle more nearly corresponded than with those in Jerusalem. It was from Alexandria that the Epistle appears first to have come to the knowledge of Christendom. Moreover, "the Epistle to the Alexandrians," mentioned in the Canon of

Muratori, may possibly be this Epistle to the Hebrews. He addresses the Jews as peculiarly "the people of God" (Heb. 2:17; 4:9; 13:12), "the seed of Abraham," that is, as the primary stock on which Gentile believers are grafted, to which Rom. 11:16–24 corresponds; but he urges them to come out of the carnal earthly Jerusalem and to realize their spiritual union to "the heavenly Jerusalem" (Heb. 12:18–23; 13:13).

The use of Greek rather than Hebrew is doubtless due to the Epistle being intended, not merely for the Hebrew, but for the Hellenistic Jew converts, not only in Palestine, but elsewhere; a view confirmed by the use of the Septuagint. Bengel thinks, probably (compare 2 Pet. 3:15, 16, explained above), the Jews primarily, though not exclusively, addressed, were those who had left Jerusalem on account of the war and were settled in Asia Minor.

The notion of its having been originally in Hebrew arose probably from its Hebrew tone, method, and topics. It is reckoned among the Epistles, not at first generally acknowledged, along with James, Second Peter, Second and Third John, Jude, and Revelation. A beautiful link exists between these Epistles and the universally acknowledged Epistles. Hebrews unites the ordinances of Leviticus with their antitypical Gospel fulfillment. James is the link between the highest doctrines of Christianity and the universal law of moral duty–a commentary on the Sermon on the Mount–harmonizing the Decalogue law of Moses, and the revelation to Job and Elias, with the Christian law of liberty. Second Peter links the teaching of Peter with that of Paul. Jude links the earliest unwritten to the latest written Revelation. The two shorter Epistles to John, like Philemon, apply Christianity to the minute details of the Christian life, showing that Christianity can sanctify all earthly relations.

A. R. Faussett

Detailed outline

I. Jesus is superior to the prophets: 1:1–4
   A. God's revelation by the prophets to the fathers: 1:1
      1. At various times.
      2. In various ways.
   B. God's revelation by His Son: 1:2–4
      1. God now has spoken through Christ: 1:2
      2. Universal dominion has been given the Son: 1:2
      3. Christ's redemptive work is accomplished: 1:3–4

II. A superior mediator: 1:3–2:18
   A. Jesus is superior to angels: 1:3–4
      1. By inheritance.
      2. By name.
   B. Christ's superiority to angels is evident in the Old Testament: 1:5–14
      1. Angels: 1:5–7
      2. The Son, Jesus Christ: 1:8–12
      3. Angels: 1:13–14
   C. (First) Warning passage: 2:1–4
      1. Exhortation: 2:1
      2. Old Testament example: 2:2
      3. Present obligation in view of this

warning: 2:3–4

D. Christ's superiority to angels is not contradicted by His humanity: 2:5–8
   1. Angels: 2:5
   2. The Son: 2:6–8

E. Christ' superiority to angels is not contradicted by His suffering: 2:9–18
   Suffering/death was necessary:
   1. To complete His identification with humanity: 2:9–13
   2. To destroy the Devil: 2:14
   3. To deliver believing men: 2:15–16
   4. To qualify Jesus as a merciful high priest: 2:17–18

III. A superior founder: Christ is superior to Moses: 3:1–4:13

A. Christ and Moses: A comparison: 3:1–6
   1. Both Christ and Moses were faithful to God: 3:1–2
   2. Christ is the builder of the house: 3:3–4
   3. Christ is the Son over the house: 3:5–6

B. (Second) Warning passage: 3:7–4:13
   1. Exhortation: 3:7–8
   2. Israel's wilderness experience: 3:8–11
      (a) Attitude of Israel: 3:8–9
      (b) Response of God: 3:10–11
   3. Warning against unbelief: 3:12–19
      (a) The warning: 3:12
      (b) Believer's response in view of the warning: 3:13
      (c) Motivation for the response: 3:14
      (d) Example of Israel: 3:15–19
   4. Warning against missing God's rest: 4:1–13
      (a) The warning: 4:1–2
      (b) Rest: 4:3–5
      (c) Unrest: 4:6–8
      (d) The rest of God: 4:9–11
      (e) Confirmation of warning by God's Word: 4:12–13

IV. A superior priesthood. Jesus is superior to Aaron: 4:14–7:28

A. Jesus is the great high priest: 4:14–16

B. The priesthood of Aaron: 5:1–4

C. The priesthood of Jesus: 5:5–10

D. (Third) Warning passage: 5:11–6:20
   1. Rebuke for spiritual immaturity: 5:11–14
   2. Encouragement toward spiritual maturity: 6:1–3
   3. Warning against the consequences of apostasy: 6:4–8
      (a) Apostasy explained: 6:4–6
      (b) The consequences of apostasy: 6:4,6
      (c) The reason for the consequences: 6:6
      (d) An illustration from nature: 6:7–8
   4. Reminder of the certainty of God's promises: 6:9–20
      (a) The persuasion: 6:9
      (b) The faithfulness of God: 6:10
      (c) The response of believers: 6:11–12
      (d) An example of the certainty of God's promises: 6:13–20
         (1) Abraham: 6:13–15
         (2) The oath: 6:16–17
         (3) Assurance of God's faithfulness: 6:18–20

E. The priesthood of Melchizedek: 7:1–28
- 1. General description: 7:1–3
- 2. Melchizedek and Abraham: 7:4–10
- 3. The Levitical priesthood: 7:11–13
- 4. The new priesthood: 7:14–17
- 5. Priesthood under the law: 7:18–21
- 6. Priesthood under the new covenant: 7:22–27
- 7. Summary of the teaching: 7:28

V. A superior ministry: The two covenants: 8:1–10:18

A. Introduction: 8:1–6
- 1. Summary of previous teaching: 8:1–2
- 2. Ministry of the high priest: 8:3–5
- 3. A more excellent ministry: 8:6

B. The two covenants: 8:7–13
- 1. The first (old) covenant: 8:7–8
- 2. The second (new) covenant: 8:8–12
  - (a) Maker: 8:8
  - (b) Covenant: 8:9–12
- 3. Contrast between the new and the old: 8:13

C. Operation of the first covenant: 9:1–10
- 1. The tabernacle: 9:1–5
- 2. The ministry of the high priest: 9:6–10

D. Operation of the new covenant: 9:11–10:18
- 1. General description: 9:11–12
  - (a) The tabernacle: 9:11
  - (b) The ministry of the high priest: 9:11–28
    - (l) In atonement for sin: 9:12–22
    - (2) In Heaven: 9:23–28
- 2. Contrasts between the old and new: 10:1–18

VI. Superior resources for faith: Practical exhortation: 10:19–13:17

A. Use the new access to God: 10:19–31
- 1. Draw near in faith: 10:19–22
  - (a) With boldness: 10:19
  - (b) Through the new and living way: 10:20
  - (c) By the high priest (Jesus): 10:20–21
  - (d) With a true heart: 10:22
  - (e) In full assurance of faith: 10:22
  - (f) With our hearts sprinkled from an evil conscience: 10:22
  - (g) With our bodies washed with pure water: 10:22
- 2. Hold on to the faith: 10:23
- 3. Encourage one another in the faith: 10:24–25

B. (Fourth) Warning passage: 10:26–31
- 1. The warning: 10:26–27
- 2. The Old Testament example: 10:28
- 3. The present situation: 10:29–31

C. Remember former experiences: 10:32–34

D. Do not throw away your confidence: 10:35

E. Be patient: 10:36–37

F. Live by faith: 10:38–11:40
- 1. The command to live by faith: 10:38–39
- 2. The definition of faith: 11:1
- 3. The function of faith: 11:2–3
- 4. Examples of faith: 11:4–38
  - (a) Abel: 11:4
  - (b) Enoch: 11:5–6
  - (c) Noah: 11:7

(d) Abraham and Sara: 11:8–19
(e) Isaac: 11:20
(f) Jacob: 11:21
(g) Joseph: 11:22
(h) Moses: 11:23–29
(i) Joshua (Jericho): 11:30
(j) Rahab: 11:31
(k) Other examples of faith: 11:32–38
5. Recipients of the promise of faith in Jesus Christ: 11:39–40
G. Endure suffering and chastening: 12:1–29
1. Examples of suffering: 12:1–3
(a) A multitude of those gone before us: 12:1
(b) Jesus: 12:2–3
2. The explanation of suffering: 12:4–11
(a) Increased resistance against sin: 12:4
(b) God loves those He disciplines: 12:5–7
(c) Only those who are not sons are not chastened: 12:8
(d) Comparison with earthly fathers: 12:9–10
(e) Results of chastening: 12:11
3. The believer's response to suffering: 12:12–17
H. (Fifth) Warning passage: 12:18–29
1. The position of Israel at Mt. Sinai: 12:18–21
2. The position of believers at Mt. Sion: 12:22–24
3. The consequent response of believers: 12:25–29
I. An exhortation to fulfill Christian responsibilities: 13:1–17
1. Social duties: 13:1–6
(a) Relationships: Let brotherly love continue: 13:1
(b) Hospitality: 3:2
(c) Remember those in prison and those who suffer: 13:3
(d) Marriage: It is honorable: 13:4
(e) Possessions: Be content with what you have: 13:5
(f) Remember God is always with you to help you: 13:5–6
2. Religious duties: 13:7–17
(a) Remember those who rule over you: 13:7
(b) Remember Jesus never changes: 13:8
(c) Do not be carried away by strange teaching: 13:9
(d) Do not be entangled in legalistic doctrines: 13:9–12
(e) Bear the reproach of the Gospel: 13:13
(f) Seek for the city which is to come: 13:14
(g) Continually offer the sacrifice of praise: 13:15
(h) Do good: 13:16
(i) Obey your rulers: 13:17
VII. Personal instructions: 13:18–25
A. A request for prayer: 13:18–19
1. For a good conscience: 13:18
2. Willingness to live honestly: 13:18
3. For an early restoration to them: 13:19
B. A prayer for the readers: 13:20–21
1. The one addressed: 13:20

2. The request: 13:21

C. An exhortation to heed the epistle: 13:22

D. Timothy's proposed visit: 13:23

E. Closing greetings: 13:24

1. To: Those who have rule over you and all the saints.

2. From: Those in Italy.

F. Benediction: 13:25

2. Helpful summaries of Hebrews

Bird's eye view

The Christian age fulfils and supercedes the Old Testament.

Reading plan

The following reading plan, taking one reading per day, enables you to read through Hebrews in thirteen days.

Hebrews 1:1–1:14

Hebrews 2:1–2:18

Hebrews 3:1–3:19

Hebrews 4:1–4:16

Hebrews 5:1–5:14

Hebrews 6:1–6:20

Hebrews 7:1–7:28

Hebrews 8:1–8:13

Hebrews 9:1–9:28

Hebrews 10:1–10:39

Hebrews 11:1–11:40

Hebrews 12:1–12:29

Hebrews 13:1–13:25

Verses to memorize

Hebrews 4:14–16

[14]Seeing then that we have a great high priest, that is passed into the heavens, Jesus the Son of God, let us hold fast our profession.

[15] For we have not an high priest which cannot be touched with the feeling of our infirmities; but was in all points tempted like as we are, yet without sin.

[16] Let us therefore come boldly unto the throne of grace, that we may obtain mercy, and find grace to help in time of need. KJV

Hebrews 4:12

For the word of God is quick, and powerful, and sharper than any two-edged sword, piercing even to the dividing asunder of soul and spirit, and of the joints and marrow, and is a discerner of the thoughts and intents of the heart. KJV

Hebrews 7:25

Wherefore he is able also to save them to the uttermost that come unto God by him, seeing he ever liveth to make intercession for them. KJV

Hebrews 11:1

Now faith is being sure of what we hope for and certain of what we do not see.

Hebrews 12:1–2

[1] Wherefore seeing we also are compassed about with so great a cloud of witnesses, let us lay aside every weight, and the sin which doth so easily beset us, and let us run with patience the race that is set before us,

[2] Looking unto Jesus the author and finisher of our faith; who for the joy that was set before him endured the cross, despising the shame, and is set down at the right hand of the throne of God. KJV

Hebrew 13:8

Jesus Christ the same yesterday, and to day, and for ever. KJV

Statistics

Nineteenth New Testament book

13 chapters

303 verses

6,913 words

Number of Old Testament quotations and allusions in Hebrews: 86.

Names/titles given

Pros Ebraious: "To Hebrews."

There are no early manuscripts to support the title given by the King James Version: "The Epistle of Paul the Apostle to the Hebrews."

3. Helpful keys to turn to in understanding Hebrews

Key words/phrases

Heaven/heavenly, 15 times

Better, 13 times

Once/once for all, 9 times

Key verses

Hebrews 11:1; 12:1, 2

Themes to study

Jesus' superiority

Faith

Eleven instances of the exhortation, "let us," found in Hebrews:

1. Let us be careful, 4:1
2. Let us labor, 4:11
3. Let us approach God's throne of grace with confidence, 4:16
4. Let us go on, 6:1
5. Let us draw near, 10:22
6. Let us hold fast, 10:23
7. Let us consider one another, 10:24
8. Let us throw off every hindrance and run with perseverance, 12:1
9. Let us worship God acceptably, 12:28
10. Let us go forth, 13:13
11. Let us offer a sacrifice of praise, 13:15

How Hebrews shows that Jesus is "better" than the Old Testament dispensation

Better revelation, Heb. 1:1–4

Better hope, Heb. 7:19

Better priesthood, Heb. 7:20–28

Better covenant, Heb. 8:6

Better promises, Heb. 8:6

Better sacrifices, Heb. 9:23

Better possessions, Heb 10:24

Better country, Heb. 11:16

Better resurrection, Heb. 11:25

Jesus in Hebrews

In Hebrews Jesus is our eternal High Priest.

Lessons to learn from Hebrews

- Warnings about the possibility of loosing one's salvation should be carefully noted.
- The Christian faith embraces both trust in God and practical action.

4. Studying Hebrews chapter by chapter

Hebrews 1

Matthew Henry's introduction

In this chapter we have a twofold comparison:

I. Between the evangelical and legal dispensation; and the excellency of the gospel above that of the law is asserted and proved, vv. 1–3.

II. Between the glory of Christ and that of the highest creatures, the angels; where the pre-eminence is justly given to the Lord Jesus Christ, and clearly demonstrated to belong to him, v. 4, to the end.

Dr. Adam Clarke's analysis of chapter

Different discoveries made of the Divine will to the ancient Israelites by the prophets, 1.

The discovery now perfected by the revelation of Jesus Christ, of whose excellences and glories description is given, 2–13.

Angels are ministering spirits to the heirs of salvation, 14.

A detailed analysis of chapter

The supremacy of the Son of God in all his work. (1–3)

His superiority over all the holy angels. (4–14)

Key verse

Verse 3: "The Son is the radiance of God's glory and the exact representation of his being, sustaining all things by his powerful word."

Key word / key phrase

Verse 2, "spoken to us by his Son."

Key event / key person / key theme

Christ is superior to angels.

Key thought

Verse 3, "at the right hand," is the place of power; "sat down," indicates that Christ's work is finished. He is now ruling with God.

Key thing to look out for

Jesus is God's last word to humankind.

Key Bible cross-reference

Verse 5. See Psalm 2:7.

Key "by way of explanation"

The writer of the epistle is not known. Though the teaching is in harmony with Paul's the writing style and the emphases are not those of Paul. The writer was possibly Apollos (a name first suggested by Luther) or Barnabas.

Key "Quotable Quote"

"The great theme of the letter to the Hebrews is the finality of Jesus Christ."

John R.W. Stott

Hebrews 2

Matthew Henry's introduction

In this chapter the apostle,

I. Makes some application of the doctrine laid down in the chapter previous about the excellency of the person of Christ, both by way of exhortation and argument, vv. 1–4.

II. Enlarges further on the pre-eminence of Christ above the angels, vv. 5–9.

III. Proceeds to remove the scandal of the cross, vv. 10–15.

IV. Asserts the incarnation of Christ, taking on him not the nature of angels, but the seed of Abraham, and assigns the reason of his so doing, v. 16, to the end.

Dr. Adam Clarke's analysis of chapter

The use we should make of the preceding doctrine, and the danger of neglecting this great salvation, 1–4.

The future world is not put in subjection to the angels, but all is under the authority of Christ, 5–8.

Jesus has tasted death for every man, 9.

Nor could he accomplish man's redemption without being incarnated and without dying; by which he destroys the devil, and delivers all that believe on him from the fear of death and spiritual bondage, 10–15.

Christ took not on him the nature of angels, but the nature of Abraham, that he might die, and make reconciliation for the sins of the people, 16–18.

A detailed analysis of chapter

Do not drift away from Christ and his gospel. (1–4)

His sufferings in no way lessen his pre-eminence. (5–9)

The reason for his sufferings. (10–18)

Key verse

Verse 4: "God also testified to it by signs, wonders and various miracles, and gifts of the Holy Spirit distributed according to his will."

Key word / key phrase

Verse 3, "such a great salvation."

Key event / key person / key theme

God's program of salvation

Key thought

Verse 10, Christ's coming to earth was completed when he went through suffering (the Greek verb "to perfect" means "to complete a process".)

Key thing to look out for

The reason why Jesus can help us in our temptations.

Key Bible cross-reference

Verses 6–8. See Psalm 8:4–6.

Key "by way of explanation"

Verse 13, "I will put my trust in him." This quotation from Isaiah 8:17 demonstrates complete trust in God. This was perfectly shown throughout the life and, pre-eminently, in the death, of Jesus.

Key "Quotable Quote"

"We will trust God to the extent we fear him; to the extent we stand in absolute awe and amazement at his great power and sovereign rule over all his creation."

Jerry Bridges

Hebrews 3

Matthew Henry's introduction

In this chapter the apostle applies what he had said in the chapter previous about the priesthood of Christ,

I. In a serious pathetic exhortation that this great high priest, who was discovered to them, might be seriously considered by them, vv. 1–6.

II. He then adds many weighty counsels and cautions, v. 7, to the end.

Dr. Adam Clarke's analysis of chapter

Jesus is the High Priest of our profession, 1.

And is counted worthy of more honor than Moses, 2–6, as the Son Israelites did, and were excluded from the earthly rest in Canaan, 7–11.

We should be on our guard against unbelief, 12.

And exhort each other, lest we be hardened through the deceitfulness of sin; and we should hold fast the beginning of our confi dence to the end, and not provoke God as the Israelites did, and who were destroyed in the wilderness, 13–17.

They were promised the earthly rest, but did not enter because of unbelief, 18, 19.

A detailed analysis of chapter

Christ is superior to Moses. (1–6)

The Hebrews are warned about the sin and danger of unbelief. (7–13)

The necessity for faith in Christ, and to steadfastly follow him. (14–19)

Key verse

Verse 5: "Moses was faithful as a servant in all God's house, testifying to what would be said in the future."

Key word / key phrase

Verse 3, "worthy of greater honor than Moses."

Key event / key person / key theme

Jesus is superior to Moses

Key thought

Christians should concentrate on Christ.

Key thing to look out for

The second series of warnings found in this letter.

Key Bible cross-reference

Verse 2. See Numbers 12:7.

Key "by way of explanation"

Verse 3, Jesus is the builder, and is therefore greater than Moses who is part of the building.

Key "Quotable Quote"

"My salvation is not based on my faith; it is based on who Jesus Christ is."

Josh McDowell

Hebrews 4

Matthew Henry's introduction

The apostle, having in the previous chapter set forth the sin and punishment of the ancient Jews, proceeds in this,

I. To declare that our privileges by Christ under the gospel exceed the privileges of the Jewish church under Moses, as a reason why we should make a right improvement of them, vv. 1–4.

II. He assigns the cause why the ancient Hebrews did not profit by their religious privileges, v. 2. Then,

III. Confirms the privileges of those who believe, and the misery of those who continue in unbelief, vv. 3–10.

IV. Concludes with proper and powerful arguments and motives to faith and obedience.

Dr. Adam Clarke's analysis of chapter

As the Christian rest is to be obtained by faith, we should beware of unbelief lest we lose it, as the Hebrews did theirs, 1.

The reason why they were not brought into the rest promised to them, 2.

The rest promised to the Hebrews was a type of that promised to Christians, 3–10.

Into this rest we should earnestly labor to enter, 11.

A description of the word of God, 12, 13.

Jesus is our sympathetic High Priest, 14–15.

Through him we have confidence to come to God, 16.

A detailed analysis of chapter

Humble reverence is urged, so that none fall short of the promised rest through unbelief. (1–10)

Arguments and motives for faith and hope as we approach God. (11–16)

Key verse

Verse 1: "Therefore, since the promise of entering his rest still stands, let us be careful that none of you be found to have fallen short of it."

Key word / key phrase

Verse 10, "God's rest."

Key event / key person / key theme

The Christian's rest, and Jesus the High Priest.

Key thought

The Christian rests in the finished work of Christ. We don't have to labor to make ourselves right with God.

Key thing to look out for

The description of God's word. How can this help us?

Key Bible cross-reference

Verse 5. See Psalm 95:11.

Key "by way of explanation"

Verse 15, "tempted in every way, just as we are." Jesus' experience of temptation was the same as ours. It wasn't different because he was God.

Key "Quotable Quote"

"Sympathy with the sinner in his trial does not depend on the experience of sin, but on the experience of the temptation to sin, which only the sinless can know in its full intensity. He who falls yields before the last strain."

B.F. Westcott

Hebrews 5

Matthew Henry's introduction

In this chapter the apostle continues his discourse on the priesthood of Christ, a sweet subject, which he would not too soon dismiss. And here,

I. He explains the nature of the priestly office in general, vv. 1–3.

II. The proper and regular call there must be to this office, vv. 4–6.

III. The requisite qualifications for the work, vv. 7–9.

IV. The peculiar order of the priesthood of Christ; it was not after the order of Aaron, but of Melchisedec, vv. 6, 7, 10.

V. He reproves the Hebrews, that they had not made those improvements in knowledge which might have made them capable of looking into the more abstruse and mysterious parts of scripture, vv. 11–14.

Dr. Adam Clarke's analysis of chapter

The nature of the high priesthood of Christ; his pre-eminence, qualifications, and order, 1–10.

Imperfect state of the believing Hebrews, and the necessity of spiritual improvement, 11–14.

A detailed analysis of chapter

The ministry of a high priest is completely fulfilled in Christ. (1–10)

The Christian Hebrews reproved for their little progress in the knowledge of the gospel. (11–14)

Key verse

Verse 7: "During the days of Jesus' life on earth, he offered up prayers and petitions with loud cries and tears to the one who could save him from death, and he was heard because of his reverent submission."

Key word / key phrase

Verse 1, "Every high priest."

Key event / key person / key theme

Jesus the great High Priest

Key thought

Jesus was truly human (verses 7, 8).

Key thing to look out for

Verses 13, 14 give a definition of maturity. Mature Christians have understanding and wisdom.

Key Bible cross-reference

Verse 3. See Leviticus 9:7.

Key "by way of explanation"

Verse 14, "the mature." The writer to the Hebrews wants his readers to be among the mature who thrive on a spiritually solid diet. They should not be content to remain infantile in their spiritual understanding and knowledge.

Key "Quotable Quote"

"I've never met anyone who became instantly mature. It's a painstaking process that God takes us through, and it includes such things as waiting, failing, losing, and being misunderstood – each calling for extra doses of perseverance."

Charles Swindoll

Hebrews 6

Matthew Henry's introduction

In this chapter the apostle proceeds to persuade the Hebrews to make a better proficiency in religion than they had done, as the best way to prevent apostasy, the dreadful nature and consequences of which sin he sets forth in a serious manner (vv. 1–8), and then expresses his good hopes about them, that they would persevere in faith and holiness, to which he exhorts them, and sets before them the great encouragement they had from God, both with respect to their duty and happiness, v. 9, to the end.

Dr. Adam Clarke's analysis of chapter

We must proceed from the first principles of the doctrine of Christ unto perfection, and not lay the foundation a second time, 1–3.

Those who were once enlightened, and have been made partakers of the Holy Spirit and the various blessings of the Gospel, if they apostatize from Christ, and finally reject him as their Savior, cannot be renewed again to repentance, 4–6.

The double similitude of the ground blessed of God, and bearing fruit; and of that ground which is cursed of God, and bears briers and thorns, 7, 8.

The apostle's confidence in them, and his exhortation to diligence and perseverance, 9–12.

God's promise and oath to Abraham, by which the immutability of his counsel is shown, in order to excite our hope, 13–18.

Hope is the anchor of the soul, and enters with in the veil, 19, 20.

A detailed analysis of chapter

The Hebrews are urged to go on to maturity in their Christian belief. The consequences of apostasy, or turning back, are described. (1–8)

The apostle encourages the Christians to persevere in faith and holiness. (9–20)

Key verse

Verse 10: "God is not unjust; he will not forget your work and the love you have shown him as you have helped his people and continue to help them."

Key word / key phrase

Verse 1, "Go on to maturity."

Key event / key person / key theme

Christian maturity

Key thought

Beware: this chapter contains the severest of warnings.

Key thing to look out for

Perseverance is the order of the day.

Key Bible cross-reference

Verse 19. See Leviticus 16:2.

Key "by way of explanation"

Verses 4–6 refer to people who have come under the influence of the Christian faith – and may be professing church-goers – but are not real Christians, but people whose basic inner relationship to God is unloving. Note that to love is omitted from the list in verses 4, 5 (cf. verse 10).

Key "Quotable Quote"

"Faith is the Christian's foundation, hope is his anchor, death is his harbor, Christ is his pilot, and heaven is his country."

Jeremy Taylor

Hebrews 7

Matthew Henry's introduction

The doctrine of the priestly office of Christ is so excellent in itself, and so essential a part of the Christian faith, that the apostle loves to dwell on it. Nothing made the Jews so fond of the Levitical dispensation as the high esteem they had of their priesthood, and it was doubtless a sacred and most excellent institution; it was a very severe threatening denounced against the Jews (Hos. 3:4), that the children of Israel should abide many days without a prince or priest, and without a sacrifice, and with an ephod, and without teraphim. Now the apostle assures them that by receiving the Lord Jesus they would have a much better high priest, a priesthood of a higher order, and consequently a better dispensation or covenant, a better law and testament; this he shows in this chapter, where,

I. We have a more particular account of Melchisedec, vv. 1–3.

II. The superiority of his priesthood to that of Aaron, vv. 4–10.

III. An accommodation of all to Christ, to show the superior excellency of his person, office, and covenant, v. 11, to the end.

Dr. Adam Clarke's analysis of chapter

About the greatness of Melchisedec, after whose order Christ is a high priest, 1–4.

The Levites had authority to take tithes of the people; yet Abraham, their representative, paid tithes to Melchisedec, 5–10.

Perfection cannot come by the Mosaic law, else there could be no need for another priest after the order of Melchisedec, according to the prediction of David in Psalm 110., which priest is sprung from a tribe to which the priesthood, according to the law, did not appertain; but Christ is a priest for ever, not according to the law, but after the order of an endless life, 11–17.

The law, therefore, is disannulled, because of its unprofitableness and imperfection; and Christ has an unchangeable priesthood, 18–24.

He is therefore able always to save them that come unto him, being in every respect a suit able Savior; and he has offered up himself for the sins of the people, 25–27.

The law makes those priests who have infirmity; but he who is consecrated by the oath is per fect, and endures for ever, 28.

A detailed analysis of chapter

The priesthood of Melchizedek and Christ are compared. (1–3)

Christ's priesthood is superior to the levitical priesthood. (4–10)

This is applied to Christ. (11–25)

The Church should be encouraged in their faith and hope from this. (26–28)

Key verse

Verse 27: "Unlike the other high priests, he does not need to offer sacrifices day after day, first for his own sins, and then for the sins of the people. He sacrificed for their sins once for all when he offered himself."

Key word / key phrase

Verse 1, "This Melchizedek."

Key event / key person / key theme

Melchizedek

Key thought

The mysterious Melchizedek is introduced (see Genesis 14:18–20).

Key thing to look out for

Jesus and Melchizedek are compared.

Key Bible cross-reference

Verse 21. See Psalm 110:4.

Key "by way of explanation"

Verse 1, "This Melchizedek was king . . . and priest." As both king and priest, Melchizedek prefigured these two ministries that particularly apply to Jesus.

Key "Quotable Quote"

"Christ has been too long locked up in the mass or in the Book: let him be your prophet, priest and king. Obey him."

George Fox

Hebrews 8

Matthew Henry's introduction

In this chapter the apostle pursues his former subject, the priesthood of Christ. And,

I. He sums up what he had already said, vv. 1, 2.

II. He sets before them the necessary parts of the priestly office, vv. 3–5. And,

III. Largely illustrates the excellency of the priesthood of Christ, by considering the excellency of that new dispensation or covenant for which Christ is the Mediator, v. 6, to the end.

Dr. Adam Clarke's analysis of chapter

The sum, or chief articles, of what the apostle has spoken, about the eternal priesthood of Christ, 1–5.

The excellency of the new covenant beyond that of the old, 6–9.

The nature and perfection of the new covenant stated from the predictions of the prophets, 10–12.

By this new covenant the old is abolished, 13.

A detailed analysis of chapter

Christ's priesthood is superior to Aaron's. (1–6)

The superiority of the new covenant over the old covenant. (7–13)

Key verse

Verse 13: "By calling this covenant "new," he has made the first one obsolete; and what is obsolete and aging will soon disappear."

Key word / key phrase

Verse 8, "I will make a new covenant."

Key event / key person / key theme

The new covenant

Key thought

The limited value of the first covenant.

Key thing to look out for

What was so special about the new covenant?

Key Bible cross-reference

Verse 1. See Psalm 110:1.

Key "by way of explanation"

Verse 8, "I will make a new covenant." This covenant will enable God's people to delight in doing his will, to have close fellowship with him, and to serve him with a renewed heart.

Key "Quotable Quote"

"In the first covenant, works were required as the condition of life; in the second, they are required only as the signs of life."

Thomas Watson

Hebrews 9

Matthew Henry's introduction

The apostle, having declared the Old-Testament dispensation antiquated and vanishing away, proceeds to let the Hebrews see the correspondence there was between the Old Testament and the New; and that whatever was excellent in the Old was typical and representative of the New, which therefore must as far excel the Old as the substance does the shadow. The Old Testament was never intended to be rested in, but to prepare for the institutions of the gospel. And here he treats,

I. Of the tabernacle, the place of worship, vv. 1–5.

II. Of the worship and services performed in the tabernacle, vv. 6, 7.

III. He delivers the spiritual sense and the main design of all, v. 8, to the end.

Dr. Adam Clarke's analysis of chapter

Of the first covenant, and its ordinances, 1.

The tabernacle, candlestick, table, show bread, veil, holy of holies, censer, ark, pot of manna, Aaron's rod, tables of the covenant, cherubim of glory, and mercy seat, 2–5.

How the priests served, 6, 7.

What was signified by the service, 8–10.

The superior excellency of Christ's ministry and sacrifice, and the efficacy of his blood, 11–26.

As men must once die and be judged, so Christ was once offered to bear the sins of many, and shall come without a sin-offering, a sec ond time, to them that expect him, 27, 28.

A detailed analysis of chapter

The Jewish tabernacle and its worship. (1–5)

Its meaning is explained. (6–10)

The worship of the tabernacle is fulfilled in Christ. (11–22)

The necessity and power of Christ's priesthood and sacrifice. (23–28)

Key verse

Verse 5: "Above the ark were the cherubim of the Glory, overshadowing the atonement cover."

Key word / key phrase

Verse 28, "so Christ was sacrificed once to take away the sins of many people; and he will appear a second time, not to bear sin, but to bring salvation to those who are waiting for him."

Key event / key person / key theme

A superior sacrifice

Key thought

With the coming of Christ, the old sacrificial system is fulfilled and abolished.

Key thing to look out for

In what ways was the death of Christ superior to the old tabernacle rituals?

Key Bible cross-reference

Verse 7. See Leviticus 16:2–34.

Key "by way of explanation"

Verse 12, "once for all." In contrast to the daily and yearly sacrifices, Jesus' sacrifice of himself for the sins of the world happened just once, but is effective for all time. The "atonement cover" (verse 5) was a slab of gold on top of the ark on which blood was sprinkled once a year on the Day of Atonement.

Key "Quotable Quote"

"When Christ's hands were nailed to the cross, he also nailed your sins to the cross."

Bernard of Clairvaux

Hebrews 10

Matthew Henry's introduction

The apostle knew very well that the Hebrews, to whom he wrote, were strangely fond of the Levitical dispensation, and therefore he fills his mouth with arguments to wean them from it; and in order thereto proceeds in this chapter,

I. To lay low the whole of that priesthood and sacrifice, vv. 1–6.

II. He raises and exalts the priesthood of Christ very high, that he might effectually recommend him and his gospel to them, vv. 7–18.

III. He shows to believers the honors and dignities of their state, and calls them to suitable duties, v. 19, to the end.

Dr. Adam Clarke's analysis of chapter

The insufficiency of the legal sacrifices to take away sin, 1–4.

The purpose and will of God, as declared by the Psalmist, relative to the salvation of the world by the incarnation of Christ; and our sanctification through that will, 5–10.

Comparison between the priesthood of Christ and that of the Jews, 11–14.

The new covenant which God promised to make, and the blessings of it, 15–17.

The access which genuine believers have to the holiest by the blood of Jesus, 18–20.

Having a High Priest over the Church of God, we should have faith, walk uprightly, hold fast our profession, exhort and help each other, and maintain Christian communion, 21–25.

The danger and awful consequences of final apostasy, 26–31.

In order to our perseverance, we should often reflect on past mercies, and the support afforded us in temptations and afflictions; and not cast away our confidence, for we shall receive the promise if we patiently ful fill the will of God, 32–37.

The just by faith shall live; but the soul that draws back shall die, 38.

The apostle's confidence in the believing Hebrews, 39.

A detailed analysis of chapter

The insufficiency of sacrifices for taking away sin, and the necessity and power of the sacrifice of Christ. (1–18)

An argument for holy boldness in the believer's access to God through Jesus Christ, And for steadfastness in faith, and mutual love. (19–25)

The danger of apostasy. (26–31)

The sufferings of believers, and the need to persevere. (32–39)

Key verse

Verse 12: "But when this priest had offered for all time one sacrifice for sins, he sat down at the right hand of God."

Key word / key phrase

Verse 14, "he has made perfect."

Key event / key person / key theme

The finality of Jesus' sacrifice

Key thought

The curtain in the temple is identified with the body of Jesus.

Key thing to look out for

Christians are called to persevere in their faith.

Key Bible cross-reference

Verses 5–7. See Psalm 40:6–8.

Key "by way of explanation"

Verse 20, "the curtain, that is, his body." Mark 15:38 states that immediately after Jesus died on the cross the curtain which cut off the holy of holies in the temple from the holy place was "torn in two from top to bottom." The way into the very presence of God was now open to all.

Key "Quotable Quote"

"Let none therefore presume on past mercies, as if they were out of danger."

John Wesley

Hebrews 11

Matthew Henry's introduction

The apostle having, in the previous chapter, recommended the grace of faith and a life of faith as the best preservative against apostasy, he now enlarges on the nature and fruits of this grace.

I. The nature of it, and the honor it reflects on all who live in the exercise of it, vv. 1–3.

II. The great examples we have in the Old Testament of those who lived by faith, and died and suffered extraordinary things by the strength of his grace, vv. 4–38. And,

III. The advantages that we have in the gospel for the exercise of this grace above what those had who lived in the times of the Old Testament, vv. 39, 40.

Dr. Adam Clarke's analysis of chapter

A definition of faith, 1, 2.

What are its immediate objects, 3.

What are its effects, instanced in Abel, 4.

In Enoch, 5, 6.

In Noah, 7.
In Abraham, 8–10.
In Sara, 11.
In their righteous posterity, 12–16.
In Abraham's offering of his son Isaac, 17–19.
In Isaac, 20.
In Jacob, 21.
In Joseph, 22.
In Moses, 23–28.
In the Israelites in the wilderness, 29.
In the fall of Jericho, 30.
In Rahab, 31.
In several of the judges, and in David, Samuel, and the prophets, 32–34.
The glorious effects produced by it in the prim itive martyrs, 35–40.

A detailed analysis of chapter

The nature and power of faith described. (1–3)
This is illustrated in the lives of different people, from Abel to Noah. (4–7)
By Abraham and his descendants. (8–19)
By Jacob, Joseph, Moses, the Israelites, and Rahab. (20–31)
By other Old Testament believers. (32–38)
Something better. (39, 40)

Key verse

Verse 1: "Now faith is being sure of what we hope for and certain of what we do not see."

Key word / key phrase

Verse 4, "By faith."

Key event / key person / key theme

Examples of faith

Key thought

A galaxy of faithful Old Testament followers of God are detailed to encourage us in our faith.

Key thing to look out for

They all lived by faith in God, but this was expressed in a variety of ways.

Key Bible cross-reference

Verse 4. See Genesis 4:3–10.

Key "by way of explanation"

Verse 5, "By faith Enoch was taken from this life." Enoch was "translated" to heaven, as was Elijah. He did not experience death in the normal way. This he did, "by faith."

Key "Quotable Quote"

"Do not be troubled because you must live by faith, nor grow weary because hope is deferred. Your reward is certain; it is preserved for you in him who created all things."

Peter Chrysologus

Hebrews 12

Matthew Henry's introduction

The apostle, in this chapter, applies what he has collected in the chapter foregoing, and makes use of it as a great motive to patience and perseverance in the Christian faith and state, pressing home the argument,

I. From a greater example than he had yet mentioned, and that is Christ himself, vv. 1–3.

II. From the gentle and gracious nature of the afflictions they endured in their Christian course, vv. 4–17.

III. From the communion and conformity between the state of the gospel-church on earth and the triumphant church in heaven, v. 18, to the end.

Dr. Adam Clarke's analysis of chapter

Having so many incitements to holiness, patience, and perseverance, we should lay aside every hindrance, and run with patience the race that is set before us, taking our blessed Lord for our example, 1–4.

These sufferings are to be considered as fatherly chastisements from God, and to be patiently submitted to on account of the benefits to be derived from them, 5–11.

They should take courage and go forward, 12, 13.

Directions to follow peace with all men, and to take heed that they fall not from the grace of God, 14, 15.

References to the case of Esau, 16, 17.

The privileges of Christians, compared with those of the Jews, by which the superior excellence of Christianity is shown, 18–24.

They must take care not to reject Jesus, who now addressed them from heaven, and who was shortly to be their Judge, 25–27.

As they were called to receive a kingdom, they should have grace, whereby they might serve God acceptably, 28, 29.

A detailed analysis of chapter

An exhortation to be constant and persevere, and the example of Christ is set out, and the gracious purpose of God in all the sufferings believers endured. (1–11)

Peace and holiness are commended, with warnings about despising spiritual blessings. (12–17)

The New Testament dispensation is shown to be much more excellent than the Old. (18–29)

Key verse

Verse 7: "Endure hardship as discipline; God is treating you as sons."

Key word / key phrase

Verse 2, "fix our eyes on Jesus."

Key event / key person / key theme

How to live by faith

Key thought

We can keep going with joyful, thankful and reverent hearts, because we are traveling to the glorious heavenly Jerusalem where Jesus is at the right hand of God.

Key thing to look out for

What view are Christians to take of hardship?

Key Bible cross-reference

Verse 20. See Exodus 19:12, 13.

Key "by way of explanation"

Verse 1, "surrounded by such a great cloud of witnesses." The people listed in chapter 11 are now pictured as spectators in a great athletics arena. They encourage us in our pilgrimage and we are to toss off all unnecessary and sinful baggage for the race.

Key "Quotable Quote"

"True progress quietly and persistently moves along without notice."

Francis de Sales

Hebrews 13

Matthew Henry's introduction

The apostle, having treated largely of Christ, and faith, and free grace, and gospel privileges, and warned the Hebrews against apostasy, now recommends several excellent duties to them, as the proper fruits of faith (vv. 1–17); he then bespeaks their prayers for him, and offers up his prayers to God for them, gives them some hope of seeing himself and Timothy, and ends with the general salutation and benediction.

Dr. Adam Clarke's analysis of chapter

Exhortations to hospitality to Strangers, 1, 2.

Kindness to those in bonds, 3.

About marriage, 4.

Against covetousness, 5, 6.

How they should imitate their teachers, 7, 8.

To avoid strange doctrines, 9.

Of the Jewish sin-offerings, 10, 11.

Jesus suffered without the gate, and we should openly confess him and bear his reproach, 12, 13.

Here we have no permanent residence; and while we live should devote ourselves to God, and live to do good, 14–16.

We should obey them that have the rule over us, 17.

The apostle exhorts them to pray for him, that he might be restored to them the sooner, 18, 19.

Commends them to God in a very solemn prayer, 20, 21.

Entreats them to bear the word of exhortation, mentions Timothy, and concludes with the apostolic benediction, 22–25.

A detailed analysis of chapter

Exhortations about various duties, and the need to be content with God's providence. (1–6)

Respect the instructions of faithful pastors. Warnings against being led astray by false teaching. (7–15)

Further exhortations to duties that relate to God, to our neighbor, and to those set over us in the Lord. (16–21)

This letter should be taken seriously. (22–25)

Key verse

Verse 9: "Do not be carried away by all kinds of strange teachings."

Key word / key phrase

Verse 1, "Keep on loving each other."

Key event / key person / key theme

An exhortation to love

Key thought

"This world is not our home."

Key thing to look out for

Reasons why the Christian must not be afraid or discouraged.

Key Bible cross-reference

Verse 5. See Deuteronomy 31:6.

Key "by way of explanation"

Verse 9, "by grace, not by ceremonial foods." This verse states categorically that faith in Jesus has done away with any need to keep ceremonial food laws. Christians now life "by grace."

Key "Quotable Quote"

"Salvation is by grace through faith; yet we must work out our own salvation."

Richard J. Foster

5. Select bibliography for Hebrews

Bruce, E. F. *The Epistle to the Hebrews*. Grand Rapids: Eerdmans, 1964.

Calvin, J. *The Epistle of Paul the Apostle to the Hebrews and the First and Second Epistles of St. Peter*. Edinburgh: Oliver and Boyd, 1963.

Guthrie, D. *The Letter to the Hebrews*. Leicester and Grand Rapids: Inter-Varsity and Eerdmans, 1983.

Hughes, P. E. *A Commentary on the Epistle to the Hebrews*. Grand Rapids: Eerdmans, 1977.

Tasker, R. V. G. *The Gospel in the Epistle to the Hebrews*. London: Tyndale, 1950.

Westcott, B. F. *The Epistle to the Hebrews*. London: MacMillan, 1892.

James

1. Book by book: Introduction to James

Introduction

Authenticity

This called by Eusebius ([*Ecclesiastical History*, 2.23], about the year 330 A.D.) the first of the Catholic Epistles, that is, the Epistles intended for general circulation, as distinguished from Paul's Epistles, which were addressed to particular churches or individuals. In the oldest manuscripts of the New Testament extant, they stand before the Epistles of Paul. Of them, two only are mentioned by Eusebius as universally acknowledged (*Homologoumena*), namely, the First Epistle of Peter, and the First Epistle of John. All, however, are found in every existing manuscript of the whole New Testament.

It should not surprise us that Epistles not addressed to particular churches (and particularly one like that of James, addressed to the Israelite believers scattered abroad) should be for a time less known. The first mention of James' Epistle by name occurs early in the third century, in Origen (*Commentary on John* 1:19, 4.306), who was born about 185, and died A.D. 254. Clement of Rome ([*First Epistle to the Corinthians,* 10); compare James 2:21, 23; [*First Epistle to the Corinthians,* 11); compare James 2:25; Heb. 11:31) quotes it. So also Hermas (*Shepherd*) quotes James 4:7. Irenaeus (*Against Heresies*, 4.16.2) is thought to refer to James 2:23. Clement of Alexandria commented on it, according to Cassiodorus. Ephrem the Syrian (*Against the Greeks*, 3.51) quotes James 5:1. An especially strong proof of its authenticity is afforded by its forming part of the old Syriac version, which contains no other of the disputed books (*Antilegomena*, [Eusebius, *Ecclesiastical History*, 3.25]), except the Epistle to the Hebrews. None of the Latin fathers before the fourth century quote it; but soon after the Council of Nicea it was admitted as canonical both by the East and West churches, and specified as such in the Councils of Hippo and Carthage (397 A.D.). This is just what we might expect; a writing known only partially at first, when subsequently it obtained a wider circulation, and the proofs were better known of its having been recognized in apostolic churches, having in them men endowed with the discernment of spirits, which qualified them for discriminating between inspired and uninspired writings, was universally accepted. Though doubted for a time, at last the disputed books (James, Second Peter, Second and Third John, Jude, and Revelation) were universally accepted, so that no argument for the Old Testament Apocrypha can be drawn from their case: as to it the Jewish Church had no doubt; it was known not to be inspired.

Luther's objection

Luther's objection to James' letter ("an Epistle of straw, and destitute of an evangelic character") was due to his mistaken idea that it (James 2:14–26) opposes the doctrine of justification by faith, and not by deeds, taught by Paul. But the two apostles, while looking at justification from distinct standpoints, perfectly harmonize and mutually complement the definitions of one another. Faith precedes love and the works of love; but without them it is dead. Paul regards faith in the justification of the sinner before God; James, in the justification of the believer evidently before men. The error which James meets was the Jewish notion that their possession and knowledge of the law of God would justify them, even though they disobeyed it (compare James 1:22 with Rom. 2:17–25). James 1:3; 4:1, 12 seem plainly to allude to Rom. 5:3; 6:13; 7:23; 14:4. Also the tenor of James 2:14–26 on "justification," seems to allude to Paul's teaching, so as to correct false Jewish notions of a different kind from those which he combated, though not unnoticed by him also (Rom. 2:17, etc.).

Author

Paul (Gal. 2:9) arranges the names "James, Cephas, John," in the order in which their Epistles stand. James who wrote this Epistle (according to most ancient writers) is called (Gal. 1:19), "the Lord's brother." He was son of Alpheus or Cleopas (Luke 24:13–18) and Mary, sister of the Virgin Mary. Compare Mark 15:40 with John 19:25, which seems to identify the mother of James the Less with the wife of Cleopas, not with the Virgin Mary, Cleopas' wife's sister. Cleopas is the Hebrew, Alpheus the Greek mode of writing the same name. Many, however, as Hegesippus (Eusebius, *Ecclesiastical History*, 23.1), distinguish the Lord's brother from the son of Alpheus. But the Gospel according to the Hebrews, quoted by Jerome, represents James, the Lord's brother, as present at the institution of the Eucharist, and therefore identical with the apostle James. So the Apocryphal Gospel of James. In Acts, James who is put foremost in Jerusalem after the death of James, the son of Zebedee, is not distinguished from James, the son of Alpheus. He is not mentioned as one of the Lord's brethren in Acts 1:14; but as one of the "apostles" (Gal. 1:19). He is called "the Less" (literally, "the little," Mark 15:40), to distinguish him from James, the son of Zebedee. Alford considers James, the brother of the Lord, the author of the Epistle, to have been the eldest of the sons of Joseph and Mary, after Jesus (compare Matt. 13:55), and that James the son of Alpheus is distinguished from him by the latter being called "the Less," (that is, junior). His arguments against the Lord's brother, the bishop of Jerusalem, being the apostle, are:

The Lord's brethren did not believe on Jesus at a time when the apostles had been already called (John 7:3, 5), therefore none of the Lord's brethren could be among the apostles (but it does not follow from John 7:3 that no one of them believed).

The apostles' commission was to preach the Gospel everywhere, not to be bishops in a particular locality (but it is unlikely that one not an apostle should be bishop of Jerusalem, to whom even apostles yield deference, Acts 15:13, 19; Gal. 1:19; 2:9, 12. The Savior's last command to the apostles collectively to preach the Gospel everywhere, is not inconsistent with each having a particular sphere of labor in which he should be a missionary bishop, as Peter is said to have been at Antioch).

He was surnamed "the Just." It needed special wisdom so to preach the Gospel as not to disparage the law. As bishop of Jerusalem writing to the twelve tribes, he sets forth the Gospel in its aspect of relation to the law, which the Jews so reverenced. As Paul's Epistles are a commentary on the doctrines flowing from the death and resurrection of Christ, so James's Epistle is closely linked with His teaching during His life on earth, especially His Sermon on the Mount. In both, the law is represented as fulfilled in love: the very language is palpably similar (compare James 1:2 with Matt. 5:12; James 1:4 with Matt. 5:48; James 1:5; 5:15 with Matt. 7:7–11; James 2:13 with Matt. 5:7; 6:14, 15; James 2:10 with Matt. 5:19; James 4:4 with Matt. 6:24; James 4:11 with Matt. 7:1, 2; James 5:2 with Matt. 6:19). The whole spirit of this Epistle breathes the same Gospel-righteousness which the Sermon on the Mount inculcates as the highest realization of the law. James's own character as "the Just," or legally righteous, disposed him to this coincidence (compare James 1:20; 2:10; 3:18 with Matt. 5:20). It also fitted him for presiding over a Church still zealous for the law (Acts 21:18–24; Gal. 2:12). If any could win the Jews to the Gospel, he was most likely who presented a pattern of Old Testament righteousness, combined with evangelical faith (compare also James 2:8 with Matt. 5:44, 48). Practice, not profession, is the test of obedience (compare James 2:17; 4:17 with Matt. 7:2–23). Sins of the tongue, however lightly regarded by the world, are an offense against the law of love (compare James 1:26; 3:2–18 with Matt. 5:22; also any swearing, James 5:12; compare Matt. 5:33–37).

The absence of the apostolic benediction in this Epistle is probably due to its being addressed, not merely to the believing, but also indirectly to unbelieving, Israelites. To the former he commends humility, patience, and prayer; to the latter he addresses awful warnings (James 5:7–11; 4:9; 5:1–6).

James was martyred at the Passover. This Epistle was probably written just before it. The destruction of Jerusalem foretold in it (James 5:1, etc.), ensued a year after his martyrdom, A.D. 69.

Hegesippus (quoted in Eusebius [*Ecclesiastical History,* 2.23]) narrates that he was set on a pinnacle of the temple by the scribes and Pharisees, who begged him to restrain the people who were in large numbers embracing Christianity. "Tell us," they said in the presence of the people gathered at the feast, "which is the door of Jesus?" James replied with a loud voice, "Why ask ye me about Jesus the Son of man? He sitteth at the right hand of power, and will come again on the clouds of heaven." Many then cried, "Hosanna to the Son of David." But James was thrown down by the Pharisees. He prayed: "Father, forgive them, for they know not what they do," he was stoned and beaten to death with a fuller's club. The Jews, we know from Acts, were exasperated at Paul's rescue from their hands, and therefore determined to wreak their vengeance on James. The publication of his Epistle to the dispersed Israelites, to whom it was probably carried by those who came up to the feasts, made him obnoxious to them, especially to the higher classes, because it foretold the woes soon about to fall on them and their country. Their taunting question, "Which is the door of Jesus?" (that is, by what door will He come when He returns?), alludes to his prophecy, "the coming of the Lord draweth nigh . . . behold the Judge standeth before the door" (James 5:8, 9). Heb. 13:7 probably refers to the martyrdom of James, who had been so long bishop over the Jewish Christians at Jerusalem, "Remember them which have (rather, 'had') the rule (spiritually) over you, who have spoken unto you the word of God; whose faith follow, considering the end of their conversation."

His inspiration as an apostle is expressly referred to in Acts 15:19, 28, "My sentence is," etc.: "It seemed good to the Holy Ghost, and to us," etc. His episcopal authority is implied in the deference paid to him by Peter and Paul (Acts 12:17; 21:18; Gal. 1:19; 2:9). The Lord had appeared especially to him after the resurrection (1 Cor. 15:7). Peter in his First Epistle (universally from the first received as canonical) tacitly confirms the inspiration of James's Epistle, by incorporating with his own inspired writings no less than ten passages from James. The "apostle of the circumcision," Peter, and the first bishop of Jerusalem, would naturally have much in common. Compare James 1:1 with 1 Pet. 1:1; James 1:2 with 1 Pet. 1:6; 4:12, 13; James 1:11 with 1 Pet. 1:24; James 1:18 with 1 Pet. 1:3; James 2:7 with 1 Pet. 4:14; James 3:13 with 1 Pet. 2:12; James 4:1 with 1 Pet. 2:11; James 4:6 with 1 Pet. 5:5, 6; James 4:7 with 1 Pet. 5:6, 9; James 4:10 with 1 Pet. 5:6; James 5:20 with 1 Pet. 4:6. Its being written in the purest Greek shows it was intended not only for the Jews at Jerusalem, but also for the Hellenistic, that is, Greek-speaking, Jews.

Style

The style is short and curt. A Hebraic character pervades the Epistle, as appears in the occasional poetic parallelisms (James 3:1–12). Compare "assembly": Greek, "synagogue," James 2:2, Margin. The images are analogical arguments, combining at once logic and poetry. Eloquence and persuasiveness are prominent characteristics.

The similarity to Matthew, the most Hebrew of the Gospels, is just what we might expect from the bishop of Jerusalem writing to Israelites. In it the higher spirit of Christianity is seen putting the Jewish law in its proper place. The law is enforced in its everlasting spirit, not in the letter for which the Jews were so zealous. The doctrines of grace, the distinguishing features of Paul's teaching to the Hellenists and Gentiles, are less prominent as being already taught by that apostle. James complements Paul's teaching, and shows to the Jewish Christians who still kept the legal ordinances down to the fall of Jerusalem, the spiritual principle of the law, namely, love manifested in obedience. To sketch "the perfect man" continuing in the Gospel law of liberty, is his theme.

A. R. Faussett

Detailed outline

I. Introduction: 1:1
- A. From: James, a servant of God and of the Lord Jesus Christ: 1:1
- B. To: The twelve tribes scattered among the nations: 1:1

II. Faith in suffering: 1:1–18
- A. Response to suffering: Joy: 1:2
- B. Benefits of suffering: 1:3–4
- C. The proper response to suffering: 1:5
  1. Wisdom from God: 1:5
  2. Stable faith: 1:6–7
  3. Single minded: 1:8
  4. Right response whether exalted or humbled: 1:9–11
- D. The blessing of suffering: 1:12
- E. The source of temptation: 1:13–18
  1. Not God: 1:13
  2. How we are tempted: 1:14–15
  3. We are to understand that: 1:16–18
     - (a) God sends only good and perfect gifts: 1:17
     - (b) God: 1:17–18
       - (1) Is the Father of the heavenly lights: 1:17
       - (2) Who does not change
       - (3) Gives us birth through the word of truth: 1:18
       - (4) Wants us to be his first fruits: 1:18

III. Faith at work: 1:19–4:12
- A. Faith makes a change: 1:19–21
  1. What we should be: 1:19–20
     - (a) Swift to hear: 1:19
     - (b) Slow to speak: 1:19
     - (c) Slow to become angry: 1:19–20
  2. What we should get rid of: 1:21
  3. What we should incorporate in our lives: The Word: 1:21
- B. Faith is in doing, not hearing only: 1:22–25
  1. We deceive ourselves if we are hearers only: 1:22
  2. The example of a man looking into a mirror: 1:23–25
- C. Faith is seen by control of the tongue: 1:26–27
  1. The necessity of controlling the tongue: 1:26
  2. Pure religion before God: 1:27
- D. Faith does not show favoritism: 2:1–13
- E. The faith that saves: 2:14–26

1. Faith, without deeds, is dead: 2:14–17
2. The relationship of faith and deeds: 2:18
3. Examples of faith and deeds: 2:20–25
(a) Abraham: 2:21–24
(b) Rahab: 2:25
4. Faith without deeds is dead: 2:26

F. Faith controls the tongue: 3:1–13
1. The tongue is the most difficult to control: 3:1–2
2. Examples of natural control: 3:3–4
3. The power of the tongue: 3:5–12

G. Faith and factions among believers: 3:14–4:12
1. Division among believers is not of God: 3:14
2. Wisdom of the world: 3:15–16
(a) Its description: 3:15
(b) Its results: 3:16
3. The wisdom from God is: 3:17
4. Faith brings righteousness and peace: 3:18
5. Divisions come from your desires: 4:1–6
(a) Such desire hinders prayer: 4:2–3
(b) It hinders relationship with God: 4:5–6
6. Correcting divisions: 4:7–12
(a) Submit to God: 4:7
(b) Resist the Devil: 4:7
(c) Draw close to God: 4:8
(d) Cleanse and purify yourself: 4:8
(e) Reflect true sorrow and repentance: 4:9
(f) Humble yourselves: 4:10
(g) Do not speak evil of others: 4:11
(h) Do not judge others: 4:11–12

IV. Faith and the future: 4:13–5:12

A. We cannot be assured of the future: 4:13–14

B. Only God knows the future: 4:15

C. When we boast in the future, it is evil: 4:16–17

D. The future of the rich: 5:1–6
1. They will experience misery: 5:1
2. Riches will perish: 5:1–3
3. Their fraudulent ways are noted by God: 5:4
4. They have lived in evil: 5:5–6
(a) In pleasure: 5:5
(b) In the ways of their own heart: 5:5
(c) Condemning and killing the just: 5:6

E. The believer's preparation for the future: 5:7–12
1. Wait patiently for the coming of the Lord: 5:7–8
2. Establish your hearts: 5:8
3. Do not hold grudges: 5:9
4. The prophets are examples about suffering: 5:10
5. Endure with joy, as did Job: 5:11
6. Do not swear, but mean what you say: 5:12

V. Faith and Christian relationships: 5:13–20

A. Response to the afflicted: 5:13

B. Response to the happy: 5:13

C. Response to the sick: 5:14–15
1. Call for the elders of the church: 5:14
2. Let them anoint and pray over the sick: 5:14

3. The prayer of faith will save the sick: 5:15
4. The Lord will raise him up: 5:15
5. If he has committed sins, they will be forgiven: 5:15

D. Response to sins in others: 5:16–18
1. Confess sins to each other: 5:16
2. Pray for one another, that you may be healed: 5:16
3. Elijah as an example of such effective prayer: 5:16–18

E. Response to the person who wanders from the truth: 5:19–20
1. Convert him: 5:19
2. Save his soul from death: 5:20

2. Helpful summaries of James

Bird's eye view

The Christian life is more than a mere profession of faith as it includes doing good deeds.

Reading plan

The following reading plan, taking one reading per day, enables you to read through James in five days.

James 1:1–1:27
James 2:1–2:26
James 3:1–3:18
James 4:1–4:17
James 5:1–5:20

Verses to memorize

James 1:19–20

Wherefore, my beloved brethren, let every man be swift to hear, slow to speak, slow to wrath: For the wrath of man worketh not the righteousness of God. KJV

James 1:21

Wherefore lay apart all filthiness and superfluity of naughtiness, and receive with meekness the engrafted word, which is able to save your souls. KJV

James 1:22

But be ye doers of the word, and not hearers only, deceiving your own selves. KJV

James 4:7

Submit yourselves therefore to God. Resist the devil, and he will flee from you. KJV

James 4:17

Therefore to him that knoweth to do good, and doeth it not, to him it is sin. KJV

Statistics

Twentieth New Testament book
5 chapters
108 verses
2,309 words
Number of Old Testament quotations and allusions in James: 16.

Names/titles given

Jakobou Epistole: Epistle of James.

3. Helpful keys to turn to in understanding James

Key word/phrase

Deeds
Be ye doers of the Word

Key verses

James 1:19–22; 2:20

Themes to study

The Old Testament teaching that illustrates James' teaching.

Jesus in James

In James Jesus is our Example.

Lessons to learn from James

- Wealthy Christians should never put any trust in their riches.
- No kind of discrimination against the poor should be tolerated.

4. Studying James chapter by chapter

James 1

Matthew Henry's introduction

After the inscription and salutation (v. 1) Christians are taught how to conduct themselves when under the cross. Several graces and duties are recommended; and those who endure their trials and afflictions as the apostle here directs are pronounced blessed and are assured of a glorious reward, vv. 2–12.

But those sins which bring sufferings, or the weakness and faults men are chargeable with under them, are by no means to be imputed to God, who cannot be the author of sin, but is the author of all good, vv. 13–18.

All passion, and rash anger, and vile affections, ought to be suppressed. The word of God should be made our chief study: and what we hear and know of it we must take care to practice, otherwise our religion will prove but a vain thing. To this is added an account in which pure religion consists, vv. 19–27.

Dr. Adam Clarke's analysis of chapter

He addresses the dispersed of the twelve tribes, 1.

Shows that they should rejoice under the cross, because of the spiritual good which they may derive from it, especially in the increase and perfecting of their patience, 2–4.

They are exhorted to ask wisdom of God, who gives liberally to all, 5.

But they must ask in faith, and not with a doubting mind, 6–8.

Directions to the rich and the poor, 9–11.

The blessedness of the man that endures trials, 12.

How men are tempted and drawn away from God, 13–15.

God is the Father of lights, and all good pro ceeds from him, 16–18.

Cautions against hasty words and wrong tem pers, 19–21.

We should be doers of the word, and not hear ers merely, lest we resemble those who, beholding their natural face in a glass, when it is removed forget what manner of people they were, 22–24.

We should look into the perfect law of liberty, and continue therein, 25.

The nature and properties of pure religion, 26, 27.

A detailed analysis of chapter

How to ask for God's help when suffering trials|, and how to behave in prosperous and in

adverse circumstances. (1–11)
Look on all evil as coming from ourselves, and all good from God. (12–18)
The necessity of keeping a quick temper in check, and of receiving the word of God with meekness. (19–25)
The difference between hypocrisy and real religion. (26, 27)

Key verse
Verse 2: "Consider it pure joy, my brothers, whenever you face trials of many kinds."

Key word / key phrase
Verse 12, "perseveres under trial."

Key event / key person / key theme
Overcoming temptation

Key thought
Christians must do what God tells them to do. It is not enough merely to listen.

Key thing to look out for
How does a Christian cope with trials?

Key Bible cross-reference
Verse 1. See Matthew 13:55.

Key "by way of explanation"
Verse 5, "wisdom." In the Bible, wisdom is practical. It means having insight into the principles by which God wants his people to live, and also knowing how they work out in the decisions and choices of everyday life. A breakdown of the principles is given in 3:17, 18.

Key "Quotable Quote"
"Though Satan instills his poison, and fans the flames of our corrupt desires within us, we are yet not carried by any external force to the commission of sin, but our own flesh entices us, and we willingly yield to its allurements."
John Calvin

James 2

Matthew Henry's introduction
In this chapter the apostle condemns a sinful regarding of the rich, and despising the poor, which he imputes to partiality and injustice, and shows it to be an acting contrary to God, who has chosen the poor, and whose interest is often persecuted, and his name blasphemed, by the rich, vv. 1–7.
He shows that the whole law is to be fulfilled, and that mercy should be followed, as well as justice, vv. 8–13.
He exposes the error and folly of those who boast of faith without works, telling us that this is but a dead faith, and such a faith as devils have, not the faith of Abraham, or of Rahab, v. 11, to the end.

Dr. Adam Clarke's analysis of chapter
We should not prefer the rich to the poor, nor show any partiality inconsistent with the Gospel of Christ, 1–4.
God has chosen the poor, rich in faith, to be heirs of his kingdom, even those whom some among their brethren despised and oppressed, 5, 6.
They should love their neighbor as themselves, and have no respect of people, 7–9.

He who breaks one command of God is guilty of the whole, 10, 11.

They should act as those who shall be judged by the law of liberty; and he shall have judg ment without mercy, who shows no mercy, 12, 13.

Faith without works of charity and mercy is dead; nor can it exist where there are no good works, 14–20.

Abraham proved his faith by his works, 21–24.

And so did Rahab, 25.

As the body without the soul is dead, so is faith without good works, 26.

A detailed analysis of chapter

All professions of faith are vain, if they do not result in love and justice to others. (1–13)

The necessity of good works to demonstrate the sincerity of faith, which otherwise will be of no more benefit than the faith of devils. (14–26)

Key verse

Verse 5: "Listen, my dear brothers: Has not God chosen those who are poor in the eyes of the world to be rich in faith and to inherit the kingdom he promised those who love him?"

Key word / key phrase

Verse 1, "don't show favoritism."

Key event / key person / key theme

Faith and discrimination and good deeds

Key thought

"Love your neighbor" is the standard to live up to.

Key thing to look out for

The relationship between good deeds and faith.

Key Bible cross-reference

Verse 8. See Leviticus 19:18.

Key "by way of explanation"

Verse 8, "royal law." The law of love is here called the "royal law" for two reasons. First, love is the source of all law. Second, love is the supreme law and is superior to all other laws.

Key "Quotable Quote"

"Jesus said the first commandment is to love the Lord your God. The second is to love your neighbor as in fact you love yourself. He did not say as a third commandment to love yourself."

John R.W. Stott

James 3

Matthew Henry's introduction

The apostle here reproves ambition, and an arrogant magisterial tongue; and shows the duty and advantage of bridling it because of its power to do mischief. Those who profess religion ought especially to govern their tongues, vv. 1–12.

True wisdom makes men meek, and avoiders of strife and envy: and hereby it may easily be distinguished from a wisdom that is earthly and hypocritical, v. 13, to the end.

Dr. Adam Clarke's analysis of chapter

They are exhorted not to be many masters, 1.

And to bridle the tongue, which is often an instrument of much evil, 2–12.

The character and fruits of true and false wisdom, 13–18.

James 4

Matthew Henry's introduction

In this chapter we are directed to consider,

I. Some causes of contention, besides those mentioned in the previous chapter, and to watch against them, vv. 1–5.

II. We are taught to abandon the friendship of this world, so as to submit and subject ourselves entirely to God, vv. 4–10.

III. All detraction and rash judgment of others are to be carefully avoided, vv. 11, 12.

IV. We must preserve a constant regard, and pay the utmost deference to the disposals of divine Providence, v. 13, to the end.

Dr. Adam Clarke's analysis of chapter

The origin of wars and contentions, and the wretched lot of those who are engaged in them, 1, 2.

Why so little heavenly good is obtained, 3.

The friendship of the world is enmity with God, 4, 5.

God resists the proud, 6.

Men should submit to God, and pray, 7, 8.

Should humble themselves, 9, 10.

And not speak evil of each other, 11, 12.

The impiety of those who consult not the will of God, and depend not on his providence, 13–15.

The sin of him who knows the will of God, and does not do it, 16, 17.

A detailed analysis of chapter

Warnings against proud behavior, and the harm done by an uncontrolled tongue. (1–12)

The superiority of heavenly wisdom especially when contrasted with worldly wisdom. (13–18)

Key verse

Verse 10: "Out of the same mouth come praise and cursing. My brothers, this should not be."

Key word / key phrase

Verse 9, "With the tongue."

Key event / key person / key theme

Controlling the tongue and producing wisdom

Key thought

How to gain victory over the tongue.

Key thing to look out for

Wisdom unpacked.

Key Bible cross-reference

Verse 9. See Genesis 1:26.

Key "by way of explanation"

Verse 6, "the tongue . . . is itself set on fire by hell." The tongue hurts the one who speaks, as well as those on the receiving end. "Hell itself" – all evil has its source in the devil.

Key "Quotable Quote"

"The proof that you have God's Spirit in your life is not that you speak in an unknown tongue, but that you know how to control the tongue that you do know about."

J. Sidlow Baxter

James 5

Matthew Henry's introduction

In this chapter the apostle denounces the judgments of God on those rich men who oppress the poor, showing them how great their sin and folly are in the sight of God, and how grievous the punishments would be which should fall on themselves, vv. 1–6.

Hereon, all the faithful are exhorted to patience under their trials and sufferings, vv. 7–11.

The sin of swearing is cautioned against, v. 12.

We are directed how to act, both under afflic tion and in prosperity, v. 13.

Prayer for the sick, and anointing with oil, are prescribed, vv. 14, 15.

Christians are directed to acknowledge their faults one to another, and to pray one for another, and the efficacy of prayer is proved, vv. 16–18.

And, lastly, it is recommended to us to do what we can for bringing back those that stray from the ways of truth, vv. 19, 20.

Dr. Adam Clarke's analysis of chapter

The profligate rich are in danger of God's judgments, because of their pride, fraudulent dealings, riotous living, and cruelty, 1–6.

The oppressed followers of God should be patient, for the Lord's coming is nigh; and should not grudge against each other, 7–9.

They should take encouragement from the example of the prophets, and of Job, 10, 11.

Swearing forbidden, 12.

Directions to the afflicted, 13–15.

They should confess their faults to each other, 16.

The great prevalence of prayer instanced in Elijah, 17, 18.

The blessedness of converting a sinner from the error of his way, 19, 20.

A detailed analysis of chapter

God's judgments on rich unbelievers. (1–6)

Be patient and meek under trials. (7–11)

Warnings against swearing. Prayer in every situation. Christians should confess their sins to each other. (12–18)

The happiness of being the means of the conversion of a sinner. (19, 20)

Key verse

Verse 13: "Is any one of you in trouble? He should pray. Is anyone happy? Let him sing songs of praise."

Key word / key phrase

Verse 17, "he prayed earnestly."

Key event / key person / key theme

The triumph of faith

Key thought

The rich come under fire.

Key thing to look out for

What to do when suffering comes.

Key Bible cross-reference

Verse 20. See Proverbs 10:12.

Key "by way of explanation"

Verse 9, "Don't grumble." The Bible is totally against the widespread practice of grumbling. Here, James is telling his readers not to grumble against their fellow-Christians.

Key "Quotable Quote"

"At the earlier Methodist class meetings, members were expected every week to answer some extremely personal questions, such as the following: Have you experienced any particular temptations during the past week? How did you react or respond to those temptations? Is there anything you are trying to keep secret, and, if so, what? At this point, the modern Christian swallows hard! We are often coated with a thick layer of reserve and modesty which covers 'a multitude of sins' – usually our own. Significantly, James 5:16–20, the original context of that phrase, is the passage which urges, 'Confess your sins to one another, and pray for one another, that you may be healed.'"

Michael Griffiths

5. Select bibliography for James

Hort, F. J. A. *The Epistle of James*. London: Macmillan, 1909.

Mayor, J. B. *The Epistle of St. James*. 3rd. ed. Grand Rapids: Zondervan, 1954.

Manton, Thomas, London, 1651.

Moo, D. J. *The Letter of James*. (Tyndale New Testament Commentaries) Leicester/Grand Rapids: InterVarsity/Eerdmans, 1985.

Tasker, R. V. G. *The General Epistle of James*. TNTC. Grand Rapids: Eerdmans, 1956.

1 Peter

1. Book by book: Introduction to 1 Peter

Introduction

Authenticity

Its genuineness is attested by 2 Pet. 3:1. Also by Polycarp (in Eusebius [*Ecclesiastical History*, 4.14]), who, in writing to the Philippians, quotes many passages: in the second chapter he quotes 1 Pet. 1:13, 21; 3:9; in the fifth chapter, 1 Pet. 2:11. Eusebius says of Papias (*Ecclesiastical History*, 3.39) that he, too, quotes Peter's First Epistle. Irenaeus (*Against Heresies*, 4.9.2) expressly mentions it; and in (4.16.5), 1 Pet. 2:16. Clement of Alexandria (*Miscellanies*, 1.3, p. 544), quotes 1 Pet. 2:11, 12, 15, 16; and (p. 562), 1 Pet. 1:21, 22; and (4, p. 584), 1 Pet. 3:14–17; and (p. 585), 1 Pet. 4:12–14. Origen (in Eusebius [*Ecclesiastical History*, 6.25]) mentions this Epistle; in (*Homily 7, on Joshua*, vol. 2, p. 63), he mentions both Epistles; and he mentions 1 Pet. 3:18–21. Tertullian (*Antidote to the Scorpion's Sting*, 12), quotes expressly 1 Pet. 2:20, 21; and (*Antidote to the Scorpion's Sting*, 14), 1 Pet. 2:13, 17. Eusebius states it as the opinion of those before him that this was among the universally acknowledged Epistles. The Peschito Syriac Version contains it. The fragment of the canon called Muratori's omits it. Excepting this, and the Paulician heretics, who rejected it, all ancient testimony is on its side. The internal evidence is equally strong. The author calls himself the apostle Peter, 1 Pet. 1:1, and "a witness of Christ's sufferings," and an "elder," 1 Pet. 5:1. The energy of the style harmonizes with the warmth of Peter's character; and, as Erasmus says, this Epistle is full of apostolic dignity and authority and is worthy of the leader among the apostles.

Peter

Simon, Or Simeon, was born in Bethsaida, on the Sea of Galilee, son of Jonas or John. With his father and his brother Andrew he was a fisherman at Capernaum, where he later lived. He was a married man, and tradition represents his wife's name as Concordia or Perpetua. Clement of Alexandria says that she suffered martyrdom, her husband encouraging her to be faithful unto death, "Remember, dear, our Lord." His wife's mother was healed of a fever by Christ. He was brought to Jesus by his brother Andrew, who had been a disciple of John the Baptist, but was pointed to the Savior as "the Lamb of God" by his master (John 1:29). Jesus, on first seeing him, gave him the name by which he is most often known, indicative of his subsequent character and work in the Church, "Peter" (Greek) or "Cephas" (Aramaic), a stone (Matt. 4:18). He did not join our Lord finally until a subsequent period.

The leading incidents in his apostolic life are well known: his walking on the troubled waters to meet Jesus, but sinking because he doubted (Matt. 14:30); his bold and clear acknowledgment of the divine person and office of Jesus (Matt. 16:16; Mark 8:29; John 11:27), notwithstanding the difficulties in the way of such belief, whence he was then also designated as the stone, or rock (Matt. 16:18); but his rebuke from his Lord when he opposed Christ speaking of his coming passion and death (Matt. 16:22); his passing from one extreme to the opposite, in reference to Christ's offer to wash his feet (John 13:8, 9); his self-confident assertion that he would never forsake his Lord, whatever others might do (Matt. 26:33), followed by his base denial of Christ thrice with curses (Matt. 26:75); his deep penitence; Christ's full forgiveness and prophecy of his faithfulness unto death, after he had received from him a profession of "love" as often repeated as his previous denial (John 21:15–17). These incidents illustrate his character as zealous, pious, and ardently attached to the Lord, but at the same time impulsive in feeling, rather than calmly and continuously steadfast. Prompt in action and ready to avow his convictions boldly, he was hasty in judgment, precipitate, and too self-confident in the assertion of his own steadfastness; the result was that, though he abounded in animal courage, his moral courage was too easily overcome by fear of man's opinion.

A wonderful change came over him by his restoration after his fall, through the grace of his risen Lord. His zeal and ardor became sanctified, being chastened by a spirit of unaffected humility. His love to the Lord was, if possible, increased, while his mode of manifesting it now was in doing and suffering for His name, rather than in loud protestations. Thus, when imprisoned and tried before the Sanhedrim for preaching Christ, he boldly avowed his determination to continue to do so. He is well called "the mouth of the apostles." His faithfulness led to his apprehension by Herod Agrippa, with a view to his execution, from which, however, he was delivered by the angel of the Lord.

After the ascension he took the lead in the Church; and on the descent of the Holy Spirit at Pentecost, he exercised the designed power of "the keys" of Christ's kingdom, by opening the door of the Church, in preaching, for the admission of thousands of Israelites; and still more so in opening (in obedience to a special revelation) an entrance to the "devout" (that is, Jewish proselyte from heathendom) Gentile, Cornelius: the forerunner of the harvest gathered in from idolatrous Gentiles at Antioch. This explains in what sense Christ used as to him the words, "On this rock I will build my Church" (Matt. 16:18), namely, on the preaching of Christ, the true "Rock," by connection with whom only he was given the designation: a title shared in common on the same grounds by the rest of the apostles, as the first founders of the Church on Christ, "the chief corner-stone" (Eph. 2:20). A name is often given in Hebrew, not that the person is actually the thing itself, but has some special relation to it; as Elijah means Mighty Jehovah, so Simon is called Peter "the rock," not that he is so, save by connection with Jesus, the only true Rock (Is. 28:16; 1 Cor. 3:11). As subsequently he identified himself with "Satan," and is therefore called so (Matt. 16:23), in the same way, by his clear confession of Christ, the Rock, he became identified with Him, and is accordingly so called (Matt. 16:18). It is certain that there is no instance on record of Peter's having ever claimed or exercised supremacy; on the contrary, he is represented as sent by the apostles at Jerusalem to confirm the Samaritans baptized by Philip the deacon; again at the council of Jerusalem, not he, but James the president, or leading bishop in the Church of that city, pronounced the authoritative decision: Acts 15:19, "My sentence is," etc. A kind of primacy, doubtless (though certainly not supremacy), was given him on the ground of his age, and prominent earnestness, and boldness in taking the lead on many important occasions. Hence he is called "first" in enumerating the apostles. Hence, too, arise the phrases, "Peter and the Eleven," "Peter and the rest of the apostles"; and Paul, in going up to Jerusalem after his conversion, went to see Peter in particular.

Once only he again betrayed the same spirit of vacillation through fear of man's reproach which had caused his denial of his Lord. Though at the Jerusalem council he advocated the exemption of Gentile converts from the ceremonial observances of the law, yet he, after having associated in closest intercourse with the Gentiles at Antioch, withdrew from them, through dread of the prejudices of his Jewish brethren who came from James, and timidly dissembled his conviction of the religious equality of Jew and Gentile; for this Paul openly withstood and rebuked him: a plain refutation of his alleged supremacy and infallibility (except where specially inspired, as in writing his Epistles). In all other cases he showed himself to be, indeed, as Paul calls him, "a pillar" (Gal. 2:9). Subsequently we find him in "Babylon," whence he wrote this First Epistle to the Israelite believers of the dispersion, and the Gentile Christians united in Christ, in Pontus, Galatia, Cappadocia, Asia, and Bithynia.

Jerome (*On Illustrious Men*, 1) states that "Peter, after having been bishop of Antioch, and after having preached to the believers of the circumcision in Pontus, etc. (plainly inferred from 1 Pet. 1:1), in the second year of Claudius went to Rome to refute Simon Magus, and for twenty-five years there held the episcopal chair, down to the last year of Nero, that is, the fourteenth, by whom he was crucified with his head downwards, declaring himself unworthy to be crucified as his Lord, and was buried in the Vatican, near the triumphal way." Eusebius (*Chronicles, Anno* 3), also asserts his episcopate at Antioch; his assertion that Peter founded that Church contradicts Acts 11:19–22. His journey to Rome to oppose Simon Magus arose from Justin's story of the statue found at Rome (really the statue of the Sabine god, Semo Sanctus, or Hercules, mistaken as if Simon Magus were worshipped by that name, "Simoni Deo Sancto"; found in the Tiber in 1574, or on an island in the Tiber in 1662), combined with the account in Acts 8:9–24. The twenty-five years' bishopric is chronologically impossible, as it would make Peter, at the interview with Paul at Antioch, to have been then for some years bishop of Rome! His crucifixion is certain from Christ's prophecy, John 21:18, 19. Dionysius of Corinth (in Eusebius [*Ecclesiastical History*, 2.25]) asserted in an epistle to the Romans, that Paul and Peter planted both the Roman and Corinthian churches, and endured martyrdom in Italy at the same time. So Tertullian (*Against Marcion*, 4.5, and *The Prescription against Heretics*, 36, 38). Also Caius, the presbyter of Rome, in Eusebius (*Ecclesiastical History*, 2.25) asserts that some memorials of their martyrdom were to be seen at Rome on the road to Ostia. So Eusebius (*Ecclesiastical History*, 2.25, and *Demonstration of the Gospel*, 3.116). So Lactantius (*Of the Manner in Which the Persecutors Died*, 2). Many of the details are palpably false; whether the whole be so or not is dubious, considering the tendency to concentrate at Rome events of interest (Alford). What is certain is, that Peter was not there before the writing of the Epistle to the Romans (A.D. 58), otherwise he would have been mentioned in it; nor during Paul's first imprisonment at Rome, otherwise he would have been mentioned in some one of Paul's many other Epistles written from Rome; nor during Paul's second imprisonment, at least when he was writing the Second Epistle to Timothy, just before his martyrdom. He may have gone to Rome after Paul's death, and, as common tradition represents, been imprisoned in the Mamertine dungeon, and crucified on the Janiculum, on the eminence of St. Pietro in Montorio, and his remains deposited under the great altar in the center of the famous basilica of St. Peter. Ambrose (*Epistles*, 33 p. 1022) relates that St. Peter, not long before his death, being overcome by the solicitations of his fellow Christians to save himself, was fleeing from Rome when he was met by our Lord, and on asking, "Lord, whither goest Thou?" received the answer, "I go to be crucified afresh." On this he returned and joyfully went to martyrdom. The church called "Domine quo vadis" on the Appian Way, commemorates the legend. It is not unlikely that the whole tradition is built on the connection which existed between Paul and Peter. As Paul, "the apostle of the uncircumcision," wrote Epistles to Galatia, Ephesus, and Colosse, and to Philemon at Colosse, making the Gentile Christians the people prominently addressed, and the Jewish Christians subordinately so; so, vice versa, Peter, "the apostle of the circumcision," addressed the same churches, the Jewish Christians in them primarily, and the Gentile Christians also, secondarily.

Readers

The heading, 1 Pet. 1:1, "to the elect strangers (spiritually pilgrims) of the dispersion" (Greek), clearly marks the Christians of the Jewish dispersion as prominently addressed, but still including also Gentile Christians as grafted into the Christian Jewish stock by adoption and faith, and so being part of the true Israel. 1 Pet. 1:14; 2:9, 10; 3:6; 4:3 clearly prove this. Thus he, the apostle of the circumcision, sought to unite in one Christ Jew and Gentile, in this way promoting the same work and doctrine as Paul the apostle of the uncircumcision. The provinces are named by Peter in the heading in the order proceeding from northeast to south and west. Pontus was the country of the Christian Jew Aquila. To Galatia Paul paid two visits, founding and confirming churches. Crescens, his companion, went there about the time of Paul's last imprisonment, just before his martyrdom. Ancyra was subsequently its ecclesiastical metropolis. Men of Cappadocia, as well as of "Pontus" and "Asia," were among the hearers of Peter's effective sermon on the Pentecost whereon the Spirit descended on the Church; these probably brought home to their native land the first tidings of the Gospel. Proconsular "Asia" included Mysia, Lydia, Caria, Phrygia, Pisidia, and Lyaconia. In Lycaonia were the churches of Iconium, founded by Paul and Barnabas; of Lystra, Timothy's birthplace, where Paul was stoned at the instigation of the Jews; and of Derbe, the birthplace of Gaius, or Caius. In Pisidia was Antioch, where Paul was the instrument of converting many, but was driven out by the Jews. In Caria was Miletus, containing doubtless a Christian Church. In Phrygia, Paul preached both times when visiting Galatia in its neighborhood, and in it were the churches of Laodicea, Hierapolis, and Colosse, of which last Church Philemon and Onesimus were members, and Archippus and Epaphras leaders. In Lydia was the Philadelphian Church, favorably noticed in Rev. 3:7, etc.; that of Sardis, the capital, and of Thyatira, and of Ephesus, founded by Paul, and a scene of the labors of Aquila and Priscilla and Apollos, and subsequently of more than two whole years' labor of Paul again, and subsequently censured for falling from its first love in Rev. 2:4. Smyrna of Ionia was in the same quarter, and as one of the seven churches receives unqualified praise. In Mysia was Pergamos. Troas, too, is known as the scene of Paul's preaching and raising Eutychus to life (Acts 20:6–10), and of his subsequently staying for a time with Carpus (2 Tim. 4:13). Of "Bithynia," no Church is expressly named in Scripture elsewhere. When Paul at an earlier period "assayed to go into Bithynia" (Acts 16:7), the Spirit suffered him not. But afterwards, we infer from 1 Pet. 1:1, the Spirit did impart the Gospel to that country, possibly by Peter's ministry, In government, these several churches, it appears from this Epistle (1 Pet. 5:1, 2, "Feed," etc.), were much in the same states as when Paul addressed the Ephesian "elders" at Miletus (Acts 20:17, 28, "feed") in very similar language; elders or presbyter-bishops ruled, while the apostles exercised the general superintendence. They were exposed to persecutions, though apparently not systematic, but rather annoyances and reproach arising from their not joining their heathen neighbors in riotous living, into which, however, some of them were in danger of falling. The evils which existed among themselves, and which are therefore reproved, were ambition and lucre-seeking on the part of the presbyters (1 Pet. 5:2, 3), evil thoughts and words among the members in general, and a want of sympathy and generosity towards one another.

Purpose

Peter's object seems to be, by the prospect of their heavenly portion and by Christ's example, to hold out consolation to the persecuted, and prepare them for a greater approaching ordeal, and to exhort all, husbands, wives, servants, presbyters, and people, to carry out their duties, so as to give no handle to the enemy to reproach Christianity, but rather to win them to it, and so to establish them in "the true grace of God wherein they stand" (1 Pet. 5:12).

We may divide the Epistle into: (I) The inscription (1 Pet. 1:1, 2). (II) The stirring-up of a pure feeling in believers as born again of God. By the motive of hope to which God has regenerated us (1 Pet. 1:3–12); bringing forth the fruit of faith, considering the costly price paid for our redemption from sin (1 Pet. 1:14–21). Being purified by the Spirit unto love of the brethren as begotten of God's eternal word, as spiritual priest-kings, to whom alone Christ is precious (1 Pet. 1:22; 2:10); after Christ's example in suffering, maintaining a good conversation in every relation (1 Pet. 2:10; 3:14), and a good profession of faith as having in view Christ's once-offered sacrifice, and His future coming to judgment (1 Pet. 3:15; 4:11); and exhibiting patience in adversity, as looking for future glorification with Christ, (1) in general as Christians, 1 Pet. 4:12–19; (2) each in his own sphere, 1 Pet. 5:1–11. "The title "Beloved" marks the separation of the second part from the first, 1 Pet. 2:11; and of the third part from the second, 1 Pet. 4:12" [Bengel). (III). The conclusion.

Date and place of writing

It was clearly before the open and systematic persecution of the later years of Nero had begun. That this Epistle was written after Paul's Epistles, even those written during his imprisonment at Rome, ending in A.D. 63, appears from the acquaintance which Peter in this Epistle shows he has with them. Compare 1 Pet. 2:13 with 1 Tim. 2:2–4; 1 Pet. 2:18 with Eph. 6:5; 1 Pet. 1:2 with Eph. 1:4–7; 1 Pet. 1:3 with Eph. 1:3; 1 Pet. 1:14 with Rom. 12:2; 1 Pet. 2:6–10 with Rom. 9:32, 33; 1 Pet. 2:13 with Rom. 13:1–4; 1 Pet. 2:16 with Gal. 5:13; 1 Pet. 2:18 with Eph. 6:5; 1 Pet. 3:1 with Eph. 5:22; 1 Pet. 3:9 with Rom. 12:17; 1 Pet. 4:9 with Phil. 2:14; Rom. 12:13 and Heb. 13:2; 1 Pet. 4:10 with Rom. 12:6–8; 1 Pet. 5:1 with Rom. 8:18; 1 Pet. 5:5 with Eph. 5:21; Phil. 2:3, 5–8; 1 Pet. 5:8 with 1 Thess. 5:6; 1 Pet. 5:14 with 1 Cor. 16:20.

Moreover, in 1 Pet. 5:13, Mark is mentioned as with Peter in Babylon. This must have been after Col. 4:10 (A.D. 61–63), when Mark was with Paul at Rome, but intending to go to Asia Minor. Again, in 2 Tim. 4:11 (A.D. 67 or 68), Mark was in or near Ephesus, in Asia Minor, and Timothy is told to bring him to Rome. So that it is likely it was after this, namely, after Paul's martyrdom, that Mark joined Peter, and consequently that this Epistle was written. It is not likely that Peter would have entrenched on Paul's field of labor, the churches of Asia Minor, during Paul's lifetime. The death of the apostle of the Gentiles, and the consequent need of someone to follow up his teachings, probably gave occasion to the testimony given by Peter to the same churches, collectively addressed, on behalf of the same truth. The relation in which the Pauline Gentile churches stood towards the apostles at Jerusalem favors this view. Even the Gentile Christians would naturally look to the spiritual fathers of the Church at Jerusalem, the center whence the Gospel had emanated to them, for counsel wherewith to meet the pretensions of Judaizing Christians and heretics; and Peter, always prominent among the apostles in Jerusalem, would even when elsewhere feel a deep interest in them, especially when they were by death bereft of Paul's guidance. Birks (*Horæ Evangelicæ*) suggests that false teachers may have appealed from Paul's doctrine to that of James and Peter. Peter then would naturally write to confirm the doctrines of grace and tacitly show there was no difference between his teaching and Paul's. Birks prefers dating the Epistle A.D. 58, after Paul's second visit to Galatia, when Silvanus was with him, and so could not have been with Peter (A.D. 54), and before his imprisonment at Rome, when Mark was with him, and so could not have been with Peter (A.D. 62); perhaps when Paul was detained at Cæsarea, and so debarred from personal intercourse with those churches. I prefer the view previously stated. This sets aside the tradition that Paul and Peter suffered martyrdom together at Rome. Origen's and Eusebius' statement that Peter visited the churches of Asia in person seems very probable.

Place of writing

The place of writing was doubtless Babylon on the Euphrates (1 Pet. 5:13). It is most improbable that in the middle of writing matter-of-fact communications and greetings in a remarkably plain Epistle, the symbolical language of prophecy (namely, "Babylon" for Rome) should be used. Josephus (*Antiquities,* 15.2.2; 3.1) states that there was a great multitude of Jews in the Chaldean Babylon; it is therefore likely that "the apostle of the circumcision" (Gal. 2:7, 8) would at some time or other visit them. Some have maintained that the Babylon meant was in Egypt because Mark preached in and around Alexandria after Peter's death, and therefore it is likely he did so along with that apostle in the same region previously. But no mention elsewhere in Scripture is made of this Egyptian Babylon, but only of the Chaldean one. And though towards the close of Caligula's reign a persecution drove the Jews thence to Seleucia, and a plague five years after still further thinned their numbers, yet this does not preclude their return and multiplication during the twenty years that elapsed between the plague and the writing of the Epistle. Moreover, the order in which the countries are enumerated, from north-east to south and west, is such as would be adopted by one writing from the Oriental Babylon on the Euphrates, not from Egypt or Rome. Indeed, Cosmas Indicopleustes, in the sixth century, understood the Babylon meant to be outside the Roman empire. Silvanus, Paul's companion, became subsequently Peter's, and was the carrier of this Epistle.

Style

Fervor and practical truth, rather than logical reasoning, are the characteristics, of this Epistle, as they were of its energetic, warm-hearted writer. His familiarity with Paul's Epistles shown in the language accords with what we should expect from the fact of Paul's having "communicated the Gospel which he preached among the Gentiles" (as revealed specially to him) to Peter among others "of reputation" (Gal. 2:2). Individualities occur, such as baptism, "the answer of a good conscience toward God" (1 Pet. 3:21); "consciousness of God" (Greek), 1 Pet. 2:19, as a motive for enduring sufferings; "living hope" (1 Pet. 1:3); "an inheritance incorruptible, undefiled, and that fadeth not away" (1 Pet. 1:4); "kiss of charity" (1 Pet. 5:14). Christ is viewed less in relation to His past sufferings than as at present exalted and hereafter to be manifested in all His majesty. Glory and hope are prominent features in this Epistle (1 Pet. 1:8), so much so that Weiss entitles him "the apostle of hope." The realization of future bliss as near causes him to regard believers as but "strangers" and "sojourners" here. Chastened fervor, deep humility, and ardent love appear, just as we should expect from one who had been so graciously restored after his grievous fall. "Being converted," he truly does "strengthen his brethren." His fervor shows itself in often repeating the same thought in similar words.

In some passages he shows familiarity with the Epistle of James, the apostle of special weight with the Jewish legalizing party, whose inspiration he thus confirms (compare 1 Pet. 1:6, 7 with James 1:2, 3; 1 Pet. 1:24 with James 1:10; 1 Pet. 2:1 with James 1:21; 1 Pet. 4:8 with James 5:20, both quoting Prov. 10:12; 5:5 with James 4:6, both quoting Prov. 3:34). In most of these cases Old Testament quotations are the common ground of both. "Strong susceptibility to outward impressions, liveliness of feeling, dexterity in handling subjects, dispose natures like that of Peter to repeat afresh the thoughts of others" (Steiger).

The diction of this Epistle and of his speeches in Acts is very similar: an undesigned coincidence, and so a mark of genuineness (compare 1 Pet. 2:7 with Acts 4:11; 1 Pet. 1:12 with Acts 5:32; 1 Pet. 2:24 with Acts 5:30; 10:39; 1 Pet. 5:1 with Acts 2:32; 3:15; 1 Pet. 1:10 with Acts 3:18; 10:43; 1 Pet. 1:21 with Acts 3:15; 10:40; 1 Pet. 4:5 with Acts 10:42; 1 Pet. 2:24 with Acts 3:19, 26).

There is, too, a recurrence to the language of the Lord at the last interview after His resurrection, recorded in John 21:15–23. Compare "the Shepherd . . . of . . . souls," 1 Pet. 2:25; "Feed the flock of God," "the chief Shepherd," 1 Pet. 5:2, 4, with John 21:15–17; "Feed My lambs . . . sheep"; also "Whom . . . ye love," 1 Pet. 1:8; 2:7, with John 21:15–17; "lovest thou Me?" and 2 Pet. 1:14, with John 21:18, 19. Wiesinger well says, "He who in loving impatience cast himself into the sea to meet the Lord, is also the man who most earnestly testifies to the hope of His return; he who dated his own faith from the sufferings of his Master, is never weary in holding up the suffering form of the Lord before his readers to comfort and stimulate them; he before whom the death of a martyr is in assured expectation, is the man who, in the greatest variety of aspects, sets forth the duty, as well as the consolation, of suffering for Christ; as a rock of the Church he grounds his readers against the storm of present tribulation on the true Rock of ages."

A.R. Faussett

Detailed outline

I. Greeting: 1:1–2
  A. From Peter, an apostle of Jesus: 1:1
  B. To the elect, scattered throughout: 1:1
    1. Pontus.
    2. Galatia.
    3. Cappadocia.
    4. Asia.
    5. Bithynia.
II. Comfort and reassurance in suffering: 1:3–25
  A. Reassurance in the facts of the Gospel: 1:3–12
    1. The source of salvation: 1:3
      (a) Elected by God the Father.
      (b) Redeemed by the Lord Jesus Christ.
      (c) Sanctified by the Spirit.
    2. The description of salvation: 1:3–5
  B. Reassurance based on the benefits of suffering: 1:6–12
    1. Joy in spite of temptations: 1:6
    2. Praise, honor, and glory: 1:7
    3. Joy based on relationship to Jesus: 1:8
    4. Assurance of the faith: Salvation of the soul: 1:9–12
      (a) Sought by the prophets: 1:9–10
      (b) Their source: Christ: 1:11
      (c) Their summary: 1:11–12
      (d) Sought by the angels: 1:12
  C. Reassurance based on a proper response to suffering: 1:14–17
  D. Reassurance based on redemption: 1:18–25
    1. We were not redeemed with corruptible things: 1:18
    2. We were redeemed with the precious blood of Christ: 1:19–20
    3. Basis for assurance in times of suffering: 1:21–23
    4. Assurance of redemption based on His Word: 1:24–25
III. The Christian response to suffering: 2:1–3:13
  A. Response to sin: 2:1
  B. Response to the Word of God: 2:2
  C. Response to the Son of God: 2:3–10
  D. Response in ourselves: 2:11
  E. Response to the unsaved: 2:12
  F. Response to civil authorities: 2:13–17
  G. Response to employers: 2:18–20
  H. Response based on Christ's example: 2:21–25
  I. Response to family: 3:1–12
    1. The wife: 3:1–6
    2. The husband: 3:7
    3. The entire family: 3:8–12
IV. The discipline of suffering: 3:13–4:19.
  A. Suffering for righteousness brings joy and a good conscience: 3:13–17
  B. Suffering justifies the sinner: 3:18–22
  C. Suffering conforms you to the example of Jesus: 4:1–6
  D. Suffering anticipates the second coming of Jesus: 4:7
  E. Suffering develops spiritual qualities: 4:8–11
    1. Love: 4:8
    2. Forgiveness for sin: 4:8
    3. Hospitality: 4:9
    4. Good stewardship of gifts and ministries: 4:10–11

F. Suffering multiplies future rewards: 4:12–13
G. Suffering glorifies the Lord: 4:14–16
H. Suffering purifies the saints: 4:17–19.

V. Summary statement of the believer's attitude towards suffering: 4:19.

VI. Continue to serve, despite suffering: 5:1–9
A. Serving as shepherd: The elders of the church: 5:1–4
1. Feed the flock of God: 5:2
2. Take oversight willingly, not by constraint: 5:2
3. Do not serve just for monetary reward: 5:2
4. Be of a ready mind: 5:2
5. Be examples, not lords over the flock: 5:3
6. The Chief Shepherd rewards: 5:4
B. Serving as servants: Both young and old: 5:5–7
1. Younger submit to elder: 5:5
2. Each be subject to other: 5:5
3. Be humble: 5:5–6
(a) God resists the proud and gives grace to the humble: 5:5
(b) If we are humble, we will be exalted: 5:6
4. Cast all care on Him because He cares for you: 5:7
C. Serving as a soldier: 5:8–9
1. The Enemy: The Devil is like a roaring lion: 5:8
2. The soldier's attitudes: 5:8
(a) We should be sober: 5:8
(b) We should be vigilant: 5:8
3. Strategy against the enemy: 5:9
(a) We should resist in the faith: 5:9
(b) We endure suffering as other Christians do: 5:9

VII. Conclusion: 5:10–14
A. Benediction: 5:10–11
1. The benefits of suffering in Jesus. You will be: 5:10
(a) Perfected.
(b) Established.
(c) Strengthened.
(d) Settled.
2. To God be glory and dominion for ever: 5:11
B. Personal greetings: 5:12–14
1. Silvanus: 5:12
2. The church at Babylon: 5:13
3. Marcus, my son: 5:13
4. Greet one another with a kiss: 5:14
5. A final blessing of peace to those in Jesus: 5:14

2. Helpful summaries of 1 Peter

Bird's eye view

Peter writes to encourage and strengthen fellow Christians.

Reading plan

The following reading plan, taking one reading per day, enables you to read through 1 Peter in five days.

1 Peter 1:1–1:25
1 Peter 2:1–2:25
1 Peter 3:1–3:22
1 Peter 4:1–4:19
1 Peter 5:1–5:14

Verses to memorize

1 Peter 4:12–13

Beloved, think it not strange about the fiery trial which is to try you, as though some strange thing happened unto you: But rejoice, inasmuch as ye are partakers of Christ's ufferings; that, when his glory shall be revealed, ye may be glad also with exceeding joy. KJV

1 Peter 5:6–7

Humble yourselves therefore under the mighty hand of God, that he may exalt you in due time: Casting all your care on him; for he careth for you. KJV

Statistics

Twenty-first New Testament book

5 chapters

105 verses

2,482 words

Number of Old Testament quotations and allusions in 1 Peter: 20.

Names/titles given

Petrous A: "First of Peter."

3. Helpful keys to turn to in understanding 1 Peter

Key word

Suffer, 15 times

Key verses

1 Peter 4:12, 13

Themes to study

Grace and mercy

Love

Glory

Jesus in 1 Peter

In 1 Peter Jesus is our living hope.

Peter's descriptions of Jesus

Jesus, the source of hope, 1:3.

Jesus, the sacrificial Lamb, 1:19.

Jesus, the chief cornerstone, 2:6.

Jesus, the perfect example, 2:21.

Jesus, the ideal sufferer, 2:23.

Jesus, the bearer of our sins, 2:24.

Jesus, the shepherd of our souls, 2:25.

Jesus, the exalted Lord, 3.22.

Lessons to learn from 1 Peter

- Persecuted Christians should focus more strongly than ever on Jesus.
- We do not belong to this world, but are just pilgrims passing through, on our way to heaven.

4. Studying 1 Peter chapter by chapter

1 Peter 1

Matthew Henry's introduction

The apostle describes the people to whom he writes, and salutes them (vv. 1, 2), blesses God for their regeneration to a lively hope of eternal salvation (vv. 3–5), in the hope of this salvation he shows they had great cause of rejoicing, though for a little while they were in heaviness and affliction, for the trial of their faith, which would produce joy unspeakable and full of glory, vv. 6–9.

This is that salvation which the ancient prophets foretold and the angels desire to look into, vv. 10–12.

He exhorts them to sobriety and holiness, which he presses from the consideration of the blood of Jesus, the invaluable price of man's redemption (vv. 13–21), and to brotherly love, from the consideration of their regeneration, and the excellency of their spiritual state, vv. 22–25.

Dr. Adam Clarke's analysis of chapter

Of the people to whom this epistle was directed, and their spiritual state, 1, 2.

He describes their privileges, and thanks God for the grace by which they were preserved faithful in trials and difficulties, 3–5.

The spiritual benefit they were to receive out of their afflictions, 6, 7.

Their love to Christ, 8.

And the salvation they received through believ ing, 9.

This salvation was predicted by the prophets, who only saw it afar off and had only a fore taste of it, 10–12.

They should take encouragement, and be obe dient and holy, 13–16.

Thy should pray, and deeply consider the price at which they were purchased, that their faith and hope might be in God, 17–21.

As their souls had been purified by obeying the truth through the Spirit, they should love each other with a pure and fervent love, 22, 23.

The frailty of man, and the unchangeableness of God, 24, 25.

A detailed analysis of chapter

The apostle blesses God for his special benefits through Christ. (1–9)

Salvation by Christ foretold in ancient prophecy. (10–12)

All are exhorted to be holy. (13–16)

Obey the truth and love the brethren. (17–25)

Key verse

Verse 6: "In this you greatly rejoice, though now for a little while you may have had to suffer grief in all kinds of trials."

Key word / key phrase

Verse 3, "a living hope."

Key event / key person / key theme

The Christian hope

Key thought

Salvation was the theme of the Old Testament.

Key thing to look out for

All Christians are called to be holy. What help does this chapter give to the Christian who is traveling along "the highway of holiness" (Isaiah 35:8)?

Key Bible cross-reference

Verse 16. See Leviticus 11:44, 45.

Key "by way of explanation"

Verse 16, "Be holy, because I am holy." This is

a pivotal quotation from the Old Testament. To be holy means to be set apart, and in a Christian context this means to be separated from sin and to be dedicated to God.

Key "Quotable Quote"

"If we are born again of the Spirit of God, our one desire is a hunger and thirst after nothing less than holiness, the holiness of Jesus, and he will satisfy it."

Oswald Chambers

1 Peter 2

Matthew Henry's introduction

The general exhortation to holiness is continued, and enforced by several reasons taken from the foundation on which Christians are built, Jesus Christ, and from their spiritual blessings and privileges in him.

The means of obtaining it, the word of God, is recommended, and all contrary qualities are condemned, vv. 1–12.

Particular directions are given how subjects ought to obey the magistrates, and servants their masters, patiently suffering in well doing, in imitation of Christ, v. 13, to the end.

Dr. Adam Clarke's analysis of chapter

We should lay aside all evil dispositions, and desire the sincere milk of the word, that we may grow thereby, 1–3.

And come to God to be made living stones, and be built up into a spiritual temple, 4, 5.

The prophecy of Christ as chief corner stone, precious to believers, but a stumbling stone to the disobedient, 6–8.

True believers are a chosen generation, a royal priesthood, 9, 10.

They should abstain from fleshly lusts, 11.

Walk uprightly among the Gentiles, 12.

Be obedient to civil authority, according to the will of God, 13–15.

Make a prudent use of their Christian liberty, 16.

Fear God and honor the king, 17.

Servants should be subject to their masters, and serve them faithfully, and suffer indignities patiently, after the example of Christ, 18–23.

Who bore the punishment due to our sins in his own body on the tree, 24.

They were formerly like sheep going astray, but are now returned unto the Shepherd and Bishop of their souls, 25.

A detailed analysis of chapter

Desire to grow spiritually. (1–10)

Live good lives in this corrupt world. (11,12)

Submit to the authorities. (13–17)

Servants should submit to their masters. (18–25)

Key verse

Verse 2: "Like newborn babies, crave pure spiritual milk, so that by it you may grow up in your salvation."

Key word / key phrase

Verse 5, "like living stones."

Key event / key person / key theme

Living stones, slaves of God, and the example of Jesus' suffering

Key thought

Peter lists the things Christians need to get rid of so they can grow in the Christian life.

Key thing to look out for

Peter explains how Christians should be linked up with each other.

Key Bible cross-reference

Verse 3. See Psalm 34:8.

Key "by way of explanation"

Verse 9, "chosen people." Paul is by no means the only person to speak about election and predestination. Just as Israel was chosen by God in Old Testament times, (see Isaiah 43:10,20), so in the New Testament God's followers are said to be called, chosen, and elected by God himself.

Key "Quotable Quote"

"We were enemies of God through sin, and God had appointed the sinner to die. There must needs therefore have happened one of two things; either that God, in his truth, should destroy all men, or that in his loving-kindness he should cancel the sentence. But behold the wisdom of God; he preserved both the truth of his sentence, and the exercise of his loving-kindness. Christ took our sins 'in his body on the tree, that we by his death might die to sin, and live unto righteousness' (1 Peter 2:24)."

St. Cyril of Jerusalem

1 Peter 3

Matthew Henry's introduction

Here the apostle describes the duties of husbands and wives one to another, beginning with the duty of the wife, vv. 1–7.

He exhorts Christians to unity, love, compassion, peace, and patience under sufferings; to oppose the slanders of their enemies, not by returning evil for evil, or railing for railing, but by blessing; by a ready account of their faith and hope, and by keeping a good conscience, vv. 8–17.

To encourage them to this, he proposes the example of Christ, who suffered, the just for the unjust, but yet punished the old world for their disobedience, and saved the few who were faithful in the days of Noah, v. 18, to the end.

Dr. Adam Clarke's analysis of chapter

The duty of wives to their husbands, how they are to be adorned, and be in subjection as Sarah was to Abraham, 1–6.

The duty of husbands to their wives, 7.

How to obtain happiness, and live a long and useful life, 8–11.

God loves and succors them that do good; but his face is against the wicked, 12, 13.

They should suffer persecution patiently, and be always ready to give a reason of the hope that is in them; and preserve a good con science, though they suffered for righteous ness, 14–17.

Christ suffered for us, and was put to death in the flesh, but quickened by the Spirit, 18.

How he preached to the old world, while Noah was preparing the ark, 19, 20.

The salvation of Noah and his family a type of baptism, 21.

Christ is ascended to heaven, all creatures being subject to him, 22.

A detailed analysis of chapter

The duties of wives and husbands. (1–7)

Christians should be prepared to suffer for doing good. (8–22)

Key verse

Verse 8: "Finally, all of you, live in harmony with one another; be sympathetic, love as brothers, be compassionate and humble."

Key word / key phrase

Verse 14, "if you should suffer."

Key event / key person / key theme

How to suffer

Key thought

The gentle and quiet spirit should not only characterize wives (verse 4) – but all Christians (verses 8,15).

Key thing to look out for

What advice does Peter give about witnessing to non-Christians?

Key Bible cross-reference

Verse 6. See Genesis 18:12.

Key "by way of explanation"

There are different opinions about the meaning of verses 18–22; "spirits in prison" may mean angels who had rebelled against God, since "spirits" by itself never refers to human beings, but only to supernatural beings. "Preached" probably means "announced Christ's victory," rather than "evangelized."

Key "Quotable Quote"

"How is it that nobody has dreamed up any moral advances since Christ's teaching?"

Michael Green

1 Peter 4

Matthew Henry's introduction

The work of a Christian is twofold–doing the will of God and suffering his pleasure. This chapter directs us in both. The duties we are here exhorted to employ ourselves in are the mortification of sin, living to God, sobriety, prayer, charity, hospitality, and the best improvement of our talents, which the apostle presses on Christians from the consideration of the time they have lost in their sins, and the approaching end of all things, vv. 1–11.

The directions for sufferings are that we should not be surprised at them, but rejoice in them, only take care not to suffer as evil-doers. He intimates that their trials were near at hand, that their souls were in danger as well as their bodies, and that the best way to preserve their souls is to commit them to God in well-doing.

Dr. Adam Clarke's analysis of chapter

We should suffer patiently, after the example of Christ, 1.

And no longer live according to our former cus tom, but disregard the scoffs of those who are incensed against us because we have forsaken their evil ways, who are shortly to give account to God for their conduct, 2–5.

How the Gospel was preached to Jews and Gentiles, 6.

As the end of all things was at hand, they should be sober, watchful, charitable, benev olent, good stewards of the bounty of Providence; and, when called to instruct others, speak as the oracles of God, 7–11.

Of the persecutions and trials which were com ing on them, and how they were to suffer so as not to disgrace their Christian character, 12–16.

Judgment was about to begin at the house of God, and even the righteous would escape with difficulty from the calamities coming on the Jews; but they must continue in well-doing, and thus commit the keeping of their souls to their faithful Creator, 17–19.

A detailed analysis of chapter

Reflect on Christ's sufferings as you consider your own purity and holiness. (1–6)
The end of all things is a good reason to be sober, alert and prayerful. (7–11)
Suffer for being a Christian. (12–19)

Key verse

Verse 7: "The end of all things is near. Therefore be clear minded and self-controlled so that you can pray."

Key word / key phrase

Verse 13, "you participate in the sufferings of Christ."

Key event / key person / key theme

Suffering as a Christian

Key thought

"The end is near." (Christ's incarnation marked the beginning of "these last times" 1:20).

Key thing to look out for

Verse 11, the purpose and guiding principle of the Christian's actions.

Key Bible cross-reference

Verse 8. See Proverbs 10:12.

Key "by way of explanation"

Verse 4, "they heap abuse on you." Some fear that if they stand out in the crowd they will be made fun of. "Quite right," declares Peter. One reason you are likely to suffer is for steering clear of the wild and reckless living of the world.

Key "Quotable Quote"

"The Church is to develop a Christian counter-culture with its own distinctive goals, values, standards, and lifestyle – a realistic alternative to the contemporary technocracy which is marked by bondage, materialism, self-centeredness, and greed."

John R.W. Stott

1 Peter 5

Matthew Henry's introduction

In which the apostle gives particular directions, first to the elders, how to behave themselves towards their flock (vv. 1–4); then to the younger, to be obedient and humble, and to cast their care on God, vv. 5–7.

He then exhorts all to sobriety, watchfulness against temptations, and steadfastness in the faith, praying earnestly for them; and so concludes his epistle with a solemn doxology, mutual greetings, and his apostolic benediction.

Dr. Adam Clarke's analysis of chapter

Directions to the elders to feed the flock of God, and not to be lord over God's heritage, that when the chief Shepherd does appear, they may receive a crown of glory, 1–5.

The young are to submit themselves to the elder, and to humble themselves under the mighty hand of God, and cast all their care on him, 6–7.

They should be sober and watchful, because their adversary the devil is continually seek ing their destruction, whom they are to resist, steadfast in the faith, 8, 9.

They are informed that the God of all grace had called them to his eternal glory, 10–11.

Of Silvanus, by whom this epistle was sent, 12.

Greetings from the Church at Babylon, 13.

The apostolic benediction, 14.

A detailed analysis of chapter

Elders exhorted and encouraged. (1–4)

Younger Christians are to submit to their elders, and to yield with humility and patience to God, and to be sober, alert, and steadfast in faith. (5–9)

Prayers for their growth. (10–14)

Key verse

Verse 7: "Cast all your anxiety on him because he cares for you."

Key word / key phrase

Verse 6, "humble yourselves."

Key event / key person / key theme

Submit to God

Key thought

How to be a shepherd of God's flock.

Key thing to look out for

How to beat the devil.

Key Bible cross-reference

Verse 5. See Proverbs 3:34.

Key "by way of explanation"

Verse 8, "alert." Peter knew what it was not to be alert when he fell asleep in the Garden of Gethsemane, Matthew 26:36–46.

Key "Quotable Quote"

"Satan does not care what we do so long as we do not alert people to their sin. Our work is to wake people up."

Catherine Booth

5. Select bibliography for 1 and 2 Peter

Best, E. *1 Peter*. London: Marshall, Morgan & Scott, 1971.

Calvin, John. *Calvin's Commentaries: The Epistle of Paul The Apostle to the Hebrews and The First and Second Epistles of St. Peter*. Translated by W. B. Johnston. Edited by D. W. and T. F. Torrance. Grand Rapids: Eerdmans, 1963.

Cranfield, C. E. B. *The First Epistle of Peter*. London: SCM, 1950.

Grudem, W. *1 Peter*. (Tyndale New Testament Commentaries) Leicester: InterVarsity; Grand Rapids: Eerdmans, 1988.

Kelly, J. N. D. *The Epistles of Peter and of Jude*. New York: Harper & Row, 1970.

Stibbs, Alan M. *The First Epistle General of Peter*. TNTC. Grand Rapids: Eerdmans, 1959.

2 Peter

1. Book by book: Introduction to 2 Peter

Introduction

Authenticity

If not a gross imposture, its own internal witness is unequivocal in its favor. It has Peter's name and apostleship in its heading: not only his surname, but his original name Simon, or Simeon, he thus, at the close of his life, reminding his readers who he originally was before his call. Again, in 2 Pet. 1:16–18, he mentions his presence at the Transfiguration, and Christ's prophecy of his death! and in 2 Pet. 3:15, his brotherhood with Paul. Again, in 2 Pet. 3:1, the author speaks of himself as author of the former Epistle: it is, moreover, addressed so as to include (but not to be restricted to) the same people as the first, whom he presupposes to be acquainted with the writings of Paul, by that time recognized as "Scripture" (2 Pet. 3:15, "the long-suffering of God," compare Rom. 2:4). This necessarily implies a late date, when Paul's Epistles (including Romans) already had become generally diffused and accepted as Scripture in the Church. The Church of the fourth century had, besides the testimony which we have of the doubts of the earlier Christians, other external evidence which we have not, and which, doubtless, under God's overruling providence, caused them to accept it. It is hard to understand how a book palpably false (as it would be if Peter be not the author) could have been accepted in the Canon as finally established in the Councils of Laodicea, A.D. 360 (if the fifty-ninth article be genuine), Hippo, and Carthage in the fourth century (393 and 397). The whole tone and spirit of the Epistle disprove its being an imposture. He writes as one not speaking of himself, but moved by the Holy Spirit (2 Pet. 1:21). An attempt at such a fraud in the first ages would have brought only shame and suffering, alike from Christians and heathen, on the perpetrator: there was then no temptation to pious frauds as in later times. That it must have been written in the earliest age is plain from the wide gulf in style which separates it and the other New Testament Scriptures from even the earliest and best of the post-apostolic period. Daille well says, "God has allowed a fosse to be drawn by human weakness around the sacred canon to protect it from all invasion."

Traces of acquaintance with it appear in the earliest Fathers. Hermas (Similitudes, 6.4) (compare 2 Pet. 2:13), Greek, "luxury in the day . . . luxuriating with their own deceivings"; and (Shepherd, Vision 3.7), "They have left their true way" (compare 2 Pet. 2:15); and (Shepherd, Vision 4.3), "Thou hast escaped this world" (compare 2 Pet. 2:20). Clement of Rome, (Epistle to the Corinthians, 7.9; 10), as to Noah's preaching and Lot's deliverance, "the Lord making it known that He does not abandon those that trust in Him, but appoints those otherwise inclined to judgment" (compare 2 Pet. 2:5, 6, 7, 9). Irenaeus, a.d. 178 ("the day of the Lord is as a thousand years"), and Justin Martyr seem to allude to 2 Pet. 3:8. Hippolytus (On Antichrist), seems to refer to 2 Pet. 1:21, "The prophets spake not of their own private (individual) ability and will, but what was (revealed) to them alone by God." The difficulty is, neither Tertullian, Cyprian, Clement of Alexandria, nor the oldest Syriac (*Peschito*) version (the later Syriac has it), nor the fragment known as Muratori's Canon, mentions it. The first writer who has expressly named it is Origen, in the third century (*Homily on Joshua*; also *Homily 4 on Leviticus*, and *Homily 13 on Numbers*), who names it "Scripture," quoting 2 Pet. 1:4; 2:16; however (in Eusebius [*Ecclesiastical History*, 6.25]), he mentions that the Second Epistle was doubted by some. Firmilian, bishop of Cappadocia, in Epistle to Cyrpian speaks of Peter's Epistles as warning us to avoid heretics (a monition which occurs in the Second, not the First Epistle). Now Cappadocia is one of the countries mentioned (compare 1 Pet. 1:1 with 2 Pet. 3:1) as addressed; and it is striking, that from Cappadocia we get the earliest decisive testimony. "Internally it claims to be written by Peter, and this claim is confirmed by the Christians of that very region in whose custody it ought to have been found" (Tregelles).

The books being disputed (*Antilegomena*), as distinguished from those universally recognized (*Homologoumena*), are Epistles Second Peter, James, Second and Third John, Jude, the Apocalypse, Epistle to Hebrews (compare Eusebius [*Ecclesiastical History*, 3.3,25]). The Antilegomena stand in quite a different class from the Spurious; of these there was no dispute, they were universally rejected; for example, the Shepherd of Hermas, the Revelation of Peter, the Epistle of Barnabas. Cyril of Jerusalem (A.D. 348) enumerates seven Catholic Epistles, including Second Peter; so also Gregory of Nazianzen (A.D. 389), and Epiphanius (A.D. 367). The oldest Greek manuscripts extant (of the fourth century) contain the Antilegomena. Jerome (*On Illustrious Men*), conjectured, from a supposed difference of style between the two Epistles, that Peter, being unable to write Greek, employed a different translator of his Hebrew dictation in the Second Epistle, and not the same as translated the First into Greek. Mark is said to have been his translator in the case of the Gospel according to Mark; but this is all gratuitous conjecture. Much of the same views pervade both Epistles. In both alike he looks for the Lord's coming suddenly, and the end of the world (compare 2 Pet. 3:8–10 with 1 Pet. 4:5); the inspiration of the prophets (compare 1 Pet. 1:10–12 with 2 Pet. 1:19–21; 3:2); the new birth by the divine word a motive to abstinence from worldly lusts (1 Pet. 1:22; 2:2; compare 2 Pet. 1:4); also compare 1 Pet. 2:9 with 2 Pet. 1:3, both containing in the Greek the rare word "virtue" (1 Pet. 4:17 with 2 Pet. 2:3).

It is not strange that distinctive peculiarities of style should mark each Epistle, the design of both not being the same. Thus the sufferings of Christ are more prominent in the First Epistle, the object there being to encourage thereby Christian sufferers; the glory of the exalted Lord is more prominent in the Second, the object being to communicate fuller "knowledge" of Him as the antidote to the false teaching against which Peter warns his readers. Hence His title of redemption, "Christ," is the one employed in the First Epistle; but in the Second Epistle, "the Lord." Hope is characteristic of the First Epistle; full knowledge, of the Second Epistle. In the First Epistle he puts his apostolic authority less prominently forward than in the Second, in which his design is to warn against false teachers. The same difference is observable in Paul's Epistles. Contrast 1 Thess. 1:1; 2 Thess. 1:1; Phil. 1:1, with Gal. 1:1; 1 Cor. 1:1. The reference to Paul's writings as already existing in numbers, and as then a recognized part of Scripture (2 Pet. 3:15, 16), implies that this Epistle was written at a late date, just before Peter's death.

Striking verbal coincidences occur: compare 1 Pet. 1:19, end, with 2 Pet. 3:14, end; "His own," Greek, 2 Pet. 1:3, 2 Pet. 2:16; 3:17 with 1 Pet. 3:1, 5. The omission of the Greek article, 1 Pet. 2:13 with 2 Pet. 1:21; 2:4, 5, 7. Moreover, two words occur, 2 Pet. 1:13, "tabernacle," that is, the body, and 2 Pet. 1:15, "decease," which at once remind us of the transfiguration narrative in the Gospel. Both Epistles refer to the deluge, and to Noah as the eighth that was saved. Though the First Epistle abounds in quotations of the Old Testament, whereas the Second contains none, yet references to the Old Testament occur often (2 Pet. 1:21; 2:5–8, 15; 3:5, 6, 10, 13). Compare Greek, "putting away," 1 Pet. 3:21, with 2 Pet. 1:14; Greek, "pass the time," 1 Pet. 1:17, with 2 Pet. 2:18; "walked in," 1 Pet. 4:3, with 2 Pet. 2:10; 3:3; "called you," 1 Pet. 1:15; 2:9; 5:10, with 2 Pet. 1:3.

Moreover, more verbal coincidences with the speeches of Peter in Acts occur in this Second, than in the First Epistle. Compare Greek, "obtained," 2 Pet. 1:1 with Acts 1:17; Greek, "godliness," 2 Pet. 1:6, with Acts 3:12, the only passage where the term occurs, except in the Pastoral Epistles; and 2 Pet. 2:9 with Acts 10:2, 7; "punished," 2 Pet. 2:9, with Acts 4:21, the only places where the term occurs; the double genitive, 2 Pet. 3:2, with Acts 5:32; "the day of the Lord," 2 Pet. 3:10, with Acts 2:20, where only it occurs, except in 1 Thess. 5:2.

The testimony of Jude, Jude 17, 18, is strong for its genuineness and inspiration, by adopting its very words, and by referring to it as received by the churches to which he, Jude, wrote, "Remember the words which were spoken before of the apostles of our Lord Jesus Christ; how that they told you there should be mockers in the last time, who should walk after their own ungodly lusts." Jude, therefore, must have written after Second Peter, to which he plainly refers; not before, as Alford thinks. No less than eleven passages of Jude rest on similar statements of Second Peter. Jude 2, compare 2 Pet. 1:2; Jude 4, compare 2 Pet. 2:1; Jude 6, compare 2 Pet. 2:4; Jude 7, compare 2 Pet. 2:6; Jude 8, compare 2 Pet. 2:10; Jude 9, compare 2 Pet. 2:11; Jude 11, compare 2 Pet. 2:15; Jude 12, compare 2 Pet. 2:17; Jude 16, compare 2 Pet. 2:18; Jude 18, compare 2 Pet. 2:1; 3:3. Just in the same way Micah, Mic. 4:1–4, leans on the somewhat earlier prophecy of Isaiah, whose inspiration he thereby confirms. Alford reasons that because Jude, in many of the passages akin to Second Peter, is fuller than Second Peter, he must be prior. This by no means follows. It is at least as likely, if not more so, that the briefer is the earlier, rather than the fuller. The dignity and energy of the style is quite consonant to what we should expect from the prompt and ardent foreman of the apostles. The difference of style between First and Second Peter accords with the distinctness of the subjects and objects.

Date

The date of 2 Peter, from what has been said, would be about A.D. 68 or 69, about a year after the first, and shortly before the destruction of Jerusalem, the typical precursor of the world's end, to which 2 Pet. 3:10–13 so solemnly calls attention, after Paul's ministry had closed (compare Greek aorist tense, "wrote," past time, 2 Pet. 3:15), just before Peter's own death. It was written to include the same people, and perhaps in, or about the same place, as the first. Being without greetings of individuals, and entrusted to the care of no one church, or particular churches as the first is, but directed generally "to them that have obtained like precious faith with us" (2 Pet. 1:1), it took a longer time in being recognized as canonical. Had Rome been the place of its composition or publication, it could hardly have failed to have had an early acceptance–an incidental argument against the tradition of Peter's martyrdom at Rome. The remote scene of its composition in Babylon, or else in some of the contiguous regions beyond the borders of the Roman empire, and of its circulation in Cappadocia, Pontus, etc., will additionally account for its tardy but at last universal acceptance in the catholic Church. The former Epistle, through its more definite address, was earlier in its general acceptance.

Purpose

In 2 Pet. 3:17, 18 the twofold purpose of the Epistle is set out; namely, to guard his readers against "the error" of false teachers, and to exhort them to grow in experimental "knowledge of our Lord and Savior" (2 Pet. 3:18). The ground on which this knowledge rests is stated, 2 Pet. 1:12–21, namely, the inspired testimony of apostles and prophets. The danger now, as of old, was about to arise from false teachers, who soon were to come among them, as Paul also (to whom reference is made, 2 Pet. 3:15, 16) testified in the same region. The grand antidote is "the full knowledge of our Lord and Savior," through which we know God the Father, partake of His nature, escape from the pollutions of the world, and have entrance into Christ's kingdom. The aspect of Christ presented is not so much that of the past suffering, as of the future reigning, Savior, His present power, and future new kingdom. This aspect is taken as best fitted to counteract the theories of the false teachers who should "deny" His Lordship and His coming again, the two very points which, as an apostle and eye-witness, Peter attests (His "power" and His "coming"); also, to counteract their evil example in practice, blaspheming the way of truth, despising governments, slaves to covetousness and filthy lusts of the flesh, while boasting of Christian freedom, and, worst of all, apostates from the truth. The knowledge of Christ, as being the knowledge of "the way of righteousness," "the right way," is the antidote of their bad practice. Hence "the preacher" of righteousness, Noah, and "righteous Lot," are instanced as escaping the destruction which overtook the "unjust" or "unrighteous"; and Balaam is instanced as exemplifying the awful result of "unrighteousness" such as characterized the false teachers. Thus the Epistle forms one connected whole, the parts being closely bound together by mutual relation, and the end corresponding with the beginning; compare 2 Pet. 3:14, 18 with 2 Pet. 1:2, in both "grace" and "peace" being connected with "the knowledge" of our Savior; compare also 2 Pet. 3:17 with 2 Pet. 1:4, 10, 12; and 2 Pet. 3:18, "grow in grace and knowledge," with the fuller 2 Pet. 1:5–8; and 2 Pet. 2:21; and 2 Pet. 3:13, "righteousness," with 2 Pet. 1:1; and 2 Pet. 3:1 with 2 Pet. 1:13; and 2 Pet. 3:2 with 2 Pet. 1:19.

The germs of Carpocratian and Gnostic heresies already existed, but the actual manifestation of these heresies is spoken of as future (2 Pet. 2:1, 2, etc.): another proof that this Epistle was written, as it professes, in the apostolic age, before the development of the Gnostic heresies in the end of the first and the beginning of the second centuries. The description is too general to identify the heresies with any particular one of the subsequent forms of heresy, but applies generally to them all.

Though altogether distinct in aim from the First Epistle, yet a connection may be traced. The neglect of the warnings to circumspection in the walk led to the evils foretold in the Second Epistle. Compare the warning against the abuse of Christian freedom, 1 Pet. 2:16 with 2 Pet. 2:19, "While they promise them liberty, they themselves are the servants of corruption"; also the caution against pride, 1 Pet. 5:5, 6 with 2 Pet. 2:18, "they speak great swelling words of vanity."

A. R. Faussett

Detailed outline

- I. Introduction: 1:1–2
  - A. From Peter, a servant and apostle: 1:1
  - B. To those who have also received a precious faith: 1:1
  - C. Grace and peace: 1:2
- II. Proclamation of the power of God in the face of false teachers: 1:3
- III. The promises of God: 1:4
- IV. The principles of God: 1:5–9
  - A. To be developed with diligence: 1:5
  - B. The principles listed: 1:5–7
  - C. The value of these principles. They will make you: 1:8
    1. Abound spiritually.
    2. Fruitful in the knowledge of Jesus.
  - D. Problems without such principles: 1:9
    1. No spiritual vision.
    2. No spiritual memory.
- V. God's calling: 1:10–12
  - A. Be eager to make your calling sure: 1:10
  - B. If you do these things, you will never fall: 1:10
  - C. You will be assured entrance into the everlasting Kingdom: 1:11
  - D. You will be established in truth: 1:12
- VI. The revelation to the Apostle of God: 1:13–15

VII. The Word of God: 1:16–21
  A. Not based on fables, but on eyewitness accounts: 1:16
  B. Based on the deity of Christ: 1:17
  C. Based on a sure Word of prophecy: 1:19.
  D. Not based on individual interpretation: 1:20
  E. Based on the inspiration of the Holy Spirit: 1:21

VIII. Warning against false teachers: 2:1–3:4
  A. The identity of the enemies: 2:1–9
    1. Present days: False teachers: 2:1–3
    2. Former days: 2:1–9
      (a) False prophets: 2:1
      (b) The wicked angels: 2:4
      (c) Those living in Noah's day: 2:5
      (d) Those living in Lot's day: 2:6–9
  B. Description of the enemies of God (false teachers): 2:10–19.
  C. Destiny of the enemies: 2:20–22

IX. Warning against apostasy: 3:1–18
  A. The definition of apostasy: 3:1–4
    1. Predicted by the prophets: 3:1–2
    2. Apostasy is scoffing at the promise of the coming of Jesus: 3:4
  B. An answer to apostasy: 3:5–13
    1. They deliberately forgot God's actions: 3:5–6
    2. The future annihilation of the present world: 3:7–8,10
    3. God has His own timetable for fulfilling His plan: 3:8
    4. The salvation of lost souls: 3:9
    5. The "day of the Lord" will come unexpectedly: 5:10
    6. His plan will culminate with a new creation: 3:13
  C. The believer's response in the face of apostasy: 3:14–18
    1. Be found of Him in peace: 3:14
    2. Spotless: 3:14
    3. Blameless: 3:14
    4. The Lord's patience means salvation: 15–16
    5. Guard against error of lawless people: 3:17
    6. Grow in grace: 3:18
    7. Grow in the knowledge of the Lord: 3:18

X. Conclusion: 3:18

2. Helpful summaries of 2 Peter

Bird's eye view

Peter uses the Word of God to counter false teachers.

Reading plan

The following reading plan, taking one reading per day, enables you to read through 2 Peter in three days.

2 Peter 1:1–1:21
2 Peter 2:1–2:22
2 Peter 3:1–3:18

Verses to memorize

2 Peter 1:21

For the prophecy came not in old time by the will of man: but holy men of God spake as they were moved by the Holy Ghost. KJV

2 Peter 3:9

The Lord is not slack about his promise, as some men count slackness; but is longsuffering to us-ward, not willing that any should perish, but that all should come to repentance. KJV

2 Peter 3:18

But grow in grace, and in the knowledge of our Lord and Savior Jesus Christ. To him be glory both now and for ever. Amen. KJV

Statistics

Twenty-second New Testament book

3 chapters

61 verses

1,559 words

Names/titles given

Petrous B: "Second of Peter."

3. Helpful keys to turn to in understanding 2 Peter

Key word/phrase

Knowledge

Full knowledge of God

Key verse

2 Peter 3:2

Themes to study

The evidence of eyewitnesses

The Word of God

The end of the age

Jesus in 2 Peter

In 2 Peter Jesus is our strength.

Lessons to learn from 2 Peter

- False teachers should not be tolerated.
- All Christians should be growing towards spiritual maturity.

4. Studying 2 Peter chapter by chapter

2 Peter 1

Matthew Henry's introduction

In this chapter we have,

I. An introduction, or preface, making way for, and leading to, what is principally designed by the apostle, vv. 1–4.

II. An exhortation to advance and improve in all Christian graces, vv. 5–7.

III. To enforce this exhortation, and engage them seriously and heartily to comply with it, he adds,

A. A representation of the very great advantage which will thereby accrue to them, vv. 8–11.

B. A promise of the best assistance the apostle was able to give to facilitate and forward this good work, vv. 12–15.

C. A declaration of the certain truth and divine origin of the gospel of Christ, in the grace whereof they were exhorted to increase and persevere.

Dr. Adam Clarke's analysis of chapter

The apostolic address, and the people to whom the epistle was sent described by the state into which God had called, and in which he had placed, them, 1–4.

What graces they should possess in order to be fruitful in the knowledge of God, 5–8.

The miserable state of those who either have not these graces, or have fallen from them, 9.

Believers should give diligence to make their calling and election sure, 10, 11.

The apostle's intimations of his speedy dissolu tion, and his wish to confirm and establish those Churches in the true faith, 12–15.

The certainty of the Gospel, and the convincing evidence which the apostle had of its truth from being present at the transfiguration, by which the word of prophecy was made more sure, 16–19.

How the prophecies came, and their nature, 20, 21.

A detailed analysis of chapter

Exhortations to make one's calling and election certain. (1–11)

The apostle looks forward to his approaching death. (12–15)

He confirms the truth of the gospel, and of Christ's coming as Judge. (16–21)

Key verse

Verse 21: "For prophecy never had its origin in the will of man, but men spoke from God as they were carried along by the Holy Spirit."

Key word / key phrase

Verse 10, "your calling and election."

Key event / key person / key theme

The prerequisites for a fruitful Christian life.

Key thought

God's power has given Christians all they need (verse 3) – but this has to be worked out in practical ways.

Key thing to look out for

The vital importance of prophecy.

Key Bible cross-reference

Verses 17, 18. See Mark 9:2–7.

Key "by way of explanation"

Verse 16, "cleverly invented stories." Peter denies that his teaching about Jesus has anything to do with fabricated stories. But Peter's words indicate that weird and wonderful stories purporting to be about Jesus were circulating in Peter's day. Peter was an eyewitness of the transfiguration (verses 16,17).

Key "Quotable Quote"

"It is not the brains that matter most, but that which guides them – the character; the heart, generous qualities, progressive ideas."

Feodor Dostoevesky

2 Peter 2

Matthew Henry's introduction

The apostle, having in the previous chapter exhorted them to proceed and advance in the Christian race, now comes to remove, as much as in him lay, what he could not but apprehend would hinder their complying with his exhortation. He therefore gives them fair warning of false teachers, by whom they might be in danger of being seduced. To prevent this,

I. He describes these seducers as impious in themselves, and very pernicious to others, vv. 1–3.

II. He assures them of the punishment that shall be inflicted on them, vv. 3–6.

III. He tells us how contrary the method is which God takes with those who fear him, vv. 7–9.

IV. He fills up the rest of the chapter with a further description of those seducers of whom he would have them beware.

Dr. Adam Clarke's analysis of chapter

False teachers foretold, who shall bring in destructive doctrines and shall pervert many, but at last be destroyed by the judgments of God, 1–3.

Instances of God's judgments in the rebellious angels, 4.

In the antediluvians, 5.

In the cities of Sodom and Gomorrah, 6–8.

The Lord knoweth how to deliver the godly, as well as to punish the ungodly, 9.

The character of those seducing teachers and their disciples; they are unclean, presumptuous, speak evil of dignities, adulterous, covetous, and cursed, 10–14.

Have forsaken the right way, copy the conduct of Balaam, speak great swelling words, and pervert those who had escaped from error, 15–19.

The miserable state of those who, having escaped the corruption that is in the world, have turned back like the dog to his vomit, and the washed swine to her wallowing in the mire, 20–22.

A detailed analysis of chapter

Believers are warned against false teachers. These teachers will be punished. (1–9)

The wicked work of false teachers. (10–16)

They pretend to be free and pure. (17–22)

Key verse

Verse 1: "But there were also false prophets among the people, just as there will be false teachers among you."

Key word / key phrase

Verse 2, "there were also false prophets."

Key event / key person / key theme

False teachers condemned

Key thought

Peter describes the destruction false teachers bring in their wake.

Key thing to look out for

Peter's knock-out onslaught on false teachers.

Key Bible cross-reference

Verse 6. See Genesis 19:24.

Key "by way of explanation"

Verse 1: history is repeating itself, but how much worse these new false prophets are, in view of the fact that they have known Christ (verse 20).

Key "Quotable Quote"

"The soul which is possessed of this rich treasure of contentment, is like Noah in the ark, that can sing in the midst of a deluge."

Thomas Watson

2 Peter 3

Matthew Henry's introduction

I. The apostle drawing towards the conclusion of his second epistle, begins this last chapter with repeating the account of his design and scope in writing a second time to them, vv. 1–2.

II. He proceeds to mention one thing that induced him to write this second epistle, namely, the coming of scoffers, whom he describes, vv. 3–7.

III. He instructs and establishes them in the coming of our Lord Jesus Christ to judgment, vv. 8–10.

IV. He sets forth the use and improvement which Christians ought to make of Christ's second coming, and that dissolution and renovation of things which will accompany that solemn coming of our Lord, vv. 11–18.

Dr. Adam Clarke's analysis of chapter

The apostle shows his design in writing this and the preceding epistle, 1, 2.

Describes the nature of the heresies which should take place in the last times, 3–8.

A thousand years with the Lord are but as a day, 9.

He will come and judge the world as he has promised, and the heavens and the earth shall be burnt up, 10.

How those should live who expect these things, 11, 12.

Of the new heavens and the new earth, and the necessity of being prepared for this great change, 13, 14.

About some difficult things in St. Paul 's epistles, 15, 16.

We must watch against the error of the wicked, grow in grace, and give all glory to God, 17, 18.

A detailed analysis of chapter

Christ's final coming as Judge. (1–4)

He will appear when he is not expected. The world will be destroyed by fire. (5–10)

So we must be holy and stand firm in the faith. (11–18)

Key verse

Verse 10: "But the day of the Lord will come like a thief."

Key word / key phrase

Verse 3, "in the last days."

Key event / key person / key theme

Confidence in Jesus' return

Key thought

God's view of time differs from ours.

Key thing to look out for

There is only one sure way not to be carried along by the evil world.

Key Bible cross-reference

Verse 3. See Jude 18.

Key "by way of explanation"

Verse 18. "knowledge." The false teachers were probably peddling an early form of Gnosticism, which taught that there was a "secret knowledge" not available to ordinary believers. In contrast, Peter says that Christians should be always growing in their knowledge of Jesus who is both their Lord and Savior. That is the only knowledge they need.

Key "Quotable Quote"

"In Christ crucified is the true theology and the knowledge of God."

Martin Luther

5. Select bibliography for 2 Peter

Calvin, John. *Calvin's Commentaries: The Epistle of Paul The Apostle to the Hebrews and The First and Second Epistles of St. Peter*. Translated by W. B. Johnston. Edited by D. W. and T. F. Torrance. Grand Rapids: Eerdmans, 1963.

Green, Michael. *The Second Epistle of Peter and the Epistle of Jude*. Grand Rapids: Eerdmans, 1968.

1 John

1. Book by book: Introduction to 1 John

Introduction

Author

Polycarp, the disciple of John (*Epistle to the Philippians*, 7), quotes 1 John 4:3. Eusebius (*Ecclesiastical History*, 3.39) says of Papias, a hearer of John, and a friend of Polycarp, "He used testimonies from the First Epistle of John." Irenaeus, according to Eusebius (*Ecclesiastical History*, 5.8), often quoted this Epistle. So in his work *Against Heresies* (3.15; 5, 8) he quotes from John by name, 1 John 2:18, etc.; and in (3.16,7), he quotes 1 John 4:1–3; 5:1, and 2 John 7, 8. Clement of Alexandria (*Miscellanies*, 2.66, p. 464) refers to 1 John 5:16, as in John's larger Epistle. See other quotations (*Miscellanies*, 3.32,42; 4.102). Tertullian (*Against Marcion*, 5.16) refers to 1 John 4:1, etc.; (*Against Praxeas*, 15), to 1 John 1:1. See his other quotations (*Against Praxeas*, 28; *Against the Gnostics*, 12). Cyprian (*Epistles*, 28), quotes as John's, 1 John 2:3, 4; and (*On the Lord's Prayer*, 5) quotes 1 John 2:15–17; and (*On Works and Alms*, 3), 1 John 1:8; and (*On the Advantage of Patience*, 2) quotes 1 John 2:6. Muratori's *Fragment on the Canon of Scripture* states, "There are two of John (the Gospel and

Epistle?) esteemed Catholic," and quotes 1 John 1:3. The Peschito Syriac contains it. Origen (in Eusebius [*Ecclesiastical History*, 6.25]) speaks of the First Epistle as genuine, and "probably the second and third, though all do not recognize the latter two"; on the Gospel of John, (*Commentary on John*, 13.2), he quotes 1 John 1:5. Dionysius of Alexandria, Origen's scholar, cites the words of this Epistle as those of the Evangelist John. Eusebius (*Ecclesiastical History*, 3.24), says, John's first Epistle and Gospel are acknowledged without question by those of the present day, as well as by the ancients. So also Jerome (*On Illustrious Men*). The opposition of Cosmas Indicopleustes, in the sixth century, and that of Marcion because our Epistle was inconsistent with his views, are of no weight against such irrefragable testimony.

The internal evidence is equally strong. Neither the Gospel, nor this Epistle, can be pronounced an imitation; yet both, in style and modes of thought, are evidently of the same mind. The individual notices are not so numerous or obvious as in Paul's writings, as was to be expected in a Catholic Epistle; but such as there are accord with John's position. He implies his apostleship, and perhaps alludes to his Gospel, and the affectionate tie which bound him as an aged pastor to his spiritual "children"; and in 1 John 2:18, 19; 4:1–3, he alludes to the false teachers as known to his readers; and in 1 John 5:21 he warns them against the idols of the surrounding world. It is no objection against its authenticity that the doctrine of the Word, or divine second Person, existing from everlasting, and in due time made flesh, appears in it, as also in the Gospel, as opposed to the heresy of the Docetæ in the second century, who denied that our Lord is come in the flesh, and maintained He came only in outward semblance; for the same doctrine appears in Col. 1:15–18; 1 Tim. 3:16; Heb. 1:1–3; and the germs of Docetism, though not fully developed till the second century, were in existence in the first. The Spirit, presciently through John, puts the Church beforehand on its guard against the coming heresy.

Readers

Augustine (*The Question of the Gospels*, 2.39), says this Epistle was written to the Parthians. Bede, in a prologue to the seven Catholic Epistles, says that Athanasius attests the same. By the Parthians may be meant the Christians living beyond the Euphrates in the Parthian territory, outside the Roman empire, "the Church at Babylon elected together with (you)," the churches in the Ephesian region, the quarter to which Peter addressed his Epistles (1 Pet. 5:12). As Peter addressed the flock which John subsequently tended (and in which Paul had formerly ministered), so John, Peter's close companion after the ascension, addresses the flock among whom Peter had been when he wrote. Thus "the elect lady" (2 John 1) answers "to the Church elected together" (1 Pet. 5:13). See further confirmation of this view in Introduction to Second John. It is not necessarily an objection to this view that John never is known to have personally ministered in the Parthian territory. For neither did Peter personally minister to the churches in Pontus, Galatia, Cappadocia, Asia, Bithynia, though he wrote his Epistles to them. Moreover, in John's prolonged life, we cannot dogmatically assert that he did not visit the

Parthian Christians, after Peter had ceased to minister to them, on the mere ground of absence of extant testimony to that effect. This is as probable a view as Alford's, that in the passage of Augustine, "to the Parthians," is to be altered by conjectural emendation; and that the Epistle is addressed to the churches at and around Ephesus, on the ground of the fatherly tone of affectionate address in it, implying his personal ministry among his readers. But his position, as probably the only surviving apostle, accords very well with his addressing, in a Catholic Epistle, a cycle of churches which he may not have specially ministered to in person, with affectionate fatherly counsel, by virtue of his general apostolic superintendence of all the churches.

Time and place of writing

This Epistle seems to have been written after his Gospel as it assumes the reader's acquaintance with the Gospel facts and Christ's speeches, and also with the special aspect of the incarnate Word, as God manifest in the flesh (1 Tim. 3:16), set forth more fully in his Gospel. The tone of address, as a father addressing his "little children" (the continually recurring term, 1 John 2:1, 12, 13, 18, 28; 3:7, 18; 4:4; 5:21), accords with the view that this Epistle was written in John's old age, perhaps about A.D. 90. In 1 John 2:18, "it is the last time," probably does not refer to any particular event (as the destruction of Jerusalem, which was now many years past) but refers to the nearness of the Lord's coming as proved by the rise of Antichristian teachers, the mark of the last time. It was the Spirit's purpose to keep the Church always expecting Christ as ready to come at any moment. The whole Christian age is the last time in the sense that no other dispensation is to arise till Christ comes. Compare "these last days," Heb. 1:2. Ephesus may be conjectured to be the place whence it was written. The controversial allusion to the germs of Gnostic heresy accord with Asia Minor being the place, and the last part of the apostolic age the time, of writing this Epistle.

Contents

The main in the letter is fellowship with the Father and the Son (1 John 1:3). Two principal divisions may be noted:

1 John 1:5–2:28: the theme of this portion is stated at the outset, "God is light, and in Him is no darkness at all"; consequently, in order to have fellowship with Him, we must walk in light (1 John 1:7); connected with which in the confession and subsequent forgiveness of our sins through Christ's propitiation and advocacy, without which forgiveness there could be no light or fellowship with God: a farther step in thus walking in the light is, positively keeping God's commandments, the sum of which is love, as opposed to hatred, the acme of disobedience to God's word: negatively, he exhorts them according to their several stages of spiritual growth, children, fathers, young men, in consonance with their privileges as forgiven, knowing the Father, and having overcome the wicked one, not to love the world, which is incompatible with the indwelling of the love of the Father, and to be on their guard

against the Antichristian teachers already in the world, who were not of the Church, but of the world, against whom the true defense is, that his believing readers who have the anointing of God, should continue to abide in the Son and in the Father.

The second division (1 John 2:29–5:5) discusses the theme with which it opens, He is righteous; consequently (as in the first division), "every one that doeth righteousness is born of Him." Sonship in us involves our purifying ourselves as He is pure, even as we hope to see, and therefore to be made like our Lord when He shall appear; in this second, as in the first division, both a positive and a negative side are presented of "doing righteousness as He is righteous," involving a contrast between the children of God and the children of the devil. Hatred marks the latter; love, the former: this love gives assurance of acceptance with God for ourselves and our prayers, accompanied as they are (1 John 3:23) with obedience to His great commandment, to "believe on Jesus, and love one another"; the seal (1 John 3:24) of His dwelling in us and assuring our hearts, is the Spirit which He hath given us. In contrast to this (as in the first division), he warns against false spirits, the notes of which are, denial of Christ, and adherence to the world. Sonship, or birth of God, is then more fully described: its essential feature is unslavish, free love to God, because God first loved us, and gave His Son to die for us, and consequent love to the brethren, grounded on their being sons of God also like ourselves, and so victory over the world; this victory being gained only by the man who believes in Jesus as the Son of God.

The conclusion establishes this last central truth, on which rests our fellowship with God, Christ's having come by the water of baptism, the blood of atonement, and the witnessing Spirit, which is truth. As in the opening he rested this cardinal truth on the apostles' witness of the eye, the ear, and the touch, so now at the close he rests it on God's witness, which is accepted by the believer, in contrast with the unbeliever, who makes God a liar. Then follows his closing statement of his reason for writing (1 John 5:13; compare the corresponding 1 John 1:4, at the beginning), namely, that believers in Christ the Son of God may know that they have (now already) eternal life (the source of "joy," 1 John 1:4; compare similarly his object in writing the Gospel, John 20:31), and so have confidence as to their prayers being answered (corresponding to 1 John 3:22 in the second part); for instance, their intercessions for a sinning brother (unless his sin be a sin unto death). He closes with a brief summing up of the instruction of the Epistle, the high dignity, sanctity, and safety from evil of the children of God in contrast to the sinful world, and a warning against idolatry, literal and spiritual: "Keep yourselves from idols."

Though the Epistle is not directly polemical, the occasion which suggested his writing was probably the rise of Antichristian teachers; and, because he knew the spiritual character of the several classes whom he addresses, children, youths, fathers, he feels it necessary to write to confirm them in the faith and joyful fellowship of the Father and Son, and to assure them of the reality of the things they believe, that so they may have the full privileges of believing.

Style

He is especially fond of aphorism and repetition. His tendency to repeat his own phrase, arises partly from the affectionate, hortatory character of the Epistle; partly, also, from its Hebraistic forms abounding in parallel clauses, as distinguished from the Grecian and more logical style of Paul; also, from his childlike simplicity of spirit, which, full of his one grand theme, repeats, and dwells on it with fond delight and enthusiasm. Moreover as Alford well says, the appearance of uniformity is often produced by want of deep enough exegesis to discover the real differences in passages which seem to express the same. Contemplative, rather than argumentative, he dwells more on the general, than on the particular, on the inner, than on the outer, Christian life. Certain fundamental truths he recurs to again and again, at one time enlarging on, and applying them, at another time repeating them in their condensed simplicity. The thoughts do not march onward by successive steps, as in the logical style of Paul, but rather in circle drawn round one central thought which he reiterates, ever reverting to it, and viewing it, now under its positive, now under its negative, aspect. Many terms which in the Gospel are given as Christ's, in the Epistle appear as the favorite expressions of John, naturally adopted from the Lord. Thus the contrasted terms, "flesh" and "spirit," "light" and "darkness," "life" and "death," "abide in Him": fellowship with the Father and Son, and with one another," is a favorite phrase also, not found in the Gospel, but in Acts and Paul's Epistles. In him appears the harmonious union of opposites, adapting him for his high functions in the kingdom of God, contemplative repose of character, and at the same time ardent zeal, combined with burning, all-absorbing love: less adapted for active outward work, such as Paul's, than for spiritual service. He handles Christian verities not as abstract dogmas, but as living realities, personally enjoyed in fellowship with God in Christ, and with the brethren. Simple, and at the same time profound, his writing is in consonance with his spirit, unrhetorical and undialectic, gentle, consolatory, and loving: the reflection of the Spirit of Him on whose breast he lay at the last supper, and whose beloved disciple he was. Ewald in Alford, speaking of the "unruffled and heavenly repose" which characterizes this Epistle, says, "It appears to be the tone, not so much of a father talking with his beloved children, as of a glorified saint addressing mankind from a higher world. Never in any writing has the doctrine of heavenly love–a love working in stillness, ever unwearied, never exhausted–so thoroughly approved itself as in this Epistle."

John's place in building up the church

As Peter founded and Paul propagated, so John completed the spiritual building. As the Old Testament puts prominently forward the fear of God, so John, the last writer of the New Testament, gives prominence to the love of God. Yet, as the Old Testament is not all limited to presenting the fear of God, but sets forth also His love, so John, as a representative of the New Testament, while breathing so continually the spirit of love, gives also the plainest and most awful warnings against sin, in accordance with his original character as Boanerges, "son of thunder." His mother was Salome, mother of the sons of

Zebedee, probably sister to Jesus' mother (compare John 19:25, "His mother's sister," with Matt. 27:56; Mark 15:40), so that he was cousin to our Lord; to his mother, under God, he may have owed his first serious impressions. Expecting as she did the Messianic kingdom in glory, as appears from her petition (Matt. 20:20–23), she doubtless tried to fill his young and ardent mind with the same hope. Neander distinguishes three leading tendencies in the development of the Christian doctrine, the Pauline, the Jacobean (between which the Petrine forms an intermediate link), and the Johannean. John, in common with James, was less disposed to the intellectual and dialectic cast of thought which distinguishes Paul. He had not, like the apostle of the Gentiles, been brought to faith and peace through severe conflict; but, like James, had reached his Christian individuality through a quiet development: James, however, had passed through a molding in Judaism previously, which, under the Spirit, caused him to present Christian truth in connection with the law, in so far as the latter in its spirit, though not letter, is permanent, and not abolished, but established under the Gospel. But John, from the first, had drawn his whole spiritual development from the personal view of Christ, the model man, and from intercourse with Him. Hence, in his writings, everything turns on one simple contrast: divine life in communion with Christ; death in separation from Him, as appears from his characteristic phrases, "life, light, truth; death, darkness, lie." "As James and Peter mark the gradual transition from spiritualized Judaism to the independent development of Christianity, and as Paul represents the independent development of Christianity in opposition to the Jewish standpoint, so the contemplative element of John reconciles the two, and forms the closing point in the training of the apostolic Church" (Neander).

A. R. Faussett

Detailed outline

- I. Introduction: 1:1–4
  - A. John is writing about what he has seen: 1:1
  - B. True fellowship: 1:2–3
  - C. His purpose in writing: 1:4
- II. The conditions for true fellowship in Jesus: 1:5–10
  - A. Conformity to the standard of God's Word: 1:5–7
  - B. Confession of sin: 1:8–10
- III. The correct behavior for those in the true fellowship of believers: 2:1–29
  - A. Imitate the spiritual example set by Jesus: 2:1–11
    - 1. The principle of imitation: 2:1–2
    - 2. The pattern for imitation: 2:3–6
    - 3. The proof of proper imitation: 2:7–11
  - B. The need for separation: 2:12–17
    - 1. Spiritual maturity: 2:12–14
    - 2. Separation from worldliness: 2:15–17
  - C. The creed for our conduct: 2:18–29
    - 1. The necessity for a creed: 2:18–21
    - 2. The nature of the creed: 2:22–29
- IV. The characteristics of true Christian fellowship: 3:1–24
  - A. Purity: 3:1–3
  - B. Righteousness and love: 3:4–18
  - C. Confidence: 3:19–21
  - D. Obedience: 3:22–24

V. Enemies of the true fellowship of believers: 4:1–21
  A. False prophets: 4:1–6
    1. How to recognize them: 4:2–3
    2. How to overcome them: 4:4
    3. They are of the world: 4:5
    4. We are of God: 4:6
  B. False profession of a loving spirit: 4:7–21
    1. Perfect love described: 4:7–17
    2. A false profession of a loving spirit: 4:18–21
VI. The reason for maintaining true fellowship: 5:1–21
  A. Faith in Jesus is seen by obeying God: 5:1–5
  B. Faith in Jesus brings eternal life: 5:6–12
  C. Faith in Jesus brings confidence in approaching God: 5:13–15
  D. Faith in Jesus is proved by conquering sin: 5:16–21

2. Helpful summaries of 1 John

Bird's eye view

Because of God's character, of light and righteousness, Christians are to love God and their fellow Christians.

Reading plan

The following reading plan, taking one reading per day, enables you to read through 1 John five days.

1 John 1:1–1:10
1 John 2:1–2:29
1 John 3:1–3:24
1 John 4:1–4:21
1 John 5:1–5:21

Verses to memorize

1 John 1:9

If we confess our sins, he is faithful and just to forgive us our sins, and to cleanse us from all unrighteousness. KJV

1 John 2:15–17

[15] Love not the world, neither the things that are in the world. If any man love the world, the love of the Father is not in him.
[16] For all that is in the world, the lust of the flesh, and the lust of the eyes, and the pride of life, is not of the Father, but is of the world.
[17] And the world passeth away, and the lust thereof: but he that doeth the will of God abideth for ever. KJV

1 John 3:1–3

[1] Behold, what manner of love the Father hath bestowed on us, that we should be called the sons of God: therefore the world knoweth us not, because it knew him not.
[2] Beloved, now are we the sons of God, and it doth not yet appear what we shall be: but we know that, when he shall appear, we shall be like him; for we shall see him as he is.
[3] And every man that hath this hope in him purifieth himself, even as he is pure. KJV

1 John 4:10–11

[10] Herein is love, not that we loved God, but that he loved us, and sent his Son to be the propitiation for our sins.
[11] Beloved, if God so loved us, we ought also to love one another. KJV

1 John 4:19

We love him, because he first loved us. KJV

Statistics

Twenty-third New Testament book

5 chapters

105 verses

2,523 words

Number of Old Testament quotations and allusions in 1 John: 6.

Names/titles given

Ioannou A: "First of John."

"The letter of certainties."

3. Helpful keys to turn to in understanding 1 John

Key words

Fellowship

Know

Love

Key verses

1 John 5:11–13

Themes to study

Life

Light and truth

Sin

The world

Positive statements about Jesus

Assurance

The phrase "we/you know" which occurs frequently in 1 John underlines what Christians are said to know for certain:

- We know that a righteous life is a sign of regeneration, 2:29; 5:18
- We know that when Jesus comes we will be like him, 3:2
- We know that Jesus came to take away our sins, 3:5
- We know that brotherly love shows that we have passed from death to life, 3:14
- We know that Jesus lives in us by his Spirit, 3:24
- We known that we have eternal life, 5:13
- We know that our prayers are answered by God, 5:15

Jesus in 1 John

In 1 John Jesus is our life.

Lessons to learn from 1 John

- We should be joyful in our assurance in being God's children.
- Our world is constantly under Satan's influences, which must be resisted.

4. Studying 1 John chapter by chapter

1 John 1

Matthew Henry's introduction

Evidence given about Christ's person and excellency, vv. 1, 2. The knowledge thereof gives us communion with God and Christ (v. 3), and joy, v. 4. A description of God, v. 5. How we are thereon to walk, v. 6. The benefit of such walking, v. 7. The way to forgiveness, v. 9. The evil of denying our sin, vv. 8–10.

Dr. Adam Clarke's analysis of chapter

The testimony of the apostle concerning the reality of the person and doctrine of Christ; and the end for which he bears this testimony, 1–4.

God is light, and none can have fellowship with him who do not walk in the light; those who walk in the light are cleansed from all unrighteousness by the blood of Christ, 5–7.

No man can say that he has not sinned; but God is faithful and just to cleanse from all unrighteousness them who confess their sins, 8–10.

A detailed analysis of chapter

Christ is the Word of life. (1–4)

To have fellowship with God holiness is essential. (5–10)

Key verse

Verse 7: "But if we walk in the light, as he is in the light, we have fellowship with one another, and the blood of Jesus, his Son, purifies us from all sin."

Key word

"Fellowship" in verses 3, 6, 7.

Key event / key person / key theme

John insists on the flesh and blood reality of the Incarnation.

Key thought

Verse 8, some false teachers claimed they were above the ordinary laws of morality. John's answer is a categorical denial.

Key thing to look out for

The ways in which John emphasizes that Jesus was a real human being.

Key Bible cross-reference

Verse 1. See John 1:2.

Key "by way of explanation"

See 2:19, "they went out from us." John is writing to answer the claims of false teaching which was probably an early form of Gnosticism. Gnostics believed they had secret knowledge which gave them enlightenment. They thought that matter was evil, and therefore denied that the Word was made flesh. Cerinthus, a heretical teacher in the time of John, taught that Christ only *seemed* to have a real body.

Key "Quotable Quote"

"Thus we learn that we only make due progress in the knowledge of the Word of the Lord when we become really humbled and groan under the burden of our sins and learn to flee to God's mercy and find rest in nothing except his fatherly favor."

John Calvin

1 John 2

Matthew Henry's introduction

Here the apostle encourages against sins of infirmity (vv. 1, 2), shows the true knowledge and love of God (vv. 3–6), renews the precept of fraternal love (vv. 7–11), addresses the several ages of Christians (vv. 12–14), warns against worldly love (vv. 15–17), against seducers (vv. 18, 19), shows the security of true

Christians (vv. 20–27), and advises to abide in Christ, vv. 28, 29.

Dr. Adam Clarke's analysis of chapter

He exhorts them not to sin; yet encourages those who may have fallen, by the hope of mercy through Christ, who is a propitiation for the sins of the whole world, 1, 2.

He who knows God keeps his commandments; and he who professes to abide in Christ ought to walk as Christ walked, 3–6.

The old and new commandment, that we should walk in the light, and love the brethren, 7–11.

The apostle's description of the different states in the family of God; little children, young men, and fathers; and directions to each, 12–15.

A statement of what prevails in the world, 16, 17.

Cautions against antichrists, 18–23.

Exhortations to persevere in what they had received, and to continue to follow that anointing of the Divine Spirit, by which they could discern all men, and know all things necessary to their salvation, and proper to prepare them for eternal glory, 24–29.

A detailed analysis of chapter

Christ's atonement helps in the battle against sin. (1, 2)

Salvation results in obedience, and love for the brethren. (3–11)

Christians are spoken of as little children, young men, and fathers. (12–14)

All are warned against the love of this world, and against false teaching. (15–23)

They are encouraged to stand firm in faith and holiness. (24–29)

Key verse

Verse 9: "Anyone who claims to be in the light but hates his brother is still in the darkness."

Key word / key phrase

Verse 3, "obey his commands."

Key event / key person / key theme

Obeying and loving God, and dealing with heretics

Key thought

Here is an acid test for you: Do you hate any fellow-Christian?

Key thing to look out for

Here is another awkward question: Do you love aspects of the world's ways and values?

Key Bible cross-reference

Verse 7. See John 13:34.

Key "by way of explanation"

Verse 15, "the world" refers to any society where people live in opposition, or indifference, to God. It is characterized by sensuality, greed, and pride. It is ruled over by the devil.

Key "Quotable Quote"

"The corridors of the New Testament reverberate with dogmatic affirmations beginning 'We know,' 'We are sure,' 'We are confident.' If you question this, read the First Epistle of John in which verbs meaning 'to know' occur about forty times. They strike a note of joyful assurance which is sadly missing from many parts of the Church today and which needs to be recaptured."

John R.W. Stott

1 John 3

Matthew Henry's introduction

The apostle here magnifies the love of God in our adoption, vv. 1, 2. He thereon argues for holiness (v. 3), and against sin, vv. 4–19. He presses brotherly love, vv. 11–18. How to assure our hearts before God, vv. 19–22. The precept of faith, v. 23. And the good of obedience, v. 24.

Dr. Adam Clarke's analysis of chapter

The extraordinary love of God towards mankind, and the effects of it, 1–3.

Sin is the transgression of the law, and Christ was manifested to take away our sins, 4–6.

The children of God are known by the holiness of their lives, the children of the devil by the sinfulness of theirs, 7–10.

We should love one another, for he that hateth his brother is a murderer; as Christ laid down his life for us, so we should lay down our lives for the brethren, 11–16.

Charity is a fruit of brotherly love; our love should be active, not professional merely, 17, 18.

How we may know that we are of the truth, 19–21.

They whose ways please God, have an answer to all their prayers, 22.

The necessity of keeping the commandment of Christ, that he may dwell in us and we in him by his Spirit, 23, 24.

A detailed analysis of chapter

The apostle states that the love of God makes believers his children. (1, 2)

Live as God's children. (3–10)

Love for the brethren is a characteristic of genuine Christians. (11–15)

That love is described and seen by its actions. (16–21)

Grow in faith, love, and obedience. (22–24)

Key verse

Verse 11: "This is the message you heard from the beginning: We should love one another."

Key word / key phrase

Verse 11, "love one another."

Key event / key person / key theme

Living as God's children.

Key thought

To the question, "How can I keep going as a Christian?" John answers, "Remember how much God the Father has loved you."

Key thing to look out for

To the question, "What characteristics should I be displaying as a Christian?" John answers, "you should believe in Jesus Christ and you should be showing Christian love to your fellow-Christians" (verse 23).

Key Bible cross-reference

Verse 1: See John 1:12.

Key "by way of explanation"

Verse 17, "the love of God." The love that God pours into the hearts and lives of believers by the Holy Spirit enables Christians to love one another. To the question, "What is this love like?" John answers that it is exemplified in the life and death of Jesus Christ (verse 16).

Key "Quotable Quote"

"Fellowship is the sharing of the divine life and communion of the Father and the Son."

R.W. Orr

1 John 4

Matthew Henry's introduction

In this chapter the apostle exhorts to try spirits (v. 1), gives a note to try by (vv. 2, 3), shows who are of the world and who of God (vv. 4–6), urges Christian love by divers considerations (vv. 7–16), describes our love to God, and the effect of it, vv. 17–21.

Dr. Adam Clarke's analysis of chapter

We must not believe every teacher who professes to have a Divine commission to preach, but try such, whether they be of God; and the more so because many false prophets are gone out into the world, 1.

Those who deny that Jesus Christ is come in the flesh have the spirit of antichrist, 2, 3.

The followers of God have been enabled to discern and overcome them, 4–6.

The necessity of love to God and one another shown, from God's love to us, 7–11.

Though no man hath seen God, yet every genuine Christian knows him by the spirit which God has given him, 12, 13.

The apostles testified that God sent his Son to be the saviour of the world; and God dwelt in those who confessed this truth, 14, 15.

God is love, 16.

The nature and properties of perfect love, 17, 18.

We love him because he first loved us, 19.

The wickedness of pretending to love God while we hate one another, 20, 21.

A detailed analysis of chapter

Believers warned against those who falsely claim to have God's Spirit. (1–6)

Brotherly love is encouraged. (7–21)

Key verse

Verse 13: "We know that we live in him and he in us, because he has given us of his Spirit."

Key word / key phrase

Verse 1, "test the spirits."

Key event / key person / key theme

Testing the spirits, and the proof of love

Key thought

"Don't believe everything you are told. Test the spirits."

Key thing to look out for

John's reasons for the pre-eminence of love.

Key Bible cross-reference

Verse 12. See John 1:18.

Key "by way of explanation"

Verse 6: "we" refers to the apostles (1:1–3). The tests of authenticity are: to acknowledge the pre-existence of Christ (he came); his humanity (in the flesh); his continuing reality (has come, i.e. he is still here verse 2); and to accept the witness of John and the other apostles.

Key "Quotable Quote"

"The proper Christian attitude to sin is not to deny it but to admit it, and then to receive the forgiveness which God has made possible and promises to us. If we confess our sins, acknowledging before God that we are sinners not only by nature (sin) but by practice also (our sins), God will both forgive us our sins and purify us from all unrighteousness (1 John. 1:9). In the first phrase sin is a debt which he remits and in the second a stain which he removes."

John R.W. Stott

1 John 5

Matthew Henry's introduction

In this chapter the apostle asserts,

I. The dignity of believers, v. 1.

II. Their obligation to love, and the trial of it, vv. 1–3.

III. Their victory, vv. 4, 5.

IV. The credibility and confirmation of their faith, vv. 6–10.

V. The advantage of their faith in eternal life, vv. 11–13.

VI. The audience of their prayers, unless for those who have sinned unto death, vv. 14–17.

VII. The preservation from sin and Satan, v. 18.

VIII. Their distinction from the world, v. 19.

IX. Their true knowledge of God (v. 20), on which they must depart from idols, v. 21.

Dr. Adam Clarke's analysis of chapter

He that believeth is born of God; loves God and his children; and keeps his commandments, which are not grievous, 1–3.

Faith in Christ overcomes the world, 4, 5.

The three earthly and heavenly witnesses, 6–9.

He that believeth hath the witness in himself, 10.

God has given unto us eternal life in his Son, 11, 12.

The end for which St. John writes these things, 13–16.

The sin unto death, and the sin not unto death, 16, 17.

He that is born of God sinneth not, 18.

The whole world lieth in the wicked one, 19.

Jesus is come to give us understanding, that we may know the true God, 20.

All idolatry to be avoided, 21.

A detailed analysis of chapter

Brotherly love is the result of the new birth. (1–5)

Jesus, the Son of God, is the true Messiah. (6–8)

Eternal life is God's gift through Christ. (9–12)

The assurance of God listening to and answering prayer. (13–17)

The happy state of true believers, and a command to renounce all idolatry. (18–21)

Key verse

Verse 13: "I write these things to you who believe in the name of the Son of God so that you may know that you have eternal life."

Key word / key phrase

Verse 11, "God has given us eternal life."

Key event / key person / key theme

Grounds for assurance

Key thought

It is no good to know about Jesus, you must believe in him personally at first hand.

Key thing to look out for

Verse 13, John's purpose in writing his letter.

Key Bible cross-reference

Verse 11. See John 3:36.

Key "by way of explanation"

Verses 18–20. John concludes with four great things that we know. First, we know we do not want to carry on sinning as before, verse 18; second, that we are God's children, verse 19; third, that the devil controls the world; and fourth, we know that our understanding comes from Jesus, verse 20. Verse 16, the sin that leads to death may be the deliberate and constant rejection of light.

Key "Quotable Quote"

"Over and above your intelligent apprehension of it, over and above your intelligent and intellectual deduction of it, there is a direct and immediate assurance given by the Holy Ghost who sheds abroad the love of God in your heart. You are overwhelmed by it, it is poured out in your heart, and there is no uncertainty any more."

D. Martyn Lloyd-Jones

5. Select bibliography for 1 John

Boice, James Montgomery. *The Epistles of John*. Grand Rapids: Zondervan, 1979.

Bruce, F. F. *The Epistles of John: Introduction, Exposition, and Notes*. Grand Rapids Eerdmans, 1970.

Harrison, E. F. *Introduction to the New Testament*. Grand Rapids: Eerdmans, 1964.

Marshall, I. H. *The Epistles of John*. NIC. Grand Rapids: Eerdmans, 1978.

Ross, A. *The Epistles of James and John*. NIC. Grand Rapids: Eerdmans, 1954.

Stott, J. R. W. *The Epistles of St. John*. TNTC. Grand Rapids: Eerdmans, 1964.

Westcott, B. F. *The Epistles of St. John: The Greek Text with Notes and Essays*. London: Macmillan, 1883.

2 and 3 John

1. Book by book: Introduction to 2 John and 3 John

Introduction

Authenticity

That these two Epistles were written by the same author appears from their similarity of tone, style, and sentiments. That John, the beloved disciple, was the author of the Second and Third Epistles, as of the First Epistle, appears from Irenaeus (*Against Heresies*, 1.16.3), who quotes 2 John 10, 11; and in (3.16.8), he quotes 2 John 7, mistaking it, however, as if occurring in First John. Clement of Alexandria (A.D. 192) (*Miscellanies*, 2.66), implies his knowledge of other Epistles of John besides the First Epistle; and in fragments of his *Adumbrations* (p. 1011), he says, "John's Second Epistle which was written to the virgins (Greek, *"parthenous"*; perhaps *Parthos* is what was meant) is the simplest; but it was written to a certain Babylonian named the Elect lady." Dionysius of Alexandria (in Eusebius [*Ecclesiastical History*, 7.25]) observes that John never names himself in his Epistles, "not even in the Second and Third Epistles, although they are short Epistles, but simply calls himself the presbyter, a confutation of those who think John the apostle distinct from John the presbyter. Alexander of Alexandria cites 2 John 10, 11, as John's (Socrates, *Ecclesiastical History*, 1.6). Cyprian (*About the Baptism of Heretics*), in referring to the bishops at the Council of Carthage, says, "John the apostle, in His Epistle, has said, if any come to you" (2 John 10); so that this Epistle, and therefore its twin sister, Third John, was recognized as apostolic in the North African Church. The Muratori fragment is ambiguous. The Second and Third Epistles were not in the Peschito or old Syriac version; and Cosmas Indicopleustes in the sixth century says that in his time the Syriac Church only acknowledged three of the Catholic Epistles, First Peter, First John, and James. But Ephrem the Syrian quotes the Second Epistle of John. Eusebius (*Ecclesiastical History*,) reckons both Epistles among the Antilegomena or controverted Scriptures, as distinguished from the Homologoumena or universally acknowledged from the first. Still his own opinion was that the two minor Epistles were genuine, remarking, as he does in *Demonstration of the Gospel* (3.5), that in John's "Epistles" he does not mention his own name, nor call himself an apostle or evangelist, but an "elder" (2 John 1; 3 John 1). Origen (in Eusebius [*Ecclesiastical History*, 6.25]) mentions the Second and Third Epistles, but adds, "not all admit (implying that most authorities do) their genuineness." Jerome (*On Illustrious Men*, 9) mentions the two latter Epistles as attributed to John the presbyter, whose sepulcher was shown among the Ephesians in his day. But the designation "elder" was used of the apostles by others (for example, Papias, in Eusebius [*Ecclesiastical History*, 3.39]), and is used by Peter, an apostle, of himself (1 Pet. 5:1). Why, then, should not John also use this designation of himself, in consonance with the humility which leads him not to name himself or his apostleship even in the First Epistle? The Antilegomena were generally recognized as canonical soon after the Council of Nicea (A.D. 325). Thus Cyril of Jerusalem, a.d. 349, enumerates fourteen Epistles of Paul, and seven Catholic Epistles. So Gregory of Nazianzen, in A.D. 389. The Councils of Hippo, 393, and Carthage, 397, adopted a catalogue of New Testament books exactly agreeing with our canon. So our oldest extant Greek manuscripts. The Second and Third Epistles of John, from their brevity (which Origen notices), and the private nature of their contents, were less generally read in the earliest Christian assemblies and were also less quoted by the Fathers; hence arose their non-universal recognition at the first. Their private nature makes them the less likely to be spurious, for there seems no purpose in their forgery. The style and coloring too accord with the style of the First Epistle.

Readers

The Third Epistle is directed to Gaius or Caius; whether Gaius of Macedonia (Acts 19:20), or Gaius of Corinth (Rom. 16:23; 1 Cor. 1:14), or Gaius of Derbe (Acts 20:4), it is hard to decide. Mill believes Gaius, bishop of Pergamos (Apostolic Constitutions, 7.40), to be the person addressed in 3 John 1.

The address of the Second Epistle is more disputed. It opens, "The elder unto the Elect lady" (2 John 1). And it closes, "The children of thy elect sister greet thee" (2 John 13). Now, 1 Pet. 1:1, 2, addresses the elect in Asia, etc., and closes (1 Pet. 5:13), "The Church that is at Babylon, elected together with you, saluteth you." Putting together these facts, with the quotations (above) from Clement of Alexandria, and the fact that the word "Church" comes from a Greek word (*kyriake*) cognate to the Greek for "lady" (*kyria*; "belonging to the Lord," *kyrios*); Wordsworth's view is probable. As Peter in Babylon had sent the greetings of the elect Church in the then Parthian (see above on Clement of Alexandria) Babylon to her elect sister in Asia, so John, the metropolitan president of the elect Church in Asia, writes to the elect lady, that is, Church, in Babylon. Neander, Alford, and others, think the Greek "*kyria*" not to mean "lady," but to be her proper name; and that she had a "sister, a Christian matron," then with John.

Date and place of writing

Eusebius (*Ecclesiastical History*, 3.25) relates that John, after the death of Domitian, returned from his exile in Patmos to Ephesus, and went on missionary tours into the heathen regions around, and also made visitations of the churches around, and ordained bishops and clergy. Such journeys are mentioned, 2 John 12; 3 John 10, 14. If Eusebius be right, both Epistles must have been written after the Apocalypse, in his old age, which harmonizes with the tone of the Epistles, and in or near Ephesus. It was on one of his visitation tours that he designed to rebuke Diotrephes (3 John 9, 10).

A. R. Faussett

Detailed outline

2 John

I. Introduction: Greeting: 1–3
 A. From: The elder, John: 1
 B. To: The chosen lady: 1-2
 C. He sends from God the Father and the Son Jesus Christ: 3
  1. Grace.
  2. Mercy.
  3. Peace.

II. Exhortation to love: 4–6
 A. Walk in truth: 4
 B. Walk in love: 5
 C. Walk in His commandments: 6

III. Warning against false doctrine and false teachers: 7–11
 A. The confession of false teachers: 7
 B. The consequences of believing false teachers: 8–9
  1. Losing spiritual things previously achieved in their lives: 8
  2. Transgressing by not abiding in Christ's teaching: 9
  3. Taking part in their evil deeds: 10–11

IV. Conclusion: 12–13
 A. John hopes to come to visit them: 12
 B. John sends greetings from the members of a sister church: 13

3 John

I. Introduction: 1–2
 A. From: The elder, John: 1
 B. To: My dear friend Gaius: 1
 C. John's wish for him: spiritual health: 2

II. The believer's relationship to truth: 3–4
 A. It should be in them: 3
 B. They should walk in truth: 3
 C. When we walk in truth it brings joy to our spiritual leaders: 4

III. The believer's relation to other fellow Christians: 5–8
 A. They are to minister to brethren and strangers: 5
 B. They should be known to the church for their love: 6
 C. They are to work together for the truth: 8

IV. The believer's relationship to good and evil: 9–12
 A. Diotrephes as an example of evil: 9–10
 B. The proper response to such evil: 11
  1. Do not follow evil: 11
  2. Follow what is good: 11
 C. Demetrius: An example of good: 12
  1. Had a good testimony of all men.
  2. Was aligned with the truth of God's Word.
  3. Had a good reputation with the God appointed leadership.

V. Conclusion: 13–14
 A. John hoped to pay a visit: 13–14
 B. He sends: 14
  1. Peace.
  2. Greetings from his friends to Gaius and the church.
 C. He asks Gaius to greet his friends by name: 14

2. Helpful summaries of 2 and 3 John

Bird's eye view

2 John

A warning against heretics and mixing with false teachers.

3 John

A plea for Christian hospitality.

Reading plan

The following reading plan, taking one reading per day, enables you to read through 2 and 3 John in one day.

2 John 1:1–3 John 1:14

Statistics

2 John

Twenty-fourth New Testament book

1 chapter

13 verses

303 words

The New Testament book with the least number of verses in it.

3 John

Twenty-fifth New Testament book

1 chapter

14 verses

299 words

The New Testament book with the least number of words in it.

Names/titles given

Ioannou B: “Second of John.”

Ioannou G: “Third of John.” (Gamma is the third letter in the Greek alphabet.)

3. Helpful keys to turn to in understanding 2 and 3 John

Key words

Love in 2 John

Truth in 3 John

Key verses

Verse 6 in 2 John

Verse 4 in 3 John

Themes to study

2 John

How to combat false teachers.

3 John

How God’s servants should be supported.

Jesus in 2 John

In 2 John Jesus is the truth.

Jesus in 3 John

In 3 John Jesus is the way to God.

Lessons to learn from 2 and 3 John

2 John

We should take trouble to constantly follow God’s commands and maintain our love for fellow Christians.

3 John

Truth should be nurtured, while heresy should be exposed.

4. Studying 2 and 3 John verse by verse

2 John

Matthew Henry’s introduction

The apostle here salutes an honorable matron and her children, vv. 1–3. Recommends to them faith and love, vv. 5, 6. Warns them of deceivers (v. 7), and to take heed to themselves, v. 8. Teaches how to treat those who bring not the doctrine of Christ, vv. 10, 11. And, referring other things to personal discourse, concludes the epistle, vv. 12, 13.

Dr. Adam Clarke's analysis of chapter

The apostle's address to a Christian matron and her children, 1–3.

He rejoices to find that certain of her family had received, and continued to adorn, the truth; and he exhorts them to continue to love one another according to the commandment of Christ, 4–6,

And particularly cautions them against deceivers, and to so watch, that they might not lose the benefit of what they had received, 7, 8.

The necessity of abiding in the doctrine of Christ, 9.

He cautions them against receiving, or in any way forwarding, those who did not bring the true doctrine of Christ, 10, 11.

Excuses himself from writing more largely, and purposes to pay her and family a visit shortly, 12, 13.

A detailed analysis of chapter

The apostle greets the chosen lady and her children. (1–3)

He states his joy in their faith and love. (4–6)

He warns them against those who are out to deceive them. (7–11)

His conclusion. (12,13)

Key verse

Verse 7: "Many deceivers, who do not acknowledge Jesus Christ as coming in the flesh, have gone out into the world."

Key word / key phrase

Verse 6, "you walk in love."

Key event / key person / key theme

Faith and love

Key thought

John links up truth, obedience, and love.

Key thing to look out for

"Use your wits," says John, "don't have open house to your enemies."

Key Bible cross-reference

Verse 5. See John 13:34.

Key "by way of explanation"

Verse 10, "take him into your house." In those days it was usual for traveling Christian teachers to be given hospitality in Christian homes. Verse 1, "chosen lady" could refer to an individual or a church (see 1 Peter 5:13).

Key "Quotable Quote"

"If a man be gracious and courteous to strangers, it shows he is a citizen of the world and that his heart is no island, cut off from other islands, but a continent that joins them."

Francis Bacon

3 John

Matthew Henry's introduction

In this epistle the apostle congratulates Gaius on the prosperity of his soul (vv. 1, 2), on the fame he had among good Christians (vv. 3, 4), and on his charity and hospitality to the servants of

Christ, vv. 5, 6. He complains of contemptuous treatment by an ambitious Diotrephes, (vv. 9, 10), recommends Demetrius, (v. 12), and expresses his hope of visiting Gaius shortly, vv. 13, 14.

Dr. Adam Clarke's analysis of chapter

The apostle's address to Caius, and his good wishes for his prosperity in body and soul, 1, 2.

He commends him for his steadiness in the truth, and his general hospitality, especially to the itinerant evangelists, 3–8.

Speaks of the bad conduct of Diotrephes; his abuse of his power in the Church; and his slander of the apostles, 9, 10.

Exhorts Caius to avoid his example, and to follow what is good, 11.

Commends Demetrius, 12.

Excuses himself from writing more fully, and proposes to pay him a visit shortly, 13, 14.

A detailed analysis of chapter

A warning against taking sides with Diotrephes, but a commendation for Demetrius, a man of excellent character. (9–12)

He hopes to see Gaius soon. (13,14)

Key verse

Verse 8: "We ought therefore to show hospitality to such men so that we may work together for the truth."

Key word / key phrase

Verse 11, "do not imitate what is evil."

Key event / key person / key theme

Imitate what is good

Key thought

Genuine Christian teachers should never be cold-shouldered.

Key thing to look out for

What are the qualities for which John praises Gaius?

Key Bible cross-reference

Verse 1: See Acts 19:29.

Key "by way of explanation"

Verse 6 "send them on their way," that is, with practical help – food, money, perhaps letters of introduction.

Key "Quotable Quote"

"In the midst of the suffocating self-love of our modern and postmodern culture, the Bible is clear that our real hunger is to know the one true God revealed in its pages. Only in doing so will we satisfy our cravings for security and find the purpose for which we exist, hope, and be able to live free from slavery to self love."

Scott J. Hafemann

5. Select bibliography for 2 and 3 John

See Select bibliography for 1 John.

Jude

1. Book by book: Introduction to Jude

Introduction

Author

He calls himself in the address "the servant of Jesus Christ, and brother of James." See Introduction to the Epistle of James, in proof of James the apostle, and James the Lord's brother, the bishop of Jerusalem, being one and the same person. Gal. 1:19 alone seems to me to prove this. Similarly, Jude the brother of our Lord, and Jude the apostle, seem to be one and the same. Jerome ( ), rightly maintains that by the Lord's brethren are meant his cousins, children of Mary and Cleophas (the same as Alphæus). From 1 Cor. 9:5 (as "brethren of the Lord" stands between "other apostles" and "Cephas"), it seems natural to think that the brethren of the Lord are distinguished from the apostles only because all his brethren were not apostles, but only James and Jude. Jude's reason for calling himself "brother of James," was that James, as bishop of Jerusalem, was better known than himself. Had he been, in the strict sense, brother of our Lord, he probably would have so entitled himself. His omission of mention of his apostleship is no proof that he was not an apostle; for so also James omits it in his heading; and Paul, in his Epistles to the Philippians, Thessalonians, and Philemon, omits it. Had the writer been a counterfeiter of the apostle Jude, he would doubtless have called himself an "apostle." He was called also Lebbæus and Thaddeus, probably to distinguish him from Judas Iscariot, the traitor. Lebbæus, from Hebrew "*leeb,*" "heart," means courageous. Thaddeus is the same as Theudas, from Hebrew "*thad,*" the "breast." Luke and John, writing later than Matthew, when there would be no confusion between him and Judas Iscariot, give his name Judas. The only circumstance relating to him recorded in the Gospels occurs in John 14:22, "Judas saith unto Him, not Iscariot, Lord, how is it that Thou wilt manifest Thyself unto us, and not unto the world?" Jerome (*Commentary on Matthew*) says that he was sent to Edessa, to Abgarus, king of Osroene, or Edessa, and that he preached in Syria, Arabia, Mesopotamia, and Persia, in which last country he suffered martyrdom. The story is told on Eusebius' authority, that Abgarus, on his sickbed, having heard of Jesus' power to heal, sent to beg Him to come and cure him, to which the Lord replied, praising his faith, that though he had not seen the Savior, he yet believed; adding, "As for what thou hast written, that I should come to thee, it is necessary that all those things for which I was sent should be fulfilled by Me in this place, and that having filled them I should be received up to Him that sent Me. When, therefore, I shall be received into heaven, I will send unto thee some one of My disciples who shall both heal thy distemper and give life to thee and those with thee." Thomas is accordingly said to have been inspired to send Thaddeus for the cure and baptism of Abgarus. The letters are said to have been shown Thaddeus among the archives of Edessa. It is possible such a message was verbally sent, and the substance of it registered in writing afterwards (compare 2 Kings 5:1–27; and Matt. 15:22).

Hegesippus (in Eusebius [*Ecclesiastical History*, 3.20]) states that when Domitian inquired after David's posterity, some grandsons of Jude, called the Lord's brother, were brought into his presence. Being asked as to their possessions, they said that they had thirty-nine acres of the value of nine thousand denarii, out of which they paid him taxes, and lived by the labor of their hands, a proof of which they gave by showing the hardness of their hands. Being interrogated as to Christ and His kingdom, they replied that it was not of this world, but heavenly; and that it would be manifested at the end of the world, when He would come in glory to judge the living and the dead.

Authenticity

Eusebius (*Ecclesiastical History*, 3.25), reckons it among the Antilegomena or controverted Scriptures, "though recognized by the majority." The reference to the contest of Michael, the archangel, with the devil, for the body of Moses, not mentioned elsewhere in the Old Testament, but found in the apocryphal "Book of Enoch," probably raised doubts as to its authenticity, as Jerome (*On Illustrious Men*, 4) says. Moreover, its not being addressed to one particular Church, or individual, caused it not to be so immediately recognized as canonical. A counterfeiter would have avoided using what did not occur in the Old Testament, and which might be regarded as apocryphal.

As to the book of Enoch, if quoted by Jude, his quotation of a passage from it gives an inspired sanction only to the truth of that passage, not to the whole book; just as Paul, by inspiration, sanctions particular sentiments from Aratus, Epimenides, and Menander, but not all their writings. I think, rather as there is some slight variation between Jude's statement and that of the book of Enoch, that Jude, though probably not ignorant of the book of Enoch, stamps with inspired sanction the current tradition of the Jews as to Enoch's prophecies; just as Paul mentions the names of the Egyptian magicians, "Jannes and Jambres" (2 Tim. 3:8), not mentioned in the Old Testament. At all events, the prophecy ascribed to Enoch by Jude was really his, being sanctioned as such by this inspired writer. So also the narration as to the archangel Michael's dispute with Satan about the body of Moses, is by Jude's inspired authority (Jude 9) declared true. The book of Enoch is quoted by Justin Martyr, Irenaeus, Clement of Alexandria, etc. Bruce, the Abyssinian traveler, brought home three copies of it in Ethiopic, from Alexandria, of which Archbishop Lawrence, in 1821, gave an English translation. The Ethiopic was a version from the Greek, and the Greek doubtless a version from the Hebrew, as the names of the angels in it show. The Apostolic Constitutions, Origen (*Against Celsus*), Jerome, and Augustine, pronounce it not canonical. Yet it is in the main edifying, vindicating God's government of the world, natural and spiritual, and contradicting none of the Scripture statements. The name Jesus never occurs, though "Son of man," so often given to Messiah in the Gospels, is frequent, and terms are used expressive of His dignity, character, and acts, exceeding the views of Messiah in any other Jewish book. The writer seems to have been a Jew who had become thoroughly imbued with the sacred writings of Daniel. And, though many coincidences occur between its sentiments and the New Testament, the Messianic portions are not distinct enough to prove that the writer knew the New Testament. Rather, he seems to have immediately preceded Christ's coming, about the time of Herod the Great, and so gives us a most interesting view of believing Jews' opinions before the advent of our Lord. The Trinity is recognized (Enoch 60:13,14). Messiah is "the elect One" existing from eternity (Enoch 48:2,3,5); "All kings shall fall down before Him, and worship and fix their hopes on this Son of man" (Enoch 61:10–13). He is the object of worship (Enoch 48:3,4); He is the supreme Judge (Enoch 60:10,11; 68:38,39). There shall be a future state of retribution (Enoch 93:8,9; 94:2,4; 95; 96; 99; 103); The eternity of future punishment (Enoch 103:5). Volkmar, in Alford, thinks the book was written at the time of the sedition of Barchochebas (A.D. 132), by a follower of Rabbi Akiba, the upholder of that impostor. This would make the book Antichristian in its origin. If this date be correct, doubtless it copied some things from Jude, giving them the Jewish, not the Christian, coloring.

Eusebius (*Demonstration of the Gospel*, 3.5) remarks, it accords with John's humility that in Second and Third John he calls himself "the elder." For the same reason James and Jude call themselves "servants of Jesus Christ." Clement of Alexandria (Adumbrations, in *Epistle of Jude*, p. 1007) says, "Jude, through reverential awe, did not call himself brother, but servant, of Jesus Christ, and brother of James."

Tertullian (*On the Apparel of Women*, 3) cites the Epistle as that of the apostle James. Clement of Alexandria in Miscellanies (3.2.11) quotes Jude 8, 17 as Scripture, in The Instructor (3.8.44), Jude 5. The Muratori fragment asserts its canonicity (Routh, *Sacred Fragments*, 1.306). Origen (*Commentary on Matthew* 13:55) says, "Jude wrote an Epistle of few lines, but one filled full of the strong words of heavenly grace." Also, in his *Commentary on Matthew* 22:23, Origen quotes Jude 6; and on Matthew 18:10, he quotes Jude 1. He calls the writer "Jude the apostle," in the Latin remains of his works (compare Davidson, Introduction to the New Testament, vol. 3, p. 498). Jerome (*On Illustrious Men*, 4) reckons it among the Scriptures. Though the oldest manuscripts of the Peschito omit it, Ephrem the Syrian recognizes it. Wordsworth reasons for its genuineness thus: Jude, we know, died before John, that is, before the beginning of the second century. Now Eusebius (*Ecclesiastical History*, 3.32) tells us that James was succeeded in the bishopric of Jerusalem by Symeon his brother; and also that Symeon sat in that see till a.d. 107, when as a martyr he was crucified in his hundred twentieth year. We find that the Epistle to Jude was known in the East and West in the second century; it was therefore circulated in Symeon's lifetime. It never would have received currency such as it had, nor would Symeon have permitted a letter bearing the name of an apostle, his own brother Jude, brother of his own apostolic predecessor, James, to have been circulated, if it were not really Jude's.

Readers

The references to Old Testament history, Jude 5, 7, and to Jewish tradition, Jude 14, etc., make it likely that Jewish Christians are the readers to whom Jude mainly (though including also all Christians, Jude 1) writes, just as the kindred Epistle, Second Peter, is addressed primarily to the same group of people;

compare Introduction to First Peter and Introduction to Second Peter. The people stigmatized in it were not merely libertines (as Alford thinks), though no doubt that was one of their prominent characteristics, but heretics in doctrine, "denying the only Lord God, and our Savior Jesus Christ." Hence he urges believers "earnestly to contend for the faith once delivered unto the saints" (Jude 3). Insubordination, self-seeking, and licentiousness, the fruit of Antinomian teachings, were the evils against which Jude warns his readers; reminding them that, to build themselves in their most holy faith, and to pray in the Holy Spirit, are the only effectual safeguards. The same evils, along with mocking skepticism, shall characterize the last days before the final judgment, even as in the days when Enoch warned the ungodly of the coming flood. As Peter was in Babylon in writing 1 Pet. 5:13, and probably also in writing Second Peter (compare Introduction to First Peter and Introduction to Second Peter), Jude addressed his Epistle primarily to the Jewish Christians in and about Mesopotamian Babylon (a place of great resort to the Jews in that day), or else to the Christian Jews dispersed in Pontus, Galatia, Cappadocia, Asia, and Bithynia (1 Pet. 1:1), the people addressed by Peter. For Jude is expressly said to have preached in Mesopotamia (Jerome, *Commentary on Matthew*), and his Epistle, consisting of only twenty-five verses, contains in them no less than eleven passages from Second Peter (see my Introduction to Second Peter for the list). Probably in Jude 4 he witnesses to the fulfillment of Peter's prophecy, "There are certain men crept in unawares, who were before of old ordained (rather as Greek, "forewritten," that is, announced beforehand by the apostle Peter's written prophecy) to this condemnation, ungodly men denying the only Lord God, and our Lord Jesus Christ." Compare 2 Pet. 2:1, "There shall be false teachers among you who privily shall bring in damnable heresies, even denying the Lord that bought them, and bring on themselves swift destruction." Also Jude 17, 18 plainly refers to the very words of 2 Pet. 3:3, "Remember the words which were spoken before of the apostles of our Lord Jesus; how they told you there should be mockers in the last time who should walk after their own ungodly lusts." This proves, in opposition to Alford, that Jude's Epistle is later than Peter's (whose inspiration he thus confirms, just as Peter confirms Paul's, 2 Pet. 3:15, 16), not vice versa.

Time and place of writing

Alford thinks, that, considering Jude was writing to Jews and citing signal instances of divine vengeance, it is very unlikely he would have omitted to allude to the destruction of Jerusalem if he had written after that event which uprooted the Jewish polity and people. He conjectures from the tone and references that the writer lived in Palestine. But as to the former, negative evidence is doubtful; for neither does John allude in his Epistles, written after the destruction of Jerusalem, to that event. Mill fixes on A.D. 90, after the death of all the apostles save John. I incline to think from Jude 17, 18 that some time had elapsed since the Second Epistle of Peter (written probably about A.D. 68 or 69) when Jude wrote, and, therefore, that the Epistle of Jude was written after the destruction of Jerusalem.

A. R. Faussett

Detailed outline

I. Introduction: Greeting: 1–2
 A. From: Jude: 1
  1. Brother of James.
  2. Bondservant of Jesus Christ.
 B. To those: 1
  1. Sanctified by God.
  2. Preserved in Christ.
  3. Called.

II. Purpose: 3
 A. Common salvation.
 B. That they fight for the faith.

III. Characteristics of false teachers: 4
 A. Crept in unawares.
 B. Ordained to condemnation.
 C. Ungodly men.
 D. Turning God's grace to lasciviousness.
 E. Denying the Lord Jesus Christ.

IV. Three historical records: 5–7
 A. Israel: Once saved, afterward destroyed: 5
 B. Angels: Left first estate, reserved in chains: 6
 C. Sodom and Gomorrah: 7

V. Description of false teachers: 8–10 (continued description from verse 4)
 A. Filthy dreamers: 8
 B. Defile the flesh: 8
 C. Despise dominion: 8
 D. Speak evil of dignities: 8–10
  1. Michael the archangel and the devil: 9
  2. These men speak evil: 10
 E. Corrupt natural things: 10

VI. Description of these evil men by example: 11
 A. They followed the way of Cain.
 B. They followed the error of Balaam.
 C. They were destroyed in Korah's rebellion.

VII. Description of these evil men: 12–13
 A. Blemishes: 12
 B. Waterless Clouds:12
 C. Dead Trees: 12
 D. Wild Waves: 13
 E. Wandering Stars: 13

VIII. Future judgment: 14–15
 A. The messenger: Enoch: 14
 B. The message: 15

IX. Description of evil men continued: 16
 A. Murmurers.
 B. Complainers.
 C. Walking after their own lusts.
 D. People who boast.
 E. Flatters.

X. Remember: Jesus warned of these men: 17–19
 A. Mockers would come in the last time: 18
 B. They would walk after their own ungodly lusts: 18
 C. They would separate themselves (groups, cliques): 19
 D. They would be sensual: 19
 E. They would not have the Spirit of God: 19

XI. Four point plan for avoiding the deception of these evil men: 20–21
 A. Build up yourself in the faith: 20
 B. Pray in the Holy Spirit: 20
 C. Keep yourself in the love of God: 21
 D. Look for the return of the Lord Jesus Christ: 21

XII. Our response to these evil men: 22–23
 A. On some have compassion: 22

1. The weak and the deliberately evil.

B. Others save with fear: 23

XIV. Closing benediction: 24–25

A. What He does for us now: He is able to keep us from falling: 24

B. What He will do later: Present us faultless: 24

1. Before the presence of His glory.
2. With exceeding great joy.

C. To the only wise God our Savior, now and forever, be: 25

1. Glory.
2. Majesty.
3. Dominion.
4. Power.

Contents

The writer begins his Epistle with the regular address and apostolic blessing, 1, 2.

He informs his readers that he felt it incumbent on him to warn them against certain intruders, who deny Christ, lead lascivious lives and will certainly be punished like the people delivered from Egypt, the fallen angels and the cities of the plain, 3–7.

These intruders are further described as defilers of the flesh and as despisers and blasphemers of heavenly dignities, and the woe is pronounced on them, 8–11.

After giving a further description of their debauchery, the author exhorts the readers to be mindful of the words of the apostles, who had spoken of the appearance of such mockers, 12–19.

Admonishing them to increase in faith and to keep themselves in the love of God, and giving them directions as to the correct behavior towards others, he concludes his Epistle with a doxology, 20–25.

2. Helpful summaries of Jude

Bird's eye view

A letter warning the Christian church against false and immoral teachers.

Reading plan

The following reading plan enables you to read through Jude in one day.

Jude 1:1–1:25

Verses to memorize

Jude 24–25

To him who is able to keep you from falling and to present you before his glorious presence without fault and with great joy— to the only God our Savior be glory, majesty, power and authority, through Jesus Christ our Lord, before all ages, now and forevermore! Amen.

Statistics

Twenty-sixth New Testament book

1 chapter

25 verses

613 words

Names/titles given

Iouda: "Of Jude."

3. Helpful keys to turn to in understanding Jude

Key word

Kept

Key verse

Jude verse 24

Themes to study

- Sin is always punished.
- How false teachers and their teaching can be exposed.

Jesus in Jude

In Jude Jesus preserves us.

Lessons to learn from Jude

- Eroneous teaching and ungodly behavior should be opposed.
- God's promises are the firm foundation on which we stand.

4. Studying Jude verse by verse

Matthew Henry's introduction

We have here,

I. An account of the penman of this epistle, a character of the church, the blessings and privileges of that happy society, vv. 1, 2.

II. The occasion of writing this epistle, v. 3.

III. A character of evil and perverse men, who had already sprung up in that infant state of the church, and would be succeeded by others of the like evil spirit and temper in after-times, v. 4.

IV. A caution against hearkening to and following after such, from the severity of God towards the unbelieving murmuring Israelites at their coming out of Egypt, the angels that fell, the sin and punishment of Sodom and Gomorrah, vv. 5–7.

V. To these the apostle likens the seducers against whom he was warning them, and describes them at large, (vv. 8–13).

VI. Then (as specially suitable to his argument) he cites an ancient prophecy of Enoch foretelling and describing the future judgment, vv. 14, 15.

VII. He enlarges on the seducers' character, and guards against the offence which honest minds might be apt to take at the so early permission of such things, by showing that it was foretold long before that so it must be, vv. 16–19.

VIII. Exhorts them to perseverance in the faith, fervency in prayer, watchfulness against falling from the love of God, and a lively hope of eternal life, vv. 20, 21.

IX. Directs them how to act towards the erroneous and scandalous, vv. 22, 23. And,

X. Closes with an admirable doxology in the last two verses.

Dr. Adam Clarke's analysis of chapter

The address and apostolic benediction, 1, 2.

The reasons which induced Jude to write this epistle, to excite the Christians to contend for the true faith, and to beware of false teachers, lest, falling from their steadfastness, they should be destroyed after the example of backsliding Israel, the apostate angels, and the inhabitants of Sodom and Gomorrha, 3–7.

Of the false teachers, 8.

Of Michael disputing about the body of Moses, 9.

The false teachers particularly described: they are like brute beasts, going the way of Cain, run after the error of Balaam, and shall per ish, as did Korah in his gainsaying, 10, 11.

Are impure, unsteady, fierce, shameless, 12, 13.

How Enoch prophesied of such, 14, 15.

They are farther described as murmurers and complainers, 16.

We should remember the cautions given unto us by the apostles who foretold of these men, 17–19.

We should build up ourselves on our most holy faith, 20, 21.

How the Church of Christ should treat such, 22, 23.

The apostle's farewell, and his doxology to God, 24, 25.

A detailed analysis of chapter

Greeting and warning of danger. (1–4)

Danger from false teachers, and the punishment which will fall on them and their followers. (5–7)

A dreadful description of these "dreamers". (8–16)

Believers warned against being surprised that such deceivers are in their fellowship. (17–23)

The letter ends with an encouraging doxology, or words of praise. (24,25)

Key verse

Verse 24: "To him who is able to keep you from falling and to present you before his glorious presence without fault and with great joy."

Key word / key phrase

Verse 24, "keep you from falling."

Key event / key person / key theme

Persevere

Key thought

Christians must be on the watch for immoral and godless men who have slipped unnoticed into the Christian fellowship.

Key thing to look out for

Verses 20,21. Advice on how to withstand this evil teaching.

Key Bible cross-reference

Verse 9. See Zechariah 3:2.

Key "by way of explanation"

Verse 4, "a license for immorality." These perverse people argued that they could commit immorality with impunity as it was God's business to forgive them. Jude and 2 Peter are very similar, and it appears that one writer borrowed heavily from the other in order to counter similar false teachings. It is possible that the writer was Jude, the brother of Jesus.

Key "Quotable Quote"

"When you shall see the wicked heresy, which is the army of Antichrist, standing in the holy places of the Church, then let those who are in Judea head for the mountains, that is, those who are Christians should head for the Scriptures. For the true Judea is Christendom, and the mountains are the Scriptures of the prophets and apostles."

John Chrysostom

5. Select bibliography for Jude

Bauckham, R. J. *Jude-2 Peter*. Waco: Word, 1983.

Kelly, J. N. D. *The Epistles of Peter and of Jude*. New York: Harper & Row, 1970.

Manton, Thomas. *Commentary on Jude*. London, 1658.

Revelation

1. Book by book: Introduction to Revelation

Introduction

Authenticity

The author calls himself John (Rev. 1:1, 4, 9; 2:8). Justin Martyr (*Dialogue with Trypho*, p. 308) (a.d. 139–161) quotes from the Apocalypse, as John the apostle's work, the prophecy of the millennium of the saints, to be followed by the general resurrection and judgment. This testimony of Justin is referred to also by Eusebius (*Ecclesiastical History,* 4.18). Justin Martyr, in the early part of the second century, held his controversy with Trypho, a learned Jew, at Ephesus, where John had been living thirty or thirty-five years before: he says that "the Revelation had been given to John, one of the twelve apostles of Christ." Melito, bishop of Sardis (about a.d. 171), one of the seven churches addressed, a successor, therefore, of one of the seven angels, is said by Eusebius (*Ecclesiastical History*, 4.26) to have written treatises on the Apocalypse of John. The testimony of the bishop of Sardis is the more impartial, as Sardis is one of the churches severely reproved (Rev. 3:1). So also Theophilus of Antioch (about a.d. 180), according to Eusebius (*Ecclesiastical History*, 4.26), quoted testimonies from the Apocalypse of John. Eusebius says the same of Apollonius, who lived in Asia Minor in the end of the second century. Irenaeus (about a.d. 180), a hearer of Polycarp, the disciple of John, and supposed by Archbishop Ussher to be the angel of the Church of Smyrna, is most decided again and again in quoting the Apocalypse as the work of the apostle John (*Against Heresies*, 4.20.11; 4.21.3; 4.30.4; 5.36.1; 5.30.3; 5.35.2). In (5.30.1), alluding to the mystical number of the beast, six hundred sixty-six (Rev. 13:18), found in all old copies, he says, "We do not hazard a confident theory as to the name of Antichrist; for if it had been necessary that his name should be proclaimed openly at the present time, it would have been declared by him who saw the apocalyptic vision; for it was seen at no long time back, but almost in our generation, towards the end of Domitian's reign." In his work *Against Heresies*, published ten years after Polycarp's martyrdom, he quotes the Apocalypse twenty times, and makes long extracts from it, as inspired Scripture. These testimonies of people contemporary with John's immediate successors, and more or less connected with the region of the seven churches to which Revelation is addressed, are most convincing. Tertullian, of North Africa (about A.D. 220), (*Against Marcion*, 3.14), quotes the apostle John's descriptions in the Apocalypse of the sword proceeding out of the Lord's mouth (Rev. 19:15), and of the heavenly city (Rev. 21:1–27). Compare *On the Resurrection of the Flesh* (27); *A Treatise on the Soul*, (8, 9, etc.); *The Prescription against Heretics*, (33). The Muratori fragment of the canon (about a.d. 200) refers to John the apostle writing to the seven churches. Hippolytus, bishop of Ostia, near Rome (about A.D. 240) (On Antichrist, p. 67), quotes Rev. 17:1–18, as the writing of John the apostle. Among Hippolytus' works, there is specified in the catalogue on his statue, a treatise "on the Apocalypse and Gospel according to John." Clement of Alexandria (about a.d. 200) (*Miscellanies*, 6.13), alludes to the twenty-four seats on which the elders sit as mentioned by John in the Apocalypse (Rev. 4:5); also, (*Who Is the Rich Man Who Shall Be Saved*? 42), he mentions John's return from Patmos to Ephesus on the death of the Roman tyrant. Origen (about A.D. 233), (*Commentary on Matthew*, in Eusebius *Ecclesiastical History*, 6.25), mentions John as the author of the Apocalypse, without expressing any doubts as to its authenticity; also, in *Commentary on Matthew*, (16.6), he quotes Rev. 1:9, and says, "John seems to have beheld the Apocalypse in the island of Patmos." Victorinus, bishop of Pettau in Pannonia, who suffered martyrdom under Diocletian in a.d. 303, wrote the earliest extant commentary on the Apocalypse. Though the Old Syriac Peschito version does not contain the Apocalypse, yet Ephrem the Syrian (about A.D. 378) frequently quotes the Apocalypse as canonical, and ascribes it to John.

Canonicity and inspiration

Its canonicity and inspiration (according to a scholium of Andreas of Cappadocia) are attested by Papias, a hearer of John, and associate of Polycarp. Papias was bishop of Hierapolis, near Laodicea, one of the seven churches. Wordsworth conjectures that a feeling of shame, on account of the rebukes of Laodicea in Revelation, may have operated on the Council of Laodicea, so as to omit Revelation from its list of books to be read publicly. The Epistle of the churches of Lyons and Vienne to the churches of Asia and Phrygia (in Eusebius, [*Ecclesiastical History,* 5.1–3]), in the persecution under Marcus Aurelius (A.D. 77) quotes Rev. 1:5; 3:14; 14:4; 22:11, as Scripture. Cyprian (about A.D. 250) also, in Epistle 13, quotes Rev. 2:5 as Scripture; and in Epistle 25 he quotes Rev. 3:21, as of the same authority as the Gospel. (For other instances, see Alford's *Prolegomena*, from whom mainly this summary of evidence has been derived). Athanasius, in his *Festival Epistle*, enumerates the Apocalypse among the canonical Scriptures, to which none must add, and from which none must take away. Jerome (*Epistle to Paulinus*) includes in the canon the Apocalypse, adding, "It has as many mysteries as words. All praise falls short of its merits. In each of its words lie hid manifold senses." Thus an unbroken chain of testimony down from the apostolic period confirms its canonicity and authenticity.

The Alogi (Epiphanius, *Heresies*, 51) and Caius the Roman presbyter (Eusebius, *Ecclesiastical*

History, 3.28), towards the end of the second and beginning of the third century, rejected John's Apocalypse on mere captious grounds. Caius, according to Jerome (*On Illustrious Men*), about A.D. 210, attributed it to Cerinthus, on the ground of its supporting the millennial reign on earth. Dionysius of Alexandria mentions many before his time who rejected it because of its obscurity and because it seemed to support Cerinthus' dogma of an earthly and carnal kingdom; whence they attributed it to Cerinthus. This Dionysius, scholar of Origen, and bishop of Alexandria (A.D. 247), admits its inspiration (in Eusebius [*Ecclesiastical History*, 7.10]), but attributes it to some John distinct from John the apostle, on the ground of its difference of style and character, as compared with John's Gospel and Epistle, as also because the name John is several times mentioned in the Apocalypse, which is always kept back in both the Gospel and Epistle; moreover, neither does the Epistle make any allusion to the Apocalypse, nor the Apocalypse to the Epistle; and the style is not pure Greek, but abounds in barbarisms and solecisms. Eusebius wavers in opinion (*Ecclesiastical History*, 24.39) as to whether it is, or is not, to be ranked among the undoubtedly canonical Scriptures. His antipathy to the millennial doctrine would give an unconscious bias to his judgment on the Apocalypse. Cyril of Jerusalem (A.D. 386), (*Catechetical Lectures*, 4.35,36), omits the Apocalypse in enumerating the New Testament Scriptures to be read privately as well as publicly. "Whatever is not read in the churches, that do not even read by thyself; the apostles and ancient bishops of the Church who transmitted them to us were far wiser than thou art." Hence, we see that, in his day, the Apocalypse was not read in the churches. Yet in *Catechetical Lectures,* 1.4 he quotes Rev. 2:7, 17; and in *Catechetical Lectures,* 1; 15.13 he draws the prophetical statement from Rev. 17:11, that the king who is to humble the three kings (Dan. 7:8, 20) is the eighth king. In *Catechetical Lectures*, 15 and 27, he similarly quotes from Rev. 12:3, 4. Alford conjectures that Cyril had at some time changed his opinion, and that these references to the Apocalypse were slips of memory whereby he retained phraseology which belonged to his former, not his subsequent views. The sixtieth canon (if genuine) of the Laodicean Council in the middle of the fourth century omits the Apocalypse from the canonical books. The Eastern Church in part doubted, the Western Church, after the fifth century, universally recognized, the Apocalypse. Cyril of Alexandria (*On Worship,* 146), though implying the fact of some doubting its genuineness, himself undoubtedly accepts it as the work of St. John. Andreas of Caesarea, in Cappadocia, recognized as genuine and canonical, and wrote the first entire and connected commentary on, the Apocalypse. The sources of doubt seem to have been, (1) the antagonism of many to the millennium, which is set forth in it; (2) its obscurity and symbolism having caused it not to be read in the churches, or to be taught to the young. But the most primitive tradition is unequivocal in its favor. In a word, the objective evidence is decidedly for it; the only arguments against it seem to have been subjective.

The personal notices of John in the Apocalypse occur Rev. 1:1, 4, 9; Rev. 22:8. Moreover, the writer's addresses to the churches of Proconsular Asia (Rev. 2:1) accord with the concurrent tradition, that after John's return from his exile in Patmos, at the death of Domitian, under Nerva, he resided for long, and died at last in Ephesus, in the time of Trajan (Eusebius, *Ecclesiastical History*, 3.20,23). If the Apocalypse were not the inspired work of John, purporting as it does to be an address from their superior to the seven churches of Proconsular Asia, it would have assuredly been rejected in that region; whereas the earliest testimonies in those churches are all in its favor. One person alone was entitled to use language of authority such as is addressed to the seven angels of the churches–namely, John, as the last surviving apostle and superintendent of all the churches. Also, it accords with John's manner to assert the accuracy of his testimony both at the beginning and end of his book (compare Rev. 1:2, 3, and 22:8, with John 1:14; 21:24; 1 John 1:1, 2). Again, it accords with the view of the writer being an inspired apostle that he addresses the angels or presidents of the several churches in the tone of a superior addressing inferiors. Also, he commends the Church of Ephesus for trying and convicting "them which say they are apostles, and are not," by which he implies his own undoubted claim to apostolic inspiration (Rev. 2:2), as declaring in the seven epistles Christ's will revealed through him.

Style

As to the difference of style, as compared with the Gospel and Epistle, the difference of subject in part accounts for it, the visions of the seer, transported as he was above the region of sense, appropriately taking a form of expression abrupt, and unbound by the grammatical laws which governed his writings of a calmer and more deliberate character. Moreover, as being a Galilean Hebrew, John, in writing a Revelation akin to the Old Testament prophecies, naturally reverted to their Hebraistic style.

Alford notices, among the features of resemblance between the styles of the Apocalypse and John's Gospel and Epistle:

(1) the characteristic appellation of our Lord, peculiar to John exclusively, "the Word of God" (Rev. 19:13; compare John 1:1; 1 John 1:1).

(2) the phrase, "he that overcometh" (Rev. 2:7, 11, 17; 3:5, 12, 21; 12:11; 15:2; 17:14; 21:7; compare John 16:33 1 John 2:13, 14; 4:4; 5:4, 5).

(3) The Greek term (*alethinos*) for "true," as opposed to that which is shadowy and unreal (Rev. 3:7, 14; 6:10; 15:3; 16:7; 19:2, 9, 11; 21:5; 22:6). This term, found only once in Luke (Luke 16:11), four times in Paul (1 Thess. 1:9; Heb. 8:2; 9:24; 10:22), is found nine times in John's Gospel (John 1:9; 4:23, 37; 6:32; 7:28; 8:16; 15:1 John 17:3; 19:3, 5), twice in John's First Epistle (1 John 2:8; 5:20), and ten times in Revelation (Rev. 3:7, 14; 6:10; 15:3; 16:7; 19:2, 9, 11; 21:5 Rev. 22:6).

(4) The Greek diminutive for "Lamb" (*arnion*, literally, "lambkin") occurs twenty-nine times in the Apocalypse, and the only other place where it occurs is John 21:15. In John's writings alone is Christ called directly "the Lamb" (John 1:29, 36). In 1 Pet. 1:19, He is called "as a lamb without blemish," in allusion to Is. 53:7. So the use of "witness," or "testimony" (Rev. 1:2, 9; 6:9; 11:7, etc.; compare John 1:7, 8, 15, 19, 32; 1 John 1:2; 4:14; 5:6–11). "Keep the word," or "commandments" (Rev. 3:8, 10; 12:17; compare John 8:51, 55; 14:15). The assertion of the same thing positively and negatively

(Rev. 2:2, 6, 8, 13; 3:8, 17, 18; compare John 1:3, 6, 7, 20; 1 John 2:27, 28). Compare also 1 John 2:20, 27 with Rev. 3:18, as to the spiritual anointing. The seeming solecisms of style are attributable to that, inspired elevation which is above mere grammatical rules, and are designed to arrest the reader's attention by the peculiarity of the phrase, so as to pause and search into some deep truth lying beneath. The vivid earnestness of the inspired writer, handling a subject so transcending all others, raises him above all servile adherence to ordinary rules, so that at times he abruptly passes from one grammatical construction to another, as he graphically sets the thing described before the eye of the reader. This is not due to ignorance of grammar, for he "has displayed a knowledge of grammatical rules in other much more difficult constructions" (Winer). The connection of thought is more attended to than mere grammatical connection. Another consideration to be taken into account is that two-fifths of the whole being the recorded language of others, he moulds his style accordingly. Compare Tregelles' Introduction to Revelation from Heathen Authorities.

Tregelles well says (*New Testament Historic Evidence*), "There is no book of the New Testament for which we have such clear, ample, and numerous testimonies in the second century as we have in favor of the Apocalypse. The more closely the witnesses were connected with the apostle John (as was the case with Irenaeus), the more explicit is their testimony. That doubts should prevail in after ages must have originated either in ignorance of the earlier testimony, or else from some supposed intuition of what an apostle ought to have written. The objections on the ground of internal style can weigh nothing against the actual evidence. It is in vain to argue, *a priori*, that John could not have written this book when we have the evidence of several competent witnesses that he did write it."

Revelation and the rest of the Bible

Gregory of Nyssa calls Revelation "the last book of grace." It completes the volume of inspiration, so that we are to look for no further revelation till Christ Himself shall come. Appropriately the last book completing the canon was written by John, the last survivor of the apostles. The New Testament is composed of the historical books, the Gospels and Acts, the doctrinal Epistles, and the one prophetical book, Revelation. The same apostle wrote the last of the Gospels, and probably the last of the Epistles, and the only prophetical book of the New Testament. All the books of the New Testament had been written, and were read in the Church assemblies, some years before John's death. His life was providentially prolonged that he might give the final attestation to Scripture. About the year A.D. 100, the bishops of Asia (the angels of the seven churches) came to John at Ephesus, bringing him copies of the three Gospels, Matthew, Mark, and Luke, and desired of him a statement of his apostolic judgment about them; whereon he pronounced them authentic, genuine, and inspired, and at their request added his own Gospel to complete the fourfold aspect of the Gospel of Christ: compare Muratori (*Fragment on the Canon of Scripture*); Eusebius (*Ecclesiastical History*, 3.24); Jerome (*Commentary on Matthew*); Victorinus (*On the Apocalypse*); Theodoret (*Ecclesiastical History*, 39). A Greek divine, quoted in Allatius, calls Revelation "the seal of the whole Bible." The canon would be incomplete without Revelation. Scripture is a complete whole, its component books, written in a period ranging over one thousand five hundred years, being mutually connected. Unity of aim and spirit pervades the entire, so that the end is the necessary sequence of the middle, and the middle of the beginning. Genesis presents before us man and his bride in innocence and blessedness, followed by man's fall through Satan's subtlety, and man's consequent misery, his exclusion from Paradise and its tree of life and delightful rivers. Revelation presents, in reverse order, man first liable to sin and death, but afterwards made conqueror through the blood of the Lamb; the first Adam and Eve, represented by the second Adam, Christ, and the Church. His spotless bride, in Paradise, with free access to the tree of life and the crystal water of life that flows from the throne of God. As Genesis foretold the bruising of the serpent's head by the woman's seed (Gen. 3:15), so Revelation declares the final accomplishment of that prediction (Rev. 19:1–20:15).

Place and time of writing

The best authorities among the Fathers state that John was exiled under Domitian (Irenaeus (*Against Heresies*, 5; 30); Clement of Alexandria; Eusebius (*Ecclesiastical History*, 3.20). Victorinus says that he had to labor in the mines of Patmos. At Domitian's death, A.D. 95, he returned to Ephesus under the Emperor Nerva. Probably it was immediately after his return that he wrote, under divine inspiration, the account of the visions vouchsafed to him in Patmos (Rev. 1:2, 9). However, Rev. 10:4 seems to imply that he wrote the visions immediately after seeing them. Patmos is one of the Sporades. Its circumference is about thirty miles. "It was fitting that when forbidden to go beyond certain bounds of the earth's lands, he was permitted to penetrate the secrets of heaven" (Bede, *Explanation of the Apocalypse* on chap. 1). The following arguments favor an earlier date, namely, under Nero: (1) Eusebius (*Demonstration of the Gospel*) unites in the same sentence John's banishment with the stoning of James and the beheading of Paul, which were under Nero. (2) Clement of Alexandria's story of the robber reclaimed by John, after he had pursued, and with difficulty overtaken him, accords better with John then being a younger man than under Domitian, when he was one hundred years old. Arethas, in the sixth century, applies the sixth seal to the destruction of Jerusalem (A.D. 70), adding that the Apocalypse was written before that event. So the Syriac version states he was banished by Nero the Cæsar. Laodicea was overthrown by an earthquake (A.D. 60) but was immediately rebuilt, so that its being called "rich and increased with goods" is not incompatible with this book having been written under the Neronian persecution (A.D. 64). But the possible allusions to it in Heb. 10:37; compare Rev. 1:4, 8; 4:8; 22:12; Heb. 11:10; compare Rev. 21:14; Heb. 12:22, 23; compare Rev. 14:1; Heb. 8:1, 2; compare Rev. 11:19; 15:5; 21:3; Heb. 4:12; compare Rev. 1:16; 2:12, 16; 19:13, 15; Heb. 4:9; compare Rev. 20:1–15; also 1 Pet. 1:7, 13; 4:13, with Rev. 1:1; 1 Pet. 2:9 with Rev. 5:10; 2 Tim. 4:8, with Rev. 2:26, 27; 3:21; 11:18; Eph. 6:12, with Rev. 12:7–12; Phil. 4:3, with Rev. 3:5; 13:8; 17:8; 20:12,

15; Col. 1:18, with Rev. 1:5; 1 Cor. 15:52, with Rev. 10:7; 11:15–18, make a date before the destruction of Laodicea possible. Cerinthus is stated to have died before John; as then he borrowed much in his Pseudo-Apocalypse from John's, it is likely the latter was at an earlier date than Domitian's reign. See Tilloch's *Introduction to Apocalypse*. But the Pauline benediction (Rev. 1:4) implies it was written after Paul's death under Nero.

Readers

The inscription states that it is addressed to the seven churches of Asia, that is, Proconsular Asia. John's reason for fixing on the number seven (for there were more than seven churches in the region meant by "Asia," for instance, Magnesia and Tralles) was doubtless because seven is the sacred number implying totality and universality: so it is implied that John, through the medium of the seven churches, addresses in the Spirit the Church of all places and ages. The Church in its various states of spiritual life or deadness, in all ages and places, is represented by the seven churches, and is addressed with words of consolation or warning accordingly. Smyrna and Philadelphia alone of the seven are honored with unmixed praise, as faithful in tribulation and rich in good works. Heresies of a decided kind had by this time arisen in the churches of Asia, and the love of many had waxed cold, while others had advanced to greater zeal, and one had sealed his testimony with his blood.

Purpose

It begins with admonitory addresses to the seven churches from the divine Son of man, whom John saw in vision, after a brief introduction which sets forth the main subject of the book, namely, to "show unto His servants things which must shortly come to pass" (the first through third chapters). From the fourth chapter to the end is mainly prophecy, with practical exhortations and consolations, however, interspersed, similar to those addressed to the seven churches (the representatives of the universal Church of every age), and so connecting the body of the book with its beginning, which therefore forms its appropriate introduction.

Three schools of interpreters exist:

The Preterists, who hold that almost the whole has been fulfilled.

The Historical Interpreters, who hold that it comprises the history of the Church from John's time to the end of the world, the seals being chronologically succeeded, by the trumpets and the trumpets by the bowls.

The Futurists, who consider almost the whole as yet future, and to be fulfilled immediately before Christ's second coming.

The first theory was not held by any of the earliest Fathers, and is only held now by Rationalists, who limit John's vision to things within his own horizon, pagan Rome's persecutions of Christians, and its consequently anticipated destruction. The Futurist school is open to this great objection: it would leave the Church of Christ unprovided with prophetical guidance or support under her fiery trials for 1700 or 1800 years. Now God has said, "Surely He will do nothing, but He revealeth His secrets unto His servants the prophets" (Amos 3:7). The Jews had a succession of prophets who guided them with the light of prophecy: what their prophets were to them, that the apocalyptic Scriptures have been, and are, to us.

Alford, following Isaac Williams, draws attention to the parallel connection between the Apocalypse and Christ's discourse on the Mount of Olives, recorded in Matt. 24:4–28. The seals plainly bring us down to the second coming of Christ, just as the trumpets also do (compare Rev. 6:12–17; 8:1, etc.; Rev. 11:15), and as the vials also do (Rev. 16:17): all three run parallel, and end in the same point. Certain "catchwords" (as Wordsworth calls them) connect the three series of symbols together. They do not succeed one to the other in historical and chronological sequence, but move side by side, the subsequent series filling up in detail the same picture which the preceding series had drawn in outline. So Victorinus (on Rev. 7:2), the earliest commentator on the Apocalypse, says, "The order of the things said is not to be regarded, since often the Holy Spirit, when He has run to the end of the last time, again returns to the same times, and supplies what He has less fully expressed." And Primasius (*Commentary on the Apocalypse*), "In the trumpets he gives a description by a pleasing repetition, as is his custom."

At the very beginning, John hastens, by anticipation (as was the tendency of all the prophets), to the grand consummation. Rev. 1:7, "Behold, He cometh with clouds," etc. Rev. 1:8, 17, "I am the beginning and the ending . . . the first and the last." So the seven epistles exhibit the same anticipation of the end. Rev. 3:12, "Him that overcometh, I will write on Him the name of my God, and the name of the city of my God, which is new Jerusalem, which cometh down out of heaven"; compare at the close, Rev. 21:2. So also Rev. 2:28, "I will give him the morning star"; compare at the close, Rev. 22:16, "I am the bright and morning star."

Again, the earthquake that ensues on the opening of the sixth seal is one of the catchwords, that is, a link connecting chronologically this sixth seal with the sixth trumpet (Rev. 9:13; 11:13): compare also the seventh vial, Rev. 16:17, 18. The concomitants of the opening of the sixth seal, it is plain, in no full and exhaustive sense apply to any event, save the terrors which shall overwhelm the ungodly just before the coming of the Judge.

Again, the beast out of the bottomless pit (Rev. 11:7), between the sixth and seventh trumpets, connects this series with the section, twelfth through fourteenth chapters, about the Church and her adversaries.

Again, the sealing of the 144,000 under the sixth seal connects this seal with the section, the twelfth through fourteenth chapters.

Again, the loosing of the four winds by the four angels standing on the four corners of the earth, under the sixth seal, answers to the loosing of the four angels at the Euphrates, under the sixth trumpet.

Moreover, links occur in the Apocalypse connecting it with the Old Testament. For instance, the "mouth speaking great things" (Dan. 7:8 Rev. 13:5), connects the beast that blasphemes against God, and makes war against the saints, with the little horn (Dan. 7:21; Rev. 13:6, 7), or at last king, who, arising after the ten kings, shall speak against the Most High, and wear out the saints (Dan. 7:25); also, compare the "forty-two months" (Rev. 13:5), or "a thousand two hundred and threescore days" (Rev. 12:6), with the "time, times, and the dividing of time," of Dan. 7:25. Moreover, the "forty-two months," Rev. 11:2, answering to Rev. 12:6; 13:5, link together the period under the sixth trumpet to the section, Rev. 12:1–14:20.

Auberlen observes, "The history of salvation is mysteriously governed by holy numbers. They are the scaffolding of the organic edifice. They are not merely outward indications of time, but indications of nature and essence. Not only nature, but history, is based in numbers. Scripture and antiquity put numbers as the fundamental forms of things, where we put ideas." As number is the regulator of the relations and proportions of the natural world, so does it enter most frequently into the revelations of the Apocalypse, which sets forth the harmonies of the supernatural, the immediately Divine. Thus the most supernatural revelation leads us the farthest into the natural, as was to be expected, seeing the God of nature and of revelation is one. Seven is the number for perfection (compare Rev. 1:4; 4:5, the seven Spirits before the throne; also, Rev. 5:6, the Lamb's seven horns and seven eyes). Thus the seven churches represent the Church catholic in its totality. The seven seals (Rev. 5:1), the seven trumpets (Rev. 8:2), and the seven vials (Rev. 17:1), are severally a complete series each in itself, fulfilling perfectly the divine course of judgments. Three and a half implies a number opposed to the divine (seven), but broken in itself, and which, in the moment of its highest triumph, is overwhelmed by judgment and utter ruin. Four is the number of the world's extension; seven is the number of God's revelation in the world. In the four beasts of Daniel (Dan. 7:3) there is a recognition of some power above them, at the same time that there is a mimicry of the four cherubs of Ezekiel (Ezek. 10:9), the heavenly symbols of all creation in its due subjection to God (Rev. 4:6–8). So the four corners of the earth, the four winds, the four angels loosed from the Euphrates, and Jerusalem lying "foursquare" (Rev. 21:16), represent world-wide extension. The sevenfoldness of the Spirits on the part of God corresponds with the fourfold cherubim on the part of the created. John, seeing more deeply into the essentially God-opposed character of the world, presents to us, not the four beasts of Daniel, but the seven heads of the beast, whereby it arrogates to itself the sevenfold perfection of the Spirits of God; at the same time that, with characteristic self-contradiction, it has ten horns, the number peculiar to the world power. Its unjust usurpation of the sacred number seven is marked by the addition of an eighth to the seven heads, and also by the beast's own number, six hundred sixty-six, which in units, tens, and hundreds, verges on, but falls short of, seven. The judgments on the world are complete in six: after the sixth seal and the sixth trumpet, there is a pause. When seven comes, there comes "the kingdom of our Lord and His Christ." Six is the number of the world given to judgment. Moreover, six is half of twelve, as three and a half is the half of seven. Twelve is the number of the Church: compare the twelve tribes of Israel, the twelve stars on the woman's head (Rev. 12:1), the twelve gates of new Jerusalem (Rev. 21:12, 21).

Six thus symbolizes the world broken, and without solid foundation. Twice twelve is the number of the heavenly elders; twelve times twelve thousand the number of the sealed elect (Rev. 7:4): the tree of life yields twelve manner of fruits. Doubtless, besides this symbolic force, there is a special chronological meaning in the numbers; but as yet, though a commanded subject of investigation, they have received no solution which we can be sure is the true one. They are intended to stimulate reverent inquiry, not to gratify idle speculative curiosity; and when the event shall have been fulfilled, they will show the divine wisdom of God, who ordered all things in minutely harmonious relations, and left neither the times nor the ways haphazard.

The arguments for the year-day theory are as follows: Dan. 9:24, "Seventy weeks are determined on," where the Hebrew may be seventy sevens; but Mede observes, the Hebrew word means always seven of days, and never seven of years (Lev. 12:5; Deut. 16:9, 10, 16). Again, the number of years' wandering of the Israelites was made to correspond to the number of days in which the spies searched the land, namely, forty: compare "each day for a year," Num. 14:33, 34. So in Ezek. 4:5, 6, "I have laid up on thee the years of their iniquity, according to the number of the days, three hundred and ninety days . . . forty days: I have appointed thee each day for a year." John, in Revelation itself, uses days in a sense which can hardly be literal. Rev. 2:10, "Ye shall have tribulation ten days": the persecution of ten years recorded by Eusebius seems to correspond to it. In the year-day theory there is still quite enough of obscurity to exercise the patience and probation of faith, for we cannot say precisely when the 1260 years begin: so that this theory is quite compatible with Christ's words, "Of that day and hour knoweth no man" (Matt. 24:36; Mark 13:32). However, it is a difficulty in this theory that "a thousand years," in Rev. 20:6, 7, can hardly mean one thousand by three hundred sixty days, that is, three hundred sixty thousand years. The first resurrection there must be literal, even as Rev. 20:5 must be taken literally, "the rest of the dead lived not again until the thousand years were finished" (Rev. 20:5). To interpret the former spiritually would entail the need of interpreting the latter so, which would be most improbable; for it would imply that "the rest of the (spiritually) dead lived not (spiritually)" until the end of the thousand years, and then that they did come spiritually to life. 1 Cor. 15:23, "they that are Christ's at His coming," confirms the literal view.

A. R. Faussett

Contents of Revelation

After the introduction and the apostolic blessing, 1:1–8, the book contains seven visions or series of visions, extending from 1:9–22:7, followed by a conclusion, 22:8–21.

I. The first Vision, 1: 9–3:22.

This vision is of the glorified Christ in the middle of the Church, directing John to write letters of reproof, of warning, of exhortation and of consolation to seven representative churches of proconsular Asia, viz. to Ephesus, Smyrna, Pergamus, Thyatire, Sardis, Philadelphia and Laodicea.

II. The second Vision, 4:1–8:1.

This vision reveals God as ruling the world's destiny, and the Lamb as taking the book of the divine decrees and breaking the seven seals of which each one represents a part of God's purpose, the first four referring to the terrestrial, and the last three to the celestial sphere. Between the sixth and seventh seals an episode is introduced to show the safety of the people of God amid the judgments that are inflicted on the world.

III. The third Vision, 8:2–11:19.

This vision shows us seven angels, each one having a trumpet. After an angel has offered up the prayers of the saints to God, the seven angels blow their trumpets, and each trumpet is followed by a vision of destruction on the sinful world, the destruction of the last three being more severe than that of the first four. Between the sixth and seventh trumpets there is again an episode describing the preservation of the Church.

IV. The fourth Vision, 12:1–14: 20.

This vision describes the conflict of the world with the Church of God. The Church is represented as a woman bringing forth the Christ, against whom the dragon representing Satan wages war. In successive visions we behold the beasts which Satan will employ as his agents, the militant Church, and the advancing stages of Christ's conquest.

V. The fifth Vision, 15:1–16:21.

This vision once more reveals seven angels, now having seven vials or bowls containing the last plagues or judgments of God. First we have a description of the Church that triumphed over the beast, glorifying God; and this is followed by a picture of the sevenfold judgment of God on the world, represented by the seven vials.

VI. The sixth Vision, 17:1–20:15.

This vision reveals the harlot city Babylon, the representative of the world, and the victory of Christ over her and over the enemies that are in league with her, the great conflict ending in the last judgment.

VII. The seventh Vision, 21:1–22: 7.

This vision discloses to the eye the ideal Church, the new Jerusalem, and pictures in glowing colors her surpassing beauty and the everlasting, transcendent bliss of her inhabitants.

The book closes with an epilogue in which the seer describes its significance and urges the readers to keep the things that are written on its pages, 22:7–21.

Louis Berkhof

Detailed outline

Part One: The Past: "Things which thou hast seen" 1:1–20

I. Introduction: 1:1–3

II. Salutation: 1:4–6

III. Theme of the Revelation: 1:7–8

IV. Author: John 1:9–10

V. John's vision of the Lord: 1:10–18

A. His Person: Alpha and Omega, the Lord: 1:11

B. His position: In the middle of the churches (candlesticks): 1:12–13

C. His characteristics: 1:13–16

D. His message: 1:17–20

Part Two: The Present: "Things which are" 2:1–3:22

I. Messages to the churches: 2:1–3:22

A. Ephesus: 2:1–7

B. Smyrna: 2:8–11

C. Pergamos: 2:12–17

D. Thyatira: 2:18–29

E. Sardis: 3:1–6

F. Philadelphia: 3:7–13

G. Laodicea: 3:14–22

Part Three: The Future: "Things which shall be hereafter" 4:1–22:5

I. The control of events in the end time: 4:1–5:14

A. The Throne of God: 4:1–11

B. The Scroll: 5:1–5

C. The Lamb: 5:6–14

II. The wrath of the Lamb: 6:1–19:21

A. The seven seal judgments: 6:1–11:19

1. The first seal: 6:1–2

2. The second seal: 6:3–4

3. The third seal: 6:5–6

4. The fourth seal: 6:7–8

5. The fifth seal: 6:9–11

6. The sixth seal: 6:12–17

7. An interlude: 7:1–17

(a) On earth: The sealing of the servants of God: 7:1–8

(b) In Heaven: The singing of the servants of God: 7:9–17

8. The seventh seal: 8:1–11:19, consisting of seven trumpets:

(a) First trumpet: 8:7

(b) Second trumpet: 8:8–9

(c) Third trumpet: 8:10–11

(d) Fourth trumpet: 8:12–13

(e) Fifth trumpet: 9:1–12

(f) Sixth trumpet: 9:13–21

(g) Interlude: 10:1–11:14.

Seven events occur between the 6th and 7th trumpets.

(h) Seventh trumpet: 11:15–19

III. Prophecies: 12:1–14:20

A. The woman: 12:1–6

B. War in heaven: 12:7–12

C. War on earth: 12:13–17

D. The beast from the sea: 13:1–10

E. The beast from the earth: 13:11–18

F. The 144,000: 14:1–5

G. The announcements of the three angels: 14:6–13

H. The harvest judgment: 14:14–20

IV. Seven bowls of judgment: 15:1–19:6

A. Preparation for the bowl judgments: 15:1–8

B. The first bowl: 16:1–2

C. The second bowl: 16:3

D. The third bowl: 16:4–7

E. The fourth bowl: 16:8–9
F. The fifth bowl: 16:10–11
G. The sixth bowl: 16:12–16
H. The seventh bowl: 16:17–21
I. Overthrow of the great prostitute: 17:1–18
J. Description of the great prostitute: 17:1–6
K. Destruction of the great prostitute: 17:7–19
L. Overthrow of Babylon the Great: 18:1–19:6
M. Babylon the Great is destroyed: 18:1–8
N. Earth mourns Babylon the Great's destruction: 18:9–19
O. Heaven rejoices in Babylon the Great's destruction: 18:20–19:6

VIII. Prophecies about the second coming: 19:7–21
A. The marriage supper of the Lamb: 19:7–10
B. The second coming of Jesus: 19:11–21

IX. Prophecies about the millennium: 20:1–15
A. Satan is bound for 1,000 year: 20:1–3
B. Satan's 1,000 year reign: 20:4–6
C. Satan is released and the rebellion: 20:7–9
D. Satan's eternal torment: 20:10
E. The great white judgment throne: 20:11–15

X. Prophecies about the eternal state: 21:1–22:5
A. The creation of the new heaven and the new earth: 21:1
B. New Jerusalem descends: 21:2–8
C. Description of New Jerusalem: 21:9–22:5

Conclusion: Closing exhortations: 22:6–21

2. Helpful summaries of Revelation

Bird's eye view

The spiritual battle that takes place in every age.

Reading plan

The following reading plan, taking one reading per day, enables you to read through Revelation in nineteen days.

Revelation 1:1–1:20
Revelation 2:1–2:29
Revelation 3:1–3:22
Revelation 4:1–5:14
Revelation 6:1–6:17
Revelation 7:1–7:17
Revelation 8:1–8:13
Revelation 9:1–9:21
Revelation 10:1–11:19
Revelation 12:1–12:18
Revelation 13:1–13:18
Revelation 14:1–14:20
Revelation 15:1–16:21
Revelation 17:1–17:18
Revelation 18:1–18:24
Revelation 19:1–19:21
Revelation 20:1–20:15
Revelation 21:1–21:27
Revelation 22:1–22:21

Verses to memorize

Revelation 3:20

Behold, I stand at the door, and knock: if any man hear my voice, and open the door, I will come in to him, and will sup with him, and he with me. KJV

Revelation 4:11

Thou art worthy, O Lord, to receive glory and honor and power: for thou hast created all things, and for thy pleasure they are and were created. KJV

Revelation 21:4

And God shall wipe away all tears from their eyes; and there shall be no more death, neither sorrow, nor crying, neither shall there be any more pain: for the former things are passed away. KJV

Revelation 21:6

And he said unto me, It is done. I am Alpha and Omega, the beginning and the end. I will give unto him that is athirst of the fountain of the water of life freely. KJV

Statistics

Twenty-seventh New Testament book

22 chapters

404 verses

12,000 words

Number of Old Testament quotations and allusions in Revelation: 249.

Names/titles given

Greek title: *Apokalypsis Ioannou*: "Revelation of John."

First verse: *Apokalypsis Iesou Christoue*: "Revelation of Jesus Christ."

"Revelation of Jesus Christ by God."

"Apocalypse of John"

"Apocalypse of St. John the Divine"

"The book of the unveiling of the future."

"The seal of the whole Bible."

This book is sometimes called "Revelations" but this is quite wrong.

3. Helpful keys to turn to in understanding Revelation

Key words

Overcome

Seven

Key verses

Revelation 1:19; 19:11–15

Themes to study

The names and titles given to Jesus.

History is in God's hands.

The main different ways in which the book of Revelation should be interpreted.

"Sevens" in the book of Revelation

Seven churches in Asia: 1:4,11

Seven spirits: 1:4

Seven golden candlesticks (churches): 1:12,20

Seven stars (angels/messengers): 1:16,20

Letters to seven churches: 2:1–3:22

Seven lamps: 4:5

Seven seals: 5:1; 6:1–8:1

Seven horns: 5:6

Seven eyes: 5:6

Seven trumpets: 8:2–11:9

Seven thunders: 10:3–4

7,000 killed: 11:13

Seven heads: 12:3

Seven crowns: 12:3

Seven angels: 15:1

Seven plagues of God's wrath: 15:1–16:21
Seven mountains: 17:9
Seven kings: 17:10
Seven "beatitudes" (see below)

The seven "beatitudes" of Revelation

The book of Revelation records seven times that the Lord promises to bless his people. These are called the beatitudes of Revelation.

1.3

Blessed is he that readeth, and they that hear the words of this prophecy, and keep those things which are written therein: for the time is at hand. KJV

14:13

Blessed are the dead which die in the Lord from henceforth: Yea, saith the Spirit, that they may rest from their labors; and their works do follow them. KJV

16:15

Blessed is he that watcheth, and keepeth his garments, lest he walk naked, and they see his shame. KJV

19:9

Blessed are they which are called unto the marriage supper of the Lamb. KJV

20:6

Blessed and holy is he that hath part in the first resurrection: on such the second death hath no power, but they shall be priests of God and of Christ, and shall reign with him a thousand years. KJV

22:7

Blessed is he that keepeth the sayings of the prophecy of this book. KJV

22:14.

Blessed are they that do his commandments, that they may have right to the tree of life, and may enter in through the gates into the city. KJV

Pictures of heaven in Revelation

No sea, Rev. 21:1
No sorrow, Rev. 21:4
No pain, Rev. 21:4
No crying, Rev. 21:4
No death, Rev. 21:4
No curse, Rev. 22:3
No night, Rev. 22:5

Descriptions of those who have received salvation

"Dressed in white," Rev. 3:4; 7:13
"Washed their robes and made them white in the blood of the Lamb," Rev. 7:14
"they are before the throne of God," Rev. 7:15
"Never again will they hunger," Rev. 7:16
"For the Lamb at the center of the throne will be their shepherd," Rev. 7:17
"they may have the right to the tree of life," Rev. 22:14

Revelation and the Old Testament

Over five hundred allusions and quotations to the Old Testament have been identified in the book of Revelation.

Revelation's opening vision
1:12–18
See Ex. 25:31

The throne in heaven
4:1–5, 14
See Is. 6; Ezek. 1:27–28; 10:2, 20; Dan. 7:9–10; Zech. 4:10.

The four horsemen

6:1–8

See Zech. 1:8; 6:1–8; Ezek. 14:21; Jer. 15:2–3

The great earthquake

6:12–17

See Joel 2:30–31; Is. 2:19; 34:4; Hos. 10:8; Ezek. 32:7.

The sealing of God's people

7:1–8

See Ezek. 9:4

The vision of the redeemed

7:9–17

See Zech. 3:4; Is. 1:18; 49:10.

The four trumpets

8:7–12

See Joel 2:1; Ex. 9:24; 7:17–21; 10:21–23.

The three Woes

8:13–9:21

See Is. 14:12, 31; Joel 2:1–11.

The Temple measured

11:1–2

See Zech. 2:1–5; Ezek. 40:5f.

The two witnesses

11:3–13

See Zech. 4:11; Mal. 4:5.

The dragon and the beasts

12:-13:18

See Dan. 7:1–12:13.

War in heaven

12:7–9

Isa.14:12

The great harvest

14:14–20

See Joel 3:13; Is. 63:1–6.

The fall of Babylon

18:1–3

See Is. 21:9; Jer. 51:7,8,13; Nah. 3:4.

Lament over Babylon

18:4–24

See Ex. 26:1–28:6; Is. 13; 14; 34; Jer.50:51.

The marriage of the Lamb

19:5–9

See Hos. 2:19; Is. 54:1–8.

Gog and Magog

See Ezek. 38:1–39:29

The last judgment

20:11–15

See Dan. 7:9–10; 12:1–2.

The new Jerusalem

21:1–22:5

See Is. 65:17; 64:4; Ezek. 40:1–48:35; Zech. 14:8, 11.

Jesus in Revelation

In Revelation Jesus is our Coming King.

Descriptions of Jesus in Revelation

Jesus is the faithful Witness, 1:5.

Jesus is the Alpha and Omega, 1:8.

Jesus is the Lion of the tribe of Judah, 5:5.

Jesus is the Lamb, 17:14.

Jesus is the Word of God, 19:13.

Jesus is the King of kings and Lord of lords, 19:16.

Lessons to learn from Revelation

- History, as well as the present and the future, are in God's hands.
- God is, and will be our judge, and the judge of the world.
- We should increasingly long to be with Jesus in heaven.

4. Studying Revelation chapter by chapter

Revelation 1

Matthew Henry's introduction

This chapter is a general preface to the whole book, and contains,

I. An inscription, declaring the original and the design of it, vv. 1, 2.

II. The apostolic benediction pronounced on all those who shall pay a due regard to the contents of this book, vv. 3–8.

III. A glorious vision or appearance of the Lord Jesus Christ to the apostle John, when he delivered to him this revelation, v. 9, to the end.

Dr. Adam Clarke's analysis of chapter

The preface to this book, and the promise to them who read it, 1–3.

John's address to the seven Churches of Asia, whose high calling he particularly mentions; and shows the speedy coming of Christ, 4–8.

Mentions his exile to Patmos, and the appear ance of the Lord Jesus to him, 9–11.

Of whom he gives a most glorious description, 12–18.

The command to write what he saw, and the explanation of the seven stars and seven golden candlesticks, 19, 20.

A detailed analysis of chapter

The divine origin, the purpose, and the importance of this book. (1–3)

The apostle John greets the seven churches of Asia. (4–8)

Declares when, where, and how, the revelation was made to him. (9–11)

His vision, in which he saw Christ. (12–20)

Key verse

Verse 1: "The revelation of Jesus Christ, which God gave him to show his servants what must soon take place."

Key word / key phrase

Verse 1, "The revelation of Jesus Christ."

Key event / key person / key theme

John's vision

Key thought

In Revelation symbolism and metaphor are used to express God's final victory over all evil.

Key thing to look out for

Each aspect of the vision of Jesus is drawn from the Old Testament, notably Daniel 7. What is the overwhelming impression?

Key Bible cross-reference

Verse 4. See Exodus 3:14.

Key "by way of explanation"

Verse 8, "the Alpha and the Omega." This is the name given to Jesus. "Alpha" and "Omega" were the first and last letters of the Greek alphabet. Jesus rules everything, including history. The book may have been written about AD 95. John received this vision when he had been exiled to the Aegean island of Patmos.

Key "Quotable Quote"

"Christ is the Alpha and the Omega of the Bible, from the first verse in Genesis to the last verse in Revelation."

Octavius Winslow

Revelation 2

Matthew Henry's introduction

The apostle John, having in the previous chapter written the things which he had seen, now proceeds to write the things that are, according to the command of God (1:19), that is, the present state of the seven churches of Asia, with which he had a particular acquaintance, and for which he had a tender concern. He was directed to write to every one of them according to their present state and circumstances, and to inscribe every letter to the angel of that church, to the minister or rather ministry of that church, called angels because they are the messengers of God to mankind. In this chapter we have,

I. The message sent to Ephesus, vv. 1–7.

II. To Smyrna, vv. 8–11.

III. To Pergamos, vv. 12–17.

IV. To Thyatira, vv. 18–29.

Dr. Adam Clarke's analysis of chapter

The epistle to the Church of Ephesus, commend ing their labor and patience, 1–3.

And, reprehending their having left their first love, exhorting them to repent, with the promise of the tree of life, 4–7.

The epistle to the Church of Smyrna, commend ing their piety, and promising them support in their tribulation, 8–11.

The epistle to the Church of Pergamos, com mending their steadfastness in the heavenly doctrine, 12, 13.

And reprehending their laxity in ecclesiastical discipline, in tolerating heretical teachers in the Church, 14, 15.

The apostle exhorts them to repent, with the promise of the white stone and a new name, 16, 17.

The epistle to the Church of Thyatira, with a commendation of their charity, faith, and patience, 18, 19.

Reprehending their toleration of Jezebel, the false prophetess, who is threatened with grievous punishment, 20–23.

Particular exhortations and promises to this Church, 24–29.

A detailed analysis of chapter

To the Church at Ephesus; (1–7)

To the Church at Smyrna; (8–11)

To the Church at Pergamos; (12–17)

To the Church at Thyatira. (18–29)

Key verse

Verse 10: "Be faithful, even to the point of death, and I will give you the crown of life."

Key word / key phrase

Verse 7, "he who has an ear, let him hear."

Key event / key person / key theme

Letters to the first four of the seven churches

Key thought

Verse 2, the early Christians had to test the authenticity of the teaching of those who professed to teach in the name of Christ.

Key thing to look out for

Note the different reasons why each church is commended.

Key Bible cross-reference

Verse 8. See Isaiah 44:6.

Key "by way of explanation"

Each letter follows a pattern: the risen Christ, with a title taken from the opening, speaks to the church. He describes the church, giving a specific message. The letter ends with a warning to listen, and an encouragement to those who conquer. The letters reveal the pressure the churches were under to conform to the society around them.

Key "Quotable Quote"

"It is a bad world, an incredibly bad world. But I have discovered in the midst of it a quiet and holy people who have learned a great secret. They have found a joy which is a thousand times better than any pleasure of our sinful life. They are despised and persecuted, but they care not. They have overcome the world. These people are the Christians – and I am one of them."

Cyprian

Revelation 3

Matthew Henry's introduction

Here we have three more of the epistles of Christ to the churches:

I. To Sardis, vv. 1–6.

II. To Philadelphia, vv. 7–13.

III. To Laodicea, v. 14, to the end.

Dr. Adam Clarke's analysis of chapter

The epistle to the Church of Sardis, 1–6.

The epistle to the Church of Philadelphia, 7–13.

The epistle to the Church of Laodicea, 14–22.

A detailed analysis of chapter

Letters to the Church at Sardis (1–6);
at Philadelphia (7–13);
and Laodicea. (14–22)

Key verse

Verse 20: "Here I am! I stand at the door and knock. If anyone hears my voice and opens the door, I will come in and eat with him, and he with me."

Key word / key phrase

Verses 1, 8, 15, "I know."

Key event / key person / key theme

The last three of the seven letters to the churches

Key thought

Verse 14. We can rely absolutely on the witness of Christ.

Key thing to look out for

Note the different reasons why the six churches are reprimanded.

Key Bible cross-reference

Verse 7. See Isaiah 22:22.

Key "by way of explanation"

Verse 9, "synagogue of Satan." This refers to the aggressive Jews who attacked the beliefs of the early Christians. Each message matches the situation of the church. Laodicea was the wealthiest city in Asia (verse 14). Its water supply was drawn from hot springs five miles to the south, and the water was tepid by the time it reached Laodicea.

Key "Quotable Quote"

"Blessed is the soul at whose door Christ stands and knocks. Our door is faith. That is the door by which Christ enters."

Ambrose of Milan

Revelation 4

Matthew Henry's introduction

In this chapter the prophetical scene opens; and, as the epistolary part opened with a vision of Christ (ch. 1.), so this part is introduced with a glorious appearance of the great God, whose throne is in heaven, compassed about with the heavenly host. This discovery was made to John, and in this chapter he,

I. Records the heavenly sight he saw, vv. 1–7. And then,

II. The heavenly songs he heard, v. 8, to the end.

Dr. Adam Clarke's analysis of chapter

John sees the throne of God in heaven sur rounded by twenty-four elders; and four living creatures, full of eyes; which all join in giving glory to the Almighty, 1–11.

A detailed analysis of chapter

A vision of God on his glorious throne, around which were twenty-four elders and four living creatures. (1–7)

Songs of worship. (8–11)

Key verse

Verse 6: "In the center, around the throne, were four living creatures, and they were covered with eyes, in front and in back."

Key word / key phrase

Verse 2, "a throne in heaven."

Key event / key person / key theme

God's throne

Key thought

The activity in heaven is worship.

Key thing to look out for

What are the overwhelming impressions that you receive from this account of worship in heaven?

Key Bible cross-reference

Verse 5. See Exodus 19:16.

Key "by way of explanation"

Verse 7. Compare this verse with the vision Ezekiel was given of four living creatures in Ezekiel 1:6,10, where each creature had four faces, that of a human, lion, ox, and eagle.

Key "Quotable Quote"

"Worship is a meeting at the center so that our lives are centered on God and not lived eccentrically. People who do not worship are swept into a vast restlessness."

Eugene H. Peterson

Revelation 5

Matthew Henry's introduction

In the previous chapter the prophetical scene was opened, in the sight and hearing of the apostle, and he had a sight of God the Creator and ruler of the world, and the great King of the church. He saw God on the throne of glory and government, surrounded with his holy ones, and receiving their adorations. Now the counsels and decrees of God are set before the apostle, as in a book, which God held in his right hand; and this book is represented,

I. As sealed in the hand of God, vv. 1–9.

II. As taken into the hand of Christ the Redeemer, to be unsealed and opened, v. 6, to the end.

Dr. Adam Clarke's analysis of chapter

The book sealed with seven seals, which no being in heaven or earth could open, 1–3.

Is at last opened by the Lion of the tribe of Judah, 4–8.

He receives the praises of the four living crea tures and the twenty-four elders, 9, 10.

And afterwards of an innumerable multitude, who acknowledge that they were redeemed to God by his blood, 11, 12.

And then, of the whole creation, who ascribe blessing, honor, glory, and power to God and the Lamb for ever, 13, 14.

A detailed analysis of chapter

A book sealed with seven seals, which could only be opened by Christ. (1–7)

All honor is given to him, as he is worthy to open the scroll. (8–14)

Key verse

Verse 6: "Then I saw a Lamb, looking as if it had been slain, standing in the center of the throne, encircled by the four living creatures and the elders."

Key word / key phrase

Verse 1, "sealed with seven seals."

Key event / key person / key theme

The scroll of destiny

Key thought

The Lamb is the only one worthy to open the scroll of destiny.

Key thing to look out for

The reason why the Lamb is worthy.

Key Bible cross-reference

Verse 5. See Genesis 49:9.

Key "by way of explanation"

The major framework of the book consist of a series of sevens (seven standing for completeness): seven churches; the seven seals, seven trumpets and seven bowls (chapters 2–16). The seals, trumpets and bowls describe judgments.

Key "Quotable Quote"

"The last book of the Bible takes the entire biblical revelation and reimages it in a compelling, persuasive, evangelistic vision which has brought perseverance, stamina, joy and discipline to Christians for centuries."

Eugene H. Peterson

Revelation 6

Matthew Henry's introduction

The book of the divine counsels being thus lodged in the hand of Christ, he loses no time, but immediately enters on the work of opening the seals and publishing the contents; but this is done in such a manner as still leaves the predictions very abstruse and difficult to be understood. Hitherto the waters of the sanctuary have been as those in Ezekiel's vision, only to the ankles, or to the knees, or to the loins at least; but here they begin to be a river that cannot be passed over. The visions which John saw, the epistles to the churches, the songs of praise, in the two previous chapters, had some things dark and hard to be understood; and yet they were rather milk for babes than meat for strong men; but now we are to launch into the deep, and our business is not so much to fathom it as to let down our net to take a draught. We shall only hint at what seems most obvious. The prophecies of this book are divided into seven seals opened, seven trumpets sounding, and seven vials poured out. It is supposed that the opening of the seven seals discloses those providences that concerned the church in the first three centuries, from the ascension of our Lord and Savior to the reign of Constantine; this was represented in a book rolled up, and sealed in several places, so that, when one seal was opened, you might read so far of it, and so on, till the whole was unfolded. Yet we are not here told what was written in the book, but what John saw in figures enigmatical and hieroglyphic; and it is not for us to pretend to know "the times and seasons which the Father has put in his own power."

In this chapter six of the seven seals are opened, and the visions attending them are related; the first seal in vv. 1, 2, the second seal in vv. 3, 4, the third seal in vv. 5, 6, the fourth seal in vv. 7, 8, the fifth seal in vv. 9–11, the sixth seal in vv. 12, 13, etc.

Dr. Adam Clarke's analysis of chapter

What followed on the opening of the seven seals. The opening of the first seal; the white horse, 1, 2.

The opening of the second seal; the red horse, 3, 4.

The opening of the third seal; the black horse and the famine, 5, 6.

The opening of the fourth seal; the pale horse, 7, 8.

The opening of the fifth seal; the souls of men under the altar, 9–11.

The opening of the sixth seal; the earthquake, the darkening of the sun and moon, and falling of the stars, 12–14.

The terrible consternation of the kings and great men of the earth, 15–17.

A detailed analysis of chapter

The opening of the seals. The first, second, third, and fourth. (1–8)

The fifth. (9–11)

The sixth. (12–17)

Key verse

Verse 11: "Then each of them was given a white robe, and they were told to wait a little longer, until the number of their fellow servants and brothers who were to be killed as they had been was completed."

Key word / key phrase

Verse 1, "opened the first of the seven seals."

Key event / key person / key theme

Six seals opened, revealing future events

Key thought

The terror on the earth because of God's judgment.

Key thing to look out for

Why had the martyrs been slain?

Key Bible cross-reference

Verse 8. See Ezekiel 14:21. Four horses: see Zechariah 6.

Key "by way of explanation"

The breaking of the first four seals brings in the four horsemen, with a deadly role to play. "The appearance of the horsemen marks 'the beginning of birth pangs" which herald the winding up of the first age (Mark 13:8)" (F.F. Bruce).

Key "Quotable Quote"

"I tell you, brethren, if mercies and if judgments do not convert you, God has no other arrows in his quiver."

Robert Murray M'Cheyne

Revelation 7

Matthew Henry's introduction

The things contained in this chapter came in after the opening of the six seals, which foretold great calamities in the world; and before the sound of the seven trumpets, which gave notice of great corruptions arising in the church: between these comes in this comfortable chapter, which secures the graces and comforts of the people of God in times of common calamity. We have,

I. An account of the restraint laid on the winds, vv. 1–3.

II. The sealing of the servants of God, vv. 4–8.

III. The songs of angels and saints on this occasion, vv. 9–12.

IV. A description of the honor and happiness of those who had faithfully served Christ, and suffered for him, v. 13, etc.

Dr. Adam Clarke's analysis of chapter

The four angels holding the four winds of heaven, 1.

The angel with the seal of the living God, and sealing the servants of God out of the twelve tribes, whose number amounted to one hun dred and forty-four thousand, 2–8.

Besides these, there was an innumerable multi tude from all nations, who gave glory to God and the Lamb, 9–12.

One of the elders shows who these are, and describes their most happy state, 13–17.

A detailed analysis of chapter

A pause between two great periods. (1–3)

The peace, happiness, and safety of the saints, as seen in an angel's sealing 144,000. (4–8)

A song of praise. (9–12)

The blessedness and glory of those that suffered martyrdom for Christ. (13–17)

Key verse

Verse 10: "And they cried out in a loud voice: 'Salvation belongs to our God, who sits on the throne, and to the Lamb.'"

Key word / key phrase

Verse 4, "144,000."

Key event / key person / key theme

Sealing and martyrs

Key thought

The "seal" is the Name and "Name" denotes character (14:1; 22:4). The people who belong to God are protected during the coming judgments.

Key thing to look out for

The description of the new age (15–17) (cf. Isaiah 40:11; 25:8; 40:10) when believers will serve God.

Key Bible cross-reference

Verse 1: See Jeremiah 49:36.

Key "by way of explanation"

Verse 4, "1444,000." This is a symbolic number and stands for faithful believers. It is a "great multitude" and consists of people from "every nation, tribe, people, and language," verse 9. Verse 1, the winds are the wins of judgment.

Key "Quotable Quote"

"It is the happiness of heaven to have God be all in all."

Jeremiah Burroughs

Revelation 8

Matthew Henry's introduction

We have already seen what occurred on opening six of the seals; we now come to the opening of the seventh, which introduced the sounding of the seven trumpets; and a direful scene now opens. Most expositors agree that the seven seals represent the interval between the apostle's time and the reign of Constantine, but that the seven trumpets are designed to represent the rise of antichrist, some time after the empire became Christian.

In this chapter we have,

I. The preface, or prelude, to the sounding of the trumpets, vv. 1–6.

II. The sounding of four of the trumpets, v. 7, etc.).

Dr. Adam Clarke's analysis of chapter

The opening of the seventh seal, 1.

The seven angels with the seven trumpets, 2–6.

The first sounds, and there is a shower of hail, fire, and blood, 7.

The second sounds, and the burning mountain is cast into the sea, 8, 9.
The third sounds, and the great star Wormwood falls from heaven, 10, 11.
The fourth sounds, and the sun, moon, and stars are smitten; and a threefold wo is denounced against the inhabitants of the earth, because of the three angels who are yet to sound, 12, 13.

A detailed analysis of chapter

The seventh seal is opened and seven angels appear with seven trumpets, ready to proclaim God's purposes. (1, 2)

Another angel throws down fire on the earth, which produces terrible storms of judgment. (3–5)

The seven angels prepare to sound their trumpets. (6)

Four sound them. (7–12)

Another angel announces greater woes to come. (13)

Key verse

Verse 2: "And I saw the seven angels who stand before God, and to them were given seven trumpets."

Key word / key phrase

Verse 1, "the seventh seal."

Key event / key person / key theme

The seventh seal, the censer, and the first four trumpets.

Key thought

Verse 1. In silent suspense heaven waits the final judgment, but the opening of the seventh seal introduces further judgments.

Key thing to look out for

The way in which all creation suffers as the result of human sin.

Key Bible cross-reference

Verse 7. See Exodus 9:23–25.

Key "by way of explanation"

Verse 2, "seven trumpets." In the Old Testament trumpets were used to herald some important event or to give instructions to troops in battle.

Key "Quotable Quote"

"God hath appointed a day, wherein he will judge the world by Jesus Christ, when every one shall receive according to his deeds; the wicked shall go into everlasting punishment; the righteous, into everlasting life."

Southern Baptist Theological Seminary

Revelation 9

Matthew Henry's introduction

In this chapter we have an account of the sounding of the fifth and sixth trumpets, the appearances that attended them, and the events that were to follow; the fifth trumpet (vv. 1–12), the sixth, v. 13, etc..

Dr. Adam Clarke's analysis of chapter

The fifth angel sounds, and a star falls from heaven to earth, 1.

The bottomless pit is opened, and locusts come out on the earth, 2, 3.

Their commission, 4–6.

Their form, 7–10.

Their government, 11, 12.

The sixth angel sounds, and the four angels bound in the Euphrates are loosed, 13–15.

The army of horsemen, and their description, 16–19.

Though much evil is inflicted on men for their idolatry, 20, 21.

A detailed analysis of chapter

The fifth trumpet and the star falling from heaven; the opening of the bottomless pit, out of which come swarms of locusts. (1–12)

The sixth trumpet is followed by the freeing of four angels bound in the great river Euphrates. (13–21)

Key verse

Verse 11: "They had as king over them the angel of the Abyss, whose name in Hebrew is Abaddon, and in Greek, Apollyon."

Key word / key phrase

Verse 1, "the Abyss," (the dwelling-place of demons)

Key event / key person / key theme

The fifth and sixth trumpet

Key thought

These malign demon-horsemen released from the Abyss wreak hideous destruction (the fire, smoke and sulfur, verse 8, betray their origin).

Key thing to look out for

Even facing God's judgment some refused to repent (verse 20).

Key Bible cross-reference

Verse 2. See Genesis 19:28.

Key "by way of explanation"

Verse 1, "sounded his trumpet." The seven trumpets of chapters 8 – 9, and also of 11:15–19 announce the plagues. These are worse than the seals, but not as bad as the bowls. Verse 11, "Abaddon," and "Apollyon" both mean destruction.

Key "Quotable Quote"

"The law opens not nor makes visible God's grace and mercy, or the righteousness whereby we obtain everlasting life and salvation, but our sins, our weakness, death, God's wrath and judgment."

Martin Luther

Revelation 10

Matthew Henry's introduction

This chapter is an introduction to the latter part of the prophecies of this book. Whether what is contained between this and the sounding of the seventh trumpet (11:15) be a distinct prophecy from the other, or only a more general account of some of the principal things included in the other, is disputed by our curious enquirers into these abstruse writings. However, here we have,

I. A remarkable description of a very glorious angel with an open book in his hand, vv. 1–3.

II. An account of seven thunders which the apostle heard, as echoing to the voice of this angel, and communicating some discoveries, which the apostle was not yet allowed to write, v. 4.

III. The solemn oath taken by him who had the book in his hand, vv. 5–7.

IV. The charge given to the apostle, and observed by him, vv. 8–11.

Dr. Adam Clarke's analysis of chapter

The description of a mighty angel with a little book in his hand, 1, 2.

The seven thunders, 3, 4.

The angel swears that there shalt be time no longer, 5–7.

John is commanded to take the little book and eat it; he does so, and receives a commission to prophesy to many peoples, 8–11.

A detailed analysis of chapter

The angel of the covenant presents a little open book, which is followed by seven thunders. (1–4)

At the end of the following prophecies, time should be no more. (5–7)

A voice directs the apostle to eat the book (8–10);

and tells him he must prophesy further. (11)

Key verse

Verse 11: "You must prophesy again about many peoples, nations, languages and kings."

Key word / key phrase

Verse 9, "the little scroll."

Key event / key person / key theme

The little scroll

Key thought

The contents of the scroll were sweet, because they were God's word, but bitter to digest because they concerned judgment (cf. Ezekiel 3:3,14).

Key thing to look out for

The contents of the scroll are given in Revelation 11:1–13.

Key Bible cross-reference

Verses 5–7. See Exodus 20:11.

Key "by way of explanation"

Verse 9, "Take it and eat it." John had to read, mark, learn and inwardly digest the contents of the scroll. See Psalm 119:103.

Key "Quotable Quote"

"Even if I were attempting to study the Scriptures and nothing else, from boyhood to decrepit old age, with the utmost leisure, the most unwearied zeal, and with talents greater than I possess, I would still be making progress in discovering their treasures."

Augustine of Hippo

Revelation 11

Matthew Henry's introduction

In this chapter we have an account,

I. Of the measuring–reed given to the apostle, to take the dimensions of the temple, vv. 1, 2.

II. Of the two witnesses of God, vv. 3–13.

III. Of the sounding of the seventh trumpet, and what followed on it, v. 14, etc.

Dr. Adam Clarke's analysis of chapter

The command to measure the temple, 1,2.

The two witnesses which should prophesy twelve hundred and sixty days, 3.

The description, power, and influence of these witnesses, 4–6.

They shall be slain by the beast which shall arise out of the bottomless pit, and shall arise again after three days and a half, and ascend to heaven, 7–12.

After which shall be a great earthquake, 13.

The introduction to the third wo, 14.

The sounding of the seventh angel, and the four and twenty elders give glory to God, 15–19.

A detailed analysis of chapter

The state of the Church is represented by a temple which is measured. (1,2)

Two witnesses prophesy is sackcloth. (3–6)

They are killed, after which they arise and ascend to heaven. (7–14)

The seventh trumpet. (15–19)

Key verse

Verse 4: "These are the two olive trees and the two lamp stands that stand before the Lord of the earth"

Key word / key phrase

Verse 3, "my two witnesses."

Key event / key person / key theme

The two witnesses and the seventh trumpet

Key thought

It has been suggested that verses 1–4 refer to the literal Jerusalem temple and a period when its outer court was occupied by Rome (the 42 months). This historical event is moved into John's apocalyptic vision – the temple is now the people of God.

Key thing to look out for

The reasons for praising God.

Key Bible cross-reference

Verse 1. See Ezekiel 40:3.

Key "by way of explanation"

Verse 3, "1,260 days." In verse 2 there are said to be "42 months." The 1,260 days are made up of 30 days, that is 42x30=1,260. This period of time was a symbol (taken from Daniel) for a period of Gentile domination.

Key "Quotable Quote"

"Man's chief work is the praise of God."

Augustine of Hippo

Revelation 12

Matthew Henry's introduction

It is generally agreed by the most learned expositors that the narrative we have in this and the two following chapters, from the sounding of the seventh trumpet to the opening of the vials, is not a prediction of things to come, but rather a recapitulation and representation of things past, which, as God would have the apostle to foresee while future, he would have him to review now that they were past, that he might have a more perfect idea of them in his mind, and might observe the agreement between the prophecy and that Providence that is always fulfilling the scriptures. In this chapter we have an account of the contest between the church and antichrist, the seed of the woman and the seed of the serpent.

I. As it was begun in heaven, vv. 1–11.

II. As it was carried on in the wilderness, v. 12, etc.

Dr. Adam Clarke's analysis of chapter

The woman clothed with the sun, and in travail, 1, 2.

The great red dragon waiting to devour the child as soon as born, 3, 4.

The woman is delivered of a son, who is caught up unto God; and she flees to the wilderness, 5, 6.

The war in heaven between Michael and the dragon, 7, 8.

The dragon and his angels are overcome and cast down to the earth; whereon the whole heavenly host give glory to God, 9–11.

The dragon, full of wrath at his defeat, perse cutes the woman, 12, 13. She flees to the wilderness, whither he attempts to pursue her; and he makes war with her seed, 14–17.

A detailed analysis of chapter

A description of the messianic community and of Satan, represented by a woman and a great red dragon. (1–6)

Michael and his angels fight against the devil and his angels, who are defeated. (7–12)

The dragon persecutes the Church. (13, 14)

His unsuccessful attempt to destroy her. He renews his war against her descendants. (14–17)

Key verse

Verse 9: "The great dragon was hurled down – that ancient serpent called the devil, or Satan, who leads the whole world astray. He was hurled to the earth, and his angels with him."

Key word / key phrase

Verse 1, "a woman clothed with the sun."

Key event / key person / key theme

The woman, war in heaven and on earth

Key thought

The victory of Christ and ruin of Satan (the dragon).

Key thing to look out for

The reason for the devil's fury (verse 12) and the believers' victory (verse 11).

Key Bible cross-reference

Verse 5. See Psalm 2:9.

Key "by way of explanation"

Verse 3. In the Old Testament dragons are used metaphorically to stand for God's enemies. The woman probably symbolizes the true Israel, out of which the Messiah came (verse 5).

Key "Quotable Quote"

"In the buzzing, booming confusion of good and evil, blessing and cursing, rest and conflict, St John discovers pattern and design. He hears rhythms. He discovers arrangement and proportion. He communicates an overpowering sense of an ending."

Eugene H. Peterson

Revelation 13

Matthew Henry's introduction

We have, in this chapter, a further discovery and description of the church's enemies: not other enemies than are mentioned before, but described after another manner, that the methods of their enmity may more fully appear. They are represented as two beasts; the first you have an account of (vv. 1–10) the second, v. 11, etc. By the first some understand Rome pagan, and by the second Rome papal; but others understand Rome papal to be represented by both these beasts, by the first in its secular power, by the second in its ecclesiastical.

Dr. Adam Clarke's analysis of chapter

The beast rising out of the sea with seven heads, ten horns, and ten crowns, 1. His description, power, blasphemy, cruelty, 2–10.

The beast coming out of the earth with two horns, deceiving the world by is false mira cles, and causing every one to receive his mark in their right hand, 11–17.

His number, 666. 18.

A detailed analysis of chapter

A wild beast rises out of the sea, to whom the dragon gives his power. (1–10)

Another beast, which has two horns like a lamb, but speaks as a dragon. (11–15)

It makes everyone worship its image, and receive its mark, as people who are given over to it. (16–18)

Key verse

Verse 6: "He opened his mouth to blaspheme God, and to slander his name and his dwelling place and those who live in heaven."

Key word / key phrase

Verse 1, "a beast coming out of the sea."

Key event / key person / key theme

The beast from the sea, and from the land

Key thought

The evil power of the beast out of the sea (perhaps the Roman Empire), and the beast out of the earth (may be the false prophet, 16:13). Today the beast might be said to represent totalitarian world power; and the prophet, false religion.

Key thing to look out for

The qualities needed by Christians (verses 10, 18; also 14:12)

Key Bible cross-reference

Verses 1–7. See Daniel 7.

Key "by way of explanation"

Verse 13, "miraculous signs" do not always come from God and are not always intended to bring him glory, but rather, to deceive his followers. See Deuteronomy 13:1–3; Matthew 24:24.

Key "Quotable Quote"

"Nothing great was ever done without much enduring."

Catherine of Siena

Revelation 14

Matthew Henry's introduction

After an account of the great trials and sufferings which the servants of God had endured, we have now a more pleasant scene opening; the day begins now to dawn, and here we have represented,

I. The Lord Jesus at the head of his faithful followers, vv. 1–5.

II. Three angels sent successively to proclaim the fall of Babylon and the things antecedent and consequent to so great an event, vv. 6–13.

III. The vision of the harvest, v. 14, etc.

Dr. Adam Clarke's analysis of chapter

The Lamb on mount Sion, and his company and their character, 1–5.

The angel flying in the midst of heaven, with the everlasting Gospel, 6, 7.

Another angel proclaims the fall of Babylon, 8.

A third angel denounces God's judgments against those who worship the beast or his image, 9–11.

The patience of the saints, and the blessedness of them who die in the Lord, 12, 13.

The man on the white cloud, with a sickle, reaping the earth, 14–16.

The angel with the sickle commanded by another angel, who had power over fire, to gather the clusters of the vines of the earth, 17, 18.

They are gathered and thrown into the great winepress of God's wrath, which is trodden without the city, and the blood comes out 1600 furlongs, 19, 20.

A detailed analysis of chapter

Those who remain faithful to Christ praise God. (1–5)

Three angels; one proclaiming the everlasting gospel; another, the downfall of Babylon; and a third, the dreadful wrath of God on the worshipers of the beast. The happy state of those who die in the Lord. (6–13)

A vision of Christ with a sickle, and of a harvest ready to be cut down. (14–16)

The symbol of a ripe grape harvest, trodden in the wine-press of God's wrath. (17–20)

Key verse

Verse 1: "Then I looked, and there before me was the Lamb, standing on Mount Zion, and with him 144,000 who had his name and his Father's name written on their foreheads."

Key word / key phrase

Verse 1, "the Lamb."

Key event / key person / key theme

The vision of the Lamb and of the harvest

Key thought

An interlude to encourage believers. There is victory and rest for those who remain faithful.

Key thing to look out for

Note what can be gleaned about the 144,000 (the true followers) verses 1–5. (Verse 4 probably symbolizes purity of heart.)

Key Bible cross-reference

Verse 1: See Ezekiel 9:4.

Key "by way of explanation"

Verse 10, "cup of wrath." In the Old Testament, God's wrath is often pictured as a cup full of wine which has to be drunk. See Psalm 75:8; Jeremiah 25:15.

Key "Quotable Quote"

"Jesus is our mouth, through which we speak to the Father; He is our eye, through which we see the Father; He is our right hand through which we offer ourselves to the Father. Unless He intercedes, there is no intercourse with God."

Ambrose

Revelation 15

Matthew Henry's introduction

Hitherto, according to the judgment of very eminent expositors, God had represented to his servant, John,

I. The state of the church under the pagan powers, in the six seals opened; and then,

II. The state of the church under the papal powers, in the vision of the six trumpets that began to sound on the opening of the seventh seal: and then is inserted.

III. A more general and brief account of the past, present, and future state of the church, in the little book, etc. He now proceeds,

IV. To show him how antichrist should be destroyed, by what steps that destruction should be accomplished, in the vision of the seven vials. This chapter contains an awful introduction or preparation for the pouring out of the vials, in which we have,

A. A sight of those angels in heaven who were to have the execution of this great work, and with what acclamations of joy the heavenly hosts applauded the great design, vv. 1–4.

B. A sight of these angels coming out of heaven to receive those vials which they were to pour out, and the great commotions this caused in the world, v. 5, etc.

Dr. Adam Clarke's analysis of chapter

The seven angels with the seven last plagues, 1.

The sea of glass, and those who had a victory over the beast, 2.

The song of Moses and the Lamb, 3, 4.

The temple in heaven opened, 5.

Seven angels come out of the temple, who receive from one of the four living creatures seven golden vials full of the wrath of God, 6–8.

A detailed analysis of chapter

A song of praise is sung by the Church. (1–4)

Seven angels with the seven plagues. To them one of the living creatures gives seven golden bowls full of God's wrath. (5–8)

Key verse

Verse 2: "And I saw what looked like a sea of glass mixed with fire and, standing beside the sea, those who had been victorious over the beast and his image and over the number of his name."

Key word / key phrase

Verse 3, "the song of the Lamb."

Key event / key person / key theme

The victory song of the redeemed

Key thought

After the song comes a further unfolding of God's purposes and judgment ("was opened" verse 5).

Key thing to look out for

What we are told here about the nature of God.

Key Bible cross-reference

Verse 5. See Exodus 38:21.

Key "by way of explanation"

Verse 3, "song of Moses." This is recorded in Exodus 15 and Deuteronomy 32. The song of Moses and the "song of the Lamb" both express God's triumph over his enemies. Verse 2. They were victorious because they did not worship the beast or let themselves be marked with his number (13:15–17).

Key "Quotable Quote"

"By engaging with the power of the devil, the fear of death, and the pains of hell, Christ gained the victory, and achieved a triumph, so that we now fear not in death those things which our Prince has destroyed."

John Calvin

Revelation 16

Matthew Henry's introduction

In this chapter we have an account of the pouring forth of these vials that were filled with the wrath of God. They were poured out on the whole antichristian empire, and on every thing appertaining to it.

I. On the earth, v. 2.
II. On the sea, v. 3.
III. On the rivers and fountains of water, v. 4. Here the heavenly hosts proclaim and applaud the righteousness of the judgments of God.
IV. The fourth vial was poured out on the sun, v. 8.
V. The fifth on the seat of the beast.
VI. The sixth on the river Euphrates.
VII. The seventh in the air, on which the cities of the nations fell, and great Babylon came in remembrance before God.

Dr. Adam Clarke's analysis of chapter

The angels are commanded to pour out their vials on the earth, 1.

The first pours out his vial on the earth, by which a grievous sore is produced, 2.

The second angel pours out his trial on the sea, and it is turned into blood, 3.

The third angel pours out his vial on the rivers and fountains, and they are turned also into blood, 4–7.

The fourth angel pours out his vial on the sun, and men are scorched with fire, 8, 9.

The fifth angel pours out his vial on the throne of the beast, 10, 11.

The sixth angel pours out his vial on the river Euphrates, 12.

Three unclean spirits come out of the mouth of the beast, dragon and false prophet: and go forth to gather all the kings of the world to battle, in the place called Armageddon, 13–16.

The seventh angel pours out his vial on the air, on which followed thunders, lightnings, earth-quakes, and extraordinary hail, 17–21.

A detailed analysis of chapter

The first bowl is poured out on the earth, the second on the sea, the third on the rivers and fountains. (1–7)

The fourth on the sun, the fifth on the throne of the beast. (8–11)

The sixth on the great river Euphrates. (12–16)

And the seventh into the air, after which will follow the destruction of all antichristian enemies. (17–21)

Key verse

Verse 16: "Then they gathered the kings together to the place that in Hebrew is called Armageddon."

Key word / key phrase

Verse 1, "pour out the seven bowls."

Key event / key person / key theme

The bowls of God's anger

Key thought

These judgments are similar to the previous judgments but more severe because they affect the whole area.

Key thing to look out for

"More terrible than the plagues themselves is the way in which those on whom they fall are but hardened in their impenitence." (F.F. Bruce)

Key Bible cross-reference

Verse 10. See Exodus 10:21.

Key "by way of explanation"

Verse 16, "Armageddon." This depicts the unspecified place where the final battle to overthrow evil will take place.

Key "Quotable Quote"

"The existence of evil is not so much an obstacle to faith in God as a proof of God's existence, a challenge to turn toward that in which love triumphs over hatred, union over division, and eternal life over death."

N.A. Berdyaev

Revelation 17

Matthew Henry's introduction

This chapter contains another representation of those things that had been revealed before about the wickedness and ruin of antichrist. This antichrist had been before represented as a beast, and is now described as a great whore. And here,

I. The apostle is invited to see this vile woman, vv. 1, 2.

II. He tells us what an appearance she made, vv. 3–6.
III. The mystery of it is explained to him, vv. 7–12. And,
IV. Her ruin foretold, v. 13, etc.

Dr. Adam Clarke's analysis of chapter

The judgment of the great whore, which sits on many waters, 1, 2.
Her description, name, and conduct, 3–6.
The angel explains the mystery of the woman, of the beast, 7–18.

A detailed analysis of chapter

One of the angels who had the bowls explains the meaning of the previous vision of the antichristian beast that was to reign 1260 years, and then to be destroyed. (1–6)
The angel interprets the mystery of the woman, and the beast that had seven heads and ten horns. (7–18)

Key verse

Verse 17: "For God has put it into their hearts to accomplish his purpose by agreeing to give the beast their power to rule, until God's words are fulfilled."

Key word / key phrase

Verse 1, "punishment of the great prostitute."

Key event / key person / key theme

Overthrow of the great prostitute

Key thought

What effect do the descriptions of evil in this book have on us?

Key thing to look out for

How can we best fight evil and promote good?

Key Bible cross-reference

Verse 4. See Jeremiah 51:7.

Key "by way of explanation"

Verse 14, "Lord of lords and King of kings." In the middle of great evil God's power and sovereignty are reflected in this title of his. Verse 5, "Mystery," that is, the name is to be understood symbolically. In Revelation Babylon refers to Rome.

Key "Quotable Quote"

"People account it a great thing to have friendship and fellowship with an earthly king; how incomparably greater is the privilege of having fellowship and friendship with God, who is the King of kings, and the Lord of lords."

Tikhon of Zadonsk

Revelation 18

Matthew Henry's introduction

We have here,

I. An angel proclaiming the fall of Babylon, vv. 1, 2.
II. Assigning the reasons of her fall, v. 3.
III. Giving warning to all who belonged to God to come out of her (vv. 4, 5), and to assist in her destruction, vv. 6–8.
IV. The great lamentation made for her by those who had been large sharers in her sinful pleasures and profits, vv. 9–19.

V. The great joy that there would be among others at the sight of her irrecoverable ruin, v. 20, etc.

Dr. Adam Clarke's analysis of chapter

A luminous angel proclaims the fall of Babylon, and the cause of it, 1–3.

The followers of God are exhorted to come out of it, in order to escape her approaching punishment, 4–8.

The kings of the earth lament her fate, 9, 10. The merchants also bewail her, 11.

The articles in which she trafficked enumerated, 12–16.

She is bewailed also by shipmasters, sailors, 17–19.

All heaven rejoices over her fall, and her final desolation is foretold, 20–24.

A detailed analysis of chapter

Another angel from heaven proclaims the fall of mystical Babylon. (1–3)

A voice from heaven admonishes the people of God in case they take part in her plagues. (4–8)

The lamentations over her. (9–19)

The Church called on to rejoice in her utter ruin. (20–24)

Key verse

Verse 1: "After this I saw another angel coming down from heaven. He had great authority, and the earth was illuminated by his splendor."

Key word / key phrase

Verse 2, "Fallen is Babylon."

Key event / key person / key theme

Babylon's fall

Key thought

Rome's great wealth came from exploitation of others and callous indifference to people's needs (verse 13).

Key thing to look out for

There are parallels between Rome and Western society. What can Christians do?

Key Bible cross-reference

Verse 11. See Ezekiel 27:31.

Key "by way of explanation"

Verse 2, "Fallen is Babylon." Babylon stands for any political system that opposes God. It stands for political power, decadence, and hatred of God's faithful followers. Here Babylon's fall is celebrated.

Key "Quotable Quote"

"To comment in detail on this severe and vivid poetry would be like trying to analyze every note in a piece of music: we wouldn't hear the tune. It is best simply to read it, perhaps aloud, and sense how tragic, how poignant, how catastrophic and inevitable is the collapse of a world power which overreaches itself."

Stephen Travis

Revelation 19

Matthew Henry's introduction

In this chapter we have,

I. A further account of the triumphant song of

angels and saints for the fall of Babylon, vv. 1–4.

II. The marriage between Christ and the church proclaimed and perfected, vv. 5–10.

III. Another warlike expedition of the glorious head and husband of the church, with the success of it, v. 10, etc.

Dr. Adam Clarke's analysis of chapter

The whole heavenly host give glory to God, because he has judged the great whore, and avenged the blood of his saints, 1–6.

The marriage of the Lamb and his bride, 7–9.

John offers to worship the angel, but is pre vented, 10.

Heaven is opened, and Jesus the Word of God appears on a white horse; he and his armies described, 11–16.

An angel in the sun invites all the fowls of heaven to come to the supper of the great God, 17, 18.

The beast, the false prophet, and the kings of the earth, gather together to make war with him who sits on the white horse; but they are all discomfited, and utterly destroyed, 19–21.

A detailed analysis of chapter

Joy at God's victory over Babylon. (1–5)

The marriage of the Lamb. (6–10)

A vision of Christ going out to destroy the beast and his armies. (11–21)

Key verse

Verse 6: "Then I heard what sounded like a great multitude, like the roar of rushing waters and like loud peals of thunder, shouting: "Hallelujah! For our Lord God Almighty reigns."

Key word / key phrase

Verse 7, "the wedding of the Lamb."

Key event / key person / key theme

The marriage of the Lamb, and the rider on the white horse

Key thought

These hymns of praise should be used in our own worship and prayers.

Key thing to look out for

What do verses 11–16 show about Christ?

Key Bible cross-reference

Verses 7–9. See Mark 2:19; 2 Corinthians 11:2; Ephesians 5:25–27.

Key "by way of explanation"

Verses 11–16 give a symbolic picture of Christ in his Second Coming. The white horse is a symbol of victory. Verses 7–21 are a further reference to the Battle of Armageddon (see 16:14–16).

Key "Quotable Quote"

"Praise is a soul in flower."

Thomas Watson

Revelation 20

Matthew Henry's introduction

This chapter is thought by some to be the darkest part of all this prophecy: it is very probable that the things contained in it are not yet accomplished; and therefore it is the wiser way to content ourselves with general observations, rather than to be positive and particular in our explications of it. Here we have an account,

I. Of the binding of Satan for a thousand years, vv. 1–3.

II. The reign of the saints with Christ for the same time, vv. 4–6.

III. Of the loosing of Satan, and the conflict of the church with Gog and Magog, vv. 7–10.

IV. Of the day of judgment, v. 11, etc.

Dr. Adam Clarke's analysis of chapter

An angel binds Satan a thousand years, and shuts him up in the bottomless pit, 1–3.

They who were beheaded for the testimony of Jesus, who have part in the first resurrection, and shall reign with Christ a thousand years, 4–6.

When the thousand years are expired, Satan shall be loosed out of his prison, shall go forth and deceive the nations, and shall gather Gog and Magog from the four corners of the earth, 7, 8.

These shall besiege the holy city; but fire shall come down from heaven and consume them, and they and the devil be cast into a lake of fire, 9, 10.

The great white throne, and the dead, small and great, standing before God, and all judged according to their works, 11, 12.

The sea, death, and hades, give up their dead, and are destroyed; and all not found in the book of life are cast into the lake of fire, 13–15.

A detailed analysis of chapter

Satan is bound and the martyrs reign. (1–6)

Satan set free. Gog and Magog. (7–10)

The last judgment. (11–15)

Key verse

Verse 1: "And I saw an angel coming down out of heaven, having the key to the Abyss and holding in his hand a great chain."

Key word / key phrase

Verse 2, "He seized the dragon."

Key event / key person / key theme

Binding Satan and the reign of the martyrs, Gog and Magog, and the final judgment

Key thought

Satan will finally be utterly defeated, and all humankind will be judged. This is a judgment of each individual.

Key thing to look out for

Verses 11–15, the scene is awesome in its grandeur and gravity. What is the basis of the judgment?

Key Bible cross-reference

Verses 11, 12. See Daniel 7:9, 10.

Key "by way of explanation"

Verse 4, "those who had been beheaded." This refers to Christian martyrs of all ages. Gog and Magog represent all the nations who make one final attack on God. Verse 2 "thousand years": the millennium. There are different views about the order of events, the meaning of the "thousand years" and "the first resurrection."

Key "Quotable Quote"

"In order to avoid lying to our interrogators or deceiving them, we freely go to our deaths confessing Christ."

Justin Martyr

Revelation 21

Matthew Henry's introduction

Hitherto the prophecy of this book has presented to us a very remarkable mixture of light and shade, prosperity and adversity, mercy and judgment, in the conduct of divine Providence towards the church in the world: now, at the close of all, the day breaks, and the shadows flee away; a new world now appears, the former having passed away. Some are willing to understand all that is said in these last two chapters of the state of the church even here on earth, in the glory of the latter days; but others, more probably, take it as a representation of the perfect and triumphant state of the church in heaven. Let but the faithful saints and servants of God wait awhile, and they shall not only see, but enjoy, the perfect holiness and happiness of that world. In this chapter you have,

I. An introduction to the vision of the new Jerusalem, vv. 1–9.

II. The vision itself, v. 10, etc.

Dr. Adam Clarke's analysis of chapter

The new heaven and the new earth, 1.

The new Jerusalem, 2.

God dwells with men; the happy state of his followers, 3–7.

The wretched state of the ungodly, 8.

An angel shows John the holy city, the New Jerusalem, 9, 10.

Her light, wall, gates, and foundations, described, 11–21.

God and the Lamb are the temple and light of it, 22, 23.

The nations and kings of the earth bring their glory and honor to it; the gates shall never be shut, nor shall any defilement enter into it, 24–27.

A detailed analysis of chapter

A new heaven, and new earth: the new Jerusalem where God dwells, and all sorrow is banished from his people. (1–8)

Its heavenly origin, glory, and secure defense. (9–21)

More details about the new Jerusalem. (22–27)

Key verse

Verse 6: "It is done. I am the Alpha and the Omega, the Beginning and the End. To him who is thirsty I will give to drink without cost from the spring of the water of life."

Key word / key phrase

Verse 1, "a new heaven and a new earth."

Key event / key person / key theme

The new Jerusalem

Key thought

In the new Jerusalem God will be fully with his people. (To John a city was a place of community and happiness).

Key thing to look out for

What are the characteristics of the new Jerusalem?

Key Bible cross-reference

Verse 1. See Isaiah 65:17.

Key "by way of explanation"

Verse 4, "wipe every tear." In heaven, not only will tears be wiped away, but all reasons for crying will be a thing of the past. See 7:17; Isaiah 25:8. "No more sea," the Jews were afraid of the sea.

Key "Quotable Quote"

"Heaven is that state where we will always be with Jesus, and where nothing will separate us from him any more."

William Barclay

Revelation 22

Matthew Henry's introduction

In this chapter we have,

I. A further description of the heavenly state of the church, vv. 1–5.

II. A confirmation of this and all the other visions of this book, vv. 6–19.

III. The conclusion, vv. 20, 21.

Dr. Adam Clarke's analysis of chapter

The river of the water of life, 1.

The tree of life, 2.

There is no curse nor darkness in the city of God, 3–5.

The angel assures John of the truth of what he has heard, and states that the time of the ful filment is at hand, 6, 7.

He forbids John to worship him, 8, 9.

Again he states that the time of the fulfilment of the prophecies of this book is at hand, 10–12.

Christ is Alpha and Omega, 13.

The blessedness of those who keep his com mandments; they enter through the gates into the city, 14.

All the unholy are excluded, 15.

Christ sent his angel to testify of those things in the Churches, 16.

The invitation of the Spirit and the bride, 17.

A curse denounced against those who shall either add to or take away front the prophecies of this book, 18, 19.

Christ cometh quickly, 20.

The apostolic benediction, 21.

A detailed analysis of chapter

A description of the heavenly city, using the symbols of water and the tree of life, and of the throne of God and the Lamb. (1–5)

The truth and certain fulfillment of all the prophetic visions. The Holy Spirit, and the bride, the Church, issue their invitation, and say, "Come." (6–19)

The closing blessing. (20, 21)

Key verse

Verse 8: "I, John, am the one who heard and saw these things. And when I had heard and seen them, I fell down to worship at the feet of the angel who had been showing them to me."

Key word / key phrase

Verse 1, "the river of the water of life."

Key event / key person / key theme

The river of life

Key thought

Jesus is coming.

Key thing to look out for

What does it mean for me to live in the light of Revelation 21 and 22?

Key Bible cross-reference

Verse 3. See Zechariah 14:11.

Key "by way of explanation"

Verse 2, "tree of life." The description of the tree of life in this chapter should be compared with Genesis 2:9; 3:22 and Ezekiel 47:12.

Key "Quotable Quote"

"I hope that the day is near at hand when the advent of the great God will appear, for all things everywhere are boiling, burning, moving, falling, sinking, groaning."

Martin Luther

5. Select bibliography for Revelation

Beasley-Murray, G. R. *The Book of Revelation.* New Century Bible Commentary. Grand Rapids: Eerdmans, 1981.

Caird, G. B. *The Revelation of St. John the Divine.* Harper's New Testament Commentaries. New York: Harper & Row, 1966.

Guthrie, D. *The Relevance of John's Apocalypse.* Exeter: Paternoster; Grand Rapids: Eerdmans, 1987.

Hendriksen, W. *More than Conquerors.* Grand Rapids: Baker, 1939.

Ladd, G. E. *A Commentary on the Revelation of John.* Grand Rapids: Eerdmans, 1972.

Morris, L. *The Revelation of St. John.* 2d ed. Grand Rapids: Eerdmans, 1987.

Mounce, R. H. *The Book of Revelation. The New International Commentary on the New Testament.* Grand Rapids: Eerdmans, 1977.